TULSIAN'S

BUSINESS AND CORPORATE LAWS

Dr. P.C. TULSIAN

M.Com., Ph.D., FCA, PGDFM

Additional Director (Former)
Board of Studies
The Institute of Chartered Accountants of India
Head
Department of Commerce
Ramjas College
University of Delhi
DELHI

S. CHAND
PUBLISHING

S Chand And Company Limited
(ISO 9001 Certified Company)

S. CHAND
PUBLISHING

S Chand And Company Limited

(ISO 9001 Certified Company)

Head Office: Block B-1, House No. D-1, Ground Floor, Mohan Co-operative Industrial Estate, New Delhi – 110 044 | Phone: 011-66672000

Registered Office: A-27, 2nd Floor, Mohan Co-operative Industrial Estate, New Delhi – 110 044
Phone: 011-49731800

www.**schandpublishing.com**; e-mail: **info@schandpublishing.com**

Branches

Chennai	:	Ph: 23632120; chennai@schandpublishing.com
Guwahati	:	Ph: 2738811, 2735640; guwahati@schandpublishing.com
Hyderabad	:	Ph: 40186018; hyderabad@schandpublishing.com
Jalandhar	:	Ph: 4645630; jalandhar@schandpublishing.com
Kolkata	:	Ph: 23357458, 23353914; kolkata@schandpublishing.com
Lucknow	:	Ph: 4003633; lucknow@schandpublishing.com
Mumbai	:	Ph: 25000297; mumbai@schandpublishing.com
Patna	:	Ph: 2260011; patna@schandpublishing.com

First Edition 2011

ISBN: 978-81-219-3641-5 **Product Code:** H8BCL48GLAW10ENAA11O

PRINTED IN INDIA

By Vikas Publishing House Private Limited, Plot 20/4, Site-IV, Industrial Area Sahibabad, Ghaziabad – 201 010 and Published by S Chand And Company Limited, A-27, 2nd Floor, Mohan Co-operative Industrial Estate, New Delhi – 110 044.

Preface

This book adopts a fresh and novel approach to the study of Law keeping in view the specific requirements of the candidates appearing for the Law Paper of B.Com, BBA, M.Com, MBA and Professional Courses. It has been written in a **Teach Yourself Style** strictly following a student-friendly approach, and is essentially meant to serve as a **Tutor at home**. The important features of this book include:

(a) COVERAGE OF THE BOOK

Broadly the coverage would enable the reader in understanding:

(i) The Indian Contract Act, 1872
(ii) The Sale of Goods Act, 1930
(iii) The Indian Partnership Act, 1932
(iv) The Negotiable Instruments Act, 1881
(v) The Information Technology Act, 2000 [As Amended by the Information Technology (Amendement) act, 2008, w.e.f. 27.10.2009]
(vi) The Payment of Bonus Act, 1965
(vii) The Payment of Gratuity Act, 1972
(viii) The Employee's P.F. & Misc. Provisions Act, 1952
(ix) The Companies Act, 1956 [Sec 1 to Sec 197]

(b) PEDAGOGICAL FEATURES OF THE BOOK

- **Simple Language:** The Text is presented in the simplest language "meant to serve beginners".
- **Heading for each Paragraph:** Each paragraph has been arranged under a suitable heading for easy retention of concepts.
- **Tabular Form:** Wherever possible the text matter relating to a particular topic/sub-topic has been presented in a Tabular Form.
- **Eye-catching Screens:** All Important Equations, Formulae, Figures and Practical Steps have been presented in screen format to catch the eye.
- **Uniform Format of Chapter:** Each chapter has been uniformly organised under four headings, viz., Text supported by suitable Illustrations, Solved Problems, True/False Questions and Exercises.

(c) DISTINCTIVE FEATURES OF THE BOOK

- **50 Exhibits:** To acquaint students with various important matters.
- **150 Illustrations:** To aid better understanding of the text
- **150 Practical (Solved) Problems:** Along with necessary working notes and alternative solutions (if any).
- **250 Very Short Answer Type Questions:** To enable students to test their understanding of the subject.

- **250 Short Answer Type Questions:**
- **150 Essay Type Questions:**
- **350 True/False Questions:**

REVISION ONE DAY BEFORE EXAMINATION

Dr. P.C. Tulsian
pctulsian@gmail.com

Acknowledgements

I wish to express my sincere thanks to several individuals who have been a source of inspiration and support personally and professionally including Dr. R.P. Tulsian, Dr. Renu Gupta, Dr. Tanushree Jain, Dr. Naresh Gupta, Dr. Amit Singhal, Dr. J.B. Gupta, Dr. M.M. Goyal, Dr. S.C. Garg, Dr Madhu Aggarwal, Dr. Rajeev Goyal, Dr. S.N. Gupta, Dr. S.S. Lamba, Dr. Sarita Jain, Dr. Usha Jain, Dr. V.K. Aggarwal, Dr. V.P. Bansal, Dr. Vibha Jain, Dr. Savita Gopal, Dr. S.C. Gupta, Dr. S.P. Gupta, Dr. Madhu Gupta, Dr. Sushma Aggarwal, Dr. Manju Gupta, Dr. C.P. Gupta, Dr. S.Z.H. Zaidi. CA M.K. Aggarwal, CA S.K. Aggarwal, CA N.D. Gupta, CA Naveen Gupta, CA Ashish Gupta, CA M.K. Sharda, CA Rajeev Rastogi. CA Atual Gupta, CA Kuldeep Bhardwaj, CA Neeraj Chabra, CA Kishore Paul, CA Pradeep Narang, CA S.K. Gupta, CA R. Devarajan, CA Tapas Dutta, CA Arnav Chakrabarty, CA Seema Gupta, CA Shilpa Aggarwal, CA Vishal Pandey, MS. Nidhi Singh, Dr. N.N. Sen Gupta, Prof. J.P. Sharma, Dr. Harpal Singh, Dr. P.P. Joshi and Dr. P.T. Giridharan.

Special word of thanks is also due to my favourite students **Vishal Pandey and Prarthna Mittal** who provided incisive comments and useful feedback.

I must conclude that this book would never have been written without the support, encouragement and prodding of my family members. Many thanks to them.

Any criticisms or suggestions for further improvement of the book will be gratefully acknowledged and appreciated.

Dr. P.C. Tulsian

pctulsian@gmail.com

This Page has been intentionally left blank

Contents

SECTION A BUSINESS LAWS

SECTION B INDUSTRIAL LAWS

SECTION C THE COMPANIES ACT, 1956

REVISION ONE DAY BEFORE EXAMINATION

APPENDICES

SECTION A

Business Laws

The Indian Contract Act, 1872

1. Meaning and Essentials of Contract
2. Offer and Acceptance
3. Capacity of Parties
4. Consideration
5. Free Consent
6. Legality of Object and Consideration, and Agreements Opposed to Public Policy
7. Void Agreement and Contingent Contracts
8. Performance of a Contract
9. Discharge of a Contract
10. Remedies for Beach of Contract
11. Quasi-Contracts
12. Indemnity and Guarantee
13. Bailment and Pledge
14. Contract of Agency

The Sale of Goods Act, 1930

15. The Sale of Goods Act, 1930

The Indian Partnership Act, 1932

16. The Indian Partnership Act, 1932

The Negotiable Instruments Act, 1881

17. The Negotiable Instruments Act, 1881 (Part I)
18. The Negotiable Instruments Act, 1881 (Part II)

The Information Technology Act, 2000 [As Amended by the Information Technology (Amendement) act, 2008, w.e.f. 27.10.2009]

19. The Information Technology Act, 2000

SECTION B

Industrial Laws

CHAPTER

1 Meaning and Essentials of Contract

1.0 WHAT IS LAW ?

1.1 **Law means a 'set of rules'.**

1.2 Broadly Speaking, Law may be defined as the rules of conduct recognised and enforced by the state to control and regulate the conduct of people, to protect their property and contractual rights with a view to securing justice, peaceful living and social security.

1.3 Since the value system of society keeps on changing, the law also keeps on changing according to the changing requirements of the society.

1.4 There are several branches of law such as International law, Constitutional law, Criminal law, Civil law etc. Every branch of law regulates and controls a particular field of activity.

2.0 WHY SHOULD ONE KNOW LAW ?

2.1 One should know the law to which he is subject because ***ignorance of law is no excuse.***

2.2 **Examples** *Example I* – if *X* is caught travelling in a train without ticket, he cannot plead that he was not aware of the rule regarding the purchase of ticket and therefore, he may be excused. *Example II* – if *Y* is caught driving scooter without driving license, he cannot plead that he was not aware of the traffic rule regarding the obtaining of a driving license and therefore, he may be excused.

3.0 WHAT IS MERCANTILE LAW (OR COMMERCIAL LAW) ?

3.1 Mercantile law is not a separate branch of law.

3.2 Basically, it is a part of civil law which deals with the rights and obligations of mercantile persons arising out of mercantile transactions in respect of mercantile property.

3.3 It includes laws relating to various contracts, partnership, companies, negotiable instruments, insurance, carriage of goods, arbitration etc.

4.0 WHAT ARE THE SOURCES OF MERCANTILE LAW ?

4.1 In India, mercantile law is basically an adaptation of the English Law with some modifications and reservations which are necessitated by the peculiar conditions prevailing in India.

4.2 The main sources of the Indian mercantile law are as follows.

1. **English Mercantile Law** English laws are the primary sources of Indian Mercantile Law. English laws are based on customs and usages of merchants in England.

2. **Indian Statute Law** The various Acts passed by the Indian Legislature are the main sources of mercantile law in India, e.g. Indian Contract Act, 1872, The Sale of Goods Act, 1930, The Indian Partnership Act, 1932, The Negotiable Instruments Act 1881, The Companies Act, 1956.
3. **Judicial Decisions** The past judicial decisions of English courts and Indian courts are also one of the sources of law. Wherever the law is silent on a point, the judge has to decide the case according to the principle of equity, justice and good conscience. The past judicial decisions are followed by the courts while deciding similar cases before them.
4. **Customs and Usages** The customs and usages of a trade are also one of the sources of mercantile law in India. These customs and usages govern the merchants of a trade in their dealings with each other. Some Acts passed by the Indian Legislature recognises the importance of such customs and usages. For example, Section 1 of the Indian Contract Act, 1872 provides "nothing contained therein shall affect any usage of custom of trade . . ." Similarly, Section 1 of The Negotiable Instruments Act, 1881 provides "nothing contained therein shall affect any local usage relating to instrument in an oriental language."

5.0 WHAT IS THE LAW OF CONTRACT ?

5.1 The law of contract is contained in the Indian Contract Act, 1872 which—

(a) deals with the general principles of law governing all contracts, and

(b) covers the special provisions relating to special contracts like Bailment, Pledge, Indemnity, Guarantee and Agency.

5.2 The law of Contract is applicable not only to business but also to all day-to-day personal dealings. In fact, each one of us enter into a number of contracts from sunrise to sunset.

5.3 Examples of Contract

1. when you purchase a newspaper, you enter into a contract with the vendor of newspaper.
2. when you purchase milk, you enter into a contract with the milkman.
3. when you purchase bread and butter, you enter into a contract with the vendor of bread and butter.
4. when you ride a bus, you enter into a contract with the transport company.

5.4 The general law of contract relates to the essentials of a valid contract, the rules for performance and discharge of a contract and the remedies available to the aggrieved party in case of breach of contract.

6.0 WHAT IS CONTRACT ?

6.1 According to Section 2(h) of the Indian Contract Act, 1872, "**An agreement enforceable by law is a contract**." In other words, an agreement which can be enforced in a court of law is known as a contract.

6.2 On analyzing this definition of contract, it appears that a contract must have the following **two** elements:

1. An agreement, and
2. Enforceability of an agreement.

6.3 In the form of an equation, it can be shown as under:

Contract = An Agreement + Enforceability of an agreement

Now the question arises, 'What is an Agreement?' and What is Enforceability of an agreement?

6.4 What is an Agreement ?

According to Section 2(h) of the Indian Contract Act, 1872, "**An agreement enforceable by law is a contract**." In other words, an agreement which can be enforced in a court of law is known as a contract.

According to Section 2(e) of the Indian Contract Act, 1872, "**Every promise and every set of promises forming the consideration for each other is an agreement**." Now the question arises, 'What is promise?' According to Section 2(b) of the Indian Contract Act, 1872, "**A proposal when accepted, becomes a promise**."

Example: *X offers to sell his car for Rs 1,00,000 to Y. Y accepts this offer. This offer after acceptance becomes promise and this promise is treated as an agreement between X and Y.*

In other words, an agreement consists of an offer by one party and its acceptance by the other. In the form of an equation, it can be shown as under:

Agreement = Offer (or Proposal) + Acceptance of Offer (or Proposal)

6.5 WHAT IS AN ENFORCEABILITY OF AGREEMENT ?

1. An agreement is said to be enforceable by law if it creates some legal obligation. In other words, the parties to an agreement must be bound to perform their promises and in case of default by either of them, must intend to sue.
2. In commercial or business agreements the usual presumption is that the parties intend to create legal relations.

   Example: *X offers to sell his car to Y for Rs 1,00,000. Y accepts this offer. Such an agreement between X and Y is a contract because it creates legal obligation. In this agreement, if X refuses to sell or Y refuses to buy, the other party can file a suit in the court of law for the breach of the contract.*
3. In case of social or domestic agreements, the usual presumption is that the parties do not intend to create legal relations.

   Example: *X invites his friend Y to a dinner and Y accepts the invitation. If Y fails to turn up for dinner, X cannot go to the court to claim his loss.*

   Similarly, in case of domestic arrangements, parties to agreement do not intend to sue each other so as to make such agreements unenforceable by law, e.g. in *Balfour* v. *Balfour* (1919) 2 K.B. 571, a promise by the husband to pay his wife £ 30 every month was held unenforceable as the parties never intended it to be attended by legal obligations.

Thus, in the form of a graphic representation, the contract can be expressed as under:

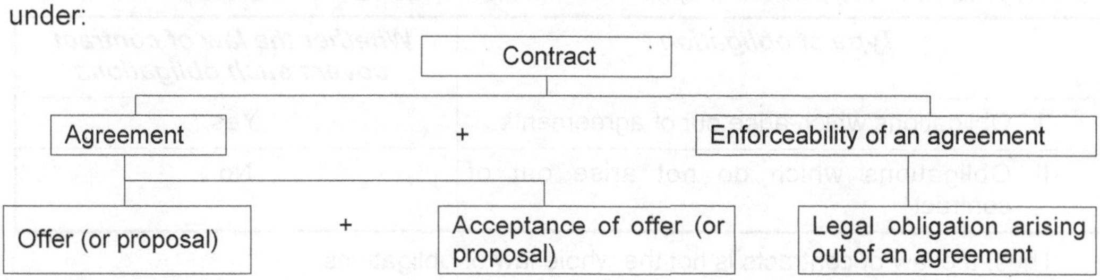

7.0 THE LAW OF CONTRACT IS NOT THE WHOLE LAW OF AGREEMENTS NOR IS IT THE WHOLE LAW OF OBLIGATIONS

7.1 "The law of contracts is not the whole law of agreements."

(*a*) The law of contracts is the law of only those agreements which create legal obligations (i.e. an obligation which is enforceable by law). An obligation is the duty to do or not to do certain act. In other words, the law of contract is concerned with only those agreements where the parties have the intention to create legal obligations (i.e. the parties are bound to do or not to do certain act). In business or commercial agreements, the usual presumption is that the parties intend to create legal obligations.

Example: *X offers to sell his car to Y for Rs 1,00,000. Y accepts this offer. In this agreement if there is default by either party, an action for breach of contract can be enforced through a court of law provided all the essential elements of a valid contract are present in this agreement.*

(*b*) The law of contract is not the law of those agreements which do not create legal obligations. In other words, the law of contract is not concerned with those agreements where the parties do not have the intention to create legal obligations. In social, domestic, moral or religious agreements, the usual presumption is that the parties do not intend to create legal obligations.

Example: *X invites Y to dinner. Y accepts the invitation but fails to turn up. Here, X cannot sue Y for damages because the parties to this agreement do not intend to create legal obligations.*

Thus, the whole position may be summarised as under:

Type of agreement	*Whether the law of contract covers such agreements*
I. Agreements where the parties intend to create legal obligations, e.g. business agreements	Yes
II. Agreements where the parties do not intend to create any legal obligation, e.g. social agreements	No

Thus, the law of contracts is not the whole law of agreements.

7.2 "The law of contracts is not whole law of obligations."

The law of contracts is the law of only those obligations which arise out of agreements. The law of contracts is not concerned with those obligations which do not arise out of agreements. For example, obligation to maintain wife and children, obligation arising from judgment of courts, obligations arising from torts or civil wrong.

Thus, the whole position may be summarised as under:

Type of obligation	*Whether the law of contract covers such obligations*
I. Obligations which arise out of agreements	Yes
II. Obligations which do not arise out of contract	No

Thus, the law of contracts is not the whole law of obligations.

8.0 DISTINCTION BETWEEN AN AGREEMENT AND A CONTRACT

An agreement differs from a contract in the following respects:

Basis of distinction	*An agreement*	*A contract*
1. What constitute?	Agreement = Offer + Acceptance	Contract = Agreement + its enforceability.
2. Creation of legal obligation	An agreement may or may not create a legal obligation.	A contract necessarily create a legal obligation.
3. One in other	Every agreement need not necessarily be a contract.	All contracts are necessarily agreements.
4. Binding	Agreement is not concluded or a binding contract.	Contract is concluded and binding on the concerned parties.

9.0 WHAT ARE THE DIFFERENT TYPES OF CONTRACTS ?

The various bases on which the contracts can be classified are discussed below:

9.1 Contracts on the Basis of Creation

(a) Express Contract	Express contract is one which is made by words spoken or written. **Example I:** X says to Y "Will you buy my car for Rs 1,00,000?" Y says to X "I am ready to buy your car for Rs 1,00,000." It is an express contract made orally. **Example II:** *X writes a letter to Y, "I offer to sell my car for Rs 1,00,000 to you." Y send a letter to X, "I am ready to buy your car for Rs 1,00,000." It is an express contract made in writing.*
(b) Implied Contract	An implied contract is one which is made otherwise than by words spoken or written. It is inferred from the conduct of a person or the circumstances of the particular case. **Example I:** *A transport company runs buses on different routes to carry passengers. This is an implied offer by transport company. X boards a bus. This is an implied acceptance by X. Now, there is an implied contract and X is bound to pay the prescribed fare.* **Example II:** *X, a coolie in uniform picks up the baggage of Y to carry it from railway platform to the taxi without being asked by Y to do so and Y allows it. In this case there is an implied offer by the coolie and an implied acceptance by the passenger. Now, there is an implied contract between the coolie and the passenger and the passenger is bound to pay for the services of the coolie.*
(c) Tacit Contract	A tacit contract is one which is inferred from the conduct of parties. **Example I:** Withdrawing cash throught ATM **Example II:** Sale by fall of hammer at an auction sale

9.2 Contracts on the Basis of Execution

(a) Executed Contract	It is a contract in which both the parties to the contract have **performed** their respective obligations under the contract. **Example:** *X offers to sell his car to Y for Rs 1,00,000. Y accepts X 's offer. X delivers the car to Y and Y pays Rs 1,00,000 to X. It is an executed contract.*
(b) Executory Contract	It is a contract in which both the parties to the contract have **still to perform** their respective obligations. **Example:** *X offers to sell his car to Y for Rs 1,00,000. Y accepts X's offer. If the car has not yet been delivered by X and the price has not yet been paid by Y, it is an executory contract.*
(c) Partly Executed and Partly Executory Contract	It is a contract in which **one of the parties** to the contract has **performed** his obligation and the **other party** has **still to perform** his obligation. **Example:** *X offers to sell his car to Y for Rs 1,00,000 on a credit of one month. Y accepts X's offer. X delivers the car to Y. Here, the contract is executed as to X and executory as to Y.*
(d) Unilateral Contract	An Unilateral contract is one sided contract in which only **one party has to perform** his promise or obligation to do or forebear.
(e) Bilateral Contract	A bilateral contract is one in which **both the parties have to perform** their respective promises or obligations to do *or* forebear.

9.3 Contracts on the Basis on Enforceability

(a) Valid Contract	A contract which satisfies all the conditions prescribed by law is a valid contract. **Example:** *X offers to marry Y. Y accepts X's offer. This is a valid contract.*
(b) Void Contract	The term 'Void Contract' is a contradiction in terms. But according to Section 2(j) of the Indian Contract Act, 1872, **"A contract which ceases to be enforceable by law becomes void when it ceases to be enforceable."** In other words, a void contract is a contract which was valid when entered into but which subsequently became void due to impossibility of performance, change of law or some other reason. **Example:** *X offers to marry Y. Y accepts X's offer. Later on Y dies. This contract was valid at the time of its formation but became void on the death of Y.*
(c) Void Agreement	According to Section 2(g), **"An agreement not enforceable by law is said to be void."** Such agreements are *void-ab-initio* which means that they are unenforceable right from the time they are made.

	Example: *An agreement with a minor or a person of unsound mind is void-ab-initio because a minor or a person of unsound mind is incompetent to contract.* Thus, a void agreement never matures into a contract.
(d) Voidable Contract	According to Section 2(i) of the Indian Contract Act, 1872, **"an agreement which is enforceable by law at the option of one or more of the parties thereon but not at the option of the other or others"**, is a voidable contract. In other words, "A voidable contract is one which can be set aside or repudiated or avoided at the option of the aggrieved party." Until the contract is set aside or repudiated by the aggrieved party, it remains a valid contract. *For example*, a contract is treated as voidable at the option of the party whose consent has been obtained by coercion or undue influence or fraud or misrepresentation. **Example:** *X threatens to kill Y if he does not sell his house for Rs 1,00,000 to X. Y sells his house to X and receives payment. Here, Y's consent has been obtained by coercion and hence this contract is voidable at the option of Y, the aggrieved party. If Y decides to avoid the contract, he will have to return Rs 1,00,000 which he had received from X. If Y does not exercise his option to repudiate the contract within a reasonable time and in the meantime, Z purchases that house from X for Rs 1,00,000 in good faith, Y cannot repudiate the contract.* **Note:** In case of voidable contract, if the aggrieved party decides to repudiate the contract, the party rescinding the contract must restore the benefit received by him under the contract to the person from whom the benefit was received and the other party is freed from his obligation to perform the contract. [Section 64]
(e) Illegal Agreement	An illegal agreement is one the object of which is unlawful. Such an agreement cannot be enforced by law. Thus, illegal agreements are always void *ab-initio* (i.e. void from the very beginning). **Example:** *X agrees to pay Y Rs 1,00,000 if Y kills Z. Y kills Z and claims Rs 1,00,000. Y cannot recover from X because the agreement between X and Y is illegal as its object is unlawful.* ***Effect on collateral agreements*** In case of illegal agreements, even the collateral agreements become void. **Example:** *If in the above example, X borrows Rs 1,00,000 from W who is aware of the purpose of the loan, the main agreement between X and Y is illegal and the agreement between X and W which is collateral to the main agreement is also void. Hence, W cannot recover the money from X.*
(f) Unenforceable Contract	It is a contract which is actually valid but cannot be enforced because of some technical defect (such as not in writing, under stamped). Such contracts can be enforced if the technical defect involved is removed.

	Example: *An oral agreement for arbitration is unenforceable because the law requires that an arbitration agreement must be in writing. If the oral agreement for arbitration is reduced to writing, it will become enforceable.*

9.4 Distinction between Void Agreement and Voidable Contract

Void agreement differs from voidable contract in the following respects:

Basis of Distinction	*Void agreement*	*Voidable contract*
1. Void ab-initio	It is void from the very beginning.	It is valid when made and continues to remain valid till it is repudiated by the aggrieved party.
2. Which essential element of contract is missing	Enforceability by law is missing.	Free consent of a party is missing.
3. Enforceability	It cannot be enforced by any party.	It continues to be enforceable if the aggrieved party does not repudiate the contract.
4. Right of third party	Third party does not acquire any rights.	A third party who purchases goods in good faith and for consideration before the contract is repudiated, acquires good title to those goods.
5. Effect of lapse of reasonable time	Even on the expiry of a reason-able time, it can never become a valid contract.	On the expiry of a reasonable time, it may become a valid contract if the aggrieved party does not repudiate the contract within reasonable time.
6. Damages	The question of damages does not arise.	The aggrieved party can claim damages.

9.5 Distinction between Void Agreement and Illegal Agreement

Void agreements differ from the Illegal Agreements in the following respects:

Basis of Distinction	*Void agreement*	*Illegal agreement*
1. Void/illegal	All void agreements need not necessarily be illegal.	All illegal agreements are always void.
2. Effect on colla-teral agreements	The collateral agreements do not become void.	The collateral agreements also become void.
3. Restoration of benefit received	If a contract becomes void subsequently, the benefit received must be restored to the other party.	The money advanced or thing given can not be claimed back.

10.0 ESSENTIALS OF A VALID CONTRACT

10.1 According to Section 10, **"All agreements are contracts if they are made by the free consent of the parties competent to contract, for a lawful consideration and with a lawful object and are not hereby expressly declared to be void."**

10.2 The analysis of the provisions of Section 10 shows that a valid contract must have the following essential elements:

1. **Proper Offer and Acceptance** There must be at least two parties—one making the offer and the other accepting it. Such offer and acceptance must be valid. An offer to be valid must fulfil certain conditions, such as it must intend to create legal relations, its terms must be certain and unambiguous, it must be communicated to the person to whom it is made, etc. An acceptance to be valid must fulfil certain conditions, such as it must be absolute and unqualified, it must be made in the prescribed manner, it must be communicated by an authorised person before the offer lapses.

2. **Intention to Create Legal Relationship** There must be an intention among the parties to create a legal relationship. In case of social or domestic agreements, the usual presumption is that the parties do not intend to create legal relationship but in commercial or business agreements, the usual presumption is that the parties intend to create legal relationship unless otherwise agreed upon.

   Example: *X invited Y to a dinner. Y accepted the invitation. It is a social agreement. If X fails to serve dinner to Y, Y cannot go to the courts of law for enforcing the agreement. Similarly, if Y fails to attend the dinner, X cannot go to the courts of law for enforcing the agreement.*

   But even a business agreement may not be enforceable by law where the agreement so provides e.g. in *Rose & Frank Co.* v. *Crompton Bros.* (1925) A.C. 445, the agreement entered into stated that it will not be subject to legal jurisdiction in the law courts, the agreement was not enforceable by law as the parties never agreed to create legal obligations despite being a business agreement.

3. **Capacity of Parties** The parties to an agreement must be competent to contract. In other words, they must be capable of entering into a contract. According to Section 11 of Indian Contract Act, 1872, **"every person is competent to contract who is of the age of majority according to the law to which he is subject and who is of sound mind and is not disqualified from contracting by any law to which he is subject."** In other words, the person must be **major**, must be of **sound mind** and must **not be declared disqualified** from contracting by any law to which he is subject. If the parties to agreement are not competent to contract, then no valid contract comes into existence.

   Example: *X, a minor borrowed Rs 8,000 from Y and executed mortgage of his property in favour of the lender. This was not a valid contract because X is not competent to contract. Therefore, the mortgage was not valid and the money advanced to minor could not be recovered.*

4. **Lawful Consideration** An agreement must be supported by lawful consideration. Consideration means something in return. According to Section 23 of the Indian Contract Act, 1872, **"the consideration is considered lawful unless it is forbidden by law or is fraudulent or involves or implies injury to the person or property of another or is immoral or is opposed to public policy."**

Example I: *X agrees to sell his car to Y for Rs 1,00,000. Here, Y 's promise to pay Rs 1,00,000 is the consideration for X's promise to sell the car and X's promise to sell the car is the consideration for Y 's promise to pay Rs 1,00,000.*

Example II: *X promises to drop prosecution which he has initiated against Y for robbery and Y promises to restore the value of things taken. The agreement is void because the consideration is unlawful.*

5. **Free Consent** There must be free consent of the parties to the contract. According to Section 14, **"Consent is said to be free when it is not caused by (i) coercion, (ii) undue influence, (iii) fraud, (iv) misrepresentation, or (v) mistake".** If the consent of the parties is not free, then no valid contract comes into existence.

   Example: *X threatens to kill Y if he does not sell his house to X. Y agrees to sell his house to X. In this case, Y's consent has been obtained by coercion and therefore, it cannot be regarded as free.*

6. **Lawful Object** The object of the agreement must be lawful. According to Section 23 of the Indian Contract Act, 1872, **"the object is considered lawful unless it is forbidden by law or is fraudulent or involves or implies injury to the person or property of another or is immoral or is opposed to public policy."**

   Example I: *X, Y and Z enter into an agreement for the division among them of gains acquired or to be acquired by them by fraud. The agreement is void because its object is unlawful.*

   Example II: *X lets a flat on hire to Y, a prostitute, knowing that it would be used for immoral purposes. The agreement is void because its object is for immoral purposes.*

7. **Agreement not Expressly Declared Void** The agreement must not have been expressly declared void under the provisions of Sections 24 to 30 of the Indian Contract Act, 1872. Under these provisions, agreement in restraint of marriage, agreement in restraint of legal proceedings, agreement in restraint of trade and agreement by way of wager have been expressly declared void.

   Example I: *X promised to marry none else except Y and in default pay her Rs 1,00,000. X married to Z and Y sued X for the recovery of Rs 1,00,000. It was held that Y was not entitled to recover anything because this agreement was in restraint of marriage and as such void.*

   Example II: *X and Y carried on business in Chandni Chowk area of Delhi. X promised to stop business in that locality if Y paid Rs 1,00,000. X stopped his business but Y did not pay him the promised money. It was held that X was not entitled to recover anything because the agreement was in restraint of trade and as such void.*

8. **Certainty of Meaning** The terms of the agreement must be certain and unambiguous. According to Section 29 of the Indian Contract Act, 1872, **"agreements the meaning of which is not certain or capable of being made certain are void."**

   Example: *X a dealer in different types of oils agreed to sell 100 tonnes of oil to Y. This agreement is void on the ground of uncertainty because it is not clear what kind of oil is intended to be sold.*

   If, however, the meaning of the agreement could be made certain from the circumstances of the case, it will be treated as a valid contract.

Example: *X who is a dealer in mustard oil, agreed to sell 100 tonnes of oil to Y. This agreement is valid because the meaning of the agreement could be easily ascertained from the circumstances of the case.*

9. **Possibility of Performance** The terms of the agreement must be such as are capable of performance. According to Section 56, **"an agreement to do an impossible act is void."**

   Example I: *X agrees with Y to discover treasure by magic and Y agrees to pay Rs 1,000 to X. This agreement is void because it is an agreement to do an impossible act.*

   Example II: *X agrees with Y to enclose some area between two parallel lines and Y agrees to pay Rs 1,000 to X. This agreement is void because it is an agreement to do an impossible act.*

10. **Legal Formalities** The agreement must comply with the necessary formalities as to writing, registration, stamping etc. if any required in order to make it enforceable by law.

   Example I: *An oral agreement for arbitration is unenforceable because the law requires that arbitration agreement must be in writing.*

   Example II: *An oral agreement for sale of immovable property is unenforceable because the law requires that such agreement must be in writing and registered.*

   Conclusion All the aforesaid elements must be present in an agreement in order to create a valid contract. If any one of them is missing or absent, the agreement will not be enforceable by law.

PRACTICAL PROBLEMS

PROBLEM 1

X invites *Y* to dinner. *Y* accepts the invitation but fails to turn up. Can *X* sue *Y* for the damage?

Solution

X cannot claim any damages from *Y* because the agreement between *X* and *Y* is not enforceable by law. It is a social agreement and the usual presumption in such agreement is that the parties do not intend to create legal relationship.

PROBLEM 2

X makes a promise to his wife *Y* to give her pocket money of Rs 1,000 per month. After 6 months, he stops making the payment. Can *Y* claim damages from *X*.

Solution

Y cannot claim any damages from *X* because the agreement between *X* and *Y* is not enforceable by law. It is a social agreement and the usual presumption in such agreement is that the parties do not intend to create legal relationship.

PROBLEM 3

X promises *Y* to give a diamond ring at the time of his marriage. *X* fails to give the ring. Can *Y* claim the ring?

Solution

Y cannot claim the diamond ring because there is no consideration from *Y*.

PROBLEM 4

X polished *Y*'s shoes without being asked by *Y* to do so. *Y* does not make any attempt to stop *X* from polishing the shoes. Is *Y* bound to make payment to *X*?

Solution

Y is bound to pay because he has accepted *X*'s implied offer by conduct (i.e. by not stopping *X* from polishing the shoes).

PROBLEM 5

X agrees to marry *Y*. *Y* dies before the marriage takes place. Is it a void agreement?

Solution

It is not a void agreement. It is a void contract because it was valid when it was entered into but subsequently became void on the death of *Y*.

PROBLEM 6

X agreed to sell a particular horse to *Y*. Later on, it was discovered that the horse was dead at the time of making the contract. Advise the parties.

Solution

The agreement is void because both the parties were under a mistake of fact regarding existence of the subject matter.

PROBLEM 7

X agrees to let his flat to *Y* for use as a gambling den on a monthly rent of Rs 10,000. After 3 months, *Y* stops making the payment of rent. Advise *X*.

Solution

X cannot recover anything. The agreement between *X* and *Y* is void because the object of the agreement is unlawful.

PROBLEM 8

X agrees to pay Rs 1,00,000 to *Y* if *Y* does not marry throughout his life. *Y* promises not to marry at all but later on *X* refuses to pay Rs 1,00,000. Advise *Y*.

Solution

Y cannot recover anything. The agreement between *X* and *Y* is in restraint of marriage which has been expressly declared void under Section 26.

PROBLEM 9

X threatens to kill *Y* if he (*Y*) does not sell his house to *X* for Rs 1,00,000. *Y* agrees. *X* borrows Rs 1,00,000 from *Z* who is also aware of the purpose of the loan. What is the nature of the agreement between *X* and *Y*, and *X* and *Z*?

Solution

The contract between *X* and *Y* is a contract which is voidable at the option of *Y* because *Y*'s consent is not free as it has been obtained by coercion. The contract between *X* and *Z* is a valid contract because the object of contract (i.e. borrowing for the purchase of a house) is lawful.

PROBLEM 10

X agrees to pay *Y* Rs 1,00,000 if *Y* kills *Z*. To pay *Y*, *X* borrows Rs 1,00,000 from *W* who is also aware of the purpose of the loan. *Y* kills *Z* but *X* refuses to pay. *X* also refuses to repay the loan to *W*. Advise *Y* and *W*.

Solution

The agreement between *X* and *Y* is an illegal agreement because its object is unlawful. Hence, *Y* cannot recover anything from *X*. Since the main agreement between *X* and *Y* is illegal, the agreement between *X* and *W* which is collateral to the main agreement is also void and hence *W* cannot recover anything from *X*.

TRUE OR FALSE QUESTIONS

State with reasons whether the following statements are True or False:

1. Law is the body of principles enforced by judiciary.
2. Indian mercantile law is primarily an adaptation of the English law.
3. Mercantile law is applicable to business community only.
4. Customs and usages are an important source of mercantile law.
5. Law of contract is the whole law of agreements.
6. Law of contract is the whole law of obligations.
7. All contracts are agreements.
8. All agreements are contracts.
9. In social agreements, the usual presumption is that the parties intend to create legal obligations.
10. In business agreements, the usual presumption is that the parties do not intend to create legal obligations.
11. Express contract is made by words in writing only.
12. Implied contract is made by words spoken only.
13. A contract where both the parties have fulfilled their respective obligations is called an 'Executory contract'.
14. A contract is not void from its inception.
15. A contract can be void *ab-initio.*
16. A contract is usually treated as voidable when the consent of a party has not been free.
17. A voidable contract also remains enforceable by law.
18. Collateral transactions to a void agreement also become void.
19. Collateral transactions to an illegal agreements do not become void.
20. An unenforceable contract can be enforced if the technical defect involved is removed.
21. A valid contract may be voidable at the option of aggrieved party.
22. A valid agreement may be voidable at the option of aggrieved party.

Answers

1. True	2. True	3. False	4. True
5. False	6. False	7. True	8. False
9. False	10. False	11. False	12. False
13. False	14. True	15. False	16. True

17. True if the aggrieved party does not repudiate the contract; false if the aggrieved party repudiates the contract.
18. False 19. False 20. True 21. True
22. False

VERY SHORT ANSWER TYPE QUESTIONS

1. Define Agreement.
2. Define Contract.
3. What is enforceability of an agreement?
4. What is the usual presumption in social or domestic agreements?
5. What is the usual presumption in commercial or business agreements?
6. What is an 'Express Contract'?
7. What is an 'Implied Contract'?
8. Define 'Executed Contract'.
9. Define 'Executory Contract'.
10. What is meant by 'Partly Executed and Partly Executory Contract'?
11. What is meant by a Valid Contract?
12. Define 'Void Contract'.
13. Define 'Void Agreements'.
14. What is 'Voidable Contract'?
15. What is Illegal Agreement?
16. What is 'Unforceable Contract'?

SHORT ANSWER TYPE QUESTIONS

17. Enumerate the essentials of a valid contract.
18. Distinguish between the following:
    (a) Implied Contract and Express Contract
    (b) Executory Contract and Executed Contract
    (c) Void Contract and Voidable Contract
    (d) Void Contract and Void Agreement
    (e) Void Agreement and Illegal Agreement
19. Comment on the following statements:
    (a) All contracts are agreements but all agreements are not contracts.
    (b) The law of contract is not the whole law of agreements nor is it the whole law of obligations.
    (c) In commercial and business agreements the presumption is that the parties intend to create legal relations.

ESSAY TYPE QUESTIONS

20. (a) Define Contract.
    (b) Explain the essentials of a valid contract.

CHAPTER 2 Offer and Acceptance

1.0 OFFER

1.1 Meaning An offer is the starting point in the making of an agreement. An offer is also called 'proposal'. According to Section 2(a) of The Indian Contract Act, 1872, "**A person is said to have made the proposal when he signifies to another his willingness to do or to abstain from doing anything with a view to obtaining the assent of that offer to such act or abstinence.**"

1.2 Essential Elements An offer involves the following ***essential elements***:

(a) It must be made by one person to another person. In other words, there can be no proposal by a person to himself.

Example: *X says to Y that he wants to sell his car to himself for Rs 1 lakh. There is no proposal because there can be no proposal by a person to himself.*

(b) It must be an expression of readiness or willingness to do (i.e. a positive act) or to abstain from doing something (i.e. a negative act).

Example I: *X offers to sell his car to Y for Rs 1 lakh. It is a positive act on the part of X.*

Example II: *X offers not to file a suit against Y if Y pays X the outstanding amount of Rs 1,00,000. It is a negative act on the part of X.*

(c) It must be made with a view to obtain the consent of that other person to proposed act *or* abstinence.

Example: *X jokingly says to Y "I am ready to sell my car for Rs 1,000." Y, knowingly that X is not serious in making the offer, says "I accept your offer." In this case, X's offer was not the real offer as he did not make it with a view to obtain the consent of Y.*

2.0 OFFERER (OR 'PROMISOR') AND OFFEREE (OR PROMISEE)

2.1 Meaning of Offerer The person making the proposal is called the 'offerer' *or* 'proposer'.

2.2 Meaning of Offeree The person to whom the proposal is made is called the 'offeree' *or* 'proposee'.

Example: *X says to Y, "I want to sell my car to you for Rs 1 lakh." Here, 'to sell car' is an offer or proposal. X who has made the offer is called offeror or promisor. Y to whom the offer has been made is called the offeree or proposee.*

3.0 HOW TO MAKE AN OFFER ?

An offer can be made by any act which has the effect of communicating it to another person. An offer may, *either* be an 'express offer' *or* 'implied offer'.

3.1 Express Offer An express offer is one which is made by words spoken or written.

Example I *X says to Y, "Will you purchase my car for Rs 1,00,000?"*

Example II *X writes to Y in a letter, "I want to sell my house for Rs 2,00,000."*

Example III *X advertises in a newspaper, "I will pay Rs 1,000 to anyone who traces my missing nephew".*

3.2 Implied Offer An implied offer is one which is made otherwise than in words. In other words, it is inferred from the conduct of the person or the circumstances of the particular case.

Example I *A transport company runs buses on different routes to carry passengers. This is an implied offer by the transport company to carry passengers for a certain fare.*

Example II *A bid at an auction is an implied offer to buy.*

4.0 TO WHOM AN OFFER IS MADE ?

An offer may be 'specific' or 'general'.

4.1 Specific Offer A specific offer is one which is made to a definite person *or* particular group of persons. A specific offer can be accepted only by that definite person *or* that particular group of persons to whom it has been made.

Example *X offers to buy car from Y for Rs 1.0 lakh. This offer is a specific offer which has been made to a definite person Y. No person other than Y can accept this offer.* [*Boulton v. Jones*]

Similarly an offer made to a company is an offer to a group of persons and hence a specific offer.

4.2 General Offer A general offer is one which is made to the world at large *or* public in general. A general offer can be accepted by any person by fulfilling the terms of the offer. In case of general offer, the contract is made with person who having the knowledge of the offer comes forward and acts according to the conditions of the offer.

Example I *X advertised in the newspaper that he would pay Rs 5,000 to anyone who traces his missing boy. Y, who knew about the reward traced that boy and sent a telegram to X that he had found his son. It was held that X was entitled to receive the amount of reward.* [*Harbhajan Lal v. Harcharan Lal* (*AIR All 539*)]

Example II *Carbolic Smoke Ball Co. advertised in the newspaper that it would pay Rs 1,000 to anyone who contracts influenza after using the smoke ball of the company according to the printed instructions. Mrs Carlil uses the smoke ball according to the printed directions but subsequently contracted influenza. On a suit for the reward she was held entitled to recover the same because she had accepted the offer by fulfilling the terms of the offer.* [*Carlil v. Carbolic Smoke Ball Co.*]

5.0 WHAT ARE THE LEGAL RULES FOR A VALID OFFER ?

An offer to be valid must fulfil the conditions discussed below :

5.1 Intention to Create Legal Relationship An offer must intend to create legal relations. An offer must be such that when accepted, it will create legal relationship among the parties.

The question whether or not the parties have intention to create legal relationship can be answered with reference to type and terms of agreement and the circumstances under which the agreement is made. (As discussed in the last chapter.)

5.2 Certain and Unambiguous Terms The terms of the offer must be certain and unambiguous and not vague. If the terms of the offer are vague, no contract can be entered into because it is not clear as to what exactly the parties intended to do.

Example I *X offers to sell to Y "a 100 tons of oil." If X is a dealer in coconut oil and mustard oil, his offer is not certain because it is not clear whether he wants to sell coconut oil or mustard oil. But if X is a dealer in coconut oil only, it is clear that he wants to sell coconut oil. Hence, the offer is certain.*

Example II *X offers to sell to Y his car for Rs 1,00,000 or Rs 1,50,000. Here X's offer is not certain because it is not clear which of the two prices was to be given by Y.*

Note: If the terms of the offer are capable of being made certain, the offer is not regarded as vague. *For example*, *X* offers to sell to *Y* "a 100 tons of coconut oil." Here, the offer cannot be said to be uncertain on the ground that it is not clear what price is to be given for oil because in such a case if such an offer is accepted by *Y*, *Y* has to give only a reasonable price.

5.3 Different from a Mere Declaration of Intention The offer must be distinguished from a mere declaration of intention. Such statement or declaration merely indicates that an offer may be made or invited in future.

Example I *A father wrote to his would be son-in-law that his daughter would have a share of what he left after the death of his wife. It was held that the letter was a mere statement of intention and not an offer.* [*Farine v. Fickar*]

Example II *X, a broker of Mumbai wrote to Y a merchant of Ghaziabad stating the terms on which he is willing to do business. It was held that the letter was a mere statement of intention and not an offer.* [*Devidatt v. Shriram*]

Example III *A notice that the goods stated in the notice will be sold by tender does not amount to an offer to sell.* [*Spencer v. Harding*]

Example IV *An auctioneer advertised in a newspaper that a sale of office furniture will be held on a particular day. Mr X with the intention to buy furniture came from a distant place for the auction but the auction was cancelled. It was held that Mr X cannot file a suit against the auctioneer for his loss of time and expenses because the advertisement was merely a declaration of intention to hold auction and not an offer to sell.* [*Harris v. N. Nickerson*]

5.4 Different from an Invitation to Offer An offer must be distinguished from an invitation to offer. In case of an invitation to offer, the person making an invitation invites others to make an offer to him. It is prelude to an offer inviting negotiations or preliminary discussions.

Example I *Goods were displayed in the shop for sale with price tags attached on each article and self service system was there. One customer selected the goods but the owner refused to sell. It was held that the display of goods was only an invitation to offer and the selection of the goods was an offer by the customer to buy and refusal by owner was rejection of the offer and hence there was no contract and customer had no right to sue the owner.* [*Pharmaceutical Society of Great Britain v. Boots Cash Chemists Ltd.*]

Example II *A prospectus issued by a company for subscription of its shares and debentures is only an invitation to general public to make an offer to buy the shares/debentures which may or may not be accepted by the company.*

Similarly, an advertisement inviting quotations of lowest price in response to an enquiry amounts to invitation to offer but not an offer capable of acceptance, e.g. in Harvey v. Facie (1893), X sent a telegram to Y asking "Will you sell us Bumper Hall Penn? Telegraph Lowest Cash Price." Y replied through a telegram "Lowest Price for Bumper Hall Penn £900." X replied telegraphically stating "We agree to buy Bumper Hall Penn for £900 asked by you." Held, the quotation of price by Y was a mere invitation to offer. Consent of X to purchase the estate for £900 was an offer.

Distinction between Offer and Invitation to offer

Basis of Distinction	*Offer*	*Invitation to offer*
1. Meaning	Where a person shows his willingness to enter into a contract, it is called as an offer.	Where a person invites others to make an offer to him, it is called as an invitation to offer.
2. Purpose	An offer is made by a person with the purpose of entering into a contract.	The purpose of making an invitation to offer is to receive the offers or to negotiate the terms on which the person making the invitation is willing to contract.
3. Legal effect	An offer, if acted upon (*i.e.,* accepted), results in a contract.	An invitation to offer, if acted upon, only results in making of an offer.

5.5 Communication An offer must be communicated to the person to whom it is made. An offer is complete only when it is communicated to the offeree. One can accept the offer only when he knows about it. Thus, an offer accepted without its knowledge does not confer any legal rights on the acceptor.

Example I *G sent his servant L to trace his lost nephew. When the servant had left, G announced a reward of Rs 500 to anyone who traces the missing boy. L found the boy and brought him home. When L ca*greement + its enforce*d a suit against G to recover the reward. It was held that L was not entitled the reward because he did not know about the reward when he found the missing boy.* [*Lalman Shukla* v. *Gauri Dutt*]

Example II *S offered a reward to anyone who traces his lost dog. F brought the dog without any knowledge of the offer of reward. It was held that F was not entitled to the reward because F cannot be said to have accepted the offer which he did not know.* [*Fitch* v. *Snedakar*]

5.6 No Term the Non-compliance of which Amounts to Acceptance The offer must not contain a term the non-compliance of which would amount to acceptance. It means that while making the offer, the offerer can not say that if offer is not accepted before a certain date, it will be presumed to have been accepted.

An offer cannot impose the burden on the offeree to reply. Acceptance can not be presumed merely by silence.

Example *X writes a letter to Y. I offer to sell my horse for Rs 1,00,000. If I do not receive your reply by Friday next, I shall assume that you have accepted the offer Y* *does not reply. There is no contract since acceptance was not communicated by Y to X [Felthouse v. Bindley]*

5.7 Communication of Special Terms or Standard Form Contracts The special terms of the offer must also be communicated along with the offer. If the special terms of the offer are not communicated, the offeree will not be bound by those terms. The question of special terms arises generally in case of standard form of contracts. Standard contracts are made with big companies such as insurance companies, railways, shipping companies, banking companies, hotel companies, dry cleaning companies. Since such companies are in position to exploit the weakness of general public by including certain terms in the contract which may limit their liabilities, it is provided that the special terms of the offer must be brought to the notice of general public.

Example I *X purchased a steamer ticket for travelling from Dablin to White Haven and on the back of the ticket, certain conditions were printed one of which excluded the liability of the company for loss, injury or delay to the passengers or his luggage. X never looked at the back of the ticket and there was nothing to draw his attention to the conditions printed on the back side. His luggage was lost due to the negligence of the servants of the shipping company. It was held that X was entitled to claim compensation for the loss of his luggage in spite of the exemption clause because there was no indication on the face of the ticket to draw his attention to the special terms printed on the back of the ticket.* [*Handerson v. Stevenson*]

Example II *P deposited his bags in the cloakroom at a railway station. On the face of the receipt the words 'see back' were printed. One of the conditions printed on the back was 'the liability of the railway company shall be limited for any package to $10'. P's bag was lost and P claimed the actual value of bag amounting to $24. P admitted knowledge of the condition printed on the back but denied having read it. It was held that P could recover only $10 because the railways had given reasonable sufficient notice on the face of the ticket as to the existence of conditions.* [*Parker v. S.E. Rail Co.*]

Notes:

(i) In case the special conditions are printed in a language which the offeree does not understand, it is the offeree's duty to ask for the translation of the condition before accepting the offer and if he does not ask, it shall be presumed that he knows them and he will be bound by them.

(ii) The special terms and conditions must be brought to the knowledge of the offeree before the contract is concluded and not afterwards. A subsequent communication will not bind the acceptor unless he himself agrees thereto. For example, Mr *X* and Mrs *X* hired a room in hotel for a week. When they entered the room, they found a notice on the wall disclaiming the owner's liability for damages, loss or theft of articles. Some of their items were stolen. It was held that owner was liable because the notice was not a part of the contract as it came to the knowledge of the customer after the contract was entered into. [*Olley* v. *Marlborough Court Ltd.*]

(iii) The special terms and conditions must be reasonable. What is reasonable is a question of facts. If terms and conditions are unreasonable, the other party will not be bound by them. For example, if a dry cleaner limits his liability to 25% of the market price of the article in case of loss, the customer will not be bound by this condition because it means that the dry cleaner can purchase garments at 25% of the market price. In *Lily White Drycleaners* v. *Munnuswamy* AIR 1966 (Mad.), the receipt issued by the drycleaner stated that the drycleaner would be liable only to the extent of 10 times the drycleaning charges in the event of any damage to the clothes. Held, such a clause was unreasonable and opposed to public policy, and therefore, couldn't bind the parties.

6.0 CROSS OFFERS

6.1 Meaning Two offers which are similar in all respects made by two parties to each other, in ignorance of each other's offer are known as 'cross offers'.

6.2 Effect Cross offers do not amount to acceptance of one's offer by the other. Hence, no contract is entered into on cross offers.

Example *X of Agra sends a letter by post to Y of Delhi offering to sell his car for Rs 1 lakh. The letter is posted on 1st January and the same day, Y of Delhi sends a letter by post to X of Agra offering to buy X's car for Rs 1 lakh. These two letters cross each other. Y's letter is merely an offer and not the acceptance of X's letter. Here, both the parties are making offer and no party has accepted the offer. Therefore, no contract has been entered into. If they want to enter into a contract, at least one of them must send his acceptance to the offer made by the other.*

7.0 STANDING OFFER/OPEN OFFER/CONTINUING OFFER

7.1 Meaning An offer of a continuous nature is known as 'standing offer'.

7.2 Nature A standing offer is in the nature of a tender. 7.3 It is the same thing as an invitation to an offer.

7.3 Contract A contract is said to have been entered into only when an order is placed on the basis of the tender.

Example *X Ltd. requires a large quantity of certain goods during the 12 months period and gives an advertisement inviting tender in the leading newspaper. Z submitted the tender to supply those goods at a specific rate. Z's tender is accepted or approved. Now, Z's tender becomes a standing offer. Each order given by X Ltd. will be an acceptance of the offer.*

8.0 MEANING OF ACCEPTANCE

8.1 Acceptance means giving consent to the offer. It is an expression by the offeree of his willingness to be bound by the terms of the offer. According to Section 2(b) of the Indian Contract Act, 1872, "**A proposal is said to be accepted when the person to whom the proposal is made signifies his assent thereto. A proposal when accepted becomes a promise**." In other words, an acceptance is the consent given to offer.

Example *X offers to sell his car to Y for Rs 1,00,000. Y agrees to buy the car for Rs 1,00,000. Y's act is an acceptance of X's offer.*

9.0 WHO CAN ACCEPT AN OFFER ?

In general, an offer can be accepted only by the person or persons to whom it is made. The specific answer to this question can be given with reference to type of offer as under:

9.1 In case of Specific Offer An offer made to a definite person or particular group of persons (called specific offer) can be accepted only by that definite person or that particular group of persons to whom it has been made and none else.

Example *X sold his business to Y but this fact was not known to an old customer Z. Z placed an order for certain goods to X by name. Y supplied those goods to Z. It was held that there was no contract between Y and Z because Z never made any offer to Y.* [*Boulton* v. *Jones*]

9.2 In case of General Offer An offer made to the world at large or public in general (called general offer) can be accepted by any person having knowledge of the offer by fulfilling the terms of the offer.

Example *A company advertised that it would pay $100 to anyone who contracts influenza after using the smoke balls of the company according to the printed directions. Mrs Carlil used the smoke balls according to the printed directions but subsequently she contracted influenza. She filed a suit for the reward. It was held that she was entitled to recover the reward because she had accepted the offer by complying with the terms of the offer.* [*Carlil* v. *Carbolic Smoke Ball Company*]

10.0 HOW TO MAKE AN ACCEPTANCE ?

Like an offer, an acceptance may also be *either* an 'implied acceptance' *or* 'express acceptance'.

10.1 Express Acceptance An express acceptance is one which is made by words spoken or written.

Example *X says to Y, "Will you purchase my car for Rs 1,00,000?" Then Y says, "I am ready to purchase your car for Rs 1,00,000."*

10.2 Implied Acceptance An implied acceptance is one which is made otherwise than in words. In other words, it is inferred from the conduct of the person or the circumstances of the particular case.

Example *A transport company runs buses on different routes to carry passengers. X, a passenger boards the bus. X's act is an implied acceptance by X and he is bound to pay the fare.*

11.0 WHAT ARE THE LEGAL RULES FOR A VALID ACCEPTANCE ?

An acceptance to be valid must fulfil certain conditions which are discussed below.

11.1 Absolute and Unqualified According to Section 7(1) of the Indian Contract Act, 1872, "**In order to convert a proposal into a promise, the acceptance must be absolute and unqualified.**" It means, that an offer must be accepted as it is without any reservation, variation or condition. A qualified and conditional acceptance amounts to marking of a counter offer which puts an end to the original offer and it cannot be revived by subsequent acceptance.

Example I *X offered to sell his car for Rs 1,00,000 to Y. Y agreed to buy it for Rs 90,000. Y's act is a counter offer and not an acceptance of X's offer. Now, if Y accepts the original offer to buy the car for Rs 1,00,000, X will not be bound to sell the car because Y's counter offer has put an end to the original offer.* [*Nihal Chand* v. *Amar Nath*]

Example II *X offered to sell two plots of land to Y at a certain price. Y accepted the offer for one plot. It was held that the acceptance was not valid because it was not for the whole of the offer.* [*Bhawan* v. *Sadula*]

Example III *At an auction sale, X's bid was provisionally accepted at an auction sale. The acceptance was subject to confirmation. X withdrew his bid before confirmation. It was held that X could withdraw his bid before confirmation because the acceptance was not absolute but subject to confirmation.*

11.2 Manner According to Section 7(2) of the Indian Contract Act, 1872, the acceptance of an offer must be given in the following manner.

(a) If the proposal does not prescribe the manner in which it is to be accepted.	The offer must be accepted in some usual and reasonable manner.
(b) If the proposal prescribes the manner in which it is to be accepted	The offer must be accepted in the prescribed manner.

Consequences of not accepting the offer in the prescribed manner: If the offer is not accepted in the prescribed manner, the offerer may approve or reject such acceptance. If the offerer wants to reject it, he must inform the acceptor within a reasonable time that he is not bound by acceptance because it is not in the prescribed manner. If he does not do so within a reasonable time the presumption will be that he doesn't mind the offer being accepted in a different mode and will be bound by such acceptance.

Example *X of Agra sends a letter by post to Y of Delhi offering to sell his car for Rs 1,00,000 and also writes "send your acceptance by telegram." Y sends his acceptance by an ordinary letter. X can reject such acceptance on the ground that it was not accepted in the prescribed manner. But if he does not inform Y within the reasonable time, he shall be deemed to have accepted such acceptance and a valid contract will be formed between X and Y.*

11.3 Communication The acceptance must be signified (i.e. indicated or declared). In other words, the acceptance is complete only when it has been communicated to the offerer. A mere mental determination to accept is no acceptance in the eyes of law unless there is some external manifestation of that determination by words or conduct.

Example *X offered to supply coal to a Railway Company. The manager of the company accepted the offer and put it in the drawer of his table and forgot all about it. It was held that no contract was made because acceptance was not communicated. (Brogden v. Metropolitan Railway Co.]*

Note: In case of acceptance made by post, the proposer becomes bound by the acceptance as soon as the properly addressed and stamped letter of acceptance is duly posted even if such letter of acceptance is lost or delayed in post.

11.4 By Whom Acceptance must be communicated by the offeree himself or by a person who has the authority to accept. In other words, if acceptance is communicated by an unauthorised person, it will not give rise to legal relations.

Example *P applied for the post of a headmaster in a school. The managing committee passed a resolution approving P to the post but this decision was not communicated to P. But one member of the managing committee in his individual capacity and without any authority informed P about the decision. Subsequently, the managing committee cancelled its resolution and appointed someone else. P filed a suit for breach of contract. It was held that P's suit was not maintainable because there was no communication of acceptance as he was not informed about his appointment by some authorised person. [Powell v. Lee]*

***Note*:** The communication of acceptance is not necessary in case of unilateral contracts where the offerer prescribed a particular mode of acceptance. In such cases, it is sufficient if that prescribed mode is followed as in case of *Carlil* v. *Smoke Ball Co.* and *Har Bhajan Lal* v. *Harcharn Lal.*

11.5 To Whom Acceptance must be communicated to the offerer himself. In other words, if acceptance is communicated to an unauthorised person, it will not give rise to legal relations.

Example *F offered by a letter to buy his nephew's horse for $30 saying "If I hear no more about him, I shall consider the horse mine." The nephew sent no reply at all but told B his auctioneer, not to sell that particular horse as he intended to sell that horse to F. B sold the horse by mistake. It was held that F will not succeed because his nephew had not communicated acceptance to him. [Felthouse v. Bindley]*

11.6 Time Limit The acceptance must be given within the time prescribed (if any) or within a reasonable time (if no time is prescribed). What is reasonable time depends upon the facts and circumstances of the case.

Example *An offer to buy shares of a company was made in June but the acceptance was communicated in November, it was held that the offerer was not bound by the acceptance because the acceptance was not given within a reasonable time. [Ramsgate Victoria Hotel Co. v. Montefiore]*

11.7 Before Lapse of Offer The acceptance must be given before the offer lapses or is withdrawn. In other words, if an acceptance is made after the lapse or withdrawal of the offer, it will not give rise to legal relations.

Example *X offered by a letter to sell his car for Rs 1,00,000. Subsequently, X withdrew his offer by a telegram which was duly received by Y. After the receipt of telegram, Y sent his acceptance to X. In this case, the acceptance is invalid because it was made after the effective withdrawal of the offer.*

11.8 Mode of Acceptance—Acceptance may be given by performance of condition or acceptance of consideration.

12.0 PROVISIONS RELATING TO COMMUNICATION OF OFFER AND ACCEPTANCE

The communication of offer and acceptance must complete so as to bind the concerned parties because as soon as the communication is complete the parties loose the right of withdrawal or revocation. The legal provisions relating to the communication of offer and acceptance are as under:

12.1 When is Communication of Offer Complete ?

The communication of offer is complete when it comes to the knowledge of the person to whom it is made. In case an offer is made by post, its communication will complete when the letter containing the offer reaches the offeree.

Example *X of Agra sends a letter by post to Y of Delhi offering to sell his car for Rs 1,00,000. The letter is posted on 1st January and this letter reaches on 7th January. The communication of the offer is complete on 7th January.*

Note: An offer accepted without its complete communication does not bind the offerer.

Example *In case of Lalman v. Gauri Dutt, G sent his servant L to trace his lost nephew. When the servant had left, G announced a reward to anyone who traces the boy. L found the boy and brought him home. When L came to know of the reward, he claimed the reward. It was held that L was not entitled to the reward because he did not know about the offer when he found the missing boy.*

11.1 When is Communication of Acceptance Complete ?

The communication of acceptance is complete at different times for the proposer and acceptor. The rules regarding the communication of acceptance are as under:

The communication of acceptance is complete...	*When does the communication of acceptance complete...*
(i) ***As against the proposer***	When it is put in a course of transmission to him, so as to be out of the power of the acceptor. In case of acceptance made by post, the proposer becomes bound by the acceptance as soon as the properly addressed and stamped letter of acceptance is duly posted even if such letter of acceptance is lost or delayed in post.
(ii) ***As against the acceptor***	When it comes to the knowledge of the proposer. In case of acceptance made by post, the acceptor becomes bound by the acceptance only when the letter of acceptance is actually received by proposer.

Note: The time gap between the date on which the letter of acceptance is posted and the date on which the letter of acceptance is received by the proposer, can be utilized by the acceptor to withdraw his acceptance by a speedier mode of communication so that the revocation notice reaches the proposer before the letter of acceptance.

Example *X of Agra sends a letter by post to Y of Delhi offering to sell his car for Rs 1,00,000. The letter is posted on 1st January and this letter reaches Y on 7th January. Y sends his acceptance by post on 10th January but X receives this letter of acceptance on 15th January. In this case the legal position relating to the communication of offer and acceptance is as under.*

Communication	*When does the communication*	*Reason*
(*a*) ***Communication of offer***	7th January	The letter containing the offer reaches the offeree on 7th January.
(*b*) ***Communication of acceptance as against the prposer***	10th January	The letter of acceptance is posted on 10th January.
(*c*) ***Communication of acceptance as against the acceptor***	15th January	The letter of acceptance is received by the proposer on 15th January

After posting the letter of acceptance on 10th January, *Y* can withdraw his acceptance by a speedier mode of communication so that the revocation notice reaches the proposer before the letter of acceptance.

12.3 Position of Contracts over telephone/telex/fax A contract by telephone/telex/fax is treated on the same principle as an oral agreement made between two parties when they are face to face with each other. In such cases, the contract will complete only when the acceptance is received by the proposer and not when it is transmitted by the acceptor. Therefore, the acceptor must ensure that his acceptance is properly received by the proposer.

Example *X made an offer to Y over telephone. While Y was conveying his acceptance, the line went dead and X could not hear anything. In this case, there was no contract at that moment.*

Note: In case of contracts over telephone, telex or fax, the question of revocation (i.e. withdrawal of acceptance) does not arise because there is instantaneous communication of the offer and its acceptance (i.e. the offer is made and accepted at the same time).

13.0 PROVISIONS RELATING TO REVOCATION OF OFFER AND ACCEPTANCE

13.1 Meaning of Revocation The term 'revocation' means 'taking back' or 'withdrawal'.

13.2 What is the Time Limit within which Offer can be Revoked ?

According to Section 5 of the Indian Contract Act, a proposal may be revoked at any time before the communication of its acceptance is complete as against the proposer, but not afterwards. We know that communication of acceptance is complete as against the proposer when a properly addressed and stamped letter of acceptance is duly posted by the acceptor. Hence, an offer can be revoked at any time before the letter of acceptance is duly posted by the acceptor. Thus, the proposer may revoke his offer by a speedier mode of communication which will reach before the letter of acceptance is posted by the acceptor.

Example *X of Agra offers by a letter dated 1st January sent by post to sell his car to Y of Delhi for Rs. 1,00,000. Y accepts the offer on 7th January at 1 p.m. by letter sent by post. Here, X may revoke his offer at any time before 1 p.m. on 7th January but not afterwards.*

***Notes*:**

(i) Revocation must always be expressed.

(ii) Revocation must move from the offerer himself or a duly authorised agent.

(iii) Notice of revocation of a general offer must be given through the same channel by which the original offer was made.

(iv) Offer cannot be revoked even if the letter of acceptance is lost or delayed in transit.

13.3 What is the Time Limit within which Acceptance can be Revoked ?

According to Section 5 of the Indian Contract Act, "An acceptance may be revoked at any time before the communication of the acceptance is complete as against the acceptor, but not afterwards." We know that communication of acceptance is complete as against the acceptor when the letter of acceptance is actually received by the proposer. Hence, an acceptance can be revoked at any time before the letter of acceptance is actually received by the proposer. Thus an acceptor may revoke his acceptance by a speedier mode of communication which will reach before the letter of acceptance is received by the proposer.

Example *X of Agra offers by a letter dated 1st January sent by post to sell his car to Y of Delhi for Rs 1,00,000. Y accepts the offer on 7th January at 1 p.m. by a letter sent by post. X receives the letter of acceptance on 15th January at 3 p.m. Here, Y may revoke his acceptance at any time before 3 p.m. on 15th January but not afterwards.*

Acceptance is to Offer what a Lighted Match is to a Train of Gunpowder ?

The position relating to revocation of proposal and acceptance has been described by Anson in the following words,

"Acceptance is to offer what a lighted match is to a train of gunpowder. It produces something which can not be recalled or undone."

This statement primarily holds good under English law.

Here, **Gunpowder = Offer and Lighted Match = Acceptance**

When a lighted match is shown to a train of gunpowder, it explodes and something happens which cannot be undone. Similarly, an offer once accepted cannot be revoked. But so long a lighted match is not shown, the gunpowder remains inert and can be removed, similarly an offer can be revoked before it is accepted.

Similarly, once acceptance is given it cannot be revoked. But under Indian Contract Act, acceptance can be revoked by resorting to quicker means of communication so that the offerer learns about it before acceptance. Thus, the above statement doesn't hold in relation to revocation of acceptance under Indian law.

13.4 Simultaneous Delivery of Letter of Acceptance and the Telegram Containing Revocation of Acceptance In case the letter of acceptance and the telegram containing revocation of acceptance are delivered to the proposer at the same time, the formation of contract depends upon the fact which one is read first by the offerer. The contract shall be said to have been formed if the letter of acceptance is read first but shall not be said to have been formed if the telegram containing revocation of acceptance is read first. Generally, it is presumed that a man of ordinary prudence will first read the telegram. Hence the revocation will be quite effective.

13.5 No Revocation in case of Contract over Telephone or Telex or Fax In case of contracts over telephone or telex or fax, the question of revocation does not arise because there is instantaneous communication of the offer and its acceptance (i.e. the offer is made and accepted at the same time).

13.6 When is Communication of Revocation complete [Section 4] ?

The communication of revocation is complete at different times for person who makes it and the person to whom it is made. The rules regarding the communication of revocation are as under:

The communication of revocation is complete . . .	***When does the communication of revocation complete . . .***
(*i*) **As against the person who makes it**	When it is put in a course of transmission to the person to whom it is made so as to be out of the power of the person who makes it.
(*ii*) **As against the person to whom it is made**	When it comes to his knowledge.

Example *X proposes by letter to sell his car to Y for Rs 1,00,000. Y accepts X's proposal by a letter sent by post. If X revokes his proposal by telegram, the revocation of offer is complete as against X when the telegram is dispatched and it is complete as against Y when Y receives the telegram. If Y revokes his acceptance by telegram, the revocation of acceptance is complete against Y when the telegram is despatched and as against X when it reaches him.*

Conclusion :

1. **Revocation of offer binds the offeree only if it comes to his knowledge before the completion of its acceptance against the offeror.**

2. **Revocation of Acceptance binds the offeror only it comes to his knowledge before the completion of its acceptance against the offeree.**

14.0 WHEN DOES AN OFFER COME TO AN END ? (LAPSE OF AN OFFER)

An offer must be accepted before it lapses (i.e. comes to an end). An offer may come to end in any of the following ways:

14.1 By Revocation An offer lapses if the offerer revokes the offer before its acceptance by the offeree. According to Section 5 of the Indian Contract Act, a proposal may be revoked at any time before the communication of acceptance is complete as against the proposer but not afterwards.

Example I *X of Agra offers by a letter dated 1st January sent by post to sell his car to Y of Delhi for Rs 1,00,000. Y accepts the offer on 7th January at 1 p.m. by a letter sent by post. Here, X may revoke his offer at any time before 1 p.m. on 7th January but not afterwards.*

Example II *At an auction sale, the highest bidder can revoke his offer to buy before the fall of the hammer.*

14.2 By Lapse of Time An offer lapses if it is not accepted within the fixed time (if any prescribed in the offer) *or* within reasonable time (if no time is prescribed in the offer).

Example *An offer to buy shares of a company was made in June but the acceptance was communicated in November. It was held that offer to buy shares had lapsed because it was not accepted within a reasonable time.* [*Ramsgate Victoria Hotel Co.* v. *Montefiore*]

14.3 By Death or Insanity of the Offeror or Offeree An offer lapses if—

(*a*) the fact of death or insanity of offeror comes to the knowledge of the acceptor before he makes his acceptance.

(b) the offeree dies or becomes insane before accepting the offer because an offer can be accepted only by the offeree and not by any other person.

Notes : If the offer is accepted in ignorance of the death or insanity of the offerer, there will be a valid contract. It may be noted that in English law the death of the offerer terminates the offer even if acceptance is made in ignorance of the death.

14.4 By Failure to Accept condition Precedent An offer lapses if it is accepted without fulfilling the conditions of the offer.

Example *X offered to sell his car to Y for Rs 1,00,000 subject to the condition that Y should pay an advance of Rs 20,000 before a certain date. Y accepted the offer but did not send an advance of Rs 20,000. In this case, the offer has lapsed because the advance was not paid.*

14.5 By Counter Offer An offer lapses if the counter offer is made because a counter offer amounts to rejection of the original offer. Counter means making a fresh offer instead of accepting the original offer.

Example *X offered to sell his car to Y for Rs 1,00,000. Y said that he would buy it for Rs 90,000. X refused to sell for Rs 90,000. Subsequently, Y offered to buy the car for Rs 1,00,000. Here, Y's offer to buy for Rs 90,000 is a counter offer which terminates the original offer. Y's second offer to buy for Rs 1,00,000 is a fresh offer and not an acceptance of the original offer.* [*Hyde* v. *Wrench*]

14.6 By not Accepting in the Prescribed Mode or usual Mode An offer if it is not accepted in the specific manner (if any, prescribed in the offer) or in some usual and reasonable manner (if no manner has been prescribed in the offer).

Example *X offered to sell his car to Y for Rs 1,00,000 and wrote to Y "Send your acceptance by telegram." Y sent acceptance by an ordinary letter. X can reject such acceptance.*

14.7 By Rejection of Offer by Offeree An offer lapses if it is rejected by the offeree and offeree communicates his refusal to the offeror. An offer is said to be rejected if the offeree expressly rejects it or accepts it subject to certain conditions. It may be noted that once an offer is rejected, it can not be revived subsequently.

14.8 By Subsequent illegality or Destruction of Subject Matter of the Offer An offer lapses if it becomes illegal or the subject matter is destroyed before its acceptance by offeree.

Example I *X of Delhi offered supply of 100 tons of sugar to Y at Mumbai on a certain date. Before this offer is accepted by Y, the Central Government issued an order prohibiting the inter-state movement of sugar. Here, X's offer has come to an end.*

Example II *X of Delhi offered to sell his car to Y of Agra for Rs 1,00,000. Before the offer is accepted by Y, the car is destroyed by fire. Here X's offer has come to an end.*

PRACTICAL PROBLEMS

PROBLEM 1

X advertises in a newspaper that he would pay Rs 1,00,000 to anyone who traces his missing son. *Y* traced that boy and claimed the amount of reward. State whether *Y* is entitled to receive the amount of reward if (a) he did not know about the reward, (b) if he knew about the reward?

Solution

(a) *Y* is not entitled to receive the amount of reward because there can be no valid acceptance without the knowledge of the offer. [Leading case: *Lalman Shukla* v. *Gauri Dutt*]

(b) *Y* is entitled to receive the amount of reward because *Y* has accepted the general offer by tracing the missing son. [*Har Bhajan Lal* v. *Harcharan Lal*]

PROBLEM 2

Mr. X promises to pay Rs 1,000 per month to Mrs *X* but fails to pay the promised amount. Mrs *X* filed a suit against her husband for breach of this agreement. Will she succeed?

Solution

She will not succeed because it was a social agreement and the parties never intended to create any legal relations. [*Leading case: Balfour* v. *Balfour*]

PROBLEM 3

X Ltd. was appointed as an agent by *Y* Ltd. by an agreement. One of the clauses of the agreement provided, "This agreement is not entered into as a formal or legal agreement and shall not be subject to legal jurisdiction in the law courts." Is this agreement a valid contract?

Solution

This agreement is not a legally binding contract because there was no intention to create relations. [Leading case: *Rose & Frank Company* v. *Crompton Brothers*]

PROBLEM 4

X wrote to *Y*, his would be son-in-law, that his daughter would have a share of what he left after the death of his wife. Is the letter a valid offer by *X* to *Y*?

Solution

The letter was a mere statement of intention and not an offer at all. [*Farina* v. *Fickus*]

PROBLEM 5

X, a broker of Mumbai wrote to *Y*, a merchant of Ghaziabad stating the terms on which he is willing to do business. Is the letter a valid offer by *X* to *Y*?

Solution

The letter was a mere statement of intention and not an offer at all. [*Devidatt* v. *Shriram*]

PROBLEM 6

A notice that the goods stated in the notice will be sold by tender. Is the notice a valid offer to sell?

Solution

The notice was mere a statement of intention and not an offer to sell. [*Spencer* v. *Harding*]

PROBLEM 7

X, gave an advertisement in a newspaper that a sale of office furniture by auction will be held at 2 p.m. On 9th August 1997 at 'Pragati Maidan, Stall No. 420, New Delhi.' *Y* from Mumbai reached New Delhi on the appointed date and time but *X* had cancelled the auction sale. Advise *Y*.

Solution

Y cannot file a suit against *X* for his loss of time and expenses because the advertisement was merely an invitation to offer and not an offer to sell. [Leading case: *Harris* v. *Nickerson*]

PROBLEM 8

X delivered a coat to *Y*, a dry cleaner for dry cleaning and took the receipt. On the back of the receipt, certain conditions were printed in English language. One of the conditions printed on the back was "the liability of the dry cleaner company shall be limited to the 50% of the cost of the goods." *X* never looked at the back of the receipt. *X*'s coat was lost and *X* claimed the actual value of the coat. Discuss the legal position in each of the following alternative cases:

Case (*a*) If there was nothing on the face of the receipt to draw the attention to the conditions printed on the back side and *X* was a graduate in English.

Case (*b*) If on the face of the receipt, the words 'See Back' were printed in English but *X* did not read it.

Solution

Case (*a*) *X* was entitled to claim compensation for the loss of his coat because there was no indication on the face of the ticket to draw his attention to the special terms printed on the back of the ticket. [*Handerson* v. *Stevenson*]

Case (*b*) *X* was entitled to claim only 50% of the cost of the coat because there was sufficient notice on the face of the ticket as to the existence of the conditions.

PROBLEM 9

Mr. *X* and Mrs *X* hired a room in a hotel for a week. When they entered the room, they found a notice on the wall disclaiming the owner's liability for damages, loss or theft of articles. Some of their items were stolen. Discuss the legal position.

Solution

The owner of the hotel was liable because the special terms (i.e. notice) were communicated after the formation of the contract. [Leading case: *Olley* v. *Marlborough Court Ltd.*]

PROBLEM 10

X sold his business to *Y* but this fact was not known to an old customer *Z*. *Z* placed an order for certain goods to *X* by name. *Y* supplied the goods to *Z*. Is there a valid contract?

Solution

There was no contract at all between *Y* and *Z* because *Z*'s offer was a specific offer to *X* and *X* alone could accept it. [Leading case: *Boulton* v. *Jones*]

PROBLEM 11

X offered to sell his car for Rs 1,00,000 to *Y*. *Y* replies "I will pay Rs 90,000 for it." *X* refuses to sell at this price. *Y* then attempts the original offer but *X* refuses to sell his car. Discuss the legal position.

Solution

Y's first reply is a counter offer and not an acceptance of *X*'s offer and has put an end to the original offer. After having made the counter offer, *Y* cannot accept the original offer which has already come to an end. Hence, *X* is not bound to sell his car to *Y*.

[Leading case: *Nihal Chand* v. *Amar Nath*]

PROBLEM 12

X offered to sell two plots of land to *Y* at a certain price. *Y* accepted the offer for one plot. Is there a valid contract?

Solution

This is not a contract at all because the acceptance was not valid as it was not for the whole of the offer. [*Bhawan* v. *Sadula*]

PROBLEM 13

F offered by a letter to buy his nephew's horse for Rs 100 saying "If I hear no more about him, I shall consider the horse mine." The nephew sent no reply at all but told *B* his auctioneer not to sell that particular horse as he intended to sell that horse to *F*. *B* sold the horse by mistake. *F* filed a suit against *B*. Will he succeed?

Solution

F will not succeed because his nephew had not communicated acceptance to him.

[*Felthouse v. Bindley*]

PROBLEM 14

X made an offer to buy shares of *Y* Ltd. on 10th January 1997 but the allotment was made on 10th July 1997. Is *X* bound by the acceptance?

Solution

X is not bound by the acceptance because the acceptance was not given with in a reasonable time. [*Ramsgate Victoria Hotel Co.* v. *Montefore*]

PROBLEM 15

X of Agra sends a letter by post to *Y* of Delhi offering to sell his car for Rs 1,00,000. This letter is posted on 1st January and reaches *Y* on 7th January *Y* sends his acceptance by post on 10th January but *X* receives this letter of acceptance on 15th January. Answer each of the following questions.

(a) When is the communication of offer complete?

(b) When is the communication of acceptance complete as against the offerer?

(c) When is the communication of acceptance complete as against the acceptor?

(d) If *X* sends a telegram on 8th January revoking his offer, and this telegram reaches *Y* before the letter of the acceptance is posted. Is revocation of offer is valid?

(e) If *Y* sends a telegram on 14th January revoking his acceptance and this telegram reaches *X* before the letter of acceptance is received by *X*. Is revocation of acceptance is valid?

Solution

(a) The communication of offer is complete on 7th January because the letter containing the offer reaches the offeree on 7th January.

(b) The communication of acceptance is complete as against the offerer on 10th Jan. because the letter of acceptance is posted on 10th January.

(c) The communication of acceptance is complete as against the acceptor, on 15th Jan. because the letter of acceptance is received by the offerer on 15th January.

(d) *X*'s revocation is valid because *X* can revoke his offer at any time before the letter of acceptance is posted by the offeree.

(e) *Y*'s revocation is valid because *Y* can revoke his acceptance at any time before the letter of acceptance is received by the offerer.

TRUE OR FALSE QUESTIONS

State with reasons whether the following statements are True or False:

1. An express offer must be in writing.
2. A bid at an auction is an express offer.
3. An advertisement to pay reward to anyone who traces the missing boy of the advertiser is a specific offer.
4. An advertisement to sell goods by auction is an offer.
5. An advertisement offering reward to anyone who finds the lost dog of the advertiser is not an offer.
6. An acceptance of an invitation for dinner does not create any legal obligations.
7. Special terms and conditions of an offer may be communicated later on.
8. If the offeree remains silent, it means that he has accepted the offer.
9. A specific offer can be accepted by anyone.
10. A general offer can be accepted by anyone.
11. In social agreements, the usual presumption is that the parties do not intend to create legal relations.
12. In commercial agreements, the usual presumption is that parties intend to create legal relations.
13. A notice that the goods stated in the notice will be sold by tender amounts to an offer to sell.
14. The offer must not contain any term the non-compliance of which would amount to an acceptance.
15. Two offers which are similar in all respects made by two different parties to one person are known as cross offers.
16. A standing offer is in the nature of a tender.
17. A standing offer is an invitation to offer.

18. A counter offer amounts to rejection of original offer.
19. If counter offer is not accepted, the original offer can be accepted.
20. Acceptance may be communicated by any person.
21. Communication of offer is complete when the properly addressed and stamped letter of offer is duly posted by the offerer.
22. Communication of acceptance is complete when it comes to the knowledge of the offerer.
23. An offer can be revoked at any time before its acceptance is complete as against the offeree.
24. An acceptance can be revoked at any time before the letter of acceptance reaches the offerer.
25. The communication of acceptance is complete as against the acceptor when it is put into a course of transmission.
26. Death or insanity of the proposer automatically revokes the proposal.
27. Crossing of letters of offer in the post for the sale and purchase of the same article constitute a valid agreement.
28. A proposal may be revoked by the proposer before the posting of the letter of acceptance by the acceptor.
29. If an offer is made in the form of a promise in return for any act, the performance of that act even without any communication thereof is to be treated as an acceptance of the offer.
30. Acceptance can be made even without the knowledge of the offer.
31. An agreement with intention to create legal liability is not enforceable by law.
32. A valid contract results from identical cross offers.

Answers

1. False	2. False	3. False	4. False
5. False	6. True	7. False	8. False
9. False	10. True	11. True	12. True
13. False	14. True	15. False	16. True
17. True	18. True	19. False	20. False
21. False	22. False	23. False	24. True
25. False	26. False	27. False	28. True
29. True	30. False	31. False	32. False

VERY SHORT ANSWER TYPE QUESTIONS

1. What is an offer?
2. Who is called an offerer?
3. Who is called an offeree?
4. What is meant by an express offer?
5. What is meant by an implied offer?
6. What is meant by specific offer?

7. What is meant by general offer?
8. What are cross offers?
9. What is 'standing offer'?
10. What is acceptance?
11. What is an 'express acceptance'?
12. What is an 'implied acceptance'?
13. What happens if an offer is not accepted in the prescribed mode?
14. What happens if the acceptance is not made according to the mode prescribed?

SHORT ANSWER TYPE QUESTIONS

1. How can an offer be made?
2. To whom an offer can be made?
3. How can an offer be accepted?
4. Who can accept an offer?
5. When is communication of offer complete?
6. When is communication of acceptance complete as against the offerer?
7. When is communication of acceptance complete as against the acceptor?
8. When is communication of revocation complete?
9. Is there any limit of time after which an offer cannot be revoked?
10. Is there any limit of time after which an acceptance cannot be revoked?
11. When does an offer come to an end?
12. Can the following be regarded as offer?
    (a) An advertisement to sell goods by auction.
    (b) An advertisement by a Company for subscribing to its shares.
    (c) An advertisement offering reward to anyone who finds the lost dog of the advertiser.
    (d) Display of goods with price tags attached to them in the showcase.
    (e) A catalogue of goods for sale.
13. Comment on the following statements:
    (a) An invitation to offer is an offer.
    (b) Acceptance must be something more than a mere mental assent.
    (c) There cannot be a contract to make a contract.
    (d) Acceptance is to offer what a lighted match is to a train of gunpowder.
    (e) An acceptance to be effective must be communicated to the offerer.
14. Write short notes on the following:
    (a) Counter offer
    (b) Cross offer
    (c) Standing offer
    (d) Lapse of offer
    (e) General offer
    (f) Implied offer

(g) Implied acceptance
(h) Invitation to offer
(i) Contracts over telephone
(j) Contracts by post

15. Distinguish between the following:
    (a) Offer and invitation to offer
    (b) Offer and mere statement of intention
    (c) Counter offer and Cross offers
    (d) Revocation of offer and lapse of offer

ESSAY TYPE QUESTIONS

1. (a) What is an offer?
   (b) When does it complete?
   (c) Discuss the legal rules of a valid offer.
2. (a) What is an acceptance?
   (b) How can an offer be accepted?
   (c) Discuss the legal rules of a valid acceptance.
3. Explain briefly the legal provisions relating to the communication of offer.
4. Explain briefly the legal provisions relating to the communication of acceptance.
5. How and on what grounds does an offer stand revoked? Is there any limit of time after which an offer cannot be revoked?
6. How can an acceptance be revoked? Is there any limit of time after which an acceptance cannot be revoked?

CHAPTER

3 Capacity of Parties

1.0 WHO IS COMPETENT TO CONTRACT ?

1.1 According to Section 11 of the Indian Contract Act, 1872, "Every person is competent to contract who is of the age of majority according to the law to which he is subject, and who is of sound mind, and is not disqualified from contracting by any law to which he is subject."

1.2 **Three Tests** All the three tests (*viz.* age, soundness, disqualification) must be applied to determine whether a person is competent to contract or not. The following table summarises the result of these tests.

	Test to check competency	*The person is competent to contract*	*The person is not competent to contract in the following cases*						
I.	***Whether he is of the age of majority***	Yes	Yes	Yes	No	No	No	Yes	No
II.	***Whether he is of sound mind***	Yes	Yes	No	Yes	No	Yes	No	No
III.	***Whether he is not disqualified from contracting***	Yes	No	Yes	Yes	Yes	No	No	No

2.0 AGREEMENTS WITH A MINOR

2.1 Who is Minor ?

A minor is a person who has not attained majority. According to Section 3 of the Indian Majority Act, 1875, a person is deemed to have attained majority as under:

(a)	**Where a guardian of a minor's person or property is appointed under the Guardian and Wards Act, 1890**	On completion of 21 years
(b)	**Where minor's property has passed under the superintendence of the court of wards**	On completion of 21 years
(c)	**In other cases**	On completion of 18 years

2.2 Position of Agreements by a Minor

The law protects minor's rights because they are not mature and may not possess the capacity to judge what is good and what is bad for them. The position of agreements with or by a minor may be summarised as under:

1. **Validity** An agreement with a minor is void *ab-initio*
   [Leading case Law *Mohiri Bibee* v. *Dharmodas Ghosh*]

   Facts D, a minor borrowed a sum from *M* by executing a mortgage of his property in favour of *M*. Subsequently, *D* sued for setting aside the mortgage. The privy council held that Sections 10 and 11 of the Indian Contract Act make the minor's agreement void and therefore the mortgage was not valid. *M* prayed for refund of the amount by the minor. It was held that the money advanced to minor cannot be recovered because minor's agreement was void.

2. **No Estoppel** A minor is not estopped from setting up the plea of minority. He may plead infancy to escape from being liable. In *G. Bhimappa Meti* v. *Balangowda Bhimangowda*; the Bombay High Court held that "Where an infant represents fraudulently or otherwise that he is of age and thereby induces another to enter into a contract with him, he in an action founded on the contract, is not estopped from setting up infancy."

3. **In case of fraudulent representation of age by minor** According to Sections 30 and 33 of the Specific Relief Act, 1963, in case of a fraudulent misrepresentation of his age by the minor inducing the other party to enter into a contract, the court may award compensation to the other party. The Lahore High Court in *Khan Gul* v. *Lakha Singh* held that where the contract is set aside, the *status quo ante* should be restored and the court may direct the minor on equitable grounds to restore the money or property to the other party if the money or property could be traced.

4. **No Ratification on attaining the age of majority** An agreement with a minor cannot be ratified even after he attains majority. Ratification relates back to the date of the making of the agreement and therefore an agreement which was then void cannot be made valid by subsequent ratification. In *Indran Ramaswamy* v. *Anthaoppa,* a person on attaining majority, gave a promissory note in satisfaction of one executed by him for money borrowed when he was a minor. It was held that the claim under the promissory note could not be enforced because there was no consideration.

5. **Contract for supply of necessaries**

   (a) A person who has supplied the necessaries to a minor or to those who are dependent on him is entitled to be reimbursed from the property of such minor. [Section 68]

   (b) ***Meaning of necessaries:*** The term necessaries includes articles required to maintain a particular person in the state, degree and station in life in which he is. In India, food, clothing, shelter, education and marriage of a female have been held to be necessaries.

   (c) Section 68 covers the reimbursement for the supply of such items or loans for the same. *Example:* In case of *Nash* v. *Inman*, a minor bought eleven fancy coats from *N* for his own use. It was held that eleven coats at a time cannot be a necessity. Section 68 also covers the rendering of necessary services to a minor. *For example*, the lending of a money to a minor for the purpose of defending him in prosecution is deemed to be a service rendered to the minor.

   (d) '***Claim against property and not against person***' A claim for the payment of necessaries supplied can be made against the minor's property and not against the minor personally. In other words, a minor cannot be asked to expend labour in exchange.

(e) ***Liability of minor's guardian*** The parent or guardian of a minor cannot be held liable unless those goods/services are supplied/rendered to a minor as the agent of the parent or guardian.

6. **Contract by minor's guardian** The contracts entered into on behalf of a minor by his guardian or manager of his estate can be enforced by or against the minor if the contract (a) is within the scope of the authority of guardian or manager, and (b) is for the benefit of the minor. [*Subramanyam* v. *Subba Rao*]. It may also be noted that his guardian cannot enter into a valid contract for purchase of the immovable property for his/her service.
7. **Contract for the benefit of a minor** A minor can be a promisee. In *Raghva Chariar* v. *Srinivasa,* the Madras High Court held that a mortgage executed in favour of a minor who has advanced the mortgage money is enforceable by him or by any other person on his behalf. Similarly, in case of sale of goods by a minor, he is entitled to recover the price from the buyer. Thus, he may be a promisee but not promisor on a promissory note or a drawer but not drawee on a bill of exchange.
8. **Minor as a partner** A minor cannot become a partner in a partnership firm. However, according to Section 30 of Indian Partnership Act 1932, with the consent of all the partners for the time being be admitted to the benefits of partnership. In other words, he can share the profits without incurring any personal liability.
9. **Minor as an agent** A minor can act as an agent and bind his principal by his acts without incurring any personal liability.
10. **Minor as a shareholder or member of a company** A minor can become a shareholder or member of a Company if (a) the shares are fully paid up and (b) the articles of association do not prohibit so.
11. **Minor as an insolvent** A minor cannot be declared insolvent because he is not competent to contract.
12. **Minor as an Apprentice**—A minor can be apprentice if he is of at least 14 years of age.
13. **Minor as guarantor**—A mind can not be a guarantor.
14. **Validity of minor's agreement jointly with a major person** The agreements made by a minor jointly with a major person are void vis-a-vis the minor but can be enforced against the major person who has jointly promised to perform.
15. **Minor's liability in Tort** A minor may be held liable in Tort (civil wrong). But if in the course of doing what he is entitled to do under the contract, he is found guilty of negligence, he cannot be made liable on tort if he is not liable on the contract, e.g. in *Burnard* v. *Huggis*, a minor hired a horse promising not to jump it. He lent the horse to his friend who used the horse against the instructions and this led to the death of the horse. The minor was held liable on Tort. But in another case a horse was hired for riding. The horse was injured due to over-riding. The minor could not be held liable since the injury resulted from negligence in the course of what he was entitled to do under the contract. Since he was not liable on the contract himself, he could not be held liable in tort too. (*Jennings* v. *Randall*).

3.0 POSITION OF PERSONS OF UNSOUND MIND

3.1 Who is a Person of Unsound Mind ?

According to Section 12 of the Indian Contract Act, "A person is said to be of sound mind for the purpose of making a contract, if at the time when he makes it, is capable—

(a) to understand the terms of the contract,

(b) to form a rational judgment as to its effect upon his interests."

Thus, if a person is not capable of both, he is said to have suffered from unsoundness of mind. The examples of persons having an unsound mind include idiots, lunatics and drunken persons. A person who is so mentally deficient by birth as to be incapable of ordinary reasoning or rational conduct is said to be an 'idiot'. A person affected by lunacy is said to be 'lunatic'. A person can become lunatic at any stage of his life.

3.2 Position of a Person Who is Usually of Unsound Mind but Occasionally of Sound Mind	He may make a contract when he is of sound mind." **Example.** *A patient in a lunatic asylum who is at intervals of sound mind may contract during those lucid intervals.*
3.3 Position of a Person Who is Usually of Sound Mind but Occasionally of Unsound Mind	He may not make a contract when he is of unsound mind." **Example.** *A sane man who is so drunk that he cannot understand the terms of a contract or form a rational judgment as to its effect on his interest, cannot enter into contract whilst such drunkenness lasts.*

Thus, a person can enter into contract only when he is of sound mind.

3.4 Burden of Proof

The law presumes that every person is of sound mind.

The rules regarding the burden of proof are summarised as under:

Case	*The burden of proof lies on . . .*
I. Where a person is usually of sound mind	The burden of proving that he was of unsound mind at the time of contract lies on the person who challenges the validity of contract.
II. Where a person is usually of unsound mind	The burden of proving that he was of sound mind at the time of contract, lies on the person who affirms it.
III. In case of drunkenness or delirium from fever or other causes	The burden of proving that he was delirious from fever or was so drunk at the time of contract, lies on the person who challenges the validity of the contract.

3.4 Position of Agreements with Persons of Unsound Mind

The position of agreements of persons of unsound mind is summarised as under:

Persons of unsound mind	*Capacity to enter into contract*
I. Lunatic (i.e. a person who is mentallyderanged due to some mental strain or other personal experience but who has some lucid intervals of sound mind)	
(a) ***While he is of unsound mind***	He cannot enter into any contract. Any agreement entered into by him during this period is altogether void and he cannot be held liable thereon.
(b) ***While he is of sound mind***	He can enter into a valid contract and he is liable for such contracts.
II. Idiots (i.e. a person who is permanently of unsound mind)	He cannot enter into any contract. Any agreement entered into by him is altogether void and he is not liable thereon.
III. Drunken person (i.e. a sane person who is delirious from fever or who is so drunk that he cannot understand the terms of a contract or form a rational judgment as to its effect on his interest)	He cannot contract while such delirium or drunkenness lasts.

Exceptions The position of contracts with persons of unsound mind is identical with that of contracts with a minor. Thus, the position of contracts with persons of unsound mind is as under:

(a) He may enforce a contract for his benefit;

(b) His properties shall be attachable for realisation of money due against him for the supply of necessaries to him or to any of his dependents.

4.0 PERSONS DISQUALIFIED BY LAW

Besides minors and persons of unsound mind, there are others who are disqualified from contracting under the provisions of some other laws. Such persons have been discussed below:

4.1 Alien Enemy

(a) An alien is a person who is the citizen of a foreign country. An alien may either an alien friend or an alien enemy.

(b) An alien whose country is at peace with the Republic of India is called as alien friend. He has usually the full contractual capacity.

(c) An alien whose country is at war with the Republic of India is called an alien enemy. His contractual capacity can be summarised as under:

I. Position of contracts during the war	An alien enemy can *neither* enter into any contract *nor* can be sued in an Indian Court except by licence from the Central Government.

II. Position of contracts entered into before the war	
(a) ***If such contracts are against the public policy or are such that may benefit the enemy***	(a) Such contracts stand dissolved.
(b) ***If such contracts are not against public policy***	(b) Such contracts are merely suspended for the duration of the war and revived after the war is over unless they have already become time barred under the Law of Limitation Act.

Example *X, an Indian, carries on a business in Pakistan. He enters into a contract with Y who carries on business in India. Immediately after the formation of the contract, a war broke out between India and Pakistan. In this case, X becomes an alien enemy though he is Indian and the contract between X and Y (if not against the public policy) will be suspended for the duration of the war and revived after the war is over.*

4.2 Foreign Sovereigns and Ambassadors They **can enter into contracts** and enforce those contracts in our courts but they **cannot be sued** in our courts without the sanction of the Central Government unless they choose to submit themselves to the jurisdictions of our Courts.

Notes:

(i) An ex-king can be sued in our Courts.

(ii) Where a foreign sovereign etc. enter into a contract through an agent residing in India, the agent shall be held liable on the contract.

4.3 Convicts A person is called a convict during his period of sentence. His contractual capacity is summarised as under:

I. ***During the period of sentence***	He cannot enter into any contract.
II. ***After the expiration of the period of sentence or when he is on parole.***	He can enter into a contract. He can sue on a contract.

4.4 Company under the Companies Act or Statutory Corporation under the Special Act of Parliament The contractual capacity of the company and the statutory corporation is summarised as under:

I. ***In case of a Company***	Its contractual capacity is determined by the 'object clause' of its Memorandum of Association.
II. ***In case of Statutory Corporation***	Its contractual capacity is determined by the statute creating it.

Any act done in excess of the power given is *ultra vires* (i.e. beyond power) and hence void.

4.5 Insolvents When a person's debts exceed his assets, he is adjudged insolvent and his property stands vested in the Official Receiver or OfficialAssignee appointed by the Court. Such person—

(i) cannot enter into contracts relating to his property,

(ii) cannot sue,

(iii) cannot be sued.

Note: When the insolvent is discharged, the aforesaid disqualification is removed.

PRACTICAL PROBLEMS

PROBLEM 1

D, a minor, borrowed a sum from *M* by executing a mortgage of his property in favour of *M*. Subsequently, *D* sued for setting aside the mortgage. Is mortgage valid? Can *M* recover the sum advanced to *D*?

Solution

Section to which the given problem relates: Section 10 and Section 11.

Decision: The mortgage was not valid and the money advanced to minor cannot be recovered.

Reason: A minor is not competent to contract and hence minor's contract is void.

[**Leading case:** *Mohiri Bibee* v. *Dharmodas Ghosh*]

PROBLEM 2

X, on attaining majority, gave a promissory note in the satisfaction of one executed by him for money borrowed when he was a minor. Is this promissory note valid?

Solution

Sections to which the given problem relates: Section 10 and Section 11.

Decision: The promissory note is not valid and hence cannot be enforced.

Reason: There was no consideration.

[**Leading case:** *Ramaswamy* v. *Anthaoppa*]

PROBLEM 3

X, executed a mortgage in favour of *Y*, a minor who has advanced the money. Is this mortgage valid?

Solution

The mortgage is valid and hence the money advanced to *X* can be recovered.

Reason: A minor can be a promisee.

[**Leading case:** *Raghva Chariar* v. *Srinivasa*]

PROBLEM 4

X, a guardian, on behalf of *Y*, a minor, entered into a contract with *Z* for the purchase of a movable property for the benefit of the minor. Is the contract valid?

Solution

Section to which the given problem relates: Section 10 and Section 11.

Decision: This contract is valid provided this contract is within the scope of the authority of guardian.

Reason: This contract is for the benefit of minor.

[**Leading case:** *Subramanayan* v. *Subba Rao*]

PROBLEM 5

X, a minor entered into contract with *Y* to supply food and clothes to his dependents. *Y* supplied the same but *X* refused to pay for the same. Can *Y* recover anything?

Solution

Section to which the given problem relates: Section 68.

Decision: *Y* is entitled to be reimbursed from the property of such minor.

Reason: A person who has supplied the necessaries to a minor or those who are dependents on him is entitled to be reimbursed from the property of such minor.

PROBLEM 6

X, a guardian, on behalf of *Y*, her minor daughter, entered into a contract with *Z* whereby *Z* promised to marry her. Later on *Z* refused to marry. Can *Y* sue *Z* for damages?

Solution

Sections to which the given problem relates: Sections 10 and 11.

Decision: *Y* can sue *Z* for damages.

Reason: This contract was for the benefit of minor and a minor can be promisee.

[**Leading case:** *Mohiri Bibee* v. *Dharmodas Ghosh*]

PROBLEM 7

X agreed to sell his property worth about Rs 1,00,000 for Rs 10,000 only. *X*'s mother proved that *X* was a congenital idiot, incapable of understanding the transaction. Is this sale valid?

Solution

Section to which the given problem relates: Section 12.

Decision: This sale is void.

Reason: *X* was incapable of exercising his own judgment as to whether the act he is about to do is in his interest or not.

TRUE OR FALSE QUESTIONS

State with reasons whether the following statements are True or False:

1. A minor who is of sound mind is competent to contract.
2. A major who is of unsound mind is not competent to contract.
3. A contract with a minor is voidable at the option of the minor.
4. The court shall not award any compensation to the other party even in case of a fraudulent misrepresentation of his age by the minor.
5. An agreement with a minor can be ratified after he attains majority.
6. An agreement made by a minor with a major person can *neither* be enforced against the minor person *nor* against the major person.
7. A minor together with two major persons can form a partnership.
8. A minor can act as principal.
9. A minor cannot act as an agent.
10. A minor can be shareholder even if the shares are partly paid up.
11. A minor can also be declared as insolvent.
12. A minor can be a payee of a cheque.
13. A minor cannot recover the price of his goods sold on credit to a major person.

14. The contracts entered into on behalf of a minor by his guardian cannot be enforced against the minor.
15. A contract entered into on behalf of a minor by his guardian for the purchase of immovable property for the benefit of the minor is valid.
16. A minor is personally liable for the necessaries supplied to him or his dependents.
17. Guardian of a minor shall not be held liable for necessaries supplied to minor or his dependents.
18. A person who is usually of an unsound mind cannot enter into contract even when he is of a sound mind.
19. A person who is usually of a sound mind cannot enter into contract when he is of unsound mind.
20. A person of sound mind can make a valid contract even when he is so drunk that he is incapable of forming a rational judgment.
21. An idiot can never enter into a contract.
22. A lunatic can never enter into a contract.
23. An alien friend can acquire property in India.
24. A convict cannot enter into a contract even when he is on parole.
25. When a person is declared an insolvent, he cannot be sued.

Answers

1. False	2. True	3. False	4. False
5. False	6. False	7. False	8. False
9. False	10. False	11. False	12. True
13. False	14. False	15. False	16. False
17. True	18. False	19. True	20. False
21. True	22. False	23. True	24. False
25. True			

VERY SHORT ANSWER TYPE QUESTIONS

1. Is a minor who is of sound mind competent to contract?
2. What are necessaries?
3. Can a minor be promisee?

SHORT ANSWER TYPE QUESTIONS

1. Who is competent to contract?
2. State the effect on a contract where a minor, a party to the contract is guilty of deliberate misrepresentation with regard to his age.
3. Name the persons who are treated as persons of unsound mind.
4. Name the persons forbidden under other laws for the time being in force, to enter into contracts.

ESSAY TYPE QUESTIONS

1. (a) Who is competent to contract?

   (b) Discuss briefly the position of a minor with regard to the contracts entered into by him.

2. (a) Who are treated as persons of unsound mind?

   (b) State the legal position of contracts with such persons.

3. (a) Who are treated as persons disqualified by law other than minor and persons of unsound mind?

   (b) State the legal position of contracts with such persons.

CHAPTER 4 Consideration

1.0 WHAT IS CONSIDERATION ?

1.1 Consideration is one of the essential elements of a valid contract.

1.2 The term 'consideration' means something in return, i.e. *quid-pro-quo*. What is 'something' has been explained by Justice Lush J. in a leading English case *Currie* v. *Misa* as under:

"A valuable consideration in the sense of the law, may consist *either* in some right, interest, profit or benefit accruing to the one party *or* some forbearance, detriment, loss or responsibility given, suffered or undertaken by the other."

1.3 Thus, consideration must result in a benefit to the promisor, and a detriment or loss to the promisee or a detriment to both.

1.4 Section 2(d) of the Indian Contract Act, 1872 defines consideration as under:

"When, at the desire of the promisor, the promisee or any other person has done or abstained from doing, or does or abstains from doing, or promises to do or abstain from doing something, such act or abstinence or promise is called a consideration for the promise."

Example I *X promises to deliver his good to Y and Y promises to pay Rs 1,000 on delivery. In this case, the consideration for each of these promises is as under:*

Promise	*Consideration*
For X's promise	Y's promise to pay Rs 1,000 on delivery
For Y's promise	X's promise to deliver his goods.

Example II *X owes Y Rs 10,000. Y promises X not to file a suit against him for one year on X's agreeing to pay him Rs 500 more. In this case, the consideration for each of the promise is as under:*

Promise	*Consideration*
For X's promise	Forbearance on the part of Y to file a suit
For Y's promise	X's promise to pay Rs 500 more

2.0 ESSENTIAL ELEMENTS OF VALID CONSIDERATION

On the basis of definition of consideration as per Section 2(d), the essential elements of valid consideration are discussed below:

2.1 **It must be given only at the Desire of the Promisor** An act constituting consideration must have been done at the desire or request of the promisor. Thus, an act done at the desire of a third party or without the desire of the promisor cannot constitute a valid consideration.

Example I *A's son is lost and B goes in search for him. Can B claim remuneration from A, (a) if B does this act voluntarily, (b) if B does this act at the request of A, (c) if B does this act at the request of C?*

Case	*Decision and reason*
(a) If *B* does this act voluntarily	B cannot claim remuneration from *A* because he has not done at A's request.
(b) If *B* does this act at the request of *A*	B can claim remuneration from *A* because he has done at A's request.
(c) If *B* does this act at the request of *C*	B cannot claim remuneration from *A* because he has not done at A's request.

Example II *X spent Rs 1,00,000 on the construction of shops at the request of the collector of the District. In consideration of this Y a shopkeeper promised to pay some money to X. It was held that this agreement was void being without consideration because X had constructed the shops at the request of collector and not at the desire of Y. [Durga Prasad v. Baldeo]*

2.2 It may move from any Person An act constituting consideration may be done by the promisee himself or any other person (i.e. stranger to consideration). Thus, it is immaterial who furnishes the consideration and therefore, may move from the promisee or any other person who may be stranger to the contract.

Thus, privity of consideration is not required.

Example *X, by a deed of gift transferred certain property to her daughter Y with a direction that Y should pay Z an annuity. On the same day, Y executed a deed in writing in favour of Z and agreed thereby to pay the annuity. Later, Y refused to pay the annuity on the plea that no consideration had moved from Z. It was held that Z was entitled to maintain suit because a consideration need not necessarily move from the promisee, it may move from any other person (i.e. X in the present case). [Chinnayya v. Ramayya]*

2.3 It may be Past or Present or Future The consideration may be past, present or future.

Past Consideration	The consideration which has already moved before the formation of agreement. **Example** *X renders some service to Y at Y's request in the month of May. In June, Y promises to pay X Rs 1,000 for his past services. Past services amount to past consideration. X can recover Rs 1,000 from Y.*
Present Consideration	The consideration which moves simultaneously with the promise, is called present consideration. **Example** *In case of cash sale, promise to pay the price and promise to deliver the goods are performed simultaneously.*
Future Consideration	The consideration which is to be moved after the formation of agreement is called future consideration. **Example** *X promises to deliver certain goods to Y after 10 days and Y promises to pay after 10 days from the date of delivery.*

Tutorial Note: The English Law does not recognise the past consideration.

2.4 It must be of Some Value The consideration need not be adequate to the promise but it must be of some value in the eye of the law. It is understood in the sense of something in return and that something can be anything, adequate or grossly inadequate. According to Explanation 2 of Section 25, an agreement to which the consent of the promisor is freely given is not void merely because the consideration is inadequate; but the inadequacy of the consideration may be taken into account by the Court in determining the question whether the consent of the promisor was freely given.

Example *A agrees to sell a horse worth Rs 1,000 for Rs 10. A denies that his consent to the agreement was freely given. The inadequacy of the consideration is a fact which the Court should taken into account in considering whether or not A's consent was freely given.*

2.5 It must be Real and not Illusory The consideration must be real and not illusory. (*i.e.,* existing only in name)

Example I *X engages Y for doing a certain work and promises to pay reasonable remuneration. This promise is not enforceable because the consideration is uncertain.*

Example II *X promises to put life into Y's dead wife and Y promises to pay Rs 1,00,000. This agreement is void because consideration is physically impossible to perform.*

2.6 Something other than the Promisor's Existing Obligation The act constituting consideration must be something which the promisor is not already bound to do because a promise to do what a promisor is already bound to do adds nothing to the existing obligation.

Example I *X promises Y, his advocate, to pay an additional sum if the suit was successful. The suit was declared in favour of X but X refused to pay additional sum. It was held that Y could not recover additional sum because the promise to pay additional sum was void for want of consideration as Y was already bound to render his best services under the original agreement. [Ramchandra Chintamana v. Kalu Raju]*

Example II *X had received summons to appear before a court of law as witness on behalf of Y who promised to pay some money for his trouble. It was held that the promises to pay money was void for want of consideration because X was under a legal duty to appear as witness before court of law. [Collins v. Godefrey]*

2.7 Lawful The consideration must *neither* be unlawful *nor* opposed to public policy.

Example I *X promises Y to pay Rs 1,000 to beat Z, Y beats Z and claims Rs 1,000 from X, X refuses to pay. Y cannot recover because the agreement is void on the ground of unlawful consideration.*

Example II *X promises Y to obtain an employment in the public service and Y promises to pay Rs 1,000 to X. The agreement is void on the ground of unlawful consideration.*

3.0 STRANGER TO CONSIDERATION CAN SUE BUT A STRANGER TO A CONTRACT CAN NOT SUE

3.1 A Stranger to Consideration can sue

A stranger to consideration can sue because the consideration can be furnished or supplied by any person whether he is the promisee or not.

3.2 A Stranger to contract can not sue—A stranger to a contract cannot sue because of the absence of privity of contract (i.e. relationship subsisting between the parties to a contract).

Example I *X owes Y Rs 1,00,000 and sells his property to Z. Z promises to pay off X's debt to Y. Z fails to pay. Y cannot sue Z because he is a stranger to a contract.*

Example II *X bought tyres from Dunlop Rubber Co. and sold them to Y, a sub-dealer who agreed with X not to sell below Dunlop's list price and to pay to Dunlop Co. Rs 150 as damages on every tyre he undersold. Y sold two tyres at less than the list price and thereupon, Dunlop Co. sued him for the breach. It was held that the Dunlop Co. could not maintain the suit because it was a stranger to the contract. [Dunlop P. Tyre Co. Ltd. v. Selfridge & Co. Ltd.]*

3.3 Exceptions to Rule 'A stranger to a contract can not sue'.

The rule that a stranger to a contract cannot sue, is subject to the following exceptions:

1. **In case of Trusts** The beneficiary (i.e. the person for whose benefit the trust has been created) may enforce the contract.

   Example I *X transferred certain properties to be held by Y for the benefit of Z. Z can enforce the agreement even though he is not a party to the agreement. [M.K. Rapai v. John]*

   Example II *X sent an insured parcel to Y. On loss of such parcel, Y sued the post office. It was held that Y was entitled to sue though he was stranger to the contract because on receipt of such article, the post office becomes a trustee for the addressee. [Amir Ullah v. Central Govt.]*

   Example III *X, the father of a minor daughter D, and Y, the father of a minor son S, entered into an agreement of marriage for D and S on the condition that after the marriage, Y would pay his daughter-in-law D, Rs 500 as kharch-e-paan daan (betel box money). After the marriage took place, X died. On Y's refusal to pay the agreed amount to D, the Court held that D was entitled to recover the amount as a beneficiary of trust even if she was a stranger to the contract between X and Y. [Khwaja Mohd. v. Hussaini Begum (1910) 37.1A 152]*

2. **In Case of Family Settlement** The person for whose benefit the provision is made under family arrangements may enforce the contract.

   Example *A provision of marriage expenses of a female member was made in a Joint Hindu Family. On partition, the female member sued for such expenses. It was held that she was entitled to sue. [Rakhmanbai v. Govind]*

3. **Acknowledgment** The person who becomes an agent of third party by acknowledgment or otherwise, can be sued by such third party.

   Example *X* receives Rs 1,000 from *Y* for paying the same to *Z*. *X* acknowledges this receipt to *Z*. *Z* can recover the amount from *X* because *X* will be regarded as *Z*'s agent. [*Surjan* v. *Nanat*]

4. **Assignment of a Contract** Where a benefit under a contract has been assigned, the assignee can enforce the contract subject to all equities between the original parties to the contract e.g. the assignee of an insurance policy.

4.0 CONTRACTS WITHOUT CONSIDERATION

4.1 General Rule 'No Consideration, No Contract

According to Section 25, **an agreement made without consideration is void.**

4.2 **Example** *Abdul Aziz* v. *Mazum Ali*, a promise to donate Rs 500 towards construction of a mosque was held unenforceable as it was a gratuitous promise lacking consideration.

4.3 But gratuitous promise shall be enforceable by law if the promisee on the faith of such promise suffered a liability as suffering of detriment forms a valid consideration [*Kedarnath* v. *Gorie Mohd.*]

4.4 **Exceptions to the General Rule "No Consideration, No Contract"**

The following are the exceptions to the general rule No Consideration, No Contract:

1. **Agreements made on Account of Natural Love and Affection [Section 25(1)]** Such agreement made without consideration is valid if:

   (i) it is expressed in writing,

   (ii) it is registered under the law,

   (iii) it is made on account of love and affection, and

   (iv) it is between parties standing in a near relation to each other.

   Note: Mere Nearness of relation by itself does not necessarily imply natural love and affection.

   Example I *A Hindu husband by a registered document promised to pay his wife Rs 1,000 per month as her pin-pocket money. This agreement is valid.*

   Example II *A Hindu husband by a registered document, after referring to quarrels and disagreements between himself and his wife, promised to pay his wife Rs 1,000 p.m. for her maintenance. It was held that this agreement was void because there was no natural love and affection. [Rajlakhi Devi v. Bhoot Nath Mookherjee]*

2. **Promise to Compensate for Past Voluntary Services [Section 25(2)]** Such promise made without consideration is valid if:

   (i) it is a promise to compensate (wholly or in part); and

   (ii) the person who is to be compensated has already done something voluntarily or has done something which the promisor was legally bound to do.

   Example I *X finds Y's purse and gives it to him. Y promises to give Rs 500 to X. This is a valid contract even though the consideration did not move at the desire of Y, the promisor.*

   Example II *X, a neighbour helped putting down the fire in Y's house. Afterwards, Y promised X to give Rs 1,000. This is a valid contract even though the consideration did not move at the desire of the promisor.*

   Example III *X, supported Y's infant son. Y promised to pay X's expenses in so doing. This is a valid contract. Here, X has done that act which Y was legally bound to do.*

3. **Promise to Pay Time Barred Debt [Section 25(3)]** Such promise without consideration is valid if:

   (i) it is made in writing,

   (ii) it is signed by the debtor or his agent, and

   (iii) it relates to a debt which could not be enforced by a creditor because of the Law of Limitation Act.

Note: According to The Law of Limitation Act, a debt which remains unpaid or unclaimed for a period of 3 years becomes a time barred debt which is legally not recoverable. But a promissory note issued in personal capacity by the wife of a debtor to pay his time barred debt of her husband is not enforceable [Pestonjee v. Bai Meharbai]

4. **Completed Gifts [Explanation to Section 25]** The gifts actually made by a donor and accepted by the donee are valid even without consideration. Thus, a completed gift needs no consideration.

   Example *X transferred some property to Y by a duly written and registered deed as a gift. This is a valid contract even though no consideration moved.*

5. **Agency [Section 185]** No consideration is necessary to create an agency.
6. **Gratuitous Bailment**—No Consideration is necessary for gratuitous bailment.

PRACTICAL PROBLEMS

PROBLEM 1

X promises to donate Rs 10,000 towards the repairs of a temple. *X* does not pay. Can the trustees recover the promised amount from *X* (a) if they have not incurred any liability on the faith of the *X*'s promise, (b) if they have incurred any liability on the faith of this promise.

Solution

Case (a)

Decision: The trustees cannot recover the promised amount from *X*.

Reason: The agreement is void in the absence of any consideration.
[**Leading case:** *Abdul Aziz* v. *Masum Ali*]

Case (b)

Decision: The trustees can recover the promised amount from *X*.

Reason: The agreement is valid because it was supported by consideration in the form of a detriment to the trustees who had incurred liability on the faith of the promise made by *X*.

[**Leading case:** *Kedar Nath v. Gorie Mohammad*]

PROBLEM 2

X, a Hindu husband executed a registered document in favour of *Y*, his wife, whereby he promised to pay her Rs 1,000 per month. Later, *X* did not pay. Can *Y* recover from *X* (a) if this promise was made without any disagreement and quarrels between them? (b) if this promise was made after disagreement and quarrels between them?

Solution

Section to which the given problem relates: Section 25(1).

Case (a)

Decision: *Y* could recover from *X*.

Reason: The agreement was valid because it was made on account of natural love and affection between *X* and *Y*.

Case (b)

Decision: *Y* could not recover from *X*.

Reason: The agreement was void because it was not made an account of natural love and affection between *X* and *Y*.

[**Leading case:** *Rajlakhi Devi* v. *Bhoot Nath Mookherjee*]

PROBLEM 3

X supports *Y*'s infant son without being asked to do so. *Y* promises to pay *X* Rs 10,000 for doing so. Later, *Y* refuses to pay. Can *X* recover the promised amount from *Y*?

Solution

Section to which the given problem relates: Section 25(2).

Decision: *X* can recover the promised amount from *Y*.

Reason: *X* has done something which the promisor was legally bound to do.

PROBLEM 4

X owes *Y* Rs 10,000 but this debt is time barred. In a birthday party of *Z*, who is a friend of *X* and *Y*, *X* promises *Y* to pay this debt. Later, *X* refuses to *Y*. Can *Y* recover the promised amount from *X*?

Solution

Section to which the given problem relates: Section 25(3).

Decision: *Y* cannot recover anything from *X*.

Reason: *X*'s promise was *neither* in writing *nor* signed by him or his agent.

PROBLEM 5

X gifted Rs 50,000 to *Y* his neighbour's wife by executing a registered gift deed without any consideration. There is no near relation between *X* and *Y*. Is this gift valid?

Solution

Section to which the given problem relates: Explanation I to Section 25.

Decision: The gift is valid.

Reason: A completed gift needs no consideration and need not be a result of natural love and affection or near relation.

PROBLEM 6

X promises to make a gift of Rs 50,000 to *Y*, his neighbour's wife. Is this promise valid?

Solution

Section to which the given problem relates: Explanation I to Section 25.

Decision: A promise to gift is not valid.

Reason: This agreement is void for want of consideration and at the same time, there is only a promise to gift and not a completed gift.

PROBLEM 7

X, who was badly in need of money offered to sell his car worth Rs 1,00,000 to *Y* for Rs 10,000. Before the car was delivered, *X* received an offer of Rs 20,000 and refused to carry out the contract on the ground of inadequacy of consideration. Is *X* liable to *Y* for damages?

Solution

Section to which the given problem relates: Explanation 2 to Section 25.

Decision: *X* is liable to *Y* for damages.

Reason: An agreement to which the consent of the party is freely given is not void merely because the consideration is inadequate.

PROBLEM 8

X, a client promises to pay *Y*, his advocate Rs 10,000 in addition to his fees if he succeeds. *X* succeeds but refuses to pay Rs 10,000. Can *Y* recover from *X*?

Solution

Decision: *Y* cannot recover the additional sum of Rs 10,000.

Reason: *X*'s promise to pay the additional sum was without any consideration. The consideration must be something which the promisor is not already bound to do. Here, *Y* was bound to render the best of his services under the original contract.

[**Leading case:** *Ramchandra Chintaman v. Kalu Raju*]

TRUE OR FALSE QUESTIONS

State with reasons whether the following statements are 'True' or 'False'.

1. An act constituting consideration must have been done at the desire of the promisor or any other person.
2. An act constituting consideration must be done by the promisee only.
3. Consideration must result in a benefit to both parties.
4. Consideration must result in a detriment to both parties.
5. Consideration must result in a benefit to the promisor and a detriment to promisee.
6. Consideration may result in a detriment to both parties.
7. Past consideration is no consideration in India.
8. Consideration must be adequate.
9. An agreement to which the consent of the promisor is freely given is not void merely because the consideration is inadequate.
10. The inadequacy of the consideration may be taken into account by the Court in determining the question whether the consent of the promisor was freely given.
11. Consideration must be something which a promisor is not already bound to do.
12. A stranger to consideration can sue.
13. A stranger to a contract cannot sue.
14. In case of trusts, the beneficiary being a stranger to a contract cannot sue.
15. An assignee cannot enforce the contract because he is a stranger to a contract.
16. Nearness of relation by itself does not necessarily import natural love and affection.
17. Natural love and affection by itself does not necessarily import nearness of relation.
18. A promise made without consideration to compensate the person who has already done something voluntarily is valid if it is made in writing.

19. A verbal promise to pay a time barred debt is valid.
20. Completed gifts need no consideration.
21. Completed gifts without consideration are valid only if they are out of natural love and affection, and near relation.
22. A promise to gift to wife is valid.
23. No consideration is required to create an agency.
24. If the promisee undertakes a liability on the faith of a promise made by a promisor to contribute to charity, the contract is valid.

Answers

1. False	2. False	3. False	4. False
5. False	6. True	7. False	8. False
9. True	10. True	11. True	12. True
13. True	14. False	15. False	16. True
17. True	18. False	19. False	20. True
21. False	22. False	23. True	24. True

VERY SHORT ANSWER TYPE QUESTIONS

1. Define Consideration.
2. What is meant by 'Stranger to Consideration'?
3. What is meant by 'Stranger to Contract'?
4. What is meant by 'Privity of Contract'?
5. What is meant by 'Privity of Consideration'?

SHORT ANSWER TYPE QUESTIONS

1. Comment on the following statements:
   (a) No consideration, No contract.
   (b) Insufficiency of consideration is immaterial but an agreement without consideration is void.
   (c) A stranger to consideration can sue.
   (d) A stranger to a contract cannot sue.

ESSAY TYPE QUESTIONS

1. (a) Define Consideration.
   (b) What are the essential elements of a valid consideration?
2. (a) Explain the rule that a stranger to a contract cannot sue with the help of an illustration.
   (b) Are there any exceptions to this rule?
3. (a) Explain the rule 'No consideration, No contract'.
   (b) Are there any exceptions to this rule?

CHAPTER

5 Free Consent

1.0 CONSENT

1.1 What is the Meaning of Consent ?

The consent means an act of assenting to an offer. *According to Section 13*, "**Two or more persons are said to consent when they agree upon the same thing in the same sense.**" Thus, consent involves identity of minds in respect of the subject matter of the contract. In English Law, this is called '*consensus-ad-idem*'.

1.2 What is the Effect of Absence of Consent ?

When there is no consent at all, the agreement is void *ab-initio*, i.e. it is not enforceable at the option of either party.

Example I *X has one Maruti car and one Fiat car. He wants to sell Fiat car. Y does not know that X has two cars. Y offers to buy X's Maruti car for Rs 50,000. X accepts the offer thinking it to be an offer for his Fiat car. Here, there is no identity of mind in respect of the subject matter. Hence there is no consent at all and the agreement is void ab-initio.*

Example II *X, an illiterate woman, signed a gift deed thinking that it was a power of attorney. This gift deed was not explained to her. It was held that her mind did not go with that writing and she never intended to sign a gift deed. Hence, there was no consent at all and the agreement was void ab-initio. [Bala Devi v. S. Majumdar]*

2.0 FREE CONSENT

2.1 What is the Meaning of Free Consent ?

Free consent is one of the essential elements of a valid contract as it is evidenced by Section 10 which provides that all agreements are contracts if they are made by the free consent of the parties . . .

According to Section 14, "**Consent is said to be free when it is not caused by (a) coercion, or (b) undue influence, or (c) fraud, or (d) misrepresentation, or (e) mistake**".

2.2 What is the Effect of Absence of Free Consent ?

When there is consent but it is not free (i.e. when it is caused by coercion or undue influence or fraud or misrepresentation), the contract is usually voidable at the option of the party whose consent was so caused.

Example *X threatens to kill Y if he does not sell his house to X. Y agreed to sell his house to X. In this case, Y's consent has been obtained by coercion and therefore, it cannot be regarded as free.*

3.0 COERCION

3.1 What is the Meaning of Coercion ?

Coercion means compelling a person to enter into a contract under a pressure or a threat. *According to Section 15*, a contract is said to be caused by coercion when it is obtained by—

(a) committing any act which is forbidden by the Indian Penal Code; or

(b) threatening to commit any act which is forbidden by the Indian Penal Code; or

(c) unlawful detaining of any property; or

(d) threatening to detain any property.

Example I *X beats Y and compels him to sell his car for Rs 50,000. Here, Y 's consent has been obtained by coercion because beating someone is an offence under the Indian Penal Code.*

Example II *A Hindu widow of 13 years was forced to adopt a boy under threat that her husband's dead body would not be allowed to be removed if she does not adopt the boy. She adopted the boy. Here, widow's consent has been obtained by coercion because preventing the dead body from being removed for cremation is an offence under Section 297 of the Indian Penal Code. [Ranganayakamma v. Alwar Setti]*

Note: The Indian Penal Code need not be in force at place where the coercion is employed and at the time when coercion is employed.

3.2 Against Whom/by Whom Coercion may be Exercised ?

Coercion may proceed from any person (whether a party to contract or stranger) and may be directed against any person (whether a party to contract or stranger)

Example I *X threatens to kill Z, Y's son, if Y refuses to sell his house to him. Y agrees to sell his house. Here, Y's consent has been obtained by coercion though Z is a stranger to the contract.*

Example II *X threatens to kill Y if Y refuses to sell his house to Z. Y agrees to sell his house. Here, Y's consent has been obtained by coercion though X is a stranger to the contract.*

3.3 What is the Effect of Threat to File a Suit ?

A threat to file a suit (whether civil or criminal) does not amount to coercion unless the suit is on false charge. Threat to file a suit on false charge is an act forbidden by the Indian Penal Code and thus will amount to an act of coercion.

3.4 What is the Effect of Threat to Commit Suicide ?

A 'suicide' and a 'threat to commit suicide' are not punishable but an attempt to commit suicide is punishable under the Indian Penal Code. It does not mean that 'suicide' and threat to commit suicide are permitted by Indian Penal Code. The question whether a 'threat to commit suicide' amounts to coercion or not was considered by **Madras High Court** in the case of *Chikham Ammiraju* v. *Seshamma*. In this case, a person threatened to commit suicide if his wife and son did not execute a release deed in favour of his brother in respect of certain property. It was ***held*** **that *though a threat to commit suicide is not punishable under the Indian Penal Code, it is deemed to be forbidden by that code*.** Hence, the threat to commit suicide amounted to coercion and the release deed was therefore, voidable.

Duress V. Coercion: The English law uses the term 'duress' for coercion. However, the two are different in the following way:

(a) Duress does not include detaining of property or threat to detain property.

(b) Duress can be employed only by a party to the contract or his agent.

3.5 What are the Effects of Coercion ?

The effects of coercion are as follows:

Effects	*Provision*
(a) Option of aggrieved party to avoid the contract	When consent to an agreement is obtained by coercion, the contract is voidable at the option of the party whose consent was obtained by coercion (also called aggrieved party). [Section 19]
(b) Obligation of aggrieved party to restore benefit	The party rescinding a voidable contract shall restore the benefit received by him under the contract, to the person from whom the benefit was received. [Section 64]
(c) Obligation of other party to repay or return	A person to whom money has been paid or anything delivered under coercion, must repay or return it. [Section 72]

Example I *X threatens to kill Y if he does not sell his house for Rs 1,00,000 to X. Y sells his house to X and receives the payments. Here, Y's consent has been obtained by coercion. Hence, this contract is voidable at the option of Y. If Y decides to avoid the contract, he will have to return Rs 1,00,000 which he had received from X.*

Example II *A railway company refused to deliver certain goods to the consignee, except upon the payment of an illegal charge for carriage. The consignee pays the sum charged in order to obtain the goods. He is entitled to recover so much of the charge as was illegally excessive.*

3.6 On Whom Burden or Onus of Proof Lies

The burden of proving that consent was obtained by coercion, and the aggrieved party would not have entered into contract had coercion not been employed, lies on the party intending to avoid the contract.

4.0 UNDUE INFLUENCE

4.1 What is the Meaning of Undue Influence ?

The term 'undue influence' means dominating the will of the other person to obtain an unfair advantage over the other. According to Section 16(1), a contract is said to be induced by undue influence—

(a) where the relations subsisting between the parties are such that one of them is in a position to dominate the will of the other, and

(b) the dominant party uses that position to obtain an unfair advantage over the other.

4.2 When a Person is Deemed to be in a Position to Dominate the will of another ?

According to Section 16(2), a person is deemed to be in a position to dominate the will of another in the following three circumstances:

Circumstances	*Examples*
(a) Where he holds a real or app- arent authority over the other	Master and servant, parent and child, Income Tax Officer and assessee, Principal and a temporary teacher
(b) Where he stands in a fiduciary relation to the other	Trustee and beneficiary, spiritual adviser (Guru) and his disciples, solicitors and client, guardian and ward
(c) Where he makes a contract with with a person whose mental capacity is temporarily or permanently affected by reason of age, illness or mental or bodily distress	Medical attendant and patient

4.3 In Which cases there is No Presumption of Domination of Will ?

According to judicial decisions held in various cases, there is no presumption of undue influence in the following relationships:

(a) Husband and wife (other than pardanashin)

(b) Landlord and tenant

(c) Creditor and debtor

Example I *X advanced Rs 10,000 to his son Y during his minority and obtained upon Y's coming of age, a bond from Y for Rs 1,00,000. Here, there is misuse of parental influence.*

Example II *A poor Hindu widow agreed to pay interest at 100% p.a. because she needed the money to establish her right of maintenance. It was held that the lender was in position to dominate the will of widow. [Ranee Annpurni v. Swaminath]*

Example III *A devotee gifted her property to her spiritual guru to secure benefits to her soul in next world. It was held that spiritual guru was in position to dominate the will of devotee. [Mannu Singh v. Umadat Pandey]*

Example IV *X, an illiterate old man of about 90 years, physically infirm and mentally in distress, executed a gift deed of his properties in favour of Y his nearest relative who was looking after his daily needs and managing his cultivation. It was held that Y was in a position to dominate the will of X. [Sher Singh v. Prithi Singh]*

4.4 What is the Effect of Undue Influence ?

When consent to an agreement is caused by undue influence, the contract is voidable at the option of the party whose consent was so caused.

Discretion of Court Any such contract may be set aside *either* absolutely *or*, if the party who was entitled to avoid it has received any benefit thereunder, upon such terms and conditions as the court may seem just.

Example I *A's son forged B's name to a promissory note. B, under threat of prosecuting A's son, obtains a bond from A, for the amount of the forged note. If B sues on this bond, the court may set the bond aside.*

Example II *A, a moneylender, advances Rs 10,000 to B, an agriculturist, and by undue influence, induces B to execute a bond for Rs 20,000 with interest at 6 per cent per month. The court may set the bond aside, ordering B to repay Rs 10,000 with such interest as may seem just.*

4.5 On Whom the Burden of Proof Lies ?

When a contract is avoided on the ground of undue influence, the liabilities of dominant party and weaker party to prove are as under:

The **weaker party** has to prove—	**In case of unconscionable transaction, the dominant party** has to prove that such contract was not induced by undue influence.
(a) that the other party was in a position to dominate the wil	
(b) that the other party actually used his influence to obtain an unfair advantage	**Note:** *A transaction is said to be unconscionable if the dominant party makes an exorbitant profit of the other's distress.*
(c) that the transaction is unconscionable (unreasonable)	

Example *X was in great need of money. The market rate of interest prevailing at that time was 15% to 24%. A lender agreed to grant the loan at 30% because of stringency in the money market. This cannot be called as unconscionable transaction merely because of an unusual high rate of interest. However, if the lender agreed to grant the loan at a rate which is so high (say 75% or 100%) then the Court considers it unconscionable, and the transaction will be called unconscionable.*

4.6 How can Presumption of Undue Influence be Rebutted ?

The presumption of undue influence can be rebutted by showing—

(a) that the dominant party has made a full disclosure of all the facts to the weaker party before making the contract;

(b) that the price was adequate; and

(c) that the weaker party was in receipt of competent independent advice before entering into the contract.

4.7 What is the Position of Contracts with Pardanashin Woman ?

Meaning of Pardanashin Woman: A woman who observes complete seclusion (i.e. who does not come in contact with people other than her family members) is called pardanashin woman.

Legal Presumption: A contract with a pardanashin woman is presumed to have been induced by undue influence.

Burden of Proof: The other party who enters into a contract with a pardanashin woman must prove—

(a) that he made full disclosure of all the facts to her;

(b) that she understood the contracts and the implications of the contract;

(c) that she was in receipt of competent independent advice before entering into the contract.

5.0 COMPARISON BETWEEN COERCION AND UNDUE INFLUENCE

5.1 Similarities: In case of both coercion and undue influence, the consent is not free and the contract is voidable at the option of the aggrieved party.

5.2 Distinction: Coercion differs from the undue influence in the following respects:

Basis of Distinction	*Coercion*	*Undue Influence*
1. Relevant Sec.	Sec. 15	Sec. 16
2. Relationship	Parties to a contract **may or may not be related** to each other.	Parties to a contract are **related** to each other under some sort of relationship.
3. Consent	Consent is obtained by giving a threat of **an offence or committing an offence**	Consent is obtained by **dominating the will.**
4. Nature of Pressure	It involves **physical** pressure.	It involves **moral** pressure.
5. Who can exercise	It can be exercised even by a **stranger** to the contract.	It can be exercised only by a **party to a contract** and not by a stranger.
6. Restoration of benefit	The aggrieved party who is rescinding the contract has to return the benefit received to the other party under Sec. 64.	The aggrieved party may or may not be required to return the benefit in whole or in part as per Court's direction.
7. Presumption	Coercion has to be proved by the aggrieved party alleging it in. It is not presumed by the law.	It may be presumed by the law under certain circumstances. The party against whom such presumption lies must disprove it.
8. Nature of liability	The party committing the crime may be punishable under I.P.C	It doesn't involve any criminal liability

6.0 FRAUD

6.1 What is the Meaning of Fraud ?

The term 'fraud' means a false representation of fact made wilfully with a view to deceive the other party.

Section 17 defines the fraud as follows:

'Fraud' means and includes any of the following acts committed by a party to a contract, or with his connivance, or by his agent, with intent to deceive another party thereto or his agent, or to induce him, to enter into the contract:

1. **the suggestion, as to a fact, of that which is not true, by one who does not believe it to be true**; e.g. *X* sells to *Y* locally manufactured goods as imported goods charging a higher price, it amounts to fraud.
2. **the active concealment of a fact by one having knowledge or belief of the fact.** Mere concealment is no fraud. But where steps are taken by a seller concealing some material facts so that the buyer even after a reasonable examination cannot trace the defects, it will amount to fraud, e.g. *X* a furniture

dealer, conceals the cracks in furniture sold by him by using some packing material and polishing it in such a way that the buyer even after reasonable examination cannot trace the defect, it would tentamount to fraud through active concealment.

3. **a promise made without any intention of performing** it; e.g. in *Shireen* v. *John*, AIR (1952) Punj 227, a man and a woman underwent a ceremony of marriage with the husband not regarding it as a real marriage. Held, the husband had no intention to perform the promise from the time he made it and hence the consent of the wife was obtained under fraud.
4. **any such act or omission as the law specially declares to be fraudulent**, e.g. under Companies Act and Insolvency Acts, certain kinds of transfers have been declared to be fraudulent.
5. **any other act fitted to deceive**. It covers those acts which deceive but are not covered under any other clause.

6.2 What are the Essential Elements of Fraud ? On the basis of aforesaid definition of fraud, the essential elements of fraud are as follows:

1. **By a party to a contract:** The fraud must be committed by a party to a contract or by anyone with his connivance or by his agent. Thus, the fraud by a stranger to the contract does not affect the validity of the contract.

   Example *The directors of a company issued a prospectus containing false statements. A shareholder who had subscribed for the shares on the faith of the prospectus wanted to avoid the contract. It was held that he could do so because the false statement made by directors amounted to fraud. [Reese River Silver Mining Co. v. Smith]*

2. **False representation:** There must be a false representation and it must be made with the knowledge of its falsehood. Where the representation was true at the time when it was made but becomes untrue before the contract is entered into and this fact is known to the party who made the representation, it must be corrected. If it is not so corrected, it will amount to a fraud.

   Example I *X fraudulently informs Y that X's estate is free from encumbrance. On the faith of X's statement, Y buys the estate. Actually the estate is subject to mortgage. Here, Y may avoid the contract because X with the intention to deceive Y induced Y to enter into a contract.*

   Example II *On 1st January X correctly informs Y that the monthly sales of his business are Rs 1,00,000. In May the contract of sale of business was signed. During this period the monthly sales decreased to Rs 50,000. It was held that Y was entitled to avoid the contract because X's failure to disclose the fall in monthly sales amounted to fraud. [With V O' Flanagan]*

3. **Representation as to fact:** The representation must relate to a fact. In other words, a mere opinion, a statement of expression or intention does not amount to fraud.
4. **Actually deceived:** The fraud must have actually deceived the other party who has acted on the basis of such representation. In other words, an attempt to deceive the other party by which the other party is not actually deceived, is not a fraud.

   Example *X had a defective cannon. In order to conceal the defect, he put a metal plug on it. Y bought this cannon without examining. When Y used it, it burst. Y refused to pay the balance. It was held that Y was liable to pay as he* *was not actually deceived by fraud because he would have bought it even if no deceptive plug was inserted. [Horsefull v. Thomas]*

5. **Suffered loss:** The party acting on the representation must have suffered some loss.

   Conclusion : Fraud is said to have taken place where a party to the contract (Not stranger) made a false representation as to the fact with the knowledge of its falsehood with a view to deceive the other party who actually acted on the faith of such representation and suffered a loss.

6.3 What are the Effects of Fraud ?

The effects of fraud are as follows:

1. **Right to Rescind the Contract** The party whose consent was caused by fraud can rescind (cancel) the contract but he cannot do so in the following cases:
   - (i) where silence amounts to fraud, the aggrieved party cannot rescind the contract if he had the means of discovering the truth with ordinary diligence;
   - (ii) where the party gave the consent in ignorance of fraud;
   - (iii) where the party after becoming aware of the fraud takes a benefit under the contract;
   - (iv) where an innocent third party before the contract is rescinded acquires for consideration some interest in the property passing under the contract,
   - (v) where the parties cannot be restored to their original position.
2. **Right to Insist Upon Performance** The party whose consent was caused by fraud may, if he thinks fit, insist that the contract shall be performed and that he shall be put in the position in which he would have been if the representation made had been true.

   Example *A fraudulently informs B that A's estate is free from encumbrance. B thereupon buys the estate. The estate is subject to a mortgage. B may either avoid the contract, or may insist on its being carried out and the mortgage-debt redeemed.*
3. **Right to Claim Damages** The party whose consent was caused by fraud, can claim damages if he suffers some loss.

6.4 Does Silence amount to Fraud ?

6.4.1 General Rule According to explanation to Section 17, "Mere silence as to facts likely to affect the willingness of a person to enter into a contract is not fraud."

Example I *A sells, by auction, to B a horse which A knows to be unsound. A says nothing to B about the horse's unsoundness. This is not fraud by A.*

Example II *A and B, being traders, enter upon a contract. A has private information of a change in prices which would affect B's willingness to proceed with the contract. A is not bound to inform B.*

Example III *In Shri Krishna v. Kurukshetra University (AIR 1976 SC 376) a candidate failed to mention the fact of shortage of attendance in the examination form, It was held that there was no fraud.*

6.4.2 Exceptions to the General Rule The general rule that silence does not amount to fraud has the following exceptions :

Where the circumstances of the case are such that, regard being had to them, it is the duty of the person keeping silence to speak. Such duty arises in the following two cases:

(i) **Where parties stand in fiduciary relationship like parent-child, trustee-beneficiary.**

Example *A sells by auction to B, a horse which A knows to be unsound. B is A's daughter and has just come of age. Here, the relation between the parties would make it A's duty to tell B if the horse is unsound.*

(ii) **Where the silence itself is equivalent to speech**.

Example *B says to A, "If you do not deny it, I shall assume that the horse is sound." A says nothing. Here A's silence is equivalent to speech. If the horse turns out to be vicious A can be held liable for fraud.*

(iii) **Half Truth:** Half truth is worse than a blatant lie. Partial truthful disclosures may easily deceive the other party, e.g. prospectus of a company disclosing only average dividend declared by the company in the last 5 years instead of the actually declining dividends over that period is a glaring example of half truth amounting to fraud.

7.0 MISREPRESENTATION

7.1 What is the Meaning of Misrepresentation ?

The term 'Misrepresentation' means a false representation of fact made innocently or non-disclosure of a material fact without any intention to deceive the other party. Section 18 defines the term 'misrepresentation' as follows:

"Misrepresentation" means and includes—

1. the positive assertion, in a manner not warranted by the information of the person making it, of that which is not true, though he believes it to be true;
2. any breach of duty which, without an intent to deceive, gains an advantage to the person committing it, or any one claiming under him, by misleading another to his prejudice or to the prejudice of anyone claiming under him;
3. causing, however innocently, a party to an agreement, to make a mistake as to the substance of the thing which is the subject of the agreement.

7.2 What are the Essential Elements of Misrepresentation ?

On the basis of the aforesaid definition of misrepresentation, the essential elements of misrepresentation are discussed below:

1. **By a party to a contract:** The representation must be made by a party to a contract or by anyone with his connivance or by his agent. Thus, the representation by a stranger to the contract does not affect the validity of the contract.
2. **False representation:** There must be a false representation and it must be made without the knowledge of its falsehood i.e. the person making it must honestly believe it to be true.
3. **Representation as to fact:** The representation must relate to a fact. In other words, a mere opinion, a statement of expression or intention does not amount to misrepresentation.

   Example *X sold his Hotel to Y and stated that a part of the hotel is occupied by a tenant who is most desirable. In fact the rent from the tenant could only be* *recovered under pressure and was currently much in arrear. It was held that Y was entitled to avoid the contract because X's statement amounted to misrepresentation. [Smith's case]*

4. **Object:** The representation must be made with a view to inducing the other party to enter into contract but without the intention of deceiving the other party.
5. **Actually acted:** The other party must have acted on the faith of the representation.

   Example I *X says to Y who intends to purchase his land, "My land produces 2 tons of rice per acre." X believes the statement to be true although he has no sufficient ground for the belief. Y purchases X's land believing X's statement. Later on, Y finds that the land produces only 1.5 tons of rice per acre. Here X's representation is misrepresentation.*

   Example II *The prospectus of a company contained a statement that the company had been authorised by Special Act of the Parliament to use steam or mechanical power for running the trains. In fact, the authority to use the steam was subject to the approval of the 'Board of Trade'. But this fact was not mentioned in the prospectus. The Board of Trade did not approve the use of steam, and consequently the company wound up. The shareholders of the company filed a suit against the directors for fraud. But the court held that they were not liable for fraud. The directors were not guilty of fraud, as they honestly believed that once the Parliament had authorised the use of steam, the consent of the Board of Trade practically concluded. [Derry v. Peek]*

   Conclusion : Misrepresentation is said to have taken place where a party to the contract (not stranger) made a false representation as to the fact without the knowledge of its falsehood without the intention of deceiving the other party who actually acted on the faith of such representation.

7.3 What are the Effects of Misrepresentation ? [Section 19]

The effects of misrepresentation are as follows:

1. **Right to Rescind the Contract** The party whose consent was caused by misrepresentation can rescind (cancel) the contract but he cannot do so in the following cases:
   (i) where the party whose consent was caused by misrepresentation had the means of discovering the truth with ordinary diligence;
   (ii) where the party gave the consent in ignorance of misrepresentation;
   (iii) where the party after becoming aware of the misrepresentation, takes a benefit under the contract;
   (iv) where an innocent third party, before the contract is rescinded, acquires for consideration some interest in the property passing under the contract;
   (v) where the parties cannot be restored to their original position.

Example *X, leads Y erroneously to believe that 1000 mounds of indigo are made annually at X's factory. Y examines the accounts of X's factory which show that only 800 mounds of indigo have been made. After this Y buys the factory. Here, the contract is not voidable on account of X's misrepresentation because Y after becoming aware of misrepresentation takes the benefit under the contract.*

2. **Right to Insist upon Performance** The party whose consent was caused by misrepresentation may if he thinks fit, insist that the contract shall be performed, and that he shall be put in the position in which he would have been if the representation made had been true.

8.0 COMPARISON BETWEEN FRAUD AND MISREPRESENTATION

8.1 Similarities There are basically two similarities in case of fraud and misrepresentation as follows:

(a) In both the cases, a false representation is made by a party;

(b) In both the cases, the contract is voidable at the option of the party whose consent is obtained by fraud or misrepresentation.

8.2 Distinction Fraud differs from misrepresentation in the following respects:

Basis of Distinction	*Fraud*	*Misrepresentation*
1. *Intention*	A wrong representation is made wilfully with the intention to deceive the other party.	A wrong representation is made innocently, i.e., without any intention to deceive the other party.
2. *Knowledge of falsehood*	The person making the wrong statement does not believe it to be true.	The person making the wrong statement believes it to be true.
3. *Right to claim damages.*	The aggrieved party can claim damages.	The aggrieved party cannot claim damages.
4. *Availability of means to discover the truth*	Except where silence amounts to fraud, the contract is voidable even if the aggrieved party had the means of discovering the truth with ordinary diligence.	The aggrieved party cannot avoid the contract if he had the means of discovering the truth with ordinary diligence.

9.0 MISTAKE

9.1 What is the Meaning of Mistake ?

A mistake is said to have occurred where the parties intending to do one thing by error do something else. Mistake is an erroneous belief concerning something.

9.2 What are the Types of Mistake ?

The mistake can be of following two types:

Mistake of Law

Type of mistake of law	*Effect*
(a) Mistake of Indian Law	The contract is **not voidable** because everyone is supposed to know the law of his country.
(b) Mistake of Foreign Law	A mistake of foreign law is treated as mistake of fact, i.e. the contract is void if both the parties are under a mistake as to a foreign law because one cannot be expected to know the law of other country.

Mistake of Fact Mistake of fact can be *either* bilateral mistake *or* unilateral mistake.

9.3 ***Bilateral Mistake*** The term 'bilateral mistake' means where both the parties to the agreement are under a mistake. According to Section 20, "Where both the parties to an agreement are under a mistake as to a matter of fact essential to the agreement, the agreement is void." Thus, the agreement is void if :

(i) **Both the parties are under a mistake**

(ii) **Mistake is of fact but not of law.**

According to explanation to Section 20, "An erroneous opinion as to the value of the thing which forms the subject matter of the agreement is not to be deemed a mistake as to a matter of fact."

Example *X buys a painting believing it to be worth Rs 50,000 while in fact it is worth only Rs 5,000. The contract is not void.*

(iii) **Mistake relates to an essential fact.**

Example I *A agrees to sell to B a specific cargo of goods supposed to be on its way from England to Mumbai. It turns out that, before the date of the bargain, the shop conveying the cargo had been cast away and the goods lost. Neither party was aware of facts. The agreement is void.*

Example II *A agrees to buy from B a certain horse. It turns out that the horse was dead at the time of the bargain, though neither party was aware of the fact. The agreement is void.*

Example III *A, being entitled to an estate for the life of B, agrees to sell it to C. B was dead at the time of the agreement, but both parties were ignorant of the fact. The agreement is void.*

Bilateral Mistake as to the Subject Matter: An **agreement is void** where there is a bilateral mistake as to the subject matter. A bilateral mistake as to the subject matter includes the following:

(i) Mistake as to the existence of subject matter
(ii) Mistake as to the quantity of subject matter
(iii) Mistake as to the quality of subject matter
(iv) Mistake as to the price of subject matter
(v) Mistake as to the identity of subject matter
(vi) Mistake as to the title of subject matter

Example I *A agrees to buy from B a certain horse. It turns out that the horse was dead at the time of bargain though neither party was aware of the fact. The agreement is void because there is bilateral mistake as to the existence of subject matter.*

Example II *A agrees to buy from B all his horses believing that B has two horses but B actually has three horses. The agreement is void because there is bilateral mistake as to the quantity of subject matter.*

Example III *A agrees to buy a particular horse from B. Both believe it to be a race horse but it turns to be a cart horse. The agreement is void because there is bilateral mistake as to the quality of the subject matter.*

Example IV *A agrees to buy a particular horse from B who mentioned in his letter the price as Rs 1,150 instead of 5,150. The agreement is void because there is bilateral mistake as to the price of the subject matter.*

Example V *A agrees to buy from B a certain horse. B has one race horse and one cart horse. A thinks that he is buying race horse but B thinks that he is selling cart horse. The agreement is void because there is bilateral mistake as to the identity of subject matter.*

Example VI *A agrees to buy a particular horse from B. That horse is already owned by A. The agreement is void because there is bilateral mistake as to the title of the subject matter.*

Bilateral Mistake as to the Possibility of Performance: The **agreement is void** where there is a bilateral mistake as to the possibility of performance. In other words, where the parties to an agreement believe that the agreement is capable of performance, while in fact it is not so, the agreement is treated as void. The impossibility may *either* be physical *or* legal.

9.4 ***Unilateral Mistake*** The term 'unilateral mistake' means where only one party to the agreement is under a mistake. According to Section 22, "A **contract is not voidable** merely because it was caused by one of the parties to it being under a mistake as to matter of fact."

Example *X sold Oats to Y by sample and Y, thinking that they were old Oats, purchased them. In fact, the Oats were new. It was held that Y was bound by the contract. [Smith v. Hughes]*

Exceptions: The agreement is void where a unilateral mistake relates to the identity of the person contracted with or as to the nature of the contract.

Example I *One Blenkarn, knowing that Blenkarn & Co. was a reputed customer of Lindsay & Co., placed an order with Lindsay & Co. by imitating the signatures of Blenkarn. The goods were then sold to Cundy, an innocent buyer. A suit was filed by Lindsay & Co. against Cundy for recovery of goods. It was held that there was no contract between Lindsay & Co. and Blenkarn as Lindsay & Co. never intended to contract with Blenkarn and as such, Cundy did not get a good title and hence he must return the goods or make payment of goods. [Cundy v. Lindsay & Co.]*

Example II *A woman by falsely misrepresenting her to be wife of a well known Baron (a millionaire) obtained two pearl necklaces from a firm of jewellers on the pretext of showing them to her husband before buying. She pledged them with a broker, who in good faith paid her Rs 1,00,000. A suit was filed by the jeweller against the broker. It was held that there was no contract between the jeweller and the woman as the jeweller never intended to contract with her and as such, the broker did not get a good title and hence he must return the goods. [Lake v. Simmons]*

Example III *S knew that on account of his criticism of the plays in the past, he would not be allowed entry to the performance of a play at the theatre. The managing director of the theatre gave instructions that ticket should not be sold to S. S, however, obtained a ticket through one of his friends. On being refused admission to the theatre, he sued for damages for breach of contract. It was held that there was no contract between the theatre company and S as the theatre company never intended to contract with S. [Said v. Butt]*

Example IV *An old illiterate man was induced to sign a Bill of Exchange by means of a false representation that it was a mere guarantee. It was held that he was not liable for the Bill of Exchange because he never intended to sign a Bill of Exchange. [Foster v. Mackinnon]*

But the contract shall be valid and binding in spite of the mistake as to the identity of the parties in all those cases where the parties were willing to enter into contract with any person. Thus, if the mistake only relates to the attributes or motives of the person such as creditworthiness, it will not make the contract void. It may at the most make it voidable for fraud, e.g. in ***Phillips* v. *Brooks***. One Mr North entered a Jeweller's shop, selected a ring which the jeweller agreed to sell against payment by cheque which North signed in the name of Sir G B, a man of credit and standing. North pledged the ring with Brooks. In the meanwhile the cheque got dishonoured. It was held that the contract between North and the Jeweller was valid as the jeweller agreed to sell goods to the very person who entered the shop. Thus, the contract had been made before the goods were delivered to North. As the contract was induced by fraud, the jeweller could rescind the contract. However, the pledge made by North was valid. The jeweller's right was only confined to filing a suit against North to recover damages.

9.5 What are the Effects of Mistake ?

The effects of mistake are as follows:

(a) In case of Bilateral Mis-take as to essential fact	The agreement is void.
(b) In case of Unilateral Mis-take	
(i) as to the identity of the person contracted with	The agreement is void.
(ii) as to the nature of contract	The agreement is void.
(iii) as to other matter	The agreement is not void
(c) Obligation of aggrieved party	He must restore any benefit received by him under the contract to the other party from whom the benefit had been received [Section 64]
(d) Obligation of other party	The person to whom money has been paid or anything delivered by mistake must repay or return it. [Section 72]

10.0 DISTINCTION BETWEEN VOID AND VOIDABLE CONTRACT

Basic of Distinction	*Void Contract*	*Voidable Contract*
1. *Meaning*	A contract which ceases to be enforceable by law becomes void when it ceases to be enforceable. [Sec. 2 (j)]	An agreement which is enforceable by law at the option of one or more of the parties thereto, but not at the option of the other or others, is a voidable contract. [Sec. 2(i)]
2. *Right to Recind the contract*	No Question arises	The party whose consent was not free has the right to rescind the contract.

3. ***Sue for Performance of contract***	No party can sue the other party for claiming the performance of a void contract.	If the aggrieved party does not, within reasonable time, exercise its right to avoid the contract, any party can sue the other for claiming the performance of the contract.
4. ***Reason***	A contract becomes void due to change in law or change in circumstances beyond the contemplation of parties.	A contract becomes a voidable contract if the consent of a party was not free.
5. ***Right to Claim Damages***	No party can claim damages for non-performance of a void contract.	A party whose consent was not free may claim damages.

PRACTICAL PROBLEMS

PROBLEM 1

X beats *Y* and compels him to sell his house for Rs 1,00,000. *Y* agrees to sell his house to *Y*. *Y* signs the necessary documents for the sale of house and receives the payment. Later on, *Y* wants to avoid the contract? Will he succeed?

Solution

Sections to which the given problem relates: Sections 15 and 72.

Decision: *Y* can avoid the contract on the ground of coercion but he will have to return Rs 1,00,000 which he has received from *X*.

Reason: *Y*'s consent is not free as it has been obtained by committing an act which is forbidden by the Indian Penal Code.

PROBLEM 2

X threatens to kill *Y* if he does not sell his house to *X* for Rs 1,00,000. *Y* assigns the necessary documents for the sale of house and receives the payment. Later on, *Y* wants to avoid the contract. Will he succeed?

Solution

Sections to which the given problem relates: Sections 15 and 72.

Decision: *Y* can avoid the contract on the ground of coercion but he will have to return Rs 1,00,000 which he has received from *X*.

Reason: *Y*'s consent is not free as it has been obtained by giving a threat to commit an act which is forbidden by the Indian Penal Code.

PROBLEM 3

X threatens to kill *Y*'s son if *Y* does not sell his house to *X* for Rs 1,00,000. *Y* signs the necessary documents for the sale of house and receives the payment. Later on, *Y* wants to avoid the contract. Will he succeed?

Solution

Sections to which the given problem relates: Sections 15 and 72.

Decision: *Y* can avoid the contract on the ground of coercion but he will have to return Rs 1,00,000 which he has received from *X*.

Reason: *Y*'s consent is not free as it has been obtained by committing an act which is forbidden by the Indian Penal Code.

PROBLEM 4

X threatens to kill *Y*'s son if *Y* does not sell his house to *Z* for Rs 1,00,000. *Y* signs the necessary document for the sale of house and receives the payment. Later on, *Y* wants to avoid the contract. Will he succeed?

Solution

Sections to which the given problem relates: Sections 15 and 72.

Decision: *Y* can avoid the contract on the ground of coercion but he will have to return Rs 1,00,000 which he has received from *X*.

Reason: *Y*'s consent is not free as it has been obtained by committing an act which is forbidden by the Indian Penal Code.

PROBLEM 5

X, an agent, refused to hand over the account books of *Y*, the principal to the new agent appointed in his place unless the principal released him from all liabilities. The principal had to give a release deed as demanded. Is this release deed binding upon the principal?

Solution

Section to which the given problem relates: Section 15.

Decision: *Y* can avoid the contract on the ground of coercion.

Reason: *Y*'s consent is not free as it has been obtained by unlawful detaining of the property (i.e. account books).

[Leading case: *Muthia* v. *Karuppan*]

PROBLEM 6

The Government of a State gave a threat of attachment against the property of *Y* for the recovery of a fine due from *Y*'s son. *Y* paid the fine. Advise *Y*.

Solution

Section to which the given problem relates: Section 15.

Decision: *Y* could recover the amount paid on the ground of coercion.

Reason: *Y*'s consent is not free as it has been obtained by threatening to detain an property unlawfully.

[Leading case: *Bansraj* v. *The Secretary of State*]

PROBLEM 7

X, by a threat to commit suicide induced *Y*, his wife, and *Z*, his son, to execute a release deed in favour of his brother in respect of certain property. Are *Y* and *Z* bound by such release deed?

Solution

Section to which the given problem relates: Section 15.

Decision: *Y* and *Z* are not bound by such release deed.

Reason: The consent of *Y* and *Z* is not free as it has been obtained by threatening to commit an act which is deemed to be forbidden by the Indian Penal Code.

[**Leading case:** *Ammiraju* v. *Seshamma*]

PROBLEM 8

X, an illiterate old man of about 90 years, physically infirm and mentally in distress, executed a gift deed of his properties in favour of *Y* his nearest relative who was looking after his daily needs and managing his cultivation. Is *X* bound by this gift deed.

Solution

Section to which the given problem relates: Section 16(2).

Decision: No. *X* is not bound by this gift deed.

Reason: *Y*'s consent is not free as it has been obtained by exercising undue influence because *Y* was in position to dominate the will of *X*.

[**Leading case:** *Sher Singh* v. *Prithi Singh*]

PROBLEM 9

X, a poor Hindu widow, was in great need of money to establish her right to maintenance. She took a loan of Rs 1,500 bearing a rate of interest of 100% p.a. Is this transaction an unconscionable?

Solution

Section to which the given problem relates: Section 16(3).

Decision: This transaction appears to be an unconscionable.

Reason: Not only the rate of interest is too high but also the lender has used the circumstances of poor Hindu widow to obtain an unfair advantage.

[**Leading case:** *Ranee Annapurni* v. *Swaminatha*]

PROBLEM 10

X sells by auction to *Y* a horse which *X* knows to be unsound. The horse appears to be sound but *X* knows about the unsoundness of the horse. Is this contract valid in each of the following alternative cases:

Case (*a*) *X* says nothing about the unsoundness of the horse to *Y*.

Case (*b*) If *X* says nothing about it to *Y* who is *X*'s daughter who has just come of age.

Case (*c*) If *Y* says to *X* "If you do not deny it, I shall assume that the horse is sound." *X* says nothing.

Solution

Section to which the given problem relates: Section 17.

Case (*a*)

Decision: This contract is valid.

Reason: Mere silence as to the facts likely to affect the willingness of a person to enter into a contract is not fraud. Here, it is not the duty of the seller to disclose defects.

Case (*b*)

Decision: This contract is not valid.

Reason: It becomes *X*'s duty to tell *Y* about the unsoundness of the horse because a fiduciary relationship exists between *X* and his daughter *Y*. Here, *X*'s silence is equivalent to speech and hence amounts to fraud.

Case (c)

Decision: This contract is not valid.

Reason: Here, *X*'s silence is equivalent to speech and hence amounts to fraud.

PROBLEM 11

X chartered a ship to *Y* which was described in the 'Charter party' and was represented to him as being not more than 2,800 tonnage register. It turned out that the registered tonnage was 3,045 tons. *Y* refused to accept the ship in fulfilment of the charter party. Is *Y*'s action valid?

Solution

Section to which the given problem relates: Section 18.

Decision: *Y* was entitled to avoid the Chartered party.

Reason: *X* made erroneous statements as to tonnage.

[**Leading case:** *The Oceanic Steam Navigation Co.* v. *Soonderdas Dhrumsy*]

PROBLEM 12

X is having two horses, a white and another black. *X* offers to sell his black horse to *Y*. *Y* not knowing that *X* has two horses, thinks of white horse and agrees to buy the horse. Is this agreement valid?

Solution

Section to which the given problem relates: Section 20.

Decision: This agreement is void.

Reason: Both the parties to an agreement are under a mistake as to a matter of fact essential to the agreement.

PROBLEM 13

X offers to sell his black horse to *Y*. *Y* agrees to buy that horse. It turns out that the horse was dead at the time of bargain though neither party was aware of the fact. Is this agreement valid?

Solution

Section to which the given problem relates: Section 20.

Decision: This agreement is void.

Reason: Both the parties to an agreement are under a mistake as to a matter of fact essential to the agreement.

PROBLEM 14

X buys a painting believing it to be worth Rs 1,00,000 while in fact it is worth only Rs 10,000. Is it a valid contract?

Solution

Section to which the given problem relates: Explanation to Section 20.

Decision: This contract is valid.

Reason: An erroneous opinion as to the value of the thing which forms the subject matter of the agreement is not treated as mistake relating to a matter of fact. Here, *X* will have to blame himself for ignorance of the true value of the painting.

PROBLEM 15

X offers to sell a painting to *Y* which *X* knows is the copy of a well-known master piece. *Y*, thinking that the painting is the original one, decides to buy it at a very high price. Is this a valid contract?

Solution

Section to which the given problem relates: Explanation to Section 20.

Decision: This contract is valid.

Reason: An erroneous opinion as to the value of the thing which forms the subject matter of the agreement is not treated as mistake relating to a matter of fact. Here, *X* will have to blame himself for ignorance of the true value of the painting.

PROBLEM 16

P inquired about the price of rifles from *H* suggested that he might buy fifty rifles. On receiving the quotation, *P* telegraphed "Send three rifles". But because of the mistake of the telegraph authorities, the message transmitted was "Send the rifles". *H* despatched fifty rifles. *P* accepted three rifles and returned the remaining forty-seven rifles. Is this agreement valid?

Solution

Section to which the given problem relates: Section 20.

Decision: This agreement is void.

Reason: Both the seller and the buyer made a mistake regarding the quantity of the subject matter.

[Leading case: *Henked* v. *Pape*]

PROBLEM 17

X entered into a contract for the hiring of a room for witnessing the coronation procession of Edward VII. Unknown to both the parties, the procession had already been cancelled. Is this contract valid?

Solution

Section to which the given problem relates: Section 20.

Decision: This agreement is void on the ground of impossibility of performance of contract.

Reason: Both the parties are under a mistake as to the possibility of performance.

[Leading case: *Griffith* v. *Brymer*]

PROBLEM 18

X sold oats to *Y* by sample and *Y*, thinking that they were old oats, purchased them. In fact, the oats were new. Is *Y* bound by the contract?

Solution

Section to which the given problem relates: Section 22.

Decision: *Y* is bound by the contract.

Reason: A contract is not voidable because of unilateral mistake (i.e. mistake by only one party to the agreement) as to the matter of fact. Here, *Y* will have to blame himself for ignorance or wrong judgment.

[Leading case: *Smith* v. *Hughes*]

PROBLEM 19

One Blenkarn, knowing that Blenkarn & Co. was a reputed customers of Lindsay & Co., placed an order with Lindsay & Co. by imitating the signature of Blenkarn & Co. The goods were then sold to Cundy, an innocent buyer. A suit was filed by Lindsay & Co. against Cundy for recovery of goods. Discuss the legal position.

Solution

Section to which the given problem relates: Section 72.

Decision: Cundy didn't get a good title and hence he must return the goods or make payment for the same.

Reason: There was no contract between Lindsay & Co. and Cundy as Lindsay never intended to contract with Blenkarn.

[**Leading case:** *Cundy* v. *Lindsay & Co.*]

PROBLEM 20

A woman by falsely misrepresenting her to be wife of a well-known Baron (a millionaire), obtained two pearl necklaces from a firm of jewellers on the pretext of showing them to her husband before buying. She pledged them with a broker, who in good faith paid her Rs 1,00,000. A suit was filed by the jeweller against the broker. Discuss the legal position.

Solution

Section to which the given problem relates: Section 72.

Decision: Broker did not get a good title and hence he must return the goods.

Reason: There was no contract between the jeweller and the woman as jeweller never intended to contract with her.

[**Leading case:** *Lake* v. *Simmons*]

PROBLEM 21

S knew that on account of his criticism of the plays in the past, he would not be allowed entry to the performance of a play at the theatre. The managing director of the theatre gave instructions that no ticket should be sold to *S*. *S*, however, obtained a ticket through one of his friends. On being refused admission to the theatre, he sued for damages for breach of contract. Discuss the legal position.

Solution

Section to which the given problem relates: Section 22.

Decision: *S* is not entitled to claim any damages.

Reason: There was no contract between the theatre company and *S* as the theatre company never intended to contract with *S*.

[**Leading case:** *Said* v. *Butt*]

PROBLEM 22

X, an old illiterate man, was induced to sign a Bill of Exchange by means of a false representation that it was a mere guarantee. Discuss the legal position.

Solution

Section to which the given problem relates: Section 22.

Decision: *X* is not liable for the bill of exchange.

Reason: *X* never intended to sign a bill of exchange.

[**Leading case:** *Foster* v. *Mackinnon*]

TRUE OR FALSE QUESTIONS

State with reasons whether the following statements are True or False:

1. The Indian Penal Code must be in force in place where the coercion is employed.

2. An act of coercion must necessarily proceed from a party to the contract.
3. An act of coercion must necessarily be against the promisor.
4. A threat to file a civil suit does not amount to coercion.
5. A threat to file a criminal suit amounts to coercion.
6. A threat to file a suit on false charges amounts to coercion.
7. A threat to commit suicide does not amount to coercion.
8. A contract is void if the consent of a party to an agreement is obtained by coercion.
9. Undue influence involves use of physical pressure.
10. There is a presumption of undue influence between creditor and debtor.
11. There is no presumption of undue influence between a husband and wife.
12. A contract is void if the consent of a party to an agreement is obtained by undue influence.
13. Undue influence can be exercised by a stranger to a contract.
14. Silence always amounts to fraud.
15. A contract is void if the consent of a party to an agreement is obtained by fraud.
16. In case of fraud, the aggrieved party cannot sue for damages.
17. A mere attempt to deceive is fraud.
18. If there is no damage, there is no fraud.
19. The aggrieved party in case of active fraud loses the right to rescind the contract if he had the means of discovering the truth by ordinary diligence.
20. The aggrieved party in case of misrepresentation can rescind the contract even if he had the means of discovering the truth by ordinary diligence.
21. Ignorance of law is no excuse.
22. The contract will be void if both the parties are under a mistake as to a foreign law.
23. The contract will be voidable if the parties are under a mistake as to the Indian law.
24. Where both the parties to an agreement are under a mistake as to a matter of fact essential to the agreement, the contract is voidable.
25. A contract is void if one of the parties to the contract is under a mistake of fact.
26. A contract is voidable if there is a mistake as to the identity of the person contracted.

Answers

1. False	2. False	3. False	4. True
5. False	6. True	7. False	8. False
9. False	10. False	11. True	12. False
13. False	14. False	15. False	16. False
17. False	18. False	19. False	20. False
21. True	22. True	23. False	24. False
25. False	26. False		

VERY SHORT ANSWER TYPE QUESTIONS

1. Define consent.
2. What is coercion?
3. On whom the burden of proof lies in case of coercion?
4. What is undue influence?
5. What is unconscionable transaction?
6. Can the presumption of undue influence be rebutted?
7. What is fraud?
8. What is misrepresentation?
9. What is mistake?
10. What is mistake of fact?
11. What is bilateral mistake?
12. What is unilateral mistake?

SHORT ANSWER TYPE QUESTIONS

1. Comment on the following statements:
   (a) A threat to commit suicide amounts to coercion.
   (b) Mere silence as to facts is not fraud.
   (c) Ignorance of law is no excuse.
2. Distinguish between the following:
   (a) Coercion and undue influence.
   (b) Fraud and misrepresentation.
   (c) Unilateral mistake and bilateral mistake.
3. State the effects of coercion.
4. State the effects of undue influence.
5. When is a party said to be in a position to dominate the will of another?
6. State the effects of fraud.
7. State the circumstances under which the right of an aggrieved party to rescind the contract is lost in case of fraud.
8. State the effects of misrepresentation.
9. State the effects of mistake of law.
10. State the effect of mistake of fact.
11. Write short notes on the following:
    (a) Contracts made with a pardanashin woman
    (b) Free consent
    (c) Coercion
    (d) Undue influence
    (e) Fraud
    (f) Misrepresentation
    (g) Mistake

ESSAY TYPE QUESTIONS

1. (a) Define Consent.
   (b) When is consent said to be free?
2. (a) Define Coercion.
   (b) State the effects of coercion on the validity of a contract.
   (c) Does a threat to commit suicide amount to coercion?
   (d) On whom the burden of proof lies in case of coercion?
3. (a) Define Undue Influence.
   (b) When is a person deemed to be in position to dominate the will of another?
   (c) What is an unconscionable transaction?
   (d) On whom the burden of proof lies in case of undue influence?
4. (a) Define Fraud.
   (b) Does silence amount to fraud?
   (c) State the effects of fraud.
5. (a) Define Misrepresentation.
   (b) State the effects of misrepresentation.
6. (a) Define 'Mistake'.
   (b) Explain and illustrate the effects of various types of mistake.
7. "Law Relating to mistake is a comedy of errors." Explain.

CHAPTER

6 Legality of Object and Consideration, and Agreements Opposed to Public Policy

1.0 WHAT ARE THE CIRCUMSTANCES UNDER WHICH THE OBJECT OR CONSIDERATION IS DEEMED TO BE UNLAWFUL ?

The object and the consideration of an agreement must be lawful, otherwise, the agreement is **void**. According to Section 23 of The Indian Contract Act, 1872, the consideration or the object of an agreement is unlawful in the following cases:

1.1 If it is Forbidden by Law If the object or the consideration of an agreement is the doing of an act which is forbidden (i.e. prohibited) by law, the agreement is void. An act is said to be forbidden by law when it is punishable *either* by the criminal law of the country *or* by special legislation.

Example I *A promises B to drop a prosecution which he has instituted against B for robbery, and B promises to restore the value of the things taken. The agreement is void, as its object is unlawful. [William v. Bayley]*

Example II *X granted a loan to the guardian of a minor to enable him to celebrate the minor's marriage. It was held that X could not recover back because agreement is void as its object (i.e. minor's marriage) is illegal. [C. Srinivas v. K. Raja Rama Mohana Rao]*

Example III *A promises to obtain for B an employment in the public service, and B promises to pay Rs 1,000 to A. The agreement is void as the consideration for it is unlawful.*

Example IV *X, a Hindu already married and his wife alive, entered into a marriage agreement with Y an unmarried girl. This agreement is void because the second marriage is forbidden by Hindu Law.*

1.2 If it Defeats the Provisions of any Law If the object or the consideration of an agreement is of such nature that, if permitted, it would defeat the provisions of any law, the agreement is **void**.

Example I *A's estate is sold for arrears of revenue under the provisions of an Act of the Legislature, by which a defaulter is prohibited from purchasing the estate. B, upon an understanding with A, becomes the purchaser, and agrees to convey the estate to A, upon receiving from him the price which B has paid. The agreement is void as it tenders the transaction, in effect, a purchase by the defaulter, and would so defeat the object of the law.*

Example II *X borrowed Rs 1,00,000 from Y and agreed not to raise any objection as to the limitation and that Y may recover the amount even after the expiry of limitation period. This agreement is void as it defeats the provisions of the Law of Limitation Act. [Rama Murthi v. Goppayya]*

1.3 If it is Fraudulent If the object of an agreement is to defraud others, the agreement is **void**.

Example I *A, B and C enter into an agreement of the division among them of gains acquired, or be acquired, by them by fraud. The agreement is void, as its object is unlawful.*

Example II *A, being agent for a landed proprietor, agrees for money, without the knowledge of his principal, to obtain for B a lease of land belonging to his principal. The agreement between A and B is void, as it implies a fraud by concealment by A, on his principal.*

1.4 If it Involves or Implies Injury to a Person or Property of Another If the object of an agreement is to injure a person or the property of another, the agreement is **void**.

Example I *X borrowed Rs 100 from Y and executed a bond under which he promised to work for Y without pay for 2 years and agreed to pay interest at 10% per month and the principal amount at once. It was held that the agreement was void because it involved injury to X. [Ramsaroop v. Bansi Mandar]*

Example II *X promised to pay Rs 10,000 to Y when he agreed to publish a libel (i.e. defamatory article against someone). It was held that Y could not recover the amount because the agreement was void as it involved injury to someone. [Clay v. Yates]*

1.5 If the Court Regards it as Immoral or Opposed to Public Policy If the object or consideration is immoral or is opposed to the public policy, the agreement is **void**.

Example I *A, who is B's mukhtar, promises to exercise his influence, as such, with B in favour of C, and C promises to pay Rs 1,000 to A. The agreement is void, because it is immoral.*

Example II *A agrees to let her daughter to hire to B for concubinage. The agreement is void because it is immoral, though the letting may not be punishable under the Indian Penal Code (45 of 1860).*

Example III *X let a flat to Y on a monthly rent of Rs 10,000. Y was a prostitute and used the flat for prostitution and did not pay the rent. X cannot recover the rent if he knew the purpose otherwise he can. [Pearce v. Brooks]*

Example IV *X gave Rs 1,00,000 to Y a married woman to obtain a divorce from her husband. X agreed to marry her as soon as she obtained a divorce. It was held that X could not recover back the amount because the agreement was void as its object was immoral. [Baivijli v. Hamda Nagar]*

Example V *Agreements for past or future cohabitation are void because the consideration which is immoral at the time when it passes cannot become legal by passage of time [S. Yellappa v. Y. Sabu (Bombay High Court)]*

2.0 ILLEGAL AGREEMENTS

2.1 What is the Meaning of Illegal Agreements ?

Illegal agreements are those agreements which are—

(a) **void *ab-initio***, i.e. void from the very beginning, and

(b) punishable by the criminal law of the country or by any special legislation/regulation.

2.2 What are the Effects of Illegal Agreements

The effects of illegal agreements are as under:

(a) The **collateral** transactions to an illegal agreement **also** become **illegal** and hence cannot be enforced.

(b) No action can be taken for the recovery of money paid or property transferred under an illegal agreement and for the breach of an illegal agreement.

(c) In case of an agreement containing the promise, some part of which is legal and other part illegal, the legal position is as under:

	Case	*Provision*
1.	**If the illegal part cannot be separated from the legal part**	The whole agreement is altogether illegal.
2.	**If the illegal part can be separated from the legal part**	The Court will enforce the legal part and reject the illegal part.

Example I *X promises to pay Y Rs 1,000 if Y beats Z. Y beats Z and claims Rs 1,000 but X refuses to pay. Y cannot recover from X because the agreement between X and Y is illegal.*

Example II *X pays Y Rs 1,000 to beat Z. Y does not beat. X cannot recover from Y because the agreement between X and Y is illegal.*

Example III *X lent Rs 1,00,000 to Y to enable him to purchase certain smuggled goods from Z. X cannot recover the amount from Y if he knows the Y's purpose of borrowing.*

3.0 WHAT IS THE NATURE OF AGREEMENTS IF ONE OF THE SEVERAL CONSIDERATIONS OR OBJECTS IS UNLAWFUL ?

According to Section 24, if one of the several considerations or objects of an agreement is unlawful, the agreement is **void**.

Example *A promises to superintend, on behalf of B, a legal manufacturer of indigo and illegal traffic of other articles. B promises to pay to A, a salary of Rs 10,000 a year. The agreement is void, the object of A's promise and the consideration for B's promise being in part unlawful.*

4.0 WHAT ARE THE AGREEMENTS OPPOSED TO PUBLIC POLICY ?

It is not easy to define the term 'Public policy' with any degree of precision because 'public policy' by its very nature, is highly uncertain and keeps on fluctuating with the passage of time. An agreement which conflicts with morals of the time and contravenes any established interest of society may be said to be opposed to public policy. In India, it has been left to Court to hold any contract as unlawful on the ground of being opposed to public policy.

The following agreements have been held to be opposed to public policy:

4.1 Agreements of Trading with Enemy All agreements made with an alien enemy are illegal on the ground of public policy.

4.2 Agreement for Stifling Prosecution An agreement for stifling prosecution is illegal on the ground of public policy.

Example *X, who knows that Y has committed a murder, receives Rs 7,00,000 from Y in consideration of not exposing Y. This agreement is illegal.*

4.3 Agreements in the Nature of Maintenance and Champerty Maintenance is an agreement whereby one party having no interest in suit, agrees to assist another to maintain suit. *For example*, *X* promises to pay *Y* Rs 5,000 if *Y* files a suit against *Z*. This is a maintenance agreement.

Champerty is an agreement whereby one party agrees to assist another in recovering property and in turn is to share in the proceeds of the action.

Example *X, agreed to pay Rs 10,000 to Y to enable him to file a suit for the recovery of his property and Y promised to give him 3/4th share in the property, if recovered. The agreement was held to be champertous and void. [Nuthahi Venkataswami v. Katta Nagi]*

Position in England: Both of these agreements are declared illegal and void.

Position in India: All of these agreements are not illegal. The Court may refuse to enforce such agreements if its object is not bonafied or the terms of reward are unreasonable in the opinion of court.

4.4 Agreement for the Sale/Transfer of Public Offices and Titles The agreements for the sale or transfer of public offices or to obtain public titles like Padma Shree, are illegal on the ground of public policy.

Example *X promises to pay Y Rs 50,000 if Y secures him an employment in Govt. service. This agreement is opposed to public policy.*

4.5 Agreements in Restraint of Parental Rights An agreement which prevents a parent to exercise his right of guardianship, is void on the ground of public policy.

Example *G, a father having two sons, agreed to transfer guardianship in favour of A and also agreed not to revoke the transfer during his life. Subsequently, he filed a suit for the recovery of boys. It was held that he had a right to revoke his authority and get back his children. [Giddu Narayanish v. Mrs Annie Besant]*

4.6 Agreements in Restraint of Personal Liberty An agreement which unduly restricts the personal liberty of any person is void on the ground of public policy.

Example *X borrowed Rs 1,00,000 from Y on the promise that he would not, without the Y's written permission leave his job, borrow money, dispose of his property or change his residence. It was held that the agreement was illegal on the ground of public policy. [Harwood v. Miller's Timber and Trading Co.]*

4.7 Agreement Tending to Create Monopoly An agreement which tends to create monopoly is void on the ground of public policy.

Example *A local body granted a monopoly to X to sell vegetables in a particular locality. This agreement is void on the ground of being opposed to public policy.*

4.8 Agreements Interfering with Course of Justice An agreement which interferes with course of justice is void on the ground of being opposed to public policy.

4.9 Marriage Brokerage Contracts A marriage contract is one whereby one or more persons receives money or money's worth in consideration of marriage.

4.10 Agreement in Restraint of Marriage [Section 26] Every agreement in restraint of marriage of any person other than a minor is void.

4.11 Agreement in Restraint of Trade [Section 27] Every agreement by which anyone is restrained from exercising a lawful profession, trade or business of any kind, is to that extent void.

4.12 Agreement in Restraint of Legal Proceeding [Section 28] An agreement which restricts a party absolutely from enforcing his legal rights arising under a contract or an agreement which curtails the period of limitation within which the legal rights may be enforced is void.

Note: The agreements referred to in 4.10, 4.11 and 4.12 have been discussed in detail in Chapter 7.

PRACTICAL PROBLEMS

PROBLEM 1

X granted a loan to *Y* a guardian of a minor to enable him to celebrate the minor's marriage. Can *X* recover his loan from *Y*?

Solution

Section to which the given problem relates: Section 23.

Decision: *X* cannot recover his loan from *Y*.

Reason: The agreement is void because its object (i.e. minor's marriage in contravention of the Child Marriage Restraint Act) is unlawful.

[**Leading case:** *C. Srinivas* v. *K. Raja Ram Mohan*]

PROBLEM 2

X promises to drop prosecution which he has instituted against *Y* for robbery and *Y* promises to restore the value of the things taken. Is this agreement valid?

Solution

Section to which the given problem relates: Section 23.

Decision: This agreement is void.

Reason: The object of this agreement is unlawful.

[**Leading case:** *William* v. *Bayley*]

PROBLEM 3

X's estate is sold for arrears of revenue under the provisions of an Act of the Legislature, by which a defaulter is prohibited from purchasing the estate. *Y*, upon the understanding with *X*, becomes the purchaser and agrees to convey the estate to *X* for the price which *Y* has paid. Is this agreement valid?

Solution

Section to which the given problem relates: Section 23.

Decision: The agreement is void.

Reason: This agreement results in an indirect purchase by the defaulter and hence it defeats the object of the law by which a defaulter is prohibited from purchasing the estate.

PROBLEM 4

X, *Y* and *Z* enter into an agreement for the division among them of gains acquired or to be acquired by them by fraud. Is this agreement valid?

Solution

Section to which the given problem relates: Section 23.

Decision: This agreement is void.

Reason: The object of this agreement is unlawful as it is fraudulent.

PROBLEM 5

X borrowed Rs 1,000 from *Y*. *X* executed a bond promising to work for *Y* without pay for 2 years and in case of default agreed to pay interest at 10% per month and the principal amount at once. Is this agreement valid?

Solution

Section to which the given problem relates: Section 23.

Decision: This agreement is void.

Reason: The object of this agreement is unlawful as it involves an injury to another person.

[**Leading case:** *Ram Saroop* v. *Bansi Mandar*]

PROBLEM 6

X let a flat on hire to *Y*, a prostitute, knowing that it would be used for immoral purposes. Is this agreement void?

Solution

Section to which the given problem relates: Section 23.

Decision: The agreement is void.

Reason: The object of this agreement is immoral.

[**Leading case:** *Pearce* v. *Brooks*]

PROBLEM 7

X promises to supervise the business on behalf of *Y*, a licensed manufacturer of some permissible chemicals and some contraband items. *Y* promises to pay *X* a salary of Rs 30,000 per month. Is this agreement valid?

Solution

Section to which the given problem relates: Section 24.

Decision: The agreement is void.

Reason: The object of *X*'s promise and the consideration for *Y*'s promise being in part unlawful.

PROBLEM 8

X, knowing that *Y* has committed a murder, obtains a promise from *Y* to pay him (*X*) Rs 5,00,000 in consideration of not exposing *Y*. Is this agreement valid?

Solution

Section to which the given problem relates: Section 23.

Decision: The agreement is void.

Reason: This agreement is opposed to public policy as it is for stifling prosecution.

PROBLEM 9

X promises to pay *Y* Rs 1,00,000 if *Y* secures him an employment in the public service. Is this agreement valid?

Solution

Section to which the given problem relates: Section 23.

Decision: The agreement is void.

Reason: The agreement is opposed to public policy as it is for the sale of public office.

PROBLEM 10

X promises to pay Rs 1,00,000 to *Y* in order to induce him to retire so as to provide room for *X*'s appointment to the public office held by *Y*. Is this agreement valid?

Solution

Section to which the given problem relates: Section 23.

Decision: The agreement is void.

Reason: The agreement is opposed to public policy as it is for the sale of public office.

[**Leading case:** *Venkataramanaya* v. *J.M. Labo*]

PROBLEM 11

X, a father having two minor sons agreed to transfer their guardianship in favour of Mrs. *Y* and also agreed not to revoke the transfer. Subsequently, he filed a suit for the recovery of the boys and declaration that he was the rightful guardian. Discuss the legal position.

Solution

Section to which the given problem relates: Section 23.

Decision: The agreement is void and hence *X* had the right to revoke his authority and get back the children.

Reason: This agreement is opposed to public policy as it is in restraint of parental rights.

[**Leading case:** *Giddu Narayanish* v. *Mrs. Annie Basant*]

TRUE OR FALSE QUESTIONS

State with reasons whether the following statements are True or False:

1. If the object of an agreement is to defraud other, the agreement is voidable at the option of other party.
2. The collateral transaction to an illegal agreement also becomes illegal.
3. In India, the categories of contract that are opposed to public policy are limited and exhaustive.
4. Dowry provided voluntarily by the father of daughter is not unlawful.
5. Every agreement in restraint of the marriage of any person is void.
6. Every agreement in restraint of trade is altogether is void.
7. Agreement in restraint of legal proceeding is altogether void.

Answers

1. False	2. True	3. False	4. False
5. False	6. False	7. True	

VERY SHORT ANSWER TYPE QUESTIONS

1. What is an illegal agreement?
2. What is the nature of agreement if its consideration or object is unlawful?

SHORT ANSWER TYPE QUESTIONS

1. Enumerate the circumstances under which the object or consideration of a contract is deemed to be unlawful.
2. Enumerate any ten agreements that are considered opposed to public policy.

ESSAY TYPE QUESTIONS

1. Under what circumstances is the object or consideration of a contract deemed unlawful? Illustrate with examples.
2. (a) What is an illegal agreement?

   (b) What are the effects of illegality?
3. "No action is allowed on an illegal agreement." Comment and state the exceptions (if any) to this rule.
4. Discuss the doctrine of public policy. Give examples of agreements that are contrary to public policy.

CHAPTER 7 Void Agreement and Contingent Contracts

1.0 WHAT IS THE MEANING OF VOID AGREEMENTS ?

1.1 According to Section 2(g) of the Indian Contract Act, 1872, a void agreement is an agreement which is not enforceable by law. The agreements which are not enforceable by law right from the time when they are made, are *void-ab-initio*.

1.2 The following types of agreements have expressly been declared void under various sections of the Indian Contract Act.

1. Agreements by or with persons incompetent to contract (Sections 10 & 11).
2. Agreements entered into through a mutual mistake of fact between the parties (Section 20).
3. Agreement, the object or consideration of which is unlawful (Section 23).
4. Agreement, the consideration or object of which is partly unlawful (Section 24).
5. Agreement made without consideration (Section 25).
6. Agreements in restraint of marriage (Section 26).
7. Agreements in restraint of trade (Section 27).
8. Agreements in restraint of legal proceedings (Section 29).
9. Wagering agreement (Section 30).
10. Impossible agreement (Section 56).
11. An agreement to enter into an agreement in the future.

Agreements from Nos 1 to 5 have already been discussed in earlier chapters. The other agreements are discussed in this chapter.

2.0 WHAT IS THE NATURE OF AGREEMENTS IN RESTRAINT OF MARRIAGE ?

According to Section 26 of the Indian Contract Act, every agreement in restraint of the marriage of any person other than a minor is void.

Example I *X promised to marry Y only and none else, and to pay Rs 2,000 in default. X married Z and Y sued X for recovery of Rs 2,000. It was held that Y could not recover anything because the agreement was in restraint of marriage. [Lowe v. Peers]*

It may be noted that an agreement which provides for a penalty upon remarriage may not be considered as a restraint of marriage.

Example II *An agreement between two co-widows that if one of them remarried, she should forfeit her right to her share in the deceased husband's property, was not void because no restraint was imposed upon either of the two widows from remarrying. [Roa Rani v. Gulab Rani]*

Example III *Nikah Nama (i.e. a marriage agreement in Muslims) which authorises wife to divorce herself and to claim maintenance from the husband on his marrying* *a second wife, was not void because no restraint was imposed upon husband from marrying a second wife. [Badu v. Badarannessa]*

3.0 WHAT IS THE NATURE OF AGREEMENTS IN RESTRAINT OF TRADE ?

3.1 Legal Position According to Section 27 of Indian Contract Act, 1872, "**every agreement by which anyone is restrained from exercising a lawful profession, trade or business of any kind, is to that extent void.**" This is because Article 19(g) of the Constitution of India regards the freedom of trade and commerce as a right of every individual. Therefore, no agreement can deprive or restrain a person from exercising such a right.

3.2 Burden of Proof Where an agreement is challenged on the ground of its being in restraint of trade, the party supporting the contract must show that the restraint is reasonably necessary to protect his interests, and the party challenging the contract must show that the restraint is injurious to the public.

3.3 Meaning of Expression 'that Extent' The expression 'that extent' may be interpreted in the sense that only that portion of such agreement is void which is considered *either* as unreasonable *or* as opposed to public policy being in restraint of trade. The rest of the agreement would continue to be valid.

Example I *In Patna city, 29 out of 30 manufacturers of combs agreed with R to supply him combs and not to anyone else. R was free to reject goods if he found that there was no market for them. It was held that the agreement was in restraint of trade and was thus void. [Shaikh Kalu v. Ram Saran Bhagat]*

Example II *X and Y carried on business in a certain locality in Kolkata. X promised to stop business in that locality if Y paid him Rs 1,000. X stopped his business but Y did not pay him the promised money. It was held that X could not recover anything from Y because the agreement was in restraint of trade and was thus void. [Madhub Chander v. Raj Coomer]*

Example III *An agreement restraining a servant from competing for 5 years after the period of service, was held as void. [Brahamputra Tea Co. v. E. Scarth]*

3.4 Exceptions to the Rule that "An Agreement in Restraint of Trade is Void" The exceptions here mean the cases where agreements in restraint of trade are not considered as void. Such exceptions are discussed below.

I. Exceptions Under Statutory Provisions

(a) ***Sale of Goodwill [Exception 1 to Section 27]*****:** An agreement which restrains the seller of a goodwill from carrying on a business is valid if all the following conditions are fulfilled:

(i) Such restriction must relate to a similar business.

(ii) Such restriction must be within specified local limits.

(iii) Such restriction must be for the time so long as the buyer or any person deriving title to the goodwill from him, carries on a like business in the specified local limits.

(iv) Such specified local limits must be reasonable having regard to the nature of the business.

Thus, the buyer of goodwill may restrain the seller for carrying on any business similar to the one sold by him within a certain vicinity and for a certain period of time provided the restrictions in regard to time and vicinity are found reasonable.

(b) ***Partners' Agreements:*** The Indian Partnership Act, 1932, recognises the following agreements in restraint of trade as valid:

(i) *Restriction on existing partner* [*Section 11(2)*]—A partner shall not carry on any business other than that of the firm while he is a partner.

(ii) *Restriction on outgoing partner* [*Section 36(2)*]—An outgoing partner may agree with his partners that he will not carry on any business similar to that of the firm within a specified period or within specified local limits. Such agreement shall be valid only if the restrictions are reasonable.

(iii) *Restriction on partners upon or in anticipation of the dissolution of the firm* [*Section 54*]—Partners may, upon or in anticipation of the dissolution of the firm, make an agreement that some or all of them will not carry on a business similar to that of the firm within a specified period or within specified local limits. Such agreement shall be valid only if the restrictions are reasonable.

(iv) *Restriction in case of sale of goodwill* [*Section 55(3)*]—A partner may upon the sale of the goodwill of a firm, make an agreement that such partner will not carry on any business similar to that of the firm within a specified period or within specified local limits. Such agreement shall be valid if the restrictions are reasonable.

II. Exceptions Under Judicial Interpretations

(a) **Trade Combinations:** Trade combinations which have been formed to regulate the business or to fix prices are not void, but the trade combinations which tend to create monopoly and which are against the public interest are void.

Example I *An agreement among four ginning factories to fix uniform rate for ginning cotton and to divide the profits in a certain proportion is not void because such agreements are neither in restraint of trade nor opposed to public policy. [Haribhai v. Sharafali]*

Example II *An agreement by two firms to avoid competition is void because it tends to create monopoly and is against the public interest. [Jai Ram v. Kahna Ram]*

Example III *An agreement between certain persons to carry on business with the members of their caste only is void. [Vaithelinga v. Saminada]*

Example IV *An agreement among some ice manufacturing companies not to sell ice below a minimum price and to divide the profits in a certain proportion is not void because such agreement was made to regulate the business and not to restrain it. [S.B. Fraser & Co. v. Bombay Ice Mfg. Co.]*

(b) ***Sole Dealing Agreements:*** An agreement to deal in the products of a single manufacturer or to sell the whole produce to a single dealer are valid if their terms are reasonable.

Example I *An agreement by a person to sell all the mica produced by him to the plaintiffs and not to any other firm, and not to keep any in stock, is valid. [Subha Naidu v. Haj Badsha Sahib]*

Example II *An agreement by a buyer of goods for Delhi market, not to sell them in Kolkata, is valid.*

Example III *X, a seller of immitation jewellery in England sold his business to Y and agreed not to deal for two years (a) in immitation jewellery in England, (b) in real jewellery in certain foreign countries. The first promise was held lawful,* *the second promise was held as void because the restraint was unreasonable having regard to the nature of business.*

(c) ***Service Agreements:*** A clause in service agreement may or may not be in restraint of trade. An analysis of some of the clauses of service agreement is as under:

Clause	*Whether held as restraint of trade*
(i) A clause to serve the employer for a stipulated period.	Such agreements if reasonable, do not amount to restraint of trade and hence, are enforceable.
(ii) A clause to prevent the employee from accepting any other engagement during his employment.	Such agreements do not amount to restraint of trade and hence, are enforceable. **Example** *Doctors employed in Govt. service are usually not allowed to carry on private practice.*
(iii) A clause to prevent the employee from accepting a similar engagement after the termination of his services.	
(a) *If a restraint is intended only to protect an employer against an employee making use of trade secrets learned by him in the course of his employment.*	(a) Such agreements do not amount to restraint of trade and hence, are enforceable by law. **Example** *An employee who possesses certain trade secrets, agreed not to carry on the similar business during 5 years after the termination of service [Forster & Sons Ltd. v. Suggett]*
(b) *If a restraint is intended to serve any other purpose (say, to avoid competition)*	(b) Such agreements amount to restrain of trade and hence, are not enforceable by law. **Example** *An agreement to restraint a servant from competing for 5 years after the period of service, is void [Brahamputra Tea Co. v. E. Scarth]*

4.0 WHAT IS THE POSITION OF AGREEMENTS IN RESTRAINT OF LEGAL PROCEEDINGS ?

According to Section 28, the following two agreements amount to restraint of legal proceedings and are thus, void to that extent.

4.1 Agreements Restricting Enforcement of Rights An agreement by which any party is restricted absolutely from enforcing his legal rights under or in respect of any contract is void to that extent.

Example *A clause in a contract provided that no action should be brought upon it in case of breach. Such a clause is void because it restricts both the parties from enforcing their legal rights.*

There are **two Exceptions** to the above rule:

Exception I An agreement between two or more persons to refer to arbitration any dispute which may arise between them, is not illegal.

Exception II An agreement in writing between two or more persons to refer to arbitration any dispute which has already arisen, is not illegal.

***Note*:** Where two courts have jurisdiction to try a suit, an agreement between the parties that the suit should be filed in one of those courts alone and not in the other is not invalid. [*C. Milton & Co.* v. *Ojha Automobile Co.*]

However, an agreement not to go in appeal to a higher court against the judgement of a lower court, does not amount to restraint of legal proceedings.

4.1 Agreements Limiting the Period of Limitation An agreement which limits the time within which an action may be brought so as to make it shorter than that prescribed by the Law of Limitation, is void because its object is to defeat the provisions of law.

Example *A clause in a contract provides that no action should be brought after two years. Such a clause is void because it limits the period of limitation to two years which is less than the period of limitation (i.e. three years) prescribed by the law of limitation.*

5.0 WHAT IS THE MEANING OF NATURE OF UNCERTAIN AGREEMENTS ?

An uncertain agreement means an agreement the meaning of which is not certain or capable of being made certain. Such agreements are void.

Example I *A agrees to sell to B "a hundred ton of oil." There is nothing whatever to show what kind of oil was intended. The agreement is void for uncertainty.*

Example II *A agrees to sell to B a hundred ton of oil of a specified description, known as an article of commerce. There is no uncertainty here to make the agreement void.*

Example III *A, who is a dealer in coconut oil, agrees to sell to B "100 ton of oil." The nature of A's trade implies that A intends to sell 100 tons of coconut oil. Hence, there is no uncertainty.*

Example IV *A agrees to sell to B "all the grain in my granary at Ramnagar." There is no uncertainty since it is possible to determine the quantity of grain lying at A's granary at Ramnagar.*

Example V *A agrees to sell to B "100 tons of rice at a price to be fixed by C." As the price is capable of being made certain, there is no uncertainty here to make the agreement void.*

Example VI *A agrees to sell to B "my white horse for Rs 5,000 or 10,000." There is nothing to show which of the two prices was to be given. The agreement is void.*

Example VII *An agreement to grant a lease when no date of commencement is expressly or impliedly fixed is void because it is not certain when the period of lease shall commence.*

Example VIII *A agrees to sell to B 10 tons of Punjab wheat. But the price is not indicated. Such agreement is not void because in such a case, a reasonable price shall be payable according to Section 2 of the Sale of Goods Act, 1930.*

Example IX *X agreed to buy a horse from Y for Rs 5,000 and to pay Rs 100 more if the horse proved lucky. It was held that the agreement was void because there was no mechanism to determine what luck bad or good the horse had brought to the buyer. [Guthing v. Lynn]*

Example X *X agreed to pay Rs 10,000 when he was able to pay. It was held that the agreement was void for uncertainty. [Pushpabala v. LIC of India]*

Example XI *X agrees to agree in future. Such agreement is void because there is no certainty whether the parties will agree under the future circumstances.*

6.0 WAGERING AGREEMENTS (SEC. 30)

6.1 What is the Meaning of Wagering Agreements ?

An agreement between two persons under which money or money's worth is payable, by one person to another on the happening or non-happening of a future uncertain event is called a wagering event. Such agreements are chance oriented and therefore, completely uncertain.

Example *X promises to pay Rs 1,000 to Y if it rained on a particular day, and Y promises to pay Rs 1,000 to X if it did not. Such agreement is a wagering agreement.*

6.2 What are the Essentials of a Wagering Agreement ?

The aforesaid definition highlights the following essentials of a wagering agreement:

(a) ***Promise to Pay Money or Money's Worth:*** The wagering agreement must contain a promise to pay money or money's worth.

(b) ***Uncertain Event:*** The performance of the promise must depend upon the determination of an uncertain event. An event is said to be uncertain when it is yet to take place or it might have already happened but the parties are not aware of its result.

(c) ***Mutual Chances of Gain or Loss:*** Each party must stand to win or lose upon the determination of an uncertain event. If either of the parties may win but cannot lose, or may lose but cannot win, it is not a wagering agreement.

(d) ***Neither Party to have Control over the Event:*** Neither party should have control over the happening of the event one way or the other.

(e) ***No other Interest in the Event:*** Neither party should have interest in the happening or non-happening of the event other than the sum or stake he will win or lose.

6.3 What are the Examples of Wagering Agreements ?

(a) An agreement to settle the difference between the contract price and market price of certain goods or shares on a particular day.

(b) A lottery (i.e. a game of chance). But parties running a Government approved lottery cannot be prosecuted.

(c) An agreement to buy a lottery ticket.

(d) A crossword puzzle in which prizes depend upon correspondence of the competitor's solution with a previously prepared solution kept with the Editor of newspapers is a lottery and hence a wagering transaction [*State of Bombay* v. *R.M.D. Chamarbaugwala*]. But a crossword puzzle is generally a game of skill and intelligence and hence not a wager.

6.4 What are the Examples of Transactions which are not held wagers ?

(a) Prize competitions which are games of skill, e.g. picture puzzles, athletic competitions. For example, an agreement to enter into a wrestling event in which winner was to be rewarded by the entire sale proceeds of tickets, was held not to be a wagering contract. [*Babasaheb* v. *Rajaram*]

(b) According to the Prize Competition Act, 1955, prize competition in games of skill are not wagers provided the prize money does not exceed Rs 1,000.

(c) An agreement to contribute to a plate or prize of the value of above Rs 500 to be awarded to the winner of a horse race. [Section 30]

(d) Contracts of insurance.

6.5 What are the Effects of Wagering Agreements ?

The effects of wagering agreements are given as under:

(a) Agreements by way of wager are void in India.

(b) Agreements by way of wager have been declared illegal in the states of Maharashtra and Gujarat.

(c) No suit can be filed to recover the amount won on any wager.

(d) Transaction which are collateral to wagering agreements are not void in India except in the states of Maharashtra and Gujarat.

(e) Transactions which are collateral to wagering agreements are illegal in the states of Maharashtra and Gujarat.

Example *A Cricket match is to be held between India and Pakistan. X agrees to pay Rs 1,00,000 to Y if India wins the match and agrees to deposit the money with Z a third person of confidence for this purpose. X borrows Rs 1,00,000 from W. The implications of this case are summarised as under:*

(a) The agreement between *X* and *Y* is a wagering agreement because the performance of an agreement depends upon the happening or non-happening of a future uncertain event and each party stands to win or loose.

(b) If India wins the match, *Y* (a winner) cannot recover the amount but *X* (a looser) can recover if the amount has not been paid to *Y*. Thus, a winner cannot recover the amount but a looser can if the amount has not been paid to the winner.

(c) If India wins the match and *Z* (a stakeholder) pays the money to *Y* (a winner), *X* (a looser) cannot recover it from *Z*. [*Bridger* v. *Savage*]

(d) The agreement between *X* and *W* which is a collateral to wagering agreement, is valid in India except in the States of Maharashtra and Gujarat. Thus, *W* can recover the money from *X* if the agreement between *X* and *Y* is entered into in India except in the States of Maharashtra and Gujarat but *W* cannot recover the money from *X* if the agreement between *X* and *Y* is entered into in the States of Maharashtra or Gujarat.

7.0 DISTINCTION BETWEEN CONTRACTS OF INSURANCE AND WAGERING AGREEMENT

The contracts of insurance differ from the wagering agreements in the following respects:

Basis of Distinction	*Contracts of Insurance*	*Wagering Agreement*
1. *Insurable interest*	Person having an insurable interest can insure his life or property.	Parties to a wagering agreement need not have insurable interest.
2. *Actual amount payable*	In case of contracts of insurance except life	In case of wagering agreement, the actual

	insurance, the actual amount payable need not necessarily be the full amount for which the property is insured.	amount payable is usually fixed.
3. ***Beneficial/against public policy***	These are regarded as beneficial to the public policy.	These are considered to be against public policy.
4. *Gamble*	Such agreements do not tantamount to gambling as they involve the element of invest ment and protection.	Being chance oriented, these are closer to gambling.

8.0 SPECULATIVE TRANSACTION

Speculative transaction is one in which mutual intention of parties is to settle the transaction *either* by actual delivery of goods *or* by payment of difference in price on settlement date. Speculative transaction is generally valid. If, however the mutual intention is only to settle the transaction by payment of difference in price on settlement date, the transaction would be wagering agreement which would be void.

9.0 COMPARISON BETWEEN WAGERING AGREEMENT AND ILLEGAL AGREEMENTS

9.1 Similarity– Both Wagering Agreements and Illegal Agreements are void in India.

9.2 Distinction– Transactions which are collateral to wagering agreements are not void in India (except in the States of Maharastra & Gujrat) but transactions which are collateral to Illegal agreements are void.

10.0 WHAT IS THE NATURE OF AGREEMENTS CONTINGENT ON IMPOSSIBLE EVENTS ?

According to Section 36 of the Indian Contract Act, 1872 "Contingent agreements to do or not to do anything, if an impossible event happens are void whether the impossibility of the event is known or not to the parties to the agreement at the time when it is made".

Example *A agrees to pay Rs 1000 if B marries C (a Hindu) who is already married to D. This agreement is void since happening of an event is impossible.*

11.0 WHAT IS THE NATURE OF AGREEMENTS TO DO IMPOSSIBLE ACTS ?

According to Section 56 of the Indian Contract Act, 1872, "**An agreement to do an impossible act is void**."

Example I *A undertakes to put life into the dead wife of B. This agreement is void since the act is impossible at the time of making agreement.*

Example II *A (a Hindu who is already married) agrees to marry B. This agreement is void since the act is impossible at the time of making agreement.*

12.0 WHAT IS PRINCIPLE OF RESTITUTION

12.1 Meaning of Restitution means "return or restoration of benefit." The provisions relating to 'restitution' are given below:

Case	*Provision*
(a) When a person at whose option a contract is voidable rescinds it [Section 64].	The party rescinding a voidable contract must restore the benefit to the person from whom he has received it.
(b) When an agreement is discovered to be void or the contract becomes void [Section 65].	The person who has received any benefit or advantage under such agreement or contract must restore it or compensate for it to the person from whom he has received it.

Example I *A, a singer contracts with B the manager of a theatre to sing at his theatre for two nights every week during the next two months and B agrees to pay her Rs 100 for each night's performance. On the sixth night, A wilfully absent herself from the theatre and B in consequence rescinds the contract, B must pay A for the five nights on which she had sung.*

Example II *A contracts to sing for B on a specified day and receives an advance of Rs 1,000 but is unable to sing due to serious illness on that day. Since the contract has become void. A must return Rs 1,000 to B.*

12.2 Non-applicability of the Principle of Restitution

The principle of restitution does not apply to contracts which are void *ab-initio* with the exception where the minor has entered into agreement by misrepresenting his age.

Example I *X pays Rs 1,000 to Y to beat Z. Y does not beat Z. X claims Rs 1,000 from Y. X can not recover anything because this agreement is void ab-initio.*

Example II *X advances Rs 10,000 to Y a married woman to enable her to obtain a divorce from her husband. Y agrees to marry X as soon as she obtained a divorce. Y obtains the divorce but refuses to marry X. X can not recover anything from Y because this agreement is void ab-initio. [Baiviji v. Hamda Nagar]*

Example III *X advances Rs 10,000 to Y a married woman, if Y marries X in the event of death of Y's husband. Subsequently, Y's husband died but Y refused to marry X. X cannot recover anything from Y because this agreement is void ab-initio.*

13.0 CONTINGENT CONTRACT

13.1 What is the Meaning of a Contingent Contract ? [Section 31]

A 'contingent contract' is a contract to do or not to do something if some event, collateral to such contract, does or does not happen. Insurance contracts provide the best example of contingent contracts.

Example I *A contracts to pay B Rs 10,000 if B's house is burnt. This is a contingent contract.*

Example II *A promises to pay B Rs 1 crore if a certain ship does not return within a year.*

13.2 What are the Essential Features of a Contingent Contract ?

The essential features of a Contingent Contract are discussed below.

(a) ***Dependence on a Future Event:*** The performance of a contingent contract depends upon the happening or non-happening of some future event.

(b) ***Collateral Event:*** The event must be collateral to the contract.

(c) ***Uncertain Event:*** The event must be uncertain.

Note: *The performance of a contingent contract must depend upon the happening or non-happening of an event and not on the mere will of the promisor. For example, if A promises to pay B Rs 10,000 if he so chooses, it is not a contingent contract.*

13.3 What are the Rules Regarding Contingent Contracts ?

The various rules regarding the enforcement of contingent contract are given below:

Kind of Contingent Contract	*Rule regarding enforcement*
1. Contracts contingent upon the happening of an uncertain future event. [Section 32]	Such contracts cannot be enforced by law unless and until that event has happened. If the event becomes impossible, such contracts become void. **Example I** *A makes a contract with B to buy B's horse if A survives C. This contract cannot be enforced by law unless and until C dies in A's life-time.* **Example II** *A makes a contract with B to sell a horse to B at a specified price, if C, to whom the horse has been offered, refuses to buy him. The contract cannot be enforced by law unless and until C refuses to buy the horse.* **Example III** *A contracts to pay B a sum of money when B marries C. C dies without being married to B. The contract becomes void.*
2. Contracts contingent upon the non-happening of a certain future event. [Section 33]	Such contracts can be enforced when the happening of that event becomes impossible and not before. **Example** *A agrees to pay B a sum of money if a certain ship does not return. This ship is sunk. The contract can be enforced when the ship sinks.*
3. Contracts contingent upon the future conduct of a living person. [Section 34]	If the uncertain event is the future conduct of a living person, such event shall be considered impossible if that such person does anything by which it becomes impossible to perform the contract within any definite time. **Example** *A agrees to pay B a sum of money if B marries C. C marries D. The marriage of B to C must now be considered impossible, although it is possible that D may die, and that C may afterwards marry B.*

4. Contracts contingent upon the happening of an uncertain specified event within a fixed time. [Section 35]	Such contracts become void if before the expiry of fixed time— (a) such event does not happen, or (b) such event becomes impossible. **Example** *A promises to pay B a sum of money if a certain ship returns within a year. The contract may be enforced if the ship returns within the year, and becomes void if the ship is burnt within the year.*
5. Contracts contingent upon the non-happening of an uncertain specified event within a fixed time. [Section 35]	Such contracts can be enforced by law if before the expiry of fixed time— (a) such event does not happen, or (b) it becomes certain that such event will not happen. **Example** *A promises to pay B a sum of money if a certain ship does not return within a year. The contract may be enforced if the ship does not return within the year, or is burnt within the year.*
6. Agreements contingent upon impossible events. [Section 36	Such agreements are void whether the impossibility of the event is known or not to the parties to the agreement at the time when it is made. **Example I** *A agrees to pay B Rs 1,000 if two straight lines should enclose a space. The agreement is void because two straight lines can never enclose a space.* **Example II** *A agrees to pay B, Rs 1,000 if B will marry A's daughter C. C was dead at the time of the agreement. The agreement is void because B's marriage with C can never take place.*

14.0 DISTINCTION BETWEEN A WAGERING AGREEMENT AND A CONTINGENT CONTRACT

A wagering agreement differs from a contingent contract in the following ways:

Basis of Distinction	*Wagering Agreement*	*Contingent Contract*
1. ***Reciprocal promises***	It consists of reciprocal promises.	It may or may not consists of reciprocal promises.
2. ***Void/valid***	It is **void**.	It is **valid**.
3. ***Main/Collateral Future Event***	Future event is **essential** to the contract.	Future event is **collateral** to the contract.
4. ***Nature***	It is always of a **contingent nature.**	It may **not be of a wagering nature.**

5. *Interest of parties*	Its parties have **no other interest** in the subject matter of the agreement except winning or losing of wagering amount.	Its parties may **have other interest as well.**

PRACTICAL PROBLEMS

PROBLEM 1

X promised to marry *Y* only and none else, and to pay Rs 1,00,000 in default. *X* married *Z*. *Y* claimed Rs 1,00,000 but *X* refused to pay. State the legal position.

Solution

Section to which the given problem relates: Section 26.

Decision: *Y* cannot recover anything from *X*.

Reason: The agreement between *X* and *Y* was in restraint of marriage.

PROBLEM 2

X employed *Y*. The terms of service agreement are—

(a) The employee has to serve the organisation for 5 years.

(b) The employee shall not accept any other similar engagement during the term of agreement.

(c) The employee shall not accept similar engagement after the termination of services.

(d) The employee shall not compete with his employer after the termination of services.

State the legal position of the terms of service agreement.

Solution

Section to which the given problem relates: Section 27.

Decision: First two terms (a) and (b) are not in restraint of trade and hence valid. Last two terms (c) and (d), are restraint of trade and hence void.

PROBLEM 3

X and *Y* were rival traders in South Delhi. *X* agreed to pay *Y* Rs 5,00,000 if *Y* closes his business in that locality. *Y* accordingly did so but *X* refused to pay. Can *Y* claim Rs 5,00,000?

Solution

Section to which the given problem relates: Section 27.

Decision: *Y* cannot claim anything from *X*.

Reason: The agreement between *X* and *Y* was in restraint of trade.

[**Leading case:** *Madhub Chander* v. *Raj Coomar*]

PROBLEM 4

X sold his business including goodwill to *Y* for Rs 5,00,000 by an agreement. The agreement provided that *X* shall not engage himself in the similar business in the whole of India for the next 10 years. *X* started the same business in the same city after 1 month. State the legal position.

Solution

Section to which the given problem relates: Section 27.

Decision: *Y* cannot take any legal action against *X*.

Reason: The agreement between *X* and *Y* was in restraint of trade because the limits were unreasonable.

PROBLEM 5

A clause in a life insurance policy was that "no suit to recover under the policy shall be brought after one year from the date of death of assured." *X* died and his legal representatives filed a suit to recover the assured sum after two and half years. Is this suit maintainable?

Solution

Section to which the given problem relates: Section 28.

Decision: This suit is maintainable.

Reason: The clause in policy is void because it curtailed the prescribed period of limitation (which is 3 years) according to Law of Limitation Act.

PROBLEM 6

X agrees to sell to *Y* "100 tons of oil."

State the legal position of this agreement in each of the following alternative cases:

Case (a) If *X*, who is a dealer in coconut oil only, decides to sell @ Rs 10,000 per ton.

Case (b) If *X* is a dealer in coconut oil and price is not fixed.

Case (c) If *X* is a dealer in coconut oil and price is to be fixed by *Z*.

Case (d) If *X* who is a dealer in coconut oil agrees to sell at Rs 10,000 per ton or Rs 11,000 per ton.

Case (e) If *X* is a dealer in coconut oil and mustard oil.

Solution

Section to which the given problem relates: Section 29.

Case	*Decision*	*Reason*
(a)	Valid	There is no uncertainty as to the description of oil because the nature of *X*'s trade indicates that this contract is for sale of coconut oil.
(b)	Valid	There is no uncertainty because in this case a reasonable price shall be payable according to Section 2 of the Sale of Goods Act, 1930.
(c)	Valid	There is no uncertainty because in this case the price fixed by *Z* shall be payable.
(d)	Void	There is no certainty as to which of the two price shall be payable.
(e)	Void	There is no certainty as to which of the two oils has been sold.

PROBLEM 7

X instructed *Y* to enter on his behalf a wagering transaction. *Y* lost Rs 10,000 in that transaction and paid from his pocket. *Y* claimed Rs 10,000 from *X* who refused on the ground of wagering transaction. State the legal position if wagering transaction was entered into (a) Delhi (b) Mumbai (c) Ahmedabad.

Solution

Section to which the given problem relates: Section 30.

Decision: *Y*'s transaction is collateral to the main transaction (i.e. wagering transaction).

Case (a): *Y* can recover Rs 10,000 from *X* because the collateral transaction to the main transaction which is void in Delhi, is not affected at all.

Cases (b) and (c): *Y* cannot recover Rs 10,000 from *X* because the collateral transaction to the main transaction which is illegal in the state of Maharashtra and Gujarat, is also affected.

[Leading case: *Daya Ram* v. *Murli Dhar*]

PROBLEM 8

M lost a sum of Rs 8,500 to L & Co. on bets on horse races, and on his failure to pay was reported to the race course club. *M* subsequently executed in favour of L & Co. a Hundi for Rs 8,500 in consideration of their withdrawing his name from the club and thereby his being posted as a defaulter. When L & Co. demanded the payment. *M* pleaded that the consideration was unlawful. Decide.

Solution

Section to which the given problem relates: Section 30.

Decision: *M* shall be liable to pay.

Reason: A wagering contract being void only does not affect collateral transactions.

PROBLEM 9

A agrees to pay *B* Rs 50,000 if *B* marries *C* within 1 year. State the legal position in each of the following alternative case:

Case (a) If *B* marries *C* after 1 year.

Case (b) If *B* marries *C* within 1 year.

Case (c) If *B* marries *D* within 6 months of agreement.

Case (d) If *B* marries *D* within 6 months of agreement. Subsequently, *D* dies and *B* marries *C* within 6 months of marriage *D*.

Solution

Case (a)

Section to which the given problem relates: Section 35.

Decision: *B* cannot recover anything from *A*.

Reason: The contract becomes void on the expiry of 1 year.

Case (b)

Section to which the given problem relates: Section 32.

Decision: *B* can recover Rs 50,000 from *A*.

Reason: The contract can be enforced by law when the event has happened (i.e. the marriage of *B* to *C*).

Case (c)

Section to which the given problem relates: Sections 34, 35.

Decision: *B* cannot recover anything from *A*.

Reason: The contract becomes void because the event (i.e. the marriage of *B* to *C*) has become impossible.

Case (d)

Section to which the given problem relates: Section 32.

Decision: *B* can recover Rs 50,000 from *A* when he marries *C*.

Reason: The contract can be enforced by law when the event has happened (i.e., the marriage of *B* to *C*).

PROBLEM 10

A agrees to pay *B* Rs 1,00,000 if a certain ship returns within a year. State the legal position in each of the following alternative cases:

Case (*a*) If the ship returns within the year.

Case (*b*) If the ship returns after the expiry of 1 year.

Case (*c*) If the ship is burnt within the year.

Solution

Section to which the given problem relates: Section 35.

***Case* (*a*)**

Decision: *B* can recover Rs. 1,00,000 from *A*.

Reason: The contract can be enforced by law when the event has happened (i.e., return of ship).

***Case* (*b*)**

Decision: *B* cannot recover anything from *A*.

Reason: The contract becomes void on the expiry of the fixed time if the event does not happen.

***Case* (*c*)**

Decision: *B* cannot recover anything from *A*.

Reason: The contract becomes void when such event becomes impossible.

PROBLEM 11

A agrees to pay *B* Rs 1,00,000 if a certain ship does not return within a year. State the legal position in each of the following alternative cases:

Case (*a*) If the ship does not return within a year.

Case (*b*) If the ship returns within a year.

Case (*c*) If the ship is burnt within a year.

Solution

Section to which the given problem relates: Section 35.

***Case* (*a*)**

Decision: *B* can recover Rs 1,00,000 from *A*.

Reason: The contract can be enforced on the expiry of the fixed time since the ship has not returned within a year.

***Cases* (*b*)**

Decision: *B* cannot recover anything from *A*.

Reason: The Contract becomes void because the ship has returned within a year.

***Cases* (*c*)**

Decision: *B* can recover Rs. 1,00,000 from *A*.

Reason: The Contract can be enforced since it has become certain that the ship will not return.

PROBLEM 12

A agreed to pay *B* Rs 50,000 if *B* marries *C*. *C* was already married to *D* at the time of agreement. State the legal position.

Solution

Section to which the given problem relates: Section 36.

Decision: Such agreement is void and hence not enforceable by law.

Reason: Marriage of *B* to *C* is impossible at present.

TRUE OR FALSE QUESTIONS

State whether the following statements are True or False:

1. The performance of a contingent contract depends upon the happening of some future event.
2. The performance of a contingent contract depends upon the non-happening of some future event.
3. The event in a contingent contract must be essential to the contract.
4. The event in a contingent contract may be certain or uncertain.
5. The performance of a contingent contract must not depend upon mere will of the promisor.
6. Contracts contingent upon the happening of an uncertain future event becomes voidable at the option of promisee if that event becomes impossible.
7. Contracts contingent upon the non-happening of a certain future event cannot be enforced if the happening of that event becomes impossible.
8. Contracts contingent upon the happening of an uncertain specified event within a fixed time can become void only after the expiry of the fixed time.
9. Contracts contingent upon the non-happening of an uncertain specified event within a fixed time can be enforced only after the expiry of the fixed time.
10. Agreements contingent upon impossible events are void only if the impossibility of the event is known to the parties to the agreements at the time when these are made.

Answers

1. False	2. False	3. False	4. False
5. True	6. False	7. False	8. False
9. False	10. False		

VERY SHORT ANSWER TYPE QUESTIONS

1. Define Void Agreements.
2. Define Uncertain Agreements.
3. Define Wagering Agreements.
4. Give an example of agreements contingent on impossible acts.
5. What is meant by restitution?
6. State whether the party who has received some benefit under the following is bound to restore it to the other party in each of the following alternative cases?
   (a) under a voidable contract
   (b) under an agreement discovered to be void
   (c) under a contract which becomes void
   (d) under a void agreement

7. What is a contingent contract?
8. State whether the event in a contingent contract is main or collateral.
9. State whether the event in a contingent contract is certain or uncertain.
10. State whether the agreements contingent upon impossible events are void or voidable.

SHORT ANSWER TYPE QUESTIONS

1. Comment on the following statements:
   (a) An agreement is restraint of trade is void.
   (b) Wagering agreements do not cover the insurance contracts.
2. Distinguish between the following:
   (a) Void Agreements and Void Contracts
   (b) Void Agreements and Illegal Agreements
   (c) Void Contracts and Voidable Contracts
   (d) Wagering Agreements and Insurance Contracts
3. Write short notes on the following:
   (a) Void Agreements
   (b) Wagering Agreements
   (c) An agreements in restraint of trade
   (d) Restitution
4. Enumerate the agreements which have been expressly declared void by the Indian Contract Act, 1872.
5. Distinguish between wagering agreement and contingent contract.
6. Write short note on 'contingent contracts'.

ESSAY TYPE QUESTIONS

1. "An agreement in restraint of trade is void." Examine this statement mentioning exceptions, if any.
2. (a) What are agreements by way of wagers?
   (b) State the legal effects of such agreements.
   (c) Is a contract of insurance a wager?
3. (a) What are contingent contracts?
   (b) State the rules regarding enforcement of such contracts. Give illustrations also.

CHAPTER

8 Performance of a Contract

1.0 WHAT IS THE MEANING OF PERFORMANCE ?

1.1 Performance of the contract is one of the various modes of discharge of the contract.

1.2 A contract is said to have been performed when the parties to a contract *either* perform *or* offer to perform their respective promises.

1.3 *According to section, 37*, "**The parties to a contract must *either* perform *or* offer to perform their respective promises, unless such performance is dispensed with or excused under the provisions of this Act, or of any other law.**"

2.0 WHAT ARE THE TYPES OF PERFORMANCE OF THE CONTRACT ?

There may be **two** types of performance as follows:

2.1 **Actual Performance** Where a promisor has made an offer of performance to the promisee and the offer has been accepted by the promisee, it is called an actual performance.

Example *X contracted to deliver to Y at his warehouse on 1st October, 100 bales of cotton of a particular quality. X brought the cotton of requisite quality to the appointed place on the appointed day during the business hours, and Y took the delivery of goods. This is an actual performance.*

2.2 **Attempted Performance (or Tender or Offer to Perform)** Where a promisor has made an offer of performance to the promisee, and the offer has not been accepted by the promisee, it is called an attempted performance (Section 38).

Example *If in the aforesaid example, Y refused to take the delivery of goods, it is a case of attempted performance because X has done what he was required to do under the contract.*

3.0 WHAT ARE THE EFFECTS OF TENDER ?

There are **two effects** of tender as under:

3.1 The promisor is not responsible for non-performance.

3.2 The promisor does not loose his rights under the contract.

4.0 WHAT ARE THE TYPES OF TENDER ?

There can be two types of tender as follows:

Types of tender	*Meaning*	*Effects*
I. **Tender of goods or services**	Where the promisor offers to deliver the goods or services but the promisee refuses to accept the delivery.	(a) Goods or services need not be offered again. (b) Promisor may sue the promisee for non-performance. (c) Promisor is discharged from his liability.

II. Tender of money	Where the promisor offers to pay the amount but the promisee refuses to accept the same.	(a) Promisor is not discharged from his liability to pay the amount. (b) Promisor will not be liable for interest from the date of a valid tender.

5.0 WHAT ARE THE ESSENTIALS OF A VALID TENDER ?

The essentials of a valid tender are discussed below:

5.1 Unconditional It must be unconditional. Tender is said to be unconditional when it is made in accordance with the terms of the contract.

Example *X offers to deliver 100 bales of cotton to Y if Y sells his one machine to X. It is a conditional tender and hence invalid.*

5.2 At Proper Time It must be at proper time, i.e. at the stipulated time (if there is an agreement as to time) or during business hours (if there is no agreement as to time). Tender of goods or money before the due date is also not a valid tender.

5.3 At Proper Place It must be at proper place, i.e. at the stipulated place (if there is an agreement as to place) or at promisee's business place (if there is business) or at promisee's residence (if there is no business place).

5.4 Reasonable Opportunity to Promisee It must give a reasonable opportunity to the promisee of ascertaining that the goods offered are the same as the promisor is bound to deliver.

5.5 For Whole Obligation It must be for the whole obligation and not for a part of the whole obligation. However, a minor deviation from the terms of the contract may not render the tender invalid.

Example *Delivery of 100.10 tons of wheat in a contract for 100 tons of wheat is a valid tender but delivery of 120 tons of wheat is invalid tender.*

5.6 To Proper Person It must be made to the promisee or his duly authorised agent. In case of several joint promisees, a tender made to one of them has the same legal consequences as tender to all of them.

5.7 Of Exact Amount and in Legal Tender In case of tender of money, it must be of exact amount and in legal tender.

6.0 WHAT IS THE EFFECT OF REFUSAL OF PARTY TO PERFORM PROMISE WHOLLY ?

When a party to a contract has refused to perform or disabled himself from performing his promise in its entirety, the promisee may put an end to the contract, unless he has signified, by words or conduct, his acquiescence in its continuance. [Sec. 39]

Example I *A, a singer enters into a contract with B, the manager of a theatre, to sing at his theatre two nights in every week during the next two months, and B engages to pay her Rs 100 for each night's performance. On the sixth night, A wilfully absents herself from the theatre. B is at liberty to put an end to the contract.*

Example II *A, a singer enters into a contract with B, the manager of a theatre, to sing at his theatre two nights every week during the next two months and B engages to pay her at the rate of Rs 100 for each night. On the sixth night, A wilfully absents herself. With the assent of B, A sings on the seventh night. B has* *signified his acquiescence in the continuance of the contract, and cannot now put an end to it, but is entitled to compensation for damage sustained by him through A's failure to sing on the sixth night.*

7.0 WHO MAY DEMAND PERFORMANCE OF A CONTRACT ?

The following persons may demand performance of a contract:

7.1 Promisee Promisee can only demand the performance of the promise under a contract. *For example*, *X* promises *Y* to pay Rs 1,000 to *Z*. It is only *Y* who can demand performance and not *Z*.

7.2 Legal Representative In case of death of the promisee, his legal representative can demand performance unless a contrary intention appears from the contract *or* the contract is of a personal nature. *For example*, *X* promises to marry *Y* on the specified day. *Y* dies before the specified day. The legal representatives of *Y* cannot demand performance of the promise from *X* because the contract is of personal nature.

7.3 Third Party A third party can also demand the performance of the contract in some exceptional cases like beneficiary in case of trust, the person for whose benefit the provision is made in family arrangements.

7.4 Joint Promisees In case of several promisees, unless a contrary intention appears, the performance can be demanded by the following persons:

Case	***Who can demand the performance of promise***
I. In case all the promisees are alive	All the promisees jointly.
II. In case of death of any of joint promisees	Representatives of deceased promisee jointly with the surviving promisee(s).
III. In case of death of all joint promisees	Representatives of all of them jointly.

Example *X promises Y and Z jointly to repay loan of Rs 1,000 on a specified day. Y dies before that specified day. Y's representative jointly with Z can demand the performance from X on specified day. If Y and Z die before that specified day, the representatives of Y and Z jointly can demand the performance from X on specified day.*

8.0 WHO MAY PERFORM THE CONTRACT ?

A contract may be performed by the following persons:

8.1 Promisor If it appears from the nature of the case that it was the intention of the parties to any contract that any promise contained in it must be performed by the promisor himself, such promise must be performed by the promisor.

Example I *X promises to marry Y. X must perform this promise personally.*

Example II *X promises to paint a picture for Y. X must perform the promise personally.*

8.2 Promisor's Agent If it was not the intention of the parties that the promise must be performed by the promisor himself, such contracts can be performed by the promisor himself or any competent person employed by him.

Example *A promises to pay B a sum of money. A may perform this promise either by personally paying the money to B, or by causing it to be paid to B by another, and if A dies before the time appointed for payment, his representatives must perform the promise, or employ some proper person to do so.*

8.3 Legal Representatives In case of death of promisor, his legal representative can perform the contract unless a contrary intention appears or the contract is of personal nature.

Example *X promises to marry Y. X dies. X's legal representatives cannot perform this promise.*

8.4 Third Party A contract can be performed by a third party if the promisee accepts the arrangement. According to Section 41, when a promisee accepts performance of the promise from a third person, he cannot afterwards enforce it against the promisor.

8.5 Joint Promisors In case of several promisors, unless a contrary intention appears, the following persons must perform the promise:

Case	*Who must perform the promise*
I. In case all the promisors are alive	All the promisors jointly.
II. In case of death of any of joint promisors	Representatives of the deceased promisor jointly with the surviving promisor(s).
III. In case of death of all joint promisors	Representatives of all of them jointly.

Example *X and Y jointly promise to repay a loan of Rs 1,000 on a specified day. X dies before that specified day. X's representative jointly with Y must perform the promise on the specified day.*

9.0 DEVOLUTION OF JOINT LIABILITIES AND JOINT RIGHTS

9.1 What is the Meaning of Devolution ?

Devolution means passing over from one person to another.

9.2 What is the Meaning of Devolution of Joint Liabilities ? [Section 42]

The liabilities of joint promisors pass to their legal representatives (in case of death). In case of several promisors, the persons who are liable to perform the promise are given in Para 8.0.

9.3 What are the Rules Regarding the Performance of Joint Promise [Sections 43 and 44]

The rules regarding the performance of joint promises are as follows:

(a) Joint and Several Liability of Joint Promisors In the absence of express agreement to the contrary, the promisee may compel anyone or more of such joint promisors to perform the whole of the promise.

Example *A, B and C jointly promise to pay D Rs 3,000. D may compel either A or B or C to pay him Rs 3,000.*

(b) Joint Promisor's Right to Claim Contribution Each of the joint promisors may compel every other joint promisor to contribute equally with himself to the performance of the promise, unless a contrary intention appears from the contract.

Example *A, B and C jointly promise to pay D a sum of Rs 3,000. C is compelled to pay the whole. A is insolvent, but his assets are sufficient to pay one-half of his debts. C is entitled to receive Rs 500 from A's estate and Rs 1,250 from B.*

(c) Joint Promisor's Duty to Share Loss from Default in Contribution If any of the joint promisors makes default in such contribution, the remaining joint promisor must bear the loss arising from such default in equal shares.

Example *A, B and C are under a joint promise to pay D Rs 3,000. C is unable to pay anything and A is compelled to pay the whole. A is entitled to receive Rs 1,500 from B.*

(d) Effect of Release of One Joint Promisor A release of one of such joint promisors by the promisee, does not discharge the other joint promisors *neither* does it free the joint promisor so released from responsibility to the other joint promisors.

Example *A, B and C jointly promise to pay D Rs 3,000. D releases A from his liability and sues B and C for payment. Here, neither B and C are released from their liability to D nor A is released from his liability to B and C for contribution.*

However, under English law, the liability of joint promisors is only joint and not joint and several and therefore, the release of one of the joint promisors shall relieve all the other promisors of their liability.

9.4 What is the Meaning of Devolution of Joint Rights ? [Section 45]

When a person has made a promise to two or more persons jointly, then, unless a contrary intention appears from the contract, the right to claim performance rests, as between him and them, with them during their joint lives, and, after the death of any of them, with the representative of such deceased person jointly, with the survivor or survivors and after the death of the last survivor, with the representatives of all jointly. *Refer to Para 8.5.*

Example *A, in consideration of Rs 5,000 lent to him by B and C, promises B and C jointly to repay them that sum with interest on a day specified. B dies. The right to claim performance rests with B's representative jointly with C during C's life, and, after the death of C, with the representatives of B and C jointly.*

10.0 WHAT ARE THE RULES AS TO TIME AND PLACE OF PERFORMANCE ?

The various rules regarding the time and place of performance are given below:

Case	*Rule*
1. **Where the time for performance is not specified in a contract and the promisor has undertaken to perform without application by the promisee.**	The contract must be performed within a reasonable time. The question 'What is reasonable time' is a question of fact [Section 46].
2. **Where the time for performance is specified in a contract and the promisor has undertaken to perform it without application by the promisee.**	The promisor must perform his promise on that particular day during the usual business hours and at a place where the promise ought to be performed [Section 47].

3. Where the time for performance is specified in a contract and the promisor has not undertaken to perform it without application by the promisee.	The promisee must apply for performance at a proper place and within usual business hours [Section 48].
4. Where the place for performance is not specified in a contract and the promise is to be performed without application by the promisee.	The promisor must apply to the promisee to appoint a reasonable place for the performance and to perform the promise at such place [Section 49].
5. Where the promisee prescribes the manner or time for performance.	The promise must be performed in the manner and at the time prescribed by the promisee [Section 50].

Example I *B owes A Rs 2,000. A desires B to pay the amount to A's account with C, a banker. B who also banks with C, orders the amount to be transferred from his account to A's credit, and this is done by C. Afterwards, and before A knows of the transfer, C fails. There has been a good payment by B.*

Example II *A and B are mutually indebted. A and B settle an account by setting off one item against another, and B pays A the balance found to be due from him upon such settlement. This amounts to payment by A and B, respectively, of the sums which they owed to each other.*

Example III *A owes B Rs 2,000. B accepts some of A's goods in reduction of the debt. The delivery of the goods operates as a part payment.*

Example IV *A desires B, who owes him Rs 100, to send him a note for Rs 100 by post. The debt is discharged as soon as B posts a letter containing the note duly addressed to A.*

11.0 IS TIME AN ESSENCE OF CONTRACT ?

11.1 Meaning of Time as Essence of Contract

Time is an essence of a contract means that it is essential for the parties to a contract to perform their respective promises within the specified time.

11.2 Cases where Time is considered to be Essence of Contract

In the following cases, time is usually considered to be the essence of contract:

(a) Where the parties have expressly agreed to treat the time as the essence of the contract.

(b) Where the non-performance at the specified time operates as an injury to the party.

(c) Where the nature and necessity of the contract requires the performance of the contract within the specified time.

11.3 Presumption as to Time as Essence of Contract

In commercial or mercantile contracts	*In non-commercial or non-ssmercantile contracts*
(a) Time fixed for the delivery of goods is considered to be the essence of a contract.	(a) Usually, the presumption is that time is not the essence of a contract.

(b) Time fixed for the payment of the price is not considered to be the essence of a contract.	*For example*, in case of the sale of an immovable property, time is presumed to be not the essence of a contract.

11.4 What are the Consequences of Non-performance of Contract within Specified Time ?

The consequences of non-performance of a contract within the specified time depends upon whether the time is essence of the contract or not:

When time is essence of a contract	*When time is not essence of a contract*
(a) The contract becomes voidable at the option of the promisee.	(a) The contract does not become voidable at the option of the promisee.
(b) If performance beyond the specified time is accepted, the promisee cannot claim compensation for any loss occasioned by the non-performance of the promise at the agreed time unless at the time of such acceptance, he gives notice to the promisor of his intention to do so.	(b) The promisee is entitled to claim compensation for any loss occasioned to him by non-performance of the promise at the agreed time.

12.0 RECIPROCAL PROMISES

12.1 What is the Meaning of Reciprocal Promises ?

Promises which form the consideration or part of the consideration for each other, are called 'reciprocal promises'. [Section 2(f)]

Example *In a contract for sale, A promises to deliver the goods to B at a fixed price and B promises to give security for the payment of the price. Such promises are called reciprocal promises.*

12.2 What are the Types of Reciprocal Promises ?

Lord Mansfield in *Jones* v. *Barkley* case have classified the reciprocal promises as under:

Types of Reciprocal Promises	*Meaning*
(a) **Mutual and Independent**	When the promises are to be performed by each party independently, without waiting for the other party to perform his promise.
(b) **Mutual and Dependent**	When the performance of one party depends on the prior performance of the other party.
(c) **Mutual and Concurrent**	When the promises are to be performed simultaneously.

12.3 What are Rules Regarding Performance of Reciprocal Promises ?

The rules regarding the performance of reciprocal promises are as follows:

(a) **Regarding Simultaneous Performance [Section 51]** When a contract consists of reciprocal promises to be simultaneously performed, the promisor need not perform his promise unless the promisee is ready and willing to perform his reciprocal promise.

Example I *A and B contract that A shall deliver goods to B to be paid for by B on delivery. A need not deliver the goods unless B is ready and willing to pay for the goods on delivery. B need not pay for the goods, unless A is ready and willing to deliver them on payment.*

Example II *A and B contract that A shall deliver goods to B at a price to be paid in instalments, the first instalment to be paid on delivery. A need not deliver unless B is ready and willing to pay the first instalment on delivery. B need not pay the first instalment, unless A is ready and willing to deliver the goods on payment of the first instalment.*

(b) **Regarding Order of Performance [Section 52]** Where the order in which reciprocal promises are to be performed is expressly fixed by the contract, they must be performed in that order, and where the order is not expressly fixed by the contract, they must be performed in the order which the nature of the transaction requires.

Example I *A and B contract that A shall build a house for B at a fixed price. A's promise to build the house must be performed before B's promise to pay for it.*

Example II *A and B contract that A shall make delivery of his stock-in-trade to B at a fixed price, and B promises to give security for the payment of the money. A's promise need not be performed until the security is given, because the nature of the transaction requires that A should have security before he delivers up his stock.*

(c) **Effects of Preventing the Performance [Section 53]** When a contract contains reciprocal promises, and one party to the contract prevents the other from performing his promise, the contract becomes voidable at the option of the party so prevented; and such party is entitled to compensation from the other party for any loss which he may sustain in consequence of the non-performance of the contract.

Example *A and B contract that B shall execute certain work for A, for Rs 1,000. B is ready and willing to execute the work accordingly, but A prevents him from doing so. The contract is voidable at the option of B; and, if he elects to rescind it, he is entitled to recover from A compensation for any loss which he has incurred by its non-performance.*

(d) **Effects of non-performance in case of Mutual and Dependent Reciprocal Promises [Section 54]** Where the performance of one party depends on the prior performance of the other party and the party who is liable to perform first, fails to perform it, then such party cannot claim the performance from the other party and must make compensation to the other party for any loss which the other party may sustain by the non-performance of the contract.

Example I *A hires B's ship to take in and convey, from Kolkata to Mauritius a cargo, to be provided by A, B receiving a certain freight for its conveyance. A does not provide any cargo for the ship. A cannot claim the performance of*

B's promise, and must make compensation to B for the loss which B sustains by the non-performance of the contract.

Example II *A contracts with B to execute certain builder's work for a fixed price, B supplying the scaffolding and timber necessary for the work. B refuses to furnish any scaffolding or timber. A need not execute the work, and B is bound to make compensation to A for any loss caused to him by the non-performance of the contract.*

Example III *A contracts with B to deliver to him, at a specified price, certain merchandise on board of a ship which cannot arrive for a month, and B engages to pay for the merchandise within a week from the date of the contract. B does not pay within the week. A's promise to deliver need not be performed, and B must make compensation.*

Example IV *A promises B to sell him 1000 bales of merchandise to be delivered next day, and B promises A to pay them within a month. A does not deliver according to his promise. B's promise to pay need not be performed, and A must make compensation.*

(e) **Effect of Promise to do Legal and Illegal things [Section 57]** Where persons reciprocally promise, firstly, to do certain things which are legal, and secondly, under specified circumstances, to do certain other things which are illegal, the first set of promises is a contract, but the second is a void agreement.

Example *A and B agree that A shall sell B a house for Rs 10,000 but that, if B uses it as a gambling house, he shall pay Rs 50,000 for it.*

The first set for reciprocal promises, namely to sell the house and to pay Rs 10,000 for it, is a contract. The second set is for an unlawful object, namely, that B may use the house as a gambling house and is a void agreement.

(f) **Effect of alternative Promise being Illegal [Section 58]** In the case of an alternative promise, one branch of which is legal and the other illegal, the legal branch alone can be enforced.

Example *A and B agree that A shall pay B Rs 1,000 for which B shall afterwards deliver to A either rice or smuggled opium. This is a valid contract to deliver rice, and a void agreement as to the opium.*

13.0 ASSIGNMENT OF CONTRACTS

13.1 What is the Meaning of Assignment of Contracts ?

Assignment of a contract means transfer of contractual rights and liabilities to a third party.

13.2 What are the Modes of Assignment of Contracts ?

Assignment of a contract may take place in the following ways:

(a) Assignment by act of parties

(b) Assignment by operation of law

(a) **Assignment by Act of Parties** Assignment by act of parties takes place when the parties to a contract themselves make the assignment. Such an assignment is subject to the following rules:

Case	Rule
I. Assignment of Contractual Liabilities	
(a) *In case the contractual obliga-tion involves personal skill or taste or ability (e.g. contract to marry)*	(a) Such obligation cannot be assigned.
(b) *In other cases*	
(i) If the contract expressly or impliedly provides that the contract shall be performed by the promisor only	(i) Such obligation cannot be assigned.
(ii) If the contract does not ex-pressly or impliedly provide that the contract shall be performed by the promisor only	(ii) The promisor or his representative may employ a competent person to perform such obligation [Section 40] but even the promisor remains liable to the promisee for proper perform-ance.
(iii) By novations	(iii) The promisor may transfer his liability to a third party with the consent of promisee and the transferee by entering into a tripartite agreement.
II. Assignment of Contractual Rights	
(a) *In case of contractual rights involving personal skill*	(a) Such rights cannot be assigned.
(b) *In other cases*	(b) Such rights can be assigned subject to all equities between the original parties.
(c) *Actionable claims (i.e. claim to any debt [except a secured debt) or to any beneficial interest in movable property e.g. book debts, right of action arising out of a contract etc.].*	(c) Such claims can always be assigned by an instrument in writing. Notice of such assignment must also be given to the debtor.

(b) Assignment by Operation of Law Assignment by operation of law takes place when the law intervenes. Such assignment takes place in the following cases:

Case	Rule
I. **In case of death of any party**	The rights and obligations (other than those of personal nature) of the deceased party pass on to his legal representatives.
II. **In case of insolvency of any party**	The rights and obligations (other than those of personal nature) of the insolvent party pass on to the Official Receiver or Assignee.

Example I *X promises to marry Y. Here, neither X can assign his obligation nor Y can assign his right because the contract is of personal nature.*

Example II *X owes Y Rs 10,000 and Z owes X Rs 10,000. Here X cannot compel Y to recover the amount from Z. However, he can transfer his liability to Z with the consent of Y and Z. Y can also transfer his right to a third party to recover the amount from X.*

13.3 Assignment and Succession

Under succession, both benefits and burden attached to the contract devolve upon the legal heir. A son succeeding his father's estate shall be liable to meet the debts and liability of his father to the extent of the property inherited. However, in assignment, only the benefit of a contract can be assigned and not the liabilities attached thereto.

Why this is so? This is because when liability is assigned, a third party gets involved therein. Thus a debtor cannot relieve himself of his liability to creditor by assigning to someone else his obligation to repay the debt.

On the other hand, if a creditor assigns the benefit of a promise, he thereby entitles the assignee to realise the debt from the debtor but where the benefit is coupled with a liability or when a personal consideration has entered into the making of the contract then the benefit cannot be assigned. In *Zaffer Mehar Ali* v. *Budge Budge Jute Mills Company Ltd. 33 Cal., X* agreed to sell certain gunny bags to *Y*, which were to be delivered in monthly instalments for a period of 6 months and the contract contained certain options for the buyer as regards quality and packing. It was held that the clause as to the buyer's option did not preclude from assigning the contract.

Distinction between Succession and Assignment

Basis of distinction	*Succession*	*Assignment*
1. *Meaning*	The transfer of rights and liabilities of a deceased person to his legal representative is called as succession.	The transfer of rights by a person to another person is called as assignment.
2. *What can be transferred ?*	All the **rights and liabilities** of a person are transferred.	Only **rights** can be assigned.
3. *Notice*	Notice of succession is not required to be given to any person.	Notice of assignment is required to be given to the creditor.

4. *Time when takes place*	It takes place on the death of a person.	it takes place during the lifetime of a person.
5. *Written document*	It does not require any written document.	It requires execution of an assignment deed.
6. *Voluntary Act*	Succession is not a voluntary act.	Assignment is a voluntary act of the parties.
7. *Consideration*	Consideration is **not required** for succession	Consideration is **must** for assignment.

14.0 APPROPRIATION OF PAYMENT [SECTIONS 59–61]

14.1 What is the Meaning of Appropriation of Payment ?

Appropriation of payment means application of payment to a particular debt.

14.2 What are the Rules Regarding Appropriation of Payments ?

Where a debtor owes several distinct debts to a creditor and makes payment to a creditor, the following various rules regarding appropriation of payments shall apply :

Case	*Rule*
I. **Where debt to be discharged is indicated,** *(i.e. where a debtor who owes several distinct debts to one creditor, makes a payment to the creditor either with express intimation or under circumstances implying that the payment is to be applied to the discharge of some particular debt.)*	**The payment, if accepted must be applied accordingly.** (a) *A* owes *B*, among other debts, Rs 1,000 upon a promissory note, which falls due on the first June. He owes *B* one other debt of that amount. On the first June, *A* pays to *B* Rs 1,000. The payment is to be applied to the discharge of the promissory note. (b) *A* owes to *B*, among other debts, the sum of Rs 567. *B* writes to *A* and demands payment of this sum. *A* sends to *B* Rs 567. This payment is to be applied to the discharge of the debt of which *B* had demanded payment.
II. **Where debt to be discharged is not indicated,** (*i.e. where the debtor who owes several distinct debts makes a Payment to a the creditor but does not indicate the debt for which the payment is to be applied and there are no circumstances indicating the debt for which the payment is to be applied.)*	The creditor has **option to apply** the payment to any lawful debt due from the debtor even if it is a time barred debt. But he cannot apply to a disputed debt.

III. Where neither party makes any appropriation *(i.e. where the debtor who owes several distinct debts makes a payment to a the creditor but does not indicate the debt for which the payment is to be applied)*	The payment shall be applied in discharge of the debts **in order of time** whether or not they are time barred. If the debt are of equal standing, the payment shall be applied in discharge of each, proportionately. In other words all payments shall be applied towards the payment of first debt till it gets extinguished. Similarly, all subsequent payments applied towards second debt till it gets fully paid and so on and so forth.

14.3 Rule in Clayton's Case This rule applies where parties have a running account between them. According to this rule, in the absence of any contract to the contrary, an item of receipt side must be appropriated against the items of payment side in order of date.

PRACTICAL PROBLEMS

PROBLEM 1

W promises *X*, *Y* and *Z* jointly to repay a sum of Rs 9,000. Who can demand the performance of the promise in each of the following alternative cases:

(a) If *X* dies (b) If *Y* dies (c) If *Z* dies (d) If *X*, *Y* and *Z* die?

Solution

Section to which the given problem relates: Section 45.

Decision:

Case (*a*) Legal representatives of *X* jointly with *Y* and *Z*

Case (*b*) Legal representative of *Y* jointly with *X* and *Z*

Case (*c*) Legal representatives of *Z* jointly with *X* and *Y*

Case (*d*) Legal representatives of *X*, *Y* and *Z* jointly

PROBLEM 2

X, *Y* and *Z* jointly promise to pay Rs 9,000 to *W*. Who is liable to pay the amount to *W* in each of the following alternative cases:

Case (*a*) If *X* dies, *Case* (*b*) *X*, *Y* and *Z* die?

Solution

Section to which the given problem relates: Section 42.

Decision:

Case (*a*) Legal representatives of *X* jointly with *Y* and *Z*.

Case (*b*) Legal representatives of *X*, *Y* and *Z* jointly.

PROBLEM 3

X, Y and *Z* jointly promise to pay Rs 9,000 to *W*. Can *W* compel *X* to pay him in full?

Solution

Section to which the given problem relates: Section 43, Para 1.

Decision: *W* can compel *X* to pay him in full.

Reason: In the absence of an express agreement to the contrary, the promisee may compel anyone or more of such joint promisors to perform the whole of the promise.

PROBLEM 4

X, Y and *Z* jointly promise to pay Rs 9,000 to *W*. *W* compelled *X* to pay the whole amount. Can *X* recover anything from *Y* and *Z* (a) if both *Y* and *Z* are solvent, (b) if *Y* is solvent and *Z* being insolvent pays only 60 paise in a rupee.

Solution

Section to which the given problem relates: Section 43.

Decision:

Case (*a*) *X* can recover Rs 3,000 each from *Y* and *Z*.

Case (*b*) *X* can recover Rs 1,800 from *Z* and 3,600 from *Y*.

PROBLEM 5

X owes *Y* three sums, one for Rs 2,000 which is barred by limitation, second for Rs 3,000 which is not barred, and third for Rs 4,000 which is not barred. *X* sends Rs 1,000 to *Y*. Can *Y* appropriate Rs 1,000 towards Rs 2,000 (a) if *X* gives no direction in this regard (b) if *X* asks *Y* to appropriate Rs 1,000 towards the third debt of Rs 4,000?

Solution

Section to which the given problem relates: Section 59.

Decision:

Case (*a*) *Y* can appropriate Rs 1,000 towards Rs 2,000.

Case (*b*) *Y* cannot appropriate Rs 1,000 towards Rs 2,000. He must appropriate Rs 1,000 towards Rs 4,000 only because the creditor is bound to follow the instruction of debtor regarding application of the payment.

PROBLEM 6

X owes *Y* Rs 1,000 and *Z* owes *X* Rs 1,000. Can *Y* recover Rs 1,000 from *Z* (a) if no agreement has been entered into between *X, Y* and *Z* (b) if *Y* accepts *Z* as his debtor in pursuance of an agreement entered into between *X, Y* and *Z*?

Solution

Section to which the given problem relates: Section 62.

Decision:

Case (*a*) *Y* cannot recover from *Z* because there is privity of contract between *Y* and *Z*.

Case (*b*) *Y* can recover from *Z* because *X*, the promisor has transferred his liability by novation (i.e. by tripartite agreement between promisor, promisee and transferee)

TRUE OR FALSE QUESTIONS

State with reasons whether the following statements are 'True' or 'False':

1. Tender means actual performance.
2. Tender of money discharges the debtor from his liability to pay the debt.
3. Conditional offer of performance is a valid tender.
4. An offer to perform promise in part is a valid tender.
5. In case of several joint promisees, the performance of the contract may be demanded by any of them.
6. In case of several joint promisors, the promisee can demand the performance from anyone or more of joint promisors.
7. Unless otherwise agreed, each of a joint promisor cannot compel other joint promisors to contribute equally to the performance of the promise.
8. Unless otherwise agreed, if anyone of the joint promisor makes default in making the payment, the other joint promisor must share the loss arising from such default equally.
9. When a promisee releases one of the joint promisors, the released joint promisor remains no longer liable to contribute to the other joint promisors.
10. Where time for performance is specified and the promise is to be performed on demand by the promisee, the promisor must apply for the performance.
11. Where no place for performance is specified and the promise is to be performed without demand by the promisee, the promisor must apply for the performance.
12. Where time is the essence of the contract and the promisor fails to perform his promise in time, the contract becomes void.
13. Where a promisee accepts the performance from a third person, even then he can compel the promisor to perform the promise again.
14. Promises forming consideration for each other are called joint promises.
15. Promises which are to be performed simultaneously are called mutual and independent.
16. Where one party to a reciprocal promise prevents the other from performing his promise, the contract becomes void.
17. All contractual obligations can be assigned by executing an instrument in writing.
18. A promisor can compel the promisee to accept a third person as the promisor in this place.
19. The assignee takes assignment subject to all equities between the original parties.
20. An actionable claim can always be assigned.
21. Assignment by operation of law takes place only in case of death of any party.
22. The creditor has always a discretion to apply the payment made by a debtor towards any debt.
23. In the absence of any direction by debtor, a creditor cannot apply the payment towards a time barred debt.
24. In the absence of any specific appropriation by *either* party, the money received must first be applied towards the payment of principal and then towards the payment of interest.

Answers

1. False	2. False	3. False	4. False
5. False	6. True	7. False	8. True
9. False	10. False	11. True	12. False
13. False	14. False	15. False	16. False
17. False	18. False	19. True	20. True
21. False	22. False	23. False	24. False

VERY SHORT ANSWER TYPE QUESTIONS

1. What do you understand by performance of a contract?
2. What is meant by tenders?
3. Is performance of a contract by a third party valid?
4. Define the term 'reciprocal promise'.
5. What is meant by 'assignment of contracts?'
6. What is meant by 'appropriation of payment?'
7. When joint promisors are liable under the Indian Contract Act?

SHORT ANSWER TYPE QUESTIONS

1. Comment on the following:
   (a) Time is the essence of a contract. Comment.
   (b) Tender is attempted performance.
   (c) Appropriation is a right primarily of the debtor and for his benefit.
2. Write short notes on the following:
   (a) Time as essence of contract
   (b) Appropriation of payment
   (c) Assignment of contract
   (d) Reciprocal promises
   (e) Valid tender or attempted performance
   (f) Joint promise
3. Distinguish between Assignment and Succession.

ESSAY TYPE QUESTIONS

1. (a) What do you understand by performance of a contract?
   (b) Explain the rules of law relating to time and place of performance of a contract.
2. (a) What is meant by tender?
   (b) What are the essentials of a valid tender?
3. (a) Who can demand performance of the contract?

(b) Who should perform a contract?

(c) Is performance of a contract by a third party valid?

4. (a) When is time deemed to be the essence of a contract in the performance of the contract?

   (b) What are the consequences of non-performance of contract within specified time?

5. (a) Discuss the provisions relating to the rights and liabilities of joint promisors.

   (b) Discuss the provisions relating to the joint rights.

6. (a) Define the term 'reciprocal promise'.

   (b) State the rules for the performance of reciprocal promises.

7. (a) What is meant by 'assignment of contracts'?

   (b) Discuss the law relating to assignment of contracts.

8. (a) What is meant by appropriation of payment?

   (b) State the rules regarding appropriation of payment.

CHAPTER

9 Discharge of a Contract

1.0 WHAT IS THE MEANING OF DISCHARGE OF A CONTRACT ?

Discharge of a contract means termination of the contractual relations between the parties to a contract. A contract is said to be discharged when the rights and obligations of the parties under the contract come to an end.

2.0 WHAT ARE THE MODES OF DISCHARGE OF CONTRACT ?

A contract may be discharged in various modes shown on next page.

3.0 WHAT IS THE MEANT BY DISCHARGE OF PERFORMANCE ?

A contract can be discharged by performance in any of the following ways:

3.1 By Actual Performance A contract is said to be discharged by actual performance when the parties to the contract perform their promises in accordance with the terms of the contract.

3.2 By Attempted Performance or Tender A contract is said to be discharged by attempted performance when the promisor has made an offer of performance (i.e. a Valid Tender) to the promisee but it has not been accepted by the promisee.

4.0 WHAT IS MEANT BY DISCHARGE BY MUTUAL AGREEMENT ?

Since a contract is created by mutual agreement, it can also be discharged by mutual agreement. A contract can be discharged by mutual agreement in any of the following ways:

4.1 Novation [Section 62] Novation means the substitution of a new contract for the original contract. Such a new contract may be *either* between the same parties *or* between different parties. The term of contracts may *or* may not be changed. The consideration for the new contract is the discharge of the original contract.

Example I *A owes money to B under a contract. It is agreed between A, B and C that B shall henceforth accept C as his debtor, instead of A. The old debt of A to B no longer exists and a new debt from C to B has been contracted.*

Example II *A owes B Rs 10,000. A enters into an agreement with B, and gives B a mortgage of his (A's) estate for Rs 5,000 in place of the debt of Rs 10,000. This is a new contract and extinguishes the old.*

4.2 Rescission [Section 62] Rescission means cancellation of the contract by any party or all the parties to a contract.

Example *X promises Y to sell and deliver 100 Bales of cotton on 1st October at his godown and Y promises to pay for goods on 1st Nov. X does not supply the goods. Y may rescind the contract.*

4.3 Alteration [Section 62] Alteration means a change in the terms of a contract with mutual consent of the parties. Alteration discharges the original contract and creates a new contract. However, parties to the new contract must not change.

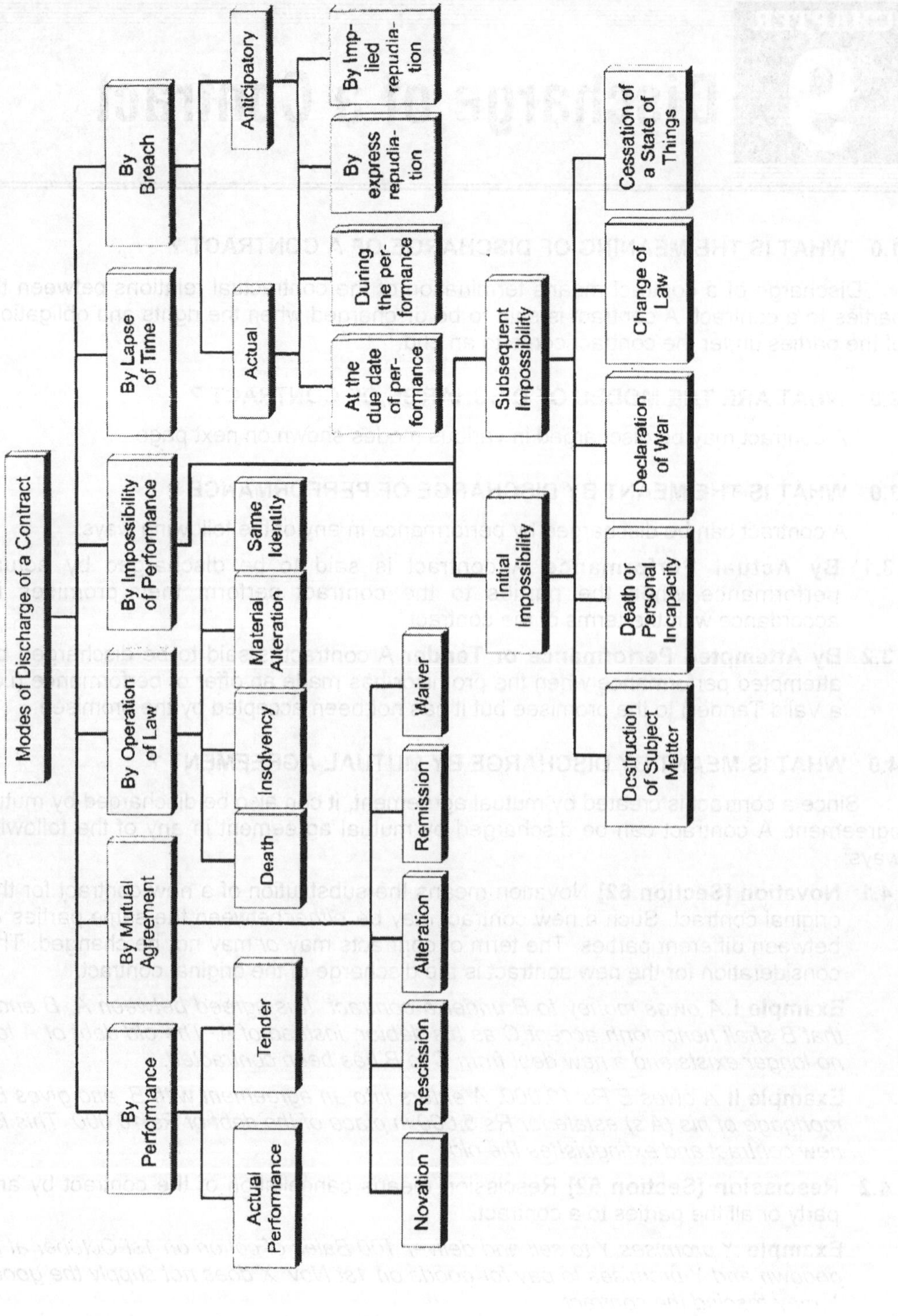
Modes of Discharge of a Contract
By Performance
By Mutual Agreement
By Operation of Law
By Impossibility of Performance
By Lapse of Time
By Breach
Actual Performance
Tender
Novation
Rescission
Alteration
Remission
Waiver
Death
Insolvency
Material Alteration
Same Identity
Initial Impossibility
Subsequent Impossibility
Destruction of Subject Matter
Death or Personal Incapacity
Declaration of War
Change of Law
Cessation of a State of Things
Actual
Anticipatory
At the due date of performance
During the performance
By express repudiation
By Implied repudiation

Example *X promises to sell and deliver 100 bales of cotton on 1st October and Y promises to pay for goods on 1st November Afterwards, X and Y mutually decide that the goods shall be delivered in five equal instalments at Z 's godown. Here, original contract has been discharged and a new contract has come into effect.*

4.4 Remission [Section 63] Remission means acceptance by the promisee of a lesser fulfillment of the promise made. According to Section 63, "Every promisee—

- may dispense with or remit, wholly or in part, the performance of the promise made to him, or
- may extend the time for such performance, or
- may accept any other consideration than agreed to in the contract instead of it any satisfaction which he thinks fit."

No consideration is necessary for remission.

Example I *A promises to paint a picture for B. B afterwards forbids him to do so. A is no longer bound to perform the promise.*

Example II *A owes B Rs 5,000. A pays to B, and B accepts, in satisfaction of the whole debt, Rs 2,000 paid at the time and place at which Rs 5,000 were payable. The whole debt is discharged.*

Example III *A owes B Rs 5,000. C pays to B Rs 1,000, and B accepts them in satisfaction of his claim on A. This payment is a discharge of the whole claim.*

Example IV *A owes B, under a contract a sum of money, the amount of which has not been ascertained. A, without ascertaining the amount, gives to B, and B, in satisfaction thereof, accepts the sum of Rs 2,000. This is a discharge of the whole debt, whatever may be its amount.*

Example V *A owes B Rs 2,000, and is also indebted to other creditors. A makes an arrangement with his creditors, including B, to pay them a composition of 50 paise in a rupee upon respective demands. Payment to B of Rs 1,000 is a discharge of B's demand.*

4.5 Waiver Waiver means intentional relinquishment of a right under the contract. Thus, it amounts to releasing a person of certain legal obligation under a contract, e.g. *X* promises to supply goods to *Y*. Subsequently, *Y* exempts *X* from carrying out the promise. This amounts to waiving the right of performance on the part of *Y*.

4.6 Distinction Between Novation and Alteration

Basis of Distintion	*Novation*	*Alteration*
1. *Parties*	The parties of contract may or may not be changed.	The parties to contract must not change.
2. *Terms*	The terms of contract may or may not be changed.	The terms of contract are changed.

5.0 WHAT IS MEANT BY DISCHARGE BY OPERATION OF LAW ?

A contract may be discharged by operation of law in the following cases:

5.1 By Death of the Promisor A contract involving the personal skill or ability of the promisor is discharged automatically on the death of the promisor.

5.2 By Insolvency When a person is declared insolvent, he is discharged from his liability up to the date of his insolvency.

5.3 By Unauthorised Material Alteration If any party makes any material alteration in the terms of the contract without the approval of the other party, the contract comes to an end.

5.4 By the Identity of Promisor and Promisee When the promisor becomes the promisee, the other parties are discharged.

Example *X draws a bill receivable on Y who accepts the same. X endorses the bill in favour of Z who in turn endorses in favour of Y. Here, Y is both promisor and promisee and hence the other parties are discharged.*

6.0 WHAT IS MEANT BY DISCHARGE BY IMPOSSIBILITY OF PERFORMANCE ?

The effects of impossibility of the performance of a contract may be discussed under the following **two** heads:

6.1 Effects of Initial Impossibility

6.2 Effects of Supervening Impossibility

6.3 Effects of Initial Impossibility [Section 56, Paras 1 and 3] Initial impossibility means the impossibility existing at the time of making the contract. The effects of initial impossibility are as follows:

Case	*Effect*
I. Where both the promisor and promisee know about the initial impossibility	Such agreement is void *ab-initio.* **Example** *X undertakes to put life into the dead wife of Y. This agreement is void.*
II. Where both the promisor and promisee do not know about the initial impossibility	Such agreement is void on the ground of mutual mistake. **Example** *X agrees to sell his horse to Y. Unknown to both the parties, the horse was dead at the time of making the agreement. This agreement is void.*
III. Where the promisor alone knowsabout the initial impossibility	Such promisor must compensate for any loss which such promisee sustains through the non-performance of the promise. **Example** *A contracts to marry B, being already married to C, and being forbidden by the law to which he is subject to practise polygamy. A must make compensation to B for the loss caused to her by the non-performance of his promise.*

6.4 Effects of Supervening Impossibility [Section 56, Para 2] Supervening impossibility means impossibility which does not exist at the time of making the contract but which arises subsequently after the formation of the contract and which makes the performance of the contract impossible or illegal. The effects of supervening impossibility are as under:

Case	*Effect*
I. Where an act becomes impossible after the contract is made	The contract to do such an act becomes void when the act becomes impossible. [Section 56, Para 2]
II. Where an act becomes unlawful by reason of some event beyond the control of promisor	The contract to do such an act becomes void when the act becomes unlawful. [Section 56, Para 2]

III. Where the promisor alone knows about the impossibility	Such promisor must compensate the promisee for any loss which such promisee might have suffered on account of non-performance of the promise. [Section 56, Para 3]
IV. Where an agreement is discovered to be void or where a contract becomes void	Any person who has received any benefit under such agreement or contract is bound to restore it or to make compensation for it, to the person from whom he received it. [Section 65] **Example** *X contracts to sing for Y at a concert for Rs 1,000 which is paid in advance. X is too ill to sing. X must refund Rs 1,000 to Y.*

7.0 CASES WHEN A CONTRACT IS DISCHARGED ON THE GROUND OF SUPERVENING IMPOSSIBILITY

A contract is discharged by supervening impossibility in the following cases:

7.1 Destruction of Subject Matter The contract is discharged if the subject matter of the contract is destroyed after the formation of the contract without any fault of either party.

Example I *X agreed to sell his crop of wheat. The entire crop was destroyed by fire though no fault of the party. The contract was discharged.*

Example II *A music hall was rented out for a series of concerts on certain days. The hall caught fire before the date of first concert. It was held, the contract has become void on ground of supervening impossibility.*

7.2 Death or Personal Incapacity The contract is discharged on the death or incapacity or illness of a person if the performance of a contract depends on his personal skill or ability.

Example *X agreed to sing on a specified day. X fell seriously ill and could not perform on that day. The contract was discharged.*

7.3 Declaration of War The pending contracts at the time of declaration of war are *either* suspended *or* declared as void.

Example *X contracts to take in cargo for Y at a foreign port. X's government afterwards declares war against the country in which the port is situated. The contract becomes void when the war is declared.*

7.4 Change of Law The contract is discharged if the performance of the contract becomes impossible or unlawful due to change in law after the formation of the contract.

Example *X agreed to sell his land to Y. After the formation of the contract, the Government issued a notification and acquired the land. The contract was discharged. [Shyam Sunder v. Durga]*

7.5 Non-existence or Non-occurrence of a Particular State of Things Necessary for Performance The contract is discharged if that particular state of thing which forms the basis of a contract, ceases to exist or occur.

Example I *X and Y contract to marry each other. Before the time fixed for the marriage. X goes mad. The contract becomes void.*

Example II *X hired a room from Y for viewing the coronation process of King Edward VII. The procession was cancelled because of King's illness. It was held that X was not liable to pay the room rent because the procession which formed the basis of the contract did not occur. (Krell v. Henry)*

8.0 CASES WHEN THE CONTRACT IS NOT DISCHARGED ON THE GROUND OF SUPERVENING IMPOSSIBILITY

Impossibility of performance is, as a rule, not an excuse from performance. It means that when a person has promised to do something, he must perform his promise unless the performance becomes absolutely impossible. A contract is not discharged by the supervening impossibility in the following cases:

8.1 Difficulty of Performance A contract is not discharged simply on the ground that its performance has become more difficult, more expensive or less profitable than that agreed at the time of its formation.

Example *X agreed to supply coal within a specified time. He failed to supply in time because of government's restriction on the transport of coal from collieries. Here X will not be discharged because the coal was available in the open market from where X could have obtained it.*

8.2 Commercial Impossibility A contract is not discharged simply on the ground of commercial impossibility, i.e. when the contract becomes commercially unviable or unprofitable.

Example *X, a furniture manufacturer agreed to supply certain furniture to Y at an agreed rate. Afterwards, there was a sharp increase in the rates of the timber and rates of wages. Since, it was no longer profitable to supply at the agreed rate, X did not supply. X will not be discharged on the ground of commercial impossibility.*

8.3 Default of a Third Party A contract is not discharged if it could not be performed because of the default of a third party on whose work the promisor relied.

Example *X entered into a contract with Y for the sale of goods to be manufactured by Z, a manufacturer of those goods. Z did not manufacture those goods. X will not be discharged and will be liable to Y for damages.*

8.4 Strikes, Lockouts and Civil Disturbances A contract is not discharged on the grounds of strikes, lockouts and civil disturbances unless otherwise agreed by the parties to the contract.

Example *X agreed to supply to Y certain goods to be imported from Algeria. The goods could not be imported due to riots in that country. It was held that this was no excuse for non-performance of the contract. [Jacobs v. Credit Lyonnais]*

8.5 Partial Impossibility A contract is not discharged simply on the ground of impossibility of some of the objects of the contract.

Example *X agreed to let a boat to H (i) to view the naval review at the coronation of king and (ii) to cruise round the fleet. Due to the illness of the king, the naval review was cancelled but the fleet was assembled and the boat could have been used to cruise round the fleet. It was held that the contract was not discharged. [H.B. Steamboat Co. v. Hutton]*

9.0 WHAT IS MEANT BY DISCHARGE BY LAPSE OF TIME ?

A contract is discharged if it is not performed or enforced within a specified period, called period of limitation. The Limitation Act, 1963 has prescribed the different periods for different contracts, e.g. period of limitation for exercising right to recover a debt is 3 years, and to recover an immovable property is 12 years. The contractual parties cannot exercise their rights after the expiry of period of limitation.

Example *On 1st July 20X1 X sold goods to Y for Rs 1,00,000 and Y has made no payment till August 20X4. State the legal position as on 1st August 20X4 if no credit period was allowed (b) if 2 months credit period was allowed.*

Solution:

Case (*a*) The contract is discharged by lapse of time (i.e. 3 years) from 1st July 20X1 because the debt has become time barred and hence *X* cannot exercise his right to recover this debt.

Case (*b*) The contract is not discharged by lapse of time because the period of limitation is yet to expire on 31st August 20X4 (i.e. 3 years from the expiry of the credit period).

10.0 WHAT IS MEANT BY DISCHARGE BY BREACH OF CONTRACT ?

A contract is said to be discharged by breach of contract if any party to the contract refuses or fails to perform his part of the contract or by his act makes it impossible to perform his obligation under the contract. A breach of contract may occur in the following two ways:

10.1 Anticipatory Breach of Contract Anticipatory breach of contract occurs when the party declares his intention of not performing the contract before the performance is due.

10.2 Actual Breach of Contract Actual breach of contract occurs in the following two ways:

(*i*) ***On Due Date of Performance:*** If any party to a contract refuses or fails to perform his part of the contract at the time fixed for performance, it is called an actual breach of contract on due date of performance.

(*ii*) ***During the Course of Performance:*** If any party has performed a part of the contract and then refuses or fails to perform the remaining part of the contract, it is called an actual breach of contract during the course of performance.

11.0 CONSEQUENCES OF BREACH OF CONTRACT

The aggrieved party (i.e. the party not at fault)—

(a) is discharged from his obligation, and

(b) is entitled to proceed against the party at fault.

The various remedies available to an aggrieved party have been discussed in detail in the next chapter.

PRACTICAL PROBLEMS

PROBLEM 1

X undertakes to put life into the dead wife of *Y* and takes his fees Rs 5,000 in advance. *X* fails to do so. *Y* claims Rs 5,000. Is *Y*'s claim valid?

Solution

Section to which the given problem relates: [Section 56 (Para 1), and Section 65].

Decision: *Y*'s claim is void.

Reason: (a) The agreement is void *ab-initio* [Section 56 (Para 2)].

(b)The person who received any advantage under a void agreement, is bound to restore it [Section 65].

PROBLEM 2

X of Delhi agreed to sell 100 bales of cotton @ Rs 1,000 per bale and to deliver within a fortnight at buyer's godown at Lahore. *X* failed to supply these goods. State the legal position in each of the following alternative cases:

Case (*a*) If, unknown to both the parties, the goods were destroyed by fire at the time of agreement.

Case (*b*) If *X* knew that goods were destroyed by fire at the time of agreement.

Case (*c*) If the goods were destroyed by fire after the formation of agreement.

Case (*d*) If war is declared between India and Pakistan.

Case (*e*) If these goods were to be manufactured by *Z* who is ready to supply @ Rs 1,100 per bale because of unexpected increase in the cost of material and labour.

Case (*f*) If these goods were to be manufactured by *Z* who did not manufacture those goods.

Case (*g*) If these goods could not be delivered because of strike of transport operators.

Solution

Section to which the given problem relates: Section 56.

Decision and Reason:

Case (*a*) The contract is void on the ground of mutual mistake.

Case (*b*) The contract is void but *X*, the promisor, must compensate the buyer for the promisee for any loss which such promisee sustains through the non-performance of the promise.

Case (*c*, *d*) The contract has become void on the ground of supervening possibility.

Case (*e*) The contract is not discharged because of commercial impossibility.

Case (*f*) The contract is not discharged because of default of third party.

Case (*g*) The contract is not discharged because of non-performance due to strikes, lock-out or civil disturbances.

PROBLEM 3

Mr *X*, a Hindu contracts to marry *Y* a muslim. State the legal position in each of the following alternative cases:

Case (*a*) If Mr *X* is already married to *Z* who lives with *X*;

Case (*b*) If Mr *X* goes mad before the date fixed for marriage;

Case (*c*) If Mr *X* dies before the date fixed for marriage.

Solution

Section to which the given problem relates: Section 56.

Decision and Reason:

Case (*a*) The contract is void *ab-initio* because such contract is forbidden by law. *X* must compensate *Y* for the loss caused to her by the non-performance of the promise.

Case (*a*) The contract becomes void because of change in the state of things which formed the basis of the contract.

Case (*c*) The contract is discharged on the death of *X*.

PROBLEM 4

X, a singer enters into a contract with *Y*, the manager of a theatre, to sing at his theatre two nights every week during the next two months and *Y* engages to pay her at the rate of Rs 100 for each night on completion of the contract. State the legal position in each of the following alternative cases:

Case (*a*) On sixth night if *X* wilfully absents herself from the theatre and wants to sing on the seventh night but *Y* does not allow her to sing on the seventh night.

Case (*b*) On the sixth night if *X* wilfully absents herself from the theatre and *Y* allows *X* to sing on seventh night.

Case (*c*) On sixth night, *X* is too ill to sing.

Case (*d*) On sixth night, *X* dies before she sings.

Solution

Section to which the given problem relates: Sections 39, 56.

Decision and Reason:

Case (*a*) *Y* can rescind the contract and can claim the damages for the breach of contract [Section 39].

Case (*b*) *Y* cannot rescind the contract but can claim the compensation for the damages sustained by him through *X*'s failure to sing on the sixth night [Section 39].

Cases (*c*, *d*) *X* is discharged on the sixth night because of her incapability to sing and *Y* cannot claim the compensation for the damages sustained by him through *Y*'s failure to sing on the sixth night.

PROBLEM 5

On 1st June, *X* contracted to supply *Y* 1000 cubic feet of Finland Timber @ Rs 500 per cubic feet to be delivered at Mumbai from 1st July to 30th September. On 15th June, *X* informs that he could not supply those goods. The rates of timber per cubic feet on various dates were—on 15th June Rs 1,200, on 1st July Rs. 1,300, on 30th September Rs. 1,400. State the legal position in each of the following alternative cases:

Case (*a*) If *Y* filed a suit for breach of contract on 15th June.

Case (*b*) If *Y* filed a suit for breach of contract on 30th September

Case (*c*) If on 29th September the import of such goods was banned and *Y* filed a suit for breach of contract on 30th September

Solution

Section to which the given problem relates: Sections 73 and 56.

Decision and Reason:

Case (*a*) *Y* is entitled to claim Rs 7,00,000 being the difference between the market price on the date of repudiation of contract (i.e. on 15th June) and the contract price [Section 73].

Case (*b*) *Y* is entitled to claim Rs 9,00,000 being the difference between the market price on the date of repudiation of contract (i.e. on 30th September) and the contract price [Section 73].

Case (*c*) *Y* is not entitled to claim anything because the contract has already been discharged by supervening illegality [Section 56].

TRUE OR FALSE QUESTIONS

State with reasons whether the following statements are True or False.

1. Substitution of a new contract in place of an existing contract is called alteration.
2. Cancellation of contract is called remission.
3. In case the goods are sold on credit and a debt is not recovered within three years from the date of grant of credit, the debt becomes time barred and is discharged by lapse of time.
4. The death of the promisor always discharges the contract.
5. The insolvency of the promisor discharges the contract.
6. An agreement to do an impossible act is voidable at the option of the promisee.
7. Where initial impossibility is unknown to both the parties, the contract will not be void.
8. When the performance of a contract becomes subsequently impossible or unlawful, the contract becomes voidable at the option of promisee.
9. When a contract becomes void, any person who had received any advantage under such contract must restore it.
10. Impossibility of performance is not an excuse for non-performance of a contract.
11. Commercial impossibility makes the contract void.
12. A contract which could not be performed because of a default by a third person on whose work the promisor relied, becomes void.
13. Discharge of contract by anticipatory breach of contract takes place when the performance is due.

Answers

1. False	2. False	3. False	4. False
5. True	6. False	7. False	8. False
9. True	10. True	11. False	12. False
13. False			

VERY SHORT ANSWER TYPE QUESTIONS

1. What do you understand by performance of a contract?
1. What is discharge of a contract?
2. What is meant by discharge of a contract by tender?
3. What is meant by 'Novation'?
4. What is meant by 'Rescission'?
5. What is meant by 'Alteration'?
6. What is meant by 'Remission'?
7. When is a contract is said to discharged by lapse of time?
8. What is the period of limitation for exercising the right to recover an immovable property?
9. What is the period of limitation for exercising the right to recover a debt?

10. Does the death of the promisor discharge the contract in all cases?
11. Does the insolvency of the promisor discharge the contract in all cases?
12. What is meant by supervening impossibility?
13. What is meant by discharge of contract by anticipatory breach of contract?

SHORT ANSWER TYPE QUESTIONS

1. Comment on the following:
   (a) Impossibility of performance is as a rule not an excuse for non-performance of a contract. Discuss.
   (b) Commercial impossibility is not a valid excuse for the non-performance of a contract.
   (c) The death of the promisor discharges the contract.
   (d) The insolvency of the promisor discharges the contract.
2. Distinguish between the following:
   (a) Novation and Alteration
   (b) Novation and Rescission
   (c) Initial Impossibility and Supervening Impossibility.
3. Write short notes on the following:
   (a) Discharge of a contract by tender
   (b) Discharge of a contract by consent
   (c) Novation of a contract
   (d) Discharge of a contract by lapse of time
   (e) Discharge of a contract by operation of law
   (f) Doctrine of Supervening Impossibility
   (g) Effects of Supervening Impossibility
   (h) Discharge of a contract by breach.

ESSAY TYPE QUESTIONS

1. (a) What is discharge of a contract?
   (b) What are the various ways in which a contract may be discharged?
2. Explain with examples the doctrine of supervening impossibility.

CHAPTER

10 Remedies for Breach of Contract

1.0 WHAT IS THE MEANING OF BREACH OF CONTRACT ?

A breach of contract occurs if any party refuses or fails to perform his part of the contract or by his act makes it impossible to perform his obligation under the contract. In case of breach, the aggrieved party (i.e. the party not at fault) is relieved from performing his obligation and gets a right to proceed against the party at fault. A breach of contact may arise in two ways, (a) anticipatory breach and (b) actual breach.

2.0 ANTICIPATORY BREACH OF CONTRACT

2.1 What is the Meaning of Anticipatory Breach of Contract ?

Anticipatory breach occurs when the party declares his intention of not performing the contract before the performance is due. Thus, when a party refuses to perform a contract even before it is due for performance, it is called anticipatory breach.

2.2 Modes of Declaring an Intention not Performing the Contract

A party may declare his intention of not performing the contract in the following two ways:

(a) **When a party to a contract has refused to perform his promise.**

Example *X, a farmer agrees to sell to Y his entire crop of 10 tons of wheat @ Rs 8,000 per ton to be delivered on 20th October. On 1st October, X informs Y that he is not going to supply the goods. X has committed anticipatory breach of contract by express repudiation.*

(b) **When a party to a contract has disabled himself from performing his promise in its entirety.**

Example *X, a farmer agrees to sell to Y his entire crop of 10 tons of wheat @ Rs 8,000 per ton to be delivered on 20th October. On 1st October, X sold his entire crop to Z @ Rs 10,000 per ton. X has committed anticipatory breach of contract by implied repudiation.*

2.3 What are the Options Available to Aggrieved Party ?

In case of anticipatory breach, the aggrieved party has the following two options:

Option I. He can rescind the contract and claim damages for breach of contract without waiting until the due date for performance, or

Option II. He may treat the contract as operative and wait till the due date for performance and claim damages if the promise still remains unperformed.

2.4 What are the Consequences of Treating Contract as Operative ?

In case of anticipatory breach, if the aggrieved party treats the contract as operative and waits till the due date for performance, the consequences will be as follows:

(a) The promisor may perform his promise on or before the due date of performance and the promisee will be bound to accept the performance.

(b) The promisor may take advantage of the discharge by supervening impossibility arising between the date of breach and the due date of the performance and in such a case, the promisee shall lose his right to sue for damages.

Example *X, a farmer agreed to sell to Y his entire crop of wheat @ Rs 8,000 per ton to be delivered on 20th October. On 1st October, X informed Y that he was not going to supply the goods. Y decided not to rescind the contract on 1st October and to wait till 20th October. On 19th October, the entire crop was destroyed by fire without the fault of either party. Since the contract had become void on the ground of impossibility of performance, Y had lost his right to sue X for damages.*

2.5 What is the Amount of Damages ?

The amount of damages in each of the options exercised by an aggrieved party will be calculated as under:

Option exercised	*Amount of damages*
I. **When the aggrieved party rescinds the contract at the date of breach**	The amount of damages will be equal to the difference between the price prevailing on the date of breach and the contract price.
II. **When the aggrieved party does not rescind the contract at the date of breach**	The amount of damages will be equal to the difference between the price prevailing on the due date of performance and the contract price.

Example *X, a farmer, agreed to sell to Y his entire crop of 10 tons of wheat @ Rs 8,000 per ton to be delivered on 20th October. On 1st October, X informed Y that he was not going to supply the goods. Calculate the amount of damages which could be recovered by Y from X (a) if Y rescinded the contract on 1st October when the market price of wheat was Rs 10,000 per ton, (b) If Y did not rescind the contract on 1st October and waited till 20th October when the market price of wheat was Rs 12,000 per ton.*

Case	*A* *Market Price per ton*	*B* *Contract Price per ton*	*C = A – B* *Difference per ton*	*D* *Qty. in tons*	*E = C × D* *Amount of Damages*
(a) If Y rescinded the contract	Rs 10,000	Rs 8,000	Rs 2,000	10	Rs 20,000
(b) If Y did not rescind the contract	Rs 12,000	Rs 8,000	Rs 4,000	10	Rs 40,000

3.0 ACTUAL BREACH OF CONTRACT

3.1 What is the Meaning of Actual Breach of Contract ?

Actual breach of contract may take place in any of the following two ways:

(i) On due Date of Performance If any party to contract refuses or fails to perform his part of the contract at the time fixed for performance, it is called an actual breach of contract on due date of performance.

Example *X agreed to sell to Y 10 tons of wheat @ Rs 8,000 per ton to be delivered in two equal instalments on 20th October and on 21st October. On 20th October, X refused to deliver the goods. It is an actual breach of contract on due date of performance.*

(i) During the Course of Performance *If any party has performed a part of the contract and then refuses or fails to perform the remaining part of the contract, it is called an actual breach of contract during the course of performance.*

Example *X agreed to sell to Y 10 tons of wheat @ Rs 8,000 per ton to be delivered in two equal instalments on 20th October and 21st October. On 20th October, X delivered 5 tons and refused to deliver remaining 5 tons. It is an actual breach of contract during the course of performance.*

3.2 Consequences of Actual Breach [Section 55]

The consequences of actual breach depends upon whether the time was the essence of the contract or not. The consequences in both the cases may be summarised as under:

	Where time is the essence of a contract	***Where time is not the essence of a contract***
I. Whether the contract becomes voidable at the option of the promisee.	**Yes**	**No**
II. Whether the promisee is entitled to claim the compensation for any loss occasioned to him by the non-performance of the promise at the stipulated time		
(i) *Where performance beyond the stipulated time is not accepted*	**Yes**	**Yes**
(ii) *Where performance beyond the stipulated time is accepted*	**No**, unless the promisee gives notice to the promisor of his intention to do so.	**No**, unless the promisee gives notice to the promisor of his intention to do so.

Example *X, a singer, enters into a contract with Y, the manager of a theatre, to sing at his theatre two nights in every week for the next two months. Y agrees to pay her Rs 100 for each performance. On the sixth night, X wilfully absents herself from the theatre.*

In this case, Y has the following two options:

(a) Y may rescind the contract and claim compensation for the loss occasioned to him by X's failure to sing on the sixth night.

(b) Y may permit X to sing on the seventh night and claim compensation for loss from X by giving a notice to X of his intention to do so.

4.0 REMEDIES FOR BREACH OF CONTRACT

4.1 What is the Meaning of Remedy ?

A remedy is the course of action available to an aggrieved party (i.e. the party not at default) for the enforcement of a right under a contract.

4.2 What are the Remedies for Breach of Contract ?

The various remedies available to an aggrieved party are as follows:

1. Rescission of Contract [Section 39] Rescission means a right not to perform obligation.

In case of breach of a contract, the promisee may put an end to the contract. In such a case, the aggrieved party is discharged from all the obligations under the contract and is entitled to claim compensation for the damage which he has sustained because of the non-performance of the contract.

Example *X agrees to supply 10 tons of wheat to Y on 20th October. Y promises to pay for the goods on its receipt. X does not supply the goods on the due date. Here, Y is discharged from the liability of paying the price. Y is entitled to rescind the contract and to claim compensation for the damage which he has sustained because of non-supply of goods on the due date.*

2. Suit for Damages Damages are monetary compensation allowed for loss suffered by the aggrieved party due to breach of a contract. The object of awarding damages is not to punish the party at fault but to make good the financial loss suffered by the aggrieved party due to the breach of contract.

In India, the rules relating to damages are based on the judgement in English case of *Hadley* v. *Baxendale*. The facts of this case were: *H*'s mill was stopped due to the breakdown of a shaft. He delivered the shaft to *B*, a common carrier, to be taken to a manufacturer to copy it and make a new one. *H* had not made it known to *B* that delay would result in a loss of profits. By some neglect on the part of *B*, the delivery of the shaft was delayed in transit beyond a reasonable time. Held, *B* was not liable for loss of profits during the period of delay as the circumstances communicated to *B* did not show that a delay in the delivery of shaft would entail loss of profits to the mill. The following rule of law was laid down in this case: 'Where two parties have made a contract which one of them has broken, the damages which the other party ought to receive in respect of such breach of contract should be such as may fairly and reasonably be considered *either* arising naturally i.e., according to the usual course of things, from such breach of contract itself, *or* such as may reasonably be supposed to have been in the contemplation of both parties, at the time they made the contract, as the probable result of the breach of it.

Compensation for Loss or Damage Caused by Breach of Contract [Section 73] Section 73, of the Indian Contract Act which deals with compensation for loss or damage caused by breach of contract is based on the judgement in the above case. It states that the aggrieved party may claim the damages as follows:

(a) Such damages which naturally arose in the usual course of things from such breach. This relates to ordinary damages arising in the usual course of things.

(b) Such damages which the parties knew, when they made the contract, to be likely to result from the breach. This relates to special damages.

(c) The aforesaid compensation is not to be given for any remote or indirect loss or damage sustained by reason of the breach, and

(d) Such compensation for damages arising from breach of quasi contract shall be same as in any other contract.

(*a*) *Ordinary Damages* Ordinary damages are those which naturally arise in the usual course of things from such breach. These damages can be recovered if the following two conditions are fulfilled:

(i) The aggrieved party must suffer by breach of contract, and

(ii) The damages must be proximate (i.e. direct) consequence of the breach of contract and not the indirect consequence.

Measure of Ordinary Damages: In a contract for the sale of goods, the measure of ordinary damages is the difference between the contract price and the market price of such goods on the date of breach.

Example *On 1st December, X contracted to sell and deliver 50 tons of wheat @ Rs. 8,000 per ton to Y on 1st January. On 20th December Y, afterwards, contracted to sell those goods to Z at Rs 10,000 per ton. X failed to deliver goods on 1st January when the price of the wheat was Rs 9,500 per ton. Y is entitled to recover Rs 75,000 [i.e (Rs 9,500 – Rs 8,000) × 50]. Y is not entitled to recover Rs 1,00,000 as profit which would have arisen to Y from the sale to Z because the profit is the indirect consequence of the breach of contract.*

(*b*) *Special Damages* Special damages are those which may reasonably be supposed to have been in the contemplation of both parties as the probable result of the breach of a contract.

Condition for Recovery of Special Damage—These damages can be recovered if the special circumstances which would result in a special loss in case of breach of a contract are communicated to the promisor, e.g. loss of profits on account of default by the other party to the contract can be claimed only when an advance notice of such damages has been given before.

Example I *A, a builder, contracts to erect and finish a house by the first of January, in order that B may give possession of it at that time to C, to whom B has contracted to let it. A is informed of the contract between B and C. A builds the house so badly that, before the first of January it falls down, and has to be rebuilt by B, who, in consequence, loses the rent which he was to have received from C, and is obliged to make compensation to C for the breach of his contract. A must make compensation to B for the cost of rebuilding the house, for the rent lost, and for the compensation made to C.*

Example II *A delivers to B, a common carrier, a machine to be delivered without delay, to A's mill informing that his mill has stopped for want of the machine. B unreasonably delays the delivery of machine, and A, in consequence, loses a profitable contract with the Government. A is entitled to receive from B, by way of compensation, the average amount of profit, which would have been made by the working of the mill during the time that delivery of it was delayed, but not the loss sustained through the loss of the Government contract.*

(*c*) *Exemplary or Punitive or Vindictive Damages* Exemplary damages are those which are in the nature of punishment. The court may award these damages in case of (i) a breach of promise to marry, where damages shall be calculated on the basis of mental injury sustained by the aggrieved party, (ii) Wrongful dishonour of a cheque by a banker. In case of wrongful dishonour of a cheque, the rule is smaller the amount of the cheque, larger will be the amount of damages awarded. A trader may recover such damages as wrongful dishonour of cheque shall adversely affect his goodwill but a non-trader whose cheque is wrongfully dishonoured will have to prove the loss of goodwill before claiming such damages.

(*d*) ***Nominal Damages*** Nominal damages are those which are awarded where there is only a technical violation of a legal right but the aggrieved party has not in fact suffered any loss because of breach of contract. These damages are called nominal because they are very small, say, one rupee. The court may or may not award these nominal damages.

(*e*) ***Damages for Inconvenience and Discomfort*** If a party has suffered physical inconvenience and discomfort due to breach of contract, that party can recover the damages for such inconvenience and discomfort.

Example *H with his wife and children booked a ticket for a midnight train, to be transported to a particular place where he lived. They were, however, transported to a wrong place and they had to walk several miles on a drizzling night and as a result, his wife caught cold and he had to incur some medical expenses. It was held that he could recover compensation for inconvenience and not for medical expenses for the sickness of his wife because it was very remote consequence. [Hobbs v. London & S.W. Rail Co.]*

(*f*) ***Liquidated Damages and Penalty*** When the parties to a contract at the time of formation of contract, specify a sum which will become payable by the party responsible for breach, such specified sum is called:

(i) ***Liquidated Damages*** if the specified sum represents a fair and genuine pre-estimate of the damages likely to result due to breach;

(ii) ***Penalty*** if the specified sum is disproportionate to the damages likely to result due to breach.

In India, there is no distinction between penalty and liquidated damages. The Courts in India allow only reasonable compensation not exceeding the sum specified in the contract. [Section 74].

But under English law, liquidated damages are enforceable and not penalty.

(*g*) ***Stipulation for Interest*** The stipulations for interest may or may not be in the nature of a penalty. If the stipulation for interest is in the nature of a penalty, the court may award reasonable compensation only. On the basis of various judicial pronouncements, the following guidelines may be adopted to decide whether a particular stipulation for interest is in the nature of a penalty or not:

Stipulation	***Whether the stipulation is in the nature of a penalty or not***
(i) For payment of interest in case of default	It is not in the nature of a penalty if the interest is reasonable.
(ii) For payment of increased interest from the date of the contract	It is always in the nature of a penalty.
(iii) For payment of increased interest from the date of default only	It may or may not be in the nature of a penalty depending on the terms and circumstances of the case.
(iv) For payment of compound interest on default at the same rate as simple interest	It is not in the nature of a penalty.

(v) For payment of compound interest on default at the rate higher than that of simple interest	It is in the nature of a penalty.
(vi) For payment of interest at a rate lower than that of original rate if interest is paid on due date	It is not in the nature of a penalty.

(h) Forfeiture of Security Deposit (or Earnest Money) A clause in a contract which provides for forfeiture of security deposit in the event of failure to perform is in the nature of a penalty. In such cases, the court may award reasonable compensation only.

3. Suit for Specific Performance Suit for specific performance means demanding the court's direction to the defaulting party to carry out the promise according to the terms of the contract.

Cases where suit for specific performance is maintainable

(i) Where Actual damages arising from breach are not measurable

(ii) Where Monetary compensation is not an adequate remedy.

Example *X agreed to sell an old painting to Y for Rs 50,000. Subsequently, X refused to sell the painting. Here, Y may file a suit against X for the specific performance of the contract.*

Cases where suit for specific performance is not maintainable.

(i) Where the damages are considered as an adequate remedy.

(ii) Where the contract is of personal nature, e.g. contract to marry.

(iii) Where the contract is made by a company beyond its powers as laid down in its Memorandum of Association.

(iv) Where the court cannot supervise the performance of the contract.

(v) Where one of the parties is a minor.

(vi) Where the contract is inequitable to either party.

4. Suit for Injunction Suit for injunction means demanding court's stay order. Injunction means an order of the court which prohibits a person to do a particular act. Where a party to a contract does something which he promised not to do, the court may issue an order prohibiting him from doing so.

Example *W agreed to sing at L's theatre only during the contract period. During the contract period, W made contract with Z to sing at another theatre and refused to perform the contract with L. It was held that W could be restrained by injunction from singing for Z. [Lumely v. Wagner]*

5. Suit for Quantum Meruit Quantum Meruit means as much as is earned. Right to Quantum Meruit means a right to claim the compensation for the work already done. (For more details, see the next chapter.)

Example *C an owner of a magazine engaged P to write a book to be published by instalments in his magazine. After a few instalments were published, the publication of the magazine was stopped. It was held that P could claim payment for the part already published. [Planche v. Calburn]*

PRACTICAL PROBLEMS

PROBLEM 1

X contracts to repair *Y*'s house in a certain manner and receives payment in advance. *X* repairs the house but not according to the contract. *Y* incures Rs 1,000 to remedy the defect. Can *Y* recover Rs 1,000 from *X*.

Solution

Section to which the given problem relates: Section 73.

Decision and Reason: *Y* can recover Rs 1,000 from *X* because he suffered the loss which naturally arose in the usual course of things from such a breach.

PROBLEM 2

X sells certain merchandise to *Y* warranting it to be of a particular quality, and *Y* in reliance upon this warranty, sells it to *Z* with a similar warranty. The goods prove to be not according to the warranty, and *Y* becomes liable to pay *Z* Rs 1,000 by way of compensation. Can *Y* recover Rs 1,000 from *X*?

Solution

Section to which the given problem relates: Section 73.

Decision and Reason: *Y* can recover Rs 1,000 from *X* because the damages were the direct consequence of the breach of contract.

PROBLEM 3

X contracts to pay a sum of money to *Y* on a day specified. *X* does not pay the money on that day. *Y* in consequence of not receiving the money on that day, is unable to pay his debt and is totally ruined. Discuss the legal position.

Solution

Section to which the given problem relates: Section 73.

Decision and Reason: *Y* will not be able to recover anything except the principal sum together with interest up to the date of payment because *Y*'s insolvency is an indirect consequence of breach of contract.

PROBLEM 4

X contracts to sell and deliver 500 bales of cotton to *Y* on a fixed day. *X* knows nothing of *Y*s mode of conducting business. *X* breaks his promise and *Y*, having no cotton is obliged to close his mill. Is *X* responsible to *Y*?

Solution

Section to which the given problem relates: Section 73.

Decision and Reason: *X* is not responsible to *Y* for the loss caused to *Y* by the closure of the mill because it is an indirect consequence of the breach of the contract.

PROBLEM 5

A, a ship owner, contracts with *B* to convey him from Kolkata to Sydney in *A*'s ship, sailing on the first of January, and *B* pays to *A*, by way of deposit, one-half of his passage-money. The ship does not sail on the first of January, and *B*, after being, in consequence, detained in Kolkata, for sometime, and thereby put to some expense, proceeds to Sydney in another vessel, and, in consequence, arriving too late in Sydney, loses a sum of money. Is *A* liable to pay anything to *B*?

Solution

Section to which the given problem relates: Section 73 .

Decision and Reason: *A* is liable to repay to *B* deposit with interest, and the expense to which he is put by his detention in Kolkata, and the excess, if any, of the passage-money paid for the second ship over that agreed upon for the fist, but not the sum of money which *B* lost by arriving in Sydney too late.

PROBLEM 6

X contracts with *Y* to pay Rs 1,000 if he fails to pay *Y* Rs 500 on a given day. *X* fails to pay Rs 500 on that day. Can *Y* recover Rs 1,000?

Solution

Section to which the given problem relates: Section 74.

Decision and Reason: *Y* is entitled to recover from *X* such compensation not exceeding Rs 1,000 as the court considers reasonable because in case of stipulation for penalty, the aggrieved party is entitled to receive only reasonable compensation not exceeding the sum specified in the contract.

PROBLEM 7

X borrows Rs 1,00,000 from *Y* @ 12% p.a. interest payable by five half-yearly instalments of Rs 20,000 each. State the legal position in each of the following alternative stipulations:

Case (*a*) "In case of default in payment of any instalment, interest rate shall be raised to 15% p.a."

Case (*b*) "In case of default in payment of any instalment, interest rate shall be raised to 75% from the date of default."

Case (*c*) "In case of default in payment of any instalment, the interest shall be calculated @ 12% p.a. on monthly compounding basis."

Case (*d*) "In case of default in payment of any instalment, the interest shall be calculated @ 15% p.a. on monthly compounding basis."

Case (*e*) "In case of no default, the interest rate shall be 9% p.a.

Case (*f*) "In case of default in payment of any instalment, the whole sum shall become due."

Solution

Section to which the given problem relates: Section 74.

Decision and Reason:

Cases (*a*), (*b*) *and* (*d*) *Y* is entitled to recover from *X* such compensation as the court considers reasonable because the stipulation is in the nature of a penalty.

Cases (*c*) *and* (*e*) *Y* is entitled to recover from *X* as per stipulation because the stipulation is not in the nature of a penalty.

Case (*f*) The contract may be enforced according to its terms because the stipulation is not in the nature of a penalty.

PROBLEM 8

X borrows Rs 100 from *Y* and gives him a bond for Rs. 200 payable by five yearly instalments of Rs. 40 with a stipulation that in default of payment of any instalment, the whole shall become due. Discuss the legal position.

Solution

Section to which the given problem relates: Section 74.

Decision and Reason: *Y* is entitled to recover from *X* such compensation as the court considers reasonable because the stipulation is in the nature of a penalty.

PROBLEM 9

X lends Rs 10,000 to *Y* without interest for one month with a stipulation that in case of default, interest shall be payable. State the legal position if rate of interest is (a) 2% p.m. (b) 3% p.m.

Solution

Section to which the given problem relates: Section 74.

Decision and Reason:

Case (a) *X* is entitled to recover from *X* as per stipulation because the stipulation is not in the nature of a penalty.

Case (b) *X* is entitled to recover from *Y* such compensation as the court considers reasonable because the stipulation is in the nature of a penalty.

PROBLEM 10

A, a singer, contracts with *B*, the manager of a theatre, to sing at his theatre for two nights in every week during the next two months and engages to pay her Rs 100 for each night's performance. On the sixth night, *A* wilfully absents herself from the theatre, and *B*, in consequence, rescinds the contract.

Solution

Section to which the given problem relates: Section 75.

Decision and Reason: *B* is entitled to claim compensation for the damage which he has sustained through the non-fulfilment of the contract because a person who rightfully rescinds a contract is entitled to compensation for any damage which he has sustained through the non-fulfilment of the contract.

PROBLEM 11

X contracted with *Y* to write a book in 12 volumes for Rs 1,00,000 payable on the completion of the whole work. Discuss the legal position in each of the following alternative cases:

(a) If after completion and delivery of six volumes, *Y* abandoned the publication.

(b) If after completion and delivery of six volumes, *X* died.

Solution

Case (a) *X* is entitled to claim compensation for the work already done on quantum meruit basis.

[**Leading case:** *Planche* v. *Colburn*]

Case (b) *X*'s legal representatives are not entitled to claim compensation for the work already done by *X* because the contract to write a book in 12 volumes is an indivisible contract.

PROBLEM 12

X bought a horse with a warranty that it was free from any disease. The horse was suffering from a disease at the time of sale. As a result, not only that horse died but infected other horses also. Discuss the legal position.

Section to which the given problem relates: Section 73.

Decision and Reason: *X* is entitled to claim not only the loss occasioned by the death of the horse bought but the entire loss which occurred as a result of the breach of warranty.

[Leading case: *Smith* v. *Green*]

TRUE OR FALSE QUESTIONS

State with reasons whether the following statements are True or False:

1. Anticipatory breach of a contract takes place at the time when the performance is due.
2. Actual breach of a contract may take place during the performance of the contract.
3. In case of anticipatory breach of contract, the aggrieved party must rescind the contract and sue for damages for breach of contract at the time of such breach.
4. In case of anticipatory breach of contract, if the promisee decides not to rescind the contract, the contract shall remain alive for the benefit of both the parties.
5. In case of actual breach of a contract, the contract becomes void if the time is the essence of the contract.
6. In case of actual breach of a contract, if performance beyond stipulated time is accepted, the promisee can claim the compensation for any loss occasioned by the non-performance of the promise at the stipulated time if he gives notice of his intention to do so.
7. The aggrieved party has a right to refuse to accept monetary compensation and insist on specific performance of a contract by the promisor.
8. Specific performance can be granted in case of contract to marry.
9. Suit for specific performance can be filed where a party does something which he promised not to do.
10. Suit upon *quantum meruit* can be filed in case of incomplete and indivisible contract.
11. Ordinary damages are available only when the contract provides therefor.
12. Special damages are available as a matter of statutory right.
13. Special damages can be claimed whether or not the special circumstances are communicated to the promisor.
14. Exemplary damages are available only in case of a breach of promise to marry.
15. In case of wrongful dishonour of a cheque, the rule is smaller the amount, smaller will be the amount of damages and *vice versa*.
16. The damages which are awarded in case of breach of contract whereby no loss is caused, are called "punitive damages".
17. Liquidated damages need not be specified at the time of formation of contract.
18. Liquidated damages is a sum which is disproportionate to the damages likely to occur.
19. Penalty payable by party guilty of breach cannot be decided at the time of formation of contract.
20. Penalty is not enforceable in India.

21. Penalty is a fair and genuine pre-estimate of the damages likely to result due to breach.
22. The aggrieved party is entitled to claim the highest of the amount of penalty or actual compensation.

Answers

1. False	2. True	3. False	4. True
5. False	6. True	7. False	8. False
9. False	10. False	11. False	12. False
13. False	14. False	15. False	16. False
17. False	18. False	19. False	20. False
21. False	22. False		

VERY SHORT ANSWER TYPE QUESTIONS

1. What is a breach of contract?
2. What is an actual breach of contract?
3. When does an actual breach of contract take place?
4. What is meant by 'remedy'?
5. What is 'rescission of contract'?
6. What are 'ordinary damages'?
7. How are 'ordinary damages measured'?
8. What are 'special damages'?
9. What are 'exemplary damages'?
10. Explain 'nominal damages'?
11. What are 'liquidated damages'?
12. What is 'penalty'?
13. Is the distinction between 'liquidated damages' and 'penalty' recognised in India?
14. Is stipulation for payment of interest in case of default a penalty?
15. Is stipulation for payment of interest at a higher rate from the date of contract in case of default, a penalty?
16. Is stipulation for payment of interest at a higher rate from the date of default, a penalty?
17. Is stipulation for payment of compound interest in case of default at the same rate than that of simple interest, a penalty?
18. Is stipulation for payment of compound interest in case of default at a higher rate than that of simple interest a penalty?
19. Is stipulation for payment of interest in case of no default at a rate lower than that originally agreed, a penalty?
20. Is a clause in a contract providing for forfeiture of earnest money in the event of failure to perform a penalty?
21. What is specific performance?
22. What is an injunction?
23. What is *quantum meruit*?

SHORT ANSWER TYPE QUESTIONS

1. State the options available to a promisee in case of an anticipatory breach of contract.
2. State the consequences of not rescinding a contract at the time of anticipatory breach of contract.
3. State the consequences of actual breach of a contract.
4. State the importance of time in case of actual breach of a contract.
5. Enumerate the remedies for breach of a contract.
6. Comment on the following:
   (a) Damages for breach of contract are granted by way of compensation and not by way of punishment.
   (b) If a contract is broken, the law will endeavour, so far as money can do it, to place the injured party in the same position as if the contract had been performed.
7. Distinguish between the following:
   (a) Ordinary damages and liquidated damages
   (b) Liquidated damages and penalty
   (c) Actual breach of contract and anticipatory breach of contract
8. Write short notes on the following:
   (a) Liquidated damages (b) Exemplary damages (c) Penalty (d) Nominal damages (e) Special damages (f) Specific performance.

ESSAY TYPE QUESTIONS

1. (a) What is a breach of contract?
   (b) What do you understand by an anticipatory breach of contract?
   (c) State the rights of the promisee in case of anticipatory breach.
2. State the principles on which damages are assessed for breach of contract.
3. What remedies are available to an aggrieved party on the breach of contract?
4. State the circumstances under which a party is not entitled to specific performance.
5. State briefly whether all stipulations for payment of interest are in the nature of a penalty. Give examples also.
6. Examine critically the rule in *Hadley* v. *Baxendale* and indicate to what extent the said rule is applicable in India.
7. Explain special damages, exemplary damages, nominal damages, liquidated damages, specific performance, injunction, quantum meruit, penalty.

CHAPTER 11 Quasi-Contracts

1.0 WHAT IS THE MEANING OF QUASI-CONTRACTS

1.1 A Quasi-contract is not a contract at all because one or the other essentials for the formation of a contract are absent.

1.2 It is an obligation imposed by law upon a person for the benefit of another even in the absence of a contract.

1.3 It is based on the principle of equity, which means no person shall be allowed to unjustly enrich himself at the expense of another.

1.4 Such obligations are called quasi-contracts or implied contracts because the outcome of such obligations resemble those created by a contract.

2.0 WHAT ARE THE FEATURES OF A QUASI-CONTRACT

The salient features of a quasi contract are as under:

(a) It is imposed by law and does not arise from any agreement.

(b) The duty of a party and not the promise of any party is the basis of such contract.

(c) The right under it is always a right to money and generally, though not always, to a liquidated sum of money.

(d) The right under it is available against specific person(s) and not against the world.

(e) A suit for its breach may be filed in the same way as in case of a complete contract.

3.0 DISTINCTION BETWEEN QUASI-CONTRACTS AND CONTRACTS

Quasi-contracts differ from other contracts in the following respects:

Basis of distinction	*Quasi-contract*	*Contract*
1. *Essential for the formation of a valid contract*	The essentials for the formation of a valid contract are absent.	The essentials for the formation of a valid contract are present.
2. *Obligation*	Obligation is imposed by law.	Obligation is created by the consent of the parties.

4.0 SIMILARITY BETWEEN QUASI-CONTRACTS AND CONTRACTS

The outcome of quasi-contracts resemble that created by a contract. So far as claim for damages are concerned, there is a similarity between a Quasi-contracts and contract because in case of breach of a quasi-contract, Section 73 provides for the same remedies as provided in case of breach of a contract.

5.0 WHAT ARE THE KINDS OF QUASI-CONTRACTS

The various kinds of Quasi-contracts are discussed below:

5.1 Right to Recover the Price of Necessaries Supplied [Section 68] The person who has supplied the necessaries to a person who is incompetent to contract or anyone who is dependent on such incompetent person, is entitled to claim their price from the property of such incapable person.

Example I *A supplies B, a lunatic, with necessaries suitable to his condition in life. A is entitled to be reimbursed from B's property.*

Example II *A supplies the wife and children of B, a lunatic, with necessaries suitable to their condition in life. A is entitled to be reimbursed from B's property.*

Notes: 1. If money has been advanced in like circumstances for the purchase of necessaries, its reimbursement can also be claimed u/s 68.

2. Necessities mean necessities suitable to the conditions in the life of the person to whom such necessities are supplied.

5.2 Right to Recover Money Paid for Another Person [Section 69] A person who is interested in the payment of money for which another person is legally bound to pay, and who therefore pays it, is entitled to recover the payment made from the person who was legally bound to pay.

Example I *B holds land in Bengal, on a lease granted by A, a Zamindar. The revenue payable by A to the Government being in arrears, his land is advertised for sale by the Government. Under the revenue law, the consequence of such sale will be the annulment of B's lease. B, to prevent the sale and the consequent annulment of his own lease, pays the Government the sum due from A. A is bound to make good to B the amount so paid.*

Example II *The goods belonging to A were wrongfully attached in order to realise arrears of Government revenue due by G. A paid the amount to save the goods from sale. It was held that A was entitled to recover the amount from G. [Abid Hussain v. Ganga Sahai]*

5.3 Right to Recover for Non-Gratuitous Act [Section 70] Such right to recover arises if the following **three** conditions are satisfied:

(i) The thing must have been done or delivered lawfully;

(ii) The person who has done or delivered the thing, must not have intended to do so gratuitously; and

(iii) The person for whom the act is done/to whom thing is delivered must have enjoyed the benefit of the act done/thing delivered.

Example I *A, a tradesman, leaves goods at B 's house by mistake. B treats the goods as his own. He is bound to pay A for them.*

Example II *A saves B 's property from fire. A is not entitled to compensation from B, if the circumstances show that he intended to act gratuitously.*

5.4 Responsibility of Finder of Goods [Section 71] A person who finds goods belonging to another, and takes them into his custody, is subject to the same responsibility as a bailee.

Example *X a guest found a diamond ring at a birthday party of Y. X told Y and other guests about it. He has performed his duty to find the owner. If he is not able to find the owner he can retain the ring as bailee.*

5.5 Right to Recover from a Person to whom Money is Paid or thing is Delivered, by Mistake or Under Coercion [Section 72] A person to whom money has been paid, or anything delivered by mistake or under coercion, must repay or return it.

Example I *A and B jointly owe Rs 100 to C. A alone pays the amount to C, and B, not knowing this fact, pays Rs 100 over again to C. C is bound to repay the amount to B.*

Example II *A railway company refuses to deliver up certain goods to the consignee, except upon the payment of an illegal charge for carriage. The consignee pays the sum charged in order to obtain the goods. He is entitled to recover so much of the charge as was illegally excessive.*

Notes:

(i) Section 72 is wide enough to cover not only a mistake of fact but also a mistake of law. [*Sales Tax Officer* v. *Kanhaiya Lal Mukand Lal*]

(ii) The expression 'coercion' occurring in Section 72 is not governed by the definition of this term given u/s 15. It is to be interpreted in its popular sense to mean oppression, extortion or such other means. [*Seth Kanhaiya Lal* v. *National Bank of India*]

6.0 COMPENSATION FOR FAILURE TO DISCHARGE OBLIGATION CREATED BY QUASI-CONTRACTS [SECTION 73]

When an obligation created by a Quasi-contract is not discharged, the injured party is entitled to receive the same compensation from the party in default as if such person had contracted to discharge it and had broken his contract.

7.0 QUANTUM MERUIT

7.1 Meaning of *Quantum Meruit*

The term '*quantum meruit*' means as much as merited or 'as much as earned'. In other words, it means payment in proportion to the amount of work done. Generally, one cannot claim performance from another unless one has performed his obligation in full but in certain cases, a person who has performed some work under a contract can claim remuneration for the work which he has already done. The right to claim on '*quantum meruit*' does not arise out of a contract as the right to damages does. It is a claim on the quasi contractual obligations which is implied by the circumstances. The claim for *quantum meruit* arises only when the original contract is discharged.

7.2 Cases in which the Claim of *Quantum Meruit* Arise

The various cases in which the claim of *quantum meruit* arise are discussed below:

(a) In Case of Void Agreement, or Contract that becomes Void [Section 65] When an agreement is discovered to be void, or when a contract becomes void, any person who has received any advantage under such agreement or contract is bound to restore it, or to make compensation for it, to the person from whom he received it.

Example I *A pays B, Rs 1,000 in consideration of B's promise to marry C, A's daughter. C is dead at the time of the promise. The agreement is void but B must repay A Rs 1,000.*

Example II *A contracts with B to deliver to him 250 maunds of rice before the 1st of May. A delivers 130 maunds only before that day, and none after. B retains the 130 maunds after the first of May. He is bound to pay A for them.*

Example III *A, a singer contracts with B, the manager of a theatre, to sing at his theatre for two nights in every week during the next two months, and B engages to pay her Rs 100 for each night's performance. On the sixth night, A wilfully absents herself from the theatre, and B, in consequence rescinds the contract. B must pay A for the five nights on which she had sung.*

Example IV *A contracts to sing for B for Rs 1,000 which are paid in advance. A is too ill to sing. A is not bound to make compensation to B for the loss of the profits which B would have made if A had been able to sing, but must refund to B Rs 1,000 paid in advance.*

(b) In Case of Non-gratuitous Act [Section 70] The obligation to pay arises if the following three conditions are satisfied:

(i) The thing must have been done or delivered lawfully;

(ii) The person who had done or delivered the thing must not have intended to do so gratuitously; and

(iii) The person for whom the act is done must have enjoyed the benefit of the Act.

Example *A, a tradesman leaves goods at B 's shop by mistake. B treats the goods as his own. He is bound to pay A for them.*

(c) In Case of Act Preventing the Completion of Contract If a party does not complete the contract or prevents the other party to complete the contract, the aggrieved party can sue on *quantum meruit*.

Example *C an owner of a magazine engaged P to write a book to be published as series in his magazine. After a few series were published, the publication of the magazine was stopped. It was held that P could claim payment on quantum meruit for the part already published. [Planche v. Calburn]*

(d) In Case of Divisible Contract The party at default may sue on a *quantum meruit* if the following conditions are satisfied:

(i) If the contract is divisible; and

(ii) If the party not at default has enjoyed benefits of the part performance.

Example *S agreed to construct a house for H for Rs 965 but he abandoned this contract after having done the work worth Rs 333. Afterwards, H got the work completed. It was held that S could not recover anything for the work done because he was entitled to the payment only on the completion of the work.*

(e) In Case of Indivisible Contract Performed Completely but Badly The party at default may claim the lumpsum *less* deduction for bad work if the following conditions are satisfied:

(i) If the contract is indivisible;

(ii) If the contract is for lumpsum;

(iii) If the contract is completely performed; and

(iv) If the contract is performed badly.

Example *X agreed to decorate Y's flat for a lumpsum of Rs 20,000. X did the complete work but Y complained of faulty workmanship. It costs Y another Rs 3,000 to remedy the defect. It was held that X could recover only Rs 17,000 from Y. [Hoenig v. Issacs (1952)]*

PRACTICAL PROBLEMS

PROBLEM 1

X supplied rice and wheat worth Rs. 20,000. *Y* supplied a mobile phone worth Rs 30,000 and *Z* lent Rs 50,000 for the purchase of necessaries to the wife and children of *M*, a minor. *M* had assets worth Rs 1,00,000. Can *X*, *Y* and *Z* recover anything from *M*?

Solution

Section to which the given problem relates: Section 68.

Decision and Reason: *X* and *Z* can recover from the *Z*'s assets because *X* supplied necessaries and *Z* lent for the purchase of necessaries but *Y* cannot recover anything because he has not supplied necessaries.

PROBLEM 2

P left his carriage on *D*'s premises and *D*s landlord seized the carriage for non-payment of the rent. *P* paid the rent to obtain the release of his carriage. Could *P* recover the amount from *D*?

Solution

Section to which the given problem relates: Section 69.

Decision and Reason: *P* could recover the amount from *D* because he made the payment which *D* was bound by law to pay.

[**Leading case:** *Exall* v. *Patridge*]

PROBLEM 3

X saved *Y*s house from fire. Can *X* claim compensation from *Y* on the ground that *Y* enjoyed the benefit of *X*'s act?

Solution

Section to which the given problem relates: Section 70.

Decision and Reason: *Y* cannot claim compensation from *Y* unless the circumstances show that he did not intend the act gratuitously.

PROBLEM 4

X picked up a diamond from the floor of *Y*s shop and handed it over to *Y* to keep it till owner is founded, *Y* did his best to find out the owner but true owner could not be found. After sometime, *X* offered *Y* the lawful charges incurred by *Y* for finding out the true owner and asked him to return the diamond to him. *Y* refused to do so. Discuss the legal position.

Solution

Section to which the given problem relates: Sections 71 and 168.

Decision and Reason: *Y* must return the diamond to *X* because *X* was entitled to retain it against the whole world except the true owner.

PROBLEM 5

X owes Baburam and pays to Rambabu by mistake. Discuss the rights of *X* and Baburam.

Solution

Section to which the given problem relates: Section 72.

Decision and Reason: Rambabu must repay the money to *X* because money was paid by mistake. Baburam cannot recover from Rambabu because there is no privity of contract between Baburam and Rambabu.

PROBLEM 6

X engaged *Y* to write a book to be published as series in a magazine. The magazine was abandoned after a few issues. Can *Y* recover anything from *X*.

Solution

Y can recover compensation for the work done by him on *quantum meruit* basis. [*Planche* v. *Colburn*]

PROBLEM 7

X is employed as a managing director in a company. After he rendered service for sometime, it is found that the Board of Directors was not competent to appoint him as such. Can *X* recover anything from the company?

Solution

X can recover compensation for the work done by him on *quantum meruit* basis. [*Craven Ellis* v. *Canons Ltd.*]

PROBLEM 8

X agreed to construct a house for *Y* for Rs. 1,00,000 but after having done three forth of the work, he abandons the contract. *Y*, afterwards, completed the house. Can *X* recover anything from *Y*?

Solution

X cannot recover anything from *Y* because the contract is indivisible. [*Sumpter* v. *Hedges*]

PROBLEM 9

X decorated *Y*'s house for a lumpsum of Rs 20,000. The work is done but *Y* complains of faulty workmanship. *Y* spent Rs 5,000 to remedy the defect. Can *X* recover anything from *Y*?

Solution

X can recover only Rs 15,000 (i.e. Rs 20,000 *less* Rs. 5,000) from *Y* because the contract is indivisible but has been completely performed.

TRUE OR FALSE QUESTIONS

State whether the following statements are True or False:

1. In quasi-contracts, the promise to pay is based on express agreement.
2. A minor is personally responsible for necessaries supplied to his dependent.
3. The essentials for the formation of a valid contract are present in quasi-contracts.
4. An agreement void *ab-initio* cannot be a quasi-contract.
5. A finder of lost goods is just like a bailee.
6. A finder of goods is the next best owner to the real owner.
7. The finder of goods may sue the true owner for expenses incurred by him in respect of the goods.

8. The finder of goods may sue the owner for a specific award (if any) offered by owner.
9. A person cannot recover from another an amount paid under a mistake of law.
10. When an indivisible contract is partly performed in accordance with the terms of contract, the party at default can claim compensation on *quantum meruit* basis.
11. When an indivisible contract is completely performed but badly, the party at default cannot recover anything.
12. The right to claim *quantum meruit* arises out of the contract.
13. The right to claim on *quantum meruit* arises only in case of quasi-contracts.

Answers

1. False	2. False	3. False	4. True
5. True	6. True	7. True	8. True
9. False	10. False	11. False	12. False
13. False			

VERY SHORT ANSWER TYPE QUESTIONS

1. What are Quasi-contracts?
2. Are Quasi-contracts outcome of contracts?
3. What do you understand by '*Quantum Meruit*'?
4. Does the right to claim on *Quantum Meruit* arise out of the contract?

SHORT ANSWER TYPE QUESTIONS

1. Enumerate the quasi-contracts dealt with under the Indian Contract Act, 1872.
2. Enumerate the cases in which the claim on the *Quantum Meruit* basis arises.

ESSAY TYPE QUESTIONS

1. (a) What are the Quasi-contracts?
   (b) Discuss the Quasi-contracts dealt with under the Indian Contract Act, 1872.
2. (a) Who is finder of lost goods?
   (b) What are the obligations of a finder of goods?
   (c) What are the rights of a finder of goods?
   (d) When can a finder sell the goods?
3. (a) What is meant by '*Quantum Meruit*'?
   (b) Explain the cases in which the claim on quantum meruit basis arises.

CHAPTER 12 Indemnity and Guarantee

1.0 INTRODUCTION

1.1 The Contract of Indemnity and Contract of Guarantee are specific types of Contract.

1.2 The specific provisions relating to these contracts are contained in Sections 124 to 147 of the Indian Contract Act, 1872.

1.3 In addition to these specific provisions, the general principles of contracts are also applicable to such specific contracts.

2.0 A CONTRACT OF INDEMNITY

2.1 **Meaning of Indemnity** The term 'indemnity' means to make good the loss or to compensate the party who has suffered some loss.

2.2 **Meaning of Contract of Indemnity [Section 124]** A "contract of indemnity" is a contract by which one party promises to save the other from loss caused to him by the conduct of the promisor himself, or by the conduct of any other person.

Example *A contracts to indemnify B against the consequences of any proceedings which C may take against B in respect of a certain sum of Rs 200. This is a contract of indemnity.*

2.3 **Two parties to a Contract of Indemnity.** There are two parties to a Contract of Indemnity—Indemnifier and Indemnity-Holder.

(a) **Meaning of Indemnifier** The person who promises to make good the loss is called the 'indemnifier'. In the aforesaid example, *A* is the indemnifier.

(b) **Meaning of Indemnity-Holder** The person whose loss is to be made good is called 'indemnity-holder'. In the aforesaid example, *B* is the indemnity-holder.

2.4 **Mode of Contract of Indemnity** A contract of indemnity may be express or implied.

(a) A contract of indemnity is said to be express when a person expressly promises to compensate the other from loss.

(b) A contract of indemnity is said to be implied when it is to be inferred from the conduct of the parties or from the circumstances of the case.

Example *X an auctioneer, sold certain goods at the instruction of Y. Later on, it is discovered that the goods belonged to Z and not Y. Z recovered damages from X for selling his goods. Here, X is entitled to recover the compensation from Y because there was an implied promise to compensate the auctioneer for any loss which he may suffer on the defective title of goods sold by auction. [Adamson v. Jarvis]*

2.5 **Essential Elements of Contract of Indemnity** In addition to the implied or express promise to indemnify, all the essentials of a valid contract must also be present.

Example *X asks Y to beat Z and promises to indemnify Y against the consequences. Y beats Z and is fined Rs 1,000. Y cannot claim this amount from X because the object of the agreement was unlawful.*

2.6 Rights of Indemnity Holder [Section 125] An indemnity holder is entitled to recover the following amounts from the indemnifier provided he acts within the scope of his authority.

(a) ***All damages*** which he is compelled to pay in any suit in respect of any matter to which the promise to indemnify applies;

(b) ***All costs*** which he is compelled to pay, in bringing or defending such suit

Condition : (a) he did not contravene the orders of the promisor, and acted as it would have been prudent for him to act in the absence of any contract of indemnity, or (b) the promisor authorized him to bring or defend the suit.

(c) ***All sums*** which he has paid under the terms of any compromise of any such suit

Condition : (a) the compromise was not contrary to the orders of the promisor, and was one which it would have been prudent for the promisee to make in the absence of any contract of indemnity, or

(b) the promisor authorized him to compromise the suit.

2.7 Whether Contract of Indemnity Covers the Cases of Loss Caused by the Events or Accidents which do not Depend upon the Conduct of the Promisor or any other Person

(a) If the definition of contract of indemnity as per Section 124 is strictly interpreted, it would not cover the cases of loss caused by the events or accidents which do not depend upon the conduct of the promisor or any other person. In other words, contracts of insurance would be outside the purview of the contract of indemnity.

(b) Since the intention of law makers had never been to exclude the contracts of insurance from the purview of contracts of indemnity, the courts in India have decided to apply the same equitable principles that the courts in England do. As per English law, a contract of indemnity is defined as "a promise to save another harmless from loss caused as a result of a transaction entered into at the instance of the promisor." This definition covers a promise to make good the loss arising from any cause whatsoever.

(c) Thus, Indian courts follow the English law in respect of contract of indemnity which covers the contracts of insurance also.

2.8 When does the Liability of Indemnifier Commence ? Although The Indian Contract Act, 1872 is silent on the time of commencement of liability of indemnifier but on the basis of judicial pronouncement of courts, it can be said that the liability of an indemnifier commences **as soon as the liability of the indemnity-holder becomes absolute and certain**. In other words, if the indemnity-holder has incurred an absolute liability even though he has himself paid nothing, he is entitled to ask the indemnifier to indemnify him.

Example *X promises to compensate Y for any loss that he may suffer by filing a suit against Z. The court orders Y to pay Z damages of Rs 5,000. As the loss has become certain, Y may claim the amount of loss from X and pass it on to Z.*

3.0 A CONTRACT OF GUARANTEE

3.1 Meaning of a Contract of Guarantee [Section 126] A contract of guarantee is a contract to perform a promise or discharge the liability of a third person in case of his default.

Example *X and his friend Y enter a shop and X says to Z "Supply the goods required by Y and if he does not pay you, I will." It is a contract of guarantee.*

3.2 Three Parties to a Contract of Guarantee There are three parties to a contract of Guarantee—Principle debtor, Creditor and Surety.

(a) Meaning of Principal Debtor [Section 126] The person in respect of whose default the guarantee is given is called the 'Principal debtor'. *Y* is the principal debtor in the aforesaid example.

(b) Meaning of Creditor [Section 126] The person to whom the guarantee is given, is called the 'creditor'. *Z* is the creditor in the aforesaid example.

(c) Meaning of Surety [Section 126] The person who gives the guarantee is called the 'Surety'. *X* is the surety in the aforesaid example.

3.3 Essential Features of a Contract of Guarantee The essential features of a contract of guarantee are as follows.

(a) Tripartite Agreement A contract of guarantee is a tripartite agreement between the principal debtor, creditor and surety. There are three contracts as under:

(i) Contract between creditor and the principal debtor out of which the guaranteed debt arises.

(ii) Contract between surety and the principal debtor by which the principal debtor undertakes to indemnity the surety if surety is required to pay.

(iii) Contract between surety and the creditor by which the surety guarantees to pay the principal debtor's debt if the principal debtor fails to pay.

(b) Consent of Three Parties There must be consent of all the three parties.

Example *X sells and delivers goods to Y. X afterwards requests Z to pay in default of Y. Z agrees to do so. Here, Z cannot become surety without the consent of Y.*

(c) Existence of a Liability There must be an existing liability or a promise whose performance is guaranteed. Such liability or promise must be enforceable by law. Hence, guarantee can be given only for liability or promise which is enforceable by law. *For example*, guarantee given for a time-barred debt is invalid since time-barred debt is not legally enforceable. But there is an exception to this rule. The exception is a guarantee given for minor's debt. Though minor's debt is not enforceable by law, yet the guarantee given for minor's debt is valid.

Example *X took a loan of Rs 10,000 from Y on 1st Jan. 1993 and paid nothing on account of interest and principal. On 2nd Jan. 1996, Z gave the guarantee to Y for the payment of Rs 10,000 due from X. This is not a valid contract of guarantee because the primary liability between X and Y is a time barred debt which is not enforceable by law.*

(d) Essentials of a Valid Contract All the essentials of a valid contract must be present in a contract of guarantee. However, the following points are worth noting in this regard:

(i) The principal debtor need not be competent to contract. In case the principal debtor is not competent to contract, the surety would be regarded as the principal debtor and would be personally liable to pay.

(ii) Surety need not be benefited. According to Section 127, "Anything done, or any promise made, for the benefit of the principal debtor, may be a sufficient consideration to the surety for giving the guarantee."

Example I *B requests A to sell and deliver to him goods on credit. A agrees to do so, provided C guarantees the payment of the price of the goods. C promises to guarantee the payment in consideration of A's promise to deliver the goods. This is a sufficient consideration for C's promise.*

Example II *A sells and delivers goods to B. C, afterwards, requests A to forbear to sue B for the debt for a year, and promises that if he does so, C will pay for them in default of payment by B. A agrees to forbear as requested. This is a sufficient consideration for C's promise.*

Example III *A sells and delivers goods to B. C, afterwards, without consideration, agrees to pay for them in default of B. The agreement is void.*

(iii) A guarantee need not be in writing. According to Section 126, a guarantee may be *either* oral *or* written.

(e) Guarantee not to be Obtained by Misrepresentation [Section 142] Any guarantee which has been obtained by means of misrepresentation made by the creditor, or with his knowledge and assent, concerning a material part of the transaction, is invalid.

(f) Guarantee not to be Obtained by Concealment [Section 143] Any guarantee which the creditor has obtained by means of keeping silence as to material circumstances is invalid.

Example I *A engages B as clerk to collect money for him. B fails to account for some of his receipts, and A in consequence calls upon him to furnish security for his duty accounting. C gives his guarantee for B's duty accounting. A does not acquaint C with B's previous conduct. B afterwards makes a default. The guarantee is invalid.*

Example II *A guarantees to C payment for iron to be supplied by him to B to the amount of 2,000 tons. B and C have privately agreed that B should pay Rs 500 per ton beyond the market price, such excess to be applied in liquidation of an old debt. This agreement is concealed from A. A is not liable as a surety.*

(g) The liability of the principal debtor is primary.

(h) The liability of surety is secondary and conditional and arises only if the principal debtor makes a default.

3.4 Is a Contract of Guarantee a Contract of *Uberrimae Fidei?*

(a) A contract of guarantee is **not** a contract of *uberrimae fidei* (i.e. a contract of absolute good faith) and hence, it is not necessary for the principal debtor or the creditor to disclose all the material facts to the surety before he enters into a contract. For example, in case of guarantee given to a bank, bank need not inform the surety of matters affecting the credit of principal debtor.

(b) However, the provisions of Sections 142 and 143 give some protection to the surety by making the following guarantee as invalid.

(a) a guarantee obtained by misrepresentation

(b) a guarantee obtained by concealment of material facts.

3.5 Distinction between a Contract of Indemnity and a Contract of Guarantee

Basis of Distinction	*Contract of Indemnity*	*Contract of Guarantee*
1. No. of Parties	There are ***two*** parties—indemnifier and the indemnity-holder.	There are ***three*** parties—principal debtor, creditor and surety.
2. No. of Contracts	There is only ***one*** contract between indemnifier and indemnity-holder.	There are ***three*** contracts, one between creditor and principal debtor, second between surety and principal debtor, and third between surety and the creditor.
3. Undertaking	The ***indemnifier*** undertakes to save the indemnity-holder from any loss.	The ***surety*** undertakes for the payment of debts of principal debtor.
4. Nature of liability	The liability of indemnifier is ***primary and unconditional.***	The liability of surety is ***secondary and conditional.*** Surety's liability is secondary in the sense that the primary liability is of principal debtor. Surety's liability is conditional in the sense that it arises only on default of principal debtor.
5. Nature of event	The liability arises only on the happening of a contingency.	The liability arises only on the non-performance of an existing promise or non-payment of an existing debt.
6. Request	The indemnifier need not act at the request of indemnity-holder.	The surety acts at the request of the principal debtor.
7. Right to sue	The indemnifier cannot sue a third party in his own name because of absence of privity of contract between him and a third party. He can sue the third party in his own name if there in an assignment in his favour.	A surety, on discharging the debt of principal debtor, can sue the principal debtor in his own name.

4.0 EXTENT OF SURETY'S LIABILITY

4.1 General Rule—Equal to that of Principal Debtor. In the absence of a contract to the contrary, the liability of a surety is co-extensive with that of the principal debtor. It means that the liability of a surety is equal to that of the principal debtor unless otherwise agreed.

Example *A guarantees to B the payment of a bill of exchange by C, the acceptor. The bill is dishonoured by C. A is liable not only for the amount of the bill, but also for any interest and charges which may have become due on it.*

4.2 Can Surety's liability be limited ? The liability of the surety may be made less than that of the principal debtor by an express contract to that effect.

Example *X lends Rs 10,000 to Y and Z gives guarantee for Rs 4,000 only. If Y makes a default, Z shall be liable only for Rs 4,000.*

4.3 When does the Surety's liability commence ? The liability of the surety arises immediately when a default is made by the principal debtor. The creditor can sue the surety without suing the principal debtor.

4.4 Can Surety's liability be conditional ? If there is a condition precedent for surety's liability, the surety would be liable only when the such condition is fulfilled. According to Section 144, where a person gives a guarantee upon a contract that a creditor shall not act upon it until another person has joined in it as co-surety, the guarantee is not valid if that person does not join.

Example *X requires a loan of Rs 1,00,000 and requests Y and Z to give guarantee. Y and Z agree to do so. Y signs but Z does not sign the necessary documents. Y is not liable because a condition precedent to Y's guarantee that repayment of loan shall be guaranteed by Y and Z, has not been fulfilled.*

5.0 KINDS OF GUARANTEE

Guarantee may be classified under the following two categories:

5.1 Specific guarantee 5.2 Continuing guarantee

Let us discuss these categories in detail.

5.1 Specific Guarantee

(a) ***Meaning of Specific Guarantee***–A guarantee which extends to a single debt or specific transaction is called a specific guarantee.

(b) ***Surety's Liability***–A surety's liability comes to an end when the guaranteed debt is duly discharged or the promise is duly performed.

Example I *X guarantees payment to Y of the price of the five bags of flour to be delivered by Y to Z and to be paid for in a month. Y delivers five bags to Z, Z pays for them. This is a contract of specific guarantee because X intended to guarantee only for the payment of price of the first five bags of flour to be delivered at one time. [Kay v. Groves]*

Example II *X gave his godown to Y on a lease for 10 years on a lease rent of a Rs 12,000 p.a. Z guaranteed that Y would fulfil his obligations. This is a contract of specific guarantee because the lease for 10 years is entirely an indivisible transaction and cannot be classified as a series of distinct transactions.*

5.2 Continuing Guarantee

(a) ***Meaning of Continuing Guarantee*** *[Section 129]* A guarantee which extends to a series of transactions is called a 'continuing guarantee'.

(b) ***Surety's Liability***–A surety's liability continues until the revocation of the guarantee.

Example I *On S's recommendation, C employed P for the collection of rent from his tenants. S promised to make good any default made by P. This is a contract of continuing guarantee.*

Example II *A guarantees payment to B, a tea-dealer to the extent of Rs 100, for any tea he may supply to C from time to time. B supplies C with tea to the above value of Rs 100, and C pays B for it. Afterwards, B supplies C with tea to the value of Rs 200. C fails to pay. The guarantee given by A was a continuing guarantee, and he is accordingly liable to B to the extent of Rs 100.*

(c) A continuing guarantee may be given for a part of the entire debt or for the entire debt subject to a limit.

Example *X gives guarantee for the loans given by Y to Z. Z owes Rs 1,00,000 to Y. X may give this guarantee in the following forms:*

Form (a): I guarantee the payment of the loan of Rs 60,000 by *Y* to *Z*

Form (b): I guarantee the payment of the loan by *Y* to *Z* subject to the limit of Rs 60,000

The distinction between these two forms becomes clear when *Z* becomes insolvent. Let us suppose that *Z* becomes insolvent and his estate pays 30 paise in a rupee. In this case, the rights of *X* and *Y* will be as under:

Right	*In case of guarantee for a part of debt [Form (a)]*	*In case of guarantee for the entire debt subject to a limit [Form (b)]*
Right of Y	*Y* can recover Rs 60,000 from *X* and Rs 12,000 (being 30% of the balance of Rs 40,000) from *Z*s estate.	*Y* can recover Rs 60,000 from *X* and Rs 30,000 (being 30% of the entire debt of Rs 1,00,000) from *Z*s estate.
Right of X	After paying Rs 60,000 to *Y*, *X* can recover Rs 18,000 (being 30% of Rs 60,000) from *Z*s estate.	*X* will not get anything from *Z*s estate till the entire debt of Rs 1,00,000 is paid to *Y*.

(d) **Revocation of Continuing Guarantee** A continuing guarantee as to future transactions may be revoked in any of the following ways:

(i) **By Notice of Revocation [Section 130]** A continuing guarantee may at any time be revoked by the surety as to the future transactions by notice to the creditor. However, the surety remains liable for the past transactions which have already taken place.

Example *X gives guarantee to the extent of Rs 60,000 for the loans given from time to time by Y to Z. Y gave a loan of Rs 20,000 to Z. Afterwards, X gives notice of revocation. X is discharged from all liability to Y for any loan granted after the revocation of guarantee but he is liable to Y for Rs. 20,000 on default of Z.*

(ii) **By Death of Surety [Section 131]** In the absence of any contract to the contrary, the death of surety operates as a revocation of a continuing guarantee as to the future transactions taking place after the death of surety. However, the surety's estate remains liable for the past transactions which have already taken place before the death of surety.

(iii) **By Modes of Discharging the Surety** A continuing guarantee is also revoked in the same manner in which the surety is discharged such as:

(a) Novation [Section 62]

(b) Variance in terms of contract [Section 133]

(c) Release or discharge of principal debtor [Section 134]
(d) When the creditors enter into an arrangement with the principal debtor [Section 135]
(e) Creditor's act or omission impairing surety's eventual remedy [Section 139]
(f) Loss of security [Section 141]

These modes have been discussed in detail in Para 7.2

6.0 RIGHTS OF A SURETY

After discharging the liability of the principal debtor, the surety gets various rights shown below:

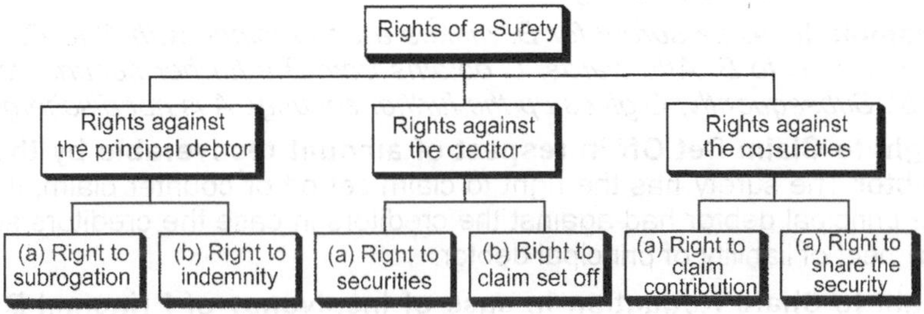

Let us discuss them one by one.

6.1 Rights Against the Principal Debtor

(a) Right to Subrogation [Section 140] On payment of the guaranteed debt or performance of the guaranteed duty, the surety acquires all the rights which the creditor had against the principal debtor. Thus, the surety steps into the shoes of creditor.

(b) Right to Indemnity [Section 145] In every contract of guarantee there is an implied promise by the principal debtor to indemnify the surety, and the surety is entitled to recover from the principal debtor whatever sum he has **rightfully** paid under the guarantee, but **not** those sums which he had paid **wrongfully.**

Example I *B is indebted to C, and A is surety for the debt. C demands payment from A, and on his refusal sues him for the amount. A defends the suit, having reasonable grounds for doing so, but he is compelled to pay the amount of the debt with costs. He can recover from B the amount paid by him for costs, as well as the principal debt.*

Example II *C lends B a sum of money, and A, at the request of B, accepts a bill of exchange drawn by B upon A to secure the amount. C, the holder of the bill, demands payment of it from A, and on A's refusal to pay sues him upon the bill. A, not having reasonable grounds for so doing, defends the suit, and has to pay the amount of the bill and costs. He can recover from B the amount of the bill, but not the sum paid for costs, as there was no real ground for defending the action.*

Example III *A guarantees to C, to the extent of Rs 2,000, payment for rice to be supplied by C to B. C supplies to B rice of less amount than Rs 2,000 but obtains from A payment of the sum of Rs 2,000 in respect of the rice supplied. A cannot recover from B more than the price of the rice actually supplied.*

6.2 Rights Against the Creditor

(a) Right to Securities held by creditor [Section 141] A surety is entitled to the benefit of every security which the creditor has against the principal debtor at

the time when the contract of suretyship is entered into, whether the surety knows of the existence of such security or not; and if the creditor loses, or, without the consent of the surety, parts, with such security, the surety is discharged to the extent of the value of the security.

Example I *C advances to B his tenant, Rs 2,000 on the guarantee of A. C has also a further security for Rs 2,000 of B's furniture. C cancels the security of B's furniture. B becomes insolvent, and C sues A on his guarantee. A is discharged from liability to the amount of the value of the furniture.*

Example II *C, a creditor, whose advances to B is secured by a decree, receives also a guarantee for that advance from A. C, afterwards, takes B's goods in execution under the decree, and then, without the knowledge of A, withdraws the execution. A is discharged.*

Example III *A, as surety for B, makes a bond jointly with B to C, to secure a loan from C to B. Afterwards, C obtains from B a further security for the same debt. Subsequently, C gives up the further security. A is not discharged.*

(b) **Right to Claim Set Off in respect of amount recoverable by the Principal Debtor** The surety has the right to claim set off or counter claim, if any, which the principal debtor had against the creditors in case the creditors sues him for payment of liability of principal debtor.

(c) **Right to Share Reduction in case of Insolvency of Principal Debtor.** The surety has the right to claim proportionate reduction in his liability if the principal debtor becomes insolvent.

6.3 Rights Against Co-sureties

(a) **Meaning of Co-sureties** When the same debt or duty is guaranteed by two or more persons, such persons are called as 'co-sureties'.

(b) **Right to Claim Contribution** If a co-surety pays more than his proportionate share of liability, he has a right to claim contribution from the other co-surety or co-sureties.

(c) **Right to Share the Security** If a co-surety obtains any security of principal debtor, the other co-surety (or co-sureties) has (or have) a right to share such security.

(d) **Liability of Co-sureties** The liability of co-sureties is summarised as under:

Where there is no contract to the contrary	***Where the co-sureties have agreed to guarantee different sums***
The co-sureties are liable to contribute equally to the extent of default of principal debtor [Section 146]	The co-sureties are liable to contribute equally subject to the maximum amount guaranteed by each one. [Section 147] They are not liable in proportion to the amount guaranteed by them.

(e) **Matters Immaterial for the aforesaid Principal** The aforesaid principal regarding the liability of co-sureties is applicable—

(a) whether the sureties are liable jointly or severally.

(b) whether the sureties are liable under the same or different contracts.

(c) whether the sureties are liable with or without the knowledge of each other.

Example I *A, B and C are sureties to D for a sum of Rs 3,000 lend to E. E makes default in payment. A, B and C are liable, as between themselves to pay Rs 1,000 each.*

Example II *A, B and C are sureties to D for a sum of Rs 1,000 lent to E, and there is a contract between A, B and C that A is to be responsible to the extent of one-quarter, B to the extent of one quarter, and C to the extent of one half. E makes default in payment. As between the sureties, A is liable to pay Rs 250, B Rs 250 and C Rs 500.*

Example III *A, B and C as sureties for D, enter into three separate bonds, of different amounts—A for Rs 10,000, B for Rs 20,000 and C for Rs 40,000. The liability of A, B, C will be as under if D makes default to the extent of (a) Rs 30,000 (b) Rs 40,000 (c) Rs 70,000.*

	A's liability	*B's liability*	*C's liability*
Case (a)			
(i) Equal share in default (Rs 30,000/3)	10,000	10,000	10,000
(ii) Maximum amount guaranteed	10,000	20,000	40,000
(iii) Actual liability [least of (i) & (ii)]	10,000	10,000	10,000
Case (b)			
(i) Equal share in default (Rs 40,000/3)	13,333	13,333	13,334
(ii) Maximum amount guaranteed	10,000	20,000	40,000
(iii) Actual liability of *A* [least of (i) & (ii)]	10,000	—	—
(iv) Equal share in remaining default to be shared by remaining co-sureties (Rs 40,000—Rs 10,000/2)	—	15,000	15,000
(v) Actual liability of *B* & *C* [least of (ii) & (iv)]	—	15,000	15,000
Case (c)			
(i) Equal share in default (Rs 70,000/3)	26,666	26,667	26,667
(ii) Maximum amount guaranteed	10,000	20,000	40,000
(iii) Actual liability of *A* & *B* [least of (i) & (ii)]	10,000	20,000	—
(iv) Remaining default to be shared by remaining co-surety (Rs 70,000—Rs 10,000—Rs 20,000)	—	—	40,000
(v) Actual liability of *C* [least of (ii) & (iv)]	—	—	40,000

Thus, as between the co-sureties, there is equality of burden and benefit.

(f) Effect of Release of One Co-surety [Section 138] Where there are co-sureties, a release by the creditor of one of them does not discharge the others; neither does it free the surety so released from his responsibility to the other sureties. However, under English law the release of one co-surety shall release all the other co-sureties since the liability of co-sureties under English law is only joint and not joint and several.

7.0 DISCHARGE OF SURETY

7.1 Meaning of Discharge of Surety A surety is said to be discharged when his liability as surety comes to an end.

7.2 Modes of Discharge of Surety The various modes of discharge of a surety are discussed below.

I. By Revocation of Contract of Guarantee

(a) By Notice [Section 130] A specific guarantee may be revoked by a surety by notice to the creditor if the liability of the surety has not yet accrued. A continuing guarantee may at any time be revoked by the surety as to future transactions by notice to the creditor. However, the surety remains liable for the past transactions which have already taken place.

(b) By the Death of Surety [Section 131] In the absence of any contract to the contrary, the death of a surety operates as a revocation of a continuing guarantee as to future transactions taking place after the death of surety. However, the deceased surety's estate remains liable for the past transactions which have already taken place before the death of the surety but will not be liable for the transactions taking place after the death of surety even if the creditor has no notice of surety's death.

(c) By Novation [Section 62] The surety under original contract is discharged if a fresh contract is entered into *either* between the same parties *or* between other parties, the consideration being the mutual discharge of the old contract.

II. By Conduct of Creditor

(a) By Variance in terms of Contract [Section 133] The surety is discharged as to transactions subsequent to the variance if any variance is made in the terms of the contract between the principal debtor and the creditor, without the surety's consent.

Example I *A becomes surety to C for B's conduct as a manager in C's bank. Afterwards, B and C contract, without A's consent, that B's salary shall be raised, and that he shall become liable for one-fourth of the losses on overdrafts. B allows a customer to overdraw, and the bank loses a sum of money. A is discharged from his suretyship by the variance made without his consent, and is not liable to make good this loss.*

Example II *C agrees to appoint B as his clerk to sell goods at a yearly salary, upon A's becoming surety to C for B's duly accounting for money received by him as such clerk. Afterwards, without A's knowledge or consent, C and B agree that B should be paid by a commission on the goods sold by him and not by a fixed salary. A is not liable for subsequent misconduct of B.*

Example III *C contracts to lend B Rs 5,000 on 1st March. A guarantees repayment. C pays Rs 5,000 to B on the 1st January. A is discharged from his liability as the contract has been varied inasmuch as C might sue B for the money before the first of March.*

But variation which is not substantial or material or which is beneficial to the surety will not discharge him of his liability. In *M.S. Anirudhan* v. *Thomco's Bank*, the surety guaranteed overdraft provided by the bank to the principal-debtor only upto Rs 25,000. Subsequently since the bank was willing to provide overdraft only upto Rs 20,000, the principal debtor reduced the amount in the guarantee form to Rs 20,000. On default by the principal debtor the court held the surety liable as the alteration was beneficial to him and it was not of a substantial nature.

(b) By Release or Discharge of Principal Debtor [Section 134] The surety is discharged if the creditor

(i) makes a fresh contract with the principal debtor, by which the principal debtor is released, or

(ii) does any act or omissions, the legal consequence of which is the discharge of the principal debtor.

Example I *A contracts with B for a fixed price to build a house for A within a stipulated time, B supplying the necessary timber. C guarantees A's performance of the contract. B omits to supply the timber. C is discharged from his suretyship.*

Example II *A contracts with B to grow a crop of wheat on A's land and to deliver it to B at a fixed rate, and C guarantees A's performance of this contract. B diverts a stream of water which is necessary for irrigation of A's land, and thereby prevents him from raising the wheat. C is no longer liable for his guarantee.*

Example III *A gives guarantee to C for goods to be supplied by C to B. C supplies goods to B, and afterwards B becomes embarrassed and contracts with his creditors (including C's) to assign to them his property in consideration of their releasing him from their demands. Here, B is released from his debt by the contract with C, and A is discharged from his suretyship.*

(c) By Arrangement [Sec. 135] The surety is discharged if the creditor makes a composition with, or promises to give time to, or not to sue the principal debtor without surety's consent in a contract with Principal Debtor.

Cases where surety is not discharged

(i) Where a contract to give time to the principal debtor is made by the creditor with a third person, and not with the principal debtor, the surety is not discharged. [Sec. 136]

Example *C, the holder of an overdue bill of exchange drawn by A as surety for B, and accepted by B, contracts with M to give more time to B. A is not discharged.*

(ii) Mere forbearance on the part of the creditor to sue the principal debtor or to enforce any other remedy against him, does not, in the absence of any provision in the guarantee to the contrary, discharge the surety.

Example *B owes to C a debt guaranteed by A. The debt becomes payable. C does not sue B for a year after the debt has become payable. A is not discharged from his suretyship.*

(iii) Where there are co-sureties, the release by the creditor of one of them does not discharge the other nor does it free the surety so released from his responsibility to the other sureties. [Section 138]

(d) By Creditor's Act or Omission Impairing Surety's Eventual Remedy [Section 139] The surety is discharged if a creditor does any act which is inconsistent with the rights of the surety, or omits to do an act which is his duty to the surety requires him to do, and the eventual remedy of the surety himself against the principal debtor is thereby impaired.

Example I *B contracts to build a ship for C for a given sum, to be paid by instalments as the work reaches certain stage. A becomes surety to C for B's due performance of the contract. C, without the knowledge of A, pre-pays to B the last two instalments. A is discharged by this prepayment.*

Example II *C lends money to B on the security of a joint and several promissory note, made in C's favour by B, and by A as surety for B, together with a bill of sale of B's furniture, which gives power to C to sell the furniture, and apply the proceeds in discharge of the note. Subsequently, C sells the furniture, but, owing to his misconduct and willful negligence, only a small price is realized. A is discharged from liability on the note.*

Example III *A puts M as apprentice to B, and gives a guarantee to B for M's fidelity. B promises on his part that he will at least once a month, see M make up the cash. B omits to see this done as promised, and M embezzles. A is not liable to B on his guarantee.*

(e) By Loss of Security [Section 141] The surety is discharged from liability to the extent of the value of security, if the creditor loses, or without the consent of the surety, parts with security given to him.

Example *A gave a loan to B on the guarantee of C as well as on the mortgage of B's furniture. Afterwards, A cancels the mortgage. B becomes insolvent and A sues C on this guarantee. C is discharged from liability to the value of furniture.*

III. By Invalidation of Contract

(a) Guarantee Obtained by Misrepresentation [Section 142] Any guarantee which has been obtained by means of misrepresentation made by a creditor or with his knowledge and assent, concerning a material part of the transaction, is invalid.

(b) Guarantee Obtained by Concealment [Section 143] Any guarantee which a creditor has obtained by means of keeping silence to material circumstances is invalid.

Example *X employs Y as a clerk to collect money for him. Y fails to account for some of his receipts and X, in consequence calls upon Z to furnish security for his duly accounting. Z gives guarantee for Y's duly account. X does not inform Z about Y's previous conduct. Y, afterwards, makes default. Z is not liable because the guarantee was obtained by concealment of facts.*

(c) Failure of a person to Join as Co-surety [Section 144] Where a person gives a guarantee upon a contract that a creditor shall not act upon it until another person has joined in it as co-surety, the guarantee is not valid if that person does not join.

PRACTICAL PROBLEMS

PROBLEM 1

A, *B*, *C* and *D* enter in a shop. *A* says to the trader, "supply the goods required by *B* and if he does not pay, I will." *C* says to the trader, "Let *D* have the required goods. I will see that you are paid." State the nature of the contract between *A* and *B* and that of between *C* and *D*.

Solution

The contract between *A* and *B* is a contract of guarantee but between *C* and *D* is a contract of indemnity.

PROBLEM 2

X, an auctioneer, sold certain goods on the instructions of *Y*. Later on, it is discovered that the goods belonged to *Z* and not to *Y*. *Z* recovered damages from *X* for selling his goods. Can *X* recover the compensation from *Y*?

Solution

X is entitled to recover the compensation from *Y* because there was an implied promise to compensate the auctioneer for any loss which he may suffer on the defective title for goods sold by auction. [*Adamson* v. *Jarvis*]

PROBLEM 3

X asks *Y* to beat *Z* and promises to indemnify *Y* against the consequences. *Y* beats *Z* and is fined Rs 1,000. Can *Y* claim Rs 1,000 from *X*?

Solution

Y cannot claim Rs 1,000 from *X* because the object of the agreement was unlawful.

PROBLEM 4

C sells and delivers goods to *P*. Is the agreement of guarantee valid in each of the following alternative cases:

Case (*a*): If *S* afterwards agrees to pay for the goods in default of *P*.

Case (*b*): If *S* afterwards requests *C* to allow a credit period of 1 year to *P* and promises that if *C* does so, he will pay for the goods if *P* defaults. *C* agrees to allow as requested.

Solution

Section to which the given problem relates: Section 127.

Decision and Reason:

Case (*a*): The agreement of guarantee is void because such agreement was without any consideration.

Case (*b*): The agreement of guarantee is valid because credit period allowed was a sufficient consideration for *S*'s promise.

PROBLEM 5

C agrees to sell goods to *P* on the guarantee of *S* for payment of the price of goods in default of *P*. Is the agreement of guarantee valid in each of the following alternative cases:

Case (*a*): If *C* is a minor

Case (*b*): If *S* is a minor

Case (*c*): If *P* is a minor

Solution

Case (*a*): The agreement of guarantee is void because a creditor is incompetent to contract.

Case (*b*): The agreement of guarantee is void because the surety is incompetent to contract.

Case (*c*): The agreement of guarantee is valid because the incapability of principal debtor does not affect the validity of agreement of guarantee.

PROBLEM 6

S gives guarantee for the loans given by *C* to *P*. *P* owes Rs 1,00,000 to *C*. *P* becomes insolvent and a dividend of 20 paise in a rupee is declared. Discuss the rights of *C* and *S* if (a) *S* gives the guarantee for the payment of the loan of Rs 60,000 (b) *S* gives the guarantee for the payment of the loan subject to a limit of Rs 60,000.

Solution

Right	In case of guarantee for *a part of debt [Case (a)]*	In case of guarantee for the entire *debt subject to a limit [Case (b)]*
Right of *C*	*C* can recover Rs 60,000 from *S* and Rs 8,000 (being 20% of the balance of Rs 40,000) from *P*s estate	*C* can recover Rs 60,000 from *S* and Rs 20,000 (being 20% the entire debt of Rs 1,00,000) from *P*s estate.
Right of *S*	After paying Rs 60,000 to *C*, *S* can recover Rs 12,000 (being 20% of Rs 60,000) from *P*s estate.	*S* will not get anything from *P*s estate till the entire debt of Rs 1,00,000 is paid to *C*.

PROBLEM 7

S_1, S_2 and S_3 are sureties to *C* for a sum of Rs 4,000 lent to *P*. *P* makes a default to the extent of Rs 3,000. Discuss the liability of sureties in each of the following alternative cases:

Case (*a*): If there is no contract between sureties.

Case (*b*): If there is a contract between sureties that S_1 to be responsible to the extent of one-quarter, S_2 to be responsible to the extent of one quarter and S_3 to be responsible to the extent of two quarter.

Case (*c*): If sureties enter into three separate security bonds of different amounts—S_1, Rs 700, S_2 Rs 1,100, and S_3 Rs 1,200.

Solution

Section to which the given problem relates: Sections 146 and 147.

Decision and Reason:

Case (*a*): S_1, S_2 and S_3 are liable to pay Rs 1,000 each because in the absence of any contract to the contrary, sureties are liable to contribute equally to the extent of default.

Case (*b*): S_1, S_2 and S_3 are liable to pay Rs 750, Rs 750 and Rs 1,500, respectively, because co-sureties are liable to contribute according to the terms of contract.

Case (*c*): S_1 is liable to pay Rs 700 (being least of one third of Rs 3,000 and Rs 700), S_2 is liable to pay Rs 1,100 (being least of one half of Rs 2,300 and Rs 1,100) and S_3 is liable to Rs 1,200 (being least of Rs 1,200 and Rs 1,200).

Reason: Co-sureties are liable to pay equally subject to the maximum amount guaranteed by each one.

PROBLEM 8

S_1, S_2 and S_3 as sureties for *P* enter into three separate bonds of different amounts—S_1 for Rs 10,000, S_2 for Rs 20,000 and S_3 for Rs 40,000. Discuss the liability of sureties if *P* makes default to the extent of (a) Rs 30,000 (b) Rs 40,000 (c) Rs 70,000.

Solution

Refer to Solution to Example III on page 12-10.

PROBLEM 9

C agreed to sell a colour TV set to *P* under a hire-purchase agreement on guarantee of *S* and a pledge of *P*s furniture. The terms were: hire-purchase price Rs 24,000 payable in 12 monthly instalments, ownership to be transferred on the payment of last instalment. State whether *S* is discharged in each of the following alternative cases:

Case (*a*): If after seven months, *P* stopped paying the instalments. *C* sued *P* for the payment of arrears and *S* then gave a notice revoking his guarantee for the remaining months.

Case (*b*): If after seven months, *S* died.

Case (*c*): If *C* without the knowledge of *S* agreed to increase the number of monthly instalments from 12 to 24 of Rs 1,000 each.

Case (*d*): If *C* terminated this agreement and entered into a fresh contract with *P* taking a security bond from *Z*.

Case (*e*): If *C* without the knowledge of *S*, allowed *P* further time for payment of one of the instalments.

Case (*f*): If *C* did not sue for a year after the debt has become payable.

Case (*g*): If *C* without the knowledge of *S* transferred the ownership before the payment of last instalment.

Case (*h*): If, on the instalments being in arrears for 3 months, *C* terminated the contract and seized the goods.

Case (*i*): If *C* without the knowledge of *S* cancelled the pledge. *P* became insolvent and *C* sued *S* for his guarantee.

Case (*j*) : If a contract to give time to the P is made by C with T.

Solution

Case	*Decision*	*Reason*
(a)	*S* is not discharged from his liability.	*S* could not revoke his guarantee for the remaining months because the hire-purchase agreement was an entire indivisible transaction and could not be classified as a series of transaction. In other words, this contract was a contract of specific guarantee and not of continuing guarantee [Section 130]
(b)	*S*'s estate is liable.	Death operates as a revocation of the continuing guarantee and not of a specific guarantee [Section 131]
(c)	*S* is discharged from his liability.	The terms of the contract have been varied without the surety's consent [Section 133]
(d)	*S* is discharged from his liability.	The original agreement has been terminated by *C* [Section 134]
(e)	*S* is discharged from his liability.	The creditor has given further time to the principal debtor without the surety's consent [Section 135]
(f)	*S* is not discharged from his liability.	Mere forbearance on the part of the creditor to sue the principal debtor does not discharge the surety [Section 137]
(g)	*S* is discharged from his liability.	The creditor has transferred the ownership before the payment of the last instalments [Section 139]
(h)	*S* is discharged from his liability.	The creditor has terminated the agreement and seized the goods [Section 139]
(i)	*S* is discharged from liability to the extent of the value of furniture.	The creditor has cancelled the pledge the extent of the value of furniture. [Section 141]
(j)	*S* is not discharged from his liability.	Contract to give time between creditor and third person does not discharge the surety. [Sec. 136]

PROBLEM 10

S stands as a surety for the good conduct of *P* who is employed in a Bank on a monthly salary of Rs 5,000. Discuss the liability of *S* in each of the following alternatives cases:

Case (*a*): Two months after, *S* gave notice revoking his guarantee. Five months after it is discovered that *P* has been continuously misappropriating Rs 1,000 per month.

Case (*b*): Two months after *P*s employment, *S* dies. Five months after it is discovered that *P* has been continuously misappropriating Rs 1,000 per month.

Case (*c*): Two month after *P*s employment, bank requested *P* to accept a salary of Rs 4,000 and *P* agrees to accept. Five months after, it is discovered that *P* has been continuously misappropriating Rs 1,000 per month.

Case (*d*): *P* misappropriates Rs 1,000 but the bank excuses him without informing *S* of *P*s misconduct. *P* again misappropriates Rs 5,000. Bank asks *S* to pay Rs 5,000.

Solution

Case	*Decision*	*Reason*
(a)	*S* is liable to Pay only Rs. 2000	Surety remains liable for the transactions already entered into prior to notice revoking guarantee [Section 130]
(b)	*S*'s estate is liable to pay only Rs. 2,000	Surety's estate remains liable for the transactions already entered into prior to the death of surety [Section 131]
(c)	*S* is liable to pay only Rs. 2,000	Surety is discharged as to the transactions subsequent to the variance in terms of contract [Section 133]
(d)	*S* is not liable to pay anything	Surety is discharged because the creditor failed to inform surety of *P*s misconduct [Section 139]

TRUE OR FALSE QUESTIONS

State with reasons whether the following statements are True or False.

1. A contract of indemnity is not a contingent contract.
2. A contract of insurance is a contract of indemnity.
3. Indemnity is given by repayment after payment by the indemnity-holder.
4. An indemnifier can sue the third party in his own name.
5. A contract of guarantee cannot be oral.
6. In a contract of guarantee, the principal debtor can not be minor.
7. In a contract of guarantee, the surety need not be benefitted.
8. A guarantee for payment of a time barred debt is valid.
9. A contract of guarantee is a contract of *uberrimae fidei*.
10. The liability of surety is primary.
11. The liability of surety is co-extensive with that of the liability of the principal debtor.
12. If the principal debtor cannot be held liable then the surety will also not be liable.
13. Creditor is bound to proceed first against the principal debtor before suing the surety.
14. A fidelity guarantee is a continuing guarantee.
15. A continuous guarantee can never be revoked.
16. A continuing guarantee cannot be given for a part of the entire debt.
17. A continuing guarantee can be given for the entire debt subject to a limit.

18. A specific guarantee cannot be revoked by notice even if the liability has not accrued.
19. A continuing guarantee can be revoked as to the past transaction by giving notice to the creditor.
20. The death of a surety puts an end to the contract of guarantee.
21. Surety's estate will be liable for the transactions taking place after the death of surety if the creditor had no knowledge of surety's death.
22. On payment of the guaranteed debt or performance of the guaranteed duty, the surety steps into the shoes of creditor.
23. In every contract of guarantee, there is implied contract of indemnity.
24. After the discharge of liability of principal debtor, the surety has right to only those securities which were given by the principal debtor to the creditor at the time of contract of guarantee.
25. Between co-sureties, there is equality of burden and benefit.
26. Co-sureties who have given guarantee for different amounts share the liability proportionately.
27. A variance in terms of contract without surety's consent, discharge the surety as to all transactions.
28. Discharge of principal debtor by operation of law operates as discharge of the surety.
29. A release by the creditor of one of the co-sureties discharges the other co-sureties.
30. A release by the creditor of one of the co-sureties frees the surety so released from his responsibility to other sureties.
31. A contract between the creditor and the third party to allow more time to the principal debtor discharges the surety.
32. Forbearance by the creditor to sue the principal debtor discharges the surety.
33. Guarantee obtained by misrepresentation is invalid.
34. Guarantee obtained by concealment of material facts is invalid.

Answers

1. False	2. True	3. False	4. False
5. False	6. False	7. True	8. False
9. False	10. False	11. True	12. False
13. False	14. True	15. False	16. False
17. True	18. False	19. False	20. True
21. False	22. True	23. True	24. False
25. True	26. False	27. False	28. False
29. False	30. False	31. False	32. False
33. True	34. True		

VERY SHORT ANSWER TYPE QUESTIONS

1. What is a contract of indemnity?
2. Who is an indemnity-holder?
3. Who is an indemnifier?

4. Is a contract of indemnity a contingent contract?
5. Is a contract of insurance a contract of indemnity?
6. What is the time of commencement of the indemnifier's liability?
7. What is a contract of guarantee?
8. Who is a principal debtor?
9. Who is a surety?
10. Who is a creditor?
11. Can there be oral guarantee?
12. Is it necessary for the surety to be benefitted?
13. Can the principal debtor be minor?
14. Can the surety be minor?
15. What is a specific guarantee?
16. What is a continuing guarantee?
17. Can a continuing guarantee be for a part of the entire debt?
18. Can a specific guarantee be revoked?
19. Can a continuing guarantee be revoked?
20. Enumerate the rights of a surety against the principal debtor.
21. Enumerate the rights of a surety against the creditor.
22. Enumerate the rights of a surety against the co-sureties.
23. Is the liability of surety primary?
24. Is the liability of co-sureties proportionate?
25. Enumerate the modes of discharge of a surety by revocation of guarantee.
26. Enumerate the modes of discharge of a surety by the conduct of the creditor.
27. Enumerate the modes of invalidation of the contract of guarantee.

SHORT ANSWER TYPE QUESTIONS

1. Comment on the following statements:
   (a) A contract of indemnity is a contingent contract.
   (b) The liability of surety is co-extensive with that of the principal debtor.
   (c) Surety is a favoured debtor.
   (d) A surety is undoubtedly and not unjustly an object of some favour both at law and at equity.
   (e) Between co-sureties, there is equality of burden and benefit.
   (f) The liability of surety is secondary.
   (g) The death of a surety puts an end to the contract of indemnity.
   (h) In every contract of guarantee, there is an implied contract of indemnity.
2. Distinguish between the following:
   (a) A contract of indemnity and a contract of guarantee.
   (b) Specific guarantee and continuing guarantee.

3. Write short notes on the following:
   (a) Continuing guarantee
   (b) Nature and extent of surety's liability
   (c) Rights of surety against principal debtor
   (d) Invalid guarantee
   (e) Right to subrogation.

ESSAY TYPE QUESTIONS

1. (a) Define a contract of indemnity.
   (b) Is a contract of indemnity a contingent contract?
   (c) Is a contract of insurance a contract of indemnity?
   (d) What are the rights of an indemnity-holder?
   (e) What is the time of commencement of an indemnifier's liability?
2. (a) Define a contract of guarantee.
   (b) Can there be oral guarantee?
   (c) State the essential features of a contract of guarantee.
   (d) When is a contract of guarantee held to be invalid?
3. Explain the nature and extent of surety's liability.
4. (a) What is a continuing guarantee?
   (b) How is it different from specific guarantee?
   (c) How is it revoked?
5. State the rights of a surety against (i) the principal debtor, (ii) the creditor, and (iii) co-sureties.
6. State the circumstances in which surety is discharged from his liability.

CHAPTER 13

Bailment and Pledge

1.0 INTRODUCTION

The Indian Contract Act, 1872 deals with the general rules relating to bailment but does not deal with all types of bailment for which separate acts have been enacted, for example, The Carrier Act 1865, The Railways Act, 1890, The Carriage of Goods by Sea Act, 1925.

2.0 MEANING OF BAILMENT

2.1 Meaning of Bailment [Section 148] The word 'Bailment' is derived from a French word 'baillier' which means 'to deliver'. *According to Section 148*, a "bailment" is **"the delivery of goods by one person to another for some purpose, upon a contract that they shall, when the purpose is accomplished, be returned or otherwise disposed off according to the directions of the person delivering them."**

Explanation If a person already in possession of the goods of another contracts to hold them as a bailee, he thereby becomes the bailee, and the owner becomes the bailor of such goods, although they may not have been delivered by way of bailment.

The person delivering the goods is called the 'bailor'.

The person to whom the goods are delivered is called the 'bailee'.

2.2 Examples of Bailment:

(a) *X* who is going out of station delivers a horse to *Y* for proper care.

(b) *X* lends a horse to *Y* for his riding only without charge.

(c) *Y* hires a horse from *X* for riding.

(d) *X* delivers a horse to a doctor, *Y*, for medical treatment.

(e) *X* sells a horse to *Y* who leaves the horse in the possession of *X*.

2.3 Essential Elements of a Bailment The essential elements of a bailment are as follows:

(a) Agreement There must be an agreement between the bailor and the bailee. This agreement may be *either* express *or* implied. However, a bailment may be implied by law also. *For example*, bailment between a finder of goods and owner of goods.

(b) Delivery of Goods There must be delivery of goods. It means that the possession of goods must be transferred. In this connection, the following points may be noted:

(i) **Voluntary Delivery**—The delivery **must be voluntary**; *for example*, the delivery of jewellery by its owner to a thief who shows a revolver, does not create a bailment because the delivery is not voluntary.

(ii) **Modes of Delivery**—Delivery may be **actual or constructive**.

Actual Delivery: A delivery is said to be actual where the goods are physically handed over by one person to another. *For example*, delivery of a car for repair to a workshop dealer.

Constructive Delivery *[Section 149]:* A delivery is said to be constructive where it is made by doing anything which has the effect of putting goods in the possession of the intended bailee or of any person authorized to hold them on his behalf. For example, delivery of the key of a car to a workshop dealer for the repair of car.

(c) Purpose The delivery of goods must be for some intended purpose. *For example*, wrong delivery of goods to Jaipur Golden Roadways instead of Patel Roadways, does not create any bailment.

(d) Return of Specific Goods After the accomplishment of purpose or after the expiry of period of the bailment, the goods which form the subject matter of a bailment must be (i) returned to the bailor *or* (ii) otherwise disposed off according to the directions of the bailor,

Note : The same goods (which were delivered by bailor to bailee) must be returned in their original form or desired form (if any required by the bailor). Thus, goods must be returned in specie (same) though they may undergo a change of form.

Example I *Delivery of old gold jewellery to a banker for safe custody creates a bailment because same old gold jewellery in its original form is to be returned.*

Example II *Delivery of old gold jewellery to a goldsmith for melting and making new one out of it also creates a bailment even though the same old gold is returned in the form of new jewellery.*

2.4 Distinction between A Contract of Bailment and A Contract of Sale

A contract of bailment differs from a contract of sale in the following respects:

Basis of Distinction	*Bailment*	*Sale*
1. *Transfer of ownership/ possession*	There is only a transfer of possession of goods from the bailor to the bailee.	There is a transfer of ownership of goods from the seller to the buyer.
2. *Consideration*	The consideration need not be passed between bailor and bailee.	The consideration in terms of price must be passed between seller and buyer.
3. *Return of goods*	The bailee must return the goods to the bailor on the fulfillment of the purpose for which the bailment is made.	There is no question of such return of goods in contract of sale.

3.0 KINDS OF BAILMENT

The various types of bailment have been shown below:

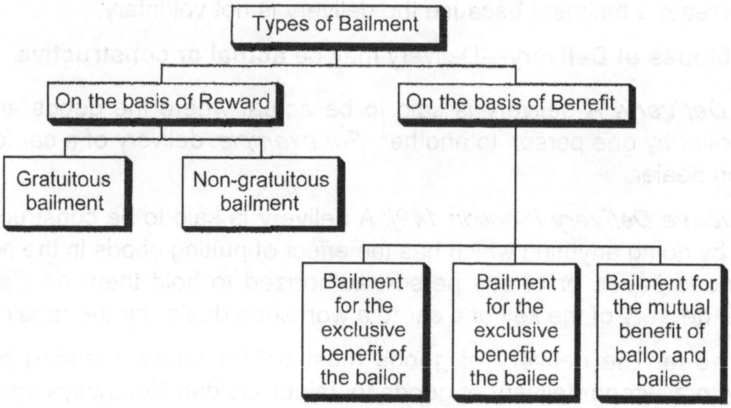

Let us discuss them one by one.

3.1 Bailment on the Basis of Reward

Type	*Meaning*	*Example*
(a) ***Gratuitous bailment***	It is a contract of bailment where no consideration passes between the bailor and the bailee.	X lends a horse to Y for his riding without any charge.
(b) ***Non-gratuitous bailment***	It is a contract of bailment where some consideration passes between the bailor and the bailee.	*Y* hires a horse from *X*.

3.2 Distinction between a Gratuitous and Non-gratuitous Bailment

A gratuitous bailment can be distinguished from a non-gratuitous bailment as follows:

Basis of Distinction	*Gratuitous bailment*	*Non-gratuitous bailment*
1. *Consideration*	No consideration passes between the bailor and the bailee.	Some consideration passes between the bailor and the bailee.
2. *Benefit*	It is for the exclusive benefit of the bailor or bailee.	It is for the exclusive benefit of the bailor and bailee.
3. *Liability of bailor for unknown defects [Section 151]*	The bailor is not liable to the bailee for the loss due to defect in the goods if he does not know those defects.	The bailor is liable to the bailee for the loss due to defects in the goods whether he knows those defects or not.
4. *Bailor's duty to bear expenses [Section 158]*	The bailor must repay to the bailee all the necessary expenses which the bailee has already incurred for the purposes of bailment.	The bailor must repay to the bailee only the extraordinary expenses which the bailee has already incurred for the purpose of bailment.

5. ***Bailment for a specified period/purpose***	It can be terminated at any time even though the bailment was for a specified period or specified purpose.	It is terminated on the expiry of specified period or on the fulfillment of the specified purpose.
6. ***Effect of death of bailor/bailee***	It is terminated by the death of bailor or bailee	It is not termminated by the death of bailor or bailee.

3.3 Bailment on the Basis of Benefit

Type	*Meaning*	*Example*
(a) ***Bailment for the exclusive benefit of the bailor***	It is a contract of bailment which is executed only for the benefit of the bailor and the bailee does not derive any benefit form it.	*X* who is going out of station, delivers a horse to *Y* for proper care.
(b) ***Bailment for the exclusive benefit of the bailee***	It is a contract of bailment which is executed only for ther benefit of the bailee and the bailor does not derive any benefit from it.	*X* lends a horse to *Y* for his riding without any charge.
(c) ***Bailment for the mutual benefit***	It is a contract of bailment which is executed for the mutual benefit of bailor and bailee.	*Y* hires a horse from *X*.

4.0 DUTIES OF A BAILOR

The various duties of a bailor are as follows:

4.1 Duty to Disclose Defects [Section 151]

In case of Gratuitous Bailment	*In case of Non-gratuitous Bailment*
The bailor must disclose all the known defects in the goods— (i) which materially interfere with the use of them, *or* (ii) expose the bailee to extraordinary risks.	The bailor must disclose all the faults whether known to him or not.
Effect of Non-disclosure: If the bailor does not disclose such defects and the bailee suffers some loss due to such defects, the bailor is liable to bailee for such loss.	***Effect of Non-disclosure:*** If the bailee suffers any loss due to any defect in the goods, the bailor is liable to bailee for such loss whether he knows those defects or not.

Example I *X delivered a horse to Y for his own riding without any charge. The horse runs away. Y is thrown and injured. State the legal position in each of the following alternative case:*

Case (*a*): If *X* did not know that the horse was vicious.

Case (*b*): If *X* disclosed the fact that the horse was vicious.

Case (*c*): If *X* did not disclose the fact known to him that the horse was vicious.

Solution: The bailment in the given problem is gratuitous bailment and, hence the legal position is as under:

Case (*a*): *X* is not liable to *Y* for loss because he did not know the defect.

Case (*b*): *X* is not liable to *Y* for such loss because he disclosed the known defect.

Case (*c*): *X* is liable to *Y* for such loss because he did not disclose the known defect.

Example II *If in Example I, X charge Rs 100 from Y, will your answer be same?*

Solution: Then, it becomes a case of non-gratuitous bailment and hence the legal position will be changed as under:

In all cases, *X* is liable to *Y* for such loss because bailor is liable to bailee for any loss arising due to all defects whether he knows or not.

4.2 Duty to Bear Expenses [Section 158]

In case of Gratuitous Bailment	*In case of Non-gratuitous Bailment*
The bailor must repay to the bailee **all** the ***necessary expenses*** (whether ordinary or extraordinary) which the bailee has already incurred for the purpose of bailment.	The bailor must repay to the bailee all the ***extraordinary expenses*** which the bailee has incurred for the purpose of bailment. **Note** : Ordinary Expenses are to be borne by bailee.

Example *X delivered a horse to Y. Y incurred Rs 100 as feeding expenses and Rs 200 as medical expenses when the horse became sick. State the legal position (a) if nothing was charged by either party, (b) if X charged Rs 500 from Y.*

Solution:

Case (*a*): It is a case of gratuitous bailment where *X* (the bailor) must repay Rs 300 to *Y* (the bailee) because the bailor is bound to bear all expenses incurred by the bailee for the purpose of bailment.

Case (*b*): It is a case of non-gratuitous bailment where *X* (the bailor) must repay Rs 200 to *Y* (the bailee) because the bailor is bound to bear all extraordinary expenses (and not ordinary expenses) incurred by the bailee for the purpose of bailment.

4.3 Duty to Indemnify the Bailee in Case of Premature Termination of Gratuitous Bailment [Section 159] A gratuitous bailment may be terminated by the bailor at anytime even though the bailment was for a specified time or purpose. The bailor must indemnify the bailee in case the loss arising due to premature termination of the bailment exceeds the benefits actually derived by the bailee.

4.4 Duty to Indemnify the Bailee against the Defective Title of the Bailor [Section 164] The bailor is responsible to the bailee for any loss which the bailee may suffer because of the defective title of the bailor.

Example *Y asks X, his friend to give him horse for one hour. X, instead of his own horse, delivers Z's horse to Y. While Y was riding, Z catches Y and hands him over the police custody. Y is entitled to recover from X all costs which he had to incur in getting out of this situation.*

4.5 Duty to Receive Back the Goods [Section 164] The bailor must receive back the goods when the bailee, in accordance with the terms of bailment, returns the goods to him. If the bailor refuses to receive back the goods, he must repay to the bailee all the expenses which the bailee has incurred for the safe custody of goods.

Example *X lent a horse to Y for five days. On the expiry of five days, X refused to receive back the horse but two days thereafter, he agreed to receive back the horse. During these two days, Y incurred Rs 100 as feeding expenses. X must repay Rs 100 to Y.*

4.6 Duty to Bear the Risk of Loss [Section 152] The bailor must bear the risk of loss of goods provided the bailee has taken all reasonable steps to protect the goods from loss.

Example *X lent a horse to Y for five days. On third day, the horse became sick and was hospitalised but died. Y is not liable to X for this loss.*

5.0 DUTIES OF A BAILEE

The various duties of a bailee are as follows:

5.1 Duty to take Care of the Goods Bailed [Sections 151 and 152]

In the absence of any Special Contract	*In case of Special Contract*
The bailee is bound to take as much care of the goods bailed to him as a man of ordinary prudence would, under similar circumstances take of his own goods of the same bulk, quality and value as the goods bailed. If he has taken care as an ordinary prudent person, he is not responsible for the loss, destruction, or deterioration of the goods bailed.	The bailee is bound to take as much care as provided by the term of contract. If he has taken the amount of care described in the special contract, he is not responsible for the loss, destruction, or deterioration of the goods bailed.

Note: The bailee is bound to take care whether the bailment is gratuitous or non-gratuitous.

Example *X, who was going out of station delivered a horse to his friend Y for safe custody for 5 days without any charge. The horse became sick on second day but Y did not bother about any medical treatment of the hose. The horse died. Y was liable as he failed to exercise reasonable care.*

5.2 Duty not to Make any Unauthorised Use of Goods [Section 154] The bailee must use the goods bailed according to the conditions of the bailment. If he does not use the goods bailed according to the conditions of the bailment, he is liable to make compensation to the bailor for any damage (due to any reason) arising to the goods from or during such use of them.

Example *X lends a horse to Y for his own riding only. Y allows Mrs Y to ride the horse. Mrs Y rides with care but the horse accidentally falls and is injured. Y is liable to make compensation to X for the injury to the horse.*

5.3 Duty not to Mix Bailor's Goods with his Own Goods [Sections 155 to 157] The bailee must not mix bailor's goods with his own goods. In case of mixing, the following provisions shall apply.

Case	*Provision*
I. In case of mixture with bailor's consent [Section 155]	The bailor and the bailee shall have an interest in proportion to their respective shares in the mixture thus produced.
II. In case of mixture without bailor's consent when the goods can be separated [Section 156]	The property in the goods remains with the parties respectively, but the bailee is bound to bear the expenses of

	separation or division and any damage arising from the mixture.
III. In case of mixture without bailor's consent when the goods cannot be separated [Section 157]	The bailor is entitled to be compensated by the bailee for the loss of the goods.

Example I *A bails 100 bales of cotton marked with a particular mark to B. B without A's consent mixes the 100 bales with other bales of his own, bearing a different mark. A is entitled to have his 100 bales returned, and B is bound to bear all the expenses incurred in the separation of the bales, and any other incidental damage.*

Example II *A bails a barrel of imported flour worth Rs 45 to B. B, without A's consent mixes the flour with Punjabi flour of his own, worth only Rs 25 a barrel. B must compensate A for the loss of his flour.*

5.4 Duty to Return the Goods [Sections 160 and 161] The bailee must return or deliver the goods according to the bailor's directions without demand, after the accomplishment of purpose or after the expiry of period of bailment. If he fails to do so, he is responsible to the bailor for any loss, destruction or deterioration of the goods from that time.

Example *X lent a horse to Y for 5 days. On the expiry of 5 days, Y did not return the horse. The horse died without any fault on part of Y. Y was responsible to X for the loss.*

5.5 Duty to Return Accretions to the Goods [Section 163] In the absence of any contract to the contrary, the bailee is bound to deliver to the bailor, or according to his directions, any increase or profit which may have accrued from the goods bailed.

Example *A leaves a cow in the custody of B to be taken care of. The cow has a calf. B is bound to deliver the calf as well as the cow to A.*

5.6 Duty not to Set Up any Adverse Title The bailee must not do any act which is inconsistent with the title of the bailor. He must not set up his own title or a third party's title on the goods bailed to him.

6.0 RIGHTS OF A BAILOR

Basically, the duties of a bailee are the rights of a bailor and the bailor can enforce his rights against the bailee by suing him in case of a default. The various rights of a bailor are as follows:

6.1 Right to Claim Damages in Case of Negligence [Section 152] If the bailee has not taken reasonable care (in the absence of any special contract) or special care (in case of special contract to that effect), the bailor has a right to claim damages for the loss, destruction or deterioration of the goods bailed.

6.2 Right to Terminate the Contract in Case of Unauthorised Use [Section 153] If the bailee does any act in respect of goods bailed, which is inconsistent with the conditions of the bailment, the bailor has a right to terminate the contract of bailment.

6.3 Right to Claim Compensation in Case of Unauthorised Use [Section 154] If the bailee does not use the goods bailed according to the conditions of the bailment, the bailor has a right to claim compensation from bailee for any damage arising to the goods from or during such use of them.

6.4 Right to Claim the Separation of Goods in Case of Unauthorised Mixture [Section 156] If the bailee, without the consent of the bailor mixes bailor's goods with his own goods and the goods can be separated, the bailor has a right to claim his goods after separation.

6.5 Right to Claim Compensation in Case of Unauthorised Mixture of Goods which cannot be Separated [Section 157] If the bailee, without the consent of the bailor mixes bailor's goods with his own goods and the goods cannot be separated, the bailor has a right to claim compensation from bailee for the loss of the goods.

6.6 Right to Demand Return of Goods [Section 160] The bailor has a right to demand return of goods after the accomplishment of the purpose or after the expiry of period of bailment.

6.7 Right to Claim Compensation in Case of Unauthorised Retention of Goods [Section 161] If the bailee does not return or deliver the goods according to the bailor's directions, after the accomplishment of purpose or after the expiry of period of bailment, the bailor has a right to claim compensation for any loss, destruction or deterioration of the goods from that time.

6.8 Right to Demand Accretion to Goods [Section 163] In the absence of contract to the contrary, the bailor has a right to demand any increase or profit which may have accrued from the goods bailed.

7.0 RIGHTS OF A BAILEE

Basically, the duties of a bailor are the rights of a bailee, and a bailee can enforce his rights against the bailor by suing him in case of default. The various rights of a bailee are as follows:

7.1 Right to Claim Damages [Section 150]

In case of Gratuitous Bailment	*In case of Non-gratuitous Bailment*
If the bailor does not disclose the defect in the goods which are known to him and the bailee suffers some loss due to such defects, the bailee has a right to claim damages.	If the bailee suffers any loss due to any defect in the goods, the bailee has a right to claim damages.

7.2 Right to Claim Reimbursement of Expenses [Section 158]

In case of Gratuitous Bailment	*In case of Non-gratuitous Bailment*
The bailee has a right to claim reimbursement of all the necessary expenses (**whether Ordinary or Extraordinary**) which he has already incurred for the purpose of bailment.	The bailee has a right to claim reimbursement of all the **extra-ordinary expenses** which the bailee has already incurred for the purpose of bailment.

7.3 Right to be Indemnified in Case of Premature Termination of Gratuitous Bailment [Section 159] The bailee has a right to be indemnified in case the loss arising due to premature termination of the gratuitous bailment exceeds the benefits actually derived by him.

7.4 Right to Recover Loss in Case of Bailor's Defective Title [Section 164] The bailee has a right to be indemnified in case he suffers any loss because of the defective title of the bailor.

7.5 Right to Recover Loss in Case of Bailor's Refusal to take the Goods Back [Section 164] The bailor has a right to be indemnified in case he suffers any loss because of bailor's refusal to take the goods back.

7.6 Right to Deliver Goods to Anyone of the Joint Bailors [Section 165] In the absence of any contract to the contrary, the bailee has a right to deliver back the goods to anyone of the joint owners or may deliver the goods back according to the directions of one joint owner without the consent of all [Section 165].

7.7 Right to Deliver the Goods to Bailor in Case of Bailor's Defective Title [Section 166] If the bailor has no title to the goods, and the bailee, in good faith, delivers them back to, or according to the directions of the bailor, the bailee is not responsible to the owner in respect of such delivery.

7.8 Right to Particular Lien [Section 170] Where the bailee has, in accordance with the purpose of the bailment, rendered any service involving the exercise of labour or skill in respect of the goods bailed, he has, in the absence of a contract to the contrary, a right to retain such goods until he receives due remuneration for the services he has rendered in respect to them.

Example I *A delivers a rough diamond to B, a jeweller, to be cut and polished which is accordingly done. B is entitled to retain the stone till he is paid for the services he has rendered.*

Example II *A gives cloth to B, a tailor, to make into a coat. B promises A to deliver the coat as soon as it is finished, and to give a three months credit for the price. B is not entitled to retain the coat until he is paid.*

8.0 LIEN

8.1 Meaning of Lien

Lien means the right of a person having possession of goods belonging to another to retain those goods until the satisfaction of sum claimed by the person in possession of the goods. It may be noted that the possession of goods must be lawful and continuous. *For example*, *X* took *Y*'s godown on a rent of Rs 5,000 p.m. on an agreement that *X* can at any time deposit or take out his goods from the godown. After six months, *X* stopped paying the rent. *Y* auctioned *X*'s goods and claimed lien. *Y* cannot claim lien because it was agreed that *X* can take out his goods whenever he wanted.

8.2 Types of Lien

A lien may be *either* a particular lien *or* a general lien.

(a) Particular Lien [Section 170] A particular lien is a right to retain only those goods in respect of which some charges are due. This right is available only if the following conditions are fulfilled:

(a) The bailee must have rendered some service involving the exercise of labour or skill in respect of the goods bailed.

(b) The bailee must have rendered the service in accordance with the purpose of the bailment.

(c) The goods must be in the possession of the bailee.

(d) There must not exist any contract for payment of price in future.

(e) The labour and skill must have been used so as to confer an additional value on the article.

Note: The bailee has a right to recover the charges for the services performed even if the goods are destroyed or stolen without any fault on his part.

Example *X gives a piece of cloth to Y, a tailor, to make a coat. Y promises X to deliver the coat as soon as it is finished. Y is entitled to retain the coat till he is paid for (if he has not allowed any credit period) but is not entitled to retain the coat (if he has allowed one month's credit for the payment).*

(b) General Lien [Section 171] A general lien is a right to retain all the goods as a security for the general balance of account until the full satisfaction of the claims due whether in respect of those goods or other goods. In the absence of a contract to the contrary, general lien is available only to bankers, factors, wharfingers, attorneys of a High Court (only for non-payment of their professional fees) and policy brokers. The general lien is available to other persons only when there is an express contract to that effect.

Example *X deposited US 64 units and shares of Reliance Industries Ltd. as security with Citi Bank and took a loan against the shares of Reliance Industries Ltd. Citi Bank may retain both the securities until its claims are fully satisfied.*

8.3 Distinction between Particular Lien and General Lien

Basis of Distinction	*Particular lien*	*General lien*
1. ***Goods in respect of which lien is available***	It is available against those goods in respect of which some charges are due.	It is available against all goods whether in respect of which claims are due or not.
2. ***Purpose***	It is available only for non-payment of remuneration for the services.	It is available for a general balance of account.
3. ***To whom available in the absence of contract to contrary***	It is available to **every bailee** to whom the goods have been bailed.	It is available only to **specific bailees** like bankers, factors, Wharfingers, attorneys of High Court and policy brokers.
4. ***Rendering of service***	It is available only when some service involving the exercise of labour or skill has been rendered.	It is available even when no such service has been rendered.
5. ***Purpose of delivery of goods***	The purpose of delivery of goods is to confer an additional value as the goods bailed.	The purpose of delivery of goods is to deposit the goods as security.

9.0 RIGHTS OF BAILOR AND BAILEE AGAINST WRONGDOER

9.1 Rights of Bailor and Bailee against Wrongdoer [Section 180] If a third party wrongfully deprives a bailee of the use or possession of the goods bailed, or does them any injury, the bailee is entitled to such remedies as the owner might have used in the like case if no bailment had been made; and *either* the bailor *or* the bailee may bring a suit against a third person for such deprivation or injury.

9.2 Apportionment of Relief or Compensation Obtained by such suits [section 181] Whatever is obtained by way of relief or compensation in any such suit shall, as between the bailor and the bailee, be dealt with according to their respective interests.

Example *X delivered a TV to Y for repairs. Z forcefully takes possession of TV from Y's shop. In this case, either X or Y may sue Z. If Y files the suit, he shall hand over the amount received after deducting his repair charges to X.*

10.0 FINDER OF GOODS

10.1 Meaning of Finder of Goods Finder of goods is the person who finds some goods which do not belong to him.

Example *If X finds a purse or a diamond ring or a watch, which does not belong to him, he will be called as finder of goods.*

10.2 Rights of a Finder of Goods The rights of a finder of goods are as follows:

(a) Right to Lien [Section 168] The finder of goods has a right to retain the goods found until he receives the compensation for trouble and expenses voluntarily incurred by him—

(i) to preserve the goods and

(ii) to find out the owners.

It may be noted that the finder of goods has **no right to sue the owner** for such compensation.

(b) Right to Sue for Reward [Section 168] Where the owner has offered a specific reward for the return of goods lost, the finder has a right to sue the owner for such reward and to retain the goods until he receives it.

(c) Right to Sell [Section 169] A finder of goods has a right to sell the goods found under the following circumstances:

(i) If the owner cannot with reasonable diligence be found; or

(ii) If the owner when found, refuses to pay the lawful charges of the finder; or

(iii) If the goods are in danger of perishing or of losing the greater part of their value; or

(iv) If the lawful charges of the finder in respect of goods found, amount to two-third of its value.

10.3 Duties of a Finder of Goods [Section 171] A finder of goods is subject to the same responsibility as a bailee. The duties of a finder of goods are as follows:

(a) Duty to take Reasonable Care The finder of goods must take reasonable care of the goods found like a person of ordinary prudence.

(b) Duty not to Use for Personal Purpose The finder of goods must not use the goods found for personal purpose.

(c) Duty not to Mix with his Own Goods The finder of goods must not mix the goods found with his own goods.

(d) Duty to Find the Owner The finder of goods must find the owner of the goods found and return those goods to him, of course subject to his lien. For example, *X*, a guest, found a diamond ring at a birthday party of *Y*. *X* told *Y* and few other guests about it. He has performed his duty to find the owner. If he is not able to find the owner, he can retain the ring as bailee.

11.0 TERMINATION OF BAILMENT

11.1 Termination of every Contract of Bailment (whether Gratuitous or not) Every contract of bailment comes to end under the following circumstances:

(a) **On the Expiry of Fixed Period** A bailment is terminated on the expiry of fixed period if the goods are bailed for a fixed period.

(b) **On Fulfilment of the Purpose** A bailment is terminated on the fulfilment of the purpose if the goods are bailed for a specific purpose.

(c) **Inconsistent Use of Goods** A bailment may be terminated if the bailee does not use the goods according to the conditions of the bailment.

(d) **Destruction of the Subject Matter of Bailment** A bailment is terminated if the subject matter of the bailment (i) is destroyed, or (ii) becomes incapable of being used for bailment because of some change in the nature of goods.

11.2 Termination of Gratuitous Bailment A contract of gratuitous bailment is terminated in the following circumstances also.

(a) **Before the Expiry of a Fixed Period** A gratuitous bailment may be terminated by the bailor at any time even though the bailment was for a fixed period. However, the bailor is required to idemnify the bailee in case the loss due to premature termination exceeds the benefit actually derived by the bailee.

(b) **On Death of Bailor/Bailee** A gratuitous bailment is terminated by the death of *either* the bailor *or* bailee.

12.0 PLEDGE

12.1 Meaning of Pledge (or Pawn) [Section 172] The bailment of goods as security for payment of a debt or performance of a promise is called pledge (or pawn).

Example *X borrows Rs 1,00,000 from Citi Bank and keeps his shares as security for payment of a debt. It is a contract of pledge.*

12.2 Meaning of a Pawnor (or Pledgor) [Section 172] The person who delivers the goods as security for payment of a debt or performance of a promise is called the Pawnor or Pledgor. In the aforesaid example, *X* is the pawnor.

12.3 Meaning of Pawnee (or Pledgee) [Section 172] The person to whom the goods are delivered as security for payment of a debt or performance of a promise is called the Pawnee or Pledgee. In the aforesaid example, Citi Bank is the pawnee.

12.4 Special Feature of Pledge It is the special property in goods and not the general property in goods, which is transferred to the pledgee. General property means the ownership of goods and special property means the possession of goods.

Example *A producer of a film borrowed Rs 10,00,000 from a financier-distributor and agreed to deliver the final prints of the film when ready. This agreement was not a pledge because there was no actual transfer of possession. [Revenue Authority v. Sudarshan Pictures]*

12.5 Distinction between Pledge and Bailment

Basis of Distinction	*Pledge*	*Bailment*
1. Purpose	Pledge is bailment of goods for a specific purpose, i.e. repayment of a debt or performance of a duty.	Bailment is for a purpose of any kind.

2. Right to use	Pawnee cannot use the goods pledged.	Bailee can use the goods as per terms of bailment.
3. Right to sell	Pawnee can sell the goods pledged after giving notice to the pawnor in case of default by the pawnor.	Bailee can *either* retain the goods *or* sue the bailor for his dues.

It may be noted that every pledge involves bailment but every bailment does not amount to pledge.

12.6 Distinction between Pledge and Hypothecation Hypothecation is also one of the modes of providing security. However, it is different from pledge in the following respects:

Basis of Distinction	*Pledge*	*Hypothecation*
1. Possession of goods	Borrower transfers the possession of goods.	Borrower does not transfer the possession of goods.
2. Right to deal with the goods	Borrower has no right to deal with the goods pledged.	Borrower has a right to deal with the goods hypothecated.

13.0 RIGHTS OF A PAWNEE

A pawnee has almost the same rights as those of a bailee. His rights are as follows:

13.1 Rights of Retainer [Section 173] The pawnee has right to retain the goods pledged,

(i) for payment of the debt or the performance of the promise

(ii) for the interest of the debt, and

(iii) all necessary expenses incurred by him in respect of the possession or for the preservation of the goods pledged.

13.2 Right to Recover Reimbursement of Extraordinary Expenses [Section 173] The pawnee has right to recover from the pawnor extraordinary expenses incurred by him for the preservation of the goods pledged.

13.3 Right to Sue Pawnor [Section 176] The pawnee has right to sue the pawnor. If the pawnor makes default in payment of the debt or performance of the promise.

13.4 Right to Sell [Section 176] The pawnee has a right to sell the goods pledged after giving a reasonable notice of the intended sale, to the pawnor, if the pawnor makes default in payment of the debt or performance of the promise. Any **loss** from such sale is **recoverable** from the pawnor but **profits** resulting therefrom is **returnable** to the pawnor.

13.5 Right Against True Owner [Section 178A] The pawnee acquires a good title to the goods provided he acts in good faith and without notice of the pawnor's defect of title. When the pawnor has obtained possession of the goods pledged by him under a contract voidable under Section 19 or 19-A but the contract has not been rescinded at the time of the pledge.

14.0 DUTIES OF A PAWNEE

The pawnee has almost the same duties as those of the bailee. His duties are as follows:

14.1 Duty to take Reasonable Care of the Goods Pledged The pawnee must take reasonable care of the goods pledged.

14.2 Duty not to make Unauthorised Use of Goods The pawnee must not make unauthorised use of the goods pledged.

14.3 Duty not to Mix Goods Pledged with his Own Goods The pawnee must not mix the goods pledged with this own goods.

14.4 Duty to Return Goods The pawnee must return the goods pledged on the repayment of the debt or on the performance of the promise.

14.5 Duty to Return Accretions to the Goods The pawnee must return the accretions (if any) to the goods pledged.

15.0 RIGHTS OF A PAWNOR

The duties of a pawnee are basically the rights of a pawnor. He has the following rights:

15.1 Right to get Pawnee's Duties Duly Enforced The pawnor has the right to get pawnee's duties duly enforced (for example, right to get back the goods pledged, right to receive any accretions to the goods pledged).

15.2 Right to Redeem [Section 177]

Meaning of Redemption—Redemption means right to recover back the goods by making payment of the debt or performance of promise.

Time for Redemption—The pawnor may excessive the right of redemption :

(a) before the expiry of fixed time or

(b) after the expiry of fixed time provided—

(i) the pawnee has not sold the goods

(ii the pawnor pays the pawnee all expenses arising on account of this default.

16.0 DUTIES OF A PAWNOR

Basically, the pawnor has the following duties:

16.1 Duty to Comply with the Terms of Pledge The pawnor must comply with the terms of pledge. He must repay the debt on the stipulated date or perform the promise at the stipulated time.

16.2 Duty to Compensate the Pawnee for Extraordinary Expenses [Section 175] The pawnor must compensate the pawnee for any extraordinary expenses incurred by him for preserving the goods pledged.

16.3 Duty to Pay the Loss on Sale [Sec. 176] The pawnor must pay the loss on sale if the pawnee sells the goods due to default by pawnor.

16.4 Duty to Disclose all Faults in Goods The pawnor must disclose all the faults which

(a) are material for use of the goods

(b may put the pawnee to extraordinary risks

16.5 Duty to Indemnity against Defective Title The pawnor must indemnity the pawnee if loss is caused to the pawnee due to defect in pawnor's title to goods.

17.0 PLEDGE BY NON-OWNERS

According to the general rule, only the true owner can pledge the goods but under the following cases, even a non-owner can make a valid pledge:

17.1 Pledge by a Mercantile Agent [Section 178] If a mercantile agent acts unauthorisedly against the instructions of his principle, the pledge made shall be valid if the following conditions are fulfilled:

(i) The pawnor must be a mercantile agent. According to Section 2(a) of the Sale of Goods Act, 'Mercantile Agent' means an agent having in the customary course of business as such agent authority *either* to sell goods *or* to raise money on the security of goods.

(ii) Mercantile agent must be in possession of goods or documents of title to goods.

(iii) Mercantile agent must be in possession with the consent of the owner.

(iv) Pledge must have been made by the mercantile agent, when acting in the ordinary course of business of a mercantile agent.

(v) The pawnee must have acted in good faith.

(vi) The pawnee must not have the notice that the pawnor has no authority to pledge.

17.2 Pledge by Person in Possession under Voidable Contract [Section 178A] The pledge by a person in possession under voidable contract (as per Section 19 or 19A of the Indian Contract Act) is valid if the following conditions are fulfilled:

(i) The pledge is made before the contract is rescinded e.g. in *Phillips* v. *Brooks* (1919), the pledge by North who acted fraudulently, was held to be valid.

(ii) The pawnee has acted in good faith.

(iii) The pawnee has no knowledge of the defective title of the pawnor.

17.3 Pledge where Pawnor has a Limited Interest [Section 179] Pledge by a person who has only a limited interest in the goods is valid to the extent of that interest. *For example*, a finder of goods, a mortgagee or a person having lien over the goods may make a valid pledge of such goods to the extent of his interest in the goods.

17.4 Pledge by a Co-owner in Possession Pledge by a co-owner is valid if the following conditions are fulfilled:

(i) The goods must be owned by more than one person.

(ii) The goods must be in the possession of one of the co-owners.

(iii) Such sole possession must be with the consent of other owners.

17.5 Pledge by Seller or Buyer in Possession [Section 30 of Sale of Goods Act, 1930] A pledge by a seller who is in possession of goods after sale with the consent of buyer or by a buyer who is in possession of goods before sale with the consent of seller, is valid if the following conditions are fulfilled:

(i) The pawnee must act in good faith.

(ii) The pawnee must not have knowledge of the defect in title of the pawnor.

Example *X sold goods to Y who left the goods with X who then pledged those goods with Z who acted in good faith and has no notice of prior sale. Such pledge is valid.*

PRACTICAL PROBLEMS

PROBLEM 1

Mrs *X* delivered her old gold jewellery to her husband Mr *X* a goldsmith for the purpose of making new one out of it. Is there a contract of bailment?

Solution

Section to which the given problem relates: Section 148.

Decision: There is a contract of bailment.

Reason: All the essential of a valid bailment are present (i.e., contract, delivery, purpose and return of goods).

PROBLEM 2

Mrs *X* delivered her old gold jewellery to Mr *X*, a goldsmith for the purpose of making new one out of it. Every evening she used to receive the unfinished jewellery and to put it into a box kept at Mr *X*'s shop. She kept the key of that box with herself. One night, the jewellery was stolen from the box. Was there a contract of bailment?

Solution

Section to which the given problem relates: Section 148.

Decision: There was no contract of bailment.

Reason: The goldsmith (bailee) had redelivered the jewellery bailed to the lady (bailor).

[Leading case: *Kaliaperumal Pillai* v. *Visalakshmi*]

PROBLEM 3

X hires a motor launch from *Y* for holiday on a river. The launch caught fire and *X* was unable to extinguish it as the fire fighting equipment was out of order which *Y* did not know. As a result, *X* injured and suffered loss. Who is liable and why?

Solution

Section to which the given problem relates: Section 150.

Decision: *Y* is liable to *X* for loss.

Reason: In case of non-gratuitous bailment, the bailor is responsible for all defects in the goods which he knows or not.

[Leading case: *Read* v. *Dean*]

PROBLEM 4

X delivered some cattle to *Y* for feeding grass in *Y*'s farmhouse against some payment. Without any negligence on *Y*'s part, a cattle was stolen. *Y* did not inform the owner or the police or make any effort to recover the cattle because he thought it would be useless to do so. Who is liable and why?

Solution

Section to which the given problem relates: Section 151.

Decision: *Y* is liable to *X* for such loss.

Reason: *Y* (the bailee) failed to take reasonable care of the goods bailed.

[Leading case: *Coldman* v. *Hill*]

PROBLEM 5

X entered a restaurant for dinner. His coat was taken by a waiter who hung it on a hook behind *X*. When *X* rose to leave, the coat was not on the hook. Who is responsible and why?

Solution

Section to which the given problem relates: Section 151.

Decision: The proprietor of the restaurant is responsible to *X* for such loss.

Reason: The proprietor (the bailee) failed to take reasonable care of the goods bailed.

[**Leading case:** *Ultzen* v. *Nicols*]

PROBLEM 6

X lends a horse to *Y* for his riding only. *Y* allows Mrs *Y*, his wife who is an expert rider, to ride the horse. Mrs *Y* rides with care, but the horse accidentally falls and is injured. Who is liable for the injury caused to the horse?

Solution

Section to which the given problem relates: Section 154.

Decision: *Y* is liable to *X* for the injury caused to the horse.

Reason: *Y* (the bailee) has not used the goods bailed according to the conditions of the bailment.

PROBLEM 7

X delivered some books to *Y* for the purpose of binding. *Y* neglected to return them even after the expiry of a reasonable time. One night a fire broke out in *Y*s shop without any negligence on *Y*s part and the books were destroyed. Who was liable and why?

Solution

Section to which the given problem relates: Section 161.

Decision: *Y* was liable to *X* for the loss.

Reason: *Y* (the bailee) failed to deliver the books within a reasonable time.

[**Leading case:** *Shaw & Co.* v. *Symmons & Sons*]

PROBLEM 8

X took *Y*s motorcar garage for 2 years on a monthly rent of Rs 1,000. *X* was entitled to take the car out of garage as and when he wanted. After 6 months, *X* stopped the payment of rent. *Y* detained the car at the garage until payment of arrears of rent. Advise *X*.

Solution

Section to which the given problem relates: Section 170.

Decision: *Y* had no lien.

Reason: As per the contract, *X* was entitled to take car away as and when he wanted.

[**Leading case:** *Hatton* v. *Car Maintenance Co.*]

PROBLEM 9

Subhash Ghai, a film producer, borrowed Rs 10,00,000 from Amitabh Bachchan, a financier-distributor, and agreed to deliver the final prints of the film when ready. Was the agreement a pledge?

Solution

Section to which the given problem relates: Section 172.

Decision: The agreement was not a pledge.

Reason: There was no actual transfer of possession.

[**Leading case:** *Revenue Authority* v. *Sudarshan Pictures*]

PROBLEM 10

On 1st Jan., 2009 *X* borrows Rs 1,00,000 from *Y* on the security of shares. On 1st June 2009, *X* borrows another sum of Rs 50,000. *X* repays the first debt in full. Can *Y* retain the shares against his claim for the repayment of the second loan?

Solution

Section to which the given problem relates: Section 174.

Decision: *Y* can retain the shares against his claim for the repayment of the second loan.

Reason: The pawnee's right of retainer over the pledged goods extends to subsequent advances also.

PROBLEM 11

X, a doctor by the exercise of undue influence persuades *Y*, his patient to sell a valuable gold watch to him for Rs 500. *X* obtained the possession of the watch and pledges it with *Z*, who does not know about the defective title of *X*. Is this a valid pledge?

Solution

Section to which the given problem relates: Section 178A.

Decision: This is a valid pledge.

Reason: A pledge by a person in possession of goods under a voidable contract is valid if the contract has not been rescinded before the contract of pledge and the pawnee has acted in good faith and without notice of the pawnor's defect of title.

PROBLEM 12

X finds a defective watch lying on a road. He gets it repaired for Rs 100 and pledges with *Y* for Rs 300. Later on when *Z* the true owner, came to know about this, he sued *Y* to recover his watch. Can *Z* recover his watch?

Solution

Section to which the given problem relates: Section 179.

Decision: *Z* can recover his watch only on paying Rs 100 to *Y* (the pawnee).

Reason: A pledge by a person having a limited interest in the goods is valid to the extent of that interest.

TRUE OR FALSE QUESTIONS

State with reasons whether the following statements are 'True' or 'False':

1. Bailment can be of immovable property also.
2. In bailment, the delivery of goods must be actual.
3. Gold jewels delivered to a bank for safe custody is not a contract of bailment.
4. Placing of ornaments in a bank locker is a contract of bailment.
5. In case of non-gratuitous bailment, no consideration is involved.
6. Gratuitous bailment is for the mutual benefit of bailor and bailee.
7. Non-gratuitous bailment is for the exclusive benefit of *either* bailor *or* bailee.

8. The bailor is not responsible for those defects in the goods which are not known to him.
9. The bailor must repay to the bailee all the necessary expenses which the bailee has already incurred for the purpose of bailment.
10. The bailor must repay to the bailee all the extraordinary expenses which the bailee has already incurred for the purpose of bailment.
11. If the bailee makes unauthorised use of goods, the contract of bailment becomes void.
12. In the absence of a contract to the contrary, the bailee may deliver back the goods to anyone of the joint bailors with the consent of all.
13. To claim the right of lien, the possession must be rightful and continuous.
14. A bailee is entitled to a general lien.
15. A banker is entitled to a particular lien.
16. A person who takes an animal for feeding has a particular lien.
17. A surgeon who has treated the animals has a general lien.
18. A third person who wrongfully deprives the bailee of the use of possession of the goods bailed, can be sued by bailee only.
19. A finder of goods may sue the owner for compensation for trouble and expenses voluntarily incurred by him in finding the owner and in preserving the goods found.
20. A finder of goods may sue the owner for the award (if any offered on the lost goods).
21. A finder of goods may sell the goods found if the lawful charges for preserving the goods amount to one third of the value of goods.
22. A bailment for a fixed period can be terminated at any time.
23. A bailment is terminated by the death of *either* the bailor *or* the bailee.
24. In a pledge, a general property passes to the pawnee.
25. Pledge is a special kind of bailment.
26. A pledge can also be created of immovable property.
27. In pledge, the creditor has the right to use the goods pledged.
28. In hypothecation, the debtor has the right to use the goods hypothecated.
29. In pledge, the pawnee has the right to retain the goods pledged but has no right to sell the goods pledged.
30. In bailment, the bailee has the right to sell the goods bailed but has no right to retain the goods bailed.
31. The liability of the finder of goods is same as of a bailee.
32. A valid pledge cannot be made by persons who are not owners of goods.
33. Bailee need not return accretions to the goods to the bailor on the completion of the contract of bailment.
34. A pledge of documents of title to goods by a mercantile agent is a valid pledge.

Answers

1. False	2. False	3. False	4. False
5. False	6. False	7. False	

8. True for gratuitous bailment and false for non-gratuitous bailment
9. True for gratuitous bailment and false for non-gratuitous bailment.

10. True	11. False	12. False	13. True
14. False	15. False	16. False	17. False
18. False	19. False	20. True	21. False

22. True for gratuitous bailment and false of non-gratuitous bailment.
23. True for gratuitous bailment and false for non-gratuitous bailment.

24. False	25. True	26. False	27. False
28. True	29. False	30. False	31. True
32. False	33. False	34. True	

VERY SHORT ANSWER TYPE QUESTIONS

1. Define bailment.
2. Can a bailment be of immovable property?
3. Who is a 'bailor'?
4. Who is a 'bailee'?
5. What is gratuitous bailment?
6. What is non-gratuitous bailment?
7. Define 'lien'.
8. Define 'general lien'.
9. What is a 'particular lien'?
10. What is the nature of bailee's lien?
11. What is the nature of lien of finder of goods?
12. Is the liability of the finder of goods same as of a bailee?
13. Who are entitled to general lien?
14. Is every bailment terminated by the death of the bailor or bailee?
15. Define pledge.
16. Who is a 'pawnor'?
17. Who is a 'pawnee'?
18. What is the nature of pawnee's lien?
19. What is the nature of property which passes to the pawnee?
20. Is pledge a bailment?
21. Can a pledge be created of immovable property?
22. Has a bailee a right to sell the goods bailed?
23. Has a pawnee right to sell the goods pledged?
24. Can a valid pledge be created by non-owners?
25. Can there be a pledge of documents of title to goods?

SHORT ANSWER TYPE QUESTIONS

1. Comment on the following statements:
   (a) The position of a finder of goods is exactly that of a bailee.
   (b) Pledge can be made even by non-owners of goods.
   (c) In bailment, delivery of goods must be voluntary.
   (d) The bailor is not responsible for those defects in the goods, which are not known to him.
   (e) The bailor must repay to the bailee all the necessary expenses which the bailee has already incurred for the purpose of bailment.
   (f) The bailor may terminate the bailment even before the term of bailment.
   (g) A bailment is terminated by the death of the bailor or bailee.
2. Distinguish between the following:
   (a) Bailment and Sale
   (b) Bailment and Pledge
   (c) Gratuitous Bailment and Non-gratuitous Bailment
   (d) General Lien and Particular Lien
3. Write short notes on the following:
   (a) Pledge by non-owners
   (b) Position of Finder of lost goods
   (c) Lien
   (d) Termination of bailment.
   (e) Pledge by a Mercantile Agent

ESSAY TYPE QUESTIONS

1. (a) Define Bailment
   (b) Discuss the essential elements of a contract of bailment.
2. (a) Who is a 'bailee'?
   (b) State briefly his rights and obligations.
3. (a) Who is a 'bailor'?
   (b) State briefly his rights and duties.
4. When does a bailment come to an end?
5. (a) What is meant by the 'lien'?
   (b) Distinguish between 'general lien' and 'particular lien'.
   (c) In what category would you place the following lien?
   (i) Bailee's lien (ii) Banker's lien (iii) Lien of finder of lost goods
6. (a) Define 'pledge'.
   (b) Discuss the essential elements of a pledge.

7. (a) Who is a 'pawnee'?
   (b) State briefly his rights and duties.
8. (a) Who is a 'pawnor'?
   (b) State briefly his rights and duties.
9. (a) Who is a 'finder of goods'?
   (b) State briefly his rights and obligations.
   (c) What is the nature of the lien he has over the goods?
10. When is a pledge created by non-owners valid?
11. When a pledger fails to redeem his pledge, what right does the pledgee have in the pledge?

CHAPTER 14 Contract of Agency

1.0 INTRODUCTION

Since it is not always possible for a person to do everything by himself, it becomes necessary to delegate some of the acts to be performed by another person. Such another person is called an agent. The person represented is called the principal. The law relating to agency is contained in Chapter X (Sections 182 to 238) of the Indian Contract Act, 1872.

2.0 MEANING OF CONTRACT OF AGENCY

2.1 By a contract of agency, a person employs another person to do any act for him or to represent him in dealing with third persons so as to bind himself by the acts of such another person.

2.2 The law of agency is based on the following general rules:

(i) Whatever the principal can do by himself, he may get the same done through an agent, except when the act involved is of personal nature e.g. the principal cannot ask his agent to become insolvent on his behalf or to marry on his behalf.

(ii) What a person does by another, he does by himself. Thus, the acts of the agent are the acts of the principal.

3.0 AGENT

3.1 **Meaning of an Agent [Section 182]** An agent is a person employed to do any act for another *or* to represent another in dealings with third persons. Thus, an agent establishes a contract between such another person and third person.

3.2 **Who may be an Agent [Section 184]** Any person (whether he has contractual capacity or not) may become an agent. Thus, a minor or a person of unsound mind can also become an agent.

3.3 **Agent's Responsibility to his Principal [Section 184]** An agent who is of the age of majority and of sound mind is responsible to his principal. Thus, an agent who is minor or a person of unsound mind is not liable to principal.

Example *X hands over to Y, a minor, a TV set worth Rs 18,500 and instructs him not to sell below Rs 19,000. Y sells the same to Z for Rs 18,000. X will be responsible to Z for the act of Y but Y himself will not be responsible to X since he has no contractual capacity.*

3.4 Distinction between an Agent and Servant

An agent differs from a servant in the following respects:

Basis of Distinction	An Agent	Servant
1. Authority to create contractual relationship	He has the authority to create contractual relationship between the principal and a third party.	He ordinarily has no such authority.
2. Work of several persons	He may work for several principal at a time.	He ordinarily works only for one master.
3. Remuneration	He usually gets commission.	He usually gets salary or wages.

3.5 Distinction between an Agent and Independent Contractor

An agent differs from an Independent Contractor in the following respects:

Basis of Distinction	An Agent	Independent Contractor
1. Control and supervision	He works under the control and supervision of the principal	He works independently of the control of the person for whom he does the work.
2. Personal liability	He is not personally liable for all acts done by him within the scope of his authority.	He is personally liable for all acts done by him.
3. Remmuneration	He usually gets commission.	He usually gets the fixed contracted amount or amount at a fixed contracted rate.

4.0 PRINCIPAL

4.1 Meaning of Principal [Section 182] Principal is the person for whom act is done by an agent *or* who is represented in dealings with third persons by an agent.

4.2 Who may employ an Agent [Section 183] Any person who is of the age of majority according to the law to which he is subject, and who is of sound mind, may employ an agent. Thus, a minor or a person of unsound mind cannot appoint an agent. It has been held that a guardian of a minor can appoint an agent to minor. [*Madan Lal* v. *Bheru Lal*]

5.0 IS CONSIDERATION FOR AGENCY NECESSARY [SECTION 185]

No consideration is necessary to create an agency. Thus, a contract of agency constitutes an exception to the general rule contained in Section 25 that no contract can be valid unless it is entered into for a consideration. It means that there can be a gratuitous contract of agency and a gratuitous agent will be as much bound by his acts as a paid agent.

6.0 TEST OF AGENCY

The true test of agency lies in answering the question whether a person has the capacity to create contractual relationship between the principal and a third party and to bind the principal by his acts. If the answer to this question is yes, there exists the relationship of agency, otherwise not.

7.0 MODES OF CREATION OF AGENCY

The various modes to create the contract of agency are shown below:

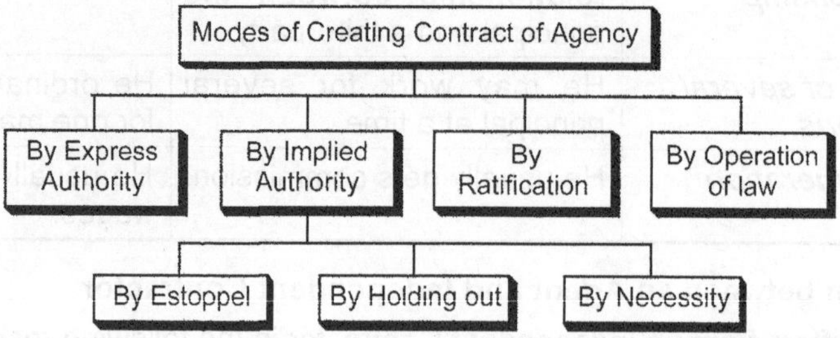

7.1 Agency by Express Authority [Sections 186 and 187] An agency by express authority arises when an express authority is given to the agent by spoken *or* written words.

Example *X who owns a shop, appoints Y to manage his shop by executing a power of attorney in Y's favour. Here, the relationship of principal and agent has been created between X and Y by an express authority.*

7.2 Agency by Implied Authority [Section 187] An agency which has to be understood from the conduct and behaviour of the parties is called implied agency. It is to be inferred from the circumstances of the case and things spoken *or* written, *or* the ordinary course of dealing may be accounted as circumstances of the case.

Example *A owns a shop in Shimla, living himself in Calcutta, and visiting the shop occasionally. The shop is managed by B, and he is in the habit of ordering goods from C in the name of A for the purposes of the shop and of paying for them out of A's funds with A's knowledge. B has an implied authority from A to order goods from C in the name of A for the purposes of the shop.*

Implied agency includes the following:

(a) Agency by Estoppel [Sec. 237] Agency by estoppel arises where a person by his words or conducts induces third persons to believe that a certain person is his agent. The person who induces as such is estopped or prevented from denying the truth of agency.

Example *X tells Y in the presence and within the hearing of Z that he (X) is Z's agent. Z does not contradict this statement. Later on Y enters into a contract with X believing that X is Z's agent. In such a case Z is bound by this contract and in a suit between Z and Y, Z cannot be permitted to say that X was not his agent, even though X was not actually his agent.*

(b) Agency by Holding Out Agency by holding arises when a person by his past affirmative or positive conduct leads third person to believe that person doing some act on his behalf is doing with authority.

Example *X allows Y, his servant to purchase goods for him on credit from Z and later on pays for them. One day X pays cash to Y to purchase goods. Y misappropriates the money and purchases goods on credit from Z. Z can recover the price of his goods from X because X had held out Y as his agent on earlier occasions.*

(c) Agency by Necessity Agency by necessity arises under the following two conditions:

(i) There is an actual and definite necessity for acting on behalf of the principal, and

(ii) It is impossible to communicate with the principal and obtain his consent.

Note: The act must have been done in the best interest of the principal.

Example I *X consigned some vegetables from Delhi to Bombay by a truck. The truck met with an accident. The vegetable being perishable were sold by the transporter. This sale is binding on X. In this case, the transporter became an agent by necessity. [Sim & Co. v. Midland Rly Co.]*

Example II *X stored some furniture in Y's house free of charge. After three years, Y needed the space occupied by the furniture. He obtained X's address from his bank and wrote two letters to him but he received no reply. Y then sold the furniture. It was held that the sale was not binding on the owner because there was no emergency which required the sale of furniture. [Sachs v. Milkos]*

7.3 Agency by Ratification [Section 196]

(a) Meaning–Agency by ratification is said to arise when a person, on whose behalf the acts are done without his knowledge or authority, expressly or impliedly accepts such acts. Thus, when the principal approves an act of the agent who never had the authority to undertake such an act, it is called Ratification. It is also known as *ex-post facto* agency i.e. agency arising after the event.

(b) Effect of Ratification [Section 196] The effect of ratification is to make the agent's unauthorised acts as authorised as if they had been performed with the principal's authority. It may also be noted that **ratification is tantamount to prior authority**. This means that the **ratification relates back to the date when the act was done by the agent and not to the date when the act was ratified by the principal**. Hence, the agency is deemed to have come into existence from the time when the agent first acted and not from the time when the principal ratified the act.

Example *X the managing director of a company, without prior authority from the company accepted an offer made by Y on behalf of the company. Y later on revoked the offer but the company ratified X's acceptance. It was held that Y is bound by ratification because ratification related back to the time of X's acceptance. [Bolton Partner v. Lambert]*

(c) Mode of Ratification [Section 197] Ratification may be express or may be implied by the conduct of the person on whose behalf the acts are done.

Example I *A, without authority, buys goods for B. Afterwards B sells them to C on his own account; B's conduct implies a ratification of the purchases made for him by A.*

Example II *A, without B's authority, lends B's money to C. Afterwards B accepts interest on the money from C. B's conduct implies a ratification of the loan.*

(d) Essentials of a Valid Ratification [Sections 198 to 200] The essentials of a valid ratification are as follows:

(i) ***Full Knowledge [Section 198]:*** No valid ratification can be made by a person whose knowledge of the facts of the case is materially defective.

Example *X instructed Y to arrange a house on a reasonable rent in Bombay. Y lets out his own house at a rent which is much higher than the prevailing rentals in that* *area. X started living in the house. Later on X came to know that the house belonged to Y. X's ratification is not binding upon himself. [Damodharan Das v. Sheoram Dass]*

(ii) ***Whole Transaction [Section 199]:*** The ratification must be made for the whole transaction and not for a part of transaction. When a person ratifies a part of the unauthorised transaction, it is treated as the ratification of whole transaction.

Example *X, without Y's authority buys 100 bales of cotton. Y wants to ratify this transaction to the extent of 60 bales and reject the rest. Y cannot do so. If he does so, it will be treated as the ratification of whole transaction of 100 bales.*

(iii) ***No Damage to Third Party [Section 200]:*** An act which has the effect of subjecting a third person to damages or of terminating any right or interest of a third person, cannot be ratified.

Example I *X is in possession of a horse belonging to Y. Z without Y's authority demands on behalf of Y the delivery of that horse. X refuses to deliver the horse to Z. Y cannot ratify the demand made by Z so as to make X liable for damages for his refusal to deliver.*

Example II *X holds a flat on a lease from Y. The lease is terminable on 3 months' notice. Z, without Y's authority gives notice of termination of lease to X. Y cannot ratify the notice given by Z so as to be binding on X.*

(iv) ***Act on Behalf of Another Person:*** The acts done by an agent on behalf of another person can only be ratified. Thus, the acts done by the agent in his own name cannot be ratified.

Example *X, without Y's authority or knowledge buys 100 bales of cotton on behalf of Y and buys 50 bales of cotton in his personal name from Z on different dates. Subsequently, the prices of cotton go up. Y wants to ratify the purchase of 150 bales of cotton. He can ratify only the purchase of 100 bales made on his behalf and not the purchase of 50 bales. [Keighley Maxted & Co. v. Durant]*

(v) ***Acts within Principal's Power:*** Only those acts which are within the principal's power can be ratified. Thus, an act which is beyond the competence of a principal cannot be ratified.

Example *A director of a non-trading and non-banking company borrowed Rs 1,00,000 on behalf of the company. The company cannot ratify such act of director because it is ultra-vires the Company (i.e. beyond the power of the company).*

(vi) ***Lawful Acts:*** Only those acts which are lawful can be ratified.

Example *X forges Y's signature on a cheque and withdraws Rs 1,000 from Y's bank account. Subsequently, Y ratifies the act of withdrawing money. Such ratification is not valid because forgery is an offence.*

(vii) ***Existence of Principal:*** The principal must be in existence at the time when the act is done in his name.

Example *The promoters of a company enter into contract for a company before its incorporation. The company after incorporation, cannot ratify such contracts because the company was not in existence at the time when the contract was entered into [Kelner v. Baxter].*

(viii) ***Contractual Capacity:*** The principal must have contractual capacity both at the time of contract and at the time of ratification.

Example *A minor on attaining majority cannot ratify the contracts made on his behalf during his minority.*

(ix) ***Within Reasonable Time:*** The ratification must be done within a reasonable time, otherwise it will not be binding.

Example *X without authority from Y insured his goods against fire. After the policy was taken, the goods were destroyed by fire subsequent to the fire, Y ratified X's act of insuring the goods and accepted the insurance policy. It was held that the ratification made by Y was not valid because X's act should have been ratified before the loss of goods. [Grover and Grover Ltd v. Mathews]*

(x) ***Communication:*** The ratification must be communicated to the third party so as to be binding on the third party.

7.4 Agency by Operation of Law Agency by operation of law is said to arise where the law treats one person as an agent of another.

Example *On formation of a partnership, every partner becomes the agent of other partner. Such agency is said to be arisen by operation of law.*

8.0 AGENCY RELATIONSHIP BETWEEN HUSBAND AND WIFE

The question whether and to what extent a wife can pledge her husband's credit, may be discussed as under:

Case	***Provision***
1. Where wife lives with her husband	There is a legal presumption that a wife has authority to pledge her husband's credit for necessaries. But the legal presumption can be rebutted in the following cases:
	(a) Where the goods purchased on credit are not necessaries.
	(b) Where the wife is given sufficient money for purchasing necessaries.
	(c) Where the wife is forbidden from purchasing anything on credit or contracting debts.
	(d) Where the trader has been expressly warned not to give credit to his wife.
2. Where the wife lives apart for no fault on her part	A wife has authority to pledge her husband's credit for necessaries. This legal presumption can be rebutted only in cases (a) and (b), and not in cases (c) and (d).
3. Where wife lives apart for no fault on her husband's part	A wife has no authority to pledge her husband's credit even for necessaries.

Example *X was the manager of a hotel where his wife Y was working as manageress. They were living together in the same hotel but they did not have any domestic establishment of their own. Y purchased some clothes from Z on credit. Z demanded the payment from X. It was held that X was not liable to pay because there was no domestic establishment of their own. [Debenham v. Mellon]*

9.0 CLASSIFICATION OF AGENTS

The classification of agents has been shown below:

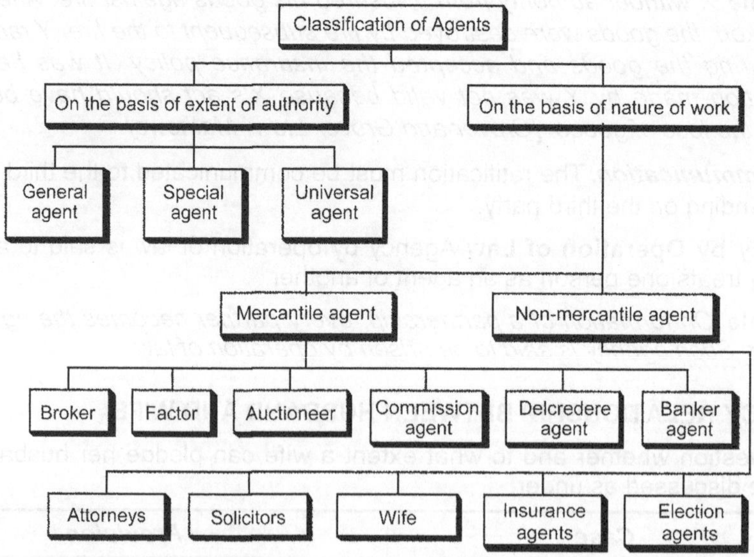

Let us discuss them one by one.

9.1 General Agent A general agent is one who has authority to do all acts in the ordinary course of trade or profession. The authority of a general agent is continuous unless it is terminated.

9.2 Special Agent A special agent is one who has authority to do a particular act in a particular transaction. The authority of a special agent is limited to that particular act only and his authority comes to an end when that act for which authority was given is performed.

9.3 Universal Agent A universal agent is one who has authority to do all acts which the principal can lawfully do and delegate. He has an unlimited authority to bind the principal.

9.4 Mercantile or Commercial Agent 'Mercantile agent' means an agent having the authority to—

- sell the goods;
- consign the goods for the purposes of sale
- buy the goods;
- raise money on the security of goods

acting as mercantile agent in the ordinary course of business.

9.5 Broker A broker is one who negotiates and makes contracts between the principal and the third party. He is not entrusted with the possession of goods and hence he has no lien on the goods.

9.6 Factor A factor is one who is entrusted with the possession of goods and who has the authority to buy, sell or otherwise deal with the goods or to raise money on their security. He has a general lien on the goods.

9.7 Auctioneer An auctioneer is one who is entrusted with the possession of goods for sale at a public auction. He has only a particular lien on the goods for his charges.

9.8 Commission Agent The term 'commission agent' is a general term which is used in practice even for a factor or broker.

9.9 Del-credere Agent A del-credere agent is one who gives guarantee to his principal to the effect that the third person with whom he enters into contracts shall perform his obligation. He gives such guarantee for an extra remuneration which is called the Del-credere Commission. *For example*, an agent who also undertakes the risk of bad debts due to the insolvency of customers to whom the goods were sold on credit, will be called the del-credere agent.

9.10 Banker Banker acts as an agent of the customer when he collects cheques or drafts or bills or buys or sells securities on behalf of his customers. He has a general lien in respect of the general balance of account.

9.11 Non-mercantile Agent An agent who does not deal in mercantile transactions. These include attorneys, solicitors, guardian, promoters, wife, etc.

10.0 EXTENT OF AGENT'S AUTHORITY

10.1 Meaning of Agent's Authority An agent's authority means the ***capacity of the agent to bind his principal.***

10.2 Meaning of Extent of Agent's Authority Extent of agent's authority means the ***scope of authority*** of an agent. In other words, it means what a person can do as an agent on behalf of his principal. Extent of agent's authority may be discussed under normal circumstances and emergency circumstances.

10.3 Extent of Agent's Authority under Normal Circumstances [Section 188] An agent having an authority to do an act has authority to do every lawful thing which is necessary in order to do such act. An agent having an authority to carry on a business, has authority to do every lawful thing necessary for the purpose or usually done in the course of conducting such business.

Example I *A is employed by B, residing in London, to recover at Bombay a debt due to B. A may adopt any legal process necessary for the purpose of recovering the debt, and may give a valid discharge for the same.*

Example II *A appoints B, his agent to carry on his business of a ship-builder. B may purchase timber and other materials, and hire workmen for the purpose of carrying on the business.*

10.4 Extent of Agent's Authority in Emergency [Section 189] An agent has authority, in an emergency, to do all such acts for the purpose of protecting his principal from loss as would be done by a person of ordinary prudence, in his own case, under similar circumstances.

Example I *A consigns provisions to B at Calcutta, with directions to send them immediately to C, at Cuttack. B may sell the provisions at Calcutta, if they will not bear the journey to Cuttack without spoiling.*

Example II *Where butter was in danger of becoming useless owing to delay in transit and it was impossible to obtain instructions of the principal, the railway company sold the butter for the best available price. It was held that the principal was bound by this sale. [Sim & Co. v. Midland Rail Co.]*

11.0 DELEGATION OF AUTHORITY OF AGENT

11.1 Can an Agent Delegate his Authority [Section 190] The answer to this question is given by the Latin maxim ***'delegatus non potest delegare'***, which means that a delegate cannot further delegate. In other words, a person to whom powers have been delegated cannot delegate them to another. In case of an agency, the agent cannot further delegate his authority because he himself is a person to whom authority has been delegated by the principal. In the root of agency lies the confidence which a principal reposes in his agent but may not like to repose in the sub-agent who is literally a stranger to him. Section 190 of the Act embodies this principal which provides that ***an agent cannot lawfully employ another to perform acts which he has expressly or impliedly undertaken to perform personally.***

11.2 Exceptions to the General Rule [Section 190] There are some exceptions to the general rule that a delegate cannot further delegate, as follows:

(a) Where the custom of the trade permits delegation, e.g. Article clerks employed by a Chartered Accountant.

(b) Where the nature of the agency requires delegation.

(c) Where the principal permits delegation.

(d) Where the principal knows that the agent intends to delegate but does not object to it.

(e) Where an emergency requires delegation.

(f) Where the duties of the agent do not require any personalised skill, confidence or discretion and the work involved is of routine nature.

11.3 Meaning of Sub-agent [Section 191] A sub-agent is a person who is employed by the original agent and who acts under the control of the original agent in the business of agency. Thus, a sub-agent is the agent of the original agent. As between the original agent and the sub-agent, the relationship is that of the principal and agent.

11.4 Effects of Appointment of Sub-agent [Sections 192 and 193] The effects of appointment of a sub-agent may be discussed under the following two heads:

(i) in case of proper appointment

(ii) in case of improper appointment

Basis of Comparison	***Where a sub-agent is properly appointed [Section 192]***	***Where a sub-agent is not properly appointed [Section 193]***
1. Is principal bound	The principal **is bound** to third parties by the acts of sub-agent.	The principal **is not bound** to third parties by the acts of sub-agent.
2. Is original agent responsible for acts of sub-agent	The original agent is responsible **to the principal** for the acts of sub agent.	The original agent is responsible for the acts of sub-agent **both to the principal and to the third parties.**
4. Is sub-agent responsible	The sub-agent is responsible to the original agent but **not to the principal except in case of fraud or wilful wrong.**	The sub-agent is responsible to the original agent but **not to the principal even in cases of fraud or wilful wrong.**

Note: The acts done by a properly appointed sub-agent in the name of original principal may be ratified by the original principal.

11.5 Meaning of Substituted Agent [Section 194] A substituted agent is a person who is named by the agent holding an express or implied authority to name another person, to act for the principal in the business of the agency. Such person is an agent of the principal for such part of the business of the agency as is entrusted to him.

Example I *A directs B, his solicitor, to sell his estate by auction, and to employ an auctioneer for this purpose. B names C, an auctioneer, to conduct the sale, C is not a sub-agent, but A's agent for the conduct of the sale.*

Example II *A authorizes B, a merchant in Calcutta, to recover the money due to A from C Co. B instructs D, a solicitor to initiate legal proceedings, against C & Co., for the recovery of the money. D is not a sub-agent but is a solicitor for A.*

11.6 Agent's Duty in Naming such Person [Section 195] In selecting such agent for his principal, an agent is bound to exercise the same amount of discretion as a man of ordinary prudence would exercise in his own case; and if he does this, he is not responsible to the principal for the acts or negligence of the agent so selected.

Example I *A instructs B, a merchant, to buy a ship for him. B employs a sub-surveyor of good reputation to choose a ship for A. The surveyor makes the choice negligently, and the ship turns out to be unseaworthy and is lost. B is not, but the surveyor is, responsible to A.*

Example II *A consigns goods to B, a merchant, for sale. B, in due course employs an auctioneer in good credit to sell the goods of A, and allow the auctioneer to receive the proceeds of sale. The auctioneer afterwards becomes insolvent without having accounted for the proceeds. B is responsible to A for the proceeds.*

11.7 Distinction between Sub-Agent and Substituted Agent

Basis of Distinction	*Sub-agent*	*Substituted agent*
1. Work	He works under the control of original agent.	He works under the control of principal.
2. Privity	There is no privity of contract between a sub-agent and principal and hence both cannot sue each other except that in case of fraud or willful wrong committed by a properly appointed sub-agent, the principal can sue sub-agent.	There is a privity of contract between a substituted agent and principal hence both can sue each other.
3. Original agent's responsibility	The original agent is responsible for the acts or negligence of the sub-agent.	The original agent is not responsible for the acts or negligence of the substituted agent if in selecting such agent he has exercised the same amount of diligence as a man of ordinary prudence would exercise in his own case.

12.0 RIGHTS OF AN AGENT

The rights of an agent are as follows:

12.1 Right of Retainer [Section 217] An agent has the right to retain, out of any sum received on account of the principal in the business of the agency, all money due to himself in respect of the following:

(i) advance made by him;

(ii) expenses properly incurred by him in conducting such business;

(iii) such remuneration as may be payable to him for acting as an agent.

12.2 Right to Receive Remuneration [Sections 219 and 220] The agent has the right to receive agreed remuneration (if there is an agreement to that effect) or usual remuneration as per the custom of the trade in which he has been employed (if there is no agreement to that effect).

When Agent's Remuneration becomes Due: In the absence of any special contract, payment for the performance of any act is not due to the agent until the completion of such act; but an agent may retain the money received by him on account of goods sold, although the whole of the goods consigned to him for sale may not have been sold, or the sale may not be actually complete.

Now the question arises, 'when does the act complete?' This is a question of fact depending upon the facts and circumstances of each case. In general, the act shall be deemed to have completed when the agent has done what he had undertaken to do even though the contract is not completed.

Example *X, an agent introduced a customer to purchase the principal's property. The sale was settled and earnest money was paid. The sale could not complete because of customer's inability to pay. State whether the agent was entitled to remuneration if (a) he was appointed to sell a property on the terms that he would be paid commission on the completion of sale, (b) he was appointed to introduce a customer to purchase the principal's property.*

Solution:

Decision:

Case (a): The agent was not entitled to remuneration because the sale had not been completed. [*Luxor* (*Eastbourne*) *Ltd.* v. *Cooper*]

Case (b): The agent was entitled to remuneration because he did what he was required to do, i.e. to introduce a customer to buy the principal's property. [*Sheikh Farid Baksh* v. *Hargulal Singh*]

Agent not Entitled to Remuneration for Business Misconducted: An agent who is guilty of misconduct in the business of the agency is not entitled to any remuneration in respect of that part of the business which he has misconducted.

Example I *(a) A employs B to recover Rs 1,00,000 from C, and to invest it in good security. B recovers Rs 1,00,000 and invested Rs 90,000 on good security, but invested Rs 10,000 on security which he ought to have known to be bad, whereby A loses Rs 2,000. B is entitled to remuneration for recovering Rs 1,00,000 and for investing Rs 90,000. He is not entitled to remuneration for investing the Rs 10,000 and he must make good Rs 2,000 to B.*

Example II *A employs B to recover Rs 1,000 from C. Through B's misconduct the money is not recovered. B is entitled to no remuneration for his services, and must make good the loss.*

12.3 Right of Lien [Section 221] In the absence of any contract to contrary, an agent has right to retain goods, papers and other property whether movable or immovable, of the principal received by him, until the amount due to him for commission, disbursement and services in respect of the same has been paid or accounted for to him. Thus, this right of lien arises—

(i) only if there is no contract to the contrary,

(ii) only in respect of those properties the possession of which has been lawfully acquired by the agent,

(iii) only in respect of those properties in respect of which some amount is due to the agent.

Thus, this lien is only a particular lien.

12.4 Right to be Indemnified against Consequences of Lawful Acts [Section 222] An agent has right to be indemnified by the Principal against the consequences of all lawful acts done in exercise of the authority conferred upon him.

Example I *B, at Singapore, under instructions from A of Calcutta, contracts with C to deliver certain goods to him. A does not send the goods to B and C sues B for breach of contract. B informs A of the suit, and A authorises him to defend the suit. B defends the suit, and is compelled to pay damages and costs and incurs expenses. A is liable to B for such damages, costs and expenses.*

Example II *B, a broker at Calcutta, by the orders of A, a merchant there contracts with C for the purchase of 10 casks of oil for A. Afterwards, A refuses to receive the oil, and C sues B. B informs A, who repudiates the contract altogether. B defends, but unsuccessfully, and has to pay damages and costs and incurs expenses. A is liable to B for such damages, costs and expenses.*

No liability of employer of agent to do a criminal act [Section 224]: Where one person employs another to do an act which is criminal, the employer is not liable to the agent, *either* upon an express *or* implied promise, to indemnify him against the consequences of that act.

Example I *A employs B to beat C, and agrees to indemnify him against all consequences of the act. B thereupon beats C and has to pay damages to C for so doing. A is not liable to indemnify B for these damages.*

Example II *B, the proprietor of a newspaper, publishes at A's request, a libel upon C, in the paper, and A agrees to indemnify B against all the expenses of publication and all costs and damages of any action in respect thereof, B is sued by C and has to pay damages, and also incurs expenses. A is not liable to B upon the indemnity.*

12.5 Right to be Indemnified against Consequences of Acts done in Good Faith [Section 223] An agent has right to be indemnified by the principal against the consequences of act done in good faith that causes an injury to the rights of third person.

Example I *A, a decree-holder and entitled to execution of B's goods, requires the officer of the court to seize certain goods, representing them to be the goods of B. The officer seizes the goods and is sued by C, the true owner of the goods. A is liable to indemnify the officer for the sum which he is compelled to pay to C, in consequences of obeying A's directions.*

Example II *B, at the request of A, sells goods in possession of A, but which A had no right to dispose of. B does not know this, and hands over the proceeds of the sale to A. Afterwards C, the true owner of the goods, sues B and recovers the value of the goods and costs. A is liable to indemnify B for what he has been compelled to pay to C and for B's own expense.*

12.6 Right to Receive Compensation for Injury caused by Principal's Neglect [Section 225] An agent has right to claim compensation for injury caused by the principal's neglect or want of skill.

Example *A employs B as a breach layer in building a house and puts up the scaffolding himself. The scaffolding is unskilfully put up, and B is in consequence hurt. A must make compensation to B.*

13.0 DUTIES OF AN AGENT

The various duties of an agent are as follows:

13.1 To Conduct business as per Directions or Custom of Trade [Section 211] An agent is bound to conduct the business of his principal according to principal's directions or the custom of trade (in the absence of principal's directions).

Consequences of not performing this duty: When the agent acts otherwise, and any loss is incurred, he must make it good to his principal and if any profit accrues, he must account for it.

Example I *A, an agent who was asked to insure the goods, failed to do so and the goods were destroyed by fire. A was liable to compensate his principal for the loss suffered by him. [Pannalal Jankidas v. Mohan Lal]*

Example II *A, an auctioneer, contrary to the usual custom accepted a bill of exchange in payment of the price of goods sold and the bill was dishonoured. A was liable to compensate his principal for the amount of the bill.*

13.2 To Conduct business with Reasonable Care and Skill [Section 212] An agent is bound to conduct the business of the agency with reasonable care and skill.

Consequences of not performing this duty: The agent must compensate the principal in respect of the direct consequences of his own neglect, want of skill or misconduct but not in respect of loss or damage which are indirectly or remotely caused by such neglect, want of skill or misconduct.

Example I *A, an agent for the sale of goods, having authority to sell on credit, sells to B on credit, without making the proper and usual enquiries as to the solvency of B. B, at the time of such sale is insolvent. A must make compensation to this principal in respect of any loss thereby sustained.*

Example II *A, an insurance-broker employed by B to collect an insurance on a ship, omits to see that the usual clauses are inserted in the policy. The ship is afterwards lost. In consequences of the omission of the clauses nothing can be recovered from the insurers. A is bound to make good the loss to B.*

13.3 To Render Proper Accounts [Section 213] An agent is bound to render proper accounts to his principal on demand.

13.4 To Communicate with Principal [Section 214] An agent is bound to use all reasonable diligence to establish contact with his principal to obtain his instructions.

13.5 To Disclose all Material Circumstances and to obtain Principal's Consent in Personal Dealings [Sections 215 & 216] An agent is bound to disclose all material circumstances which have come to his knowledge on the subject, to the principal and obtain his consent if he desires to deal on his own account in the business of agency.

Consequences of not performing this duty:

(i) The principal may repudiate the transaction and disclaim all losses [Section 215].

(ii) The principal is entitled to claim from the agent any benefit which may have resulted to him from the transaction [Section 216].

Example I *A directs B to sell A's estate. B buys the estate for himself in the name of C. A, on discovering that B bought the estate for himself, may repudiate the sale, if he can show that B has dishonestly concealed any material fact, or that the sale has been disadvantageous to him.*

Example II *A directs B to sell A's estate. B, on looking over the estate before selling it, finds a mine on the estate which is unknown to A. B informs A that he wishes to buy the estate for himself, but conceals the discovery of the mine. A allows B to buy in ignorance of the existence of the mine. A on discovering that B knew of the mine at the time he bought the estate, may either repudiate or adopt the sale at his option.*

Example III *A directs B, his agent to buy a certain house for him. B tells A it cannot be bought and buys the house for himself. A may, on discovering that B has bought the house, compel him to sell it to A at the price he gave for it.*

Example IV *X directed Y an auctioneer to sell his goods. Y sold those goods to Z and received some secret commission from Z in addition to the normal commission from X. It was held that Y was bound to hand over the X the secret commission received from Z [Andreson v. Ramsay & Co.]*

13.6 To Pay Sum Received for Principal [Section 218] The agent is bound to pay to his principal all sums received on his account. However, an agent may retain, out of such sums all moneys due to himself in respect of advances made or expenses properly incurred by him in conducting such business, and also such remuneration as may be payable to him for acting as an agent.

13.7 To Protect and Preserve the Interest [Section 209] When an agency is terminated by the principal dying or becoming of unsound mind, the agent is bound to take, on behalf of the representative of his late principal, all reasonable steps for the protection and preservation of the interests entrusted to him.

13.8 Not to Delegate Authority [Section 190] An agent cannot lawfully employ another to perform acts which he has expressly or impliedly undertaken to perform personally unless custom of trade or the nature of the agency so requires.

14.0 PERSONAL LIABILITY OF AN AGENT

14.1 General Rule [Section 230] In the absence of any contract to that effect, an agent cannot personally enforce contract entered into by him on behalf of his principal, nor is he personally bound by them.

14.2 When the Agent becomes Personally Liable The circumstances under which an agent becomes personally liable are as follows:

(a) **In case of Foreign Principal [Section 230]** Where the contract is made by an agent for the sale or purchase of goods for a merchant residing abroad, in the absence of any contract to the contrary, it is presumed that the agent is personally liable for such contracts.

(b) **In case of Undisclosed Principal [Section 230]** Where the contract is made by an agent for an undisclosed principal, in the absence of any contract to the contrary, it is presumed that the agent is personally liable.

(c) **In case of Incompetent Principal [Section 230]** Where a contract is made by an agent for a person who cannot be sued (e.g. minor, lunatic, foreign ambassador), in the absence of any contract to the contrary, it is presumed that the agent is personally liable.

(d) **In case of Principal not in Existence** Where a contract is made for a non-existent principal. *For example,* Where a contract is made by the promoter for a company not yet incorporated, the promoters are personally liable.

(e) **In case of Acts not Ratified [Section 235]** A person untruly representing himself to be the authorised agent of another, and thereby inducing a third person to deal with him as such agent, is liable, if his alleged employer does not ratify his acts, to make compensation to the other in respect of any loss or damage which he has incurred by so dealing.

(f) **In case of Acts in his Own Name** Where a contract is made by an agent without disclosing that he is contracting as an agent, the agent is personally liable.

Example *X took a loan from Y by executing a hundi in Y's favour. X did not sign the hundi as agent of the firm nor did he disclose to Y the name of his principal. The agent was held personally liable. [Trilok Chand v. Rameshwar Lal]*

(g) **In case of Express Agreement** Where a contract made by an agent specifically provides for the personal liability of the agent, the agent will be personally liable.

(h) **In case of Custom or Usage of Trade** Where there is a custom or usage of trade making the agent personally liable, in the absence of any contract to the contrary, the agent is personally liable.

Example *X, a share broker purchased 100 shares @ Rs 100 per share and sold the same shares @ Rs 90 per share on behalf of Y who refused to give the difference. X is personally liable because it is a custom that a share broker is personally liable for the contracts entered into by him.*

15.0 RIGHTS OF PERSON DEALING WITH AGENT

15.1 Rights of Person Dealing with Agent Personally Liable [Section 233] In cases where the agent is personally liable, a person dealing with him may hold *either* him *or* his principal *or* both of them liable.

Example *A enters into a contract with B to sell him 100 bales of cotton, and afterwards discovers that B was acting as agent for C. A may sue either B or C, or both, for the price of the cotton.*

15.2 Consequences of Inducing Agent or Principal to Act on Belief that Principal or Agent will be held Exclusively Liable [Section 234] When a person who has made a contract with an agent induces the agent to act upon the belief that the principal only will be held liable, or induces the principal to act upon the belief that the agent only will be held liable, he cannot afterwards hold liable the agent or principal respectively.

16.0 POSITION OF PRINCIPAL

The position of principal in respect of contracts entered into by an agent may be discussed under the following heads:

(a) Where the principal is named i.e. where both the existence and the name of the principal are disclosed;

(b) Where the principal is unnamed i.e. where only the existence of the principal has been disclosed but not his name;

(c) Where the principal is undisclosed i.e. where both the existence and the name of the principal are not disclosed.

Let us discuss the position of the principal under the various heads one by one.

(a) Where the Principal is Named

Acts of Agent	*Position of Principal*
(a) For acts done within the scope of his actual or ostensible authority [Section 226]	The principal is bound by such acts as if the acts had been done by the principal. **Example** *A, being B's agent, with authority to receive money on his behalf, receives from C a sum of money due to B. C is discharged of his obligation to pay the sum in question to B.*
(b) For unauthorised acts when agent exceeds his authority and the unauthorised acts can be separated from authorised acts [Section 227]	The principal is bound by his authorised acts only when agent exceeds his authority. **Example** *A being owner of a ship and cargo, authorised B to procure an insurance for Rs 4 crores on the ship. B procured an insurance for Rs 4 crores on the ship and another for the like sum on the cargo. A is bound to pay the premium for the policy on the ship, but not the premium for the policy on the cargo.*
(c) For unauthorised acts when agent exceeds his authority and the unauthorised acts can not be separated from authorised acts.	The principal is not bound to recognise the entire transaction. **Example** *A authorises B to buy 500 sheep for him. B buys 500 sheep and 200 lambs for one sum of Rs 6,000. A may repudiate the whole transaction.*
(d) For notice or information given to agent [Section229]	The principal is bound by the notice given to, or information obtained by the agent in the course of business of agency if it had been given to or obtained by the principal. **Example** *A is employed by B to buy from C certain goods of which C is the apparent owner. B had some claim against C which he wanted to set off against the price of goods. Can B claim set off if (a) in the course of negotiation, A came to know that the goods really belonged to D and B was ignorant of that fact. (b) A was, before he was employed by B, a servant of C and then learnt that goods really belonged to D and B was ignorant of that fact.* ***Solution:*** (a) No, because *B* was bound by the knowledge of *A*. (b) Yes, because *B* was not bound by the knowledge of *A* as *A* obtained the knowledge as *C*'s servant and not as *B*'s agent.

(e) For inducting third persons to believe that agent's unauthorised acts were authorised [Section 237]	The principal is bound by agent's unauthorised acts if he has, by words or conduct, induced such third persons to believe that agent's unauthorised acts were authorised acts. **Example I** *A* consigns goods to *B* for sale, and gives him instructions not to sell under a fixed price. *C*, being ignorant of *B*'s instructions enters into a contract with *B* to buy the goods at a price lower than the reserved price. *A* is bound by the contract. **Example II** *A* entrusts *B* with negotiable instruments endorsed in blank. *B* sells them to *C* in violation of private orders from *A*. The sale is good.
(f) For misrepresentation made or fraud committed by agent in matters falling within agent's authority [Section 238]	The principal is liable for such misrepresen tation made or fraud committed. **Example I** *A*, being *B*'s agent for the sale of goods, induces *C* to buy them by misrepresentation. The contract is voidable, as between *B* and *C*, at the option of *C*. **Example II** *A, the captain of B's ship, signs bills of lading without having received on board the goods mentioned therein. The bills of lading are void as between B and the pretended consignor.*
(g) For misrepresentation or fraud committed by an agent in matters not falling within agent's authority [Section 238]	The principal is not liable for such misrepresentation or fraud committed.

(b) Where the Principal is Unnamed

The principal is bound by the acts of an agent done within the scope of actual or ostensible authority of the agent unless the circumstances of the case suggest the personal liability of the agent. If an agent refuses to disclose his principal's identity, then he becomes personally liable.

(c) Where Principal is Undisclosed

In case an agent makes a contract with a person who *neither* knows, *nor* has reason to suspect that he is an agent, the position of principal, agent and the third party may be discussed as under:

Position of Principal	*Position of Agent*	*Position of Third Party*
1. He may obtaimed the performance of the contract subject	1. He has all rights of an agent as against the principal.	1. He has as against the principal same rights as he would have had as against

to right and obligations subsisting between the agent and the other contracting party. 2. *He can be sued by the third party.*	2. He is personally liable to the third party. 3. He can be sued by the third party. 4. He can sue the third party.	the agent if the agent had been the principal. 2. He may refuse to fulfil the contract under the following circumstances: (a) If the principal discloses himself before the contract is completed, and (b) If he can show that if he had known who was the principal or if he had known that the agent was not a principal, he would not have entered into the contract. 3. He can sue *either* principal *or* agent *or* both.

Example *A, who owes Rs 500 to B, sells Rs 1,000 worth of rice to B. A is acting as agent for C in the transaction, but B has no knowledge, nor reasonable ground of suspicion that such is the case. C cannot compel B to take the rice without allowing him to set-off A's debt.*

17.0 TERMINATION OF AGENCY

17.1 Meaning of Termination of Agency Termination of agency implies the end of the relationship of principal and agent.

17.2 Modes of Termination of Agency The various modes in which the agency may be terminated are given on next page:

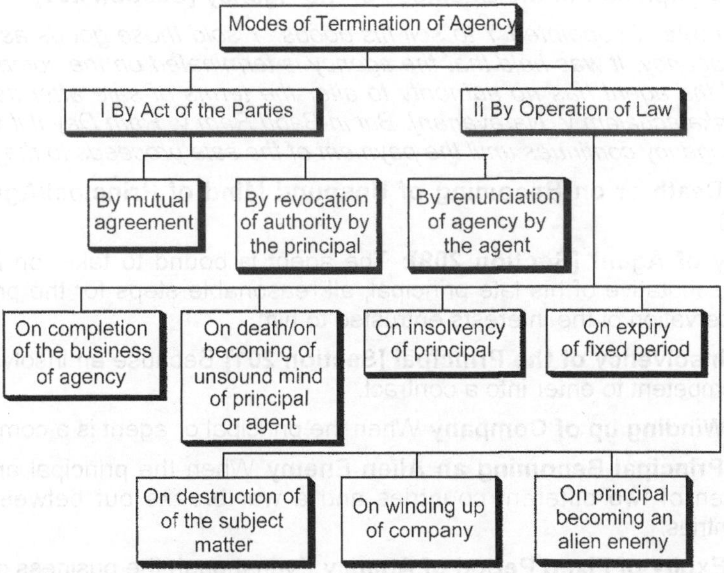

Let us discuss them one by one.

I. Termination of Agency by Act of the Parties

(a) By Mutual Agreement An agency is terminated if the principal and agent mutually agree to do so.

(b) By Revocation of Authority by the Principal An agency is terminated if the principal revokes the authority of his agent. It may be noted that the principal may revoke the authority of his agent at any time before the authority has been exercised so as to bind the principal.

(c) By Renunciation of Agency by the Agent The agency is terminated if the agent himself renounces the business of agency.

Provisions relating to Revocation or renunciation [Sections 205, 206 and 207]

(i) ***Compensation for Revocation of Agency for fixed period by Principal, or Renunciation by Agent [Section 205]:*** Where there is an express or implied contract that the agency should be continued for any period of time, the principal must make compensation to the agent, or the agent to the principal, as the case may be, for any previous revocation or renunciation of the agency without sufficient cause [Section 206].

(ii) ***Notice of Revocation or Renunciation [Section 206]:*** Reasonable notice must be given of such revocation or renunciation, otherwise the damage thereby resulting to the principal or the agent, as the case may be, must be made good to the one by the other.

(iii) ***Revocation and Renunciation may be Expressed or Implied [Section 207]:*** Revocation and renunciation may be expressed or may be implied in the conduct of the principal or agent, respectively.

Example *A empowers B to let A's house. Afterwards A lets it himself. This is an implied revocation of B's authority.*

II. Termination of Agency by Operation of Law

An agency is automatically terminated

(a) On Completion of the Business of the Agency [Section 201]

Example *X appointed Y to sell his goods. Y sold those goods as per terms of the agency. It was held that the agency is terminated on the completion of sale and the agent has no authority to alter the terms of sale after its completion. [Venkatachalam v. Narayanan]. But in Babu Ram v. Ram Dayal it was held that the agency continues until the payment of the sale proceeds to the principal.*

(b) On Death or on Becoming of Unsound Mind of Principal/Agent [Section 201]

Duty of Agent [Section 209]: The agent is bound to take, on behalf of the representative of his late principal, all reasonable steps for the protection and preservation of the interests entrusted to him.

(c) On Insolvency of the Principal [Section 201] Because an insolvent person is incompetent to enter into a contract.

(d) On Winding up of Company When the principal or agent is a company.

(e) On Principal Becoming an Alien Enemy When the principal and agent are citizen of two different countries and a war breaks out between these two countries.

(f) On Expiry of Fixed Period of Agency Even though the business of the agency has not yet completed.

(g) On Destruction of the Subject-matter

17.3 Effective Time of Termination of Agent's Authority [Section 208]

Party	*Time when termination of agent's authority takes place*
I. As regards the agent	When the agent comes to know that his authority has been terminated.
II. As regards the third persons	When they come to know that the agent's authority has been revoked.
III. As regards the sub-agent	When the original agent comes to know that his authority has been terminated.

Thus, termination may be effective at a different time as regards the agent and as regard, the third persons.

Example I *A directs B to sell goods for him and agrees to give B five per cent commission on the price fetched by the goods. A, afterwards, by a letter, revokes B's authority. B, after the letter is sent but before he receives it, sells the goods for Rs 10,000. The sale is binding on A and B is entitled to Rs 500 as his commission.*

Example II *A, at Madras, by letter, directs B to sell for him some cotton lying in a warehouse in Bombay and afterwards by a letter, revokes his authority to sell, and directs B to send the cotton to Madras. B, after receiving the second letter, enters into a contract with C, who knows of the first letter, but not of the second, for the sale of him of the cotton. C pays B the money, with which B absconds. C's payment is good, as against A.*

Example III *A directs B, his agent, to pay certain money to C. A dies and D being A's executor takes out probate of his will. B, after A's death, but before hearing of it, pays the money to C. The payment is good as against D, the executor.*

18.0 IRREVOCABLE AGENCY

18.1 Meaning of Irrevocable Agency The term 'Irrevocable Agency' means an agency which cannot be revoked or terminated by the principal.

18.2 Circumstances when the Agency is Irrevocable [Sections 202 and 204] The circumstances when the agency is irrevocable are as follows:

(a) Where the Agency is Coupled with Interest [Section 202]

Meaning of Agency Coupled with Interest An agency is said to be coupled with interest when the object of creating the agency is to secure some benefit to the agent in addition to his remuneration as agent. It may be noted that an agency cannot be said to be agency coupled with interest in the following cases:

(i) where the interest of the agent arises after the creation of agency;

(ii) where the agency secures a benefit to the agent incidentally though the agency was not created for this object.

No Termination of Agency coupled with Interest [Section 202]: Where the agent has himself an interest in the property which forms the subject matter of the agency, the agency cannot, in the absence of an express contract, be terminated to the prejudice of such interest.

Example I *X consigned 100 bags of wheat to Y who has advanced Rs 10,000 to X. X authorised Y to sell the wheat and to pay himself Rs 10,000 out of the* *proceeds of wheat. Later on, X directed Y not to sell the wheat. Ignoring X's direction, Y sold the wheat to recover Rs 10,000. X could not revoke his authority because the agency was coupled with interest. Hence, Y could sell the wheat.*

Example II *X consigned 100 bags of wheat to Y and authorised Y to sell the wheat. Later on Y advanced Rs 10,000 to X which X failed to pay. X directed Y not to sell the wheat. Ignoring X's directions, Y sold the wheat to recover Rs 10,000. X could revoke his authority because the agency was not coupled with interest. Hence Y could not sell the wheat. [Smart v. Sandars]*

(b) Where the Agent has partly Exercised his Authority [Section 204] The principal cannot revoke the authority given to his agent after the authority has been partly exercised, so far as regards such acts and obligations as arise from acts already done in the agency. Thus, the principal cannot revoke the agent's authority for the acts already done.

Example *A authorises B to buy 1,000 bales of cotton on account of A, and to pay for it out of A's money remaining in B's hands. B buys 1,000 bales of cotton in A's name, and so as not to render himself personally liable for the price, A cannot revoke B's authority to pay for the cotton.*

(c) Where the Agent has Incurred a Personal Liability The principal cannot revoke the agent's authority for the authorised acts in respect of which the agent has already incurred a personal liability.

Example *A authorises B to buy 1,000 bales of cotton on account of A, and to pay for it out of A's money remaining in B's hands. B buys, 1,000 bales of cotton in his own name, so as to make himself personally liable for the price. A cannot revoke B's authority so far as regards payment for the cotton.*

PRACTICAL PROBLEMS

PROBLEM 1

X appoints the following persons. State whether they can be called as agent of *X*.

(a) *A* to cook food for *X* and *X*'s family on a monthly salary of Rs 1,000.
(b) *B* to furnish kitchen in his house for Rs 10,000.
(c) *C* to buy utensils for his kitchen for an agreed commission of 5% on purchases.
(d) Mrs *X* to buy provisions for his kitchen without any commission on purchases.
(e) *D* to advise on financial matters.

Solution

(a) No, because *A* is servant.
(b) No, because *B* is an independent contractor.
(c) Yes, because *C* is authorised to establish contract between *X* and a third party (i.e. supplier of utensils).
(d) Yes, because Mrs *X* is authorised to establish contract between *X* and a third party (i.e. supplier of provisions).
(e) No, because *D* is not authorised to establish contract between *X* and a third party.

PROBLEM 2

Can the following persons appoint an agent?

(a) A minor who is of sound mind

(b) A lunatic who is major
(c) Guardian of a minor who is of sound mind
(d) A lunatic who is minor

Solution

Section to which the given problem relates: Section 183.

Decision and Reason:

(a) No, because he is not of the age of majority and hence he does not have contractual capacity.
(b) No, because he is not of sound mind and hence he does not have contractual capacity.
(c) Yes, because he has a contractual capacity.
(d) No, because he does not have contractual capacity.

PROBLEM 3

Can the following persons be appointed as an agent?
(a) A minor who is of sound mind
(b) A lunatic who is a major
(c) A guardian of a minor who is of sound mind

Solution

Section to which the given problem relates: Section 184.

Decision and Reason: Yes, because no person is debarred from being appointed as an agent whether he has contractual capacity or not.

PROBLEM 4

Mrs *X* purchased some goods forming part of necessaries on Mr *X*'s credit from *Y*. State whether Mr *X* is liable to *Y* in each of the following alternative cases:

Case (a) If Mrs *X* lives with Mr *Y*

Case (b) If Mrs *X* lives apart for no fault on her part

Case (c) If Mrs *X* live apart for no fault on part of Mr *X*

Solution

Cases (a) & (b) Yes, because there is a legal presumption that a wife has authority to pledge her husband's credit for necessaries.

Case (c) No, because there is no legal presumption under this case.

PROBLEM 5

State with reasons whether each of the following ratification are valid or invalid:

(a) *X* accepts interest from *C* to whom money was lent by *X*'s agent without *X*'s authority.
(b) *X* sells goods which were purchased by *X*'s agent without *X*'s authority.
(c) *X* ratifies his agent's acceptance of an offer made by *B*, a third party after the revocation of offer by *B*.
(d) *X* ratifies the purchase of goods by *Y*, his agent who bought those goods in his own name without *X*'s authority.
(e) *X* a minor, on attaining majority ratifies the contracts made on his behalf during his minority.
(f) *X* ratifies half of the purchase of goods by *Y*, his agent who bought those goods on behalf of *X* but without *X*'s authority.

(g) *X* ratifies the notice of termination of lease given by *Y* his agent without *X*'s authority.

(h) *X* ratifies the act of *Y* who withdrew money after forging *X*'s signature.

(i) A new company ratifies the contracts entered into by the promoters.

(j) A company ratifies the act done by a director on behalf of a company which is *ultra-vires* the company.

Case	*Decision*	*Reason*
(a)	Valid	*X*'s conduct implies a ratification of loan. [Section 197]
(b)	Valid	*X*'s conduct implies a ratification of purchase. [Section 197]
(c)	Valid	Ratification relates back to the time of acceptance by his agent. [Section 196]
(d)	Invalid	Acts done by an agent in his own name cannot be ratified. [Section 196]
(e)	Invalid	Principal ratifying the act must have contractual capacity both at the time when the act was done and at the time of ratification.
(f)	Valid	Ratification of a part of transaction amounts to ratification of whole transaction. [Section 199]
(g)	Invalid	An act which causes any damage to third party and terminates any right or interest of a third party cannot be ratified. [Section 200]
(h)	Invalid	An unlawful act cannot be ratified.
(i)	Invalid	The Company (principal) was not in existence when the contracts were entered into by the promoters.
(j)	Invalid	The Company (principal) cannot ratify the act which is beyond its powers.

PROBLEM 6

X instructed *Y*, a transporter, to send the consignment of tomatoes to Calcutta. After covering the half distance, *Y* found that tomatoes will not bear the journey to Calcutta without spoiling and sold at half the market price for good tomatoes. *X* sued *Y*. Discuss the legal position.

Solution

Section to which the given problem relates: Section 189.

Decision: The sale by *Y* is binding on *X* and *Y* is not liable to *X*.

Reason: *Y* a carrier acted as an agent by necessity.

PROBLEM 7

X, a driver of a bus requested a passenger to drive the bus to its destination. He drove the bus negligently and injured *Z*. Is the owner of a bus liable?

Solution

Section to which the given problem relates: Section 190.

Decision: The owner is not liable to *Z*.

Reason: The driver cannot delegate his authority.

PROBLEM 8

X the principal, instructed *Y* his agent to insure the goods. *Y* failed to do so and the goods are destroyed by fire. Is *Y* liable to *X*?

Solution

Section to which the given problem relates: Section 211

Decision: *Y* is liable to compensate *X* for the loss.

Reason: *Y* has not acted according to *X*'s directions.

PROBLEM 9

X, the principal, instructed *Y* his agent to put goods in *Z*'s warehouse. *Y* puts half of the goods in *Z*'s warehouse and the balance in another equally safe warehouse. All the goods were destroyed by fire without any negligence on part of *Y*. Is *Y* liable to *X*?

Solution

Section to which the given problem relates: Section 211.

Decision and Reason:

(a) *Y* is not liable for the loss of goods put in *Z*'s warehouse because he acted according to the directions of his principal.

(b) *Y* is liable for the loss of goods put in another warehouse because he has not acted according to the directions of his principal.

PROBLEM 10

Y, a broker sold goods of *X*, his principal on credit. Before making the payment, *Z* became insolvent. State whether *Y* is liable to *X* in each of the following alternative cases:

Case (a) If *X* instructed *Y* not to sell on credit and *Z* was a reputed party.

Case (b) If *X* did not instruct *Y* whether or not to sell on credit but in the agency business it is not the custom to sell the goods on credit.

Case (c) If *Y* having authority to sell on credit sold to *Z* after making proper enquiries as to the solvency of *Z*.

Case (d) If *Y* having authority to sell on credit sold to Z without making proper enquiries as to the solvency of *Z*.

Solution

Case (a): **Section to which the given problem relates:** Section 211.

Decision: *Y* is liable to *X* for the loss.

Reason: *Y* has not acted according to the directions of his principal.

Case (b): **Section to which the given problem relates:** Section 211.

Decision: *Y* is liable to *X* for the loss.

Reason: *Y* has not acted according to the custom prevailing in the business of agency.

Case (c): **Section to which the given problem relates:** Section 212.

Decision: *Y* is not liable to *X* for the loss.

Reason: *Y* has acted with reasonable care and skill and diligence.

Case (d): **Section to which the given problem relates:** Section 212.

Decision: *Y* is liable to *X* for the loss.

Reason: *Y* has acted negligently.

PROBLEM 11

X directs *Y* to sell his estate for not less than Rs 1,00,000. *Y* on looking over the estate before selling it, finds a mine on the estate which is unknown to *A*. *Y* buys the estate himself and hands over Rs 1,00,000 to *X* who is quite satisfied with the price. *Y* resold the estate for Rs. 1,50,000 after three months. Discuss the legal position in each of the following alternative cases.

Case (a): *Y* informs *X* that he wishes to buy the estate for himself but conceals the discovery of the mine.

Case (b): *Y* informs *X* that there exists a mine in the estate but conceals the fact that he wishes to buy.

Case (c): *Y* informs that there exists a mine in the estate and he wishes to buy the estate for himself.

Solution

Case (a): **Section to which the given problem relates:** Sections 215 and 216.

Decision and Reason: On discovery that *Y* knew of the mine at the time he bought the estate, *X* has two rights—

(i) He may repudiate or adopt the sale at his option because *Y* concealed the existence of mine [Section 215]

(ii) If he adopts the sale, he is entitled to claim Rs. 50,000 because the principal is entitled to claim from the agent any benefit which may have resulted to him from the personal transaction in the business of the agency [Section 216]

Case (b): **Section to which the given problem relates:** Sections 215 and 216.

Decision and Reason: On discovery that *Y* himself bought the estate, *X* has two rights:

(i) He may repudiate or adopt the sale at his option because *Y* did not obtain *X*'s consent [Section 215]

(ii) If he adopts the sale, he is entitled to claim Rs 50,000 because the principal is entitled to claim from the agent any benefit which may have resulted to him form the personal transaction in the business of the agency [Section 216]

Case (c): **Section to which the given problem relates:** Sections 215 and 216.

Decision and Reason: *X* is bound by the sale.

(i) *X* cannot repudiate the sale because *Y* has obtained *X*'s consent and has not concealed any material fact [Section 215]

(ii) *X* is not entitled to claim Rs 50,000 because *Y* has obtained *X*'s consent [Section 216]

PROBLEM 12

X appointed *Y*, an auctioneer, to sell certain goods. *Y* sold goods to *Z* and received Rs 500 as secret commission from *Z* in addition to Rs 1,000 as normal commission from *X*. Discuss the rights of *X*.

Solution

X has the following two options:

(i) he may repudiate the sale and recover Rs 1,000, or

(ii) he may recover Rs 1,500. [*Andrews* v. *Ramsay & Co.*]

PROBLEM 13

X directs *Y* his solicitor to sell his estate by auction. *Y* employs *Z*, an auctioneer, to sell the goods of *X*. *Z* became insolvent without having accounted for the proceeds of sale. Discuss the legal position (a) if *Y* selected *Z* after proper enquiries, (b) if *Y* selected *Z* without making proper enquiries.

Solution

Section to which the given problem relates: Section 195.

Decision and Reason:

Case (a): *Z* is responsible to *X* because *Y* exercised the reasonable care and skill in selecting a substituted agent.

Case (b): *Y* is responsible to *X* because *Y* did not exercise the same amount of discretion as a man of ordinary prudence would exercise in his own case, in selecting a substituted agent.

PROBLEM 14

Y under instructions from *X*, his principal contracted with *Z* for the sale of 100 bags of wheat. Afterwards, *X* refused to deliver the wheat and *Z* sued *Y* for breach of contract. *Y* defended the suit and was compelled to pay damages, costs and incure expenses. Is *X* liable to *Y* for such damages, costs and expenses?

Solution

Section to which the given problem relates: Section 222.

Decision: *X* is liable to *Y* for such damages, costs and expenses.

Reason: The employer of an agent is bound to indemnify him against the consequences of all lawful acts done by such agent in exercise of his authority.

PROBLEM 15

Y, under instruction from *X* his principal, sold 100 bags of wheat in possession of *X* which *X* had no right to dispose off. *Y* did not know this and handed over the proceeds of sale to *X*. Afterwards, *Z* the true owner of the goods sued *Y* and recovered the proceeds and costs. Is *X* liable to *Y* for proceeds and costs?

Solution

Section to which the given problem relates: Section 223.

Decision: *X* is liable to *Y* for proceeds and costs.

Reason: The employer of an agent is bound to indemnify him against the consequences of bonafide acts a done by the agent.

PROBLEM 16

Y, the proprietor of a newspaper published at *X*'s request a libel upon *Z* in the paper and *X* agreed to indemnify *Y* against the consequences of the publication. *Y* was sued by *Z* and had to pay damages and also incurred expenses. Is *X* liable to *Y* for such damages and expenses?

Solution

Section to which the given problem relates: Section 224.

Decisions: *X* is not liable to *Y* for such damages and expenses.

Reason: The employer is not liable to indemnify the agent against the consequences of a criminal acts.

PROBLEM 17

Y being *X*'s agent, with authority to receive money on his behalf receives from *Z* a sum of money due to *X*. Is *Z* discharged of his obligation?

Solution

Section to which the given problem relates: Section 226.

Decision: *Z* is discharged of his obligation.

Reason: Receipt by agent operates as receipt by his principal.

PROBLEM 18

X, being owner of a ship and cargo, authorises *Y* to procure an insurance on the ship. *Y* procures insurance on the ship as well as cargo. State the legal position in each of the following alternative cases:

Case (a) If two separate insurance policies are issued viz one for ship and another for cargo.

Case (b) If one comprehensive insurance policy is issued for both ship and cargo.

Solution

***Case (a)* Section to which the given problem relates:** Section 227.

Decision: *X* is bound to pay the premium for the policy on the ship but not the premium for the policy on the cargo.

Reason: The principal is bound by the agent's authorised acts only where the agent exceeds his authority and the authorised acts can be separated from unauthorised acts.

***Case (b):* Section to which the given problem relates:** Section 228.

Decision: *X* is not bound to recognise the transaction.

Reason: The principal is not bound to recognise the transaction where the agent exceeds his authority and the authorised acts cannot be separated from unauthorised acts.

Note: However, *X* may ratify the unauthorised act and accept the comprehensive policy [Section 196].

PROBLEM 19

Z owes Rs 1,000 to *X* and *X* instructs *Y* to buy Rs 5,000 worth of wheat from *Z*. *Y* buys the goods from *Z*. *Y* knows that the goods really belonged to *M* but *X* is ignorant of that fact. *X* claims set off of Rs 1,000 while making the payment of the price of the wheat. State the legal position in each of the following alternative cases:

Case (a): If in the course of dealing for sale, *Y* comes to know that goods really belonged to *M*.

Case (b): If *Y* was, before he was employed by *X*, a servant of *Z* and then came to know that the goods really belonged to *M*.

Solution

Section to which the given problem relates: Section 229.

Decision and Reason:

Case (a): *X* cannot claim set off of Rs 1,000 due from *Z* against the price of the goods because information obtained by the agent operates as information obtained by the principal.

Case (b): *X* can claim set off of Rs 1,000 due from *Z* against the price of goods because *Y* obtained the information as an employee of *Z* and not as agent of *X* and hence, *Y*'s knowledge does not operate as information obtained by *X*.

PROBLEM 20

Y, who owes Rs 1,000 to *Z*, sells Rs 5,000 worth of wheat to *Z*. *Z* claims set off of Rs 1,000 while making the payment of the price of the wheat. State the legal position in each of the following alternative cases:

Case (a): If *Z* knows that *Y* is acting as agent for *X*.

Case (b): If *Z* knows that *Y* is acting as agent but does not know who is the principal.

Case (c): If *Z neither* knows *nor* has reason to suspect that *Y* is acting as agent.

Solution

Cases (a)* and *(b)

Section to which the given problem relates: Section 226.

Decision: *Z* cannot claim set off of Rs 1,000 while making the payment of the price of the wheat.

Reason: Sale by *Y* has established a contract between *X* and *Z* and hence *X* is the person who is entitled to claim the price of the goods.

***Case (c):* Section to which the given problem relates:** Section 232.

Decision: *Z* can claim set off of Rs 1,000.

Reason: *X* can obtain the performance of the contract only subject to the rights and obligations subsisting between the agent and the other party to the contract.

PROBLEM 21

Y buys Rs 5,000 worth of wheat from *Z* and pays Rs 1,000 as advance. *Z* wants to sue for the price. Name the person who can be sued by *Z* in each of the following alternative cases:

Case (a): If *Z* knows that *Y* is acting an agent for *X*.

Case (b): If *Z* knows that *Y* is acting as an agent but does not know who is the principal.

Case (c): If *Z* *neither* knows *nor* has reason to suspect that *Y* is acting as an agent.

Solution

Case (a): **Section to which the given problem relates:** Section 226.

Decision: *Z* can sue *X* only.

Reason: Purchase by *Y* has established a contract between *X* and *Z* and hence *X* is the person who can be sued for the price of goods.

Cases (b) and (c):

Section to which the given problem relates: Section 233.

Decision: *Z* can sue *X* or *Y* or both of them.

Reason: Where the agent does not disclose the name of the principal, the agent is presumed to be personally liable and where the agent is personally liable, a person dealing with him may hold *either* him *or* his principal *or* both of them liable.

PROBLEM 22

X consigned goods to *Y* for sale and instructed him not to sell under a fixed price. *Z* being ignorant of *X*'s instructions enters into a contract with *Y* to buy the goods at a price lower than the reserved price. Is *X* bound by the contract?

Solution

Section to which the given problem relates: Section 237.

Decision: *X* is bound by contract.

Reason: The principal is bound by the unauthorised acts of the agent if he has induced a third person to believe that agent's unauthorised acts were authorised.

[***Note:*** *X* can however claim damages from *Y*.]

PROBLEM 23

Y being *X*'s agent for the sale of goods, induces *Z* to buy them by misrepresentation which he was not authorised by *X* to make. State the legal position.

Solution

Section to which the given problem relates: Section 238.

Decision: The contract is voidable, as between *X* and *Z* at the option of *Z*.

Reason: Misrepresentation made by agent in respect of authorised acts operates as misrepresentation by the principal.

PROBLEM 24

X, an Indian, appoints *Y*, a Pakistani citizen as his agent for 1 year on 1st Jan. 2009 to sell his goods. On the same day, by a letter he directs his agent (a) to insure the goods, (b) not to sell for less than a certain price, and (c) not to sell on credit. Discuss the legal position in each of the following alternative cases:

Case (a): If *X* himself sells these goods on 5th Jan. 2009.

Case (b): If *Y* himself renounces the agency on 5th Jan. 2009.

Case (c): If *X* and *Y* mutually agree to terminate the agency on 5th Jan. 2009.

Case (d): If goods for the sale of which agency was created have already been sold.

Case (e): If *X* dies or becomes of unsound mind.

Case (f): If *Y* dies or becomes of unsound mind.

Case (g): If *X* becomes insolvent.

Case (h): If 1 year expired on 31.12.2009.

Case (i): If goods for the sale of which agency was created are destroyed by fire.

Case (j): If a war breaks out between India and Pakistan.

Case (k): If *X* dies but before the fact of his death becomes known to *Y*, *Y* sells the goods to *Z* who is not aware of *X*'s death.

Case (l): If *X* dies and after the fact of his death becomes known to *Y*, *Y* sells the goods to *Z* who is not aware of *X*'s death.

Solution

Case (a) to Case (j): The agency terminates in all these cases [Section 201].

Case (k): The sale is binding of *X*'s executors because as regards the agent, the termination of agency is effective from the time when it comes to the knowledge of the agent [Section 208].

Case (l): The sale is binding on *X*'s executors because as regards the third parties, the termination of agency is effective from the time when it comes to the knowledge of the third party [Section 208].

PROBLEM 25

X consigned 100 bags of wheat to *Y* who had advanced Rs 10,000 to *X*. *X* authorised *Y* to sell the wheat and to pay himself Rs 10,000, out of the proceeds of wheat. Later on, *X* directed *Y* not to sell the wheat. Ignoring *X*'s directions, *Y* sold the wheat to recover Rs 10,000. Is this sale binding on *X*?

Solution

Section to which the given problem relates: Section 202.

Decision: This sale is binding on *X*.

Reason: *X* could not revoke his authority because the agency was coupled with interest.

PROBLEM 26

What would be the decision if in problem 25, *X* died before directing *Y* not to sell and after the fact of his death becomes known to *Y*, *Y* sold the wheat?

Solution

Decision : The sale is binding on *X*'s executors, because an agency coupled with interest cannot be terminated by the death of the principal.

PROBLEM 27

X consigned 100 bags of wheat to *Y* and authorised *Y* to sell the wheat. Later on, *Y* advanced Rs 10,000 to *X* which *X* failed to pay; *X* directed *Y* not to sell the wheat. Ignoring *X*'s directions, *Y* sold the wheat to recover Rs 10,000. Is this sale binding on *X*?

Section to which the given problem relates: Section 202.

Decision: No.

Reason: *X* could revoke his authority because the agency was not coupled with interest, the agent's interest arose after the creation of agency.

[Leading Case: *Smart* v. *Sandars*]

PROBLEM 28

X authorises *Y* to buy 100 bags of wheat on account of *X* and to pay for it out of *X*'s money remaining in *Y*'s hands. *Y* buys 100 bags of wheat and after the dealing receives *X*'s letter revoking *Y*'s authority. State the legal position (a) if *Y* buys in *X*'s name (b) if *Y* buys in his own name.

Solution

Section to which the given problem relates: Section 204.

Decision: The purchase is binding on *X*.

Reason:

Case (a): The principal cannot revoke the agent's authority after the authority has been partly exercised.

Case (b): The principal cannot revoke the agent's authority for the authorised acts in respect of which the agent has already incurred a personal liability.

PROBLEM 29

X offered to buy certain flats from *Y*. *X* made an enquiry from *Z* the property manager of *Y* whether all the tenants were paying their rents regularly. *Z* informed that the tenants were paying rents regularly with immaterial exceptions. This statement was false. Is *Y* liable for *Z*'s false statement?

Solution

Section to which the given problem relates: Section 238.

Decision: *Y* is liable for *Z*'s false statement.

Reason: Misrepresentation made by agent in respect of authorised acts operates as misrepresentation by the principal.

[***Leading Case:*** *London Country Freehold and Household Properties Ltd.* v. *Barkerlay Property and Insurance Co Ltd.*]

TRUE OR FALSE QUESTIONS

State with reasons whether the following statements are 'True' of 'False':

1. An agent is a servant.
2. An agent is an independent contractor.
3. A minor can *neither* be agent *nor* be a principal.
4. A minor can be a principal but cannot be an agent.
5. A minor can be an agent but cannot be a principal.
6. A contract of agency may be created expressly but not impliedly.
7. Consideration for agency is necessary.
8. A gratuitous contract of agency is invalid.
9. The principal is liable for all acts of his agent.
10. An agent can exceed his authority in an emergency.
11. A delegate cannot further delegate.

12. An agent cannot appoint a sub-agent.
13. Ratification is tantamount to prior authority.
14. He who acts through an agent is himself acting.
15. In general, a sub-agent is not directly under the control of the principal.
16. There is no privity of contract between a substituted agent and the principal.
17. The act of the agent to be ratified must not be illegal.
18. For valid ratification, the principal must be competent to contract at the time of ratification.
19. A forgery of signature when ratified, conveys good title.
20. A part of transaction can also be ratified.
21. The lien existing in favour of an agent is generally a general lien.
22. The principal may revoke agency for future acts only.
23. An agency is always revocable.
24. Where the interest of the agent arises after the creation of agency, the agency is said to be coupled with interest.
25. An agency coupled with interest is irrevocable.
26. Termination of agency may be effective at a different time as regards the agent and as regards the third parties.
27. Revocation of agency must be express and not implied.
28. Notice of revocation of agency must be given in all cases.
29. The principal must make compensation to the agent whenever he revokes the authority of his agent.
30. The termination of the authority of an agent causes the termination of the authority of all sub-agents appointed to him.
31. A substituted agent is not appointed by the agent.
32. The acts of sub-agent may be ratified by the principal when he purports to act in his name.
33. An agent entitled to collect debts for his principal and to receive amount for him is not a bailee.

Answers

1. False	2. False	3. False	4. False
5. True	6. False	7. False	8. False
9. False	10. True	11. True	12. False
13. True	14. True	15. True	16. False
17. True	18. False	19. False	20. False
21. False	22. True	23. False	24. False
25. True	26. True	27. False	28. False
29. False	30. True	31. False	32. False
33. False			

VERY SHORT ANSWER TYPE QUESTIONS

1. Define an agent.
2. Who may be an agent?
3. Is agent responsible to his principal?
4. Define 'principal'.
5. Who may employ an agent?
6. Is consideration for agency necessary?
7. Can there be gratuitous contract of agency?
8. Is gratuitous agent is liable like a non-gratuitous agent?
9. What is the true test of agency?
10. What is meant by an agent's implied authority?
11. Can an agent exceed his authority in an emergency?
12. Can a wife pledge her husband's credit?
13. Define sub-agent.
14. Define substituted agent
15. Who is a disclosed principal?
16. Who is an undisclosed principal?
17. Who is a named principal?
18. What is effect of death of principal on a contract of agency?
19. When does termination of agency takes effect?
20. Does the termination of agency terminate sub-agency?

SHORT ANSWER TYPE QUESTIONS

1. Comment on the following:
   (a) Ratification is tantamount to prior authority.
   (b) An agency coupled with interest is revocable.
   (c) A delegate cannot further delegate.
   (d) An agency is always revocable.
   (e) He who acts through an agent, is himself acting.
2. Distinguish between the following:
   (a) Sub-agent and substituted Agent
   (b) Agent and Servant
   (c) Agent and an Independent Contractor
   (d) Broker and Factor
3. Write short notes on the following:
   (a) Agency by Express Authority
   (h) Agency relationship between husband and wife

(b) Agency by Implied Authority
(c) Agency by Estoppel
(d) Agency by Holding out
(e) Agency by Necessity
(f) Agency by ratification
(g) Essentials of a valid ratification
(i) Sub-agent
(j) Substituted agent
(k) Undisclosed principal
(l) Irrevocable agency
(m) Agency coupled with interest

ESSAY TYPE QUESTIONS

1. (a) Define 'agent' and 'principal'
   (b) Who may be an agent?
   (c) Who can employ an agent?
   (d) Is consideration for agency necessary?
   (e) What is the true test of agency?
2. Explain the various modes of creation of agency.
3. What is agency by ratification? What are requisites of a valid ratification?
4. To what extent a wife can pledge her husband's credit when (i) she lives with him (ii) she lives separately.
5. Define a sub-agent. When can an agent appoint a sub-agent?
6. Explain the rights of an agent against his principal.
7. State the duties of an agent to his principal.
8. State the circumstances under which an agent may be held personally liable.
9. State the rights of an agent, principal and third parties if an agent acts for (a) disclosed principal (b) named principal and (c) undisclosed principal.
10. Describe the various modes by which the authority of an agent may be terminated.
11. (a) State the effect of death, insanity and insolvency of the principal or agent on a contract of agency.
    (b) When does termination of agency takes effect?
    (c) When is an agency irrevocable?

CHAPTER

15 The Sale of Goods Act, 1930

1.0 INTRODUCTION

1.1 Till 1930, transactions relating to sale and purchase of goods were regulated by the Indian Contract Act, 1872.

1.2 In 1930, Sections 76 to 123 of the Indian Contract Act, 1872 were repealed and a separate Act called 'The Indian Sale of Goods Act, 1930 was passed.

1.3 It came into force on 1st July 1930. With effect from 22nd September, 1963, the word 'Indian' was also removed. Now, the present Act is called 'The Sale of Goods Act, 1930'.

1.4 What is the territory to which this Act applies ?

This Act extends to the whole of India except the State of Jammu and Kashmir.

1.5 Do the provisions of the India Contract Act, 1872 still apply to contracts for Sale of Goods ?

According to Section 3, "**the provisions of the Indian Contract Act, 1872 still continue to apply to contracts for the sale of goods except where 'The Sale of Goods Act', 1930 provides for the contrary**".

2.0 WHAT IS THE SCOPE OF THE ACT ?

2.1 The Sale of Goods Act deals with 'sale' but not with 'mortgage' (which is dealt with under the Transfer of Property Act, 1882) or 'pledge' (which is dealt with under the Indian Contract Act, 1872).

2.2 This Act deals with 'goods' but not with other movable property, e.g., actionable claims and money.

2.3 In other words, this Act does not deal with movable property other than goods, and immovable property.

3.0 WHAT IS THE MEANING OF CONTRACT OF SALE ?

3.1 *According to Section 4(1) of the Sale of Goods Act, 1930*, "**contract of sale of goods is a contract whereby the seller transfers or agrees to transfer the property in goods to the buyer for a price.**"

3.2 'Contract of Sale' is a generic term which includes both a sale as well as an agreement to sell.

4.0 WHAT ARE THE ESSENTIAL ELEMENTS OF CONTRACT OF SALE ?

The aforesaid definition clearly indicates the following essential elements

1. Seller and Buyer	There must be a seller as well as a buyer. 'Buyer' means a person who buys or agrees to buy goods [Section 2(1)]. 'Seller' means a person who sells or agrees to sell goods [Section 2(13)]. A person cannot be a seller as well as a buyer as a person cannot buy his own goods. That is why

	distribution of goods among partners on account of dissolution of a firm does not amount to a sale of goods because the partners are joint owners and they cannot be both sellers and buyers [*State of Gujarat* v. *Raman Lal & Co.*]. However, one part owner may be a seller and another part owner may be buyer. Where a person's goods are sold under an execution of decree, a bankrupt may also buy back his own goods from his trustee. [*King* v. *England*]
2. Goods	There must be some goods. 'Goods' means every kind of movable property other than actionable claims and money and includes stock and shares, growing crops, grass and things attached to or forming part of the land which are agreed to be severed before sale or under the contract of sale [Section 2(7)]. It may be noted that the contract relating to actionable claims, immovable property and services are not covered by this Act. ***Notes:*** (i) The 'actionable claims' mean a claim which can be enforced through the courts of Law, e.g. a debt due from one person to another is an actionable claim. (ii) The 'money' here means the legal tender (i.e. currency of the country) and not old coins.
3. Transfer of Property	Property means the general property in goods, and not merely a special property [Section 2(11)]. General property in goods means ownership of the goods. Special property in goods means possession of goods. Thus, there must be *either* a transfer of ownership of goods *or* an agreement to transfer the ownership of goods. The ownership may transfer either immediately on completion of sale or sometime in future in agreement to sell.
4. Price	There must be a price. Price here means the money consideration for a sale of goods [Section 2(10)]. When the consideration is only goods, it amounts to a 'barter' and not sale. When there is no consideration, it amounts to gift and not sale. However, the consideration may be partly in money and partly in goods because the law does not prohibit as such. [*Shelden* v. *Cox*]
5. Essential Elements of a Valid Contract	In addition to the aforesaid specific essential elements, all the essential elements of a valid contract as specified under Section 10 of Indian Contract Act, 1872 must also be present since a contract of sale is a special type of a contract. For example, an agreement to sell smuggled gold is not valid because its object is unlawful.[*Refer to Practical Problem 1*]

5.0 WHAT ARE THE FORMALITIES OF A CONTRACT OF SALE ? [SECTION 5]

In connection with the formalities of a contract of sale, the provisions of Section 5 specifically provide only for the following **three** matters:

1. Offer and Acceptance	A contract of sale is made by an offer to buy or sell the goods for a price and acceptance of such offer.

2. Delivery and Payment	The contract of sale may provide for any of the following combinations:		
	Option	***Delivery***	***Payment***
	I	Immediate	Immediate
	II	Immediate	By Instalments
	III	Immediate	At some future date
	IV	By instalments	By Instalments
	V	By instalments	Immediate
	VI	By instalments	At some future date
	VII	At some future date	At some future date
	VIII	At some future date	Immediate
	IX	At some future date	By Instalments
3. Express or Implied	A contract of sale may be implied from the conduct of parties or express (*i.e.* written or oral or partly written or oral)		
	It may be noted that an offer by word of mouth may be accepted in writing and an offer in writing may be accepted by word of mouth.		

6.0 WHAT DOES 'CONTRACT OF SALE' INCLUDE ?

The term 'Contract of Sale' includes both a 'sale' and 'agreement to sell' as shown below:

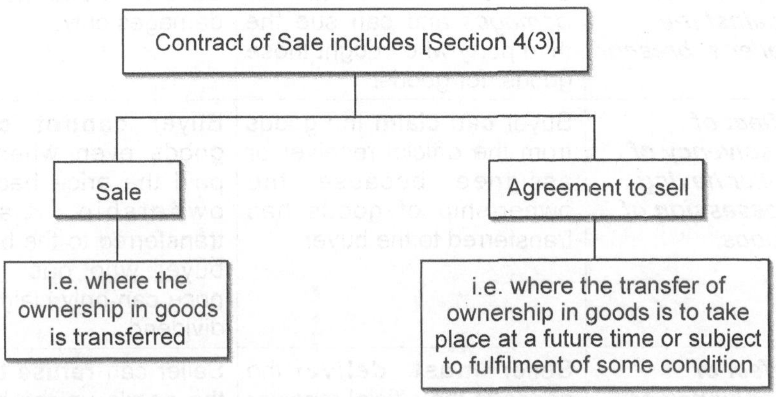

7.0 WHEN DOES AGREEMENT TO SELL BECOME SALE ?

An agreement to sell becomes a sale when the time elapses or the conditions are fulfilled subject to which the ownership in the goods, is to be transferred.

8.0 DISTINCTION BETWEEN SALE AND AGREEMENT TO SELL

A 'Sale' and an 'Agreement to Sell' can be distinguished as follows:

Basis of distinction	***Sale***	***Agreement to sell***
1. ***Transfer of ownership***	Transfer of ownership of goods takes place **immediately.**	Transfer of ownership of goods is to take place at a **future time** or subject to fulfilment of some condition.

2. *Executed Contract or Executory Contract*	It is an **executed** contract because nothing remains to be done.	It is an **executory** contract because something remains to be done.
3. *Conveyance of property*	Buyer **gets a right to enjoy** the goods against the whole world including seller. There-fore, a sale creates **jus in rem** (Right against property).	Buyer does **not get such right** to enjoy the goods. It only creates **jus in personam** (Right against the person).
4. *Transfer of Risk*	Transfer of *risk of loss of goods takes place* **imme-diately** because ownership is transferred. As a result, in	Transfer of risk of loss of goods **does not take place** because ownership is not transferred. As a result, in case of destruction of goods, the loss shall be borne by the seller even though the goods are in the possession of the buyer.
5. *Rights of seller against the buyer's breach*	Seller can *sue* the buyer *for the* **price** even though the goods are in his possession.	Seller can sue the buyer *for* **damages** even though the goods are in the possession of the buyer.
6. *Rights of buyer against the seller's breach*	Buyer can sue the seller *for damages* and can sue the third party who bought those goods, for goods.	Buyer can sue the seller for damages only.
7. *Effect of insolvency of seller having possession of goods*	Buyer **can claim** the goods from the official receiver or assignee because the owner-ship of goods has transferred to the buyer.	Buyer **cannot claim** the goods even when he has paid the price because the ownership has not transferred to the buyer. The buyer who has paid the price can only claim rateable dividend.
8. *Effect of insolvency of the buyer before paying the price*	Seller **must deliver** the goods to the official receiver or assignee because the owner-ship of goods has transferred to the buyer. He can only claim rateable dividend for the unpaid price.	Seller can **refuse to deliver** the goods unless he is paid full price of the goods because the ownership has not transferred to the buyer.

9.0 DISTINCTION BETWEEN SALE AND HIRE-PURCHASE AGREEMENT

9.1 Meaning of Hire-purchase Agreement Hire-purchase agreement means an agreement under which goods are let on hire and under which the hirer has an option to purchase them in accordance with the terms of the agreement and includes the agreement under which:

(i) Possession of goods is delivered by the owner thereof to a person on condition that such person pays the agreed amount in periodical instalments;

(ii) the property in the goods is to pass to such a person on the payment of the last instalment; and

(iii) such a person has a right to terminate the agreement at any time before the property so passes.

9.2 True Test of Hire-purchase Agreement If in an agreement the person taking the goods has an option to terminate the agreement at any time before the transfer of ownership of goods, it will be an agreement of hire purchase. If, in an agreement, the person taking the goods has no option to terminate the agreement, it will be a contract of sale even if the price is payable in instalments. [*Lee* v. *Butler*]

Example *X takes the delivery of a furniture from Y under an agreement which provides for (a) an immediate down payment of Rs 300, (b) the balance by way of 12 monthly instalments of Rs 100 each, (c) transfer of ownership on the payment of last instalment, (d) Y's right to or possess the goods in case of non-payment of instalments due. Before the 12th instalment was paid, X sold the furniture to Z. Can Y recover the furniture from Z ? State your answer in each of the following cases:*

Case (*a*): If the agreement does not provide for any other stipulation.

Case (*b*): If the agreement also provides that *X* can return the goods.

Solution:

Case (*a*): *Y* cannot recover the furniture from *Z* because it was a contract of sale (as *X* was not having any option to return but was under compulsion to buy) and not hire-purchase agreement.

Case (*b*): *Y* can recover the furniture from *Z* because it was a hire-purchase agreement (as *X* was having an option to return) and hence, *X* was not having any title to it.

9.3 Distinction between a Sale and Hire-purchase Agreement A 'Sale' can be distinguished from a hire-purchase agreement as under:

Basis of Distinction	*Sale*	*Hire-purchase agreement*
1. *Regulating Law*	All contracts of sale are governed by **Sale of Goods Act, 1930.**	The Hire-purchase agreements are governed by **Hire Purchase Act, 1972.**
2. *Nature of Contract*	It is **contract of sale.**	It is an **agreement of hiring** and hence an agreement to sell.
3. *Possession of goods*	Possession of goods need **not necessarily** be transferred immediately.	Possession of goods is necessarily **transferred** immediately.
4. *Transfer of ownership of goods*	Ownership of goods is transferred **immediately.**	Ownership of goods is transferred **on the payment of the last instalment** when the option to purchase is exercised.

5. *Right to terminate*	The buyer has **no right** to terminate the contract of sale.	The hirer has **right** to terminate the agreement at any time before the ownership is transferred.
6. *Right to repossess the goods*	The seller has **no right** to repossess the goods. He can sue for price.	The hire-vendor has a **right** to repossess the goods if the hirer defaults.
7. *Transfer of good title to third party*	The buyer **can transfer** a good title to third party because ownership of goods has been transferred.	The hirer **cannot transfer** a good title to third party because ownership of goods has not been transferred.
8. *Compulsion as to be in writing*	A contract of sale **need not** necessarily be in writing.	The hire-purchase agreement **must be in writing.**
9. *Benefits of implied conditions and warranties under the Sale of Goods Act*	The benefits of implied conditions and warranties are **available.**	The benefits of implied conditions and warranties are **not available.**
10. *Value Added Tax (VAT)*	In case of sale of taxable goods, VAT is **levied.**	In case of hire of even taxable goods, VAT is **not levied.**
11. *Treatment of payment made by instalment*	The payment made by the buyer is treated as payment towards the **price** of goods.	The payment made by the hire purchases is treated as **hire charges** for the use of goods till the option to purchase the goods is exercised.

10.0 DISTINCTION BETWEEN SALE AND CONTRACT FOR WORK AND LABOUR

In a contract for work and labour, the rendering of the service and exercise of skill is the essence of contract even though there may be delivery of goods. In a contract of sale, the delivery of goods is the essence of the contract although some labour on the part of the seller might also have been exercised. It may be noted that the Sale of Goods Act does not apply to contracts for skill and labour.

Example I *X engaged an artist to paint a portrait and supplied canvas, paint and other necessary articles. It was a contract for work and labour and not a contract of sale because the substance of the contract was the artist's skill and not the delivery of material. [Robinson v. Graves]*

Example II *X purchased a portrait painted by a famous artist. It was a contract of sale and not a contract for work and labour because the substance of the contract was the delivery of portrait.*

Example III *A restaurant provides food and drinks to its customers in the restaurant. It is essentially in the nature of service and not a transaction of sale because the customers come there not to buy the food and drinks but to find bodily satisfaction that service of food in the setting of a restaurant can afford to give. [Northern India Caterers (India) Ltd. v. Lt. Governor of Delhi].*

Example IV *A customer takes home a supply of certain food and drinks from the restaurant. It is a contract of sale and not a contract of work and labour because the substance of the contract is the delivery of foods and drinks.*

Example V *The contract for the construction of coaches on the underframes supplied by the Railways was held to be a contract for work and labour and not for sale. [State of Gujarat v. Variety Body Builders (1976) S.C. 2108]*

Example VI *A dentist agreed to supply an artificial denture to fit the mouth of a patient, material being wholly supplied by the Dentist. Held, it was a contract of sale. (Lee v. Griffin)*

11.0 MEANING AND TYPES OF GOODS

11.1 What is the Meaning of Goods ? [Section 2(7)]

Goods means every kind of movable property other than actionable claims and money, and includes the following:

(a) Stock and shares

(b) Growing crops, grass and thing attached to or forming part of the land which are agreed to be served before sale or under the Contract of Sale.

Examples of Goods: Old rare coins, stock, shares, debentures, goodwill, patents, trademark, copyright, water, gas, electricity, grass, growing crops, trees to be cut and their log wood delivered etc.

Things excluded from the term 'goods': The term 'goods' does not include the following:

(a) Actionable claim, which means a claim to any debt or any beneficial interest in movable property not in possession. Such claims cannot be sold or purchased like goods, they can only be assigned, e.g., a debt due from one person to another;

(b) Money, which means the legal tender and not the old rare coins;

(c) Immovable property.

11.2 What are the Types of Goods ? [Section 6]

The goods which form the subject of a contract of sale may be classified into following categories as shown below:

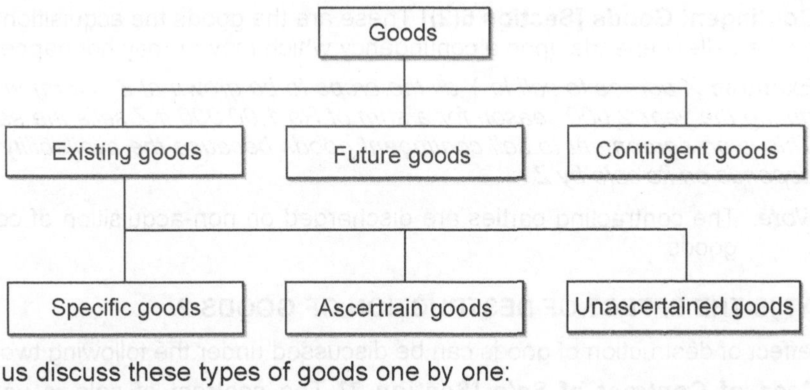

Let us discuss these types of goods one by one:

(a) Existing Goods Existing goods mean the goods which are *either* owned *or* possessed by the seller at the time of contract of sale. The existing goods may be specific or ascertained or unascertained as follows:

(i) ***Specific Goods* [*Section* 2(14)]:** These are the goods which are identified and agreed upon at the time when a contract of sale is made—For example, a specified TV, VCR, Car, Ring.

(ii) ***Ascertained Goods:*** Goods are said to be ascertained when out of a mass of unascertained goods, the quantity extracted for is identified and set aside for a given contract. Thus, when part of the goods lying in bulk are identified and earmarked for sale, such goods are termed as ascertained goods.

(iii) ***Unascertained Goods:*** These are the goods which are not identified and agreed upon at the time when a contract of sale is made. e.g. goods in stock or lying in lots.

Example *X goes to a Maruti car showroom where 10 Maruti cars have been displayed. X agrees to buy one Maruti car 800 and the seller agrees to sell. Here, 10 cars will be classified as under:*

I. 10 cars are unascertained goods before the identification of a particular car to be sold.

II. 9 cars are unascertained goods after the identification of 1 particular car to be sold. Such one particular car to be sold is an ascertained goods.

III. 1 particular car identified and agreed upon at the time when the contract of sale is made is specific goods and other 9 cars are unascertained goods.

(b) Future Goods [Section 2(6)] Future goods mean goods to be manufactured or produced or acquired by the seller after the making of the contract of sale. There can be an agreement to sell only. There can be no sale in respect of future goods because one cannot sell what he does not possess.

Example *X agrees to sell to Y all the crops to be grown at his farm in Haryana during the year 2,000 season for a sum of Rs 1,00,000. This is an agreement to sell future goods and not a sale.*

Notes: (i) The contracting parties are not discharged on non-acquisition or non-production of future goods.

(ii) The future goods are *neither* in existence *nor* in possession of the seller at the time of contract of sale whereas the unascertained goods are in existence and in possession of the seller at the time of contract of sale.

(c) Contingent Goods [Section 6(2)] These are the goods the acquisition of which by the seller depends upon a contingency which may or may not happen.

Example *X agrees to sell to Y all the crops to be grown at Z's farm in Haryana during the year 2,000 season for a sum of Rs 1,00,000 if Z sells the same to X. This is an agreement to sell contingent goods because the availability of crops depends on its sale by Z.*

Note: The contracting parties are discharged on non-acquisition of contingent goods.

12.0 WHAT IS THE EFFECT OF DESTRUCTION OF GOODS ?

The effect of destruction of goods can be discussed under the following two heads:

12.1 In Case of Contract of Sale [Section 7] The contract of sale is void if the following **three** conditions are satisfied:

(i) There must be a contract of sale for specific goods.

(ii) The goods must have perished or become so damaged as no longer to answer to their description in the contract, before making of the contract.

(iii) The seller must not be aware about the destruction of goods.

The aforesaid provision is based on the principle of impossibility of performance of the contract.

Example *X sold to Y all 700 bags of cement lying in his Delhi's godown. State the legal position (I) if unknown to X, all bags had been stolen before the contract was made, (II) if unknown to X, the cement had becomes stone as a result of heavy rainfall, (III) if unknown to X, 109 bags had been stolen at the time of making the contract.*

Solution:

Case I: The contract, is void because the goods have perished before making of the contract.

Case II: The contract is void because the goods became so damaged as no longer to answer to their description.

Case III: The contract has become void and *Y* cannot be compelled to accept 591 bags because the contract was indivisible.

[*Barrow Lane & Ballard Ltd* v. *Phillips & Co*]

12.2 In Case of an 'Agreement to Sell' [Section 8] An agreement to sell becomes void if the following **four** conditions are satisfied:

(i) There must be an agreement to sell specific goods;

(ii) The goods must have perished or become so damaged as no longer to answer to their description in the agreement;

(iii) There must not be any fault of seller or buyer;

(iv) The risk must not have passed to the buyer, i.e. the goods must have perished before the agreement to sell becomes sale.

Example I *X agrees to sell a particular horse to Y on the expiry of 8 days. The horse was delivered on trial for 8 days. However, the horse died on the third day, without any fault of either seller or buyer. This agreement became void and X could not recover the price from Y. [Elphick v. Barnes]*

Example II *X agrees to sell some specific goods to Y on the expiry of 8 days. However, the goods were requisitioned by the Government on the third day. This agreement becomes void.*

Example III *X agreed to sell to Y 10 tons of potatoes to be grown on his land. X sowed sufficient land to grow more than 10 tons of potatoes. But without any fault on X 's part, a disease attacked the crop and only about eight tons of potatoes could be grown. It was held that the agreement to sell has become void. [Howell v. Coupland]*

***Note*:** The provision of Sections 7 and 8 are applicable only in case of specific goods and not in case of unascertained goods. If unascertained goods are destroyed *either* before *or* after making the agreement, the contract shall not become void. An agreement to sell certain unascertained goods shall not become void even if the entire stock of unascertained stock is destroyed. For example, *X* agrees to sell 100 bags of cement out of 700 bags lying in his godown. The entire cement had become stone. The contract is not void because the contract was for unascertained goods and not for specific goods. Hence, *X* must deliver 100 bags of cement or pay damages for the breach.

13.0 PRICE OF GOODS

Meaning of Price	Price means the money consideration for a sale of goods.
Modes of Determining Price	There are **three** modes of determining the price as under: (a) It may be fixed by the contract; or (b) It may be left to be fixed in an agreed manner, or (c) It may be determined by the course of dealing between the parties. Thus, the price need not necessarily be fixed at the time of sale.
Consequences of not Determining the Price	Where the price is not determined in accordance with Section 9(1), the buyer must pay the seller a reasonable price. What is a reasonable price is a question of fact dependent on the circumstances of each particular case. It may be noted that a reasonable price need not be market price.
Consequences of not Fixing Price by Third Party	The agreement to sell goods becomes void if the following two conditions are fulfilled. (a) If such agreement provides that the price is to be fixed by the valuation of a third party, and (b) If such third party cannot or does not make such valuation.
Duty of Buyer	A buyer who has received and appropriated the goods, must pay a reasonable price therefor.
Right of Party not at Fault	Where such a third party is prevented from making the valuation by fault of the seller or buyer, the party not at fault may maintain a suit for damages against the party in fault. **Example** *X agrees to sell 100 bags of cement to Y at a price to be fixed by Z and to be delivered in 4 equal instalments. Y receives a delivery of 25 cement bags. State the legal position (a) if Z refuses to value the goods and fix the price, (b) if Z is prevented from fixing the price by the fault of X, (c) if Z is prevented for fixing the price by the fault of Y.* ***Solution:*** *Case (a)*: The agreement to sell becomes void. But *Y* must pay a reasonable price for 25 cement bags. *Case (b)*: The agreement to sell becomes void. But *Y* must pay a reasonable price for 25 cement bags. However, *Y* may maintain a suit for damages against *X*. *Case (c)*: The agreement to sell becomes void. But *Y* must pay a reasonable price for 25 cement bags. However, *X* may maintain a suit for damages against *Y*.

Earnest v. Advance Payment	Earnest means security for the due performance of the contract. Advance payment means the payment of the price of the goods in advance which is to be adjusted against the ultimate total price of the goods. If the contract is not or cannot be performed by the fault of the buyer, the seller may forfeit the earnest and not the advance payment. The party not at fault may maintain a suit for damages against the party in fault.

14.0 IS STIPULATION AS TO TIME AN ESSENCE OF CONTRACT ?

Stipulation as to time of payment is not deemed to be an essence of a contract of sale unless a different intention appears from the terms of the contract. [Section 11]

Other Stipulation as to Time Whether any other stipulation as to time is of the essence of the contract or not depends on the terms of the contract.

15.0 CONDITIONS AND WARRANTIES

It is usual for both seller and buyer to make representations to each other at the time of entering into a contract of sale. Some of these representations are mere opinions which do not form a part of contract of sale. Whereas some of them may become a part of contract of sale. Representations which become a part of contract of sale are termed as stipulations which may rank as condition and warranty *e.g.* a mere commendation of his goods by the seller doesn't become a stipulation and gives no right of action to the buyer against the seller as such representations are mere opinion on the part of the seller. But where the seller assumes to assert a fact of which the buyer is ignorant, it will amount to a stipulation forming an essential part of the contract of sale.

Meaning of Stipulation	A stipulation in a contract of sale of goods may be a condition or warranty [Section 12(1)].
Meaning of Condition	A condition is a stipulation— (a) which is essential to the main purpose of the contract, and (b) the breach of which gives the aggrieved party a right to terminate the contract. [Section 12(2)]. **Example** *X asked a car dealer to suggest him a car suitable for touring purposes. The dealer suggested a 'Buggati Car'. Accordingly, X purchased it but found it unsuitable for touring purpose. In this case, suitability of car for touring purpose was a condition of contract. X was, therefore entitled to reject the car and have refund of the price paid. [Baldry v. Marshall]*
Meaning of Warranty	A warranty is a stipulation— (a) which is collateral to the main purpose of the contract, and (b) the breach of which gives the aggrieved party a right to claim damages but not a right to reject goods and to terminate the contract. [Section 12(3)]. **Example** *X asked a car dealer to suggest him a good car and while suggesting the car, the dealer said that it could*

	run for 20 km per litre of petrol. But the car could run only 15 kms per litre of petrol. In this case, the statement made by the seller was a warranty. X was, therefore not entitled to reject the car but he was entitled to claim the damages.
How to Determine	Whether stipulation is a contract of sale is condition or a warranty depends in each case on the construction of the contract. Stipulation may be a condition though called a warranty in the contract.

15.1 Distinction Between Condition and Warranty

A condition can be distinguished from a warranty as under:

Basis of Distinction	***Condition***	***Warranty***
1. ***Essential vs. Collateral***	It is a stipulation which is essential to the main purpose of the contract.	It is a stipulation which is only collateral to the main purpose of the contract.
2. ***Right in case of breach***	The aggrieved party can terminate the contract.	The aggrieved party can claim damages but cannot termi-nate contract.
3. ***Treatment***	A breach of condition can be treated as a breach of war-ranty. For example, a buyer may like to retain the goods and claim only damages.	A breach of warranty cannot be treated as a breach of condition.

15.2 When Condition to be treated as Warranty ? [Section 13]

In the following three cases, a breach of a condition is treated as a breach of a warranty:

(a) where the buyer waives a condition; once the buyer waives a condition, he cannot insist on its fulfilment e.g. accepting defective goods or beyond the stipulated time amounts to waiving a condition.

(b) where the buyer elects to treat breach of the condition as a breach of warranty; e.g. where he claims damages instead of repudiating the contract.

(c) where the contract is not severable and the buyer has accepted the goods or part thereof, the breach of any condition by the seller can only be treated as a breach of warranty. It can not be treated as a ground for rejecting the goods unless otherwise specified in the contract. Thus, where the buyer after purchasing the goods finds that some condition is not fulfilled, he cannot reject the goods. He has to retain the goods entitling him to claim damages.

16.0 EXPRESS AND IMPLIED CONDITIONS AND WARRANTIES

In a contract of sale of goods, conditions and warranties may be express or implied.

(a) **Express Conditions and Warranties** These are expressly provided in the contract. **For example**, a buyer desires to buy a SONY TV Model No. 2062. Here, model no. is an express condition. In an advertisement for Khaitan fans, guarantee for 5 years is an express warranty.

(b) **Implied Conditions and Warranties** These are implied by law in every contract of sale of goods unless a contrary intention appears from the terms of the contract. The various implied conditions and warranties have been shown below.

Implied Conditions and Warranties

Implied Conditions

- **(a) Conditions as to title [Section 14(a)]**
- **(b) Conditions in case of sale by description [Section 15]**
- **(c) Conditions in case of sale by sample [Section 17]**
- **(d) Conditions in case of sale by description and sample [Section 15]**
- **(e) Conditions as to quality or fitness [Section 16(1)]**
- **(f) Condition as to merchantable quality [Section 16(2)]**
- **(g) Condition as to wholesome-ness**
- **(h) Condition implies by custom [Section 16(3)]**

Implied Warranties

- **(a) Warranty as to quiet possession [Section 14(b)]**
- **(b) Warranty of freedom from encumbrances [Section 14(c)]**
- **(c) Warranty as top quality or fitness for particular purpose annexed by uisage of trade [Section 16(3)]**

17.0 WHAT ARE THE IMPLIED CONDITIONS ?

17.1 Condition as to Title [Section 14(a)] There is an implied condition on the part of the seller that (i) in the case of a sale, he has a right to sell the goods, and (ii) in the case of an agreement to sell, he will have a right to sell the goods at the time when the property is to pass.

Note: The term 'right to sell' is wider than 'right to pass ownership'.

Example I *X purchased a car from Y. After 6 months Z, the true owner of car, demanded it from X. X had to return it to its true owner. X was entitled to recover the full price even though several months had passed. [Rowland v. Divall]*

Example II *X purchased from Y tins of condensed milk bearing the label 'N BRAND.' It is proved that there was an infringement of trademark. X had to remove the labels and sold the tin at a loss. X was entitled to sue Y for breach of implied condition that Y had the right to sell. [Niblett Ltd. v. Confectioner's Materials Co.]*

Example III *X (a buyer in Chor Bazaar) purchased some stolen goods from Y, a thief. Z, the true owner of stolen goods, demanded it from X. X had to return it to its true owner. X is not entitled to sue Y because the knowledge of the buyer has negatived the implied condition as to title.*

17.2 Sale by Description [Section 15] Where there is a contract of sale of goods by description, there is an implied condition that the goods shall correspond with description. The main idea is that the goods supplied must be same as were described by the seller. Sale of goods by description include many situations as under:

(i) **Where the buyer has never seen the goods and buys them only on the basis of description given by the seller.**

Example *X bought a reaping machine from Y who described it to be one year old and used only to cut 50 to 60 acres but X found that the machine extremely old. X was entitled to reject the machine because machine did not correspond with the description given by the seller. [Varley v. Whipp.]*

(ii) **Where the buyer has seen the goods but he buys them only on the basis of description given by the seller.**

Example *The buyer bought after seeing certain goods which were described by the seller as "dating from seventeenth century" but he found them of eighteenth century. The buyer was entitled to reject the goods because goods did not correspond with the description given by the seller. [Nicholson and Venn v. Smith Marriott]*

(iii) **Where the method of packing has been described.**

Example *X purchased from Y 5000 tins of canned fruit to be packed in cases each containing 50 tins but Y supplied cases containing 25 tins. X was entitled to reject the goods because the goods were not packed according to the description. [Moore & Co. v. Landauer & Co.]*

Note: If the goods do not correspond with the description but such goods are fit for buyer's purpose, even then the buyer may reject the goods and the seller cannot take the defence by saying that the goods will serve the buyer's purpose. [*Arcos* v. *Ranaason & Sons*]

17.3 Sale by Sample [Section 17] A contract of sale is a contract for sale by sample when there is a term in the contract, express or implied, to that effect. Such sale by sample is subject to the following **three** conditions:

(i) The goods must correspond with the sample in quality.

(ii) The buyer must have a reasonable opportunity of comparing the bulk with the sample.

(iii) The goods must be free from any defect which renders them unmerchantable and which would not be apparent on reasonable examination of the sample. Such defects are called latent defects and are discovered when the goods are put to use. It may be noted that the seller cannot be held liable for apparent or visible defects which could be easily discovered by an ordinary prudent person.

Example *X bought from Y certain quantity of worsted coating equal to sample. The coating was equal to sample but due to a latent defect, the cloth was found to be unfit for making coats. The buyer was entitled to reject the goods because the defect contained in the sample was not apparent on reasonable examination of the sample. [Drummond & Sons v. Van Ingen]*

17.4 Sale by Sample as well as by Description [Section 15] If the sale is by sample as well as by description, the goods must correspond with the sample as well as the description.

Example *X bought from Y foreign refined rapeseed oil which was warranted to be equal to sample. The oil supplied was equal to the sample. The sample was actually a mixture of rapeseed oil and hemp oil. X was entitled to reject the goods because the goods supplied did not correspond with the description. [Nichol v. Godts]*

17.5 Condition as to Quality or Fitness [Section 16(1)] There is no implied condition as to the quality or fitness for any particular purpose of goods supplied under a contract of sale. In other words, the buyer must satisfy himself about the quality as well as the suitability of the goods. This is expressed by the maxim *caveat emptor* (let the buyer beware).

Exception to this Rule: There is an implied condition that the goods shall be reasonably fit for a particular purpose described if the following **three** conditions are satisfied:

(i) **The particular purpose for which goods are required must have been disclosed (expressly or impliedly) by the buyer to the seller.**

Note: This condition need not be fulfilled if the goods can be used only for a particular purpose.

(ii) **The buyer must have relied upon the seller's skill or judgement.**

(iii) **The seller's business must be to sell such goods.**

Note: This condition cannot be invoked against a casual seller.

Example I *X purchased a hot water bottle from Y, retail chemist. X asked Y if it would stand boiling water. The Chemist told him that the bottle was meant to hold hot water. The bottle burst when water was poured into it and injured his wife. The chemist is liable to refund the price and pay damages because bottle was unfit for the purpose for which it was purchased.* *[Priest v. Last]*

Example II *X asked a car dealer to suggest him car suitable for touring purposes. The dealer suggested a 'Buggati Car.' Accordingly, X purchased it but found it unsuitable for touring purpose. The car dealer is liable for breach of condition as to fitness because X who relied upon his skill and judgement is entitled to reject the car and have refund of the price paid.* *[Baldry v. Marshall]*

Example III *X bought a refrigerator without asking the dealer whether it is fit to make ice. Refrigerator failed to make ice. The dealer is liable to refund the price because refrigerator was unfit for the purpose for which it was meant for and the buyer was not required to disclose this particular purpose.*

[Evens v. Stelle Benjamin]

Example IV *X bought a set of false teeth from Y a Dentist. But the set was not fit for X's mouth. X rejected the set of teeth and claimed the refund of price. It was held that X was entitled to do so as the only purpose for which he wanted the set of teeth was not fulfilled.* *[Dr. Baretto v. T.R. Pruce]*

Circumstances under which Condition as to Fitness not Applicable [Provision to Section 16(1)]:

(i) **Where the buyer fails to disclose to the seller any abnormal circumstances.**

Example *X bought tweed coat and found unfit for her abnormally sensitive skin. The seller was not liable because the cloth was fir for anyone with a normal skin and she did not inform the seller about her abnormally sensitive skin.*

[Griffiths v. Peter Conway Ltd.]

(ii) **Where the buyer buys a specified article under its patent or other trade name and does not rely upon the skill and judgement of the seller.**

Example *X asks a chemist to supply 'Bournvita' as health drink. He found no improvement in his health in spite of its prolonged use. He is not entitled to claim any compensation because there was no condition as to fitness because goods are bought under patent name.*

Tutorial ***Note:*** *The implied condition as to fitness for a particular purpose applies to goods whether or not the buyer has examined the goods.*

17.6 **Condition as to Merchantable Quality [Section 16(2)]** Where the goods are bought by description from a seller who deals in goods of that description (whether he is the manufacturer or producer or not), there is an implied condition that the goods shall be of merchantable quality. The expression 'merchantable quality' means that the quality and condition of the goods must be such that a man of ordinary prudence would accept them as the goods of that description. Goods must be free from any latent or hidden defects.

Example I *X bought from a dealer a bottle of wine. While opening its cork in the normal manner, the bottle broke off and injured X's hands. X was entitled to claim damages because the bottle was not of merchantable quality.*

[Morelli v. Fitch & Gibbons]

Example II *X a dealer sold a plastic catapult to B. While using the catapult in the usual manner, it broke due to the fact that the materials used in its manufacture were unsuitable. As a result the boy who was using was blinded in one eye. The seller was liable because the goods were not of merchantable quality.*

[Godley v. Perry]

Example III *X bought some cooking coal from Y a coal dealer for his domestic use. However, the coal contained an explosive substance which exploded and caused injury to X. It was held that the coal was not of merchantable quality as it was not fit for using as cooking coal. X was entitled to claim damages from Y.*

[Wilson v. Rickett Cackerrel & Co.]

Circumstances under which Condition as to Merchantable Quality not Applicable [Provision to Section 16(2)]: There shall be no implied conditions as regards defects which the buyer could have discovered if the buyer has examined the goods.

Example *X purchased glue from Y. The glue was packed in barrels and every facility was given to X for its examination but X did not examine the contents. X could not reject the goods by saying that they are not merchantable because opportunity of examining the goods was given to X but he did not examine.*

[Thornett & Fehs v. Beers & Sons]

Notes: (i) The implied condition as to merchantable quality applies to goods whether or not the goods are sold under a patent or trade name.

(ii) The implied condition as to merchantable quality applies to goods whether or not the buyer relies on the skill and judgement of the seller.

17.7 **Condition as to Wholesomeness** In case of eatables or provisions or foodstuffs, there is an implied condition as to wholesomeness. Condition as to wholesomeness means that the goods shall be fit for human consumption.

Example *X bought milk from Y's dairy. The milk contained typhoid terms. X's wife consumed milk, became infected and died. Y was liable for damages because the milk was not fit for human consumption* *[Frost v. Aylesbury Dairy Co. Ltd.]*

17.8 **Condition Implied by Custom [Section 16(3)]** Condition as to quality or fitness for a particular purpose may be annexed by the usage of trade.

Example *X sold certain drugs by auction to Y. In case of sale by auction, there was a trade custom to declare any sea damage in the goods. But the goods were sold without such declaration. Such goods were found to be sea damaged. It was held Y could reject the goods and claim the refund of the price because the sale without such declaration meant that the goods were free from any sea damage.*

[Jones v. Bowden]

18.0 WHAT ARE THE IMPLIED WARRANTIES ?

18.1 Warranty as to Quiet Possession [Section 14(b)] There is an implied warranty that the buyer shall have and enjoy quiet possession of the goods. The reach of this warranty gives buyer a right to claim damages from the seller.

Example *X sold a second hand Radio to Y who spent Rs 100 on the repairs of this radio. This radio was seized by the police as it was a stolen one. Y filed a suit against X for the recovery of damages for breach of warranty of quite possession including the cost of repairs. It was held that Y was entitled to recover the same*

[Mason v. Burmingham]

18.2 Warranty of Freedom from Encumbrances [Section 14(c)] There is an implied warranty that the goods are free from any charge or encumbrance in favour of any third person if the buyer is not aware of such charge or encumbrance. The breach of this warranty gives buyer a right to claim damages from the seller.

Example *X borrowed Rs 500 from Y and hypothecated his radio with Y as security. Later on X sold this radio to Z who bought in good faith. Here, Z can claim damages from X because his possession is disturbed by Y having a charge.*

18.3 Warranty as to Quality or Fitness for a Particular Purpose which may be Annexed by the Usage of Trade [Section 16(3)]

18.4 Warranty to Disclose Dangerous Nature of Goods In case of goods of dangerous nature the seller must disclose or warn the buyer of the probable danger. If the seller fails to do so, the buyer may make him liable for breach of implied warranty.

Example *X purchased a tin of disinfectant powder which required to be opened with special care. X's wife while opening the tin was injured as the powder flew into her eyes. Held, the seller was liable for the injury sustained by X's wife because of breach of warranty*

[Clarke v. Army and Navy Cooperative Society Ltd. (1903) 1 KB 155]

19.0 MEANING AND EXCEPTION TO THE DOCTRINE OF CAVEAT EMPTOR

Meaning	The expression 'Caveat Emptor' means 'let the buyer beware.' The doctrine of caveat emptor has been given in the first para of Section 16 which reads as under: "*Subject to the provisions of this Act and any other law for the time being in force, there is no implied warranty or condition as to the quality or fitness for any particular purpose of goods supplied under a contract of sale*". In other words, it is not part of the seller's duty to point out defects of the goods which he offers for sale, rather it is the duty of the buyer to satisfy himself about the quality as well as the suitability of the goods. **Example** *Pigs were sold subject to all faults and the seller knew that the pigs were suffering from swine-fever but he did not inform the buyer about this defect. The seller was not liable for damages because there was no implied warranty.* *[Ward v. Hobbs]*

Exceptions	The doctrine of caveat emptor is subject to the following exceptions: **(a) In Case of Misrepresentation by the Seller** Where the seller makes a misrepresentation and the buyer relies on that representation. **(b) In Case of Concealment of Latent Defect** Where the seller knowingly conceals a defect which would not be discovered on a reasonable examination. **(c) In Case of Sale by Description [Section 15]** Where the goods are sold by description and the goods supplied by the seller do not correspond to the description. **(d) In Case of Sale by Sample [Section 17]** Where the goods are sold by sample and the goods supplied by the seller do not correspond with the sample. **(e) In Case of Sale by Sample as well as Description [Section 15]** Where the goods are sold by sample as well as description and the goods supplied do not correspond with sample as well as description. **(f) Fitness for a Particular Purpose [Section 16(1)]** Where the seller or a manufacturer is a dealer of the type of goods sole by him and the buyer has disclosed the purpose for which goods are required and relied upon the seller's skill or judgement. **(g) Merchantable Quality [Section 16(2)]** Where the goods are bought by description from a seller who deals in goods of that description (whether he is the manufacturer *or* producer *or* not), there is an implied condition that goods shall be of merchantable quality.
Relevance	The rule of Caveat Emptor appeared to play an important role in the past when trade was conducted on local scale and the buyer had every opportunity to examine the goods before buying. However, in the modern context, the rigours of the rule have been mitigated because of global dimensions of trade, government legislations on consumer protection, professional management, intense competition and consumer awareness. In fact, the rule of caveat emptor should be replaced by the rule of ***'caveat vendor'*** (*Let the seller beware*).

20.0 WHAT IS THE MEANING AND SIGNIFICANCE OF PASSING OF PROPERTY ?

20.1 Meaning of Passing of Property

Passing of property implies transfer of ownership and not the physical possession of goods. For example, where a principal sends goods to his agent, he merely transfers the physical possession and not the ownership of goods. Here, the principal is the owner of the goods but is not having possession of goods and the agent is having possession of goods but is not the owner.

20.2 Significance of Passing of Property

The time of transfer of ownership of goods decides various rights and liabilities of the seller and the buyer. Thus, it becomes very important to know the exact time of transfer of ownership of goods from seller to buyer to answer the following questions:

(*a*) ***Who shall bear the risk:*** It is the owner who has to bear the risk and not the person who merely has the possession.

(*b*) ***Who can take action against third party:*** It is the owner who can take action and not the person who merely has the possession.

(*c*) ***Whether a seller can sue for price:*** The seller can sue for the price only if the ownership of goods has been transferred to the buyer.

(*d*) ***In case of insolvency of a buyer whether the official receiver or assignee can take the possession of goods from seller:*** The Official Receiver or Assignee can take the possession of goods from seller only if the ownership of goods has been transferred to the buyer.

(*e*) ***In case of insolvency of a seller whether the official receiver or assignee can take the possession of goods from buyer:*** The official receiver or assignee can take the possession of goods from buyer only if the ownership of goods has not been transferred to the buyer.

21.0 WHAT ARE THE RULES RELATING TO THE TRANSFER OF OWNERSHIP OF SPECIFIC GOODS OR ASCERTAINED GOODS ?

21.1 Meaning of Specific Goods [Section 2(14)] Specific goods mean goods identified and agreed upon at the time when a contract of sale is made.

21.2 General Rule [Section 19(1)] The ownership of specific goods or ascertained goods is transferred to the buyer at such time as the parties intend it to be transferred.

21.3 Ascertainment of the Intention [Sections 19(2), 19(3), 20, 21, 22, 23] For the purpose of ascertaining the intention of the parties, regard shall be had to the terms of the contract, the conduct of the parties and the circumstances of the case [Section 19(2)]. Unless a different intention appears, the following rules are applicable [Section 19(3)]:

Case	***Time when the ownership is transferred***
I. Where there is an unconditional contract for sale of specific goods in a deliverable state [Section 20] ***Notes:*** *(i) Unconditional contract means a contract containing no condition regardingthe transfer of ownership.* *(ii) Deliverable state means such state that the buyer would be bound to take delivery of the goods under the contract.* *(iii) It is immaterial whether the time of payment of the price or the delivery of goods, or both is postponed.*	When the contract is made. [*Refer to Example I*]

II. Where there is a contract for sale of specific goods not in a deliverable state [Section 21]	When the goods are put into a deliverable state and the buyer has notice thereof. [*Refer to Example II*] ***Note:*** Where the seller undertakes to put the goods on rail or any other means of transportation, the ownership shall remain with the seller till the goods are loaded. [*Underwood Ltd.* v. *Burgh*]
III. Where there is a contract for sale of specific goods in a deliverable state but the seller has to do some act to ascertain the price [Section 22]	When the seller has done that act to ascertain the price and the buyer has notice thereof. [*Refer to Example III*]

Example I *X bought from Y a heap of wheat the weight of which is 1,000 kg at the rate of Rs 8 per kg, and agrees to pay the price on the first day of the next month and the wheat is to be delivered at X's godown on the following day. A fire broke out and the entire quantity of wheat was destroyed. In this case X is liable to pay the price because the ownership of wheat has transferred from Y to X on making the contract even though the price has not been paid and the goods have not been delivered.*

Example II *X bought from Y a heap of wheat (weight 100 kg) at the rate of Rs 8 per kg, and Y had to put the wheat in bags to deliver it to X. Y filled some bags in X's presence, but before the remainder could be filled, a fire broke out and the entire quantity of wheat was destroyed. In this case, X is liable to pay the price for the wheat which was put into bags because the ownership in respect of these goods has passed when Y has put the wheat in bags and the buyer has notice thereof.*
[Rugg v. Minett]

Example III *X bought from Y a heap of wheat at a rate of Rs 8 per kg and Y had to weigh the wheat. Before weighing was completed, the wheat was destroyed by fire. In this case, X is not liable to pay the price because the ownership of goods has not passed from Y to X.* *[Zagury v. Furnell]*

22.0 WHAT ARE THE RULES RELATING TO THE TRANSFER OF OWNERSHIP OF UNASCERTAINED GOODS AND FUTURE GOODS ?

22.1 Meaning of Unascertained Goods Unascertained goods means goods which have not been identified and agreed upon at the time when contract of sale is made.

22.2 Meaning of Future Goods [Section 2(6)] Future goods means goods to be manufactured or produced or acquired by the seller after the making of the contract of sale.

22.3 Rules [Sections 18 and 23] The ownership of unascertained goods is transferred to the buyer when the following **two** conditions are fulfilled:

(a) the goods must have been ascertained.

Note: Ascertainment is the process of identifying the goods to be sold to the buyer. It is an unilateral act and is usually done by the seller alone.

(b) the goods must have been unconditionally appropriated by the seller or the buyer with the consent of the other.

Notes: (i) Appropriation means an act involving the selection of goods with the intention of using the goods in performance of the contract.

(ii) The consent of the seller or the buyer as to appropriation may be express or implied and may be given before or after the appropriation is made.

(iii) Where the seller delivers the goods to the buyer or to a carrier or other bailee (whether named by the buyer or not) for the purpose of transmission to the buyer and does not reserve the right of disposal, he is deemed to have unconditionally appropriated the goods to the contract.

(iv) The contract to sell unascertained goods is not a complete sale. It is merely an agreement to sell.

Example I *X agreed to sell 100 bags of wheat to Y out of his stock of 500 bags. A fire broke out and the entire quantity of wheat was destroyed. State who shall bear the loss and why in each of the following alternative cases?*

(a) If no bag had been separated before fire for the purposes of delivery to *Y*;

(b) If 100 bags had been separated before fire with *Y*'s consent.

Solution:

Case (*a*): *X* shall bear the loss because the ownership has not transferred to *Y* as the goods were not ascertained.

Case (*b*): *Y* shall bear the loss because the ownership has transferred to *Y* as the goods were ascertained.

Example II *X agreed to sell to Y the oil to be produced by him. The oil was filled by X into the bottles supplied by Y. Here, the ownership passed when the oil was filled into the bottles because the buyer gave his consent to the appropriation by supplying the bottles.* *[Langton v. Higgins]*

23.0 WHAT ARE THE RULES RELATING TO THE TRANSFER OF OWNERSHIP OF GOODS SENT 'ON APPROVAL' OR 'ON SALE OR RETURN' BASIS ?

23.1 **Meaning** Goods sent 'on approval' or 'on sale or return' basis mean those goods in respect of which the buyer has option *either* to return *or* retain.

23.2 **Rules** The various rules relating to the transfer of ownership of such goods have been given below.

Case	*Time when the ownership is transferred*
(a) **When the buyer signifies his approval or acceptance**	When the approval or acceptance is communicated to the seller.
(b) **When the buyer does some act adopting the transaction**	When the act of adoption is done.
(c) **When the buyer fails to return the goods**	
(i) *If a time has been fixed for the return of goods*	On the expiry of fixed time.
(ii) *If no time has been fixed for the return of goods*	On the expiry of the reasonable time. ***Note:*** What is a reasonable time is a question of fact depending upon the facts and circumstances of each case.

Example I *X delivers some goods to Y on "Sale or return" for 7 days. State the legal position in each of the following alternative cases:*

Case (*a*) such goods are destroyed by fire on the third day itself without any fault of *Y*.

Case (*b*) *Y* informs *X* on telephone on the third day itself that he has accepted the goods and immediately after the receiver is put off, the goods are destroyed by fire.

Case (*c*) such goods are further delivered by *Y* on the third day itself to *Z* and then by *Z* to *A* on similar terms. The goods are stolen while in the custody of *A*.

Case (*d*) *Y neither* returns *nor* gives notice of rejection even after the expiry of 7 days. Goods are destroyed by fire on the eighth day.

Case (*e*) *Y* retains the goods but gives the notice of rejection on the expiry of 7 days. Goods are destroyed by fire on the eighth day.

Solution:

Case (*a*): *X* shall bear the loss because the ownership has not yet passed to the buyer. [*Elphick* v. *Barnes*]

Case (*b*): *Y* shall bear the loss because the ownership has passed to the buyer.

Case (*c*): *X* can recover the loss from *Y* because the ownership passed to *Y* as *Y* has adopted the transaction by delivering the goods to *Z*. *Y* can recover the loss from *Z* because the ownership has passed to *Z* as *Z* has adopted the transaction by delivering the goods to *A*. *Z* cannot recover the loss from *A* because the ownership has not yet passed.

[*Genn* v. *Winkel*]

Case (*d*): *Y* shall bear the loss because the ownership has passed to the buyer.

Case (*e*): *X* shall bear the loss because the ownership has not yet passed.

Example II *X delivered some jewellery to Y on 'sale or return' without specifying any time for its return in case of non-acceptance. State the legal position in each of the following alternative cases:*

Case (*a*) If *Y* pledges the jewellery with *Z*.

Case (*b*) If *X* makes it clear that the goods are to remain his property until paid for. Before *Y* pays the price, he pledges the jewellery with *Z*.

Case (*c*) If *Y neither* accepts *nor* rejects within one month and after a month a burglary takes place in *Y*'s house and the jewellery is stolen.

Solution:

Case (*a*): *X* can recover the price of the jewellery from *Y* because ownership has passed to *Y* as *Y* had adopted the transaction by pledging the jewellery with *Z*. But *X* cannot recover the jewellery from *Z*.

[*Kirkham* v. *Attenborough*]

Case (*b*): *X* can recover the jewellery from *Z* because the pledge was not valid as the ownership has not yet transferred to *Y*. [*Weiner* v. *Smith*]

Case (*c*): *X* can sue *Y* for the price of the jewellery because a reasonable time to reject has expired. As such, the ownership has transferred to *Y*.

[*Hooghly Chinsurah Municipality* v. *Spence Ltd.*]

24.0 RESERVATION OF RIGHT OF DISPOSAL

24.1 Can a Seller Reserve the Right of Disposal of the Goods ? [Section 25(1)]

Where there is a contract for the sale of specific goods or where goods are subsequently appropriated to the contract, the seller may reserve the right of disposal of the goods until certain conditions are fulfilled.

24.2 When Ownership is transferred in Case of Reservation of Right of Disposal ? [Section 25(1)]

In such a case, the ownership of goods will not be transferred to the buyer until the conditions imposed by the seller are fulfilled even if the goods have already been delivered to the buyer or to a carrier or other bailee for the purpose of transmitting the same to the buyer.

24.3 What are the Modes of Reservation ?

The seller may reserve the right of disposal of goods *either* expressly *or* by implication. In the following **two** cases, the seller is deemed to have reserved the right of disposal to himself.

(a) **In case of Goods Deliverable to the Order of Seller or his Agent [Section 25(2)]** Where the goods are shipped or delivered to a railway administration for carriage and by the bill of lading or railway receipt, as the case may be, they are deliverable to the order of seller or his agent.

Example *X sold some goods to Y with the terms that the goods shall be sent by railway. The goods were destroyed in the course of journey. State the legal position (i) if railway receipt is taken in the name of X, (ii) if railway receipt is taken in the name of Y but is sent through Bank, (iii) if railway receipt is taken in the name of Y and is sent to him.*

Solution:

Cases (*i*) and (*ii*): *X* will have to bear the loss because the ownership has not yet been transferred. [*General Papers Ltd.* v. *P. Mohideen & Sons*]

Case (*iii*): *Y* will have to bear the loss because the ownership has already been transferred.

(b) **In case of Drawing a Bill of Exchange [Section 25(3)]** Where the seller of goods draws on the buyer for the price of the goods and sends the bill of exchange together with the bill of lading or railway receipt, the ownership of goods will not be transferred to the buyer until the buyer honours the bill of exchange. The buyer must return the bill of lading or the railway receipt if he does not honour the bill of exchange, and if he wrongfully retains the bill of lading or the railway receipt, the ownership of goods will not be transferred.

Example *X sold some goods to Y, took the bill of lading in Y's name and drew a Bill of Exchange on Y and delivered bill of lading and Bill of exchange to his banker with the instruction to deliver the bill of lading to Y on his accepting and paying the amount of the bill. Initially, Y refused to accept the offer and sold the goods to Z. It was held that the banker was liable to Y for making the wrongful sale to Z because the ownership was transferred to Y when he offered to pay the amount.*

[Mirabita v. Imperial Ottoman Bank]

25.0 DOES RISK PRIMA FACIE PASS WITH PROPERTY

25.1 Meaning of General Rule

Risk means the liability to bear the loss if the goods are lost or damaged. The general rule is that the risk follows ownership. In other words, risk and ownership go together. This general rule implies that it is the owner of the goods who has to bear the loss and not the person who merely has the possession of goods. Thus, this general rule can be summarised as under:

Case	*Party who has to bear the loss*
(a) If the ownership has not been transferred to the buyer.	The seller has to bear the loss because he is the owner at the time of loss.
(b) If the ownership has been transferred to the buyer	The buyer has to bear the loss because he is the owner at the time of loss. It is immaterial whether delivery has been made or not.

Example I *X selects some books from Y's books shop and agrees to pay the price after 20 days and the books are to be delivered at X's house on the following day. These books were destroyed as a result of fire in the shop. The loss is to be borne by X because at the time of loss of books, he had become the owner of the books even if the delivery has not been made and the price has not been paid.*

Example II *X selects some books from Y's book shop and asks the seller whether he can return after 2 days if he does not like. The seller agrees but asks the buyer to deposit the price of those books. The buyer agrees thereto. On the very same day, the books were destroyed as result of fire in X's house. The loss is to be born by Y because at the time of loss of books, he was the owner of the books even if the delivery has been made.*

25.2 Exceptions to the General Rule 'Risk Follows Ownership'

The general rule that the risk follows the ownership is subject to the following two exceptions:

(a) Agreement to the Contrary Where the parties have made an agreement to the contrary.

Example *X sold goods to Y with the term that the goods shall be sent by railway and during the transit the goods shall be the property of the seller but they shall be at the risk of the buyer. During the transit the goods were destroyed by an accident. Here Y will have to bear the loss though the ownership of the goods is with X.* *[M. Champalal v. C.P. Shah]*

(b) Delayed Delivery Where the delivery has been delayed through the fault of *either* buyer *or* seller, the party in fault has to bear the loss which might not have occurred but for such fault.

Example *X contracted to sell 100 tons of apple juice to Y. X crushes the apples, puts juice in corks and keeps them ready for delivery. Y took the delivery of part of the juice but made a default to accept the remaining juice. The juice became unfit for consumption. Y will have to bear the loss.*

[Demby Hamilton & Co. Ltd. v. Barden]

(c) Usage of Trade Risk and ownership may be separated by usage of trade.

No Effect on Duties as a Bailee: This general rule shall not affect the duties or liabilities of the seller or the buyer as bailee of goods for the other party even when the risk has passed.

26.0 IS SALE BY NON-OWNERS VALID?

26.1 Meaning of General Rule

The general rule is expressed by the latin maxim "*Namo dat quod non habet,*" which means that "no one can give what he does not himself possess." If the seller's title to the goods is defective, the buyer's title will also be defective because the buyer acquires his title to the goods from the seller. Hence, the seller cannot give a better title to the buyer than he himself has.

Example *X stole a TV and delivered it to Y, an auctioneer. Y sold the TV to Z at auction. It was held that Z obtained no title to the TV because X had no title to it. [Leo v. Byes]*

26.2 Exceptions to the General Rule 'Namo Dat Quod Non Habet'

The circumstances under which a seller can give a better title than what he himself has are discussed below:

Exception to the general rule	*Conditions to be fulfilled before a buyer gets a good title to the goods*
(a) Sale by a Mercantile Agent [Section 27]	(i) The agent must be in possession of goods or a document title (e.g., Railway receipt, Bill of Lading) to the goods with the consent of the owner. (ii) The agent must have sold the goods in the ordinary course of business as a mercantile agent. (iii) The buyer must have acted in good faith. (iv) The buyer must have no knowledge that the seller had no authority to sell. **Example** *P, the owner of the car instructed an agent A to sell his car at not less than Rs 50,000. But A sold the car to B for Rss40,000 and misappropriated the money. B acted in good faith and without notice of the above instruction to agent. Here, B got a good title to the car and the real owner P cannot recover the car from B.* *[Folkes v. King]*
(b) Sale by one of the Joint Owners [Section 28]	(i) The joint owner must be in the sole possession of goods with the consent of other co-owners. (ii) The buyer must have bought the goods in good faith. (iii) The buyer must have no knowledge that the seller had no authorityto sell. **Example** *X, Y and Z were the co-owners of some goods. X was in the possession of those goods with the consent of Y and Z. X sold those goods to B who bought them in good faith and without notice that X had no authority to sell. In this case, B got a good title to the goods and Y and Z cannot recover the goods from B.*
(c) Sale by a Person in possession under voidable contract	(i) The seller must be in possession of goods under a contract voidable u/s 19 or 19A of Indian Contract Act, 1872 on ground of coercion, undue influence, misrepresentation or fraud.

<table>
<tr><td></td><td>(ii) The goods must have been sold before the contract is rescinded.
(iii) The buyer must have bought the goods in good faith.
(iv) The buyer must have no knowledge that the seller's title is defective.
Example X, by fraud obtained the possession of a diamond ring from Y. X sold the ring to B before Y rescinded the contract. B bought the ring in good faith and without notice of X's defective title. B got a good title and Y cannot recover the ring from B. [Phillips v. Brooks]</td></tr>
<tr><td>(d) Sale by a Seller in possession after sale [Section 30(1)]</td><td>(i) The seller must be in possession of goods or of a document of title to the goods, in the capacity of a seller and not in any other capacity such as bailee.
(ii) The buyer must have bought the goods in good faith.
(iii) The buyer must have no knowl- edge about the previous sale.
Example X sold two TV sets to Y with the terms that one to be delivered immediately and another to be delivered after 2 days. Later on, Y delivered the first TV to X for some minor repair. X resold the first TV to P and the second to Q. Both P and Q bought in good faith and without notice of the previous sale.
Here, Q got a good title to the TV but P did not get good title because X was in the possession of TV in the capacity of a bailee and not in the capacity of a seller.</td></tr>
<tr><td>(e) Sale by a Buyer in possession before the transfer of ownership [Section 30(2)]</td><td>(i) The buyer must be in possession of the goods or a document of title to the goods, with the consent of the original seller and must have bought or agreed to buy the goods.
(ii) The new buyer must have bought the goods in good faith.
(iii) The new buyer must have no knowledge about any lien or other right of the original seller in respect of goods.
Example X takes the delivery of a furniture from Y under an agreement which provides for (a) an immediate down payment of Rs 300, (b) the balance by way of 12 monthly instalments of Rs 100 each, (c) transfer of ownership on the payment of last instalment, (d) Y's right to repossess the goods in case of non-payment of</td></tr>
</table>

	instalments due. Before the 12th instalment was paid, X sold the furniture to Z. Can Y recover the furniture from Z? State your answer in each of following cases. *Case (a):* If the agreement does not provide for any other stipulation. *Case (b):* If the agreement also provides that *X* can return the goods. ***Solution:*** *Case (a): Y* cannot recover the furniture from *Z* because it was a contract of sale (as *X* was not having any option to return but was under compulsion to buy) and not hire-purchase agreement. *Case: (b): Y* can recover the furniture from *Z* because it was a hire-purchase agreement (as *X* was having an option to return) and hence, *X* was not having any title to it. ***Note:*** A buyer (being hirer in case of a hire purchase agreement) cannot transfer a valid title to the new buyer because an 'option to buy does not amount to an 'agreement to buy'.
(f) Sale by an Unpaid Seller [Section 54(3)]	An unpaid seller must have exercised his right of lien or stoppage in transit.
(g) Sale by a Finder of Goods [Section 169 of Indian Contract Act 1872]	(i) The owner cannot be found with reasonable diligence; or (ii) The owner, if found refuses to pay the lawful charges of finder; or (iii) If the goods are in danger of perishing or of losing the greater part of its value; or (iv) If the lawful charges of the finder in respect of the thing found amounts to two third of its value.
(h) Sale by a Pawnee or Pledgee	(i) The pawnor or pledger must have made a default in the payment of the debt or the performance of the promise at the stipulated time.
	(ii) The pawnee or pledgee must have given a reasonable notice to the pawnor or pledger.
(i) Sale by Official Receiver or Assignee or Liquidator	The involvement person must be the owner of goods.
(j) Sale by Owner by Estoppel	The owner of the goods by his statement or conduct must have lead the buyer to believe that the seller has the authority to sell.

	Example *X told Y, a buyer in the presence of Z that he (X) is the owner of the TV. But Z remained silent though the TV belonged to him. Y bought the TV from X. Here, Y will get a valid title to the TV even though X had no title to the TV because Z by his own conduct is prevented from denying X's authority to sell the TV.*

27.0 DELIVERY

27.1 Meaning of Delivery [Section 2(2)]

Delivery means the voluntary transfer of possession from one person to another.

27.2 Mode of Delivery [Section 33]

Delivery of goods may be made—

(a) by doing anything which the parties agree shall be treated as delivery, or

(b) by doing anything which has the effect of putting the goods into the buyer's or his authorised agent's possession.

27.3 Types of Delivery

The delivery of goods may be of the following three types:

Actual Delivery	Delivery is said to be actual where the goods are physically handed over to the buyer or his authorised agent. **For example**, *X* sells to *Y* 100 bags of wheat lying in *Z*'s warehouse. *X* orders *Z* to deliver the wheat to *Y*. *Z* delivers to *Y*. In this case there is an actual delivery of goods.
Symbolic Delivery	Delivery is said to be symbolic where some symbol of the real possession or control over the goods is handed over to buyer. **For example**, *X* sells to *Y* 100 bags of wheat lying in *Z*'s warehouse and hands over the key of *Z*'s warehouse to *Y*. In this case, there is symbolic delivery of goods.
Constructive Delivery	Delivery is said to be constructive where a person who is in possession of the goods, acknowledges to hold the goods on behalf of the buyer. **For example**, *X* sells to *Y* 100 bags of wheat lying in *Z*'s warehouse. *Y* orders *Z* to deliver the wheat to *Y*. *Z* agrees to hold the 100 bags of wheat on behalf of *Y* and makes the necessary entry in his books. In this case, there is constructive delivery of goods.

27.4 Rules as to Delivery [Sections 32 to 39]

The various rules as to delivery have been discussed below:

1. **Payment and Delivery to be Concurrent [Section 32]** Unless otherwise agreed, delivery of the goods and payment of the price are concurrent conditions, that is to say, the seller must be ready and willing to give possession of the goods to the buyer and the buyer must be ready and willing to pay the price.
2. **Mode of Delivery [Section 33]** Delivery must have the effect of putting the goods into the buyer's or his authorised agent's possession.

3. **Effect of Part Delivery [Section 34]** A delivery of part of goods with an intention of giving the delivery of the whole amounts to the delivery of the whole for the purpose of transfer of ownership of goods, but a delivery of part of goods with an intention of separating it from the whole lot does not amount to the delivery of the whole of the goods.
4. **Buyer to Apply for Delivery [Section 35]** Unless otherwise agreed, the seller of the goods is not bound to deliver them until the buyer applies for delivery.
5. **Place of Delivery [Section 36(1)]** The various rules as to the place of delivery are summarised as under:

Case	*Place at which goods are to be delviered*
1. ***Where there is a contract as to the place of delivery***	At the agreed place.
2. ***Where there is no contract as to the place of delivery***	
(a) In case of sale	At the place at which the goods are at the time of sale.
(b) In case of an agreement to sell	
(i) in respect of existing goods	At the place at which the goods are at the time of agreement to sell.
(ii) in respect of future goods	At the place at which the goods are manufactured or produced.

6. **Time of Delivery [Section 36(2)]** The various rules as to the time of delivery are summarised as under:

Case	*Time within which goods are to be delivered*
(a) Where there is a contract as to the time of delivery	Within the time agreed.
(b) Where there is no contract as to the time of delivery	Within the reasonable time. *Note:* What is a reasonable time is a question of fact depending upon the facts and circumstances of each case.

7. **Delivery when the Goods are in Possession of a Third Party [Section 36(3)]** Where the goods at the time of sale are in the possession of a third person, there is no delivery by seller unless and until such third person acknowledges to the buyer that he holds the goods on his behalf. However, this provision shall not affect the operation of the issue or transfer of any document of title to goods.
8. **Demand of Delivery to be Treated as Ineffectual [Section 36(4)]** Demand or tender of delivery may be treated as ineffectual unless made at a reasonable hour. What is a reasonable hour is a question of fact.
9. **Expenses of Delivery [Section 36(5)]** Unless otherwise agreed, the expenses of putting the goods into a deliverable state shall be borne by the seller.

10. **Delivery of Wrong Quantity [Section 37]** Subject to any usage of trade, special agreement or course of dealing between the parties, the rules as to the delivery of wrong quantity are summarised below:

Case	*Rights available to the buyer*
I. Short delivery, i.e., where the seller delivers a quantity of goods less than contracted for	(a) The buyer may accept the goods so delivered, or (b) The buyer may reject the goods.
II. Excess delivery, i.e., where the seller delivers a quantity of goods larger than contracted for	(a) The buyer may accept the goods so delivered, (b) The buyer may reject the whole, or (c) The buyer may accept the contracted. quantity and reject the excess.
III. Mixed delivery, i.e., where the seller delivers the goods contracted for mixed with goods of different description ***Note:*** *The mixing of goods with inferior quality does not amount to mixing of goods of different description. [Harnarain v. M/s Radha Krishan Naraindas]*	(a) The buyer may reject the whole, or (b) The buyer may accept the goods which are in accordance with the contract and reject the rest.

Notes: (i) The buyer may not be allowed to reject the goods in case of negligible short or excess delivery.

(ii) In case of short or excess delivery if the buyer rejects the whole quantity, the contract is not treated as cancelled. The seller still has the right to tender again the quantity of goods as per contract and the buyer is bound to accept the same.

[*Vilas Udyog Ltd.* v. *Prag Vanaspati Products*]

11. **Delivery by Instalments [Section 38]** Unless otherwise agreed, the buyer of goods is not bound to accept delivery by instalments.

The question whether the aggrieved party can repudiate the whole contract or not depends upon the terms of the contract and the circumstances of each case where—

(i) The goods are to be delivered in instalments;

(ii) The instalemnts are to be separately paid for;

(iii) The seller makes no delivery or defective delivery in respect of one or more instalments, or the buyer neglects or refuses to take delivery of or pay for one or more instalments.

12. **Delivery to Carrier or Wharfinger [Section 39]** Where the seller is authorised or required to send the goods to the buyer, delivery of the goods to carrier (whether named by the buyer, or not) for the purpose of transmission to the buyer, or delivery of the goods to wharfinger custody, is *prima facie* deemed to be a delivery of the goods to the buyer [Section 39(1)]. The seller is further required to perform the following two duties also.

(a) ***To make a reasonable contract with the carrier or wharfinger:*** Unless otherwise authorised by the buyer, the seller shall make a reasonable contract with the carrier or wharfinger on behalf of the buyer. If the seller omits to do so, and the goods are lost or damaged in course of transit or whilst in the custody of the wharfinger, the buyer may decline to treat the delivery to the carrier or wharfinger as a delivery to himself, or may hold the seller irresponsible for damages [Section 39(2)].

(b) ***To give notice to the buyer to enable him to insure the goods:*** Unless otherwise agreed, where goods are sent by the seller to the buyer by a route involving sea transit, in circumstances in which it is usual to insure, the seller must inform the buyer to enable him to insure them during their sea transit, and if the seller fails to do so, the goods shall be deemed to be at his risk during such transit [Section 39(3)].

Example *X agrees to sell 100 tons of 'Basmati' rice to Y at Rs 40,000 per ton. State the legal position in each of the following alternative cases:*

Case (*a*) If *X* delivers 8 tons of Basmati rice.

Case (*b*) If *X* delivers 12 tons of Basmati rice.

Case (*c*) If *X* delivers 10 tons of Basmati rice and 2 tons of Dehraduni rice.

Case (*d*) If *X* delivers 10 tons of Basmati rice of which 2 tons of inferior quality.

Case (*e*) If *X* delivers 8 tons of Basmati rice in April and the remaining 2 tons in the first week of May.

Case (*f*) If *X* delivers 10 tons of Basmati rice at *Y*'s godown. *Y* refuses to accept them and *neither* returns *nor* informs the seller that he refused to accept the goods.

Case (*g*) If *X* delivers 10 tons of Basmati rice at *Y*'s godown. *Y* refuses to accept them and inform the seller about his intention but does not return the goods.

Case (*h*) If *X* is ready to deliver but *Y* refuses to take delivery and repudiates the contract.

Case (*i*) If *X* delivers 10 tons of Basmati rice and *Y* resells the rice to *Z*. When the rice are delivered to *Y*, he inspected a sample of it and sends it to *Z*. *Z* rejects it as not having according to sample. *Y* rejects the goods.

Case (*j*) If *X* delivers 10 tons 1 kg of Basmati rice and does not charge the buyer with excess quantity.

Solution:

Case (*a*): *Y* has two options: (i) he can reject the goods or (ii) he can accept the goods. [*Beck etc.* v. *Synzmanoski*]

Case (*b*): *Y* has three options, (i) he can reject the whole, (ii) he can accept the whole, or (iii) he can accept 10 tons and can reject 2 tons. If he accepted 12 tons, he must pay for them at the contract rate. [*Cunliffe* v. *Harrison*]

Case (*c*): *Y* has two options: (i) he can reject the whole or (ii) he can accept 10 tons of Basmati rice and can reject 2 tons of Dehraduni rice. [*London Plywood Ltd.* v. *Nasik Oak Ltd.*]

Case (d): *Y* has two options: (i) he can accept the whole, or (ii) he can accept 8 tons of Basmati rice of superior quality and can reject 2 tons of Basmati rice of interior quality.

It may be noted that *Y* cannot reject the whole because mixing of goods with inferior quality does not amount to mixing of goods of different description. [*Harnarain* v. *M/s Radha Krishan Naraindas*]

Case (e): *Y* can reject the whole lot of 10 tons because he is not bound to accept delivery in instalments. [*Renter* v. *Sala*]

Case (f): *Y* is deemed to have accepted the goods after a lapse of reasonable time.

Case (g): *Y* is not deemed to have accepted the goods because he has informed the seller about his intention.

Case (h): *X* can sue *Y* for price and for damages.

Case (i): *Y*'s act in inspecting the sample and then sending the rice to *Z* was an acceptance and he could not afterwards reject it.

[*Perkins* v. *Bell*]

Case (j): *Y* is not entitled to reject the whole quantity of what because the excess delivery of 1 kg was so trivial as to be wholly insignificant.

[*Shipton Anderson & Co.* v. *Weil Brothers & Co. Ltd.*]

27.5 Acceptance of Delivery [Section 42]

Delivery does not amount to acceptance of goods. Acceptance is something more than mere receipt of goods by the buyer. It means the final assent by the buyer that he has received the goods under, and in performance of the contract of sale. The buyer is deemed to have accepted the goods under the following circumstances:

(a) When he intimates to the seller that he has accepted the goods, or

(b) When the goods have been delivered to him and he does any act in relation to them which shows that he has accepted them (for example resale or pledge of goods by buyer), or

(c) When he does not inform the seller that he has rejected the goods and retains the goods beyond a reasonable time.

27.6 Duties and Liabilities of Buyer [Sections 43 and 44]

The duties and liabilities of buyer in various cases are as under:

Case	*Duties and liabilities of buyer*
(a) Where the goods are deliviered to the buyer and he refuses to accept them	The buyer must inform the seller that he refuses to accept them.
(b) Where the seller is ready and willing to deliver the goods and requests the buyer to take delivery and the buyer does not, take delivery of goods within a reasonable time after such request.	The buyer is liable to the seller for— (i) any loss caused by his neglect or refusal to take delivery, and (ii) a reasonable charge for the care and custody of goods.

28.0 WHAT IS THE MEANING OF AN UNPAID SELLER?

The seller of goods is deemed to be 'unpaid seller'—

(a) When the whole of the price has not been paid or tendered.

(b) When a bill of exchange or other negotiable instrument (such as cheque) has been received as conditional payment, and it has been dishonoured [Section 45(1)].

The term 'seller' includes any person who is in the position of a seller (for instance, an agent of the seller to whom the bill of lading has been endorsed, or a consignor or agent who has himself paid, or is directly responsible for the price) [Section 45(2)].

Notes: (i) The seller shall be called an unpaid seller even when only a small portion of the price remains to be paid.

(ii) It is for the non-payment of the price and not for other expenses, that a seller is termed as an unpaid seller.

(iii) Where the goods have been sold on credit, the seller cannot be called as an unpaid seller during the credit period unless the buyer becomes insolvent. On the expiry of credit period if the price remains unpaid, then only the seller will become an unpaid seller.

(iv) Where the full price has been tendered by the buyer and the seller has refused to accept it, the seller cannot be called as unpaid seller.

Example *State whether the seller is an unpaid seller or not in each of the following alternative cases:*

Case (*a*) *X* sold some goods to *Y* for Rs 10,000. *Y* paid Rs 9,900 but failed to pay the balance.

Case (*b*) *X* sold some goods to *Y* for Rs 10,000 and received a cheque for the full price as conditional payment. On presentment, the cheque was dishonoured by the Bank.

Case (*c*) *X* sold some goods to *Y* for Rs 10,000 on a credit of one month. One month has not yet expired.

Case (*d*) *X* sold some goods to *Y* for Rs 10,000 on a credit of one month and one month has expired and the price remains unpaid.

Case (*e*) *X* sold some goods to *Y* for Rs 10,000 on a credit of one month. *Y* became insolvent during the period of credit.

Solution:

Case (a): *X* is an unpaid seller because the full price has not been paid.

Case (b): *X* is an unpaid seller because the cheque received as conditional payment has been dishonoured.

Case (c): *X* is not an unpaid seller because the credit period has not yet expired and the buyer has not yet become insolvent.

Case (d): *X* is an unpaid seller because the price remains unpaid even after the expiry of credit period.

Case (e): *X* is an unpaid seller because the buyer has become insolvent.

28.1 Rights of an Unpaid Seller [Sections 46–52, 54–56, 60–61]

The rights of an unpaid seller can broadly be classified under the following two categories:

I. Rights against the goods

II. Rights against the buyer personally

The various rights of an unpaid seller have been shown.

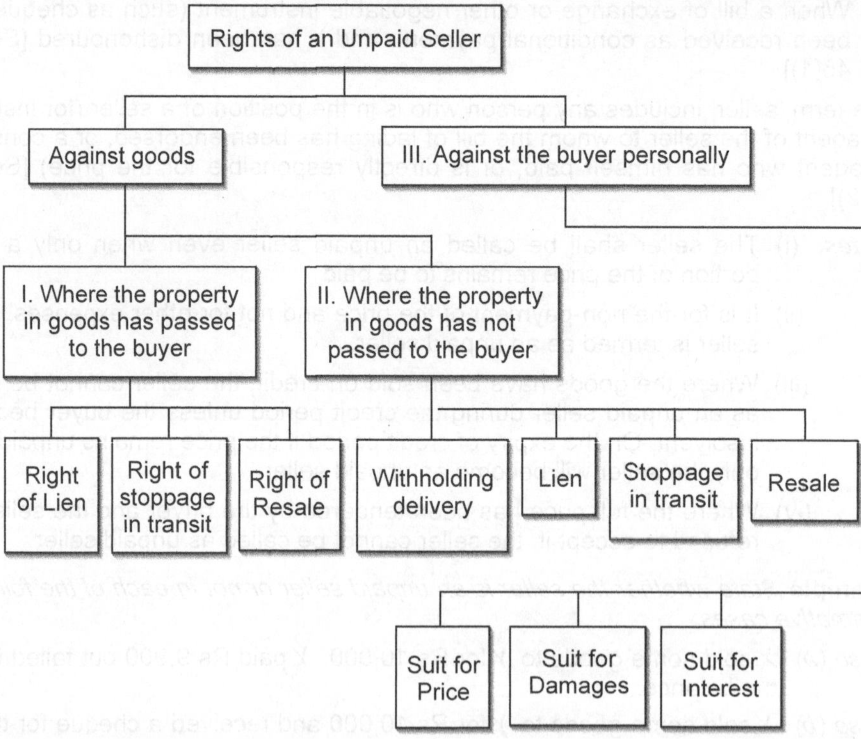

29.0 RIGHT OF LIEN

29.1 Meaning of Right of Lien

The right of lien means the right to retain the possession of the goods until the full price is received.

29.2 Three Circumstances Under Which Right of Lien can be Exercised [Section 47(1)]

The unpaid seller of goods who is in possession of them is entitled to retain possession of them until payment or tender of the price in the following cases, namely:

(i) Where the goods have been sold without any stipulation to credit;

(ii) Where the goods have been sold on credit, but the term of credit has expired; and

(iii) Where the buyer becomes insolvent.

29.3 Other Provisions regarding right of lien [Sections 47(2), 48, 49(2)]

(i) The seller may exercise his right of lien, even if he possesses the goods as agent or bailee for buyer [Section 47(2)].

(ii) Where an unpaid seller has made part delivery of the goods, he may exercise his right of lien on the remainder, unless such part delivery has been made under such circumstances as to show an agreement to waive the lien [Section 48]. In other words, in case of part delivery, this right of lien can be exercised only where part delivery is not intended as delivery of the whole.

(iii) The seller may exercise his right of lien even though he has obtained a decree for the price of the goods [Section 49(2)].

29.4 Circumstances under which Right of Lien is lost [Sections 49(1) and 53(1)]

The unpaid seller losses his right of lien in the following cases:

(i) When he delivers the goods to a carrier or other bailee for the purpose of transmission to the buyer without reserving the right of disposal of the goods [Section 49(1)(a)].

(ii) When the buyer or his agent lawfully obtains possession of the goods [Section 49(1)(b)].

(iii) When the seller waives his right of lien [Section 49(1)(c)].

(iv) When the buyer disposes of the goods by sale or in any other manner with the consent of the seller [Section 53(1)].

(v) Where document of title to goods has been issued or lawfully transferred to any person as buyer or owner of the goods and that person transfers the document by way of sale, to a person who takes the document in good faith and for consideration. [Proviso to Section 53(1)].

Example *State whether a right of lien can be exercised in each of the following alternative cases:*

Case (*a*) *X* sold goods to *Y* for Rs 10,000 without any stipulation as to credit and the price remains unpaid.

Case (*b*) *X* sold goods to *Y* for Rs 10,000 on a credit of 1 month and the period of credit has expired.

Case (*c*) *X* sold goods to *Y* for Rs 10,000 on a credit of 1 month and *Y* became insolvent during the period of credit.

Case (*d*) *X* of Delhi, sold goods to *Y* of Mumbai for Rs 10,000 and delivered the same to the railway for the purpose of transmission to the buyer. The railway receipt was taken in the name of *Y* and sent to *Y*.

Case (*e*) *X* sold goods to *Y* for Rs 10,000 and *Y*'s agent lawfully took the delivery of goods.

Case (*f*) *X* sold goods to *Y* for Rs 10,000 and expressly waived his right of lien.

Case (*g*) *X* sold 10 tons of wheat to *Y* for Rs 1,00,000 and *Y* resold 8 tons of wheat out of 10 tons to *Z*. *Y* instructed *X* to deliver 8 tons of wheat to *Z*. *Y* then became insolvent.

Case (*h*) *X* of Delhi sold some goods to *Y* of Mumbai and took the railway receipt in his own name and sent the railway receipt to his agent.

Case (*i*) *X* of Delhi sold some goods to *Y* of Mumbai and took the railway receipt in the name of *Y* and it was sent by *X* to his agent.

Solution:

Case (*a*): Yes, because the price has not been paid.

Case (*b*): Yes, because the term of credit has expired and the price remains unpaid.

Case (*c*): Yes, because the buyer has become insolvent.

Case (*d*): No, because the delivery to the carrier *prima facie* amounts to the delivery to the buyer himself and the right of disposal of the goods has not been reserved as the railway receipt has been sent to buyer [Section 49(1)(a)].

Case (*e*): No, because buyer's agent has lawfully taken the delivery of the goods [Section 49(1)(b)].

Case (*f*): No, because seller has waived his right of lien [Section 49(1)(c)].

Case (*g*): *X* can exercise his right of lien only against 2 tons of wheat and not against 8 tons of wheat.

Case (*h*): Yes, because the seller is deemed to have reserved the right of disposal of the goods by sending the railway receipt to his own agent.

Case (*i*): Yes, because the seller is deemed to have reserved the right of disposal by sending the railway receipt to his own agent.

30.0 RIGHT OF STOPPAGE OF GOODS IN TRANSIT

30.1 Meaning of Right of Stoppage of Goods in Transit

The right of stoppage in transit means the right of stopping the goods while they are in transit, to regain possession and to retain them till the full price is paid. Lord Cairns LJ in case of *Schotsmans* v. *Lances and Yorks Rly.* had made the following observation in this regard:

"The essential feature of stoppage in transit is that the goods should be in the possession of a middleman or some other person intervening between the vendor who has parted with and the purchaser who has not received them."

30.2 Conditions under which Right of Stoppage in Transit can be Exercised [Section 50]

The unpaid seller can exercise the right of stoppage in transit only if the following conditions are fulfilled:

(i) The seller must have parted with the possession of goods, i.e., the goods must not be in the possession of seller.

(ii) The goods must be in the course of transit.

(iii) The buyer must have become insolvent.

Note: The buyer is said to be insolvent when he has ceased to pay his debts in ordinary course of business, or cannot pay his debts as they become due, whether he has committed an act of insolvency or not.

Note: The seller's right of stoppage in transit is based on the principle that one man's goods shall not be applied to the payment of other man's debt.

[*Lord Reading in Booth Steamship Co Ltd.* v. *Cargo Fleet Iran Co.*]

30.3 Duration of Transit [Section 51(1)]

Goods are deemed to be in course of transit from the time when they are delivered to a carrier or other bailee for the purpose of transmission to the buyer, until the buyer or his agent in that behalf takes delivery of them from such carrier or other bailee.

Note: The carrier must hold the goods in the capacity of an independent person and not in the capacity of an agent for the seller or buyer. If the carrier holds the goods as an agent for the seller, there is no question of exercising the right of stoppage in transit because the seller can exercise his right of lien. If the carrier holds the goods as an agent for the buyer, the seller cannot exercise the right of stoppage in transit because the delivery to the carrier amounts to delivery to buyer.

30.4 Circumstances under which Right of Stoppage is Lost [Sections 51 and 53(1)]

The right of stoppage in transit is lost when transit comes to an end. Transit comes to an end in the following cases:

(i) If the buyer or his agent in that behalf obtains delivery of the goods before their arrival at the appointed destination [Section 51(2)].

(ii) If, after the arrival of the goods at the appointed destination, the carrier or other bailee acknowledges to the buyer or his agent that he holds the goods on his behalf and continues in possession of them as bailee for the buyer or his agent, even if a further destination for the goods may have been indicated by the buyer [Section 51(3)].

(iii) When goods are delivered to a ship chartered by the buyer, it is a question depending on the circumstances of the particular case, whether goods are in the possession of the master as a carrier or as agent of the buyer [Section 51(5)].

(iv) Where the carrier or other bailee wrongfully refuses to deliver the goods to the buyer or his agent in that behalf [Section 51(6)].

(v) Where part delivery of the goods has been made to the buyer or his agent in that behalf, the remainder of the goods may be stopped in transit and such part delivery has not been given in such circumstances as to show an agreement to give up possession of the whole of the goods [Section 5 1(7)].

(vi) Where the sub-sale or other disposition by the buyer has been done with seller's consent [Section 53(1)].

(vii) Where a document of title to goods (e.g., bill of lading or railway receipt) has been issued or lawfully transferred to any person as buyer and that person transfers the document by way of sale to a person who takes the document in good faith and for consideration [Provision to Section 53(1)].

30.5 How to Exercise Right of Stoppage in Transit [Section 52(1)]

The unpaid seller may exercise his right of stoppage in transit in anyone of the following two ways:

(i) by taking actual possession of the goods, or

(ii) by giving notice of his claim to the carrier or other bailee who possesses the goods.

Such notice may be given *either* to the person in actual possession of the goods *or* to his principal. In the latter case, the notice to be effectual shall be given at such time and in such circumstances that the principal, by the exercise of reasonable diligence, may communicate it to his servant or agent in time to prevent a delivery to the buyer.

30.6 Duty of Carrier [Section 51(2)]

When notice of stoppage in transit is given by the seller to the carrier or other bailee in possession of the goods, he shall redeliver the goods to or according to the directions of the seller. The expenses of such redelivery shall be borne by the seller.

31.0 DISTINCTION BETWEEN RIGHT OF LIEN AND RIGHT OF STOPPAGE IN TRANSIT

Basis of Distinction	*Right of Lien*	*Right of Stoppage in transit*
1. *Possession of goods*	The goods must be in actual possession of the seller.	The goods must be in the possession of a carrier or other bailee who is acting as an independent person.
2. *Solvency*	The right can be exercised even when the buyer is solvent but refuses to pay the price.	This right can be exercised only when the buyer has become insolvent.
3. *End vs. Commencement on delivery to carrier*	This right comes to an end when the seller delivers the goods to a carrier.	This right commences only when the seller delivers the goods to a carrier.
4. *Purpose*	The purpose of right is to retain possession of the goods.	The purpose of this right is to regain the possession of the goods.
5. *Mode of exercising the right*	This right can be exercised by the seller himself.	This right can be exercised by the seller through the carrier or the other bailee.

Right of Stoppage in Transit as an Extension of the Right of Lien: The right of stoppage in transit is an extension of the right of lien in the sense that the right of stoppage in transit begins when the right of lien ends and the purpose of the right of stoppage in transit is to regain possession of the goods.

32.0 EFFECT OF SUB-SALE OR PLEDGE BY BUYER

32.1 General Rule The unpaid seller's right of lien or stoppage in transit is not affected by any sale or other disposition of the goods by the buyer [Section 52(1)].

Example *X sold 10 tons of wheat to Y for Rs 1,00,000. Y resold 8 tons of wheat out of 10 tons to Z and instructed X to deliver 8 tons of wheat to Z. X delivered 5 tons of wheat to Z. Later on when Y did not pay the price, X refused to make further deliveries to Z. It was held that X was entitled to refuse further delivery of oil to Z.*

[Mordaunt Bros. v. The British Oil & Cake Mills Ltd.]

32.2 ***Exceptions to the General Rule:*** There are **two** exceptions to the aforesaid rule as under:

1. Where the sub-sale or other disposition by the buyer has been done with the consent of the seller;
2. Where a document of title to goods (e.g., bill of lading or railway receipt) has been issued or lawfully transferred to any person as buyer and that person transfers the document by way of sale to a person who takes the document in good faith and for consideration.

33.0 RIGHTS OF UNPAID SELLER IN CASE OF TRANSFER OF DOCUMENT BY WAY OF PLEDGE

(i) Where the transfer was by way of pledge or other disposition for value, the unpaid seller's right of lien or stoppage in transit can only be exercised subject to rights of the transferee.

(ii) Where the transfer is by way of pledge, the unpaid seller may require the pledgee to have the amount secured by the pledge satisfied in the first instance, as far as possible, out of any other goods or securities of the buyer in the hands of the pledgee and available against the buyer.

Example *X of Delhi sold some goods to Y of Mumbai and took the railway receipt in the name of Y and sent to Y. State whether a right of stoppage in transit can be exercised in each of the following alternative cases:*

Case (*a*) Before the goods reach Mumbai, *Y* became insolvent.

Case (*b*) When the goods reached Mumbai, *Y* asked the railways to carry them to Calcutta. In the meantime *Y* became insolvent.

Case (*c*) When the goods reached Mumbai, the railway officials inform *Y* that the goods are lying at the station at *Y*'s risk. *Y* became insolvent in the meantime.

Case (*d*) *Y* handed over railway receipt to *Z* in return for a loan. *Z* took the railway receipt in good faith and for consideration. Before the goods reach Mumbai, *Y* became insolvent.

Case (*e*) Before the goods reach Mumbai, *Y* became insolvent. *Y* assigned the railway receipt for Rs 10,000 to *Z* who knew about the *Y*'s insolvency.

Case (*f*) *Y* assigned the railway receipt to *Z* to borrow Rs 10,000 on the security of railway receipt. Before the goods reach Mumbai, *Y* became insolvent.

Solution:

Case (*a*): Yes, because the goods are still in transit [Section 50].

Case (*b*): No, because the transit came to an end when *Y* asked the railways to carry the goods to Kolkata [Section 51(2)].

Case (*c*): No, because the transit came to end when the railway official informed *Y* that the goods are lying at *Y*'s risk [Section 51(3)].

Case (*d*): No, because the transfer was by way of sale and *Z* took the railway receipt in good faith and for valuable consideration and hence, *Z* got a good title [Section 53(1)].

Case (*e*): Yes, because *Z* has not acted in good faith and hence, *Z* did not get a good title [Section 53(1).

Case (*f*): Yes, but subject to rights of *Z*. In other words, *X* can get back the railway receipt after paying Rs 10,000 to *Z* [Section 53(2)].

34.0 RIGHT OF RESALE [SECTIONS 46(1) AND 54]

34.1 *What are circumstances under which an unpaid seller can resell the goods.*

An unpaid seller can resell the goods under the following **three** circumstances:

(i) Where the goods are of a perishable nature.

(ii) Where the seller expressly reserves a right of resale if the buyer commits a default in making the payment.

Note: As a result of this resale, the original contract will be terminated but the seller will have a right to claim damages [Section 54(4)].

(iii) Where the unpaid seller who has exercised his right of lien or stoppage in transit gives a notice to the buyer about his intention to resell and buyer does not pay or tender within a reasonable time.

34.2 ***Effects of Resale with or without Notice [Sections 54(2) and (3)]:*** The effects of resale with or without notice are summarised as under:

Rights	*In case of resale after notice*	*In case of resale without notice*
I. Unpaid seller's right to recover the loss on the sale	Available	Not available
II. Original buyer's right to recover the profit on resale	Not available	Available
III. New buyer's (who buys in resale) right to acquire a good title	Available	Available

Example *X sold 10 tons of rice to Y at a rate of Rs 40,000 per ton on a credit of one month. One month expired but Y did not pay. State the legal position in each of the following alternative cases:*

Case (*a*) If *X* resold 10 tons of rice to *Z* at a rate of Rs 50,000 per ton after giving a notice of resale to *Y*.

Case (*b*) If *X* resold 10 tons of rice to *Z* at a rate of Rs 30,000 per ton after giving a notice of resale to *Y*.

Case (*c*) If *X* resold 10 tons of rice to *Z* at a rate of Rs 50,000 per ton without giving a notice of resale to *Y*.

Case (*d*) If *X* resold 10 tons of rice to *Z* at a rate of Rs 30,000 without giving a notice of resale to *Y*.

Solution:

Case (*a*): *X* is entitled to keep the profit of Rs 1,00,000 with himself because the buyer cannot be allowed to take advantage of his own wrong i.e., breach of contract [Section 54(2)]. *Z* shall get a good title against *Y* [Section 54(3)].

Case (*b*): *X* is entitled to recover the loss of Rs 1,00,000 from *Y* [Section 54(2)]. *Z* shall get an good title against *Y* [Section 54(3)].

Case (*c*): *Y* is entitled to the profit of Rs 1,00,000 [Section 54(2)]. However, *Z* shall get a good title against *Y* [Section 54(3)].

Case (*d*): *X* is not entitled to recover the loss of Rs 1,00,000 [Section 54(2)]. However, *Z* shall get a good title against *Y* [Section 54(3)].

35.0 RIGHTS AGAINST THE GOODS WHERE THE PROPERTY IN THE GOODS HAS NOT PASSED TO THE BUYER

Where the property in goods has not passed to the buyer, the unpaid seller has, in addition to his other remedies, a right of withholding delivery similar to and co-extensive with his rights of lien and stoppage in transit where the property has passed to the buyer [Section 46(2)].

36.0 RIGHTS AGAINST THE BUYER PERSONALLY

In addition to the rights against the goods, unpaid seller has the following rights against the buyer personally:

1. Suit for Price [Sec. 55(1)]	Where under a contract of sale, the property in the goods has passed to the buyer and the buyer wrongfully neglects or refuses to pay for the goods according to the terms of the contract, the seller may sue him for the price of goods. Where under a contract of sale the price is payable on a certain day irrespective of delivery and the buyer wrongfully neglects or refuses to pay such price, the seller may sue him for the price although the property in the goods has not passed and the goods have not been appropriated to the contract.
2. Suit for Damages for Non-acceptance [Sec. 56]	Where the buyer wrongfully neglects or refuses to accept the goods and pay for the goods, the seller may sue him for damages for non-acceptance of the goods.
3. Suit for Damages for Repudiation of the Contract [Sec. 60]	Where buyer repudiates the contract before the due date of delivery, the seller may *either* treat the contract as subsisting and wait till the due date of delivery *or* he may treat the contract as rescinded and sue for damages for the breach.
4. Suit for Interest [Sec. 61(2)]	In case of breach of contract on the part of the buyer, while filing a suit for the price, the seller may sue the buyer for interest from the date of the tender of the goods or from the date on which the price was payable.

37.0 RIGHTS OF BUYER

The following rights are available to the buyer:

1. Suit for Damages for Non-delivery [Sec. 57]	Where the seller wrongfully neglects or refuses to deliver the goods to the buyer, the buyer may sue the seller for damages for non-delivery.
2. Suit for Specific Performance [Sec. 58]	In any suit for breach of contract to deliver specific or ascertained goods, the court may direct that the contract shall be performed specifically.
3. Suit for Breach of Warranty [Sec. 59]	Where there is a breach of warranty by the seller, or where the buyer elects or is compelled to treat any breach of a condition on the part of the seller as a breach of warranty, the buyer is not by reason only of such breach of warranty entitled to reject the goods, but he may— (i) set up against the seller the breach of warranty in diminution or extinction of the price; or (ii) sue the seller for damages for breach of warranty. ***Note:*** The fact that a buyer has set up a breach of warranty in diminution or extinction of the price does not prevent him from suing for the same

	breach of warranty if he suffered further damage. [Section 59(2)] **Example** *X sold a second hand Radio to Y who spent Rs 100 on the repair of this radio. This radio was seized by the police as it was a stolen one. Y filed a suit against X for recovery of damages for breach of warranty of quite possession including the cost of repairs. It was held that Y was entitled to recover the same. [Mason v. Burmingham]*
4. Right to Treat the Contract as Rescinded or Operative in Case of Repudiation of Contract by Seller before due Date [Sec. 60]	Where seller repudiates the contract before the date of delivery, the buyer may *either* treat the contract as subsisting and wait till the date of delivery, *or* he may treat the contract as rescinded and sue for damages for the breach.
5. Suit for Interest [Sec. 61(2)]	In case of breach of the contract on the part of the seller, the buyer may sue the seller for interest from the date on which the payment was made.

38.0 AUCTION SALE [SECTION 64]

38.1 Meaning of Auction Sale

Auction sale means a public sale where intending buyer assemble at one place and offer the price at which they are ready to buy the goods. The offer of the price is known as 'bid' and the person making the bid is known as the 'bidder.' The owner of the goods may himself sell them by auction or appoint a person to sell the goods by auction on his behalf. The person so appointed is known as 'auctioneer.' The relationship between the owner of the goods and the auctioneer is that of the principal and agent. In an auction the goods are sold to the highest bidder. It may be noted that an advertisement to sell the goods by auction is simply an invitation to the public to make offers and not an offer to sell. That is why the intending buyers have no right to sue the auctioneer if auctioneer cancels or postpones the sale by auction.

38.2 Rules Regarding Sale by Auction [Section 64]

The various rules regarding sale by auction are given as follows:

Separate Contract	Where goods are put up for sale in lots, each lot is *prima facie* deemed to be the subject of a separate contract of sale [Section 64(1)].
Completion of Sale	A sale is complete when the auctioneer announces its completion by the fall of the hammer or in other customary manner. *For example*, by saying one, two and three, or by shouting going, going, gone etc. [Section 64(2)].
Right to Withdraw bid	Until the announcement of completion of sale is made, any bidder may withdraw his bid [Section 64(2)].
Seller's Right to bid	A right to bid may be reserved expressly by or on behalf of the seller and, where such right is expressly so reserved, the seller or anyone person on his behalf may bid at the auction [Section 64(3)].

Fraudulent Sale	Where a sale is not notified to be subject to a right to bid on behalf of the seller, it shall not be lawful for the seller to bid himself or to employ any person to bid at such sale, or for the auctioneer knowingly to take any bid from the seller or any such person, and any sale contravening the rule may be treated as fraudulent by the buyer [Section 64(4)].
Reserve Price	A sale may be notified to be subject to a reserve or upset price [Section 64(5)]. The term 'reserve' or 'upset' price may be defined as the minimum price below which the auctioneer will not sell the goods put up for auction sale.
Voidable Sale	If a seller makes use of pretended bidding to raise the price, the sale is voidable at the option of the buyer [Section 64(6)].

Notes: (i) An auctioneer can refuse to accept even the highest bid because 'bid' is only an offer which may or may not be accepted by the auctioneer.

(ii) An agreement between the bidders not to bid against each other is called the knock-out agreement. Under such agreement, it is agreed that only one person will bid and anything obtained by him shall be shared by all privately. Such agreements are lawful unless the intention of the parties to the agreement is to defraud a third party.

(iii) Damping, which is intended to discourage the bidders from bidding is an unlawful act.

(iv) Puffers (also known as By-bidders or White Bonnets or Decoy Ducks) are persons who are appointed by the seller for the purpose of raising the price. The seller can appoint only one puffer.

Example *At an auction sale, C made the highest bid for an article of P. State the legal position in each of the following alternative cases:*

Case (*a*) If *C* withdrew the bid before the fall of the hammer though he knew that one of the condition of the sale was 'bid once made cannot be withdrawn'.

Case (*b*) If *P* refused to accept the highest bid. The sale was not notified subject to a reserve price.

Case (*c*) If *P* appointed two persons *A* and *B*, to bid on his behalf. The sale was notified subject to a right to bid.

Case (*d*) If *C* was allowed to take it away on (i) giving a cheque for the price (ii) signing an agreement that ownership should not pass to him until the cheque was cleared. The cheque was dishonoured but in the meantime *C* sold the article to *Z*.

Case (*e*) If the sale was notified subject to a reserve price and the auctioneer by mistake accepted the *C*'s highest bid (which was lower than the reserve price) by striking the hammer. Later, auctioneer refused to deliver the goods.

Solution:

Case (*a*): *C*'s bid was an offer to buy and he was entitled to withdraw his bid before the sale is completed as per express provision of Section 64(2) [*Payne* v. *Cave*]. Such a condition in an auction sale was inoperative because it was against the provisions of the law. [*Champa Lal* v. *Jaigopal*]

Case (b): *C*'s bid was an offer to buy which may or may not be accepted by the auctioneer. Hence, *P* could refuse to accept the highest bid. [*Fenwick* v. *Macdonald*]

Case (c): It amounts to fraud and sale is voidable at the option of the buyer because the seller could appoint only one person to bid on his behalf. [Section 64(3) and Section 64(6)]. Here intention of the seller was not to protect his interest but to raise the price. [*Thornett* v. *Haines*]

Case (d): *Z* had a good title because the property passed to *C* on the fall of the hammer [*Dennant* v. *Skinner*]. The ownership of specific goods in a deliverable state passes on the completion of contract of sale.

Case (e): The sale was not valid and *C* was not entitled to goods. It was held that the auctioneer could not effectively accept such a bid (which was lower than reserve price) because he could not make a contract so as to bind his principal to accept less than the reserve price. [*Manas* v. *Fortesque*]

38.3 What are the Liabilities of an Auctioneer ?

On the basis of various decisions taken by the court, it can be said that an auctioneer is liable for damages in the following cases:

(a) If the auctioneer had no authority to sell the goods. [*Anderson* v. *Creall & Sons Ltd.*]

(b) If there is a defect in principal's title. [*Benton* v. *Compbell Parker & Co.*]

(c) If the auctioneer refuses to give the possession on the payment of the price.

(d) If the buyer's possession is disturbed by his principal or himself.

PRACTICAL PROBLEMS

PROBLEM 1

State whether each of the following transaction is a contract of sale under the Sale of Goods Act, 1930.

(a) A partner agreed to sell his goods to the firm.

(b) A partner agreed to buy goods from the firm.

(c) *X* is the owner of some goods, but he is not aware of this fact. *Y* pretends to be the owner of these goods and sells them to *X*.

(d) *X*, *Y* and *Z* are joint owners of some furniture and with the consent of *Y* and *Z*, the furniture was kept in possession of *X*. *X* buys *Y*'s share from him.

(e) *X* agreed to sell a set containing 100 new currency notes of Rs 500 each for Rs 50,000 to *Y*.

(f) *X* agreed to sell 100 silver coins for Rs 10,000 to *Y*.

(g) *X* agreed to sell 100 shares for Rs 10,000 to *Y*.

(h) *X* agreed to sell his building for Rs 1,00,000 to *Y*.

(i) *X* agreed to sell the goodwill of his proprietorship firm for Rs 1,00,000 to *Y*.

(j) *X* agreed to transfer some jewellery to his prospective wife Mrs. Kajol on account of love and affection.

(k) *X* agreed to exchange with *Y* 100 kg of rice (valued at Rs 20 per kg) for 200 kg of wheat (valued at Rs 10 per kg).

(l) *X* agreed to exchange with *Y* 100 kg of rice (valued at Rs 20 per kg) for 200 kg of wheat (valued at Rs 12 per kg and pay the difference in cash.

(m) *X* agreed to pledge his goods valued at Rs 1,00,000 with *Y*.

(n) *X* engaged an artist to paint a portrait, canvas and other materials were to be supplied by *A* to painter.

(o) *X* agreed to buy a painting from an artist.

(p) Supply of wagons or coaches on the under frame supplied by the Railways.

(q) *X* delivered a manuscript to *Y* for printing. *Y* agreed to use his own ink and paper for printing the book.

(r) *X* supplied a piece of cloth to a tailor to make a suit for him. The tailor agreed to supply the lining material and buttons.

(s) Supply of food by a hotel company to its resident customers, where no rebate is allowed if food is not taken by the customers.

(t) *X* sold a car to *Y*, on the payment of Rs 6,000 per month for 36 months at the end of which the ownership of the car will be transferred to *Y*. It was agreed that *X* can recover the car if *Y* makes a fault.

Solution

Section to which the given problem relates: Section 4.

Decision and reason.

Case	*Decision*	*Reason*
(*a*)	Yes	because there are two distinct parties—the firm being buyer and the partner being seller.
(*b*)	Yes	because there are two distinct parties—the firm being seller and the partner being buyer.
(*c*)	No	because there are not two distinct parties—buyer and seller. A person cannot buy his own goods. [Leading case: *Bell* v. *Lever Bros Ltd.*]
(*d*)	Yes	because a part-owner may sell to another part-owner as per the express provision of Section 4.
(*e*)	No	because money has been specifically excluded from the definition of 'goods'. Hence, the new currency notes cannot be the subject-matter of the contract of sale.
(*f*)	Yes	because old rare coins can be the subject-matter of the contract of sale. The term 'goods' excludes money which means current money and not old rare coins.
(*g*)	Yes	because shares can be the subject-matter of the contract of sale. The term 'goods' specifically includes stock and shares.
(*h*)	No	because immovable property cannot be the subject-matter of the contract of sale of goods. The immovable property does not fall in the definition of the term 'goods'.
(*i*)	Yes	because goodwill can be the subject-matter of the contract of sale. The term 'goods' includes goodwill as well.
(*j*)	No	because the consideration is not money but love and affection. Thus, it amounts to a gift and not sale.
(*k*)	No	because the consideration is not money but goods. Thus, it amounts to a barter and not sale.
(*l*)	Yes	because there is nothing in law to prevent the consideration from being partly in money and partly in goods. [Leading case: *Shelden* v. *Cox*]

(*m*)	No	because the property involved in this case is a special property and not general property.
(*n*)	No	because it is a contract for work and labour and not contract of sale. In this case rendering of service and exercise of skill is the essence of contract and the delivery of the goods is merely ancillary to the contract. [Leading case: *Robinson* v. *Graves*]
(*o*)	Yes	because it is contract of sale. In this case, delivery of the goods is the essence of contract.
(*p*)	No	because it is a contract of work and labour and not a contract of sale. In this case, rendering of service and exercise of skill is the essence of contract and the delivery of the goods is merely ancillary to the contract.
(*q*)	No	because it is contract of work and labour and not a contract of sale. In this case, rendering of service and exercise of skill is the essence of contract and the delivery of the goods is merely ancillary to the contract.
(*r*)	No	because it is contract of work and labour and not a contract of sale. In this case rendering of service and exercise of skill is the essence of contract and the delivery of the goods is merely ancillary to the contract.
(*s*)	No	because supply of food is essentially in the nature of service and not a transaction of sale because there is an indivisible contract of multiple services. [Leading case: *Associated Hotels of India* v. *Excise and Taxation officer*]
(*t*)	Yes	because *X* did not have any option to return, but was under compulsion to buy. Hence, it is not a hire purchase agreement. [Leading case: *Lee* v. *Butler*]

PROBLEM 2

State whether the following contracts of sale amount to sale or an 'agreement to sell'.

***Case* (*a*)**: *X* entered into a contract for sale of the entire crop of rice that would yield on his farm.

***Case* (*b*)**: *A* railway administration entered into a contract for sale of coal-ash that might accumulate during the period of contract.

***Case* (*c*)**: *X* entered into a contract for sale of some goods in a particular ship to be delivered on the arrival of the ship.

***Case* (*d*)**: *X* entered into a contract for sale of a painting only if *Z*, its present owner, sells it to him.

Solution

	***Cases* (*a*) *and* (*b*)**	***Cases* (*c*) *and* (*d*)**
Relevant Section	Section 6(3)	Section 6(2)
Decision and Reason	The contract amounted to an agreement to sell because the subject matter of the contract is future goods which can be the subject-matter of an agreement to sell only.	The contract amounted to an agreement to sell because the subject matter of the contract is contingent goods which can be the subject-matter of an agreement to sell only.

PROBLEM 3

X agreed to sell to *Y* a parcel of 700 bags of groundnuts lying in his godown. Unknown to *X*, 109 bags had been stolen at the time of contract. *X* tendered delivery of 591 bags. *Y* declined to accept. State the legal position.

Solution

Relevant Section	Section 7
Decision	The contract of sale has become void and thus, *Y* cannot be compelled to accept 591 bags.
Reason	There was a contract for sale of an indivisible lot of specific goods and some goods are destroyed at the time when the contract was made without the knowl-edge of the seller. [Leading case: *Barrow Lane & Ballard Ltd.* v. *Phillips & Co.*]

PROBLEM 4

X agreed to sell a horse to *Y* on condition that *Y* will keep it for 10 days on trial basis and have the option to return on the expiry of 10 days, if he does not find it suitable. However, the horse dies on the third day, without any fault of either the seller or buyer. State the legal position.

Solution

Relevant Section	Section 8
Decision	The agreement to sell has become void and thus, the seller could not recover the price from the buyer.
Reason	There was an agreement to sell specific goods which are destroyed before it becomes a sale without any fault of seller or buyer.

PROBLEM 5

X entered into on a contract for the sale of 100 bags of wheat out of 1,000 bags lying in his godown. Unknown to *X*, the entire stock was destroyed by fire. *X* declined to deliver. State the legal position.

Solution

Relevant Section	Section 7
Decision	*X* must deliver 100 bags of wheat or pay damages for the breach.
Reason	There was a contract for the sale of unascertained goods and not specific goods and hence the contract did not become void.

TRUE OR FALSE QUESTIONS

State giving reasons whether each of the following statements is 'True' or 'False':

1. A contract of sale of goods includes the sale of goods and not an agreement to sell goods.
2. The consideration for the contract of sale can be partly in money and partly in goods.
3. The subject matter of the contract of sale can be all movable goods.
4. In a sale the property in goods is transferred when the buyer pays the price.
5. A sale by a partner of a firm to his firm is void.
6. Future goods cannot be the subject-matter of sale.
7. In case of destruction of unascertained goods, the contract becomes void.
8. In case of contract of sale of goods, price of the goods must be fixed at the time of sale.

9. Parties to a contract of sale can get the price of goods fixed by third parties.
10. Where the price is not determined in any manner, the buyer must pay the seller the market price of the goods.
11. Stipulation as time of payment is deemed to be essence of a contract of sale unless otherwise agreed.
12. A stipulation the breach of which gives the aggrieved party a right to terminate the contract is called a warranty.
13. A breach of warranty can be treated as a breach of condition in some cases.
14. In a contract of sale by sample the bulk of goods must correspond to *either* sample *or* merchantability.
15. In a contract of sale by description and by sample, the bulk of goods must correspond to *either* description *or* sample.
16. In a contract for sale of goods there is no implied condition or warranty as to the quality of the goods or their fitness for any particular purpose.
17. A seller need not disclose the defect of his goods to the buyer before sale.
18. The implied condition as to fitness for a particular purpose does not apply to goods if the buyer had examined the goods.
19. The implied condition as to merchantable quality applies to goods whether or not the buyer has examined the goods.
20. The term property in goods and possession of goods mean the same thing.
21. The property in goods passes only when the goods are delivered.
22. Property in goods can pass only in case of ascertained goods.
23. Where there is an unconditional contract for sale of specific goods in deliverable state, the property in goods passes when the goods are delivered.
24. Where there is a contract for sale of specific goods not in deliverable state, the property in goods passes when the goods are put into a deliverable state whether or not the buyer has notice thereof.
25. Where there is a contract for sale of specific goods in a deliverable state but the seller has to do some act to ascertain the price, the property in goods passes when the seller has done that act to ascertain price.
26. In a contract for the sale of unascertained goods, the property in goods passes when the contract is made.
27. In case of unascertained goods, the goods can be appropriate *either* by the seller *or* the buyer with the consent of the other.
28. The consent of the seller or buyer as to appropriation of unascertained goods must be given before the appropriation is made.
29. Where the seller delivers the goods to the buyer or to a carrier or other bailee for the purpose of transmission to the buyer and reserves the right of disposal, he is deemed to have unconditionally appropriated the goods to the contract.
30. When the goods are sent on sale or return basis, the property in goods passes when the buyer retains the goods beyond a reasonable time.
31. Pledging of goods obtained on sale or return basis will complete the sale.
32. When the goods are sent on sale or return basis, the property in goods will pass when the buyer delivers that goods to a third person on the same basis.
33. Delivery of the goods to the carrier amounts to transfer of ownership to the buyer.

34. Property in goods passes to the buyer where the seller has reserved the right of disposal.
35. When the seller takes a railway receipt in the name of buyer and sends the railway receipt to his agent, he is said to have reserved the right.
36. When a bill of exchange is sent together with documents of title, the property in goods passes when the buyer honours the bill of exchange.
37. Generally, risk follows ownership whether the goods have been delivered or not and whether price has been paid or not.
38. Sale by a non-owner does not make the buyer an absolute owner of goods.
39. A seller in possession of goods under a voidable contract can pass a good title to a bonafide buyer.
40. A seller in possession of goods in the capacity of a bailee can pass a good title to bona fide buyer.
41. A joint owner in sole possession of goods with the consent of majority of other joint owners can pass a good title to a bona fide buyer.
42. Delivery means the compulsory transfer of possession from one person to another.
43. Delivery of the key of a warehouse where goods are lying amounts to symbolic delivery.
44. Unless otherwise agreed, delivery of goods and payment of the price need not be concurrent conditions.
45. A delivery of part of goods with an intention of separating it from the whole lot does not amount to the delivery of the whole of the goods.
46. In case there is no contract as to the place of delivery, the goods are to be delivered at the place of buyer.
47. In case there is no contract as to the time of delivery, the goods are to be delivered within 1 month.
48. In case of delivery of wrong quantity, the buyer may reject the whole lot.
49. Buyer must accept the delivery by instalment.
50. Delivery to a carrier is *prima facie* deemed to be a delivery to the buyer.
51. Delivery of goods amounts to acceptance of goods.
52. When goods are rejected by the buyer, he must return them to the seller.
53. Where the neglect or refusal of the buyer to take delivery amounts to a repudiation of the contract, the seller may sue the buyer only for claims and not for price.
54. The right of lien can be exercised only when the buyer has become insolvent.
55. The right of lien cannot be exercised if the seller possesses the goods as agent or bailee for buyer.
56. In case of part delivery, the unpaid seller can exercise his right of lien over the remainder even if the part delivery is intended as delivery of the whole.
57. The right of lien cannot be exercised when the unpaid seller has obtained a decree for the price of the goods.
58. The right of lien is lost when the seller takes railway receipt in the name of buyer and sends the railway receipt to his agent.
59. The right of stoppage in transit can be exercised even in case of non-payment of price by buyer who is solvent.

60. The right of stoppage in transit commences only when the right of lien is lost.
61. An unpaid seller can exercise the right of stoppage in transit when the carrier holds the goods as seller's agent.
62. Transit comes to an end where the carrier wrongfully refuses to deliver the goods to the buyer or his agent.
63. Transit does not come to an end when the goods are delivered to a ship.
64. In case of part delivery, the unpaid seller can exercise his right of stoppage-in-transit over the remainder if the part delivery is not intended as delivery of the whole.
65. The right of stoppage in transit is lost when the unpaid seller gives his consent to the sale by the buyer.
66. Where the transfer of documents of title was by way pledge, the unpaid seller's right of lien or stoppage-in-transit can only be exercised subject to right of the transferor.
67. An unpaid seller is bound to resale the goods.
68. The unpaid seller must give a notice of resale to the buyer irrespective of the nature of goods.
69. Where the seller has expressly reserved the right of resale, the unpaid seller need not give any notice of the resale to the buyer.
70. Where a notice of resale has been given to the buyer and there is loss on resale, the unpaid seller can recover it from the buyer.
71. If notice of resale is not given, the new buyer will not get a good title.
72. The relationship between the owner of the goods and the auctioneer is that of the principal and agent.
73. A seller cannot reserve a right to bid at an action.
74. Where the right to bid at an auction is expressly reserved by the seller, the seller or anyone person on his behalf may bid the auction.
75. An auction sale cannot be subject to a reserve price.
76. In an auction sale, a bid once given cannot be withdrawn.
77. An auctioneer can refuse to accept even the highest bid.
78. In an auction sale, bidder can enter into an agreement to keep the bid low by eliminating competition amongst them.

Answers

1. False	2. True	3. False	4. False
5. False	6. True	7. False	8. False
9. True	10. False	11. False	12. False
13. False	14. False	15. False	16. True
17. True	18. False	19. False	20. False
21. False	22. True	23. False	24. False
25. True	26. False	27. True	28. False
29. False	30. True	31. True	32. True
33. False	34. False	35. True	36. True
37. True	38. True	39. True	40. False
41. False	42. False	43. True	44. False

45. True	46. False	47. False	48. True
49. False	50. True	51. False	52. False
53. False	54. False	55. False	56. False
57. False	58. False	59. False	60. True
61. False	62. True	63. False	64. True
65. True	66. False	67. False	68. False
69. True	70. True	71. False	72. True
73. False	74. True	75. False	76. False
77. True	78. True		

VERY SHORT ANSWER TYPE QUESTIONS

1. Define a 'contract of sale'.
2. Does the term 'contract of sale' include an agreement to sell?
3. When does an agreement to sell become sale?
4. Can a contract of sale be implied from the conduct of parties?
5. Can a contract of sale be partly in writing and partly by words of mouth?
6. Can an offer to sell by words of month be accepted in writing?
7. Can an offer in writing be accepted by words of mouth?
8. What is the true test of hire-purchase agreement?
9. What is a contract for work and labour?
10. Is a contract for work and labour covered under the Sale of Goods Act, 1930?
11. Define the term 'goods'.
12. Do old rare coins constitute goods?
13. Do actionable claims constitute goods?
14. Do money other than old rare coins constitute goods?
15. Do immovable property constitute goods?
16. Do all movable property constitute goods?
17. What is meant by 'existing goods'?
18. What is meant by 'specific goods'?
19. What is meant by 'ascertained goods'?
20. What is meant by 'unascertained goods'?
21. Define 'future goods'.
22. Define 'contingent goods'.
23. What is the effect of destruction of specific goods on contract of sale?
24. What is the effect of destruction of specific goods on an agreement to sell?
25. What is the effect of destruction of unascertained goods on a contract of sale?
26. Define 'condition' in a contract of sale of goods.
27. What is a 'warranty' in a contract of sale of goods?

28. What is meant by 'passing of property'?
29. What is meant by '*nemo dat quid non-habet*'?
30. What is meant by delivery of goods?
31. What is symbolic delivery?
32. What is constructive delivery?
33. Define an unpaid seller.
34. What is a 'right of lien'?
35. What is a 'right of stoppage of goods in transit'?
36. Is the unpaid seller bound to return the surplus realised on resale of goods?
37. What in an auction sale?
38. What is a bid?
39. Define 'bidder'.
40. Define 'auctioneer'.
41. What is a 'reserve price'?
42. What is a knock-out agreement?
43. Is a knock-agreement lawful?
44. What is damping?
45. Is damping lawful?
46. Can a seller appoint any person to bid on his behalf in auction?
47. Can a bidder withdraw his bid?
48. Can an auctioneer refuse to accept even a highest bid?
49. Can the seller fix a reserve price in an auction sale?

SHORT ANSWER TYPE QUESTIONS

1. Enumerate the implied conditions and implied warranties.
2. What is meant by 'sale by description'?
3. What is meant by 'sale by sample'?
4. What is meant by 'sale by sample as well as by description'?
5. What is meant by 'condition as to quality or fitness'?
6. State the conditions to be satisfied to avail of the condition as to fitness.
7. State two cases where the condition as to fitness may not be applicable.
8. What is meant by 'condition as to merchantable quality'?
9. When can a breach of condition be treated as a breach of warranty?
10. What is doctrine of 'caveat emptor'?
11. Enumerate the exceptions to the doctrine of caveat emptor.
12. State the reason of knowing the exact moment when property in goods passes to the buyer.
13. 'State the rules relating to transfer of property of specific goods from seller to buyer.

14. State the rules relating to transfer of property of unascertained goods from seller to buyer.
15. State the rules relating to transfer of property of goods delivered on approval or on sale or return basis.
16. Does delivery of goods to a carrier amount to transfer of ownership?
17. What is meant by reservation of right of disposal?
18. Enumerate the circumstances when a non-owner can transfer a better title than what he himself possess.
19. Explain the rules regarding place of delivery.
20. Explain the rules regarding delivery of wrong quantity.
21. Explain the rules regarding delivery by instalments.
22. Explain the rules regarding delivery by a carrier or wharfinger.
23. When the buyer is said to have accepted the goods?
24. State the rights of seller when the buyer refuses or neglects to take delivery of the goods.
25. Enumerate the rights of an unpaid seller.
26. State the circumstances under which an unpaid seller can exercise his right of lien.
27. State the circumstances under which an unpaid seller cannot exercise his right of lien.
28. State the conditions under which an unpaid seller can exercise his right of stoppage of goods in transit.
29. State the circumstances under which an unpaid seller loses his right of stoppage of goods is transit.
30. How is stoppage in transit effected?
31. What are the effects of sub-sale or pledge by buyer on the unpaid seller's right of lien and stoppage in transit?
32. When can an unpaid seller resell the goods?
33. State the circumstances under which a notice of resale is not required to be given.
34. State the effects of resale of goods with or without notice under the circumstances when a notice is required to be given.
35. State the rights of an unpaid seller against the buyer personally.
36. State the rights of a buyer against the seller.
37. Comment on the following statements:
    (a) In a contract for the sale of goods there is no implied condition or warranty as to the quality of the goods or their fitness for any particular purpose.
    (b) The seller of goods is not bound to disclose defects in the goods that he intends to sell.
    (c) No seller of goods can transfer better title to the buyer of the goods than he himself possesses.
    (f) Risk *prima facie* passes with ownership.
    (g) The fact that the buyer of the goods has received the goods does not mean that he has accepted them.
    (h) Delivery does not amount to acceptance of goods by buyer.

(i) Delivery of goods to a carrier amounts to delivery to the buyer.
(j) Delivery of goods to a carrier amounts to transfer of ownership.
(k) Right of stoppage in transit is an extension of the right of lien.
(l) In case of 'sale by sample as well as buy description', the goods must not only correspond to the sample but also to the description.
(m) The condition as to merchantability extends only to the latent defects.

38. Distinguish between the followings:
(a) A Sale and an Agreement of Sell.
(b) A Sale and Hire-Purchase Agreement.
(c) A Sale and a Contract for work and labour.
(d) Future goods and Contingent Goods.
(e) Ascertained goods and Unascertained Goods.
(f) Specific goods and Ascertained goods.
(g) Condition and Warranty.
(h) Symbolic Delivery and Constructive Delivery.
(i) Part Delivery and Instalment Delivery.
(j) Right of lien and Right of Stoppage in transit.

ESSAY TYPE QUESTIONS

1. (a) Define a contract of sale.
(b) Explain the essentials of a valid contract of sale.
(c) How is a contract of sale different from an agreement to sell?
2. (a) How is a contract of sale made? State briefly with illustrations the necessary formalities of such a contract.
3. (a) Explain the term 'goods as defined in, the Sale of Goods Act, 1930.
(b) What are the various types of goods?
4. What is the effect of destruction of specific goods?
5. (a) Distinguish between condition and warranty.
(b) Briefly discuss the implied conditions and warranties in a contract of sale.
(c) Under what circumstances does a condition descend to the level of a warranty?
6. (a) What is the doctrine of 'caveat emptor'?
(b) What are the exceptions to this rule?
7. (a) What is a 'sale by sample'?
(b) Explain the implied conditions inherent in a sale by sample.
8. (a) Why is it important to know the exact time when the property in goods passes from a seller to buyer?
(b) Explain with example, the rules governing the transfer of ownership of goods from seller to buyer.
9. What are the rules for ascertaining the intention of the parties as to the time when the property in specific goods is to pass to the buyer?

10. "No seller of goods can give the buyer of goods a better title to those goods than what he himself possesses." Examine this statement and mention whether there are any exceptions to this rule.
11. What is meant by reservation of the right of disposal in a contract of sale of goods?
12. Explain in brief the rules relating to the delivery of goods.
13. Explain with examples the rules relating to (a) part delivery, (b) delivery by instalments, and (c) delivery of wrong quantity.
14. Define an unpaid seller. Explain his right (i) against the goods and (ii) against the buyer personality.
15. (a) What is meant by the right of lien in respect of sale of goods?
    (b) Under what circumstances this right can be exercised?
    (c) When is this right lost?
    (d) What is the effect of sub-sale or pledge on this right?
16. (a) What is meant by the right of stoppage in transit in respect of sale of goods?
    (b) Under what conditions this right can be exercised?
    (c) When is this right lost?
    (d) How is this right effected or exercised?
    (e) What is effect of sub-sale or pledge on this right?
17. When can a seller resell the goods?
18. (a) What is an auction sale?
    (b) Explain in brief the rules applicable to an auction sale.

CHAPTER 16

The Indian Partnership Act, 1932

1.0 INTRODUCTION

1.1 Partnership is one of the specific contracts which were part of the Indian Contract Act, 1872.

1.2 In 1930, however, the provisions relating to partnership contract were repealed and a separate Act called the Indian Partnership Act, 1932 was passed which is in force till today.

1.3 What is the Territory to which the Act applies?

It extends to the whole of India except the State of Jammu and Kashmir.

1.4 When the Act came into force?

It has come into force on the 1st day of October 1932 except Section 69, which came into force on the 1st day of October 1933.

1.5 Do the Provisions of the Indian Contract Act, 1872 apply to firms?

The provisions of the Indian Contract Act, 1872 also apply to firms except where The Indian Partnership Act, 1932, specifically provides to the contrary [Section 3].

2.0 WHAT IS PARTNERSHIP ?

"Partnership is the relation between two or more persons who have agreed to share the profits of a business carried on by all or any of them acting for all." [Section 4]

3.0 WHAT ARE THE ESSENTIAL ELEMENTS OF PARTNERSHIP ?

3.1 Two or more Persons There must be at least two persons to form a partnership and all such persons must be competent to contract. According to Section 11 of the Indian Contract Act, 1872, every person except the following, is competent to contract:

(i) Minor

(ii) Persons of unsound mind (e.g. lunatics, idiots), and

(iii) Persons disqualified by any law to which they are subject (e.g., alien enemies, insolvents).

Example: Three brothers, *X* (age 19 years), *Y* (age 18 years) and *Z* (age 17 years), decide to form a partnership with a provision that *Z* will share the profits only.

Solution : Section to which given Problem relates: Section 4.

Decision	No.
Reason	All the persons entering into partnership agreement must be competent to contract. *Z* is not competent to contract because he is a minor. It may be noted that no partnership can be formed with a minor partner but after the formation

	of partnership, a minor can be admitted to the benefits of partnership with the consent of all other partners of the firm as per the provisions of Section 30 of the Act.
Leading Case Law	*Shivaram* v. *Gauri Shankar*

3.2 Agreement There must be an agreement to form a partnership. This agreement may be express (whether written or oral) or implied. This essential element is further clarified under Section 5. Section 5 provides that the relation of partnership arises from contract and not from status. That is why, a Hindu undivided family carrying on a family business is not considered a partnership. The reason is that the coparceners of a Hindu undivided family acquire interest in the business because of their status (i.e., birth) in the family and not because of any agreement between them. Thus, partnership is voluntary and contractual in nature.

3.3 Business There must exist a business. According to Section 2(b), the term 'Business' includes every trade, occupation and profession. For example, when two or more persons agrees to share the income of a joint property (e.g., rent from a building), it does not amount to a partnership because there does not exist any business. Similarly, an association created for charitable, religious or social purpose cannot be regarded as partnership because there does not exist any business. It may also be noted that an agreement to carry on business at a future time does not result in partnership unless that time arrives and the business is started. [*R.R. Sarna,* v. *Reuben*]

Example : Ten major persons form an association to which each member contributes Rs 10,000. The purpose is to produce medicines for free distribution to poor patients. Is there a valid partnership?

Solution : Section to which the given Problem relates: Section 4.

Decision	No.
Reason	There is no intention to carry on the business and to share the profits thereof.

3.4 Sharing of Profits There must be sharing of profits. Sharing of profits does not necessarily imply sharing of losses as well. That is why there are minor partner and partner in profits only. It may also be noted that sharing of profits is a *prima facie* evidence and not a conclusive evidence of partnership. That is why, everyone who shares the profits of business need not necessarily be a partner. **For example**, a manager who receives a particular share in the profits of a business as part of his remuneration, is simply an employee and not a partner (for more details, see Explanations I and II to Sec. 6 discussed in para 7.2).

3.5 Mutual Agency There must exist a mutual agency relationship among the partners. 'Mutual Agency' relationship means that each partner is both an agent and a principal. Each partner is an agent in the sense that he has the capacity to bind other partners by his acts done. Each partner is a principal in the sense that he is bound by the acts of other partners. Such mutual agency relationship in case of a firm of *X*, *Y* and *Z* has been shown on next page.

The mutual relationship of agency is emphasised in Section 18 of the Indian Partnership Act, which reads as under:

"Subject to the provision of this Act, a partner is the agent of the firm for the business of the firm."

Moreover, the use of the words 'carried as by all or by any of them acting for all, in Section 4 of the Act clearly emphasises agency relationship.

Mutual Agency Relationship in Case of a Firm of *X*, *Y* and *Z*			
	When *X* does an act	**When *Y* does an act**	**When *Z* does an act**
Who is an Agent	*X*	*Y*	*Z*
Who are Principles	*Y* and *Z*	*X* and *Z*	*X* and *Y*

Because of the existence of mutual agency relationship amongst the partners, the law of partnership is also regarded as an extension of the general law of agency. It may be noted that the mutual agency relationship distinguishes a partnership from co-ownership and simple agreement for sharing profits.

Example : *X*, *Y* and *Z* agreed to share the profits and losses and to carry on the business by all or anyone acting for all for mutual benefits and gain. The management and control was entrusted in *X* with power to restrict the right of *Y* and *Z*. Is there a valid partnership?

Solution : Section to which the given Problem relates: Section 4.

Decision	Yes.
Reason	All the essential elements of partnership exist under the partnership agreement.
Leading Case Law	*K.D. Kamath Co.* v. *Commission of Income Tax* (1972) 82, ITR 680 (SC)

4.0 MEANING OF 'PARTNER', 'FIRM' AND 'FIRM NAME'

Partner	Persons who have entered into partnership with one another are called individually 'partners'.
Firm	Persons who have entered into partnership with one another are called collectively 'a firm'.
Firm Name	The name under which their business is carried on is called the 'firm name'.

5.0 WHAT IS THE MAXIMUM LIMIT ON NUMBER OF PARTNERS ?

According to Section 11 of the Companies Act, 1956, the maximum limit is as under:

In case of a partnership firm carrying on a banking busines	10
In case of a partnership firm carrying on any other business	20

If the number of partners exceeds the aforesaid limit, the partnership firm becomes an illegal association.

Note: These statutory limits do not appy to a Hindu Undivided Family. However in case of amalgamation of two or more families these limit apply.

[*Refer to Practical Problems 4 to 7*]

6.0 NATURE OF A PARTNERSHIP FIRM

6.1 A partnership firm is not a person in the eyes of law [except under Section 2(31) of the Income Tax Act, 1961]. It has no separate legal entity apart from the partners constituting it [*Malabar Fisheries Co.* v. *CIT*].

6.2 Thus, firm themselves cannot enter into a contract for partnership though their partners can. **For example,** two firms, namely, M/s A&B and M/s X&Y, themselves cannot form a new partnership though the partners of the individual firms can form a partnership.

7.0 WHAT IS THE TEST OF PARTNERSHIP ?

7.1 Legal Position

According to Section 6, "In determining whether a group of persons is or is not a firm, regard shall be had to the real relation between the parties as shown by all relevant facts taken together." The real relation between the partners can be ascertained as under:

I. If there is an express contact.	The real relation is ascertained from the terms of partnership contract.
II. If there is no express contract.	The real relation is ascertained from all the rele-vant factors such as contract of parties, books of accounts, statement of employees etc.

Section 6 is based on the principle laid down in an important case of *Cox* v. *Hickman* (1860). The analysis of this section reveals that the following is the true test of partnership:

(a) The partnership is determined from the real relation between partners and such relation must show the existence of mutual agency relationship, and

(b) The sharing of profit is *prima facie* evidence but not a conclusive test of partnership.

A group of persons shall be regarded as partnership if the real relation between the partners shows that all essential elements of partnership are present.

7.2 Cases where the Partnership Relation does not Exist

The **two** cases where the partnership relation does not exist are given below:

(a) Joint owners of some property sharing profits or gross returns arising from the property [Explanation 1 to Section 6].

Example *X and Y jointly purchased a building and contributed capital equally to convert the building into a hotel. They let it out on a rent of Rs 1,00,000 per annum and share the rental income equally.*

Decision: *X* and *Y* are regarded as co-owners and not partners.

Reason: *X* and *Y* do not have mutual agency relationship.

[**Leading case:** *Govind Nair* v. *Maga*]

(b) Persons sharing the profits but not having mutual agency [Explanation II to Section 6] The sharing of profits is *prima facie* evidence. This statement is true in the sense that some persons though sharing the profits of a business, are not regarded as partners since they do not have mutual agency relationship. Such persons are:

(i) a lender of the firm (who has lent money) who receives a share of profits; [*Mollow March & Co.* v. *The Court of Wards*]

(ii) a widow or child of a deceased partner who receives a share of profits; [*I.T. Commissioner* v. *Kesharmal Keshardeo*]

(iii) a servant or an agent who receives a share of profits as part of his remuneration; and [*Munshi Abdul Latif* v. *Gopeshwar Chattora*]

(iv) a person who receives a share of profits in consideration of sale of business or goodwill of the business. [*Rawlinson* v. *Clarke*]

Conclusion: The true test of partnership is not the sharing of profits but the existence of mutual agency relationship, i.e., the capacity of a partner to bind other partners by his acts done in firm's name and be bound by the acts of other partners in firm's name. [*Refer to Practical Problems 8 to 16*]

7.3 Who are not Partners?

In addition to the persons sharing the profits but not having mutual agency relationship (as listed in aforesaid Para (b)), the following persons are not treated as partners:

(a) Members of a Hindu undivided family (HUF) carrying on family business.

(b) Burmese Buddhist husband and wife carrying on a business.

7.4 Conclusion

Thus, partnership can be presumed when (a) there is an agreement to share the profits of a business and (b) the business must be carried on by all or by any of them acting for all. Even when the exclusive power and control is vested with one partner under an agreement, partnership shall be presumed to exist.

[*K.D. Kamath & Co.* v. *Commmissioner of Income. Tax,* 1972, 82 ITR 680 (SC)]

8.0 DISTINCTION BETWEEN PARTNERSHIP AND CO-OWNERSHIP

8.1 Meaning of Co-ownership

Co-ownership means joint ownership of some property. The two or more persons who own some property jointly are called co-owners. As per Explanation I to Section 6, the joint owners of some property sharing profits or gross returns arising from the property do not become partners.

Example *Two sons who inherit a building from their father, let it out on a rent of Rs 10,000 per annum and share the rental income equally, are regarded as co-owners. If, however, they enter into an agreement to run a hotel in that building and share the income thereof, they will be regarded as partners.*

8.2 Distinction The partnership and co-ownership can be distinguished as under:

Basis of Distinction	*Partnership*	*Co-ownership*
1. *Agreement*	It arises from an agreement.	It may or may not arise from agreement.
2. *Business*	It is formed to carry on a business.	It may or may not involve carrying on a business.
3. *Profit or loss*	It involves profit or loss.	It may or may not involve profit or loss.
4. *Mutual agency*	Partners have a mutual agency relationship.	Co-owners do not have a mutual agency relationship.
5. *Name of persons involved*	The persons who form partnership are called partners.	The persons who own some property jointly are called co-owners.

6. ***Maximum limit***	The maximum limit of partners is 10 for a banking business and 20 for any other business.	There is *no* maximum *limit* of co-owners.
7. ***Transfer of interest***	A partner *cannot transfer* his share to a stranger without the consent of other partners.	A co-owner *can transfer* his share to a stranger without the consent of other co-owners.
8. ***Right to claim partition***	A partner has *no right* to claim partition of property but he can sue the other partners for the dissolution of the firm and accounts.	A co-owner *has* the *right* to claim partition of property.
9. ***Lien on property***	A partner has a lien on the partnership property for expenses incurred by him on behalf of the firm.	A co-owner has *no* such *lien.*

9.0 DISTINCTION BETWEEN PARTNERSHIP AND HINDU UNDIVIDED FAMILY

9.1 Meaning of Hindu Undivided Family (HUF)

(a) According to the Hindu Law, "Hindu undivided family is a family which consists of all persons lineally descended from a common ancestor and includes their wives and unmarried daughters."

(b) Three successive generations in the male line (son, grandson, and great-grandson) who inherit the ancestral property are called 'Coparceners'.

(c) The property which a man inherits from any of his three immediate male ancestors (i.e., his father, grandfather and great grandfather), is called 'ancestral property'.

(d) There are two schools of Hindu Law—Dayabhaga and Mitakshara.

(e) Under Dayabhaga School of Law, which is applicable to West Bengal and Assam, a son acquires an interest in the ancestral property only after the death of his father.

(f) Under Mitakshara School of Law, which is applicable to whole of India (except West Bengal and Assam), each son acquires by birth an interest in the ancestral property.

9.2 Distinction The partnership and Hindu undivided family can be distinguished as under:

Basis of Distinction	*Partnership*	*Hindu Undivided Family*
1. Agreement	It arises from an agreement.	It arises by status or operation of law.
2. Regulating law	It is governed by the Indian Partnership Act, 1932.	It is governed by Hindu Law.
3. Name of the persons involved.	The persons who form partnership are called 'partners'.	The persons who are the members of the HUF are called 'Coparceners'.

4. Maximum limit	The maximum limit of partner is 10 for a banking business and 20 for any other business.	There is no maximum limit of coparceners.
5. Admission of new members	A person can be admitted to the existing partnership with the consent of all other partners.	A male person becomes a member merely by his birth.
6. Minor members	A minor can be admitted to the benefits of partnership with the consent of all the partners.	A male minor becomes a member merely by his birth.
7. Female members	A female can become a full fledged partner.	A female does not become member merely by her birth.
8. Implied authority	Each partner has implied authority to bind the firm by acts done in the ordinary course of the business of the firm.	Only the *Karta* has implied authority.
9. Liability of members	The liability of all the partners is unlimited.	Only *Karta's* liability is unlimited and the liability of the other coparceners is limited only to their shares in the family property.
10. Right to demand accounts	Each partner has a right to inspect and copy the account books and ask for the account of profits and losses.	The coparceners have no right to aks for the account of past dealings.
11. Effect of death of a member	Unless otherwise agreed partnership is dissolved on the death of any partner.	The Hindu undivided family continues to operate even after the death of a coparcener.

10.0 DISTINCTION BETWEEN PARTNERSHIP AND COMPANY

10.1 Meaning of Company

A company is an artificial person created by law having separate legal entity, perpetual succession, and a common seal.

10.2 Distinction between Partnership and Company

Basis of Distinction	*Partnership*	*Company*
1. *Legal entity*	A firm doesn't enjoy separate legal existence. Partners are collectively termed as a firm and individually as partners.	It has a separate legal existence. A company is separate from its members.
2. *Liability*	The liability of partners is unlimited.	Liability of its members is limited to the extent of the value of shares held by them.

3. ***Tenure***	It does not enjoy a long lease of life. Death, sickness, retirement of partners may affect its existence so as to dissolve it. Dissolution may take place on flimsy grounds.	It enjoys perpetual existence. Even an atom bomb cannot destroy a company unless it is wound up under the due process of law. Winding up may take years.
4. ***Number of members***	Minimum number of partners is 2. Maximum may be 10 (in case of banking business) or twenty (in case of non-banking business).	A public company must have a minimum 7 members to start with. However, there is no limit on the maximum number of members of a company.
5. ***Transfer of interest***	A partner cannot transfer his share without the consent of other partners.	A member may transfer his share's as and when he likes. There is no restriction on transfer of shares.
6. ***Agency***	Each partner represents the other partners so as to bind and be bound to others.	There is no agency relationship among members of a company as they do not bind each other with their actions.
7. ***Distribution of profits***	Profits are distributable among partners as per the partnership deed.	There is no such compulsion that profits must be distributed. Only when the dividends are declared that the members get a share of profits.
8. ***Management***	The entire management lies with all the partners.	Members cannot participate in management unless appointed as directors. However, members may attend and vote at meetings while making the appointment of Directors, Auditors etc.
9. ***Property***	Property of the firm is the joint property of all its partners.	Property of the company is not the property of its members as the company and members have separate legal existence.
10. ***Remedy of creditors***	The creditors of the firm can proceed against the partners jointly & severally	The creditors of a company can proceed only against the company and not against its members.

11. *Contract*	A partner can not contract with the firm.	A member can contract with the company
12. *Restriction on Authority*	Restrictions on partner's authority do not bind the outsiders)	Such restrictions contained in Articles bind the outsiders
13. **Compulsory Audit**	Audit is not compulsory	Audit is compulsory

11.0 DISTINCTION BETWEEN PARTNERSHIP AND CLUB

11.1 Meaning of Club

A club is an association of persons aimed at promoting non-profit making objects like culture, health, recreation etc.

11.2 Distinction between Partnership and Club

Basis of Distinction	***Partnership***	***Club***
1. ***Objects***	It has business oriented ob-jects aimed at profit sharing.	It is not aimed at making profits and hence has no business interests.
2. ***Number of members***	Membership limited to 10 or 20 depending upon the nature of business.	There is no limit on the number of its members.
3. *Tenure*	Change in membership affe-cts its existence and therefore generally does not enjoy a long tenure.	Change in membership does not affect its existence.
4. *Agency*	It is based on agency relationship among partners.	A member of a club is not agent of other members and therefore they do not bind each other with their acts.

12.0 PARTNERSHIP DEED

Meaning	The document which contains the term of a partnership as agreed among the partners is called 'partnership deed'. The deed is required to be duly stamped as per the Indian Stamp Act, 1889 and duly signed by all the partners.
Why necessary	A partnership is formed by an agreement. This agreement may be express (i.e., oral or in writing) or implied. Though the law does not expressly require that the partnership agreement should be in writing, it is desirable to have it in writing in order to avoid any dispute with regard to the terms of the partnership.

Contents	The partnership deed contains various provisions relating to various matters such as: (a) Name of the firm. (b) Names and addresses of all partners (c) Nature and place of business (d) Date of commencement of partnership (e) Duration of partnership (f) Amount of capital of each partner (g) Profit sharing ratio (h) Interest on capital (i) Interest on drawings (j) Interest on loan advanced by a partner to the firm (k) Salary or commission payable to any partner (l) Method of valuation of goodwill and other assets and liabilities in case of admission or retirement or death of a partner (m) Settlement of accounts in case of retirement/death of a partner or dissolution of firm
What must not contain	The partnership deed must not contain any term which is in contravention with the provisions of the Indian Partnership Act.
Variation	The terms laid down in the partnership deed may be varied with the consent of *all* the partners.

13.0 REGISTRATION

13.1 Meaning of Registration

Registration means getting the partnership registered with the Registrar of Firm of the area in which the place of business of the firm is situated or proposed to be situated.

13.2 What is the Procedure for Registration ?

The practical steps involved in the registration of a firm are given below:

Practical Steps Involved in the Registration of a Firm

Step 1 : *Obtain a Statement in the prescribed form from the office of the Registrar of Firms of the area in which any place of business of the firm is situated or proposed to be situated.*

Step 2 : *State the following information in the statement:*

(a) the name of the firm;
(b) the principal place of the firm;
(c) the names of other places where the firm carries on business;
(d) the date when each partner joined the firm;
(e) the names in full and permanent addresses of the partner;
(f) the duration of the firm.

Step 3 : *Get the statement duly verified and signed by all the partners or by their duly authorised agents.*

Step 4 : *File the Statement alongwith prescribed fees with the Registrar of the Firms of the area.*

Step 5 : *Obtain a Certificate from the Registrar.*

Note: When the Registrar is satisfied that the provisions of Section 58 have been duly complied with, he shall record an entry of the Statement in the register called 'Register of Firms' and file the statement. He shall then issue a certificate of registration [Section 59].

It may be noted that if any change is made in the particulars filed with the Registrar, the same should be duly notified to the Registrar so that he can incorporate the same in the 'Register of Firms'.

13.3 When can a firm be registered ?

Since the registration of a firm is not compulsory, it can be effected at any stage, i.e., at the time of its formation or at anytime thereafter. Section 69(2) provides that no suit can be filed by or on behalf of an unregistered firm in a court. This means the firm must be got registered before any suit is filed in a court.

13.4 When does Registration becomes Effective ?

Registration becomes effective from the date of filing of the duly signed and verified statement alongwith the prescribed form and not from the date of issue of certificate of registration since the act of the Registrar in recording an entry of the statement in the Register of Firms is only a clerical act.

[*J.R. and O.M. Contractors* v. *Income Tax Commissioner*]

13.5 Is the Registration of Firm Compulsory ?

Under the Indian Partnership Act 1932, the registration of a firm is not compulsory. But, indirectly, by creating certain liabilities (also termed as effects of non-registration u/s 69) from which an unregistered firm suffers, the law has made the registration of firms desirable. **The effects of non-registration of a firm are as follows:**

(*a*) ***No suit by a partner against the firm or the other partner [Section 69(1)]*** A partner of an unregistered firm cannot file a suit against the firm or any partner of the firm to enforce any right arising from contract. *For example,* if a partner of an unregistered firm is not paid his share of profits, he cannot claim it through the court.

Note: Section 69(1) prohibits the institution of civil suit and not the criminal suit.

(*b*) ***No suit by the firm against third parties [Section 69(2)]*** An unregistered firm cannot file a suit against a third party to enforce any right arising from contract. *For example*, if an unregistered firm has sold some goods to a customer, it cannot file a suit against the customer for the recovery of the price of goods. On the other hand, if any unregistered firm has purchased some goods from a supplier, such supplier can file a suit against the firm for the recovery of the price of goods. Thus, it is only a suit by the unregistered firm or its partners against a third party, which is prohibited and not a suit by the third party against the unregistered firm or its partners. It may be noted that this disability can be removed by getting the firm registered before filing the suit. In case of *Puran Mal* v. *Central Bank of India*, it was held that a subsequent registration could not cure the defect that existed at the time of filing the suit.

(*c*) ***No right to claim set off in excess of Rs 100 [Section 69(3)]*** An unregistered firm or any partner thereof cannot claim a set off (if value exceeds Rs 100) in proceeding instituted against the firm by a third party to enforce a right arising from a contract. *For example*, if an unregistered firm owes Rs 10,000 to *X*, a third party, *X* owes Rs 1,000 to such firm, *X* files a suit against the firm for the recovery of Rs 10,000. In this case, an unregistered firm cannot say that Rs 1,000 should be adjusted against Rs 10,000.

13.6 What are the Rights not Affected by Non-registration ?

(*a*) ***Rights of unregistered firm or partners thereof***

(i) Right of firm or partner of a firm having no place of business in India. [Section 69(4)(a)].

(ii) Right to file a suit or claim of set-off if the value of suit does not exceed Rs 100 [Section 69(4)(b)].

(iii) Right of a partner to sue (a) for the dissolution of the firm, (b) for the accounts of a dissolved firm, or (c) for claiming share of the assets of a dissolved firm [Section 69(3)(a)].

(iv) Right to enforce a right arising otherwise than out of a contract, e.g. infringement of a Patent right by a third party. The firm may file a suit to restrain the third party from misusing the Patent right.

(*b*) ***Right of a third party to file a suit against the unregistered firm or partners thereof.***

(*c*) ***Power of an Official Assignee or Receiver or Court to realise the property of an insolvent partner [Section 69(3)(b)].***

Example *X and Y purchased a taxi and they were plying it in partnership. The firm was not registered. After 1 year, X sold the taxi without Y's consent and did not pay anything to Y. Y filed a suit against X to recover his share in the sale proceeds. X defended the suit on the ground that the firm was not registered. It was held that the suit was maintainable because it was for the realisation of the assets of a dissolved firm.* *[Basant Lal v. Chiranjit Lal]* [*Refer to Practical Problems 17 to 22*]

14.0 WHAT ARE THE TYPES OF PARTNERSHIP ON THE BASIS OF ITS DURATION

On the basis of duration, the partnership can be *either* Partnership at will *or* Particular Partnership.

Partnership at Will [Sec. 7]	When there is no provision in partnership agreement for duration of the partnership, the partnership is called 'Partnership at Will'. A partnership at will may be dissolved by any partner by giving a notice in writing to *all other* partners of his intention to dissolve the firm.
Particular Partnership [Sec. 8]	When a partnership is formed for a specific venture or for a particular period, the partnership is called a 'Particular Partnership'. Such partnership comes to an end on the completion of the venture *or* on the expiry of the period. If such partnership is continued after the expiry of term or completion of the venture, it is deemed to be a partnership at will. A particular partnership may be dissolved before the expiry of the term *or* completion of the venture only by the mutual consent of *all* the partners.

15.0 WHAT ARE THE TYPES OF PARTNERS ?

A person who deals or intends to deal with a firm, must know who the partners are and to what extent each partner is liable. To ascertain the extent of partner's liability, it becomes necessary to know the various types of partners which are given as follows:

TYPES OF PARTNERS

Actual or Ostensible Partner	*Sleeping or Dormant Partner*	*Nominal Partner*	*Partner in Profits only*	*Sub-partner*
He takes an active part in the conduct of the business.	He does not take an active part in the conduct of the business.	He lends his name to the firm without having any real interest in the firm. He *neither* contributes to the capital *nor* shares the profits or takes part in the conduct of the business of the firm.	He shares the profits only and not losses.	He is a third person with whom a partner agrees to share his profits derived from the firm.
He alongwith other partners is liable to third parties for all the acts of the firm.	He alongwith other partners is liable to third parties for the acts of the firm.	He alongwith other partners is liable to third parties for all acts of the firm as if he is an actual partner.	He alongwith other partners is liable to third parties for all the acts of the firm.	He has no right against right against the firm nor is he liable for the acts of the firm.
He must give public notice of his retirement.	He need not gives public notice of his retirement.	He must give public notice of his retirement.	He must give public notice of his retirement.	There is no question of public notice at all since he is a third person and not a partner
His insanity or permanent incapacity to perform his duties may be a ground for the dissolution of the firm.	His insanity or permanent incapacity to perform his duties is no ground for the dissolution of the firm.	His insanity or permanent incapacity to perform his duties is no ground for the dissolution of the firm.	His insanity or permanent incapacity to perform his duties may be a ground for the dissolution of the firm.	His insanity or permanent incapacity to perform his duties is no ground for the dissolution of the firm since he is a third person and not a partner.

16.0 PARTNER BY ESTOPPEL OR HOLDING OUT

16.1 Two Conditions for Partner by Estapple or Holding out

A person is held liable as a partner by estoppel or holding out if the following two conditions are fulfilled:

(a) He must have represented himself to be a partner by word spoken or written or by his conduct (such type of representation may be called as active representation), or

He must have knowingly permitted himself to be represented as a partner (such type of representation may be called as tacit representation); and

(b) The other person acting on the faith of such representation must have given credit to the firm. It is immaterial whether the person so representing to be a partner, is aware or not that the representation has reached the other person.

Example I *Ram, a sole proprietor of Ram Shyam & Co. employed Shyam as manager. Ram introduced Shyam as his partner to S, a supplier of goods. Shyam remained silent. Treating Shyam a partner S supplied the goods on credit. Ram failed to pay the price of goods. S filed a suit against both Ram and Shyam for the recovery of the price. Here, Shyam is liable as a partner by holding out because he has knowingly permitted himself to be represented as a partner and the S the supplier has acted on the faith of such representation.* *[Martyn v. Grag]*

Example II *Patudi, a renowned sportsman assumed the honorary presidentship of a publishing business which brings out a sports magazine because other partners requested him to do. S a supplier gave credit to this firm in the bona fide belief that Patudi was a partner in a firm. Here, Patudi is liable as a partner by holding out because he has knowingly permitted himself to be represented as a partner and the supplier has acted on the faith of such representation.*

16.2 Position of a Retiring Partner as Partner by Holding Out [Section 28(2)]

Where, after the retirement of a partner, the firm uses the retired partner's name as a partner, the retired partner who has not given public notice of his retirement, is held liable on grounds of holding out to third parties who give credit to the firm on the faith that he is still a partner.

16.3 Exceptions to the Principle of Holding Out [Sections 28(2) and 34]

The principle of holding out does not apply in the following cases:

(a) Where, after the death of a partner, the firm uses the deceased partner's name as a partner, the estate of the deceased partner or his legal representatives cannot be held liable for acts of the firm done after his death. It may be noted that a public notice of a partner's death is not required.

(b) The estate of the insolvent partner cannot be held liable for the acts of the firm done after the date of the order of adjudication [Section 34]. It may be noted that a public notice of a partner's insolvency is not required.

17.0 POSITION OF MINOR AS A PARTNER

17.1 Can a minor enter into a Partnership agreement ?

Since a minor is not capable of entering into a contract, an agreement by or with a minor is void *ab-initio* (*Mohni Bibi* v. *Dharamdas Ghosh*). Since partnership is formed by an agreement, a minor cannot enter into a partnership agreement.

17.2 Can a minor be admitted as Partner ?

on the basis of the general rule that a minor cannot be a promisor, but can be a promisee or a beneficiary, Section 30 of the Indian Partnership Act 1932, provides as under:

"**With the consent of *all* the partners for the time being, a minor may be admitted to the benefits of partnership.**"

An analysis of the above provision highlights the following three conditions:

(a) Before admission of a minor as a partner, there must be an existence of partnership;

(b) There must be mutual consent of *all* the partners;

(c) A minor can be admitted only to the benefits of partnership.

Note: There cannot be a partnership consisting of all the minors or of one major and all other minors. [*Shivaram* v. *Gaurishanker*]

17.3 What are the Rights and Liabilities of a Minor Partner before Attaining Majority ?

Rights	*Liabilities*
(a) He has a right to share the profits and property of the firm in accordance with the agreement. [Section 30(2)]	(a) He is liable only to the extent of his share in the profits and the property of the firm. He is not personally liable to third parties. [Section 30(3)]
(b) He has a right to have access to, and inspect and copy, any of the accounts of the firm. But he does not enjoy such rights in respect of books other than account books. [Section 30(2)]	(b) He cannot be declared insolvent on declaration of firm's insolvency, his share vests in the Official Receiver or Official Assignee.
(c) He has a right to file a suit for his share of profits or the property of the firm when he is not given his due share of profits. However, he can exercise this right only when he decides to sever his connections with the firm [Section 30(4)].	

17.4 What are the Rights and Liabilities of a Minor Partner on Attaining Majority ?

Within six months of date of his attaining majority or date of his obtaining knowledge that he had been admitted to the benefits of firm, whichever is later, the minor partner has to exercise his option whether or not to become a partner. Such option is required to be exercised by giving a public notice within the said six months. If he fails to give a public notice, he is deemed to have become a partner in the firm on the expiry of the said six months [Section 30(5)]. The various rights and liabilities of a minor partner on his attaining majority are given below:

When he elects to become a partner	*When he elects not to become a partner*
(a) He becomes personally liable to third parties for all acts of the firm since he was admitted to the benefits of partnership [Section 30(7)(a)].	(a) His rights and liabilities continue to be those of minor up to the date of giving public notice [Section 30(8)(a)].
(b) His share in the property and profits of the firm remains the same as he was entitled as a minor [Section 30(7)(b)].	(b) His share is not liable for any acts of the firm done after the date of the public notice [Section 30(8)(b)].
	(c) He is entitled to sue the partners for his share of the property and profits in the firm [Section 30(8)(c)].

18.0 PROPERTY OF THE FIRM [Sec. 14 & 15]

Meaning	Unless otherwise agreed by the partners, the property of the firm includes: (a) all properties, rights and interests originally brought to the common stock of the firm, (b) the property acquired by purchase or otherwise by or for the firm, (c) the property acquired with money belonging to the firm, and (d) the goodwill of the business of the firm. The Act does not define the term goodwill. But it is understood in the sense of value of reputation of the firm judged in respect of its capacity to bring super profits due to general public patronage. It is a part of the partnership property and can be sold either separately or alongwith the other property of the firm [Section 55(1)]. **Example** *X, Y and Z are partners. X bought three plots of land—one in firm's name, one in his own name, one in the name of a fictitious person with money belonging to the firm. All the plots of land will be treated as the property of the firm.*
Use	Unless otherwise agreed by the partners, the property of the firm shall be held and used by the partners exclusively for the purposes of the business of the firm. [*Refer to Practical Problem 23*]

19.0 MUTUAL RIGHTS AND DUTIES

19.1 Provisions which Govern Rights & Duties of Partners

The mutual rights and duties of partners are governed by (a) the Partnership Agreement and (b) the Partnership Act. The various provisions of the Partnership Act governing the mutual rights and duties of partners are summarised below:

Provisions of Sections 9 and 10	*Provisions of Sections 11, 12, 16 to 25*
(a) These provisions lay down the *mandatory* duties of partners	(a) These provisions lay down the *general* rights and duties.
(b) These provisions *cannot be changed* by an agreement amongst the partners.	(b) These provisions *can be changed* by an agreement amongst the partners

19.2 What are the Mandatory Duties of Partners ? [Sections 9 and 10]

The mandatory duties are:

1. to carry on the business of the firm to the greatest common advantage,
2. to be just and faithfull to each other, i.e. every partner should act in good faith. Good faith requires that a partner should not deceive the other partner by concealment of material facts.
3. to render true accounts and full information of all things affecting the firm to any partner or his legal representative.
4. to indemnify (i.e., to make good or to compensate) the firm for loss caused to it by his fraud in the conduct of the business of the firm.

Note: These mandotary duties can not be changed by mutual agreement amongst partners.

19.3 What are the General Duties of Partners ?

The general duties of partners as provided in the Act are subject to the agreement by partners. These can be changed by an agreement amongst the partners. Unless otherwise agreed by the partners, every partner has the following duties:

1. ***To attend deligently [Section 12(b)]:*** Every partner is bound to attend deligently (i.e. carefully) to his duties in the conduct of his business.
2. ***Not to claim remuneration for taking part [Section 13(a)]:*** A partner is not entitled to receive remuneration for taking part in the conduct of the business.
3. ***To contribute equally to the losses [Section 13(b)]:*** A partner must contribute equally to the losses sustained by the firm.
4. ***To indemnify the firm [Section 13(f)]:*** A partner must indemnify (i.e., compensate) the firm for any loss suffered by the firm due to his wilful neglect in the conduct of the business of the firm. The term 'wilful neglect', is something more than a mere 'negligence' and has been described as 'culpable negligence'.
5. ***To hold and use firm's property for business purpose [Section 15]:*** The partners must hold and use the firm's property for the purposes of the business.
6. ***To account for and pay the personal profits from transactions of firm etc. [Section 16(a)]:*** Every partner must account for and pay to the firm the profits earned by him from any transaction of the firm or from the use of firm's property, business connection or name. If a partner is entrusted with the job of buying sugar for the firm and he supplies sugar to the firm at a higher price from personal supplies held by him, he is liable to account for profits made (*Bentlay* v. *Crawen* (1853)18 Beave.
7. ***To account for and pay the personal profits from a competing business [Section 16(b)]:*** Every partner must account for and pay all profits earned by him in the competing business. It may be noted that Section 11(2) permits the partners to enter an agreement restraining a partner from carrying on any business other than the business of the firm so long as he is a partner.

[*Refer to Practical Problems 24 to 27*]

19.4 What are the Rights of Partners ?

The rights of partners as provided in the Act are subject to the agreement by partners. These can be changed by an agreement amongst the partners. Unless otherwise agreed by the partners, every partner has the following rights:

1. ***Right to take part [Section 12 (a)]:*** Every partner has a right to take part in the conduct of the business.
2. ***Right to express opinion [Section 12(c)]:*** Every partner has the right to express his opinion before the matter is decided. **All matters *except the change in the nature of the business,* may be decided by a *majority*** of the partners. The change in the nature of the business may be made only with the *unanimous consent* of all the partners.
3. ***Right to have access to books [Section 12(d)]:*** Every partner has a right to have access to and to inspect and copy any of the books of the firm.
4. ***Rights to share profits equally [Section 13(b)]:*** A partner is entitled to share the profits of the business of the firm equally.
5. ***Right to receive interest on capital out of profits [Section 13(c)]:*** If the partnership agreement provides for the payment of interest on capital, the

interest on capital shall be payable only out of profits. In other words, if there are losses, interest on capital will not be allowed.

6. ***Right to claim interest on advances [Section 13(d)]:*** A partner is entitled to claim interest on advances made by him to the firm @ 6% p.a. Interest on advances is payable whether there are profits or losses. It may be noteod that the partner is not entitled to interest after the date of dissolution of firm unless otherwise agreed.
7. ***Right to be indemnified [Section 13(e)]:*** A partner has a right to recover from the firm the payments made and liabilities incurred by him:
   (i) in the ordinary and proper conduct of the business, and
   (ii) in doing act in emergency for the purpose of protecting the firm from loss if he has acted in a manner as a person of ordinary prudence would have acted in similar circumstances in his own case.
8. ***Right to prevent the introduction of a new partner [Section 31]:*** Every partner has the right to prevent the introduction of a new partner without the consent of all the existing partners.
9. ***Right to retire [Section 32]:*** Every partner has the right to retire with the consent of all other partners and in the case of a partnership at will, by giving notice to that effect in writing to all the other partners.
10. ***Right not to be expelled [Section 33]:*** Every partner has the right not to be expelled from the firm by any majority of partners unless such power is conferred by partnership agreement and is exercised in good faith. Thus expulsion may be exercised subject to the following conditions.
    (a) It must be approved by majority of the partners.
    (b) It must be exercised in good faith without any private animosity.
    (c) The concerned partner must be given an opportunity to make a representation.
11. ***Right to carry on competing business [Section 36(1)]:*** Every outgoing partner has a right to carry on a competing business and to advertise such business. But, he cannot (i) use the firm's name, (ii) represent the firm, or (iii) solicit the firm's customers.
12. ***Right to share subsequent profits [Section 37]:*** Every outgoing partner or the estate of any partner who ceased to be a partner has the right to claim *either* a share in the subsequent profits of the firm *or* interest @ 6% p.a. on his share in the firm's property till the accounts are finally settled.
13. ***Right to dissolve the partnership [Section 40]:*** Every partner has the right to dissolve the partnership with the consent of all partners and in the case of a partnership at will, by giving notice to that effect in writing to all the other partners.

20.0 RELATION OF PARTNERS WITH THIRD PARTIES [SECTION 18]

The relations of partners with third parties are governed by the mutual agency relationship existing among the partners. According to Section 18, "every partner is an agent of the firm for the purposes of the business of the firm." In other words, every partner has the capacity to bind other partners by his acts done in firm's name. Therefore, all partners are liable to third parties for the acts of every partner done for the purpose of the business of the firm. [*Refer to Practical Problem 28*]

21.0 IMPLIED AUTHORITY OF A PARTNER [SECTION 19]

21.1 Meaning of Implied Authority

The authority of a partner means the capacity of a partner to bind the firm by his act. This authority may be express or implied. The authority conferred on a partner by mutual agreement is called 'express authority'. The authority conferred on a partner by the provisions of Section 19 of the Indian Partnership Act is called 'implied authority'. Reading together Sections 19(1) and 22. Implied authority covers those acts of partners which fulfill the following three conditions:

(a) The act must relate to the normal business of the firm;

(b) The act must have been done in the usual way of carrying on the business of the firm;

(It may be noted that the question as to what is usual and what is unusual in a business depends on the nature of business and the usage of trade, e.g. taking loan is considered as usual activity in case of a trading concern but unusual activity in case of a professional concern of solicitors.)

(c) The act must be done in the firm's name or in any other manner expressing or implying an intention to bind the firm.

A firm was engaged in trapping elephants. One of the partners of the firm hired out an elephant without the consent of the other partners. Held, the act fell within the implied authority of the partner (*Mathuranath* v. *Bageshwari Rani*).

Example *A, B, C, D and E are partners of a banking firm. State the legal position of firm for the following acts of partners:*

(a) *A* borrows money in the name of the firm,

(b) *B* orders for a certain quantity of wine, on the firm's letter head.

(c) *C* receives money from a borrower of a firm and utilised this amount for personal use without informing other partners about the receipt of this money.

(d) *D* borrows money on his own credit by giving his own promissory note and utilises subsequently this amount for firm's use.

Solution

Analysis of Partner's Acts whether Satisfying the Conditions of Sec. 19

Partner's act	***Whether the act done relates to the normal business of the firm***	***Whether the act has been done in the usual way***	***Whether the act has been done in firm's name or with an intention to bind firm***
A's act	Yes	Yes	Yes
B's act	No	Yes	Yes
C's act	Yes	Yes	Yes
D's act	Yes	Yes	No

Decision and reason:

(a) The firm is liable for the acts of *A* and *C*. Their acts fall within the scope of implied authority because all the conditions of Section 19 have been fulfilled.

(b) The firm is not liable for the acts of *B* and *D*. Their acts do not fall within the scope of implied authority because all the conditions of Section 19 have not been fulfilled.

21.2 What are the Acts within the Implied Authority ?

An implied authority of a partner of a trading firm include the following acts:

(a) To purchase goods of the kind that are used in the business of the firm;

(b) To sell the goods of the firm;

(c) To settle accounts with the persons dealing with the firm;

(d) To receive payment of the debts due to the firm and issue receipts for the same;

(e) To engage servants for the business of the firm;

(f) To engage a lawyer to defend an action brought against the firm;

(g) To borrow money for the purpose of the firm's business;

(h) To pledge the goods of the firm as security for the repayment of borrowings made for the purpose of firm's business;

(i) To draw, accept, endorse Bill of Exchange and other negotiable instruments in the name of the firm.

21.3 Restrictions on the Implied Authority of a Partner [Sections 19 and 20]

The restrictions on the implied authority of a partner may be discussed under the following two heads:

(I) Statutory Restrictions and (II) Restrictions imposed by mutual agreement.

I. Statutory Restrictions [Section 19(2)] In the absence of any usage or custom of trade to the contrary, the implied authority of a partner does not empower him to do the following acts namely—

(a) To submit a dispute to arbitration relating to the business of the firm;

(b) To open a Bank Account on behalf of the firm in partner's own name;

(c) To compromise or relinquish any claim or portion of the claim by the firm;

(d) To withdraw a suit or proceedings filed on behalf of the firm;

(e) To admit any liability in a suit or proceedings against the firm;

(f) To acquire immovable property on behalf of the firm;

(g) To transfer immovable property belonging to the firm; and

(h) To enter into partnership on behalf of the firm. [*Refer to Practical Problem 30*]

Note: A partner can do any of the above-mentioned acts only if he is expressly authorised to do that act or the usage or custom of the trade permits him to do that act.

For example, a partner may open a Bank Account on behalf of the firm in his own name if he is expressly authorised to do so by mutual agreement.

Liability of the Firm for the Restricted Acts of Partner

The firm is not liable to third party for the above mentioned restricted acts of a partner whether or not the person dealing with the firm knew about such restrictions.

II. Restrictions Imposed by Mutual Agreement [Section 20] The partners of a firm by mutual agreement may extend or restrict the scope of implied authority of any partner. But a third party is not bound by any such restriction unless it has the knowledge of such restriction. In other words, the firm is liable to third party only if the third party has no knowledge of the restrictions.

Example *X, Y and Z are partners in a trading firm. They decide that no partner shall have the right to borrow beyond Rs 20,000 without the consent of other partners. X* *without consulting Y and Z borrows from W Rs 25,000 in the name of the firm and utilised the same in paying of the firm's debts. The firm is liable to pay W if W is unaware of the restriction but it will not be liable to pay W if W was aware of such restriction.*

21.4 Implied Authority and Third Parties [Sections 20, 23 to 27]

All partners are liable to third parties for all acts of a partner which fall within the scope of his implied authority. Their liability to third parties in various cases are summarised as under:

(a) Effect of Restriction on Implied Authority [Section 20] The partners of a firm by mutual agreement, may extend or restrict the scope of implied authority of any partner. But, the third party is not bound by any restriction imposed on the implied authority of a partner unless it has the knowledge of such restriction. For example, *X*, *Y* and *Z* are partners in a trading firm. By an agreement, they decided that no partner shall have the right to buy goods beyond the value of Rs 1,00,000 without the consent of other partners. A third party who had no knowledge of such restriction sold goods worth Rs 2,00,000 to *X* who did not consult his other partners about this transaction. The firm is liable to pay the full amount to the third party.

Note: The above-mentioned extension or restriction is only possible with the consent of all the partners. Any one partner or even a majority of the partners, cannot restrict or extend the implied authority. [*Refer to Practical Problem 31*]

(b) Effect of Admissions by a Partner [Section 23] Any admission or representation (e.g., acknowledgement signed by a partner) by a partner is sufficient evidence against the firm if the following two conditions are fulfilled:

(i) Such admission or representation must relate to the affairs of the firm; and

(ii) Such admission or representation must be made in the ordinary course of business.

Notes:

(a) In the opinion of the Calcutta, Bombay and Allahabad High Courts, an acknowledgement signed by a partner in connection with partnership debt will extend the period of limitation against the firm under the Limitation Act. The High Court of Madras, however, has taken the view that the special authority must be proved.

(b) The provisions of Section 23 would not apply after the dissolution of the firm [*Premji Dossa* 10 Bombay 358].

(c) Effect of Notice to an Acting Partner [Section 24] Any notice to a partner operates as a notice to the firm if the following three conditions are fulfilled:

(i) Such notice must relate to the affairs of the firm;

(ii) Such notice must be given to a working partner and not to a sleeping partner.

(iii) There must not be any fraud committed by the partners and the third party against the firm. [*Refer to Practical Problem 33*]

(d) Contractual Liability [Section 25] Every partner is liable jointly with other partners and also severally (i.e., individually) for all those acts of the firm which have been done while he was a partner.

Example *X, Y and Z were partners in a firm when infringement of a trademark took place. X retired. Later on, damages arising out of the alleged infringement arose after the dissolution of the firm. It was held that all the partners who were members* *of the firm at the time when infringement of a trademark took place, were liable. [Thomas Bear & Sons v. Ralia Ram]* *[Refer to Practical Problem 35]*

(e) Liability of the Firm for Wrongful Acts of a Partner [Section 26] The firm is liable to the same extent as the partner for any loss or injury caused to any third party or any penalty by the wrongful act or omission of a partner if *either* of the following two conditions is fulfilled:

(i) Such wrongful act or omission must have been done by a partner while he was acting in the ordinary course of business of the firm, or

(ii) Such wrongful act or omission must have been done by a partner with the authority of the other partners.

Note: *The term 'wrongful act' includes fraud or negligence of the partners.*

Example *X, Y, Z are partners in a magazine business. X allows the publication of a defamatory article about a prominent person 'Sharad Pawar', without checking its validity. Sharad Pawar files a suit against the firm. The firm will be liable for this act of the editor partner on the following two grounds:*

(i) Such act caused loss of goodwill to Sharad Pawar,

(ii) Such act was done in the usual course of business.

[Refer to Practical Problem 36]

(f) Liability of Firm for Misappropriation by Partner [Section 27] The firm is liable to the third parties in the following two cases of misappropriation by a partner:

Case	***Condition***
(a) ***Where a partner receives money or property from a third person and misapplies it.***	The receipt of money or other property by a partner must be an act within the scope of his apparent authority.
(b) ***Where a firm, in the course of its business, receives money or property from a third person and the same is misapplied by any of its partners.***	The partner must have misapplied while the property was in the custody of firm.

Notes:

(i) The provisions of Section 26 deals with general wrongful act or defaults of a partner, whereas Section 27 deals with one particular wrong, i.e. misapplication of money or property by a partner.

(ii) Under Clause (a) of Section 27, it is not necessary that the property must have actually come into the custody of the firm whereas under Clause (b) of Section 27, it is necessary.

Example *X, Y and Z are partners in a trading firm. W, a debtor of the firm, repays his debt of Rs 5,000 to X who does not inform Y and Z about the repayment and misuses the money. W would be discharged of the debts on account of payment made to X because whatever is done by a partner, in the ordinary course of partnership business and within the scope of his authority, is deemed to have been done by him only as an agent for the other partners and it is immaterial whether or not the other partners have notice of this act.*

[Refer to Practical Problems 37 and 38]

Partner's Authority in an Emergency [Section 21]

A partner's authority in an emergency covers those acts which fulfil the following two conditions:

(a) The act must be done to protect the firm from loss; and

(b) The act must be such as a prudent man would undertake under similar circumstances in his own case.

It may be noted that these acts do not form part of the implied authority of the partner but, nevertheless, they would bind the firm. A partner's authority in an emergency is similar to that of an agent in similar circumstances u/s 189 of the Indian Contract Act.

Example *X, Y and Z are partners in a trading firm. By an agreement, they decided that no partner would have authority to sell goods of the firm above the value of Rs 50,000 without the consent of other partners. Owing to a sudden slump in the market, the prices crashed. One partner, in order to save the firm from loss, sold all the stock worth Rs 5,00,000 without consulting any other partner. Such an act would bind the firm.*

22.0 RECONSTITUTION OF A FIRM

The reconstitution of a firm takes place when there is any change in the composition of the partnership. The various ways in which a firm is reconstituted are shown below:

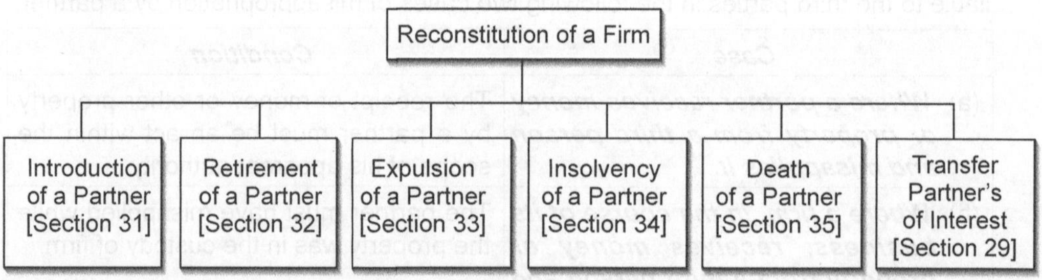

22.1 Introduction of a Partner [Section 31] Subject to provisions of Section 30 (regarding minor partner), a person may be admitted as a partner *either*—

(i) with the consent of all the existing partners, or

(ii) in accordance with a contract already entered into between the existing partners for the admission of a new partner.

Example *The partnership agreement between X and Y provides that X could introduce into partnership any of his sons on attaining the age of majority. X decides to admit his son (who has attained majority) as a partner. Y refused to consent, Y's consent is not required since the clause in the partnership agreement operated as a consent [Leading case: Byrne v. Reid]*

Liability of an Incoming Partner for Firm's Acts done before his Admission An incoming partner is not liable for all the acts of the firm done before his admission. This general rule has two exceptions which are as follows:

(i) An incoming partner is liable for the acts done before his admission if (a) the new firm assumes the liabilities of the old firm, and (b) the creditors accept the new firm as their debtor and discharge the old firm from its liability.

(ii) A minor who, on attaining majority decides to become a partner, is liable for all acts of the firm done since he was admitted to the benefits of partnership.

Liability of an Incoming Partner for Firm's Acts done after his Admission An incoming partner is liable for all the acts of the firm done after his admission.

22.2 Retirement of a Partner [Section 32] A partner may be retire from the firm in any of the following ways:

(i) with the consent of all the other partners; or
(ii) in accordance with an express agreement among the partners; or
(iii) in the case of partnership at will, by giving a notice to all other partners of his intention to retire.

Note: In case of a partnership at will, a partner may retire by notice even if the pending contracts have not been completed. [Keshav Lal v. Bhai Lal]

Liabilities of a Retiring Partner The liabilities of a retiring partner may be discussed as under:

(a) ***For Firm's acts before his retirement [Section 32(2)]***	He continues to be liable to third party unless he is discharged for the same by a tripartite agreement between him, third party and the partners of the reconstituted firm.
(b) ***For Firm's acts after his retirement [Section 32(3), (4)]***	He continues to be liable to third party (other than one who deals with the firm without knowing that he was a partner) until public notice of his retirement is given *either* by himself *or* any of the other partners. This liability of a retiring partner is based on the principle of holding out.

Rights of a Retiring Partner [Sections 36 and 37] A retiring partner has the following two rights:

(a) ***Right to carry on competing business [Section 36]***	He may carry on a business competing with that of the firm and may advertise such business but unless otherwise agreed he cannot— (i) use the firm's name; (ii) represent himself as carrying on firm's business; (iii) solicit the old customers.
(b) ***Right in case of no final settlement of accounts [Section 37]***	He at his option, is entitled to claim, *either* of the following: (i) such share of profits earned after his retirement which is attributable to the use of his share of the property of the firm, or (ii) Interest at the rate of 6% p.a. on the amount of his share in the property. ***Notes:*** This right is available to a retiring partner even if only a part of his property is used in the business. [*Ramakrishna Ayyar* v. *Muthu-swami Ayyar*] This right is also available to the legal representatives of a deceased partner.

[*Refer to Practical Problems 42 to 44*]

22.3 Expulsion of a Partner [Section 33] A partner may be expelled if the following four conditions are satisfied:

(a) **Express Power**	The power to expel a partner must have existed in a contract between the partners;
(b) **By Majority**	The power must have been exercised by a majority of the partners, and
(c) **Good Faith**	The power must have been exercised in good faith without any private animosity.
(d) **Opportunity**	The affected partner must be given an opportunity to make a representation before being dismissed.

The expulsion, without the satisfaction of the aforesaid conditions, is said to be an irregular expulsion which is null and void. The partner who has been wrongly expelled, has a right to claim re-instalment as a partner and not to recover damages for wrongful expulsion.

The rights and liabilities of an expelled partner are the same as those of a retired partner. [Section 33(2)]

22.4 Insolvency of a Partner [Section 34] The effects resulting from the insolvency of a partner are summarised below:

(a) He ceases to be a partner on the date of the order of adjudication;

(b) Unless otherwise agreed, the firm is dissolved; [Section 42(d)]

(c) His estate is not liable for firm's acts done after the date of the order;

(d) Firm is not liable for his acts done after the date of the order.

Note: No public notice is required on the insolvency of a partner.

[Section 45] *[Refer to Practical Problem 45]*

22.5 Death of a Partner [Sections 35 and 42(c)] Unless otherwise agreed by the partners, a firm is dissolved on the death of a partner [Section 42(c)]. Where under the contract a firm is not dissolved by the death of a partner, the estate of the deceased partner is not liable for any act of the firm done after the date of his death [Section 35].

Note: No public notice is required on the death of a partner. [Section 45]

Example *X was a partner in a firm. The firm ordered goods in X's life time but the delivery of the goods was made after X's death. In such a case, X's estate would not be liable for this debt because there was no debt due in respect of such goods in X's life time.* *[Leading case: Bagel v. Miller]*

22.6 Rights of Transferee of a Partner's Share [Section 29] A partner may transfer his interest in the firm by sale, mortgage or charge fully or partially. The rights of such a transferee are as follows:

(a) ***During the continuance of the partnership***	He is entitled to receive the share of the profits of the transferring partner and the account of profits agreed to by the partners. He is not entitled (a) to interfere with the conduct of the business (b) to require accounts; (c) to inspect the books of the firm.

(b) ***On the dissolution of firm or on the retirement of the transferring partner***	He is entitled to receive (a) the share of the assets of the transferring partner and (b) an account as from the date of the dissolution for the purpose of ascertaining the share.

Sub-partnership: A sub-partnership arises when a partner of a firm agrees to share his share in the firm, with a stranger. It was assumed in *Venkatratnam* v. *Venkatratnam* (A.I.R. 1944, Madras, 394) that a sub-partner is a transferee within the meaning of Section 29. Thus, the rights of a sub-partner are the same as those of a transferee of partner's share under Section 29.

22.7 Effect of the Change in the Constitution of the Firm on Continuing Guarantee [Section 38] A continuing guarantee is a guarantee which extends to a series of transactions. Unless otherwise agreed by the partners, a continuing guarantee given to a firm or to a third party in respect of the transaction of a firm is revoked as to the future transactions from the date of any change in the constitution of the firm.

[*Refer to Practical Problem 47*]

22.8 Rights and Duties of Partners After Change in the Firm [Section 17] The rights and duties of the partners of the reconstituted firm shall be the same as they were before the change in the firm. Section 17 provides for the following **three types of changes** in the firm:

(a) Where there is a change in the Constitution of the firm. [Section 17(a)]

(b) Where the firm continues after the expiry of the term of the firm. [Section 17(b)]

(c) Where the firm carries on an additional undertaking. [Section 17(c)]

23.0 DISSOLUTION OF FIRM [SECTIONS 39 TO 47]

23.1 Meaning of Dissolution The term 'dissolution' stands for discontinuation. Under the Indian Partnership Act, 1932, the dissolution may be *either* of Partnership *or* of a firm.

23.2 Meaning of Dissolution of Partnership Dissolution of partnership refers to the change in the existing relations of the partners. The firm continues its business after being reconstituted. This may happen on admission, retirement or death of a partner or change in profit sharing ratio in the firm

Example *X, Y and Z are partners in a firm. X retires. The partnership between X, Y and Z comes to an end and new partnership between Y and Z comes into existence. This new partnership between Y and Z shall be known as 'reconstituted firm'. Thus, on retirement of partner, the old partnership stands dissolved, but the firm continues its business with the remaining partners Y and Z.*

23.3 Meaning of Dissolution of Firm Dissolution of a firm means the dissolution of partnership between all the partners of a firm. In such a situation, the business of the firm is discontinued, its assets are realised, the liabilities are paid off and the surplus (if any) is distributed among the partners according to their rights.

23.4 Distinction between Dissolution of Partnership and Dissolution of a Firm The dissolution of a partnership and dissolution of a firm can be distinguished as follows:

Basis of Distinction	*Dissolution of Partnership*	*Dissolution of Firm*
1. *Termination of old partnership and formation of new partnership*	Old partnership comes to an end a new partnwership comes into exisxtence.	Old partnership comes to an end but no new partnership comes into existence.
2. *Constitution of business under firm's name*	The business continues under firm's name.	The business does not continue under firm's name.
3. *Revalution vs. Realisation*	Revalution account is prepared.	Under firm's dissolution, Realisation account is prepared.

Thus, dissolution of firm involves dissolution of partnership but dissolution of partnership may not lead to dissolution of firm.

23.5 What are the Modes of Dissolution of a Firm ? [Sections 40 to 44] The dissolution of a firm may take place *either* without the order of the court *or* by an order of the court. The circumstances under which dissolutions take place are shown below :

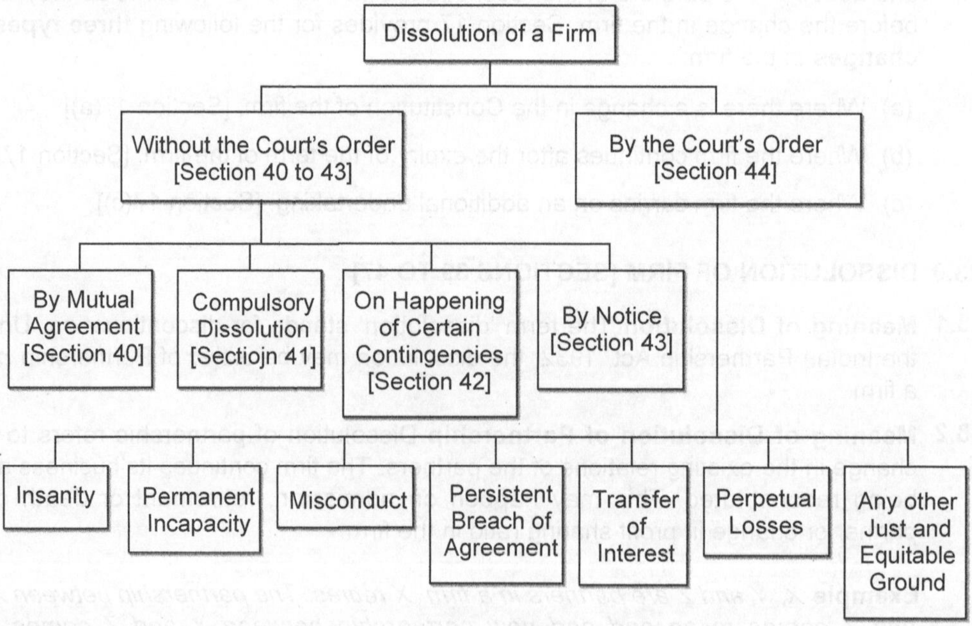

23.6 Dissolution without the Court's Order [Sections 40 to 43] Dissolution of firm without the Court's order may take place in the following ways:

1. ***Dissolution by Mutual Agreement* [*Section 40*]:** A firm may be dissolved by mutual agreement among all the partners.

   Note: Even a firm for a fixed duration may be dissolved by mutual agreement.
   [*Refer to Practical Problem 48*]

2. ***Compulsory Dissolution* [*Section 41*]:** A firm is compulsorily dissolved in the following two circumstances:

   (a) If all the partners, or all but one partner of the firm are declared insolvent;

[The reason is that there must be at least two persons to continue a firm and such persons must be competent to contract].

(b) If some event takes place which makes it unlawful for the firm's business to be carried on.

Example *X a resident in India and Y a resident in Pakistan, are partners in a trading firm. War breaks out between India and Pakistan. In such a situation, on outbreak of war, it becomes unlawful for the business of the firm to be carried on.*

Note: The illegality of one or more business but not all businesses would not necessitate the dissolution of the firm.

[*Refer to Practical Problems 49(a), (b) and 50*]

3. ***Dissolution on the happening of certain Contingencies* [*Section 42*]*:*** Unless otherwise agreed by partners, a firm is dissolved on the happening of any of the following four contingencies:
   (a) On the expiry of the fixed term for which the firm was constituted;
   (b) On completion of the venture(s) or undertaking(s) for which the firm was constituted;
   (c) On the death of a partner; and
   (d) On the insolvency of a partner.

   Note: If all the partners or all but one partner of the firm are dead, the firm shall be compulsorily dissolved even if the partnership agreement provided that the firm shall not be dissolved on the death of a partner. The reason is that there must be at least two partners to continue a firm.

   [*Refer to Practical Problems 49(c) and 51*]

4. ***Dissolution by Notice* [*Section 43*]*:*** Where the partnership is at will, the firm may be dissolved by any partner giving notice in writing to all other partners of his intention to dissolve the firm. The firm is dissolved from the date of dissolution mentioned in the notice or if no date is mentioned, as from the date of the communication of the notice.

   Note: Notice once given cannot be withdrawn without the consent of all other partners. [*Jones* v. *Lloyd*] [*Refer to Practical Problem 52*]

23.7 What are the Grounds for Dissolution by the Court's Order ?

This section deals with those grounds on which the court may, on the receipt of petition by a partner, order for the dissolution of the firm. These grounds are:

1. ***Insanity [Section 44(a)]:*** When a partner has become of unsound mind, the court may allow dissolution of the firm on a suit by any partner of the firm. However, temporary sickness is no ground for dissolution of partnership. Similarly, a dormant partner's insanity will be no ground to seek dissolution under this head as such partner has hardly any duties to perform.

   Note: In this particular case only, the petition may be filed *either* by any other partner *or* the next friend of the insane partner.

2. ***Permanent Incapacity [Section 44(b)]:*** When a partner [i.e., an active partner and not a sleeping partner] has become permanently incapable of performing his duties as a partner, any other partner may apply for dissolution. Such permanent incapacity may result from physical disablement, illness etc.

3. ***Misconduct [Section 44(c)]:*** When a partner is guilty of misconduct which is likely to adversely affect the carrying on of the business, the court may allow dissolution. The court may order the dissolution of a firm on account of

misconduct of any partner other than the one filing a suit for dissolultion. It is not necessary that the misconduct must relate to the business of the firm e.g. in *Carmichael* v. *Evans* (1. Ch. 486), a partner of the firm was convicted on account of travelling without ticket in Rail, the court ordered the firm to be dissolved on petititon by other partners as such act of the partner was detrimental to the interest of the firm.

Similarly, in *Abbot* v. *Grump* (1870) 5 Bang. L.R. 109, the court ordered the firm to be dissolved on account of adultery committed by one partner against the wife of the other partner. Dissolution was ordered as such act of adultry would adversely affect the mutual trust and confidence among partners.

4. ***Persistent Breach of Agreement [Section 44(d)]:*** When a partner willfully or persistently (i.e., frequently) commits breach of agreement in matters relating to the business of the firm, any other partner may seek for dissolution of the firm. Embezzlement, fraudulent breach of trust, or keeping erroneous accounts may be sufficient ground for the court to order dissolution of the firm, e.g. a partner as a matter of routine holding more cash than allowed under the partnership deed, refusal to show accounts despite repeated requests, would be a sufficient ground to uphold dissolution. However, the partner seeking dissolution must not be a party to such misconduct.

5. ***Transfer of Interest [Section 44(e)]:*** When a partner has transferred the *whole* of his interest in the firm to a third party *or* allowed his share to be charged on account of a decree passed by a court towards payment of liabilities of that partner *or* allowed his share to be sold in the recovery of arrears of land revenue, it would be sufficient to attract dissolution.

6. ***Perpetual Losses:*** Where the business of the firm cannot be carried on except at a loss, the court may order dissolution of the firm.

7. ***Any other Just and Equitable Ground [Section 44(f)]:*** Where the court is satisfied that it is just and equitable to dissolve the firm it may allow dissolution using its discretionary power to meet the ends of justice. Examples of such grounds include continued quarrelling between the partners, refusal to meet on matters of business. Complete deadlock in management due to partners not on speaking terms or lack of confidence and good faith between partners.

Note: The right of a partner to file a suit for dissolution on any of the above seven grounds cannot be excluded by any agreement to the contrary.

[*Hardit Singh* v. *Mukha Singh*] [*Refer to Practical Problem 53*]

24.0 WHAT ARE THE RIGHTS OF A PARTNER ON DISSOLUTION ?

The various rights of a partner on dissolution are as follows:

24.1 Partner's General Lien [Section 46]: Every partner or his representative is entitled—

(i) to have the firm's property applied in payment of the firm's debts, and

(ii) to have the surplus distributed amongst the partners or the representatives according to their respective rights.

24.2 Right to Claim the Return of Premium on Premature Winding Up [Section 51]: If a partner joined a firm for a fixed term and had paid a premium and the firm is dissolved before the fixed term, he is entitled to return of the premium. The amount of premium will depend upon (i) the terms upon which he became a partner, and (ii) the length of the time during which he was a partner. However, such a partner cannot claim any return of the premium in the following three circumstances:

(i) When the dissolution is due to the death of partner;

(ii) When the dissolution is mainly due to the misconduct of the partner who paid the premium; or

(iii) The dissolution is according to an agreement which had no provision for the return of premium or any part thereof. [*Refer to Practical Problem 54*]

24.3 Rights of a Partner in Case of Dissolution on Account of Fraud or Misrepresentation [Section 52]: Where the partnership is rescinded on grounds of fraud or misrepresentation, the aggrieved partner, besides other rights under other provisions, has the following rights:

(i) He has a right of lien on the surplus assets after the payment of firm's debts, for any sum paid by him for purchase of a share in the firm or for any capital contributed by him;

(ii) He is entitled to rank as a creditor of the firm in respect of any payment made by him towards firm's debts;

(iii) He is entitled to be indemnified by the partner(s) guilty of fraud or misrepresentation against all the debts of the firm.

24.4 Right to Restrain from Use of Firm Name or Firm Property [Section 53]: Unless otherwise agreed by the partners, every partner or his representative may restrain any other partner or his representative from carrying on a similar business in the firm name or from using the property of the firm for his own benefit till the affairs of the firm are completely wound up.

25.0 WHAT ARE THE LIABILITIES OF A PARTNER ON DISSOLUTION ?

The various liabilities of a partner on dissolution are as follows:

25.1 Continuing Liability for Acts of Partners Done After Dissolution [Section 45] Until a public notice is given of dissolution, the partners continue to be liable for any act done by any of them after dissolution and such act is deemed to be an act done before the dissolution.

Example *X, Y and Z are partners in a trading firm. They executed a dissolution deed to dissolve the firm as from 1st March but did not give public notice till 31st March. On 20th March, X borrowed Rs 20,000 in the firm's name. The firm is liable.*

Exceptions The following shall not be liable for acts done after the dissolution of the firm even though the public notice has not been given:

(i) the estate of a deceased partner;

(ii) the estate of an insolvent partner;

(iii) a sleeping or dormant partner who has retired from the firm.

[*Refer to Practical Problem 55*]

25.2 Continuing Authority of Partners After Dissolution [Section 47] After the dissolution of a firm, the authority of a partner to bind the firm and the other mutual rights and obligations of the partners continue, so far as may be necessary—

(i) to wind up the affairs of the firm, and

(ii) to complete the unfinished transactions pending at the date of dissolution.

26.0 SETTLEMENT OF ACCOUNTS [SECTIONS 48, 49 AND 55]

Unless otherwise agreed by the partners, the accounts of a dissolved firm shall be settled according to the provisions of Sections 48, 49 and 55. These provisions are as follows:

26.1 Treatment of Losses [Section 48(a)] Losses including deficiencies of capital are to be paid in the following manner:

(i) First out of profits;

(ii) Then out of capital;

(iii) Lastly by partners individually in their profit-sharing ratio. [Section 48(a)]

[*Refer to Practical Problem 56*]

26.2 Application of Assets [Section 48(b)] The assets of the firm (including the sums, if any, contributed by the partners to make up the deficiencies of capital) shall be applied in the following manner and order:

(i) in paying firm's debts to the third parties;

(ii) in paying to each partner rateably what is due to him on account of advances;

(iii) in paying to each partner rateably what is due to him on account of capital;

(iv) the residue, if any, shall be divided among the partners in their profit-sharing ratio. [Section 48(b)]. [*Refer to Practical Problem 57*]

26.3 Payment of Firm's Debts and Partner's Private Debts [Section 49] Where there are firm's debts and partner's private debts, the following provisions shall apply:

(i) Firm's property shall be applied first in payment of firm's debts then the surplus, if any, shall be applied in the payment of partner's private debts to the extent to which the concerned partner is entitled to share in the surplus; and

(ii) Partner's private property shall be applied first in payment of his private debts and the surplus, if any, in payment of firm's debts if firm's liabilities exceed the firm's assets. [Section 49] [*Refer to Practical Problem 58*]

26.4 Distinction between Firm's Debts and Private Debts

Firm's Debts and Private Debts can be distinguished as under:

Basis of Distinction	*Firm's Debts*	*Private Debts*
1. *Who incurs*	Firm's debts are incurred by the firm.	Private debts are incurred by a partner in the individual capacity of a household and not in the capacity capacity of a partner of a firm.
2. *Who is liable*	For firm's debts, jointly and severally liable.	For private debts, only the debts, all partners are concerned partner is liable.
3. *Application of Firm's Property*	For firm's debts, firm's property shall be applied first.	For private debts, only the share of concerned partner in the excess of firm's property over firm's debts can be applied.
4. *Application of Private Property*	For firm's debts, only the excess of of partner's private property over his private debts canbe applied.	For private debts, private property shall be applied first.

26.5 Treatment of Loss Arising due to Insolvency of a Partner

The Capital Account of a partner may show a debit balance after making all adjustments (including the share of any profit or loss on realisation and the receipts from his private estate, if any). It may be noted that the private estate of each partner is applied first to pay off his private debts and the surplus (i.e. excess of private estate over private debts), if any, is applied to pay off the fim's debts. If a partner having a debit balance in his Capital Account is unable to bring in the necessary cash to make up the deficiency, he is said to be an insolvent partner. The irrecovered debit balance is called the loss arising due to the insolvency of a partner. Now the question arises, should this loss be regarded as an ordinary loss (which is shared by the partners in their profit sharing ratio) or an extraordinary one? This issue was involved in the leading case of *Garner* v. *Murray* (1904).

26.6 Decision in *Garner* v. *Murray*

Justice Joyee held that the loss arising due to the insolvency of a partner must be distinguished from an ordinary loss (including realisation loss). Unless otherwise agreed, the decision in *Garner* v. *Murray* requires—

(a) that the solvent partners should bring in cash equal to their respective shares of the loss on realisation;

(b) that the solvent partners should bear the loss arising due to the insolvency of a partner in the ratio of their Last Agreed Capitals.

The Last Agreed Capital should be interpreted as under:

Case	*Meaning of Last Agreed Capital*
(a) In case of Fixed Capitals	Last Agreed Capital means the Fixed Capital (as given in the Balance Sheet) without any adjustment.
(b) In case of Fluctuating Capitals	Last Agreed Capital means the Capital after making adjustments for past accumulated reserves, profits or losses, drawings, interest on capitals, interest on drawings, remuneration to a partner, etc. to the date of dissolution but before making adjustment for profit or loss on realisation.

27.0 SALE OF GOODWILL [SECTION 55]

Unless otherwise agreed by the partners, the goodwill shall be included in the assets and may be sold *either* separately *or* alongwith other property of the firm. In case of sale of goodwill of dissolved firm, the rights of buyer and seller are as under:

Rights of a Buyer	*Rights of a Seller*
(i) to use the firm's name.	**(i) to carry on a business competing with that of the buyer.**
(ii) to represent himself carrying on the as business of the old firm.	**(ii) to advertise such business.**
(iii) to solicit the old customers	**But subject to agreement between him and the buyer, he is not entitled (a) to use the firm's name, (b) to represent himself as carrying on business of the old firms, or (c) to solicit the old customers.**

It may be noted that any partner may enter into an agreement with the buyer of goodwill that such partner will not carry on any business similar to that of the dissolved firm within a specified period or within the specified local limits. Such agreement shall be valid if restrictions imposed are reasonable.

Note: Though such an agreement is in restraint of trade and is void under Section 27 of the Indian Contract Act but Section 55(3) of the Indian Partnership Act permits and declares such agreements as valid. *[Refer to Practical Problem 59]*

28.0 PUBLIC NOTICE [SECTION 72]

28.1 When a Public Notice is required to be given ?

A public notice is required to be given in the following three cases:

(a) on the retirement or expulsion of a partner, or

(b) on the dissolution of the firm,

(c) on the election to become or not to become a partner by a minor on his attaining majority.

28.2 When a Public Notice is not required to be given ?

A public notice is not required to be given in the following two cases:

(a) on the death of a partner;

(b) on the insolvency of a partner.

28.3 What is the Mode of giving Public Notice ?

The mode of giving public notice is given as under:

In case of a Registered Firm	*In case of an Unregistered Firm*
(a) It must be given by publication in the Official Gazette.	(a) It must be given by publication in the Official Gazette.
(b) It must be given by publication in at least one vernacular newspaper circulating in the district where the firm to which it relates has its place or principal place of business.	(b) It must be given by publication in at least one vernacular newspaper circulating in the distinct where the firm to which it relates has its place or principal place of business.
(c) It must be given to the Registrar of Firms.	

28.4 What are the Consequences of not giving a Public Notice ?

If a public notice is not given in cases in which it is required to be given, the consequences will be as follows:

Case	*Consequences*
(a) On Election to become or not to become a Partner by a Minor on his attaining majority	Minor is deemed to have become a partner on the expiry of 6 months [Section 30(5)].
(b) On Retirement of a Partner	Retiring partner and the other partners continues to be liable as partner to the third parties for firm's acts done after retirement [Section 32(3)].

(c) On Expulsion of a Partner	The expelled partner and the other partners continue to be liable to third parties for firm's acts done after his expulsion [Section 33(2)].
(d) On Dissolution of a Firm	All the partners continue to be liable to third parties for firm's acts done after the dis-solution of firm [Section 45].

PRACTICAL PROBLEMS

PROBLEM 1

Two brothers *X* (age 18 years), *Y* (age 17 years), decide to form a partnership. Can they do so?

Solution: Section to which the given Problem relates: Section 4.

Decision	No.
Reason	There must be at least two persons and such persons must be competent to contract. In the given case, *Y* is not competent to contract because he is a minor. Hence, there is only one person *X* who alone cannot form a partnership.
Leading Case Law	*Shivaram* v. *Gauri Shankar*

PROBLEM 2

Three brothers, *X* (age 19 years), *Y* (age 18 years) and *Z* (age 17 years), decide to form a partnership with a provision that *Z* will share the profits only.

Solution

Section to which given Problem relates: Section 4.

Decision	No.
Reason	All the persons entering into partnership agreement must be competent to contract. *Z* is not competent to contract because he is a minor. It may be noted that no partnership can be formed with a minor partner. but after the formation of partnership, a minor can be admitted to the benefits of partnership with the consent of all other partners of the firm as per the provisions of Section 30 of the Act.
Leading Case Law	*Shivaram* v. *Gauri Shankar*

PROBLEM 3

Ten major persons form an association to which each member contributes Rs 10,000. The purpose is to produce medicines for free distribution to poor patients. Is there a valid partnership?

Solution

Section to which the given Problem relates: Section 4.

Decision	No.
Reason	There is no intention to carry on the business and to share the profits thereof.

PROBLEM 4

Two manufacturing firms, each having twenty members, amalgamate their business. Can contracts entered into by the amalgamated firm be enforced by the firm?

Solution

Section to which the given Problem relates: Section 11 of the Companies Act, 1956.

Decision	No.
Reason	The amalgamated firm is an illegal association because such firm consists of 40 persons which exceeds the statutory limit of 20 persons.

PROBLEM 5

Two banking firms, each having ten members, amalgamate their business. Can contracts entered into by the amalgamated firm be enforced by the firm?

Solution

Section to which the given Problem relates: Section 11 of the Companies Act, 1956.

Decision	No.
Reason	The amalgamated firm is an illegal association because such a firm consists of 20 persons which exceeds the statutory limit of 10 persons.

PROBLEM 6

A Hindu undivided family consisting of 11 major members and 2 minor members, carries on a family banking business.

(a) Is there anything wrong?

(b) Can such members be called partners?

Solution

Part (a)

Section to which the given Problem relates: Section 11 of the Companies Act, 1956.

Decision: No.

Reason: The statutory limit of 10 persons does not apply to a joint family.

Part (b)

Section to which the given Problem relates: Section 5.

Decision: No.

Reason: The relation of partnership arises from contract and not from status. Such members are called coparceners.

PROBLEM 7

Two Hindu undivided families—one consisting of 11 major members and 2 minor members, and other one consisting of 6 major members and 2 minor members amalgamate their business. Can contracts entered into by the amalgamated firm be enforced by the firm?

Solution

Section to which the given Problem relates: Section 11 of the Companies Act, 1956.

Decision	Yes.
Reason	The amalgamated firm is not an illegal association because such firm consists of 17 major members which does not exceed the statutory limit of 20 members.

PROBLEM 8

X, *Y* and *Z* agreed to share the profits and losses and to carry on the business by all or anyone acting for all for mutual benefits and gain. The management and control was entrusted in *X* with power to restrict the right of *Y* and *Z*. Is there a valid partnership?

Solution

Section to which the given Problem relates: Section 4.

Decision	Yes.
Reason	All the essential elements of partnership exist under the partnership agreement.
Leading Case Law	*K.D. Kamath Co.* v. *Commission of Income Tax* (1972) 82, ITR 680 (SC)

PROBLEM 9

X and *Y* agreed to share the profits of a business carried on by all or any of them acting for all. Later on, *Z* lent Rs 1,00,000 to the firm on the condition that he will take 25% share in profits. Can *Z* be regarded as a partner?

Solution

Section to which the given Problem relates: Sections 4 and 6.

Decision	No.
Reason	Sharing of profit, which is a *prima facie* evidence, exists, but the mutual agency relationship among *X*, *Y* and *Z*, which is a conclusive evidence, does not exist.
Leading Case Law	*Mollow March & Co.* v. *The Court of Wards*

PROBLEM 10

X, a contractor, appointed *Y* one of his servants to manage his business of loading and unloading railway wagons. *Y* was to receive 50% of the profits of the business and also to bear the losses, if any. Is *Y* a partner of *X*?

Solution

Section to which the given Problem relates: Sections 4 and 6.

Decision	No.
Reason	Sharing of profit which is a *prima facie* evidence, exists but the mutual agency relationship among *X* and *Y*, which is a conclusive evidence, does not exist. Here, *Y* is an agent of *X* but *X* is not an agent of *Y*.
Leading Case Law	*Munshi Abdul Latif* v. *Gopeshwar Chattoraj*

PROBLEM 11

X, *Y* and *Z* were partners in a firm. *X* died. It was agreed that the widow of *X* would receive 10% share of profits of business as annuity. Is the widow of *X* a partner?

Solution

Section to which the given Problem relates: Sections 4 and 6.

Decision	No.
Reason	Sharing of profit, which is a *prima facie* evidence, exists but the mutual agency relationship among *X*, *Y* and widow of *X*, which is a conclusive evidence, does not exist.
Leading Case Law	*I.T. Commissioner* v. *Kesharmal Keshardeo*

PROBLEM 12

X and *Y* who jointly own a house, let it out on rent of Rs 10,000 p.a., and share the rental income equally. Can *X* and *Y* be regarded as partners?

Solution

Section to which the given Problem relates: Explanation 1 to Section 6.

Decision	No.
Reason	*X* and *Y* are merely co-owners who are sharing the gross returns arising from a joint property.
Leading Case Law	*Govind Nair* v. *Maga*

PROBLEM 13

X and *Y* who jointly own a house, converted that house into a hotel after investing Rs 1,00,000 each. *X* manages the hotel and meet all expenses and retains half of gross earnings and hands over the other half to *Y*. Can *X* and *Y* be regarded as partners?

Solution

Section to which the given Problem relates: Explanation 1 to Section 6.

Decision	No.
Reason	*X* and *Y* are merely co-owners who are sharing the gross returns arising from a joint property.
Leading Case Law	*Govind Nair* v. *Maga*

PROBLEM 14

An unregistered firm sold goods to *W* on credit. On the expiry of the term of credit, the firm filed a suit against *W* for the recovery of the amount due from *W*. Will the firm succeed? What difference would it make if immediately after filing the suit, the firm got itself registered?

Solution

First Part

Section to which the given Problem relates: Section 69(2).

Decision: No.

Reason: The firm is not registered at the time of institution of the suit.

Second Part

It would not make any difference because the subsequent registration cannot cure the initial defect.

PROBLEM 15

X, *Y* and *Z* are partners in a registered firm. *X* died. The firm filed a suit against *W* in the name and on behalf of firm without notifying to the Registrar of firms about the changes in the constitution of the firm. Is the suit maintainable?

Solution

Section to which the given Problem relates: Section 69(2).

Decision	Yes.
Reason	Both the requirements of Section 69(2) have been complied with (i) the suit must be instituted by or on behalf of the firm which had been registered; (ii) the persons suing must have been shown as partners in the Register of Firms. Persons suing means all the partners at the date of instituting the suit.
Leading Case Law	*Durga Das* v. *Preete Shah*

PROBLEM 16

X, *Y* and *Z* are partners in a registered firm. *X* died and *D* was admitted as a partner. The firm filed a suit against *W* in the name and on behalf of firm without notifying to the Registrar of Firms about the changes in the constitution of the firm. Is the suit maintainable?

Solution

Section to which the given Problem relates: Section 69(2).

Decision	No.
Reason	First requirement of Section 69(2) that the suit must be instituted by or on behalf of the firm which had been registered, had been complied with, whereas the second requirement of Section 69(2) that all the partners at the date of instituting the suit have been shown in the Register of Firms, had not been complied with.
Leading Case Law	*V.S. Behal* v. *Kapur & Co.*

PROBLEM 17

An unregistered firm sold goods worth Rs 1,000 to *W* who gave a cheque which was dishonoured. *X*, a partner demanded money from *W* who paid only 50%. In the meantime, the firm was dissolved. *X* sued *W* for the recovery of the balance. Will *X* succeed?

Solution

Section to which the given Problem relates: Section 69(3).

Decision	Yes.
Reason	Non-registration of firm does not affect the right of a partner to realise the property of a dissolved firm.

PROBLEM 18

X and *Y* are in partnership for refining sugar. *Y* was appointed to buy sugar for the firm. Without the knowledge of *X*, he supplied his own sugar to the firm at market price and made a huge gain. Is he accountable to firm for profit he makes?

Solution

Section to which the given Problem relates: Section 16(a).

Decision	Yes.
Reason	Subject to contract between the partners, if a partner derives any profit for himself from any transaction of the firm, he must account for the profit and pay it to the firm.
Leading Case Law	*Bentley* v. *Craven*

PROBLEM 19

X, *Y* and *Z* are partners in a trade. *Z* without the knowledge of *X* and *Y*, obtains for his own sole benefit a lease of the house in which the partnership business is carried on. Are *X* and *Y* entitled to participate in the benefit of the lease?

Solution

Section to which the given Problem relates: Section 16(a).

Decision	Yes.
Reason	Subject to contract between the partners, where a partner derives any profit for himself from the use of the property of the firm, he must account for the profit and pay it to the firm.
Leading Case Law	*Featherstonhaugh* v. *Fenwick*

PROBLEM 20

X and *Y* are in partnership for supplying meat to the government. Subsequently, it is found out that *X* is engaged with *Z* in the supplying of meat to the same government. Can he retain the profits made out of the second engagement?

Solution

Section to which the given Problem relates: Section 16(b).

Decision	No.
Reason	Subject to contract between the partners, if a partner carries on competing business, he must account for and pay to the firm all profits made by him in that business.
Leading Case Law	*Loch* v. *Lynam*

PROBLEM 21

A, *B*, *C*, *D* and *E* are partners. *A* and *B* executed a promissory note in favour of *C* agreeing to pay him a certain sum due to him on taking partnership accounts. Are *D* and *E* bound by the promissory note?

Solution

Section to which the given Problem relates: Section 18.

Decision	No.
Reason	The principle of agency is applicable only to the act done by partners for the purpose of the business of the firm.
Leading Case Law	*Hoshiar Singh* v. *Udairam*

PROBLEM 22

X, *Y* and *Z* were partners when an infringement of a trademark by the firm took place. *X* retired and damages arose after the dissolution of the firm. Are all partners liable for damages?

Solution

Section to which the given Problem relates: Section 25.

Decision	Yes.
Reason	Every partner is liable jointly and severally for all acts of the firm done while he is a partner.
Leading Case Law	*Thomas Bear & Sons* v. *Ralia Ram*

PROBLEM 23

X, *Y* and *Z* were partners when goods were sent to a firm on approval. Goods not required were returned after the dissolution of the firms. Are all partners liable for goods accepted?

Solution

Section to which the given Problem relates: Section 25.

Decision	Yes.
Reason	Every partner is liable jointly and severally for all acts of the firms done while he is a partner.
Leading Case Law	*Mayadas* v. *Marley*

PROBLEM 24

It was in the course of the business of a firm of grain merchants to obtain by legitimate means information in regard to contracts made by competing firms and one of the partners obtained such information by bribing a clerk of a competitor in the business. Consequently, competitor lost some business and sued the firm for damages. Will the competitor succeed?

Solution

Section to which the given Problem relates: Section 26.

Decision	Yes.
Reason	The firm is liable for the wrongful act of partner done in the ordinary course of the business.
Leading Case Law	*Hamlyn* v. *Houston & Co.*

PROBLEM 25

A, B, C and *D* are partners in a firm of solicitors. *A* receives money from a client *X* for the purpose of making a specific investment. *A* never invests it but applies it to his own use. The other partners are not aware of this transaction. Is the firm liable for *A*'s act?

Solution

Section to which the given Problem relates: Section 27.

Decision	Yes.
Reason	The firm is liable for misapplication of money by a partner who received while acting within the scope of his apparent authority.
Leading Case Law	*Blair* v. *Bromley*

PROBLEM 26

X and *Y* are partners of a banking firm. *X* receives certain securities from a customer for safe custody and puts in the safe custody of the firm. *Y* disposes off those securities and applies the money for his own use. Is the firm liable for *Y*'s act?

Solution

Section to which the given Problem relates: Section 27.

Decision	Yes.
Reason	The firm is liable for the misapplication of property by a partner if the property was in the custody of the firm.
Leading Case Law	*Devaynes* v. *Noble*

PROBLEM 27

Pataudi, a renowned sportsman assumed the honorary presidentship of a publishing business bringing out a sports magazine becasue other partners requested him to do so. A supplier gave credit to the firm in the bona fide belief that Pataudi was a partner in the firm. Is Pataudi liable to the supplier?

Solution

Section to which the given Problem relates: Section 28.

Decision	Yes.
Reason	Pataudi is a partner by estoppel. Both the conditions of Section 28 are fulfilled. (i) Pataudi has knowingly permitted himself to be represented as a partner (ii) Supplier has acted on the faith of such representation.
Leading Case Law	*Lake* v. *Duke of Argyll*

PROBLEM 28

A, B, C and *D* were partners in a firm. One of the terms of partnership deed was that *A* could introduce into partnership any of his sons on their attaining the age of 18. *A*'s son attained the age of 18 and he proposed to make him a partner. *C* and *D* objected to admission of *A*'s son. Is admission of *A*'s son jusitified?

Solution

Section to which the given Problem relates: Section 31(1).

Decision	Yes.
Reason	Admission is in accordance with a contract already entered into.
Leading Case Law	*Byrne* v. *Reid*

PROBLEM 29

X, *Y* and *Z* are partners. The firm ordered goods. Thereafter *X* died. The delivery of the goods was made after *X*'s death. Is *X*'s estate liable for the debt?

Solution

Section to which the given Problem relates: Section 35.

Decision	No.
Reason	There was no debt in respect of goods in *X*'s life time.
Leading Case Law	*Bagel* v. *Miller*

PROBLEM 30

A became surety to the firm of 'NC Mookerji' for *B*'s conduct as cashier to the firm. The constitution of the firm subsequently underwent a change. Two sons of N. Mookerji were admitted as partners and its name was altered to "N. Mookerji and Sons". Subsequently *B* defalcated. Is *A* liable for *B*s defalcation?

Solution

Section to which the given Problem relates: Section 38.

Decision	No.
Reason	*A* continuing guarantee is revoked as to the future transactions from the date of any change in the constitution of the firm.

PROBLEM 31

X, *Y* and *Z* are partners in a firm. State whether the court may pass an order for dissolution of a firm in each of the following alternative cases:

Case (*a*): If *X* (an active partner) becomes insane and the suit is filed by the *X*'s next friend who is not a partner.

Case (*b*): If *X* (a dormant partner) becomes insane and the suit is filed by *Y*.

Case (*c*): If *X* had an attack of paralysis and the suit is filed by *Y*. According to doctors, paralysis was of a temporary nature and the patient's condition was improving.

Case (*d*): If *X* has adulterous relations with *Y*s wife.

Case (*e*): If *X* was convicted of travelling on a railway without a ticket and with intent to defraud.

Case (*f*): If *X* has adulterous relations with *W*s wife.

Case (g): If *X* has adulterous relation with *W*s wife who is a regular patient of medical firm of *X*, *Y* and *Z*.

Case (*h*): If *X* omitted to enter a particular receipt of money in the books of accounts.

Case (i): If *X* continuously omits to enter receipts of money in the books of accounts.

Case (j): If *X* transferred the whole of his interest in a firm to a third party.

Case (k): *X*, *Y* and *Z* enter into a partnership agreement for 20 years. The business resulted in a loss each year. *X* and *Y* decide to dissolve the firm as the business cannot be carried on except at a loss. *Z* objects. *X* filed a suit.

Case (l): *X*, *Y* and *Z* are partners in a firm and are not on speaking terms with each other.

Solution

Section to which the given Problem relates: Section 44.

Case	*Decision and Reason*
(*a*)	The court may pass an order for dissolution when a partner has become of unsound mind. The suit can be filed by the next friend of such partner or any other partner.
(*b*)	The court may not pass an order for dissolution because such a partner does not take an active part in the conduct of firm's business.
(*c*)	The court will not pass an order for dissolution because incapacity of a partner was of a temporary nature. **Leading Case:** *Whitwell* v. *Arthur*
(*d*)	The court will pass an order for dissolution because *X*'s conduct is likely to affect prejudicially the carrying on of the business because this destroys the mutual confidence between *X* and *Y*. **Leading Case:** *Abbot* v. *Crump*
(*e*)	The court will pass an order for dissolution because *X*'s conviction was for dishonesty which is likely to affect prejudicially the carrying on of the business. **Leading Case:** *Carmichael* v. *Evans*
(*f*)	The court may not pass an order for dissolution as *X*'s conduct does not affect prejudicially the carrying on of the business. **Leading Case:** *Snow* v. *Milform*
(*g*)	The court will pass an order for dissolution since *X*'s conduct is likely to affect prejudicially the carrying on of medical profession. **Leading Case:** *Snow* v. *Milform*
(*h*)	The court may not pass an order for dissolution since there is no persistent breach.
(*i*)	The court will pass an order for dissolution since there was persistent breach.
(*j*)	The court will pass an order for dissolution since *X* has transferred the whole of his interest in a firm to a third party.
(*k*)	The court will pass an order for dissolution because the business has been running at loss and it cannot be carried on except at a loss.
(*l*)	The court will pass an order for dissolution because absence of speaking terms is sufficient ground to justify dissolution.

TRUE OR FALSE QUESTIONS

State giving reasons whether each of the following statements is True or False:

1. A partnership can be formed with a minor.
2. There can be no partnership without express agreement.
3. A partnership can be formed for a charitable purpose.

4. A partnership can be formed for carrying on a profession.
5. Sharing of profits of a business implies sharing of its losses as well.
6. Sharing of profits is a conclusive evidence of a partnership.
7. Mutual agency is a *prima facie* evidence of a partnership.
8. Business of the firm must be carried on by majority of the partners.
9. The members of a joint Hindu family carrying on family business are called partners.
10. The maximum limit on number of members of a Joint Hindu family carrying on family banking business is 10.
11. Burmese Buddhist husband and wife carrying on a business are not regarded as partners.
12. Co-ownership is not necessarily the result of agreement.
13. Co-ownership necessarily involves profit or loss.
14. Co-ownership necessarily involves carrying on of a business.
15. A co-owner is an agent of the other co-owners.
16. A co-owner has no lien on the joint property for expenses.
17. A co-owner has no right to claim partition of joint property.
18. In co-ownership, there is no maximum limit of co-owners.
19. Mitakshra School of Hindu Law is applicable to Bengal and Assam.
20. Dayabhaga School of Hindu Law is applicable to the whole of India except Bengal and Assam.
21. A male person becomes a member in joint Hindu family on his birth under Mitakshra School of Hindu Law.
22. A male person becomes a member in joint Hindu family only on the death of the father under Dayabhaga School of Hindu Law.
23. The liability of the *Karta* is unlimited, whereas the other coparceners are liable only to the extent of their share in the family business.
24. If a coparcener takes part in the act performed or a transaction entered into by the *Karta*, the liability of that coparcener will be unlimited.
25. It is compulsory to have a partnership deed.
26. The partnership deed must be signed by the majority of the partners.
27. The terms laid down in the partnership deed may be varied by the consent of majority of the partners.
28. It is compulsory for a partnership firm to get itself registered.
29. Registration of firm provides protection to the outsiders dealing with the firm.
30. A partner of an unregistered firm cannot file a civil suit against the firm or other partner(s).
31. An unregistered firm can file a suit against a third party to enforce any right arising from contract if the value of a suit exceed Rs 100.
32. A third party cannot file a suit against an unregistered firm or its partners.
33. An unregistered firm can file a suit against a third party if the value of suit does not exceed Rs 100.

34. A partner of an unregistered firm can file a suit for the dissolution of firm.
35. A partner of dissolved unregistered firm can file a suit for the recovery of money from firm's debtors.
36. In case of an unregistered firm, the official assignee or receiver can realise the property of an insolvent partner.
37. Partnership at will is for an indefinite period.
38. Partnership at will can be dissolved simply by any partner giving notice in writing to any of the other partners.
39. Partnership for a fixed period cannot be dissolved before the expiry of fixed period.
40. Partnership for a fixed period can be dissolved only with the consent of majority of the partners.
41. A firm has no legal existence apart from the partners.
42. A minor can become a partner.
43. A minor can be admitted to the benefits of partnership with the consent of majority of the partners.
44. A minor cannot take part in the conduct of the firm's business.
45. A minor has a right to have access to and inspect and copy any of the books of the firm.
46. A minor has a right to file a suit for his share of profits or the property of the firm when he is not given his due share of the profit without severing his connections with the firm.
47. A minor is personally liable to the third parties.
48. A minor cannot be declared insolvent in the event of firm's failure to pay off its debts.
49. A minor must give a public notice if he elects to become a partner.
50. A minor need not give a public notice if he does not elect to become a partner.
51. If a minor on attaining majority, elects to become a partner, he becomes only personally liable to third parties for those acts of the firm which are done after the date of his becoming partner.
52. The mutual rights and duties of partners are governed by the partnership agreement only.
53. All partners are not bound to carry on the business of the firm to the greatest common advantage.
54. All partners are bound to be just and faithful to each other.
55. All partners are bound to render true accounts and full information of all things affecting the firm to any partner but not to his legal representative.
56. Every partner shall indemnify the firm for any loss caused to it by his fraud in the conduct of the business of the firm.
57. The contract between the partners cannot provide that a partner shall not carry on any business other than that of the firm while he is a partner.
58. Every partner cannot take part in the conduct of the business.
59. Every partner is bound to attend diligently to his duties in the conduct of the business.
60. Every partner has the right to express his opinion before the matter is decided.

61. Any difference arising as to ordinary matter connected with the business must be decided with the consent of all the partners.
62. A change in the nature of the business can be made with the consent of majority of the partners.
63. Every partner has a right to have access to and to inspect and copy only the accounts books of the firm.
64. Even in the absence of any contract between the partners, a working partner is entitled to receive or remuneration for taking part in the conduct of the business.
65. In the absence of any contract between the partners, the partners are entitled to share the profits and losses in the ratio of their capitals.
66. Where a partner is entitled to interest on capital, such interest shall be payable as a charge against the profits.
67. Where a partner makes advances to the firm over and above the amount of capital, he is entitled to claim the interest thereon at the rate of 6% p.m.
68. Every partner has a right to be indemnified by the firm in respect of payments made and liabilities incurred by him in the ordinary and proper conduct of the business.
69. Every partner shall indemnify the firm for any loss caused to it by his wilful neglect in the conduct of the business of the firm.
70. Property belonging to a partner who enters into an existing partnership constitute firm's property.
71. Capital originally brought to the stock of the firm constitutes firm's property.
72. Any property used for the purpose of the business of the firm constitutes firm's property.
73. Property of the firm shall be held and used by the partner exclusively for the purposes of the business.
74. Subject to contract between the partners, if a partner carries on any business whether or not competing with that of the firm, he must account for and pay to the firm all profits made by him in that business.
75. Subject to contract between the partners, mutual right and duties of the partners in the reconstituted firm remain the same as they were immediately before the change.
76. A partner is the agent of the firm for the purposes of the business of the firm.
77. The authority of a partner to bind the third party is called his implied authority.
78. Implied authority of a partner does not empower him to file a suit on behalf of the firm.
79. Implied authority of a partner does not empower him to submit a dispute relating to the business of the firm to arbitration.
80. Implied authority of a partner does not empower him to acquire/transfer any movable property on behalf of the firm.
81. Implied authority can be restricted or extended by mutual agreement.
82. In case of an emergency, in order to prevent losses to the firm, a partner may exceed his implied or express authority.
83. In order to bind a firm, an act must be done in the firm name or in any other manner expressing or implying an intention to bind the firm.

84. An admission or representation made by a partner concerning the affairs of the firm is an evidence against the firm whether or not it is made in the ordinary course of business.
85. Notice to any partner, of any matter relating to the affairs of the firm operates as notice to the firm except in the case of fraud on the firm committed by or with the consent of the partner.
86. Every partner is jointly and severally liable to third parties.
87. For wrongful acts of a partner, the firm is liable to the same extent as the partner.
88. The transferee is bound to accept the account of profits agreed to by the partners.
89. During the continuance of the firm, the transferee is entitled to receive the share of the assets of the firm to which the transferring partner is entitled.
90. A person can be introduced as partner into a firm with the consent of majority of the partners.
91. A partner may retire with the consent of majority of the partners.
92. A partner in a particular partnership can retire from the firm by giving notice in writing to the Registrar of firms of his intention to retire.
93. A partner in a partnership at will can retire from the firm by giving notice in writing to any of the partners, of his intention to retire.
94. Public notice of retirement must be given by the retired partner only.
95. A partner can be expelled from a firm only with the consent of all other partners.
96. An insolvent partner ceases to be a partner on the date on which an application for insolvency is made.
97. The estate of an insolvent partner continues to be liable to third parties for firm's acts done after the date on which the orders of adjudication is made if public notice is not given.
98. The estate of a deceased partner continues to be liable to third parties for firm's acts done after the death if public notice is not given.
99. An outgoing partner may carry on a business competing with that of the firm and he may advertise such business.
100. A continuing guarantee is revoked as to the future transactions from the date of any change in the constitution.
101. Dissolution of the firm necessarily means the dissolution of partnership.
102. A firm may be dissolved with the consent of majority of the partners.
103. A firm is compulsorily dissolved by the adjudication of a partner as an insolvent even if there are other two partners who are solvent.
104. A firm carrying on more than one adventures is compulsorily dissolved by the illegality of at least one adventure.
105. Unless otherwise agreed, a firm is dissolved by the death of a partner.
106. Where the partnership is at will, the firm may be dissolved by any partner giving notice in writing to the Registrar of firms of his intention to dissolve the firm.
107. Where a partner has become of unsound mind, the suit for dissolution may be brought by a friend of that partner.
108. Where a partner has become permanently incapable of performing his duties as partner, he may file a suit for dissolution.
109. A partnership for a fixed term cannot be continued after the expiry of that term.

110. Partnership constituted for a particular venture is dissolved on the completion of such venture unless otherwise agreed.
111. When a partner has transferred the whole of his interest to a third party, the other partners can sue for dissolution.
112. In the event of continued losses, the court may dissolve any partnership other than partnership for a fixed term.
113. Partners continue to be liable to third party for firm's acts done after dissolution whether or not a public notice is given.
114. After the dissolution of a firm, the authority of each partner to bind the firm does not continue at all.
115. Losses, including deficiencies of capital shall be paid first out of capital.
116. Firm's assets shall be applied first in payment of private debts of a partner.
117. A partner's private assets shall be applied first in payment of firm's debts.
118. If a partner derives any profit for himself from any transaction of the firm undertaken after the firm is dissolved under any circumstance and before its affairs have been completely wound up, he must account for the profit and pay it to the firm.
119. If a partner starts any business of the same nature and competing with that of the firm, after the firm is dissolved on account of death of a partner and before its affairs have been completely wound up, he must account for and pay to the firm all profits made by him in that business.
120. Where a partner has paid a premium on entering into partnership for a fixed term, he is entitled to the repayment of proportionate premium on any premature dissolution.
121. Where the goodwill of a dissolved firm is sold, the partners of the dissolved firm cannot carry on a business competing with that of the buyer of goodwill.
122. Public notices relating to unregistered firm must also be communicated to Registrar of firms.
123. Public notices relating to unregistered firm must be published in Official Gazettes only.
124. Any surplus left after payment of firm's debts is divided among all the partners in their profit sharing ratio.
125. Any deficiency of partner's capital arising on the insolvency of a partner is shared by the solvent partners in the ratio of their Capital just standing prior to dissolution according to *Garner* v. *Murray Rule*.

Answers

1. False	2. False	3. False	4. True
5. True	6. False	7. False	8. False
9. False	10. False	11. True	12. True
13. False	14. False	15. False	16. True
17. False	18. True	19. False	20. False
21. True	22. True	23. True	24. True
25. False	26. False	27. False	28. False
29. False	30. True	31. False	32. False

33. True	34. True	35. True	36. True
37. True	38. False	39. False	40. False
41. True	42. False	43. False	44. True
45. False	46. False	47. False	48. True
49. False	50. False	51. False	52. False
53. False	54. True	55. False	56. True
57. False	58. False	59. True	60. True
61. False	62. False	63. False	64. False
65. False	66. False	67. False	68. True
69. True	70. False	71. True	72. False
73. True	74. False	75. True	76. True
77. False	78. False	79. True	80. False
81. True	82. True	83. True	84. False
85. False	86. True	87. True	88. True
89. False	90. False	91. False	92. False
93. False	94. False	95. False	96. False
97. False	98. False	99. True	100. True
101. True	102. False	103. False	104. False
105. True	106. False	107. True	108. False
109. False	110. True	111. True	112. False
113. False	114. False	115. False	116. False
117. False	118. False	119. False	120. False
121. False	122. False	123. False	124. False
125. True			

VERY SHORT ANSWER TYPE QUESTIONS

1. Define partnership.
2. Is it necessary to have a partnership agreement?
3. Is it necessary to have a partnership agreement in writing?
4. Can a partnership agreement be implied by conduct of partners?
5. What is the minimum limit of persons to form a partnership?
6. What is the maximum limit on number of partners?
7. Can a partnership be formed for a charitable or religious purpose?
8. Can a partnership be formed to carry on profession?
9. Does the sharing of profits of a business imply sharing of its losses?
10. What is mutual agency relationship?
11. What is co-ownership?
12. Is co-ownership necessarily the result of an agreement?
13. Does co-ownership necessarily involve profit or loss?
14. Can one co-owner without the consent of the others, transfer his interest to a stranger?

15. Is co-owner an agent of the other co-owner?
16. Does co-ownership necessarily involve carrying on of a business?
17. What is the maximum limit of co-owners in co-ownership?
18. Does a co-owner have right to claim partition of property owned with other co-owner?
19. Does a co-owner have lien on the property owned in common for expenses incurred by him?
20. What is Hindu undivided family?
21. Who are called 'coparceners'?
22. What is an 'Ancestral property'?
23. Name the two schools of Hindu Law.
24. Name the school of Hindu Law which is applicable to West Bengal and Assam.
25. Name the school of Hindu Law under which an interest in the ancestral property is acquired by birth.
26. Does a Hindu undivided family arise from an agreement?
27. What is the maximum limit of coparceners?
28. Does a female become member merely by her birth in a Hindu undivided family?
29. Who has implied authority in case of Hindu undivided family?
30. What is the extent of liability of members in case of Hindu undivided family?
31. What is the effect of death of a coparcener on the status of a Hindu undivided family?
32. What is a 'Partnership deed'?
33. Why is it considered desirable to have a partnership deed in writing?
34. Is it necessary to have a 'Partnership deed'?
35. Is it necessary to have a 'Partnership deed' duly stamped?
36. Is it necessary to have a 'Partnership deed' duly signed by all the partners?
37. Does the change in the terms laid down in the 'Partnership deed' require the consent of all the partners?
38. What is meant by 'Registration of firm?
39. When does the registration become effective?
40. Is the registration of firm compulsory?
41. What is 'Partnership at will'?
42. What is a 'Particular partnership'?
43. Who is called an 'Actual partner'?
44. Who is called a 'Sleeping or dormant partner'?
45. Who is called a 'Nominal partner'?
46. Who is called a 'Partner in profits only'?
47. Who is called a 'Sub-partner'?
48. Can a partnership be formed with a minor?
49. Can a minor be admitted as a partner?

50. On attaining majority, within what period a minor partner is required to exercise his option whether or not to become a partner?
51. Are the mutual rights and duties of partners governed by the partnership agreement only?
52. Can the duties of partner laid down under Sections 9 and 10 be changed by an agreement amongst the partners?
53. Define 'Authority of a partner'.
54. Define 'Express authority of a partner'.
55. Define 'Implied authority of a partner'.
56. Can the 'Implied authority of a partner' be restricted?
57. Is the third party bound by any restriction imposed on the 'Implied authority of a partner'?
58. Is an incoming partner liable for firm's acts done before his admission?
59. Is a retiring partner liable for firm's acts done after his retirement?
60. What is the right of a partner who has been wrongly expelled?
61. Is a public notice required on the expulsion of a partner?
62. Are the rights and liabilities of an expelled partner the same as those of a retired partner?
63. Is the estate of an insolvent partner liable for firm's acts done after the date of order of adjudication?
64. Is a public notice required on the insolvency of a partner?
65. Is the firm dissolved on the death of a partner?
66. Is the estate of the deceased partner liable for firm's acts done after the date of his death?
67. Is a public notice required on the death of a partner?
68. Can a partner transfer his interest partially?
69. During the continuance of the partnership, (a) Is a transferee entitled to require accounts? (b) Is a transferee bound to accept the account of profits agreed to by the partners?
70. Define sub-partnership.
71. Are the rights of a sub-partner same as those of a transferee of a partner's share?
72. What is a 'Continuing guarantee'?
73. What is the effect of the change in the constitution of the firm on continuing guarantee?
74. What is meant by 'Dissolution'?
75. What is meant by 'Dissolution of partnership'?
76. What is meant by 'Dissolution of firm'?
77. Does the illegality of one or more business but not all businesses necessitate the compulsory dissolution of a firm?
78. How can a partnership at will be dissolved?
79. Give the two examples of just and equitable grounds on which a court may order dissolution of the firm?

80. Can a return of the premium be claimed when the dissolution is due to the death of a partner?
81. Can the partner be held liable for any act done after dissolution?
82. Is a public notice required on dissolution of a firm?
83. Is the estate of a deceased partner liable for the acts done after the dissolution of firm?
84. Is the estate of an insolvent partner liable for the acts done after the dissolution of the firm?
85. Is a sleeping partner who has retired from the firm liable for acts done after the dissolution of firm?
86. Does the authority of a partner to bind the firm continue after the dissolution of a firm?
87. Can a partner being a seller of goodwill of a dissolved firm carry on a business competing with that of the buyer?
88. Is it necessary to give notice to the Registrar of Firms?

SHORT ANSWER TYPE QUESTIONS

1. Comment on the following statements:
   (a) Law of partnership is an extension of the law of agency.
   (b) Sharing of profit is a *prima facie* evidence of existence of partnership but it is not the conclusive evidence.
   (c) The relation of partnership arises from contract and not from status.
   (d) The Indian Partnership Act has effectively ensured the registration of firms without making it compulsory.
2. Distinguish between the following:
   (a) Partnership and Co-ownership
   (b) Partnership and Hindu undivided family
   (c) Registered firm and Unregistered Firm
   (d) Partnership at will and Particular Partnership
   (e) Active Partner and Sleeping Partner
   (f) Dissolution of Partnership and Dissolution of Firm
   (g) Firm's Debts and Partner's Private Debts
3. Write explanatory notes on the following:
   (a) Test of partnership
   (b) Partnership deed
   (c) Procedure for registration of a firm
   (d) Consequences of non-registration of a firm
   (e) Duration of partnership
   (f) Partner, firm and firm's name
   (g) Dormant partner
   (h) Partner in profits only
   (i) Sub-partner

(j) Partner by estoppel or holding out
(k) Rights and liabilities of a minor partner before attaining majority
(l) Rights and liabilities of a minor partner on attaining majority
(m) Mandatory duties of partners
(n) Property of the firm
(o) Implied authority of a partner
(p) Acts outside the implied authority of a partner
(q) Partner's authority in an emergency
(r) Effect of restriction of partner's implied authority by mutual agreement
(s) Effect of admission or representation by a partner
(t) Effect of notice to an acting partner
(u) Liability of partners for acts of the firm
(v) Liability of firm for wrongful acts of a partner
(w) Liability of firm for misapplication by partners
(x) Liability of an incoming partner for firm's acts done before his admission
(y) Rights of a retiring partner
(z) Expulsion of a partner
(aa) Insolvency of a partner
(ab) Rights of a transferee of partners' interest
(ac) Compulsory dissolution
(ad) Dissolution on the happening of certain contingencies
(ae) Dissolution by an order of court
(af) Liabilities of partners for acts done after dissolution
(ag) Right to get return of premium on premature dissolution
(ah) Settlement of Accounts
(ai) Rights of a partner in case of sale of goodwill after dissolution of a firm

ESSAY TYPE QUESTIONS

1. (a) Define 'Partnership'. (b) Explain the essential elements of a partnership. (c) Also explain the terms "partner", "firm" and "firm name". (d) Is there any difference between "partnership" and "firm"?
2. Explain how you will determine whether a group of persons is a partnership or not.

*3. (a) Is it compulsory for a partnership firm to get itself registered?
   (b) Explain briefly the procedure for registration of firms.
   (c) Explain the consequences of non-registration.

4. Enumerate the different types of partners and briefly explain the extent of their liabilities.
5. Explain the circumstances under which a person can be made liable as a partner even if he is not a partner.

*6. (a) Can a partnership be formed with a minor partner?

(b) Can a minor be admitted to partnership? If so, what are his rights and liabilities during minority and after he has attained majority?

7. (a) State the duties of partners which cannot be changed by an agreement amongst the partners.

(b) State the duties of partners which can be changed by an agreement amongst the partners.

(c) State the rights of partners in the absence of any express agreement.

8. In the absence of an express agreement, state the legal position regarding

(a) interest on capital of partners,

(b) interest on loan by a partner

(c) remuneration of partners,

(d) profit sharing ratio.

9. (a) What is partnership property?

(b) If a partner's property is used for the purpose of the firm's business, does it automatically become the property of the firm?

(c) State how far is the partnership property liable for the separate debts of partners.

*10. (a) What is meant by 'implied authority of a partner?'

(b) What are the statutory restrictions on the implied authority of a partner?

(c) Can the implied authority of any partner be extended or restricted?

(d) How far are third parties affected by the restrictions placed on such implied authority?

11. (a) How can a major person be admitted in an existing firm?

(b) How can a minor person be admitted in an existing firm?

(c) Is an incoming partner liable for firm's acts done before his admission? Are there exceptions?

12. (a) How can a partner retire from a firm?

(b) Is a retiring partner liable for the firm's acts done before his retirement? If so, can he be discharged from his liability towards the third parties?

(c) Is a retiring partner liable for firm's acts done after his retirement?

(d) Is the public notice of the retirement of a partner required? Who can give public notice of retirement? What are the consequences of not giving public notice in case of retirement of (i) an acting partner (ii) a dormant partner?

(e) State the rights of a retiring partner.

13. (a) Can a partner be expelled? If so, how?

(b) What are the rights and liabilities of an expelled partner?

(c) What are the rights of a partner who has been wrongly expelled?

(d) Does expulsion necessarily result in dissolution of the firm?

(e) What is meant by 'sub-partnership' and 'sub-partner'? State the rights of a 'sub-partner'.

14. (a) Does the insolvency of a partner necessarily result in dissolution of the firm?
    (b) Is the estate of an insolvent partner liable for firm's acts done after the date on which the order of adjudication is made if no public notice of insolvency is given?
15. (a) Does the death of a partner necessarily result in dissolution of the firm?
    (b) Is the estate of deceased partner liable for firm's acts done after the date of his death if no public notice of death is given?
16. (a) Can a share in a partnership be transferred like any other property?
    (b) Does the assignee of a partner's interest by sale, mortgage or otherwise enjoy the same rights and privileges as the original partner?
    (c) Does the transfer of partner's interest necessarily result in dissolution of the firm?
    (d) State the rights of transferee of partner's interest (i) during the continuance of partnership, (ii) on the dissolution of firm or on the retirement of the transferring partner.

*17. (a) What is meant by dissolution of a firm?
    (b) Under what circumstances a firm is compulsorily dissolved?
    (c) Under what circumstances a firm is dissolved on the happening of certain contingencies in the absence of any contract to the contrary?
    (d) Discuss the grounds on which a partnership firm may be dissolved by the court. Also state the person who can file a petition before the court.

18. Discuss the rights and liabilities of partners on dissolution of a firm.
19. Discuss the rights of a partner when the firm has been dissolved on the grounds of fraud or misrepresentation by a partner.
20. Discuss the provisions relating to the settlement of accounts of a firm after dissolution.
21. Who would bear and in which ratio the deficiency arising due to the insolvency of a partner?
22. (a) Can firm's assets be used to pay off partner's private debts?
    (b) Can partner's private assets be used to pay off firm's debts?
23. Where the goodwill of a dissolved firm has been sold, what are the rights of a partner of a dissolved firm?
24. (a) State the circumstances under which a public notice is required to be given under the Indian Partnership Act, 1932.
    (b) State the mode of giving public notice.
    (c) State the consequence if a public notice is not given.
    (d) Who can give a public notice?
25. State the circumstances under which unanimous consent of all partners is required.

CHAPTER 17

The Negotiable Instruments Act, 1881 (Part I)

1.0 INTRODUCTION

1.1 The Negotiable Instruments Act, 1881 came into force on 1st March, 1881.

1.2 It extends to the whole of India except the State of Jammu and Kashmir.

1.3 The Act deals with the law relating to three specific classes of Negotiable Instruments, viz. Promissory Note, Bill of Exchange and Cheque.

1.4 The Act does not apply to:

(a) Indian Paper Currency Act, 1871

(b) the local usage relating to any instrument in an oriental language (for example, *hundies*)

1.5 But where no custom is established, the Act will apply to *Hundies.*

2.0 MEANING AND CHARACTERISTICS OF NEGOTIABLE INSTRUMENT (SECTION 13)

2.1 Meaning of Negotiable Instrument [Section 13(1)] *According to Sec 13 (1),* **Negotiable Instrument means a promissory note, bill of exchange or cheque, payable either to order or to the bearer.** But, this definition does not explain the features of a Negotiable Instrument. *According to Willis*, "A negotiable instrument is one the property in which is acquired by anyone who takes it bonafide, and for value, inspite of any defect of title in the person from whom he took it." Thus, a negotiable instrument must possess **two features:**

1. The right of **ownership** contained in the instrument **can be transferred** from one person to another by mere delivery if it is payable to bearer or by endorsement and delivery if payable to order, and
2. The **transferee** taking the instrument in good faith and for consideration **gets a good title** to the same even though the title of the transferor is defective.

2.2 Essential Characteristics of a Negotiable Instrument The essential characteristics of a negotiable instrument are as follows:

(a) Payable to Order or Bearer It must be payable *either* to order *or* to bearer.

(b) Freely Transferable An instrument payable to order is negotiable by endorsement and delivery and an instrument payable to bearer is negotiable by mere delivery.

(c) Presumption as to Holder Every holder of a negotiable instrument is presumed to be a holder in due course.

(d) Title of Holder in due Course Free from all Defects A holder in due course (i.e., the person who became the possessor of negotiable instrument before maturity, for valuable consideration and in good faith) gets the instrument free from all defects in the title of the transferor.

(e) **Presumption as to Consideration** Every negotiable instrument is presumed to have been made, drawn, accepted, endorsed, negotiated or transferred for consideration.

2.3 Meaning of Negotiable Instrument Payable to Order [Explanation I to Section 13(1)] A promissory note, bill of exchange or cheque is payable to order if, ***either*** **of** the following **two conditions** is fulfilled:

(a) It must be expressed to be so payable, or

(b) It must be expressed to be payable to a particular person and it must not contain words which prohibit transfer or indicate an intention that it shall not be transferable.

2.4 Meaning of Negotiable Instrument Payable to Bearer [Explanation II to Section 13(1)] A promissory note, bill of exchange or cheque is payable to bearer if ***either*** **of** the following **two conditions** is fulfilled.

(a) It must be expressed to be so payable, or

(b) The only or last endorsement must be an endorsement in blank.

2.5 Clarification Regarding Negotiable Instruments Payable to the Order of a Specified Person [Explanation III to Section 13(1)] Where a promissory note, bill of exchange or cheque, *either* originally *or* by endorsement, is expressed to be payable to the order of a specified person and not to him or his order, it is nevertheless payable to him or his order at his option. In *Raghunath* v. *Bihari Lal*, the document signed by Raghunath stated "I promise to pay you (Bihari Lal) on demand the sum of Rs 7000", it was contended that as the document stated nothing about the amount being payable to the order of a person or to the bearer, it was not a negotiable instrument and hence not a promissory note. Held that even if the amount was payable to a specified person it was a valid promissory note.

Notes:

(i) In addition to a promissory note, bill of exchange or cheque, there may be other negotiable instruments recognised by the usage or custom or other Acts. For example, Share Warrant, Dividend Warrant, Bearer Debenture etc. Free transferability makes these instruments negotiable.

(ii) Railway Receipt (R/R), Bill of Lading, Dock Warrant, Deposit Receipts are not negotiable instruments because they cannot give a better title to the transferee than that of the transferor. *[Refer to Practical Problem 1]*

2.6 Can There be More than One Payee [Section 13(2)] A negotiable instrument may be made payable to two or more payees jointly, or it may be made payable in the alternative to one of the two, or some of the several payees.

3.0 PRESUMPTIONS AS TO NEGOTIABLE INSTRUMENTS [SECTION 118]

Until the contrary is proved, the following presumptions shall be made:

3.1 ***Of consideration:*** That every negotiable instrument was made or drawn accepted, endorsed, negotiated or transferred for consideration.

3.2 ***As to date:*** That every negotiable instrument bearing a date was made or drawn on such date.

3.3 ***As to time of acceptance:*** That every accepted bill of exchange was accepted within a reasonable time after its date and before its maturity.

3.4 ***As to time of transfer:*** That every transfer of a negotiable instrument was made before its maturity.

3.5 ***As to time of endorsement:*** That the endorsements appearing upon a negotiable instrument were made in the order in which they appear thereon.

3.6 ***As to stamp:*** That a lost promissory note, bill of exchange or cheque was duly stamped.

3.7 ***As to holder in due course:*** That the holder of a negotiable instrument is a holder in due course except where the instrument has been obtained from its lawful owner, or from any person in lawful custody thereof, by means of an offence or fraud, or has been obtained from the maker or acceptor thereof by means of an offence of fraud, or for unlawful consideration, and the burden of proving that the holder is a holder in due course lies upon him.

3.8 ***As to protest:*** In a suit upon an instrument which has been dishonoured, the Court shall, on proof of the protest, presume the fact of dishonour, unless and until such fact is disproved.

4.0 TYPES OF NEGOTIABLE INSTRUMENTS

The various types of negotiable instruments are given below:

Types of Negotiable Instruments

Type of Instrument	*Meaning*	*Example*
1. Bearer Instrument [Explanation II to Section 13(1)]	A negotiable instrument is a Bearer Instrument if : (a) It is expressed to be payable to bearer or (b) The only or last endorsement is an endorsement in blank. ***Notes:*** (i) A promissory note cannot be made payable to the bearer. (ii) A bill of exchange cannot be made payable to bearer on demand. [Section 31 of the Reserve Bank of India Act, 1934] (iii) A bearer instrument can be transferred by mere delivery.	"Pay to R or bearer" *[Refer to Practical Problem I]*
2. Order Instrument [Explanation I to Section 13(1)]	A negotiable instrument is an Order Instrument if : (a) It is expressed to be payable to order, or (b) It is expressed to be payable to a particular person and it does not contain words which prohibit	(i) "Pay to R or order" (ii) "Pay to the order of R" (iii) "Pay to R"

	transfer or indicate an intention that it shall not be transferable. ***Note:*** An order instrument can be transferred by an endorsement on it and then its delivery.	*[Refer to Practical Problem 1]*
3. Inland Instrument [Section 11]	A negotiable instrment is an inland instrment if : (a) It is drawn in India, (b) It is payable in India, or it is drawn upon any person resident in India. ***Notes:*** (i) Protest of an inland bill is optional. (ii) An inland instrument remains inland even if it has been endorsed in a foreign country.	(i) "A bill drawn in Delhi on a merchant in Agra and accepted payable in London" (ii) "A bill drawn in Delhi on a merchant in London and accepted payable in Agra." *[Refer to Practical Problem 2]*
4. Foreign Instrument [Section 12]	An instrument which is not an inland instrument is deemed to be a foreign instrument. ***Note:*** Foreign bills must be protested for dishonour if such protest is required by the law of the place where they are drawn [Section 104]	(i) "A bill drawn in Delhi on a merchant in London and accepted payable in London." (ii) "A bill drawn in London on a merchant in Agra and accepted payable in Agra." *[Refer to Practical Problem 2]*
5. Ambiguous Instruments [Section 17]	An ambiguous bill means an instrument which can be constructed *either* as a promissory note *or* a bill of exchange. Once he exercises his option, the instrument shall be thence forward treated accordingly.	(i) "A bill drawn by an agent acting within his authority upon his principal." (ii) "A bill drawn upon a fictitious person." *[Refer to practical Problem 3]*
6. Inchoate Instrument [Section 20]	A negotiable instrument is an Inchoate Instrument if : (a) it is wholly blank or partially blank, (b) it is duly stamped, (c) it is duly signed and	"A bill drawn payable to ....or order"

	(d) it is delivered by person signing such instrument to another person. **Legal Effect** : The holder gets a *prima facie* authority to make or complete the negotiable instrument, for any amount specified therein and not exceeding the amount covered by the stamp. **Liability on An Inchoate Instrument—** (a) A person other than holder in due course can recover only such amount as he was authorised to **fill.** (b) A holder in due course can recover the whole amount stated in the instrument but not exceeding the amount covered by the stamp. ***Notes:*** (i) The principal of this rule is one of estoppel. (ii) The signer is liable if the following conditions are fulfilled: (a) The blanks must be filled in and the instrument must be completed. (b) The instrument must have been delivered to the transferee. (c) The instrument must be stamped one and the stamp affixed must be sufficient to cover the amount filled in the instrument. (iii) A holder in due course can recover in excess of the amount intended to be paid by the signer provided the amount is covered by the stamp affixed on the instrument.	

	(iv) The provisions of this Section cannot be applied to a cheque which is not required to be stamped.	*[Refer to Practical Problems 4 & 5]*
7. Instruments payable on demand [Section 19 and 21]	A promissory note or bill of exchange is payable on demand if (a) no time for payment is specified, *or* (b) it is expressed to be payable on demand, or at sight or on presentment ***Notes:*** (i) A cheque is always payable on demand. (ii) 'At sight' and presentment means on demand. (iii) An instrument payable on demand may be presented for payment at anytime. (iv) An instrument payable on demand is not entitled to any days of grace.	(i) "I Promise to pay *B* Rs. 500" (ii) "I promise to pay *B* Rs. 500 on demand." (iii) "Pay *B* Rs 500 at sight." (iv) "Pay *B* Rs 500 on presentment." *[Refer to Practical problem 6]*
8. Time Instrument	Time instruments mean the instruments in which time for payment is mentioned. A promissory note or bill of exchange is a time instrument when it is expressed to be payable— (a) after a specified period (b) on a specific day (c) after sight (d) on the happening of event which is certain to happenT ***Notes:*** (i) The expression 'after sight' means— (a) in a promissory note, after presentment for sight	(i) "I promise to pay *B* Rs 500 after 3 months." (ii) "I promise to pay Rs 500 on 1st Jan., 1998." (iii) "I promise to pay *B* Rs 500 after sight" (iv) "I Promise to pay *B* Rs 500 after *C*'s death."

	(b) in a bill of exchange, after acceptance or noting for non-acceptance or protest for non-acceptance. [Section 21] (ii) A cheque cannot be a time instrument because the cheque is always payable on demand.	*[Refer to Practical Problem 6]*
9. Accommodation Bills	An accommodation bill means a bill which is drawn, accepted without consideration. Provisions relating to such bills: (a) The accommodated party cannot, after he has paid the amount of the bill, recover the amount from any person who became a party to the bill for his accommodation [Explanation 1 to Section 43] (b) The person who becomes the holder of such a bill in good faith and for consideration, after maturity, may recover the amount from any prior party [Section 59].	*X* who needs funds, draws a bill on *Y* who accepts the bill and gets the bill and gets the bill discounted with his banker and on due date remits the requisted amount to *Y* to enable him to meet the bill; such a bill is an accomodation bill. *[Refer to Practical Problems 7 to 10]*
10. Fictitious Bill	A fictitious bill is a bill in which the name of the drawer or the payee or both is fictitious. When both the drawer and payee of a bill are fictitious persons, the acceptor is liable to a holder in due course if the holder in due course can show that the signature of the supposed drawer and that of the first endorser (payee) are in the same handwriting [Section 42].	(i) A bill drawn upon *X* in favour of *P* and the drawer is fictitious person. (ii) *X* drawn a bill upon *Y* in favour of *Z* who is a fictitious person. *[Refer to Practical Problem 3]*
11. Documentary Bill	A documentary bill means a bill to which the documents of title to the goods (i.e. Railways Receipt, Bill of Lading) and other documents are attached.	
12. Clean Bill	A clean bill means a bill to which no document relating to the	

	goods (for the transaction of which the bill is being drawn) is attached.	
13. Escrow [Section 46, Para 3]	A negotiable instrument which is delivered conditionally or for a special purpose as a *collateral security* or for *safe custody* only and not for the purpose of transferring absolutely the property therein, is called 'Escrow'. The liability to pay in case of an escrow does not arise if conditions agreed upon are not fulfilled or the purpose for which the instrument was delivered is not satisfied. This however, does not affect rights of a holder in due course.	
14. Bills in sets [Section 132 & 133]	Bills of exchange drawn in parts is called bills in sets. Provisions relating to 'Bills in sets' are: (a) Each part must be numbered. (b) Each part must contain a provision that it shall continue to be payable only so long as the other parts remain unpaid. (c) Each part must contain reference to the other parts. (d) Each part must be signed and delivered by the drawer. (e) All the parts of the whole set need not be accepted. (f) When a person accepts or endorses different parts of the bill in favour of different persons, he and the subsequent endorsers of each part are liable on such parts if it were a separate bill. (g) As between holders in due course of different parts of the same set, he who first acquired title to his part is entitled to the other parts and the money represented by the bill. [Section 133]	

5.0 PROMISSORY NOTES [SECTION 4]

5.1 Meaning of Promissory Note [Section 4] *According to Section 4 of the Negotiable Instruments Act, 1881*, **"A promissory note is an instrument in writing (not being a bank note or a currency note) containing an unconditional undertaking, signed by the maker to pay a certain sum of money only to, or to the order of a certain person or to the bearer of the instrument."**

Notes:

(i) A promissory note may be payable on demand or after a definite period of time.

(ii) The words "or to the bearer of the instrument" have become inoperative in view of the provision contained in Section 31(2) of the Reserve Bank of India Act, which provides that no person in India other than Reserve Bank of India or the Central Government can make or issue promissory note payable to the bearer of the instrument.

(iii) A bank note or currency note is not a promissory note because it is money itself.

5.2 Essential Characteristics of a Promissory Note

The essential characteristics of a promissory note are as follows:

(i) In writing: It must be in writing. In other words, an oral promise does not make a promissory note since it is not an instrument.

Example *A promises to pay B a sum of Rs. 500 on telephone. This promise will not make a promissory note because it is not in writing.*

(ii) Express promise to pay: There must be an express promise to pay and not mere acknowledgement of indebtedness.

Example *State with reasons whether each of the following instruments is a Promissory Note or not:*

(a) "Mr *B*, I owe you Rs 500."

(b) "We have received the sum of Rs 500 in cash from Mr *B*."

(c) "We have received the sum of Rs 500 in cash from Mr *B*. This amount will be repaid on demand."

(d) "We promise to pay Mr *B* a sum of Rs 500".

Solution. ***Cases (a) and (b).*** These instruments are not promissory notes because there is no express promise to pay. These instruments are merely acknowledgements of indebtedness.

Cases (c) and (d). These instruments are promissory notes because there is an express promise to pay.

In *Akbar Khan* v. *Attar Singh* (ILR 1936, 17 Lahore, 557 DC) a document was made with the following words, "This receipt is hereby executed by *B*... for Rs 43,000 received from *A*, the amount to be payable after two years. Interest @ Rs 5 % to be charged". Held the instrument was not a Promissory Note as it was a mere receipt stating the terms of repayment.

(iii) Definite and unconditional promise: The promise must be definite and unconditional. It may be noted that a promise to pay is not conditional if it depends upon an event which is certain to happen but the time of its occurrence may be uncertain.

Example *State with reasons whether each of the following instruments is a Promissory Note or not:*

(a) "I promise to pay *B* Rs 500 seven days after my marriage with Madhuri or Sridevi."

(b) "I promise to pay *B* for Rs 500 on *D*'s death provided *D* leaves me enough to pay that sum".

(c) "I promise to pay Rs 500 on *D*'s death".

Solution. ***Cases (a) and (b).*** These instruments are not promissory notes because the promise to pay is not unconditional. In *Beardsley* v. *Baldwin* (1741) 93 IR 1094, a written undertaking to pay a certain amount within a specified time after defendant's marriage was not recognised as a promissory note because possibly the defendant may never marry and the sum may never become payable.

Case (c). This instrument is a promissory note because the promise to pay is unconditional as it is certain that *D* will die.

(iv) Signed by the maker: It must be signed by the maker. The purpose of signature is to authenticate the instrument. The signatures can be made on any part of the instrument.

(v) Promise to pay certain sum: The promise must be to pay a certain sum. Negotiable Instruments are meant for free circulation and if their value is not clearly mentioned on the instruments, their circulation would be materially impeded. The sum payable is also certain in the following cases:

(a) Where it is payable along with interest and *either* the amount of interest itself *or* the rate of interest is given.

(b) Where it is payable at a specified rate of exchange.

(c) Where it is payable by instalments with a provision that a default being made in payment, the unpaid balance shall become due [Section 5].

Example *State with reasons whether each of the following instruments is a Promissory Note or not:*

(a) "I promise to pay *B* Rs 500 and all other sums which shall be due to him."

(b) "I promise to pay *B* Rs 500, first deducting thereout any money which he may owe me."

(c) "I promise to pay *B* Rs 500 along with interest thereon."

Solution. The aforesaid instruments are not promissory notes because the sum payable is not certain.

(vi) Promise to pay money only: The payment must be in money and money only.

Example *State with reasons whether each of the following instruments is a Promissory Note or not:*

(a) "I promise to deliver to *B* 1000 kg of paddy."

(b) "I promise to pay *B* Rs 500 and deliver of 1000 kg of paddy."

(c) "I promise to pay *B* Rs 500 and to deliver to him by black horse on 1st January next."

Solution. The aforesaid instruments are not promissory notes because the payment is not in money and money only.

(vii) Certain payee: The payee must be certain. Where the payee is designated by description only (say captain of a particular cricket team, president of a particular club, manager of a particular bank), the promissory note is valid if the payee can be ascertained by evidence.

A promissory note cannot be made payable to the maker himself. Such a note is invalid. However, it becomes a valid promissory note if it is endorsed by the maker because it then becomes payable to bearer (if endorsed in blank) or it becomes payable to the endorsee or his order (if endorsed specially).

(viii) Duly stamped: A promissory note must be stamped with adhesive stamp or engrossed on a stamp paper of proper value. This requires the cancellation of such stamp which may be done by writing his name across the stamp or initials with the date of his writing or in any other effectual manner.

Notes:

(i) The ommission of consideration received, place and date will not invalidate the instrument.

(ii) An undated instrument will be treated as having been made on the date of delivery.

(iii) An ante-dated or post-dated instrument is not invalid.

[*Refer to Practical Problem* 13]

5.3 Two Parties to a Promissory Note There are two parties to a promissory note as under:

(a) ***The maker:*** The person who makes the promissory note is called the maker.

(b) ***The payee:*** The person to whom or to whose order the payment is to be made, is called the payee.

5.4 Specimen of a Promissory Note The usual form of a Promissory Note is given below:

Bharat Tulsian sells goods to Rahul Tulsian for Rs 10,000 to be paid 3 months after date. If Rahul Tulsian promises to pay in writing, this promise will be a promissory note.

Payee — **Specimen of a Promissory note** — Maker

Rahul Tulsian
87, Engg. Enclave, Delhi - 34
Jan. 17, 2010

Rs 1 Crore

Three months after date I promise to pay Bharat Tulsian or to his order the sum of Rupees One Crore, for value received.

To

Bhrarat Tulsian
D-3/33, Rajasthali Apartments
Pitampura
Delhi - 110 034

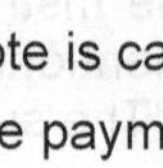

[Rahul Tulsian]

6.0 BILL OF EXCHANGE [SECTION 5]

6.1 Meaning of Bill of Exchange [Section 5] According to Section 5 of the Negotiable Instruments Act, 1881, "A bill of exchange is an instrument in writing containing an unconditional order signed by the maker directing a certain person to pay a certain sum of money only to, or to the order of a certain person or the bearer of the instrument." Thus, a bill is an order by a creditor upon his debtor requiring him to pay the money to the person specified.

Notes:

(i) A bill of exchange may be made payable to bearer on demand or after a definite period of time.

(ii) A bill of exchange cannot be made payable to bearer on demand because Section 31 of the Reserve Bank of India Act prohibits the issue of such bills of exchange.

6.2 Essential Characteristics of a Bill of Exchange The essential characteristics of a Bill of Exchange are as follows:

(i) ***In writing:*** It must be in writing.

(ii) ***Express order to pay:*** There must be an express order to pay and not a mere request to pay.

(iii) ***Definite and unconditional order:*** The order must be definite and unconditional.

(iv) ***Order to pay certain sum:*** The order must be to pay a certain sum.

(v) ***Order to pay money only:*** The order must be to pay money only.

(vi) ***Certain three parties:*** The three parties (i.e. drawer, drawee and payee) must be certain and must be mentioned in the instrument. It may be noted that the drawer and payee can be the same person but the drawer and drawee cannot be the same person.

(vii) ***Signed by the drawer:*** It must be signed by the drawer.

(viii) ***Duly Stamped:*** It must be duly stamped.

6.3 Three Parties to a Bill of Exchange There are three parties to a bill of exchange as under:

(a) ***Drawer:*** The person who draws a bill of exchange is called the drawer.

(b) ***Drawee:*** The person on whom the bill of exchange is drawn is called the drawee. He is also called as an acceptor of the Bill.

(c) ***Payee:*** The person to whom or to whose order the money is directed to be paid by the instrument, is called the payee.

6.4 Specimen of a Bill of Exchange The usual form of a Bill of Exchange is given below:

Bharat Tulsian sells goods to Rahul Tulsian for Rs 10,000 to be paid 3 months after date and buys goods from Rajat Tulsian for Rs 10,000 on similar terms. If Bharat Tulsian directs Rahul Tulsian to pay the sum of Rs 10,000 to Rajat Tulsian, this order will be a bill of exchange.

Payee

Drawee/Acceptor **Specimen of a Bill of Exchange** Drawer

Rs 10,000/- only Delhi Jan. 17, 2007 ....

Three months after date pay to Rajat Tulsian or order the sum of Rupees Ten Thousand, for value received.

Accepted
Rahul Tulsian

To

Rahul Tulsian
87, Engg. Enclave, Pitampura
Delhi - 110 034
In case of need with
Dena Bank, Pitampura Delhi - 34

[Bharat Tulsian]

7.0 ACCEPTANCE

7.1 Meaning of Acceptance A bill is said to be accepted when the drawee (i.e., the person on whom the bill is drawn), after putting his signature on it, *either* delivers it *or* gives notice of such acceptance to the holder of the bill or to some person on his behalf.

Acceptor After the drawee has accepted the bill, he is known as the acceptor. It is only the bill of exchange (other than cheque) which requires acceptance.

However, acceptance is not necessary to make a valid bill. If a bill is not accepted, it does not become invalid. It only becomes dishonoured by non-acceptance.

7.2 Acceptance in Case of Bills in Sets Where a bill is drawn in sets, the acceptance is required to be put on one part only. Where the drawee signs his acceptance on two or more parts, he may become liable on each of them respectively.

7.3 Essentials of a Valid Acceptance The essential of a valid acceptance are as follows:

(a) ***Written:*** It must be in writing and not oral.

(b) ***Signed:*** It must be signed by the drawee personally or through his duly authorised agent. [**Note :** The word 'Accepted is not legally required]

(c) ***On the bill:*** It must be on the bill whether on the face or on the back of the bill.

(d) ***Delivery:*** The drawee must *either* deliver the bill *or* give notice of his acceptance to the holder of bill or to some person on his behalf.

[*Refer to Practical Problem 14*]

7.4 Types of Acceptance Acceptance may be *either* general *or* qualified.

(a) Meaning of General Acceptance: An acceptance is said to be general when the drawee accepts the bill without qualification to the order of the drawer.

(b) Meaning of Qualified Acceptance: *An acceptance is said to be qualified when the drawee accepts the bill subject to qualification.* It may be noted that an acceptance will not be treated as a qualified acceptance unless the qualification is expressed on the bill in the clearest language. The qualification may relate to an event, amount, place, time, etc.

Circumstances indicating Qualified Acceptance

According to Section 86, an acceptance is qualified under the following circumstances:

(a) where it undertakes the payment on the happening of an event therein stated;

(b) where it undertakes the payment of part only of the sum ordered to be paid;

(c) where it undertakes the payment at a specified place of his choice and not otherwise or elsewhere;

(d) where it undertakes the payment at a time other than that at which under the order it would be legally due.

(e) where it is not signed by all drawees who are not partners.

[*Refer to Practical Problem 15*]

Effect of Qualified Acceptance

(a) the holder, may, treat the bill as dishonoured due to non-acceptance and after giving due notice of dishonour, sue the drawer and prior endorsers.

(b) If he accepts a qualified acceptance all prior parties whose consent is not obtained are discharged as against the holder and those deriving title from him.

Examples of Qualified Acceptance

(a) Accepted payable when in funds.

(b) Accepted payable on giving up bill of lading.

(c) Accepted payable when a cargo consigned to me is sold.

(d) A bill drawn for Rs 1,000 accepted for Rs 900 only.

(e) Accepted payable at Delhi only where no place of payment being specified in the order.

(f) Accepted payable at Delhi only where the place of payment specified in the order was Bombay.

(g) Accepted payable 4 months after date where the bill drawn as payable 3 months after date.

(h) Accepted by *A*, *B* and *C* where drawees were *A*, *B*, *C* and *D* who were not partners.

8.0 DISTINCTION BETWEEN BILL OF EXCHANGE AND PROMISSORY NOTE

A Bill of Exchange differs from a Promissory Note in the following respects:

Basis of Distinction	*A Bill of Exchange*	*A Promissory Note*
1. No. of Parties	There are **three** parties—drawer, drawee and payee.	There are **two** parties—maker and payee.
2. Promise/order	It contains an unconditional **order** given by a creditor to a debtor.	It contains an unconditional **promise** given by a debtor to a creditor.
3. Nature of liability	The liablity of the drawer is **secondary and conditional.**	The liability of the maker is **primary and absolute.**
4. Acceptance	It **requires** acceptance to become a valuable instrument.	It **does not require** any acceptance since it is a valuable instrument right from te beginning.
5. Same identity of payor and payee	The drawer and payee **may be** the same person.	The maker and payee **cannot be** the same person.
6. Payable to bearer	It **can be** payable to bearer. It cannot be drawen as payable to bearer on demand.	It **cannot be** payable to bearer.
7. Protest of dishonour	It **requires** the protesting for dishonour.	It **does not** *require* any protesting.
8. Notice of dishonour	Notice for dishonour **must** be given to all persons (including drawer) liable to pay.	Such notice is ***not required*** to be given to the maker.

9.0 CHEQUE [SECTION 6]

9.1 Meaning of a Cheque [Section 6] A cheque is a bill of exchange which is (a) drawn upon a specified banker, and (b) payable on demand and includes :

(i) the electronic image of truncated cheque

(ii) a cheque in electronic form.

9.2 Essential Characteristics of a Cheque The essential characteristics of a cheque are as follows:

(i) ***In writing:*** It must be in writing.

(ii) ***Express order to pay:*** There must be an express order to pay and not request to pay.

(iii) ***Definite and unconditional order:*** The order must be definite and unconditional.

(iv) ***Signed by the drawer:*** It must be signed by the drawer.

(v) ***Order to pay certain sum:*** The order must be to pay a certain sum.

(vi) ***Order to pay money only:*** The order must be to pay money only.

(vii) ***Certain three parties:*** The three parties (i.e., drawer, drawee and payee) must be certain and must be mentioned in the instrument.

In addition to the aforesaid essentials of a bill of exchange, the cheque must also satisfy the following two requirements:

(viii) ***Drawn upon a specified banker:*** It must always be drawn upon a specified banker.

(ix) ***Payable on demand:*** It must always be payable on demand.

Thus, all cheques are bills of exchange in the sense that these have all the essential elements of a bill of exchange. But all bills of exchange are not cheques because a bill of exchange becomes a cheque only when it satisfies the aforesaid two additional requirements.

Notes: (i) No acceptance of a cheque is required.

(ii) Cheque is not required to be stamped.

9.3 Three Parties to a Cheque There are three parties to a cheque as under:

(a) ***Drawer:*** The person who draws the cheque is called the drawer.

(b) ***Banker:*** The bank on which the cheque is drawn is called the drawee.

(c) ***Payee:*** The person in whose favour the cheque is drawn is called the payee. The payee may be a third party or the drawer himself.

9.4 Specimen of a Cheque

The usual form of a cheque is given below:

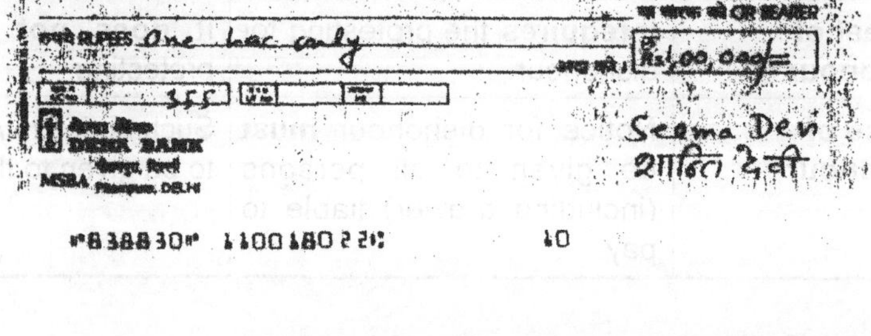

10.0 DISTINCTION BETWEEN A CHEQUE AND A BILL OF EXCHANGE

A Cheque can be distinguished from a Bill of Exchange as under:

Basis of Distinction	*A Cheque*	*A Bill of exchange*
1. Drawer	It is always drawn on a **bank.**	It can be drawn upon **any person** (Including a bank.)
2. Payable on demand	It is **always** payable on demand.	It **need not** always be payable on demand.
3. Payable to bearer on demand	It ***can be*** drawn payable to bearer on deman.	It **can not** be payable to bearer on demand [Section 31 of the Reserve Bank of India Act, 1934].
4. Acceptance	It does **not require** an acceptance.	It **requires** an acceptance of the drawee.
5. Stamp	It does **not require** a stamp.	It **requires** a stamp.
6. Three days of grace	It is **not entitled** to three days of grace.	A bill, unless payable on demand is **entitled** to three days of grace.
7. Crossing	It **can be** crossed.	It **cannot** be crossed.
8. Fixed Form	Its **fixed from** is honoured by a banker.	There is **no fixed form.**
9. Notice of dishonour	Notice of dishonour is **not required.**	Notice of dishonour is usually **required.**
10. Counter-manding	It **can be revoked** by countermanding of payment.	It **cannot be** countermanded.

11.0 CROSSING OF A CHEQUE [SECTIONS 123 TO 131A]

11.1 Meaning of Crossing Crossing means a direction to the drawee bank to pay the amount of cheque only to a banker. The crossing of a cheque is an instance of an alteration which is authorised by the Act. A cheque is said to be crossed when it bears across its face two parallel transverse lines which are usually drawn on the left hand top corner of the cheque.

11.2 Purpose of Crossing The purpose of Crossing is to direct the drawee (banker) to pay the amount of cheque only to a banker so that the party who receives the payment of the cheque can be easily traced.

11.3 Types of Crossing There are two types of Crossing, viz. general crossing and special crossing. The meaning, specimens and effects of various types of crossing have been given in Exhibits 1, 2 and 3.

Exhibit 1 Meaning, Specimen and Effects of General Crossing

Meaning	*Specimen*	*Effects*
A cheque is said to be crossed generally where it bears across its face an addition of		(i) The banker on whom it is drawn must pay only to the collecting banker.

(i) two parallel transverse lines	(two parallel lines)	(ii) The effect of the words, 'Not Negotiable' on a crossed cheque is that the title of the transferee of such a cheque cannot be better than that of the transferor of such a cheque even if the transferee is a holder in due course. It may be noted that the use of words 'Not Negotiable' does not restrict the further transferability of such a cheque but only takes away the mainfeature of negotiability. The instrument is transferred subject to equities. In other words, if the title of the endorser of such a cheque is defective then the title of endorsee will also be defective. Thus, the transferee shall get only the rights of the transferor. The transferee cannot become a holder in due course. The object of 'Not Negotiable' crossing is to protect the rights of the holder of a cheque.
(ii) the words 'and Company' between two parallel transverse lines	and Company	
(iii) the words '& Co' between two parallel transverse lines	& Co.	
(iv) the words 'Not Negotiable' between two parallel transverse lines	Not Negotiable	
(v) the words 'and Company' and 'Not Negotiable' between two parallel transverse lines	and Company Not Negotiable	
(vi) the words '& Co' and 'Not Negotiable' between two parallel transverse lines	& Co. Not Negotiable	

Exhibit 2 Meaning, Specimen and Effects of Special Crossing

Meaning	*Specimen*	*Effects*
A Cheque is said to be crossed specially where it bears across its face in addition of:		The banker on whom it is drawn must pay it only to the banker to whom it is crossed or his agent for collection.
(i) the name of a banker		
— without lines	Dena Bank	
— between two parallel transverse lines	Dena Bank	
(ii) the name of a bank with the words, 'Not Negotiable'		
— without lines	Dena Bank Not Negotiable	
— between two parallel transverse lines	Dena Bank Not Negotiable	

(iii) the name of a banker with the words 'and company' — without lines — between two parallel transverse lines	Dina Bank and Company Dina Bank and Company	
(iv) the name of a banker with the words '& Co.' — without lines — between two parallel transverse lines	Dena Bank & Co. Dena Bank & Co.	
(v) the name of a banker with the words 'Not Negotiable 'and Company' — without lines — between two parallel transverse lines	Deena Bank Not Negotiable and Company Deena Bank Not Negotiable and Company	
(vi) the name of a banker with the words 'Not Negotiable' and '& Co.' — without lines — between two parallel transverse lines.	Dena Bank Not Negotiable & Co. Dena Bank Not Negotiable & Co.	

Exhibit 3 **Meaning, Specimen and Effect of Crossing Adopted by Usage**

Meaning	***Specimen***	***Effects***
The words 'A/c Payee' are entered on the face of a cheque crossed whether generally or specially.	A/c Payee A/c Payee Not Negotiable A/c Payee only Dena Bank	The amount collected on the cheque must be credited only to the account of payee. It may be noted that though the cheque remains legally negotiable but 'A/c Payee' crossing hinders the negotiability of the cheque in practice.

Notes:

(i) Only the cheques can be crossed. The promissory notes or bills of exchange cannot be crossed.

(ii) A general crossing can be converted into special crossing but a special crossing cannot be converted into general crossing. If the holder converts the special crossing into general crossing by striking out the banker's name, it will amount to material alteration.

(iii) A special crossing can be made only once except where the second special crossing is made by a banker to another banker to act as an agent of the former.

(iv) Where a cheque contains special crossing to more than one banker, then the paying banker shall refuse to make the payment of the same. [Section 127]

11.4 Who can Cross a Cheque after Issue [Section 125] A cheque may be crossed after its issue in the following manner:

Case	*Right to cross*
1. Where a cheque is uncrossed	The holder may cross it generally or specially.
2. Where a cheque is crossed generally	The holder may cross it spe cially by adding the name of same banker.
3. Where a cheque is crossed generally or specially	The holder may add the word 'Not Negotiable'.
4. Where a cheque is crossed specially	The banker to whom it is crossed may again cross it specially to another banker (his agent) for collection.

11.5 Can a Cheque be Crossed Specially more than Once? [Section 127] A cheque cannot be crossed more than once. It is only a special crossing which may require a second crossing. This is allowed only when a Banker in whose favour a crossing is made, can once again cross it in favour of his agent for collection. Therefore, a banker is except for the above stated case, prohibited to make payment on a cheque bearing more than one crossing.

12.0 BOUNCING OR DISHONOUR OF CHEQUES

12.1 Meaning of Bouncing or Dishonour of Chques A cheque is said to be bounced or dishonoured by non-payment when the drawee of the cheque makes default in payment upon being duly required to pay the same.

12.2 Liability of Drawee on Dishonour of a Cheque [Section 31] The drawee of a cheque must compensate the drawer for any loss or damage caused by non-payment if the following **three conditions** are fulfilled:

(a) If the drawee has sufficient funds of the drawer in his hands;

(b) If the funds are properly applicable to such payment;

(c) If the drawee is duly required to pay the cheque.

Note: The drawee (i.e., paying banker) is liable to drawer and not to any other person.

12.3 Liability of Drawer on Dishonour of a Cheque [Section 138] On dishonour of a cheque, the drawer is punishable with **imprisonment** for a term upto **2 year** or with **fine not exceeding twice the amount** of a cheque or with both if the following **conditions** are fulfilled:

(a) If the cheque was drawn to discharge a **legally enforceable debt** or other liability;

(b) If the cheque is returned by the bank unpaid due to **insufficiency of funds** in the account of drawer;

(c) If the cheque has been **presented** to the bank **within** a period of **6 months** from the date on which it is drawn or within the period of its validity, whichever is earlier;

(d) If the payee or the holder in due course of the cheque has made a **demand** for the payment of the said amount of money **by giving a notice, in writing,** to the drawer of the cheque **within 30 days of the receipt of information** by him from the bank regarding the return of the cheque as unpaid; and

(e) If the drawer of such cheque has **failed to make the payment** of the said amount of money to the payee or to the holder in due course of the cheque, **within 30 days of the receipt of the said notice.**

The complaint can be made only by the payee/holder in due **within 1 month** of expiry of 30 days of receipt of notice by drawer.

12.4 Practical Illustration

Date of disonour of cheque —13th January 2009

Date of Receipt of information by payee from the

Bank regarding the return of the cheque as unpaid —17th January 2009

State whether the holder/payee of a cheque can initiate prosecution for an offence under Section 138 in the following cases:

Cases	*I*	*II*	*III*	*IV*	*V*
Purpose of drawing a cheque	To make gift	To discharge a debt	To discharge a debt	To discharge a debt	To discharge a debt
Reson for Dishonour of cheque	Insuffi-ciency of funds	Insuffi-ciency of funds	Insuffi-ciency of funds	Stop payment	Signature differs
Date of presentment of a cheque	within validity period	within validity period.	within validity period	within validity period.	within validity period
Date of demand made by payee/holder in due course of cheque	15th Feb.	15th Feb.	16th Feb.	15th Feb.	15th Feb.
Date of payment by Drawer	16th Mar.	16th Mar.	16th Mar.	16th Mar.	16th Mar.

Solution:

Case	*Whether consitute an offence u/s 138*	*Reason*
I	No	The cheque was not drawn to discharge a legally enfoceable a debt.

II	Yes	All conditions to constitute an offence u/s 138 are fulfilled
III	No	Payee/holder in due course of a cheque failed to m ake a demand within 30 days of the receipt of information from the bank regarding the return of cheque failed to make a demand within 30 days of the recipt of information from the bank regardfing the return of chequer as unpaid
IV	Yes	(a) Presumption u/s 139 follows: (b) Section 138 is a penal provision. (c) The object of Sections 130 to 142 is ensure credibility in transacting business through cheque *[Modi Cements Ltd. vs. Kuchi Kumar Nandi (1998) SC]*
V	No	The cheque is not returned by the bank unpaid due to insufficiency of funds in the account of the drawers

12.5 Judical Rulings

1. The holder/payee of a cheque cannot initiate prosecution for an offence u/s 138 for its dishonour for the second time if he had no initiate such prosecution on the earlier cause of action.

   [*Sadanandan Bhadran v. Madhavan Sunil Kumar* (1998) (SC)]

2. Where a company committed an offence u/s 138, then not only the company but also every person who at the time when the offence was committed was incharge of and was responsible to the comany shall be deemed to be guilty of the offence [*K.P.G. Nair vs. Jindal Menthol Indian Ltd.* (2001) (SC)]
3. If the drawer is to be held criminally liable, the cheque must be presented personally or through the collecting bank of payee/holder, at the bank on which the cheque is drawn within 6 months from the date on which it is shown to how been issued. [*Shri Ishar Alloy Steel Ltd v. jayaswale Neco Ltd.* (2001) (SC)]
4. A pay order was helf to be a cheque to lodge a complaint u's 138.

   [*Pubjab & Sind Bank v. Vinkar Sakari Bank Ltd.* (2001) (SC)]

12.6 Cases in which a Banker *must* Refuse to Honour a Customer's Cheque

A banker *must* refuse to honour a customer's cheque in the following cases:

1. ***Stop payment:*** When the banker receives instructions from the customer not to honour (i.e. stop payment) a particular cheque issued by him.
2. ***Garnishee order:*** When the banker receives a Garnishee Order, i.e., a prohibiting order by any court attaching the money in the customer's account.
3. ***Death:*** When the banker receives a notice of the death of his customer.
4. ***Insolvency:*** When the banker receives a notice of the insolvency of his customer.
5. ***Insanity:*** When the banker receives a notice of the insanity.
6. ***Assignment:*** When the banker receives a notice of assignment of his credit balance from a customer.

7. ***Defect in title:*** When the banker suspects or has reason to believe that the title of the person presenting the cheque is defective.
8. ***Loss of Cheque:*** When the banker receives a notice of loss of cheque from his customer.
9. ***Material alteration:*** When there is a material alteration in the cheque and such alteration has not been authenticated by his customer by putting his signature.
10. ***Different signature:*** When the signature of the drawer does not tally with the specimen signature kept by the bank.
11. ***Notice of closure:*** When the banker receives a notice in respect of closure of account.
12. ***Irregular endorsement:*** When there is an irregular endorsement.

12.7 Cases in which a Banker *may* Refuse to Honour a Customer's Cheque A banker *may* refuse to honour a customer's cheque in the following cases:

1. ***Insufficient funds:*** When funds in the customer's account are insufficient to honour the cheque presented.
2. ***Funds not applicable:*** When funds in the customer's account are not applicable for the cheque presented.
3. ***Presentment at different branch:*** When the cheque is presented at the branch other than the branch where the customer who has issued the cheque, has the account.
4. ***Presentment after banking hours:*** When the cheque is presented after the banking hours.
5. ***Stale cheque*:** When the cheque is presented after 6 months from the date of its issue.
6. ***Post dated cheque:*** When the cheque is presented before the actual date on which it is written to be payable.
7. ***Undated cheque*:** When the cheque is undated [*Griffith* v. *Dalton* (1940)]

13.0 'HOLDER' AND 'HOLDER IN DUE COURSE'

13.1 Meaning of Holder [Section 8] A person is called holder of a negotiable instrument if he satisfies the following **two** conditions:

(a) he must be entitled to the possession of the instrument in his own name; and

(b) he must be entitled to receive/recover the amount due on the instrument from the parties liable under the instrument.

Thus, Holder means the bearer of the bearer instrument and the endorsee or payee of the order instrument. He must be a *dejure* holder and not a *defacto* holder. He should be the owner thereof at law, whatever be his position in equity. It may be noted that under English Law, actual possession of the instrument is essential to be a Holder but such physical possession is not necessary under the Negotiable Instruments Act.

Example *X advanced Rs. 10,000 to Y who executed a promissory note in the name of Z a benamidar. On Maturity Y failed to pay the amount due and X brought an action against Y. It was held that X could not recover the amount because he was not entitled to the promissory note in his own name. [Sarjoo Prasad v. Ramapayari Debi]*

Note: Only a holder can bring a legal action to recover the amount due on the instrument.

Holder in case of loss or destruction: Where a note, bill or cheque is lost or destroyed, its holder is the person who was entitled to the instrument in his own name at the time of such loss or destruction. For example, the finder of a lost instrument payable to bearer, or a person in wrongful possession of such instrument is not a holder. Similarly, an agent holding an instrument for his principal will also not be a holder of it although he may receive its payment.

13.2 Meaning of Holder in due Course [Section 9] A person is called a holder in due course if he satisfies the following conditions:

(a) He must be a **holder**.

(b) He must have become, ***for consideration, either*** the possessor of the instrument if payable to bearer, *or* payee *or* endorsee thereof if payable to order. Such consideration must not be unlawful and need not be adequate.

(c) He must have obtained the instrument ***before its maturity***. He must become the holder before the amount becomes payable thereon. A person taking the bill or note on the day on which it becomes payable is not a holder as he takes it after it has become payable since the instrument may be discharged at any time on that day.

(d) He must have obtained the instrument ***in good faith***, i.e. without having sufficient cause to believe that any defect existed in the title of the person from whom he derived his title.

(e) He must receive the instrument **complete and regular on the face of it**, e.g. in *Arab Bank Ltd*. v. *Ross* (1952) 2Q.B.216; the payee in the promissory note was described as F and F.N. & Co., whereas endorser endorsed the note as F and F.N. omitting the words 'company'. Held, the endorsee did not constitute to be a holder in due course since the endorser and the payee appeared to be different person making the instrument not complete and regular on the face of it.

13.3 Privileges of Holder in due Course [Sections 20, 36, 42, 43, 46, 53, 58, 120, 121] A holder in due course gets title to a negotiable instrument free from equities. His privileges under the Act are as follows:

Privileges of Holder in due Course

Case	*Privileges*
1. In case of Inchoate Stamped Instrument [Section 20]	He can recover the whole amount stated in the Inchoate Instrument but not exceeding the amount covered by the stamp. A person signing the instrument cannot say that the instrument has not been filled in accordance with the authority given by him.
2. Liability of prior parties [Section 36]	Every prior party to a negotiable instrument is liable thereon to a holder in due course until the instrument is duly satisfied.
3. In case of fictious parties to bill [Section 42]	The acceptor of a bill cannot as against a holder in due course say that the other parties to the bill were fictitious if the holder in due course can show that the signature of the supposed drawer and that of the first endorser are in the same handwriting.

4. In case of instruments without consideration [Section 43]	He can recover the amount due on such instruments, from the transferor or any prior party thereto for consideration.
5. In case of conditional delivery [Section 46]	In case a bill or note is negotiated to a holder in due course, the other parties to the bill or note cannot avoid liability on the ground that the delivery of the instrument was conditional or for a special purpose only.
6. Protection to subsequent holders [Section 53]	A holder who derives title from a holder in due course has the same rights as that of holder in due course. Thus, once the instrument passes through the hands of a holder in due course, it is purged (i.e. cured) of all prior defects.
7. In case of instrument obtained by unlawful means or for unlawful consideration [Section 58]	The person liable to pay an instrument cannot, as a holder in due course, say that the instrument had been lost or obtained from him by means of an offence of fraud or for an unlawful consideration.
8. Estopple against denying original validity of instrument [Section 120]	The maker of a note, the drawer of a bill or cheque and acceptor of a bill for the honour of the drawer, cannot deny the validity of the instrument as originally made or drawn when a suit is filed by a holder in due course for the recovery of the amount due on the instrument.
9. Estoppel against denying capacity of payee to endorse [Section 121]	The maker of a note and acceptor of a bill payable to order, cannot deny the payee's capacity at the date of the note or bill, to indorse the same when a suit is filed by a holder in due course for the recovery of the amount due on the instruments.

[Refer to Practical Problem 12]

13.4 Distinction between a Holder and a Holder in due Course A holder can be distinguished from a holder in due course as under:

Basis of Distinction	*Holder*	*Holder in due course*
1. Consideration	He may become the possessor or payee of an instrument **even without** consideration.	He acquires possession **for consideration.**
2. Possessor Before maturity	He **need not** become the possessor before the maturity of the instrument.	He must become the possessor **before** the maturity of the instrument.
3. Good faith	He **need not** become the possessor in good faith	He **must** become the possessor in good faith, i.e. without having sufficient

		cause to believe that any defect existed in the transferor's title.
4. Right to have better title than that of transferor	He **cannot** have a better title than of transferor.	He **can have** a better title than that of transferor.
5. Right to enforce rigthts against all prior parties.	He **cannot** enforce his rights against all the prior parties. He can recover the amount from a person who has signed it and also from the trasferror from whom he obtained.	He **can** enforce his rights against all the prior parties.
6. Privilleges	He **does not enjoy** all the privileges available to holder in due course	He **enjoys** some privileges under the Act, for example under Sections 20, 36, 42, 43, 46, 58, 120, 121.

14.0 MATURITY OF A NEGOTIABLE INSTRUMENT [SECTIONS 22 TO 25]

14.1 Meaning of Maturity [Section 22] The maturity of a promissory note or bill of exchange is the date on which it falls due for payment.

14.2 Three Days of Grace [Section 22] Every instrument payable otherwise than on demand is entitled to 3 days of grace.

14.3 Calculation of Date of Maturity [Sections 23 to 25] The date of maturity in various cases is calculated as under:

Case	*Date of Maturity*
1. In case of bill or note payable on a specified day.	3rd day after specified day.
2. In case of bill or note payable on stated number of months after date [Section 23]	3rd day after the date on which the period of the bill or note shall expire. ***Note:*** The period shall expire on that day of the month which corresponds with the day on which the bill is dated. If the month in which the period terminates has no corresponding day, the period shall be deemed to expire on the last day of such a month.
3. In case of bill payable on a stated number of months after sight and accepted for honour [Section 23]	3rd day after the date on which the period of the bill or note shall expire. ***Note:*** The period shall expire on that day of the month which corresponds with the day on which the bill is accepted for honour. If the month in which the period terminates has no corresponding day, the period shall be deemed to expire on the last day of such month.

4. In case the day on which a note or bill is at maturity, is a public holiday [Section 25]	The immediately preceding business day. ***Note:*** The expression public holidays includes Sundays and any other day declared by the Central Government by notification in the Official Gazette to be a public holiday.
5. In case the day or which a note or bill is at maturity is an emergency/unforeseen public holiday.	The immediately following business day.

Note: The day on which the bill/note is drawn or presented for acceptance, sight or the day on which the event happens, must be excluded. [Section 24]

14.4 Practical Illustration

Find out the date of maturity of the following Bills Receivable:

Bill No.	*Date of drawing*	*Date of acceptance*	*Payable*
A-1	31.01.2007	02.02.2007	1 month after date
A-2	29.01.2007	03.02.2007	30 days after due date
A-3	29.01.2007	02.02.2007	1 months after date
A-4	12.07.2007	14.07.2007	1 month after date
A-5	27.06.2007	28.06.2007	3 months after date
A-6	28.09.2007	01.10.2007	2 months after sight
A-7	23.12.2007	24.12.2007	1 month
A-8	02.01.2008	03.01.2008	On demand
A-9	05.01.2008	06.01.2008	At sight
A-10	10.01.2008	11.01.2008	On presentment

Drawer demanded the amount of the last three bills on 24th Jan. 1999.

Solution:

Bill No.	*Date of drawing*	*Date of maturity*	*Remarks*
A-1	31.01.2007	03.03.2007	
A-2	29.01.2007	03.03.2007	
A-3	29.01.2007	31.03.2007	Since 1st April (being a bank holiday) is a public holiday.
A-4	12.07.2007	14.08.2007	Since 15th Aug. (being Independence Day) is a public holiday.
A-5	27.06.2007	29.09.2007	Since 30th Sept., (being a bank holiday) is a public holiday.
A-6	28.09.2007	04.12.2007	
A-7	23.12.2007	25.01.2008	Since 26th Jan. (being Republic Day) is a public holiday.

A-8	02.01.2008	24.01.2008	
A-9	05.01.2008	24.01.2008	
A-10	10.01.2008	24.01.2008	

Notes: (i) Three days of grace have been considered in case of bills after date and bills after sight, to ascertain the date of maturity.

(ii) The term of a 'bill after sight' commences from the date of acceptance.

15.0 PAYMENT IN DUE COURSE [SECTION 10]

A payment is said to be in due course if the following ***three*** conditions are fulfilled:

(a) ***The payment must be in accordance with the apparent tenor of the instrument*** i.e. payment according to whatever is apparently written on the instrument. *For example*, a payment of post-dated cheque before maturity is not according to the tenor of the instrument. But where an instrument has been endorsed payment to the endorsee will be in due course. In *Dena Bank* v. *K. K. Alex*, payment on a traveller cheque was made to a wrong person who forged the signatures of the holder while collecting payment, the payment was not held to be in due course.

(b) ***The person to whom payment is made must be in possession of the instrument.***

(c) ***The payment must be made in good faith***, without negligence and under circumstances which do not afford a reasonable ground for believing that the person to whom it is made is not entitled to receive the amount. The party making payment should be acting under the belief that the payment has been made to the person genuinely entitled to receive it. Thus, if there are suspicious circumstances and the person making payment doesn't make the necessary inquiry, the payment is not in due course.

16.0 PAYMENT OF AMOUNT DUE AND INTEREST [SECTIONS 78 TO 80]

16.1 To whom the Payment must be Made [Section 78] In order to discharge the maker or acceptor, the payment of the note, bill or cheque must be made to the holder.

16.2 Payment of Interest [Sections 79 to 80] The payment of interest shall be calculated as under:

Case	*Interest*
I. When the rate of interest is specified [Section 79]	The interest shall be calculated at the rate specified on the amount due: (i) from the date of instrument until tender of realisation of such amount, or (ii) from the date of the instrument until such date after the institution of suit to recover such amount as the Court directs.

II. When no rate of interest is specified [Section 80]	The interest shall be calculated at the rate of 18% p.a. on the amount due from the date at which the same ought to have been paid until tender or realization of such amount or until such date as the court directs.

Note: When the party charged is the endorser of an instrument dishonoured by non-payment, he is liable to pay interest only from the time that he receives notice of dishonour. [Explanation to Section 80]

17.0 CAPACITY AND AUTHORITY OF A PERSON TO BE A PARTY TO A NEGOTIABLE INSTRUMENT [SECTIONS 26 TO 28]

17.1 Meaning of Capacity Capacity here means competence to contract so as to bind oneself.

17.2 Who can bind and be bound [Section 26] Every person capable of contracting, according to the law to which he is subject, may bind himself and be bound by the making, drawing, acceptance, endorsement, delivery and negotiation of a promissory note, bill of exchange or cheque.

17.3 Position of Minor [Section 26] A minor may draw, endorse, deliver and negotiate such instrument so as to bind all parties, except himself.

In order words, the instrument will be valid and binding on all parties except minor.

Note: It is the estate of a minor (not the minor as person) which is liable for debts arising out of 'necessaries' supplied to minor.

[*Refer to Practical Problem 11*]

17.4 Can Liability Under Instrument be Incurred through an Agent [Section 27] Every person capable of binding himself or of being bound, as mentioned in Section 26, may so bind himself or be bound by a duly authorised agent acting on his behalf.

17.5 Does an Agent's General Authority include an Authority to Accept or Endorse a Bill [Section 27] A general authority to transact business and to receive and discharge debts does not confer upon an agent the power of accepting or endorsing bills of exchange so as to bind his principal.

17.6 Does an Agent's Authority to Draw a Bill include an Authority to Endorse [Section 27] An authority to draw bill of exchange does not of itself impart an authority to endorse.

17.7 Liability of an Agent [Section 28] An agent who signs his name on a promissory note, bill of exchange or cheque without indicating thereon that he signs as an agent, or that he does not intend thereby to incur personal responsibility, is liable personally on the instrument.

Exception to the aforesaid rule: An agent is not personally liable to those who induced him to sign upon the belief that the principal only would be held liable.

Note: The mere signature of an agent in his own name with the word 'agent' added does not exempt him from personal liability [*Liverpool Bank* v. *Walter*]

Example of agent's signature

When an agent is personally liable	*When an agent is not personally liable*
RAM *Partner* *Ram & Co.*	*For and on behalf of Ram & CO.* Ram *Partner*

18.0 PROTECTION TO PAYING BANKER AND COLLECTING BANKER [SECTIONS 85, 85A, 126, 131]

18.1 Protection to Paying Banker [Section 85]

(a) Meaning of Paying Banker: A paying banker is one who makes the payment of a cheque on behalf of his customer.

(a) Essential Conditions for Protection to Paying Banker [Section 85]: The essential conditions for protection to paying banker in respect of payment of various types of cheques are summarised below:

Type of Cheque	*Conditions for Protection*
1. Cheques payable to order [Section 85(1)]	The paying banker is discharged if *payment is made in due course. **Notes:** (i) Such protection is also available even when the endorsement subsequently turns out to be a forgery or the endorsement may have been made by payee's agent without his authority. (ii) Such protection is also available in respect of drafts drawn by one branch of a bank on another payable to order. [Section 85A]
2. Cheques originally payable to bearer [Section 85(2)]	The Paying banker is discharged if (a) Payment is made in due course (b) Payment is made to the bearer of the cheque. **Note:** Such protection is also available even when the endorsement whether in full or in blank which restricts or excludes further indorsement appears on such cheque.
3. Cheques Crossed Generally [Section 126]	The Paying Banker is discharged if— (a) Payment is made in due course (b) Payment is made to a banker
4. Cheques Crossed Specially [Section 126]	The Paying Banker is discharged if— (a) *payment is made in due course. (b) payment is made to a banker to whom cheque is crossed or his agent for collection.

5. Cheques which do not appear to be crossed or where crossing is obliterated.	The paying banker is discharged, if *payment is made in due course.

* Payment in due course means payment accordance with the apparent tenor of the instrument in good faith and without negligence to any person in possession thereof under circumstances which do not afford a reasonable ground for believing that he is not entitled to receive payment of the amount therein mentioned. [Section 10]

Notes: Even though the banker is protected for having made pay ment of the cheque to a wrong person, the true owner of the cheque is entitled to recover the amount of the cheque from the person who had no title to the cheque.

18.2 Circumstances under which Paying Banker is liable [Sec. 129]

The paying banker becomes liable to the true owner of the cheque for any loss suffered by him in the following circumstances:

(a) If the paying banker makes the payment of a cheque containing general crossing to any person other than a banker.

(b) If the paying banker makes the payment of a cheque containing special crossing to any banker other than the specified banker to whom the cheque is crossed. [Section 129]

18.3 Protection to Collecting Banker [Section 131]

(a) Meaning of Collecting Banker: A collecting banker is one who receives the payment of a crossed cheque on behalf of his customer.

(a) Essential Conditions for Protection to Collecting Banker: In case the title to the cheque proves defective, the collecting banker shall not incur any liability to the true owner of the cheque for having received payment thereof if the following conditions are fulfilled:

(a) if the collecting banker has acted in good faith:

(b) if the collecting banker has acted without negligence.

(c) if the collecting banker has received the payment on behalf of a customer as an agent for collection and not on his own behalf as a holder.

(d) if the collecting banker has received the payment only for a crossed cheque.

Notes: (i) Such protection is also available even when the collecting banker has credited his customer's account with the amount of the cheque before receiving the payment thereof. [Explanation to Section 131]

(ii) Such protection is also available in respect of any draft as defined in Section 85A [Section 131A] *[Refer to Practical Problem 17]*

19.0 NEGOTIATION AND ASSIGNMENT [SECTIONS 14, 47, 48, 60]

A negotiable instrument may be transferred *either* by negotiation *or* by assignment.

19.1 Meaning of Negotiation [Section 14] An instrument is said to be negotiated when a negotiable instrument is transferred to any person so as to constitute that person the holder of the instrument.

Thus, the essence of the negotiation is that it must be made with the intention of transferring a title of the instrument to the transferee.

Example *X was the holder of a cheque of Rs. 10,000 payable to bearer. He delivered this cheque to Y to keep it in his (Y) safe custody. In this case there is no negotiation of cheque from X to Y because the transfer of the cheque to Y makes him a bailee only and not the holder of the cheque.*

19.2 How to Effect Negotiation There are two methods of transfer by negotiation as follows:

(i) ***Negotiation by delivery [Section 47]:*** A *bearer* instrument is negotiable by voluntary delivery thereof. Thus, the instrument must be actually delivered and the delivery must also be voluntary.

Example *X was the holder of a cheque for 10,000 payable to bearer. He kept the cheque in his safe. Y, a thief stolen the cheque from X's safe. In this case, there is no negotiation of the cheque from X to Y because the cheque was not voluntarily delivered to Y. It may also be noted that if Y delivers this cheque for some consideration to Z who receives the same in good faith and before maturity. Z will become the holder in due course and will be entitled to receive the amount of the instrument. [Section 58]*

(ii) ***Negotiation by endorsement and delivery [Section 48]:*** An *order* instrument is negotiable by endorsement and delivery thereof. Thus, a mere indorsement (i.e., signing of a negotiable instrument for the purpose of negotiation) does not amount to negotiation unless there is delivery of the same.

19.3 Duration of Negotiability [Section 60] A negotiable instrument may be negotiated:

(a) by person other than the maker, drawer or acceptor until payment.

(b) by the maker, drawee or acceptor until maturity.

19.4 Meaning of Assignment An instrument is said to be assigned when a negotiable instrument is transferred by means of a written and registered document under the provisions of the Transfer of Property Act, 1882. The person who transfers his right to recover the payment of a debt is called an assignor and the person to whom such rights are transferred is called an assignee. The assignee takes the instrument subject to all equities which arise between the party liable and the assignor. Thus, the assignee gets the rights of the assignor only. He does not get the rights of a holder in due course.

19.5 Distinction between Negotiation and Assignment Negotiation can be distinguished from assignment as under:

Basis of Distinction	*Negotiation*	*Assignment*
1. Consideration	Consideration is **presumed.** [Section 118]	Consideration is to be **proved.**
2. How to effect	Bearer instruments are negotiated by mere delivery, and order instruments are negotiated by endorsement and delivery.	Assignment is done always by means of a written and registered document under the provisions of Transfer of Property Act, 1882.
3. Scope	Negotiation can be done in respect of **negotiable instruments only.**	Assignment can be done in case of **other documents** in addition to negotiable instruments.

4. Notice	Notice of transfer to the debtor by the transferee is **not necessary.**	An assignment does not bind the debtor unless notice of assignment has been given by the assignee to the debtor and the debtor in turn expressly or impliedly, has assented.
5. Better Title	The transferee **acquires** a title better than that of transferor.	The assignor does **not acquire** a title better than that of the assignor because the title of the assignee is subject to all equities in the title of assignor. In other words, assignee gets the right of assignor only.
6. Stamp Duty	It does **not require** any stamp duty.	It **requires** payment of stamp duty.

20.0 ENDORSEMENT [SECTIONS 15, 16, 50, 51, 52, 56]

20.1 Meaning of Endorsement [Section 15] The process of transferring an instrument is called an endorsement. An endorsement means signing the negotiable instrument on the back or face thereof or on a slip of paper (called allonge) annexed thereto by the holder of negotiable instrument for the purpose of negotiation. The person who endorses the instrument is called the 'endorser' and the person in whose favour the instrument is endorsed is called the 'endorsee'.

20.2 Who may Endorse/Negotiate [Section 51] Every sole maker, drawer, payee or endorsee, or all of several joint makers, drawers, payees or endorsees of a negotiable instrument may endorse and negotiate the same if the negotiability of such instrument has not been restricted or excluded as mentioned in Section 50 [Section 51]. In other words, a stranger (i.e., a person other than those stated above) cannot endorse a negotiable instrument. If a stranger endorses it, the endorsement is void and he cannot be made liable as endorser. [*Thakersey* v. *Kishandas*]

A maker or drawer or payee or endorsee may endorse or negotiate an instrument only if he is a holder thereof [Explanation to Section 51].

20.3 Essential Requirements of a Valid Endorsement The essential requirements of a valid endorsement are as follows:

(a) It must be signed on the back or face of instrument or on a slip of paper (called allonge) annexed thereto.

(b) It must be signed by the endorser.

(c) It must be completed by the delivery of the instrument.

(d) It must be made by the holder of the instrument.

20.4 Kinds of Endorsement [Sections 16, 50, 52, 56] The meaning and specimen of various kinds of endorsements have been discussed as follows:

Meaning and Specimen of Various Kinds of Endorsements

Type of Endorsement	*Meaning*	*Specimen*
1. General Endorsement or Blank Endorsement [Section 16(1) & 54]	An endorsement is said to be in blank if the endorser signs his name only. An instrument endorsed in blank becomes payable to the bearer thereof even although it was originally payable to order.	"P.C. Tulsian"
2. Special Endorsement or Full Endorsement [Section 16(1)]	An endorsement is said to be full if the endorser (a) signs his name, and (b) adds a direction to pay the amount to or to the order of a specified person. **Note:** The use of words 'or order' is not necessary.	(i) "Pay to *B* P.C. Tulsian" (ii) "Pay to *B* or order P.C. Tulsian"
3. Restrictive Endorsement [Section 50]	An endorsement is said to be restrictive if it restricts/excludes the right of further negotiation. Thus, in case of restrictive endorsement, the endorsee does not become the owner of the instrument as in case of other endorsement.	"Pay the contents to *C* only, P.C. Tulsian" "Pay *C* for my use. P.C. Tulsian" "Pay *C* or order for the account of *B*. P.C. Tulsian" "The within must be credited to C. P.C. Tulsian"
4. Partial Endorsement [Section 56]	An endorsement is said to be a partial endorsement when it purports to transfer only a part of the amount of the instrument. A partial endorsement is invalid. *Exception:* Where an instrument has been paid in part, the fact of the part payment may be endorsed on the instrument and it may then be negotiated for the residue.	In case of a Bill of Rs. 1000 "Pay Rs. 50 to *B*. P.C. Tulsian" "Pay *B* being the unpaid balance of the bill P.C. Tulsian"
5. Conditional Endorsement or Qualified Endorsement [Section 52]	An endorsement is said to be a conditional endorsement if it limits or negatives the liability of the endorser. **Examples**	

	(i) ***Sans Recourse Endorsement:*** An endorsement is said to be Sans Recourse Endorsement if the endorser relieves himself from the liability to all subsequent endorsees. **Note:** If an endorser who has excluded his own liability in this manner, afterwards becomes the holder of the instrument, all the intermediate endorsers continue to be liable to him.	"Pay *B* or order Sans Recourse P.C. Tulsian" "Pay B or order without recourse to me. P.C. Tulsian"
	(ii) ***Facultative Endorsement:*** An endorsement is said to be a Facultative Endorsement if the endorser waives any of his rights.	"Pay *B* or order at his own risk, P.C. Tulsian" "Pay B order notice of dishonur waived. P.C. Tulsian"
	(iii) ***Sanc Frais:*** An endorse ment is said to be Sans Frais endorsement if the endorser endorses the instrument in such a way that no expenses should be incurred on account of the bill.	"Pay *B* or is order sans frais. P.C. Tulsian"
	(iv) ***Contingency based Endorsement:*** An endorsement is said to be contingency based endorsement if the endorser makes his liability dependent upon the happening of an event which may or may not happen. **Note:** The condition is operative as between the endorser and endorsee. An endorsee cannot recover the amount *either* from the endorser *or* from any prior party until such event has happened. However, such endorsement does not affect the position of the party who has to pay for the instrument on its maturity.	"Pay *B* or order on the arrival of the ship at Calcutta. P.C. Tulsian" "Pay *B* or order on his marriage with *C*, P.C. Tulsian"

[Refer to Practical Problems 18 & 19]

20.5 Negotiation Back *Meaning:* An instrument is said to be negotiated back to the holder when an endorser, after he has negotiated an instrument, again becomes its holder before its maturity.

(a) ***Party who cannot be sued:*** The holder cannot enforce payment against an intermediate party to whom he was previously liable. This rule is made to prevent multiplicity of actions and it is an exception to the general rule that a holder in due course can sue all prior parties.

(b) ***Party who can be sued:*** The holder can enforce payment against an intermediate party to whom he was previously not liable.

Example I *The endorsement on a negotiable instrument are as under:*

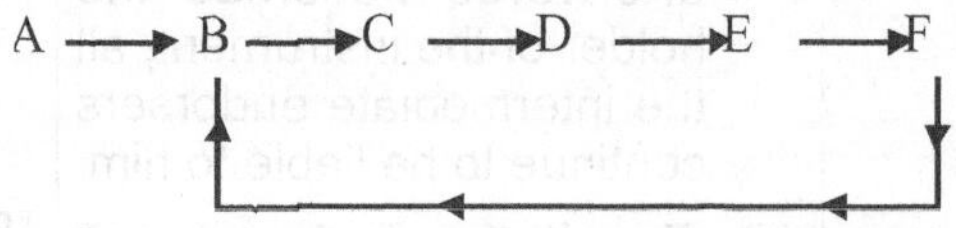

The endorsement by *F* to *B* is a 'negotiation back'. *B* cannot sue *C*, *D*, *E* or *F* but can sue *A* because *A* is prior to *B*'s original endorsement. If *B* is allowed to sue *F* then *F* could sue *E* who could sue *D* who could sue *C* who could sue *B* and this will lead to multiplicity of legal actions. The law prohibits such multiplicity of actions.

Example II *If however, B in original endorsement had signed 'Sans Recourse', there could be no circuitry of action and B could sue F, E, D or C.*

[Refer to Practical Problems 20 to 22]

21.0 RIGHTS AND OBLIGATIONS OF VARIOUS PARTIES TO AN INSTRUMENT OBTAINED BY UNLAWFUL MEANS

The rights and obligations of various parties to an instrument which has been (a) lost, or (b) obtained by fraud, or (c) obtained for unlawful consideration are summarised below:

Case	*Position of person who obtained illegally*	*Position of transferee*	*Position of true owner*	*Position of party liable to pay*
(a) If the person who obtained illegally retains the instrument.	He gets no title to it. He cannot sue any party liable for payment. he is bound to return the instrument to the ture owner.	No question	He is entitled to get back the instrument from him.	
(b) If the person who obtained illegally receives the payment of the instrument.	He is bound to return te amount to the true owner.	No question	He is entitled to recover the amount from ther person who obtained the instrument illegally.	Such party is discharged from his liability if he makes the payment of bearer instrument in due course.

(c) If the person who obtained illegally transfers a bearer instrument to a person who is not a holder in due course.		He is *neither* entitled to retain the instrument *nor* to receive the payment.	He is entitled to recover the amount from the transferee.	Such party is discharged from his liability if he makes the payment of bearer instrument in due course.
(d) If the person who obtained illegally transfers a bearer instrument to a holder in due course.	He is liable to true owner for damages.	He gets a good title to it. He is entitled both to retain the instrument and to receive the payment.	He is entitled to claim damages from the person who obtained the instrument illegally.	Such party is discharged from his liability if he makes the payment in due course.
(e) If the person who obtained illegally transfers an order instrument by making a forged endorsement.	He is liable to the party who has paid money by mistake.	He gets no legal title to it. He is *neither* entitled to retain the instrument *nor* to receive the payment even if he is a holder in due course.	He is entitled to recover the amount from the party a (except paying Banker) liable to pay.	Such party (except paying Banker who makes payment of the cheque in due course contunues to be liable to the true owner. Such party who has paid money by mistake on a forged instrument may recover it from the person to whom he has paid it [Section 72 of Indian Contract Act]

Note: When a negotiable instrument has been lost or has been obtained by means of an offence of fraud or for an unlawful consideration, no possessor or indorsee who claims through the person who found or so obtained the instrument is entitled to receive the amount due thereon unless such indorsee was a holder in due course or the possessor in the person who derived title from such a holder in due course. [Section 58] *[Refer to Practical Problems 23 to 26]*

22.0 MATERIAL ALTERATION [SECTIONS 20, 49, 87, 89, 125]

22.1 Meaning of Material Alteration An alteration is called a material alteration if (a) it alters or attempts to alter the character of the instrument or (b) it affects or is likely to affect the rights and liabilities of any of the parties to a negotiable instrument. Thus, it totally alters the business effect of the instrument. It makes the instrument speak a language other than that intended.

22.2 Examples of Material Alteration and Non-material Alteration

Material Alteration	*Non-material Alteration*
1. Alteration of date of instrument (e.g. if a bill dated 1st May, 1998) is changed to a bill dated 1st June, 1998.	1. Conversion of instrument payable to order into one payable to bearer.
2. Alteration of time of payment (e.g., if a bill payable three months after date is changed to a bill payable four months after date).	2. Conversion of instrument payable to bearer into order.
3. Alteration of place of payment (e.g., if a bill payable at Delhi is changed to bill payable at Bombay).	3. Elimination of the words 'or order' from an endorsement.
4. Alteration of amount payable (e.g., if bill for Rs 1000 is changed to a bill for Rs 2000)	4. Additional of the words 'on demand' to a note in which no time or payment is expressed.
5. Conversion of blank endorsement into special endorsement.	
6. Addition of a new party to an instrument.	
7. Alteration of one of the clauses of the instrument containing a penal action.	

[Refer to Practical Problems 27 to 28]

22.3 Material Alterations Authorised by the Act [Sections 20, 49, 125] The following material alterations have been authorised by the Act and do not require any authentication:

(a) Filling blanks of inchoate instruments [Section 20]

(b) Conversion of a blank endorsement into an endorsement in full [Section 49]

(c) Crossing of cheques [Section 125]

(d) Conversion of General Crossing into Special Crossing or 'Not Negotiable Crossing or A/c Payee Crossing (But not vice versa)

(e) Conversion of a bearer instrument into an order instrument by deleting the word 'Bearer'.

22.4 Effect of Material Alteration [Sections 87 and 88]

The effect of material alteration on liability of various parties is summarised below:

Persons	*Effect*
I. Persons who were parties at the time of alteration and did not consent to alteration.	Such persons are altogether discharged from liability under that instrument. Such persons shall not be liable even to a bonafide purchaser of the instrument having no notice of alteration. [Section 87]

II. Persons who were parties at the time of alteration and consented to alteration and persons who became parties to the instrument subsequent to the alteration.	Such persons continue to be liable under that instrument. [Section 88]

22.5 Protection to a Person Paying a Materially Altered Instrument [Section 89] The payer of a materially altered instrument is discharged from all liability on the instrument if the following two conditions are fulfilled:

(a) The alteration must not be apparent; and

(b) The payment must be made in due course.

Example *X draws a cheque for Rs. 1000 and Y, a holder without the consent of X, alters the figure 1000 into 10,000 and makes the instrument look like a cheque drawn for Rs 10,000. The banker who pays such cheque in due course is discharged from all liability under the cheque since the alteration was not apparent.*

PRACTICAL PROBLEMS

PROBLEM 1

State with reasons whether each of the following instruments is bearer or order:

(a) A bill is drawn payable to *X* or bearer.

(b) A bill is drawn payable to *X* who endorses it in blank in favour of *Y*.

(c) A bill is drawn payable to *X*.

(d) A bill is drawn payable to *X* or order.

(e) A bill is drawn payable to *X* only.

Solution

Case	*Decision*	*Reason*
(a)	Bearer instrument [Explanation II to Section 13(1)]	It is expressed to be so payable.
(b)	Bearer instrument [Explanation II to Section 13(1)]	The last endorsement is an endorsement in blank.
(c)	Order instrument [Explanation I to Section 13(1)]	It is expressed to be payable to a particular person and does not contain words which prohibit transfer or indicate an intention that it shall not be transferable.
(d)	Order instrument [Explanation I to Section 13(1)]	It is expressed to be so payable
(e)	Not a negotiable instrument at all [Explanation I to Section 13(1)]	The use of the word 'only' prohibits or indicates an intention that bill shall not be transferable.

PROBLEM 2

State with reasons whether each of the following instruments is an Inland Instrument or a Foreign Instrument:

(a) A bill drawn in Delhi upon a merchant in Agra and accepted payable in London.

(b) A bill drawn in Delhi upon a merchant in London and accepted payable in Agra.

(c) A bill drawn in Delhi upon a merchant in London and accepted payable in London.

(d) A bill drawn in London upon a merchant in Agra and accepted payable in Delhi.

(e) A bill drawn in Delhi on a merchant in Agra but endorsed in London.

(f) A bill drawn in London on a merchant in Agra and endorsed in Delhi.

Solution

Case	*Decision*	*Reason*
(a)	Inland instrument [Section 11]	It is drawn in India and the drawee is resident in India.
(b)	Inland instrument [Section 11]	It is drawn in India and is payable in India.
(c)	Foreign instrument [Section 12]	It is not accepted payable in India and at the same time its drawee is not a resident of India.
(d)	Foreign instrument [Section 12]	It is not drawn in India.
(e)	Inland instrument [Section 11]	It is drawn in India and the drawee is resident in India.
(f)	Foreign instrument [Section 12]	It is not drawn in India.

PROBLEM 3

State with reasons whether each of the following instruments is an Ambiguous Instrument or Fictitious Instrument:

(a) A bill is drawn by *A*, an agent, acting within the scope of his authority, upon his principle *P*.

(b) *X* draws a bill on *Y* who is a fictitious person and negotiates it himself.

(c) *X* draws a bill on *Y* who is a minor.

(d) A bill is drawn by Delhi branch of Dena Bank upon its Bombay branch.

(e) A bill is drawn upon *Y* who is a major person payable to *Z* who is a fictitious person.

(f) A bill is drawn upon *Y* as payable to *Z*. The drawer is a fictitious person.

Solution

Case	*Decision*	*Reason*
(a)	Ambiguous instrument [Section 17]	The drawer and the drawee are the same person.
(b)	Ambiguous instrument [Section 17]	The drawee is a fictitious person.
(c)	Ambiguous instrument [Section 17]	The drawee is incompetent to contract.
(d)	Ambiguous instrument [Section 17]	The drawer and the drawee are the same person.
(e)	Fictitious instrument [Section 42]	The payee is a fictitious person.
(f)	Fictitious instrument [Section 42]	The drawer is a fictitious person.

PROBLEM 4

State with reasons whether each of the following instruments is an Inchoate Instrument or not:

(a) *X* signs and delivers an unstamped and blank promissory note to *Y*.

(b) *X* delivers a stamped and blank promissory note to *Y* without his signature.

(c) *X* signs a stamped and blank promissory note and keeps in his safe.

(d) *X* signs and delivers a stamped and blank promissory note to *Y*.

(e) *X* signs and delivers a stamped and complete promissory note to *Y*.

Solution

Section to which the given problem relates: Section 20.

Case	*Decision*	*Reason*
(a)	No	It is not stamped.
(b)	No	It has not been signed by the maker.
(c)	No	It has not been delivered.
(d)	Yes	There is a delivery of a signed, stamped and blank instrument.
(e)	No	It is not incomplete.

PROBLEM 5

X signs his name on a blank but stamped instrument (stamp was sufficient to cover Rs 10,000). He delivers the instrument to *Y* with authority to fill upon a promissory note for Rs 8,000 only. *Y* fills the note for Rs 10,000 and endorses it to *Z* who takes in good faith for valuable consideration. Discuss the legal position.

Solution

Section to which the given problem relates: Section 20.

Decision and reason: *Z* (being a holder in due course) can recover Rs 10,000 from *X* and *Y*. But *Y* (not being a holder in due course) can recover Rs 8,000 only from *X*.

PROBLEM 6

State with reasons whether each of the following instruments is a Time Instrument or Demand Instrument:

(a) I promise to pay *B* Rs 500.

(b) I promise to pay *B* Rs 500 on demand.

(c) Pay Rs 500 at sight.

(d) Pay Rs 500 on presentment.

(e) I promise to pay *B* Rs 500 after 3 months.

(f) I promise to pay *B* Rs 500 on 1st Jan. 1997.

(g) I promise to pay Rs 500 after sight.

(h) I promise to pay *B* Rs 500 after *C*'s death.

(i) Pay *B* Rs 500 on or before 1st Jan. 1997.

Solution

Case	*Decision*	*Reason*
(a)	Demand instrument [Sections 19 and 21]	No time for payment has been specified.
(b)	Demand instrument [Sections 19 and 21]	It is expressed to be so payable.
(c)	Demand instrument [Sections 19 and 21]	The expression at right means on demand.
(d)	Demand instrument [Sections 19 and 21]	The expression 'on presentment' means on demand.
(e)	Time instrument [Section 21]	Fixed period has been specified.

(f)	Time instrument [Section 21]	A particular day has been specified.
(g)	Time instrument [Section 21]	After sight means after presentment for sight.
(h)	Time instrument [Section 21]	It is payable on the happening of an event (i.e., death) which is certain to happen.
(i)	Not a negotiable instrument at all	Time is uncertain.

PROBLEM 7

X accepts a bill for the accommodation of *A* (drawer). *A* transfers it to *B*, without consideration. *B* transfers it to *C* without consideration. *C* transfers it to *D* for value. *D* transfers it to *E*, without consideration. On the due date, the bill is dishonoured by *X*. Discuss the rights of *A*, *B*, *C*, *D* and *E*.

Solution

Section to which the given problem relates: Section 43 [Explanation I].

Decision and Reason:

(a) *E* cannot recover from *D*, *C* cannot recover from *B*, *B* cannot recover from *A*, and *A* cannot recover from *X* because a negotiable instrument without consideration creates no obligation of payment between the parties to the transaction.

(b) *D* and *E* can recover from *X*, *A*, *B* and *C* because any holder for consideration (*D*), and every subsequent holder deriving the title from him (*E*) may recover the amount due from the transferor for consideration or any prior party thereto.

PROBLEM 8

X accepts a bill for the accommodation of *A* (drawer), *A* transfers it to *B* for value. The bill is dishonoured by *X* on the due date. *B* collects the amount from *A*. Can *A* sue *X* for the recovery of the amount?

Solution

Section to which the given problem relates: Explanation I to Section 43.

Decision: *A* cannot sue *X* for the recovery of the amount in view of the specific provision to that effect provided in Explanation I to Section 43.

PROBLEM 9

X accepts a bill for the accommodation of *A* (drawer). *A* transfers it to *B* for value after maturity. *B* becomes the holder in good faith. Discuss the rights of *A* and *B*.

Solution

Section to which the given problem relates: Sections 43 and 59.

Decision and Reason:

(a) *A* cannot recover from *X* because an instrument without consideration creates no obligation between the parties to the transaction as per the provisions of Section 43.

(b) *B* can recover from *X* and *A* because a bonafide holder for value can recover from any prior party even though he acquires the instrument after maturity as per the provisions of Proviso to Section 59.

PROBLEM 10

X, on attaining the age of majority, makes a fresh promissory note in consideration of a promissory note made by him during his minority. Can a suit be maintained on the fresh promissory note?

Solution

Section to which the given problem relates: Section 43.

Decision and Reason: A suit cannot be maintained on the fresh promissory note because the fresh promissory note is void in the absence of consideration.

PROBLEM 11

X sells a TV to *M*, a minor, who pays for it by his cheque. *X* endorses the cheque to *Y* who in turn endorses it in favour of *Z*. The cheque is dishonoured. Discuss the legal position.

Solution

Section to which the given problem relates: Section 26.

Decision and Reason: (a) *Y* can enforce payment of the cheque against *X* only and not against *M* because a minor cannot bind himself. (b) *Z* can enforce payment of cheque against *X* and *Y*.

PROBLEM 12

Can an acceptor of a bill avoid his liability against a person who is a holder in due course or who derives his title from a holder in due course, on the following grounds:

(a) that the instrument has not been filled in accordance with the authority given by him.

(b) that the other parties to the bill were fictitious.

(c) that the instrument was drawn without consideration.

(d) that the delivery of the instrument was conditional.

(e) that the instrument had been lost.

(f) that the instrument was obtained from him by means of fraud.

(g) that the instrument was obtained from him for an unlawful consideration.

(h) that his signature was forged.

(i) that payee had no capacity to endorse.

Solution

Ground	*Decision*	*Explanation*
(a)	No	Privilege given to holder in due course under Section 20 provided the stamp put on the instrument was sufficient to cover the amount.
(b)	No	Privilege given to a holder in due course u/s 42
(c)	No	Privilege given to a holder in due course u/s 43
(d)	No	Privilege given to a holder in due course u/s 46
(e)	No	Privilege given to a holder in due course u/s 58
(f)	No	Privilege given to a holder in due course u/s 58
(g)	No	Privilege given to a holder in due course u/s 58
(h)	Yes	Forgery passes no title to anyone at all
(i)	No	Privilege given to a holder in due course u/s 121

Note: The aforesaid decisions also hold good for a person who derives title from a holder in due course.

PROBLEM 13

State with reasons whether each of the following instruments is a Promissory Note or not:

(a) *X* promises to pay *Y* a sum of Rs 500 on telephone.

(b) Mr *Y*, I owe you Rs 500.

(c) I have received the sum of Rs 500 in cash from Mr *Y*.

(d) I have received the sum of Rs 500 in cash from Mr *Y*. This amount will be repaid on demand.

(e) I promise to pay *Y* a sum of Rs 500.

(f) I promise to pay *Y* Rs 500 seven days after my marriage with Madhuri or Sridevi.

(g) I promise to pay *Y* Rs 500 on *Z*'s death provided *Z* leaves me enough to pay that sum.

(h) I promise to pay *Y* Rs 500 on *Z*'s death.

(i) I promise to pay Rs 500 and all other sums which shall be due to him.

(j) I promise to pay *Y* Rs 500 first deducting thereout any money which he may owe me.

(k) I promise to pay Rs 500 along with interest thereon.

(l) I promise to deliver to *Y* 1000 kg of paddy.

(m) I promise to pay *Y* Rs 500 and deliver 1000 kg of paddy.

(n) I promise to pay *Y* Rs 500 and to deliver to him my black horse on 1st January next.

(o) I promise to pay *Y* (myself) Rs 500.

(p) I promise to pay *Y* (myself) Rs 500. *Y* endorses it to *Z* or his order.

(q) I promise to pay the President of Rotary Club Delhi Rs 500.

Solution

Section to which the given problem relates: Section 4.

Case	*Decision*	*Reason*
(a)	No	It is not in writing.
(b)	No	There is no express promise to pay. It is merely an acknowledgement of debt.
(c)	No	There is no express promise to pay. It is merely an acknowledgement of debt.
(d)	Yes	There is an express promise to pay.
(e)	Yes	There is an express promise to pay.
(f)	No	Promise to pay is not unconditional.
(g)	No	Promise to pay is not unconditional.
(h)	Yes	Promise to pay is unconditional as it is certain that *D* will die.
(i)	No	The sum payable is not certain.
(j)	No	The sum payable is not certain.
(k)	No	The sum payable is not certain.
(l)	No	The payment is not in money and money only.
(m)	No	The payment is not in money and money only.
(n)	No	The payment is not in money and money only.
(o)	No	A note cannot be made payable to the maker himself.
(p)	Yes	It is payable to *Z* or to his order.
(q)	Yes	If the payee can be ascertained by evidence.

PROBLEM 14

State whether a bill can be said to have accepted by *B* in each of the following alternative cases:

(a) *B* delivers the bill confirming orally that he has accepted the bill.

(b) *B* delivers the bill after writing the words 'accepted' only.

(c) *B* delivers the bill without writing words 'accepted' but after putting his signature on the face of the bill.

(d) *B* delivers the bill without writing the words 'accepted' but after putting his signatures on the back of the bill.

(e) *B*s agent delivers the bill after putting his signature as an agent of the bill.

(f) *B* puts his signature on the bill and dies. Subsequently, the bill was delivered by *B*s heirs.

(g) *B* puts his signatures on the bill and informs the drawer that he has accepted the bill but does not deliver the bill to the drawer.

Solution

Case	*Decision*	*Reason*
(a)	No	The acceptance is not in writing.
(b)	No	The acceptance has not been signed by the drawee.
(c)	Yes	The acceptance has been signed by the drawee. The use of the word 'accepted' is not compulsory.
(d)	Yes	The acceptance is on the bill. It is immaterial whether the acceptance is on the face or back of the bill.
(e)	Yes [Section 27]	The acceptance may also be signed by a duly authorised agent.
(f)	No [Section 46]	The acceptance would not complete until there is delivery thereof.
(g)	Yes [Section 46]	The acceptance has completed on giving notice of acceptance.

PROBLEM 15

State whether a holder can refuse to take the following acceptance or not:

(a) Accepted payable when in funds.

(b) Accepted payable when a cargo consigned to me is sold.

(c) A bill drawn for Rs 5,000 but accepted for the 4,000 only.

(d) Accepted payable at Delhi when no place of payment is specified in the order.

(e) Accepted payable at Delhi only when no place of payment is specified in the order.

(f) Accepted payable at Delhi when place of payment specified in the order was Bombay.

(g) A bill drawn payable three months after date but accepted payable two months after date.

(h) A bill drawn on *X*, *Y*, and *Z* (who are not partners) but accepted by *X* only.

(i) A bill drawn on *X*, *Y* and *Z* (who are partners) but accepted by *X*.

Solution

Case	*Decision*	*Reason*
(a)	Yes	It is a qualified acceptance because it is conditional acceptance [Section 86].
(b)	Yes	It is a qualified acceptance because it is conditional acceptance [Section 86].

(c)	Yes	It is a qualified acceptance because it is a partial acceptance for a part only [Section 86].
(d)	No	It is a general acceptance and not a qualified acceptance [Section 86].
(e)	Yes	It is a qualified acceptance because of the use of the word 'only' [Section 86].
(f)	Yes	It is a qualified acceptance because it is accepted payable at a place other than specified one [Section 86].
(g)	Yes	It is a qualified acceptance because it is accepted payable at a time other than specified one [Section 86].
(h)	Yes	It is a qualified acceptance because acceptance has not been made by all drawees [Section 34].
(i)	No	It is a general acceptance because acceptance has been made by a partner [Section 34].

PROBLEM 16

A bill is drawn as "Pay to *X* or order the sum of ten thousand rupees". In the margin the amount stated is Rs 1,000. Discuss the legal position.

Solution

Section to which the given problem relates: Section 18.

Decision and reason: This bill is a valid bill for Rs 10,000 because in case of discrepancy between the amount stated in figure and in words, the amount stated in words shall be the amount of the instrument.

PROBLEM 17

A cheque is drawn upon Dena Bank. It is stolen by *X* who hands it over to *Y* who takes in good faith for valuable consideration. *Y* deposits the cheque into his own account in Canara Bank who presents it and obtains payment from Dena Bank. Discuss the legal position of paying banker, collecting banker, *Y* and true owner in each of the following alternative cases:

(a) If the cheque is payable to bearer.

(b) If the cheque is payable to bearer and is crossed generally.

(c) If the cheque is payable to bearer and is crossed generally with words 'not negotiable'.

(d) If the cheque is payable to bearer and is crossed specially with words 'Canara Bank'.

(e) If the cheque is payable to bearer and is crossed specially with words 'Allahabad Bank'.

(f) If the cheque is payable to *B* or order and *X* forges *B*s endorsement.

(g) If the drawer's signatures were forged.

Case	***Paying Banker***	***Collecting Banker***	***Y***	***True Owner***
(a)	Drawee is discharged by payment in due	Collecting banker does not incur any liability to the true opwner [Section 131]	He is not liable to true owner.J	He cann recover from *X* and not from *Y*.
(b)	-do-	-do-	-do-	-do-
(c)	-do-	-do-	He is liable to true owner because he got a defective title.	He can recover from *Y* or *X*.J

(d)	-do-	-do-		
(e)	Drawee is liable to true owner [Section 129]	Collecting banker is liable to true owner [Section 131]	He is not liable to true owner.J	He can recover from *X* only.
(f)	Drawee is discharged by payment in due course [Section 85(1)]	Collecting banker does not incur any liability to the true owner [Section 131]	He is not liable to true owner. He is not liable to true owner.	He can rexcover X or paying banker or collecting banker.
(g)	Drawee is liable to true owner because the payment is not in due course [Section 101]	Collecting banker is liable to the true owner [Section 131]	He is liable to true owner becase use forgery passes no title at all.	He can recover form *X* only. He can recover from paying banker collecting bamker or *Y*.

PROBLEM 18

B signs the following endorsements on different negotiable instruments payable to bearer. Classify the endorsements with reasons as Blank Endorsement or Full Endorsement or Restrictive Endorsement or Partial Endorsement or Conditional Endorsement. Also, state whether the following Endorsements are valid or invalid.

(a) No other words except *B*s signature.
(b) Pay *C*.
(c) Pay *C* or order.
(d) Pay *C* only.
(e) Pay *C* or order for the account of *B*.
(f) Pay *C* or order Rs 500 out of Rs 1,000.
(g) Pay *C* or order being the unpaid residue of the bill.
(h) Pay *C* or order on safe receipt of goods.
(i) Pay *C* Sans Recourse.
(j) Pay *C* Sans Frais.
(k) Pay *C*, notice of dishonour dispensed with.

Solution

Case	*Decision*	*Valid or invalid*	*Reason*
(a)	Blank Endorsement	Valid [Section 16]	No other words have been used.
(b)	Full Endorsement	Valid [Section 16]	The use of word *C*.
(c)	Full Endorsement	Valid [Section 16]	The use of word *C* or order'.
(d)	Restrictive Endorsement	Valid [Section 16]	The use of word 'only'.
(e)	Restrictive Endorsement	Valid [Section 50]	The use of word 'for the account of *B*.
(f)	Partial Endorsement	Invalid [Section 56]	The endorsement purports to transfer only a part of the amount due on instrument.
(g)	Partial Endorsement	Valid [Section 56]	The endorsement is for the unpaid balance.
(h)	Conditional Endorsement	Valid [Section 52]	The use of the words 'on safe receipt of goods'.

(i)	Conditional Endorsement	Valid [Section 52]	The use of the words 'Sans Recourse'.
(j)	Conditional Endorsement	Valid [Section 52]	The use of the words 'Sans Frais'.
(k)	Conditional Endorsement	Valid [Section 52]	The use of the words

'Notice of dishonour dispensed with'.

PROBLEM 19

B signs the following endorsements on different negotiable instruments payable to bearer. State whether each of these alternative endorsement exclude the right of further negotiation by *C* or not:

(a) "Pay the contents to *C* only"

(b) "Pay *C* for my use"

(c) "Pay *C* or order for the account of *B*"

(d) "The within must be credited to *C*"

(e) "Pay *C*"

(f) "Pay *C* value in account with the State Bank"

(g) "Pay the contents to *C*, being part of the consideration in a certain deed of assignment executed by the endorser and other".

Solution

Case	*Decision*	*Reason*
(a)	Yes	The use of the word 'only' exclude the right of further negotiation.
(b)	Yes	The use of the words 'for my use', excludes the right of the further negotiation.
(c)	Yes	The use of the words 'or order for the account of *B* excludes the right of further negotiation.
(d)	Yes	The use of the words 'must be credited to *C* excludes the right of further negotiation.
(e)	No	The endorsement does not contain words excluding the right or further negotiation.
(f)	No	The endorsement does not contain words excluding the right of further negotiation.
(g)	No	The use of the words 'others' gives the right of further negotiation.

PROBLEM 20

B accepts a bill drawn upon by *A* who endorses it to *C* who in turn endorses it to *D*, who in turn endorses it to *A*. Discuss the legal position of *A*.

Solution

A can sue *B* only because *B* is a prior party to his original endorsement. *A* cannot sue *C* or *D* because it will lead to circuitry of action (i.e., if *A* is allowed to sue *C* or *D* then *C* or *D* in turn can sue *A* because *A* is a prior party).

PROBLEM 21

B accepts a bill drawn upon *A* who endorses it with words 'Sans Recourse' to *C*, who in turn endorses it to *D*, who in turn endorses it to *A*. Discuss the legal position of *A*.

Solution

Section to which the given problem relates: Section 52.

Decision and Reason: *A* can sue *B*, *C* or *D* because it will not lead to circuitry of action as *A* at the time of the first endorsement, expressly excludes his liability by using words 'Sans recourse'.

PROBLEM 22

B accepts a bill drawn upon *A* who endorses it to *C* without consideration, and *C* endorses it to *D* in good faith for valuable consideration and *D*, in turn endorses it to *E* as a gift. *E* endorses it to *A*. Discuss the legal position of *A*.

Solution

A can sue *B* because *B* is a prior party to his original endorsement. *A* can sue *C* because *A* was not liable to *C* as the endorsement was without consideration [Section 43]. *A* cannot sue *D* or *E* because it will lead to circuitry of action.

PROBLEM 23

A bill is payable to *X* or order, *X* endorses the bill in blank. The bill is thereafter lost and comes into the hands of *Y*. Discuss the legal position in each of the following alternative cases:

(a) If *Y* receives the payment of the bill.

(b) If *Y* passes the bill by simple delivery to *Z* as a gift.

(c) If *Y* passes the bill after maturity by simple delivery to *Z* who takes the bill in good faith for valuable consideration.

(d) If *Y* passes the bill before maturity by simple delivery to *Z* who takes the bill in good faith for valuable consideration.

Solution

Section to which the given problem relates: Section 58.

Decision and Reason:

Case (a): The true owner can recover the amount from *Y* because *Y* had no title to bill.

Case (b): The true owner can recover the amount from *Y* and *Z* because *Y* and *Z* (not being holders in due course) had no title to bill.

Case (c): The true owner can recover the amount from *Y* and *Z* because *Y* and *Z* (being not holders in due course) had no title to bill.

Case (d): The true owner can recover the amount from *Y* and not from *Z* because *Z* being a holder in due course had a good title to bill.

PROBLEM 24

A bill is payable to *X* or order. The bill is thereafter lost and comes into the hands of *Y*, who forges *X*'s signature to effect an endorsement in blank. Discuss the legal position in each of the following alternative cases:

(a) If *Y* passes the bill by simple delivery to *Z* as a gift.

(b) If *Y* passes the delivery before maturity by simple delivery to *Z* who takes the bill in good faith for valuable consideration.

Solution

In both the cases, the true owner can recover from *Y* and *Z* because under forged endorsement no person, whether he is a holder in due course or not, acquires any legal title to the bill.

PROBLEM 25

A bill is payable to *X* or order, *X* endorses the bill in blank. It comes into the hands of *Y* who passes it on by simple delivery to *Z*, who forges *Y*'s signature and transfers it to *W*. Can *W* sue any of the parties to the bill?

Solution

Section to which the given problem relates: Section 58.

Decision and Reason: We can sue all the prior parties because he derives his title through the genuine endorsement by *X* and not through a forged endorsement by *Z*.

PROBLEM 26

X obtains *Y*'s acceptance to a bill by fraud. *X* endorses it to *Z* who takes it in good faith for valuable consideration. *Z* endorses the bill to *F* who knows of the fraud. Discuss the rights of *X*, *Y* and *Z*.

Solution

Section to which the given problem relates: Sections 53 and 58.

Decision and Reason:

(a) *X* cannot recover from *Y* because *X* is not a holder in due course.

(b) *Z* can recover from *X* or *Y* because *Z* is a holder in due course. [Section 58]

(c) *F* can recover from *X*, *Y* and *Z* because *F* derives the title from *Z* who is a holder in due course and at the same time *Z* is not a party to fraud. [Section 53]

PROBLEM 27

State whether the following alterations are material or not:

(a) A bill dated 1st April 1998 is changed to a bill dated 1st May 1998.

(b) A bill payable three months after date is changed to a bill payable three months after sight.

(c) A bill payable at Delhi is changed to bill payable at Bombay.

(d) A bill for Rs 1000 is changed into a bill for Rs 2000.

(e) A bill is accepted payable at Dena Bank is changed to a bill accepted payable at Canara Bank.

(f) A bill payable to *P* is changed into a bill payable to *P* and *Q*.

(g) A bill was endorsed in blank and handed over to Y, who endorsed as 'Pay to *Z* or order'.

(h) The holder of a bill inserts the words 'or order'.

(i) A bill was dated 1986 instead of 1996 and subsequently the agent of the drawer corrected the mistake.

(j) A cheque payable to bearer was converted into a cheque payable to order.

(k) Crossing a cheque.

Solution

***Cases* (*a*) *to* (*g*):** Material alterations.

***Cases* (*h*) *to* (*j*):** Non-material alterations.

***Case* (*k*):** Material alteration authorised by the Act without any authentication.

PROBLEM 28

X draws a cheque for Rs 2000 and *Y*, a holder without the consent of *X* alters the figure of Rs 2000 to Rs 20000 and makes the instrument look like a cheque drawn for Rs 20000. The banker pays the cheque in due course. Discuss the legal position of the banker.

Solution

Section to which the given problem relates: Section 89.

Decision: The banker is discharged from all liabilities.

Reason: The banker made the payment in due course and alteration was not apparent.

TRUE OR FALSE QUESTIONS

State with reasons whether the following statements are True or False:

1. All negotiable instruments are governed by the Negotiable Instruments Act.
2. A promissory note can be made originally payable to bearer.
3. A bill of exchange can be made originally payable to bearer.
4. A bill of exchange can be made originally payable to bearer on demand.
5. A bill of exchange can be made payable to bearer on demand after endorsement in blank.
6. A cheque cannot be drawn originally payable to bearer on demand.
7. A cheque is always payable on demand.
8. Every negotiable instrument is presumed by law to have been drawn for consideration.
9. A lost instrument is not presumed by law to have been duly stamped.
10. Generally, every holder of a negotiable instrument is presumed by law to be holder in due course.
11. Presumption in respect of negotiable instrument by law cannot be rebutted by the defendant.
12. In case of discrepancy between the amount written in figure and words, the amount stated in figures shall be the amount undertaken or ordered to be paid.
13. An unstamped negotiable instrument signed but blank in some respect is called an inchoate instrument.
14. A minor signing a note for necessaries is personally liable.
15. An agent signing without disclosing the name of his principal is personally liable.
16. The donee of negotiable instrument is a holder in due course.
17. Omission of the date will invalidate the negotiable instrument.
18. A person mentioned by designation will invalidate the negotiable instrument.
19. All the parts of the whole set (in case of bills in sets) must be accepted.
20. Bills in sets are used in all transactions.
21. A bill of exchange can be drawn upon a bank.
22. In a special crossing, the name of a banker must be written between two transverse parallel lines.
23. Crossing a cheque amounts to a material alteration which requires authentication.
24. A post-dated cheque is not negotiable.
25. Protection to the paying banker is available only in respect of payments of crossed cheques.

26. Protection to collecting banker is available in respect of payments received on all types of cheques.
27. All negotiable instruments are entitled to three days of grace.
28. When no interest is specified in the bill or note, the rate of interest will be 6% p.a.
29. Payee of a cheque is entitled for claiming the interest.
30. A negotiable instrument can be transferred by negotiation only.
31. A valid endorsement must be on the back of the instrument.
32. An instrument is said to be negotiated back to the holder if an endorsor or, after he has negotiated an instrument again becomes its holder after its maturity.
33. The liability of the drawer of a bill is secondary and conditional.
34. The liability of the maker of a note is primary and unconditional.
35. The acceptor would not be a prior party if he has signed the acceptance after the bill has come into the hands of the holder in due course.
36. An instrument can be negotiated by the maker of a note or the drawer or acceptor of a bill until payment.
37. An instrument can be negotiated by any person other than the maker of a note or the drawer or acceptor of a bill, until maturity.
38. A bonafide transferee for value shall get a good title even to an instrument transferred by making a forged instrument.
39. All material alterations in a cheque requires authentication.
40. The elimination of the words 'or order' or 'or bearer' amounts to material alteration requiring authentication.
41. Conversion of instrument payable to order into one payable to bearer amounts to material alteration.

Answers

1. False	2. False	3. True	4. False
5. True	6. False	7. True	8. True
9. False	10. True	11. False	12. False
13. False	14. False	15. True	16. False
17. False	18. False	19. False	20. False
21. True	22. False	23. False	24. False
25. False	26. False	27. False	28. False
29. False	30. False	31. False	32. False
33. True	34. True	35. False	36. False
37. False	38. False	39. False	40. False
41. False			

VERY SHORT ANSWER TYPE QUESTIONS

1. What is a Negotiable Instrument?
2. Can there be more than one payee in a Negotiable Instrument?
3. What is meant by maturity of a Negotiable Instrument?

4. What is meant by 'days of grace'?
5. To whom the payment of an instrument is required to be made?
6. Who can bind and be bound by drawing a negotiable instrument?
7. Can a minor draw a negotiable instrument?
8. Is a negotiable isntrument drawn by a minor valid?
9. Is a negotiable instrument drawn by a minor binding on minor?
10. Is a minor personally liable for a negotiable instrument drawn by him for necessaries supplied to him?
11. Can a liability under instrument be incurred through an agent?
12. Does an agent's general authority include an authority to accept or endorse a bill?
13. Does an agent's authority to draw a bill include an authority to endorse?
14. What is the liability of an agent signing a negotiable instrument?
15. Define promissory note.
16. Can a promissory note payable to bearer be issued by any person?
17. Define bill of exchange.
18. Can a bill of exchange payable to bearer on demand be issued by any person?
19. Define cheque.
20. What is meant by 'crossing of a cheque'?
21. What is the purpose of crossing of a Cheque?
22. What is meant by negotiation?
23. How is negotiation effected?
24. What is the duration of negotiability?
25. What is meant by assignment?
26. Define endorsement.
27. Who may endorse/negotiate?

SHORT ANSWER TYPE QUESTIONS

1. Enumerate the essential characteristics of a negotiable instrument.
2. How does the Reserve Bank of India Act restrict the negotiable instruments?
3. Explain with example the meaning of bearer instrument.
4. Explain with example the meaning of order instrument.
5. State the meaning of inland instrument with two examples.
6. State the meaning of foreign instrument with two examples.
7. Illustrate the meaning of ambiguous instruments.
8. Illustrate the meaning of Inchoate stamped instruments.
9. Explain the meaning of instruments payable on demand with at least two examples.
10. State the meaning of time instrument with at least two examples.
11. Explain the meaning and provisions relating to 'accommodation bills'.

12. What is a fictitious bill?
13. What is a documentary bill?
14. What is a clean bill?
15. What is meant by escrow?
16. Explain the meaning and provisions relating to bills in sets.
17. Explain the meaning and provisions relating to date of maturity.
18. What is meant by payment in due course?
19. Explain the provisions relating to the payment of interest.
20. Define holder.
21. Who is a holder in case of loss or destruction?
22. Define holder in due course.
23. Enumerate the privileges of a holder in due course
24. Give four points of distinction between a holder and a holder in due course.
25. Enumerate the essential characteristics of a promissory note.
26. Explain the parties to a promissory note.
27. Give a specimen of a promissory note.
28. Enumerate the essential characteristics of a bill of exchange.
29. Explain the parties to a bill of exchange.
30. Who are parties to a bill of exchange?
31. Give a specimen of a bill of exchange.
32. Explain the meaning and essentials of a valid acceptance.
33. Explain the meaning and effect of qualified acceptance with examples.
34. Enumerate the essential characteristics of a cheque.
35. Who are parties to a cheque?
36. Give a specimen of a cheque.
37. Illustrate the meaning of general crossing of a cheque.
38. Illustrate the meaning of special crossing of a cheque.
39. What is the effect of 'Not negotiable crossing'?
40. Who can cross a cheque after issue?
41. Explain the liability of a drawee on a dishonour of a cheque.
42. Explain the liability of a drawer on a dishonour of a cheque.
43. State the cases in which a banker must refuse to honour a customer's cheque.
44. State the cases in which a banker may refuse to honour a customer's cheque.
45. Explain the provisions relating to the protection to a paying banker in respect of payment of various types of cheques.
46. Explain the provisions relating to the protection to a collecting banker in respect of payment received on a crossed cheque.
47. Enumerate the essential requirements of a valid endorsement.
48. Illustrate the meaning of blank endorsement.
49. Illustrate the meaning of full endorsement.

50. Explain the meaning of restrictive endorsement with two examples.
51. Explain the meaning of partial endorsement with two examples.
52. Explain the meaning of conditional endorsement with three different examples.
53. What is meant by negotiation back? Illustrate with an example.
54. State the parties who can and who cannot be sued in case of negotiation back.
55. State the legal position of a person who obtained an instrument illegally and retains the instrument.
56. State the legal position of a person who obtained an instrument illegally and receives the payment of the instrument.
57. State the legal position of a person who obtained an instrument illegally and transfers a bearer instrument to a person who is not a holder in due course.
58. State the legal position of a person who obtained an instrument illegally and transfers a bearer instrument to a holder in due course.
59. State the legal position of a person who obtained an instrument illegally and transfers an order instrument by making a forged endorsement.
60. What is meant by material alteration?
61. Give four examples of material alterations.
62. Give four examples of non-material alterations.
63. Give three examples of material alterations authorised by the Act.
64. Explain the effect of material alteration.
65. Is a protection available to a person paying a materially altered instrument?
66. "Cheques crossed not negotiable are nevertheless negotiable". Comment.
67. "Issuing a cheque that bounces is an offence". Comment.

ESSAY TYPE QUESTIONS

1. (a) What is a negotiable instrument?
   (b) What are its essential characteristics?
   (c) How does the Reserve Bank of India Act restrict the negotiable instruments.
2. What are the legally permitted presumptions in respect of negotiable instruments?
3. (a) Define a promissory note.
   (b) What are its essential characteristics?
   (c) Give three examples each of an instrument representing a promissory note and instrument not representing a promissory note.
4. (a) Define a bill of exchange.
   (b) What are its essential characteristics?
5. (a) Define a cheque.
   (b) What are its essential characteristics?
6. (a) What is crossing of cheque?
   (b) Who can cross a cheque?
   (c) Explain various types of crossing of a cheque.
   (d) What is not negotiable crossing? What is its effect?

7. Discuss the common features of a promissory note, bill of exchange and cheque.
8. (a) What is meant by 'Payment in due course'?
   (b) To what extent is protection given to the paying and collecting banker.
9. (a) What is the liability of a banker who wrongfully refuses payment of a cheque?
   (b) When must a banker refuse to honour a customer's cheque?
   (c) When may a banker refuse to honour a customer's cheque?
10. (a) What is meant by negotiation?
    (b) How is it effected?
    (c) How is it different from assignment?
11. (a) What is an endorsement?
    (b) Explain the various types of such endorsements.
    (c) What is the effect of cancellation of endorsement by the holder?
    (d) Explain with illustrations what is meant by negotiation back.
12. (a) Define a holder in due course.
    (b) What are his privileges under the negotiable instruments act?
    (c) Distinguish betwen a holder and a holder in due course.
    (d) Can the defence (a) that one of the endorsement is forged, (b) that payee is minor, (c) that payee is insolvent be raised against him?
13. (a) What is meant by maturity of an instrument?
    (b) What is meant by days of grace?
    (c) Explain the provisions relating to the calculation of date of maturity.
14. Distinguish between the following:
    (a) A Bill of Exchange and a Promissory Note.
    (b) A Bill of Exchange and a Cheque.
    (c) A General crossing and a Special crossing.
    (d) Negotiation and Assignment.
    (e) Holder and Holder in due course.
    (f) Bearer Instrument and Order instrument.
    (g) Inland Instrument and Foreign Instrument.
    (h) Documentary bill and Clean bill.
    (i) Trade bill and Accomodation bill
    (j) Blank Endorsement and Full Endorsement
    (k) Material Alteration and Non-material Alteration.
    (l) Stale Cheque and Post-dated Cheque.
    (m) General Acceptance and qualified acceptance.
15. Comment on the following statements:
    (a) A holder in due course gets a title from all equities.
    (b) Every holder in due course is a holder, but every holder may not be a holder in due course.

(c) A cheque marked 'Not negotiable' is nevertheless negotiable.

(d) Once a bearer always a bearer.

16. Write short notes on the following:

(a) Ambiguous instruments

(b) Inchoate instruments

(c) Instruments payable on demand

(d) Time instruments

(e) Fictitious bill

(f) Escrow

(g) Bill in sets

(h) Opening of a crossed cheque

(i) Per pro endorsement

(j) Not negotiable crossing

(k) Negotiation Back

(l) Forged Instrument

(m) Holder in due course

(n) Payment in due course

(o) Acceptor for honour

(p) Maturity of a bill and Days of grace.

(q) Stale cheque

(r) Post-dated cheque

(s) Material Alteration

CHAPTER

18 The Negotiable Instruments Act, 1881 (Part II)

1.0 LIABILITIES OF VARIOUS PARTIES

1.1 Liability of Legal Representative [Section 29] A legal representative of a deceased person who signs his name to a promissory note, bill of exchange or cheque is liable personally thereon unless he expressly limits his liability to the extent of the assets received by him as such.

1.2 Liability of Drawer [Section 30] The drawer of a bill of exchange or cheque is bound, in case of dishonour by the drawee or acceptor thereof, to compensate the holder, provided due notice of dishonour has been given to or received by, the drawer as hereinafter provided. The following points are worthnoting in this regard:

(i) Notice of dishonour must be given unless it is dispensed with u/s 98.

(ii) In case of dishonour of a bill by non-acceptance, the liability of the drawer is ***primary and conditional***. The liability is primary in the sense that the drawer is liable as a principal debtor and not as surety for drawee. The liability is conditional in the sense that it arises only in the event of a dishonour by the drawee or acceptor.

(iii) In case of dishonour of a bill by non-payment, the liability of the drawer is ***secondary and conditional***. The liability is secondary in the sense that the drawer is liable as a surety for the acceptor whose liability is primary as a principal debtor. The liability is conditional in the sense that it arises only in the event of a dishonour by the drawee or acceptor.

(iv) In case of dishonour of an accommodation bill drawn for the accommodation of the drawer, in addition to his liability to the payee or holder, the drawer is bound to indemnify the acceptor if he suffers any damage on account of his acceptance.

(v) In case of dishonour of a cheque, the liability of the drawer of a cheque is primary and not secondary because the holder of a cheque has no remedy against the drawee (i.e., banker). His remedy is only against the drawer. [*Punjab National Bank* v. *Bank of Baroda*]

1.3 Liability of Drawee of a Cheque [Section 31] The drawee of a cheque must compensate the drawer for any loss or damage caused by non-payment if the following three conditions are fulfilled:

(a) If the drawee has sufficient funds of the drawer in his hands;

(b) If the funds are properly applicable to such payment;

(c) If the drawee is duly required to pay the cheque.

Notes: (i) The banker is liable if he makes the payment of a cheque on which the customer's signature is forged because such payment is without authority. [*Brewer* v. *Westminister Bank Ltd.*]

(ii) The banker is not liable if he makes the payment in due course of a cheque on which the endorsement is forged.

(iii) The banker is liable for the increased amount where the customer has drawn a cheque with reasonable precautions and the amount is increased by some dishonest person. [*Hall* v. *Fuller*]

1.4 Liability of Maker of a Note and Acceptor of Bill [Section 32] In the absence of a contract to the contrary, the maker of a promissory note and the acceptor before maturity of a bill of exchange are bound to pay the amount thereof at maturity according to the apparent tenor of the note or acceptance respectively, and the acceptor of a bill of exchange at or after maturity is bound to pay the amount thereof to the holder on demand.

In default of such payment as aforesaid, such maker or acceptor is bound to compensate any party to the note or bill for any loss or damage sustained by him and caused by such default.

1.5 Distinction between the Liability of Drawer of a Bill and Liability of Acceptor of a Bill or Maker of a Note

Basis of Distinction	*Liability of drawer*	*Liability of acceptor of bill or maker of a note*
1. *Primary or Secondary*	The liability of drawer after acceptance is secondary as surety.	The liability of acceptor of a bill or maker of a note is primary as a principal debtor.
2. *Conditional or Uncoditional*	The liability of drawer is conditional, in the sense that is arises only in the even of dishonour.	The liability of acceptor of a bill or maker of a note is unconditional and is not dependent on the notice of dishonour.

1.6 Liability of Endorser [Section 35] The endorser of a negotiable instrument must compensate the holder for any loss or damage cuased to him by the dishonour if the following conditions are fulfilled:

(a) If there is no contract to the contrary;

(b) If the instrument has been endorsed and delivered before maturity;

(c) If the endorser has not excluded his own liability or has made conditional his own liability;

(d) If due notice of dishonour has been given to, or received by such endorser.

Every endorser after dishonour is liable as upon an instrument payable on demand.

Notes: (i) The liability under this section arises out of endorsement and not on the instrument.

(ii) The liability of an endorser is conditional in the sense that it arises only in the event of dishonour.

1.7 Liability of Prior Parties to Holder in due Course [Section 36] Every prior party to a negotiable instrument is liable thereon to a holder in due course until the instrument is duly satisfied. The expression 'prior party' here means the maker or drawer, the acceptor and all the intervening indorsers.

Notes: (i) The liability of the prior parties is joint and several, i.e. the holder in due course may recover the amount from one party only or from all of them jointly.

(ii) If a holder of an accepted bill of exchange releases the acceptor from his liability then all other parties will also be discharged from liability to the holder [Sections 134 and 135]. However, in such cases, the holder may expressly reserve his right against the other parties. [Section 39]

1.8 Liability of Maker, Drawer and Acceptor as Principals and that of other Parties as Sureties [Section 37] The maker of a promissory note or cheque, the drawer of a bill of exchange until acceptance, and the acceptor are, in the absence of a contract to the contrary, respectively, liable thereon as principal debtors, and the other parties thereto are liable thereon as sureties for the maker, drawer or acceptor, as the case may be.

1.9 Liability of Prior Party as a Principal Debtor in respect of each Subsequent Party [Section 38] As between the parties so liable as sureties, each prior party is, in the absence of a contract to the contrary, also liable thereon as a principal debtor in respect of each subsequent party.

Example *A draws a bill payable to his own order on B, who accepts. A, afterwards, endorses the bill to C, C to D and D to E. As between E and B, B is the principal debtor and A, C and D are his sureties. As between E and A, A is the principal debtor and C and D are his sureties. As between E and C, C is the principal debtor and D is his surety.*

1.10 Nature of Suretyship [Section 39] When the holder of an accepted bill of exchange enters into any contract with the acceptor which, under Sections 134 or 135 of the Indian Contract Act, 1872 would discharge the other parties, the holder may expressly reserve his right to charge the other parties, and in such a case they are not discharged.

1.11 Discharge of Endorser's Liability [Section 40] Where the holder of a negotiable instrument, without the consent of the endorser, destroys or impairs the endorser's remedy against a prior party, the endorser is discharged from liability to the holder to the same extent as if the instrument has been paid at maturity.

Example *A is the holder of a bill of exchange made payable to the order of B, which contains the following endorsements in blank:*

First endorsement, "*B*"

Second endorsement, "*C*"

Third endorsement, "*D*"

Fourth endorsement. "*E*"

A strikes out, without *E*s consent, the endorsements by *C* and *D*, *A* is not entitled to recover anything from *E* because the release of principal debtor has the effect of discharging the surety. [Section 134 of the Indian Contract Act, 1872]

1.12 Effect of Forged Endorsement on Acceptor's Liability [Section 41] An acceptor of a bill of exchange already endorsed is not relieved from liability by reason that such endorsement is forged.

1.13 Liability of Acceptor of a Bill drawn in Fictitious Name [Section 42] An acceptor of a bill of exchange drawn in a fictitious name and payable to the drawer's order is not relieved from liability to any holder in due course, on the ground being that such name is fictitious.

1.14 Liability on Negotiable Instrument etc. made without Consideration [Section 43] A negotiable instrument made, drawn, accepted, endorsed or transferred without consideration or for a consideration which fails, creates no obligation of payment between the parties to the transaction. But, if any such party has transferred the instrument with or without endorsement to a holder for consideration, such holder, and every subsequent holder deriving title from him, may recover the amount due on such instrument from the transferor for consideration or any prior party thereto.These provisions are subject to the following two exceptions:

Exception I No party for whose accommodation a negotiable instrument has been made, drawn, accepted or endorsed can, if he has paid the amount thereof, recover thereon such amount from any person who became a party to such instrument for his accommodation.

Exception II No party to the instrument who has induced any other party to make, draw, accept, endorse or transfer the same to him for a consideration which he has failed to pay or perform in full, shall recover thereon an amount exceeding the value of the consideration (if any) which he has actually paid or performed.

Example *X, Y and Z are, respectively, the drawer, payee and acceptor of a bill of exchange drawn for the accommodation of X, Y endorses the bill to W for consideration W can recover the amount due on bill from X, or Y or Z. If X has paid, he cannot recover the amount from any person.*

2.0 PROPORTIONATE REDUCTION IN CASE OF PARTIAL FAILURE OF CONSIDERATION

2.1 Partial Absence or failure of Monetary Consideration [Section 44] When the consideration for which a person signed a promissory note, bill of exchange or cheque consisted of money, and was originally absent in part or has subsequently failed in part, the sum for which a holder standing in immediate relation with such signer is entitled to receive from him is proportionally reduced.

Explanation The drawer of a bill of exchange stands in immediate relation with the acceptor. The m of a promissory note, bill of exchange or cheque stands in immediate relation with the payee, and the endorser with his endorsee. Other signers may by agreement stand in immediate relation with a holder.

Example *A draws a bill on B for Rs. 500 payable to the order of A. B accepts the bill but subsequently dishonours it by non-payment. A sues B on the bill. B proves that it was accepted for value as to Rs. 400 and as an accommodation to the plaintiff as to the residue. A can only recover Rs. 400.*

2.2 Partial Failure of Consideration not Consisting of Money [Section 45] Where a part of the consideration for which a person signed a promissory note, bill of exchange or cheque, though not consisting of money, is ascertainable in terms of money without collateral enquiry, and there has been a failure of that part, the sum for which a holder standing in immediate relation with such signer is entitled to receive from him is proportionally reduced.

3.0 PRESENTMENT FOR ACCEPTANCE [SECTIONS 61 TO 63]

3.1 Meaning of Presentment Presentment means placing negotiable instrument before a drawee for acceptance or for sight or for payment.

3.2 Provisions Relating to Presentment for Acceptance The various provisions relating to the presentment for acceptance are summarised below:

Provisions Relating to Presentment for Acceptance

Matter	*Provision*
1. When presentment is necessary	Presentment for acceptance is necessary— (a) Where a bill is payable after sight, and (b) where a bill expressly stipulates that is shall be presented for acceptance. *[Refer to Practical Problem 1]*
2. By whom	Presentment for acceptance must be made by the person entitled to demand acceptance, i.e., holder or his duly authorised agent.
3. To whom	Presentment must be made to the drawee of a bill of exchange.
4. Hours and day for presentment	Presentment for acceptance mt be made during business hours on a business day.
5. Time for presentment	The bill must be presented for acceptance within a specified time (or reasonable time if no time is specified) after it is drawn.
6. Place of presentment	The bill must be presented for acceptance at a specified place (or at the place of business or at the usual residence of the drawee if no place is specified).
7. Drawee's time for delibration [Section.63]	The holder must, if so required by the drawee of a bill of exchange presented to him for acceptance, allow the drawee 48 hours (exclusive of public holidays) to consider whether he will accept it.
8. When presentment is excused [Section 61]	Presentmentfor acceptance is excused— (a) if the drawee cannot be found even after a reasonable search; (b) if the draweeis a fictitious person; (c) if the drawee is incompetent to contract.
9. Effect of non-presentment	Where presentment is essential but presentment is not made, all parties liable on the instrument are discharged from the liability on the instrument to the person making such default.
10. Mode of service of presentment	A presentment thorugh post office by means of a registered letter is sufficient if authorised by agreement or usage.

3.3 Presentment of Promissory Note for Sight [Section 62] A promissory note, payable at a certain period after sight, must be presented to the maker thereof for sight (if he can, after reasonable search, be found) by a person entitled to demand payment, within a reasonable time after it is made and during business hours on a business day. In default of such presentment, no party thereto is liable thereon to the person making such default.

Object: Such presentment is required to fix the maturity of the note.

4.0 PRESENTMENT FOR PAYMENT [SECTIONS 64 TO 76]

4.1 Meaning of Presentment for Payment Presentment for payment implies presenting an instrument to the party for payment.

4.2 Provisions Relating to the Presentment for Payment The various provisions relating to the presentment for payment are summarised below:

Provisions relating to Presentment for Payment

Matter	*Provision*
1. Negotiable instruments in which required [Section 64]	Presentment for payment must be made in respect of all instruments except a promissory note payable on demand and which is not payable at a specified place. [*Refer to a Practical Problem 2*]
2. By whom [Section 64]	Presentment for payment must be made by the holder or his duly authorised agent.
3. To whom [Sections 64 and 75]	Presentment for payment must be made to— (a) the maker, acceptor or drawee; (b) the duly authorised agent of maker, acceptor or drawee; (c) legal representative in case of death. (d) assignee in case of insolvency.
4. Hours for presentment [Section 65]	Presentment for payment must be made during usual business hours and, if at a banker's place, it must be within banking hours.
5. Time for presentment [Sections 66, 67, 74]	(a) A negotiable instrument payable on demand must be presented for payment within a reasonable time after it is received by the holder. [Section 74] (b) A promissory note or bill of exchange, made payable at a specified period after date or sight thereof, must be presented for payment at maturity. [Section 66](c) A promissory note payable by instalments must be presented for payment on the third day after the date fixed for payment of each instalment. [Section 67]
6. Place of presentmen [Section 68, 69, 70, 71]	The instrument must be presented for payment at a specified place (or at the place of business or at the usual residence of the maker, acceptor or drawee thereof as the case may be.) ***Note:*** If the maker, drawee, or acceptor of a negotiable instrument has no known place of business or fixed residence, and no place is specified in the instrument for presentment for acceptance or payment, such presentment may be made to him in person wherever he can be found. [Section 71]

7. Presentment of cheque [Sections 72 and 73]	A cheque must be presented— (a) in order to charge the drawer at the bank upon which it is drawn before the relation between the drawer and his banker has been altered to the pre- judice of the drawer (b) in order to charge any person except the drawer, within a reasonable time after delivery thereof by such person.
8. Excuse for delay [Section 75 A]	Delay in presentment for acceptance or payment is excused if the delay is caused by circumstances beyond the control of the holder, and not imputable to his default, misconduct or negligence. When the cause of delay ceases to operate, presentment must be made within a reasonable time.
9. Effect of Non-presentation	Where presentment is essential but presentment is not made, all parties (other than the maker of a promissory note, acceptor of a Bill of Exchange or drawee of cheque) liable as the instrument are discharged from their liability to the holder making such default.

4.3 When Presentment for Payment is Unnecessary? [Section 76] No presentment for payment is necessary, and the instrument is dishonoured at the due date for presentment in any of the following cases:

(i) if the maker, drawee or acceptor intentionally prevents the presentment of the instrument, or

(ii) if the instrument is payable at his place of business, and he closes such place on a business day during the usual business hours, or

(iii) if the instrument is payable at some other specified place and *neither* he *nor* any person authorised to pay it attends at such place during the usual business hours, or

(iv) if the instrument is not payable at any specified place, and he cannot after due search be found;

(v) as against any party sought to be charged therewith, if he has engaged to pay notwithstanding non-presentment;

(vi) as against any party if, after maturity, with knowledge that the instrument has not been presented, he makes a part-payment on account of the amount due on the instrument, or promises to pay the amount due thereon in whole or in part; or otherwise waive his right to take advantage of any default in presentment for payment;

(vii) as against the drawer, if the drawer could not suffer damage for want of such presentment.

Note: The presentment for payment is not excused only because of the party to whom the presentment has to be made has gone abroad. *[Phillips* v. *Astling]*

5.0 ACCEPTANCE FOR HONOUR [SECTIONS 108 TO 112]

5.1 Meaning of Acceptance for Honour [Sections 108 to 110] An acceptance is said to be an acceptance for honour if the following conditions are fulfilled:

(a) The bill must have been noted or protested for non-acceptance or for better security;

(b) The acceptance must be made for the honour of any party already liable under the bill;

(c) The acceptance must be made by any person who is already not liable under the bill;

(d) The acceptance must be made with the consent of the holder of the bill;

(e) The acceptance must be made in writing on the bill;

(f) The person desiring to accept for honour must have declared that he accepts under protest, the protested bill, e.g. accepted upon protest.

Note: Where the acceptance does not express for whose honour it is made, it shall be deemed to be made for the honour of the drawer. [Section 110]

5.2 Meaning of Acceptor for Honour The person who accepts the bill for the honour is called the acceptor for honour.

5.3 Rights and Liabilities of Acceptor for Honour The rights and liabilities of acceptor for honour are as follows:

(a) An acceptor for honour binds himself to all parties subsequent to the party for whose honour he accepts to pay the amount of the bill if the drawee does not pay [Section 111]

(b) Such party and all prior parties are liable in their respective capacities to compensate the acceptor for honour for all losses or damages sustained by him in consequence of such acceptance. [Section 111]

(c) But an acceptor for honour is not liable to the holder of the bill unless it is presented, or (in case the address given by such acceptor on the bill is a place other than the place where the bill is made payable) forwarded for presentment, not later than the day next after the day of its maturity. [Section 111]

(d) An acceptor for honour cannot be charged unless the bill has, after its maturity, been presented to the drawee for payment, and has been dishonoured by him, and noted or protested for such dishonour. [Section 112]

6.0 PAYMENT FOR HONOUR [SECTIONS 113 AND 114]

6.1 Meaning of Payment for Honour [Section 113] A payment is said to be 'payment for honour' if the following conditions are fulfilled:

(a) The bill must have been noted or protested for non-payment;

(b) The payment must be made for the honour of any party already liable under the bill;

(c) The payment must be made by any person whether he is already liable on the bill or not;

(d) The person paying or his agent must have declared before Notary Public the party for whose honour he pays;

(e) Such declaration must have been recorded by such Notary Public.

6.2 Meaning of Payer for Honour The person who buys the bills for honour is called the 'payer for honour'.

6.3 Rights of Payer for Honour [Section 114] The payer for honour is entitled:

(a) to all rights of a holder on the bill:

(b) to recover all sums paid by him together with the interest and all expenses properly incurred in making such payment from the party for whose honour he pays and all the parties prior to such party.

7.0 DISHONOUR OF A BILL [SECTIONS 76, 91 TO 98, 105, 106]

7.1 A Bill of Exchange (excluding cheques) may be dishonoured by (a) non-acceptance or (b) by non-payment.

7.2 It is to be noted that a promissory note or cheque can be dishonoured by non-payment only because a promissory note or cheque does not require any acceptance.

7.3 Meaning of Dishonour by Non-acceptance [Section 91] A bill of exchange is said to be dishonoured by non-acceptance in anyone of the following circumstances:

(a) If the drawee does not accept it within **48 hours** from the time of presentment.

(b) If all the drawees (who are not partners) (in case there are more than one drawee) do not accept.

(c) When the drawee is incompetent to contract.

(d) When the drawee is a fictitious person.

(e) When the drawee gives a qualified acceptance and the holder does not give his consent to qualified acceptance.

(f) When the drawee cannot be found after reasonable search.

(g) When the presentment for acceptance is excused and the bill is not accepted.

7.4 Drawee in case of Need Where a drawee in case of need is named in a bill of exchange, or any endorsement thereon, the bill is not dishonoured until it has been dishonoured by such drawee. [Section 115] His liability arises only when the bill is not honoured by the drawee named in the bill.

7.5 Meaning of Dishonour by Non-payment [Sections 76 and 92] An instrument is said to be dishonoured by non-payment in any one of the following circumstances:

(a) When the party primarily liable (i.e., the maker of the note or acceptor of the bill or drawee of the cheque) makes default in payment upon being duly required to pay the same. [Section 92]

(b) When the presentment for payment is excused and the instrument when overdue remains unpaid. [Section 76]

7.6 Distinction between Dishonour by Non-acceptance and by Non-payment On dishonour by non-acceptance, the drawee cannot be sued because he is not a party to the bill, whereas on dishonour by non-payment, the drawee can be sued.

8.0 NOTICE OF DISHONOUR [SECTIONS 93-98]

8.1 Provisions Relating to Notice of Dishonour [Sections 93-97] The various provisions relating to the notice of dishonour are summarised below:

Provisions Relating to the Notice of Dishonour

Matter	*Provisions*
1. Notice by whom [Section 93]	Notice of dishonour must be given by the holder or by a party liable on the instrument.
2. Notice to whom [Section 93, 94, 97]	Notice of dishonour must be given— (a) to all parties (other than the maker of a note or drawee of a bill or cheque) whom the holder seeks to make severally or jointly liable, or (b) to the duly authorised agents of the aforesaid party or parties, or (c) to legal representatives in case of death or (d) to Receiver or Official Assignee in case of insolvency.
3. Contents of Notice [Section 94]	Notice must inform the party to whom it is given that the instrument has been dishonoured and in what way and that he will be held liable thereon.
4. Form of Notice [Section 94]	Notice may be in any form.
5. Mode of Draft of Notice [Section 94]	Notice may be oral or written.
6. Mode of Service of Notice [Section 94]	A written notice may be sent by post and if the notice is duly directed and sent by post and miscarries, such miscarriage does not render the notice invalid.
7. Time within which Notice is to be given [Sections 94, 105 and 106]	Notice must be given within a reasonable time after dishonour.
8. Place at which notice is to be given	**Reasonable time of giving notice of dishonour—** If the holder and the party to whom notice of dishonour is given carry on business or live (as the case may be) in different places, such notice is given within a reasonable time if it is despatched by the next post or on the day next after the day of dishonour. If the said parties carry on business or live in the same place, such notice is given within a reasonable time if it is despatched in time so to reach its destination on the day next after the day of dishonour. [Section 106]
9. Transmission by party receiving notice [Section 95]	**Notes:** (i) In calculating the reasonable time, public holidays must be excluded.

	(ii) Each party is entitled to one clear day for giving notice of dishonour. (iii) One clear day is allowed for each step in the communication of notice between parties who are liable or the instrument but a holder or endorser who wants to give notice to all parties cannot claim as many days as there are endorsers. He must give notice to all within such time as is allowed to give notice to his immediate endorser. Notice must be given at the place of business or (in case such party has no place of business at the residence of the party for whom it is intended). Any party receiving notice of dishonour must, give notice of dishonour to such prior party to whom he wants to make liable within a reasonable time, unless such party otherwise receives due notice as provided by Section 93.

[*Refer to Practical Problem 3*]

8.2 Effect of Omission to give Notice of Dishonour If notice is not given to any party to whom it is required to be given, within reasonable time, such party is discharged from liability on the instrument. In fact, the liability of the drawer and that of the endorser arises only in the notice of dishonour being given to them unless the notice is excused.

8.3 When Notice of Dishonour is Unnecessary [Section 98]

No notice of dishonour is necessary—

(a) when it is dispensed with by the party entitled thereto;

(b) when the drawer of cheque has countermanded payment, notice to drawer is not required;

(c) when the party entitled to notice cannot be found after due search;

(d) when the party bound to give notice is, unable to give notice without any fault of his own;

(e) when the party charged could not suffer damage for want of notice;

(f) to charge the drawers, when the acceptor is also a drawer; (e.g., when a firm draws a Bill of Exchange on its branch);

(g) in the case of a promissory note which is not negotiable;

(h) when the party entitled to notice, knowing the facts, promises unconditionally to pay the amount due on the instrument.

9.0 RIGHTS OF HOLDER IN CASE OF INSTRUMENT ACQUIRED AFTER DISHONOUR OR AFTER MATURITY

9.1 The rights of a holder in case of an instrument acquired after dishonour or after maturity are summarised below:

In case of an instrument other than an accommodation instrument	*In case of an accommodation instrument*
Its holder has as against the other parties only the rights of his immediate transferor	Its bonafide holder for value is entitled torecover the amount from any prior party.

Example I *The acceptor of a bill of exchange, when he accepted it, deposited with the drawer certain goods as a collateral security for the payment of the bill with power to the drawer to sell the goods and apply the proceeds in discharge of the bill if it were not paid at maturity. The bill not having been paid at maturity, the drawer sold the goods and retained the proceeds but endorsed the bill to A. A's title is subject to the same objection as the drawer's title.*

Example II *X draws a bill on Y who accepts the bill just to accommodate X. X transfers the bill to Z a bonafide person for value after maturity. Z can realise the amount from Y though Z's transferor X could not, at the date of transfer, recover anything from Y.*

9.2 Duration of Negotiability [Section 60] A negotiable instrument may be negotiated:

(a) by person other than the maker, drawee or acceptor until payment.

(b) by the maker, drawee or acceptor until maturity.

10.0 NOTING AND PROTESTING [SECTIONS 99 TO 104A]

10.1 Meaning of Noting Noting is recording the fact of dishonour of a negotiable instrument on the instrument.

10.2 Who does Noting Noting is done by a person officially designated for this purpose and such person is known as Notary Public. Notary Public is appointed by the Central or State Government. The profession of notaries is regulated by the Notaries Act 1952.

10.3 Procedure and Contents of Noting [Section 99] A dishonoured bill is handed over to a notary public who presents it again for acceptance or payment as the case may be, and if the drawee or acceptor still refuses to accept or pay the bill, the notary public records (a) the date of dishonour (b) the fact of dishonour (c) the reason, if any, assigned for such dishonour and (d) Notary's charges.

10.4 Meaning of Notary's Charges The fee charged by Notary Public for noting is called Notary's Charges.

10.5 Time within which Noting is to be Done Noting must be done within a reasonable time after dishonour.

10.6 Compulsory or Optional Noting is compulsory in the case of foreign bills and is optional in case of inland bills. Since noting provides an authentic evidence of dishonour, it is better to get the dishonoured bill noted.

10.7 Meaning of Protest Protest is a formal certificate issued by the Notary Public about the fact of dishonour of a bill or note.

10.8 Time within which Protest is to be done [Section 100] Protest must be done within a reasonable time.

10.9 Meaning of Protest for better Security [Section 100] When the acceptor of a bill of exchange has become insolvent, or his credit has been publicly impeached, before the maturity of the bill, the holder may, within a reasonable time, cause a notary public to demand better security of the acceptor, and on its being refused may, within a reasonable time cause such facts to be noted and certified as aforesaid. Such certificate is called a protest for better security.

10.10 Contents of Protest [Section 101] A protest under Section 100 must contain—

(a) *either* the instrument itself, *or* a literal transcript of the instrument and of everything written or printed thereupon;

(b) the name of the person for whom and against whom the instrument has been protested;

(c) a statement that payment or acceptance, or better security, as the case may be, has been demanded of such person by the Notary Public; the terms of his answer, if any, or a statement that he gave no answer, or that he could not be found;

(d) when the note or bill has been dishonoured, the place and time of dishonour, and when better security has been refused, the place and time of refusal;

(e) the subscription of the Notary Public making the protest;

(f) in the event of an acceptance for honour or of a payment for honour, the name of the person by whom, of the person for whom, and the manner in which, such acceptance or payment was offered and effected.

A Notary Public may make the demand mentioned in clause (c) under this section *either* in person *or* by his clerk or, where authorised by agreement or usage, by registered letter.

10.11 Notice of Protest [Section 102] When a promissory note or bill of exchange is required by law to be protested, notice of such protest must be given instead of notice of dishonour, in the same manner and subject to the same conditions, but the notice may be given by the Notary Public who makes the protest.

10.12 Protest for Non-payment after Dishonour by Non-acceptance [Section 103] All bills of exchange drawn payable at some other place than the place mentioned as the residence of the drawee, and which are dishonoured by non-acceptance may, without further presentment to the drawee, be protested for non-payment, in the place specified for payment, unless paid before or at maturity.

10.13 Protest of Foreign Bill [Section 104] Foreign bills of exchange may be protested for dishonour when such protest is required by the law of the place where they are drawn.

10.14 When Noting Equivalent to Protest [Section 104A] For the purposes of this Act, where a bill or note is required to be protested within a specified time or before some further proceeding is taken, it is sufficient that the bill has been noted for protest before the expiration of the specified time or the taking of the proceeding, and the formal protest may be extended at anytime thereafter as of the date of the noting. In other words, the instrument which has been noted can be protested anytime thereafter for taking legal action against the parties.

11.0 DRAWEE IN CASE OF NEED [SECTIONS 7, 115, 116]

11.1 Meaning of Drawee in Case of Need [Section 7] When in the bill or in any endorsement thereon the name of any person is given in addition to the drawee to be resorted to in case of need, such person is called a "drawee in case of need".

11.2 Meaning of in Case of Need In case of need means in the event of the bill being dishonoured by the drawee by non-acceptance or non-payment.

11.3 Dishonour of a Bill in Case of Drawee in Case of Need [Section 115] Where a drawee in case of need is named in a bill of exchange or any endorsement thereon, the bill is not dishonoured until it has been dishonoured by drawee in case of need.

11.4 Option to Accept and Pay without Previous Protest [Section 116] A drawee in case of need may accept and pay the bill of exchange without previous protest.

11.5 Leading Decisions

(i) The failure to present the bill to the drawee in case of need absolves the drawer from liability [*Bahadur Chand* v. *Gulab Rai* A.I.R. Lah. 577]

(ii) If a bill of exchange has been duly accepted but dishonoured when presented to drawee in the first instance for payment, it cannot be validly presented for payment to the drawee in case of need if it was not first presented to him for acceptance. [*Dore* v. *Kanchiwalla & Co.* Bom. L.R. 473]

12.0 DISCHARGE OF AN INSTRUMENT

12.1 Meaning of Discharge of an Instrument An instrument is said to be discharged only when the party who is ultimately liable thereon is discharged from liability. All rights of action under the instrument are completely extinguished and the instrument ceases to be negotiable.

12.2 Modes of Discharge of an Instrument An instrument is discharged :

(a) By Payment in due Course If the maker or acceptor makes payment to the holder of the instrument at or after maturity in goodfaith and without notice of any defect in the title to the instrument,

Note: A payment before maturity does not discharge the instrument unless the instrument is cancelled or the fact of payment is recorded on the instrument.

(b) By Cancellation If the holder of an instrument cancels acceptor's or endorser's name with intent to discharge him,

(c) By Release If the holder of an instrument renounces his right against all the parties to the instrument,

(d) By Party Primarily Liable becoming Holder [Section 90] If the acceptor of a bill of exchange becomes its holder at or after maturity in his own right.

Note: This happens by 'Negotiation Back'.

13.0 DISCHARGE OF A PARITY

13.1 Meaning of Discharge of a Party A party is said to be discharged onlywhen a party or parties (other than a party ultimately liable on instrument) to a negotiable instrument is or are discharged and the instrument continues to be negotiable with the liabilities of undischarged parties attaching thereto.

13.2 Modes of Discharge of a Party [Sections 82 to 90] A party may be discharged in one of the following ways:

(a) By Payment [Section 82(c)] If the maker, acceptor or endorser makes payment to the holder of the instrument at or after maturity in goodfaith and without notice of any defect in the title to the instrument, all the parties to the instrument are discharged.

(b) By Cancellation [Section 82(a)] If the holder of an instrument cancels the name of any of the parties liable under the instrument with the intention to discharge him, such party and all subsequent parties deriving their title from such party are discharged from the liability to the holder.

Note: The cancellation of an acceptor's or maker's name means discharge of all the parties and thus operates as the discharge of the instrument. This is based upon the principle of law of guarantee that when a principal debtor is discharged, the sureties are also discharged.

(c) **By Release [Section 82(b)]** If the holder of an instrument renounces his rights against any party to the instrument, such party is discharged from the liability to the holder.

(d) **By Allowing Drawee more than 48 hours to Accept [Section 83]** If the holder of a bill allows the drawee more than 48 hours exclusive of public holidays to accept, all previous parties not consenting to the same are discharged from liability to such holder.

(e) **By Non-presentment of Cheque within a Reasonable time [Section 84]** The drawer of a cheque is discharged to the extent of the loss or damage suffered by him if the following 2 conditions are fulfilled:

(i) The cheque is not presented for payment within a reason able time of its issue, and

(ii) The drawer suffers actual damages through the delay.

Notes: (i) In determining what is a reasonable time, the nature, the nature of the instrument, the usage of trade and of Bankers and the facts of the particular case shall be considered.

(ii) The holder of the cheque shall become a creditor of such banker to the extent of such discharge and entitled to recover the amount from prior him

Example *X draws a cheque for Rs. 1,000. The bank fails before the cheque is presented. State the extent to which the drawer shall be discharged if—*

(a) *X* had Rs. 1,000 in his account when the cheque sought to be presented and the cheque is not presented within a reasonable time.

(b) *X* had Rs. 900 in his account when the cheque sought to be presented and the cheque is not presented within a reasonable time.

(c) *X* had Rs. 1,000 in his account when the cheque sought to be presented but the bank failed before the cheque could be presented within a reasonable time.

Solution:

Case (*a*) The drawer is discharged to the extent of Rs. 1,000 but the holder can proceed against the bank for the amount of the cheque.

Case (*b*) The drawer is discharged to the extent of Rs. 900 and the holder can proceed against (a) the bank for Rs. 900 and (b) the drawer for Rs. 100.

Case (*c*) The drawer is not discharged at all.

(f) **By Payment of a Cheque Payable to Order or Bearer by the Drawee Banker [Section 85]**

(i) When a cheque payable to order purports to be endorsed by or on behalf of the payee, the drawee is discharged by payment in due course [Section 85(1)]. Thus, the paying banker is protected if it makes payment of an order cheque with forged endorsement on behalf of the payee.

(ii) Where a cheque is originally expressed to be payable to bearer, the drawee is discharged by payment in due course to the bearer thereof, notwithstanding any endorsement whether in full or in blank appearing thereon, and notwithstanding that any such endorsement purports to restrict, or exclude further negotiation. [Section 85(2)]

The rule of discharge applicable to a cheque payable to order also applies to a draft drawn by one of the banks upon another payable to order or demand. [Section 85A]

(g) By Qualified Acceptance [Section 86] If a holder of a bill consents to a qualified acceptance, all previous parties whose consent is not obtained to such acceptance are discharged from liability, unless on notice given by the holders, they approve of such acceptance by the holder.

(h) By Material Alteration [Section 87] Each party not consenting to material alteration of a negotiable instrument is discharged.

Alteration by endorsee—Any such alteration, if made by an endorsee, discharges his endorser from all liability to him in respect of the consideration thereof.

(i) By Payment of an Instrument on which Alteration is not Apparent [Section 89] The payer of a materially altered instrument is discharged from all liability under the instrument if the following two conditions are fulfilled:

(i) The alteration must not be apparent, and

(ii) The payment must be made in due course.

(j) By Acceptor becoming Holder of a Bill at or after Maturity [Section 90] If a bill of exchange which has been negotiated is, at or after maturity, held by the acceptor in his own right, all right of action thereon are extinguished. This happens by 'Negotiation back'.

(k) By Operation of Law Each party is discharged—

(i) If the negotiable instrument becomes time barred under the Law of the Limitation Act,

(ii) If party is declared as an insolvent by the Court under the Law of the Insolvency,

Note: The limitation period for the recovery of debts is 3 years from the date of default.

14.0 DISTINCTION BETWEEN DISCHARGE OF AN INSTRUMENT AND DISCHARGE OF A PARTY

Discharge of an instrument differs from discharge of a party in the following respects:

Basis of Distinction	***Discharge of an Instrument***	***Discharge of a Party***
1. When takes place	When the party who is ultimately liable, is discharged from liability.	When any party or parties to an instrument is/are discharged.
2. Negotiability	The instrument ceases to be negotiable.	The instrument continues to be negotiable.

3. Extinguishment of all rights of action	All rights of action under the instrument are completely extinguished.	All rights of action under the instrument are not completely extinguished.
4. Discharge of all parties	Discharged of an instrument means discharge of all parties.	Discharge of a party does not mean discharge of all parties.

15.0 HUNDIES

15.1 Meaning of Hundi Hundi is a negotiable instrument drawn in an oriental or vernacular or local language. The Negotiable Instrument Act, 1872 is ordinarily not applicable to hundis but the parties to the Hundies may agree to be governed by the Negotiable Instrument Act. A hundi may be accepted orally as per local usage. A hundi is assignable without any regular form of endorsement. A hundi is not necessarily a bill of exchange as defined in the Act.

15.2 Types of Hundies The most common types of hundis are as follows:

Types of Hundi	*Meaning of Hundi*
(a) Shahjog Hundi	It is payable to Shah (i.e. a financier of repute) Shah, like a banker, presents the hundi when it eventually comes to him for payment to the drawee on behalf of the holders.
(b) Nam Jog Hundi	It is payable to the party named in the Hundi or his order. It is transferable by endorsement and delivery.
(c) Dhani Jog Hundi	It is payable to the Dhani or owner—a holder or bearer owner. It is transferable by mere delivery.
(d) Jokhmi Hundi	It is drawn on or against goods shipped on the vessel mentioned in the hundi and is payable only when the goods reach their destination safely. It is combination of a bill of exchange and insurance policy.
(e) Jawabee Hundi	It is in the nature of a letter or recommendation to a banker for payment of particular amount to a particular person.
(f) Zikri Hundi (or Zikri Chit)	It is in the nature of a letter of protection and is accepted for honour. It is addressed to a merchant in the town where a hundi is payable and contains a request to the merchant that he may accept the hundi in case of dishonour. It is issued to the holder of the hundi by some prior party liable thereon.
(g) Darshni Hundi	It is payable at sight and is transferable by endorsement. It is like a bill of exchange payable on demand.
(h) Miadi Hundi (or Muddati Hundi)	It is payable after a specified period of time. Usually, the interest for the period up to due date is deducted in advance. It is like a time bill of exchange.

(i) Peth	It is a duplicate copy of hundi which is issued on the loss of the original hundi.
(j) Perpeth	It is the triplicate copy of the hundi given on the loss of the peth.
(k) Khoka	It is a hundi which has already been paid and cancelled.

PRACTICAL PROBLEMS

PROBLEM 1

State whether presentment for acceptance is necessary in each of the following alternative cases:

(a) A bill payable on demand.

(b) A bill payable 30 days after date.

(c) A bill payable on 1st Jan. 1997.

(d) A bill payable 3 months after sight.

(e) A bill payable 3 months after presentment.

(f) A bill in which there is an express provision that it shall be presented for acceptance before it is presented for payment.

(g) Where the drawee cannot after reasonable search be found.

(h) Where the drawee is a fictitious person.

(i) Where the drawee is a person incapable of contracting.

Solution

Section to which the given problem relates: Section 61.

Presentment is necessary in: (d), (e), (f).

Presentment is not necessary in: (a), (b), (c), (g), (h), (i).

PROBLEM 2

State whether presentment for payment is necessary to charge the drawer of instrument in each of the following alternative cases:

(a) A promissory note payable on demand and is not payable at a specified place.

(b) A promissory note or bill of exchange payable at a specified period after date of sight thereof.

(c) A bill is not payable at a specified place and the acceptor cannot after due search be found.

(d) A bill is payable at a specified place and *neither* the acceptor *nor* any person authorised to pay is present at such place during the usual business hours.

(e) If the drawer cannot suffer any damage for want of presentment.

Solution

Section to which the given problem relates: Section 76.

Presentment is necessary: (b).

Presentment is not necessary: (a), (c), (d), (e).

PROBLEM 3

A draws a bill in favour of *B* upon *X*, *B* endorses it to *C* who, in turn endorses it to *D* who, in turn, endorses it to *E* who, in turn, endorse to *F*. On presentment for acceptance, *X* refuses to accept the bill. Who has a right of action against whom in each of the following alternative cases:

(a) If *F* gives no notice of dishonour.
(b) If *F* gives notice of dishonour only to *E*.
(c) If *F* gives notice of dishonour only to *E* and *A*.

Solution

Section to which the given problem relates: Section 93 and Section 95.

Case	*Decision*
Case (a)	*F* has no right of action against any prior party because all prior parties who do not receive the notice of dishonour are discharged. [Section 93]
Case (b)	*F* has right of action against *E* only and not against *A*, *B*, *C* or *D*.
Case (c)	*F* has right of action against *E* and *A* only and not against *B*, *C* or *D*. [Section 93]
	E has right of action against *A* and not against *B*, *C* or *D* because *A* received the notice of dishonour from *F*. [Section 95]\

TRUE OR FALSE QUESTIONS

State with reasons whether the following statements are True or False.

1. Bill payable on demand must be presented for acceptance.
2. Any person can be acceptor for honour.
3. A bill can be accepted for honour even without the consent of holder.
4. A promissory note can be accepted for honour.
5. A bill can be accepted for honour in the absence of noting or protest.
6. A payment for honour can be made only by a person who is liable as a party to the bill.
7. Notice of dishonour of a negotiable instrument can be given by any person.
8. Noting and Protesting are compulsory in the case of all bills.
9. In case of foreign bill, notice of protest and not the notice of dishonour is required to be given.
10. discharge of one or more (not all) parties to an instrument does not discharge the instrument.
11. The maker is discharged from liability to a holder of an instrument by payment only.
12. A valid discharge of promissory note takes place only when payment is made by cash.

Answers

1. False	2. False	3. False	4. False
5. False	6. False	7. False	8. False
9. True	10. True	11. False	12. False

VERY SHORT ANSWER TYPE QUESTIONS

1. What is meant by presentment for acceptance?
2. When is presentment for acceptance necessary?
3. What is meant by presentment for payment?

4. When is presentment for payment necessary?
5. Define acceptance for honour.
6. Who is an acceptor for honour?
7. Who can be an acceptor for honour?
8. Define payment for honour?
9. Who is a payer for honour?
10. Who can be payer for honour?
11. What is meant by noting?
12. What is meant by 'Notary's Charges'?
13. State the time limit within which noting is to be done.
14. Is noting compulsory?
15. What is meant by protest?
16. Define drawee in case of need.
17. What is meant by 'Discharge of a party'?
18. What is meant by 'Discharge of an instrument'?
19. What is a hundi?
20. Are hundis governed by the Negotiable Instruments Act?

SHORT ANSWER TYPE QUESTIONS

1. Distinguish between the following:
   (a) Liability of a drawer of a bill of exchange and drawer of a promissory note.
   (b) Dishonour by non-acceptance and dishonour by non-payment.
   (c) Dischage of an instrument and discharge of a party.
   (d) Noting and protest.
2. Write short notes on the following:
   (a) Acceptor for Honour
   (b) Payer for Honour
   (c) Notice of Dishonour
   (d) Noting and Protest
   (e) Drawee in case of need
   (f) Shah Jog Hundi and Zikri Hundi
3. Explain the liabilities of a drawer of a bill of exchange.
4. Explain the liabilities of a drawee of a cheque.
5. Explain the liabilities of a maker of a note or acceptor of a bill of exchange.
6. Explain the liabilities of an endorser.
7. Explain the liabilities of the prior parties to holder in due course.
8. Explain the liabilities of various parties when the instrument is lost or stolen.
9. Explain the liabilities of various parties when the instrument is obtained by fraud.
10. Explain the liabilities of various parties when the instrument is forged.

11. Explain the liabilities of various parties when the instrument is made without consideration.
12. When is presentment for acceptance not necessary?
13. State the effects of non-presentment for acceptance.
14. When is presentment for payment is not necessary?
15. Explain the rights and liabilities of an acceptor for honour.
16. Explain the rights of payer for honour.
17. What is meant by dishonour by non-acceptance?
18. What is meant by dishonour by non-payment?
19. State the effect of omission to give notice of dishonour.
20. When is notice of dishonour unnecessary?
21. State the contents of noting.
22. State the contents of protest.
23. Is noting equivalent to protest?

ESSAY TYPE QUESTIONS

1. Explain the liabilities of the following parties:
   (a) the Drawer of a bill of exchange
   (b) the Drawee of a cheque
   (c) the maker of a note or acceptor of a bill of exchange
   (d) the endorser
   (e) the prior parties to holder in due course
2. Explain the liabilities of various parties in the following cases:
   (a) when the instrument is lost or stolen
   (b) when the instrument is obtained by fraud
   (c) when the instrument is forged
   (d) when the instrument is made without consideration
3. (a) What is meant by presentment for acceptance?
   (b) When is presentment for acceptance necessary?
   (c) When is presentment for acceptance not necessary?
   (d) State the provisions regarding presentment for acceptance
   (e) State the effects of non-presentment for acceptance
   (f) State the provisions regarding presentment of promissory note for sight
4. (a) What is meant by presentment for payment?
   (b) When is presentment for payment is necessary?
   (c) When is presentment for payment is not necessary?
   (d) State the provisions regarding presentment for payment.
5. (a) Define 'acceptance for honour'.
   (b) Who is an acceptor for honour?

(c) Who can be an acceptor for honour?

(d) Explain the rights and liabilities of an acceptor for honour.

6. (a) Define 'Payment for honour'.

(b) Who is payer for honour?

(c) Who can be payer for honour?

(d) Explain the rights of payer for honour.

7. (a) What is meant by dishonour by non-acceptance?

(b) What is meant by dishonour by non-payment?

(c) Distinguish between the dishonour by non-acceptance and dishonour by non-payment.

(d) Expain the provisions relating to notice of dishonour.

(e) State the effect of ommission to give notice of dishonour.

(f) When is notice of dishonour unnecessary?

8. State the rights of holder in case of an instrument acquired after dishonour or after maturity.

9. (a) What is meant by 'Noting'?

(b) State the procedure and contents of noting.

(c) State the meaning of Notary's Charges.

(d) State the time limit within which noting is to be done.

(e) Is noting compulsory?

10. (a) What is meant by 'protest'?

(b) What is meant by 'protest for better security'?

(c) State the contents of protest.

(d) State the provisions regarding protest.

(e) Is noting equivalent to protest?

11. (a) Define Drawee in case of need.

(b) Explain the provisions regarding Drawee in case of need.

12. (a) What is meant by 'Discharge of an instrument'?

(b) Explain the various modes of discharge of an instrument.

13. (a) What is meant by 'Discharge of a party'?

(b) Explain the various modes of discharge of a party.

14. Distinguish between discharge of an instrument and discharge of a party.

15. (a) What is a Hundi?

(b) Are Hundis governed by the Negotiable Instruments Act?

(c) Explain—Shah Jog Hundi, Nam Jog Hundi, Dhani Jog Hundi, Jokhmi Hundi, Jawabee Hundi, Zikri Hundi, Darshni Hundi, Miadi Hundi, Peth, Perpeth, Khoka.

CHAPTER 19 The Information Technology Act, 2000

1.0 INTRODUCTION

Businesses and consumers are increasingly using computers to create, transmit and store information in the electronic form instead of traditional paper documents. Information stored in electronic form has many advantages. It is cheaper, easier to store, retrieve and speedier to communicate. Although people are aware of these advantages, they are reluctant to conduct business or conclude any transaction in the electronic form due to lack of appropriate legal framework. The two principal hurdles which stand in the way of facilitating electronic commerce and electronic governance are the requirements as to writing and signature for legal recognition. At present many legal provisions assume the existence of paper based records and documents and records which should bear signatures. The Law of Evidence is traditionally based upon paper based records and oral testimony. Since electronic commerce eliminates the need for paper based transactions, hence to facilitate e-commerce, and to give legal recognition to electronic records and digital signatures the need for legal changes became an urgent necessity and this gave birth to The Information Technology Act, 2000.

The United Nations Commission on International Trade Law adopted the Model Law on Electronic Commerce by resolution dated 30.1.1997. India being signatory to it had to revise its laws as per the said Model Law. Keeping in view the urgent need to bring suitable amendments in the existing laws to facilitate e-commerce and with a view to facilitate Electronic Governance, the Information and Technology Bill, 1999, was introduced in the Parliament and was passed by both the Houses of Parliament, and it received the assent of the President on the 9th June, 2000 and became THE INFORMATION TECHNOLOGY ACT, 2000 (21 of 2000).

The United Nations Commission on International Trade Law (UNCITRAL) in the year 2001 adopted the Model Law on Electronic Signatures. The General Assembly of the United Nations by its resolution No. 56/80, dated 12th December, 2001, recommended that all States accord favorable consideration to the said Model Law on Electronic Signatures. Since the digital signatures are linked to a specific technology under the existing provisions of the Information Technology Act, it has become necessary to provide for **alternate technology of electronic signatures** for bringing harmonization with the said Model Law.

2.0 WHAT IS INFORMATION TECHNOLOGY ACT ?

Information Technology Act is an Act to provide legal recognition for transactions carried out by means of electronic data interchange and other means of electronic communication, commonly referred to as "electronic commerce", which involve the use of alternatives to paper-based methods of communication and storage of information, to facilitate electronic filing of documents with the Government agencies and further to amend the Indian Penal Code, the Indian Evidence Act, 1872, the Banker's Books Evidence Act, 1891 and the Reserve Bank of Indian Act, 1934 and for matters connected therewith or incidental thereto.

3.0 WHAT ARE THE MAIN OBJECTIVES OF INFORMATION TECHNOLOGY ACT ?

The objectives of Information Technology Act are:

(i) To grant legal recognition for transactions carried out by means of electronic data interchange or electronic commerce in place of paper based method of communication.

(ii) To give legal recognition to Electronic signature for authentication of any information or matter which requires authentication under any law.

(iii) To facilitate electronic filing of documents with Government departments.

(iv) To facilitate electronic storage of data.

(v) To provide legal sanction to transfer fund electronically to and between banks and financial institutions.

(vi) To provide legal recognition for keeping books of account in electronic format by bankers.

(vii) To amend the Indian Penal Code, Indian Evidence Act, 1872, the Bankers Book Evidence Act, 1891 and RBI Act, 1934.

(viii) To provide legal infrastructure to promote e-commerce and secure information system.

(ix) To manage crimes at national and international levels by enforcing laws.

4.0 WHAT IS THE SCHEME OF THE INFORMATION TECHNOLOGY ACT ?

The scheme of the Information Technology Act is summarised follows:

No. of Chapters	XIII Ch. I to VIII relate to digital signature Ch. IX to XIII relate to penalties, offences etc.
No. of Sections	94
No. of Schedules	Four The First Schedule—Amendments to Indian Penal Code, 1860. The Second Schedule—Amendments to Indian Evidence Act, 1872 The Third Schedule—Amendments to Bankers' Books Evidence Act, 1891 The Fourth Schedule—Amendments to Reserve Bank of India Act, 1934

5.0 WHAT IS THE DATE ON WHICH THE INFORMATION TECHNOLOGY ACT CAME INTO FORCE?

The IT Act, 2000 came into force on Oct. 17, 2000.

6.0 WHAT IS THE SCOPE OF INFORMATION TECHNOLOGY ACT ?

6.1 The Information Technology Act, shall extend to the whole of India

6.2 Unless otherwise provided in the Act, it applies also to any offence or contravention thereunder committed outside India by any person.

6.3 The Act **shall not apply** to the following:

(a) a negotiable instrument as defined in Section 13 of the Negotiable Instruments Act, 1881;

(b) a Power-of-Attorney as defined in Section 1A of the Power-of-Attorney Act, 1882;

(c) a Trust as defined in section 3 of the Indian Trusts Act, 1882;

(d) a will as defined in section (h) of section 2 of the Indian Succession Act, 1925 including any other testamentary disposition by whatever name called;

(e) any contract for the sale or conveyance of immovable property or any interest in such property;

(f) any such class of documents or transactions as may be notified by the Central Government in the Official Gazette.

7.0 DEFINITIONS OF TERMS USED IN THE INFORMATION TECHNOLOGY ACT [SEC. 2(1)]

1. **"Access"**	with its grammatical variations and cognate expressions means gaining entry into, instructing or communicating with the logical, arithmetical, or memory function resources of a computer, computer system or computer network;
2. **"Addressee"**	means a person who is intended by the originator to receive the electronic record but does not include any intermediary;
3. **"Adjudicating Officer"**	means adjudicating officer appointed u/s 46(1);
4. **"Affixing Electronic Signature"**	with its grammatical variations and cognate expressions means adoption of any methodology or procedure by a person for the purpose of authenticating an electronic record by means of Electronic Signature;
5. **"Appropriate Government"**	means as respects any matter (i) enumerated in List II of the Seventh Schedule to the Constitution; (ii) relating to any State law enacted under List III of the Seventh Schedule to the Constitution, the State Government and in any other case, the Central Government;
6. **"Asymmetric Crypto System"**	means a system of a secure key pair consisting of a private key for creating a digital signature and a public key to verify the digital signature;
7. **"Certifying Authority"**	means a person who has been granted a license to issue a Electronic Signature Certificate u/s 24;
8. **"Certification Practice Statement"**	means a statement issued by a Certifying Authority to specify the practices that the Certifying Authority employs in issuing Electronic Signature Certificates;
9. **"Communication Device"**	means Cell Phones, Personal Digital Assistance (Sic), or combination of both or any other device used to communicate, send or transmit any text, video, audio, or image.

10. "Computer"	means any electronic, magnetic, optical or other high-speed data processing device or system which performs logical, arithmetic, and memory functions by manipulations of electronic, magnetic or optical impulses, and includes all input, output, processing, storage, computer software, or communication facilities which are connected or related to the computer in a computer system or computer network.
11. "Computer Network"	means the interconnection of one or more Computers or Computer systems or Communication device through- (i) the use of satellite, microwave, terrestrial line, wire, wireless or other communication media; and (ii) terminals or a complex consisting of two or more interconnected computers or communication device whether or not the interconnection is continuously maintained.
12. "Computer Resource"	means computer, communication device, computer system, computer network, data, computer database or software.
13. "Computer System"	means a device or collection of devices, including input and output support devices and excluding calculators which are not programmable and capable of being used in conjunction with external files, which contain computer programmes, electronic instructions, input data, and output data, that performs logic, arithmetic, data storage and retrieval, communication control and other functions.
14. "Controller"	means the Controller of Certifying Authorities appointed u/s 17 (7).
15. "Cyber Appellate Tribunal"	means the Cyber Appellate * Tribunal established u/s 48 (1).
16. "Cyber Café"	means any facility from where access to the internet is offered by any person in the ordinary course of business to the members of the public.
17. "Cyber Security"	means protecting information, equipment, devices, computer, computer resource, communication device and information stored therein from unauthorized access, use, disclosure, disruption, modification or destruction.
18. "Data"	means a representation of information, knowledge, facts, concepts or instructions which are being prepared or have been prepared in a formalized manner, and is intended to be processed, is being processed or has been processed in a computer system or computer network and may be in any form (including computer printouts magnetic or optical storage media, punched cards, punched tapes) or stored internally in the memory of the computer.
19. "Digital Signature"	means authentication of any electronic record by a subscriber by means of an electronic method or procedure in accordance with the provisions of Sec. 3.

20. "Digital Signature Certificate"	means a Digital Signature Certificate issued u/s 35 (4).
21. "Electronic Form"	with reference to information means any information generated, sent, received or stored in media, magnetic, optical, computer memory, micro film, computer generated micro fiche or similar device;
22. "Electronic Gazette"	means official Gazette published in the electronic form;
23. "Electronic Record"	means data, record or data generated, image or sound stored, received or sent in an electronic form or micro film or computer generated micro fiche;
24. "Electronic Signature"	means authentication of any electronic record by a subscriber by means of the electronic technique specified in the second schedule and includes digital signature.
25. "Electronic Signature Certificate"	means an Electronic Signature Certificate issued u/s 35 and includes Digital Signature Certificate"
26. "Function",	in relation to a computer, includes logic, control, arithmetical process, deletion, storage and retrieval and communication or telecommunication from or within a computer;
27. "Indian Computer Emergency Response Team"	means an agency established u/s 70B (1).
28. "Information"	includes data, message, text, images, sound, voice, codes, computer programmes, software and databases or micro film or computer generated micro fiche.
29. "Intermediary"	with respect to any particular electronic records, means any person who on behalf of another person receives, stores or transmits that record or provides any service with respect to that record and includes telecom service providers, network service providers, internet service providers, web hosting service providers, search engines, online payment sites, online-auction sites, online market places and cyber cafes.
30. "Key Pair"	in an asymmetric crypto system, means a private key and its mathematically related public key, which are so related that the public key can verify a digital signature created by the private key;
31. "Law"	includes any Act of Parliament or of a State Legislature, Ordinances promulgated by the President or a Governor, as the case may be. Regulations made by the President under Article 240, Bills enacted as President's Act under Article 357(1)(a) of the Constitution and includes rules, regulations, bye-laws and orders issued or made thereunder
32. "License"	means a license granted to a Certifying Authority u/s 24.

33. "Originator"	means a person who sends, generates, stores or transmits any electronic message or causes any electronic message to be sent, generated, stored or transmitted to any other person but does not include an intermediary.
34. "Prescribed"	means prescribed by rules made under this Act.
35. "Private Key"	means the key of a key pair used to create a digital signature.
36. "Public Key"	means the key of a key pair used to verify a digital signature and listed in the Digital Signature Certificate.
37. "Secure System"	means computer hardware, software, and procedure that -: (a) are reasonably secure from unauthorized access and misuse; (b) provide a reasonable level of reliability and correct operation; (c) are reasonably suited to performing the intended functions; and (d) adhere to generally accepted security procedures;
38. "Security Procedure"	means the security procedure prescribed u/s 16 by the Central Government.
39. "Subscriber"	means a person in whose name the Electronic Signature Certificate is issued.
40. "Verify"	in relation to a digital signature, electronic record or public key, with its grammatical variations and cognate expressions means to determine whether (a) the initial electronic record was affixed with the digital signature by the use of private key corresponding to the public key of the subscriber; (b) the initial electronic record is retained intact or has been altered since such electronic record was so affixed with the digital signature.

8.0 PROVISIONS RELATING TO ELECTRONIC SIGNATURE

8.1 Meaning of 'Electronic Signature' [Sec 2(1)(p)]

"Electronic Signature" means authentication of any electronic record by a subscriber by means of an electronic technique specified in the second schedule and includes Digital signature.

8.2 Meaning of 'Affixing Electronic Signature' [Sec. 2(1)(d)]

"Affixing Electronic Signature" means adoption of any methodology or procedure by a person for the purpose of authenticating an electronic record by means of Electronic signature.

8.3 How is Digital Signature Created? [Sec 3]

The digital signature is created in two distinct steps:

(a) **Hash Function**—First, the electronic record is converted into a message digest by using a mathematical function known as "hash function" which digitally freezes. The electronic record thus ensuring the integrity of the contents of the intended communication contained in the electronic record. Any tampering with the contents of the electronic record will immediately invalidate the digital signature.

For the purposes of this sub-section, "**hash function**" **means** an algorithm mapping or translation of one sequence of bits into another, generally smaller, set known as "hash result" such that an electronic record yields the same hash result every time the algorithm is executed with the same electronic record as its input making it computationally infeasible—

(i) to derive or reconstruct the orginal electronic record from the hash result produced by the algorithm;

(ii) that two electronic records can produce the same hash resulting using the algorithm.

(b) **Asymmetric Crypto System**—Secondly, the identity of the person affixing the digital signature is authenticated through the use of a private key which attaches itself to the message digest and which can be verified by anybody who has the public key corresponding to such private key. This will enable anybody to verify whether the electronic record is retained intact or has been tampered with since it was so fixed with the digital signature. It will also enable a person who has a public key to identify the originator of the message.

8.4 Authentication of Electronic Records

(1) Subject to the provisions of this section any subscriber may authenticate an electronic record by affixing his Digital Signature.

(2) The authentication of the electronic record shall be effected by the use of asymmetric crypto system and hash function which envelop and transform the initial electronic record into another electronic record.

(3) Any person by the use of a public key of the subscriber can verify the electronic record.

(4) The private key and the public key are unique to the subscriber and constitute a functioning key pair.

8.5 Electronic Signature [Section 3A]

(1) Notwithstanding anything contained in Sec. 3, but subject to the provisions of Sec. 3A (2) a subscriber may authenticate any electronic record by such electronic signature or electronic authentication technique which-

(a) is considered reliable ; and

(b) may be specified in the Second Schedule

(2) For the purposes of this section any electronic signature or electronic authentication technique shall be considered reliable if-

(a) the signature creation data or the authentication data are, within the context in which they are used, linked to the signatory or , as the case may be, the authenticator and of no other person;

(b) the signature creation data or the authentication data were, at the time of signing, under the control of the signatory or, as the case may be, the authenticator and of no other person;

(c) any alteration to the electronic signature made after affixing such signature is detectable

(d) any alteration to the information made after its authentication by electronic signature is detectable; and

(e) it fulfills such other conditions which may be prescribed.

(3) The Central Government may prescribe the procedure for the purpose of ascertaining whether electronic signature is that of the person by whom it is purported to have been affixed or authenticated

(4) The Central Government may, by notification in the Official Gazette, add to or omit any electronic signature or electronic authentication technique and the procedure for affixing such signature from the second schedule;

Provided that no electronic signature or authentication technique shall be specified in the Second Schedule unless such signature or technique is reliable

(5) Every notification issued u/s 3A (4) shall be laid before each House of Parliament

9.0 PROVISIONS RELATING TO ELECTRONIC GOVERNANCE

The Act contains the following provisions to facilitate e-governance:

9.1 Legal Recognition of Electronic Records [Sec. 4]

Where any law provides that information or any other matter shall be in writing or in the typewritten or printed form, then, notwithstanding anything contained is such law, such requirement shall be deemed to have been satisfied if such information or matter is—

(a) rendered or made available in an electronic form; and

(b) accessible so as to be usable for a subsequent reference.

9.2 Legal Recognition of Digital Signatures [Sec. 5]

Where any law provides that information or any other matter shall be authenticated by affixing the signature or any document shall be signed or bear the signature of any person then, notwithstanding anything contained in such information or matter is authenticated by means of digital signature affixed in such manner as may be prescribed by the Central Government.

Explanation—For the purposes of this Section, "signed", with its grammatical variations and cognate expressions, shall, with reference of a person, mean affixing of his handwritten signature or any mark on any document and the expression "signature" shall be construed accordingly.

9.3 Use of Electronic Records and Electronic Signature in Government and its Agencies [Sec. 6]

This Section lays down the foundation of electronic governance.

Where any law provides for—

(i) the filing of any form, application or any other document with any office, authority, body or agency owned or controlled by the appropriate Government in a particular manner;

(ii) the issue or grant of any licence, permit, sanction or approval by whatever name called in a particular manner;

(iii) the receipt or payment of money in a particular manner,

then, notwithstanding anything contained in any other law for the time being in force, such requirement shall be deemed to have been satisfied in such filing, issue of grant, receipt or payment, as the case may be, is effected by means of such electronic form as may be prescribed by the appropriate Government.

The appropriate Government may, by rules, prescribe—

(i) the manner and format in which such electronic records shall be filed, created or issued;

(ii) the manner or method of payment of any fee or charges for filling, creation or issue of any electronic record under clause (a) stated above.

9.4 Delivery of Services by Service Provider [Section 6A]

(1) The appropriate Government may, for the purposes of this Chapter and for efficient delivery of services to the public through electronic means authorize, by order, any service provider to set up, maintain and upgrade the computerized facilities and perform such other services as it may specify, by notification in the Official Gazette.

Explanation : For the purposes of this section, service provider so authorized includes any individual, private agency, private company, partnership firm, sole proprietor form or any such other body or agency which has been granted permission by the appropriate Government to offer services through electronic means in accordance with the policy governing such service sector.

(2) The appropriate Government may also authorize any service provider authorized u/s 6A (1) to collect, retain and appropriate service charges, as may be prescribed by the appropriate Government for the purpose of providing such services, from the person availing such service.

(3) Subject to the provisions of u/s 6A (2), the appropriate Government may authorize the service providers to collect, retain and appropriate service charges under this section notwithstanding the fact that there is no express provision under the Act, rule, regulation or notification under which the service is provided to collect, retain and appropriate e-service charges by the service providers.

(4) The appropriate Government shall, by notification in the Official Gazette, specify the scale of service charges which may be charged and collected by the service providers under this section: Provided that the appropriate Government may specify different scale of service charges for different types of services.

9.5 Retention of Electronic Records [Sec. 7]

Where any law provides that documents records or information shall be retained for any specific period, then, that requirement shall be deemed to have been satisfied if such documents, records or information are retained in the electronic from, if—

(i) the information contained therein remains accessible so as to be usable for a subsequent reference;

(ii) the electronic records is retained in the format in which it was originally generated, sent or received or in a format which can be demonstrated to represent accurately the information originally generated sent or received:

(iii) the details which will facilitate the identification of the origin, destination date and time of despatch or receipt of such electronic record are available in the electronic record.

Exception—This section does not apply—

(a) to any information which is automatically generated solely for the purpose of enabling an electronic record to be despatched or received.

(b) to any law that expressly provides for the retention of documents, records or information in the form of electronic records.

9.6 Audit of Documents etc in Electronic form [Section 7A]

Where in any law for the time being in force, there is a provision for audit of documents, records or information, that provision shall also be applicable for audit of documents, records or information processed and maintained in electronic form.

9.7 Publication of Rules, Regulations, etc., in Electronic Gazette [Sec. 8]

Where any law provides that any rule, regulation, order, buy-law notification or any other matter shall be published in the Official Gazette, then, such requirement shall be deemed to have been satisfied if the same is published in the Official Gazette or electronic Gazette.

Date of Publication—The date of publication shall be deemed to be the date of the Gazette which was first published in any form.

Note: Electronic Gazette means Official Gazette published in the electronic form [Sec. 2(1)(s)]

9.8 No Right to insist that the Document should be accepted in Electronic Form [Sec. 9]

Sections 6, 7 and 8 shall not confer right upon any person to insist that any Ministry or Department of the Central Government or the State Government or any authority or body established by or under any law or controlled or funded by the Central or State Government should accept, issue, create, retain and preserve any document in the form of electronic records or effect any monetary transaction in the electronic form.

9.9 Power of Central Government to make Rules [Sec. 10]

The Central Government may make rules in respect of digital signature prescribing—

(a) the type of electronic signature;

(b) the manner and format in which the electronic signature shall be affixed;

(c) the manner or procedure which facilitates identification of the person affixing the electronic signature;

(d) control processes and procedures to ensure adequate integrity, security and confidentiality or electronic records or payments; and

(e) any other matter which is necessary to give legal effect to electronic signatures.

9.10 Validity of contracts formed through electronic means [10A]

Where in a contract formation, the communication of proposals, the acceptance of proposals, the revocation of proposals and acceptances, as the case may be, are expressed in electronic form or by means of an electronic record, such contract shall not be deemed to be unenforceable solely on the ground that such electronic form or means was used for that purpose.

10.0 WHEN SHALL THE TRANSMISSION OF AN ELECTRONIC RECORD BE ATTRIBUTED TO THE ORIGINATOR? [SEC. 11]

10.1 An electronic record shall be attributed to the originator if it is sent—

(a) by the originator himself;

(b) by a person who has the authority to act on behalf of the originator in respect of that electronic record; or

(c) by an information system programmed by or on behalf of the originator to operate automatically.

10.2 Originator [Sec. 2(1)(za)]. It means a person who sends, generates, stores or transmits any electronic message or cause any electronic message to be sent, generated, stored or transmitted to any other person but does not include an *intermediary*.

10.3 Intermediary [Sec. 2(1)(w)]. Intermediary, with respect to any particular electronic message, means any person who on behalf of another person receives, stores or transmits the message or provides any service with respect to that message.

10.4 Addressee [Sec. 2(1)(b)]. It means a person who is intended by the originator to receive the electronic record but does not include any intermediary.

11.0 WHAT ARE PROVISIONS RELATING TO THE ACKNOWLEDGEMENT OF RECEIPT?

11.1 How to Make Acknowledgement? [Sec. 12(1)]

Where the originator has not agreed with the addressee that the acknowledgement of receipt of electronic record be given in a particular form or by a particular method. An acknowledgement may be given by—

(a) any communication by the addressee, automated or otherwise; or

(b) any conduct of the addressee, sufficient to indicate to the originator that the electronic record has been received [Sec. 12(1)]

11.2 Binding Effect [Sec. 12(2) & 12(3)]

(a) **In case of stipulation by the originator**—Where the originator has stipulated that the electronic record shall be binding only on receipt of an acknowledgement of such electronic record by him, then unless acknowledgement has been so received, the electronic record shall be deemed to have been never sent by the originator. [Sec. 12(2)].

(b) **In case of no stipulation by the originator**—Where the originator has not stipulated that the electronic record shall be binding only on receipt of such acknowledgement, and the acknowledgement has not been received by the originator within the time specified or agreed or, if no time has been specified or agreed to within a reasonable time, then the originator may give notice of the addressee stating that no acknowledgement has been received by him and specifying a reasonable time by which the acknowledgement must be received by him and if no acknowledgement is received within the aforesaid time limit he may after giving notice to the addressee, treat the electronic record as though it has never been sent. [Sec. 12(3)].

12.0 HOW TO DETERMINE TIME AND PLACE OF DESPATCH AND RECEIPT OF ELECTRONIC RECORD [SEC. 13]

Time of Despatch	Unless otherwise agreed between the originator and the addressee the dispatch of an electronic record occurs when it enters a computer resource outside the control of the originator.
Time of Receipt	Unless otherwise agreed between the originator and the addressee the time of receipt of an electronic record shall be determined as follows:

	(a) if the addressee had designated a computer resource for the purpose of receiving electronic records— (i) receipt occurs at the time when the electronic record enters the designated computer resource; or (ii) if the electronic record is sent to a computer resource of the addressee that is not the designated computer resource, receipt occurs at the time when the electronic record is retrieved by the addressee; (b) if the addressee has not designated a computer resource along with specified timings, if any, receipt occurs when the electronic record enters the computer resource of the addressee.
Place of Despatch and Receipt	Unless otherwise agreed between the originator and the addressee, an electronic record is deemed to be dispatched at the place where the originator has his place of business, and is deemed to be received at the place where the addressee has his place of business. For the purposes of this Section— (a) if the originator or the addressee has more than one place of business, the principal place of business, shall be the place of business; (b) if the originator or the addressee does not have a place of business, his usual place or residence shall be deemed to be the place of business; (c) "usual place of residence", in relation to a body corporate, means the place where it is registered.

13.0 WHEN SHALL AN ELECTRONIC RECORD BE DEEMED TO BE A SECURE ELECTRONIC RECORD? [SEC. 14]

Where any security procedure has been applied to an electronic record at a specific point of time, then such record shall be deemed to be a secure electronic record from such point of time to the time of verification.

14.0 WHEN SHALL AN ELECTRONIC SIGNATURE BE DEEMED TO BE A SECURE ELECTRONIC SIGNATURE [SECTION 15]

An electronic signature shall be deemed to be a secure electronic signature if-

(i) the signature creation data, at the time of affixing signature, was under the exclusive control of signatory and no other person; and

(ii) the signature creation data was stored and affixed in such exclusive manner as may be prescribed

Explanation- In case of digital signature, the "signature creation data" means the private key of the subscriber

15.0 SECURITY PROCEDURES AND PRACTICES [SECTION 16]

The Central Government may for the purposes of sections 14 and 15 prescribe the security procedures and practices Provided that in prescribing such security procedures and practices, the Central Government shall have regard to the commercial circumstances, nature of transactions and such other related factors as it may consider appropriate.

16.0 WHAT ARE THE PROVISIONS RELATING TO THE APPOINTMENT OF CONTROLLER AND OTHER OFFICERS [SEC. 17]

Who Can Appoint?	The Central Government may, by notification in the Official Gazette appoint a Controller of Certifying Authorities for the purposes of this Act and may also by the same or subsequent notification appoint such number of Deputy Controllers; Assistant Controllers and other officers & employees as it deems fit.
Functions	(a) The Controller shall discharge his functions under this Act subject to the general control and directions of the Central Government. (b) The Deputy Controllers and Assistant Controllers shall perform the functions assigned to them by the Controller under the general superintendence and control of the Controller.
Qualifications etc.	The qualifications, experience and terms and conditions of service of Controller, Deputy Controller and Assistant Controllers and other officers & employees shall be such as may be prescribed by the Central Government.
Place of Office	The Head Office and Branch Office of the office of the Controller shall be at such places as the Central Government may specify, and these may be established at such places at the Central Government may think fit.
Seal of Office	There shall be a seal of the Office of the Controller.

17.0 WHAT ARE THE FUNCTIONS OF CONTROLLER? [SEC. 18]

The Controller may perform all or any of the following functions, namely;

(a) exercising supervision over the activities of the Certifying Authorities;

(b) certifying public keys of the Certifying Authorities;

(c) laying down the standards to be maintained by the Certifying Authorities;

(d) specifying the qualifications and experience which employees of the Certifying Authorities should possess;

(e) specifying the conditions subject to which the Certifying Authorities shall conduct their business;

(f) specifying the contents of written, printed or visual materials and advertisements that may be distributed or used in respect of a Digital Signature Certificate and the public key;

(g) specifying the form and content of a Digital Signature Certificate and the key;

(h) specifying the form and manner in which accounts shall be maintained by the Certifying Authorities;

(i) specifying the terms and conditions subject to which auditors may be appointed and the remuneration to be paid to them;

(j) facilitating the establishment of any electronic system by a Certifying Authority either solely or jointly with other Certifying Authorities and regulation of such systems;

(k) specifying the manner in which the Certifying Authorities shall conduct their dealings with the subscribers;

(l) resolving any conflict of interest between the Certifying Authorities and the subscribers;

(m) laying down the duties of the Certifying Authorities;

(n) maintaining a database containing the disclosure record of every Certifying Authority containing such particulars as may be specified by regulations which shall be accessible to public.

18.0 WHAT ARE THE PROVISIONS RELATING TO RECOGNITION OF FOREIGN CERTIFYING AUTHORITIES? [SEC. 19]

Power of Controller	Subject to such conditions and restrictions as may be specified by regulations, the Controller may with the previous approval of the Central Government, and by notification in the Official Gazette, recognize any foreign Certifying Authority as a Certifying Authority for the purposes of this Act.
Validity of DSC	Where any Certifying Authority is recognised under sub-sections (1), the Digital Signature Certificate issued by such Certifying Authority shall be valid for the purposes of the Act.
Revocation	The controller may if he is satisfied that any Certifying Authority has contravened any of the conditions and restrictions subject to which it was granted recognition under section 19(1) he may, for reasons to be recorded in writing, by notification in the Official Gazette, revoke such recognition.

19.0 WHO CAN APPLY FOR A LICENCE TO ISSUE ELECTRONIC SIGNATURE CERTIFICATES? [SEC. 21]

Who can Apply	Any person may make an application, to the Controller, for a licence to issue Electronic Signature Certificate, provided he fulfils such requirements with respect to qualifications, expertise, manpower, financial resources and other infrastructure facilities, which are necessary to issue Digital Signature Certificates as may be prescribed by the Central Government.
Restriction on Licence	A licence granted under this Section shall— (a) be valid for such period as may be prescribed by the Central Government; (b) not be transferable or heritable; (c) be subject to such terms and conditions as may be specified by the regulations [Sec. 21(3)]

20.0 WHAT ARE THE PROVISIONS RELATING TO APPLICATION FOR LICENCE? [SEC. 22 AND SEC. 24]

Form of Application	Every application for issue of a licence shall be in such form as may be prescribed by the Central Government.
Enclosures	Every application for issue of a licence shall be accompanied by— (a) a certification practice statement; (b) a statement including the procedures with respect to identification of the applicant; (c) payment of such fees, not exceeding Rs 25,000 as may be prescribed by the Central Government; (d) such other documents, as may be prescribed by the Central Government
Meaning of Certification Practice Statement	It means a statement issued by a Certifying Authority to specify the practices that it employs in issuing Digital Signature Certificates." Basically it specifies a set of rules and requirements which are to be followed by a Certifying Authority (CA) in its operations and issuing certificates.
Power of Controller	The controller may, on receipt of an application for a licence to issue Electronic Signature Certificate, after considering the documents accompanying the application and such other factors, as he deems fit, grant the licence or reject the application.
Opportunity	However, no application shall be rejected under this Section unless the applicant has been given a reasonable opportunity of presenting his case.

21.0 WHAT ARE THE PROVISIONS RELATING TO RENEWAL OF LICENCE? [SEC. 23]

Form	An application for renewal of a licence shall be in the prescribed form.
Fee	Such application shall be accompanied by such **fees, not exceeding Rs 5,000** as may be prescribed by the Central Government
Period	Such application shall be made **at least 45 days before** the date of expiry of the period of validity of the licence.

22.0 WHAT ARE THE PROVISIONS RELATING TO SUSPENSION OF LICENCE? [SEC. 25]

Circumstances	The Controller may, if he is satisfied after making an inquiry, revoke the licence where a Certifying Authority has,— (a) made a statement in, or in relation to, the application for the issue or renewal of the licence, which is incorrect or false in material particulars; (b) failed to comply with the terms and conditions subject to which the licence was granted;

	(c) failed to maintain the standards specified u/s 30 (d) contravened any provision of this Act, rule, regulation or order made there- under.
Opportunity	No licence shall be revoked unless the Certifying Authority has been given a reasonable opportunity of showing cause against the proposed revocation.
Power to Suspend	The Controller may, if he has reasonable cause to believe that there is any ground for revoking a licence under section 25(1), by order suspend such licence pending the completion of any inquiry ordered by him.
Suspension Period	No licence shall be suspended for a period exceeding 10 days unless the Certifying Authority has been given a reasonable opportunity of showing cause against the proposed suspension.
No Issue of DSC during Suspension	No Certifying Authority whose licence has been suspended shall issue any Digital Signature Certificate during such suspension.
Notice of Suspension or Revocation of Licence	(a) Where the licence of the Certifying Authority is suspended or revoked, the Controller shall publish notice of such suspension or revocation as the case may be, in the database maintained by him. (b) Where one or more repositories are specified, the Controller shall publish notices of such suspension or revocation, as the case may be, in all such repositories, (c) However, the database containing the notice of such suspension or revocation, as the case may be, shall be made available through a website which shall be accessible round the clock. (d) However, that the Controller may, if he considers necessary, publicize the contents of the data-base in such electronic or other media, as he may consider appropriate.

23.0 WHAT ARE THE POWERS OF CONTROLLER? [SEC. 27, 28, 68(1) & 69(1)]

The Controller of Certifying Authorities has the power—

1. To authorise, in writing, the Deputy or the Assistant Controller or any officer to exercise any of his powers [Sec. 27].
2. To take up for investigation any contravention of the Act or rules or regulations made thereunder. He may authorise any officer also in this behalf [Sec. 28(1)].
3. To exercise himself or through an authorised officer like powers which are conferred on Income-tax Authorities under Chapter XIII of the Income-tax Act, 1961 [Sec. 28(2)].
4. To have access to any computer system, any apparatus, data or any other material connected with such system, for the purpose of searching or causing a search to be made for obtaining any information or data contained in or available to such computer system if the Controller has reasonable cause to

suspect that any contravention of the provisions of this Act, rules or regulations made thereunder has been committed. [Sec 29(1)]

5. To direct any person incharge of, or otherwise concerned with the operation of, the computer system, data apparatus or material, to provide him with such reasonable technical and other assistance as he may consider necessary. [Sec. 29(2)]
6. To direct by order, a Certifying Authority or any employee of such Authority to take such measures or cease carrying on such activities as specified in the order, if those are necessary to ensure compliance with the provisions of the Act, rules or any regulations made thereunder [Sec. 68(1)].
7. To direct by order, any agency of the Government to intercept any information transmitted through any "computer resource" (i.e., computer, computer system and computer network, etc.), if it is necessary or expedient in the interest of the sovereignty or integrity of Inida, the security of the State, friendly relations with foreign States or public order or for preventing incitement to the commission of any cognizable *officence* [Sec. 69(1)].

24.0 WHAT ARE THE PROCEDURES TO BE FOLLOWED BY CERTIFYING AUTHORITY? [SEC. 30]

Meaning of Certifying Authority	The person to whom a licence has been granted by the Controller to issue Digital Signature Certificates is termed as a Certifying Authority [Sec. 2(1)(g)].
Procedure to be followed	Every Certifying Authority shall follow certain procedures relating to security of system, in performance of its services. It is required, to,— (a) make use of hardware, software, and procedures that are secure from instrusion and misuse; (b) provide a reasonable level of reliability in its services which are reasonably suited to the performance of intended functions; (c) adhere to security procedures to ensure that the secrecy and privacy of the digital signatures are assured; and (d) observe such other standards as may be specified by regulations. (e) be the repository of all Electronic Signature Certificates issued under this Act (f) publish information regarding its practices, Electronic Signature Certificates and current status of such certificates;

25.0 WHAT ARE THE DUTIES OF CERTIFYING AUTHORITY? [SEC 31 TO SEC 34]

The Certifying Authority has the duty:

1. To ensure that every person employed or otherwise engaged by it complies, in the course of his employment or engagement, with the provisions of the Act, rules, regulations and orders made thereunder (Sec. 31).

2. To display its licence at a conspicuous place of the premises in which it carries on its business (Sec. 32).
3. To surrender the licence to the Controller immediately after its suspension or revocation [Sec. 33(1)].
4. To disclose in the manner specified by the regulations—
   (i) the use
   (a) its Electronic Signature Certificate which contains the public key corresponding to the private key used by the Certifying Authority to digitally sign another Electronic Signature Certificate;
   (b) any certification practice statement relevant thereto;
   (c) notice of the revocation or suspension of its Certifying Authority certificate, if any; and
   (d) any other fact that materially and adversely affects either the reliability of a Electronic Signature Certificate, which that Authority has issued, or the Authority's ability to perform its services [Sec. 34(1)].
5. To make reasonable efforts to notify any person who is likely to be affected by the occurrence of any event which, in the opinion of the Certifying Authority, may materially and adversely affect the integrity of its computer system or the conditions subject to which a Digital Signature Certificate was granted [Sec 34(1)].
6. To act in accordance with the procedure specified in its 'certification practice statement' to deal with such event or situation [Sec. 34(2)].

26.0 WHAT ARE THE PROVISIONS RELATING TO APPLICATION FOR THE ISSUE OF ELECTRONIC SIGNATURE CERTIFICATE [SEC. 35 (1) TO 35(3)]

26.1 Any person may make an application **to the Certifying Authority** for the issue of a Electronic Signature Certificate in such form as may be prescribed by the Central Government.

26.2 Such application must be **accompanied by**:

(a) such **fee not exceeding Rs 25,000** as may be prescribed by the Central Government. However, different fees may be prescribed for different classes of applicants.

(b) a '**certification practice statement**' or where there is no such statement, a statement containing such particulars, as may be specified by regulations.

27.0 WHAT ARE THE PROVISIONS RELATING TO GRANT OF CERTIFICATE ? [SEC 35(4)]

Power of Certifying Authority	On receipt of an application for the issue of Electronic Signature Certificate, the Certifying Authority may, after consideration of the 'certification practice statement' or the other statement referred u/s 35(3) and after making such enquiries as it may deem fit, grant the Electronic Signature Certificate or for reasons to be recorded in writing, reject the application.
Conditions	No Electronic Signature Certificate shall be granted unless the Certifying Authority is satisfied that— (a) the applicant holds the private key corresponding to

	the public key to be listed in the Digital Signature Certificate; (b) the applicant holds a private key, which is capable of creating a digital signature; (c) the public key to be listed in the certificate can be used to verify a digital signature affixed by the private key held by the applicant.

28.0 WHAT ARE THE REPRESENTATIONS UPON ISSUANCE OF DIGITAL SIGNATURE CERTIFICATE? [SEC. 36]

While issuing a Digital Signature Certificate, the Certifying Authority shall certify that—

(a) it has complied with the provisions of this Act and the rules and regulations made thereunder;

(b) it has published the Digital Signature Certificate or otherwise made it available to such person relying on it and the subscriber has accepted it;

(c) the subscriber holds the private key corresponding to the public key, listed in the Digital Signature Certificate;

(d) the subscriber's public key and private key constitute a functioning key pair; and

(e) the information contained in the Digital Signature certificate is accurate;

(f) it has no knowledge of any material fact, which if it had been included in the Digital Signature Certificate would adversely affect the reliability of the representations made in clauses (a) to (d);

(g) the subscriber holds a private key which is capable of creating a digital signature;

(h) the public key to be listed in the certificate can be used to verify a digital signature affixed by the private key held by the subscriber.

29.0 WHAT ARE THE PROVISIONS RELATING TO SUSPENSION OF DIGITAL SIGNATURE CERTIFICATE? [SEC. 37]

Circumstances	The Certifying Authority which has issued a Digital Signature Certificate may suspend such Digital Signature Certificate,— (a) on receipt of a **request** to that effect from— (i) the subscriber listed in the Digital Signature Certificate; or (ii) any person duly authorised to act on behalf of that subscriber; (b) if it is of **opinion** that the Digital Signature Certificate should be suspended in public interest.
Period of Suspension	A Digital Signature Certificate shall not be suspended for a period exceeding 15 days unless that subscriber has been given an opportunity of being heard in the matter.
Communication	On suspension of a Digital Signature Certificate under this Section, the Certifying Authority shall communicate the same to the subscriber.

30.0 WHAT ARE THE CIRCUMSTANCES FOR REVOCATION OF DIGITAL SIGNATURE CERTIFICATE? [SEC. 38]

Circumstances	A Certifying Authority may revoke a Digital Signature Certificate issued by it— (a) where the subscriber or any other person authorised by him makes a **request** to that effect; or (b) upon the **death** of the subscriber; or (c) upon the **dissolution** of the firm or winding up of the company where the subscriber is a firm or a company. (d) where it is of **opinion** that— (i) a material fact represented in the Digital Signature Certificate is false or has been concealed; (ii) a requirement for issuance of the Digital Signature Certificate was not satisfied; (iii) the Certifying Authority's private key or security system was compromised in a manner materially affecting the Digital Signature Certificate's reliability; (iv) the subscriber has been declared insolvent or dead or where a subscriber is a firm or a company, which has been dissolved, wound-up or otherwise ceased to exist.
Opportunity	A Digital Signature Certificate shall not be revoked unless the subscriber has been given an opportunity of being heard in the matter. [Sec 38(3)]
Communication	On revocation of a Digital Signature Certificate under this Section, the Certifying Authority shall communicate the same to the subscriber. [Sec 38(4)]
Publication of Notice	1. Where a Digital Signature Certificate is suspended or revoked under Section 37 or Section 38, the Certifying Authority shall publish a notice of such suspension or revocation, as the case may be, in the repository specified in the Digital Signature Certificate for publication of such notice. 2. Where one or more repositories are specified, the Certifying Authority shall publish notices of such suspension or revocation, as the case may be, in all such repositories.

31.0 WHAT ARE THE DUTIES OF SUBSCRIBERS? [SEC 40 TO SEC 42]

The Subscribers have the following duties:

Generating Key Pair	Where any Digital Signature Certificate, the public key of which corresponds to the private key of that subscriber which is to be listed in the Digital Signature Certificate, has been accepted by a subscriber, the subscriber must generate that key pair by applying the security procedure.

Acceptance of Digital Signature Certificate	A subscriber shall be deemed to have accepted a Digital Signature Certificate if he publishes or authorises its publication: (a) to one or more persons: (b) in a repository, or if he otherwise demonstrates his approval in any manner. **Subscriber representation**. By accepting a Digital Signature Certificate the subscriber certifies to all who reasonably rely on the information contained therein that— (a) he holds the private key corresponding to the public key listed in the Digital Signature Certificate and is entitled to hold the same; (b) all his representations to the Certifying Authority and all material relevant information contained in the Certificate are true; (c) all information in the Certificate that is within his knowledge is true.
Control of Private Key	Every subscriber must exercise reasonable care to retain control of the private key corresponding to the public key listed in his Digital Signature Certificate and take all steps to prevent its disclosure [Sec 42(1)]
Communication	If the private key corresponding to the public key listed in the Digital Signature Certificate has been compromised, then, the subscriber must communicate the same without any delay to the Certifying Authority in the prescribed manner. He shall be liable till he has so communicated. [Sec 42(2)].
Prescribed Duties	In respect of Electronic Signature Certificate the subscriber must perform such duties as may be prescribed [Section 40A].

32.0 WHAT IS THE PENALTY FOR DAMAGE TO COMPUTER, COMPUTER SYSTEM. ETC? [SEC. 43]

A person shall be liable to pay damages by way of compensation **not exceeding Rs 1 crore** to the person so affected, if he without permission of the owner or any other person who is incharge of a computer, computer system or computer network.

(a) accesses or secures access to such computer, computer system or computer network, or computer resource;

(b) downloads, copies or extracts any data, computer database or information from such computer, computer system or computer network including information or data held or stored in any removable storage medium;

(c) introduces or causes to be introduced any computer contaminant or computer virus into any computer, computer system or computer network.

(d) damages or causes to be damaged any computer, computer system or computer network, data, computer database or any other programmes residing in such computer, computer system or computer network;

(e) disrupts or causes disruption of any computer, computer system or computer network;

(f) denies or causes the denial of access to any person authorised to access any computer, computer system or computer network by any means;

(g) provides any assistance to any person to facilitate access to a computer, computer system or computer network in contravention of the provisions of this Act, rules or regulations made thereunder;

(h) charges the services availed of by a person to the account of another person by tampering with a manipulating any computer, computer system, or computer network.

(i) destroys, deletes or alters any information residing in a computer resource or diminishes its value or utility or affects it injuriously by any means.

(j) Steals, conceals, destroys or alters or causes any person to steal, conceal, destroy or alter any computer source code used for a computer resource with an intention to cause damage.

Explanation—For the purposes of this Section—

(i) "**computer contaminant**" **means** any set of computer instructions that are designed—

(a) to modify, destroy, record, transmit data or programme residing within a computer, computer system or computer network; or

(b) by any means to disturbt the normal operation of the computer, computer system, or computer network;

(ii) "**computer database**" **means** a representation of information, knowledge, facts, concepts or instructions in text, image, audio, video that are being prepared or have been prepared in a formalised manner or have been produced by a computer, computer system or computer network and are intended for use in a computer, computer system or computer network;

(iii) "**computer virus**" **means** any computer instruction, information, data or programme that destroys, damages, degrades or adversely affects the performance of a computer resource or attaches itself to another computer resource and operates when a programme, data or instruction is executed or some other event takes place in that computer resource;

(iv) "**damage**" **means** to destroy, alter, delete, add, modify or rearrange any computer resource by any means.

(v) **"Computer Source code"** means the listing of programmes, computer commands, design and layout and programme analysis of computer resource in any form.

33.0 COMPENSATION FOR FAILURE TO PROTECT DATA

Where a body corporate, possessing, dealing or handling any sensitive personal data or information in a computer resource which it owns, controls or operates, is negligent in implementing and maintaining reasonable security practices and procedures and thereby causes wrongful loss or wrongful gain to any person, such body corporate shall be liable to pay damages by way of compensation, to the person so affected.

Explanation: For the purposes of this section

(i) **"body corporate"** means any company and includes a firm, sole proprietorship or other association of individuals engaged in commercial or professional activities

(ii) **"reasonable security practices and procedures"** means security practices and procedures designed to protect such information from unauthorized access, damage, use, modification, disclosure or impairment, as may be specified in an agreement between the parties or as may be specified in any law for the time being in force and in the absence of such agreement or any law, such reasonable security practices and procedures, as may be prescribed by the Central Government in consultation with such professional bodies or associations as it may deem fit.

(iii) **"sensitive personal data or information"** means such personal information as may be prescribed by the Central Government in consultation with such professional bodies or associations as it may deem fit.

Section 46 confers the power to adjudicate contravention under the Act to an officer not below than the rank of a Director to the Government of India or an equivalent officer of a State Government. Such appointment shall be made by the Central Government. In order to be eligible for appointment as an adjudicating officer, a person must possess adequate experience in the field of Information Technology and such legal or judicial experience as may be prescribed by the Central Government. The adjudicating officer so appointed shall be responsible for holding an inquiry in the prescribed manner after giving reasonable opportunity of being heard and thereafter, imposing penalty where required.

34.0 PENALTY FOR DEFAULTS [SEC 44 AND SEC 45]

Default	*Maximum Penalty*
1. *For failure to furnish any document, return or report to the Controller or the Certifying Authority [Sec. 44(a)]*	Rs 1,50,000 for each default
2. *For failure to file any return or furnish any information, books or other documents within the specified time [Sec. 44(b)]*	Rs 5,000 for every day during which such failure continues
3. *For failure to maintain books of account or records [Sec. 44(c)]*	Rs 10,000 for every day during which the failure continues
4. *For the contravention of any rules or regulations for which no specific penalty has been separately provided [Sec. 45]*	The person who contravens shall be liable to pay a compensation not exceeding Rs 25,000 to the person affected by such contravention or a penalty not exceeding Rs 25,000

35.0 ADJUDICATION [SEC 46 AND SEC 47]

35.1 Who can be Appointed Adjudicating Officer? [Sec. 46(1)]

For the purpose of adjudging whether any person has committed a contravention of any of the provisions of this Act or of any rule, regulation, direction or order made thereunder the Central Government shall appoint any officer (a) who is not below the rank of a Director to the Government of India or an equivalent officer of a State

Government (b) who possesses such experience in the field of Information Technology and legal or judicial experience as may be prescribed by the Central Government.

Where more than one adjudicating officers are appointed, the Central Government shall specify by order the matters and places with respect to which such officers shall exercise their jurisdiction.

The adjudicating officer appointed u/s46 (1) shall exercise jurisdiction to adjudicate matters in which the claim for injury or damage does not exceed Rs. 5 crores.

Provided that the jurisdiction in respect of claim for injury or damage exceeding Rs. 5 crores shall vest with the competent court Sec. 46 (1A)

35.2 What are the Powers of Adjudicating Officer? [Sec. 46(2), Sec. 46(5)]

(a) The adjudicating officer shall, after giving the person referred to above, give a reasonable opportunity for making representation in the matter and if, on such inquiry, he is satisfied that the person has committed the contravention, he may impose such penalty or award such compensation as he thinks fit in accordance with the provisions of that Section.

(b) Every adjudicating officer shall have the powers of a civil court which are conferred on the Cyber Appellate Tribunal under sub-section (2) of Section 58, and—

- (i) all proceedings before it shall be deemed to be judicial proceedings within the meaning of Sections 193 and 228 of the Indian Penal Code, 1860:
- (ii) shall be deemed to be civil court for the purposes of Sections 345 and 346 of the Code of Criminal Procedure, 1973.
- (iii) shall be deemed to be a Civil Court for purposes of order XXI of the Civil Procedure Code, 1908.

35.3 What are the Factors to be taken into account by the Adjudicating Officer? (Sec. 47)

While adjudging the quantum of compensation the adjudicating officer shall have due regard to the following factors, namely:

(a) the amount of gain of unfair advantage, wherever quantifiable, made as a result of the default;

(b) the amount of loss caused to any person as a result of the default;

(c) the repetitive nature of the default.

36.0 THE CYBER REGULATIONS APPELLATE TRIBUNAL

36.1 Who can establish Cyber Appellate Tribunal? [Sec. 48]

The Central Government shall, by notification, establish one or more appellate tribunals to be known as the Cyber Regulations Appellate Tribunal. It shall also specify, in the notification the matters and places in relation to which the Cyber Appellate Tribunal may exercise jurisdiction.

36.2 Composition of Cyber Appellate Tribunal [section 49]

(1) The Cyber Appellate Tribunal shall consist of a Chairperson and such number of other Members, as the Central Government may, by notification in the Official Gazette, appoint.

(2) The selection of Chairperson and Members of the Cyber Appellate Tribunal shall be made by the Central Government in consultation with the Chief Justice of India.

(3) Subject to the provisions of this Act-

(a) the jurisdiction, powers and authority of the Cyber Appellate Tribunal may be exercised by the Benches thereof

(b) a Bench may be constituted by the Chairperson of the Cyber Appellate Tribunal with one or two members of such Tribunal as the Chairperson may deem fit.

Provided that every Bench shall be presided over by the Chairperson or the Judicial Member appointed u/s 50(3).

(c) the Benches of the Cyber Appellate Tribunal shall sit at New Delhi and at such other places as the Central Government may, in consultation with the Chairperson of the Cyber Appellate Tribunal, by notification in the Official Gazette, specify.

(d) the Central Government shall, by notification in the Official Gazette, specify the areas in relation to which each Bench of the Cyber Appellate Tribunal may exercise its jurisdiction

(4) Notwithstanding anything contained in sub-section (3), the Chairperson of the Cyber Appellate Tribunal may transfer a Member of such Tribunal from one Bench to another Bench

(5) If at any stage of the hearing of any case or matter, it appears to the Chairperson or a Member of the Cyber Appellate Tribunal that the case or matter is of such a nature that it ought to be heard by a Bench consisting of more Members, the case or matter may be transferred by the Chairperson to such Bench as the Chairperson may deem fit.

36.3 Qualifications for Appointment as Chairperson and Members of Cyber Appellate Tribunal [section 50]

(1) A person shall not be qualified for appointment as a Chairperson of the Cyber Appellate Tribunal unless he is, or has been, or is qualified to be, a Judge of a High Court;

(2) The Members of the Cyber Appellate Tribunal, except the Judicial Member to be appointed u/s 50 (3), shall be appointed by the Central Government from amongst persons, having special knowledge of and professional experience in, information technology, telecommunication, industry, management or consumer affairs. Provided that a person shall not be appointed as a Member, unless he is, or has been, in the service of the Central Government or a State Government, and has held the post of Additional secretary to the Government of India or any equivalent post in the Central Government or State Government for a period of at least two years or joint secretary to the Government of India or any equivalent post in the Central Government or State Government for a period of at least seven years.

(3) The Judicial Members of the Cyber Appellate Tribunal shall be appointed by the Central Government from amongst persons who is or has been a member of the Indian Legal Service and has held the post of Additional Secretary for a period of not less than one year or Grade I post of that service for a period of not less than five years.

36.4 Term of Office, Conditions of Service etc of Chairperson and Members [Section 51]

(1) The Chairperson or Member of the Cyber Appellate Tribunal shall hold office for a term of 5 years from the date on which he enters upon his office or until he attains the age of 65 years, whichever is earlier.

(2) Before appointing any person as the Chairperson or Member of the Cyber Appellate Tribunal, the Central Government shall satisfy itself that the person does not have any such financial or other interest as is likely to affect prejudicially his functions as such Chairperson or Member.

(3) An officer of the Central Government or State Government on his selection as the Chairperson or Member of the Cyber Appellate Tribunal, as the case may be, shall have to retire from service before joining as such Chairperson or Member.

36.5 Salary, Allowance and other Terms and Conditions of Service of Chairperson and Member [Section 52]

The salary and allowances payable to, and the other terms and conditions of service including pension, gratuity and other retirement benefits of, the Chairperson or a Member of Cyber Appellate Tribunal shall be such as may be prescribed.

36.6 Powers of Superintendence, Direction, etc [Section 52A]

The Chairperson of he Cyber Appellate Tribunal shall have powers of general superintendence and directions in the conduct of the affairs of that Tribunal and he shall, in addition to presiding over the meetings of the Tribunal, exercise and discharge such powers and functions of the Tribunal as may be prescribed.

36.7 Distribution of Business among Benches [Section 52B]

Where Benches are constituted, the Chairperson of the Cyber Appellate Tribunal may, by order, distribute the business of that Tribunal amongst the Benches and also the matters to be dealt with by each Bench.

36.8 Powers of the Chairperson to transfer cases [Section 52C]

On the application of any of the parties and after notice to the parties, and after hearing such of them as he may deem proper to be heard, or suo motu without such notice, the Chairperson of the Cyber Appellate Tribunal may transfer any case pending before one Bench, for disposal to any other Bench.

36.9 Decision by majority [Section 52D]

If the Members of a Bench consisting of two Members differ in opinion on any point, they shall state the point or points on which they differ, and make a reference to the Chairperson of the Cyber Appellate Tribunal who shall hear the point or points himself and such point or points shall be decided according to the opinion of the majority of the Members who have heard the case, including those who first heard it.

36.10 Filling up of Vacancies [Section 53]

Sec. 53 provides that in the situation of any vacancy occurring in the office of the Presiding officer of Cyber Regulations Tribunal, the Central Government shall appoint another person in accordance with the provisions of this Act.

If, for reason other than temporary absence, any vacancy occurs in the office of the Chairperson or Member as the case may be of a Cyber Appellate Tribunal, then the Central Government shall appoint another person in accordance with the provisions of this Act to fill the vacancy and the proceedings may be continued before the Cyber Appellate Tribunal from the stage at which the vacancy is filled.

36.11 Resignation and Removal [Section 54]

(1) The Chairperson or Member of the Cyber Appellate Tribunal may, by notice in writing under his hand addressed to the Central Government, resign his office:

However, the said Chairperson or Member shall, unless he is permitted by the Central Government to relinquish his office sooner, continue to hold office until the expiry of three months from the date of receipt of such notice or until a person duly appointed as his successor enters upon his office or until the expiry of his term of office, whichever is the earliest.

(2) The Chairperson or Member of a Cyber Appellate Tribunal shall not be removed from his office except by an order by the Central Government on the ground of proved misbehaviour or incapacity after an inquiry made by a Judge of the Supreme Court in which the Chairperson or Member concerned has been informed of the charges against him and given a reasonable opportunity of being heard in respect of these charges.

(3) The Central Government may, by rules, regulate the procedure for the investigation of misbehaviour or incapacity of the aforesaid Chairperson or Member.

36.12 Orders constituting Appellate Tribunal to be final and not to invalidate its proceedings [Section 55]

No order of the Central Government appointing any person as the Chairperson or Member of a Cyber Appellate Tribunal shall be called in question in any manner and no act or proceeding before a Cyber Appellate Tribunal shall be called in question in any manner on the ground merely of any defect in the constitution of a Cyber Appellate Tribunal.

36.13 Staff of the Cyber Appellate Tribunal [Section 56]

(1) The Central Government shall provide the Cyber Appellate Tribunal with such officers and employees as the Government may think fit.

(2) The officers and employees of the Cyber Appellate Tribunal shall discharge their functions under general superintendence of the Presiding Officer.

(3) The salaries and allowances and other conditions of service of the officers and employees of the Cyber Appellate Tribunal shall be such as may be prescribed by the Central Government.

37.0 WHAT ARE THE PROVISIONS RELATING TO AN APPEAL TO CYBER REGULATIONS APPELLATE TRIBUNAL? [SEC. 57]

Who can	Any person aggrieved by an order made by Controller or an adjudicating officer under this Act may prefer an appeal to a Cyber Appellate Tribunal having jurisdiction in the manner. However no appeal shall lie from an order made by an adjudicating officer with the consent of the parties [sec. 57(1) & (2)]
Period	Every appeal shall be filed within a period of **45 days** from the date on which a copy of the order made by the Controller or the adjudicating officer is received by the person aggrieved and it shall be in such form and be accompanied by such fee as may be prescribed. However, the Cyber Appellate Tribunal may entertain an appeal after the expiry of the said period of forty-five days if it is satisfied that there was sufficient cause for not filing it within that period.
Opportunity	On receipt of an appeal, the Cyber Appellate Tribunal may, after giving the parties to the appeal, an opportunity of being

	heard, pass such orders thereon as it thinks fit, confirming modifying, or setting aside the order appealed against.
Time Limit for Disposal	The appeal shall be dealt with by it as expeditiously as possible and endeavour shall be made by it to dispose of the appeal finally **within 6 months** from the date of receipt of the appeal.
Duty to Send a Copy of Order	The Cyber Appellate Tribunal shall send a copy of every order made by it to the parties to the appeal and to the concerned controller or adjudicating officer.
Who can Present case	The appellant may either appear in person or authorise one or more legal practitioners or any of its officers to present his or its case before the Cyber Appellate Tribunal.

38.0 WHAT ARE THE PROVISIONS RELATING TO PROCEDURE AND POWER OF THE CYBER APPELLATE TRIBUNAL? [SEC. 58]

Is CRAT Bound by CPC ?	The Cyber Appellate Tribunal shall not be bound by the procedure laid down by the Code of Civil Procedure, 1908. It shall however, be guided by the principles of natural justice, provisions of the Act and rules made thereunder. Natural justice means to act in good faith, fairly, justly and impartially and never arbitrarily. It shall have powers to regulate its own procedure including the place at which it shall have its sittings.
Powers	The Cyber Appellate Tribunal shall have, for the purpose of discharging its functions under this Act, the same powers as are vested in a civil court the Code of Civil Procedure, 1908, while trying a suit in respect of the following matters, namely: (a) summoning and enforcing the attendance of any person and examining him on oath: (b) requiring the discovery and production of documents of other electronic records; (c) receiving evidence on affidavits; (d) issuing commission for the examination of witnesses of documents; (e) reviewing its decisions; (f) dismissing an application for default or deciding it *ex-parte*; (g) any other matter which may be prescribed.
Nature of Proceeding	Every proceeding before the Cyber Appellate Tribunal shall be deemed to be a judicial proceeding within the meaning of Sections 193 and 228, and for the purposes of Section 196 of the Indian Penal Code.
Nature of CRAT	The Cyber Appellate Tribunal shall be deemed to be a civil court for the purposes of Section 195 and Chapter XXVI of the Code of Criminal Procedure, 1973.

39.0 SHALL A CIVIL COURT HAVE JURISDICTION? [SEC. 61]

No Court shall have jurisdiction	to entertain any suit or proceeding in respect of any matter which an adjudicating officer appointed under this Act or the Cyber Appellate Tribunal constituted under this Act is empowered by or under this Act to determine; and

No Injunction	No Injunction shall be granted by any court or other authority in respect of any action taken or to be taken in pursuance of any power conferred by or under this Act. Injunction is a specific order of the court directing the defendant to refrain from doing certain act. Provided that the court may exercise jurisdiction in cases where the claim for injury or damage suffered by any person exceeds the maximum amount which can be awarded under this Chapter.
Appeal Against the Order of CRAT	Any person aggrieved by any decision or order of the Cyber Appellate Tribunal may file an appeal to the High Court within **60 days** from the date of communication of the decision or order of the Cyber Appellate Tribunal to him on any question of fact or law arising out of such order. However, the High Court may, if it is satisfied that the appellant was prevented by sufficient cause from filling the appeal within the said period allow it to be filed within a further period not exceeding 60 days.

40.0 WHAT ARE THE PROVISIONS RELATING TO COMPOUNDING OF CONTRAVENTIONS? [SEC. 63]

Power to Compound	Any contravention under the Act may, either before or after the institution of adjudication proceedings, be compounded by the Controller or such other officer as may be specially authorized by him in this behalf or by the adjudicating officer, as the case may be subject to such conditions he may impose.
Maximum Penalty	The compounded sum shall not in any case, exceed the maximum amount of the penalty which may be imposed under this Act for the contravention so compounded. **Exception.** The above provisions shall not apply to a person who commits the same or similar contravention within a period of 3 years from the date on which the first contravention committed by him, was compounded. **Explanation.** For the purposes of this Section, any second or subsequent contravention committed after the expiry of a period of 3 years from the date on which the contravention was previously compounded shall be deemed to be a first contravention.
No Further Proceeding	Where any contravention has been compounded, no proceeding or further proceeding as the case may be, shall be taken against the person guilty of such contravention in respect of the contravention so compounded.

41.0 HOW CAN PENALTY BE RECOVERED? [SEC. 64]

A penalty imposed under this Act, if it is not paid, shall be recovered as an arrear of land revenue and the licence or the Digital Signature Certificate, as the case may be, shall be suspended till the penalty is paid.

42.0 WHAT ARE THE PROVISIONS RELATING TO TAMPERING WITH COMPUTER SOURCE DOCUMENTS? [SEC. 65]

If any person knowingly, or intentionally conceals, destroys or alters or intentionally or knowingly causes another to conceal, destroy or alter any computer source code used for a computer. Computer programme computer system or computer network, when the computer source code is required to be kept or maintained by law for the time being in force, he shall be punishable **with imprisonment up to 3 years, or with fine up to Rs 2,00,000 or with both.**

Explanation—For the purposes of this Section, "computer source code" means the listing of programmes, computer commands design and layout and programme analysis of computer resource in any form.

43.0 WHAT ARE THE PROVISIONS RELATING TO COMPUTER RELATED OFFENCES ? [SECTION 66]

If any person, dishonestly, or fraudulently, does any act referred to in section 43, he shall be punishable with imprisonment for a term which may extend to two 3 years or with fine which may extend to Rs. 5 Lakhs or with both.

Explanation: For the purpose of this section,- the word "dishonestly" and the word "fraudulently" shall have the meaning assigned to u/s 24 and 25 of IPC respectively.

43.1 Punishment for sending offensive messages through communication service, etc. [Section 66A]

Any person who sends, by means of a computer resource or a communication device,-

(a) any **information** that is grossly offensive or has menacing character; or

(b) any **information** which he knows to be false, but for the purpose of causing annoyance, inconvenience, danger, obstruction, insult, injury, criminal intimidation, enmity, hatred, or ill will, persistently **by making** use of such computer resource or a communication device,

(c) any electronic mail or electronic mail message for the purpose of causing annoyance or inconvenience or to deceive or to mislead the addressee or recipient about the origin of such messages shall be punishable with imprisonment for a term which may extend to three years and with fine.

Explanation : For the purposes of this section, terms "Electronic mail" and "Electronic Mail Message" means a message or information created or transmitted or received on a computer, computer system, computer resource or communication device including attachments in text, image, audio, video and any other electronic record, which may be transmitted with the message.

43.2 Punishment for dishonestly receiving stolen computer resource or communication device [Section 66B]

Whoever dishonestly receives or retains any stolen computer resource or communication device knowing or having reason to believe the same to be stolen computer resource or communication device, shall be punished with imprisonment of either description for a term which may extend to three years or with fine which may extend to Rs. 1 lakh or with both.

43.3 Punishment for identity theft [Section 66C]

Whoever, fraudulently or dishonestly make use of the electronic signature, password or any other unique identification feature of any other person, shall be punished with imprisonment of either description for a term which may extend to three years and shall also be liable to fine which may extend to Rs. 1 lakh.

43.4 Punishment for cheating by personation by using computer resource [Section 66D]

Whoever, by means of any communication device or computer resource cheats by personation, shall be punished with imprisonment of either description for a term which may extend to three years and shall also be liable to fine which may extend to Rs. 1 lakh rupees.

43.5 Punishment for violation of privacy [Section 66E]

Whoever, intentionally or knowingly captures, publishes or transmits the image of a private area of any person without his or her consent, under circumstances violating the privacy of that person, shall be punished with imprisonment which may extend to three years or with fine not exceeding two lakh rupees, or with both

Explanation - For the purposes of this section--

(a) **"transmit"** means to electronically send a visual image with the intent that it be viewed by a person or persons;

(b) **"capture"**, with respect to an image, means to videotape, photograph, film or record by any means;

(c) **"private area"** means the naked or undergarment clad genitals, pubic area, buttocks or female breast;

(d) **"publishes"** means reproduction in the printed or electronic form and making it available for public;

(e) **"under circumstances violating privacy"** means circumstances in which a person can have a reasonable expectation that--

(i) he or she could disrobe in privacy, without being concerned that an image of his private area was being captured; or

(ii) any part of his or her private area would not be visible to the public, regardless of whether that person is in a public or private place.

43.6 Punishment for cyber terrorism [Section 66F]

(1) Whoever,-

(A) with intent to threaten the unity, integrity, security or sovereignty of India or to strike terror in the people or any section of the people by –

(i) denying or cause the denial of access to any person authorized to access computer resource; or

(ii) attempting to penetrate or access a computer resource without authorisation or exceeding authorized access; or

(iii) introducing or causing to introduce any Computer Contaminant and by means of such conduct causes or is likely to cause death or injuries to persons or damage to or destruction of property or disrupts or knowing that it is likely to cause damage or disruption of supplies or services essential to the life of the community or adversely affect the critical information infrastructure specified u/s 70, or

(B) knowingly or intentionally penetrates or accesses a computer resource without authorization or exceeding authorized access, and by means of such conduct obtains access to information, data or computer database that is restricted for reasons of the security of the State or foreign relations; or any restricted information, data or computer database, with reasons to believe that such information, data or computer database so obtained may be used to cause or likely to cause injury to the interests of the sovereignty and integrity of India, the security of the State, friendly relations with foreign States, public order, decency or morality, or in relation to contempt of court, defamation or incitement to an offence, or to the advantage of any foreign nation, group of individuals or otherwise, commits the offence of cyber terrorism.

(2) Whoever commits or conspires to commit cyber terrorism shall be punishable with imprisonment which may extend to imprisonment for life'.

44.0 WHAT ARE THE PROVISIONS RELATING TO PUBLISHING OF INFORMATION WHICH IS OBSCENE IN ELECTRONIC FORM? [SEC. 67]

Whoever publishes or transmits or causes to be published in the electronic form, any material which is lascivious or appeals to the prurient interest or if its effect is such as to tend to deprave and corrupt persons who are likely, having regard to all relevant circumstances, to read, see or hear the matter contained or embodied in it, shall be punished. On first conviction he shall be punishable with imprisonment up to 3 years and with fine up to Rs 5,00,000 rupees. In the event of a second or subsequent conviction he shall be punishable with imprisonment up to 5 years and also with fine up to Rs 10,00,000.

Important to Note—It is only the publishing or transmitting of obscenity which is an offence, and not its possession.

44.1 Punishment for Publishing or Transmitting of Material Containing Sexually Explicit Act, etc. in Electronic form [Section 67A]

Whoever publishes or transmits or causes to be published or transmitted in the electronic form any material which contains sexually explicit act or conduct shall be punished on first conviction with imprisonment of either description for a term which may extend to **5** years and with fine which may extend to Rs. 10 Lakhs and in the event of second or subsequent conviction with imprisonment of either description for a term which may extend to **7 years** and also with fine which may extend to Rs. 10 Lakhs.

Exception: This section and Sec. 67 does not extend to any book, pamphlet, paper, writing, drawing, painting, representation or figure in electronic form-

(i) the publication of which is proved to be justified as being for the public good on the ground that such book, pamphlet, paper, writing, drawing, painting, representation or figure is in the interest of science, literature, art, or learning or other objects of general concern; or (ii) which is kept or used bona fide for religious purposes.

44.2 Punishment for Publishing or Transmitting of Material Depicting Children in Sexually Explicit Act, etc. in Electronic form [Section 67B]

Whoever,-

(a) publishes or transmits or causes to be published or transmitted material in any electronic form which depicts children engaged in sexually explicit act or conduct or

(b) creates text or digital images, collects, seeks, browses, downloads, advertises, promotes, exchanges or distributes material in any electronic form depicting children in obscene or indecent or sexually explicit manner or

(c) cultivates, entices or induces children to online relationship with one or more children for and on sexually explicit act or in a manner that may offend a reasonable adult on the computer resource or

(d) facilitates abusing children online or

(e) records in any electronic form own abuse or that of others pertaining to sexually explicit act with children, shall be punished on first conviction with imprisonment of either description for a term which may extend to five years and with a fine which may extend to ten lakh rupees and in the event of second or subsequent conviction with imprisonment of either description for a term which may extend to seven years and also with fine which may extend to ten lakh rupees:

Provided that the provisions of Sec. 67 and Sec. 67A and this section does not extend to any book, pamphlet, paper, writing, drawing, painting, representation or figure in electronic form-

(i) The publication of which is proved to be justified as being for the public good on the ground that such book, pamphlet, paper writing, drawing, painting, representation or figure is in the interest of science, literature, art or learning or other objects of general concern; or

(ii) which is kept or used for bonafide heritage or religious purposes

Explanation : For the purposes of this section, "children" means a person who has not completed the age of 18 years.

45.0 PRESERVATION AND RETENTION OF INFORMATION BY INTERMEDIARIES [SECTION 67 C]

(1) Intermediary shall preserve and retain such information as may be specified for such duration and in such manner and format as the Central Government may prescribe.

(2) Any intermediary who intentionally or knowingly contravenes the provisions of sub section (1) shall be punished with an imprisonment for a term which may extend to three years and shall also be liable to fine.

46.0 POWER OF CONTROLLER TO GIVE DIRECTIONS [SECTION 68]

Section 68 provides that the controller may give directions to a Certifying Authority or any employee of such authority to take such measures or cease carrying on such activities as specified in the order, so as to ensure compliance with this law. If any person fails to comply, he shall be liable to imprisonment upto 3 years or fine upto Rs.2 lakhs, or both. As per ITAA 2008, Sec. 68 is given as under:

(1) The Controller may, by order, direct a Certifying Authority or any employee of such Authority to take such measures or cease carrying on such activities as specified in the order if those are necessary to ensure compliance with the provisions of this Act, rules or any regulations made there under.

(2) Any person who **intentionally or knowingly** fails to comply with any order u/s 68(1) shall be guilty of an offence and shall be liable on conviction to imprisonment for a term not exceeding two years or to a fine not exceeding one lakh rupees or to both.

47.0 POWERS TO ISSUE DIRECTIONS FOR INTERCEPTION OR MONITORING OR DECRYPTION OF ANY INFORMATION THROUGH ANY COMPUTER RESOURCE [SECTION 69]

Section 69 empowers the Controller, it he is satisfied that it is necessary or expedient so to do in the interest of sovereignty and integrity of India, security of the

State, friendly relation with foreign states or public order, to intercept any information transmitted through any computer system or computer network. As per ITAA 2008, Sec. 69 is given as follows:

(1) Where the central Government or a State Government or any of its officer specially authorized by the Central Government or the State Government, as the case may be, in this behalf may, if is satisfied that it is necessary or expedient to do in the interest of the sovereignty or integrity of India, defense of India, security of the State, friendly relations with foreign States or public order or for preventing incitement to the commission of any cognizable offence relating to above or for investigation of any offence, it may, subject to the provisions of u/s 69 (2), for reasons to be recorded in writing, by order, direct any agency of the appropriate Government to intercept, monitor or decrypt or cause to be intercepted or monitored or decrypted any information transmitted received or stored through any computer resource.

(2) The Procedure and safeguards subject to which such interception or monitoring or decryption may be carried out, shall be such as may be prescribed.

(3) The subscriber or intermediary or any person in charge of the computer resource shall, when called upon by any agency which has been directed u/s 69 (1), extend all facilities and technical assistance to -

   (a) provide access to **or secure access to** the computer resource generating, transmitting, receiving or storing such information; or

   (b) intercept or monitor or decrypt the information, **as the case may be**; or

   (c) provide information stored in computer resource.

(4) The subscriber or intermediary or any person who fails to assist the agency referred to in u/s 69 (3) shall be punished with an imprisonment for a term which may extend to seven years and shall also be liable to fine.

48.0 POWER TO ISSUE DIRECTIONS FOR BLOCKING FOR PUBLIC ACCESS OF ANY INFORMATION THROUGH ANY COMPUTER RESOURCE [SECTION 69A]

(1) Where the Central Government or any of its officer specially authorized by it in this behalf is satisfied that it is necessary or expedient so to do in the interest of sovereignty and integrity of India, defense of India, security of the State, friendly relations with foreign states or public order or for preventing incitement to the commission of any cognizable offence relating to above, it may subject to the provisions of u/s 69A (2) for reasons to be recorded in writing, by order direct any agency of the Government or intermediary to block access by the public or cause to be blocked for access by public any information generated, transmitted, received, stored or hosted in any computer resource.

(2) The procedure and safeguards subject to which such blocking for access by the public may be carried out shall be such as may be prescribed.

(3) The intermediary who fails to comply with the direction issued u/s 69A (1) shall be punished with an imprisonment for a term which may extend to seven years and also be liable to fine.

49.0 POWER TO AUTHORIZE TO MONITOR AND COLLECT TRAFFIC DATA OR INFORMATION THROUGH ANY COMPUTER RESOURCE FOR CYBER SECURITY [SECTION 69B]

(1) The Central Government may, to enhance Cyber Security and for identification, analysis and prevention of any intrusion or spread of computer contaminant in the country, by notification in the official Gazette, authorize any agency of the

Government to monitor and collect traffic data or information generated, transmitted, received or stored in any computer resource.

(2) The Intermediary or any person in-charge of the Computer resource shall when called upon by the agency which has been authorized u/s 69B (1), provide technical assistance and extend all facilities to such agency to enable online access or to secure and provide online access to the computer resource generating, transmitting, receiving or storing such traffic data or information.

(3) The procedure and safeguards for monitoring and collecting traffic data or information, shall be such as may be prescribed.

(4) Any intermediary who intentionally or knowingly contravenes the provisions of u/s 69B (2) shall be punished with an imprisonment for a term which may extend to 3 years and shall also be liable to fine.

Explanation : For the purposes of this section,

(i) **"Computer Contaminant"** shall have the meaning assigned to it in Sec. 43

(ii) **"traffic data"** means any data identifying or purporting to identify any person, computer system or computer network or location to or from which the communication is or may be transmitted and includes communications origin, destination, route, time, date, size, duration or type of underlying service or any other information.

50.0 PROTECTED SYSTEM [SECTION 70]

Sec.70 empowers the appropriate Government to declare by notification any computer, computer system or computer network to be a protected system. Any unauthorized access of such systems will be punishable with imprisonment which may extend to ten years or with fine.

(1) The appropriate Government may, by notification in the Official Gazette, declare any computer resource which directly or indirectly affects the facility of Critical Information Infrastructure, to be a protected system.

Explanation : For the purposes of this section, "Critical Information Infrastructure" means the computer resource, the incapacitation or destruction of which , shall have debilitating impact on national security, economy, public health or safety.

(2) The appropriate Government may, by order in writing, authorize the persons who are authorized to access protected systems notified u/s 70(1)

(3) Any person who secures access or attempts to secure access to a protected system in contravention of the provisions of this section shall be punished with imprisonment of either description for a term which may extend to ten years and shall also be liable to fine.

(4) The Central Government shall prescribe the information security practices and procedures for such protected system.

51.0 NATIONAL NODAL AGENCY [SECTION 70A]

(1) The Central Government may, by notification published in the official Gazette, designate any organization of the Government as the national nodal agency in respect of Critical Information Infrastructure Protection.

(2) The national nodal agency designated u/s 70A (1) shall be responsible for all measures including Research and Development relating to protection of Critical Information Infrastructure.

(3) The manner of performing functions and duties of the agency referred to in sub-section (1) shall be such as may be prescribed.

52.0 INDIAN COMPUTER EMERGENCY RESPONSE TEAM TO SERVE AS NATIONAL AGENCY FOR INCIDENT RESPONSE [SECTION 70B]

(1) The Central Government shall, by notification in the Official Gazette, appoint an agency of the government to be called the Indian Computer Emergency Response Team.

(2) The Central Government shall provide the agency referred to in u/s 70B (1) with a Director General and such other officers and employees as may be prescribed.

(3) The salary and allowances and terms and conditions of the Director General and other officers and employees shall be such as may be prescribed.

(4) The Indian Computer Emergency Response Team shall serve as the national agency for performing the following functions in the area of Cyber Security,-

- (a) collection, analysis and dissemination of information on cyber incidents
- (b) forecast and alerts of cyber security incidents
- (c) emergency measures for handling cyber security incidents
- (d) coordination of cyber incidents response activities
- (e) issue guidelines, advisories, vulnerability notes and white papers relating to information security practices, procedures, prevention, response and reporting of cyber incidents
- (f) such other functions relating to cyber security as may be prescribed

(5) The manner of performing functions and duties of the agency referred to in u/s 70B (1) shall be such as may be prescribed.

(6) For carrying out the provisions of u/s 70B (4), the agency referred to in u/s 70B (1) may call for information and give direction to the service providers, intermediaries, data centers, body corporate and any other person

(7) Any service provider, intermediaries, data centers, body corporate or person who fails to provide the information called for or comply with the direction u/s 70B (6), shall be punishable with imprisonment for a term which may extend to 1 year or with fine which may extend to Rs. 1 lakh or with both.

(8) No Court shall take cognizance of any offence under this section, except on a complaint made by an officer authorized in this behalf by the agency referred to in u/s 70B (1).

53.0 WHAT IS THE PENALTY FOR MISREPRESENTATION? [SEC.71]

Whoever makes any misrepresentation to, or suppresses any material fact from, the Controller or the Certifying Authority for obtaining any licence or Digital Signature Certificate, as the case may be, shall be punished with imprisonment for a term upto 2 years, *or* with fine upto Rs 1,00,000 *or* with both.

54.0 WHAT IS THE PENALTY FOR BREACH OF CONFIDENTIALITY AND PRIVACY? [SEC. 72]

If any person who, in pursuance of any of the powers conferred under this Act, rules or regulations made thereunder, has secured access to any electronic record, book, register, correspondence, information, documents or other material without the consent of the person concerned, discloses such electronic record, book, register, correspondence, information, document or other material to any other person he shall be punished with imprisonment for a term upto 2 years, *or* with fine upto Rs 1,00,000 *or* with both.

55.0 PUNISHMENT FOR DISCLOSURE OF INFORMATION IN BREACH OF LAWFUL CONTRACT [SECTION 72A]

Save as otherwise provided in this Act or any other law for the time being in force, any person including an intermediary who, while providing services under the terms of lawful contract, has secured access to any material containing personal information about another person, with the intent to cause or knowing that he is likely to cause wrongful loss or wrongful gain discloses, without the consent of the person concerned, or in breach of a lawful contract, such material to any other person shall be punished with imprisonment for a term which may extend to three years, or with a fine which may extend to five lakh rupees, or with both.

56.0 WHAT IS THE PENALTY FOR PUBLISHING FALSE ELECTRONIC SIGNATURE CERTIFICATE ? [SEC. 73]

Probibition	No person shall publish a Electronic Signature Certificate or otherwise make it available to any other person with the knowledge that— (a) it has not been issued by the Certifying Authority, or (b) it has not been accepted by the subscriber; or (c) the certificate has been revoked or suspended.
Exception to Sec. 73	The above provision shall not apply if the publication is for the purpose of verifying a digital signature created prior to such suspension or revocation.
Penalty	Any person, who contravenes the above provisions, shall be punished with imprisonment for a term upto 2 years, *or* with fine upto Rs 1,00,000 *or* with both.

57.0 WHAT IS THE PENALTY FOR PUBLICATION FOR FRAUDULENT PURPOSES? [SEC. 74]

Whosoever knowingly creates, publishes or otherwise makes available a Digital Signature Certificate for any fraudulent or unlawful purpose shall be punished with **imprisonment for a term upto 2 years, *or* with fine upto Rs 1,00,000 *or* with both.**

58.0 SHALL THE PROVISIONS OF THE IT ACT APPLY FOR OFFENCE OR CONTRAVENTION COMMITTED OUTSIDE INDIA? [SEC. 75]

The provisions of this Act shall **apply also** to any offence or contravention committed **outside India** by any person irrespective of his nationality, if the act or conduct constituting the offence or contravention involves a computer; computer system or computer network located in India.

59.0 WHAT ARE THE PROVISIONS RELATING TO CONFISCATION? [SEC. 76]

Any computer, computer system floppies, compact disks, tape drives or any other accessories related thereto, in respect of which there is contravention of any provision of this Act shall be liable to confiscation.

However, where it is established to the satisfaction of the court adjudicating the confiscation that the person who is in possession, power or control of these articles is not responsible for the contravention the court may, instead of making an order for confiscation, make such other order as it may think fit.

60.0 COMPENSATION, PENALTIES OR CONFISCATION NOT TO INTERFERE WITH OTHER PUNISHMENT [SECTION 77]

No compensation awarded, penalty imposed or confiscation made under this Act shall prevent the award of compensation or imposition of any other penalty or punishment under any other law for the time being in force.

60.1 Compounding of Offences [Section 77 A]

(1) A Court of competent jurisdiction may compound offences other than offences for which the punishment for life or imprisonment for a term exceeding three years has been provided under this Act.

Provided that the Court shall not compound such offence where the accused is by reason of his previous conviction, liable to either enhanced punishment or to a punishment of a different kind.

Provided further that the Court shall not compound any offence where such offence affects the socio-economic conditions of the country or has been committed against a child below the age of 18 years or a woman.

(2) The person accused of an offence under this act may file an application for compounding in the court in which offence is pending for trial and the provisions of Sec. 265 B and 265 C of Code of Criminal Procedures, 1973 shall apply.

60.2 Offences with three years imprisonment to be cognizable [Section 77 B]

Notwithstanding anything contained in Criminal Procedure Code 1973, the offence punishable with imprisonment of three years and above shall be cognizable and the offence punishable with imprisonment of three years shall be bailable.

61.0 WHO HAS POWER TO INVESTIGATE OFFENCES? [SEC. 78]

A police officer **not below the rank of Inspector** of Police is empowered to investigate any offence under the Act.

62.0 ARE NETWORK SERVICE PROVIDERS LIABLE? [SEC. 79]

62.1 For the removal of doubts it is herby declared that **no** person providing any service as a network service provider shall be **liable** under this Act, rules or regulations made thereunder for any third party information or data made available by him if he proves that the offence or contravention was committed without his knowledge or that he had exercised all due diligence to prevent the commission of such offence or contravention.

62.2 Explanation—For the purposes of this Section,—

(a) **"network service provider"** means a intermediary;

(b) **"third party information"** means any information dealt with by a network service provider in his capacity as an intermediary.

Exemption from liability of intermediary in certain cases [Section 79]

(1) Notwithstanding anything contained in any law for the time being in force but subject to the provisions of Sec. 79 (2) and (3), an intermediary shall not be liable for any third party information, data, or communication link hosted by him.

(2) The provisions of u/s 79 (1) shall apply if-

(a) the function of the intermediary is limited to providing access to a communication system over which information made available by third parties is transmitted or temporarily stored; or

(b) the intermediary does not-

(i) initiate the transmission,

(ii) select the receiver of the transmission, and

(iii) select or modify the information contained in the transmission

(c) the intermediary observes due diligence while discharging his duties under this Act and also observes such other guidelines as the Central Government may prescribe in this behalf

(3) The provisions of u/s 79 (1) shall not apply if_

(a) the intermediary has conspired or abetted or aided or induced whether by threats or promise or otherwise in the commission of the unlawful act

(b) upon receiving actual knowledge, or on being notified by the appropriate Government or its agency that any information, data or communication link residing in or connected to a computer resource controlled by the intermediary is being used to commit the unlawful act, the intermediary fails to expeditiously remove or disable access to that material on that resource without vitiating the evidence in any manner.

Explanation : For the purpose of this section, the expression "third party information" means any information dealt with by an intermediary in his capacity as an intermediary.

63.0 EXAMINER OF ELECTRONIC EVIDENCE [SECTION 79A]

The Central Government may, for the purposes of providing expert opinion on electronic form evidence before any court or other authority specify, by notification in the official Gazette, any department, body or agency of the Central Government or a State Government as an Examiner of Electronic Evidence.

Explanation:- For the purpose of this section, "Electronic Form Evidence" means any information of probative value that is either stored or transmitted in electronic form and includes computer evidence, digital audio, digital video, cell phones, digital fax machines".

64.0 WHAT ARE THE PROVISIONS RELATING TO OFFENCES BY COMPANIES? [SEC. 85]

64.1 Where a person committing a contravention of any of the provisions of this Act or of any rule, direction or order made thereunder is a company, every person who, at the time the contravention was committed, was incharge of, and was responsible to, the company for the conduct of business of the company as well as the company shall be guilty of the contravention and shall be liable to be proceeded against and punished accordingly, unless he proves that the contravention took place without his knowledge or that he exercised all due diligence to prevent such contravention

64.2 If it is proved that the contravention has taken place with the consent or connivance of or is attributable to any neglect on the part of any director, manager, secretary or other officer of the company such person shall also be deemed to be guilty of the contravention and shall be liable to be proceeded against and punished accordingly.

64.3 Explanation—For the purposes of this Section,—

(i) "company" means any body corporate and includes a firm or other associatior of individuals; and

(ii) "director" in relation of a firm, means a partner in the firm.

65.0 WHAT IS THE CONSTITUTION OF ADVISORY COMMITTEE? [SEC. 88]

Who can Appoint	The Central Government, shall as soon as may be after the commencement of this Act, constitute a Committee called the Cyber Regulations Advisory Committee.
Composition	It shall consist of a Chairperson and such number of the official and non-official members representing the interests principally affected or having special knowledge of the subject-matter as the Central Government may deem fit.
Allowances	There shall be paid to the non-official members of such committee such travelling and other allowances as the Central Government may fix.
Functions	The Cyber Regulations Advisory Committee shall advise— (a) the Central Government either generally as regards any rules or for any other purpose connected with the Act. (b) the Controller in framing the regulations under this Act.

66.0 WHAT ARE THE PROVISIONS RELATING TO POWER OF CONTROLLER TO MAKE REGULATIONS? [SEC. 89]

How	The Controller may after consultation with the Cyber Regulations Advisory Committee and with the previous approval of the Central Government by modification in the Official Gazette, make regulations consistent with the act and the rules made thereunder to carry out the purposes of the Act.
Matters	In particular such regulations may provide for all or any of the following matters, namely: (a) the particulars relating to maintenance of database containing the disclosure record of every Certifying Authority under Section 18(m). (b) the conditions and restrictions subject to which the Controller may recognize any foreign Certifying Authority under Section 19(1); (c) the terms and conditions subject to which a licence may be granted under Section 21(3)(c); (d) other standards to be observed by a Certifying Authority under Section 30(d); (e) the manner in which the Certifying Authority shall disclose the matters specified in Section 34(1); (f) the particulars of statement which shall accompany an application under Section 35(3); (g) the manner by which the subscriber communicates the compromise of private key to the Certifying Authority under Section 42(2).

67.0 POWER OF CENTRAL GOVERNMENT TO MAKE RULES

67.1 How—The Central Government may, by notification in the Official Gazette and in the Electronic Gazette, make rules to carry out the provisions of this Act.

67.2 Matters—In particular, such rules may provide for all or any of the following matters, namely;—

(a) the conditions for considering reliability of electronic signature or electronic authentication technique u/s 3A (2).

(aa) the procedure for ascertaining electronic signature or authentication u/s 3A (3) of section 3A

(ab) the manner in which any information or matter may be authenticated by means of electronic signature u/s 5.

(b) the electronic form in which filing, issue, grant or payment shall be effected u/s 6 (1)

(c) the manner and format in which electronic records shall be filed or issued and the method of payment u/s 6 (2)

(ca) the manner in which the authorized service provider may collect, retain and appropriate service charges u/s 6A (2)

(d) the matters relating to the type of Electronic Signature, manner and format in which it may be affixed u/s 10;

(e) the manner of storing and affixing electronic signature creation data u/s 15

(ea) the security procedures and practices u/s 16

(f) the qualifications, experience and terms and conditions of service of Controller, Deputy Controllers and Assistant Controllers, other officers and employees u/s 17;

(h) the requirements which an applicant must fulfill under u/s 21 (2)

(i) the period of validity of license granted u/s 21 (3) (a)

(j) the form in which an application for license may be made u/s 22 (1)

(k) the amount of fees payable u/s 22 (2) (c)

(l) such other documents which shall accompany an application for license 22 (2) (d)

(m) the form and the fee for renewal of a license and the fee payable thereof u/s 23;

(ma) the form of application and fee for issue of Electronic Signature Certificate u/s 35

(n) the amount of late fee payable under the proviso to Sec. 23;

(o) the form in which application for issue of a Electronic Signature Certificate may be made u/s 35 (1)

(oa) the duties of subscribers under Sec. 40A

(ob) the reasonable security practices and procedures and sensitive personal data or information u/s 43A

(p) the fee to be paid to the Certifying Authority for issue of a Digital Signature Certificate u/s 35 (2)

(q) the manner in which the adjudicating officer shall hold inquiry u/s 46 (1)

(r) the qualification and experience which the adjudicating officer shall possess u/s 46 (2) (Ed: error in the act item number (vii). Bill mentions correction not in the original section-"Presiding Officer" to be replaced with "Chairman and Members")

(s) the salary, allowances and the other terms and conditions of service of the Chairman and Members u/s 52;

(t) the procedure for investigation of misbehaviour or incapacity of the Chairman and Members under sub-section (3) of Sec. 54; (Ed: Error: bill mentions corrections to (r) and (s) instead of (s) and (t)

(u) the salary and allowances and other conditions, of service of other officers and employees under sub-section (3) of Sec. 56;

(v) the form in which appeal may be filed and the fee thereof under subsection (3) of Sec. 57;

(w) the powers and functions of the Chairperson of the Cyber Appellate Tribunal u/s 52 A

(wa) the information, duration, manner and form of such information to be retained and preserved u/s 67C

(x) The Procedures and safeguards for interception, monitoring or decryption u/s 69 (2)

(xa) the procedure and safeguards for blocking for access by the public u/s 69A (2)

(xb) the procedure and safeguards for monitoring and collecting traffic data or information u/s 69B (3)

(y) the information security practices and procedures for protected system u/s 70

(ya) manner of performing functions and duties of the agency u/s 70A (3)

(yb) the officers and employees u/s 70B (2)

(yc) salaries and allowances and terms and conditions of service of the Director General and other officers and employees u/s 70B (3)

(yd) the manner in which the functions and duties of agency shall be performed u/s 70B (5)

(z) the guidelines to be observed by the intermediaries u/s 79 (4) (2)

(za) the modes or methods for encryption u/s 84A

(3) Every notification made by the Central Government u/s 70 (1) (A) and every rule made by it shall be laid, as soon as may be after it is made, before each House of Parliament, while it is in session, for a total period of thirty days which may be comprised in one session or in two or more successive sessions, and if, before the expiry of the session immediately following the session or the successive sessions aforesaid, both Houses agree in making any modification in the regulation or both Houses agree that the regulation should not be made, the regulation shall thereafter have effect only in such modified form or be of no effect, as the case may be; so, however, that any such modification or annulment shall be without prejudice to the validity of anything previously done under that regulation.

68.0 POWER OF STATE GOVERNMENT TO MAKE RULES [SECTION 90]

(1) The State Government may, by notification in the Official Gazette, make rules to carry out the provisions of this Act.

(2) In particular, and without prejudice to the generality of the foregoing power, such rules may provide for all or any of the following matters, namely_

(a) the electronic form in which filing, issue, grant receipt or payment shall be effected u/s 6 (1) (b) for matters specified in u/s 6 (2)

(3) Every rule made by the State Government under this section shall be laid, as soon as may be after it is made, before each House of the State Legislature where it consists of two Houses, or where such Legislature consists of one House, before that House.

EXERCISES

1. State the main objectives of IT Act, 2000.
2. What is the scope of IT Act, 2000?
3. Explain the meaning and creation of digital signature.
4. Explain the provisions relating to legal recognition of electronic records.
5. Explain the provisions relating to legal recognition of electronic signature.
6. Explain the provisions relating to retention of electronic records.
7. When shall the transmission of an electronic record be attributed to the originator?
8. What are the provisions relating to acknowledgement of receipt?
9. How is the time and place of dispatch and receipt of Electronic Record determined?
10. What are the provisions relating to;
    (a) Secure Electronic Record
    (b) Secure Electronic Signature
    (c) Security Procedure
11. State **any six** functions of Controller.
12. State the meaning of 'Repository' and duties of Controller to act as Repository.
13. What are the provisions relating to making of an application for licence to issue Electronic Signature Certificates?
14. State the restrictions on licence granted to issue Electronic Signature Certificates under Sec 21(3).
15. What are the provisions relating to suspension of licence?
16. (a) Define Certifying Authority.
    (b) State the procedures relating to security of system followed by Certifying Authority.
17. State the duties of Certifying Authority.

*18. What are the provisions relating to application for the issue of Electronic Signature Certificate?

*19. What are the provisions relating to grant of Electronic Signature Certificate?

*20. What are the representations upon issuance of Electronic Signature Certificate?

*21. What are the provisions relating to suspension of Electronic Signature Certificate?

*22. What are the provisions relating to revocation of Electronic Signature Certificate?

*23. Explain the duties of subscribers.

*24. Write short notes on the following:
   (a) Tempering with Computer Source Documents
   (b) Haking with Computer System
   (c) Electronic Signature and Electronic Signature Certificate
   (d) Key Pair, Private Key and Public Key
   (e) Asymmetric Crypto System
   (f) Addressee, Originator, Subscriber, Intermediary
   (g) Certifying Authority and Certification Practice Statement.
   (h) Cyber Regulation Appellate Tribunal
   (i) Advisory Committee

25. State the penalty for the following computer crimes:
   (a) Damage to Computer, Computer System etc.
   (b) Tampering with Computer Source Documents
   (c) Haking with Computer System
   (d) Publishing or transmitting or causing to be published or transmitted information which is obscene in electronic form
   (e) Securing unauthorised access to Protected System
   (f) Misrepresentation or suppressing any material
   (g) Breach of confidentiality and Privacy of electronic records etc.
   (h) Publishing False Electronic Signature Certificate
   (i) Publishing of Electronic Signature Certificate for fraudulent purpose

26. Are Network service providers liable?

27. Explain the various matters on which the Central Govt. can make rules under Sec. 87 of the I.T. Act, 2000.

28. Explain the various matters on which the Controller can make regulations under Sec. 89 of the I.T. Act, 2000.

CHAPTER 20 The Payment of Bonus Act, 1965

1.0 INTRODUCTION

1.1 What is the Object of the Payment of Bonus Act, 1965 ? [Preamble to the ACT]

The object of The Payment of Bonus Act, 1965 is to provide for the payment of bonus to persons employed in certain establishments on the basis of profits or on the basis of production or productivity and for matters connected therewith.

1.2 From which date the Payment of Bonus Act came into force ?

The Payment of Bonus Act, 1965 came into force with effect from 25-09-1965

1.3 What is the territory to which the Payment of Bonus Act Applies? [Sec. 1(2)]

The Payment of Bonus Act, 1965 extends to the **whole of India.**

2.0 WHAT ARE THE CLASSES OF ESTABLISHMENT TO WHICH THE ACT APPLIES? [SECTION (3)]

2.1 The Payment of Bonus Act applies to :

(a) every **factory**;

(b) every **other establishment** employing **at least 20 persons on any day** during an accounting year.

(c) Every other establishment employing persons between 10 and 19 if the Appropriate Govt. after giving at least 2 months' notice issues a Notification in the Official Gazette. [*Provisio to Sec. 1(3)*]

2.2 Applicability even in Case Number Falls Below 20 Persons [Section 1(5)]

An establishment to which this Act applies shall continue to be governed by this Act even if that the number of persons employed therein falls below 20 [or, as the case may be the number specified in the notification issued under the proviso to Section 1(3)]

Note: While calculating the number of persons employed, even **casual workers** will be **included**.

3.0 ESTABLISHMENT

3.1 Meaning of Establishment

Establishment means any unit, undertaking or place of business in which

(a) any commercial activity or business is carried on; *or*

(b) services are rendered under any form of business organisation.

3.2 When are Departments treated as Separate Establishments or Part of Same Establishment? [Section 3]

Case	*Treatment*
(a) Where for any accounting year a separate Balance Sheet and Profit and Loss account are prepared and maintained in respect of any such department or undertaking or branch *&* *Immediately before the commencement of that accounting year such department or undertaking or branch was not treated as part of the establishment for the purpose of computation of bonus.*	Such department or undertaking or branches shall be treated as a **separate establishment** for the purpose of computation of bonus, under this Act for that year.
(b) In any other case	Such department or undertaking or branch shall be treated as **part of the same establishment** for the purpose of computation of Bonus under the Act.

4.0 ACCOUNTING YEAR [SECTION 2(1)]

4.1 What is an Accounting Year ?

4.1

In relation to	*Accounting Year means . . .*
(i) A corporation	The year ending on the day on which the books and accounts of the corporation are to be closed and balanced;
(ii) A company,	The period for which any Profit and Loss Account of the company is prepared and is laid before its annual general meeting, whether that period is a year or not;
(iii) In any other case	(a) the year commencing on the 1st April and ending on 31st March; *or* (b) if the accounts of an establishment maintained by the employer thereof are closed and balanced on any day other than the 31st day of March, then, at the option of the employer, the year ending on the day on which its accounts are so closed and balanced.

4.2 Option to Choose Accounting Year. However, an option once exercised by the employer shall not again be exercised except with the previous permission in writing of the prescribed authority and upon such conditions as that authority may think fit.

5.0 WHO IS REGARDED AS AN EMPLOYEE? [SECTION 2(13)]

"Employee" means :

- any person **(other than an apprentice)**
- employed on a salary or wage **not exceeding Rs 10,000 per mensem**
- in any industry
- to do any work (whether skilled or unskilled, manual, supervisory, managerial, administrative, technical or clerical work)
- for hire or reward
- whether the terms of employment be express or implied.

5.1 Eligibility as Decided in Judicial Decisions

An employee in the following cases is entitled to bonus:

1. **A probationer** is an employee and as such is entitled to bonus.
   [*Bank of Madura Ltd.* v. *Employee's Union*, 1970, (2) LLJ (21)]
2. **A temporary workman** is entitled to bonus on the basis of **total number of days worked by him.**
3. A **part time employee as a sweeper** engaged on a regular basis is entitled to bonus. [*Automobile Karmchari Sangh* v. *Industrial Tribunal* [1970] 38 FJR 268]
4. An employee of a **seasonal factory** is entitled to **proportionate bonus** and not the minimum bonus as prescribed under Section 10 of the Act.
5. A **piece-rated** worker is entitled to bonus.
   [*Mathuradas Kani* v. *L.A. Tribunal* AIR [1958] SC 899].
6. A **retrenched employees** is eligible to get bonus provided he has worked for minimum qualifying period.
   [*East Asiatic Co.* (*P*) *Ltd.* v. *Industrial Tribunal* [1961] 1 LLJ 720]
7. A **dismissed employee reinstated with back wages** is entitled to bonus.
   [*Gannon India Ltd.* v *Niranjan Das* [1984] 2 LLJ 223].

6.0 WHAT ARE THE CLASSES OF EMPLOYEES TO WHICH THE ACT DOES NOT APPLY? [SECTION 32]

The classes of employees to which the Act does not apply are as follows:

1. **employees employed by any insurer** carrying on **general insurance** business
2. employees employed by the **Life Insurance Corporation of India**;
3. **seamen** as defined in Section 3(43) of the Merchant Shipping Act, 1958;
4. employees registered or listed under any scheme under the **Dock Workers** (Regulation of Employment) Act, 1948, and employed by registered or listed employers;
5. employees employed by an establishment engaged in any **industry** carried on by or under the authority of any department **of the Central Government or a State Government or a Local Authority;**

6. employees employed by—
   (a) the **Indian Red Cross Society** or any other institution of a like nature (including its branches);
   (b) universities and other **educational institutions;**
   (c) **institutions** (including hospitals, chambers of commerce and social welfare institutions) established **not for purposes of profit;**
7. employees employed by the **Reserve Bank of India;**
8. employees employed by—
   (a) the Industrial Finance Corporation of India **(IFCI)**
   (b) **any Financial Corporation** established under Section 3, or any Joint Financial Corporation established under Section 3A of the State Financial Corporation Act, 1951;
   (c) the **Deposit Insurance Corporation;**
   (d) the National Bank for Agricultural and Rural Development **(NABARD)**;
   (e) the Unit Trust of India **(UTI)**;
   (f) the Industrial Development Bank of India **(IDBI)**;
   (g) the Small Industries Development Bank of India **(SIDBI)** established under section 3 of the Small Industries Development Bank of India Act, 1989;
   (h) the National Housing Bank **(NHB)**;
   (i) any other **financial institution** (other than a banking company) being an establishment in **public sector**, which the Central Government may, by notification in the Official Gazette, specify, having regard to—
      (i) its capital structure;
      (ii) its objectives and the nature of its activities;
      (iii) the nature and extent of financial assistance or any concession given to it by the government; and
      (iv) any other relevant factor;
9. employees employed by **inland water transport establishments** operating on routes passing through any other country.

7.0 WHAT IS "SALARY OR WAGE"? [SECTION 2(21)]

7.1 "Salary or Wage" means :

- all remuneration **(other than remuneration in respect of over-time work)**
- capable of being expressed in terms of money,
- which would be payable to an employee in respect of his employment or of work done in such employment.
- if the terms of employment, express or implied were fulfilled.

7.2 Salary or Wage includes :

(a) **Dearness allowance** (*i.e.,* all cash payments, by whatever name called, paid to an employee on account of a rise in the cost of living)

(b) **Free food allowance** or free food by his employer in lieu of salary or wage.

7.3 Salary does not include–

(i) any other allowance which the employee is for the time being entitled to;

(ii) the **value of any house accommodation** *or* of supply of light, water, medical attendance *or* other amenity *or* of any service of any concessional supply of foodgrains *or* other articles;

(iii) any **travelling concession**;

(iv) any **bonus** (including incentive, production and attendance bonus);

(v) any **contribution** paid *or* payable by the employer to any **pension fund or provident fund** *or* for the benefit of the employee under any law for the time being in force;

(vi) any **retrenchment compensation** *or* any **gratuity** *or* other **retirement benefit** payable to the employee *or* any ex gratia payment made to him;

(vii) any **commission** payable to the employee;

8.0 WHO IS REGARDED AS AN 'EMPLOYER'? [SECTION 2(14)]

Type of Establishment	*Employer Includes...*
(a) *In relation to an establishment which is a factory*	(a) Owner *or* Occupier of the factory, (b) Agent of such Owner *or* Occupier, (c) Legal Representative of a deceased owner or occupier and (d) a person named as a Manager of the Factory under The Factories Act, 1948.
(b) *In relation to any other establishment*	(a) Person/The Authority having ultimate control over the affairs of the establishment (b) a Manager *or*, Managing Director to whom affairs are entrusted

9.0 WHICH IS AN APPROPRIATE GOVERNMENT? [SECTION 2(5)]

Case	*Appropriate Government*
(a) *In relation to an establishment in respect of which the appropriate Government under the Industrial Disputes Act, 1947 is the Central Government,*	(i) the Central Government.
(b) *In relation to any other establishment*	(ii) the Government of the State in which that other establishment is situated.

10.0 WHAT IS AN AWARD? [SECTION 2(9)]

"Award" means an **interim or a final determination of any industrial dispute** or of any question relating thereto by any Labour Court, Industrial Tribunal or National Tribunal constituted under the Industrial Disputes Act, 1947 or by any other authority constituted under any corresponding law relating to investigation and settlement of industrial disputes in force in a State and **includes an Arbitration Award made under** Section 10A of that Act or under that law.

11.0 WHO IS ELIGIBLE FOR BONUS? [SECTION 8 READ WITH SECTION 2(3)]

11.1 Every employee is entitled to bonus provided—

(a) he has worked in that establishment for **at least 30 working days** in the accounting year (Sec. 8), and

(b) he has been employed on a salary or wage **not exceeding Rs 10,000** per mensem (i.e., month).

12.0 WHO ARE DISQUALIFIED FROM RECEIVING BONUS? [SECTION 9]

12.1 An employee shall be disqualified from receiving bonus under this Act, if he is dismissed from service for—

(a) fraud; *or*

(b) riotous or violent behaviour while on the premises of the establishment; *or*

(c) theft, misappropriation *or* sabotage of any property of the establishment

12.2 Effects of Sec. 9

An employee who is dismissed from service on the ground of misconduct as mentioned in Section 9, is disqualified for any bonus **(whether for Current Accounting year *or* previous Accounting Year)** [*Pandian Roadways Corporation Ltd.* vs. *Presiding Officer* [1996] 2 CLR 1175 (Mad.]

13.0 PAYMENT OF MINIMUM BONUS [SECTION 10]

Every employer is bound to pay to every eligible employee (as per Sec. 8, Sec. 2(3), Sec. 9) in respect of every accounting year a minimum bonus at the following rates whether or not the employer has any allocable surplus in the accounting year:

Case	*Minimum Bonus*
(a) ***Where an employee has completed 15 years of age at the beginning of the accounting year***	8.33% of the salary or wage earned by the employee during the accounting year *or* **Rs 100** whichever is **higher**.
(b) ***Where an employee has not completed 15 years of age at the beginning of the accounting year***	8.33% of the salary or wage earned by employee during the accounting year *or* **Rs 60** whichever is **higher**.

14.0 HOW TO CALCULATE PROPORTIONATE REDUCTION IN BONUS IN CERTAIN CASES [SECTION 13]

14.1 Bonus shall be proportionately reduced if, an employee has not worked for all the working days in an accounting year.

14.2 Actual Bonus after proportionate reduction will be calculated as follows:

Case	*Actual Bonus after proportionate reduction*
(a) ***Where Minimum Bonus of Rs. 100 or Rs. 60 is higher than 8.33% of Salary or Wages***	Rs. 100 *or* Rs. 60 $\times \frac{\text{Actual No. of Working Days}}{\text{Total No. of Working Days}}$
(b) *In other cases*	8.33% of Salary/wages $\times \frac{\text{Actual No. of Working Days}}{\text{Total No. of Working Days}}$

Illustration: Number of Working Days in Establishment = 300

Name of Employee	*Age*	*Monthly Wages Rs.*	*Actual no. of days on which employee worked*	*Actual Bonus after Proportionate Reduction*
P	14	50	250	Rs 60 × 250/300 = Rs 50.00
Q	15	50	250	Rs 100 × 250/300 = Rs 83.33
R	18	3,000	250	(Rs 3,000 × 12) × 8.33% × 250/300 = Rs 2,499
S	18	10,000	250	(Rs 3,500 × 12) × 8.33% × 250/300 = Rs 2,915.50

15.0 HOW TO COMPUTE NUMBER OF WORKING DAYS? [SECTION 14]

For the purposes of Section 13, an employee shall be deemed to have worked in an establishment in any accounting year also on the days on which—

(a) **Lay off Period**–He has been laid off under an agreement or as permitted by standing orders under the Industrial Employment (Stand Orders) Act, 1946 or under the Industrial Disputes Act, 1947 or under any other law applicable to the establishment;

(b) **Leave with salary or wage**–He has been on leave with salary or wage;

(c) **Temporary Disablement**–He has been absent due to temporary disablement caused by accident arising out of and in the course of his employment; and

(d) **Maternity leave with salary or wage**–The female employee has been on maternity leave with salary or wage during the accounting year.

Notes:

(i) Where an employee was ready and willing to work but for reasons beyond his control was unable to work shall be deemed to have worked on that day.

(ii) The case where an employee was prevented from workshop by reason of an illegal order of termination has not been covered by Section 14.

16.0 PAYMENT OF MAXIMUM BONUS [SECTION 11]

16.1 When is employer Bound to pay Maximum Bonus ?

The employer is bound to pay maximum bonus where the **allocable surplus exceeds the amount of minimum bonus.** [Section 11(1)]

16.2 Computation of Allocable Surplus

In computing the allocable surplus under this section, the amount set on or the amount set off under the provisions of Section 15 shall be taken into account in accordance with the provisions of that section. [Section 11(2)]

16.3 What is Maximum Bonus?

The maximum bonus shall be an amount in proportion to the salary or wage earned by the employee during the accounting year subject to a maximum of **20%** of such salary or wage. [Section 11(1)]

16.4 Ceiling on Salary/Wage for bonus computation [Section 12]

Where the salary or wage of an employee exceeds Rs 3,500 per mensem, the bonus payable to such employee under section 10 or 11, shall be calculated as if his salary or wage were Rs 3,500.

Illustration: Salary of Employee '*X*' Rs 3,000 p.m.

Salary of Employee '*Y*' Rs 10,000 p.m.

Salary of Employee '*Z*' Rs 11,000 p.m.

Rate of Bonus is 10%. Calculate the amount of maximum bonus.

Solution:

Rate of Bonus is 10%

Bonus will be calculated as follows:

Employee *X* 3,000 × 12 × 10% = Rs 3,600

Employee *Y* 3,500 × 12 × 10% = Rs 4,200

Employee *Z* is not eligible for bonus, since his salary exceeds Rs. 10,000 u/s 8.

17.0 SPECIAL PROVISION WITH RESPECT TO PAYMENT OF BONUS LINKED WITH PRODUCTION OR PRODUCTIVITY [SECTION 31A]

Where an agreement or a settlement has been entered into by the employees with their employer for payment of an annual bonus linked with production or productivity in lieu of bonus based on profits payable under this Act, then, such employees shall be entitled to receive bonus due to them under such agreement or settlement subject to the following restrictions :

1. **Minimum Bonus**–That any such agreement or settlement shall be null and void in so far as it purports to deprive an employee of his right to receive minimum bonus u/s 10. Every eligible employee shall have a right to receive the minimum bonus as per Sec. 10 even though bonus linked with production or productivity as per agreement/settlement is less than the amount of minimum bonus.
2. **Maximum Bonus**–The bonus linked with production/productivity as per agreement/settlement **cannot be more than 20%** of salary on wage earned in accounting year.

Conclusion : The Bonus linked with production or productivity can *neither* be less than Minimum Bonus (as per Sec. 10) and *nor* be more than Maximum Bonus (as per Sec. 11)

18.0 ADJUSTMENT OF CUSTOMARY OR INTERIM BONUS AGAINST BONUS PAYABLE UNDER THE ACT [SECTION 17]

18.1 Employer's Right to deduct Customary/Interim Bonus

The employer shall be entitled to deduct the amount of bonus paid from the amount of bonus payable by him to the employee under this Act in respect of that accounting year if :

(a) an employer has paid any **Puja bonus or other customary bonus** to an employee; *or*

(b) an employer has **paid a part of the bonus** before the due date of bonus.

18.2 Employee's right to receive balance

The employee shall be entitled to receive only the balance.

19.0 DEDUCTION OF CERTAIN AMOUNTS FROM BONUS PAYABLE UNDER THE ACT [SECTION 18]

19.1 Two Conditions for Deduction

(a) An employee is **found guilty of misconduct causing, and**

(b) There is **financial loss to the employer**,

then, the employer can lawfully deduct the amount of loss from the amount of bonus payable by him to the employee under this Act in respect of **that accounting year only**

19.2 Employee's right to receive balance

The employee shall be entitled to receive only the balance.

20.0 WHAT IS THE TIME-LIMIT FOR PAYMENT OF BONUS? [SECTION 19]

All amounts payable to an employee by way of bonus under this Act must be paid in cash by his employer—

Case	*Time Limit*
(a) ***where there is a dispute regarding payment of bonus pending before any authority under Section 22***	Within **1 month** from the date on which the award becomes enforceable or the settlement comes into operation,
(b) ***in any other case***	Within a period of **8 months** from the close of the accounting year **Or** within the period extended by the Appropriate Govt. or authority upon an application made by the employers and for sufficient reasons but the total period so extended must **not exceed 2 years.**

21.0 RECOVERY OF THE BONUS DUE FROM AN EMPLOYER [SECTION 21]

1. When Section 21 Applies	Where any money is due to an employee by way of bonus from his employer under a settlement or an award or agreement and it is not paid.
2. To whom to apply	An application for the recovery of the money due is required to be made to the Appropriate Authority.
3. Who can make Application	An application for the recovery of money due can be made— (a) by the employee (including an employee who is no longer in employment) *or* (b) any person authorised by employee in writing; *or* (c) by the Assignee or Legal heir of deceased employee.
4. Time Limit within which Application is to be made	An application is to be made **within 1 year** (or time, if any, extended by Appropriate Govt. on sufficient cause being shown) from the due date of bonus.

5. Issue of Certificate of Recovery	Appropriate Govt. or Prescribed Authority (if satisfied) shall issue a Recovery Certificate to the Collector.
6. Recovery by Collector	Collector shall recover the Bonus in the same manner as an Arrears of land revenue.

22.0 AVAILABLE SURPLUS [SEC. 2(6), SEC. 5]

22.1 What is Available Surplus ? [Sec. 2(6)]

Available Surplus means the available surplus computed under section 5.

22.2 How to Compute Available Surplus ? [Sec. 5]

The Available Surplus shall be computed as follows:

Statement Showing the Computation of Available Surplus u/s 5

Particulars	*Rs*	*Rs*
A. Gross Profit as per Section 4		xxx
B. *Less*: Prior Charges u/s 6		
(a) Depreciation	xxx	
(b) Development Rebate etc.	xxx	
(c) Direct Tax as per Sec. 7	xxx	
(d) Sum specified in Third Schedule	xxx	xxx
C. *Add*: Tax saved on account of Bonus in respect of the immediately preceeding accounting year		xxx
D. Available Surplus [A – B + C]		xxx

22.3 How To Compute Gross Profits? [Section 4]

The gross profit derived by an employer from an establishment in respect of the accounting year shall be calculated as follows:

Case	*Manner of Calculation*
(a) ***In case of a Banking Company***	(a) *In the manner specified in the First Schedule*
(b) ***In any other case***	(b) *In the manner specified in the Second Schedule.*

22.4 What are the Sums Deductible from Gross Profits? [Section 6]

The following **four sums** shall be deducted from the gross profits **as prior charges,** namely:

1. **Depreciation**—Any amount by way of depreciation admissible in accordance with the provisions of the Section 32(1) of the Income-tax Act or in accordance with the provisions of the Agricultural Income-tax law, as the case may be.

   Provided that where an employer has been paying bonus to his employees under a settlement or an award or agreement made before the 29th May 1965, and subsisting on that date after deducting from the gross profits notional normal depreciation, then, the amount of depreciation to be deducted under this clause shall, at the option of such employer (such option to be exercised once and within 1 year from that date) continue to be such notional normal depreciaiton.

2. **Development Rebate etc.**—Any amount by way of development rebate or investment allowance or development allowance which the employer is entitled to deduct from his income under the Income-tax Act;
3. **Direct tax**—Subject to the provisions of Section 7, any direct tax which the employer is liable to pay for the accounting year in respect of his income, profits and gains during that year;
4. **Sum Specified in Third Schedule**—Such further sums as are specified in respect of the employer in the Third Schedule.

22.5 How is Direct Tax Payable by the Employer Calculated? [Section 7]

Any direct tax payable by the employer for any accounting year shall, subject to the following provisions, be calculated at the rates applicable to the income of the employer for that year, namely—

(a) **In calculating such tax the following shall not be taken into account**—

(i) **Brought Forward Loss**—Any loss incurred by the employer in respect of any previous accounting year and carried forward under any law for the time being in force relating to direct taxes;

(ii) **Arrears of Depreciation**—Any arrears of depreciation which the employer is entitled to add to the amount of the allowance for depreciation for any following accounting year or years under Section 32(1) of the Income-tax Act;

(iii) **Exemption u/s 84 or Deduction u/s 101**—Any exemption conferred on the employer under Section 84 of the Income-tax Act *or* of any deduction to which he is entitled under Section 101(1) of that Act, as in force immediately before the commencement of the Finance Act, 1965.

(b) **Charitable/Religious Institution to be treated as widely held company** Where the employer is a religious or a charitable institution to which the provisions of Section 32 do not apply and the whole or any part of its income is exempt from tax under the Income-tax Act, then, with respect to the income so exempted, such institution shall be treated as if it were a company in which the public are substantially interested within the meaning of that act;

(c) **Establishment income to be treated as only income in case of HUF, Individual**—Where the employer is an individual or a Hindu Undivided Family, the tax payable by such employer under the Income-tax Act shall be calculated on the basis that the income derived by him from the establishment is his only income;

(d) **No Rebate on Export Profit**—Where the income of any employer includes any profits and gains derived from the export of any goods or merchandise out of India and any rebate on such income is allowed under any law for the time being in force relating to direct taxes, then, no account shall be taken of such rabate;

(e) **No Rebate for the development of any industry (other than development rebate or investment allowance or development allowance)**—No account shall be taken of any rebate (other than development rebate or investment allowance or development allowance) or credit or relief or deduction (not here in before mentioned in this section) in the payment of any direct tax allowed under any law for the time being in force relating to direct taxes or under the relevant annual Finance Act, for the development of any industry.

23.0 WHAT IS AN ALLOCABLE SURPLUS? [SECTION 2(4)]

Case	*Allocable Surplus*
(a) ***In relation to an employer, being a company (other than banking company) which has not made the arrangements prescribed under the Income-tax Act, for the declaration and payment of the dividends payable out of its profits within India in accordance with the provisions of Section 194 of that Act,***	(a) **67%** of available surplus in an accounting year.
(b) ***In any other case***	(b) **60%** of the available surplus in an accounting year.

24.0 SET ON/SET OFF OF ALLOCABLE SURPLUS [SEC. 15]

24.1 Provisions Relating to Set on/Set off

	Provision relating to Set on	*Provision relating to Set off*
When Provision applies	The provision of set on applies where for any accounting year, the **allocable surplus** is **more than** the amount of **maximum bonus** payable to the employees in the establishment under Section 11.	The provision of set-off applies in the following cases: 1. where there is no available surplus 2. where the **allocable surplus** is **less than** the amount of **minimum bonus** payable to the employees in the establishment under Section 10 and there is no amount or sufficient amount carried forward and set on u/s 15(1), which could be utilized for the purposes of payment of the minimum bonus.
Amount which can be carried forward	The excess of allocable surplus over maximum bonus, or 20% of the total salary or wage of the employee employed in the establishment in that accounting year, whichever is lower is to be carried forward for being set on.	The deficiency or the amount of minimum bonus whichever is lower, is to be carried forward for being set-off.

Accounting Years for which amount can be carried forward	Upto 4 Accounting years	Upto 4 Accounting years
Schedule in accordance with amount can be c/f	Fourth Schedule	Fourth Schedule

Conclusions :

1. The Excess (i.e. Difference between Allocable Surplus and Maximum Bonus) not exceeding 20% of salary/wage is to be carried forward for being set on upto 4 accounting years as per Fourth Schedule.
2. The Deficiency (*i.e.* Difference between Available Surplus and Minimum Bonus) is to be carried forward for being set off upto 4 accounting years as per Fourth Schedule.

24.2 Fourth Schedule to apply to all other cases:

The principle of set on and set off as illustrated in the Fourth Schedule shall apply to all other cases not covered by Section 15(1) and (2) for the purpose of payment of bonus under this Act. [Section 15(3)]

24.3 FIFO Basis to be applied while adjusting the Amount of Set on/Set off carried forward

Where in any accounting year any amount has been carried forward and set on or set off under this section, then, in calculating bonus for the succeeding accounting year, the amount of set on or set-off carried forward from the earliest accounting year shall first be taken into account. [Section 15(4)]

Illustration : A Banking Co. provides you the following information :

	Case I	***Case II***	***Case III***
Available Surplus	Rs. 2,00,000	Rs. 1,00,000	Rs. 15,000
Minimum Bonus	Rs. 20,000	Rs. 20,000	Rs. 20,000
Maximum Bonus	Rs. 48,000	Rs. 48,000	Rs. 48,000

Calculate the amount to be carried forward for being set on/set off.

Solution :

	Case I	***Case II***
A. Allocable Surplus (60% of Available Surplus)	Rs. 1,20,000	Rs. 60,000
B. Maximum Bonus	Rs. 48,000	Rs. 48,000
C. Excess (A – B)	Rs. 72,000	Rs. 12,000
D. Amount to be c/f for being set on [Excess or Maximum Bonus w.e.l.)	Rs. 48,000	Rs. 12,000

	Case III
A. Available Surplus	Rs. 15,000
B. Minimum Bonus	Rs. 20,000
C. Deficiency [B – A]	Rs. 5,000
D. Amount to be c/f for being set-off [Deficiency or Minimum Bonus w.e.l.]	Rs. 5,000

25.0 SPECIAL PROVISIONS WITH RESPECT TO NEWLY SET UP ESTABLISHMENTS [SECTION 16]

25.1 Meaning of Newly Set up Establishment

An establishment shall not be deemed to be newly set up merely by reason of a change in its location, management name or ownership. [Explanation 1 to Section 16(1)]

25.2 Bonus to Employees of Newly set up Establishment

25.2 Bonus to Employees of Newly set up Establishment—The employees of newly set up establishment shall be entitled to be paid bonus under this Act in accordance with the provisions of Sec. 16 (1A), (1B) and (1C) as follows :

1. For the First 5 accounting years [Section 16(1A)	1. Bonus shall be payable only in respect of the accounting year in which the employer derives profit from such establishment. 2. Bonus shall be calculated in accordance with the provisions of this Act in relation to that year. 3. The provisions of Section 15 (set on/set off) shall not appy.
2. For the 6th accounting year [Section 16(1B)]	Set on or set off, shall be made in the manner illustrated in the 4th Schedule after taking into account the excess or deficiency, of the allocable surplus in respect of the 5th and 6th accounting years.
3. For the 7th accounting year [Section 16(1B)]	Set on or set off, shall be made in the manner illustrated in the 4th Schedule after taking into account the excess or deficiency, of the allocable surplus in respect of the 5th, 6th and 7th accounting years.
4. From the 8th accounting year and onwards	Section 15 shall apply as it applies in relation to any other establishment.

25.3 Manner of Reckoning first 5, 6th, 7th and 8th Accounting years

First Accounting year means the year following the accounting year in which the employer sells the goods produced or manufactured by him or renders services as the case may be, from such establishments.

25.4 Meaning of Employer deriving profit—An employer shall not be deemed to have derived profit in any accounting year unless—

(a) depreciation for such accounting year has been provided; and

(b) the arrears of depreciation and losses incurred for the previous accounting years have been fully set off against the profits. [*Explanation II to Section 16*]

25.5 Trial Period Sale Excluded–Sale of the goods produced or manufactured during the course of the trial running of any factory or of the prospecting stage of any mine or an oil-field shall not be taken into consideration.

25.6 Finality of Decision of Appropriate Govt. Where any question arises with regard to such production or manufacture, the decision of the Appropriate Government made after giving the parties a reasonable opportunity of representing the case, shall be final and shall not be called in question by any court or other authority. [*Explanation III to Section 16*]

26.0 ESTABLISHMENT IN PUBLIC SECTOR

26.1 Meaning of "Establishment in Public Sector"

Means an establishment owned, controlled or managed by—

(a) a Government company as defined in Section 617 of the Companies Act, 1956

(b) a Corporation in which **at least 40%** of its capital is held (whether singly or taken together) by—

(i) the Government; or

(ii) the Reserve Bank of India; or

(iii) a corporation owned by the Government or the Reserve Bank of India;

26.2 Two Conditions for Applicability of the Act Establishment in Public Sector

1. If in any accounting year it sells any goods produced or manufactured by it or renders any services, in competition with an establishment in private sector, **and**
2. The income from such sale or services or both is **at least 20%** of its gross income for that year.

27.0 WHAT IS AN ESTABLISHMENT IN PRIVATE SECTOR? [SECTION 2(15)]

"Establishment in private sector" means any establishment other than an establishment in public sector.

28.0 PRESUMPTION ABOUT ACCURACY OF BALANCE-SHEET AND PROFIT AND LOSS ACCOUNT OF CORPORATIONS AND COMPANIES

28.1 Conditions for Applicability of Sec. 23

(a) The employer is a corporation *or* a Non-banking Company

(b) There is dispute relating to payment of bonus *or* applicability of the Payment of Bonus Act, 1965.

(c) The dispute is filed with any Court, Arbitrator, Tribunal (*called said Authority*).

(d) Audited Balance Sheet and Profit & Loss A/c are produced before the said authority during the course of proceedings.

(e) The Balance Sheet and Profit & Loss A/c have been audited by the Comptroller and Auditor General of India (in case of Corporation) *or* an auditor qualified u/s 226.

28.2 Presumption about Balance Sheet and P & L A/c [Section 23(1)]

(a) The said authority may presume that particulars contained in such Balance Sheet and Profit and Loss Account are accurate.

(b) It shall not be necessary for the corporation or the company to prove the accuracy of such statements and particulars by the filing of an affidavit or by any other mode.

28.3 Steps to Find Out Accuracy when not Accurate

Where the said authority is satisfied that the statements and particulars contained in the Balance Sheet or the Profit and Loss Account of the corporation *or* the company are not accurate, it may take such steps as it thinks necessary to find out the accuracy of such statements and particulars. [*Proviso to Section 23(2)*]

28.4 Right of Trade Union/Employee to require any Clarification

(a) An application may be made to the said authority by any Trade Union or Employees (*where there is no trade union*) being a party to the dispute, requiring any clarification relating to any item in the Balance Sheet *or* the Profit and Loss Account,

(b) The authority (if satisfied) may, direct the corporation or, the company, to furnish to the trade union or the employees such clarification within specified time and

(c) Corporation or, the company, shall comply with such direction.

29.0 AUDITED ACCOUNTS OF BANKING COMPANIES NOT TO BE QUESTIONED [SECTION 24]

29.1 Conditions for Applicability of Sec. 24

(a) The employer is a Banking Company

(b) There is dispute relating to payment of bonus or applicability of the Payment of Bonus Act, 1965.

(c) The dispute is filed with any Court, Arbitrator, Tribunal (*called said Authority*).

(d) Audited Accounts are produced before the said authority during the course of proceedings.

(e) The Accounts have been duly audited.

29.2 Presumption about Balance Sheet and P & L A/c [Section 23(1)]

(a) The said authority may presume that particulars contained in such Balance Sheet and Profit and Loss Account are accurate.

(b) It shall not be necessary for the company to prove the accuracy of such statements and particulars by the filing of an affidavit or by any other mode.

29.3 The said authority shall not permit any trade union or employees to question the correctness of such accounts.

29.4 The trade union or the employees may be permitted to obtain from the banking company such information as is necessary for verifying the amount of bonus due under this Act.

29.5 Trade union or the employee can not be permited to obtain any information which the banking company is not compelled to furnish under the provisions of Section 34A of the Banking Regulation Act, 1949.

30.0 AUDIT OF ACCOUNTS OF EMPLOYER NOT BEING CORPORATIONS OR COMPANIES [SECTION 25]

30.1 Conditions for Applicability of Sec. 25

(a) The employer is any person other than Corporation *or* a Company

(b) There is dispute relating to payment of bonus or applicability of the Payment of Bonus Act, 1965.

(c) The dispute is filed with any Court, Arbitrator, Tribunal (called said Authority).

(d) Audited Accounts are produced before the said authority during the course of proceedings.

(e) The Accounts have been duly audited by an auditor qualified to act u/s 226.

30.3 Order for Audit of Accounts

Case	*Provision*
1. ***When the accounts produced have not been audited by auditor qualified to act u/s 226(1) and said authority is of opinion that an audit of the accounts is necessary for deciding the question referred to it. [Section 25(2)]***	1. The said authority may by order, direct the employer to get his accounts audited within specified time (extended time, if any) by such auditor(s) as it thinks fit and thereupon the employer shall comply with such direction.
2. ***Where an employer fails to get the accounts audited u/s 25(2) as per order of the said authority. [Section 25(3)]***	2. (a) The said authority may get the accounts audited by such auditor(s) as it thinks fit. (b) The expenses of, and incidental to, any audit under Section 25(3) (including the remuneration of the auditor(s) shall be determined by the said authority (which determination shall be final) and shall be paid by the employer and in default of such payment shall be recoverable from the employer like recovery of bonus u/s 21. [Section 25(5)]

31.0 MAINTENANCE OF REGISTERS, RECORDS ETC. [SECTION 26]

31.1 Duty of Employer to Prepare and Maintain Every employer shall prepare and maintain such registers, records and other documents in prescribed form and in prescribed manner.

31.2 Which Registers *According to Rule 4 of the Payment of Bonus Rules, 1965, every employer shall prepare and maintain the following registers, namely—*

(a) a **Register in Form A** showing the computation of the allocable surplus referred to in Section 2(4)

(b) a **Register in Form B** showing the set-on and set-off the allocable surplus, under Section 15

(c) a **Register in Form C** showing the details of the amount of bonus due to each of the employees, the deductions under Sections 17 and 18 and the amount actually disbursed,

31.3 What is the Time Limit for Filing Returns? [Rule 5]

Every employer shall send a **return in Form D** to the Inspector so as to reach the said Form to the Inspector **within 30 days** after the expiry of the time limit specified in Section 19 for payment of bonus.

MISCELLANEOUS PROVISIONS

32.0 NATURE OF DISPUTE UNDER THE BONUS ACT [SECTION 22]

32.1 Meaning of Dispute—Any dispute between an employer and his employees with respect to

(a) the bonus payable under this Act *or*

(b) the application of this Act to an establishment in public sector

32.2 Nature of Dispute—Such dispute shall be deemed to be an industrial dispute within the meaning of the Industrial Disputes Act, 1947 or of any corresponding law relating to investigation and settlement of industrial disputes in force in a State and the provisions of that act or, as the case may be, such law, shall, save as otherwise expressly provided, apply accordingly.

33.0 PROVISIONS RELATING TO INSPECTORS [SECTION 27]

33.1 Who can appoint Inspector ? [Section 27(1)] The Appropriate Government may, by notification in the Official Gazette appoint such persons as it thinks fit to be Inspector and may define the limits within which they shall exercise jurisdiction.

33.2 Powers of Inspectors [Section 27(2)] For the purpose of ascertaining whether any of the provisions of this Act has been complied with, an Inspector has the following powers :

(a) To require an employer to furnish such information as he may consider necessary;

(b) To enter any establishment or any premises connected therewith at any reasonable time and with such assistance, if any, as he thinks fit, and require any one found in charge thereof to produce before him for examination any accounts books, registers, and other documents relating to the employment of persons or the payment of salary or wage or bonus in the establishment;

(c) To examine the employer, his agent or servant or any other persons found in charge of the establishment or any premises connected therewith or any person whom the Inspector has reasonable cause to believe to be or to have been an employee in the establishment.

(d) To make copies of, or take extracts from any book, register or other document maintained in relation to the establishment.

(e) To exercise such other powers as may be prescribed.

33.3 Inspector Deemed to be Public Servant [Section 27(3)] Every Inspector shall be deemed to be a public servant within the meaning of the Indian Penal Code.

33.4 Duty of Persons called upon Any person directed by an Inspector to produce any accounts, books, register or other document or to give information shall be legally bound to do so.

33.5 No Power to Obtain certain information in case of Banking Co. The Inspector cannot require a banking company to furnish or disclose any statement or information or to produce, or give inspection of, any of its books of account or other documents, which a banking company cannot be compelled to furnish, disclose, produce or give inspection of, under the provisions of Section 34A of the Banking Regulation Act, 1949. [Section 27(9)]

34.0 PROVISIONS RELATING TO PENALTY [SECTION 28]

34.1 When Punishable

(a) If he contravenes any of the provisions of this Act or any rule made thereunder; or

(b) If he fails to comply with the direction or requisition made under this Act.

34.2 Punishment He shall be punishable with imprisonment for a term upto 6 months, *or* with fine upto Rs 1,000, *or* with both.

35.0 PROVISIONS RELATING TO OFFENCES BY COMPANIES [SECTION 29]

35.1 Who are Deemed to be Guilty in Case of Offence [Section 29(1)] In case of an offence by a company, the following persons shall be deemed to be guilty of the offence and shall be liable to be proceeded against and punished accordingly.

(a) Every persons who, at the time when the offence was committed was in charge of and was responsible to the company for the conduct of business of the company; and

(b) the company

35.2 When is such Person not Liable? [Provision to Section 29(1)]

Any such person shall not be liable to any punishment if he proves—

(a) that the offence was committed without his knowledge, *or*

(b) that he exercised all due diligence to prevent the commission of such offence.

35.3 When is Director, Manager, Secretary or Other Officer Liable [Section 29(2)]

In case of an offence by a company if it is proved that the offence has been committed with the consent or connivance of, or is attributable to any neglect on the part of, any director, manager, secretary or other officer of the company, such director, manager, secretary or other officer shall also be deemed to be guilty of that offence and shall be liable to be proceeded against and punished accordingly.

35.4 Meaning of 'Company' and 'Director' [Explanation to Section 29]

For the purposes of this section—

(a) "company" means any body corporate and includes a firm or other association of individuals; and

(b) "director", in relation to a firm, means a partner in the firm.

36.0 PROVISIONS RELATING TO COGNIZANCE OF OFFENCE [SECTION 30(1)]

36.1 No court shall take cognizance of any offence punishable under this Act except on complaint made by or under the authority of—

(a) Appropriate Government, or

(b) Specially authorised officer of that government who must not be

 (i) below the rank of a Regional Labour Commissioner in the case of an officer of the Central Government,

 (ii) below the rank of a Labour Commissioner in the case of an officer of the State Government

36.2 Court Eligible to Try Offence Section 30(2)

No Court inferior to that of a Presidency Magistrate or a Magistrate of the first class shall try any offence punishable under the Act.

Note: Cognizance of any offence means any act or omission made punishable by any law for the time being in force [*Section 3(38) of the General Clauses Act*]

37.0 PROTECTION OF ACTION TAKEN UNDER THE ACT [SECTION 31]

No suit, prosecution or other legal proceeding shall lie against the government or any officer of the government for anything which is in good faith done or intended to be done in pursuance of this Act or any rule made thereunder.

Note: A thing shall be deemed to be done in good faith where it is in fact done honestly, whether it is done negligently or not.

[*Section 3(22) of the General Clauses Act*]

38.0 EFFECT OF LAWS AND AGREEMENTS INCONSISTENT WITH THE ACT [SECTION 34]

Subject to the provisions of Section 31A, the provisions of this Act, shall have effect even if any inconsistent provision is contained in any other law for the time being in force or in the terms of any award, agreement, settlement or contract of service.

39.0 EFFECT OF BONUS ACT ON COAL MINES PROVIDENT FUND AND BONUS SCHEME ACT [SECTION 35]

Nothing contained in this Act shall be deemed to affect the provisions of the Coal Mines Provident Fund and Bonus Schemes Act, 1948 or of any schemes made thereunder.

40.0. POWER OF APPROPRIATE GOVERNMENT TO EXEMPT FROM PROVISIONS OF THE ACT [SEC 36]

40.1 Conditions for Exemption

The exemption shall be given only if the Appropriate government, is of opinion that it will not be in public interest to apply **all or any of the provisions** of this Act to **any establishment or class of establishments**, having regard to the financial position and other relevant circumstances of such establishment.

40.2 Publishing of Order

The order of exemption shall be published **by notification in the Official Gazette**,

40.3 Contents of Order

The order of exemption shall specify—

(i) conditions subject to which exemption is given and

(ii) period of exemption

41.0 POWER TO MAKE RULES [SECTION 38]

41.1 The Central Government may make rules for the purpose of carrying into effect the provisons of this Act and without prejudice to the generality of the foregoing power, such rules may provide for—

(a) the authority for granting permission under the proviso to Sec. 2(91) (iii)

(b) the preparation of registers, records and other documents and the form and manner in which such registers, records and documents may be maintained under Section 26;

(c) the powers which may be exercised by an Inspector under Section 27(2)

(d) any other matter which is to be, or may be, prescribed

41.2 Rule to be laid before both the Houses of Parliament [Section 38(2)] Every rule thus made is to be laid before each House of Parliament while it is in session for a total period of 30 days, which may be comprised in one session or in two or more, successive sessions.

41.2 Effect of Decision of Houses [Section 38(2)]

	Case	*Effect of decisions*
1.	***If both houses agree in making any modification in the rule***	The modified rule shall be operative.
2.	***If both houses agree that the rule should not be made***	The rule made shall not be operative.

41.3 No Effect on Act Done Previously

(a) It may be noted that any such modification or annulment shall be without prejudice to the validity of anything previously done under that rule.

(b) In other words, such modification or annulment shall not effect any previously done act under that rule.

42.0 APPLICATION OF CERTAIN LAWS NOT BARRED [SECTION 39]

Save as otherwise expressly provided, the provisions of the Payment of Bonus Act, 1965 shall be in addition to and not in derogation of the Industrial Disputes Act, 1947 or any corresponding law relating to investigation and settlement of Industrial Disputes in force in a State.

In other words, the application of certain relevant laws is not excluded.

EXERCISES

Very Short Answer Type Questions

1. What is the object of the Payment of Bonus Act, 1965?
2. When did the Payment of Bonus Act come into force?
3. State the territory to which the Payment of Bonus Act, 1965 applies.
4. (a) Who is regarded as an employee?

   (b) Is an apprentice an employee?
5. What is an 'Establishment in Private Sector?
6. Is overtime wages included in Salary or Wage of an employee
7. Does free food allowance form part of salary or wage of an employee?
8. Does any commission payable to the employee form part of salary or wage of an employee?
9. State the Schedule according to which the gross profits are computed—

   (a) in the case of a banking company;

   (b) in case of any other company
10. What is the minimum bonus payable to an employee who has completed 15 years of age?

11. What is the minimum bonus payable to an employee who has not completed 15 years of age?
12. When is an employer bound to pay maximum bonus?
13. What is the maximum amount of bonus payable to an employee?
14. What is the maximum limit of the maximum amount of bonus payable to an employee?
15. Is the amount set on or the amount set off u/s 15 required to be taken while computing the allocable surplus for determing the liability of employees to pay maximum bonus?
16. How is bonus calculated in case of an employee above salary or wage exceeds Rs 10,000 per mensem?
17. When does the provisions of set on apply?
18. What amount is to be carried forward for being set on?
19. For how many accounting years, the amount can be carried forward for being set on?
20. How is the amount carried forward for being set on utilized?
21. When does the provision of set-off apply?
22. What amount is to be carried forward for being set-off?
23. In how many accounting years, the amount can be carried forward for being set-off?
24. State the common provisions relating to both set on and set-off of allocable surplus.
25. Shall an establishment be deemed to be newly set up by reason of change in its location or management name or ownership?
26. Shall the sale of the goods produced or manufactured during the course of the trial running of any factory or of the prospecting stage of any mine or an oil field be taken into consideration for the purposes of calculating bonus in case of newly set up establishment?
27. Shall the employer of an establishment be deemed to have derived profit if—
    (a) he has not made any provisions for current years depreciation.
    (b) the arrears of depreciation and losses for the previous accounting years have not fully set off against his profits.
28. Is adjustment of customary or interim bonus paid permissible against bonus payment under the Act?
29. In an accounting year an employer has sustained financial loss due to employee misconduct. Is this amount of financial loss deductible from the amount of bonus payable to the employee?
30. Can the amount of bonus be paid in kind?
31. Can the Bonus Act be applicable to an establishment in public sector?
32. To Whom the application for the recovery of the bonus?
33. Who can make application for the recovery of the bonus?
34. State the time limit within which application for the recovery of bonus is to be made.

35. Who will issue certificate to collector for the recovery of the bonus?
36. How will the collector proceed to recover the bonus?
37. Does an employee include a person who is entitled to the payment of bonus under this act but who is no longer in employment?
38. Is the dispute with respect to bonus payable on Industrial Dispute?
39. Is the dispute with respect to application of Bonus Act to an establishment in public sector on Industrial Dispute?
40. Can the trade union or employees be permitted to question the correction of duly audited accounts of a banking company?
41. Can the trade union and employees be permited to obtain any information of the banking company?
42. What is the time limit for filing return under the payment of Bonus Act?
43. Who can appoint 'Inspector' under the payment of Bonus Act?
44. Is Inspector appointed under the Payment of Bonus Act a public servant?
45. Can an Inspector require a banking company to furnish any information?
46. What is the punishment for contravention under the Bonus Act?
47. What is the effect of laws and agreements inconsistent with the payment of Bonus Act?
48. Does the Payment of Bonus Act 1965 affect the provisions of the Coal Mines Provident Fund and Bonus Scheme Act, 1948?
49. Who can exempt any establishment from the application of all or any of the provisions of the payment of Bonus Act, 1965?
50. Who can make rules under the Payment of Bonus Act?
51. Is the rule made under the Payment of Bonus Act required to be laid before both the Houses of Parliament?
52. What is the effect of decision of Houses of Parliament on the rule made under the payment of Bonus Act?
53. Shall the modification or annulment by the Houses of parliament effect any previously done act under that rule under the Payment of Bonus Act?
54. Shall the provisions of the Payment of Bonus Act be in addition to or in derogation of the Industrial Disputes Act, 1947?

Shot Answer Type Questions

1. What kind of establishment falls within the perview of the Bonus Act?

*2. Write short notes on:

(a) Accounting year
(b) Allocable Surplus
(c) Appropriate Government
(d) An Award
(e) Employee
(f) Employer
(g) Establishment in private sector
(h) Establishment in public sector
(i) Salary or wage
(j) Available surplus

3. Who is the employer—

(a) where the establishment is a factory
(b) where the establishment is not a factory

4. State when the department undertakings, or branches
   (a) shall be treated as a seperate establishment
   (b) shall be treated as part of the same establishments
5. (a) who is eligible for Bonus?
   (b) who are disqualified from receiving bonus?
6. State the sums deducted from the gross profits as prior charges.
7. How is available surplus computed?
*8. Distinguish between 'Available Surplus' and 'Allocable Suplus'
9. How is direct tax payable by the employer to be calculated?
10. What is the minimum bonus that is payable to—
   (a) an employee who has computed 15 years of age
   (b) an employee who has not completed 15 years of age?
*11. (a) When is employer bound to pay maximum bonus
   (b) What is maximum limit of maximum bonus?
*12. How is number of working days computed?
*13. How is the proportionate deduction in bonus calculated?
*14. Explain the provisions relating to set on and set-off of allocable surplus. ***[May 2008]***
15. State the deductions which an employer can make from the amount of bonus payable to employee
16. State the time limit for payment of bonus.
17. State the conditions under which the provisions of the payment of Bonus Act be made applicable to establishment in pubic sector.
*18. State the procedure which an employee shall adopt for the recovery from his employer of the amount of bonus due to him, under the payment of Bonus Act, 1965.
19. Explain the provision relating to the presumption about accuracy of Balance Sheet and Profit and Loss Account of Corporation and Companies.
20. Explain the provisions relating to the audited accounts of Banking Companies.
21. Explain the provisions relating to the audited accounts of employers not being corporations or companies.
22. List the registers to be prepared and maintained by every employer under the Payment of Bonus Act.
23. State the time limit for filing return under the Payment of Bonus Act.
24. Explain the provisions of the payment of Bonus Act relating to the appointment, powers and functioning of the Inspector appointed under the Act.
25. Explain the provisions of the Payment of Bonus Act relating to penalty.
26. Explain the provisions of the Payment of Bonus Act relating to offences by Companies.
27. Who are deemed to be guilty in case of offences by companies?
28. When shall a person not be liable to punishment in case of offences by companies?

29. When shall director, managers, secretary or other officer be liable in case of offences by companies?
30. When can a court take cognizance of any offence punishable under the Payment of Bonus Act?
31. State the protection of action taken under the Payment of Bonus Act.
32. State the special provision with respect to payment of bonus linked with production or productivity.
33. State the provisions of the payment of Bonus Act relating to the power of exemption.
34. Explain the provisions relating to the making of rules under the Payment of Bonus Act.

CHAPTER 21 The Payment of Gratuity Act, 1972

1.0 INTRODUCTION

1.1 Meaning of Gratuity

Gratuity is a word derived from a Latin word '*Gratuitas*' which simply means a 'Gift'. Gratuity scheme is one of the social security schemes which provides for payment of a lumpsum amount by an employer to his employee for his past services.

1.2 What is the object of Gratuity Scheme ?

The object of a gratuity scheme is to provide a retiring benefit to the workmen who have rendered long and unblemished service to the employer and thereby contributed to the prosperity of the employer

[*Delhi Cloth and General Mills Co. Ltd. vs. their workers (1968) 36 FJR 247 (SC)*].

1.3 Why it became necessary to have a Central Law on the Gratuity ?

It became necessary to have a Central Law on the gratuity to ensure a uniform pattern of payment of gratuity to the employees throughout the country. The Payment of Gratuity Act, 1972 was enacted largely on the basis of the West Bengal Employees' Payment of Gratuity Act, 1971 with some modifications which were made in the light of the views expressed in the Indian Labour Conference relating to the forfeiture of gratuity in cases of dismissal for gross misconduct.

1.4 What is the Payment of Gratuity Act, 1972?

The Payment of Gratuity Act, 1972 is an Act to provide for a scheme for the payment of gratuity to employees engaged in factories, mines, oilfields, plantations, ports, railway companies, shops or other establishments and for matters connected therewith or incidental thereto.

1.5 On which Date the Payment of Gratuity Act, 1972 came into Force?

The Payment of Gratuity Act, 1972 came into force on 16.9.1972.

1.6 What is the Territory to which the Payment of Gratuity Act, 1972 extends ? [Sec. 1(2)]

- It extends to the whole of India:
- It shall not extend to the State of Jammu and Kashmir in so far as it relates to plantations or ports.

2.0 ESTABLISHMENTS TO WHICH THE PAYMENT OF GRATUITY ACT, 1972 APPLIES [SEC. 1(3)]

The Payment of Gratuity Act, 1972 shall apply to—

(a) every factory, mine, oilfield, plantation, port and railway company;

(b) every shop or establishment within the meaning of any law for the time being in force in relation to shops and establishments in a State, in which at least 10 persons are employed, or were employed, on any day of the preceding 12 months;

(c) such other establishments or class of establishments, in which at least 10 employees are employed, or were employed, on any day of the preceding 12 months, as may be specified by the Central Government by notification in the Official Gazette.

Under Sec. 1(3)(c), the Central Government has specified Motor Transport undertakings, clubs, chambers of commerce and industry, inland water transport establishments, Solicitors' Officers, Local Bodies and circus industry, in which atleast 10 persons are employed or were employed on any day of the preceding 12 months, as classes of establishments to which the Act shall apply.

Act continues to apply even after No. of Persons falls below 10 [Sec. 1(3A)]

A shop or establishment to which this Act has become applicable shall continue to be governed by this Act even if the number of persons employed therein falls below 10.

Notes :

(i) The expression 'law' used in Section 1(3)(b) means any law in respect of shops, establishments, commercial or non-commercial.

[K. Gangadar vs. Appellate Authority, (1993) 66 FLR 648 (AP)]

(ii) The provisions of Section 1(3)(b) of the Act are very much comprehensive. It also includes Municipal Board.

[Municipal Board vs. Union of India, (1993) 67 FLR 93(All)].

Three Eligibility Conditions to receive Gratuity

A person is eligible to receive gratuity under the Act if—

1. He is an employee under the definition of Section 2(e) of the Act
2. He is employed in an establishment to which the Act applies
3. He has rendered continuous service for at least 5 years except in case of death/disablement.

3.0 IMPORTANT DEFINITIONS [SEC. 2 AND 2A]

3.1 Appropriate Government [Sec. 2(1)]

Establishment	*Appropriate Govt.*
1. in relation to an establishment	
(a) belonging to, or under the control of the Central Government	Central Government
(b) having branches in more than one states	Central Government
(c) of a factory belonging to, or under the control of the Central Government	Central Government
(d) of a major port, mine oilfield or railway company	Central Government
2. in any other case	State Government

3.2 Completed Year of Service means continuous service for one year [Sec. 2(b)]

3.3 Employee [Sec. 2(e)]. "Employee" means—

- any person (**other than an apprentice**) employed on wages, in any establishment, factory, mine, oilfield, plantation, port, railway company or shop

- to do any skilled, semi-skilled, or unskilled, manual, supervisory, technical or clerical work,
- whether the terms of employment are express or implied, and
- whether or not such person is employed in a managerial or administrative capacity,
- **but does not include** any such person who holds a post under the Central Government or a State Government and is governed by any other Act or by any rules providing for payment of gratuity.

3.4 **"Employer"** means, in relation to any establishment, factory, mine, oilfield, plantation, port, railway company or shop—

(i) ***belonging to, or under the control of, the Central Government or a State Government***	• a person or authority appointed by the appropriate Government for the supervision and control of employees, or • the head of the Ministry or Department concerned, where no person or authority has been so appointed,
(ii) ***belonging to, or under the control of, any local authority***	• the person appointed by such authority for the supervision and control of employees or • the chief executive officer of the local authority, where no person has been so appointed,
(iii) ***in any other case***	• the person, who, or the authority which, has the ultimate control over the affairs of the establishment, factory, mine, oilfield, plantation, port, railway company or shop, or • a manager, managing director or any other person; to whom said affairs are entrusted.

3.5 **Factory [Sec. 2(g)]**

'Factory' means—

any premises including the precincts (adjoining area) thereof—

(i) wherein at least 10 workers are working *or* were working on any day of the preceding 12 months, *and* in any part of which a manufacturing process is being carried on with the aid of power, or is ordinarily so carried on; *or*

(ii) wherein at least 20 workers are working or were working on any day of the preceding 12 months, *and* of a manufacturing process is being carried on without the aid of power, or is ordinarily so carried on.

'Factory' does not include—

(i) a mine covered under the Mines Act, 1952;

(ii) mobile unit belonging to the armed forces of the Union;

(iii) a railway running shed;

(iv) a hotel, restaurant or eating place.

3.6 Family [Sec. 2(h)]

In the case of a male employee, Family means—	*In the case of a female employee, Family means—*
• The employee **himself**	• the employee **herself**
• **Wife** of employee	• **Husband** of employee
• Children of employee (whether married or unmarried)	• Children of employee (whether married or unmarried)
• Dependent parents of employee	• Dependent parents of employee
• Dependent parents of **wife** of employee	• Dependent parents of **husband** of employee
• Widow and children of predeceased son of employee	• Widow and children of predeceased son of employee

Inclusion of Adopted child— If the personal law of an employee permits adoption of a child;' *and* employee lawfully adopts a child, then the adopted child shall be deemed to be **included** in his/her family.

Exclusion of Adopted child—If any child of the employee is adopted by another person *and* the personal law of the person making such adoption permits such adoption, then such child shall be deemed to be **excluded** from his/her family.

3.7 Retirement means termination of the service of an employee otherwise than on superannuation [Sec. 2(q)]

3.8 Superannuation [Sec. 2(r)] In relation to an employee, means—the attainment by the employee of such age—

- as is fixed in the contract or conditions of service.
- as the age on the attainment of which the employer shall vacate the employment [Sec. 2(r)]

3.9 "Wages" means

- all emoluments which are earned by an employee
- while on duty or on leave
- in accordance with the terms and conditions of his employment and
- which are paid or are payable to him in cash and
- **includes** dearness allowance but
- **does not include** any bonus, commission, house rent allowance, overtime wages and any other allowance. [Sec 2(s)]

3.10 Continuous Service [Sec. 2A]

1. an employee shall be said to be in continuous service for a period if he has, for that period, been in uninterrupted service, including service which may be interrupted on account of sickness, accident, leave, absence from duty without leave (not being absence in respect of which an order treating the absence as break in service has been passed in accordance with the standing orders, rules or regulations governing the employees of the establishment), lay-off, strike or a lock-out or cessation of work not due to any fault of the employee, whether such uninterupted or interrupted service was rendered before or after the commencement of this Act;
2. an employee employed in a non-seasonal establishment who is not in continuous service for any period of 1 year *or* 6 months, shall be deemed to be in continuous service for 1 year *or* 6 months if the employee during immediately preceding 12/6 calendar months has actually worked under the employer for at least—

Employee	*Who is not in continuous service for 12 months*	*Who is not in continuous service for 6 months*
(a) In case of an employee employed below the ground in a mine	190 days	95 days
(b) In case of an employee employed in an establishment which works for less than 6 days in a week.	190 days	95 days
(c) In case of any other employee	240 days	120 days

3. While computing the number of days on which an employee has actually worked under an employer, include the following days :
   (i) The days during which employee has been laid-off
   (ii) The days during which employee has been on leave with full wages, earned in the previous year;
   (iii) The days during which employee has been absent due to temporary disablement caused by accident arising out of and in the course of his employment; and
   (iv) The days during which female employee has been on maternity leave not exceeding 12 weeks.
4. where an employee, employed in a seasonal establishment, is not in continuous service of 1 year or 6 months, he shall be deemed to be in continuous service under the employer for such period if he has actually worked for at least 75% of the number of days on which the establishment was in operation during such period. [Sec. 2A]

Notes :

(i) An employee who is re-employed without any break in service will be eligible for gratuity and he can not be denied to get the gratuity simply on the ground of the change in employment.
[Jeevan Lal (1929) Ltd. vs. Controlling Authority; (1982) (LLN 21)].

(ii) A retrenched employee is also entitled for gratuity
[State of Punjab vs. Labour Court (1986)].

3.11 Controlling Authority

1. Controlling Authority means an authority appointed by the Appropriate Government u/s 3 (Sec. 2(d)].
2. The Appropriate Government may, by notification, appoint any officer to be a controlling authority, who shall be responsible for the administration of this Act and different authorities may be appointed for different areas. [Sec. 3]

4.0 WHEN AND TO WHOM IS GRATUITY PAYABLE UNDER THE PAYMENT OF GRATUITY ACT, 1972? [SEC. 4(1)]

4.1 Gratuity shall be payable to an employee on the termination of his employment after he has rendered continuous service for atleast 5 years,—

(a) on his superannuation, or

(b) on his retirement or resignation, or

(c) on his death or disablement due to accident or disease:

4.2 However the completion of continuous service of 5 years shall not be necessary where the termination of the employment of any employee is due to death or disablement:

Note: 'disablement' means such disablement as incapacitates an employee for the work which he was capable of performing before the accident or disease resulting in such disablement.

4.3 **Payment to Nominee/heirs in case of death**—In the case of death of the employee, gratuity payable to him shall be paid to his nominee or, if no nomination has been made, to his heirs, and where any such nominees or heirs is a minor, the share of such minor, shall be deposited with the controlling authority who shall invest the same for the benefit of such minor in such bank or other financial institution, as may be prescribed, until such minor attains majority.

Notes :

(i) The payability of Gratuity to the employee is his right as well as the obligation of the employer. By the change of ownership, the relationship of employer and employees subsits and the new employer cannot escape from the liability of payment of gratuity to the employee.

[Pattathurila K. Damodaran vs. M. Kassim Kanju (1993) ILLJ (1211 (Ker.)].

(ii) An employee resigning from service is also entitled to gratuity.

[Texmaco Ltd. vs. Sri Ram Dham, 1992 LLR 369 (Del)].

(iii) Non acceptance of the resignation is no hurdle in the way of an employee to claim gratuity.

[Mettur Spinning Mills vs. Deputy Commissioner of Labour, (1983) II LLJ 188).

(iv) A retrenched employee is entitled to gratuity.

[State of Punjab vs. Labour Court (1980) [SLR 953].

(v) Employees employed in a temple are entitled to a gratuity.

[Administrator, Shree Jagannath Temple (1992) 65 FLR 946 (Orissa)].

(vi) An employee who is re-employed without any break in service will be eligible for gratuity. *[Jeevanlal (1929) Ltd. vs. Controlling Authority (1982) ILR N 217].*

5.0 WHAT IS THE AMOUNT OF GRATUITY PAYABLE? [SEC. 4(2)]

Case	*Amount of Gratuity Payable by Employer*
1. **In case of an employee of establishment (whether seasonal or non-seasonal), who is employed throughout the year**	
(a) *In case of monthly Rated Employee*	Last Drawn Monthly Wages × 15/26 × No. of completed years of service (including part thereof in excess of 6 months.)
(b) *In the case of a piece-rated employee*	Total wages (excluding overtime wages) for 3 months immediately preceding the termination of employment = $\frac{\text{termination of employment}}{\text{Total No. of Actual Working days of Employee in 3 months}}$ × 15/26 × No. of completed years of service (including part thereof in excess of 6 months.)

2. **In case of an employee of a seasonal establishment who is not employed throughout the year**	= Last drawn Monthly Wages × 7/26 × No. of seasons.

5.2 What is the Maximum Amount of Gratuity Payable?

The amount of gratuity payable to an employee must not exceed **Rs 10,00,000** [vide Notification S.O.1217(E) 24.5.2010]

5.3 Wages for computing the gratuity payable to an employee who is employed after his disablement [Sec. 4(4)]

Wages for computing the gratuity payable to an employee who is employed after his disablement on reduced wages shall be taken as follows:

Period	*Wages*
1. *For the period preceding his disablement*	Wages last drawn at the time of disablement
2. *For the period subsequent to his disablement*	Reduced wages last drawn at the time of termination of services.

5.4 Shall the Right of an Employee to Receive better terms of Gratuity Affected? [Sec. 4(5)]

The provisions of this Act shall not affect the right of an employee to receive better terms of gratuity under any award or agreement or contract with the employer.

Some Important Judicial Pronouncements

(i) If for the purposes of computation of quantum of the amount of gratuity the terms of agreement or settlement are better than the Act, the employee is entitled for that benefit but the maximum statutory ceiling limit as provided under section 4(3) of the Act cannot be reduced by mutual settlement or agreement [*Bharat Commerce & Industries* v. *Ramprasad*, 2001 LLR 918 (MP)]

(ii) By change of ownership, the relationship of employer and employees subsists and the new employer cannot escape from the liability of payment of gratuity to the employees.

[*Pattathurila K. Damodaran* v. *M. Kassim Kanju*, (1993) I LLJ 1211 (Ker).]

6.0 WHAT ARE THE PROVISIONS RELATING TO FORFEITURE OF GRATUITY [SEC. 4(6)]

Reason for Termination of Services	*Extent of Forfeiture of Security*
1. ***for any act, willful omission or negligence causing any damage or loss to, or destruction of, property belonging to the employer' [Sec. 4(6)(a)]***	1. The gratuity shall be forfeited to the extent of the damage or loss so caused.
2. ***for his riotous or disorderly conduct or any other act of violence on his part, or***	2. The gratuity may be wholly or partially forfeited.
3. ***for any act which constitutes an offence involving moral turpitude provided that such offence is committed by him in the course of his employment. [Sec. 4(6)(b)]***	3. The gratuity may be wholly or partially forfeited.

Some Important Judicial Pronouncements

(i) Any decision to forfeit the gratuity under this section can be taken only after affording opportunity of being heard to the employee concerned

[*Bharat Gold Mines Ltd.* v. *Regional Labour Commissioner*]

(ii) When an offence of theft under law involves moral turpitude, gratuity stands wholly forfeited in view of section 4(6) of the Act

[*Bharat Gold Mines Ltd.* v. *Regional Labour Commissioner* (*Central*), (1987) 70 FJR 11 (Karn).]

(iii) The appellant even after superannuation continued to occupy the quarter and the Government in accordance with the rules charged the penal rent from him and after adjusting other dues, the gratuity amount offered to be paid. The court held that there is no illegality in this amount of gratuity

[*Wazir Chand* v. *Union of India*, 2001 LLR 172 (SC)].

(iv) Refusal of employees to surrender land belonging to employer is not a ground to withhold gratuity

[*Travancore Playwood Industries Ltd. v. Regional Joint Labour Commissioner, (1966) II LLJ 85 (Ker).]*

(v) The right of the employer to forfeit the amount of earned gratuity of an employee whose services were terminated for any act, willful omission or negligence causing any damage to the employer is limited to the extent of the damage, and the proof of such damage.

[*Parmali Wallance Limited vs. State of M.P., (196) II LLJ 515 (MP)*]

(vi) But when an employee, who has been given the benefit of probation under Section 3 of the Probation of Offenders Act, 1958, cannot be disqualified to receive the amount of his gratuity. [S.N. Sunderson (Minerals) Ltd. *vs.* Appellate Authority-cm-Deputy Labour Commissioner, (1990) 60 FLR 6 (Summary) (M.P.)]

(vii) Withholding of gratuity is not permissible under any circumstances other than those enumerated in Section 4(6) of the Act and the right to gratuity is a statutory right and none can be deprived from such right.

[*K.C. Matthew vs. Plantation Corporation of Kerala Ltd., 2001 LLR (2) (Ker.)*]

7.0 COMPULSORY INSURANCE (SEC. 4A)

7.1 Employer's Liability to Obtain an Insurance [Sec. 4A(1)]—Every Employer is required to obtain an insurance for his liability for payment towards the gratuity from LIC or any other prescribed insurer.

7.2 Employers Exempted from Compulsory Insurance [Sec. 4A(1), 4A(2)]

1. Employer of an establishment belonging to or under the Control of the Central Govt./State Govt.
2. Employer who had already established an Approved Gratuity Fund and who desires to continue such arrangement and who has been exempted by Appropriate Govt.
3. Employer employing at least 500 persons who establishes an Approved Gratuity Fund in prescribed manner and who has been exempted by Appropriate Govt.

7.3 Compulsory Registration with Controlling Authority [Sec. 4A(3)]

Every employer shall get his establishment registered with the controlling authority in the prescribed manner, within a prescribed time and only that employer who has taken an insurance or has established an approved gratuity fund shall be registered.

7.4 Power to make Rules [Sec. 4A(4)]

The appropriate Government may make rules to provide :

(a) for the composition of the Board of Trustees of the approved gratuity fund, and

(b) for the recovery by the controlling authority of the amount of the gratuity payable to an employee from the Life Insurance Corporation of India or any other insurer with, or the Board of Trustees of the Approved Gratuity Fund.

7.5 Consequences of Default [Sec. 4A(5), (6)]

(a) If the employer fails to pay the premium to the insurance or to contribute to an approved gratuity fund, he shall be liable to pay the amount of gratuity (including interest, if any, for delayed payments) to the controlling authority.

(b) Its contravention is punishable with a fine upto Rs. 10,000 and in case of continuing offence with a further fine upto Rs. 1,000 per day for each day during which the offence continues.

7.6 Approved Gratuity shall have the same meaning as in Sec. 2(5) of the Income Tax Act, 1961

8.0 POWER OF APPROPRIATE GOVT. TO EXEMPT [SEC. 5]

The appropriate Government may, by notification, and subject to such conditions as may be specified in the notification, exempt—

(a) any establishment, factory, mine, oilfield, plantation, port, railway company or shop to which this Act applies from the operation of the provisions of this Act if, in the opinion of the appropriate Government, the employees in such establishment factory, mine, oilfield, plantation, port, railway company or shop are in receipt of gratuity or pensionary benefits **not less favourable** than the benefits conferred under this Act. [Sec. 5(1)]

(b) any employee or class of employees employed in any establishment, factory, mine, oilfield, plantation, port, railway company or shop to which this Act applies from the operation of the provisions of this Act, if, in the opinion of the appropriate Government, such employee or class of employees are in receipt of gratuity or pensionary benefits not less favourable than the benefits conferred under this Act. [Sec. 5(2)]

Can Notification be issued retrospectively ?

Yes. A notification may be issued retrospectively a date not earlier than the date of commencement of this Act, but no such notification shall be issued so as to prejudicially, affect the interests of any person.

9.0 WHAT ARE THE PROVISIONS AS TO NOMINATION [SEC. 6]

9.1 Is Nomination compulsory ?

Every employee who has completed 1 year of service, is compulsorily required to make a nomination.

9.2 Time limit within which Nomination is required to be made

The nomination must be made *within* ***30 days*** **of completion of one year of service.**

9.3 Who can be Nominee ?

(*a*) ***If, at the time of making nomination, the employee has a family,***	The nomination **must** be made in favour of one or more members of the family. (**Note :** Nomination shall be void if it is made in favour of a person who is not a member of his family).
(*b*) ***If at the time of making nomination, the employee does not have a family,***	The nomination **may** be made in favour of any person. If the employee subsequently acquires a family, such nomination shall forthwith become void, and the employee shall, *within 90 days,* make a fresh nomination in favour of one or more members of his family in duplicate on form 'G'.

9.4 Can there be more than one Nominee ?

Yes. The employee may distribute the amount of gratuity amongst more than one nominee.

9.5 Can nomination be modified ?

Yes. The nomination already made by an employee may be modified by him at any time by giving a written notice to his employer.

9.6 Consequences of death of nominee

If the nominee dies before the death of the employee, the employee shall make a **fresh nomination** in duplicate on form 'H'.

9.7 Safe Custody of Nomination

- Every nomination, fresh nomination and modification of nomination shall be sent by the employee to the employer, who shall keep the same in safe custody.
- The employer shall verify the service particulars of the employee as given in the nomination form within 30 days of the receipt of nomination form.
- The employer shall return one copy of the nomination form to the employee, as acknowledgment.

9.8 Effective date of Nomination

Nomination comes into operation from the **date of receipt** of the same by the employer.

9.9 Submission of Nomination

An employee may submit the nomination form *either* by personal service *or* by registered post with acknowledgment.

10.0 WHAT ARE THE PROVISIONS RELATING TO APPLICATION, DETERMINATION AND PAYMENT OF GRATUITY ? [SEC. 7]

10.1 Provisions relating to Application for Payment of Gratuity

Who is required to make Application ?	1. An employee who is eligible for payment of gratuity. 2. Any person authorised in writing by such employee. 3. Nominee (in case nomination exists). 4. Legal heir (in case of no nomination)

To whom Application is to be made	Application shall be made to **employer.**
Time Limit for Application	• By Nominee within 30 days from the date gratuity becomes payable • By Legal heir within 1 year from the date gratuity becomes payable • By Employee/authorised person within 30 days from the date gratuity becomes payable. **Note :** Employee may apply before 30 days of date of superannuation or retirement if such date is known in advance.
Manner of Making Application	The application shall be made **in writing.**
Form of Application	**For Nominee**—Form 'J' or Plain Paper **For Legal heirs**—Form 'K' or Plain Paper **For Others**—Form 'I'.
Content of Application	The application shall require the employer to pay the gratuity to the employee.
Manner of Presenting Application	The application shall be presented to the employer *either* by personal service *or* by registered post with acknowledgement.
Effect of Delayed Application	An Application even after the prescribed period shall also be entertained by the employer, if the sufficient case for delay has been mentioned in the application. Any dispute in this regard shall be referred to the Controlling Authority for his decision. In any case, the **claim for gratuity cannot treated as invalid** merely because the claimant failed to submit the application within the prescribed time.

10.2 Duty of Employer to Determine Gratuity and give Notice [Sec. 7(2)]

As soon as gratuity becomes payable, the employer **must (*whether an application has been made or not*)** determine the amount of gratuity and give notice in writing to the person to whom the gratuity is payable and also to the controlling authority specifying the amount of gratuity so determined.

10.3 Duty of Employer to Pay [Sec. 7(3)]

The employer must arrange to pay the amount of gratuity **within 30 days** from the date it becomes payable to the person to whom the gratuity is payable.

10.4 Duty of Employer to Pay Simple Interest in case of Default [Sec. 7(3A)]

(a) If the amount of gratuity payable is not paid by the employer within 30 days, the employer must pay, simple interest at prescribed rate from the due date of gratuity to the actual date of payment.

(b) However, no such interest shall be payable if the delay in the payment is due to the fault of the employee and the employer has obtained permission in writing from the controlling authority for the delayed payment on this ground.

11.0 NOTICE FOR PAYMENT OF GRATUITY [RULE 8]

11.1 Time Limit within which Notice must be issued

If the claim for gratuity is found admissible on verification	Within 15 days of receipt of application, the employer must issue a notice in **Form 'L'** to the applicant employee, nominee or legal heir, as the case may be, specifying the amount of gratuity payable and fixing a date, not being later than the 30th day after the date of receipt of the application, for payment thereof, or
If the claim for gratuity is not found admissible	Within 15 days of receipt of application, the employer must issue a notice in **Form 'M'** to the applicant employee, nominee or legal heir, as the case may be specifying the reasons why the claim for gratuity is not considered admissible alongwith a copy endorsed to the controlling authority.

11.2 Employer's Power to ask for Evidence

If the claimant for gratuity is a nominee or a legal heir, the employer may ask for such witness or evidence as may be deemed relevant for establishing his identity or maintainability of his claim. In that case, the time specified for issuance of notices shall be operative with effect from the date such witness or evidence, called for by the employer is furnished to the employer.

11.3 Service of Notice. The notices on Form 'L' or 'M' shall be served on the applicant *either* by personal service after taking receipt *or* by registered post with acknowledgment.

12.0 MODE OF PAYMENT OF GRATUITY [RULE 9]

12.1 The gratuity shall be paid either in **cash or in demand draft or bank cheque** to the claimant.

12.2 If the claimant desires and the amount of gratuity payable is **less than Rs. 1,000** payment may be made by **postal money order** after deducting the commission due to such postal money order from the amount payable.

12.3 The intimation about the details of payment shall be given to the controlling authority by the employer.

12.4 In case of the nominee or a legal heir, who is minor, the controlling authority shall invest the gratuity amount deposited by him for the benefit of such minor in term deposit with the State Bank of India or any of its subsidiaries or any nationalized Bank.

13.0 WHAT ARE THE PROVISIONS RELATING TO DISPUTE AS TO THE AMOUNT OF GRATUITY?

13.1 Nature of Dispute—Dispute may arise as to :

(a) the amount of gratuity payable to an employee, *or*

(b) as to the admissibility of any claim of, an employee for payment of gratuity, *or*

(c) as to the person entitled to receive the gratuity,

13.2 Employer's Duty to deposit Gratuity with Controlling Authority [Sec. 7(4)(a)]

The employer shall deposit with the controlling authority such amount as he admits to be payable by him as gratuity.

13.3 Right to make Application to Controlling Authority [Sec. 7(4)(b)]

Where there is a dispute the employer or employee or any other person raising the dispute may make an application to the controlling authority for deciding the dispute.

13.4 Power of Controlling Authority to decide the dispute etc. [Sec. 7(4)(c)(d)(e)]

1. The controlling authority shall, after due inquiry and after giving the parties to the dispute a reasonable opportunity of being heard, determine the matter or matters in dispute and if, as a result of such inquiry any amount is found to be payable to the employee, the controlling authority shall direct the employer to pay such amount or, as the case may be, such amount as reduced by the amount already deposited by the employer.
2. The controlling authority shall pay the amount deposited, including the excess amount, if any, deposited by the employer, to the person entitled thereto.
3. As soon as may be after a deposit is made under clause (a), the controlling authority shall pay the amount of the deposit—
   (i) to the applicant where he is employee; or
   (ii) where the applicant is not the employee, to the nominee or, as the case may be, the guardian of such nominee or heir of the employee if the controlling authority is satisfied that there is no dispute as to the right of the applicant to receive the amount of gratuity.
4. For the purpose of conducting an inquiry, the controlling authority shall have the following powers as are vested in a civil court,
   (a) enforcing the attendance of any person or examining him on oath;
   (b) requiring the discovery and production of documents;
   (c) receiving evidence on affidavits;
   (d) issuing commissions for the examination of witnesses.

14.0 APPLICATION TO CONTROLLING AUTHORITY FOR DIRECTION [RULE 10]

14.1 Circumstances under which the claimant can apply for Direction

The claimant (employee, nominee or legal heir, as the case may be) may, within 90 days of the occurrence of the cause for the application, apply in Form 'N' to the controlling authority for issuing a direction under the following Circumstances :

(a) If an employer refuses to accept nomination, *or*

(b) If an employer refuses to entertain an application sought to be filed for the payment of gratuity, *or*

(c) If an employer issues a notice either specifying an amount of gratuity which is considered by the applicant less than what is payable or rejecting eligibility to payment of gratuity or having received an application for the payment of gratuity and fails to issue any notice as required within the specified time (i.e. within 15 days)

14.2 Acceptance of Application after 90 days—The controlling authority may accept any application on sufficient case being shown by the applicant, after the expiry of the specified period also.

14.3 Service of Application—The said application and other relevant documents shall be presented to the controlling authority *either* by personal service *or* by registered post with acknowledgment.

15.0 PROCEDURE FOR DETAILING WITH APPLICATION FOR DIRECTION [RULE 1]

(a) On receipt of application for direction the controlling authority shall issue a notice in Form 'O' to call upon the applicant as well as the employer to appear before him on a specified date, time and place, either by himself or through his authorized representative alongwith all the relevant documents and evidences, if any.

(b) Any person desiring to act on behalf of an employer or the claimant shall present a letter of authority from the person concerned to the controlling authority alongwith a written statement explaining his interest in matter and praying for permission to act so.

(c) The controlling authority shall record the same according his approval or specifying the reasons, in case of refusal to grant the permission.

(d) A party appearing through his representative shall be bound by the acts of his representative.

(e) After completion of hearing on the date fixed, or after such further evidence, examination of documents, witnesses, hearing and enquiry, as may be deemed necessary, the controlling authority shall record his findings as to whether any amount is payable to the applicant under the Act. A copy of the finding shall be given to each of the parties.

(f) If the employer fails to appear on the specified date of hearing after due service of notice without sufficient case, the controlling authority may proceed to hear and determine the application *ex-parte* and if the applicant fails to appear on the specified date of hearing without sufficient cause, the controlling authority may dismiss the application.

(g) The order passed may be received on good cause being shown within 30 days of the said order and the application reheard after giving at least 14 days notice to the opposite party of the date fixed for rehearing of the application.

(h) The controlling authority shall record the particulars of each case in Form 'Q' and at the time of passing orders shall sign and date the particulars so recorded and shall also record the findings on the merits of the case and file it alongwith the memoranda of evidence with the order sheet.

16.0 DIRECTION FOR PAYMENT [RULE 7]

16.1 If the findings are recorded that the application is entitled for the payment of gratuity under the Act, the controlling authority shall issue a notice to the employer concerned on Form 'R' specifying the amount payable and directing payment thereof to the applicant, under intimation to the controlling authority within 30 days from the date of the receipt of the notice, by the employer.

16.2 A copy of the notice shall be endorsed to the applicant also.

17.0 RIGHT OF AGGRIEVED PERSON TO MAKE AN APPEAL [SEC. 7(7)]

17.1 Appeal within 60 days—Any person aggrieved by an order of Controlling Authority u/s 7(4) may, within **60 days** from the date of the receipt of the order, prefer an appeal to the Appropriate Government or prescribed authority.

17.2 Appeal within Extended Period—The appropriate Government or the appellate authority, as the case may be, may, if it is satisfied that the appellant was prevented by sufficient cause from preferring the appeal within the said period of 60 days, extend the said period by a further period of 60 days.

17.3 Deposit of Gratuity being Condition for an appeal by Employer—No appeal by an employer shall be admitted unless at the time of preferring the appeal, the appellant either produces a certificate of the controlling authority to the effect that the appellant has deposited with him an amount equal to the amount of gratuity required to be deposited u/s 7(4), or deposits with the appellate authority such amount.

17.4 Power to Decide upon Appeal [Sec. 7(8)]

The appropriate Government or the appellate authority, as the case may be, may, after giving the parties to the appeal a reasonable opportunity of being heard confirm modify, or reverse the decision of the controlling authority.

Some Important Judicial Pronouncements

(i) An application for condonation of delay in filing application under section 7(7) is not mandatory.

[*Nataraja Pillai* v. *Regional Jt. Labour Commissioner*, (1993) 66 FLR 413 (Ker).]

(ii) The employee's right to interest on delayed payment is statutory. [*Champaran Sugar Co. Ltd.* v. *Joint Labour Commissioner and Appellate Authority*, (1987) 54 FLR 60 (Pat) (FB).]

(iii) Under section 7(7) of the Act an appeal is maintainable only against the final order of the Controlling Authority.

[*Malabar Spg. & Wvg. Mills* v. *N.N. Nair*, (1989) 74 FJR 1989 (Ker).]

(iv) If the deposit of the amount ordered by the controlling authority is not made as provided under the second proviso to sub-section, there would be no scope for to entertain the appeal.

[*Special Officer, the Kanyakumari District Co-operative Printing Works Ltd.* v. *Appellate Authority Under Payment of Gratuity Act, Thirunelveli*, 2001 LLR 613 (Mad).]

18.0 WHAT ARE THE PROVISIONS RELATING TO RECOVERY OF GRATUITY? [SEC. 8]

If the gratuity payable under the Act is not paid by the employer within 30 days of due date of gratuity the following provisions apply:

1. **Application.**	The aggrieved person is required to make an application in Form 'T' in duplicate to the controlling authority. [Rule 19]
2. **Opportunity of being heard.**	The controlling authority before issuing a certificate must give the employer a reasonable opportunity of showing cause against the issue of such certificate.
3. **Recovery Certificate.**	The controlling authority shall issue a certificate to the controller for that amount together with the compound interest thereon at the prescribed rate from the date of expiry of the prescribed time till the actual date of payment.
4. **Maximum Interest**	The amount of interest payable must not exceed the amount of gratuity payable under this Act.
5. **Recovery by Collector**	The controller shall recover the same as arrears of land revenue and pay the same to the person entitled thereto.

Note: Interest is admissible only if a certificate for recovery of dues as a public demand has been issued; [*Charan Singh* v. *Birla Textiles*, (1988) 57 FLR 534 (SC).]

19.0 WHAT ARE THE PROVISIONS RELATING TO PENALTIES UNDER THE PAYMENT OF GRATUITY ACT, 1972? [SEC. 9]

The penalties for various defaults are as follows:

Offence	*Penalty*
1. *Any person who is responsible, for the purpose of avoiding any payment to be made by himself under this Act or of enabling any other person to avoid such payment, knowingly makes or causes to be made any false statement or false representation*	Punishable with imprisonment for a term upto 6 months or fine upto Rs. 10,000 or with both.
2. **Where the employer's offence relates to:**	
(a) *non-payment of any gratuity payable under the Act*	Employer is punishable with imprisonment for a **minimum** term of **6 months** and **maximum** term of **2 years** unless the court trying the offence, for reason to be recorded by it in writing, is of opinion that a lesser term of imprisonment or the imposition of a fine would meet the ends of justice.
(b) *any other default under the Act*	Employer is punishable for a **minimum** term of **3 months** and **maximum** term of **1 year or** with **minimum fine** of **Rs. 10,000** and **maximum fine** of **Rs. 20,000 or both.**

20.0 PROTECTION OF GRATUITY [SEC. 13]

Gratuity payable to an employee shall not be liable to attachment in execution of any decree or order of the Civil or Revenue or Criminal Court.

It is immaterial as to whether the gratuity is payable to the employee—

(a) under the Act; *or*

(b) in an establishment exempted u/s 5.

MISCELLANEOUS PROVISIONS

20.0 INSPECTORS

20.1 Appointment of Inspectors [Sec. 7A]

1. **Who can Appoint Inspectors ?** The Appropriate Government may appoint as many Inspectors, as it deems fit, for the purposes of the Act by Notification in the Official Gazette.
2. **Power to define Authority**—he Appropriate Government may, by general or special order, define the area to which the authority of an inspector so appointed shall extend and where two or more inspectors are appointed for the same area, also provide, by such order, for the distribution or allocation of work to be performed by them.
3. **Public Servant**—Every inspector shall be deemed to be a **public servant** within the meaning of Section 21 of the IPC.

20.2 Purpose of Appointment of Inspectors—Inspectors are appointed to ascertain whether or not the Provisions of the Act have been complied with by an employer.

20.3 Powers of Inspectors [Sec. 7B]

An inspector may exercise all *or* any of the following powers :

1. to require an employer to furnish such informations as he may consider necessary,
2. to enter and inspect, at all reasonable hours, any premises of or place in any factory, mine, oilfield, plantation, port, railway company, shop or other establishment to which this Act applies, for the purpose of examining any register, record or notice or other documents required to be kept or exhibited under this Act or the rules made thereunder.
3. to examine the employer or any person whom he finds in such premises or place and employee employed therein, having a reasonable cause to believe.
4. to make copies of, or take extracts from, any register, record, notice or other document, as he may consider relevant, and where he has reason to believe that any offence under this Act has been committed by an employer, search seize with such assistance as he may think fit, such register, record, notice or other document as he may consider relevant in respect of that offence.
5. to exercise such other powers as may be prescribed.

20.4 Duties of Owners, etc.

Any person required to produce any type of document or to give any information by an inspector shall be deemed to be legally bound to do so within the meaning of Sections 175 and 176 of the IPC.

20.5 Application of CCP—The provisions of the Code of Criminal Procedure, 1973 shall apply to any search or seizure under this Section as they apply to any search or seizure made under the authority of a warrant issued under Section 94 of the code.

In other words, one can say that the inspector has all the executive powers to implement the provisions of the Act.

21.0 WHO ARE CONTROLLING AUTHORITIES AND APPELLATE AUTHORITIES ?

All Assistant Labour Commissioners (Central) have been appointed as Controlling Authorities and all the Regional Labour Commissioners (Central) as Appellate Authorities.

22.0 EXEMPTION OF EMPLOYER FROM LIABILITY [SEC. 10]

22.1 Where an employer is charged with an offence punishable under this Act, he shall be entitled to have any other person whom he charges as the actual offender brought before the court at the time fixed for hearing the charge.

22.2 If the employer proves to be satisfaction of the court that he has used due diligence to enforce the execution of this Act, and the said person committed the offence in question without his knowledge, consent or connivance, the other person responsible for the occurrence shall be convicted of the offences and shall be liable to the like punishment as if he were the employer.

22.3 The employer shall be discharged from any liability under the Act in respect of such offence.

23.0 COGNIZANCE OF OFFENCES [SEC. 11]

23.1 No Court shall take cognizance of any offence punishable under this Act save on a complaint made by or under the authority of the appropriate government, provided that where the amount of gratuity has not been paid, or recovered, within 6 months from the expiry of the prescribed time, the appropriate government shall authorise the controlling authority to make a complaint against the employer.

23.2 Where upon the controlling authority shall within 15 days from the date of such authorization, make such complaint to a magistrate having jurisdiction to try the offence.

23.3 No court inferior to that of a Metropolitan Magistrate or a Judicial Magistrate of the first class shall try any offence punishable under this Act. [Sec. 11]

24.0 PROTECTION AGAINST ACTION TAKEN IN GOOD FAITH [SEC. 12]

If a controlling authority or any other person in respect of anything take any action which is in good faith done or intended to be done under this Act or any Rule or any other, no suit or other legal proceedings can be instituted against him because it will be presumed that he has taken all the actions to implement or comply the provisions of the Act on behalf of Government.

25.0 POWER TO MAKE RULES [SEC. 15]

The Appropriate Government may be notification make rules for the purpose of carrying the provisions of the Act. In exercise of this power, the Central Government has made the payment of Gratuity (Central) Rules, 1972, notified vide notification dated 16-09-1972 published in Part-II, Section 3, Sub-Section (1) of the Gazette of India, extraordinary, dated 16-09-1972.

26.0 NOTICE OF OPENING, CHANGE OR CLOSURE OF THE ESTABLISHMENT

26.1 A notice of any change in name, address, employer or nature of business shall be submitted by the employer to the controlling authority of the area within 30 days.

26.2 Where an employer intends to close down the business he shall submit a notice to the controlling authority at least 60 days before the intended closure.

27.0 DISPLAY OF NOTICE SPECIFYING NAME OF OFFICER WITH DESIGNATION

The employer shall display a notice at or near the main entrance of the establishment in bold letters in English and in the language understood by the majority of the employees specifying the name of the officer with designation authorized by the employer to receive on his behalf notices under the Acts and Rules made thereunder.

28.0 DISPLAY OF ABSTRACT OF THE ACT & RULES [SEC. 20]

The employer shall display an abstract of the Payment of Gratuity Act and the Rules made there under in English and in other language understood by the majority of the employees at the important place at or near the main entrance of the establishment in Form 'U'.

THEORETICAL QUESTIONS

1. Explain the applicability of the Payment of Gratuity Act, 1972.
2. Define the following terms under the Payment of Gratuity Act, 1972:

   (a) Employee (b) Employer (c) Wages
3. Write a short note on Continuous service under the Payment of Gratuity Act, 1972.

4. State the periods for which gratuity is payable even if employee does not actually work. *(May 2008)*
5. When and to whom gratuity is payable under the Payment of Gratuity Act, 1972 ? *[Nov. 2007]*
6. (a) What is the Rate of Gratuity payable under the Payment of Gratuity Act, 1972 for employees in seasonal establishment and other establishment ?
   (b) What is the maximum amount of gratuity payable?
7. How are wages computed in the following cases:
   (a) In case of a piece rate employee
   (b) In case of a monthly rated employee
   (c) In case of an employee who is employed after his disablement at reduced wages.
8. Explain the provisions relating to Forfeiture of Gratuity. *[May 2007]*
9. Explain the provisions relating to Payment of Gratuity.
10. Explain the provisions relating to Recovery of Gratuity.
11. Explain the provisions relating to Penalities under The Payment of Gratuity Act, 1972.
12. Explain the provisions relating to Nomination under the Payment of Gratuity Act, 1972.

CHAPTER

22 The Employees Provident Funds and Miscellaneous Provisions Act, 1952

1.0 WHAT IS THE OBJECT OF THE EMPLOYEES PROVIDENT FUNDS AND MISCELLANEOUS PROVISIONS ACT, 1952?

The objective of this Act is to provide for the institution of:

(a) Provident Fund,

(b) Family Pension Fund, and

(c) Deposit-linked Insurance Fund for the employees in factories and other establishments.

2.0 WHAT IS THE TERRITORY TO WHICH THE ACT APPLIES? [SEC. 1]

This Act extends to the whole of India except the State of Jammu and Kashmir.

3.0 WHAT ARE THE CLASSES OF ESTABLISHMENTS TO WHICH THE ACT APPLIES?

3.1 Establishments to which the EPF & MP Act applies

Subject to the exceptions contained in Section 16, this Act applies to:

(a) every establishment which is a factory engaged in any industry specified in Schedule I and which employs at least 20 persons; and

(b) any other establishment which employs at least 20 persons or class of such establishment which the Central Government may, by notification in Official Gazette specify in this behalf. Thus, this clause empowers the Central Govt. to apply this Act even to an establishment which is not factory.

Notes:

(i) An establishment employing at least 20 persons even for a single day attract the provisions of this Act.

(ii) For the purposes of counting 20 persons, casual employees are not taken into account but the temporary employee as a part of regular feature of employment are taken into account. *[Chetram Aggarwal* v. *R.P.F. Commissioner, Orissa]*

3.2 Power of Central Government to apply this Act to any other Establishment

The Central Government may apply the provisions of this act to any establishment **employing less than 20 persons** after giving **at least 2 months notice** of its intention to do so, by notification in Official Gazette.

3.3 Power of Central Provident Fund Commissioner

The Central Provident Fund Commissioner may by notification in the Official Gazette apply the provisions of this Act to the establishment where it appears to him whether on an applications made to him in this behalf or otherwise, that the employer and the majority of employees in relation to any establishment have agreed that the provisions of this Act should be made applicable to the establishment. He may apply this Act on and from the date of such agreement or from a subsequent date specified in such agreement.

3.4 Does this Act Continue to Apply in Case Number of Employees Falls below 20 Subsequently? [Section 1(5)]

An establishment to which this Act applies must continue to be governed by this Act, even if the number of persons employed therein falls at any time below 20.

4.0 WHAT ARE THE CLASSES OF ESTABLISHMENTS TO WHICH THIS ACT DOES NOT APPLY? [SEC. 16]

4.1 Establishments to which the EPF & MP Act does not apply

This Act does not apply to the following classes of establishments, namely:

(a) an establishment (i) registered under the Co-operative Societies Act, 1912 or under any other law relating to co-operative societies in any State, (ii) employing **less than 50 persons** and (iii) working **without the aid of power;** *or*

(b) any other establishment belonging to or under the control of the Central Government or a State Government and whose employees are entitled to the benefit of contributory provident fund or old age pension in accordance with any scheme or rule framed by the Central Government or the State Government governing such benefits; *or*

(c) to any other establishment set up under any Central, Provincial or State Act and whose employees are entitled to the benefits or contributory provident fund or old age pension in accordance with any scheme or rule framed under the Act governing such benefits; *or*

(d) any other newly set up establishment until the expiry of a **period of 3 years** from the date on which such establishment has been set up.

4.2 Power of Central Government to exempt certain Establishment [Sec. 16(2)]

(a) The Central Government may exempt whether prospectively or retrospectively any class of establishments (not an individual establishment unless it constitutes a class within itself) from the operation of the Act,

(b) The Central Government shall consider the financial position of the establishment or other circumstances of the case.

(c) This exemption can be granted only through notification in the Official Gazette.

5.0 DEFINITIONS [SEC. 2]

5.1 Appropriate Government [Sec. 2(a)]

Establishment	*Appropriate Govt.*
1. *In relation to an establishment belonging to, or under the control of, the Central Government.*	Central Government
2. *In relation to an establishment connected with a railway company, a major port, a mine or an oil field.*	Central Government
3. *A Controlled Industry*	Central Government
4. *In relation to an establishments having departments or branches in more than one state*	Central Government
5. *In relation to any other establishment*	State Government

5.2 Basic Wages [Section 2(b)]

"*Basic wages*" means all emoluments which are earned by an employee while on duty or on leave or on holidays with wages in either case in accordance with the terms of the contract of employment and which are **paid or payable in cash** to him, but **does not include**:

(i) the cash value of any food concessions;

(ii) any dearness allowance (that is to say all cash payments, by whatever name called, paid to an employee on account of rise in the cost of living),

(iii) house rent allowance,

(iv) overtime allowance,

(v) bonus, commission or pay and other similar allowance payable to the employee in respect of his employment or of work done in such employment; and

(vi) any presents made by the employer.

5.3 Employer [Section 2(e)]

Establishment	"*Employer*" *means* ...
(*i*) *In relation to an establishment which is a factory*	• The owner or occupier of the factory • The agent of such owner or occupier, • The legal representative of a deceased owner or occupier • A person named as manager of the factory u/s 7 of The Factories Act, 1948.
(*ii*) *In relation to any other establishment*	• The person or the authority having ultimate control over the affairs of the establishment. • A Manager or Managing Director to whom the affairs are entrusted.

5.4 Employee [Section 2(f)]

"*Employee*" means any person who is employed for wages in any kind of work, manual or otherwise, in or in connection with work of an establishment, and who gets his wages directly or indirectly from the employer, and **includes any person,**

(i) employed by or through a contractor in or in connection with the work of the establishment;

(ii) engaged as an apprentice, not being an apprentice engaged under the Apprentice Act, 1961, or under the standing orders of the establishment.

Notes:

(i) Person doing the work of writing accounts on a contract basis was held to be an employee within the meaning of Section 2(f).

[M/s Satish Plastics v. *R.P.F. Commissioner (1981)]*

(ii) A person employed through a contractor shall be treated as an employee only if he has completed the period of working days laid down in the scheme for entitling an employee to the benefits of the fund.

[Kumar Bros. (Bill) (P) Ltd. v. *R.P.F. Commissioner (1968)]*

5.5 "Exempted employee" means an employee to whom a Scheme or Insurance Scheme does not apply by reason of the exemption granted u/s 17.

5.6 "Exempted Establishment" [Section 2(fff)]

It means an establishment in respect of which an exemption has been granted u/s 17 from the operation of all or any of the provisions of any Scheme, whether such exemption has been granted to the establishment as such or to any person or to class of persons employed therein.

5.7 "Factory" [Section 2(g)]

It means any premises, including the precincts thereof, in any part of which a manufacturing process is being carried on or is ordinarily so carried on, whether with the aid of power or without the aid of power.

5.8 "Industry" [Section 2(i)]

It means industry specified in Schedule I, and includes any other industry added to the Schedule by notification u/s 4.

5.9 "Manufacture" or "Manaufacturing" [Section 2(i-c)]

It means any process for making, altering repairing, ornamenting, finishing, packing, washing, cleaning, breaking up, demolishing, otherwise treating or adapting any article or substance with a view to its use, sale, transport, delivery or disposal.

5.10 "Occupier of a Factory" [Section 2(k)]

It means the person who has ultimate control over the affairs of the factory and where the said affairs are entrusted to a managing agent, such agent shall be deemed to be the occupier of the factory.

5.11 Establishment to Include all Departments and Branches [Section 2A]

If an establishment consists of different departments or has branches whether situated in the same place or in different places, all such departments or branches shall be treated as parts of the same establishment.

6.0 POWER TO APPLY THE ACT TO AN ESTABLISHMENT WHICH HAS A COMMON PROVIDENT FUND WITH ANOTHER ESTABLISHMENT [SECTION 3]

(*a*) When an establishment covered by this Act has a common Provident Fund with another establishment immediately before the Act came into force, the Central Government has the power to direct through a notification in the Offical Gazette, that the provisions of this Act shall also apply to that another establishment.

(*b*) The Central Government has also the power, by virtue of Section 4, to add to Schedule I any other industry in respect of the employees whereof it is of the opinion that a provident fund scheme should be framed under this Act. Thereupon, the industry so added must be deemed to be an industry specified in Schedule I for the purposes of this Act. The addition is to be made through a notification in the Official Gazette and the notification is to be laid before Parliament as soon as possible after issue.

7.0 CENTRAL BOARD OF TRUSTEES [SECTION 5A & 5C]

7.1 Who may constitute Central Board ?

The Central Government may, constitute a Board of Trustees *(hereinafter in this Act referred to as the Central Board)* by notification in the Official Gazette.

7.2 Nature of Central Board

The Central Board of Trustee is a body corporate having perpetual succession and a common seal [Section 5B].

7.3 What is the Composition of Central Board?

The Central Board shall consist of the following persons, as members, namely:

1. a Chairman and a Vice-Chairman to be appointed by the Central Government;
2. the Central Provident Fund Commissioner, ex-officio;
3. not more than 15 persons appointed by the Central Government from amongst its officials;
4. not more than 15 persons, representing Government of such State as the Central Government may specify in this behalf, appointed by the Central Government;
5. 10 persons representing employers of the establishments to which the Scheme applies, appointed by the Central Government after consultation with such organisations of employers as may be recognised by the Central Government in this behalf; and
6. 10 persons representing employees in the establishments to which the Scheme applies, appointed by the Central Government after consultation with such organisations of employees as may be recognised by the Central Government in this behalf.

7.4 Matters to be Provided for by the Scheme

The scheme shall provide for the following:

1. The terms and conditions subject to which a member of the Central Board may be appointed.
2. The time, place and procedure of the meetings of the Central Board.

7.5 What are the Functions of the Central Board?

1. To administer the fund vested in it in such a manner as may be specified in the Scheme.
2. To perform such other functions as it may be required to perform by or under any provisions of the Scheme (the Family Pension Scheme and the Insurance Scheme).
3. To maintain proper accounts of its income and expenditure in such form and in such manner as the Central Government may, after consultation with the Comptroller and Auditor-General of India, specify the Scheme.
4. To submit an annual report of its work and activities to the Central Government.
5. To forward the audited accounts, audit report and comments on the reports of C.A.G to the Central Government.

7.6 Provision Relating to Audit of Accounts of Central Board

1. The accounts of the Central Board shall be audited annually by the Comptroller and Auditor-General of India (CAG) and any expenditure incurred by him in connection with such audit shall be payable by the Central Board to the C.A.G.
2. The C.A.G. and any person appointed by him in connection with the audit of the accounts of the Central Board shall have the same rights and privileges and authority in connection with such audit as the C.A.G. has, in connection with the audit of Government accounts and, in particular, shall have the right to

demand the production of books, accounts, connected vouchers, documents and papers and inspect any of the offices of the Central Board.

3. The accounts of the Central Board as certified by the C.A.G. or any other person appointed by him in his behalf together with audit report thereupon shall be forwarded to the Central Board which shall forward the same to the Central Government along with its comments on the report of the C.A.G.
4. The Central Government shall present a copy of the annual report, the audited accounts together with the report of the C.A.G. and the comments of the Central Board thereon before each House of Parliament.

7.7 Delegation of Power [Sec. 5E]—The Central Board may delegate its powers to : (a) Executive Committee, (b) State Board, (c) Chairman/other officer of the Board.

8.0 EXECUTIVE COMMITTEE [SECTION 5AA]

8.1 Who may constitute Executive Committee and for what purpose ? The Central Government may, constitute an Executive Committee **to assist the Central Board** in the performance of its functions by notification in the Official Gazette.

8.2 Composition. The Executive committee shall consist of the following persons as members, namely:

(a) a Chairman appointed by the Central Government from amongst the members of the Central Board;

(b) 2 persons appointed by the Central Government from amongst the persons referred to in Section 5A(1)(b).

(c) 3 persons appointed by the Central Government from amongst the persons referred to in Section 5A(1)(c).

(d) 3 persons representing the employers elected by the Central Board from amongst the persons referred to in Section 5A(1)(d).

(e) 3 persons representing the employees elected by the Central Board from amongst the persons referred to in Section 5A(1)(e).

(f) the Central Provident Fund Commissioner, ex-officio.

8.3 Terms and Conditions of Appointment etc. in the Scheme. The scheme shall provide—(a) The terms and conditions subject to which a member of the Central Board may be appointed or elected to the Executive Committee and (b) the time, place and procedure of the meetings of the Executive Committee.

9.0 STATE BOARD [SECTION 5B & 5C]

9.1 Who may constitute State Board ?

The Central Government may constitute a State Board of Trustees for any state in consultation with the Government of that state.

9.2 Powers of State Board

The State Board shall exercise such powers and perform such duties as the Central Government may assign to it from time to time.

9.3 Nature of State Board

The State Board is a body corporate having perpetual succession and a common seal.

10.0 APPOINTMENT OF OFFICERS [SECTION 5D]

10.1 Who can appoint Officers ?

Officer	*Who can appoint?*
1. *Central Provident Fund Commissioner (CPFC)*	1. The **Central Government shall** appoint a Central Provident Fund Commissioner who shall be the Chief Executive Officer of the Central Board. He shall be subject to the general control and superintendence of that Board.
2. *Financial Advisor and Chief Accounts Officer*	2. The **Central Government may** also appoint a Financial Advisor and Chief Accounts Officer to assist the Central Provident Fund Commissioner in the discharge of his duties.
3. *Additional CPFC, Deputy PFC, Regional PFC, Assistant PFC*	3. The **Central Board may** appoint subject to the maximum scale of pay, as may be specified in the Scheme as many Additional Central Fund Commissioners, Deputy Provident Fund Commissioners, Regional Provident Fund Commissioners and Assistant Provident Fund Commissioners as it may consider necessary for the efficient administration of the Scheme.

10.2 Appointments in Consultation with UPSC

The aforesaid appointments carrying a scale of pay equivalent to Group 'A' or Group 'B' posts under the Central Government must be made only after consultation with Union Public Service Commission. However, such consultation is not required in regard to any such appointment:

(a) for a period not exceeding 1 year; *or*

(b) if the person to be appointed is at the time of his appointment: (i) an I.A.S. officer, or (ii) in the Service of the Central Government or State Government or the Central Board in Group A *or* Group B post.

10.3 Appointment by the State Board

The State Board may, with the approval of the State Government concerned appoint such staff as it may consider necessary.

10.4 Conditions of Service

1. For Central Provident Fund Commissioner, Financial Advisor and Chief Accounts Officer	Such as may be **prescribed by the Central Government**
2. For Additional CPFC, Deputy PFC, Regional PFC, Assistant PFC and other Officers & Employees.	Such as may be **specified by the Central Board** in accordance with the rules applicable to employees of the Central Government drawing corresponding scales of pay.

10.5 Acts and Proceedings of the Central Board or its Executive Committee or State Board not to be Invalidated on Certain Grounds [Section 5DD]

No Act done or proceeding taken by the Central Board or the Executive Committee constituted under Section 5AA or the State Board shall be questioned on the ground merely of the existence of any vacancy in, or any defect in the constitution of, the Central Board or the Executive Committee or the State Board, as the case may be.

10.6 Delegation [Section 5E]

The Central Board may delegate to the Executive Committee or to the Chairman of the Board or to any of its Officers and a State Board may delegate to its Chairman or to any of its officers such of its powers and functions under this Act as it may deem necessary for the efficient administration of the Scheme. This delegation may be subject to such conditions and limitations, if any, as the said Board may specify.

11.0 PROVIDENT FUND SCHEME, PENSION SCHEME AND DEPOSIT LINKED INSURANCE SCHEME [SEC. 6, 6A]

Basis of Comparison	*Employees' Provident Fund Scheme [Sec. 5, Sec. 6]*	*Employees' Pension Scheme [Sec. 6A]*	*Employees' Deposit Linked Insurance Scheme [Sec. 6C]*
1. Who Administers the Fund ?	Central Board of Trustees	Central Board of Trustees	Central Board of Trustees
2. Matters of Scheme	The Provident Fund Scheme may provide for all or any of the matters specified in **Schedule II**	The Pension Scheme may provide for all or any of the matters specified in **Schedule III**	The Insurance Scheme may provide for all or any of the matters specified in **Schedule IV.**
3. Employer's Contribution to Fund	**Minimum**—10% of Pay	Out of Employer's contribution to PF, Employer's contribution of 8.33% shall be remitted to Pension Fund within 15 days of close of every month.	**Maximum**—1% of Pay **Present Rate**—0.5% of Pay
4. Employee's Contribution to Fund	**Minimum**—10% of pay **Maximum**—No Limit	Nil	Nil
5. Central Govt.'s Contribution to Fund	Nil	1.16% of the Pay	0.25% of Pay
6. Employer's Contribution to pay Administration charges	Nil	Nil	**Maximum**—0.25% of Pay **Present Rate**—0.01% of Pay
7. Power of Central Govt. to increase Rate of contribution	Central Govt. may increase the rate of contribution to 12% by notification in the Official Gazette	No such power exists.	No such power exists.
8. Rounding off	The contribution is to be rounded off to **nearest rupee.**	The contribution is to be rounded off to **nearest rupee.**	The contribution is to be rounded off to **nearest rupee.**

9. Pay	Pay = Basic Wage + Dearness Allowance + Retaining Allowance. **Note** : DA includes Cash Value of food concession allowed to employee.	Pay = Basic Wage + Dearness Allowance + Retaining Allowance. **Note** : DA includes Cash Value of food concession allowed to employee.	Pay = Basic Wage + Dearness Allowance + Retaining Allowance. **Note** : DA includes Cash Value of food concession allowed to employee.
10. Exemption	Not Available	Not Available	Exemption can be obtained if LIC Group Gratuity Scheme is adopted by employer. In case of exemption, only inspection charges of 0.005% of pay are payable to P.F. Authorities.
11. Benefits Under Scheme	—	**Benefits under Pension Scheme** (a) Members will get pension— • on superannuation; *or* • on retirement from service; *or* • upon permanent total disablement during employment. (b) Pension will be available to widow/widower for life or till he/she remarries. (c) Children (only 2) will be entitled to pension, upto 25 years of their age. (d) Orphans (only 2) will be entitled to pension at enhanced rate. (e) If the person is unmarried or has no family, pension is available to nominee for a specified period.	If an employee dies during employment, his nominee or family members gets accumulated balance to the credit of the employee.

12.0 SETTLEMENT OF PROVIDENT FUND CLAIMS

12.1 The Provident Fund claims complete in all respects submitted along with the requisite documents shall be settled and the benefit amount shall be paid to the beneficiaries **within 30 days** from the date of its receipt by the Commissioner.

12.2 If there is any deficiency in the claim, the same shall be recorded in writing and communicated to the applicant within 30 days from the date of receipt of such application.

12.3 In case the Commissioner fails without sufficient cause to settle a claim complete in all respects within 30 days, the Commissioner shall be liable for the delay beyond the said period and **penal interest at the rate of 12%** per annum may be charged on the benefit amount and the same shall be **deducted from the salary of the Commissioner.**

13.0 DETERMINATION OF MONEYS DUE FROM EMPLOYER [SECTION 7A]

13.1 Who Determines the Moneys Due from an Employer?

Following authorities have been empowered to determine the moneys due from an employer under the EPF Act:

1. The Central PF Commissioner
2. Additional Central PF Commissioner
3. Deputy P.F. Commissioner
4. Regional P.F. Commissioner
5. Assistant P.F. Commissioner

13.2 Matters on which Authorities Take Decisions

Usually on the following matters of quasi-judicial nature the authorities take decisions:

1. amount of contribution due.
2. the due date of contribution
3. the administrative charges.
4. amount to be transferred under Section 15 *or* Section 17 of the Act.
5. any other charges payable by the employer under the Act.

13.3 Powers to Conduct Enquiry

The authorities have been given power to conduct such enquiry as may be deemed necessary and for this they have been granted powers as are vested in a Court.

13.4 Opportunity of Representing

An order must not be made unless the employer concerned is given a reasonable opportunity of representing his case.

13.5 Officer's Power to *ex-parte* Order

Where the employer, employee or any other person who was required to attend the inquiry fails to attend such inquiry without assigning any valid reason or fails to produce any document or to file any report or return when called upon to do so, the officer conducting the inquiry may decide the applicability of the Act or determine the amount due from any employer, as the case may be, on the basis of the evidence adduced during such inquiry and other documents available on record.

13.6 Right of Employer to Apply for Setting Aside *Ex-parte* Order

(a) If an *ex-parte* order is passed against an employer he may, **within 3 months** from the date of communication of such order, apply to the officer for setting aside such order if :

(*i*) he satisfies the officer that the show cause notice was not duly served or that he could not attend/reply due to sufficient reasons.

(*ii*) he has not filed any appeal against the *ex-parte* order.

(b) No such order shall be set aside merely on the ground that there has been an irregularity in the service of show cause notice if the officer is satisfied that the employer had notice of the date of hearing and had sufficient time to appear before the officer.

(c) **Notice to be Served before Setting Aside Order**—No *ex-parte* order shall be set aside on any application unless notice thereof has been served on the opposite party.

(d) **Finality of Orders**—The order passed under this section shall be final and will not be called in question in any Court of Law.

14.0 REVIEW OF ORDER PASSED UNDER SECTION 7A [SECTION 7B]

14.1 Who can Apply for Review order to whom and within what time limit ?

Any person aggrieved by an order under Section 7A(1) may apply **within 45 days of order** for a review of that order to the officer who passed the order provided no appeal has been made against the order under this Act.

14.2 Grounds for Application for Review Order.

The grounds on which review application may be made include:

(a) discovery of new and important matter or evidence which, after the exercise of due diligence was not within his knowledge or could not be produced by him at the time when the order was made, or

(b) some mistake or error apparent on the face of the record or

(c) for any other sufficient reason,

14.3 Power to Review on own motion.

Such officer may also on his own motion review his order if he is satisfied that it is necessary to do so on any such ground.

14.4 Power to Reject.

The officer may reject the application for review if there is no sufficient ground for a review.

14.5 Rejection Order not subject to Appeal but Review Order u/s 7A subject to Appeal.

No appeal shall lie against the order of the officer rejecting an application for review, but an appeal shall lie against an order passed under review as if the order passed under review were the original order passed by him under Section 7A.

14.6 No such application shall be granted

(a) without previous notice to all the parties before him to enable them to appear and be heard in support of the order on respect of which a review is applied for, and

(b) on the ground of discovery of new matter or evidence which the applicant alleges was not within his knowledge or could not be produced by him when the order was made, without proof of such allegation.

14.7 Manner of Application.

Every application for the aforesaid review shall be filed in prescribed form and manner and within prescribed time.

15.0 DETERMINATION OF ESCAPED AMOUNT BY REOPENING THE CASE

15.1 Who can Reopen the Case ? [Section 7C]

The Officer who has passed the Order u/s 7A or u/s 7B.

15.2 Time Limit within which Case be Reopened

The case can be reopened **within 5 years** from the date of communication of the order passed u/s 7A or u/s 7B.

15.3 Grounds on which Case be Reopened

The Officer who has passed the order may reopen the case if he—

(a) has reason to believe that any amount has escaped from determination for any period because of the omission or failure on the part of the employer to disclose, all material facts necessary for determining the correct amount due from the employer.

(b) has reason to believe that any amount has escaped from determination for any period even if there has been no omission or failure on the part of the employer.

15.4 Power to Pass Appropriate Order Redetermining the Amount

The Officer may pass appropriate order redetermining the amount due from employer after giving a reasonable opportunity of representing the case to the employer.

16.0 EMPLOYEES' PROVIDENT FUND APPELLATE TRIBUNAL [SECTION 7D]

16.1 Who can constitute EPF Appellate Tribunal ? The Central Government may, by notification in the Official Gazette, constitute one or more Employees' Provident Funds Appellate Tribunal to exercise the powers and discharge the functions conferred on such Tribunal by this Act and every such Tribunal shall have jurisdiction in respect of establishments situated in areas specified in the notification.

16.2 Composition of Tribunal A Tribunal shall consist of 1 person only to be appointed by the Central Government.

A person shall be qualified for appointment as the Presiding Officer of a Tribunal only, if he is, or has been, or is qualified to be a Judge of a High Court; or a District Judge.

16.3 Powers of Tribunal (Section 7J)

(a) A Tribunal shall have power to regulate its own procedure in all matters arising out of the exercise of its powers or of the discharge of its functions including the places at which the Tribunal shall have its sittings.

(b) A Tribunal shall, have all the powers which are vested in the officers referred to in Section 7A.

(c) Any proceeding before the Tribunal shall be deemed to be a judicial proceeding.

(d) The Tribunal shall be deemed to be a Civil Court.

16.4 Right of Appellant to Take Assistance of Legal Practitioner and of Government, etc. to Appoint Presenting Officers (Section 7K)

(a) A person preferring an appeal to a Tribunal under this Act may either appear in person or take the assistance of a legal practitioner of his choice to present his case before the Tribunal.

(b) The Central Government or a State Government or any other authority under this Act may authorise one or more legal practitioner or any of its officers to act as presenting officers and every person so authorised may present the case with respect to any appeal before a Tribunal.

16.5 Orders of Tribunal (Section 7L) A Tribunal may, after giving the parties to the appeal, an opportunity of being heard, pass the following orders :

(a) confirming, modifying or annulling the order appealed against, *or*

(b) may refer the case back to the authority which passed such order with such directions as the Tribunal may think fit, for a fresh adjudication or order after taking additional evidence, if necessary.

16.6 Power to Amend Order

(a) **Time Limit**—A Tribunal may, at any time **within 5 years** from the date of its order, with a view to rectifying any mistake apparent from the record, amend its order and shall make such amendment in the order if the mistake is brought to its notice by the parties to the appeal.

(b) **Opportunity of being head**—However, an amendment which has the effect of enhancing the amount due from, or otherwise, increasing the liability of, the employer shall not be made unless the Tribunal has given notice to him of its intention to do so and has allowed him a reasonable opportunity of being heard.

(c) **Order Copy to Party**—A Tribunal shall send a copy of every order passed under this section to the parties to the appeal.

(d) **Finality of Tribunal Order**—Any order made by a Tribunal finally disposing off an appeal shall not be questioned in any court of law.

16.7 Deposit of Amount Due on Filing an Appeal (Section 7-O)

(a) Appeal by the employer can be entertained by a Tribunal only if he has deposited with it **75%** of the amount due from him as determined by an officer referred to in Section 7A.

(b) The Tribunal may, waive or reduce the amount to be deposited for reasons to be recorded in writing.

16.8 Transfer of Certain Applications to Tribunals (Section 7P) All applications which are pending before the Central Government under Section 19A, before its repeal shall stand transferred to a Tribunal exercising jurisdiction in respect of establishments in relation to which such applications had been made as if such applications were appeals preferred to the Tribunal.

16.9 Employer's Liability to Pay Simple Interest (Section 7Q) The employer shall be liable to pay simple interest at the rate of **12% per annum (or at a higher rate if any specified)** on any amount due from him under this Act from the due date till actual date of payment. However, the higher rate of interest specified in the Scheme cannot exceed the lending rate of interest charged by any scheduled bank.

17.0 MODE OF RECOVERY OF MONEY DUE FROM EMPLOYERS (SECTION 8)

(a) Any amount due from employer (which is in arrear) may be recovered in the manner specified in Section 8B to 8G.

(b) For order of demand under Section 8, it is necessary that there should be a determination of the amount due, if the liability is disputed.

(c) An order under Section 7A(3) is a condition precedent to the making of a demand under Section 8. [*A.T. Union (P.) Ltd.* v. *RPF Commissioner*]

17.1 Recovery of Moneys by Employers and Contractors (Section 8A)

(a) The amount of *employers' and employees' contribution* and *any charges on* the basis of such contribution for meeting the cost of administering the fund paid or payable by an employer in respect of an employee employed by or through a contractor may be recovered by such *employer* from the contractor.

(b) The recovery may be made by deduction from any amount payable by the contractor.

(c) The contractor in his turn may recover from such employee the employee's contribution by deducting from the basic wage, dearness allowance, any retaining allowance (if any), payable to such employee.

(d) But the **contractor cannot deduct the employer's contribution or the charges** aforesaid from the total emoluments payable to the employee; nor can he otherwise recover such contribution or charges from such employee **irrespective of whether there is any contract to the contrary.**

17.2 Issue of Certificate to the Recovery Officer (Section 8B)

(i) **Power to Issue Certificate**—The authorised officer may issue to the Recovery Officer, certificate under his signature specifying the amount of arrears u/s 8.

(ii) **Mode of Recovery**—The Recovery Officer on receipt of such certificate, shall proceed to recover by one or more of the following modes :

(a) attachment and sale of the movable or immovable property of the establishment first and then that of the employer (if required due to insufficient recovery);

(b) arrest of the employer and his detention in prison;

(c) appointing a receiver for the management of the movable or immovable properties of the establishment or, the employer.

17.3 Recovery Officer to whom Certificate is to be Forwarded (Section 8C)

The authorised officer may forward the certificate referred to in Section 8B to the Recovery Officer within whose jurisdiction :

(a) the employer carries on his business or profession or within whose jurisdiction the principal place of the establishment is situated; *or*

(b) the employer resides; *or*

(c) any movable or immovable property of the establishment or the employer is situated.

17.4 Validity of the Certificate [Section 8D]

(a) The employer cannot dispute the correctness of the amount stated in the certificate.

(b) No objection to the certificate on any other ground shall be entertained by the Recovery Officer.

(c) Authorised officer shall have power to withdraw or correct the certificate by sending an intimation to the Recovery Officer.

17.5 Stay of Proceedings under Certificate and Amendment or Withdrawal Thereof [Section 8E]

(a) The authorised officer may grant time for the payment of the amount and thereupon the Recovery Officer shall stay the proceedings until the expiry of the time so granted.

(b) The authorised officer shall keep the Recovery Officer informed of any amount paid or time granted for payment, subsequent to the issue of such certificate.

(c) The authorised officer shall stay the recovery of such part of the amount of the certificate as pertains to the said reduction for the period for which the appeal or other proceeding remains pending the amount of outstanding demand is reduced as a result of in order under appeal and order is subject matter of further proceeding under the Act.

(d) The authorised officer shall amend or withdraw the certificate if the amount of the outstanding demand is reduced as a result of final order under an appeal.

17.6 Other Modes of Recovery [Section 8F]

Even where a certificate has been issued to the Recovery Officer under Section 8B, the Central Provident Fund Commissioner or any officer authorised by the Central Board may recover the amount by any one or more of the modes provided in this section.

17.7 Recovery from any Person from whom Amount is due to the Employer Who is in Arrears

If any amount is due from any person to any employer who is in arrears, the Central Provident Fund Commissioner or any other person authorised by the Central Board in this behalf may require such person to deduct from the said amount the arrears due from such employer under this Act, and such person shall comply with any such requisition and shall pay the sum so deducted to the credit of the Central Provident Fund Commissioner or the officer so authorised, as the case may be:

However this provision shall not apply to any part of the amount exempt from attachment in execution of a decree of a Civil Court under Section 60 of the Code of Civil Procedure, 1908.

17.8 Application to the Court for Release of Money

The Central Provident Fund Commissioner or the officer authorised by the Central Board in this behalf may apply to the court in whose custody there is money belonging to the employer for payment to him of the entire amount of such money, or if it is more than the amount due, an amount sufficient to discharge the amount due.

17.9 Application of Certain Provisions of Income-tax Act [Section 8G]

The provisions of the Second and Third Schedules to the Income-tax Act, 1961 and the tax (Certificate Proceedings) Rules, 1962, as in force, from time to time, shall apply with necessary modifications as if the said provisions and the rules referred to the arrears of the amount mentioned in Section 8 of this Act instead of the income-tax.

However, any reference in the said provisions and the rules to the “assessee” shall be construed as a reference to an employer as defined in this “Act”.

18.0 FUND TO BE RECOGNISED UNDER THE INCOME-TAX ACT, 1961 [SEC. 9]

For the purposes of Income-tax Act, 1961, the Fund shall be deemed to be a Recognised Provident Fund. Even if any provision of the scheme under which the Fund is established is repugnant to any of the provisions of the Income-tax Act in this regard, the provision of the scheme remains effective and operative.

19.0 PROTECTION AGAINST ATTACHMENT OF CREDIT BALANCE IN PF A/C [SECTION 10]

The amount standing to the credit of any member in the Fund or credit of any exempted employee in provident fund

(a) shall not be capable of, being assigned or charged and

(b) shall not be liable to attachment under any decree or order of any court in respect of any debt or liability incurred by the member or the exempted employee.

(c) shall not be capable of being claimed by the Official Assignee or Official Receiver

(d) shall be free from any debt or other liability incurred by the deceased member or the nominee before the death of the member

Note : No such protection is available in respect of amount already withdrawn from PF Account.

20.0 PRIORITY OF PAYMENT OF CONTRIBUTION OVER OTHER DEBTS [SECTION 11]

If the employer is adjudged an insolvent or if the employer is a company and an order for winding thereof has been made, the amount due from the employer whether in respect of the employee's contribution or the employer's contribution must be included among the debts which are to be paid in priority to all other debts under Section 49 of the Presidency-Towns Insolvency Act, Section 61 of the Provincial Insolvency Act, Section 530 of the Companies Act, 1956, in the distribution of the property of the insolvent or the assets of the company. In other words, this payment will be a **preferential payment provided the liability therefor has accrued before this order of adjudication or winding up is made.**

21.0 EMPLOYER NOT TO REDUCE WAGE ETC. [SECTION 12]

No employer in relation to any establishment to which any Scheme applies shall by reason only of his liability for the payment of any contribution to the Funds or any charge under this act or the scheme, reduce directly or indirectly the wages of any employee or the total quantum of benefits in the nature of oldage pension, gratuity fund to which the employee is entitled under the term of his employment express or implied.

22.0 SPECIAL PROVISIONS RELATING TO EXISTING PROVIDENT FUNDS [SECTION 15]

22.1 The existing provident fund shall, pending the application of the scheme, be operated and worked as though the Act had not been enforced. Therefore, every employee who is a subscriber to the existing provident fund of an establishment, pending the application of any scheme to the establishment, continues to be entitled to the benefits accruing to him under the provident fund; and the provident fund shall continue to be maintained in the same manner and subject to the same conditions as it would have been if this act had not been passed.

22.2 On the application of the scheme to the fund already in existence, the amount standing to the credit of the employee who becomes a member shall be transferred to the fund established under the scheme.

22.3 The condition contained in the scheme shall supersede all provisions of law or deed or instrument if there is anything to the contrary.

23.0 AUTHORISING CERTAIN EMPLOYERS TO MAINTAIN PROVIDENT FUND ACCOUNTS [SEC. 16A]

1. *Conditions for Authorisation*	The Central Govt. may authorise the employer by an order in writing to maintain the PF accounts of its employees, if the following conditions are satisfied : (a) An application is made to Central Govt. for seeking permission to maintain the PF accounts. (b) The application is made by the employer and the majority of employees. (c) The establishment employs at **least 100 persons.** (d) The establishment has not committed any default in the payment of provident fund contribution or any other offence under this Act during 3 years immediately preceding the date of application.
2. *Terms and conditions of authorisation*	The employer shall— • Maintain Provident Fund Accounts • Submit Returns • Deposit the contribution (*i.e.,* the PF money shall be deposited with the PF Authorities) • Provide Facilities for Inspection • Abide by other terms and conditions.
3. *Grounds of Cancellation of Authorisation*	The authorisation made by Central Govt. may be cancelled, if the employer— (a) fails to comply with any of the terms and conditions of the authorisation; or (b) commits any offence under any provisions of the Act.
4. *Conditions for Cancellation of Authorisation*	(a) Before cancelling the authorisation, Central Govt. shall give the employer a reasonable opportunity of being heard. (b) The order of cancellation shall be in writing.

24.0 EXEMPTED ESTABLISHMENT [SEC. 17]

	Exemption from Provident Fund Scheme
1. *Who may grant Exemption ?*	The exemption may be granted by Appropriate Govt.
2. *Manner of giving Exemption*	The exemption can be given only by way of a notification in the Official Gazette.

3. ***Terms of Exemption***	• The exemption shall be subject to such conditions as may be specified in the notification. • The exemption may be given prospectively or retrospectively. • The exemption may be given from the operation of all or any of the provisions of any Scheme.
4. ***Conditions for giving exemption***	1. Appropriate Govt. must form an opinion that the rules of provident fund with respect to the rates of contribution and other provident fund benefits are **not less** favourable than those specified in the Act or the Scheme; *and* 2. Appropriate Govt. must consult the Central Board. The Central Board shall forward its views within prescribed time limit the Scheme.
5. ***Applicability of provisions on exempted establishment***	(a) The terms and conditions as may be specified in the notification granting exemption shall apply to the exempted establishment. (b) If the employer contravenes, or makes default in complying with any of the said provisions or conditions or any other provision of this Act, he shall be punishable u/s 14 as if the said establishment had not been exempted.
6. ***Duty of Employer***	The employer shall establish a Board of Trustees for the administration of the Provident Fund.
7. ***Duties of Board of Trustees***	(a) The Board of Trustees shall— (i) maintain detailed accounts to show the contributions credited, withdrawals made and interest accrued in respect of each employee; (ii) submit such returns as may be directed from time to time; (iii) invest the PF moneys in accordance with the directions issued by Central Govt. (iv) transfer, where necessary, the PF Account of any employee; and (v) perform such other duties as may be specified in the scheme. (b) If the Trustees contravene, or make default in complying with, any of the duties entrusted to them, they shall be deemed to have committed an offence under section 14 and shall be punishable accordingly.

	Exemption from Pension Scheme u/s 17(1)	***Exemption from Insurance Scheme u/s 17(2A)***
1. ***Who may Grant Exemption ?***	The exemption may be granted by the Appropriate Govt.	The exemption may be granted by the Central Provident Fund Commissioner.
2. ***Manner of Giving Exemption***	The exemption can be given only by way of notification in the Official Gazette.	The exemption can be given only by way of notification in the Official Gazette.

3. *Terms of Exemption*	Notification may specify the pattern of Investment of Pension Fund.	Notification may specify the pattern of Investment of Insurance Fund.
4. *Conditions for Exemption*	**Appropriate Govt.** must form an opinion that the pensionary benefits available to the employer are **not less favourable** than those specified under the Pension Scheme.	The **Central Provident Fund Commissioner** must form an opinion that the life insurance benefits available to employees are **more favourable** than those specified under the Insurance Scheme.

25.0 TRANSFER OF ACCOUNTS [SEC. 17A]

Where an employee of an establishment (Old) leaves his employment and obtain re-employment in another establishment (New), the following provisions are applicable as to transfer of accounts :

If Old Establishment is covered but New Establishment is not covered under P.F. Act [Sec. 7-A(1)]	*If Old Establishment is not covered but New Establishment is covered under P.F. Act [Sec. 17A(2)]*	*If both Old and New Establishment are covered under P.F. Act*
The Credit balance of his old Provident Fund A/c **shall** be transferred to his new Provident Fund A/c in New Establishment provided— (a) the employee so desires (b) the rules of Old P.F. permit such transfer **Note** : Transfer has to be made within time prescribed by the Central Govt.	The Credit balance of his old Provident Fund A/c **may** be transferred to his new Provident Fund A/c in New Establishment provided— (a) the employee so desires (b) the rules of Old P.F. permit such transfer	The Credit balance of his old Provident Fund A/c **may** be transferred to his new Provident Fund A/c in New Establishment provided— (a) the employee so desires (b) the rules of Old P.F. permit such transfer

26.0 LIABILITY IN CASE OF TRANSFER OF ESTABLISHMENT [SECTION 17B]

Where an employer transfers the establishment in whole or in part by sale, gift, lease or licence or in any other manner,

(a) The employer and the transferee shall be jointly or severally liable to pay the contribution and other sum due from the employer under any of the provisions of

(i) the Act, *or*

(ii) the Scheme, *or*

(iii) the Pension Scheme

(b) The liability is limited in respect of period **upto the date of such transfer.**

(c) The liability of the transferee shall be limited to the **value of the assets obtained** by him from such transfer.

MISCELLANEOUS PROVISIONS

27.0 INSPECTORS [SECTION 13]

27.1 Who can Appoint? The appropriate government is empowered to appoint Inspectors and to define the areas of jurisdication by notifying in the Official Gazette.

27.2 Powers of Inspectors The Inspectors have powers—

(a) to collect information and require the employer or any contractor from whom any amount is recoverable under Section 8A to furnish such information as he may consider necessary;

(b) to enter and search any establishment or any premises connected therewith at any reasonable time with necessary assistance;

(c) to require any one found in charge of the above-mentioned establishment or premises to produce before him for examination of any accounts, books, registers and other documents relating to the employment of persons or the payment of wages in the establishment;

(d) to examine, the employer or any contractor from whom any amount is recoverable under Section 8A, his agent or servant or any other person found in charge of the establishment or any premises connected therewith or whom the inspector has reasonable cause to believe to be or to have been, an employee in an establishment

(e) to make copies of, or take extract from any book, register or other document maintained in relation to the establishment and, where he has reason to believe that any offence under this Act has been committed by an employer, seize with such assistance as he may think fit, such book, register or other document or portions thereof as he may consider relevant in respect of that offence;

(f) to exercise each other powers as the scheme may provide.

Note: The provisions of the Criminal Procedure Code shall, so far as may be, apply to any search or seizure mentioned in Section 13(2). [Section 13(2B)]

28.0 PENALTIES [SECTION 14]

Who is punishable	***Penalty***
1. Any person who knowingly made or caused to be made any false statement or false representation— (a) to avoid any payment to be made by himself, *or* (b) to enable any other person to avoid such payment.	Imprisonment for a term upto **1 year** *or* Fine upto **Rs 5,000** *or* Both
2. An employer who contravenes or makes default in complying with the provisions of (a) Section 6 or Section 17 (3) (a) insofar as it relates to the payment of inspection charges, or	Maximum imprisoment for a term upto 3 years. Minimum Penalty (i) in case of, default in payment of employees' contribution deducted from his wage—1 year imprisonment and a fine of Rs 10,000
(b) Para 38 of the scheme insofar as it relates to the payment of administrative charges.	(ii) in any other case—6 months imprisonment and a fine of Rs 5,000 **Note:** The court may reduce the imprisonment for a lesser term.
3. An employer who contravenes or makes default in complying with the provisions of Section 6C *or* Section 17(3A) insofar as it relates to the payment of inspection charges.	6 months, minimum imprisonment but not exceeding 1 year and fine upto Rs 5,000 **Note:** The court may reduce the imprisonment for a lesser term.

4. Any person who contravenes or makes default in complying with any of the provisions of the Scheme, the Family Pension Scheme or the Insurance Scheme.	Imprisonment for a term upto 1 year *or* fine upto Rs 4,000 *or* Both
5. Cases where no other penalty is provided	Minimum Imprisonment—1 month Maximum Imprisonment—6 months *or* fine upto Rs 5,000 *or* Both

29.0 OFFENCES OF COMPANY [SECTION 14 A]

29.1 Meaning of Company The company means any body corporate and includes a firm and other association of individuals.

29.2 Meaning of Director The director in relation to a firm means a partner in the firm.

29.3 Who are Liable If any offence under the Act is committed by a company, following will be guilty of the offence:

(a) The company itself,

(b) The person in charge of or responsible to the company at the time when the offence was committed

Both can be proceeded against and punished for the offence.

29.4 When not Liable? The company and such person shall not be liable to any punishment if it/he proves:

(a) that the offence was committed without its/his knowledge.

(b) that it/he exercised all due diligence to prevent the commission of such offence.

If the prosecution proves that the offence: (a) was committed with the *(i)* consent; or (ii) connivance; *(b)* is attributable to any negligence on the part of a director, manager secretary or other of the company, then such director, manager, secretary or other officer shall be deemed to be guilty of the offence and liable to be proceeded against and punished accordingly.

29.5 Enhanced Punishment in Certain Cases after Previous Conviction [Section 14AA] Punishment for committing the same offence subsequently is—

(a) Imprisonment for a minimum term of 2 years but maximum term upto 5 years, and

(b) fine upto Rs 25,000.

30.0 CERTAIN OFFENCES TO BE COGNISABLE [SECTION 14AB]

An offence relating to default in payment of contribution by the employer shall be a cognisable offence. A cognisable offence is one where the police can arrest a person without warrant.

31.0 COGNISANCE AND TRIAL OF OFFENCE [SECTION 14AC]

31.1 Essential Conditions of Cognisance of Offences

The essential conditions of cognisance of offences are:

(a) There must be a report in writing of the facts constituting such offence,

(b) This report must be made with the previous sanction of the

 (i) Central Provident Fund Commissioner; *or*

 (ii) Such officer as may be authorised by the Central Government;

(c) The report must be made by an Inspector appointed under Section 13.

These conditions being co-existent, no court inferior to that of a Presidency Magistrate or a Magistrate of the first class shall try any offence under this Act, or the Scheme or the Family Pension Scheme or the Insurance Scheme.

31.2 Cognisance Means Jurisdiction or Right to Try and Determine Causes

31.3 Some Judicial Pronouncements

1. Taking cognisance occurs as soon as Magistrate, as such, applies his mind to the suspected commission of an offence [*Ajit kumar* v. *State of West Bengal* AIR 1963 S 765].
2. Sec 190 of the Code of Criminal Procedure, 1973 empowers a Magistrate of the first class to take cognisance of an offence in three ways, *viz.* (i) on complaint; (ii) on police report; and (iii) on information from any person other than a police officer or on his own knowledge. It may be noted that Section 14-AC of the Act makes it necessary that in order to launch a prosecution, the facts constituting the offence have to be stated. If the facts stated do not disclose an offence, the prosecution cannot be proceeded with also that complaint means the allegation made orally or in writing to a Magistrate (Court) with a view to his taking action under the Cr. P.C. that some person, whether known or unknown, has committed an offence but it does include the report of a police report [Gopal Das Sakseria *vs.* State of Uttar Pradesh, 1956 1 I.J. 11]

32.0 POWER TO RECOVER OR REDUCE OR WAVE DAMAGES [SECTION 14B]

32.1 Power of Central Board to Recover Damages

The Central Provident Fund Commission or any authorised officer in this behalf may recover from the employer such damages not exceeding the actual amount of arrears where the employer makes a default:

(a) In payment of contribution to the fund, Pension Fund or Insurance Fund.

(b) In transfer of accumulations required to be transferred by him u/s 15(2) or 17(5).

(c) In the payment of any charges payable under the Act, any scheme, insurance scheme or any of the conditions specified under Section 17.

32.2 Power of Central Board to Reduce/Waive

The Central Board may however, reduce or waive the damages levied under this Section in relation to an establishment which is a sick industrial company and in respect of which a scheme for rehabilitation has been sanctioned by the Board for Industrial and Financial Reconstruction (BIFR) establishment under Section 4 of the Sick Industrial Companies (Special Provisions) Act, 1985 subject to such terms and conditions as may be specified in the scheme.

32.3 Opportunity of Being Heard

However, before levying or recovering such damages, the Central Board shall give a reasonable opportunity of being heard to the employer.

32.4 Power of Court to make Orders (Section 14C)

Where an employer is convicted of an offence of making default of any one of the kinds mentioned in Section 14B above the Court may, in addition to awarding any punishment, by order in writing require him within a specified period in the order to pay the amount of contribution or transfer the accumulations, as the case may be, in respect of which the offence was committed. The period referred to in this order may, however, be extended by the Court if it thinks fit and on application in this behalf from time to time.

32.5 Impact of the Aforesaid Order of the Court

The clause in the order relating to continuance of the offence would remain suspended.

32.6 Punishment for not Complying with the Aforesaid Order of the Court

If the aforesaid order of the court is not complied with then on the expiry of the specified time, or as the case may be, the extended time, this default will be regarded as a further offence. For this further offence, the employer shall be liable to be punished with imprisonment under Section 14 and shall also be liable to a fine extending upto Rs 100 for every day after such expiry on which the order has not been complied with.

33.0 ACT TO HAVE EFFECT NOTWITHSTANDING ANYTHING CONTAINED IN THE LIFE INSURANCE CORPORATION ACT, 1956 (SEC. 17-AA)

In case of any inconsistency between this Act and LIC Act, 1956, the Employees Provident Fund, etc. Act will prevail over the provisions of the Life Insurance Corporation Act, 1956.

34.0 PROTECTION OF ACTION TAKEN IN GOOD FAITH [SECTION 18]

No suit, prosecution or other legal proceeding shall lie against the Central Government, a State Government, the Presiding Officer of a Tribunal, any authority referred to in Section 7A, an Inspector or any other person for anything which is in good faith done or intended to be done in pursuance of this Act, the Scheme, the Pension Scheme or the Insurance Scheme.

35.0 PRESIDING OFFICER AND OTHER OFFICERS TO BE PUBLIC SERVANTS [SECTION 18A]

The Presiding Officer of a Tribunal, its officers and other employees, the authorities referred to in Section 7A and every inspector shall be deemed to be public servants within the meaning of Section 21 of the Indian Penal Code.

36.0 DELEGATION OF POWERS [SECTION 19]

The appropriate government may direct that any power or authority or jurisdiction exercisable by it under this Act, the Scheme, the Pension Scheme or the Insurance Scheme shall, in relation to such matters and subject to such conditions, if any, as may be specified in the direction, be exercisable also (a) where the appropriate government is the Central Government, by such officer or authority subordinate to the Central Government or by the State Government or by such officer or authority subordinate to the State Government as may be specified in the notification; (b) where the appropriate government is a State Government by such Officer or authority subordinate to the State Government as may be specificied in the notification.

Under this section, both the Central Government and the State Government have been given a right to delegate their powers, authority or jurisdiction exercisable by them to an officer or authority subordinate to them and subject to any condition. The Central Government is also authorised to delegate the powers, etc., to the State Government.

37.0 POWER TO REMOVE DIFFICULTIES [SECTION 19A]

The Central Government may, by order, make such provisions or give such directions, not inconsistent with the provisions of this act, as appear to it to be necessary or expedient for the removal of the doubt or difficulty in respect of:

1. cases where an establishment which is a factory, is engaged in any industry specified in Schedule 1;
2. whether any particular establishment is an establishment falling within the class of establishments to which this Act applies by virtue of a notification under Section 1(3)(b);
3. the number of persons employed in an establishment; or
4. the number years which have elapsed from the date on which an establishment has been set up;
5. whether the total quantum of benefit to which an employee is entitled has been reduced by the employer.

The order of the Central Govt. shall be final.

THEORETICAL QUESTIONS

1. (a) State the object of the EPF Act.

(b) State the territory to which EPF Act applies.

***2.** (a) What are the classes of establishments to which the EPF Act (i) applies (ii) does not apply?

(b) Can the EPF Act be applied to any establishment employing less than 20 persons?

(c) Does the EPF Act continue to apply in case the number of employer falls below 20?

3. Who can exempt any class of establishments from the operations of the EPF Act and when?

4. Define the following terms as used in the Employees' Provident Fund Act :

(a) Appropriate Government

(b) Basic Wages

(c) Employer [*May 2007*]

(d) Employee

(e) Exempted Employee

(f) Exempted Establishment

(g) Factory

(h) Industry

(i) Manufacturer/Manufacturing process

(j) Occupier of a factory

5. Explain the provisions of the Employees' Provident Fund and Miscellaneous Provision Act,1952 relating to *Employees Provident Fund Scheme*.

6. Explain the provisions of the Employees' Provident Fund and Miscellaneous Provision Act, 1952 relating to *Employees Family Pension Scheme*.

7. Explain the provisions of the Employees' Provident Fund and Miscellaneous Provision Act, 1952 relating to *Employees Deposit Linked Insurance Scheme*.

***8.** (a) Who is to constitute is the Central Board of Trustees under the EPF and MP Act, 1952

(b) What is the composition of Central Board?

(c) State the functions of Central Board.

(d) State the provisions relating to Audit of Accounts of Central Board.

(e) Do this board have a perpetual succession and a common seal?

***9.** (a) How is the Executive Committee constituted under the EPF and MP Act, 1952?

(b) What is the composition of Executive Committee?

10. (a) Who is to constitute State Board of Trustees?

(b) Do this Board have a perpetual succession and a common seal?

11. Explain provisions relating to the appointment and condition of service of officers.

12. Can the Central Board/State Board of Trustees delegate their powers and function to their chairman or any other officer?

***13.** Describe the provision relating to contribution by the employees and the employee under the Employees Provident Fund and Miscellaneous Provision Act, 1952.

14. State the provisions relating to Employees' Pension Fund. [*Nov. 2007*]

15. Write a note an 'Settlement of Provident fund.'

***16.** (a) Who may determine the moneys due from an employees under the EPF and MP Act, 1952.

(b) State the factors considered by the authorities at the time of determining the amount.

17. (a) Who can apply for a review of order passed u/s 7A and when?

(b) State the grounds on which review application may be made.

18. (a) How is EPF Appellate Tribunal constituted?

(b) What is its composition?

(c) What are its powers?

19. Explain the provisions relating to mode of recovery of money due from employers.

***20.** Explain provisions relating to protection against attachment of PF. [*May 2009*]

21. State the priority of payment of PF contribution over other debts. [*Nov. 2008*]

22. Can employer reduce wages etc of an employee by reason only of his liability for the payment of any contribution to the fund.

23. (a) Who can appoint Inspectors?

(b) What are the powers of Inspectors?

24. Who can recover damages and under what circumstances?

25. Who can exempt any establishment from the operations of all any of the provisions of :

(a) Provident Fund Scheme

(b) Family Pension Scheme

(c) Insurance Scheme

***26.** State the provision of EPF and MP Act, 1952 relating to transfer of account of an employee who leaves the employment of an establishment and takes up employment in another establishment. [*May 2008*]

***27.** Explain the provision of EPF and MP Act, 1952 relating to liability of an employee in case of his transferring the establishment to another person.

SECTION C

The Companies Act, 1956

1. Definition and Nature of Company
2. Types of Companies
3. Formation of a Company
4. Memorandum of Association
5. Articles of Association
6. Prospectus
7. Allotment of Shares
8. Shares and Share Capital
9. Transfer and Transmission of Shares
10. Membership
11. Borrowing Powers and Debentures
12. Fixed and Floating Charges
13. Meetings and Procedures
14. Registers, Returns, Service and Authentication of Documents
15. Company Law in a Computerized Environment

CHAPTER 1 Definition and Nature of Company

1.0 MEANING OF COMPANY

The company is one of the form of organisation. It has its distinctive characteristics and advantages which make it suitable for different purposes.

1.1 Literary Meaning

The term 'Company' implies an association of a number of persons formed for some common object or objects.

1.2 Legal Meaning

"Company means a company formed and registered under this Act or an existing company [Sec 3(1)(i)]. An existing Company means a company formed and registered under any of the previous Companies laws" [Sec 3(1)(ii)].

The above definition is not exhaustive because it does not reveal the characteristics of the company.

Let us analyse some other definitions given in various judicial decisions to ascertain the characteristics of the company.

1.3 Meaning as per Judicial Pronouncements

1. According to Lord Justice Lindley *"By a company is meant an association of many persons who contribute money or money's worth to a common stock and employ it in some trade or business and who share the profit and loss (as the case may be) arising therefrom. The common stock so contributed is denoted in money and is the capital of the company. The persons who contribute it, or to who it belongs, are called members. The proportion of capital to which each member is entitled is his share. Shares are always transferable although the right to transfer them is often more or less restricted."*

2. According to Chief Justice Marshall *"A company is person, artificial, invisible, intangible and existing only in the eyes of law. Being a mere creature of law, it possesses only those properties which the charter of its creation confers upon it, either expressly or as incidental to its very existence."*

3. According to Lord Haney *"A company is an incorporated association which is an artifical person created by law, having a separate entity, with a perpetual succession and a common seal."*

From the above definitions, it is clear that a company has a corporate and legal personality. It is an artificial person and exists only in the eyes of law. It has an independent legal entity, a common seal and perpetual succession.

2.0 MEANING OF CORPORATION SOLE, CORPORATION AGGREGATE AND BODY CORPORATE

2.1 Meaning of Corporation Sole

Corporation Sole refers to a single person constituted as a Corporation in respect of some function or office enjoying perpetual succession and separate legal entity. *For example,* The President of India, Governor of a State, The Prime Minister of India,

2.2 Meaning of Corporation Aggregate

Corporation Aggregate refers to an association of persons constituted as a corporation enjoying perpetual succession and separate legal entity.
It includes:
(a) companies incorporated under The Companies Act, 1956
(b) companies incorporated under The Special Act of Parliament
(c) companies incorporated Outside India

2.3 Meaning of Body Corporate

(a) Body Corporate refers to an association of persons which has:
  (i) been incorporated under any law
  (ii) a separate legal entity
  (iii) perpetual succession, and
  (iv) a common seal.
(b) The term 'Body Corporate' **includes**:
  (i) companies incorporated under The Companies Act, 1956
  (ii) companies incorporated under The Special Act of Parliament
  (iii) companies incorporated Outside India
  (iv) Public Financial Institutions u/s 4A [*for example,* LIC, UTI, RBI, ICICI, IDBI]
(c) The term 'Body Corporate' **does not include**:
  (i) a Corporation Sole
  (ii) a Co-operative Society registered under any law relating to Co-operative Societies.
  (iii) Any other body corporate (not being a company as defined in this Act) which the Central Government may specify in this behalf.
  (iv) a Society registered under the Societies Registration Act 1860 [*Board of Trustees Ayurvedic and Unani Tibbia College Delhi vs State of Delhi*]

Thus, the term body corporate is much wider in concept than the word 'company'.

3.0 CHARACTERISTICS OF A COMPANY

On analysing the aforesaid definitions the following characteristics of a company are revealed:

1. An Artificial Person Created by Law A company is called an artifical person because it does not take birth like a natural person but comes into existence through law. Being the creation of law, the company possesses only those properties which are conferred upon it by its charter (i.e., Memorandum of Association). Within the limits of powers conferred by its charter, it can do all acts as a natural person can do. It may be noted that the company is an artificial legal person and not a fictitious person.

Like a natural person—

(a) The company can enter into contracts.
(b) The company can enforce the contractual rights against others.
(c) The company can sue in its own name.
(d) The company can be sued in its own name.
(e) The company can own and hold property in its own name.
(f) The company has nationality. The registration of a company in a country determines the nationality of that company to that country.
(g) The company has its own rights and liabilities.

Unlike a natural person—

(a) The company has no physical shape or form.
(b) The company can not shake by hand.
(c) The company can not marry.
(d) The company can not smile or weep.
(e) The company can not take oath.
(f) The company can not commit a crime like murder.
(g) The company has no citizenship because a citizen of a country is a personal right peculiar to human beings only.

2. Separate Legal Entity The case of *Salomon* v. *Saloman & Co. Ltd.* (1897) (AC) (22) clearly established the concept of corporate personality as distinct and different from that of its members individually and collectively (known as the Doctrine of Corporate veil).

In case of ***Saloman* v. *Salomon and Company Ltd.*** Mr. Saloman was running a shoe business in England as a sole proprietor. He formed a company known as 'Saloman and Co. Ltd.' It consisted of Saloman himself, his wife, his four sons and a daughter. The shoes business of Mr. Saloman was sold to the company for £30,000. Mr. Saloman received from the company purchase price in the form of £20,000 fully paid shares of £1 each and £10,000 in debentures which carried a floating charge over the assets of the company. One share of £1 each was subscribed for in cash by each member of Saloman's family. Saloman was the managing director of the company. During the course of business, the company became liable for some unsecrued loan. The company ran into financial difficulties after some time and went into liquidation within a year. On winding up, the assets realised £6,000. The company owed £10,000 to Mr. Saloman and £7,000 to unsecured creditors. Thus, after paying off the debenture- holder. (Mr. Saloman), nothing was left for unsecured creditors. The creditors claimed priority over the debentures contending that Mr. Saloman and Saloman and Co. Ltd. were one and the same person, the company was only a facade to defraud the innocent creditors. Mr. Saloman should not therefore, be treated as a secured creditor. *The House of Lords held* that the company had been validly constituted and it had an independent existence distinct from its members. Therefore, Mr. Saloman was entitled to be paid his dues first as a secured creditor. It was observed that the business belonged to the company and not to Mr. Saloman. The company and Mr. Saloman enjoyed separate legal entities. The fact that the members were from one single family had no bearing upon the validity of the company.

The legal status of a company has been aptly described by the Supreme Court of India in ***Tata Engineering & Locomotive Co. Ltd.* v. *State of Bihar*,** as follows:

"The corporation in law is equal to natural person and has a legal entity of its own. The entity of the corporation is entirely separate from that of its shareholder; it bears its own name and has seal of its own; its assets are separate and distinct from those of its members; it can sue and be sued exclusively for its own purpose".

Lee v Lee's Air Farming Ltd. Lee was a qualified pilot. He virtually owned all the shares and he was the director also. He was also receiving salary from the company for being a chief pilot under the company. He was killed in an air accident while working for the company. It was held that Lee was a separate person for the company he had formed. Therefore, he could be legitimately employed under the company. As he was killed in the course of employment under the company, his widow was entitled to compensation.

Bacha F. Guzdar v CIT A shareholder received dividend income from a company carrying on agricultural business. The income from agriculture business was exempt for tax. The shareholder contended that her dividend income should be treated as agricultural income and therefore exempt form tax. The court held that the company was s separate person form its members, having its own business, and its own income. The income received by the shareholders was not the same income as earned by the company.

Effects As a consequence of separate legal entity—

(a) The company may enter into contracts with its members and *vice versa*. Thus, a member can be a debtor, a creditor a director, and an employee of the company at the same time.
(b) Its member can not be held liable for the acts of the company even if he holds virtually the entire share capital.
(c) Its members cannot claim ownership right in company's assets during its lifetime or even on its winding since they are not owners.
(d) Its members can not have any insurable interest in the company's properties.
(e) Its creditors' remedy for the recovery of their debts lie only against the company and not against its members or directors.

3. Perpetual Succession The term '*perpetual succession*' means the continued existence. The continued existence of the company is not affected by a continuous change in its membership. The death, insolvency or unsoundness of mind of its members or transfer of shares by its members does not in any way affect the existence of the company. Members may come and members may go but the company goes on forever. The company can be compared with flowing river where water (members) keeps on changing continuously, still the identity of the river (company) remains the same. The company continues to exist even if all its human members die. According to Gower, 'even a hydrogen bomb cannot destory a company'. Since it is created by law, it can be brought to an end by the process of law.

Thus, a company still continue to exist for an indefinite period till it is wound up in accordance with the provisions of the Companies Act.

4. Common Seal The term '*Common Seal*' means the official signature of the company. Since the company being an artificial person can not sign its name on a document, every company is required to have its common seal with its name engraved on the same. This seal acts as the official signature of the company. Any document bearing the common seal of the company and duly witnessed by at least two directors will be binding on the company.

5. Limited Liability This specific characteristic of '*Limited Liability*' is possessed by limited companies and not by unlimited companies. In case of a *company limited by shares,* the liability of a member is limited upto the amount remaining unpaid (if any) on the shares held by a member. In case of *a company limited by guarantee,* the liability of a member is limited upto the amount guaranteed by a member. In case of company limited by guarantee and having share capital, the liability of a member is limited upto the aggregate of amount unpaid on shares held by him and amount guaranteed by him.

6. Free Transferability of Shares This specific characteristic of 'Free Transferability of Shares' is possessed by public companies and not by private companies.

The shares of a public company are freely transferable. Shares are movable property transferable in the manner provided in the Articles [Sec. 8.2]. A shareholder can transfer his shares to any person without the consent of other members. Under the articles of association, even a public limited company can put certain restrictions on the transfer of shares but it cannot altogether stop it. A shareholder of public company possessing fully paid up shares is at liberty to transfer his shares to anyone he likes in accordance with the manner provided for in the articles of association of the company.

It may be noted that although restriction on the right to transfer may be placed in certain cases (e.g. in case of partly paid up shares) but absolute right of members to transfer shares cannot be restricted and any provision in the Articles to that affect shall be void.

Section 3(1)(iii) requires a private company to put restriction on transferability of its shares.

4.0 LIFTING THE CORPORATE VEIL

4.1 Meaning of Lifting the Corporate Veil

Lifting the corporate veil means 'disregarding (or Ignoring) the corporate entity and paying regard to the individual members behind the legal facade'.

When the company starts using the corporate veil for improper conduct, or to protect fraud or to justify wrongs, the law ignores the separate legal entity of the company and looks at the real persons behind and treat the company and its members as same person.

4.2 Circumstances when the Corporate Veil can be Pierced/Lifted

The circumstances and cases in which the corporate veil can be lifted may broadly be classified as follows:

Circumstances when Corporate Veil can be Lifted

Under Express Statutory Provisions	Under Judicial Interpretations
(a) When the no. of members falls below the statutory minimum [Section 45]	(a) For determination of the character of the company
(b) Non-disclosure of Representative capacity [Section 147]	(b) For prevention of fraud or improper conduct
(c) To examine the relationship of holding and subsidiary [Section 212]	(c) For the protection of revenue
(d) To investigate into the affairs of related companies [Section. 239]	(d) When company is formed to act as an agent of its members
(e) To investigate ownership of a company [Section 247]	(e) When company is formed to avoid the welfare laws
(f) When business is carried on to defraud the creditors [Section 542]	

4.3 Cases under Express Statutory Provisions

(a) When the Number of Members Falls Below Statutory Minimum [Section 45]

If the company carries on business for more than 6 months with the number of members reduced below the statutory requirement (i.e. 2 in case of private company and 7 in case of public company), the every person who was member of the company during the time when it carried on business after those 6 months and who was aware of this fact, shall be personally liable for all debts of the company **contracted after those 6 months.**

Although the company continues to enjoy its distinct personality but loses the important feature of limited liability of the members of the company. Such a situation entitles the creditors to disregard the separate entity of the company, and the creditors can take action against the members directly.

(b) Misrepresentation in Prospectus [Sections 62 and 63]

(c) Failure to Return Application Money [Section 69 and SEBI Guidelines]

(d) Non-disclosure of Representative Capacity [Section 147(4)]

Where an officer or employee of a company enters into a contract on behalf of the company, without properly disclosing the name of the company on whose behalf he is acting, such officer or employee shall be personally liable for the amount due if the company refuses to pay it. He shall be punishable with fine upto Rs. 10,000. *For example*, a bill of exchange drawn upon a company is accepted by a director in his personal capacity i.e., without disclosing that he is accepting the bill on behalf of the company, such a director shall be personally liable for the bill.

(e) To examine the Relationship of Holding and Subsidiary Company [Section 212]

When one company controls the composition of the board of directors of another company or holds majority of its shares, the former is called the holding company and the latter as subsidiary company. In general, a subsidiary company is altogether treated as a separate entity and the holding company is not liable for its acts. But, under Section 212 of the Act, every holding company is required to disclose to its shareholders the accounts of its subsidiaries. It requires that the copies of balance sheet, profit and loss account, directors' report and auditor's report of each subsidiary company be attached to the balance sheet of the holding company. Thus, companies under the same group are treated as one entity disregarding the rule that each subsidiary company has a separate legal entity. However, Sec 212 does not require holding company to prepare Consolidated Accounts.

(f) To Investigate into Affairs of Related Companies [Section 239(7)]

According to Section 239(7) of the Act, if an inspector is appointed by the Central Government to investigate the affairs of a company, he shall also have the power to investigate into the affairs of related (subsidiary) companies in the same management. The power to do so may thus lift the corporate veil.

(g) To Investigate Ownership of a Company [Section 247]

When the Central Government feels it necessary to know about the membership of any company and also some other matters relating to the company with the object of determining true persons who are (or have been) financially interested in the success or failure of the company or who are (or have been) able to control the policy of the company, may appoint one or more inspectors to investigate and report on these matters. This will be done by lifting the corporate veil so as to find out the true persons controlling it.

(h) When Business is Carried on to Defraud the Creditors [Section 542]

According to Section 542 of the Act, if in the course of the winding up of a company, it appears that any business of the company has been carried on with the intention to defraud its creditors or any other persons, in such a case the persons who were knowingly parties to such acts may be held personally liable for any debts and other liabilities of the company. In such a situation, the court may disregard the legal entity of a company and make the fraudulent persons personally liable for the all or any of the debts of the company without any limitation of liability.

(i) Arrears of Tax

Ordinarily, only a company is liable for the debts incurred by it. However, as per Sec. 179 of the income Tax Act, 1961, all the directors of the company shall also be liable for the payment of taxes payable by the company. Similarly, Sec. 18 of the Central sales Tax Act provides that all the directors of the company shall also be liable for the payment of taxes payable by the company. However, these section apply only to a private company, that too at the time of winding up.

(j) Ultra Vires Acts

The directors of a company shall be personally liable for the *ultra vires* acts done by them on behalf of the company.

4.4 Cases under Judicial Interpretations

Besides the above-mentioned circumstances, the courts have allowed the lifting of corporate veil for proper administration of taxation laws, wealth tax law, etc. and also in some other circumstances. Let us now study some of the cases where the corporate veil was lifted.

(a) For Determination of the Character of the Company

Sometimes, particularly during the war between countries, it becomes necessary to ascertain the character of certain companies. At such times the courts are justified in lifting the corporate veil of a company which is controlled by alien enemy. In this way a company registered in India may be declared alien enemy if it is found that the persons controlling such a company are citizens of an enemy country.

In case of ***Daimler Co. Ltd.* v. *Continental Tyre and Rubber Co. Ltd.*, [(1916) 2 A.C. 207]**. A company with the name Continental Tyre and Rubber Co. Ltd. was registered in England. The object of this company was to sell tyres in United Kingdom, which were manufactured in Germany by a German company. Majority of the shares of this company were held by Germans. Besides this, all the directors of the company were German residents. When the First World War broke out, the company filed a suit to recover a trade debt. The court came to the conclusion that the company was an enemy company because the effective control of the company was in the hands of Germans who were alien enemy. Hence, the claim of the company was disallowed on the ground that it was against public policy to allow alien enemies to trade by using the corporate veil.

Similarly in case of ***Connors Bros.* v. *Connors,* [(1940) 4 All E.R. 197]** the principle was applied against the managing director who made use of his position contrary to public policy. In this case the House of Lord determined the character of the company as "enemy" company, since the persons who were *de facto* in control of its affairs, were residents of Germany, which was at war with England. The alien company was not allowed to proceed with the action, as that would have meant giving money to the enemy, which was considered as monstrous and against "public policy".

(b) For the Prevention of Fraud or Improper Conduct

The courts may lift the corporate veil if the company has been formed to avoid legal obligations or to defraud the creditors.

In the case of ***Gilford Motor Co. Ltd.* v. *Horne* [(1933)** 1 Ch. 435], Horne was appointed as a managing director of Gilford Motor Co. with the condition that he would not solicit or entice away the customers of the company, so long as he was in the employment of the company and afterwards. After leaving the company, Horne formed another company which was to carry on the same business. This new company of Horne solicited the customers of Gilford Motor Co. Ltd. In a suit filed by Gilford Motor Co. Ltd. against Horne to restrain him from soliciting the business, the court came to the conclusion that Horne had created the company for his own benefit and to solicit the customers of his employer's company. The court issued an injunction against Horne and his new company and held that the new company was a mere cloak for the purpose of enabling the defendant to commit a breach of his contract that he would not solicit the business of his employer's company.

Similarly, in case of ***Jones* v. *Lipman*, (1962)**, I.W.L.R. 832, *A* agreed to sell certain land to *B*. Pending completion of formalities of the said deal, *A* sold and transferred the land to a company which he had incorporated with a nominal capital of $100 and of which he and a clerk were the only shareholders and directors. This was done in order to escape a decree for specific performance in a suit brought by *B*. The court held that the company was the creature of A and a mask to avoid recognition and that in the eyes of equity A must complete the contract, since he had the full control of the limited company in which the property was vested, and was in a position to cause the contract in question to be completed.

(c) For the Protection of Revenue

The court may lift the corporate veil if the company has been formed to evade the tax. In case of ***Re Sir Dinshaw Manekjee Petit,*** AIR 1927 Bombay 371, the assessee, Sir Dinshaw who was a very rich man, was earning huge dividend and interest income. He formed four private companies and entered into an agreement with each company to hold a block of investment as his agent. Under the arrangement the income received was credited in company's account and the company handed the amount back to him as a loan (which was never repaid). In this way he divided his income in four parts in order to reduce his tax liability. The court ignored the corporate entity of these companies and held that the company was nothing more than the assessee himself. Sir Dinshaw was held the owner of total income and liable to pay tax.

(d) Where Company is formed to Act as an Agent of its Members

Where a company is regarded as an agent or trustee of its members or of another company, for the acts done by the company, it will be the members who would be responsible and not the company.

In case of ***Re F.G. Films Ltd.*** an American company financed and produced a film 'Mansoon' in India. But, technically, the film was made in the name of a company incorporated in England. This British company had only a capital of $100 divided into 100 shares of $1 each, of this, 90 shares were held by President of the American company. The Board of trade declined to register the film as a British film. The view of the Board of Trade was upheld by the court. The court held that the British company acted only as an agent of the American company which was the true maker of the film.

(e) When a Company is formed to avoid Welfare Laws

The courts have disregarded the separate legal personality of the company when the company's independent status was being used as a device to reduce the amount payable by the company to defeat the provisions of welfare laws, such as payment of bonus to its workmen.

In the case of ***Workmen Employed in Associated Rubber Industries Ltd., Bhavnagar* v. *The Associated Rubber Industries Ltd., Bhavnagar and Others,*** a new company was formed with no assets of its own except those transferred to it by the principal company. The new company had no business of its own, it received dividend on shares transferred to it by the principal company. Thus, the principal company was able to reduce its gross profits and consequently the amount of bonus payable to workman was also reduced. The Supreme Court rejected the independent status of the new company and directed that the amounts paid to the new company as dividend shall also be taken into account while determining the gross profits of the principal company.

The court held that "in every case where ingenuity is expected to avoid taking and welfare legislations, the court will go behind the smoke-screen and discover the true state of affairs.

Thus, in all circumstances, 'honest enterprises by means of companies are allowed but the public are protected against kiting and humbuggary.

(f) For the Protection of Public Policy

The Court shall lift the corporate veil to protect the public policy and to prevent the transaction contrary to public policy.

5.0 DISTINCTION BETWEEN A PARTNERSHIP AND A COMPANY

A partnership differs from a company in the following respects:

Basis of Distinction	*Partnership*	*Company*
1. ***Separate Legal Entity***	A firm has **no separate legal existence**. Partners are collectively termed as a firm and individually as partners.	It **has** a separate legal existence. A company is separate from the members.
2. ***Nature of Liability***	The liability of partners is **unlimited.**	Liability of its members is **limited** to the extent of unpaid amount on shares held by them in case of Company Ltd. by Shares.
3. ***Perpetual Existence***	It does not enjoy perpetual existence. Death, sickness, retirement of partners may affect its existence so as to dissolve it.	It enjoys perpetual existence. Even an atom bomb cannot destroy a company unless it is wound up under the due process of law. Winding up may take years.

(Contd.)

Basis of Distinction	***Partnership***	***Company***
4. ***Minimum No. of Members***	**Minimum** No. of partners is 2.	• A public Co. – 7. • A Pvt. Co. – 2
5. ***Maximum No. of Members***	• Banking business: 10 • Non-banking business: 20.	• Public Co. – no limit . • Pvt. – 50.
6. ***Transfer of interest***	A partner **cannot transfer** his share without the consent of other partners.	A member of a public company **may transfer** his shares as and when he likes. There is no restriction on transfer of shares.
7. ***Mutual Agency***	Mutual Agency exists among partners as they bind each other.	No Mutual agency exists among members of a company as they do not bind each other with their actions.
8. ***Distribution of Profit***	Profits are distributable among partners as per the partnership deed.	There is no such compulsion that profits must be distributed. Only when the dividends are declared that the members get a share of profits.
9. ***Management***	Partners **Participate** in management.	Members **cannot participate** in management unless appointed as directors. However, members may attempt and vote at meetings while making the appointment of Directors, Auditors, etc.
10. ***Property***	Property of the firm is the **joint property of all its partners.**	Property of the company is **not the property of its members** as the company has separate legal existence.
11. ***Remedy of Creditors***	The creditors of a firm can proceed **against the partners** jointly and severally.	The creditors of a company can proceed **only against the company** and not against its members.
12. ***Whether Creditors bound by Restriction on authority***	Restriction on a partner's authority contained in partnership contracted **do not** bind outsiders.	Restriction on authority of directors contained in Articles **bind** the outsiders because they are deemed to have the knowledge of Articles.
13. ***Compulsory audit***	Audit of a firm is **not compulsory** under The Indian Partnership Act.	Audit of a company is **compulsory** under The Companies Act.
14. ***Dissolution***	Firm can be dissolved at any time by **mutual agreement**.	A company, being the creature of law, can only be **dissolved by law**.

6.0 IS COMPANY A CITIZEN?

6.1 A Company is not a Citizen

No company can be a citizen of India since Citizenship under the Citizenship Act is available only to an individual.

6.2 No Rights of Citizens

The fundamental rights which are available only to a citizen, are not available to a company since a company is not a citizen.

6.3 A Company has other Fundamental Rights

The constitution of India grants certain fundamental rights to every person, whether a citizen or not. Thus, a company registered in India can enjoy all the fundamental rights which are available to all persons.

7.0 MEANING OF 'RELATIVE'

7.1 Specified Relationships

A person shall be deemed to be a relative of another, if—

(a) they are members of a Hindu undivided family; *or*

(b) they are husband and wife.

7.2 Relationships given in Schedule IA

Two persons shall be relatives if one is related to the other in the manner specified in Schedule IA. Schedule IA specifies the following relationships:

Relationships given in Schedule IA

Father-Mother	Son	Daughter	Brother & Sister
1. Father	7. Son	13. Daughter	19. Bother
2. Father's father	8. Son's wife	14. Daughter's husband	20. Brother's wife
3. Father's mother	9. Son's son	15. Daughter's son	21. Sister
4. Mother	10. Son's son's wife	16. Daughter's son's wife	22. Sister's husband
5. Mother's mother	11. Son's daughter	17. Daughter's daughter	
6. Mother's father	12. Son's daughter's husband	18. Daughter's daughter's husband	

Note: **Children of Brother & Sister are not relatives.**

8.0 COMPANY AS A PARTNER IN A FIRM

8.1 Can a Company become a Partner in a Firm?

A company can become a partner in a firm since it is a separate legal entity in the eyes of law. It has contractual capacity to enter into any valid contract.

8.2 Can a limited liability company have unlimited liability as a partner in a firm?

A limited liability company can have unlimited liability as a partner in a firm since it is the liability of the members of a limited company which is limited and not that of the company itself. According to Department of Company Affairs (DCA) a company can become a partner only if its Memorandum of Association specifically allows it to do so.

VERY SHORT ANSWER TYPE QUESTIONS

1. Define Company.
2. Define Corporation Sole.
3. Define Corporation Aggregate.
4. Define Body Corporate.
5. What is a Corporate Veil?
6. What is meant by 'Perpetual Succession'?
7. What is Common Seal?
8. What is meant by 'Limited Liability'?
9. What is meant by 'Free transferability of shares'?
10. Can a company acquire citizenship?
11. Can a company become partner in a partnership firm?

SHORT ANSWER TYPE QUESTIONS

1. Why is a company called an 'Artificial person'?
2. What are the acts which a company can do like a natural person?
3. What are the acts which a company cannot do like a natural person?
4. The term 'Body Corporate' is much wider concept than the term 'Company'. Explain.
5. Distinguish between the following:
   (a) Body Corporate and Company
   (b) Corporation Sole and Corporation Aggregate
   (c) Partnership and Company

LONG ANSWER TYPE QUESTIONS

1. Define a company. Explain its characteristics.
2. "A company is an artificial person created by law with a perpetual succession and a common seal." Explain.
3. "A company is a legal entity quite distinct from its members." Explain.
4. What do you understand by the concept of corporate personality? Under what circumstances is a lifting of corporate veil possible?
5. Distinguish between the partnership and a limited company.
6. Comment on the following:
   (a) "Members of a limited company may nevertheless have unlimited liability".
   (b) A limited liability company can become a partner in a firm.

7. Write short notes on the following:
   (a) One man company
   (b) Common Seal
   (c) Perpetual Succession
   (d) Lifting of corperate veil

PRACTICAL PROBLEMS

1. An English company was formed for selling in England tyres produced by a German company in Germany. The bulk of English company's shares were held by the Germen company. The overwhelming majority of the shareholders and all the directors were Germen nationals residing in Germany. The English company filed a suit during the World War I to recover a trade debt. Could the company be allowed to proceed with the action? [No]
2. H was appointed the managing director of A&Co. on the term that he must not, at any time during the tenure of his office as such, or afterwards, entice away the customers of A&Co. Subsequent to the cessation of H's employment under an agreement he set up a business in the name of H&Co. which solicited the customers of A&Co. Evidence showed that H&Co. was formed to enable H to commit a breach of his covenant against solicitation. Could H&Co. and H be restrained from doing so? [Yes]
3. *X*, having huge dividend and interest income, formed four private companies. He agreed with each of such companies to hold a block of investment as an agent for the company. The income received was credited to the accounts of the company but the company gave it back to *X* as a pretended loan. In this way, *X* divided his income with a view to reduce his tax-burden. In a legal proceeding against *X*, the court ignored the company and concerned itself directly with *X*. Could the court do so? [Yes]
4. X Ltd. was incorporated with 10 members (A to J). On 1st April 2009, the number of members reduced to 6. The debts of the company on that date were Rs. 3,00,000. On 1st Jan 2010, the number of members increased to 9. The debts of the company increased to Rs. 4,50,000 and the 4,80,000 on 30th Sept. 2009 and on 31st Dec 2009 respectively. Out of Six members, two members Mr. A and Mr. B were not aware of the fact that the number of members reduced to 6. Discuss the legal position

   [As per Sec. 45, four members (other than Mr. A and Mr. B). who were aware of reduction in No. of members are personally liable for Rs. 30,000 (Rs. 4,80,000 – Rs. 4,50,000) contracted after those 6 months,]

CHAPTER

2

Types of Companies

1.0 TYPES OF COMPANIES

The companies can be classified under the three categories as follows:

1. On the basis of incorporation
2. On the basis of liability
3. On the basis of control

The various types of companies on the aforesaid basis are shown below:

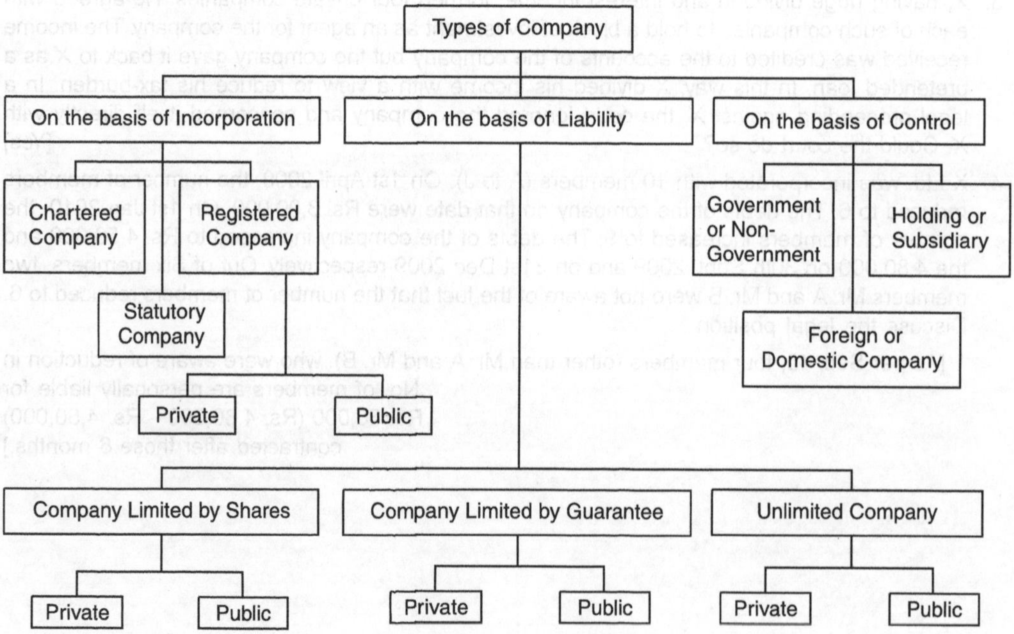

Let us discuss the various types of companies one by one.

2.0 COMPANIES ON THE BASIS OF INCORPORATION

On the basis of incorporation, companies may be divided into the following three categories:

2.1 Chartered company A company incorporated under a special charter granted by the King or Queen of England is called '**Chartered Company**'. A chartered company is regulated by its charter and the Companies Act does not apply to it. The charter also prescribes the nature of business and the powers of the company. The familiar examples of chartered company are the *East India Company* and the *Bank of England*. This type of company cannot now be formed in India.

2.2 Statutory company A statutory company is one which is created by a Special Act of Parliament or a State Legislature. Such companies are usually formed for achieving a purpose related with public utilities. The nature and powers of such companies are laid down in the Special Act under which they are created. However, the provisions of the Companies Act are also applicable to them insofar as they are consistent with the provisions of the Special Act. Such companies need not have a Memorandum of Association. A statutory company has also a separate legal entity and it is not required to use the word 'limited' after its name. The audit of such companies is conducted under the control and supervision of the Auditor General of India and the annual report of working is required to be placed before the Parliament or State legislature, as the case may be. Familiar examples of such companies are Reserve Bank of India, Unit Trust of India. The Life Insurance Corporation of India, State Trading Corporation, The Food Corporation of India, State Bank of India, etc.

2.3 Registered or Incorporated Company A registered company is one which is registered in accordance with the provisions of the Companies Act of 1956 and also includes the existing companies. By existing company we mean a company formed and registered under any of the previous laws. A registered company comes into existence only when it receives the certificate of incorporation. Registered companies are governed by the provisions of The Companies Act.

A registered Company may *either* be a private company *or* a public company.

I. Private Company [Section 3(1)(iii)] A Private Company means a company which has a minimum paid up capital of Rs 1,00,000 or such higher paid up capital as may be prescribed, and by its articles—

(a) restricts the right to transfer its shares, if any,
(b) limits the number of its members to 50, and
(c) prohibits any invitation to the public to subscribe for any shares in or debentures of the company.
(d) prohibits any invitation or acceptance of deposits from persons other than its members, directors or their relatives.

(a) Restriction on Transfer of Shares The right of transfer is generally restricted in the following manner:

(i) By authorising the directors to refuse transfer of shares to persons whom they do not approve or by compelling the shareholder to offer his shareholding to the existing shareholders first. It may be noted that it can only restrict the right of sale to a member. On this consideration, the articles usually provide that before selling or transferring his share, the directors must be communicated in writing of such intention of the shareholder.
(ii) By specifying the method for calculating the price at which the shares may be sold by one member to another. Generally, it is left to be determined either by the auditor of the company or by the company at a general meeting.
(iii) By providing that the shareholders who are employees of the company shall offer the shares to specified persons or class of persons when they leave the company's service.

Notes:

(i) The articles of a private company must provide restrictions on transferability of shares.

(ii) However, the articles can not impose absolute prohibition on transferability of shares.

(iii) The restriction must be applied uniformly on the members of the company.

(b) Limitation of Membership The articles must contain a provision whereby the company limits the number of its members to 50.

Note: For the purposes of limit of 50, **present employees** who are members and **ex-employees** who were members while in that employment and have continued to be members after the employment ceased, are **excluded** and the **joint shareholders** are counted **as a single member**.

(c) Prohibition on Making an Invitation to Public The articles must prohibit any invitation to the public to subscribe for any of its shares or debentures. Such a prohibition is necessary for the substance of the private character of the company. One should note that under Section 67, an offer or invitation to a section of the public selected as members of the company is an offer or invitation to the public or debentureholders of the company. Such an invitation to the public shall be excluded from the category of 'invitation to the public' if such offer or investigation can be properly regarded in all circumstances:

(i) as not being calculated to result directly or indirectly in the shares or debentures becoming available for subscription or purchase by person other than those receiving the offer or invitation; or

(ii) otherwise as being a domestic concern of the persons making and receiving the offer or invitation.

An offer of shares by the directors to their friends by a document marked "private and confidential not for publication" is not an invitation to the public.
[***Sharewell* vs. *Combined Incandescent Metals Syndicate,*** [1907] 23 *T.L.R.* 482]

(d) Prohibition on Invitation/Acceptance of Deposit It is desirable and advisable as a good secretarial practice to alter the articles.

Therefore, immediately by passing Special Resolution under Section 31 to provide for restriction, in particular item (d) above. If these restrictions are not there, the company will be treated as public company.

Notes:

(i) Since the above-mentioned **four restrictions** must be contained in the articles of every private limited company, it is necessary for a private company to frame its own articles. However, the articles of a private company not having share capital is not required to contain the restriction regarding the transfer of shares.

(ii) A private company may be (a) a company limited by shares, or (b) a company limited by guarantee, or (c) an unlimited company.

(iii) In case a private company is a limited company, then it must add the words '*Private Limited*' at the end of its name.

(iv) If a private company does not comply with any of the restrictions contained in the articles, it ceases to enjoy some of the privileges granted to a private company.

(v) A private company must have at least 2 directors.

II. Public Company [Section 3(1)(iv)] Public company means a company which is Either

(a) not a private company and has a minimum paid-up capital of Rs 5,00,000 or such higher paid-up capital as may be prescribed; or

(b) is a private company which is subsidiary of public company.

Notes:

(i) There is no restriction on the maximum number of members. However, the maximum number of members depends upon the number of shares allotted.

(ii) A public company may be (a) a company limited by shares, or (b) a company limited by guarantee, or (c) an unlimited company.

(iii) In case a public company is a limited company, then it must add the words '*Limited*' at the end of its name.

(iv) A public company must have at least 7 members. [Section 12(1)]

(v) A public company must have at least 3 directors.

2.4 Licensed Company or Association not for Profit [Section 25]

(a) In the case of 'association not for profit' the Central Government may by license grant that an association may be registered as a company with limited liability, without using the words 'limited' or 'private limited' as part of its name.

(b) **Conditions for obtaining licence u/s 25**

The Central Government will grant the license only if it is satisfied that:

(i) the association about to be formed as a limited company aims at the promotion of commerce, art, science, religion, charity or any other useful object;

(ii) it intends to apply its profits, if any, for promoting its objects; and

(iii) it prohibits the payment of dividend to its members.

(b) Such companies may be public or private companies and may or may not have share capital.

(d) The Central Government may impose any terms and conditions that it deems fit for the grant of the license which shall be binding on the association.

(e) The CG may grant exemptions from provisions of the Act.

(f) On registration (subject to the provisions of Section 25), it will have the same privileges and obligations as a limited company has.

(g) **Revocation of Licence** This licence may be revoked by the Central Government, if:

(a) The company violates any terms and conditions subject to which licence u/s 25 was issued.

(b) The company alters its object clause without obtaining the previous approval of Central Govt.

On revocation the Registrar shall put 'Limited' or 'Private Limited' against the company's name in the register. But before such revocation, the Central Government must give a written notice of its intention to revoke the licence and opportunity to be heard in the matter.

(h) A licensed company is not required to have minimum paid up capital.

(i) A partnership firm may become a member of a licenced company. However on dissolution, the firm shall cease to be a member.

3.0 PROVISIONS RELATING TO MINIMUM SHARE CAPITAL

3.1 Applicability

The provisions relating to minimum paid up capital apply to every company having a share capital.

- whether it is a public company or a private company;

- whether it has been incorporated before or after the commencement of Companies (Amendment) Act., 2000.

3.2 Non-applicability

The provisions relating to minimum paid up capital do not apply to:

(a) A company limited by guarantee having no share capital.

(b) A licenced company u/s 25.

3.3 Minimum Paid up Capital

(a) Every **private** company must have a minimum paid up capital of **Rs. 1 lakh** or such higher paid-up capital as may be prescribed.

(b) Every **public** company must have a minimum paid up capital of **Rs. 5 lakhs;** or such higher paid-up capital as may be prescribed.

3.4 Nature of Capital

The capital of a company may consist of preference shares or equity shares or both.

3.5 Obligation of Subscribers to Subscribe

Where a new company is proposed to be formed, the subscribers to memorandum must subscribe at least minimum paid up capital required.

4.0 COMPANIES ON THE BASIS OF LIABILITY

On the basis of liability, an incorporated company may either be (i) a company limited by shares, or (ii) a company limited by guarantee, or (iii) an unlimited company.

4.1 Company Limited by Shares [Section 12(2)(a)]

(a) A company limited by shares is a company in which the liability of its members is limited by its Memorandum to the amount (if any) unpaid on the shares respectively held by them.

(b) If a member has paid the full amount of shares, then his liability shall be nil.

For example, suppose Mr. *X* buys 1000 shares of a company of the face value of Rs 10 each. In this company his liability is fixed to the tune of Rs 10,000 only. If he paid (when called by the company) Rs 6,000 to the company. He is now liable to pay the only Rs 4,000, this being the amount unpaid on his shares. When he has paid the entire amount of Rs 10,000 (which means when his shares have been fully paid up) his liability shall be nil.

(c) The companies limited by shares may be *either* public companies *or* private companies.

(d) Thus, the two main features of a company limited by shares are as follows:

(a) The liability of its members is limited to the amount (if any) remaining unpaid on the shares held by them.

(b) Such liability can be enforced *either* during the life time of the company (by the board of Directions) *or* during the winding up of the company (by the liquidator)

4.2 Company Limited by Guarantee [Section 12(2)(b)]

(a) A company limited by guarantee is a company in which the liability of its members is limited by its Memorandum to the amount that the member has guaranteed to pay in the event of winding up of the company.

(b) Such companies are generally formed for the promotion of commerce, art, science, religion, charity or any other useful object.

(c) The companies limited by guarantee may be *either* private companies *or* public companies.

(d) Such a company may or may not have share capital.

The main features of such company are as follows:

Types of Company Limited by Guarantee	*Liability*
(i) ***Company Limited by Guarantee not having share capital***	(a) The liability of its members is limited to the amount guaranteed by them. (b) Such liability can be enforced only after the commencement of winding up of the company and not during the life time of the company.
(ii) ***Company limited by guarantee having share capital***	(a) The liability or its members is limited to following two amounts: (i) The amount (if any) remaining unpaid on the shares held by them. (ii) The amount guaranteed by them. (b) The liability in respect of guaranteed amount can be enforced only at the time of winding up of the company and not during the life time of the company.

Note: The Articles of a company limited by guarantee must state the number of members with which the company is to be registered. [Section 27(2)]

4.3 Similarity between Company Limited by Share and Company Limited by Guarantee

Both the companies are required to state in the memorandum that the members' liabilitiy is limited.

4.4 Distinction between Company Limited by Share and Company Limited by Guarantee

(a) Members of company limited by share may be called upon to discharge their liability either during the company's life time or during its winding up.

(b) Members of company limited by guarantee may be called upon to discharge their liability only after the commencemant of the winding up.

4.5 Unlimited Company [Section 12(2)(c)]

(a) An unlimited company is a company in which the liability of its members is not limited by its mermorandum. In other words, the liability of members is unlimited i.e., there is no limit on the liability of members.

(b) The members of such companies may be required to pay company's losses from their personal property.

(c) Since such companies have separate legal entity, its creditors cannot file a suit against the members directly. The creditors will have to apply to the court for the winding up of the company and then the liquidator will direct the members to contribute to the assets of the company to pay-off its liabilities.

(d) Such company may also be *either* public company *or* private company. Such company may or may not have a share capital.

Notes:

(i) Such a company must have its own Memorandum and Articles of Association.

(ii) The Articles of an unlimited company must state the number of members with which the company is to be registered. [Section 27(2)]

(iii) The Articles of an unlimited company having a share capital must also state the amount of share capital with which the company is to be registered. [Section 27(2)]

(iv) An unlimited company need not hold statutory meeting. [Section 165(1)]

(v) An unlimited company having share capital may alter its share capital without any restriction. [Section 94(1)]

(vi) An unlimited company having share capital may reduce its share capital without any restriction. [Section 100(1)]

(vii) The liability of each member extends to the whole amount of the company's debts and liabilities but he will be entitled to claim contribution from other members.

(viii) So long as the company is a going concern the liability on the shares is the only liability which can be enforced by the company, though the liability of the members is unlimited so far as creditors are concerned.
[Re Mayfair Property Co. Bartlett **v.** ***Mayfair Property*** **Co.** [1898] 2 Ch. 28].

(ix) An unlimited company can register it as a limited company if a resolution is passed to that effect [Section 98]. If the unlimited company has share capital, (a) it may increase the nominal value of its shares provided that no part of such increase shall be capable of being called up except in the event and for the purpose of the company being wound-up, or (b) to provide that a specified portion of its uncalled share capital shall not be capable of being called up except in the event and for the pureposes of the company being wound-up [Section 98].

5.0 COMPANIES ON THE BASIS OF CONTROL

On the basis of control i.e., who effectively control the affairs of the company, the companies may be grouped as follows:

5.1 Government Company

5.2 Non-Government Company

5.3 Foreign Company

5.4 Domestic Company

5.5 Holding Company

5.6 Subsidiary Company

Let us discuss these companies one by one:

5.1 Government Company According to Section 617 of the Companies Act, a government company means **"any company in which at least 51% of the paid-up share capital is held by the Central Government or by any State Government or Governments or partly by the**

Central Government and partly by one or more State Governments and includes a company which is a subsidiary of a government company as thus defined". *For example,* Indian Telephone Industry, Hindustan Aeronautics Ltd. Even a subsidiary company of a government company is regarded as a Government company. A government company registered under this Act is a non-statutory company and is not an agent of the government. Further, like any other company, it is governed by the provisions of the Companies Act. Section 620 of the Act, however, provides that the Central Government may by notification in the Official Gazette direct that any of the provisions of this Act specified in the notification—

(a) shall not apply to any government company, or

(b) shall apply to any government company, only with such exceptions, modifications and adaptations, as may be specified in the notification. A copy of such notification shall be laid before the Parliament.

Notes: Sections 618, 619 and 619(A) of the Act cannot be exempted as these sections specially deal with Government companies.

5.2 Non-government Company A company which may not be termed as a government company as defined in Section 617 is regarded as a non-government company.

5.3 Foreign Company A foreign company means **a company which is incorporated in a country outside India under the law of that country.** After the establishment of business in India, the following documents must be filed with the Registrar of companies within 30 days from the date of establishment:

(a) A certified copy of the charter or statutes under which the company is incorporated, or the memorandum and articles of the company translated into English,

(b) The full address of the registered office of the company,

(c) A list of directors and secretary of the company,

(d) The names and address of any person resident in India who is authorised to accept, on behalf of the company, service of legal process and any notice served on the company, and

(e) The full address of the company's principal place of business in India.

5.4 Domestic Company A company which cannot be termed as foreign company under the provisions of the Companies Act should be regarded as a domestic company.

5.5 Holding and Subsidiary Company

General Meaning: if one company controls another company, the controlling company may be termed as the 'Holding company' and company so controlled may be termed as a 'subsidiary company'.

Legal Meaning: Section 4(1) of the Act defines a holding company as "a company shall be deemed to be the holding company of another, if that other is its subsidiary".

Legal meaning with illustration: A company (let us call it Company *S*) is deemed to be a subsidiary of another company (let us call it Company *H*) only in the following **3 cases:**

(a) When the company (Company *H*) controls the composition of Board of Directors of other Company (Company *S*).

The company H shall be deemed to have control over the composition of the Board of directors of *S* if *H* can appoint or remove all or majority of directors of *S* without the consent or approval of any other person. Company *H* will be demeed to have the power to appoint majority of persons as directors of *S*: (i) when these persons cannot be appointed in that capacity without *H*'s consent, or (ii) when their appointments follow necessarily from their appointment as directors, manager or the holder of any office in *H* company, or (iii) when the holding company (*i.e.*, *H*) itself or its another subsidiary holds the directorship in 'S' company [Section 4(1)(a) and (2)].

(b) When the Company *H* holds more than half in the nominal value of equity share capital of Company *S*.

For the purposes of this clause,

(i) Shares held by another person as a nominee for the company or any of its subsidiaries are regarded or being held by the company.

(ii) Following shares are not regarded as being held by the company:

(i) Shares held in a fiduciary capacity (e.g. shares held in trust for an individual)

(ii) Shares held under the provisions of any debentures

(iii) Shares held as security in the ordinary course of business (which includes the lending of money)

(c) When Company *S* is a subsidiary of a Company *T*, which in turn is the subsidiary of Company *H*.

Notes:

(a) **Deemed investments of holding company:** Any shares held by a subsidiary company in any other company shall be deemed to be held by the holding company.

(b) An Indian private company which is a subsidiary of a foreign company is treated as a subsidiary of a public company if its entire share capital is not held by that foreign company either alone or together with other foreign companies. [Section 4(7)]

ILLUSTRATION

	A Ltd.	*B Ltd.*	*C Ltd.*	*D Ltd.*
Paid up Capital	Rs 5 Crore	Rs 4 Crore	Rs 3 Crore	Rs 2 Crore
Equity Shares of Rs 10 each	40,00,000	30,00,000	20,00,000	10,00,000
10% Pref. Shares of Rs 10 each	10,00,000	10,00,000	10,00,000	10,00,000

State the relationship between the companies in the following cases:

Case (a) A Ltd. holds 10,00,000 Equity shares in B Ltd. and can appoint or remove majority of directors of B Ltd. without the consent of any other person.

Case (b) A Ltd. holds 15,10,000 equity shares in B Ltd. which holds 10,00,000 equity shares in C Ltd.

Case (c) A Ltd. holds 15,10,000 equity shares in B Ltd. which holds 10,10,000 equity shares in C Ltd.

Case (d) A Ltd. holds 15,10,000 equity shares in B Ltd. which holds 10,10,000 equity shares in C Ltd. which also holds 5,05,000 equity shares in D Ltd.

Case (e) A holds 15,10,000 equity shares in B Ltd. which holds 10,10,000 equity shares in C Ltd. and holds 1,00,000 equity shares in D Ltd. C Ltd. holds 1,05,000 equity shares in D Ltd.

Solution:

Case (a) As per Sec. 4(1)(a), B Ltd. is subsidiary of A Ltd. since A Ltd. can appoint or remove majority of directors of B Ltd.

Case (b) As per Sec 4(1)(b), B Ltd. is subsidiary of A Ltd. since A Ltd. holds more than half in nominal value of equity share capital of B Ltd.

C Ltd. is not subsidiary of B Ltd. since B Ltd. does not hold more than half in nominal value of equity share capital of C Ltd.

Case (c) As per Sec 4(1)(b), B Ltd is subsidiary of A Ltd. since A Ltd. holds more than half in nominal value of equity share capital of B Ltd.

As per Sec. 4(1)(b), C Ltd. is subsidiary of B Ltd. since B Ltd. holds more than half in nominal value of equity share capital of C Ltd.

As per Sec 4(1)(c), C Ltd. which is subsidiary of B Ltd., is also subsidiary of A Ltd.

Case (d) As per Sec 4(1)(b), B Ltd is subsidiary of A Ltd. since A Ltd. holds more than half in nominal value of equity share capital of B Ltd.

As per Sec. 4(1)(b), C Ltd. is subsidiary of B Ltd. since B Ltd. holds more than half in nominal value of equity share capital of C Ltd.

As per Sec 4(1)(c), C Ltd. which is subsidiary of B Ltd., is also subsidiary of A Ltd.

As per Sec 4(1)(c), D Ltd. which is subsidiary of C Ltd., is also subsidiary of B Ltd. and A Ltd.

Case (e) As per Sec 4(1)(b), B Ltd is subsidiary of A Ltd. since A Ltd. holds more than half in nominal value of equity share capital of B Ltd.

As per Sec. 4(1)(b), C Ltd. is subsidiary of B Ltd. since B Ltd. holds more than half in nominal value of equity share capital of C Ltd.

As per Sec 4(1)(b), D Ltd. is subsidiary of B Ltd since B Ltd. along with its subsidiary (C Ltd.) holds more than half in nominal value of equity share capital of D Ltd.

As per Sec 4(1)(c), C Ltd. and D Ltd. which are subsidiaries of B Ltd. are also subsidiaries of A Ltd.

5.6 Can a Subsidiary Company become a Member of Holding Company?

According to Section 42, a body corporate cannot be a member of its holding company and any allotment and transfer of shares in a company to its subsidiary shall be void. This section shall not apply:

1. where the subsidiary company is a legal representative of a deceased member of the holding company [Section 42(2)(a)].
2. where the subsidiary is concerned as a trustee, unless the holding company or its subsidiary is beneficially interested under the trust and it is so interested only by way of security for the purposes of a transaction entered into by it in the ordinary course of a business which includes the lending of money [Section 42(2)(b)].

However, a subsidiary company may continue to be a member of its holding company if it was a member thereof either at the commencement of this Act or before becoming a subsidiary of the holding company [Section 42(3)]. But it would not except for two cases mentioned above in Section 42(2) enjoy any voting right at the holding company's meeting though it may exercise other rights of members.

Note: A subsidiary company may buy shares in its holding company under a scheme of amalgamation sanctioned by the Court. [***Himachal Telematics* v. *Himachal Futuristic Communication Ltd.***, (1996) 86 Comp. 325 (Delhi).

6.0 PUBLIC FINANCIAL INSTITUTIONS (SECTION 4A)

Under Section 4A of the Act, the following institutions are deemed to be public financial institutions:

1. The Industrial Credit and Investment Corporation of India Limited. (ICICI)
2. The Industrial Finance Corporation of India. (IFCI)
3. The Industrial Development Bank of India. (IDBI)
4. The Life Insurance Corporation of India. (LIC)
5. The Unit Trust of India. (UTI)
6. The Infrastructure Development Finance Company Limited (Included w.e.f. 31.10.1998 vide the Companies Amendment Act, 1999). (IDFCI)

The Central Government by notification in the Official Gazette is empowered to specify any other institution as Public Financial Institution if:

(a) It is constituted under any Central Act or is held or controlled by the Central Government.
(b) At least 51% of its paid up capital is controlled or held by the Central Government.

In exercise of the powers conferred under Section 4A, the Central Government has included the following institutions in the category of Public Finacial Institutions; namely:

(a) The Industrial Reconstruction Corporation of India Ltd. (IRC)
(b) The General Insurance Corporation of India (GIC)
(c) The National Insurance Company Ltd. (NIC)
(d) The New India Assurance Company Ltd. (NIAC)
(e) The Oriental Fire and General Insurance Company Ltd. (OFGIC)
(f) The Tourism Finance Corporation of India Ltd. (TFCI)
(g) The Risk Capital and Technology Finance Corporation Ltd. (RCTFC)
(h) Technology Development and Information Company of India Ltd. (TDIC)
(i) Power Finance Corporation Limited. (PFC)
(j) National Housing Bank.
(k) Small Industries Development Bank of India. (SIDBI)
(l) Rural Electrification Corporation Ltd. (REC)
(m) The Shipping Credit and Investment Company of India Ltd. (SCICI)

7.0 DISTINCTION BETWEEN PRIVATE COMPANY AND PUBLIC COMPANY

A private company differs from a public company in the following respects:

Basis of Distinction	*Public company*	*Private company*
1. *Use of the word 'Private'*	The name of the public company is ***not required*** to use the word 'Private'.	The name of the private company ***must use*** the word 'Private'.
2. *Minimum no. of members*	The minimum number of members required to form a public company is ***7***.	The minimum number of members required to form a private company is ***2***.
3. *Maximum no. of members*	There is ***no restriction*** on the maximum number of members.	The maximum limit of member ***is 50.***
4. *Minimum paid up capital*	It must have a minimum paid up capital of ***Rs 5 lakh or higher paid up capital*** as may be prescribed.	It must have a minimum paid up capital of ***Rs 1 lakh or higher paid up*** capital as may be prescribed.

(*Contd.*)

(*Contd.*)

5. ***Transferability of shares***	The right to transfer the shares is ***not restricted*** by the Articles of Association.	The right to transfer the shares is ***restricted*** by the Articles of Association.
6. ***Invitation to the public to subscribe shares/ debentures***	It ***can invite*** public to sub-scribe for its shares or debentures.	It ***cannot invite*** public to subscribe for its shares or debentures.
7. ***Invitation or Acceptance of Deposits***	It ***can invite or accept*** deposits from any person.	It ***cannot invite or accept*** deposits from persons other than its members, directors or their relatives.
8. ***Articles of association***	It ***can either frame*** its own Articles of Association *or* adopt Table 'A' as its Articles of Association.	It *has to* ***compulsorily*** frame its own articles of associations so as to include four statutory restrictions.
9. ***Delivery of prospectus/ Statement in lieu of Prospectus [Section 70]***	Prosecutes/Statement in lieu of Prospectus is ***required*** to be delivered to the Registrar before allotting shares.	Prospectus/Statement in lieu of Prospectus is ***not required*** to be delivered to the Registrar.
10. ***Offer of further shares [Section 61]***	It is ***required*** to *offer* further shares first to the existing share holders unless a special resolution is passed or approval of Central Govt. is obtained.	It ***need not offer*** further shares to the existing shareholders.
11. ***Commencement of Business [Section 149]***	It can commence its business only ***after*** obtaining the ***certificate of incorporation as well as the certificate to commence business***.	It can commence its business immediately ***after*** obtaining the ***certificate of incorporation.***
12. ***Holding of Statutory Meeting [Section 165]***	It is ***required*** to *hold* statutory meeting and to send statutory report to shareholders and file the same with Registrar.	It is ***not required*** *to hold* statutory meeting and to send statutory report to share-holders and file the same with Registrar.
13. ***Place of holding AGM [Section 166]***	It is required to hold its AGM *at* its ***registered office*** or at some other place within the city, town or village in which the registered office of the company is situated.	It can hold its AGM ***anywhere***.
14. ***Quorum [Section 174]***	There must be **at *least* 5** members personally present to constitute a valid general meeting of a public company.	There must be at ***least 2*** members personally present to constitute a valid general meeting of a private company.

(*Contd.*)

(*Contd.*)

15. ***Demand for poll [Sec. 179]***	In case of a public company, ***any member*** present in person ***or any proxy*** holding shares ***having*** at least ***1/10 of total voting power or at least Rs 50,000 paid up*** can demand for a poll.	In case of a private company **1** member present in person or by proxy (if not more than 7 such members are personally present) or **2** members (if more than 7 such members are personally present) can demand for a poll.
16. ***Appointment of Firm or Body Corporate [Sec-tion 204]***	It ***cannot*** *appoint* a firm or body corporate to an office or place of profit under the company.	It ***can appoint*** a firm a body corporate to an office or place of profit under the company.
17. ***Minimum No. of Directors [Section 252(2)]***	It must have at least ***3*** directors.	It must have at least ***2*** directors.
18. ***Retirement of Directors by Rotation [Section 255(1)]***	***Two-thirds*** of the total no. of directors of a public company *must retire* by rotation.	Its directors ***need not retire*** by rotation. There can be permanent life directors.
19. ***Statutory Notice to stand for election as director [Section 257(2)]***	Statutory notice etc. is ***required*** for a person to stand for election as a director.	Statutory notice is ***not required*** for a person to stand for election as a director.
20. ***Approval of Central Government to effect increase in no. of Directors [Section 259]***	Approval of Central Govt. is ***required*** for increase in number of directors beyond 12 or the number fixed by Articles.	Approval of Central Govt. is ***not required*** for increase in no. of directors beyond 12 or the number fixed by Article.
21. ***Appointment of Directors by single resolution [Section 263(1)]***	Two or more directors ***cannot*** be appointed by a single resolution.	Two or more directors ***can*** be appointment by a single regulation.
22. ***Filing of consent to act as director [Section 264]***	Its directors are ***required to file*** the consent to act as director within 30 days of his appointment with the Registrar.	Its directors ***need not file*** the consent to act as directors and as a result minor can also be appointed as director.
23. ***Restrictions on appointment or advertisment of directors [Section 266]***	Restrictions on appointment or advertisement of director contained in Section 266 ***apply*** to a public company.	Restrictions on appointment or advertisement of a director contained in Section 266 ***does not apply*** to a private company.
24. ***Approval of Central Govt. to modify the provisions relating to appointment [Section 268]***	Approval of Central Govt. is ***required*** to modify any provision relating to appointment of managing, whole time or non-rotational directions.	Such approval of Central Govt. is ***not required*** in case of private company.
25. ***Can Articles require to hold qualification shares [Section 273]***	The Articles of a public company can ***require*** the director to hold a qualification	The Articles of a private company ***cannot require*** a director to hold qualification shares as this provision being contrary to Sectio 273 shall be void.

(*Contd.*)

(*Contd.*)

26. ***Restrictions on powers of B.O.D. [Section 293]***	There ***are*** certain restrictions on powers of Board of Directors of a public company.	Restriction on Powers of Board of Directors ***do not apply*** to private company.
27. ***Prohibition against loan to directors [Section 295]***	There is ***prohibition*** against loan to directors of a public company.	There is ***no prohibition*** against loan to directors of a private company.
28. ***Prohibition against participation of Interested Directors [Sec. 300]***	Interested directors ***cannot*** participate in board meeting.	Interested directors ***can*** participate in board meeting.
29. ***Entry of date of birth of directors [Section 303]***	Date of birth of a director of a public company is ***required*** to be entered in the Register of Directors.	Date of Birth of a director of private company ***need not*** be entered in the register of directors.
30. ***Restrictions on remunerat-ion of directors [Section 309]***	There are ***restrictions*** on remuneration payable to directors.	There is ***no restriction*** on remuneration payable to directors.
31. ***Approval of Central Govt. to change the remuneration of directors [Section 310]***	Approval of Central Govt. is ***required*** to change the remuneration of directors.	Such *approval* of Central Govt. is ***not required*** to change the remuneration of directors.
32. ***Restrictions on appointment of M.D./WTD [Section 316]***	There are ***restrictions*** on appointment of Managing Director or whole time director of a public company.	There is ***no restriction*** on appointment of Managing Director or while time Director of a private company.
33. ***Provisions relating to ascertainment of net profit and depreciation [Section 355]***	Provision relating to method of determination of net profits and ascertainment of depreciation ***apply*** to a public company.	Provision relating to method of determination of net profits and ascertainment of depreciation ***do not apply*** to a private company.
34. ***Restriction on Inter-Company loans and inter corporate invest-ment [Section 372A]***	There are ***restrictions*** on making loans/investments by a public company to other companies.	There is ***no restriction*** as making loan investments by a private company to other companies.
35. ***Power of Central Govt. to prevent change in BOD [Section 409]***	Central Govt. ***can exercise*** its power to prevent change in board of director which is likely to affect the company prejudicially.	Central Govt. ***cannot exercise*** its power to prevent change in Board of directors which is likely to affect the company prejudicially.
36. ***Undisclosed Principal on company's behalf [Section 416]***	***No person can enter*** into contract on behalf of public company as undisclosed principal.	***A person can*** enter into contract on behalf of private company as undisclosed company and need not give intimation to other directors.

8.0 PRIVILEGES OF AN INDEPENDENT PRIVATE COMPANY

Privileges available only to an independent private company (i.e. a private company which is *not* a subsidiary of a public company) are as follows:

1. **Minimum No. of Members [Section 12(1)]** A private company can be formed with only two members.
2. **Minimum Subscription [Section 69]** A private company can allot shares without waiting for the minimum subscription to be received, since it is prohibited from offering its shares or debentures to the public.
3. **Delivery of Prospectus/Statement in Lieu of Prospectus [Section 70]** A private company need not issue and deliver prospectus/statement in lieu of prospectus to the Registrar, since it is prohibited from offering its shares/debentures to the public.
4. **Financial Assistance for Purchase of shares [Section 77]** A private company can provide financial assistance for the purchase of its own shares.
5. **Issue of Further Shares [Section 81(3)]** A private company need not offer further shares to the existing shareholders.
6. **Commencement of Business [Section 149(7)]** A private company can commence its business immediately after obtaining the certificate of incorporation.
7. **Holding of Statutory Meeting [Section 165(1)]** A private company need not hold a statutory meeting or file a statutory report with the Registrar of companies.
8. **Any Place of Annual General Meeting [Section 166]** A private company can hold its annual general meetings anywhere. It is not necessary for it to hold annual general meeting at the registered office or at some other place within the city, town or village in which the registered office of the company is situated.
9. **Provision of Section 170 to 186 to apply to General meetings [Section 170]** An independent private company can exclude the provisions of Section 170 to 186 by formulating its own provisions in its Articles to regulate its general meetings.
10. **Quorum [Section 174]** Unless otherwise provided in the Articles of a private company, only two members personally present shall form the quorum of its general meeting.
11. **Demand for Poll [Section 179]** In case of a private company one member present in person or by proxy (if not more than seven such members are personally present) or two members (if more than seven such members are personally resent) can demand for a poll.
12. **Overall Managerial Remuneration limit [Section 198]** The restrictions regarding overall managerial remuneration do not apply to an independent private company.
13. **Appointment of Firm or Body Corporate [Section 204]** The restrictions regarding the appointment of a firm or body corporate to a place of profit do not apply to an independent private company.
14. **Retirement of Directors by Rotation [Section 255(1)]** The directors of an independent company need not retire by rotation. In other words, it can have permanent life directors.
15. **No Statutory Notice to Stand for Elections as Director [Section 257(2)]** No statutory notice is required for a person to stand for elections as a director of an independent private company.
16. **No approval of Central Govt. to Effect Increase in Number of Directors [Section 259]** In case of an independent company an approval of central government is not required for increase in number of directors beyond 12 or the number fixed by the Articles.

17. **Filing of Casual Vacancies Among Directors [Section 262]** The provisions relating to filling of casual vacancies among directors do not apply to an independent private company.
18. **Appointment of Directors by Single Resolution [Section 263 (1)]** In case of an independent private company, two or more directors can be appointed by a single resolution.
19. **Filing of Consent to Act as Director [Section 264]** The directors of an independent company need not file the consent to act as directors.
20. **Restriction on Appointment or Advertisement of Directors [Section 266]** Restriction on appointment or advertisement of a director contained in Section 266 does not apply to an independent private company.
21. **No Approval of Central Govt. to modify the Provision Relating to Appointment [Section 268]** No such approval of Central Govt. is required in case of an independent company.
22. **No Approval of Central Govt. to Appoint M.D./WTD or Manager [Section 269(2)]** No such approval of Central Govt. is required in case of an independent company.
23. **Qualification Shares [Section 273]** The articles of an independent private company can not require a director to hold qualification shares as this provision being contrary to Section 273 would be void.
24. **Grounds for Disqualification of Shares [Section 274(3)]** An independent private company may by its articles provide any grounds in addition to those specified in Section 274(1), for disqualification for appointment of directors.
25. **Max No. of Directorships [Section 278]** The directorship of a private company is not includible in the maximum number of directorships that a person may hold.
26. **No Restrictions on Powers of B.O.D. [Section 293]** The restrictions on powers of B.O.D. do not apply to an independent private company.
27. **No Prohibition against Loan to Director etc. [Section 295]** There is no prohibition against loan to directors etc. in case of an independent private company.
28. **No Prohibition against Participation of Interested Director [Section 300]** An interested director of an independent private company can participate in Board meeting.
29. **No Entry of Date of Birth of Director [Section 303]** Date of Birth of a director of an independent company need not be entered in the Register of Directors.
30. **No Restriction on Remuneration of Directors [Section 309]** The restriction on remuneration of directors does not apply to an independent private company.
31. **No Approval of Central Govt. to Change the Remuneration of Directors [Section 310]** No such approval of Cental Govt. is required to change the remuneration of directors in case of an independent company.
32. **No Limit on Number of Companies of which one Person may be Appointed Managing Director [Section 316]** The provision of the Act limiting the number of companies of which one person may be appointed managing director does not apply to an independent private company.
33. **Provisions Relating to Ascertainment of Net Profits and Depreciations [Section 355]** The provisions relating to ascertainment of net profits an depreciations do not apply to an independent private company.
34. **No Restriction on Inter-company Loan and Inter-corporate Investments [Section 372A]** The restrictions on Inter-company Loan and Inter-corporate Investments do not apply to an independent private company.

35. **No Power of Central Govt. to Prevent Change in B.O.D. [Section 409]** In case of an independent private company, Central Govt. cannot exercise its power to prevent change in Board of directors which is likely to affect the company prejudicially.
36. **Undisclosed Principal on Company's Behalf [Section 416]** A person can enter into contract on behalf of an independent private company as undisclosed principal and need not give notice to the other directors.

It may be noted that the moment a private company fails to comply with any of the statutory restrictions to be contained in its articles or it becomes a subsidiary of a public company, it shall lose these special privileges.

9.0 RESTRICTIONS ON A PRIVATE COMPANY

The restrictions placed on a private company are as follows:

9.1 Restrictions to be Placed in Articles

1. Restriction on the right to transfer shares,
2. Restriction on the maximum number of the members exceeding 50, and
3. Prohibition on invitation to the public for investment in its shares or debentures.
4. Prohibition or acceptance of deposits from persons other than its members, directors and their relatives.

9.2 Other Restrictions

5. **Restriction on Issue of Share Warrants [Section 114]**—A private company cannot issue share warrants payable to bearer.
6. **Annual List of Members [Section 159 and 161]**—Public companies are required to send an annual list of their members and a summary of certain particulars to the registrar of companies. A private company is also required to send with this return, a certificate, certifying that the company has not, since the last return, made any public invitation inviting the public to subscribe for its shares or debentures. It is also required to certify that where the annual return shows the number of members of the company exceeds fifty, the excess consists of those persons who are not to be included in counting the number of fifty.
7. The member of a private company is not allowed to appoint more than one proxy to attend and vote at a meeting of the company.

10.0 CONVERSION OF A PRIVATE COMPANY INTO A PUBLIC COMPANY [SECTION 43, SECTION 44, SECTION 43B]

Conversion of a private company into a public company can take place in the following three ways:

Conversion of A Pvt. Co. into a Public Company

By Default | By Choice | By Operation of Law

Let us discuss them one by one.

10.1 Conversion by Default [Section 43]

(a) If a private company makes a default in complying with the provisions of Section 3(1)(iii), or a private company becomes a subsidiary of public company then it ceases to be a private company and is treated as a public company.

(b) Then the special privileges are not available to the company.

(c) All the provisions of a public company shall become applicable to it as if it was a public company.

(d) **Power of CLB to grant relief:**

  (i) It must however, be remembered that the Company Law Board has been given the power to grant relief in cases where it is satisfied that the default in respect of the provisions of Section 3(1)(iii) was purely accidental and not intentional.

  (ii) The Company Law Board shall grant relief on such terms and conditions as it may think just and expedient.

  (iii) The application for relief may be made by the company or any other person interested.

10.2 Conversion by Choice [Section 44]

Procedure for Conversion by Choice

In order to convert a private company into a public company, the following procedure is adopted:

1. **Convene Board Meeting** Board meeting must be convened to pass a resolution recommending the conversion of the private co. into a public co. and to fix up the time, place and agenda for convening a general meeting to alter the articles of association and the "name clause" of the memorandum.
2. **Convene General meeting** The general meeting must be covened to pass special resolution.
   (a) To alter its Articles so as to exclude—
      (i) the four restrictions of Section 3(1)(iii), and
      (ii) the provisions which may be inconsistent with the requirements of public company.
   (b) To alter name clause of the memorandum to delete the word 'private' from the name of the company.
3. **Filing of Documents** Within 30 days of passing the special resolution, the following documents must be filed with the Registrar of companies.
   (a) a copy of the special resolution regarding alteration of the articles,
   (b) a copy of the altered articles, and
   (c) a copy of the prospectus or a Statement in lieu of Prospectus in the prescribed form.
4. **Increase in No. of Members** The number of members must be increased to 7 if the existing number of members is less than 7.
5. **Increase in No. of Directors** The number of directors must be increased to 3 if the existing number of directors is less than 3.

6. **Increase in Paid-up Capital** The paid up capital must be increased to Rs 5,00,000 if the existing paid-up capital is less than Rs 5,00,000.
7. **Obtaining Fresh Certificate of Incorporation** It shall obtain fresh certificate of incorporation from the Registrar of Companies after filing the required documents.

Effects of Conversion by Choice

(a) The company becomes a public company from the date of passing the special resolution.

(b) It will have to delete the word 'private' from the name of the company.

(c) The change in its name becomes effective only on the issue of fresh certificate of incorporation.

(d) The conversion does not affect the legal personality of the company which continues to remain the same.

(e) Such conversion does not, in any way extinguishes the liability of the company, i.e. its liability remains the same as it was before conversion.

(f) Such conversion and consequent change of name would not effect the identity of the company. [***All India Reporter Ltd.* v. *Ramchandra Datar,*** AIR (1962) Bom. 292]

Note: Conversion by Operation of Law [Sec 43 B] has already been deleted.

11.0 CONVERSION OF PUBLIC COMPANY INTO A PRIVATE COMPANY

11.1 Procedure for Conversion of Public Company into a Private Company

In order to convert a public company into a private company, the following procedure is adopted:

1. **Alteration of Articles of Association [Section 31]** It shall pass a special resolution to alter its Articles so as to:
   (a) Include the four restrictions of Section 3(1)(iii).
   (b) Exclude the provisions which may be inconsistent with the requirements of private company. (e.g. Power to issue share warrants)
2. **Approval of Central Govt. [Section 31]** The approval of the Central Government must be obtained within 3 months of the date of passing the special resolution.
3. **Filling of Special Resolution within 30 days** A copy of the special resolution regarding alteration of articles alongwith explanatory statement annexed u/s 173 to the notice of meeting must be filed with the Registrar within 30 days from the date of passing the resolution.
4. **Alternation of Memorandum** It shall pass a special resolution to alter the name clause of memorandum so as to add the word 'Private' at the end of its name.
5. **Filing of the Documents** Within 1 month of the date of receipt of the order of approval, the following documents must be filed with the Registrar:
   (a) A printed copy of the altered articles and memorandum.
   (b) A certified copy of order of the Central Government.

11.2 Effects of Conversion of Public Company into a Private Company

(a) The company becomes a private company from the date of obtaining the approval of central government.

(b) It will have to reduce the number of its members to 50 if number of members is more than 50.
(c) It will have to add the word 'Private' as part the name of the company.
(d) It shall enjoy all the privileges of a private company after the conversion takes effect.
(e) Legal personality of the company continues to remain the same inspite of the conversion since the conversion of public company into private company or *vice versa* does not bring into existence a new company [*Hindustan Lever Ltd.* v. *Bombay Soda Factory*].
(f) A special resolution passed to convert a public company into private company is binding on dissenting shareholders provided it is—
   (i) bona fide,
   (ii) in the interest of company as a whole, and
   (iii) consistent with the object in the Memorandum of Association, [*Bai Rampa* v. *Master Silk Mills,* 1955].

12.0 ILLEGAL ASSOCIATION [SECTION 11]

12.1 Meaning of Illegal Association [Section 11(1) and (2)]

According to Section 11, "No company, association or partnership consisting of more than 10 persons for the purpose of carrying on the business of banking and more than 20 persons for the purpose of carrying on another business shall be formed unless it is registered as a company under this Act, or is formed in pursuance of some other Indian law."

Example I Where an unregistered association is formed for carrying on the business of banking with 8 members. Subsequently 3 more persons join the association as members. The association would become an illegal association from the moment the number of its members exceed 10.

Example II Where an unregistered association is formed for carrying on the business of non-banking with 18 members. Subsequently 3 more persons join the association as members. The association would become an illegal association from the moment the number of its members exceed 20.

Example III Where an unregistered association is formed for non-commercial purposes such as promotion of religion, art, science, charity or any other useful object, with 18 members. Subsequently 3 more persons join the association as members. The association would not become an illegal association because the limit on maximum number of members is not applicable to such associations.

Example IV Where an association is formed between three partnership firms X (having 6 persons), Y (having 7 persons), and Z (having 8 persons). Such association would be an illegal association because the limit on maximum numbers of members exceed 20.

Notes:
(i) Every person (natural or otherwise) who holds an independent position in law and in capable of entering into contract shall be counted as one person.
(ii) Two or more persons holding a share jointly are treated as a single member.

12.2 Non-Applicability of Section 11

Section 11 does not apply in the following cases:

(a) Joint Hindu Family A Joint Hindu Family may carry on any business, even for earning profits and with any number of members without being registered in pursuance of any Indian Law as required by Section 11 of the Companies Act, 1956 and yet it will not be an illegal association. But, where two joint Hindu families join hands to carry on business, the provisions of Section 11 become applicable.

However, for computing the number of members of such an association, the minor members of such families shall not be included.

Accordingly, the No. of members of the purposes of Section 11(1) & (2), would consist of not only the Kartas but also other adult members of the joint families. [*Shayam Lal* v. *Madhusudan Ray* 1959 Cal.]

(b) Stock Exchange A stock exchange is not covered by Section 11 as it is not formed for the purpose of carrying on any business.

(c) Non-profit Earning Associations All religions, charitable, literary, social, sports and other associations whose object is not to make profit are also not covered by Section 11.

12.3 Consequences of An Illegal Association [Section 11(4)]

The consequences of an illegal association are as follows:

1. **Personal Liability** Every member shall be personally liable for all the liabilities incurred in carrying on the business.
2. **Punishable with Fine** Every member shall be punishable with fine not exceeding Rs. 10,000.
3. **Cannot Sue** *Neither* such an association *nor* its members in their individual capacity can sue any outsider who has dealt with it.
4. **Cannot be sued** Such association can not be sued by its members *or* outsiders.
5. **Can not be wound up** Such an association can not be wound up under the provisions of Companies Act relating to winding up of unregulated companies as well as through court because there is nothing to dissolve at all. **[*Mewa Ram* v. *Ram Gopal*]**
6. **Cannot be made legal by subsequent reduction** Once the association contravened the provision of Section 11, it remains illegal even if there is subsequent reduction in the number of its members. In other words, the illegality of an illegal association can not be cured by subsequent reduction in the number of its members. **[*Madanlal* v. *Janki Parshad*]**
7. Such an association can not enter into any contracts since it has no legal existence.
8. No member can sue another member in respect of any matter connected with such association.
9. Outsiders can sue the members but not such association.
10. Contracts made before the registration can not be validated and issued upon by subsequent registration. **[*Gujarat Trading Co.* v. *Tricumji*]**
11. Illegality or invalidity in the constitution of an association does not effect its liability to tax or its chargeability as a unit of assessment. **[*Kumaraswamy Chettiar* v. *I.T.O.*, 1957]**
12. No suit either for administration or partition of assets of an illegal association can be filed by any member of such an association.

    In *Mewa Ram* v. *Ram Gopal*, High Court of Allahabad held that such partition of assets of an illegal association is not possible at all because a decree for partition would amount to be in substance a direction for winding up or a decree for dissolution and accounts.
13. A member of an illegal association who has paid any money to such association would be able to recover it form the director or agents or association before the money so paid has been applied to an illegal purpose. **[*Greenpur* v. *Co-operatives* (1926)]**
14. Members of an illegal association have a beneficial interest in the property belonging to such association. **[*Queen* v. *Tankard*, (1894)]**

13.0 ONE-MAN COMPANY

13.1 Meaning of One man Company

Where, virtually whole of the share capital of the company is held by one person, as was is Salomon's case, such a company is commonly called as a one-man company.

13.2 Purpose of One man Company

The main purpose of forming it is to obtain the privilege of limited liability.

13.3 Does One man Company have Separate Legal Identity?

Even if virtually whole of the share capital of the company is held by one person, such a company has a separate legal identity if it is bona fide and genuine. The principle was laid down is Salomon's and was adopted in *Lee* v *Lee's Air Farming Ltd.*

13.4 Does the Law permit one man company?

The law does not permit incorporation of one-man company. At least 2 members are required to form a private company and at least 7 members are required to form a public company (Sec. 12). Further, the minimum numbers of members must be maintained throughout the lifetime of the company.

VERY SHORT ANSWER TYPE QUESTIONS

1. What is a Private Company?
2. What is a Public Company?
3. What is meant by: 'Company limited by shares'?
4. What is meant by 'Company limited by Guarantee'?
5. What is an 'Unlimited Company'?
6. What is an 'Association not for profit'?
7. What is a 'Licensed Company'?
8. Define a Government Company.
9. Define a Foreign Company.
10. Define Holding and a Subsidiary Company.
11. What is an illegal association?
12. State the consequences of a default by a private company in complying with the provisions of Section 3(1)(iii) of the Company Act, 1956.

SHORT ANSWER TYPE QUESTIONS

1. Write a short note on 'one-may Company' and Illegal Association.
2. List any five points of distribution between a private company and public company.
3. List any five privileges available to an independent private company only.
4. What is an illegal association? What are its consequences?

LONG ANSWER TYPE QUESTIONS

1. Distinguish between private company and a public company.
2. Enumerate the privileges available to any private company.
3. Enumerate the privileges available to an independent private company only.

4. How can a private company be converted into a public company?
5. How can a public company be converted into a private company?
6. Comment on the following:
   (a) The law not only recognises a private company but also perform its benedictions on the same.
   (b) A limited company can be formed without the word 'limited' as the last word of its name'.
   (c) A subsidiary company can be the member of its holding company.
   (d) Every company must have minimum paid up capital.
   (e) Minimum paid up capital must be subscribed by the subscribers to the Memorandum of Association at the time of incorporation.
7. State the restrictions under the Companies Act, 1956 on a company becoming a member of its holding company.

PRACTICAL PROBLEMS

1. An association of 12 persons starts a banking business without being registered. Four members retire and thereafter a suit is instituted by one of the continuing members for the partition of the assets of the business. Is the suit competent? [No]
2. Two joint Hindu families carry on together a business as joint owners. The first family consists of 5 brothers and their respective sons, being 10 (including 2 minors) in number. The second family consists of the father, 6 major sons and 6 minor sons. Is the business illegal? [No if non-Banking Business, yes if Banking Business]
3. The paid up share capital of ABC (Pvt.) Limited is Rs. 50 lakhs consisting of 5,00,000 shares of Rs. 10 each fully paid, XYZ (Pvt.) Ltd and its subsidiary PQR (Pvt). are holding 1,50,000 and 1,20,000 shares in ABC (Pvt.) Limited. Examine with reference to the provisions of the Companies Act, 1956, whether ABC (Pvt.) Ltd., is a subsidiary of XYZ (Pvt.) Ltd. Would your answer be different if PQR (Pvt.) Ltd. is holding 2,70,000 shares in ABC (Pvt.) Limited and no shares are held by XYZ (Pvt.) in ABC (Pvt.) Limited.
   [(i) ABC (Pvt.) Ltd. subsidiary of XYZ (Pvt.) Ltd. as per Sec. 4(1)(b),
   (ii) ABC (Pvt.) Ltd. subsidiary of XYZ (Pvt.) Ltd. as per Sec. 4(1)(c)]
4. A Hindu undivided family consisting of 11 persons carries on banking with a view to acquiring profit for itself or its members without itself being registered under the Banking Regulation Act, 1949 (a) Will it be a legal association? (b) Will your answer be the same, if two undivided families would have carried on the said business? [(a) Yes (b) No]
5. At the inception the association was not registrable under the Act as its membership number did not exceed the statutory limit. But long thereafter the number of its members exceeded that statutory limit. Could the association continue with the business for gain without registration? [No]

CHAPTER

3 Formation of a Company

1.0 PROMOTION

1.1 Meaning of Promotion

(a) Promotion means the preliminary steps undertaken by the promoter to bring a company into existence.

(b) Promotion involves identification of a business opportunity or idea, analysis of its prospects and taking steps to implement it through the formation of a Company.

(c) ***C.W. Gerstenberg*** has defined promotion as "*the discovery of business opportunities and the subsequent organization of funds, property and managerial ability into a business concern for the purpose of making profit therefrom*".

(d) **Activities in promotion** Promotion stage comprises the following activities to be undertaken:

1. Discovery of business idea or identification of business opportunity.
2. Carrying out SWOT analysis (Strength, Weakness, Opportunities and Threats Analysis)
3. Organisation of resources.
4. Securing the cooperation of the required number of persons willing to associate themselves with the project.
5. Obtaining the consent of persons willing to act as first directors.
6. Appointing Legal Advisors.
7. Application for proposed name of the company.
8. Preparation of necessary documents like memorandum of association, articles of association.
9. Entering into preliminary contracts.
10. Filing of the necessary documents with the Registrars for Incorporation.

1.2 Meaning of Promoters

The Companies Act does not define the term promoters anywhere, it only refers to the liabilities of the promoters. A number of judicial decisions have defined the term 'promoter'.

1. ***According to L.J. Bowen,*** *the term 'promoter' is a term not of law but of business, usefully summing up in a single word, a number of business operations familiar to the commercial word by which a company is generally brought into existence.*
2. ***Lord Blackburn*** states that "*the term 'promoter' is a short and convenient way of designating those who set in motion the machinery by which the Act enables them to create an incorporated company.*"

3. ***Justice C. Cockburn*** described a promoter as "*one who undertakes to form a company with reference to a given project and to set it going, and who takes the necessary steps to accomplish that purpose.*"

Thus, a **promoter is one who identifies a business opportunity or idea, analyses its prospects and takes steps to implements it through the formation of a company**.

A company may have more than one promoter. The promoter may be an individual, firm, an association of persons or a body corporate. *For example*, J.R.D. Tata was promoter of Tata Group, G.D. Birla was promoter of Birla Group, Dhirubhai Ambani was the promoter of Reliance Group.

Whether a person is a promoter or not shall depend upon the facts and circumstances of the case.

1.3 Who are not Promoters?

Everyone who is associated with the process of the formation of a company cannot be called a promoter. The following persons cannot be called promoters:

(a) **Persons acting only in a professional capacity** [Section 62(6)]
For Example A solicitor who draws up the documents of the proposed company in his professional capacity is not a promoter in the eyes of law. Similarly, an engineer who advises on the selection of site or a valuer who helps with drawing the estimates would not be regarded as a promoter.

(b) **Merely Signatories to the Memorandum/Financier for formation expenses** A person cannot be held as promoter merely because he has signed at the foot of the memorandum or that he has provided money for the payment of formation expenses. **[*G. Tiruvengadacharir* v. *Value Muaoliar*, (1838) I.L.R. Mad. 192]**

(c) **Merely Vendors of Property** Individuals do not become promoters because they buy property, subsequently sold by them to a company at a profit even though the consideration consists of shares in the same company. But where certain persons buy property with a view to selling it later to a company to be formed by them, such persons will be regarded as promoters from the moment they took first step to carry out that object. **[*Gluckstein* v. *Barnes*, (1900) A.C. 240]**

From the above it should be clear to you that a promoter is one who performs the preliminary duties necessary to bring a company into existence. Thus, the true test to describe a person as a promoter lies in finding out whether he is keen to form a company and take steps to give it a concrete shape. Thus, whether a person is a promoter, in any particular case depends on the facts having regard to the nature of person's role and his relationship to the company that is formed.

1.4 Functions of a Promoter

The various functions performed by the promoters include the following:

1. **To Conceive Business Idea** First of all the promoters conceive the idea of business.
2. **To make Detailed Investigation** After conceiving the idea of business, they make detailed investigations to find out the weakness and strong points of the idea.
3. **To Organize the Resources** After satisfying about the profitability and feasibility of the idea, they organize the resources to convert the idea into a reality by forming a company. The steps to be taken in this regard include the following:

(i) Securing the co-operation of a the required number of persons willing to associate themselves with the project (Note: 7 persons are required to form public company and 2 persons are required to form a private company)
(ii) Appointing Legal Advisors and other experts.
(iii) Entering into preliminary contracts.
(iv) Preparing detailed financial plan.

4. **To Obtain the Consent of Persons Willing to Act as First Directors** The first directors are generally appointed by the promoters. The promoters seek the consent of some individuals whom they deem appropriate so that they agree to be the first directors.
5. **To Decide about the Name of the Company** The promoters have to seek the permission of the Registrar of companies for selecting the name of the company. The promoters usually give three names in order of preference. The promoters should ensure that the name of the company should not be identical with or should not too closely resemble the name of another existing company.
6. **To Get the Necessary Documents Prepared** The promoters on the advise of legal experts get the memorandum of association and articles of association prepared and printed.
7. **To Arrange for Filing of the Necessary Documents with the Registrar** The promoters are required to pay the stamp duty, filing fee and other charges for registration of the company. The promoters are to see that the various legal formalities for incorporating the company are complied with.

1.5 Legal Position of Promoters

The legal position of a promoter is somewhat peculiar. The promoter's legal position is that he is *neither* an agent *nor* a trustee of the company he promotes. He is not an agent because there is no principal in existence. You will recall from your exposure to the Contract of Agency that in order to be a valid contract of agency both the principal and the agent must be in existence. For the same reason, he also cannot be called the trustee of the company.

However, it does not mean that the promoters do not have any legal relationship with the proposed company. The legal position of a promoter can be correctly described by saying that **he stands in a fiduciary position (relationship of trust and confidence) in relation to the company he promotes. The fiduciary relation of a promoter really begins when the company is formed.**

Lord Cairns has rightly stated the position of promoter in *Erlanger* v. *New Sombrero Phosphate Co.,* "The promoters of company stand undoubtedly in a fiduciary position. They have in their hands the creation and moulding of the company. They have the power of defining how and when and in what shape, and under whose supervision, it shall come into existence and begin to act as a trading corporation." In fact, the promoters occupy a fiduciary position in regard to the company they promote and also the original allottees whom they induce to buy shares of the company.

1.6 Duties of Promoters

The fiduciary obligation of a promoter begins as soon as he sets out to act for or promote the company. **The fiduciary obligation of promoters means an obligation of promoters to disclose fully all material facts relating to the nature and extent of contract and profit made by them either directly or indirectly**. Such disclosure must be express and actual and not merely constructive.

The promoters in their fiduciary capacity has the following important duties:

1 **Not to make Secret Profit** A promoter cannot make any direct or indirect profits out of the promotion of the company. Since he occupies a position of a trust, it is his duty to be honest and uphold the trust of his position. The law prohibits only the making of **secret profits** by promoter (i.e. the profits not disclosed to the company) and not the disclosed profits. The promoters of a company are perfectly free to make a profit provided they disclose this fact to an independent Board of Directors. If there is no independent Board of Directors, then he must disclose the profits to the intended shareholders.

Remedies in case of secret profit When a promoter makes a secret profit, the company has the following **remedies against him:**

(a) **Recession of the Contract** The company may on learning of the secret profit, rescind the contract even though the company had adopted the contract. However, rescission must be made within a reasonable time.

(b) **Recovery of Secret Profit** The company may require the promoter to refund the amount of secret profit.

(c) **Suit for Breach of Trust** The company may sue the promoter for misfeasance, as the promoter, by making the secret profit, has defaulted in his duty towards the company.

2. **To make Full Disclosure to the Company of all Relevant Facts** Since the promoter stands in fiduciary capacity, he must make full and fair disclosure of his personal interest in a transaction with company. If he contracts to sell his own property to the company without making a full disclosure, the company may *either* repudiate the contract *or* affirm the contract and recover the profits made by the promoter. Such disclosure is ineffective if made merely to directors who are nominees of the promoters. Disclosure may be made either to an independent board, or by means of a prospectus to the prospective shareholders. If the promoter makes a secret profit the company can rescind the contract of compel him to account for it. Where all the members of a private company are cognisant of the facts, the rule would not apply.

In the case of ***Erlanger* v. *New Sombrero Phosphate Co.,*** (1878) 3 A.C. 1218.

'A' was the owner of some land. He and some of his friends, decided to form a company to manufacture microchips. They appointed the first directors of the company and *'A'* sold his own land to the company at a price higher than the actual valuation of the land. When the company was formed, the purchase agreement of land was approved at the meeting of the shareholders but the fact of *A*'s ownership and the profit made by him were not disclosed at the meeting. Subsequently when the company went into liquidation, the liquidator filed a suit against *'A'* to recover the profits made by him in the sale of land. You would observe that in this case *'A'* had defaulted in his duty to make full disclosure of all material facts and had made a secret profit out of promotion. As there was no disclosure by the promoters of the profits they were making, the company is entiled to rescind the contract. *'A'* could have retained the profit made by him if he had made a full disclosure to the directors of the company or to the shareholders of the company, all the relevant facts of the transaction including his personal interest and the profits made.

In case of Gllluckstein V Barnes A syndicate of some persons was formed with the purpose of taking over a company already in existence, named 'Olympia. The members of the syndicate purchased the debentures of 'Olympia' at a discount, and thereafter purchased the whole company of £ 1,40,000. Afterwards, 'Olympia' redeemed the debentures at par, and so the members of the syndicate made a gain of £ 20,000. Afterwards, the members of the syndicate incorporated a new company to which 'Olympia' was sold at a profit of £ 40,000. The members of the syndicate disclosed the profit of £ 40,000 made by them, but did not disclose the profit of £ 20,000. Since, disclosure was not made to the shareholders, the promoters were held liable to pay back the profit of £ 20,000 to the new company incorporated by them.

3. **To give the Benefit of Negotiations to the Company** The promoter must pass on to the company, the benefit of any negotiation or agreement that he has carried on in his capacity of a promoter. *For example*, when he has negotiated a certain price for some land for the company, he must sell the property to the company at the negotiated price. If he charges a price higher than the negotiated price, the company may rescind the contract on discovering the truth of the matter. If, due to some reason, the contract could not be rescinded, the company is entitled to claim damages from the promoters and the amount of damages shall be equal to the amount of profits made by promoters. However, it should be remembered that secret profits on the sale of property can be recovered from the promoter only when the property was bought and sold to the company while he was acting as a promoter. The promoter must act honestly and diligently to escape liability with respect to dealing with the future company and the outsiders.
4. **Duty of Promoters Towards Future Allottees** The promoters stand in a fiduciary position towards the company. It does not mean that they stand in such relation only to the company but they also stand in this position to the future allottees of shares. The promoters must ensure that the prospectus issued at their instance contains all materials facts and particulars and does not contain any mis-statements.

1.7 Liabilities of Promoters

The liabilities of the promoters under the various provisions of The Companies Act are discussed below:

1. **Liability for not Complying with the Provisions of Section 56** Section 56 explains the matters that should be stated and the reports that should be set out in the prospectus. If this provision is not complied with, the promoter may be held liable by the shareholders.
2. **Civil Liabilities for Any Untrue Statements made in the Prospectus [Section 62]** The promoter may be held liable to pay compensation to every person who subscribes for shares or debentures for any loss or damage sustained by him on account of the untrue statement made in the prospectus. Under Section 62 specific provisions have also been made of the grounds on which the promoter can avoid his liability.
3. **Criminal Liabilities for Issuing a Prospectus which Contains Untrue Statements [Section 63]** The promoter can be held criminally liable if the prospectus issued by them contained mis-statements. The punishment prescribed is imprisonment extending upto two years or a fine upto Rs 50,000 or both. The promoters may have to bear this criminal liability for misstatements unless he can prove that the untrue statement was immaterial or that he was justified in believing, because of reasonable grounds, that the statement was true at the time of issue of prospectus.
4. **Liabilities for Public Examination [Section 478]** If in the event of winding up of the company the liquidator's report alleges a fraud in the promotion or formation of the company, the promoter can also be held liable for public examination by the Court like any other director or officer of the company.

5. **Liability for Misfeasance or Breach of Trust by Misapplication of Funds [Section 543]** Like any other director or officer of the company, a promoter can also be held liable if he had misapplied or retained any of the property of the company or is found guilty of breach of trust or misfeasance in relation to the company.
6. **Liable to be Suspended from Taking Part in the Management of the Company [Section 203]** The court may suspend a promoter from taking part in the management of the company for a period of five years if he is convicted of any offence in connection with the promotion, formation or management of a company.
7. **Personally Liability for Pre-incorporation Contracts** Even the death of the promoter does not relieve him from this liability.

1.8 Legal Position of Promoter's Claim as to Expenses Incurred and Remuneration

(a) If the company, after incorporation, has not made any contract with the promoters to pay remuneration to them, following provisions shall apply:

(*i*) The promoters shall have no right to—

- receive any remuneration from the company;
- receive the expenses properly incurred by them for incorporation of the company.

(*ii*) Even where the articles provide that the company shall pay remuneration to the promoters after incorporation, such a provision in the articles is not binding on the company.

(b) If the company, after incorporation, makes a contract with the promoters to pay remuneration to them, the promoters shall have the right to—

- receive the remuneration that the company has contracted to pay;
- recover the expenses properly incurred by them for incorporation of the company.

(c) Modes of Giving Remuneration

The remuneration may be paid to the promoters in any one/more of the following ways:

(i) He may be allowed to sell his own property/business to the company for cash at a price higher than the valuation, after he has made a full disclosure about the valuation and the profit earned to an independent Board of Directors.

(ii) **Shares** He may be allotted fully paid up shares of the company at par or discount.

(iii) **Lumpsum** He may be paid a lump-sum remuneration.

(iv) **Commission** He may be given a commission at fixed rate on the shares sold by him.

(v) **Future Option** He may be given an option to subscribe for a certain number of the company's unissued shares in future at fixed price.

(d) Disclosure of Promoters' Remuneration in Prospectus

Whatever is the manner in which the company chooses to compensate for the services of the promoter, **the amount of remuneration and the manner of payment must be disclosed in the prospectus, if the remuneration is paid within two years preceding the date of the prospectus.**

2.0 PRELIMINARY CONTRACTS OR PRE-INCORPORATION CONTRACTS

2.1 Meaning of Preliminary Contracts

Preliminary contracts are those contracts which are entered into by the promoters for and on behalf of the proposed company before its incorporation. These contracts are generally entered into by the promoters to acquire some property or some rights for the proposed company. *For example*, contract with the vendor to sell his running business to the proposed company, contract for the purchase of property for the proposed company, contract for the grant of a lease for the proposed company.

2.2 Legal Position of Preliminary Contracts

The legal position of preliminary contracts can be explained as follows:

1. **The Company is not bound by the Preliminary Contracts** A company is not bound by the preliminary contracts even if (a) the company has taken the benefit of the work on its behalf under the contract (b) the contract stipulates that the company, after incorporation shall be bound by it.

   In case of ***Re English* and *Colonial Produce Ltd.,*** (1906) 2 Ch. 435, a solicitor was appointed by the promoters of the company and was instructed by them to prepare the articles and the memorandum of the company. The solicitor also paid the necessary registration fee of the company. These promoters later became the directors of the company. The solicitor sued for his expenses and the fees paid by him. It was held that since the company was not in existence when these expenses were incurred, the company is not bound to pay.

2. **The Company cannot enforce Preliminary Contracts** The company cannot enforce preliminary contracts. The company does not get a right to sue the third party for fulfilment of a preliminary contract.

   In case of ***Natal Land Co.* v. *Pauline Colliery Syndicate*** (1904) A.S. 120, the owner of a piece of land agreed to lease it to a company to be formed by promoters. The promoters later on formed a company. On some prospecting of the land, it was discovered that there was a definite possibility of striking of in that land. Subsequently 'owner' refused to grant the lease to the company. It was held that the company cannot sue 'owner' and cannot claim specific performance as it was not even in existence when the lease was signed.

   Thus, preliminary contracts can not be enforced by or against the company.

   Exception to above Principles The provisions of **Sections 15(h) and 19(e) of The Specific Relief Act, 1963** provide an important exception to the general principle 'preliminary contracts can not be enforced by or against the company'.

   According to Sections 15(h) and 19(e) of the Specific Relief Act, 1963, where the promoters of the company have entered into contracts before its incorporation, specific performance may be obtained by or against the company if—

   (a) Such contracts are for the purposes of the company.
   The term "*contracts for the purposes of the company*" means contracts which are necessary for the incorporation and working of the company. For example, contracts for the preparation and printing of the memorandum and articles or contracts for the supply of necessary raw material for the production work in the company are contracts for the purposes of the company.

   (b) Such contracts are warranted by terms of incorporation (i.e. the contract must fall within any of the clauses contained in object clause)

   (c) Such contracts are accepted by the company after its incorporation.

   (d) The acceptance of such contracts is communicated by the company to the other party to the contract.

   However, the above provisions are not applicable for:

   (a) **Contract to take shares**

   (b) **Contract to render personal services.**

3. **The Company cannot ratify the Preliminary Contracts** The company cannot ratify the preliminary contracts after incorporation because for valid ratification of a contract, the principal must have been in existence on the date when the contract is originally entered into. In case of *Kelner* v. *Baxter*, it was held as the company was not in existence when the preliminary contracts were made, it could not be bound by a purported ratification. What the company can do is to enter into a new contract with the vendors after incorporation to give effect to the terms of the contract made before incorporation.
4. **The Company cannot adopt Preliminary Contracts** The company cannot adopt preliminary contracts after its incorporation either by passing a special resolution or by making adoption of such contract as one of the objects of company in its memorandum of association. *[North Sydney Investment Company* v. *Higgins* (1999) A.C. 263]
5. **Personal Liability of the Promoter for Preliminary Contracts** The promoters are personally liable for the preliminary contracts. The reason for this is that the preliminary contract is made for a company which, as known to both the contracting parties, is as yet non-existent. The contract, therefore, is deemed to be personally entered into by the promoters and they will be held personally liable for the performance of these contracts. The promoters will continue to be personally liable until the company after its incorporation adopt preliminary contracts by entering into new contracts with the third parties on the same terms as were embodied in the original contracts.

The preliminary contracts made by the promoters generally contain a provision that if the company adopts the agreements on incorporation, the liability of the promoters shall come to an end and if the company does not adopt the preliminary contract within a specified period *either* party may rescind the contract. In such a case liability of the promoter will cease on the expiry of the specified period.

3.0 HOW TO FORM A COMPANY

The various steps involved in the formation of a company are given below:

I. Approval of Name

Step No. 1 To ascertain the availability of names apply to the Registrar of Companies of the State in which registered office is to be situated in the prescribed Form No. 1A along with a fee of Rs 500.

II. Memorandum and Articles of Association

Step No. 2 Get the Drafts of Memorandum of Association and Articles of Association **prepared**. However a public company limited by shares need not prepare its own articles. It may adopt Table A as given in Schedule I of the Act.

Step No. 3 Get the Draft of Memorandum of Association and the Articles of Association **vetted** by the Registrar.

Step No. 4 Get the Memorandum Association and Articles of Association **printed**.

Step No. 5 Get the Memorandum of Association and Articles of Association **stamped**.

Step No. 6 Get the Memorandum of Association and Articles of Association **signed** by at least 2 subscribers in case of a private company and 7 subscribers in case of a public company. Each subscriber shall also write in his own hand his address, description, occupation and number of shares subscribed for in presence of at least one witness who shall attest the signature and shall write in his own hand his address, description and occupation (if any). These documents may be signed by an agent if he is authorized to do so by a power of attorney.

Step No. 7 Ensure that Memorandum and Articles of Association are **dated** on a date after the date of stamping.

III. Consent to Act as Director in Form No. 29

Step No. 8 Get Form No. 29 (in duplicate) duly filled up and signed to accord the **consent** of a person willing to act as director if he is so appointed by the Articles of Association of a public company having share capital [Section 266].

IV. Statutory Declaration in Form No. 1

Step No. 9 Get the Statutory Declaration prepared in Form No. 1. Statutory declaration is a declaration to the effect that all the requirements of the act and rules thereunder relating to the registration of the company have been complied with. Such declaration can be signed by any one of the following persons:

(a) an advocate of the Supreme Court or of a High Court; or
(b) an attorney or a pleader entitled to appear before a High Court; or
(c) a secretary, or a chartered accountant practicing in India and who has been engaged in the formation of the company; or
(d) by a person named in the articles as a director, manager or secretary of the company.

V. Filing of Documents with Fees

Step No. 10 File the following documents with the Registrar of companies along with the forwarding application with necessary registration and filing fees:

(a) The Memorandum of Association, duly signed by the prescribed minimum number of subscribers, and duly stamped and signed by witness. [Section 33(1)(a)]
(b) The Articles of Association similarly signed, stamped and witnessed. [Section 33(1)(b)]
(c) A copy of agreement, if any, which the company purposes to enter into with any individual for appointment as its Managing Director or Whole-time Director or Manager. [Section 33(1)(c)]
(d) A copy of any other agreement, if referred to in the Memorandum and Articles of Association in that case, it will form a part of the Memorandum and Articles of Association.
(e) Power of Attorney duly stamped and signed by the subscribers authorizing a representative to make amendments and/or alterations in the Memorandum and Articles of Association at the time of registration.
(f) A Certified copy of letter of the Registrar of Companies, intimating the availability of the proposed name.
(g) Consent of director to act in Form No. 29 (in duplicate) wherever necessary).
(h) Notice of the situation of the registered office in Form No. 18 (in duplicate) wherever necessary.
(i) Particulars of Directors, Managing Director, Manager and Secretary in Form No. 32 (in duplicate) wherever necessary.
(j) Statutory Declaration in Form No. 1.

VI. Certificate of Incorporation

Step No. 11 Get the Certificate of incorporation from the Registrar

VII. Notice of Situation in Form No. 18 (May be given within 30 days of Incorporation)

Step No. 12 Get Form No. 18 (in duplicate) duly filled up and signed to give the notice of the situation of the registered office of the company if the subscribers have already chosen a registered office and they wish to give notice to the Registrar at the time of registration. *Alternatively* such notice may be given within 30 days of the incorporation of the company. [Section 146]

VIII. Particulars of Directors, Manager or Secretary in Form No. 32 (May be given within 30 days of Incorporation)

Step No. 13 Get Form No. 32 (in duplicate) duly filled up and signed to provide particulars of directors, manager or secretary if they are appointed by Articles of Association and the subscribers wish to give notice to the Registrar at the time of registration. *Alternatively,* such form may be sent within 30 days of appointment of first directors.

4.0 CERTIFICATE OF INCORPORATION

4.1 Meaning of Certificate of Incorporation

When the necessary documents have been filed with the Registrar along with the payment of requisite fee, the Registrar shall scrutinize these documents and if he is satisfied that (a) all the documents are in order, and (b) the requirements of the Act in respect of registration have been duly complied with, he shall enter the name of the company in the Register of Companies and shall issue a certificate which is termed as 'Certificate of Incorporation.'

Note: If the Registrar is of the view that there are some minor defects in any document, he may require that the defects be rectified. But, if there are some material and substantial defects, the Registrar may refuse to register the company.

4.2 Contents of Certificate of Incorporation

The certificate of incorporation contains:

(a) the name of the company,
(b) the date of its issue, and
(c) the signature of the Registrar with his seal.

This certificate is literally the birth certificate of the company evidencing that the company is born with its name on the date mentioned in the certificate.

Note: A print of this certificate is to be a part of all copies of Memorandum and Articles of association.

4.3 Conclusiveness of Certificate of Incorporation

1. According to Section 35 of the Companies Act
   Certificate of incorporation given by the Registrar of Companies in respect of any association shall be conclusive evidence that—
   (a) all the requirements of Companies Act have been complied with in respect of its registration as well as matters precedent and incidental thereto,
   (b) the association is a company authorized to be registered and duly registered under the Act.
2. **Meaning of 'conclusive evidence'** The term 'conclusive evidence' means that no inquiry shall be allowed to be made regarding the correctness or incorrectness of any particulars contained in the certificate of incorporation.

In other words, once issued, the certificate of incorporation cannot be challenged in any Court or Tribunal on any grounds whatsoever.

3. **Undisputed Validity** The certificate of incorporation shall remain valid and corporate status shall remain unaffected even in the following cases :
   (a) Where one person has signed on behalf of all the subscribers.
   (b) Where all the signatories to memorandum are minors
   (c) Where all the signatures on the memorandum are forged
   (d) Where the memorandum was altered after signing by subscribers, but before its registration
   (e) Where illegal objects are incorporated in the object clause.
4. The certificate of incorporation is also a conclusive proof of the fact that the company came into existence on the date mentioned in the certificate.

   In the case of ***Jubilee Cotton Mills Ltd.* v. *Lewis,*** the company delivered to the Registrar of Companies documents required for the registration of the company on 6th January. On 8th January, the Registrar registered the company and issued the certificate of incorporation but dated it January 6. The company allotted few shares to Mr. Lewis of 6th January. The allotment was challenged and the court was requested to declare the allotment as void. The court held that the certificate of incorporation is conclusive evidence of all that it contains. Hence, the company shall be deemed to have been formed on 6th January and allotment of shares was valid.
5. In ***Peer's case***, the memorandum was found materially altered after the signatories had signed but before registration. It was held that the corporate status remained unaffected and the certificate of incorporation was valid. Highlighting the necessity of this rule, Lord Cairns observed as follows:

   "When once the memorandum is registered and the company holds out to the world as a company undertaking business, willing to receive shareholders and ready to contract engagement, then, it would be of the most disastrous consequence if after all that has been done, any person was allowed to go back and enter into an examination of the circumstances attending the original registration and the regularity of the execution of the documents."
6. In ***Moosa Goolam Arif* v. *Ebrahim Goolam Arif,*** the memorandum of association of a public limited company was signed by 2 adult persons and guardians of other 5 minor persons. The Registrar registered the company and issued the certificate of incorporation. The incorporation of the company was challenged and the plaintiff prayed that the certificate of incorporation should be declared void. The Privy Council rejected the plea of the plaintiff and held that the certificate of incorporation was valid.
7. Certificate of incorporation is not the conclusive proof with respect to the legality of the objective of the company, mentioned in the objects clause of the Memorandum of Association. As such, if a company has been registered whose objects are illegal, the incorporation does not validate the illegal objects. In such a case the only remedy available is to wind up the company.

4.4 Effects of Registration/Incorporation

1. **Body Corporate** From the date of incorporation, the original subscribers to the memorandum as well as the other persons who may, from time to time, become

members of the company, shall constitute a body corporate by the name contained in the Memorandum of Association. [Section 34(2)]

2. The body corporate shall be capable of exercising all the functions of an incorporated company. [Section 34(2)]
3. **Perpetual Succession** The company shall have perpetual succession. [Section 34(2)] Perpetual existence shows the properties of immortality. In other words, it means that a company's existence persists irrespective of the change in the composition of its membership. It continues to exist even if all its human members are dead. The company may be compared with a flowing river where water (members) keeps as changing continuously still the identity of the river (company) remain the same. Since it is created by law, it can be put to an end only by the process of law. Thus, a company shall continue to exist indefinitely till it is wound up in accordance with the provision of the Companies Act.
4. **Common Seal** The company shall have a Common Seal. [Section 34(2)]
   Common Seal means the official signatures of the company. Any document bearing the common seal of the company and duly witnessed by at least two directors will be legally binding on the company.
5. Members are liable to contribute to the assets of the company in the events of its being wound up to the extent of their contract or guarantee as the case may be. [Section 34(2)]
6. The memorandum and articles when registered shall bind the company and members. [Sec 36(1)]
7. All money payable by any member to the company under Memorandum or Articles shall be a debt due from him to the company. [Section 36(2)]
8. The subscribers of the memorandum of a company shall be deemed to have agreed to become members of the company and on its registration, shall be entered as members in its Register of Members. [Section 41(1)]
9. A private company can commence its business immediately after obtaining the certficate of incorporation.

Judicial Rulings

1. A company on registration acquires a separate existence and the law recognises it as a legal person separate and distinct from its members
   [***State Trading Corporation of India* v. *Commercial Tax Officer,*** AIR 1963 SC 1811].
2. Merely because a company purchases all shares of another company it will not serve as a means of putting an end to the corporate character of another company because each company is a separate juristic entity
   [***Spencer & Co. Ltd. Madras* v. *CWT Madras,*** [1969] 39 Comp. Case 212].
3. Even if the entire share capital is held by the President of India it does not make a company an agent either of the President
   [***Heavy Electrical Union* v. *State of Bihar*,** AIR 1970 SC 82].

5.0 CERTIFICATE OF COMMENCEMENT OF BUSINESS

5.1 Meaning of Certificate of Commencement of Business

The certificate of commencement of business is a certificate **which entitles a company to** commence business or to exercise borrowing powers.

5.2 Company which is required to obtain Certificate of Commencement of Business

A **public company having share capital** is required to obtain certificate of commencement of business from the Registrar before it can commence its business or exercise borrowing powers.

5.3 Companies not required to Obtain Certificate of Commencement of Business

Since a private company (whether or not having share capital) and **a public company having no share capital** can commence business immediately after its incorporation, such companies are not required to obtain certificate of commencement of business.

5.4 Conditions for Obtaining the Certificate of Commencement of Business

I. ***Where a public company having share capital, has issued a prospectus—***

(a) **Allotment of Shares upto minimum subscription.** The company has allotted the shares upto the amount of minimum subscription.

(b) **Payment of Application & Allotment Money by every Director**. Every director has paid to the company, in cash, the application and allotment money on the shares taken or contracted to be taken by him in the same proportion as public.

(c) **No money is repayable**. No money is liable to be repaid to the applicants for failure to apply for or to obtain permission for the shares or debentures to be listed on any recognized stock exchange.

(d) **Filing of Declaration**. Duly verified declaration in the prescribed Form No. 19 has been filed with the Registrar. The declaration must specify that Clauses (a), (b), and (c), as above have been complied with. The declaration must be verified by one of the directors or the Secretary of the Company. Where the Company has not appointed a Secretary, the declaration may be verified by a Secretary in whole-time practice.

II. ***Where a public the company has not issued a prospectus—***

(a) **Filing of Statement in lieu of Prospectus.** The company files with the Registrar, a statement in lieu of prospectus, alongwith the report specified in Part II of Schedule III. The statement should be filed with the Registrar at least three days before the first allotment.

(b) **Payment of Application & Allotment Noney by every Director.** Every director of the company has paid to the company, in cash, the application and allotment money on the shares taken or contracted to be taken by him.

(c) **Filing of Declaration.** A duly verified declaration in the prescribed form has been filed with the Registrar at least three days before the first allotment is made. The declaration must specify that the above conditions have been complied with and must be verified by one of the directors or the Secretary of the Company. In case the company has not appointed a Secretary, the declaration may be verified by a Secretary in whole time practice. [Section 149(2)]

When the above requirements are duly fulfilled, the Registrar shall issue a certificate known as 'certificate of commencement of business'. This document certifies that the company is entitled to commence business and is also a conclusive evidence of the fact that the company is so entitled. Any contract entered into will be binding on the company.

5.5 Consequences of Default [Section 149(6)]

If any company commences business in contravention of these provisions, **every persons** who is responsible for the default shall be punishable with fine upto **Rs 50,000 for every day** during which the default continues.

5.6 Consequences of not Commencing Business within 1 year [Section 433(c)]

If any company does not commence its business within one year of its incorporation, **it is liable to be wound up by the Court under Section 433**.

5.7 Effect of Issue of Certificate to Commence Business

(a) The company can commence its business.
(b) The company can exercise borrowing powers.
(c) Provisional Contracts become automatically binding on the company.

6.0 PROVISIONAL CONTRACTS

6.1 Meaning of Provisional Contracts

Provisional Contracts are those contracts which are entered into by the company after obtaining the certificate of incorporation but before obtaining the certificate of commencement of business.

6.2 Legal Position of Provisional Contracts

(a) Before issue of Certificate to Commence Business

According to Section 149(4) such contracts are purely provisional in nature and shall not be binding on the company until the date on which it becomes entitled to commence business. Therefore, if a company enters into contract after its incorporation but never gets the certificate to commence business, contracts so entered shall not be binding upon the company. *For example*, Mr. *X*, a machinery dealer entered into a contract with the company for supplying some machinery to the company. The company went into liquidation before it could obtain the certificate of commencement of business. Mr. X will not succeed in recovering the amount from the company because the company never became entitled to commence business. [*Re Otto Electrical Co.*, (1906)]

(b) After Issue of Certificate to Commence Business

On the issue of the commencement certificate, such contracts become automatically binding on the company and need no ratification.

6.3 Applicability

Provisional contracts may exist only in case of public company having share capital as it is required to obtain a certificate to commence business.

7.0 DISTINCTION BETWEEN PRELIMINARY CONTRACTS AND PROVISIONAL CONTRACTS

Preliminary Contracts differ from Provisional Contracts in the following respects:

Basis of Distinction	*Preliminary Contracts*	*Provisional Contracts*
1. Relevant Sec.	Sec. 15 and Sec 19 of the Specific Relief Act 1963	Sec. 149 of the Companies Act, 1956
2. Time when entered into	Preliminary contracts are entered into **before the incorporation** of company.	Provisional contracts are entered into **after the incorporation** of the company but **before obtaining** the certificate to commence business
3. Legal position	• The company can **neither ratify nor adopt** such contracts. • These are not binding on a company unless the company adopts as per Specific Relief Act. 1963.	• Such contracts become automatically binding on the company on issue of certificate to commence business. • No Ratification is required.
4. Companies to which apply	These apply to **both private and public** companies.	These apply **only to public** companies having share capital.
5. Contracting Parties	These are entered into between the **promoters and outsiders**.	These are entered into between the **company and outsiders**.

VERY SHORT ANSWER TYPE QUESTIONS

1. What is meant by 'Promotion of a Company'?
2. Who are called 'Promoters'?
3. What is meant by 'Preliminary Contracts'?
4. What is meant by 'Provisional Contracts'?
5. What is meant by 'Certificate of Incorporation'?
6. What is meant by 'Certificate of Commencement of Business'?
7. From which date is a company said to be incorporated?

SHORT ANSWER TYPE QUESTIONS

1. Everyone who is associated with the process of the formation of a company is called 'promoter.' comment.
2. Enumerate the functions performed by the promoters.
3. State the legal position of promoters.
4. Enumerate the duties of promoters.
5. Enumerate the liabilities of promoters.

6. (a) Can the promoters claim as a matter of right any remuneration from the company?
   (b) Can the promoters claim remuneration if they have already entered into a contract with the prospective directors before the incorporation?
   (c) Can the promoters claim remuneration of the Articles provide that a specified sum may be paid to the promoters as remuneration?
   (d) State the various modes of giving remuneration to the promoters.
   (e) What are the disclosure requirements in respect of remuneration to promoters in prospectus?
7. Mention the documents which are filed with the registrar for incorporation.
8. (a) State the meaning and contents of certificate of incorporation.
   (b) What is meant by 'conclusiveness of certificate of Incorporation'?
9. State the effects of Registration.
10. Comment on the following:
   (a) A promoter is not a trustee or an agent of the company but he stands in a fiduciary position towards it.
   (b) The validity of a certificate of incorporation cannot be disputed on any ground whatsoever.
   (c) The services of a promoter are very peculiar.
   (d) Promoters can demand remuneration if the Articles provide for the payment thereof.
11. Distinguish between Preliminary Contracts and Provisional Contracts.

LONG ANSWER TYPE QUESTIONS

1. Explain the various functions performed by the promoters.
2. (a) Explain the duties and liabilities of promoters?
   (b) How can promoters be remunerated by the company for his work?
3. (a) What is meant by preliminary contracts?
   (b) Discuss the legal position of preliminary contracts?
   (c) Can a company rectify such contracts?
4. Enumerate the practical steps involved in the incorporation of a company.
5. (a) What is meant by 'Certificate of Commencement of Business'?
   (b) State the company which is required to obtain such certificate.
   (c) State the companies which are not required to obtain such certificate.
   (d) State the procedure for obtaining such certificate.
   (e) State the consequence of default.
   (f) State the consequence of not commencing business.
6. State the meaning and legal position of provisional contracts. Is the company required to ratify such contracts?

CHAPTER 4 Memorandum of Association

1.0 MEANING OF MEMORANDUM OF ASSOCIATION

According to Section 2(28) of The Companies Act, Memorandum means **"the memorandum of association of a company as originally framed or as altered from time to time in pursuance of any previous company laws or of this Act".** But this definition is not an exhaustive one.

The status and importance of Memorandum of Association has been clearly brought out in many decided cases as follows:

1. "*Memorandum of Association of a company contains the fundamental conditions upon which alone the company is allowed to be incorporated. These conditions are introduced for the benefit of the creditors and the outside public as well of the shareholders*". [***Guinness* v. *Land Corporation of Ireland,*** (1882) 22 Ch. D. 359]
2. "*In the case of* ***Ashbury Rly. Carriage and Iron Co.* v. *Riche,*** (1875) LR 7HL 653, ***Lord Cairns*** *observed Memorandum of association of a company is its charter and defines the limitations on the powers of the company established under the Act, that it contains in it, both that which is affirmative and that which is negative and that it states affirmatively, the ambit and extent of vitality and power which by law are given to the corporation and it states negatively that nothing shall be done beyond that ambit*".
3. *Memorandum of Association defines its relations with the outside world and the scope of its activities. Its purpose is to enable the shareholders, creditors and those who deal with the company to know that is its permitted range of activities* [***Egyptian Salt and Soda Co. Ltd.* v. *Portsaid Salt Association,*** 1931 A.C. 677].

To sum up

- **(a) Memorandum of Association is the constitution of the company which lays down the fundamental conditions upon which alone the company is allowed to be formed.**
- **(b) It defines as well as confines the powers of the company.** It not only shows the objects of formation but also determines the utmost possible scope of its operations beyond which its action cannot go. If it enters into a contract which is beyond the powers conferred on it by the memorandum, such contract will be *ultra vires* the company and hence void. Even the unanimous consent of the entire body of its members cannot ratify such contract.
- (c) It is the company's charter defining its constitution and scope of the powers with which it has been established under the Act.

2.0 PURPOSE OF MEMORANDUM OF ASSOCIATION

The Memorandum of Association is a public document which is open for inspection by any member of the public on payment of prescribed fees [Section 610]. Therefore, every person who deals with the company is presumed to have the knowledge of its contents.

The purpose of Memorandum is two-fold.

(a) First, **to enable the intending shareholders** to know the purpose for which their money is going to be used and within what field they are taking risk in making the investment.

(b) Second, **to enable the persons intending to deal** with the company to know with certainty as to whether the contractual relationship which they intend to enter into with the company is within its corporate objects or not **[*Cotman* v. *Broughman,* (1918) A.C. 514]**.

Thus, Memorandum gives protection not only to the shareholders but also to persons who intend to deal with the company.

3.0 FORM OF MEMORANDUM OF ASSOCIATION [SECTION 14]

According to Section 14, the Memorandum of Association of a company must be in one of the forms given in Schedule I as may be applicable to the case of the company or in a form as near thereto as circumstances admit.

The Tables in Schedule I to the Act specify the following forms applicable to different types of companies as under:

Table B: Memorandum of Association of a Company Limited by Shares.

Table C: Memorandum of Association of a Company Limited by Guarantee and not having a share capital.

Table D: Memorandum of Association of a Company Limited by Guarantee and having a share capital.

Table E: Memorandum of Association of an Unlimited Company.

4.0 PRINTING AND SIGNATURE OF MEMORANDUM [SECTION 15]

The memorandum must be—

(a) printed,

(b) divided into paragraphs numbered consecutively, and

(c) signed by at least 7 persons in case of a public company and by at least 2 persons in case of a private company. The persons signing the Memorandum are known as subscribers to the Memorandum.
   - — Each subscriber must give his address, description and occupation (if any).
   - — The signature of each subscriber must be attested in the presence of at least one witness.
   - — The witness must attest the signature and add his address, description and occupation (if any).

5.0 CONTENTS OF MEMORANDUM [SECTION 13]

The memorandum of association of a company must state the following clauses:

1. The Name Clause;
2. The Registered Office Clause;
3. The Objects Clause;
4. The Territorial Limit Clause;
5. The Liability Clause;
6. The Capital Clause; and
7. The Subscription Clause.

Let us know about each of the aforesaid clauses in detail.

Notes:

(i) Memorandum of Association may contain any clause in addition to the aforesaid clauses specified u/s 13.[Sec. 16(3)]

(ii) Territorial limit Clause is not required in case of a trading company.

(iii) Liability Clause and Capital Clause are not required in case of an unlimited company.

(iv) Capital Clause is not required in case of a company not having share capital.

6.0 NAME CLAUSE

1. Legal Requirements

(a) Last Word [Section 13(1)(a)] The Memorandum of every company must state the name of the company with the word "**Limited**" as the last word of the name in the case of a Public Limited Company and with "**Private Limited**" as the last words of the name in the case of a private limited company.

Exception in Case of Licensed (Associations Not for Profit) Companies [Section 25] The Central Government may by licence direct that a non-profit making association be registered as a company with limited liability without the addition of the word 'Limited' or the words 'Private limited'. A non-profit making association is an association which—

(i) is formed for promoting commerce, art, science, religion, charity or any other useful object,

(ii) intends to apply its profits/income in promoting its objects, and

(iii) prohibits the payment of any dividend to its members.

(b) Undesirable Name to be avoided [Section 20(1)] The name must not be undesriable in the opinion of Central Government.

The name shall be considered as undesirable if—

(i) It is identical with or too nearly resembles the name of an existing company [Section 20(2)(i)] or a registered trademark, or a trade mark which is subject of an application for registration of any other person under the Trade Marks Act 1999 [Section 20(2)(ii)]. However the Central government before deeming a name as undesirable under Section 20(2)(ii) consult the Registrar of Trade Mark [Section 20(3)].

In case of ***Society of Motor Manufacturers and Traders Ltd.* v. *Motor Manufacturers and Traders Mutual Assurance Co. Ltd.***, (1925) 1 Ch. 675, where a company was incorporated to conduct the business of motor vehicle assurance under a name somewhat similar to that of a motor dealer's trade protection association, the court refused an injunction to the association because the difference between the activities of the company and the association precluded any possibility of confusion.

In ***Ewing* v. *Buttercup Margarine Co.***, (1917) 2 Ch. 1, Ewing was carrying on business under the name of Buttercup Dairy Company as a wholesale and retail provision merchant. A new company, Buttercup Margarine Co., was formed with the object of manufacturing and selling margarine in wholesale. Ewing applied to the court for restraining the new company from using the name, contending that it was calculated to deceive and that people were likely to be confused into thinking of both companies as one or closely related. The court granted an injunction.

The court, however, will not grant an injunction to prevent the use of a purely descriptive word with a definite meaning and in common use.

In case of ***Aerators Ltd.* v. *Tollit*,** (1902) 2 Ch. 319, the business of the plaintiff was the sale of apparatus by which small quantities of liquids could be aerated. The defendant proposed to register a company to be called Automatic Aerators Limited, the object of which was to work under patents in respect of aeration of liquids in large quantities. The court did not grant the injunction as both companies had different patents and apparatus although the main object of both was to manufacture apparatus for the instantaneous, automatic aeration of liquids.

(ii) It is prohibited by the Emblems and Names (Prevention of Improper Use) Act, 1950. This Act prohibits the use of the name and emblems of the United Nations and the World Health Organisation, the official seal and emblems of the Central and State Governments, the Indian National Flag, the name and pictorial representation of Mahatma Gandhi and the Prime Minister of India.

(iii) It is in the contravention of the guidelines issued by the Department of Company Affairs (Govt. of India).

(c) Publication of Name and Address [Section 147]

(i) The name and the address of the registered office must be painted or affixed on the outside of every office or place of business in legible characters of one of the languages in general use in that locality.

(ii) The name and the address of the registered office must be mentioned in legible characters in all its business letters, bill heads, letter papers, notices and other official publications.

(iii) The name must be engraved in legible characters on its seal.

(iv) The name must be mentioned in all bills of exchange, hundies, promissory notes, endorsements, cheques and orders for money or goods, bills of parcels, receipts and letters of credit.

7.0 REGISTERED OFFICE CLAUSE [SECTION 13(1)(b) AND SECTION 146]

7.1 Legal Requirements

(a) Name of the State [Section 13(1)] The Memorandum of every company must state the name of the State in which the registered office of the company is to be situated. It may be noted that the exact complete address of the registered office need not be stated in the Memorandum.

(b) Time Limit within which the Company must have its Registered Office [Section 146(1)] A company must have a registered office as on date of commencement of business or within 30 days of the date of its incorporation whichever is earlier.

(c) Notice of Situation [Section 146(2)] Notice of the situation of the registered office and of every change therein must be given to the Registrar (otherwise than through a statement as to the address of the registered office in the Annual Report) within 30 days of the date of the incorporation or of the date of change.

7.2 Importance All communications and notices are to be addressed to the registered office [Section 146(1)]. Every company must keep proper books of account at its registered office [Section 209(1)]. The domicile and the nationality of the company and the jurisdiction of the court is determined by the situation of its registered office.

8.0 OBJECTS CLAUSE [SECTION 13(1)(d)]

8.1 Division of Object Clause into two Sub-Clauses

The Company registered after the commencement of the Companies (Amendment) Act, 1965 must divide its object clause into two sub-clauses, namely:

(a) Main Objects

This sub-clause covers the following two:

(i) Main Objects of the Company to be pursued on its incorporation, and

(ii) Objects incidental or ancillary to the attainment of the main objects.

(b) Other Objects

This sub-clause covers the other objects which are not included in 'Main Objects'.

Notes:

(i) If more than one activity is proposed to be pursued, a separate paragraph should be provided for each activity.

(ii) Under 'Objects incidental or ancillary to the attainment of main objects' all activities essential for the attainment of main objects such as opening of a Bank Account, Appointment of agents, officers, purchase and sale of raw material and finished goods etc., are to be included. These are also terms as *implied powers*.

(iii) The test to be applied whether a power is implied or not, is not the benefit which the transaction is expected to confer on the company but whether it can reasonably be regarded as arising from the main object of the company.

In case of ***London Country Council* v. *Attorney General*** (1902) A.C. 165, the council having a statutory power to work tramways was restrained from running omnibuses in connection with the tramways. The court held that the council could not undertake the omnibus business as it was in no way incidental to the business of working tramways, however beneficial it might prove to the original business.

In case of ***Evans* v. *Brunner Mond & Co.*** (1921) 1 Ch. 359, where a company expended money on scientific research while its main object was the business of chemical manufacturing, it was held that the act was conducive to attainment of the main object of the company and therefore very much within its powers.

(iv) Wherever the object clause includes the words such as "to do all such things as are incidental or ancillary to the attainment of the main objects", these words do not increase the area of the company's express powers as defined by the 'Main objects'. These words should be construed as being limited to the doing of such things as are legitimate necessary to the attainment of the objects previously specified.

(v) **Territorial Limit Clause**—In case of companies (other than trading corporations), with object not confined to one state, the states to whose territories the object extends, must also be mentioned. [Section 13(1)(e)].

8.2 Restrictions on the Selection of Objects

The subscribers to the memorandum may choose any 'objects' for the purposes of their company subject to the following restrictions:

(a) The objects must **not include anything** which is **illegal or contrary** to general law e.g. floating a company for dealing in lotteries [***Ex-parte More***, (1931) 2 K.B. 197].

(b) The objects must **not include anything** which is **against public policy** e.g. trading with alien enemies [***Daimler & Co.* v. *Continental Tyre Co.***, (1916) 2 A.C. 307] or objects which are in restraint of trade [***Mac. Ellis* v. *Calligot etc. Company,*** (1919) A.C. 459].

(c) The objects must **not include anything** which is **prohibited by the Companies Act, 1956**.

8.3 Importance of Objects Clause

The objects clause is of fundamental importance to its members as well as its non-members. In the *first place*, it gives protection to subscribers (members) who learn from it the purposes to which their money can be applied. In the *second place*, it gives protection to outsiders dealing with the company who learn from it what its powers are and what is the range of its activities. The narrower the objects appended in the memorandum, the lesser is the subscribers' risks, the wider these objects, the greater is the security of those who transact business with the company.

9.0 LIABILITY CLAUSE [SECTION 13(2)]

9.1 The liability clause states the nature of the liability of members.

9.2 The legal requirements regarding this clause in respect of various types of companies are as follows:

Type of company	*Legal requirement*
(a) ***In case of a company limited by shares***	Liability clause must state that the liability of its members is lim ited. It means that liability of a member is limited to the nominal value of shares held by him. In case the shares are partly paid, then no member can be called upon to pay more than the amount that remains unpaid on his shares. Thus, a member is liable to pay only the unpaid amount on his shares and no further. For example, a shareholder holds a Rs 10 share and has paid Rs 8 on its so far. He can be called upon to pay Rs 2 and nothing more. In this example, if he holds a fully paid-up share, then his liability is nil.
(b) ***In case of a company limited by guarantee***	Liability clause must state that the liability of a member is limited to the amount which he has agreed to contribute to the assets of the company in the event of winding up.
(c) ***In case of a company limited by guarantee and having share capital limited by guarantee***	Liability clause must state that— (a) the liability of its members is limited. (b) the liability of a member is limited to the amount which he has agreed to contribute to the assets of the company in the event of winding up.

Notes:

(i) **In case of an unlimited company, liability clause is not mandatory.**

(ii) In a limited company, the liability of directors or of any director or manager may be made unlimited by providing so in the memorandum. [Section 322]

(iii) Where a company has carried on business with fewer members than the statutory minimum for more than 6 months, every member who is aware of this fact is severally liable for the entire debts of the company contracted after a period of 6 months and may be severally sued therefor. [Section 45]

10.0 CAPITAL CLAUSE [SECTION 13(4)]

10.1 In case of limited companies by shares, this clause must state (a) the ***amount of share capital*** with which the company is to be registered and (b) *the* ***division thereof*** into shares of fixed amount.

10.2 Such capital is called '*Authorised*' or '*Nominal*' or '*Registered*' capital. The fixed amount of a share is known as '*Par*' or '*Nominal*' value of a share.

10.3 The stamp duty and registration fee are payable on the basis of amount of authorised capital.

Notes:

(i) In case of an **unlimited company having a share capital, the capital clause is not required** in its memorandum. But Section 27(1) provides that the amount of share capital with which the company is to be registered must be stated in the Articles of Association of an unlimited company having a share capital.

(ii) In **case of company having no share capital, the capital clause is not required in its memorandum.**

(iii) Division of the authorised capital into different classes of shares (if any) and the rights of various clauses of shareholders need not be stated in the capital clause. Instead, these details may be given in the Articles of the company.

(iv) The effect of capital clause is that the company cannot issue more shares than are authorised for the time being by the memorandum.

11.0 ASSOCIATION OR SUBSCRIPTION CLAUSE [SECTIONS 12(1), 13(4)(B), (C) AND 15(C)]

11.1 Legal Requirements

(a) There must be at least 7 subscribers (in case of a public company) or 2 subscribers (in case of a private company). [Section 12(1)]

(b) Each of the subscribers must give in his own handwriting his name with surname, address, description (by the name of father, husband or wife as the case may be). [Section 15(c)]

(c) In case of a company having share capital, each of the subscriber must also write in his own handwriting opposite to his name, the number of shares agreed to be subscribed by him. Each subscriber must take at least one share. [Section 13(4)(b), (c)]

(d) Each subscriber or his duly authorised agent must sign the memorandum of association.

(e) The signatures of the subscribers must be attested by at least one witness who must not be from among the subscribers. [Section 15(c)]

(f) Each of the witnesses must give in his own handwriting, his name, with surname, the description and occupation, if any. [Section 15(c)]

Notes:

(i) Only individuals or only a person can be a signatory to the memorandum. It follows therefore that a firm cannot be signatory to the memorandum, because it is not a person having an individuality separate from that of its partners.

(ii) Only individuals or other legal entities can be members of a company [***Ganesh Dass* v. *R.G. Cotton Mills Co.,*** [1974] C.W.N. (345)]. But under Section 25(4), a firm may continue to be member of licensed company. Thus, it is an exception to the generality of the law which precludes the firm being accepted as a share holder of a company.

11.2 Specimen of Subscription Clause in Case of Memorandum of a Company Having a Share Capital

"*We the several persons whose names and addresses are subscribed, are desirous of being formed into a company in pursuance of the Memorandum of Association and we respectively agree to take the number of shares in the capital of the company set opposite to our respective names*".

12.0 ALTERATION OF THE MEMORANDUM

A company may alter the conditions contained in this memorandum in the cases, in the mode and to the extent for which express provision is made in the Act [Section 16(1)]. Let us now discuss the procedure for making alternations in the different clauses of the memorandum.

13.0 ALTERATION OF THE NAME CLAUSE

13.1 Procedure for Changing the Name Clause

The procedure for changing the name of the company is given below:

Case	*Legal Requirements*
(i) *To delete the word 'private' on the conversion of a private company into a public company. [Proviso to Section 21]*	(a) The company may change its name by passing a **special resolution** at a general meeting of the members. (b) A **copy of resolution** is required to be filed with the Registrar within **30 days** of passing the resolution.
(ii) *To add the word 'private' on the conversion of a public company into a private company. [Proviso to Sections 21 and 31(1)]*	(a) The company may change its name by passing a **special resolution**. However, *to alter the Articles in this case*, the approval of Central Government would be necessary in addition to special resolution. (b) A **copy of resolution** is required to be filed with the Registrar within **30 days** of passing the resolution. (c) A **copy of order** of the Central Government's approval is required to be filed with the Registrar within **3 months** of the order.

(Contd.)

Case	*Legal Requirements*
(iii) ***To change the name which is identical with or too nearly resembles the name of an already registered existing company or on an application by a registered proprietor of a trade mark, is in the opinion of Central Government identical with or too nearly resembles, a registered trade mark of such proprietor under Trade Marks Act, 1999. [Section 22(1)(a)]***	(a) The company may change its name by passing an **ordinary resolution and with the previous approval** of the Central Government signified in writing. (b) A **copy of resolution** is required to be filed with the Registrar within **30 days** of passing the resolution. (c) A **copy of order** of the Central Government's approval is required to be filed with the Registrar within **3 months** of the order.
(iv) ***To change the name on direction by the Central Government within 12 months of registration of name/new name. [Section 22 (1)(b)]***	(a) The company must change its name by passing a **ordinary resolution** and **with the previous approval of** the Central Government within a period of 3 months from the date of direction or such longer period as the Central Government may think fit to allow. (b) A **copy of resolution** is required to be filed with the Registrar within **30 days** of passing the resolution. (c) A **copy of order** of the Central Government's approval is required to be filed with the Registrar within **3 months** of the order.
(v) ***To add/delete the words 'Limited' or 'Private Limited' in case of licensed companies. [Section 25(3)]***	(a) The company may change its name by passing a **special resolution.** (b) A copy of resolution is required to be filed with the Registrar within **30 days** of passing the resolution.
(vi) ***To change the name in any other case. [Section 21]***	(a) The company may change its name by passing a **special resolution** and with the written **approval of the Central Government.** (b) A copy of resolution is required to be filed with the Registrar within **30 days** of passing the resolution. (c) A copy of order of the Central Govern-ment's approval is required to be filed with the Registrar within **3 months** of the order.

Note: Application by a registered proprietor of trade mark should be considered after 5 years of coming to notice the registration of the company. [Proviso to Section 22(1)]

13.2 Registration of Change of Name [Section 23]

The provisions relating to the registration of change of name are given below:

(a) **Filing of Resolution with ROC** A **copy of the resolution** passed at the general meeting must be filed with the Registrar within **30 days** of passing the resolution.

(b) **Filing of CG's order with ROC** A copy of the order of the Central Government's approval (whenever if any required) must be filed with the Registrar within 3 months of the order.

(c) **Entry of New Name by ROC** The Registrar shall enter the new name on the Register in the place of the former name [Section 23(1)]
(d) **Issue of Fresh COI by ROC** The Registrar shall issue a fresh certificate of incorporation with the necessary alterations embodied therein. [Section 23(1)]
(e) **Effectiveness** The change of name shall be complete and effective only on the issue of such a certificate. [Section 23(1)]
(f) **Alteration in M/A by ROC** The Registrar shall also make the necessary alteration in the Memorandum of association of the company. [Section 23(2)]
(g) **No Effect on Rights/Obligation of Co.** The change of name shall not affect any right or obligations of the company. [Section 23(3)]
(h) **No Effect on Legal Proceeding by Former Name** The change of name shall not render defective any legal proceedings by or against it. Any legal proceedings which might have been continued or commenced by or against the company by its former name may be continued by its new name. [Section 23(3)]

14.0 ALTERATION OF REGISTERED OFFICE

14.1 Procedure for changing the Registered Office

The procedure for changing the registered office of the company is given below:

Case	*Legal Requirements*
(i) ***Change from one place to another within the same city, town or village [Section 146(2)]***	(a) **Board's Resolution** A resolution of the **Board of Directors** is required to be passed. (b) **Notice of New Location to ROC** Notice of new location must be given to the Registrar within 30 days of the change. [Section 146(2)]
(ii) ***Change from one city, town or village to another within the jurisdiction of the same ROC within the same State.***	(a) **Special Resolution** A special resolution is required to be passed at a general meeting of the shareholders. [Proviso to Section 146(2)] (b) **Filing of Copy of Special Resolution with ROC.** A copy of the special resolution, as aforesaid, is to be filed with the Registrar *within 30 days* in Form No. 23. (c) **Notice of New Location to ROC** Notice of the new location must be given to the Registrar within 30 days of change. [Section 146(2)]
(iii) ***Change from the jurisdiction of one ROC to the jurisdiction of another ROC within the same State.***	(a) **Special Resolution** A special resolution is required to be passed at a general meeting of the shareholders. [Proviso to Section 146(2)] (b) **Application to RD** Application is to made to Regional Director for Confirmation.

(*Contd.*)

(*Contd.*)

	(c) **Confirmation of Regional Director** The Regional Director must convey his confirmation within **4 weeks** from the date of receipt of application for such change. (d) **Filing of Copy of Special Resolution with ROC.** A copy of the special resolution, as aforesaid, is to be filed with the Registrar ***within 30 days* in Form No. 23.** (d) **Filing of Certified Copy of Confirmation together with altered Memorandum with ROC** A certified copy of the confirmation by Regional director together with a printed copy of the altered memorandum of association *must be filed* with the *Registrar of Companies* **within 2 *months* of the date of confirmation.** The Registrar is required to register the same and certify the registration within 1 month from the date of filing of the said document. The certificate shall be conclusive evidence that all the requirements of the Act with respect to the alteration and confirmation have been complied with and henceforth the memorandum as altered shall be the memorandum of the company. (e) **Notice of New Location to ROC** Notice of the new location must be given to the Registrar within 30 days of change. [Sec. 146(2)]
(iv) *Change from one state to another*	(a) **Substantive Limits Such change must be for any one of the following purposes:** (i) to carry on its business more economically or more efficiently; (ii) to attain its main purpose by new or improved means; (iii) to enlarge or change the local area of its operations; (iv) to carry on some business which under existing circumstances may conveniently or advantageously be combined with the business of the company; (v) to restrict or abandon any of the objects specified in the memorandum; (vi) to sell or dispose of the whole, or any part, of the undertaking or of any of the undertakings, of the company; or (vii) to amalgamate with any other company or body of persons. [Section 17(1)] **Procedure Limits** (b) **Special Resolution** A special resolution is required to be passed by the company at its general meeting. [Section 17(1)]

(*Contd.*)

(*Contd.*)

	(c) **Application to CLB** Application is to be made to CLB for Confirmation. (d) **Power of CLB** The C.L.B. has the power either to confirm or refuse to confirm alteration relating to the change of registered office. [Section 17(2)] (e) **Notice to Affected Parties** Notice must be given to every debenture- holder and to every other person or class of persons where interests are likely to be affected by the alterations. [Section 17(3)(a)]. However CLB may dispense with this requirement [Proviso to Section 17(3)] (f) **Notice to Govt. of State** Notice must be given to the Government of the State where the registered office is at present situated. [Rule 36 of CLB] (g) **Advertisement** The company is required to give an advertisement in the newspapers indicating the proposed change [Rule 36 of CLB] (h) *Either* dissentient creditor's (i.e. creditor who objects to the alteration) consent must be obtained or his debt or claim must be discharged or secured.

14.2 Registration of Alteration of Registered Office [Sections 18 and 19]

The company shall file with the Registers of each state:

(a) A certified copy of the order of the Company Law Board
(b) A printed copy of the altered Memorandum within 3 months from the date of order (or within time extended by CLB).
(c) The Registrar shall register the name and certify the registration within 1 month from the date of the filing of such documents. [Section 18(1)]
(d) The Registrar of the State from which such office is transferred shall send to the Registrar of the other State all documents relating to the company registered, recorded or filed in his office. [Section 18(3)]
(e) A notice of the new location of the registered office must be given to Registrar of the State in which office has been shifted within 30 days after the change of office. [Section 146(2)]

14.3 Effects of Failure to Register

(a) No such alteration shall have any effect until it has been duly registered in accordance with the provisions of Section 18. [Section 19(1)].
(b) If the certified copy of order of Company Law Board together with a printed copy of altered memorandum is not filed within 3 months from the date of order, such alteration and the order and all proceedings connected therewith shall at the expiry of 3 months become void and inoperative. [Section 19(2)].
(c) However, the Company Law Board may revive its order if: (a) sufficient cause is shown, (b) an application is made within a further period of 1 month. [Proviso to Section 19(2)]

14.4 Leading Case Laws

1. In case of ***Orient Paper Mills Limited* v. *State***, AIR (1959) Orissa 232, Orissa High Court held that the State in which the registered office of the company is situated could oppose the shifting of the registered office to place outside that State on the ground of loss of revenue and employment opportunities.
2. On the contrary, in case of ***Rank Film Distributors of India Ltd.* v. *The Registrar of Companies,*** AIR (1969) Cal. 32, the Calcutta High Court held that the State has no right to oppose the shifting of registered office from one State to another on the ground of loss of revenue. Loss of one State could be balanced by gain to another State and after all the country was one and indivisible. The consideration of loss of revenue is not only irrelevant but if it is accepted, it would deprive the company of the statutory power conferred on it by Section 17. The State may however object as a creditor in respect of arrears of revenue due to it. In case of ***Mineral Mills* v. *Government of Maharashtra*** (1975) 45 Comp. Cas. 1, the Bombay High Court also took a similar view.
3. In case of ***Orissa Chemicals and Distilleries (P) Ltd.,*** AIR (1961) Orissa [621] a company proposing to change the location of registered office from Orissa to Andhra Pradesh had relied on Section 17(1)(a) for the change on the ground of more direct and economic administration but had failed to clarify how the expenses would be curtailed or how the administration from Andhra Pradesh could be more direct while the factory was in Orissa. It was held that *bona fides* of the company's application for the change were questionable.

15.0 ALTERATION OF OBJECTS CLAUSE

Section 17 of The Companies Act lays down the substantive and procedural limits on the powers of alteration to the objects clause. These limits have been shown below:

Limits on the Power of Alteration of Objects Clause

Substantive Limits i.e. Change must be for any of the following specified purposes:

(a) to carry on its business more economically or more efficiently,
(b) to attain its main purpose by new or improved means,
(c) to enlarge or change the local area of its operations.
(d) to carry on some business which under the existing circumstance may be conveniently or advantageously combined with the business of the company.
(e) to restrict or abandon any of the objects specified in the memorandum, or
(f) to sell or dispose of the whole, or any part of the undertaking of the company,
(g) to amalgamate with any other company or body of persons.

Procedural Limits

1. Passing of the special resolution.
2. Filing within 1 month from date of resolution the following documents:
   (a) A copy of special resolution
   (b) A printed copy of altered Memorandum.

Let us discuss in detail:

15.1 Substantive Limits Section 17(1)

Section 17(1) permits a company to alter its objects clause for the under mentioned purposes only:

(a) To Carry on its Business more Economically or more Efficiently Under this clause, keeping the same business as before, the company is permitted to alter the mode of conducting the business which enables the company to do so more economically or efficiently.

In case of ***Re Scientific Poultry Breeders' Association Ltd.***, (1933) Ch. 227, the main object of the company was to encourage and improve the breeding of poultry. Its memorandum also prohibited payment of remuneration to or division of profits among the members of the governing body. When the business and membership of the company increased, it was found that members of the governing body were unable to give proper attention to the management of its affairs unless some remuneration was paid to them. It passed a special resolution for payment of equitable remuneration to the members of the governing body. When the petition was presented to the court for sanction, it was held that the alteration did not affect the main object of the company and would enable it to carry on its business more economically or efficiently.

(b) To Attain its Main Purpose by New or Improved Means Under this clause, keeping the same business as before, the company is permitted to alter the means of constructing its business which enable it to take advantage of new scientific discoveries and inventions.

(c) To Enlarge or Change the Local Area of its Operations Under this clause, keeping the same business as before the company is permitted to change the area of its operations. In case of ***Re Indian Mechanical Gold Extracting Co.,*** (1891) 3 Ch. 538, the memorandum confined the area of its operations to India. The company passed a special resolution deleting the words "in India" from the memorandum so as to enlarge its area of operation. The court confirmed the alteration on the ground that it would enable the company to enlarge its area of operations. The court also directed that the company should change its name in such a manner that it did not give the impression that its business operations were confined only to India.

(d) To Carry on some Business which under the Existing Circumstances may Conveniently or Advantageously be Combined with the Business of the Company Under this clause, keeping the same business as before the company is permitted to take up any new business which can conveniently or advantageously be combined with the existing business of the company at the date of the proposed alteration.

In case of ***Re Parent Tyre Co.,* (1923) 2 Ch. 222,** it was held that the additional business which a company, by alteration of its memorandum, may carry on may be wholly different from and bear no relation to its existing business, provided it is capable of being conveniently and advantageously combined with it. Moreover, it should not be destructive or inconsistent with the existing business. Whether a business is such or not is for the company's shareholders and managers to judge. In this case a tyre company was authorised to conduct the general business of bankers and financiers. The company in this case had never manufactured tyres as it had always been a holding company. All its funds were invested in Dunlop Rubber Co. Ltd., and it wished to spread its investment risks over a wider range of securities.

In case of ***Punjab Distillery Industries Ltd.*** v. ***Registrar of Companies,*** (1963) Comp. Cas. 81, a company which was formed for carrying on distillery business and other allied objects to that business was not permitted to undertake cinema business as the new business could not conveniently or advantageously be combined with the existing business of the company.

In case of ***Re Cyclist Touring Club,*** (1907) 1 Ch. 269, a company was incorporated to protect and promote the interests of pedal cyclists on public roads. The company passed a special resolution so as to include all vehicles including motors. The court disallowed the alteration as it was in consistent with the objects of the company because cyclists had to be protected against danger from motorists. The court held that the company would find itself in the impossible position of having to protect one class of members from another.

(e) To Restrict or Abandon any of the Objects Specified in the Memorandum Under this clause, the company is permitted to restrict or abandon any of the objects specified in the memorandum.

(f) To Sell or Dispose of the Whole or Any Part of the Undertaking Under this clause, the company is permitted to sell or dispose of the whole or any part of the undertaking of the company.

(g) To Amalgamate with any other Company or Body of Persons Under this clause, the company is permitted to amalgamate with any other company or body of persons.

15.2 Procedural Limits

The following procedure must be followed for altering the objects clause:

(a) Special Resolution

Special resolution authorising such alteration is required to be passed by the company at its general meeting. [Section 17(1)]

(b) Registration of Alteration

(i) **Filing of with ROC within 1 month** A copy of special resolution passed by the company together with a **printed copy of altered memorandum** must be filed with the Registrar within **1 month** from the date of such resolution.

(ii) The Registrar shall **register** the name and certify the registration **within 1 month** from the date of the filling of such documents. [Section 18(1)]

(iii) The **Registrar's certificate** shall be **conclusive evidence** that all the requirements with respect to alteration have been complied with and memorandum so altered shall be the memorandum of the company. The alteration is effective from the date of registration of the alteration.

15.3 Effect of Failure to Register [Section 19(2)]

If the documents required to be filled with the Registrar u/s 18 are not filed within 1 month, the alteration shall at the expiry of such period, become void and inoperative.

15.4 Steps to be taken by a Public Company for starting a Business for which there is no provision in the Main Objects Sub-Clause of the Memorandum of Association. [Section 149(2A)]

Case	*Legal Requirements*
(a) ***To Commence a new business which is not germane to the business which the company was carrying on at the commencement of Companies (Amendment) Act, 1965 in case of companies registered before the Commencement of Companies (Amendment) Act, 1965.***	(i) Special resolution is required to be passed by the company [Section 149(2A)] or Ordinary Resolution and approval of Central Government are required. [Section 149(2B)] (ii) A duly verified declaration by one of its directors or its secretary in the prescribed form is required to be filed with the registrar. [Section 149(2A)]
(b) ***To set up a business in relation to any object other than its main object or ancillary to it, in case of companies registered after the Commencement of Companies (Amendment) Act, 1965.***	Same as above.

16.0 ALTERATION OF LIABILITY CLAUSE

16.1 Effect of Increase in Members' Liability [Section 38]

The provisions relating to change of liability are given below:

Case	*Provision*
(i) ***Where the Company is neither a club nor any other association and the alteration increases his liability in any way.***	No member of the company shall be bound by such alteration unless he agrees in writing to do so *either* before *or* after the alteration.
(ii) ***Where the company is a club or any other association and the alteration requires the members to pay subscription or charges at a higher rate.***	Member is bound by such alteration even though he does not agree in writing to be bound by the alteration.

16.2 Registration of Unlimited Company as Limited Company [Section 32]

Section 32 permits the registration of an unlimited company as a limited company. The registration of an unlimited company as a limited company shall not affect any debts, liabilities, obligations or contracts incurred or entered into by or on behalf of the company before such registration.

16.3 Alteration to make the Liability of Directors Unlimited [Section 323]

A limited company, if so authorised by its articles, may alter the Memorandum by a special resolution so as to make the liability of its director or directors or manager unlimited. Any person holding the office of director or manager before the alteration shall not be bound by this alteration until the expiry of his present term or unless he has accorded his consent in writing to such alteration.

17.0 ALTERATION OF CAPITAL CLAUSE [SECTIONS 94 TO 97]

The provisions relating to the alteration of Share Capital are given below:

1. **Authority in Articles** A company may alter the capital clause of its memorandum only if it is authorised by its articles of association to do so.
2. **Manner of Alteration** A company may alter the capital clause in the following manner:
   (a) by increasing its share capital by issue of new shares; [e.g. from 1 crore to 5 crore]
   (b) by consolidating the existing shares into shares of larger amount than its existing shares; [e.g. Conversion of Shares of Rs 10 each into shares of Rs 100 each]
   (c) by Converting fully paid shares into stock or *vice versa*;
   (d) by sub-dividing the existing shares into shares of smaller amount than its existing shares; [e.g. Conversion of shares of Rs 100 each into shares of Rs 10 each]
   (e) by cancelling its unissued shares.
3. **Ordinary Resolution** An ordinary resolution is required to be passed at its general meeting.
4. **Notice to ROC within 30 Days** A notice specifying alteration made must be given to the Registrar within 30 days of alteration.
5. **Duty of Registrar** The Registrar shall make the necessary alteration in the memorandum or articles.
6. **Consequences of Default** If default is made in filing the notice as aforesaid, the company and every officer of the company who is in default shall be punishable with the fine upto Rs 500 per day during which the default continues.

18.0 DOCTRINE OF ULTRA VIRES

18.1 Meaning of Ultra Vires

The term '*ultra*' means '*beyond*' and the term '*vires*' means the '*powers*', Thus, *ultra vires* a company means '*beyond the powers of a company*'. Any act which is beyond the objects stated in the memorandum is ultra vires the company and, therefore, null and void. The company shall not be bound by such acts which are *ultra vires* the company. The purpose of the doctrine of *ultra vires* is to protect the interests of members, outsiders and creditors.

In order to protect the interest of the shareholders and the third parties which enter into contracts with the company's activities are confined to the objects given in the Memorandum of Association. It cannot do anything beyond the objects clause and if it does, it will be considered *ultra vires* (beyond capacity) and *void ab-initio*. Thus, in case of a company whatever is not permitted expressly or by implication, by the constituting instrument, is prohibited not by any express prohibition of the legislature, but by the doctrine of *ultra vires.*

18.2 Meaning of Doctrine of Ultra Vires

The term '*ultra vires*' means beyond one's power or authority. Where exercises of powers vested in a person arises, the question as to the scope of such powers becomes the matter for consideration as to whether a person is acting within the limits of authority conferred on him. If the person exercising the power goes beyond the jurisdiction of his powers, the person is said to have acted *ultra vires*. The doctrine of *ultra vires* thus contemplates two things:

1. that the person exercising the power is not having an unlimited or infinite power to do all acts or things at his will and pleasure; and

2. that the person exercising the power derived the same from some other person or persons on behalf of whom the person acts. The power may be delegated to him by an express or implied act of the said person or persons.

As far as a company is concerned, any act beyond the objects mentioned in the Memorandum of Association is *ultra vires* and void. This important rule of law was laid down in ***Ashbury Railway Carriage Co.* v. *Riche***, (1875) [L.R. 7 H.L. (653)].

The acts of the company are subject to the provisions contained in the Act in terms of which it is incorporated and its two-constitutional documents, namely, the Memorandum and Articles of Association.

18.3 Types and Validity of Ultra Vires Acts

Ulta vires acts can be divided into the following four categories:

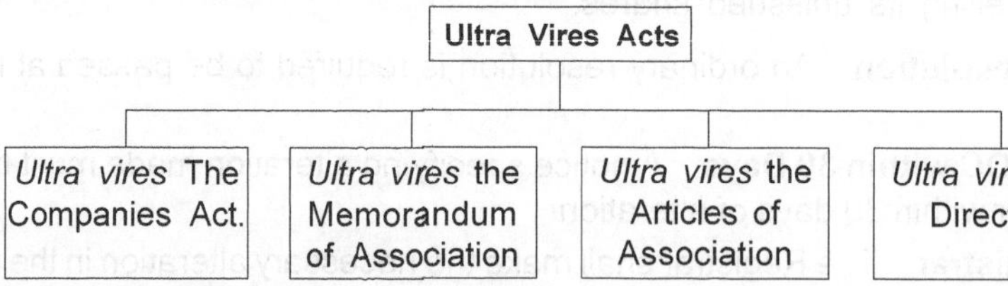

Let us discuss, these *ultra vires* acts one by one.

1. **Acts Ultra Vires The Companies Act** **Any act done contrary to or in excess of the scope of The Companies Act will be *ultra vires* the Act. Such an act shall be void and cannot be ratified even by an unanimous resolution of all the shareholders.**
   A few examples of such acts are as follows:
   (a) Payment of dividend out of capital,
   (b) Free distribution of bonus shares, and
   (c) Reducing the share capital without complying with the legal formalities.
2. **Acts Ultra Vires the Memorandum** The Memorandum defines and confines the powers of the company. The object of the company is determined by the Memorandum. A company cannot do anything which is beyond the purview of the objects clause. **Any act done in contravention of the object clause shall be *ultra vires* the Memorandum and shall be void and it cannot be ratified even by an unanimous resolution of all the shareholders.**

   The doctrine of *ultra vires* was first applied in the famous case of ***Ashbury Railway Carriage and Iron Co.* v. *Riche***. In this case the company was incorporated to make, and sell, or lend on hire, railway carriages and wagons and to carry on the business of mechanical engineers and general contractors.

   The directors of the company entered into a contract with *Riche*, a firm of Railway contractors to finance the construction of a railway line in Belgium. The contract was ratified by the company by passing a special resolution at a general meeting. Later, the contract was repudiated by the company on grounds of its being *ultra vires* and it was sued for breach of contract. The House of Lords held that the contract was *ultra vires* the Memorandum and therefore void. It could not be ratified by the shareholders, as the contract was *ultra vires* the objects clause.

   In case of ***Simpson* v. *West Minister Palace Hotel Co.***, (1861) 20 Beav. 40, a hotel company temporarily let part of its premises not required for its business. This was held to be *ultra vires.*

In case of ***Attorney General* v. *G.N. Railway Co.***, (1860) 1 Dr. & Sm. 154, a railway company was working coal mines and selling coal at a profit. This was held to be *ultra vires*.

In case of ***London Country Council* v. *Attorney General***, (1902) A.C. 165, the council having a statutory power to work tramway, proposed to run omnibuses in connection with the tramways, however beneficial it might prove the original business. It was considered *ultra vires*.

In case of ***A. Laxmanswami Mudaliar* v. *LIC of India***, contribution to a trust for promoting technical and business knowledge was held to be *ultra vires*. The court held that the power to make charitable contribution available to the company in its Memorandum does not entitle it to make grant of every kind. Such grant will be valid when it is *bona fide*, relating to company's business or welfare of employees and useful for attainment of company's own objects.

3. **Acts Ultra Vires the Articles** Acts which are *ultra vires* the Articles of Associations but are within the power of the company are termed as *ultra vires* the articles. *For example*, payment of interest on 'advance calls' at a rate higher than allowed by the articles. Such act shall also be void, but the company in General Meeting may alter the articles by a special resolution and ratify unauthorised acts with retrospective effect in accordance with the provisions of Section 31.
4. **Acts Ultra Vires the Director** Acts which are beyond the powers of the directors but are within the powers of the company are terms as acts *ultra vires* the director. Such acts are not altogether void. Such acts can be ratified and made valid by altering its Articles by a special resolution at its general meeting with retrospective effect so as to give directors the powers beyond which they have exceeded. When the acts are so ratified the company becomes liable for such acts. *For example*, if the company has power to borrow, but it restricts the authority of the directors to borrow upto a certain sum. If the directors exceed their authority and borrow more than what they are authorised to borrow, then the company may, if it wishes, ratify the directors' act, in which case the loan binds both the lender and the company as if it had been made with the company's authority in the first place.

18.4 Effects of Ultra Vires Transactions

The effects of *ultra vires* transaction are summarised as under:

1. Act which is *ultra vires* the company shall be *void-abinitio* and cannot be ratified even by an unanimous resolution of all the members.
2. The company *cannot be sued* on an *ultra vires* transactions.
3. The company *cannot sue* on an *ultra vires* transactions.
4. **Injunction** Any member can bring injunction against the company to restrain it from doing *ultra vires* acts.
5. **Personal Liability of Directors** The directors of the company can be held personally liable for any loss caused by an *ultra vires* transaction. If a director makes an *ultra vires* payment, he can be compelled to make good the funds used [***Re Sharpee***, (1892) 1 Ch. 154]. But the directors who refunded the money could get indemnity as against the person who received the payment with the knowledge that payment to him was *ultra vires*. [***Russell* v. *Wakefield Water Works Co.*** (1975) L.R. 20 Eq. 474]
6. **Liability for Breach of Warranty of Authority** The directors can be held personally liable for breach of warranty of authority if it can be established that their act amounts to an implied misrepresentation of facts and not of law.

Where the Memorandum of Association of a non-trade company did not give any power to borrow but its directors borrowed, directors are not personally liable since their act amounts to an implied misrepresentation of law as a non-trading company has no implied power to borrow.

Where the Memorandum of Association of a trading company did not give any power to borrow but its directors borrowed, directors are personally liable since their act, amounts to an implied misrepresentation of fact as a trading company has implied power to borrow.

In case of ***Weeks v. Property***, (1873): LR 8 CP 427, the directors having power to borrow up to £ 60,000, further borrowed £ 500. Loan of £500 was held to *ultra vires* and void and therefore not binding on the company. The directors were held personally liable for breach of warranty of authority.

7. **On Ultra Vires Lending by Company** If money is lent by a company having no power to lend, the company can sue the debtors for the recovery of loan since the debtors will be estopped from taking the plea that the company had no power to lend. [***Re. Coltman*** (1818) 119 Ch. D. 64]
8. **On Ultra Vires Borrowing by the Company** The effect on *ultra vires* borrowing by company depends upon whether the money borrowed has been expended or not.

   Where the company has no borrowing power, any borrowing and where the memorandum fixes a limit on borrowing powers of the Board of Directors of a Company, any borrowing in excess of that limit is known as *ultra vires borrowing.* Such borrowings are void and the securities given for them are inoperative. In such a case the lender cannot sue the company because it does not create any relation of debtor and creditor. The borrowings which are *ultra vires* cannot be ratified by a resolution passed at a general meeting.

Case	***Effect***
(a) ***If ultra vires borrowings have not been used.***	**Right of Restitution** The lender may bring injunction against the company to restrain it from using the amount of loan since the lender remains the owner of the money which is *ultra vires* the company, he can take back the property in specie. (i.e. in the same form) [***Sinclair* v. *Borughman,*** (1914) A.C. 398]
(b) ***If ultra vires borrowings have been used to pay-off lawful debt of the company.***	**Right of Subrogation** The lender steps into the shoes of paid off creditor and consequently he would be entitled to recover his loan to that extent from the company [*Naeth Building Society* v. *Luce* (1889) 43 Ch. D. 158] But he cannot claim any right to any securities held by the original creditor. [***Re. Wrexham Rly. Co.*** (1889) 1 Ch. 440].
(c) ***If ultra vires borrowings have been used for the purchase of any asset or assets.***	The lender may claim repayment of his money out of the asset or assets purchased out of his money. In addition to aforesaid rights, the lender can sue the directors for breach of warranty of authority.

9. **On Ultra Vires Torts** A company will be liable for tort of its employees if—
   (a) the tort is committed in pursuance of its stated objects, and
   (b) the tort is committed by employees within the course of their employment.

In other words, a company will not be liable for any torts committed outside its objects. For example, a company having power to run tramways, started operating omnibuses and a driver of one such bus negligently injured a person who sued the company for damages. It was held that the company could not be held liable for damages because having no existence outside the Memorandum, it could not have appointed the driver.

18.5 The Doctrine of Ultra Vires is an Illusory Protection to the Shareholders and Pitfall to Outsiders

The doctrine of *ultra vires* is intended to protect the shareholders who invest money in the capital of the company and the creditors who deal with it on the basis of range of company's permitted activities as set out in the Memorandum of Association. Any act beyond the permitted area of operation is void and has no legal effect. But the corporations have always endeavoured to escape the limitations imposed by the doctrine of *ultra vires* by drafting the objects clause of Memorandum in very wide terms be as to incorporate all conceivable objects. Alongwith the objects, they usually spell out several powers which companies will be entitled to exercise in carrying out its objects. The result is the every form of conceivable activity and power is included in the memorandum somewhere beneath the mass of words. This protects the acts of company from challenged as *ultra vires*.

Further, where any acts of the company is *ultra vires* the Articles but is *intra vires* the memorandum the company may alter its Articles and ratify the act, if the act of directors is *ultra vires* the authority delegated to them, the company may ratify such act by an ordinary or special resolution, as the case may be, provided such acts are not *ultra vires* the company.

Consequently, the protection afforded by the doctrine of *ultra vires* to the shareholders and the third parties dealing with the company has became illusory to some extent.

VERY SHORT ANSWER TYPE QUESTIONS

1. What is 'Memorandum of Association'?
2. What is 'Name Clause'?
3. (a) What is 'Registered office clause'?
   (b) Is it essential to mention the name of the city of the state in which registered office is likely to be situated?
4. (a) What is 'Objects clause'?
   (b) Enumerate the two categories of main objects.
5. What is liability clause? Name the company in which this clause is not required.
6. (a) What is capital clause?
   (b) Name the company in which case the capital clause is not required.
   (c) Is it essential to mention the division of authorised capital into different classes of shares and rights of various clauses of shareholders?
7. (a) What is subscription clause?
   (b) Can a firm be signatory to the memorandum?
8. What is meant by 'Doctrine of Ultra Vires'?

SHORT ANSWER TYPE QUESTIONS

1. State the purpose of Memorandum of Association.
2. State the form in which the Memorandum of Association must be prepared.
3. State the provisions relating to printing and signature of Memorandum.

4. State the contents of Memorandum.
5. State the legal requirements as to the name clause.
6. State the legal requirements as to the registered office clause.
7. (a) State the legal requirements as to the objects clause.
   (b) Also state the importance of object clause.
8. State the legal requirements as to the liability clause.
9. State the legal requirements as to the capital clause.
10. State the legal requirements as to the Association or Subscription clause.
11. State the procedure for changing the name of the company.
12. Comment on the following:
   (a) The memorandum is a charter of the company.
   (b) The memorandum of a company defines as well as confines its objects.
   (c) A company's object clause is of fundamental importance not only to members but also to non-members.
   (d) Act *ultra vires* the company can be made binding upon the company by a unanimous vote of all the members of the company.
   (e) The doctrine of *ultra vires* is illusory protection to the shareholders and pitfall for third parties.
   (f) Alteration of Memorandum invariably involves passing of a special resolution.
   (g) Each company must have capital, territorial and liability clause in its Memorandum.
   (h) A firm can never be a member of a company.
   (i) The authorised capital must be stated in Articles of Association
   (k) A firm can not be a signatory to Memorandum of Association.

LONG ANSWER TYPE QUESTIONS

1. Discuss the meaning, importance and contents of Memorandum of Association.
2. Explain the procedure for changing the name of the company.
3. (a) Why is it necessary to have registered office?
   (b) Explain the procedure for changing the registered office of the company.
4. (a) Explain the procedure for changing the objects clause of the Memorandum.
   (b) When does the alteration takes effect?
   (c) What is the effect of the failure to register the alteration?
5. Explain the provisions relating to:
   (a) Increase in Members' Liability.
   (b) Registration of unlimited company as limited company.
   (c) Alteration to make the liability of directors unlimited.
6. Explain the procedure for changing the capital clause of the Memorandum.
7. (a) What is 'Doctrine of Ultra Vires'?
   (b) Explain the validity of acts *ultra vires* (i) the Company (ii) Directors (iii) Articles
   (c) Explain the effects of *ultra vires* transaction.
   (d) Describe the liability of a company and its agents for *ultra vires* acts.
8. 'The doctrine of *ultra vires* is an illusory protection to the shareholders and pitfall to outsiders'. Comment.
9. Explain the importance of Registered Office Clause and Objects Clause.
10. State the procedural requirements in the following cases:
   (a) To delete the words 'Private' from the name of company.
   (b) To add the words 'Private' to the name of company.
   (c) To change the name which in the opinion of Central Govt. is identical.
   (d) To change the name of licensed company.
   (e) To change the name in any other case.
   (f) To change Registered office from one place to another within the same city.
   (g) To change Registered office from one city to another within jurisdiction of the same ROC within the same State.

(h) To change the Registered office from the jurisdiction of one ROC to the jurisdiction of another ROC within the same State.
(i) To change the Registered office from one State to another.
(j) To alter Objects Clause.
(k) To alter Liability Clause.
(l) To alter Capital Clause.

11. Follwing are the procedural legal requirements
(a) An ordinary resolution is required to be passed at the general meeting of the members.
(b) A special resolution is required to be passed at the general meeting of the members.
(c) Company Law Board's confirmation is required.
(d) Central Govt's Approval is required.
(e) A copy of special resolution passed is required to be filed with the Registrar within 30 days of passing the resolution.
(f) A certified copy of the order of Company Law board is required to be filed with the Registrar within 3 months of the order.
(g) A certified copy of the order of Central Government is required to be filed with the registrar within 3 months of the order.
(h) A printed copy of the altered memorandum is required to be filed with the Registrar.

State which of the above is/are required in each of the following cases:
(i) To change the existing name 'Jalan Ltd.' to 'Tulsian Ltd.'
(ii) To change the Registered office from Mumbai to Delhi.
(iii) To make some of other Objects as part of 'Main Objects'.
(iv) To cancell unissued shares.

CHAPTER

5 Articles of Association

1.0 MEANING OF ARTICLES OF ASSOCIATION

1.1 Legal Definition

Section 2(2) of the Companies Act defines Articles **"as the Articles of Association of a company as originally framed or as altered from time to time in pursuance of any previous companies law or of this Act".** This definition is not sufficient to explain its meaning. Let us look at some of the observations made in judicial cases.

1.2 Judicial Definitions

1. "*The Articles of Association of a company are the internal rules and regulations to the management of its internal affairs.*"
   [***Guinness* v. *Land Corporation of Ireland,*** (1882) 22 Ch. D. 349]
2. '*The articles play a part subsidiary to memorandum of association. They accept the memorandum of association as the Charter of Incorporation of the company and so accepting it, they proceed to define the duties, rights and powers of governing body as between themselves and the company at large and the mode and form in which the business of the company is to be carried on and the mode and form in which changes in the internal regulation of the company may from time to time be made.*"
   [***Ashbury Railway Carriage Co. Ltd.* v. *Riche,*** (1875) L.R. 7. H.L. 653, p. 670]
3. "*The document containing the articles of association of a company is a business document; hence it has to be construed strictly. It regulates domestic management of a company and creates certain rights and obligations between the members and the company.*" [***S.S. Rajkumar* vs. *Perfect Castings (P.) Ltd.,*** [1968] 38 Camp. Case 187]
4. The Articles of Association are in fact the bye-laws of the company according to which director and other officers are required to perform their functions as regards the management of the company, its accounts and audit.

Thus, the memorandum lays down the objects for which the company is formed, the articles lay down rules and regulations for the attainment of those objects.

2.0 WHICH COMPANIES ARE REQUIRED TO REGISTER ITS ARTICLES [SECTION 26]

According to Section 26, the following companies are required to register its Articles alongwith the memorandum of association:

1. An Unlimited Company (Whether Public or Private).
2. A Company Limited by Guarantee (Whether Public or Private).
3. A Private Company Limited by Shares.

3.0 WHICH COMPANY NEED NOT HAVE ITS OWN ARTICLES [SECTION 28]

A public company limited by shares need not necessarily have its own articles. A public company limited by shares may either have its own articles or it may adopt *either* wholly *or* partly Table A of Schedule I of the Companies Act. Even if it does register Articles of its own, Table A will still apply automatically unless it has been excluded or modified. In other words, there are three possible alternatives in which a public company limited by shares may adopt Articles of Association. These are:

(i) It may adopt Table A in full; or
(ii) It may wholly exclude Table A and set out its Articles in full; or
(iii) It may set out its own Articles and adopt part of Table A.

If such a company goes in for the first alternative, then it is not necessary to get any Articles of Association registered. It has only to endorse on the face of the Memorandum of Association that it has adopted Table A as its Articles of Association. The advantage in adopting the regulations of Table A is that its provisions are legal beyond any doubt. [***Lock* v. *Queensland Investment & Land Mortrage Co.,*** (1896) Cl. 397]

4.0 SPECIFIC REGULATION REQUIRED IN THE ARTICLES OF SPECIFIC COMPANIES

As per Section 27, the specific regulations required in the Articles of specific companies are given below:

Type of company	*Specific regulation required*
1. ***In case of an unlimited company***	Its Articles must state, (a) the **number of members** with which the company is to be registered and (b) the ***amount of share capital*** with which it is to be registered, if it has a share capital [Section 27(1)] **Note:** Its Articles must be in the Form given in **Table E.**
2. ***In case of a company limited by guarantee but not having share capital***	Its Articles must state the **number of members** with which it is to be registered. [Section 27(2)] **Note:** Its Articles must be in the Form given in **Table C.**
3. ***In case of a company limited by guarantee and having share capital***	Its Articles must state the **number of members**. [Section 27(2)] **Note:** Its Articles must be in the Form given in **Table D.**
4. ***In case of a Private Company having share capital***	Its Articles must contain the following **four restrictions** as contained in Section 3(1)(iii)— (a) Restricting the right to transfer its shares, (b) limiting the number of its members to 50 excluding the past and present employees of the company. (c) prohibiting any invitation to the public to subscribe for any shares in or debentures of the company. [Section 27(3)] (d) prohibiting any invitation or acceptance of deposits from persons other than its members, directors or their relatives.

5. ***In case of a Private Company having no share capital***	Its Articles must contain the following **three restrictions** as contained in Sub-clauses (b), (c) and (d) of Section 3(1)(iii): (a) limiting the number of its members to 50 excluding the past or present employees of the company. (b) prohibiting any invitation to the public to subscribe for any shares in or debentures of the company. (c) prohibiting any invitation or acceptance of deposits from persons other than its members, directors or their relatives.

5.0 FORM OF ARTICLES [SECTION 29]

According to Section 29, the Articles of Association of a company must be in one of the forms given in Schedule I as may be applicable to the case of the company or in a form as near thereto as circumstances admit.

The Tables in Schedule I to the Act specify the following forms applicable to different types of companies as under:

Table A: Articles of Association of a company limited by shares.

Table C: Articles of Association of a company limited by guarantee and not having a share capital.

Table D: Articles of Association of a company limited by guarantee and having a share capital.

Table E: Articles of Association of an Unlimited Company.

Note: Additional matters which are not inconsistent with the provisions contained in the form in any of the Tables C, D and E may be included in the Articles. [Proviso to Section 29]

6.0 PRINTING AND SIGNATURE OF ARTICLES [SECTION 30]

The Articles must be—

(a) printed,
(b) divided into paragraphs numbered consecutively, and
(c) signed by at least 7 persons in case of a public company and by at least 2 persons in case of a private company. The person signing the Articles are known as 'Subscribers'. Each subscriber must give his address, description and occupation (if any). The signature of each subscriber must be attested in the presence of at least one witness. The witness must attest the signature and give his address description and occupation (if any).

7.0 CONTENTS OF ARTICLES OF ASSOCIATION

The Articles of Association may contain any regulation for the attainment of objects stated in the memorandum subject to the following restrictions:

(a) The Articles must not include anything which is illegal or contrary to general law.
(b) The Articles must not include anything which is against public policy.
(c) The Articles must not include anything which is prohibited by the Companies Act, 1956.

Articles usually contain provisions relating to the following matters:

(a) Share Capital and Right of Shareholders, Variation of these rights
(b) Allotment of Shares
(c) Calls on Shares and Lien on Shares
(d) Transfer of Shares
(e) Transmission of Shares
(f) Forfeiture of Shares
(g) Conversion of Shares into Stock
(h) Share Warrants and Shares Certificates
(i) Alteration of Capital
(j) General Meeting and proceedings thereat
(k) Voting Rights, Voting and Poll and Proxies
(l) Directors, their appointment, remuneration, qualification, powers and proceedings of Board of Directors
(m) Manager/Secretary
(n) Seal
(o) Dividend and Reserves
(p) Capitalisation of Profits
(q) Accounts, Audit and borrowing powers
(r) Winding up
(s) The extent to which Table A of Schedule I of the Act is to apply or not to apply.

8.0 ALTERATION OF ARTICLES OF ASSOCIATION

Section 31 empowers the company to alter or add to its Articles. This fundamental power of the company to alter its Articles is subject to the following limitations:

1. **Special Resolution** The alteration must be affected by passing a special resolution at the general meeting of the company [Section 31(1)]. A copy of the special resolution authorising such alteration must be filed with the Registrar within 30 days of passing the resolution and a *printed copy of altered articles must be filed with the Registrar within 3 months of passing the resolution*. The effect of change must be incorporated in all copies of articles of association issued after the date of alteration. [Section 40]
2. **Approval of Central Government in Case of Conversion of Public Company into Private Company** No alteration having the effect of converting a public company into a private company shall have effect unless approved by the Central Government [Proviso to Section 31(1)]. In this case, a printed copy of the altered articles must be filed with the Registrar within 1 month of the date of receipt of the order of approval [Section 31(2A)]
3. **Valid as if Originally Contained** Any alteration made in the Article shall subject to the provisions of this Act, as valid as if originally contained in the Articles. [Section 31(2)]
4. **Not inconsistent with Any Act** The alteration must not be inconsistent with any provisions of the Companies Act or any other statute.
5. **Not Inconsistent with Memorandum** The alteration must not be inconsistent with any provisions of the Memorandum of Association. Articles being subordinate to the memorandum must not override.

6. **Not Inconsistent with CLB Order** The alteration must not be inconsistent with an order of Company Law Board.

   Where the company amends articles on order of CLB (on application u/s 397 or u/s 398 for relief in case of oppression or mismanagement), the subsequent alteration thereof which is inconsistent with such an order can be made by the company only with leave of the Company Law Board. [Section 404(1)]
7. **Not Permit any Illegal Thing** The alteration must not permit anything which is illegal.
8. **Increase in Liability of Members** No alteration having the effect of increasing the liability of a member shall be binding upon him unless he agrees in writing either before or after the alteration. However, in case of a company which is a club/any other association, the alteration requiring the member to pay subscription/charges at a higher rate shall be binding upon him although he does not agree in writing to be bound by the alteration. [Section 38]
9. **Reserve Capital** A reserve capital once created in pursuance of Section 99 cannot be unreserved but may be cancelled as a reduction of capital [***Midland Railway Carriage Wagon Co.*** (1907) W.N. 175].
10. **Retrospective Effect** The alteration may be regarded as having a retrospective effect so long as it does not affect the things already done by the company and alteration is for the benefit of the company as whole [***Allen* v. *Gold Reef of West Africa*** (1909) S.C. 732]. In the case of ***Allen* v. *Gold Reefs of West Africa,*** the original Articles gave the company a lien on all shares "not fully paid-up" for calls due to the company. '*S*' was the only member holding some fully paid-up shares, but he also owned money to the company for calls due on other shares. '*S*' died and his shares were inherited by his legal representatives. The company, thereafter, altered its Articles enabling the company to exercise lien on all shares—whether fully paid or not. Now the question arose whether the company could exercise lien even on fully paid-up shares. It was held that company could do so as it was done *bona fide* for the benefit of the company as a whole.
11. **Bona Fide** The alteration must be *bona fide* for the benefit of the company as a whole. Such alteration shall be valid even though the private interests of some members may be affected adversely. In case of ***Sidebottom* v. *Kershaw, Leese & Co., Ltd.*** (1920) 1 Ch. 154], the alteration of articles empowered the directors to require any member who carried on a business competing with that of the company to sell his shares at a fair price to persons nominated by the directors. The validity of the resolution was challenged on the ground that the alteration will not be for the benefit of the company as a whole.

    The court held that it was in the interest of the company as a whole to be protected against competition and upheld the resolution. The court was of the view that it was very much in the interest of the company as a whose to get rid of such members who were carrying on a competing business as they always had the chance to exploit the company's secrets for their personal benefit and at its cost.
12. **Must Not Constitute a Fraud on Minority** The alteration must not constitute a fraud on minority. An alteration the effect of which is to discriminate between the majority shareholders and minority shareholders so as to give the former an advantage of which the latter have been deprived, would constitute a fraud on minority.

    In case of ***Menier* v. *Hooper's Telegraph Works Ltd.,*** (1874) 9 Ch. App. 350, Two Companies *A* and *B* were in rivalry. The Majority shareholders of company A were also the shareholders of Company *B*. Company A had filed a suit against Company *B*. Later, shareholders of company A passed a resolution to compromise the action against Company *B* in such manner that the terms of compromise were favourable to Company *B* and unfavourable to Company A. The minority shareholders questioned the power of the majority to make the said compromise and the court set aside the same. It observed: "It would be a shocking thing, if that could be done and that majority should have nothing to do with it, then the majority have put something in their pockets at the expense of the minority".

Re ***Cook* v. *Deeks,*** (1916) A.C. 554, the directors of railway construction company obtained a contract in their own names to construct a railway line. The contract was obtained under circumstances which amounted to breach of trust by the directors who then used their voting powers to pass a resolution of the company declaring that the company had no interest in the contract. It was held that the benefit of the contract belongs in equity to the company and that the directors could not benefit themselves at the expense of the minority. If it were not checked, this would be tantamount to allowing a majority to oppress the minority.

In ***Brown* v. *British Abrasive Wheel Co.,*** (1919) 1 Ch. 290, the majority shareholders holding 98% of the shares were willing to subscribe further capital which the company badly needed but only if they were able to acquire the shareholdings of the minority. They passed a special resolution to alter the articles to enable them to purchase the minority shares compulsorily on certain terms. The plaintiff refused to sell its shares and challenged the validity of the majority resolution. It was decided that the alteration was not for the benefit of the company but for the benefit of the majority and accordingly an injunction was granted against the company prohibiting it from carrying out the resolution.

13. **Not Cause Breach of Contract with an Outsider** Alteration must not cause a breach of contract with an outsider. The company shall remain liable for damages for its breach.

Murac Rubber Syndicate* v. *Alperton Rubber Co. Ltd. (1915) Ch. 186. In this case an agreement was made between Company A and Company *B*. Company *A* had the right to nominate two directors on Company *B*'s board as long Company *A* held 5,000 shares in Company B. This was incorporated in the articles. Company A nominated two persons as directors and they were disapproved by Company *B*. Company *B* also made an attempt to alter the clause of articles which provided Company *A* the right of nomination. The court granted on injunction restraining Company *B* from making the said alteration on the ground that it would constitute a breach of contract with an outsider.

But later in case of ***Chittambram Chettiar* v. *Krishan Aiyanger,*** I.L.R. 30 Mad. 36, it was held that a company may alter its articles even if it causes breach of contract with the outsider. It has statutory power to do so. Where the contract with the outsider is wholly dependent on articles, alteration would be operative, and accordingly, the person accepting appointment purely on the terms of the articles takes the risk of those terms being altered, and will be bound by the altered article.

But the situation will be different if apart from the articles, there is an independent contract. In ***Southern Foundries Ltd.* v. *Shirlaw,*** *'S'* was appointed Managing Director in a company for ten years by an agreement dated 21.12.1933. Subsequently, the company was amalgamated with another company and new articles were adopted. The latter gave power to the company to dismiss a director and accordingly *S* was removed from office as director and the company treated him as having ceased to be one. He sued the company for wrongful repudiation of the contract. It was held that dismissal was breach of contract and therefore the company was liable for damages.

14. **Not to take Away Statutory Power to Alter** The powers to alter articles of association is a statutory power and it cannot be taken away by any provision in the memorandum or articles. [***Walker* v. *London Tramways Co.,*** (1879) 12 Ch. D. 705]

9.0 DISTINCTION BETWEEN MEMORANDUM AND ARTICLES

The Memorandum of Association differs from the Articles of Association in the following respects:

Basis of Distinction	*Memorandum of Association*	*Articles of Association*
1. ***Contents***	It contains the **fundamental conditions** upon which alone the company is allowed to be incorporated.	It contain the **internal rules and regulations** relating to management of internal affairs.
2. ***Fundamental/ Subordinate document***	It is **a fundamental** document.	It is **subordinate** to the Memorandum.
3. ***Compulsory or optional***	Every company **must** have its own memorandum.	A public company limited by shares **need not** have its own Articles. It may adopt Table A as its articles.
4. ***Relationship defined***	It defines the relationship between the **company and outsiders.**	It defines the relationship between the **company and its members** as members only and as **members *inter se.***
5. ***Alteration whether easy or difficult***	The memorandum **cannot be so easily** altered. The company has to follow the strict procedure for the alteration of its clauses. In some cases alteration requires the approval of the Company Law Board.	Articles can be **easily** altered by passing a special resolution.
6. ***Binding Effect of ultra vires act***	An act which is beyond the powers given in the Memorandum is *ultra vires* and **void** and it **cannot be ratified** even by the unanimous consent of all the members.	An act which is *intra vires* the Memorandum but *ultra vires* the Articles **may be ratified** by shareholders by passing a special resolution.
7. ***Outsider's Remedy in case of ultra vires contracts***	In case of the contracts *ultra vires* the memorandum, outsiders have **no remedy** against the company.	In case of contracts *ultra vires* the Articles, **outsiders can enforce** the contract against the company provided they had no knowledge of irregularity.

10.0 BINDING EFFECTS OF MEMORANDUM AND ARTICLES [SECTION 36]

Section 36 provides that the Memorandum and Articles shall, when registered, bind the company and the members thereof to the same extent as if they respectively had been signed by the company and by each member, and contained covenants on its and his part to observe all the provisions of the Memorandum and of the Articles. Thus, the Memorandum and Articles constitute a binding contract between the company and each of its members. The legal effects can be studied under the following headings:

10.1 Members Bound to the Company

Since the Memorandum and Articles constitute a contract between the members and the company, the members are bound to the company by whatever is contained in these documents. Accordingly, the company is entitled to sue its members for enforcement of the articles and can restrain its members through court from violating any provisions contained therein.

In case of ***Boreland's Trustee* v. *Steel Brothers and Co. Ltd,*** [(1901) 1 Ch. 279], the Articles of the company provided that the shares of any member who became bankrupt would be sold to other persons at a price fixed by the directors. B, a shareholder became bankrupt and his trustee in bankruptcy claimed that he was not bound by the articles and could therefore, sell those shares at their true value. But it was held, that the trustee in bankruptcy was bound by the Articles as it constituted a binding contract between the members and the company.

Similarly in case of ***Bradford Banking Company* v. *Brigs,*** (1886) 12 A.C. 29, where the articles give the company a lien upon each share for debts due by shareholders to the company, and where a shareholder mortgages his shares and the mortgagee serves notice thereof upon the company, the mortgagee would have priority over the company, only if the shareholder had incurred a liability to the company after the notice of the mortgage was given to the company. If, on the other hand, the shareholder had incurred a liability before the notice of mortgage was given to the company, the company would have the priority.

10.2 Company Bound to the Members

Since the memorandum and articles constitute a contract between members and the company, the company is bound to its members by whatever is contained in these documents. Accordingly, the members are entitled to sue the company for enforcement of the Articles and can restrain the company through court from violating any provisions contained therein. Views differ on the questions as to whether and how far the memorandum and articles bind the company to the members. The views expressed in various judicial cases are given below:

(a) "The company is bound to the extent that any member can sue it so as to prevent any beach of the article which is likely to affect his right as a member of the company". [***Hickman* v. *Kent Sheepbreeder's Association*** (1885) 1 Ch. 88]

Thus, "An individual member can file a suit against the company to enforce his individual rights e.g. right to contest election for directorship of the company, right to get back his shares wrongfully forfeited, right to receive a share certificate, notice of general meetings etc." [***Pender* v. *Lushirgton*** (1817) Ch. D. 70, ***Nogaffa* v. *Madras Race Club,*** AIR 1951 Mad. 83, ***C.L. Joseph* v. *Los,*** AIR 1965 (Ker.) 68]

(b) "The member suing in cases sues not in the rights of a member but in his own right to protect from invasion of his own individual right as a member". [***Edwards* v. *Halliwell,*** (1950) 2 All ER 1964 at p. 1067]

(c) In case of ***Johnson* v. *Lyttle Iren Agency***, (1877) 5 Ch. D. 687, a forfeiture of shares irregularly effected by a company was set aside at the instance of the aggrieved member as the company did not comply with the provisions of the Articles.

(d) In case of ***Wood* v. *Odessa Water Works,*** 6 (1884) 42, Ch. D. 636, the articles empowered the company to declare a dividend to be paid to the shareholders with the approval in the general meetings. A resolution was passed to pay the dividend by issue of debenture bonds and not in cash. At the instance of a member, the court grants an injunction restraining the director from acting on the resolution.

(e) Thus, the member can sue the company for the breach of the Articles in the following cases:

(a) When the company does an *ultra vires* illegal act,

(b) For the enforcement of personal rights e.g. right to receive declared dividend,

(c) when majority plays fraud on minority, and

(d) for submitting the petition to court for its order for preventions of oppression and mismanagement under Sections 397 and 398.

10.3 Between Members *inter se*

Although there is no express agreement between the members of the company, yet articles regulate their rights *inter se.* Such rights can only be enforced by or against a member through the company or through the liquidator representing the company but no member has as between himself and another member any right beyond that which the contract with the company gives him [***Weltan* v. *Saffary*** (1897) A.C. 315]. But the contrary view was taken in case of ***Royfield* v. *Hands and others,*** (1852) 2. W.L.R. 851. In this case, the articles provided that every member who intends to transfer his shares must inform the directors and directors must take the said shares equally between them at a fair value. The plaintiff informed the directors of his intention to transfer his shares. But the directors refused to take the shares and argued that the articles could not impose such obligation upon them in their capacity as directors. The court held that the directors were bound to take the shares since the articles imposed obligation upon them in their capacity as members and thus obligation was a personal one which could be enforced against them by other members directly without joining the company as a party.

It may also be noted that there is no privity of contract between the members, the articles constitute a contract between members only as regards matters arising out of the company relationship of members as members. They cannot regulate rights arising out of any other contracts in which other members have no interest. In case of ***Khusi Ram* v. *Hanut Mal,*** (1949) 53, C.W.N. 305, where a member had a commercial dispute of private nature with another member, an arbitration clause in the articles of the company was not allowed to be invoked.

10.4 Between the Company and Outsider

Since the memorandum and Articles do not constitute a contract between the company and outsider, an outsider is not entitled to sue the company for enforcement of the Articles even the articles provide certain rights to him. This is based on the general rule of law that a stranger to a contract can not sue.

The following case of ***Eley* v. *Positive Government Life Assurance Co. Ltd.,*** (1876) 1 Ex. D. 88 illustrates this point.

"The Articles of the company contained a provision that Eley would be the solicitor of the company for life and would not be removed from office except for misconduct. Eley acted as solicitor to the company and also became a member of the company. The company, however, terminated his services. Thereupon, he sued the company of damages for breach of contract. Held, the Articles cannot be the basis of a contract between the company and an outsider. It would be noted here that he was trying to *Exercise his Right as an Employee and not as a Member. A Person can be a Member of* the company and at the same time may be a creditor or employee of the company. In the above case, he was trying to exercise his right as an employee of the company. There was no independent contract between the company and Eley apart from whatever was contained in the Articles. Therefore, his suit was dismissed.

Similarly in case of ***Re Rotherham Alum & Co.,*** (1883) 25 D. 103, where the articles provided for remuneration to be paid to the promoters, it was held that this clause did not give any right of action to promoters against the company.

It may also be noted that where articles are deemed to have formed a part of outsider's contract with the company, the outsider is entitled to maintain a suit on the basis of that contract. In case of Re. ***New British Iron Co.,*** *(1898) 1 Ch. 324,* where an individual entered into a contract with a company to serve as a director and the articles of the company required the director to have a share qualification and fixed his remuneration, it was held that director was entitled to recover his remuneration as fixed by the articles because the terms of articles were deemed to have formed a part of his contract with the company.

Though the articles and memorandum do not constitute a contract between the company and an outsider, still the outsider is entitled to assume that all the necessary formalities have been duly compiled with in internal workings of the company. [***The Royal British Bank*** v. ***Turquand***]

11.0 MEANING OF DOCTRINE OF CONSTRUCTIVE NOTICE

(a) Since the Memorandum and Articles of Association on their registration with the Registrar become public documents and are available for public inspection in the Registrar's office on payment of prescribed fee [Section 610], every person dealing with the company is presumed to have the knowledge of the contents of these documents and also to have understood them according to their proper meaning. [***Earnest* v. *Nicholls*** (1857) 6 H.I.C. 401, ***Griffith* v. *Poget,*** (No. 2) (1877) 6 Ch. D. 517, ***Oak Bank Oil* v. *Crum,*** (1882) 8 A.C. 65]. This type of presumed knowledge of these documents is termed as 'Constructive Notice of Memorandum and Articles of Association.

(b) Accordingly, if a person supplies goods to a company in which it cannot deal according to its objects clause, he will not be able to recover the price from the company. The supplier cannot in his defence take the plea that he did not have the knowledge of the contents of the memorandum of Association of the company. Thus, if a person enters into a contract which is *ultra vires* the company, he must do so at his peril.

(c) The doctrine of constructive notice is not a positive one but a negative one like that of estopple of which it forms part. It operates only against the person who has been dealing with the company but not against the company itself. Consequently, he is prevented from alleging that he did not know that the constitution of the company rendered a particular act or particular delegation of authority *ultra vires*. Thus, **the doctrine of constructive notice protects the company and not the outsiders**. Thus, this doctrine is a 'Cloud' for the strangers.

In case of Kotla Venakataswamy v C Rammurthi

The articles of company require that all the documents and deeds of the company shall be signed by MD, the secretary and a working director of the company.

A mortgage deed was signed by the secretary and working director only.

It was held that the mortgage deed was invalid even though the plaintiff had acted in good faith and money was utilised for the benefit of the company.

12.0 PRINCIPLE OF OSTENSIBLE AUTHORITY

A third party dealing with the company in good faith, assumes that the person who is dealing with him has the required authority to deal on behalf of the company. *For example* if a person is dealing with a director in a matter in which normally a director has power to act for the company, then that person can presume that latter has 'ostensible authority' or 'apparent authority on that matter on behalf of the company. Person dealing with the company is not under obligation to inquire that whether the person to whom which he is dealing really has the authority. In such cases, it is not material whether the person had actual knowledge of company's articles. Of course, the person concern should at least have 'ostensible authority' e.g. a purchase manager can be said to have ostensible authority to issue purchase orders, but he cannot have ostensible authority to sign cheques on behalf of the company.

Notes:

(i) The director repaid their personal loan through the company's account by using company cheques. The lender knew from the cheques that the amount is from company account and not from his personal account. In this case the act of director are *ultra vires.* A director cannot be presumed to have ostensible authority to repay his personal loan from company account. Hence, lender is liable to repay the amount to the company.

(ii) A director has no ostensible authority to institute a suit on behalf of the company. Such authority has to be specifically conferred by a resolution [***Indian Commerce* v. *Swadharma Swarajya Sangha*** (1998)].

(iii) Filing of suit cannot be done without specific authority [***BOC India Ltd* v. *Zinc Products*** (1997)].

(iv) Suit filed by the secretary under general power of attorney, later ratified by Board is valid [***Turner Marrison & Co.* v. *Hunger Ford Investment,*** 42 Comp Cas 512 (SC) 85 ITR 607, AIR 1972 SC 1311].

13.0 DOCTRINE OF INDOOR MANAGEMENT

13.1 Meaning of Doctrine of Indoor Management

The doctrine of indoor management is an ***exception to the doctrine of constructive notice***. This doctrine protects the outsiders against the company by entitling them to assume that the provision of the Articles of Association have been duly complied with by the company in its internal working. This doctrine is based on the principles of justice and public convenience. In case of ***Pacific Cost Mines Ltd.* v. *Arkuthnd,*** (1971) A.C. 607, the Court held "An outsider is presumed to know the constitution of a company but not what may or may not have taken place within the doors that are closed to him." Therefore, if the contract is within the powers of the company, then company will be bound to the outsider and will not be allowed to escape liability by showing that there was some irregularly in following procedure. This is known as the Doctrine of Indoor Management or ***Rule in Royal British Bank* v. *Turquand,*** (1856) 6 E & B 327. The facts of this case are as follows:

The directors of a company were authorised by the articles to borrow on bond such sums of money, as authorised from time to time, by a resolution of the company, in General Meeting. The directors borrowed money from Turquand without any resolution of the company and issued a bond to him. **Decision**, the Court held that Turquand could sue the company on the bond, as he was entitled to assume that the resolution of the company in General Meeting authorising the directors to borrow money on the basis of bond had been passed.

Conditions for Availability of the benefit of Doctrine of Indoor Management

1. The person dealing with the company must have the knowledge of the Memorandum and Articles
2. The person dealing with the company must not have knowledge of irregularity.
3. The person dealing with the company must not be put upon an enquiry
4. There must be some procedural or internal irregularity.
5. There must not be any ultra vires act or illegality.

13.2 Exceptions to the Doctrine of Indoor Management

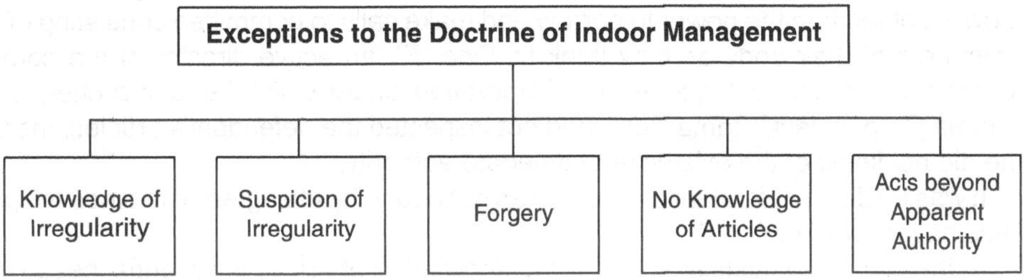

The doctrine of indoor management is subject to the following limitations:
Let us discuss these exceptions one by one.

1. **Knowledge of Irregularity**
   Where the person dealing with the company has knowledge of an internal irregularity, he cannot claim protection provided by this doctrine. The knowledge of irregularity may be actual or constructive. In the case of ***Howard* v. *Pokent Ivony Co.*** the directors were empowered to borrow money upto £1,000 and sanction of the shareholders was required for an amount in excess of this. The directors themselves lent £ 3500 to the company without the consent of the shareholders. It was held that the directors had the notice of the internal irregularity and therefore the company was liable to them only for £1,000.
2. **Suspicion of Irregularity**
   Where the person dealing with the company is put upon an enquiry, he cannot claim protection under this doctrine in the circumstances under which he would have discovered irregularity if he had made the proper enquiries. In case of ***Underwood* v. *Bank of Liverpool,*** (1924) I.K.B. 775, the sole director paid a cheque drawn in company's name, into his own bank account. It was held that the bank was put upon inquiry and was not entitled to rely upon the ostensible authority of the director. Likewise, a person dealing with the company may be put upon enquiry by reason of the unusual magnitude of the transactions having regard to the position of the agent who is acting for the company. [***Houghton & Co.* v. *Nothard Howe & Wills,*** [(1917) I.K.B. 147, 149]
3. **Forgery**
   A person dealing with the company cannot claim protection under this doctrine where forgery is involved. A company can not be held liable for forgeries committed by its officers.

In case of ***Rubben* v. *Great Fingal Consolidated,*** (1906) A.C. 439, the secretary of the company issued a share certificate in favour of Rubben by forging the signatures of two directors under the seal of the company. '*R*' wanted to be registered as a member but the company refused to register him as a member. '*R*' contended that since signatures were part of internal management and he had no means to ascertain the genuineness of the signatures, therefore he should be protected. The court held that the share certificate is not binding on the company since the **doctrine of indoor management applies to *irregularities* and *not illegalities* (i.e. forgery)**.

4. **No Knowledge of Articles**
Where the person dealing with the company has no knowledge of articles, he can not claim protection under this doctrine since this doctrine is based on the principle of estoppel and the person who did the act without consulting the Articles, can not be said to have relied upon the articles.
The company's articles contained a clause 'the directors may delegate any of their powers other than the power to borrow and make calls to committee consisting of such members of their body as they think fit. One '*T*', an active director of the company entered into a contract with '*Rama Corporation*' under which he took a cheque from 'Rama Corp.' In fact, 'Rama Corp. had not inspected the defendant's articles, therefore he did not know of the existence of delegate authority.
It was held that defendant company was not bound by the agreement since the power was never delegated to '*T*'.
In the opinion of Justice Slade, J. 'the knowledge of article is essential because the rule of 'Indoor management' is based upon the principle of estoppel. He observed, "A person who at the time of entering into a contract with a company, has the knowledge of the company's Articles of Association, cannot rely on those articles as conferring ostensible of apparent authority on the agent of the company with whom he dealt"
5. **Acts Beyond Apparent Authority**
Where an officer of the company does something, which would not ordinarily be within his powers, the person dealing with him must make proper inquiries and satisfy himself as to the officer's authority. If he fails to make proper inquiry in spite of suspicious circumstances, he cannot claim any protection under the doctrine of indoor management.

In case of ***Anand Bihari Lal* v. *Dinshaw & Co.,*** AIR (1942), the accountant of the company transferred some property of the company to the plaintiff. The transfer was held by the Court to be void, because the power to transfer property could not be considered within the apparent authority of the accountant. The plaintiff were put upon an enquiry before entering into the transaction as they should have insisted on seeing the power of attorney executed in favour of the accountant. Even a delegation clause in the Articles is not enough to validate the transaction unless the accountant was in fact authorised.

Similarly in case of ***Kredit Bank Case* v. *Scchenkers,*** (1927) K.B. 826, where a branch manager of a bank drew and endorsed bills on behalf of his company without any authority, it was held that drawing of bills was not within the ordinary ambit of power of this branch manager and company was not bound unless such authority was in fact delegated to him.

VERY SHORT ANSWER TYPE QUESTIONS

1. What is 'Articles of Association'?
2. Is it necessary for every company to have its own articles?
3. What is 'Doctrine of constructive notice'?
4. What is 'Doctrine of Indoor Management'?
5. Name the doctrine which protects company.
6. Name the doctrine which protects outsiders.
7. Name the exception to the doctrine of constructive notice.
8. Enumerate the exceptions to the doctrine of constructive notice.
9. Can articles be altered to deprive a company of its powers to amend articles?

SHORT ANSWER TYPE QUESTIONS

1. State the companies which are required to register its Articles.
2. State the companies which need not have its own Articles.
3. State the various alternatives in which a public company limited by shares may adopt Articles.
4. State the specific regulation required in the articles of:
   (a) an unlimited company,
   (b) company limited by guarantee but not having share capital,
   (c) company limited by guarantee and having share capital,
   (d) private company having share capital, and
   (e) private company having no share capital.
5. State the form in which Articles of a company must be prepared.
6. State the provision relating to printing and signature of Article.
7. State any ten contents of Articles.
8. Comment on the following:
   (a) The Articles are subordinate to and are controlled by the Memorandum of Association.
   (b) Articles constitute a contract between the member *inter se* and between the company and the members qua members.
   (c) Every person dealing with the company is deemed to have notice of the contents of its memorandum.
   (d) Doctrine of Indoor Management is an exception to the doctrine of constructive notice.
   (e) Power to alter the Articles conferred by the Companies Act is very wide yet it is subject to a large number of limitations.
   (f) The doctrine of indoor management in silver lining to strangers dealing with the company.
   (g) A company having its own Articles can adopt Table A.

LONG ANSWER TYPE QUESTIONS

1. Explain the procedure for the alteration of Articles of Association. Discuss the limits on the powers of a company to alter its Articles.
2. Distinguish between memorandum and Articles of Association.
3. Discuss the binding effects of memorandum and Articles of Association.
4. (a) Explain the doctrine of constructive notice.
   (b) Explain the doctrine of indoor management and its exceptions.
5. What is the legal effect of the Articles between—
   (a) Members and the company,
   (b) Members *inter se*, and
   (c) Company and outsiders.
6. Outline the Turquand Rule or rule in *Royal British Bank* v. *Turquand.* Are there any exceptions to this rule? If yes, discuss them also.

CHAPTER 6 Prospectus

1.0 MEANING OF PROSPECTUS [SECTION 2(36)]

According to Section 2(36) prospectus means "**any document described or issued as prospectus and includes any notice, circular, advertisement or other document inviting deposits from the public or inviting offers from the public for the subscription or purchase of any shares in, or debentures of, a body corporate.**" In simple words, the term 'Prospectus' means a document which invites deposits from the public or invites offers from the public to subscribe or buy the shares or debentures of the company. Thus, a prospectus is ***not an offer*** in itself but an ***invitation*** **to make an offer**. Application for making a deposit or for purchase of shares or debentures constitues an offer by the applicant to the company. It is only on the acceptance of the offer, by the company, a binding contract comes into existence.

The prospectus must be in writing. An oral invitation to subscribe for shares will not be considered prospectus. Television or film advertisement cannot be treated as prospectus.

2.0 MEANING OF INVITATION TO THE PUBLIC [SECTION 67]

2.1 When an Offer or Invitation is said to have been made to the Public?

From the definition of prospectus, it is clear that a document can be regarded as a prospectus only when it invites offers from the public. According to Section 67(1) and (2), the term 'public' includes any section of the public whether selected as members or debentureholder of the company concerned or as clients of the person issuing the prospects or in any other manner.

According to Section 67(3), no offer or invitation shall be treated as made to the public in *either* of the following two circumstances:

1. If it is not calculated to result in the shares/debentures becoming available by persons other than those receiving the offer or invitation.
2. If it can properly be regarded as being a domestic concern of the persons making and receiving the offer or invitation.

Thus, to determine whether or not an offer has been made to the public, the test is not who receives the offer or the invitation but who can accept it. If the invitation can be accepted by any one whether the prospectus was addressed to him or not, then it should be regarded as invitation being made to the public. If the invitation can be accepted only by those to whom it has been made, then it should not be regarded as invitation being made to the public

Examples:

(a) X Ltd. invites 50 Chartered Accountants (by sending personal communication) for subscription of its shares. It is an Invitation to public.

(b) Y Ltd. invites 40 Chartered Accountants (by sending personal communication) for subscription of its shares. It is not an invitation to the public because the invitation is made to less than 50 persons.

Judicial Rulings Some of the decided cases are given below:

(a) An offer by directors to a few of their friends, relatives, customers by sending them a copy of prospects marked "not for publication" was not considered an offer to the public. [***Sherwell* v. *Combined Incandescent Syndicate,*** (1970) W.N. 110]

(b) An offer of shares to the kith and kin of a director is not an invitation to the public. [***Rattan Singh* v. *Moga Transport,*** A.I.R. 1959 Punj, 196]

(c) A single private communication does not amount to an invitation to the public.

A managing director of a company sent to his co-director several copies of a document marked "*strictly private and confidential*" and containing particulars of a proposed issue of shares, accompanied by share application forms. One of the copies was sent by the co-director to a solicitor, who in turn, gave it to a client who passed it on to a relation. The allottee (relative of the client of the solicitor) filed a suit for compensation for the loss sustained by him by reason of an omission in the document. It was held that the document did not amount to "prospectus issued to the public", as it was marked "strictly private and confidential". [***Nash* v. *Lynde,*** (1929) A.C. 158]

2.2 When is an Offer not Treated as Private Issue? [Poviso to Section 67(3)]

If an offer is made to at least 50 persons, it will not be treated as private issue, i.e. it will be treated as public issue. However this proviso is not applicable to —

(a) Non Banking Finance Companies referred to in Section 45-I(f) at the RBI Act, orr

(b) Public Financial Institutions as defined in Section 4A of Companies Act.

Special Provisions for Non-Banking Finance Companies [NBFC] and Public Financial Institution [PFI] [Section 67 (3A)].

According to Section 67(3A), NBFC and PFI can make private offer over to 50 or more members, without issuing a prospectus as per guidelines notified by SEBI in consultation with RBI.

2.3 Meaning of the Term 'Subscription or Purchase of Shares'

The term 'subscription or 'Purchase of shares' means taking or agreeing to take shares for cash. In case of ***Government Stock and other Securities Investment Co. Ltd.* v. *Charistopper*** (*1956*), All E.R. 490, an offer was made by Company *X* to the members of Companies *Y* and *Z* to acquire all their shares in these companies in exchange for allotment of shares in the company. It was held that the offer could not be said to have been made to the public on the following two grounds:

(a) It did not invite subscription for shares since subscription means taking shares for cash (as it was an exchange offer).

(b) It could be accepted only by members to whom it was made.

2.4 Initial Offer of Securities to be in Dematerialised form in Certain Cases [Section 68B]

Every listed public company, making initial public offer or any security for a sum of rupees ten crores or more, shall issue the same only in dematerialised form by complying with the requisite provisions of the Depositories Act, 1996 and the regulations made thereunder.

3.0 SIGNIFICANCE OF PROSPECTUS

Prospectus is an important document because of the following reasons:

1. **Invitation** It serves as an invitation by the company to the public to invest through making deposit or subscribing shares or debenture.
2. **Advertisement** It acts as a medium of advertisement since it informs the public about its present operations and future prospects.
3. **Authentic Record** It serves as an authentic record of the terms and conditions of the issue of deposits, shares or debentures.
4. **Protection** It protects the interests of the investors who invest on the faith of the prospectus since any misstatement in the prospectus attracts both civil and criminal liability for persons who authorise the issue of prospectus.

4.0 WHEN PROSPECTUS IS NOT REQUIRED TO BE ISSUED [SECTION 56]

The issue of a prospectus is not necessary in the following cases:

1. Where shares/debentures are not offered to the public. [Section 56(3)]
2. Where a person is *bona fide* invited to enter into an underwriting agreement. [Section 56(3)]
3. When shares or debentures are offered to existing holders of shares or debentures. [Section 56(5)]
4. When the issue relates to shares or debentures which are uniform in all respects with shares or debentures previously issued and dealt in or quoted in a recognised stock exchange. [Section 56(5)]
5. When Shares/Debentures are issued by a Private company.

5.0 REQUIREMENTS AS TO PROSPECTUS [SECTION 55 TO 61 AND 66]

The various requirements as to issue of prospectus are given below:

1. **Dating of Prospectus [Section 55]** Every prospectus issued by the company must be dated. This date must be taken as at the date of the publication of the prospectus unless contrary is proved.
2. **Signature of Prospectus [Section 60(1)]** A copy of prospectus to be delivered to the Registrar for registration must be signed by every director or proposed director or his agent authorised in writing.
3. **Delivery of Prospectus [Section 60(1)]** A copy of prospectus must be delivered to the Registrar for registration on or before the date of publication of prospectus.
4. **Matters to be Stated on the Face of Prospectus [Section 60(2)]** Every prospectus must state on face of it—
   (a) that a copy thereof has been delivered for registration, and
   (b) the documents required to be endorsed on or attached to the copy delivered for registration.
5. **Time Limit within which Prospectus is to be Issued [Section 60(4)]** The prospectus must be issued **within 90 days** after the date on which a copy of the same is delivered to the Registrar. If it is issued after 90 days after its registration, it shall be deemed to be a prospectus a copy of which has not been delivered to the Registrar.
6. **Endorsement or Attachment** The copy of the prospectus must have endorsed on or attached to it the following:

(a) The written consent of the expert to the issue of the prospectus, if his report has been included therein and such expert must not be connected or interested in the formation, promotion or management of the company.
(b) A copy of every contract appointing or fixing the remuneration of managerial personnel.
(c) A copy of every material contract unless it is entered into in the ordinary course of business within 2 years before the date of issue of the prospectus.
(d) When the persons making the reports relating to profits and losses, assets and liabilities, etc. have made adjustments to them, a signed statement by them stating the adjustments and the reasons for the same.
(e) The written consent of the person if any named in the prospectus as the auditor, adviser, attorney, solicitor, banker of the company to act in that capacity.
(f) A duly signed report required by Part II of Schedule II relating to adjustments regarding the figures of any profits/losses, or assets or liabilities.

Penalty for Issue of Prospectus without Registration [Section 60(5)]

The company and every person who is knowingly a party to the issue of prospectus without registration shall be punishable with fine **up to Rs 50,000.**

6.0 APPROVAL OF PROSPECTUS BY VARIOUS AGENCIES

6.1 Authorities who Approve the Prospectus

The draft prospectus is required to get approved by the following authorities before it is filed with ROC for registration.

(a) All the lead managers to the issue (who must be authorised by SEBI);
(b) Each of the Stock Exchanges where the shares of the company are listed and where the shares/debentures are proposed to be listed.
(c) The lead financial institutions underwriting the issue (if applicable). (Authorised by SEBI)

6.2 Vetting by SEBI

The draft prospectus is required to get vetted by SEBI to ensure adequacy of disclosures. However, vetting by SEBI does not amount to approval of prospectus. SEBI does not take any responsibility for the correctness of the statements made or opinions expressed in the prospectus.

6.3 Duty of ROC

The ROCs must ensure that merchant bankers to the issue whether as lead manager, Co-managers, advisers or consultants are only those authorized by SEBI. Each merchant banker has been given a code number. ROC must not register a prospectus if prior registration, SEBI informs ROC that the contents of prospectus filed are in contravention of any law or statutory rules and regulations.

7.0 SHELF PROSPECTUS [SECTION 60A]

7.1 What is Shelf Prospectus?

"Shelf prospectus" means a prospectus issued by any financial institution or bank for one or more issues of the securities or class of securities specified in that prospectus.

7.2 Who is Required to File a Shelf Prospectus [Section 60A(1)]

Any public financial institution, public sector bank or scheduled bank whose main object is financing shall file a shelf prospectus.

"Financing" means making loans to or subscribing in the capital of:

(a) a private industrial enterprise engaged in infrastructural financing or,

(b) such other company as the Central Government may notify in this behalf;

7.3 Benefit of Filing Shelf Prospectus [Section 60A(2)]

A company filing a shelf prospectus with the Registrar shall not be required to file prospectus afresh at every stage of offer of securities by it within validity period of such shelf prospectus (i.e. 1 year).

7.4 Obligation to file updated Information Memorandum [Section 60A(3) and (4)]

(a) A company filing a shelf prospectus shall be required to file an information memorandum on all material facts relating to new charges created, changes in the financial positions as have occurred between the first offer of securities, previous offer of securities and the succeeding offer of securities within such time as may be prescribed by the Central Government, prior to making of a second or subsequent offer of securities under the shelf prospectus.

(b) An information memorandum shall be issued to the public along with shelf prospectus filed at the stage of the first offer of securities and such prospectus shall be valid for a period of 1 year from the date of opening of the first issue of securities under that prospectus:

Provided that where an update of information memorandum is filed every time an offer of securities is made, such memorandum together with the shelf prospectus shall constitute the prospectus.

8.0 INFORMATION MEMORANDUM [SECTION 60B]

8.1 Public Co's Option to Circulate [Section 60B(1)]

A public company making an issue of securities **may** circulate information memorandum to the public prior to filing of a prospectus.

8.2 What is Red-herring Prospectus?

"Red-herring prospectus" means a prospectus which does not have complete particulars on the price of the securities offered and the quantum of securities offered.

8.3 Obligations of Company Filing Information Memorandum

1. **To file at least 3 days before opening of offer** A company inviting subscription by an information memorandum shall be bound to file a prospectus prior to the opening of the subscription lists and the offer as a red-herring prospectus, at least 3 days before the opening of the offer.
2. **Same obligations** The information memorandum and red-herring prospectus shall carry same obligations as are applicable in the case of a prospectus.

3. **To highlight variations** Any variation between the information memorandum and the red-herring prospectus shall be highlighted as variations by the issuing company.
4. **To Intimate variations Individually** Every variation as made and highlighted in accordance with Sub-section (4) above shall be individually intimated to the persons invited to subscribe to the issue of securities.
5. **Not to Encash** In the event of the issuing company or the underwriters to the issue have invited or received advance subscription by way of cash or post-dated cheques or stock-invest, the company or such underwriters or bankers to the issue shall not encash such subscription moneys or post-dated cheques or stock-invest before the date of opening of the issue, without having individually intimated the prospective subscribers of the variation and without having offered an opportunity to such prospective subscribers to withdraw their application and cancel their post-dated cheques or stock-invest or return of subscription paid.
6. **Right to withdraw within 7 days** The applicant or proposed subscriber shall exercise his right to withdraw from the application on any intimation of variation within 7 days from the date of such intimation and shall indicate such withdrawal in writing to the company and the underwriters.
7. **Application to be Void** Any application for subscription which is acted upon by the company or underwriters or bankers to the issue without having given enough information of any variations, or the particulars of withdrawing the offer or opportunity for cancelling the post-dated cheques or stock-invest or stop payments for such payments shall be **void** and the applicants shall be entitled to receive a refund or return of its post-dated cheques or stock-invest or subscription moneys or cancellation of its application, as if the said application had never been made and the applicants are entitled to receive back their original application and interest at the rate of 15% from the date of encashment till payment of realisation.
8. **To file final Prospectus upon closing of offer** Upon the closing of the offer of securities, a final prospectus shall be filed in a case of a listed public company with the SEBI and Registrar, and in any other case with the Registrar only.
   Contents – Final prospectus shall state—
   (a) the total capital raised, whether by way of debt or share capital
   (b) the closing price of the securities
   (c) any other details as were not complete in the red-herring prospectus

9.0 DEEMED PROSPECTUS OR PROSPECTUS BY IMPLICATION OR OFFER FOR SALE [SECTION 64]

9.1 Meaning of Deemed Prospectus

Where the company allots or agrees to allot any shares or debentures to issuing house and others with a view to such shares being offered to public for sale, any document by which the offer for sale to public is made shall be deemed to be a prospectus issued by a company and all provisions applicable to prospectus shall apply with specified modification. [Section 64(1)]

9.2 Presumption as to Deemed Prospectus

Unless contrary is proved, it shall be presumed that an allotment or an agreement to allot shares or debentures to the issuing houses was made with a view to offer them to public if it is shown—

(a) that the shares were offered to the public for sale within 6 months after they were allotted or agreed to be allotted to issuing house, or

(b) that the whole consideration in respect of shares/debentures had not been received by the company. [Section 64(2)]

9.3 Contents of Deemed Prospectus

(a) The deemed prospectus issued by an issuing house u/s 64(1) must state the following matters the matters required by Section 56.

(b) The net amount of consideration received or to be received by the company in respect of these shares or debentures.

(c) The place and time at which the contract of allotment may be inspected.

10.0 APPLICATION FORMS TO BE ACCOMPANIED BY AN ABRIDGED PROSPECTUS [SECTION 56(3)]

10.1 Meaning of Abridged Prospectus

Abridged prospectus means a memorandum containing such salient features of a prospectus as may be prescribed by the Central Govt. [Section 2(1)]

10.2 Form of Abridged Prospectus

The Government has prescribed a Form 2A of abridged prospectus. The abridged prospectus and the share application form must bear the same printed number.

10.3 Abridged Prospectus to be attached to Application form

Abridged prospectus must be attached to every application form for shares in or debentures of a company.

10.4 When is Abridged Prospectus not Required

Where the form of application is issued—

(a) to person who is **bona fide** invited to enter into an underwriting agreement. [Section 56(3)(a)]

(b) in relation to shares or debentures which were not offered to the public. [Section 56(3)(b)]

(c) to existing members or debentureholders of the company whether with or without the right of renunciation. [Section 56(5)(a)]

(d) in relation to shares or debentures which are—

(i) uniform in all respects with shares or debentures previously issued, and

(ii) dealt in or quoted at a recognised stock exchange. [Section 56(5)(b)]

The logic behind the first two exceptions is that the public are not involved, hence no needs of protection. In case of last two exceptions, the offeree being already a member for the shares being quoted one, must have enough information about the company to protect himself.

10.5 Duty to Furnish Prospectus

A copy of prospectus must be furnished on a request being made by any person before the closing of the subscription list. [Provision to Section 56(3)]

10.6 Penalty for Default [Section 56(3)]

If any person acts in the contravention of the provisions of Section 56(3), he shall be punishable with fine upto Rs 50,000.

11.0 EXPERT'S CONSENT [SECTIONS 57–58–59]

11.1 Meaning of Expert [Section 59(2)]

The expression 'expert' includes an engineer, a valuer, an accountant and any other person whose profession gives authority to a statement made by him.

11.2 Expert to be Unconnected [Section 57]

The statement of an expert must not be included in the prospectus if he is in any way connected with the formation or promotion or management of the company. In other words, the person must be independent to function as an expert.

11.3 Conditions for Issue of Prospectus Containing Expert's Statement [Sec. 58]

The statement of an expert is to be included in the prospectus only if:

(a) The expert has given his written consent to the issue of the prospectus.
(b) The expert has not withdrawn such consent before the delivery of a copy of the prospectus for registration.
(c) A statement that he has given and has not withdrawn his consent, appears in the prospectus.

11.4 Penalty for Default [Section 59(2)]

Every person who is knowingly a party to the issue of prospectus in contravention of Section 57 or Section 58, shall be punishable with fine upto Rs 50,000.

11.5 Terms of Contracts Mentioned in Prospectus not to be Varied [Section 61]

A company must not vary the terms of contract mentioned in the prospectus or statement in lieu of prospectus, except with the approval of the members in general meeting.

11.6 Legal Significance [Section 56(2)]

Any condition in the prospectus which requires or binds an applicant for shares or debentures to waive compliance with any of the requirements relating to statutory matters and reports, shall be void. Similarly, the condition which has the effect of affecting him with the notice of any contract, document or a matter not specifically referred to in the prospectus, shall be void.

11.7 Expert's Right to be Indemnified [Section 62(3)]

Where an expert has given his consent to the inclusion of his report in the prospectus and has withdrawn his consent before the issue of the prospectus and inspite of this the prospects has been issued, the directors of the company and every other person who authorised the issue of the prospectus shall be liable to indemnify the expert against all damages, costs and expenses which he may have incurred on account of his being associated with the issue of the prospectus as an expert.

12.0 EFFECT OF ACCEPTING APPLICATION WITHOUT COMPLYING WITH THE REQUIREMENTS OF SECTION 56

In case the company accepts the application for shares or debentures without complying with the requirements of Section 56, the applicant can *neither* ask for the rescission of the contract *nor* the rectification of the register. But he can sue the person responsible for the issue of the prospectus for any damages which he may have suffered.
[***South of England Natural Gas and Petroleum Co.,*** (1911) Ch. 573]

13.0 MATTERS TO BE STATED IN THE PROSPECTUS [SECTION 56]

Every prospectus must state the matters specified in Part I of Schedule II and set out the reports specified in Part II and the said Part I and Part II have effect subject to provisions contained in Part III of that Schedule.

Keeping in view the requirements of Schedule II of The Companies Act, 1956 and the SEBI guidelines for disclosure and investor protection, the prospectus to be issued by companies should provide for the following matters:

1. **General Information**
   (a) Name and address of registered office of the issuer company;
   (b) Details of letter of intent/industrial licence obtained and declaration of the Central Government about non-responsibility for financial soundness or correctness of statements;
   (c) Disclaimer clause of SEBI.
   (d) Disclaimer Statement from the Issuer
   (e) Office of Board and ROC
   (f) Names of stock exchanges where listed (if applicable) and where listing applications have been made for the issue;
   (g) Provisions of Section 68A(1) of The Companies Act, 1956 regarding fictitious applications;
   (h) Minimum Subscription Clause:
      (i) **For Non-underwritten Public Issues:**
      "If the company does not receive the minimum subscription of 90% of the issued amount on the date of closure of the issue, or if the subscription level falls below 90% after the closure of issue on account of cheques having being returned unpaid or withdrawal of applications, the company shall forthwith refund the entire subscription amount received. If there is a delay beyond 8 days after the company becomes liable to pay the amount, the company shall pay interest as per Section 73 of the Companies Act 1956."
      (ii) **For Underwritten Public Issues:**
      "If the company does not receive the minimum subscription of 90% of the net offer to public including development of Underwriters within 60 days from the date of closure of the issue, the company shall forthwith refund the entire subscription amount received. If there is a delay beyond 8 days after the company becomes liable to pay the amount, the company shall pay interest prescribed under Section 73 of the Companies Act, 1956."
      For Composite Issues:

The Lead Merchant Banker shall ensure that the requirement of "minimum subscription" is satisfied both jointly and severally, i.e., independently for both rights and public issues.

If the company does not receive the minimum subscription in either of the issues the company shall refund the entire subscription received.

Note: The requirement of minimum subscription shall not be applicable to (a) offer for sale. (b) Public issues by eligible infrastructure companies.

(i) **Allotment Letters/Refund Orders** Declaration about the issue of allotment letters or refunds within a period of 10 weeks and interest in case of any delay in refund at the prescribed rate under Section 73(2)/73(2A) of the Companies Act, shall be mentioned.

(j) **Dates** Dates of opening, closing and earliest closing of the issue;

(k) **Credit Rating** Whether or not credit rating from any other recognised agency has been obtained for the proposed issue of debt (including convertible instruments) should be mentioned. If rating is obtained, it should be indicated, preferably with implications of the rating symbol. **As per SEBI guidelines, rating of a credit agency is mandatory for debentures with maturity period of more than 18 months.**

(l) Names and addresses of lead managers, co-managers, trustees (if applicable), legal advisers to the company, auditors, bankers to the issue, brokers to the issue and the secretary.

(m) **Underwriting** Underwriting arrangements made for the issue, names of underwriters, amount underwritten and declaration by Board of Directors and the lead managers that in their opinion the resources of the underwriters are sufficient to discharge their underwriting obligations.

(n) **Compliance Officer:**

   (a) The name, address, telephone number, fax and E-mail number and address of Compliance Officer.

   (b) The investor's attention shall also be invited to contact the compliance officer in case of any pre-issue/post-issue related problems such as non-receipt of letters of allotment/share certificates/refund orders/cancelled stockinvests, etc.

2. **Capital Structure of the company and Issue Details**

   (a) Authorised, issued, subscribed and paid-up capital of the company.

   (b) **Size of the issue** with break up of reservation for preferential allotment to promoters, shareholders of group/associate companies, financial institutions, mutual funds, NRI, permanent employees, etc. The lock-in-period in respect of shares/debentures to be allotted to promoters and shareholders of group and associate companies/employees/financial institutions should be mentioned. The maximum number of shares/debentures that can be allotted to each employee and the number of permanent employees in the company should be mentioned.

   (c) **Impact of Issue on Paid-up capital** (after the present issue and after conversion of debentures, if applicable.)

   (d) **Impact of Issue on Securities Premium Account** (before and after the issue)

3. **Terms of the Present Issue**

   (a) Terms of payments

   (b) Rights of the instrument holders.

(c) How to apply—availability of forms, prospectus and mode of payment.
(d) Utilisation of Issue Proceeds
(e) Any special tax benefits for company and its shareholders.

4. **Particulars of Issue**
   (a) Objects
   (b) Project cost
   (c) Means of financing
   (d) Appraisal
   (e) Deployment of funds in the project
5. **Details about the Company Management and Project**
   (a) History, main objects and present business of the company.
   (b) Subsidiaries of the company.
   (c) Promoters and their background.
   (d) Key Managerial Personnel.
   (e) Names, addresses and occupation of manager, managing director and other directors including nominee directors, whole-time directors and their directorships in other companies.
   (f) Cost of the project, Means of financing and Location of the project.
   (g) Plant and machinery for the project, technology adopted and process of manufacture.
   (h) Collaboration, performance guarantee or assistance in marketing by the collaborators.
   (i) Infrastructure facilities for raw materials and utilities like water, electricity, etc.
   (j) Schedule of implementation of the project, with separate details of land acquisition, civil work, installation of plant and machinery and the progress till the date of the prospectus.
   (k) Expected date of trial production and commercial production.
   (l) Nature of the products, consumer/industrial and end users and approach to marketing and proposed marketing set up.
   (m) Export possibilities and export obligation.
   (n) **Projections about Capacity** Expected capacity utilisation during the first 3 years from the date of commencement of production for each of the major product groups.
   (o) **Projections about Profitability** Expected year when the company would be able to earn cash profits and net profits and the expected cash profits and net profits for the next 3 years.
   (p) **Stock Market Prices** High/Low equity prices of the shares/debentures of the company for each of the last 3 years and monthly high/low prices for the last 6 months (applicable to existing listed companies).
6. **Management discussion and Analysis of the financial conditions** and result of the operations as reflected in the financial statements.
7. **Financial information of Group Companies.**
8. **Information about Companies Under the Same Management Covered u/s 370(1)(B)**
   (a) Name of the company;
   (b) Year of issue;
   (c) Type of issue (Public/Private/Composite);
   (d) Amount of issue;
   (e) Date of Closure of issue;

(f) Date of completion of delivery of share/debenture certificates/letters of allotment; and

(g) Date of completion of the project, where the object of the issue was for financing a project;

(h) Rate of dividend paid.

9. Promise vis-a-vis Performance

10. The following information shall be disclosed for all issues irrespective of the issue price:

(a) Earnings per share, i.e., EPS pre-issue for three years (as adjusted for changes in capital);

(b) P/E pre-issue and comparison thereof with industry P/E where available (giving the source from which industry P/E has been taken);

(c) average return on net worth in the last three years;

(d) minimum return on increased net worth required to maintain pre-issue EPS;

(e) Net Asset Value per share based on last balance sheet;

(f) Net Asset Value per share after issue and comparison thereof with the issue price:
Provided that the projected earnings shall not be used as a justification for the issue price in the offer document:
Provided further that the accounting ratios disclosed in the prospectus in support of basis of the issue price shall be calculated after giving effect to the consequent increase in capital on account of compulsory conversions outstanding, as well as on the assumption that the options outstanding, if any, to subscribe for additional capital will be exercised;

(g) An illustrative format of disclosure in respect of basis for issue price is given in *Schedule XV*.

(i) The issuer company and the lead merchant banker shall provide the accounting ratios as mentioned above to justify the basis of issue price:
Provided that, the lead merchant banker shall not proceed with the issue in case the accounting ratios mentioned above, do not justify the issue price.

(ii) In case of book built issues, the offer document shall state that the final price has been determined on the basis of the demand from the investors.

11. Outstanding Litigation Pertaining to:

(i) Matters likely to affect operation and finances of the company, including disputed tax liabilities; and

(ii) Criminal prosecution launched against the company and directors for alleged offences under the following statutes:
The Indian Stamp Act, 1899
The Central Excises Act, 1944
The Imports and Export (Control) Act, 1951
The Industries (Development and Regulation) Act, 1951
The Prevention of Food Adulteration Act, 1954
The Essential Commodities Act, 1955
The Companies Act, 1956
The Wealth-tax Act, 1957
The Income-tax Act, 1961
The Customs Act, 1962
The Monopolies and Restrictive Trade Practices Act, 1969

The Foreign Exchange Management Act, 1999.

12. Risk Factors and Management perception as the same, if any.

13. Disclosure on Investor Grievances and Redressal System.

14. General Information

Matters and Reports Contained in Part II of Schedule II

(a) Consent of directors, auditors, solicitors/advocates, managers to the issue, Registrar to the Issue, Bankers to the company, bankers to the issue and experts.

(b) Expert opinion obtained, if any.

(c) Change, if any, in directors and auditors during the last three years, and reasons thereof.

(d) Authority for the issue and details of resolution passed for the issue.

(e) Procedure and time of schedule for allotment and issue of certificates.

(f) Names and addresses of the company secretary, legal adviser, lead managers, co-managers, auditors, bankers to the company, bankers to the issue and brokers to the issue.

15. Financial Information

A report from the auditors on:

(a) Profits and Losses of the company (where there is no subsidiary company) and the combined profits and losses of the subsidiaries or individual profits and losses of each subsidiary for each of the five financial years preceding the issue of prospectus (where there are subsidiaries);

(b) Assets and Liabilities of the company (where there is no subsidiary company) at the last date to which the accounts are made up and the combined assets and liabilities of the subsidiaries or individually with the assets and liabilities of each subsidiary (where there are subsidiaries); and

(c) Rates of the Dividends paid by the company in respect of each class of shares for each of the five financial years preceding the issue of prospectus.

If no accounts have been made up in respect of any part of the period of five years ending three months before the date of issue of prospectus, the report should contain a statement of the fact. Further, a statement of accounts of the company should be made in respect of a part of the said period upto a date not earlier than six months of the date of issue of prospectus and the assets and liabilities position as at the end of that period. There should be a certificate from the auditors that such accounts have been examined and found correct by them.

The report should distinguish items of a non-recurring nature and indicate the nature of provisions or adjustments made or are yet to be made.

16. Statutory and other information

(a) Minimum subscription, as laid down in the SEBI guidelines.

(b) Expenses of the issue giving separately fees payable to advisers, registrars to the issue, managers to the issue and trustees for debentureholders.

(c) Underwriting commission and brokerage.

(d) Previous issue for cash or consideration otherwise than for cash.

(e) Details of public or right issue during the last 5 years:

  (i) Date of allotment and refund;

  (ii) Date of listing on the stock exchange; and

  (iii) Amount of premium or discount, if applicable.

(f) Details of premium received in respect of any issue of shares made in the two years preceding the date of issue of prospectus or to be made stating the proposed date of the issue, the reasons for differentiation of premium for different categories, if applicable and the disposal of premium received or to be received.

(g) Commission or brokerage paid on previous issue.

(h) Debentures and redeemable preference shares and other instruments outstanding on the date of prospectus and the terms of their issue.

(i) Option to subscribe. The details of options to subscribe for securities to be dealt with in a depository.

(j) Particulars of property purchased or proposed to be purchased from vendors to be paid for wholly or partly out of the proceeds of the issue and the interest of the promoters or directors in any transaction relating to the property within the last two years.

(k) Details of directors, proposed directors, whole-time directors, their remuneration, appointment and remuneration of the managing director(s).

(l) Interests of directors, their borrowing powers and qualification shares.

(m) Any amount or benefit paid or given within the two preceding years or intended to be paid or given to any promoter or officers and consideration for the payment or giving of the benefit.

(n) The dates of, parties to, and general nature of—
   (i) every contract of appointment or remuneration of a managing director or manager; and
   (ii) every other material contract, not being a contract entered into in the ordinary course of business of the company or entered into more than two years prior to the date of prospectus:

   Reasonable time and place for inspection of the contract should be provided for.

(o) Full particulars of the nature and extent of interest of every director or promoter:
   (i) in the promotion of the company; or
   (ii) in any property acquired by the company within two years of the date of the prospectus or proposed to be acquired by it.

(p) Rights of members regarding voting, dividend, lien on shares, modification of rights and forfeiture of shares/debentures.

(q) Restriction on transfer and transmission of shares/debentures and on consolidation splitting.

(r) Revaluation of assets, if any, during the last 5 years.

(s) Material Contracts and Inspection of Documents.

(t) Particulars of default in meeting statutory dues, institutional dues, dues to holders of instruments like debentures, fixed deposits and arrears of cumulative preference shares, pertaining to the company and/or other companies promoted by the same promoters, which are listed on stock exchanges.

(u) Any material development after the date of the last balance sheet and its impact on the performance and prospects of the company.

14.0 MISLEADING PROSPECTUS

14.1 Meaning of Misleading Prospectus [Section 65]

The prospectus may be described as 'misleading prospectus if it contains untrue statement. The prospectus is said to have contained untrue statement if:

(a) it contains a statement which is misleading in the form and context in which it is included,

(b) it omits any matter which is calculated to mislead.

Thus, the term 'untrue statement' has been used in a broader sense. It covers *not only false statement, but also concealment of material statements.*

14.2 Rule of Golden Legacy

Justice Kindersley, V.C. in *New Brunswick and Canada Rly. and Land Co. v. Muggeridge,* [(1860), 3 Lt 651: 30 LJ Ch. 242] observed: "*Those who issue a prospectus hold out to the public that great advantages will accrue to persons who will take shares. Public is invited to take shares on the faith of the representation contained in the prospectus. Therefore, they are bound to state everything honestly and faithfully. They must not only abstain from stating something as a fact when it is not actually so but also must not omit a fact the existence of which might in any degree affect the nature or quality of the privileges and advantages which the prospectus holds out as an inducement to take shares.*"

The above stated rule is popularly known as '**Rule of Golden Legacy**'.

Thus, there must be *neither* false statement *nor* concealment of any material fact in the prospectus.

15.0 REMEDIES IN CASE OF MISLEADING PROSPECTUS

The remedies available to person who subscribe for shares on the faith of misleading prospectus are as given below:

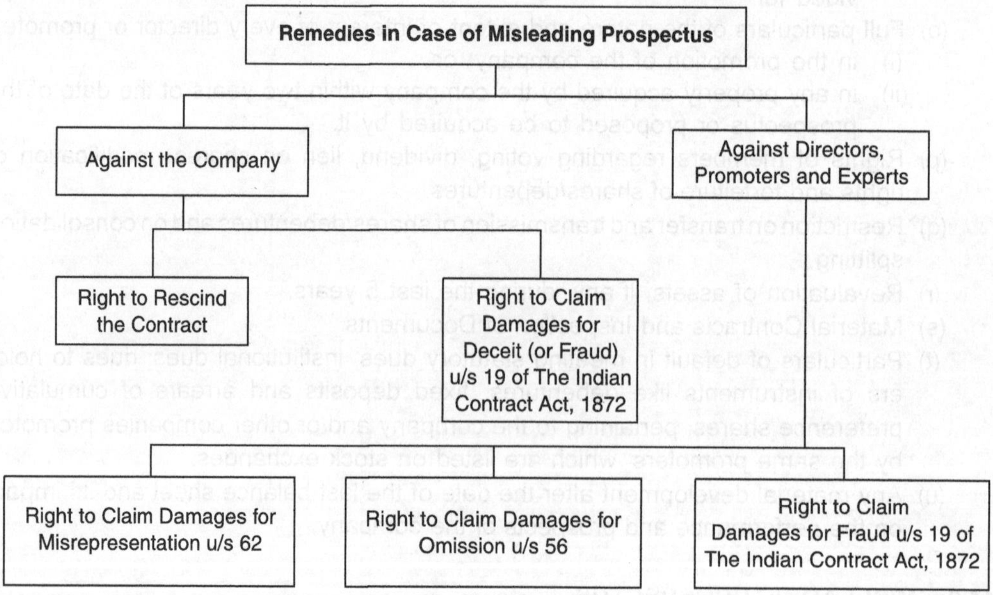

Let us discuss these remedies one by one.

15.1 Remedies Against the Company

(a) Right to Rescind the Contract to take Shares

A subscriber has a right to rescind the contract to take shares within reasonable time (but before the company goes into liquidation) if he subscribed the shares on the faith of misstatement as to material fact (whether made innocently or fraudulently).

Conditions for Right to Rescind the Contract The right to rescind the contract can be exercised subject to the following conditions:

(i) The prospectus must have been issued by the company or by someone authorised by the company in this behalf.

(ii) There must be misrepresentation or omission of a fact. In other words, a mere opinion, a statement of expression or intention does not amount to misrepresentation.

(iii) The misrepresentation must be of fact and not of law.

(iv) The misrepresentation or omission of a fact must be misleading.

In case of ***Arnison* v. *Smith,*** (1889) 40 Ch. D. 569, A statement in the prospectus that share capital has been subscribed when it has only been allotted in fully paid shares to the company's contractors, was held to be untrue.

In case of ***Rex* v. *Kylsant,*** (1932) I.K.B. 442, the company issued a prospectus which did not contain any untrue statement. One of the statements disclosed the rates of dividends paid for a number of years. This was a factual statement which was true. But the dividends had not been paid out of trading profits but out of realised capital profits. This fact was not disclosed in the prospectus. The prospectus was held to be misleading not because of what is stated but because what it concealed or omitted.

Further, if a statement was true when it was made but subsequently became untrue when shares were allotted, the contract to subscribe for shares can be rescined. [***Re Scottish Petroleum Co.,*** (1823) 23 Ch. D. 413]

(v) The *misrepresentation* must be *material* to the contract of taking shares. A fact can be considered as material if it is likely to influence the judgement of a prospective investor in deciding whether he should purchase shares in the company or refrain from doing so. In the various, judicial decisions, the misrepresentation was held to be a material facts.

(a) A statement that two leading businessmen of repute have agreed to become directors of the company when they had only expressed their willingness to help the company. [***Re Metropolitan Coal Consumer's Association,*** (1892) 3 Ch. 2]

(b) A statement that the proceeds of the issue of debentures were to be utilized for improving and developing the business whereas the real object of issuing debentures was to pay-off past liabilities. [***Edington* v. *Fitzmaurice,*** (1885) 29 Ch. D. 459]

(c) A statement that directors and their friends have subscribed a large portion of the capital of the company and that they now offer the remaining shares to the public whereas the fact was that they had only subscribed 10 shares each. [***Handerson* v. *Lacon,*** (1867) 5 Eq. 249]

(vi) The aggrieved party must have relied upon the prospectus while applying for shares. A purchaser of shares in the open market has no remedy against the company or any other persons even if he might bought the shares on the faith of misrepresentation in the prospectus. *[**Peek** v. **Gurney,*** (1870 L.R. 6 H.L. 377)]

(vii) The aggrieved party must exercise the right to rescind the contract within a reasonable time of becoming aware of a mis-statement in the prospectus and before the company goes into liquidation. *[**Shiromani Sugar Mills Ltd.** v. **Debi Prasad,** AIR* (1950) All 508]

Cases in which Right of Recession is lost

(i) **Affirmation/Addition of Contract** The aggrieved party must exercise the right to rescind the contract before he affirms his contract for purchase of shares. In the following cases, it has been held that the subscriber has affirmed the contract:

(a) where he has received dividend or paid calls [***Scholey* v. *Central Railway,*** (1868) L.R. 9 Eq. 266],

(b) where he attends and votes at general meetings [***Shrpley* v. *Louth Etc. Co.*** (1876) 2 Ch. D. 663],

(c) where he executes a transfer of his shares [***Crowley's case*** (1869) L.R. 4 Ch. App. 322].

It may be noted that a transfer of part of shares before discovery of misrepresentation does not affect his right as to the rest. [***Re Mount Morgan Etc. Ltd.,*** (1887) 56 L.T. 622].

(ii) Lapse of Reasonable Time

(iii) Commencement of Liquidation of Company

(b) Right to Claim Damages for Fraud (Deceit) u/s 19 of the Indian Contract Act, 1872

The subscriber can recover damages for any loss which he may have suffered if he was induced to take shares based on a fraudulent misrepresentation of material facts. Lord Herschall in ***Derry* v. *Peek,*** (1889) 14 A.C. 337, said: "To support an action for deceit, fraud must be proved and nothing less than fraud will do. Fraud is proved where it is shown that a false statement has been made (a) knowingly, or (b) without belief in its truth, or (c) recklessly, carelessly whether it is false or true".

Conditions for Right to claim Damages The right to claim damages may be exercised subject to the fulfilment of the following conditions:

(i) There must be fraudulent misrepresentation,

(ii) The fraudulent misrepresentation must relate to facts which are material to the contract of purchasing shares,

(iii) The aggrieved party must have actually relied on the misstatements,

(iv) The aggrieved party must have taken shares directly from the company, and

(v) The aggrieved party must have suffered some loss.

Is it essential to Rescind the contract to claim damages?

It may be noted that the right to claim damages may be exercised against the company after rescinding the contract of allotment and against the persons who authorized the issue of prospectus without rescinding the contract of allotment. The House of Lords in ***Houldsworth* v. *City Glargow Bank,*** (1880) 5 A.C. 317, held that if a shareholder wants to sue the company for damages, he must first rescind the contract. He can not sue the company for damages while he remains a shareholder.

15.2 Remedies Against Directors and Promoters

(a) Right to Claim Damages for Misrepresentation Under Section 62(1)

As subscriber has right to claim damages for any loss suffered if he subscribed for shares on the faith of prospectus containing any untrue and misleading statement.

(b) Persons liable to Compensate

(i) Every director of the company at the time of the issue of the prospectus.

(ii) Every person who has authorised himself to be named and is named in the prospectus as a director or as one having agreed to become a director, either immediately, or after an interval of time.

(iii) Every promoter of the company.

(iv) Every person who has authorised the issue of the prospectus.

Notes:

(a) The action for damages must be taken within 3 years from the date of the allotment of the shares.

(b) A shareholder who bought shares from an existing shareholders or from the share market, cannot bring an action for deceit against directors. [***Peek* v. *Gurney***]

(c) The subscribers may institute a suit for damages against those responsible for the issue of the prospectus, inspite of the fact that the contract to purchase shares has been repudiated. This is an action for deceit under the general law. [***Derry* v. *Peek***, (1889) 14 A.C. 337]

(d) The action for damages can be taken even if the remedy by way of rescission (as against the company) has been lost through negligence or even if the company goes into liquation.

Defences Available to Directors etc. [Section 62(2)]

No person shall be liable under this section, if he proves:

(i) that, he having consented to become a director, had withdrawn his consent to become director before the issue of prospectus and that it was issued without his authority; or

(ii) that the prospectus was issued without his knowledge or consent and that on becoming aware of its issue, he immediately gave reasonable public notice to that effect; or

(iii) that after the issue of the prospectus and before, allotment, he, on becoming aware of any untrue statement in it, had withdrawn his consent to the prospectus and gave reasonable public notice of the withdrawal and his reasons for doing so; or

(iv) that he had reasonable ground to believe and until allotment did believe that the statement was true. This statement pertains to every untrue statement not purporting to be made on the authority of expert or of a public official document or statement or

(v) that the statement was a correct and fair representation of the statement made by an expert and he had reasonable ground to believe and until issue of prospectus did believe that the person making the statement was competent to make it and that the expert had given his consent and had not withdrawn that consent before delivery of a copy of the prospectus for registration or to the defendant's knowledge, before allotment; or

(vi) that if the statement is a copy of or exract from an official document or is made by an official person, it was a correct and fair copy of the document or a fair representation of the statement.

15.3 Remedies Against Expert [Section 62(3)]

The form 'expert' includes an engineer, a valuer, an accountant and any other person whose profession gives authority to a statement made by him [Section 59(2)].

An expert is liable to compensate only in respect of his own untrue statement, wrong report or valuation made by him and included in the prospectus.

(a) Defences Available to an Expert

An expert shall not be liable if he proves—

(i) he withdrew his consent in writing before delivery of a copy of the prospectus for registration with the Registrar of Companies; or

(ii) he on becoming aware of the untrue statement, withdrew his consent in writing, after delivery of prospectus for registration with the Registrar of Companies but before allotment, and gave reasonable public notice of the withdrawal and his reasons therefor; or

(iii) he was competent to make the statement, and believed on reasonable grounds that it was true.

Measure of Damages The measure of damages is the loss suffered by reason of the false statement, that is to say, the difference between the value which the shares would have had if the company had processed the advantages stated in the prospectus (but not exceeding the price paid) and the true value of the shares at the time of allotment in the circumstances which in fact existed. [***McConnel* v. *Wright,*** (1903) 1 Ch. 546]

Right of Indemnity Every such director or expert who has escaped liability on the above grounds is entitled to be indemnified by other directors or experts who continue to be liable against all damages, costs and expenses which he may incur in defending himself against any legal proceedings brought against him. [Section 62(4)]

Right of Contribution If any subscriber realises any damages from any director or officer of the company for untrue statement in the prospectus, the directors and officers who authorised the issue of untrue prospectus shall contribute and pay their share of damages to the director who has made the payment. *[**Gerson* v. *Simpson,***(1903) 2 K.B. 197]

(b) Right to Claim Damages for Omission u/s 56

A subscriber has right to claim damages for omission if he proves—

(a) that there is omission of any fact required to be disclosed u/s 56 read with Schedule II.

(b) that he would not have purchased shares if there had been no such omissions, and

(c) that he has actually suffered a loss.

Notes:

(i) omission does not entitle the subscriber to rescind the contract unless it amounts to fraud or misrepresentation. *[**Shiromani Sugar Mills* v. *Debi Prasad, AIR*** (1950) All. 508]

(ii) Subscriber can sue even if omission does not make the prospectus misleading.

Defences Available to Directors and other Persons [Section 56(4)]

A director or any other person sued under this section shall not be liable, if—

(a) he proves that he had no knowledge of any matter not disclosed; or

(b) he proves that the non-compliance or contravention arose from an honest mistake of fact; or

(c) in the opinion of the court, the matter not disclosed was immaterial; or

(d) that the non-compliance or contravention ought to be excused with regard to all the circumstances of the case.

Criminal Liability for Misstatement [Section 63]

Every person who had authorised the issue of prospectus containing an untrue statement shall be punishable with imprisonment for a term upto 2 years or with fine upto Rs 5,000 or with both unless he proves either—

(a) that the statement was immaterial; or
(b) that he had reasonable ground to believe and did upto the time of issue of prospectus that the statement was true.

16.0 PENALTY FOR FRAUDULENTLY INDUCING PERSONSTOINVEST MONEY [SECTION 68]

Any person who, by making (either knowingly or recklessly) any false, deceptive or misleading statement, promise or forecast or by any dishonest concealment of material facts, induces or attempts to induce another person to enter into, or to offer to enter into—
(a) any agreement for, the acquisition, disposal, subscribing for, or underwriting shares or debentures; or
(b) any agreement for the purpose of securing any profit to any of the parties from the yield of shares or debentures, or from fluctuations in the value of shares or debentures;
shall be punishable with imprisonment for a term upto **5 years**, or with fine upto **Rs 1,00,000** or with **both**.

17.0 PERSONATION FOR ACQUISITION, ETC., OF SHARES. [SECTION 68A(1)]

Any person who—
(a) makes an application to a company for acquiring, or subscribing for, any shares therein, in a fictitious name or
(b) otherwise induces a company to allot, or register any transfer of, shares therein to him, or any other person in a fictitious name,
shall be punishable with imprisonment for a term upto 5 years.

Disclosure in Every Prospectus & Application Form [Section 68A(2)]

The provisions of Section 68A(1) must be prominently reproduced in every prospectus issued by the company and in every form of application for shares which is issued by the company to any person.

18.0 ISSUE OF SECURITIES ONLY IN DEMAT FORM [SECTION 68B]

Initial Public officer of Securities of at least Rs 10 crore must be only in Dematerialised form, by complying with the requisite provisions of the Depositories Act, 1996 and Regulations made thereunder. According to SEBI Guidelines company can make an issue of securities to the public or on right basis only in demat form, while this new section implies that only with regard to *initial offer* it should be in demat form, whereas for any subsequent issue it could be in physical form.

19.0 STATEMENT IN LIEU OF PROSPECTUS [SECTION 70]

19.1 When Required When the public company having share capital decides to raise the capital privately (say from relatives and friends) without inviting offers from the public. It is required to issue a statement in lieu of prospectus.

19.2 Contents of Statement in Lieu of Prospectus the statement in lieu of prospectus shall contain the particulars and reports as set out in Schedule III to the Companies Act.

19.3 Signature The Statement to be delivered to the Registrar for registration must be signed by every person who is named in the statement as director or proposed director or his agent authorised in writing.

19.4 Time Limit for Filing It must be delivered to the Registrar for registration at least 3 days before the allotment of the shares or debentures.

19.5 Penalty for Default The company and every director of the company, who willfully authorises or permits contravention, shall be punishable with fine upto Rs 10,000.

19.6 Liability for Misstatement The liability for any misstatement in a Statement in lieu of prospectus is the same as in case of a prospectus.

19.7 Is a Private Company Required to Issue Prospectus or Statement in Lieu of Prospectus?

A private company is *neither* required to issue a prospectus *nor* a statement in lieu of prospectus since it cannot invite public to subscribe for its shares or debentures as per restrictions of Section 3(1)(iii).

20.0 PUBLIC DEPOSITS

20.1 Meaning of Public

In general the term 'Public' includes a section of the public also. But Section 58A(1) makes a distinction between the public and the members of the company. Present and ex-employees of the company fall in the category of public.

20.2 Meaning of Deposit

'Deposit means any deposit of money including any amount borrowed by a company but **would not include**:

(a) amount received from the Central Government or State Government or Local Authority or a Foreign Government or any foreign citizen, authority or a foreign person.
(b) a loan received from any banking company.
(c) a loan received from IFCI, UTI, IDBI, LIC, or ICICI or any other financial institutions.
(d) amount received by a company from any other company provided the borrower company has not entered the field of commercial production and has not accepted any deposits from the public.
(e) any amount of security deposit received from an employee of the company.
(f) amount received as security or as an advance from any purchasing agent, selling agent during the course of business of the company.
(g) amount received as subscriptions to any shares, bonds or debentures pending allotment including the amount received as calls in advance on shares.
(h) amount received in trust or any amount in transit
(i) amount received by a public company from its directors or by a private company or a deemed public company from its shareholders or directors.
(j) amount raised by issue of bonds or secured debentures.
(k) amount brought by promoters as unsecured loans subject to certain conditions.

20.3 Conditions Subject to which Deposits may be Invited [Section 58A(2)]

(a) The deposit must be invited as per the rules of Section 58(1).
(b) An advertisement including a statement showing the financial position of the company must be issued by the company in prescribed form and prescribed manner.
(c) the company must not have not in default in the repayment of any deposit or part thereof and any interest thereupon in accordance with the terms and conditions of such deposit.

20.4 Right of Aggrieved Depositor to apply to CLB

The aggrieved depositors, whose deposits had matured after and who have not been repaid, may make an application (in triplicate) to the Company Law Board Bench (located at Delhi, Calcutta, Bombay and Madras depending upon the registered office of the company) in the prescribed Form No. 11, alongwith an application fee of Rs 50 by bank draft in favour of the "Pay and Accounts Officer, Department of Company Affairs". The application can either be filed with the concerned Bench Officer personally or sent by post.

It may be clarified that, in the following circumstances, application under Section 58A(9) of the Act will not lie:

(i) Deposit made for booking/purchase of scooter, car, etc. is not a deposit for purposes of Section 58A of the Act.
(ii) Deposits accepted by financial companies like hire purchase finance company, a housing finance company, an investment company, a loan/mutual benefit financial company, and equipment leasing company, a chit fund company or a company, which receives deposits under any scheme or arrangement by way of contribution/ subscriptions or by sale of units/certificates.
(iii) Deposits accepted by a sick industrial company covered by the Sick Industrial Companies (Special Provisions) Act, 1985, in respect of which the Board of Industrial and Financial Reconstruction (BIFR) has specifically, by order, suspended the operation of any contract, agreement, settlement, etc., under Section 22(3) of the said Act.
(iv) Deposits accepted by relief undertakings which are notified as such under the various State laws. Proceedings under Section 58A(9) of the Companies Act, 1956 shall remain stayed during the notified period.

In addition to the relief available under the Companies Act, 1956, the depositors can also take action against the defaulting companies under the normal civil law of the country.

20.5 Obligation to Repay Unrenewed Deposits [Section 58A(3)]

Every deposit accepted by a company after Sept. 1, 1989, must be repaid in accordance with terms and conditions of deposit unless renewed as per rules.

20.6 Obligation to Repay Deposits Accepted in Violation of Rules [Section 58A(4)]

Where any deposit is accepted in contravention of the rules it must be refunded within 30 days from the date of acceptance of such deposit or within such further extended time not exceeding 30 days as the Central Government may allow on sufficient cause shown by the company (Section 58A(4)).

20.7 Penalty for Default in Repayment of Deposits Accepted in Violation of Rules [Section 58A(5)]

(a) If the company fails to make repayment of deposit within the time allowed the company shall be punishable with fine which shall be at least 200% of the amount of deposit not repaid.

(b) Every officer in default shall be punishable with imprisonment up to 5 years and fine.

(c) If the fine is realised then the court shall pay an amount equal to the amount of deposit not repaid to the depositor and with that the company's liability to that extent shall stand discharged.

20.8 Penalty for Contravention Relating to the Acceptance of Deposits [Section 58A(6)]

(a) The company shall be punishable with fine which shall be at least an amount equal to the amount of the deposit so accepted.

(b) Its every officer in default shall be punishable with imprisonment for term upto 5 years and fine.

20.9 Penalty for Contravention Relating to the Invitation of any Deposit [Section 58A(6)]

(a) The company shall be punishable with fine upto 1,00,000 but five shall be at least Rs 5,000.

(b) Its every officer in default shall be punishable with imprisonment for a term upto 5 years and fine.

20.10 Companies to which Provisions of Section 58A do not Apply [Section 58A(7)]

1. A banking company
2. Such other company which the Central Government may after consultation with Reserve Bank of India specify in this behalf. The Central Government has exempted the companies which are small scale industrial units and fulfill the following conditions:
   (a) the paid up capital of the company does not exceed Rs 25 lakh
   (b) deposits are not accepted from more than 100 persons.
   (c) the deposits do not exceed Rs 20 lakh or the amount of its paid up capital, which ever is less, and
   (d) there is no invitation to public for deposits(vide Notification GSR No. 73 1E, Dt. 12-2-96).

(i) a **"Small Scale Industrial Unit"** means any industrial undertaking registered with the Directorate of Industries or Small Scale Industries, as the case may be, of the State Government and in respect of which the investment in plant and machinery is not in excess of 3 crores of rupees in value;

(ii) **"Deposit"** has the same meaning as in Clause (b) of Rule 2 of the Companies (Acceptance of Deposits) Rules, 1975.

20.11 Companies to which Provisions Except Relating to Advertisement of Section 58A do not Apply [Section 58A(8)]

The Central Government has exempted the class of companies which satisfy the eligibility criteria laid down by the Reserve Bank of India in the Non-Banking Companies (Acceptance of Deposits through commercial paper) Directives, 1989 subject to the following conditions:

(i) the companies shall comply with the terms and conditions stipulated fron time to time by the RBI.

(ii) The comlpanies shall, in their annual accounts disclose the maximum amount raised at any time during a financial year and the amount outstanding as at the end of financial year [Notification GSR1075(E), dated 29-12-1989].

20.12 Power of Company Law Board to Order Companies to Repay Deposits [Section 58A(9)]

In case a company fails to repay any deposit as per the terms and conditions of deposit, the Company Law Board is empowered to order companies to repay deposits within such time and subject to such conditions as may be specified in the order. This power may be exercised suo-moto (of its own) or on the application of a single deposit holder. But before making such an order the Company Law Board may give the company a reasonable opportunity of being heard on the matter (Section 58A(9)).

20.13 Penalty [Section 58A(10)]

Whosoever fails to comply with the orders of the Company Law Board shall be punishable with imprisonment upto 3 years and fine of at least Rs 500 for every day during which the default continues.

20.14 Nomination [Section 58A(11)]

A depositor may make a nomination and the provisions of Section 109A and B shall apply to such nomination.

21.0 THE COMPANIES (ACCEPTANCE OF DEPOSITS) RULES, 1975

21.1 Minimum Net Owned Funds The Company must have minimum net owned funds of Rs 1 crore.

21.2 Minimum Term of Deposit A company can accept or renew deposits for a minimum period of 6 months (3 months in case of deposits (upto 10%) for meeting short term requirements of funds).

21.3 Maximum Term of Deposit A company can accept or renew deposits for a maximum period of 36 months.

21.4 Maximum Limit of Deposits

Deposits	*Maximum Limit*
(a) ***In case of Govt. Company***	35% of Paid up capital and Free Reserves
(b) ***In case of any other company***	
(i) *In case of deposits received form general public*	25% of the Paid up capital and Free Reserves (10% in case of deposits for less than 12 months)
(ii) *In case of deposits received against unsecured debentures or form shareholders*	10% of the Paid up capital and Free Reserves.

21.5 Meaning of Free Reserves

(a) **Include** It includes the amount in the Securities Premium Account, Capital Redemption Reserve and Debenture Redemption Reserves and other reserves appearing in the balance sheet and created by way of appropriation from the profits of the company.

(b) **Exclude** But the term 'free reserves' would not include any reserve created:
   (i) for repayment of any future liability or for depreciation on assets or for bad debts.
   (ii) by revalution of assets (like Revaluation Reserve).

   For calculating the total paid up capital and free reserves, the following shall be deducted;
   (a) the debit balance of profit and loss account.
   (b) the balance of deferred revenue expenditure.
   (c) the balance of other intangible assets.

21.6 Maximum Rate of Interest

A company can accept or renew deposits at a rate of interest **not exceeding 11% p.a.** at rests not shorter than **monthly rests**.

21.7 Maximum Rate of Brokerage to any Broker

For Deposit upto 1 year	1%
For Deposit exceeding 1 year but not exceeding 2 years	1.5%
For Deposit exceeding 2 years	2%

21.8 Maintainance of Liquid Assets upto at least 15% of Deposits

Every company before the 30th day of April of each year must deposit or invest, as the case may be **at least 15%** of the amount of its deposits maturing during the year commencing from 1st day of April and ending on 31st day of March of the following year in any or more of the prescribed securities.

21.9 Filing of Return of Deposits with ROC and RBI on/before 30th June

A Return of Deposit in prescribed form containing information as on 31st March, duly certified by the Auditors is required to be filed with ROC and RBI on or before 30th tune.

21.10 Register of Deposits

(a) **Maintenance** The company must maintain a register of deposits at its registered office stating details about name and address of depositors, date and amount of each deposit, period of deposits, rate of interest, dates when interest will be paid and the date when each deposit shall become repayable.

(b) **Preservation** Such register must be preserved by the company **for at least 8 calendar years** from the financial year in which the latest entry was made in the register.

21.11 Advertisement

(a) In Two Newspapers Advertisement inviting deposits from public shall appear in leading **English** newspaper **and in one vernacular** newspaper circulating in the state where the registered office of the company is situated.

(b) **Under Board's Authority** The advertisement must be issued on the authority and in the name of the board of directors of the company.

(c) **Contents** It must contain the conditions subject to which deposits shall be accepted, the date on which the Board approved the text of advertisement and the prescribed information.

(d) **Validity Period of Advertisement** The advertisement for acceptance of deposits shall hold good for **6 months** from the date of the closure of financial year in which it is issued or until the date of the holding of the annual general meeting where the balance sheet is presented or where the annual general meeting is not held for any year, the latest day on which the meeting should have been held as per the Act, whichever is earlier. After the expiry of the above period the companies are required to issue a fresh advertisement for inviting further deposits.

(e) **Filing of Copy of Advertisement with ROC** No advertisement for inviting deposits can be issued unless a copy of the advertisement duly approved and signed by a majority of the directors of the company has been filed with the Ragistrar.

In case a company intends accepting deposits without an advertisement, it must file with the Registrar a copy of the statement in lieu of advertisement stating the particulars required in the advertisement and duly approved and signed by the majority of the directors of the board.

21.12 Application Form for Deposits

(a) A company can invite or renew deposits only on the form supplied by the company.

(b) The form shall contain all prescribed particulars in relation to accepting deposits specially in relation to financial position, composition of management of the company, etc. so as to enable the prospective investors to assess the risk before making deposits.

(c) It must also include declaration by the applicant that the amount is not being deposited out of funds acquired by him by borrowing or accepting deposits from any other person.

21.13 Issue of Receipts within 8 Weeks

Every company must furnish to the depositor or his agent a receipt specifying the date of deposit, name and address of depositor, amount of deposit, rate of interest payable and the date of maturity of deposit **within 8 weeks.** The receipt must be signed by a duly authorised oficer of the company.

21.14 Penalty

If a company or any other person contravenes any of thses rules for which no punishment is provided in the Act, the company and its every officer in default or such other person shall be punishable with fine upto Rs 5,000 and in case of continuing default, with a further fine upto Rs 500 per day.

21.15 Premature Repayment only after 6 months and Rate to be Reduced by 1%

(a) The deposits may be repaid before the date of maturity, but **only after 6 months** for the date of deposit.

(b) On such premature deposit, the rate of interest payable shall be reduced by 1%.

21.16 Failure to Repay Deposits

(a) If a company fails to repay the matured deposits, CLB may order the company to repay such deposit.

(b) If the company fails to pay matured deposits, **Penal interest is payable @18% (20 % in case of small depositors)** compoundable on an annual basis

22.0 "SMALL DEPOSITORS" [SECTION 58AA]

22.1 Meaning of Small Depositor

(a) A 'small depositor' means a depositor who has deposited in a financial year a sum **not exceeding Rs 20,000** in a company

(b) includes his successors, nominees and legal representatives.

(c) It does not include those depositors who renew their deposits and those depositors whose repayment is not made to death or has been stayed by a competent court.

22.2 Duty of Defaulting Company to Intimate CLB within 60 Days

Where a company fails to repay the deposit or interest thereon to any small depositor, it must give intimation on monthly basis to the Company Law Board within **60 days** of the date of default stating the names and addresses of each small depositor(s) the principal sum of deposits due to them and interest thereon.

22.3 Power of CLB to Make an Order within 30 Days

The Company Law Board on receipt of such intimation shall pass an appropriate order within **30 days** from the date of receipt of intimation from the company after giving the small depositor an oppportunity of being heard.

22.4 Restrictions on the Defaulting Company

1. **No Further Deposit** It must not accept further deposits from small depositors unless it repays all matured small deposits along with interest due thereon,
2. **Disclosure of Default in Future Advertisement & Applications** It must state in all its future advertisement and application inviting deposits the following details:
   — total number of small depositors are
   — the amount due to there in respect of which the default was committed.
3. **Applications** The fact of such waiver must be mentioned in every future advertisement and application from inviting deposits where the interest accrued as small deposits has been waived.
4. The application form inviting deposits must contain a statement that the applicant had been appraised of every past default, waiver of interest etc.
5. If the company subsequent to acceptance of small deposits avails any working capital from any bank, it must be first utilised for repaying the principal and interest due to small depositors before applying the funds for any other purpose.

22.5 Penalty for Default

The penalty for failure to comply the provisions of this section or order of CLT is subject to a fine of Rs 500 per day and imprisonment upto 3 years. Directors are also liable to be proceeded against.

23.0 NON-REFUND OF DEPOSITS TO BE COGNIZABLE. [SECTION 58AAA]

1. Any offence relating to acceptance of deposits under Section 58A or Section 58AA shall an offence cognizable under code of Criminal Procedures 1973.
2. No court shall take cognizance of any offence under this provision except on a compliant made by the Central Government or any officer authorised by it in this behalf.

24.0 PROVISIONS RELATING TO PROSPECTUS TO APPLY TO ADVERTISEMENT [SECTION 58B]

The provisions of this Act relating to a prospectus shall, so far as may be, apply to an advertisement referred to in Section 58A. But having regard to the words "so far as may be" as used in Section 58B, wherever in respect of certain matters specific provisions have been made in Section 58A or the Companies (Acceptance of Deposits) Rules, 1975, the corresponding provisions in the Act relating to prospectus would not apply to this advertisement. *For example*, Section 56(1) requires a prospectus to contain information on matters specified in Schedule II. This will not be applicable on an advertisement inviting deposits because of Rule 4 of the Companies (Acceptance of Deposit) Rules, 1975.

VERY SHORT ANSWER TYPE QUESTIONS

1. What is 'Prospectus'?
2. Where is a company not required to issue a prospectus? What is meant by 'public'?
3. What is meant by 'Invitation to the public'?
4. What is meant by 'Subscription or purchase of shares'?
5. Name the various agencies who approve the Prospectus?
6. Name the agency by whom the prospectus is to get vetted?
7. What is 'Misleading Prospectus'?
8. What is 'Rule of Golden Legacy'?
9. What is 'Statement in lieu of prospectus'?
10. Who is deemed to be an expert?
11. What is the limitation period for bringing an action against director on ground of misstatement in the prospectus?

SHORT ANSWER TYPE QUESTIONS

1. State the significance of prospectus?
2. State the requirement to prospectus?
3. What is meant by 'Deemed prospectus'?
4. 'Every application from is to be accompanied by an is Abridged Prospectus'. Comment?
5. State the provisions relating to expert's comment?
6. State the effect of accepting application form without complying with the requirements of Section 56?
7. Explain the remedies available against the company to a person who subscribe for share on the faith of misleading prospectus.
8. Explain the remedies available against the directors and experts on the faith of misleading prospectus.
9. State the defences available to directors and experts in case of misleading prospectus.

10. Write a short note on the following:
    (a) Rule of Golden Legacy.
    (b) Deemed Prospectus.
    (c) Statement in lieu of Prospectus.
    (d) Misleading Prospectus.
    (e) Application and Allotment of shares in fictitious name.
    (f) Shelf Prospectus
    (g) Abridged Prospectus

LONG ANSWER TYPE QUESTIONS

1. State the matter to be stated in the prospectus?
2. (a) What is 'Misleading Prospectus'?
   (b) Discuss the various remedies available to a person who subscribe for shares on the faith of misleading prospectus?
3. (a) Who is deemed to be an expert in relation to the prospectus of a company?
   (b) What conditions must be satisfied before a report by an expert can be published therein?
   (c) Is there any remedy available to the allottee who has been induced to take shares on the faith of an untrue statement of an expert in the prospectus?
   (d) Are there any defences available to such an expert?
4. Define 'prospectus'. Discuss briefly the contents of 'prospectus'. What guidelines have been issued by SEBI in this regard?
5. Bogo Ltd. issued a prospectus which contained some misleading statements. Mr. Yogi knowing the fact did not subscribe to the issue. But he purchased some shares from open market and claimed compensation from the company on the ground that the prospectus issued for the shares contained misleading statements. Can he succeed? Give reasons.
6. When and in what manner may a company be permitted to furnish an abridged form of prospectus? Under what circumstances such abridged prospectus is not required to be accompanied with the share application form?
7. What are the limits up to which deposits can be accepted by a non-government company?
8. State the consequences when a public company fails to pay matured deposits which it has accepted from the public. Can such a company continue to invite or accept deposits from the public?

CHAPTER

7 Allotment of Shares

1.0 MEANING OF ALLOTMENT

Allotment is the acceptance by the company of the offer to take shares made by an applicant. The term 'Allotment' means the appropriation out of the previously unappropriated capital of the company, of a certain number of shares to a person. That is why, the reissue of forfeited shares is not an allotment since reissue occurs as a result of sale of forfeited shares which had already been allotted and not allotment thereof. It is on allotment that shares come into existence. The amount payable on allotment is called 'Allotment Money'.

2.0 GENERAL PROVISIONS AS TO ALLOTMENT

Since the allotment is the acceptance of an offer to take certain number of shares, the general provisions relating to valid acceptance of an offer must be followed. The general provisions regarding allotment of shares are as follows:

1. **Proper Authority** The allotment must be made by proper authority. It is the duty of the Board of directors to allot the shares. However, the Board may delegate this authority to some other person or persons as per the provisions of the articles of association. Allotment of shares made by an improper authority will make it void.
2. **Reasonable Time** The allotment should be made within a reasonable time. The offer to take shares of the company must be accepted within a reasonable time otherwise the applicants may refuse to take shares because after a reasonable time the offer lapses. What is the 'reasonable time' is a question of fact in each case. [***Ramlgate Victoria Hotel* v. *Montefiare*,** (1866)]
3. **Communication** It must be communicated. The allotment of shares should be communicated to the applicants. Posting of a properly addressed and stamped letter of allotment will be taken as a valid communication. Even if this letter of allotment is delayed or lost in transit, the allottee will be liable, 'G' applied for certain shares in a company. The letter of allotment was despatched to him but it never reached. It was held that 'G' was liable as a shareholder (***Household Fire Insurance Co. Ltd.* v. *Grant***). A mere entry in the name of applicant on the Register of Members is not sufficient for the purpose [***Radhesham* v. *Prabhu Dayal*** A.I.R. 1936, Lah. 16]. The allotment may be communicated to the applicant either in writing or verbally or by contract. [***Gunn's* case** (1867) L.R. 3 Ch. App 40]
4. **Absolute and Unconditional** It must be absolute and unconditional. The allotment of shares must conform to the terms and conditions of the application. If the allotment is not according to the terms and conditions, the applicant may refuse to accept the shares even though allotment has been made to him. If the conditions are not fulfilled, the applicant must reject the shares promptly. His silence or acceptance will debar him from this right. Thus, where the applicant pledged his shares, he lost his right to insist on the condition. [***Hargopal* v. *People's Book of Northern India Ltd.*,** AIR 1935 Lah. 691]

In case of ***Motilal Chunilal* v. *Thakorlal***, (1912) 14 Bom. L.R. 648, an applicant was allotted certain shares in a company on the condition that he would pay for them only when the company paid dividends, it was held that he was bound by allotment even though the company went into liquidation before paying any dividend.

3.0 RESTRICTIONS AS TO THE ALLOTMENT OF SHARES BY PUBLIC COMPANIES UNDER THE COMPANIES ACT

3.1 When no Public Offer is Made [Section 70]

Where a public company does not offer its shares to the public but arranges the capital privately the company cannot proceed with the allotment unless it files with the Registrar of Companies at least 3 days before the first allotment, a statement in lieu of prospectus. If the allotment is made in contravention to this provision, it will be termed as 'irregular allotment' and it shall be voidable at the option of the allottee. In addition to this, every officer of the company, who is a party to such allotment shall be punishable with fine which may extend to Rs 10,000.

3.2 When Public Offer is Made

1. **Registration and Issue of Prospectus** Where a public company offers its shares to the public, a copy of prospectus must be filed with the Registrar for **registration on or before the date of publication of the prospectus** [Section 60(1)]. The prospectus must be **issued** to the public **within 90 days of its registration** with the registrar otherwise it will be deemed to be a prospectus a copy of which has not been delivered to the Registrar. [Section 60(4)]
2. **Time of the Opening of Subscription List** No allotment can be made until the beginning of the 5th day or such later time as may be specified in the prospectus. The 5th day is to be counted from the day when the prospectus was published in a newspaper or was otherwise notified to the public. The beginning of the fifth day is known as 'the time of the opening of the subscription lists'. The object of this provision is to enable the public to go through the contents of the prospectus and to decide whether to apply for shares.
   Vailidity The validity of an allotment shall not be affected by any contravention of the foregoing provisions of this section; but, in the event of any such contravention, the company, and every officer in default, shall be punishable with fine upto Rs 5,000. [Section 72(3)]
   Revocation of Offer An application for shares is not revocable untill the end of the 5th day from the opening of subscription list. [Section 72(5)]
3. **Time of Closing of Subscription Lists** The Companies Act is silent about the time for which the subscription list must be kept open.
   Minimum Time According to Stock Exchange regulation, where the shares are listed on any stock exchange the subscription list must be kept open for at least 3 working days and disclosure to this effect must be made in the prospectus.
   Maximum Time According to the Ministry of Finance, Stock Exchange Division, the subscription list for public issues can be kept open for a maximum period of 21 working days where the issue is not underwritten and for a maximum period of 10 working days where the issue is underwritten.

4. **Minimum Subscription in Case of First Allotment of Shares [Section 69(1)]** No allotment shall be made unless the amount stated in the prospectus as the minimum subscription has been subscribed and the sum payable on application for the stated amount has been received by the company. The minimum subscription refers to the amount which, in the opinion of directors, must be raised by issue of shares in order to provide for the following:
   (i) the purchase price of any property purchased or to be purchased which is to be met out of the proceeds of the issue of shares;
   (ii) any preliminary expenses payable by the company and any commission payable in connection with the issue of shares;
   (iii) the repayment of any money borrowed by the company in respect of any of the above two matters;
   (iv) working capital; and
   (v) any other expenditure stating the nature and purposes thereof and the estimated amount in each case.

   Note: The amount of minimum subscription shall be exclusive of any amount payable otherwise than in money.

   Position as Per SEBI Guidelines In view of the existing SEBI guidelines for the issue of shares/debentures, the aforesaid provision of The Companies Act, 1956 has practically become redundant. As per SEBI Guidelines, the minimum subscription in respect of public and right issues (excluding the offer for sale of securities) is 90% of the issued amount.

5. **Minimum Application Money [Section 69(3)]** It is the amount which is payable on each share alongwith the application for purchase of shares. The amount payable on application on each share must be at least **5% of the nominal amount of the share**.

6. **Application Money to be Deposited in a Scheduled Bank [Section 69(4)]** All the money received from applicants must be deposited in a scheduled bank.
   (a) until the certificate to commence business is received.
   (b) until the minimum subscription has been received where certificate to commence business has already been received.

7. **Refund of Application Money within 130 Days as per the Act** If minimum subscription is not received within 120 days from the date of issue of prospectus, the company must refund the application money **within 130 days without interest and with interest @ 6% p.a.** from the delayed period **beyond 130 days** from date of issue of prospectus. [Section 69(5)]

   Refund of Application Money within 78 Days as per SEBI Guidelines As per SEBI Guidelines, in case of non-receipt by the company of **90% of the issued amount** from public subscription (*plus* accepted devolvement from underwriters or from other sources in case of under subscribed issues), **within 60 days** from the date of closure of the issue, the company must refund the subscription amount in full **within 78 days without interest and with interest @ 15% p.a. for the delayed period beyond 78 days from the date of closure of the issue**.

8. **Compulsory Listing of All Public Issues [Section 73]**

   Application before Issue Every company intending to offer shares or debentures to the public for subscription by the issue of a prospectus must, before such issue, make an application to one or more recognised stock exchanges for permission for the shares or debentures intending to be so offered to be dealt with in the stock exchange or each such stock exchange. [Section 73(1)]

Name of Stock Exchange in Prospectus Where a prospectus states that an application has been made for permission for the shares or debentures offered thereby to be dealt in one or more recognised stock exchanges, such prospectus must state the name of the stock exchange or, as the case may be, each such stock exchange.

Allotment to be Void in Case of No Listing Permission Any allotment made shall be void if the permission has not been granted by the stock exchange or each such stock exchange, as the case may be, before the expiry of 10 weeks from the date of the closing of the subscription lists. However, where an appeal against the decision of any recognised stock exchange refusing permission for the shares or debentures to be dealt in on that stock exchange has been preferred under section 22 of the Securities Contracts (Regulation) Act, 1956 (42 of 1956), such allotment shall not be void until the dismissal of the appeal.

Refund within 8 Days in case of No Listing Permission Where the permission has not been applied or, such permission having been applied for, has not been granted, the company shall repay without interest all moneys received from applicants, and, if any such money is not repaid within 8 days after the company becomes liable to repay it, the company and its every director in default shall, be jointly and severally liable to repay that money with interest at such rate, not less than 4% and not more than 15%, as may prescribed for the delayed period beyond the expiry of 8th day. [Section 73(2)]

Refund within 8 Days in case of Over Subscription Where permission has been granted by the recognised stock exchange and the issue is over subscribed, the company must repay the moneys to the extent of such excess without interest, and if such money is not repaid within 8 days, from the day the company becomes liable to pay it, the company and its every director in default shall, be jointly and severally liable to repay that money with interest at such rate, not less than 4% and not more than 15%, as may be prescribed, for the delayed period beyond the expiry of 8th day. [Section 73(2A)]

Penalty If default is made in complying with the provisions of Sub-section (2A), the company and its every officer in default shall be punishable with fine upto Rs 50,000, and where repayment is not made within 6 months from the expiry of the 8th day, also with imprisonment for a term upto 1 year. [Section 73(2B)]

Application Money to be Deposited in Schedule Bank [Section 73(3)]

All application moneys received must be kept in a separate bank account maintained with a Scheduled Bank until the permission for shares to be dealt with in stock exchange has been granted, or where an appeal has been preferred against the refusal to grant such permission, until the disposal of the appeal, and where the permission has not been applied for as aforesaid or has not been granted, the money standing in such separate account must be repaid within the time and in the manner specified in Sub-section (2); and if default is made in complying with this sub-section, the company, and its every officer in default, shall be punishable with fine upto Rs 50,000. [Section 73(3)]

Restriction on Use of Application Money [Section 73(3A)]

Moneys standing to the credit of the separate bank account shall not be utilised for any purpose other than the following purposes namely:

(a) adjustment against allotment of shares, where the shares have been permitted to be dealt in on the stock exchange or each stock exchange specified in the prospectus; or

(b) repayment of moneys received from applicants in pursuance of the prospectus, where shares have not been permitted to be dealt in on the stock exchange or each stock exchange specified in the prospectus, as the case may be, or, where the company is for any other reason unable to make the allotment of share.

It will be deemed that permission has not been granted, if the application for permission, where made, has not been disposed of within the time specified in Section 73(1). [Section 73(5)]

3.3 Subsequent Allotment of Shares

The provision regarding the subsequent allotment of shares are same as discussed above except the provisions relating to minimum subscription.

4.0 IRREGULARALLOTMENT

4.1 Meaning of Irregular Allotment

An allotment is said to be irregular if it is made in contravention of the provisions of Section 69 or 70. The allotment of shares is irregular in the following, cases:

1. Where an allotment is made without receiving the minimum subscription. [Section 69(1)]
2. Where an allotment is made without receiving at least 5% of the nominal value of shares as application money. [Section 69(3)]
3. Where an allotment is made without depositing the application money in a scheduled bank. [Section 69(4)]
4. Where if the allotment is made without filing with the Registrar the 'Statement is lieu of prospectus' at least 3 days before the first allotment of shares in the case of a public company which does not invite public to subscribe its shares. [Section 70]

4.2 Effects of Irregular Allotment [Section 71]

1. **Allotment voidable [Section 71(1)]**
   An irregular allotment is voidable at the option of the applicant within the specified time given below:

Case	*Time limit within which allotment is voidable*
(a) ***Where the allotment is made before the statutory meeting***	Within 2 months after the holding of statutory meeting and not later
(b) ***Where the allotment is made after the statutory meeting***	Within 2 months after the date of allotment and not later

Notes:

(i) The allottee must inform the company that he avoids the allotment within 2 months.

(ii) It is not necessary that the allottee should commence legal proceedings within the said period provided he has given notice of avoidance within 2 months.

(iii) But Legal proceedings should be reasonably prompt thereafter if they are to be brought. [***Re National Motor Mail Coach Co.***, (1908) 2 Ch. 228]

(iv) If the applicant takes steps for avoiding the allotment within this period, it does not matter that winding up proceeding has intervened during this period. [***Blanche Fonseca* v. *Jupiter Airways Ltd.*,** AIR (1953) Bom. 407]

2. **Suit for Compensation Against the Directors [Section 71(3)]**
If any director of a company knowingly contravenes, or wilfully authorises or permits the contravention of, any of the provisions of Section 69 or Section 70 with respect to allotment, he shall be liable to compensate the company and the allottee respectively for any loss, damages or costs which the company or the allottee may have sustained or incurred thereby.
The proceedings to recover any such loss, damages or costs must be commenced before the expiration of 2 years from the date of the allotment.

Note: As the allotment is only voidable at the option of the shareholder, the shareholder may keep the shares and yet sue the directors who have knowingly contravened either of the two Sections (69 and 70) to compel them to make good the loss to him as a result of the irregular allotment.

3. **Penalty [Section 69(4) and 70(4)]**
   (a) In the event of any contravention of Section 69(4) regarding deposit of money in a scheduled Bank, every promoter, director or other person who is knowingly responsible for such contravention shall be punishable with fine upto Rs 50,000. [Section 69(4)]
   (b) If a company acts in contravention of Section 70(1) or (2), the company and its every director who wilfully authorises or permits the contravention, shall be punishable with fine upto Rs 10,000. [Section 70(4)]

5.0 RETURN OF ALLOTMENT [SECTION 75]

5.1 Meaning of Return of Allotment A report in the prescribed Form No. 2 about the allotment of shares is known as 'Return of Allotment'.

5.2 When is Return of Allotment required A company having a share capital making any allotment of its shares, is required to file the 'Return of Allotment'.

5.3 When is Return of Allotment not Required Return of allotment is not required to be filed in the following 3 cases.

(a) In case of **reissue of shares forfeited** for non-payment of calls since reissue of forfeited shares amounts to resale of shares and not the allotment of shares [Section 75(5)]
(b) In case of **issue of shares to signatories** to the Memorandum of association.
(c) In case of **allotment of debentures.**

5.4 Time Limit for Filing Return of Allotment [Section 75(3)] The company must file the return of allotment within **30 days of the allotment or period extended by the Registrar**. The period for filing return of allotment can be extended by the Registrar on an application made by the company either before or after the expiry of 30 days of allotment.

5.5 Contents of Return of Allotment

The return of allotment must contain the prescribed particulars as under:

1. ***In case shares are allotted in cash*** **[Section 75(1)(a)]**
   (a) the number and nominal amount of the shares allotted;

(b) the names, addresses and occupations of the allottees and the amount, if there be any, paid or due and payable on each shares.

But the company must not show shares as having been allotted for cash, if cash has not been actually received by it.

2. *In case **shares allotted are not bonus shares and allotted as fully or partly paid up otherwise than in cash*** [Section 75(1)(b)]. The company must produce for the inspection and examination of the Registrar the following documents.

(a) a contract in writing constituting the title of the allottee; and

(b) any contract of sale or contract of service or other consideration in respect of which the allotment was made.

These documents must be duly stamped. Also along with these documents the company must file with the Registrar:

(i) copies of the said contracts after verifying them in the prescribed manner, and

(ii) a return stating the number and nominal amount of the shares so allotted, the extent to which they are to be treated as paid-up and the consideration for which they have been allotted.

Under Rule 5 of the Companies (Central Government's) General Rules and Forms, 1956 these copies of contracts must be verified by affidavit of a responsible officer of the company. Where such a contract is not in writing, the company must within 30 days after allotment, file with the Registrar a document embodying the said particulars of the contract. The document must bear the same amount of stamp duty as would have been payable if the contract had been in writing.

3. ***In the case of issue of bonus shares* [Section 75(1)(c)(i)]:**

(a) the number and nominal amount of shares allotted,

(b) the names, addresses and occupations of the allottees, and

(c) resolution authorising the issue of bonus shares.

4. ***In the case of issue of shares at a discount* [Section 75(1)(c)(ii)].** The return must be accompanied:

(i) by a copy of the company's resolution authorising such an issue,

(ii) by copy of the order of Company Law Board which sanction the issue, and

(iii) where the maximum rate of discount exceeds 10 per cent, a copy of the Company Law Board order permitting the issue at a higher percentage.

5.6 Penalty for Default [Section 75(4)]

Case	*Penalty*
(a) ***In case of contravention of the provisions to Section 75(1)(a) regarding showing shares as having been allotted for cash if the cash has not been actually received by it.***	Every officer and every promoter who are guilty of the contravention shall be punishable with fine upto Rs 50,000.
(b) ***In case of contravention of any other provision of Section 75***	Every officer who is in default shall be punishable with fine upto Rs 5,000 for every day during which the default continues.

6.0 UNDERWRITING COMMISSION AND BROKERAGE [SECTION 76]

6.1 Meaning of Underwriting Agreement An underwriting agreement is an agreement between the company and certain party (known as underwriter) under which the latter agrees to take up the whole or part of the shares which may not be subscribed by the public for an agreed consideration (known as underwriting commission). It is in the nature of an assurance against the risk involved in placing the shares before the public.

Note: An underwriting agreement is enforceable against the executors of deceased underwriter. [***Wasner Engineering Co.*** **v.** ***Benan*** (1913) 307 L.R. 191]

6.2 Purpose for which Underwriting Commission may be Paid [Section 76(1)(a) & (b)]

A company may pay a commission to any person in consideration of—

(a) his subscribing or agreeing to subscribe, whether absolutely or conditionally, for any shares in, or debentures of, the company, or

(b) his procuring or agreeing to procure subscriptions, whether absolute or conditionals for any shares in, or debentures of, the company.

6.3 Conditions for Payment

A company may pay if the following conditions are fulfilled, namely:

(i) **Authorised by Articles** The payment of the commission must be authorised by the articles;

(ii) **Maximum Commission** The commission paid or agreed to be paid does not exceed in the case of shares, **5% of the issue price of the shares** or the amount or rate authorised by the articles, whichever is less, and in the case of debentures, **2.5% of issue the price of the debentures** are issued or the amount or rate authorised by the articles, whichever is less;

(iii) **Disclosure in Prospectus** Following must be disclosed in the prospectus:

  (a) The amount or rate per cent of the commission paid or agreed to be paid in the prospectus or in the statement in lieu of prospectus or.

  (b) The number of shares or debentures underwritten by each of the underwriters

  (c) Name and Address of the under writer(s)

(iv) **Filling of Contract with ROC** A copy of the contract for the payment of the commission must be delivered to the Registrar at the time of delivery of the prospectus or the statement in lieu of prospectus for registration.

6.4 Can Commission be Paid to Any Person on Shares or Debentures Which are not Offered to Public for Subscription?

According to Section 76(4A), no commission shall be paid to any person on shares or debentures which are not offered to the public for subscription.

Exception Proviso to Section 76(4A) provides an exception to the above rule. Accordingly, a company may pay commission to the underwriter in respect of shares or debentures already subscribed if the following two conditions are simultaneously fulfilled:

(i) where a person has subscribed or agreed to subscribe for any shares in, or debentures of, the company and before the issue of the prospectus or statement in lieu thereof any other person or persons has or have subscribed for any or all of those shares or debentures, and

(ii) that fact together with the aggregate amount of commission payable under this section in respect of such subscriptions is disclosed in such prospectus or statement.

5.5 Penalty for Default [Section 76(5)]

If default is made in complying with the provisions of this section, the company, and its every officer in default, shall be punishable with fine upto Rs 5,000.

5.6 Brokerage

Meaning Brokerage is the sum paid to a person who carries on the business of a broker for placing the shares/debentures (i.e. for finding the person who will take shares/debentures).

Lawful brokerage Section 76(3) empowers the company to pay lawful brokerage. Lawful brokerage means reasonable brokerage payable to a person carrying on the business of a broker and not to the person who had casually induced others to subscribe. [***Andreae* v. *Zinc Mines of Great Britain Ltd.,*** (1918) 2 K.B. 454]

5.7 Difference between Brokerage and Underwriting Commission

Basis Distinction	*Underwriting Commission*	*Brokerage*
1. ***Purpose of payment***	It is paid for agreeing to take up unsubscribed shares/debentures.	It is paid for procuring persons who will take shares/debentures.
2. ***Personal Liability***	Underwriter is personally liable to take up the unsubscribed shares/debenture as per agreement.	Broker is not personally liable to take up the unsubscribed shares/debentures.
3. ***Authorisation in Articles***	Required	Not Required
4. ***Maximum Rate***	Prescribed under the Act [5% of issue price of share & 2.5% of issue price of debentures]	Not Prescribed under the Act.
5. ***Payee***	Known as underwriters	Known as Broker

VERY SHORT ANSWER TYPE QUESTIONS

1. (a) What is meant by 'Allotment'?
   (b) Is the reissue of forfeited shares an allotment?
2. What is the maximum and minimum time of opening of subscription list?
3. When can application for shares be revoked?
4. What is the minimum and maximum time of closing of subscription list?
5. When is application money required to be refunded (a) without interest (b) with interest? Answer this question as per the Companies Act and as per the SEBI Guidelines.
6. When is application money required to be refunded (a) without interest (b) with interest in the following cases:
   (a) where the listing permission is not granted
   (b) where shares are oversubscribed

7. When will it be deemed that the listing permission has not been granted?
8. Is the condition of minimum subscription applicable to subsequent allotment of shares?
9. Is there any difference between the restriction applicable to first allotment of shares and subsequent allotment of shares?
10. What is "Irregular Allotment"?
11. (a) What is return of allotment?
    (b) What is the time limit to file return of allotment?
    (c) Is it required in case of re-issue of forfeited shares?
    (d) Is it required for allotment of debentures?
    (e) Is it required for allotment of shares to signatories to Memorandum?
12. (a) What is meant by 'Underwriting Agreement'?
    (b) What is meant by 'Underwriting Commission'?
    (c) What is meant by 'Brokerage'?

SHORT ANSWER TYPE QUESTIONS

1. Write short note on the following:
   (a) Minimum Subscription
   (b) Irregular Allotment
   (c) Return of Allotment
2. When is return of allotment not required?
3. Distinguish between the following:
   (a) Brokerage and underwriting commission
   (b) Void Allotment and Irregular Allotment
4. Comment on the following:
   "Commission can be paid on shares or debentures which are not offered to public for subscription."

LONG ANSWER TYPE QUESTIONS

1. Discuss the general provisions and statutory provisions on to the allotment of shares by the public company when public offer is made.
2. (a) What is an allotment of shares?
   (b) Explain the situation when allotment of shares is void, voidable and valid.
3. (a) What is 'Irregular Allotment'?
   (b) What is the effect of irregular allotment?
   (c) What are the rights of an allottee in such a situation?
4. (a) Explain the purpose for which and conditions under which a company may pay underwriter commission.
   (b) Can a company pay brokerage?

CHAPTER 8

Shares and Share Capital

1.0 MEANING OF SHARE [Sec. 2(46)]

(a) A 'Share' is smallest unit into which the capital of the company is divided.

(b) Section 2(46) of the Companies Act, 1956 defines a share as "*a share in the share capital of a company, and includes stock except where a distinction between stock and share is expressed or implied*".

For example, where a company has a share capital of Rs 1,00,000 divided into 10,000 units of Rs 10 each, then each unit of Rs 10 is called a share of Rs 10 each and a person who has taken 10 shares of that company is said to have share in the share capital of the company to the extent of Rs 100.

(c) A share represents such proportion of the interest of the shareholders as the amount paid up thereon bears to the total capital payable to the company.

(d) A share may be partly paid up or fully paid up.

(e) A share is a measure of the interest in the company's assets to which a person holding a share is entitled.

2.0 NATURE OF SHARE

(a) A share is not a sum of money but is an interest measured by a sum of money and made up of various rights contained in the contract [***Borland Trustees* v. *Steel Bros. & Co Ltd.***].

(b) A shareholder has not only contractual rights against the company but also certain other rights which accrue to him according to the provisions of the Companies Act.

(c) The shareholders even in a group are not, in the eyes of law, part owners of the undertaking. The undertaking is somewhat different from the totality of the shareholders.

3.0 NATURE OF SHARES OR DEBENTURES [SECTION 82]

The shares [or debentures] or other interest of any member in a company are the movable properties, transferable in the manner provided by the articles of the company.

4.0 NUMBERING OF SHARES [SECTION 83]

Each share (Except the shares held with a depository) in a company having a share capital must be distinguished by its appropriate number.

5.0 KINDS OF SHARE CAPITAL [SECTION 86]

The share capital of a company limited by shares shall be of two kinds only namely:

(a) Equity share capital—
   (i) with voting rights, or
   (ii) with differential rights as to dividend, voting, or otherwise in accordance with such rules and subject to such conditions as may be prescribed.

(b) Preference Share Capital.

5.1 Eligibility Conditions for Issue of Equity Shares with Differential Voting Rights

(a) ***Distributable profits*** The company must have distributable profits for 3 financial years preceding the relevant financial year.

(b) ***No default in filing requirements*** The company must not have defaulted in filing of annual accounts and annual returns for 3 financial years preceding the relevant financial year.

(c) ***No failure in payment of debts etc.*** The company must not have defaulted in—
   (i) repayment of deposits or interest thereon; *or*
   (ii) redemption of debentures (i.e., non-payment of interest on debentures does not disqualify a company from issuing shares with differential voting rights); or
   (iii) payment of dividend (i.e., non-declaration and consequent non-payment of dividend does not disqualify a company from issuing shares with differential voting rights).

(d) ***No conviction*** The company is not convicted for any offence under—
   (i) Securities and Exchange Board of Indian, 1992 (SEBI Act)
   (ii) Securities (Contracts) Regulation Act, 1956 (SCRA)
   (iii) Foreign Exchange Management Act, 1999 (FEMA)

5.2 Approval for Issue

(a) ***Articles' Authorisation*** Specific power in articles is required.

(b) ***Ordinary Resolution*** Ordinary Resolution must be passed by postal ballot if the company is listed company.

(c) ***Requirements of Notice*** The notice shall be accompanied by an explanatory statement. Contents of the explanatory statement shall be as follows:
   (i) The rate of voting right such shares shall carry.
   (ii) The scale or proportion to which the voting rights of such shares will vary.

5.3 Conditions

(a) ***Conversion not permissible*** Conversion of equity share capital with differential voting rights into equity share capital without differential voting rights or vice versa is not permissible.

(b) ***Maximum limit*** The shares with differential voting rights shall not exceed 25% of the total share capital issued.

(c) ***Rights of members*** The members holding shares with differential voting rights shall be entitled to bonus shares and right shares of the same class.

(d) ***Other rights*** The members holding shares with differential voting rights shall enjoy all other rights to which any other member is entitled to.

(e) ***Procedural requirements*** The register of member shall contain the particulars of differential rights to which the holder of such shares is entitled to.

6.0 MEANING OF AN EQUITY SHARE

(a) An equity share is a share which is not a preference share. In other words, it is a share which does not carry two preferential rights (viz., right to receive dividend and right to receive repayment of capital) attached to a preference share.

(b) The capital raised through equity shares is called equity share capital.

(c) The persons who contribute money through equity shares are called equity shareholders.

(d) ***Main features*** The main features of these shares as discussed below:

1. Payment of equity dividend is made after the payment of preference dividend.
2. Repayment of equity share capital is made after the repayment of preference share capital in the event of winding up of the company.
3. The equity shareholders generally enjoy voting rights. They have right to elect directors and to participate in the management.

Note: After the commencement of The Companies (Amendment) Act, 2000, the company can issue equity shares without voting rights.

4. The rate of equity dividend is not fixed and may vary from year to year depending upon the profits available and the decision of directors (at board meeting) and members (at annual general meeting).
5. The equity share capital is generally not redeemable during the life of the company unless the company decides to buy back its shares.
6. Equity shareholders enjoy various rights as members, which include, *inter alia*, the following rights:
   (a) Right of pre-emption in the matter of fresh issue of capital [Section 81].
   (b) Right to apply to the Court to have any variation of their rights set aside [Section 107].
   (c) Right to receive a copy of the statutory report [Section 165].
   (d) Right to apply to Central Government to call an annual general meeting when the company fails to call such a meeting [Section 167].
   (e) Right to apply to CLB for calling an extraordinary general meeting of the company [Section 186].
   (f) Right to receive copies of annual accounts along with auditor's report [Sections 210 and 219].

7.0 MEANING OF A PREFERENCE SHARE

According to Section 85 of the Companies Act, 1956, a preference share is one which carries the following two rights:

1. **a right to receive dividend** at a stipulated rate or of a fixed amount before any dividend is paid on equity shares; and
2. **a right to receive repayment of capital** on winding up of the company, before the capital of equity shareholders is returned.

8.0 KINDS OF PREFERENCE SHARES

In addition to the aforesaid two preferential rights, a preference share may carry some other rights. On the basis of additional rights, preference shares can be classified into seven types as under:

(a) **Cumulative Preference Share** is the share on which arrears of dividend accumulate. Unless stated otherwise in Articles or Terms of Issue, a preference share is always **deemed to be a cumulative share**. They carry the right to cumulative dividends if the company fails to pay the dividend in a particular year. The accumulated arrears of dividends shall be paid, if any dividend is declared in subsequent years, before any dividend is paid to the equity shareholders. If the company goes into liquidation, no arrears of dividends are payable unless either the Articles contain an express provision to this effect or such dividends have been declared. Of course the arrears of undeclared dividends shall be payable, even if the Articles are silent, out of any surplus left, after returning in full the preference and equity share capital.

(b) **Non-cumulative Preference Share** is the share on which, arrears of dividends do not accumulate as per the express provision in the Articles of Association. If no dividend is paid in any particular year, it lapses.

(c) **Participating Preference Share** is that share which, in addition to two basic preferential rights, also carries one or more of the following rights as per the articles of association:
   (i) a right to participate in the surplus profits left after paying dividend to equity shareholders; and
   (ii) a right to participate in the surplus assets left after the repayment of capital to equity shareholders on the winding up of the company.

Note: The right to participate in the surplus profits does not automatically entitle the preference shareholders to participate in the surplus assets on the winding up of the company. **[Re. *Isle of Thanet Electric Supply Co.,*** (1949) 2 All. E.R. 1060]

(d) **Non-participating Preference Share** is the share which is not a participating share. Unless stated otherwise, a preference share is always deemed to be a non-participating preference share.

(e) **Convertible Preference Share** is the share which confers on its holder a right of conversion into equity share.

(f) **Non-convertible Preference Share** is the share which does not confer on its holder a right of conversion into equity share. Unless stated otherwise, a preference share is always deemed to be a non-convertible share.

(g) **Redeemable Preference Share** is the share which is redeemable in accordance with the provisions of Section 80 and 80A of the Companies Act, 1956. Paying back of capital is called the redemption. After the commencement of the Companies (Amendment) Act, 1996, no company limited by shares shall issue any preference share which is redeemable after the expiry of a period of 20 years from the date of its issue.

(h) **Irredeemable Preference Share** is the share which is not redeemable during the life time of the company. After the commencement of the Companies (Amendment) Act, 1988, no company limited by shares can issue any preference share which is irredeemable.

(i) **Cumulative Convertible Preference Shares (CCP)** These shares were introduced in 1985. The objects of the issue of such shares should be for setting up new projects, expansion or diversification of existing projects, capital expenditure for modernisation and working capital requirements. The amount of issue of CCP shares will be to the extent the company would be offering equity shares to the public for subscription. These shares are deemed to be equity issue for the purpose of calculating debt-equity ratio. The entire issue would be convertible into equity shares between the end of 3 years and 5 years. The rate of dividend payable on CCP would be 100 per cent. The face value of these shares will ordinarily be Rs 100 each, and the holders are entitled to receive arrears of dividend, if any, even after conversion.

Important Note: Unless stated otherwise, a preference share is always deemed to be:
(a) a cumulative share
(b) a non-participating share
(c) a non-convertible share

9.0 DISTINCTION BETWEEN AN EQUITY SHARE AND A PREFERENCE SHARE

An equity share and a preference share can be distinguished as follows:

Basis of Distinction	*An Equity Share*	*A Preference Share*
1. ***Preferential right as to the payment of dividend***	Payment of equity dividend is made **after** the payment of dividend.	Payment of preference dividend is made **before** the payment of equity dividend.
2. ***Preferential right as to the repayment of capital***	Repayment of equity share capital is made **after** the repayment of preference share capital.	Repayment of preference share capital is made **before** the repayment of equity share capital.
3. ***Fluctuations in the rate of dividend***	The rate of equity dividend may **vary** from year to year depending upon the decision of directors and members.	The rate of preference dividend is **fixed.**
4. ***Arrears of dividend***	In case of an equity share, arrears of dividend **cannot accumulate** in any case.	In case of preference shares, arrears of dividend **may accumulate.**
5. ***Convertibility***	It **cannot** be convertible.	It **may be** convertible.
6. ***Redeemability***	It is **not redeemable** during the lifetime of the company unless the company decides to buy-back its shares.	It is **redeemable** during the lifetime of the company.
7. **Premium on redemption**	It **cannot carry a right** to receive premium on redemption.	It **may carry a right** to receive premium on redemption.
8. **Voting rights**	Equity shareholders generally **enjoy** voting rights.	Preference share holders **do not have** any voting rights except at their class meetings.

10.0 MEANING OF DEFERRED SHARES

Deferred shares are also known as 'founders' share' or 'Management Shares' because these shares are issued to the promoters or founders of the company. The main features of these shares are as follow:

(a) Last to Receive Dividend These shares carry the right as to the payment of dividend only after the payment of dividend on all other kinds of shares.

(b) Last to Receive Repayment of Capital Similarly in case of winding up these shares carry the right as to the repayment of capital only after the payment of capital of all other kinds of shares issued.

(c) **Disproportionate Voting Rights** These shares usually carry disproportionate voting rights so that the management may be controlled by small investment and it is for this reason that they are also known as 'Management Shares'.

No public company or private company which is subsidiary of a public company can issue deferred shares [Sections 86 and 88]. However, an independent private company is still entiltled to issue deferred shares [Section 92(2)]. Such shares are not all common now-a-days.

11.0 STOCK

11.1 Meaning of Stock

"Stock" is an aggregate of fully paid shares which have been legally consolidated. The consolidated amount is divisible into fractions of any amount, regardless of the nominal value of the shares that have been consolidated. It thus represents a part of the fully paid capital of the company.

11.2 Conditions for Conversion of Share into Stock [Sec. 94(1)(c)]

(a) A company must be limited by shares.
(b) Articles must authorise the conversion of share into stock.
(c) Ordinary resolution must be passed in a general meeting,
(d) Shares must be fully paid up.
(e) The notice of conversion must be given to the Registrar within 30 days of the conversion

Note: All the provisions which are applicable to shares only, shall cease to apply as to so much of share capital as is converted into stock. [Sec. 96]

11.3 Advantage of Stock

The main advantage claimed for stock is that it is transferable in any denomination which is not merely limited to the nominal value of the shares converted into a stock. However, this advantage may be limited by making such regulation in the Articles as contained in the proviso to Regulation 37 of Table A. Proviso to Regulation 37 runs as under: "Provided the Board may from time to time fix the minimum amount of stock transferable so however that such minimum shall not exceed the nominal amount of the shares for which the stock arose."

11.4 Distinction between Stock and Share

The difference between a share and stock may be noted as follows:

Basis of Distinction	*Share*	*Stock*
1. **Meaning**	Share represents the smallest unit into which the capital of the company is divided.	Stock represents aggregate of fully paid up shares of a member merged into one fund.
2. *Fully paid or partly paid*	Shares may be fully paid up or partly paid up.	Stock must be fully paid up.

(Conted.)

(Conted.)

Basis of Distinction	*Share*	*Stock*
3. *Transfer in fraction*	Shares transferable only in its entirety.	Stock is transferable in fraction also.
4. *Direct Issue*	Shares can be directly issued.	Stock cannot be issued directly. Stock comes into existence as a result of con version of fully paid up shares.
5. *Serial No.*	Shares are serially numbered.	Stock is not serially numbered.
6. *Article's Authorisation*	Not Required	Required

12.0 SHARE CAPITAL

12.1 Meaning of Share Capital

Share Capital means the capital raised by the issue of shares. The amounts invested by the shareholders towards the face value of shares are collectively known as 'Share Capital' which is quite distinct from the capital put in by individual shareholders.

12.2 Categories of Share Capital

The share capital is divided under the following three heads:

(a) **Authorised Capital** Authorised Capital refers to that amount which is stated in the 'Capital Clause' of the Memorandum of Association as the share capital of the company. This is the maximum limit of the company which it is authorised to raise and beyond which the company cannot raise unless the capital clause in the Memorandum is altered in accordance with the provisions of Section 94 of the Companies Act, 1956.

(b) **Issued Capital** Issued Capital refers to the nominal value of that part of authorised capital, which has been (i) subscribed for the signatories to the Memorandum of Association, (ii) allotted for cash or for consideration other than cash and (iii) allotted as Bonus shares.

(c) **Subscribed Capital** Subscribed Capital refers to the paid-up value of the issued capital.

Other terms used under the Companies Act, 1956 are:

(d) **Unissued Capital** Unissued Capital refers to that portion of the authorised capital which has not yet been issued.

(e) **Uncalled Capital** Uncalled capital refers to that portion of the issued capital which has not yet been called up by the company.

(f) **Reserve Capital** It refers to that portion of uncalled share capital which shall not be capable of being called up except in the event and for the purposes of the company being wound up (Section 99). A limited company may, by a special resolution, determine a portion of its uncalled capital as reserve capital. Reserve capital should not be confused with capital reserve.

Notes:

(i) Reserve Capital cannot be dealt with in any manner even under a power in its Memorandum of Association.

(ii) A company cannot borrow on the security of its reserve capital.

(iii) Reserve capital cannot be turned into uncalled capital without the leave of the court. It is available only for the creditors on the winding up of the company. The company can neither charge it nor cancel it in a reduction of capital. [***Re Midland Rly. Carriage Co.*** (1904) W.N. 175]

(iv) Reserve Capital is not required to be disclosed in the Balance Sheet.

12.3 Distinction Between Authorised Capital And Issued Capital

Authorised Capital and Issued Capital can be distinguished as follows:

Basis of distinction	***Authorised capital***	***Issued capital***
1. ***Meaning***	It refers to that amount which is stated in the Memorandum of Association as the share capital of the company.	It refers to the nominal value of that part of authorised capital which has been (i) subscribed for by the signatories to the Memorandum of Association, (ii) allotted for cash or consideration other than cash, (iii) allotted as Bonus issue
2. ***Determination***	Its amount is determined after considering **present and future requirements**.	Its amount is determined after considering the **present requirements**.
3. ***Disclosure in Memorandum of Association***	Its amount is **required** to be disclosed in the Memorandum of Association.	Its amount is **not required** to be disclosed in the Memorandum of Association.
4. ***Is it Basis of Stamp Duty***	Stamp Duty is **payable** on the basis of authorised capital.	**No** stamp duty is payable.
5. ***Is it Basis of Company registration fees***	Company registration fee is payable on the **basis** of authorised capital.	Issued capital is **not the basis** for registration fees.
6. ***Does the change amount to an Alteration of Memorandum***	Any change in the amount of authorised capital **amounts** to an alteration of the Memorandum of Association.	Any change in the amount of issued capital **does not amount** to an alteration of the Memorandum of Association.
7. ***Whether one can exceed other***	It **can exceed** issued capital.	It **cannot exceed** authorised capital.

Illustration 1

X Ltd. was formed with a capital of Rs 5,00,000 divided into shares of Rs 10 each. Out of these, 2,000 shares were issued to the vendors as fully paid as purchase consideration for a building acquired, 1,000 shares were issued to signatories to the Memorandum of Association as fully paid. The directors offered 6,500 shares to the public and called up Rs 6 per share and received the entire called up amount on shares allotted. Calculate Issued capital and subscribed capital in each of the following two cases:

Case (a) If the public applied for 7,000 shares.

Case (b) If the public applied for 6,000 shares.

Solution:

Case (a): Calculation of Issued Capital

	Rs
2,000 shares of Rs 10 each allotted to vendors	20,000
1,000 shares of Rs 10 each allotted to signatories to the Memorandum of Association	10,000
6,500 shares of Rs 10 each allotted to public	65,000
	95,000

Case (b): Calculation of Issued Capital

	Rs
2,000 shares of Rs 10 each allotted to vendors	20,000
1,000 shares of Rs 10 each allotted to signatories to the Memorandum of Association	10,000
6,000 shares of Rs 10 each allotted to public	60,000
	90,000

Note: The face value of shares actually allotted is considered and not the face value of shares offered.

Illustration 2

Calculate (a) Authorised Capital (b) Issued Capital (c) Unissued Capital (d) Subscribed Capital, (e) Called-up Capital, (f) Uncalled Capital (g) Paid-up Capital (h) Calls-in-arrears in each of the following alternative cases:

Case (i) X Ltd. was formed with a capital of Rs 10,00,000 divided into shares of Rs 10 each. *X* offered the entire shares and *called up fully* on application. The subscribers paid Rs 20,00,000.

Case (ii) X Ltd. was formed with a capital of Rs 10,00,000 divided into shares of Rs 10 each. It offered 90% shares and *called up fully* on application. The subscribers paid Rs 20,00,000.

Case (iii) X Ltd. was formed with a capital of Rs 10,00,000 divided into shares of Rs 10 each. It offered 90% shares and *called up fully* on application. The subscribers paid Rs 8,50,000.

Case (iv) X Ltd. was formed with a capital of Rs 10,00,000 divided into shares of Rs 10 each. It offered 90% shares and *called up* 60% on application. The subscribers paid Rs 5,10,000.

Case (v) X Ltd. was formed with a capital of Rs 10,00,000 divided into shares of Rs 10 each. It offered 90% shares called up 40% on application and 20% on allotment. The subscribers paid Rs 3,40,000 on application and Rs 1,69,000 on allotment.

Solution:

Calculation of Various Types of Capital

Type of Capital	*Case (i)*	*Case (ii)*	*Case (iii)*	*Case (iv)*	*Case (v)*
A. Authorised Capital	10,00,000	10,00,000	10,00,000	10,00,000	10,00,000
B. Issued Capital	10,00,000	9,00,000	8,50,000	8,50,000	8,50,000
C. Unissued Capital [A – B]	Nil	1,00,000	1,50,000	1,50,000	1,50,000
D. Subscribed Capital	10,00,000	9,00,000	8,50,000	5,10,000	5,09,000
E. Called-up Capital	10,00,000	9,00,000	8,50,000	5,10,000	5,10,000
F. Uncalled Capital	Nil	Nil	Nil	3,40,000	3,40,000
G. Paid-up Capital	10,00,000	9,00,000	8,50,000	5,10,000	5,09,000
H. Calls-in-arrears	Nil	Nil	Nil	Nil	1,000

12.4 Distinction Between Reserve Capital and Capital Reserve

Reserve Capital should not be confused with Capital Reserve which is created out of profits. Reserve Capital and Capital Reserve can be distinguished as folllows:

Basis of Distinction	***Reserve capital***	***Capital reserve***
1. ***Meaning***	It refers to that portion of uncalled share capital which shall not be capable of being called up except in the event and for the purpose of the company being wound up. [Section 99]	It refers to those amounts which are not regarded as free for distribution by way of dividend through Profit and Loss Account.
2. ***Creation — Optional mandatory***	It is ***not mandatory*** to create Reserve Capital.	It is ***mandatory*** to create Capital Reserve in case of profit on forfeited shares.
3. ***Disclosure in Balance Sheet***	It is ***not required*** to be disclosed in the company's Balance Sheet.	It is ***required*** to be disclosed as the 1st item under the head 'Reserves and Surplus' on the liabilities side of the Balance Sheet.
4. ***Time when it can be used***	It can be used only at the time of ***winding up***.	It can be used during the ***life*** of the company.
5. ***Realised vs. Unrealised***	It refers to the amount which has *neither been called* up ***nor*** *been* ***received***.	It (excluding items like revaluation profit) refers to that amount which has already been ***realised***.
6. ***Can it be used to write off of capital losses***	It ***cannot*** be used to write off capital losses.	It ***can*** be used to write off capital losses.
7. ***Can it be used to declare source of share bonus***	It ***cannot*** be used to declare a share bonus.	It (excluding items like revaluation profit) ***can*** be used to declare a share bonus.

13.0 ISSUE OF SHARES AT A PREMIUM [SECTION 78]

13.1 Meaning of Issue of Shares at a Premium

Shares are said to be issued at a premium when they are issued at a price higher than the face value. The excess of issue price over the face value is called as the amount of 'Securities Premium' e.g. if a share of Rs 10 is issued at Rs 15, it is said that the share has been issued at a premium of Rs 5.

13.2 Implied Power to Issue Shares at a Premium

A company may issue shares at a premium even though there is no express authority in its Articles since the company has an implied power to issue shares at a premium.

13.3 Transfer of Premium to Securities Premium Account

Where a company issues shares at a premium, whether for cash or otherwise, a sum equal to the aggregate amount or value of the premiums on those shares must be transfered to an account, to be called the Securities Premium Account. The word 'amount' refers to cash premium and the word 'value' refers to a premium other than cash. Securities issued for consideration other than cash will be treated as having been issued at a premium if the value of the assets in consideration of which they are issued is more than the nominal value of the securities.

13.4 Purposes for which Securities Premium can be utilized

(a) Though there are no restrictions in the Companies Act, 1956 on the issue of shares at a premium but there are restrictions on the application of Securities Premium. According to Section 78 of the Companies Act, 1956, the Securities Premium may be applied only for the following purposes:
   (i) To issue fully paid bonus shares to the members;
   (ii) To write off preliminary expenses of the company;
   (iii) To write off the expenses of or the commission paid or discount allowed on any issue of shares or debentures of the company.
   (iv) To provide for the premium payable on the redemption of any redeemable preference shares or of any debentures of the company;

(b) According to Sec 77A, a company may buy back its own shares or other specified securities out of Securities Premium Account.

(c) The use of Securities Premium Account for purposes other than those mentioned above requires the compliance of the provisions of the Act relating to reduction of share capital.

Notes:

(i) The amount of securities premium may be demanded alongwith the application money/allotment money/call money.

(ii) The amount of securities premium may be demanded either in lumpsum or in instalments e.g. partly with application money and balance with allotment money.

(iii) Even when the shares are issued at a premium for consideration other than cash, a sum equal to the amount of premium must be transferred to the 'Securities Premium Account'. [***Head Henry & Co. Ltd.* v. *Ropher,*** (1951) 2 All. E.R. 994]

(iv) There is no prohibition in the Act against issue of securities at different premiums. [***CIT.* v. *Standard Vacuum Oil Company,*** AIR (1966) SC 1963]

14.0 ISSUE OF SHARES AT A DISCOUNT [SECTION 79]

14.1 Meaning of Issue of Shares at a Discount

Shares are said to be issued at a discount when they are issued at a price lower than the face value. The excess of the face value over the issue price is called as the amount of discount e.g. if a share of Rs 10 is issued at Rs 9, it is said that the share has been issued at a discount of Re 1.

14.2 Six Conditions for Issue of Shares at Discount [Section 79(2)]

According to Section 79 of the Companies Act 1956, a company may issue the shares at a discount only if the following conditions are fulfilled:

(i) **Class** The shares must belong to a **class** of shares **already issued**;

(ii) **Ordinary Resolution** The issue must be authorised by an **ordinary resolution** of the company;

(iii) **Sanction** The **sanction of the *Central Government** must be obtained;

(iv) **Maximum Rate of Discount** The resolution must **specify the maximum rate of discount** at which the shares are to be issued. No resolution shall be sanctioned by the *Central Government if the maximum rate of discount specified in the resolution exceeds 10% unless it is of opinion that a higher percentage of discount may be allowed in the special circumstances of the case;

(v) **Completion of 1 year** **At least 1 year** must have elapsed since the date on which the company was entitled to commence business;

(vi) **Time Limit of Issue** The issue must be made **within 2 months** from the date of receiving the sanction of the *Central Government or within such extended time as the *Central Government may allow.

14.3 Disclosure Requirements [Section 79(4)]

Every prospectus relating to the issue of the shares shall contain particulars of the discount allowed on the issue of the shares or of so much of that discount as has not been written off at the date of the issue of the prospectus.

14.4 Consequences of Improper Issues of Shares at a Discount

1. **Penalty for Default [Section 79(4)]** In case of default, the company, and its every officer in default, shall be punishable with fine upto Rs 500.
2. **Directors Liabilities** The directors render themselves liable to compensate the company to the extent of the amount of discount. [***Hirsche* v. *Sims*,** [1894] A.C. 654].
3. **Members Liability** Even the acceptor of shares, in such a case has to pay back to the company the amount of discount if he holds the shares [***Re. Pitkin (James)*** *& Co.*, [1916] 95 L.J. Ch. 318]. This he would have to do if the conditions of Section 79 are not satisfied, despite the fact that he did not know the legal effect of his contract to take shares at a discount or that the memorandum or articles give the directors the power to issue shares at a discount [***Welden* v. *Saffery***, [1897] A.C. 229; Re ***Pitkin Supra***]. But the allottee may avoid liability to take the shares if he applies on discovery of illegality of the discount allowed without delay, before commencement of the winding up of the company, to have his name removed as a shareholder provided he has not otherwise agreed to keep the shares [Re ***Midland Electric Co.***, [1889] 60 L.T. [1892] Bom. 7].

* After the Companies (Amendment) Act, 2002

15.0 ISSUE OF SWEAT EQUITY [SECTION 79A]

15.1 Meaning of Issue of Sweat Equity

Sweat equity shares means equity shares issued by the company to employees or directors at a discount or for consideration other than cash for providing know-how or making available right in the nature of intellectual property rights or value additions, by whatever name called. (Explanation II to Section 79A)

15.2 Conditions for Issue of Sweat Equity

According to Section 79A(1), a company may issue sweat equity shares if the following conditions are fulfilled, namely:

(a) **Class** the shares must belong to a **class** of shares **already issued**;

(b) **Special Resolution** the issue must be authorised by a **special resolution** passed by the company in the general meeting;

(c) **Contents of Resolution** the resolution must **specify** the number of shares, current market price, consideration, if any, and the class or classes of directors or employees to whom such equity shares are to be issued;

(d) **Completion of 1 year** **At least 1 year** must have elapsed since the date on which the company was entitled to commence business;

(e) **As per SEBI Guidelines** the sweat equity shares of a company whose equity shares are listed on a recognised stock exchange must be issued in accordance with the regulations made by the Securities and Exchange Board of India in this behalf:

Provided that in the case of a company whose equity shares are not listed on any recognised stock exchange, the sweat equity shares are issued in accordance with the guidelines as may be prescribed.

15.3 Meaning of Company for the Purpose of Section 79A

The expression "a company means the company incorporated, formed and registered under this Act and includes its subsidiary company incorporated in a country outside India".

15.4 Applicability of Other Provisions

All the limitations, reiterations and provisions relating to equity shares shall be applicable to such sweat equity shares.

15.5 Effect of Sec. 79A

Sec. 79A applies irrespective of anything contained in Sec. 79.

16.0 CALLS ON SHARES

16.1 Meaning of Call

A call may be defined as a demand upon the shareholders to pay the whole or part of the balance remaining unpaid on their shares.

Notes:

(i) Only the registered shareholder can be made liable in respect of calls and it makes no difference whether he is a benamidar or the beneficial owner of the shares or a mere trustee. [***Murshidabad Loan Office*** v. ***Satish Chandra*** AIR, (1943) Cal. 440]

(ii) Reserve capital can be called up only in the event and for the purposes of winding up of company.

16.2 Who Can Make a Call

The following persons can make a call:

Case	*Who can make a call?*
(a) ***Before the commencement of winding up of the company***	The Board of Directors
(b) ***After the commencement of winding up of the company***	— The Court (in case of compulsory winding up by the Court ups 433) — The liquidator (in other cases of winding up)

16.3 Liability of Members in respect of a Call

All money payable by any member to the company under the Memorandum or Articles shall be a debt due from him to the company [Section 36(2)]. But the liability to pay will arise when a valid call has been made. [***Pabha Dhanabhanders Co.*** v. ***Fayezuddin***, AIR 1932 Cal. 714]

16.4 Requisites of a Valid Call

The requisites of a valid call are as follows:

1. **In accordance with the provisions of the Articles of the Company** The call must be made strictly in accordance with the provisions of the Articles. If the Articles are silent, then Regulations 13–18 of Table 'A' shall be applicable. Table 'A' provides the following regulations:

   (i) The amount of call must not exceed 25% of the nominal value of the shares;

   (ii) **At least 1 month** must have elapsed since the date which was fixed for the payment of the last preceding call.

   (iii) **At least 14 days' notice** specifying the time, place of payment and amount payable must be given to each members in the manner specified u/s 53.

   (iv) A call may be revoked as postponed at the discretion of the Board.

   (v) The joint holders of a share shall be jointly and severally liable to pay all calls in respect thereof.

Note: Any irregularity (whether material or not) in the notice of call shall invalidate the notice.

2. **Resolution of the Board of Directors** A call must be made under a resolution of the Board of Directors passed at a duly constituted meeting of the Board and not under the resolution by circulation. This **power cannot be delegated** to a director or to a committee of directors or to any other officer of the company.

   Contents of Resolution The resolution must state:

(a) time or times allowed for its payment;
(b) place of payment;
(c) the amount of the call per share.

Note: Where the directors passed a resolution fixing the amount of a call but omitted to fix the date of payment, this call was held to be invalid. [***E&W Insurance Co. Ltd.* v. *Mrs. Kamla Mehta*** AIR, (1966) Bom. 537]

2. **On Uniform Basis [Section 91]** The call must be made on a uniform basis on all shares falling under the same class. Shares of the same nominal value on which different amounts have been paid up shall not be deemed to fall under the same class. [Section 91].

   This means that if a call is made on some shareholders and not others, the call is invalid. In ***Galloway* v. *Halley Concerts Society***, (1915) 2 Ch. 233, a shareholder paid the first two calls after a great delay and neglected to pay the third call. The directors got annoyed and called upon him to pay the whole amount on his shares without making a similar call on other shareholders. The court held that the call was invalid as it did not require all the members to pay the full amount due on their shares.

4. **Bona Fide and for the Benefit of the Company** The power to make calls is a power in the nature of a trust and it must be exercised for the general benefit of the company. The amount uncalled should be called only when it is necessary for the promotion of the objects of the company.

However, if the call is made by the directors to serve their personal ends and not for the benefit of the company, shareholders can prevent its enforcement by an injunction. [***Lambus. Sambas Rubber Etc. Co.***, (1908) 1 Ch. 845]

A shareholder complaining against the director must establish *mala fide* in such a case. The court will not interfere with the discretion of the directors in making a call in the absence of proof of *mala fide*. [***Odessa Tramways Co.* v. *Mendel***, (1878) 8 Ch. D 235]

17.0 CALLS-IN-ARREARS

17.1 Meaning of Calls-in-arrears

Calls-in-arrears refer to the amount called up by the company which has not yet been paid by the shareholders till the last day fixed for the payment thereof. For example, if a company has called up a final call of Rs 2 on a share of Rs 10 each and a shareholder has not paid the final call on 100 shares held by him, then Rs 200 are said to be calls-in-arrears.

17.2 Rate of Interest on Calls-in-arrears

(a) The interest on calls-in-arrears is recoverable according to the provision in this regard contained in the Articles of the company.
(b) If the Articles are silent, Regulation 16 of Table 'A' shall be applicable which prescribes that if a sum called in respect of a share is not paid before or on the day appointed for payment thereof, the person from whom the sum is due shall pay interest thereon from the day appointed for payment thereof to the time of actual payment at 5% per annum or at such lower rate, if any, as the Board may determine and the Board shall be at liberty to waive payment of any such interest wholly or in part.

17.3 Effect of Non-Payment of a Call

(a) In the event of non-payment of a call the Board may forfeite such shares in accordance with the provisions of the Articles.
(b) If Articles are silent, Regulations 29 to 32 of Table A shall apply.

(c) Articles of company may also provide that a member who has not paid call on shares held by him shall not exercise voting rights in respect of shares held by him. [Section 181]

(d) Non-payment of a call by a person for 6 months will disqualify him from holding the office of a director of the company. [Section 274]

18.0 CALLS-IN-ADVANCE

18.1 Meaning of Calls-in-advance

Calls-in-Advance refer to the receipt of the amount which has not been called up by the company. *For example* if a company has called up a first call of Rs 3 per share and a shareholder has paid the final call of Rs 2 per share alongwith the first call on 100 shares held by him, then Rs 200 are said to be calls-in-advance.

18.2 Provisions relating to Call-in-Advance

The various provisions relating to calls-in-advance are as follows:

(i) **Authorised by Articles** A company may, if so authorised by its articles, accept from any member the whole or a part of the amount remaining unpaid on any shares held by him although no part of that amount has been called up [Section 92 (1)]. If the Articles are silent, Regulation 18(a) empowers the Board to receive the Calls-in-advance.

(ii) **No Voting Right** The member is not entitled to voting rights in respect of the moneys so paid by him until the same becomes presently payable. [Section 92(2)].

(iii) **Dividend on Call-in-advance** A company may, if so authorised by its articles, pay dividends in proportion to the amount paid-up on each share where a larger amount is paid-up on some shares than on others. [Section 93]

If the Articles are silent, then Regulation 88(2) of the Table A shall apply which does not permit so.

(iv) **Rate of Interest** The interest on calls-in-advance is payable according to the provision contained in the Articles of the company. If the Articles are silent, then the Regulation 18(b) of the Table 'A' shall be applicable which prescribes that the Board may pay interest at such rate not exceeding, (unless the company in general meeting shall otherwise direct), 6% per annum, as may be agreed upon between the Board and the members paying the sum in advance. The Board may pay such interest from the date of the receipt of such amount till the date when such amount becomes due for payment.

(v) **Payment of Interest as Charge** The payment of interest on calls-in-advance is a charge against the profits and therefore it must be paid irrespective of whether there are profits or not since the shareholders becomes the creditor of the company in respect of this amount.

(vi) **Calls-in-advance Not refundable** The amount received in advance of calls is not refundable except in the event of winding up. In the event of winding up the shareholder making the advance payment will be entitled to refund of their amount with interest before the other shareholders are paid-off.

(vii) **Extinguishment of Liability** The liability of the shareholder in respect of the call for which the amount is paid in advance is extinguished.

(viii) **Bona fide and for the Benefit of the Company** The power to accept calls-in-advance must be exercised bona fide and for the benefit of the company [*Re. Syke's case,* (1872) L.R. 13 Eq. 255]. Where the directors knew that the company was insolvent and paid the amount unpaid on their shares in advance and applied it in the payment of their own shares, they were still liable for the amount unpaid on their shares. [*Re. European Central Renil Co.,* (1872) L.R. 13 Eq. 255]

19.0 RESTRICTION ON FINANCIAL ASSISTANCE FOR THE PURCHASE OF SHARES [SECTION 77]

No public company and no private company (which is subsidiary of a public company) can give any financial assistance in any form to any person for the purchase of its own shares or shares of its holding company **except in the following 3 cases:**

1. Where a banking company lends money in the ordinary course of its business; but not on the security of its own shares.
2. Where provision of money is made by a company in accordance with any scheme to enable the trustee to purchase or subscribe fully paid shares in the company or its holding company for the benefit of employees (including director holding a salaried office or employment).
3. Where loan is made by the company to its employees (other than directors or managers) to enable them to purchase or subscribe for fully paid shares for an amount **not exceeding his salary or wages for a period of 6 months**.

Penalty In case of default, the company and its every officer in default shall be punishable with fine upto to Rs 10,000. [Section 77(4)]

20.0 BUY BACK OF SHARES [SECTION 77A]

20.1 Meaning of Buy-back of Shares

The term buy-back of shares implies the act of purchasing its own shares by a company.

20.2 Three Sources of Funds for Buy-Back [Section 77A(1)] A company may purchase its own shares or other specified securities out of—

(i) its free reserves; or
(ii) the securities premium account; or
(iii) the proceeds of any shares or other specified securities;

Provided that no buy-back of any kind of shares or other specified securities shall be made out of the proceeds of an earlier issue of the same kind of shares or same kind of other specified securities.

"Specified securities" includes employees' stock option or other securities as may be notified by the Central Government from time to time.

20.3 Buy-back from Whom? [Section 77A(5)] The buy-back may be—

(a) from the existing security holders on a proportionate basis; *or*
(b) from the open market; *or*
(c) from odd lots, that is to say, where the lot of securities of a public company, whose shares are listed on a recognised stock exchange, is smaller than such marketable lot, as may be specified by the stock exchange; *or*
(d) by purchasing the securities issued to employees of the company pursuant to a scheme of stock option or sweat equity.

20.4 Conditions for Buy-Back

1. **Authorised by Articles**—The buy-back must be authorized by the **Articles**
2. **Special Resolution/Board's Resolution**—The **special resolution** must be passed in the General Meeting of shareholders.

   OR

   The Board must pass a resolution at its meeting where the buy-back does not exceed 10% of the total equity paid up capital and free reserves of the company.
3. **Minimum Time Interval between Two buy-back**—No offer of buy back must be made within a period of 365 days from the date of preceding offer of buy-back.
4. **Overall Maximum Limit**—The buy-back of the shares must **not exceed 25%** of total paid-up capital and free reserves.
5. **Maximum Limit of Buy-back in any Financial Year**—The buy-back of equity shares in **any financial year** must not exceed 25% of its total paid up equity capital
6. **Maximum Debt-Equity Ratio**—The debt-equity ratio must **not be more than 2:1** after such buy-back.

   Here Debt = Secured + Unsecured Debt and Equity = Capital + Free Reserves Free Reserves = Free Reserves as per Sec 372A + Securities Premium as per Sec 78.
7. **Fully Paid Shares**—All the shares for buy-back must be fully paid-up.
8. **Time Limit**—The buy-back must be completed within **12 months** from the date of passing the Special Resolution/Board's Resolution.
9. **Solvency Declaration**—The company must file **solvency declaration** with the Registrar and SEBI in the form of an affidavit signed by at least two directors of the company. The affidavit must state that the Board has made full inquiry into the affairs of the company as a result of which they have formed an option that the company is capable of meeting its liabilities and will not render insolvent within a period of one year from the date of declaration adopted by the Board [77A(6)].
10. **Transfer of Certain Sums to Capital Redemption Reserve Account**—Where a company purchases its own shares out of free reserves, than a sum equal to the nominal value of the shares so purchased shall be transferred to the capital redemption reserve account referred to in Clause (d) of the proviso to Sub-section (1) of Section 80 and details of such transfer shall be disclosed in the balance sheet.
11. **As per SEBI Guidelines**—Buy-back must be as per SEBI Guidelines

20.5 Proportionate Buy-back

In case the number of securities tendered for buy-back are more than the number of securities to be bought back, the number of securities to be bought back from each member shall be determined as follows:

$$= \frac{\text{Acceptance tendered by a Member}}{\text{Total Acceptance tendered by all Members}} \times \text{No. of Securities to be bought back}$$

20.6 Extinguishment of Certificates within 7 days [Sec 77A(7)] Where a company buys-back its own shares, it must extinguish and physically destroy the securities so bought back within 7 days of the last date of completion of buy-back in the presence of merchant bankers or Registrar or Statutory auditor.

20.7 No Further Issue within a Period of 6 Months [Section 77A(8)] Where a company completes a buy-back of its shares or other specified securities under this section, it must not make further issue of same kind of shares (including allotment of further shares under section 81 (1)(a) or other specified securities *within a period of 6 months* except by way of bonus issue or in the discharge of subsisting obligations such as conversion of warrants, stock option schemes, sweat equity or conversion of preference shares or debentures into equity shares.

20.8 Register of Buy-back Securities [Section 77A(9)] Where a company buys back its securities under this section, it must maintain a register of the securities so bought, the consideration paid for the securities bought-back, the date of cancellation of securities, the date of extinguishing and physically destroying of securities and such other particulars as may be prescribed.

20.9 Filing of Buy-back Return [Section 77(A)(10)] A company must, after completion of the buy-back under this section, file with the Registrar and the SEBI, a return containing prescribed particulars.

Provided that **no return** is to be filed with the SEBI by a company whose shares are **not listed** on any recognised stock exchange.

20.10 Prohibition of Buy-back in Certain Circumstances [Section 77B] No company shall directly or indirectly purchase its own shares or other specified securities—

(a) through any subsidiary company including its own subsidiary companies; or
(b) through any investment company or group of investment companies; or
(c) if a default, by the company, in repayment of deposit or interest payable thereon, redemption of debentures or preference shares or payment of dividend to any shareholder or repayment of any term loan or interest payable thereon to any financial institutions or bank, is subsisting; or
(d) in case such company has not complied with provisions of Sections 159, 207 and 211.

20.11 Penalty for Default [Section 77A(11)] In case of default the company or its officer in default shall be punishable with imprisonment for a term upto 2 years, or with fine upto Rs 50,000 or with both.

20.12 Procedure before Buy-back [Section 77A(3)] The notice of the meeting at which special resolution is proposed to be passed must be accompanied by an explanatory statement stating—

(a) a full and complete disclosure of the all material facts;
(b) the necessity for the buy-back;
(c) the class of security intended to be purchased under the buy-back;
(d) the amount to be invested under the buy-back; and
(e) the time limit for completion of buy-back.

21.0 REDEMPTION OF REDEEMABLE PREFERENCE SHARES [SECTION 80]

21.1 Which Company can Issue Redeemable Preference Shares

A Company limited by shares may, if authorised by its Articles, issue redeemable preference shares.

21.2 Can a Company Issue Irredeemable Preference Shares after the commencement of the Companies (Amendment) Act, 1988

No Company limited by shares shall issue irredeemable preference shares. [Section 80(5A)]

21.3 What can be the Maximum Period of Redemption?

After the commencement of the Companies (Amendment) Act, 1988, no company limited by shares shall issue any preference share which is redeemable after the expiry of a period of **20 years** from the date of issue. [Section 80(5A)]

21.4 What are the Restrictions on the Redemption of Redeemable Preference Shares

According to Section 80, the redemption of preference shares is subject to the following restrictions:

(i) **Fully paid**—Such shares can be redeemed only if they are fully paid.

(ii) **Two Sources of Redeeming such shares**

Such shares can be redeemed only out of the following **two** sources:

(a) **Divisible Profits** i.e. Profit available for distribution as dividend. Some of the examples of Divisible Profits are as under:

1. General Reserve
2. Reserve Fund
3. Dividend Equalisation Fund
4. Insurance Fund
5. Workman's Compensation Fund
6. Workman's Accident Fund
7. Profit and Loss Account

(b) **Proceeds of fresh issue of shares** (whether Equity or Preference) made for the purpose of redemption.

What constitute the proceeds is explained as follows:

In case of fresh issue of shares	*What constitute the proceeds . . .*
(a) At Par	Nominal value of shares issued
(b) At Premium	Nominal value of shares issued
(c) At Discount	Net amount received (i.e. Nominal Value *less* discount on issue of shares)

Note: These shares may be Equity shares or Preference shares.

(iii) **Two Sources of providing Premium if any, payable on redemption.**

The premium, if any, payable on redemption must be provided for out of any of the following two sources:

(a) Securities Premium Account

(b) Profits (whether divisible or not) e.g. Capital Reserve

(iv) **Transfer to CRR A/c**—Where any such shares are redeemed out of divisible profits, an amount equivalent to the nominal value of the shares so redeemed, must be transferred out of divisible profits to **Capital Redemption Reserve Account**.

(v) **Utilization of CRR**—The Capital Redemption Reserve Account may be applied by the company in issuing fully paid bonus shares to the members of the company.

(vi) The provision of this Act relating to the reduction of share capital of a company shall apply to Capital Redemption Reserve Account as if it is paid up share capital of the company. [Section 80(1)(d)]

21.5 Does the Redemption of Preference Shares Constitute Reduction of Authorised Share Capital?

The redemption of preference shares by a company shall **not** be taken as reducing the amount of its authorised share capital. [Section 80(3)]

21.6 Has Company Power to Issue New Shares?

Where in pursuance of this section, a company has redeemed or is about to redeem any preference shares, it shall **have power** to issue shares upto the nominal amount of the shares redeemed or to be redeemed as if these shares have never been issued. [Section 80(4)]

21.7 Does the Issue of New Shares Constitute an Increase of Authorised Share Capital?

For the purpose of calculating the fees payable u/s 611, the share capital shall **not** be deemed to be increased by the issue of new shares before the redemption of old shares, if the old shares are redeemed within 1 month after the issue of the new shares. [Section 80(4)]

21.8 Penalties for Contravention

If a company fails to comply with the provisions of Section 80, the Company and every officer of the company who is in default shall be punishable with fine which may extend to Rs 10,000. [Section 80(6)]

22.0 FURTHER ISSUE OF CAPITAL—RIGHTS SHARES [SECTION 81]

22.1 Meaning of Pre-emptive Right

Pre-emptive rights mean that further shares must be offered to the existing equity shareholders in proportion as nearly as the circumstances admit to the capital paid up on those shares at that date. Such shares are called 'Rights Shares'.

22.2 When Pre-emptive Right is Available

Pre-emptive right is available when it is proposed to increase the subscribed capital of the company by allotment of further shares at any time **after the expiry of 2 years** from the formation of a company **or after the expiry of 1 year** from the first allotment of shares, whichever is earlier.

22.3 Provisions Applicable to Pre-emptive Rights or Right Offer

The provisions applicable to right offer are given below:

1. **Offer to be made by Notice** The right offer must be made by notice. Such notice must specify—
   (a) the number of shares offered,
   (b) the time limit (at least 15 days from date of offer) within which the offer may be accepted.
   (c) The fact that if the offer is not accepted within the specified time, it will be deemed to have been declined.

(d) Unless the articles otherwise provide, the fact that the shareholder has the right to renounce the offer in whole or in part in favour of any other person (whether members or not)

2. **Power of Board in Case of Refusal** After the expiry of the time specified in the notice aforesaid, or on receipt of earlier intimation from the person to whom such notice is given that he declines to accept the shares offered, the Board of directors may dispose of them in such manner as they think most beneficial to the company.

22.4 Circumstances Under which New Shares can be Offered to the Outsiders before Offering them to the Existing Shareholders

In the following circumstances new shares can be offered to the outsiders before offering them to the existing shareholders:

1. **Special Resolution** Where the **special resolution** to that effect is passed by the company in general meeting.
2. **Ordinary Resolution and Central Govt's Approval** Where the **ordinary resolution** to that effect is passed by the company in general meeting and the **Central Government** has sanctioned such issue after being satisfied that the proposal is most beneficial to the company.
3. **No Acceptance of Offer by Offeree/Renouncee** Where the existing shareholder to whom the offer is made or the person(s) in whose favour the renunciation if any, is made, does not accept the offer within the specified time.
4. **Allotment before expiry of Statutory Period** Where allotment of further shares is made at any time before the expiry of **2 years from the formation** of a company or before the expiry of **1 year from the first allotment** of shares, whichever is earlier.

Practical Illustration 1

Date of formation of company 1.4.20X1.
Date of first allotment of share 1.5.20X1.

State whether the further shares need to be offered to the existing shareholders under Section 81 if the date of second allotment is (a) 30.4.20X2 (b) 31.3.20X3.

Solution:

Case	*Where further shares need to be offered to the existing shareholders under Section 81*
(a)	No, since neither 1 year has expired from the date of first allotment nor 2 years have expired from the date of formation.
(b)	Yes, since 1 year has expired from the date of first allotment even though 2 years have not yet expired from the date of formation.

Practical Illustration 2

Date of formation of company 1.4.20X1
Date of first allotment of shares 1.5.20X2

State whether the further shares need to be offered to the existing shareholders under Section 81 if the date of second allotment is (a) 31.3.20X3 (b) 30.4.20X3.

Solution:

Case	*Whether further shares need to be offered to the existing shareholders under Section 81*
(a)	No, since neither 1 year has expired from the date of first allotment nor 2 years have expired from the date of formation.
(b)	Yes, since 2 years have expired from the date of formation even though 1 year has not expired from the date of first allotment.

22.5 Case where Provisions of Section 81 do not Apply [Section 81(3)]

The provisions of Section 81 do not apply—

(a) to a private company

(b) to the increase of the subscribed capital of a public company as a result of the exercise of an option attached to debentures issued or loan raised by the company. Such option must be—
   - (i) to convert such debentures or loan into shares in the company, or
   - (ii) to subscribe for shares in the company.

23.0 ISSUE OF CONVERTIBLE DEBENTURES OR RAISING OF LOANS [Sec. 81(3)] WITH AN OPTION TO CONVERT THEM INTO SHARES

23.1 Scope of Sec. 81(3)

Sec. 81(3) permits a company to—

(a) issue convertible debentures of loans; *or*

(b) issue debentures or raise loans with an option to subscribe for new shares.

23.2 Conditions of Sec. 81(3)

(a) Power in terms of issue — The terms of issue of such debentures or loans must contain term regarding conversion of such debentures of loans into shares.

(b) Approval of CG — The terms must be the approved by Central Govt. before issue of such debentures or loans. However, the approval of Central Govt. is not required if the terms are as per Central Govt. Rules.

(c) Special Resolution— The terms must be approved by a special resolution.

24.0 CONVERSION OF BORROWINGS FROM GOVERNMENT SOURCES [SEC. 81(4)]

24.1 Power of Central Govt. to order for conversion of Borrowings from Govt. Sources.

(a) The Central Govt. may make an order that—
   - (i) debentures issued to the Government by a company; or
   - (ii) loans obtained form the Government by a company

   shall be converted into shares in the company.

(b) The order of Central Govt. directing conversion shall be final and conclusive except to the extent that the company may prefer an appeal to the Court alleging that the terms and conditions of conversion are not acceptable to the company.

24.2 Terms of Conversion

(a) Central Govt. may make such an order even if the terms of issue of such debentures or loans do not contain any provision for conversion.
(b) The terms of conversion of such debentures or loans shall be such as appear reasonable to Central Govt.
(c) In determining the terms and conditions of such conversion, Central Govt. shall have due regard to the following circumstances:
- The financial position of the company
- The terms of issue of the debentures or the terms of the loans
- The rate of interest payable on the debentures or the loans
- The capital of the company, its liabilities, its reserves, its profits during the preceding 5 years
- The current market price of the shares of the company.

24.3 Conditions for Making Order of Conversion

The Central Govt. must form an opinion that it is necessary in the public interest to make an order of conversion of loans or debentures into shares.

24.4 Company's Right to Appeal to the Court within 30 days

(a) If the terms and condition of such conversion are not acceptable to the company, the company may prefer an appeal to the Court *within 30 days*
(b) The decision of the Court on such appeal shall be final and conclusive.

25.0 BONUS SHARES

25.1 Meaning of Bonus Shares

Bonus shares are the shares which are issued without any consideration by converting eligible profits or reserves into paid up share capital.

25.2 Conditions for the Issue of Bonus Shares

1. **Authorised by Articles**—The Articles must authorise to issue Bonus shares.
2. **Board's Resolution**—The Board of Directors must pass a resolution recommending its decision to issue bonus shares.
3. **Ordinary Resolution**—The members must pass an ordinary resolution at general meeting to approve Board's resolution recommending the issue of bonus shares.
4. **SEBI Guidelines**—The Bonus Issue must be an per SEBI Guidelines.
5. **Sources for issue of Bonus shares**—Bonus shares can be issue out of the following sources:
   (a) Undistributed Profits/Reserves which are available for Dividend
   (b) Securities Premium as per Sec. 78
   (c) Capital Redemption Reserve as per Sec. 80
6. **Fully Paid Shares**—Bonus shares must be fully paid up.
7. **To existing shareholders only**— Bonus shares must be issued only to the existing share holders.

25.3 Similarity Between Bonus Shares and Right Shares

Both are issued to existing shareholders. However, in certain circumstances, rights shares need not be offered to the existing shareholders.

25.4 Distinction Between Bonus Shares and Right Shares

Bonus shares differ from Right shares in the following respects:

Basis of Distinction	*Bonus Shares*	*Right Shares*
1. *Provisions Applicable*	Sec. 78, Sec. 80, Sec. 205	Sec. 81
2. *Manner of Issue*	These are issued by **Capitalizing** the accumulated profits/reserves.	These are issued by issuing **new share capital.**
3. *Consideration*	These are issued **without** any consideration.	These are issued **for cash.**
4. *T/f of Right to Receive*	Right to receive bonus shares **can not** be transferred to another person.	Right to subscribe for right shares **can be** transferred to another person.
5. *Apply*	Shareholders are **not required** to apply for bonus shares.	Shareholders are **required** to apply to subscribe for right shares.
6. *Option*	Shareholders have **no option** to receive bonus shares less than/ more than those offered.	Shareholders have an **option** to apply for right shares less than/more than those offered.
7. *Cash inflow*	There is **no** cash inflow.	There **is** cash inflow.
8. *Fully paid up*	These are always fully paid up.	These may be fully/partly paid up.
9. *Issue to Existing Shareholders*	These are always issued to existing shareholders.	These may or may not be issued to existing shareholders

26.0 ALTERATION OF SHARE CAPITAL CLAUSE [Sec. 94 to sec. 97]

The provisions relating to the alteration of Share Capital are given below:

1. **Authority in Articles** A limited company having a share capital may alter the Capital Clause of its memorandum only if it is authorised by its articles of association to do so. [Section 94(1)]
2. **Manner of Alteration** A company may alter the Capital Clause in the following manner:
   (a) by increasing its nominal share capital by issue of new shares; [e.g. from 1 crore to 5 crore]
   (b) by consolidating the existing shares into shares of larger amount than its existing shares; [e.g. Conversion of Shares of Rs 10 each into shares of Rs 100 each]
   (c) by Converting fully paid shares into stock or vice versa;
   (d) by sub-dividing the existing shares into shares of smaller amount than its existing shares; [e.g. Conversion of shares of Rs 100 each into shares of Rs 10 each]
   (e) by cancelling its unissued shares.

Note: A cancellation of shares under Section 94 shall not be deemed to a reduction of share capital within the meaning of the Act.

3. **Ordinary Resolution** An ordinary resolution is required to be passed at its general meeting. [Section 9(2)]
4. **Notice to Registrar within 30 days** A notice specifying alteration made must be given to the Registrar within 30 days of alteration. [Sections 95(1) and 97(1)]
5. **Duty of Registrar** The Registrar shall make the necessary alteration in the memorandum or articles or both. [Section 95(2)]
6. **Consequences of Default** If default is made in filing the notice as aforesaid, the company and every officer in default must be punishable with the fine upto Rs 500 for every day during which the default continues. [Sections 95(3) and 97(3)]
7. **Inapplicability of Provisions to Stock** Where a company has converted any of its shares into stock, such provisions of the Act as are applicable to shares shall cease to apply to such shares which have been converted into stock. [Section 96]
8. **Notice of Increase** Notice of increase in authorised capital or number of members beyond registered number in case of a company not limited by shares must be given to the Registrar. [Section 97]

Note: Notice of increase must be given to the registrar even when the new shares may not have been issued to any shareholder. [***Mahalaxmi Mills Co. Ltd.*** **v.** ***State,*** (1969) Comp. Case 342]

27.0 REDUCTION OF SHARE CAPITAL [SECTION 100 TO 105]

27.1 Meaning of Reduction of Share Capital

Reduction of share capital may involve reduction in respect of that portion of:

(a) issued capital which has been subscribed, called up and paid up, or
(b) issued capital which has been subscribed but not called up.

27.2 To which Company the Restriction as to Reduction of Share Capital applies

The restriction as to reduction of share capital apply to the following two companies:

(a) A company limited by shares
(b) A company limited by guarantee having share capital.

Thus, such restrictions do not apply to unlimited companies whether having share capital or not and companies limited by guarantee not having share capital.

27.3 Manner of Capital Reduction

A company may reduce its share capital in any way and in particular:

(a) by extinguishing or reducing the liability of members in respect of capital not paid up. e.g. where the shares of Rs 100 each with Rs 75 paid up are reduced to Rs 75 fully paid up shares, the shareholders are relieved from liability on the uncalled capital of Rs 25 per share.
(b) by cancelling any paid up share capital which is lost or is unrepresentated by available assets, with or without extinguishing or reducing liability of members.
(c) by paying off any paid up share capital which is in excess of the wants of the company with or without extinguishing or reducing liability.

Example I Where the fully paid shares of Rs 100 each are reduced to Rs 75 fully paid up shares and Rs 25 are returned to the members. Thus, in this case nominal value of the share is reduced and not merely the paid up value.

Example II Where the fully paid shares of Rs 100 each are reduced to Rs 75 paid up and Rs 25 are returned to the members on the condition that when required, the company may call it up again. Thus, in this case the paid up value of share is reduced and not the nominal value.

Note: Interest of creditors is really involved only in the circumstances referred to in (a) and (c).

27.4 Procedure for Reduction of Capital

The procedure for reducing the capital is given below:

1. **Authorised by Articles** The articles must authorise the company to reduce the share capital. If the articles do not so authorise, then these must be altered by a special resolution first.

   Note: It is not enough to provide this authority in the Memorandum.
2. **Special Resolution** A special resolution must be passed at a general meeting.
3. **Court's Confirmation** After passing the special resolution, the company has to apply to the court for an order confirming the reduction.

   Mandatory and Discretionary Powers of the Court The mandatory and discretionary powers of the Court are as under:

   (i) After the petition for the court's confirmation has been filed, the Court must settle the list of creditors who are entitled to object in accordance with Section 101(2)(a) (e.g. the creditors having a debt or claim admissible on a winding up). [Section 101(2)(b)]

   (ii) For settling the list of creditors, the court must ascertain the names of those creditors and the nature and amount of their debts or claims. [Section 101(2)(b)]

   (iii) The court may publish notices fixing a day or days within which the creditors not entered on the list are to claim to be so entered or are to be excluded from the right of objecting to the reduction. [Sec 101(2)(b)]

   (iv) Where a creditor entered on the list whose debt or claim is not discharged or has not determined does not consent to the reduction, the court may dispense with the consent of that creditor if the company secures the payment of his debt or claim by appropriating the full amount or the amount fixed by the court. [Section 101(2)(c)]

   (v) The court has discretionary power having regard to any special circumstances of the case to direct that the provisions of Section 101(2) shall not apply as regards any class(s) of creditors. [Section 101(3)]

Note: Special circumstances must be such as would convince the court that with reasonable foresight it can be said the proposed reduction of capital would not adversely affect the relevant creditor and would not render him any worse off than if he had attended and objected to the application for confirmation.

[***Re Lucanic Tempscule Billard Hall (London) Ltd.,*** 1965 3 All E.R. 879]

(vi) The court may make an order confirming the reduction on such terms and conditions as it think fit if the court is satisfied that either the consent of every creditor who is entitled to object to the reduction, has been obtained or his debt or claim has been discharged or has been determined or has been secured. [Section 102(1)]

(vii) The court may order that the words 'And Reduced' be added to the name of the company for a certain period. [Section 102(2)(a)]

(viii) The court may require the company to publish the reason for the reduction and the causes which led to the reduction. [Section 102(2)(b)]

4. Registration of Order and Minutes of Reduction

(i) The Registrar must register the order and minute—

(a) on the production of an order of the court confirming the reduction of the share capital, and

(b) on the delivery of a certified copy of the order and of a minute approved by the court. [Section 103(1)]

(ii) On the registration of the order and minute and not before, the resolution shall become effective. [Section 103(2)]

(iii) The notice of registration must be published in such a manner as the court may direct. [Section 103(3)]

(iv) The Registrar shall issue a certificate which shall be conclusive evidence that all the requirements of the Act as to the reduction have been complied with and that the share capital is such as is stated in the minute. [Section 103(4)]

(v) The minutes shall be deemed to be substituted for the corresponding part of the memorandum thereby altering the memorandum within the meaning of Section 40. [Section 103(5) and (6)]

5. Liability of Members in Case of Reduced Share Capital [Section 104] On the reduction of share capital the extent of the liability of any past or present member on any call or contribution shall not exceed the difference between (a) the amount already paid on the share or the reduced amount if any which is deemed to have been paid thereon by the member and (b) the amount of the shares as fixed by the minute of the reduction.

In the event any creditor entitled to object to the reduction of capital is not entered on the list of creditors by reason of his ignorance and after such reduction, the company is unable to pay his debt or claim:

(a) every member at the time of registration of court's order for reduction, shall be liable to contribute for the payment of that debt or claim an amount not exceeding the amount which he would have contributed on the day before registration of the order.

(b) In case the company is wound up, the court on the application by the creditor and on proof of his ignorance may settle a list of contributories and make and enforce calls and orders on the contributories settled on the list as if they were ordinary contributories in a winding up.

It is further provided that, if any officer of the company conceals the name of any creditor entitled to object to the reduction, he shall be liable to be punished with imprisonment up to one year, or with fine or with both [Section 105].

28.0 DISTINCTION BETWEEN REDUCTION OF SHARE CAPITAL AND DIMINUTION OF SHARE CAPITAL

Reduction of capital may involve reduction in respect of issued capital which has been subscribed but not called up and paid up, or issued capital which has been subscribed but not called up but diminuation involves cancellation of that portion of the issued capital which has not been subscribed. [Section 94(1)(e)]

Reduction of share capital differs from the diminution of share capital in the following respects:

Basis of Distinction	***Reduction of Share Capital***	***Diminution of Share Capital***
1. ***Relevant Section***	Section 100 to 104	Section 94
2. ***Which capital is involved***	It involves reduction in respect of issued capital which has been subscribed.	It involves reduction in respect of authorised capital.
3. ***Nature of resolution required***	It requires a **special** resolution. [Section 100]	It requires an **ordinary** resolution. [Section 94]
4. ***Court's Confirmation***	It **requires** Court's confirmation. [Section 101]	It **does not require** Court's confirmation [Section 94(2)]
5. ***Alteration of M/A***	It **does not involve** alteration of capital clause of M/A.	It **involves** alteration of capital clause of M/A.
6. ***Order for 'and reduced works***	The court **may order** to add the words 'And Reduced' to the name of the company. [Section 102(3)]	**No** such provision exists in this case.
7. ***Documents to be filed with the Registrar***	It requires the registration of the following with the Registrar: (a) the **court's order** confirming reduction (b) **minutes** approved by the court	It requires **only a notice** to the Registrar.
8. ***Time limit for filing the documents with the Registrar***	There is **no time limit** specified in the Act for filing the documents with the Registrar.	Notice to Registrar must be given within **30 days** from the date of cancellation.
9. ***Can Creditors object?***	**Yes.** Creditors can object since their interests are affected.	**No.** Creditors can not object since their interest are not affected.

28.1 Cases not Requiring Compliance of Sec. 100 to 104.

The compliance of Sec. 100 to 104 is not required in the following cases:

1. Purchase of own shares by a company in pursuance of an order made by CLB u/s 402 (Under section 402, the CLB has the power to direct the company to purchase the shares of any member and effect consequent reduction of capital in order to end oppression or mismanagement. The requirements of Sec. 100 to 104 are not required to be complied with in such a case).
2. Buy-back of shares u/s 77A
3. Redemption of Preference Shares u/s 80
4. Diminution or Cancellation of Capital u/s 94.
5. Forfeiture of Shares
6. Surrender of Shares

29.0 VARIATION OF SHAREHOLDERS' RIGHTS [SECTION 106 & 107]

Where the share capital of a company is divided into different classes of shares, the rights attached to the shares of any class may be varied subject to the following provisions:

1. **Authorisation or No Prohibition** There must be provision with respect to variation in the memorandum or articles or in the absence of such provision, such variation must not be prohibited by the terms of issue of the shares of that class.
2. **Written Consent of 75% Holders or Special Resolution** The rights can be varied only if—
   (a) Written consent of the holders of at least $\frac{3}{4}$th of the issued shares of that class is obtained, or
   (b) the special resolution sanctioning the variation is passed at a separate meeting of the holders of the issued shared of that class.
3. **Rights of Dissentient Shareholders [Section 107]**
   (a) The holders of at least 10% of the issued shares of that class, who did not consent to or vote in favour of the resolution for the variation, may apply to the court to have the variation cancelled. [Section 107(1)]
   (b) Such applicantion is to be made within 21 days after the consent is obtained or the resolution is passed. [Section 107(2)]
   (c) Where any such application is made, the variation shall not have effect unless and until it is confirmed by the court. [Section 107(1)]
   (d) If the court, after hearing the applicant and any other person interested in the application is satisfied that the variation would unfairly prejudice the shareholders of that class, it may disallow the variation and shall confirm the variation if not so satisfied. [Section 107(3)]
   (e) The decision of the court on any such application shall be final. [Section 107(4)]
   (f) The company must forward a copy of court's order on any such application, to the Registrar within 30 days after the service of the order on the company. If default is made, the company and every officer of the company who is in default shall be punishable with fine which may extend to Rs 500. [Section 107(5)]

Notes:

(i) Sub-division of shares is not tantamount to variation.

(ii) The variation which affects only the enjoyment of a right without modifying the right itself does not amount to variation within the meaning of Section 106.
[***Re Hindustan General Electric Corporation,*** AIR (1959) Cal. 672]

(iii) A proposed issue of new preference and ordinary capital to the ordinary stockholders does not affect the rights or privileges of the exiting preference stockholders though in fact, it lessens the latter's voting power.
[***White* v. *Bristal Aeroplane Co. Ltd.,*** (1953) 1 All E.R. 40]

(iv) Once the variation is effected in strict consonance with the provisions of Section 106, it is complete, no further steps are necessary to adopt it.
[***Re Ramuria Cotton Hills Ltd.,*** 53 C.W.N. II]

(v) In the event of the variation of right being a part of a scheme or arrangement with the intervention of the court under Section 391, Section 106 will be inapplicable.
[***Re. Hindustan General Electrical Corporation,*** ATR (1959) 190, Cal. 672]

30.0 SHARE CERTIFICATE [SECTION 113]

30.1 What is Share Certificate?

Share certificate is a document under the common seal of the company specifying that member is the holder of the specified number of the shares of the company. It is a documentary evidence of the ownership of shares.

30.2 Time of Issue of Share Certificate [Section 113]

Case	*Time*
(1) ***In case of allotment of shares. [Section 113(1)]***	Within 3 months from date of the allotment
(2) ***In case of Transfer of shares. [Section 113(1)]***	Within 2 months from date of receipt of valid application for registration of valid transfer of shares.
(3) ***In case shares are issued in demat form [Section 113(4)]***	Issue of Share Certificate is not required. However the company must intimate details of allotment of shares to depository immediately after the shares are allotted.

30.3 Penalty for Default

In case of default, the company, and its every officer in default shall be punishable with fine upto Rs 5,000 for every day during which default continues.

30.4 Object and Effect of Share Certificate [Section 84(1)]

The object and effect of share certificate are as follow:

(a) Estoppel as to Title The company is estoppel from denying the title of the shareholder on number of shares specified in the share certificate. Hence share certificate is *prima facie* evidence of the title of member to such shares.

(b) Estoppel as to Payment The company is estopped from denying that the shares are paid upto the extent stated in the share certificate.

30.5 Judicial Rulings

(i) If an officer of the company, who has no authority to issue certificates, issues a forged certificate, then there is no estoppel [***Rubben* v. *Great Fingal Consolidated***, [1906] A.C. 439; ***South London Greyhound Racecourses Ltd.* v. *Wake,*** 1931 Ch. 496].

(ii) Where a company states that shares are fully paid up, it cannot later contend that they were not, unless the person relying upon the certificate knew that the shares were not in fact fully paid up [***Bloomenthal* v. *Ford,*** [1897] A.C. 156].

(iii) The *bona fide* holder of the share certificate, who had no notice that the shares were not actually paid up fully, could sell those shares away as fully paid to a person who knew that they were not fully paid so as to give the latter a good title to shares as fully paid because the latter derived title from the transferor who had a good title [***Re. Gulabdas's,*** [1982] 17 Bom 672].

(iv) A certificate, however, does not confirm the existence of an equitable interest in the share and as such, the company owes no obligation to a person who holds such an interest. The title of mortgagee, with whom a share certificate and bank transfer have been deposited, may be defeated by the borrower selling all the shares and procuring the registration of the purchaser by obtaining a duplicate certificate. The purchaser in such cases would obtain priority over the mortgagee, since the mortagee would have no remedy against the company [***Reinford*** **v.** ***James Keith Blackman and Co.,*** [1905] 1 Ch. 296].

(v) The certificate is not conclusive proof of the title of the member, specified in the certificate, to certain shares mentioned therein. A share certificate, however cannot be described as "share". It is just *prima facie* evidence of the title to a share or shares represented by the certificate
[***Gopal Paper Mills Ltd.*** **v.** ***CIT Central Calcutta,*** [1966] 1 Com. L.J. 1 174].

30.6 Issue of duplicate Share Certificate [Section 84(2)]

A certificate may be renewed or a duplicate of a certificate may be issued if such certificate

(a) is proved to have been lost or destroyed, or
(b) having been defaced or mutilated or torn, is surrendered to the company.

Procedure for issue of duplicate share certificate:

(i) Consent of Board is given (in case of loss or destruction of certificate) or certificate in lieu of which it is being issued is surrendered to the company and is cancelled.
(ii) Payment of fees for issue of duplicate certificate is made by the shareholder. However this fee is not to exceed Rs 2 per share certificate.
(iii) Proper evidence and indemnity to the satisfaction of the company is furnished.
(iv) Out-of-pocket expenses estimated to be incurred by the company investigating the evidence, as the Board may think fit, are deposited with the company.
(v) The words "duplicate issued in lieu of share certificate No. . . ." are rubber stamped on its face and also on counterfoil. The word "Duplicate" may either be rubber stamped or punched.
(vi) Mutilated, defaced or torn certificate surrendered must be defaced by a cancellation mark and destroyed after 3 years with the authority of the Board.

30.7 Penalty for Renewing a Certificate or Issue of Duplicate Certificate by the Company with Intention of Fraudulent Motive [Section 84(3)]

If a company with intent to defraud renews a certificate or issues a duplicate thereof, the company shall be punishable with fine which may extend to Rs 10,000 and every officer of the company who is in default shall be punishable with imprisonment of a term which may extend to 6 months, or with fine which may extend to Rs 1,00,000.

30.8 Penalty for Personation of Shareholder [Section 116]

If any person impersonates or obtain certificate fraudulently, he may be liable to imprisonment up to 3 years and also fine.

30.9 Sealing and Signing of Share Certificate

According to Rule 6 of the Companies (Issue of Share Certificates) Rule, 1960, every share certificate shall be issued under the common seal of the company, which shall be affixed in presence of

(i) two directors or persons acting on behalf of the directors under a duly registered Power of Attorney.
(ii) the secretary or some other person appointed by the Board for the purpose.

Two directors or their attorney and the secretary or other person shall sign the share certificate.

In case the composition of Board permits, at least one of the aforesaid director shall be person other than the managing or whole-time director.

However in practice, where a managing or whole time director exist, the share certificate is signed by such director along with any other director.

30.10 Same Provisions Applicable to Debenture Certificate

The same provisions relating to share certificate shall equally apply to a debenture certificate. However, the **time limit for issue of a debenture certificate may be extended by CLB upto 9 months.**

31.0 SHARE WARRANT [SECTION 114 AND 115]

31.1 Meaning of Share Warrant

A share warrant is a bearer negotiable instrument which states that its bearer shall be entitled to the shares specified therein.

31.2 Which company can issue Share Warrant? [Section 114(1)]

A public company limited by shares may issue share warrant if:

(i) It is authorised by the articles.
(ii) Previous approval of Central Government has been obtained.
(iii) It is in respect of fully paid up share.
(iv) It is issued under common seal of the company.

31.3 May Company Provide for the Payment of Future Dividends on the Shares Specified in the Warrant?

Yes, the company may provide for the payment of future dividends on the shares specified in the warrant by coupons or otherwise.

31.4 Effect of Issue of Share Warrant to Bearer [Section 114(2)]

(a) A share warrant is transferrable by mere delivery.
(b) The name of the members to whom share warrant is issued shall be removed from Register of Members.
(c) The following particulars shall be entered in the Register of Members:
  (a) the fact of issue of warrant;
  (b) a statement of the shares specified in the warrant, distinguishing each share by its number; and
  (c) the date of the issue of the warrant.

31.5 Status of a Share Warrant Holder

The bearer of a share warrant is **not a member** of the company. **But if the articles** provide and subject to this Act, he shall be deemed to be member of the company for any purpose defined in the articles. [Section 115(5)]

31.6 Reconversion of Share Warrant into Shares [Section 115(2), (3), (4)]

1. The bearer of warrants shall subject to the Articles, be entitled to have his name entered as a Member in the Register of Members if—

(i) he surrenders his warrant to the company.
(ii) he pays the prescribed fees.

2. If company enters the name of the bearer of share warrant in respect of shares specified therein, without the warrant being surrendered and cancelled, then the company shall be responsible for any loss that may be occurred to any person in this regard. [Section 115(3)]
3. Until the warrant is surrendered, the particulars specificed in Section 115(1) shall be deemed to be particulars to be entered in the register of members and, on the surrender, the date of surrender shall be entered in the register of members. [Section 115(4)]

Notes: Holding of a share warrant does not operate as a qualification for being a director of a company, where such is required under the articles.

32.0 DISTINCTION BETWEEN SHARE CERTIFICATE AND SHARE WARRANT

Share certificate differ from share warrant in the following respects:

Basis of Distinction	***Share Certificate***	***Share Warrant***
1. ***Which company can issue***	It can be issued by **any** company having share capital.	It can only be issued by **public** company **limited by shares**.
2. ***Power in the articles***	Not required	Required.
3. ***Prior approval of central government***	Not required.	Required.
4. ***In respect of which shares***	Share certificate can be issued in respect of **partly paid up or fully paid** up shares.	Share warrant can be issued **only** in respect of **fully paid up** shares.
5. ***Membership***	Its holder is a **member** of the company.	Its holder is not a member of the company unless A/A provide otherwise.
6. ***Mode of Transfer***	Shares can be transferred by registering a proper transfer deed.	Shares can be transferred merely **by delivery** of share warrant.
7. ***Stamp duty***	Stamp duty is **payable** in respect of transfer of share.	**No** stamp duty is payable on transfer.
8. ***Whether Negotiable Instrument***	Share certificate is **not** a negotiable instrument.	Share warrant is a **negotiable instrument.**
9. ***Share qualification for directorship***	It **constitutes** qualification for directorship	It **does not constitute** qualification for directorship.
10. ***Petition for winding up***	Its holder **can present** petition for winding up.	Its holder of **cannot present** petition for winding up.
11. ***Time limit of Issue***	• 3 months of Allotment • 2 months of receipt of valid transfer deed	No Time limit prescribed
12. ***Dividend***	Paid of Registered holder	Paid to the Bearer of coupons attached to warrants

33.0 FORFEITURE OF SHARES

33.1 Meaning of Forfeiture of Shares

Forfeiture of shares is compulsory termination of membership of a member and confiscation of his shares as a penalty for non-payment of a call or other sum due on shares.

33.2 Power to Forfeit Shares In Articles of Association

Power to forfeit the shares can be exercised only if the Articles expressly so provide. Such power must be exercised bona fide (i.e., in good faith) and for the benefit of the company. *It must not be collusive or fraudulent.* Such power should not be exercised to expel a member or relieve a friend or relative from liability. Such power must be exercised, strictly according to be the procedure stated in the Articles.

33.3 Grounds for Forfeiture of Shares In Articles of Association

The Articles may provide for forfeiture of shares **not only for non-payment of call but also for other grounds** say non-compliance of any other arrangement according to the prescribed condition. But such grounds must not be opposed to statute or public policy. [***Calcutta Stock Exchange*** **v.** ***S.N. Nandy & Co.,*** (1950) (Cal)]

In ***Naresh Chander Sanyal*** **v.** ***The Calcutta Stock Exchange,*** (1971) (SC), where the Articles provide for forfeiture if a member failed to carry out the arrangement according to the prescribed conditions. The forfeiture was held to be valid.

33.4 Procedure for a Valid Forfeiture

Regulations 29, 30, 31 and 34 of Table A of Schedule I of the Companies Act, 1956 provides for the procedure to be followed for forfeiture:

1. **As per Articles** Power of forfeiture must be exercised only on the basis of various grounds specified in Articles.
2. **Notice** Notice must be served upon the defaulting member. Such notice must—
   (a) require the member to pay unpaid call together with an accrued interest (if any)
   (b) mention a day at least 14 days ahead from the date of service of the notice on or before which the payment is required to be made.
   (c) state that if the payment is not made on or before the date mentioned in the notice, the shares in respect of which call was made would be liable to be forfeited.

Note: A notice is deemed to be served if sent by registered post with acknowledgement due (A.D.) at the registered address of the members. But where a notice, though sent, came back unserved, the company must make enquiry at the proper address of the member whose shares are to be forfeited.

3. **Board's Resolution** The Board of directors must pass a resolution before actual forfeiture is exercised.

33.5 Effects of Forfeiture

1. On forfeiture of shares, member ceases to be a member of the company.
2. Liability of Ex-member

If the Company goes into liquidation	*Liability of Ex-Members*
(a) ***Within 1 year of forfeiture***	He may be put on 'B' list of contributories
(b) ***After 1 year but within 3 years of forfeiture***	He may be held liable as an ordinary debtor but not as a contributor.

3. **Reduction of Capital** Forfeiture of shares results in reduction of capital unless the shares are reissued.
4. Forfeited shares become the property of the company.
5. The annual return must specify the total number of shares forfeited [Section 159]

33.6 Re-issue of Forfeited Shares

1. The forfeited shares may be reissued in accordance with the provision of Articles.
2. The reissue does not amount to allotment. It is merely a sale of forfeited shares. Hence, no return is to be filed in respect of reissue of forfeited shares.
3. Re-issue price cannot be less than the amount unpaid on those shares.
4. Profit on reissue of partly paid up forfeited shares belong to the company and not to the defaulter.
5. Profit on re-issue of fully paid up forfeited shares may be refunded to the defaulter. [***Naresh Chandra Sanyal* v. *The Calcutta Stock Exchange***]

34.0 SURRENDER OF SHARES

34.1 Meaning of Surrender of Shares

Surrender of shares is voluntary return of shares for the purpose of cancellation.

34.2 Power to accept Surrender of Shares In Articles

Power to accept the surrender of shares can be exercised only if the Articles expressly so provide.

34.3 Condition for a Valid Surrender of Shares

Surrender of shares in accordance with Articles is valid—

(a) in case of partly paid up shares if it is accepted to avoid the formalities for a valid forfeiture only. [***Bellerby* v. *Rewland & Marwood's Steamship & Co. Ltd.*** (1902)]

(b) In case of fully paid up shares, if it is accepted in exchange of new shares of the same nominal value. [***Rowell* v. *John Rowell & Sons Ltd.*** (1912)]

34.4 Invalid Surrender of Shares

The surrrender of shares is invalid if—

(a) it involves reduction of share capital

(b) it amounts to a purchase by the company of its own shares

(c) it releases the member from further liability in respect of shares. [***Collector of Muradabad* v. *Equity Insurance Company,*** (1948)]

34.5 Effects of Surrender of Shares

Surrender of shares has the same effect as forfeiture of shares has.

34.6 Distinction between Forfeiture and Surrender of Shares

Forfeiture of shares differs from surrender of shares in the following respects:

Basis of Distinction	*Forfeiture of Shares*	*Surrender of Shares*
1. *Meaning*	Forfeiture of shares is **compulsory** termination of membership of a penalty for non-payment of a call.	Surrender of shares is a **voluntary** return of shares for the purposes of cancellation.
2. *Instance*	It is at the instance of **company**.	It is at the instance of **member**.
3. *Purpose*	Its purpose is **to penalise** the defaulter.	Its purpose is **to avoid the formalities** for a valid forfeiture.
4. *Notice*	Notice precedent to forfeiture is **required**.	**No** such notice is required.
5. *Provision in the Act & Table A*	Both the Act and Table A **provide** for forfeiture.	Both the Act and Table A are **silent** on surrender.

35.0 LIEN ON SHARES

35.1 Conditions for Exercising Lien

Specific provision in the articles is necessary to exercise lien on shares.

35.2 Effects of Exercise of Lien

If the shares are subject to lien, such shares cannot be sold by the shareholder.

35.3 Loss of Lien

Lien is lost if the shareholder whose shares are subject to lien applies for transfer of such shares and the company registers such transfer of shares. In this case, the transferee's title to such shares shall be free from any lien.

36.0 BOOK BUILDING

36.1 Meaning of Book Building

Book Building is a process by which the issue price of securities is determined by the issuer company and the Book Runner on the basis of bids received from various investors during bid period. The bid may vary from floor price (i.e. minimum price) to 120% of floor price. The issue price is determined after the bid closing date.

36.2 Reason for Book Building

Book Building facilitates the evaluation of the intrinsic worth of the securities and creditability of the company.

36.3 Steps in Book Building Process

1. **Book Runner**—Appoint a lead merchant banker as Book Runner.
2. **Draft Prospectus**—Prepare draft prospectus and file with SEBI.

3. **Syndicate Members**—Appoint Syndicate members to underwrite the issues to the extent of 'net offer to the public'.
4. **Circulation**—Circulate the copy of draft prospectus to the institutional investors and syndicate members.
5. **Building up an Order Book**—Build up an order book showing the demand for the securities at various prices.
6. **Issue price**—Determine the issue price.
7. **Issue size**—Determine the issue size of (a) placement portion and (b) public offer portion.
8. **Allocation**—Allocate securities to various bidders.
9. **Final Prospectus**—File the final prospectus with the Registrar of companies within 2 days of the determination of issue price and receipt of acknowledgement card from SEBI.

36.4 Advantages of Book Building Process

1. **Low Cost of Issue**—Book Building process minimises the cost of issue because of limited number of investors.
2. **No Risk**—It avoids the risk of failure of issue because of underwriting of the issue.
3. **Easy Evaluation**—It facilitates the evaluation of the intrinsic worth of the securities and creditability of the company.
4. **Realistic Issue Price**—It facilitates to determine the realistic issue price since it is based on the floor price which is fixed just 1 *or* 2 weeks before the opening of the issue.
5. **Reflects Market Price**—Since issue price is based on actual offers made by various bidders, it reflects real market price.

36.5 Limitations of Book Building Process

1. It is suitable for mega issues only.
2. There must be well organised stock exchanges.
3. Issuer company must be well known to investors.
4. There is Risk of Price Rigging on listing of securities.

37.0 DEMATERIALISATION

37.1 Meaning of Demat Shares

Demat shares represent the electronic shares standing to the credit of demat account of the holder of shares which is maintained with depository participant.

37.2 Meaning of Dematerialisation

Dematerialisation is the process of converting physical certificates into electronic holdings maintained in a demat account opened with a depository participant.

37.3 Steps in the Process of Dematerialisation

Step 1 → An investor opens a Demat Account with a Depository Participant (DP) and submits his physical certificates alongwith Dematerialisation Request Form to the DP.

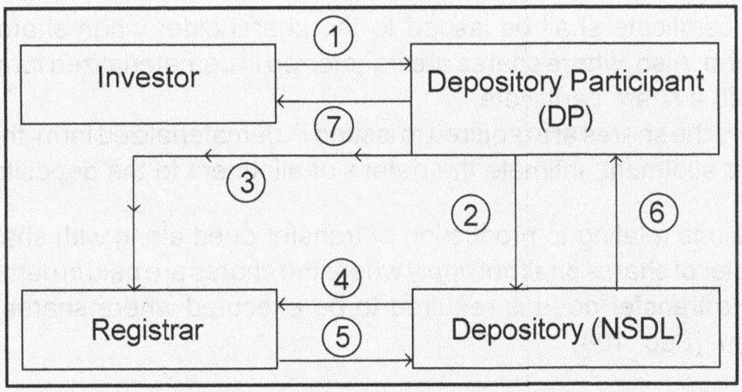

Process of Dematerialisation

Step 2 → DP intimates NSDL of the investor's request.
Step 3 → DP forwards the physical certificates to the Registrar.
Step 4 → Registrar confirms the request.
Step 5 → Registrar processes the request, updates the records and informs NSDL.
Step 6 → NSDL credits DP's Account and informs DP.
Step 7 → DP credits the investor's account and informs investor.

37.4 Meaning of Rematerialisation

Rematerialisation is the process of converting the electronic holdings into physical certificates.

37.5 Advantages of Demat Shares or Electronic Shares (E-Share)

1. No Tearing/Mutilation of Shares
2. No Risk of Loss of Shares due to theft/fire etc.
3. No Risk of Loss-in-transit
4. No Risk of Forged Certificates
5. No Risk of Bad Deliveries
6. Immediate delivery within a day after the settlement
7. Next working day settlement
8. No need to send shares for registration while buying the shares
9. No stamp duty for registration of shares in own name

Thus, E-share offers a faster, easier and safer solution to the ownership, trading and transfer of shares.

38.0 EFFECTS OF DEPOSITORY SYSTEM or DEMATERIALIZATION OF SHARES

38.1 Shares shall cease to have distinctive numbers. [Sec. 83]

38.2 The beneficial owner specified in the register maintained by the depository shall be deemed to be the member of the company. [Sec. 41]

38.3 The register and index of beneficial owners maintained by the depository shall be deemed to be the register and index of members and debentureholders. [Sec. 152A]

38.4 No share certificate shall be issued to the shareholder when shares are issued in dematerialized form. Also, where shares are transferred in dematerialized form, the transferee shall not be issued a share certificate.

However, where the shares are required to issued in dematerialized form, the company shall immediately, after allotment, intimate the details of allotment to the depository. [Sec. 113]

38.5 The provisions relating to production of transfer deed along with share certificate for effecting the transfer of shares shall not apply where the shares are held in dematerialized from. *In other words,* no transfer deed is required to be executed where shares are held in the depository system. [Sec. 108]

VERY SHORT ANSWER TYPE QUESTIONS

1. What is meant by 'Share Capital'?
2. What is meant by 'Authorised Capital'?
3. What is meant by 'Issued Capital'?
4. What is meant by 'Subscribed Capital'?
5. What is meant by 'Unissued Capital'?
6. What is meant by 'Uncalled Capital'?
7. What is meant by 'Reserve Capital'?
8. What is meant by 'Share'?
9. What is meant by 'Stock'?
10. What is meant by 'Equity Share'?
11. What is meant by 'Preference Shares'?
12. What is meant by 'Cumulative Preference Shares'?
13. What is meant by 'Non-cumulative Preference Shares'?
14. What is meant by 'Participating Preference Shares'?
15. What is meant by 'Non-Participating Preference Shares'?
16. What is meant by 'Convertible Preference Shares'?
17. What is meant by 'Non-convertible Preference Shares'?
18. What is meant by 'Cumulative Convertible Preference Share'?
19. What is meant by 'Deferred Shares'?
20. What is meant by 'Reduction of Share Capital'?
21. Name the companies to which the restriction as to reduction of share capital apply.
22. What is meant by pre-emptive right?
23. When is pre-emptive right available?
24. Is the authorisation under Articles required to issue redeemable preference shares?
25. Does the option to redeem the redeemable preference shares lie with the holders thereof?
26. Can partly paid preference shares be redeemed?
27. Name the reserve to be created on redemption of preference shares out of profits?
28. Name the resolution required to authorise (a) the alteration of capital clause; (b) the reduction of share capital.
29. Who are the creditors likely to be hit by the company's contemplated reduction?
30. (a) Can a company issue shares at premium even if there is no express authority in its Articles?
    (b) Can the shares be issued at different premiums?
    (c) Name the account to which premium received on shares must be transferred.
    (d) Can shares at a premium be issued for consideration other than cash?
31. What are sweat shares?
32. (a) What is meant by a call on share?
    (b) Who can make a call on shares before and after the commencement of winding up of a company?
    (c) What is the liability of a member in respect of a call?

33. (a) What is maximum rate of interest which is to be charged on calls-in-arrears according to Table A?
    (b) Can the directors waive the interest on calls in arrears wholly?
34. (a) Can a company accept calls-in-advance if the Articles are silent?
    (b) What is the maximum rate of interest which may be allowed on calls-in-advance according to Table A?
    (c) Is the payment of interest on calls-in-advance a charge against the profits?
    (d) Is the member entitled to voting right is respect of calls-in-advance?
    (e) Can dividend be paid on calls-in-advance?
    (f) Can call-in-advance be refunded?
35. Are there any restriction an issue of debentures at discount?
36. What are the statutory periods for the application of permission for listing and for the actual grant of the permission for listing?
37. (a) What is share certificate?
    (b) Who can sign share certificate?
    (c) State the time limit for issue of share certificate.
        (a) In case of allotment of shares
        (b) In case of transfer of shares
38. (a) What is share warrant?
    (b) Which company can issue share warrant?
    (c) How may a bearer of share warrant transfer the shares?

SHORT ANSWER TYPE QUESTIONS

1. Distinguish between the following:
   (a) Reserve Capital and Capital Reserve
   (b) Authorised Capital and Issued Capital
   (c) Share and Stock
   (d) An Equity Share and a Preference Share
   (e) Reduction of Share Capital and Diminution of a Share Capital.
2. State the nature of a share.
3. State the advantage of stock.
4. State the kinds of shares.
5. Comment on the following;
   (a) A company can offer new shares to outsiders before offering them to the existing shareholders.
   (b) Preference shareholders cannot vote on every resolution.
   (c) A public company cannot buy its own shares.
   (d) A public company cannot provide financial assistance for the purchase of its shares.
   (e) Variation of shareholders' rights is permissible only when authorised by the Memorandum or Articles.
   (f) Rights attaching the class cannot be varied after passing the special resolution at separate meeting of the shareholders of that class.
6. Write short notes on the following:
   (a) Book Building
   (b) Dematerialisation
7. Write short notes on the following:
   (a) Calls-in-arrears (b) Calls-in-advance
   (c) Lien on share
8. State two legal effects of a share certificate.
9. When can a duplicate share certificate be issued ?
10. State the conditions for the issue of share warrants.

11. Is the bearer of share warrant a member?
12. Distinguish between share certificate and share warrant.

LONG ANSWER TYPE QUESTIONS

1. Describe the various kinds of preference shares.
2. Explain the provisions relating to the alteration of share capital clause of the memorandum.
3. Explain the provision relating to the reduction of share capital.
4. Explain the liability of members in case of reduced share capital.
5. Explain the provisions relating to variation of shareholders' right's.
6. Explain the provision relating to the redemption of redeemable preference shares.
7. Explain the provisions relating to pre-emptive right?
8. (a) State the circumstances under which new share can be offered to the outsiders before offering them to the existing shareholders.
   (b) State the cases where provision of Section 81 do not apply.
9. Explain provisions relating to the conversion of loan into shares.
10. Discuss the voting rights of equity shareholder and preference shareholders.
11. (a) When does dividend on preference shares become due?
    (b) What should be the basis of voting rights of preference shareholders?
    (c) What are the restrictions on exercise of voting rights?
12. What are the restrictions on financial assistance for the purchase of shares?
13. Explain the provisions relating to buy-back of shares.
14. (a) State the conditions for the issue of shares at discount.
    (b) State the consequences of improper issue of shares at discount.
15. (a) What are sweat shares?
    (b) State the conditions for the issue of sweat shares.
16. (a) What is meant by call on shares?
    (b) Explain the requisites of a valid call on shares.
17. State the procedure for the issue of duplicate share certificates.
18. Distinguish between the following:
    (a) Share Certificate and Share Warrant
    (b) Forfeiture and Surrender of Shares
    (c) Share and Stock
19. Comment on the following:
    (a) "A director can hold a share warrant for share qualification of his directorship."
    (b) "The holder of a share warrant cannot be called as member of the company."
    (c) Surrender of shares is always lawful.
20. "Surrender is a short-cut to forfeiture". Explain
21. Explain the meaning of a share warrant. How far is the bearer of a share warrant a member of a company?
22. Explain clearly the meaning of the term share 'certificate'. What is the time limit under the provisions of the Companies Act, 1956, for the issue of such certificates for shares alloted by a company? State as to how and under what circumstances can a company issue duplicate share certificates.
23. What is meant by 'sweat equity shares'. What are the conditions to be fulfilled by a company proposing to issue 'sweat equity shares' under the Companies Act, 1956.
24. A public company proposes to purchase its own shares. State the source of funds that can be utilised by the company for purchasing its own shares and the requirements to be complied with by the company under the Companies Act before and after the shares are so purchased.

CHAPTER 9

Transfer and Transmission of Shares

1.0 MEANING OF TRANSFER OF SHARES

Transfer of Shares means the voluntary conveyance of the ownership rights from a member who wishes to cease to be a member to a person who wishes to become a member. The shares or other interests of a member of company are movable properties transferable in the manner prescribed by the Articles of the company [Section 82]. The shares in a public company are freely transferable [Sec 111A]. The articles of a public company cannot contain such absolute provision by which the right to transfer shares is altogether taken away. The right of a shareholder to transfer his shares in a company is absolute and inherent in the ownership of shares. [***Thenappa Chettiar* v. *Indian Overseas Bank Ltd.***, (1943) 13 Comp. as 2002]

2.0 PROCEDURE FOR TRANSFER OF SHARES

In addition to comply with the provisions of the Articles, the following procedure must be followed before a company can lawfully register a transfer:

1. **Prescribed Form** The instrument of transfer must be in the prescribed form i.e. Form No. 7B.
2. **Presentation to the Prescribed Authority** The instrument of transfer must be presented to the prescribed authority (i.e. the Registrar), before it is signed by the transferor or transferee and before any entry is made in it. The prescribed authority shall stamp or otherwise endorse on the instrument the date on which it is so presented.
3. **Execution** The instrument must—
   (i) be duly stamped.
   (ii) be executed by or on behalf of the transferor and the transferee
   (iii) be completed in all respects
   (iv) specify the name, address and occupation if any, of the transferee.
   (v) be signed by both the transferor and the transferee.
4. **Share Certificate/Letter of Allotment** The instrument must be accompanied by share certificate or letter of allotment (if no such certificate is in existence).
5. **Time Limit for Delivery** The instrument must be delivered to the company for registration—
   (i) In case of listed shares at any time before the date of closure of Register of Members for the first time after the date of the presentation to the prescribed authority, *or* **within 12 months** from the date of such presentation whichever is later.
   (ii) In any other case, **within 2 months** from the date of presentation to the prescribed authority.

Extension of Time Limit The Central Government is empowered to extend the aforesaid time limit on an application made *either* before *or* after the expiry of aforesaid period. [Section 108(1D)]

6. **Transfer by Legal Representative [Section 109]** A legal representative of a decreased member although he may not be a member, can validly transfer shares.
7. **Who can submit Transfer deed [Section 110]** The transfer deed may be presented to the company by the transferor or transferee.
8. **Notice in the Case of Transfer of Partly Paid Shares [Section 110]** Where the transferor makes an application for registration of partly paid shares, transfer must not be registered unless the company gives notice of the application to the transferee and the transferee makes **no objection to the transfer within 2 weeks** from the receipt of the notice. [Section 110(2)]

Note: Notice to the transferee shall be deemed to have been duly given if it is despatched by prepaid registered post to the transferee at the address given in the instrument of transfer and shall be deemed to have been duly delivered at the time at which it would have been delivered in the ordinary course of post. [Section 110(3)]

9. **Time Limit for Registration of Transfer** The Board of Directors considers the application and if found alright in all respects, registers the transfer. An endorsement is made on the back of the share certificate recognising the transferee as the new member. In Register of Members, the name of the transferer is strike off and the name of the transferee is entered. The share certificate is required to be despatched to the transferee within **2 months of the application for registration**.

3.0 NOTICE OF REFUSAL AND REMEDY AGAINST REFUSAL [SECTION 111]

1. **Notice** If a private company refuses to register a transfer, it must send the notice of refusal giving reasons to the transferor and the transferee, **within 2 months** of the date of delivery of the instrument of transfer.
2. **Remedy** The transferor or transferee may file an appeal with the Company Law Board as follows:

Refusal/failure	*Time limit for Appeal*
(a) ***Refusal to register the transfer***	Within 2 months of the receipt of notice of refusal
(b) ***Failure to register within 2 months or for not giving reason for refusal***	Within 2 months from the expiry of 2 months of date of delivery of instrument of transfer.

Note: These is no time limit in case of refusal by a public company.

3. **Penalty** For default in registration of transfer within 2 months or for not giving reason for refusal. The company and its every officer in default is punishable with fine upto Rs 500 for every day of default.
4. **Power of CLB** The Company Law Board may *either* dismiss the appeal *or* direct the company to register the transfer **within 10 days** of the receipt of the order.
5. **Penalty for Non-compliance of Order** For default in complying with the CLB order, the company and its every officer in default is punishable with fine upto Rs 10,000 and with a further fine of Rs 1,000 for every day of continuing default.

4.0 TRANSFER OF SECURITIES OF A PUBLIC COMPANY [SECTION 111A]

1. The Board of directors of a company or the concerned depository has no discretion to refuse or withhold transfer of any security. The transfer has to be effected by the company/depository automatically and immediately.
2. **Right to Appeal** Where the transfer of security effected in contravention of the SEBI Act, 1992 or SICA, 1985, a depository, company, participant or investor or SEBI may make an appeal to Company Law Board to rectify the register or records of the company or depository within 2 months from the date of transfer of securities or from the date on which the instrument of transfer or the intimation of transmission was delivered to the company as the case may be.
3. **Power of CLB** The Company Law Board—
   (a) may direct the company or the depository to rectify the register or the records of ownership if after making enquiry, if it is satisfied that the contravention has taken place.
   (b) may suspend the voting rights in respect of the securities subject to enquiry if enquiry has not yet completed.
4. **Right of Transferee** During the pendency of the application before the CLB, the transferee can transfer the security and such further transfer would entitle the transferee to voting rights also unless voting rights in case of transferee have also been suspended by CLB.

5.0 CERTIFICATE OF TRANSFER [SECTION 112]

1. **Lodging Certificate** Where a member wishes to transfer only a part of his shareholding or wishes to sell them to two or more persons, he is required to submit the share certificate with the company. This is known as lodging the certificate.
2. **Certification** Where he has already submitted the share certificate alongwith an instrument of transfer for a part of his shareholding, he may request the company to certify on the instrument of the transfer that the share certification for the shares covered by the instrument of transfer has been lodged with the company. An act of noting on the instrument that share certificate in respect of shares to be transferred has been lodged with the company is called **certification**. An instrument of transfer shall be deemed to be certified if it bears the words 'Certificate lodged' or 'Certificate deposited' the words to the like effect. [Section 112(3)(a)]

   Note: The company is under no obligation to certify any instrument of transfer of shares at all.
3. **Balance Ticket** When only a part of the shares is transferred, the company issues a ticket for the balance of shares not transferred. Such a ticket is known as 'Balance Ticket'.
4. **What Certificate represents** [Section 112(1)] Certification merely represents that the documents showing the prima facie title to the shares mentioned in the instruments have been produced to the company. It does not represent that the transferor has any title to the shares.
5. **Company's Liability** The company will be responsible for the certification only if:
   (a) the person issuing the instrument is authorised to issue such instrument on the company's behalf, and
   (b) the certificate is signed by any officer or servant of the company or any other person authorised to certify transfer on the company's behalf.

6. **Liability in Case of Wrong Certification** Where any person acts on the faith of an erroneous certification made by a company negligently, the company shall be liable to him in a manner as if the certification has been made fraudulently.

   Practical Illustration The secretary of X Ltd. after certifying the transfer negligently returns the original certificate to the transferor. If transferor pledges the same, the company shall not be liable to the pledgee because of two reasons:

   (i) it covers no duty to the pledgee,

   (ii) the immediate cause of his loss was not the issue of the certificate.
   [***Longman* v. *Bath Electric Tramways*,** (1905) Ch. 646]

6.0 BLANK TRANSFER

6.1 Meaning of Blank Transfer

A transfer of shares is said to be blank if an instrument of transfer contains only the name and signature of the transferor and does not contain the name and signature of transferee and the date of sale.

6.2 Procedure for Blank Transfer

The transferor delivers to the buyer (a) share certificate; and (b) blank transfer deed.

6.3 Effect to Blank Transfer

(a) ***Option 1 — The buyer may become the owner of such shares***

(i) The buyer does not automatically become the owner of shares on receipt of the share certificate and the blank transfer deed.

(ii) The buyer gets an implied authority to complete the transfer deed. He shall become the owner of shares only when —

- he completes the blanks in the blank transfer deed;
- he delivers the share certificate and duly filled in transfer deed to the company for effecting transfer of shares in his name; *and*
- the company registers the transfer of shares in the name of the buyer.

(iii) When the name of the buyer is registered as a shareholder by the company, he shall acquire a good title to the shares notwithstanding the fact that shares were transferred to him under a blank transfer deed.

(b) ***Option 2 — The buyer may transfer such shares***

- If the buyer does not intend to become the owner of such shares, and wants to further transfer such shares, he may do so merely by delivering the share certificate and blank transfer deed to a new buyer.
- Similarly, the new buyer has the same 2 options, i.e., to become the owner shares, or to transfer such shares to another new buyer.

6.4 Who is 'Transferee'?

(a) The list holder of blank transfer deed will become the 'transferee' of shares, and no intervening buyer of shares shall be regarded as 'transferee'.

(b) Until some buyer is registered as a shareholder, the original holder of shares (i.e., the transferor) shall continue to be the owner of the shares.

6.5 Validity Period

A blank transfer deed shall remain valid only for such period as is prescribed u/s 108.

6.6 Effects of Blank Transfers

1. Indefinite circulation of the instrument of transfer.
2. Avoidance of stamp duty on transfer.
3. Concealment of beneficial owners behind their nominees.
4. Evasion of tax by suppression of secret profit invested in holdings on blank transfer.

6.7 Present Position

Now, the blank instrument of transfer is required to be presented to the prescribed authority who will stamp the instrument alongwith the date of presentation. Such instrument can then remain in circulation for 12 months or upto the closure of the registar of members whichever is later.

7.0 FORGED TRANSFER

7.1 Meaning of Forged Transfer

The term 'forged transfer' means transfer of shares made on the basis of transfer deed on which the transferor's signatures are forged.

7.2 Forged transfer is void ab Initio

A forged transfer is a nullity (i.e., without any legal effect).

7.3 Rights of Parties

(a) The transferee does not become the owner of such shares.

(b) The original owner continues to be the shareholder.

(c) Where a company has registered the transferee as a shareholder on the basis of a forged transfer, following consequences shall follow:

   (i) The original owner can compel the company to restore his name on the register of members.

   (ii) The company may cancel the share certificate issued to the transferee, and consequently the transferee shall cease to be a member of the company.

   (iii) Where the transferee has already transferred the shares to an innocent purchaser, the position will be as follows:

   - The company can refuse to register the new purchaser of shares, as a member.
   - However, the new purchaser of shares shall have a right to claim damages for the company.
   - The company shall have a right to recover damages from the person who had lodged the forged transfer deed.

7.4 Judicial Rulings

1. If a company registers a forged transfer and removes the name of the true owner from the Register of Members, the true owner can compel the company to restore his name to the register and can claim any dividend which may not have been paid to him during the intervening period. [***Boston* v. *North Staffordshire Railway Co.*,** 38 Ch. D. 456]
2. If a company registers a forged transfer and issues a new certificate to the subsequent buyer for value acting in good faith (i.e. without the knowledge of forgery), it would be liable to compensate him since it cannot deny the liability accruing from its own act. [***Balkin Consolidated Co.* v. *Tamkinser*,** (1982) A.C. 1961]
3. If a transferee gets a certificate from the company on a forged transfer, he will be liable to indemnify the company against its liability to the true owner of the shares. [***Sheffield Corporation* v. *Barelay*,** (1905) B.C. 393]
4. If a transferee without any negligence brings about a transfer he is liable to indemnify the company against its liability to the true owner of shares.
   [***Starkey* v. *Bank of England*,** (1903) A.C. 104]
5. If a share certificate was issued fraudulently by forging the signatures of the directors, the share certificate was rendered void. Forgery is nullity and cannot be a source of a valid transfer of title and thus, it confers no rights upon a subsequent buyer and the company may deny being liable towards him.
   [***Rubben* v. *Great Fingal Consolidated Co.***]

8.0 EFFECTS OF TRANSFER

The transferee does not acquire a legal title to the shares untill his name has been entered in the Register of Members. Position during the intervening period may be summarised as follows:

1. **Legal Title** The transferor continues to the legal owner of the shares but on the principle of equity he holds them in trust for the transferee.
2. **Call** If any call is demanded by the company before transfer is registered, the transferor must pay the calls in the first instance and may later recover the amount from the transferee.
3. **Dividend** If dividends are declared and paid before transfer is registered, the company must pay it to the transferor. The tranferor is required to retain dividends where shares have been sold ex-dividend and is required to return dividends to transferee where shares have been sold-cum-dividend.
4. **Voting Rights** If voting rights are to be exercised before transfer is registered, the transferor must vote as the transferee directs where transfere has already paid the price and may vote as he likes where transferee has not paid the price.

9.0 TRANSMISSION OF SHARES [Sec 109]

9.1 Meaning of Transmission of Shares

Transmission of shares means the transfer of shares under the operation of law.

9.2 When does Transmission of Shares take place?

It takes place—

1. if a registered member dies, or
2. if a registered member is adjudged as insolvent, or

3. if a registered member being a company goes into liquidation.
4. if all the joint holders die where the shares are held jointly by 2 or more persons.

9.3 Effects of Transmission

1. Upon death, the shares of the deceased vest in his executors or administrators and the executors become liable for calls if shares are partly paid up.
2. Upon insolvency, the shares of the insolvent vest in the Official Assignee or the Receiver.
3. Upon liquidation of company, the shares vest in the Liquidator.
4. A person entitled to the shares on transmission becomes a member only when the makes an application in writing to the company and the company registers him as a member by entering his name in the Register of Members.

9.4 Other Provisions

1. No instrument of transfer is to be executed.
2. No stamp duty is payable.
3. It does not involve any consideration.
4. It is always subject to original liabilities attached to shares so transmitted.

9.5 Distinction between Transfer and Transmission

Transfer differs from transmission in the following respects:

Basis of Distinction	*Transfer*	*Transmission*
1. *Results*	Transfer is the result of *deliberate act* of a member.	Transmission is the result of *opeartion of law* on the death/insolvency of a member. or liquidation of a member being a company.
2. *Instrument of transfer*	Instrument of transfer is *required* to be executed.	*No* Instrument of transfer is required to be executed.
3. *Stamp Duty*	Stamp Duty is *payable*.	*No* Stamp Duty is payable
4. *Consideration*	It generally *involves* consideration.	It *does not involve* any consideration.

10.0 NOMINATION OF SHARES [Section 109A and 109B]

10.1 Who can make Nomination?

Every member who is an individual can make a nomination.

10.2 Who can be a Nominee?

(a) Only an individual can be nominee.
(b) Two or more individuals can be jointly made nominees.
(c) A minor can be named as a nominee provided the name of a guardian is mentioned in the nomination from, who shall be entitled to the shares until the minor becomes major.

10.3 Requirements of Valid Nomination

Nomination shall be made in prescribed form and in prescribed manner.

10.4 Time Limit for Nomination

The nomination can be made by a member at anytime.

10.5 Variation or Cancellation of Nomination

A nomination can be varied or cancelled at anytime.

10.6 Consequences in Case of Death of Member

- Shares shall vest in the nominee.
- The nomination shall be valid and effectual irrespective of anything contained in—
  (a) any other law for the time being in force; *or*
  (b) any will made by the shareholder or any other instrument.

10.7 Rights of Nominee

(a) ***Right to become a member***
- An application signed by the nominee and alongwith a death certificate of the deceased member shall be submitted to the company.
- The application shall state that the nominee has elected to become a member of the company

(b) ***Right to transfer the shares***
- A *transfer deed* signed by the nominee alongwith a death certificate of the deceased member shall be submitted to the company.
- The transfer deed signed by the nominee shall be valid even though he is not a registered shareholder.

(c) ***No right to vote at any GM*** The nominee shall not have any right to vote in the General Meeting until he is registered as a member.

11.0 RECTIFICATION OF REGISTER OF MEMBERS OF PRIVATE COMPANY

11.1 Application to Whom Application is to be made to Company Law Board.

11.2 Grounds for Rectification Without reasonable or justifiable case—
- name of person has been entered in register of members
- the name of a person has been removed from the register of members
- default or unnecessary delay is being made in entering the fact of becoming a member of cessation of membership.

11.3 Time Limit for Making Application

Application must be filed within reasonable time since no time limit has been prescribed.

12.0 RECTIFICATION OF REGISTER OF MEMBERS OF PUBLIC COMPANY

12.1 Application to Whom Application is to be made to CLB.

12.2 Grounds for Rectification The application shall be made on the ground that—

- the public company has effected the transfer of shares; but
- there was 'sufficient cause' to refuse the transfer of shares.

12.3 Time Limit for making the application The application must be made within 2 months of—

(i) date of submission of transfer deed to the company;
(ii) date of submission of intimation of transmission of shares;
(iii) transfer of shares held by a depository.

12.4 Who can make Application?

(a) The company
(b) SEBI
(c) The depository
(d) The depository participant

12.5 Rights of transferee

(a) **General Rule:** The transferee shall be entitled to exercise all the membership rights.
(b) **Exception:** CLB may make an interim order *restricting the voting rights* in respect of such shares until final disposal of the application.

VERY SHORT ANSWER TYPE QUESTIONS

1. Is registration of transfer optional with the company?
2. Can the instrument of transfer be in any form?
3. Can the instrument be signed by the transferor or can any entry be made in the instrument before it is presented to prescribed authority?
4. What is the prescribed authority required to do with the instrument?
5. What is the next step to be taken in this regard and by whom?
6. Will it be sufficient legal compliance if the instrument of transfer of shares is executed only by the transferor?
7. Is it necessary to specify the name, address and occupation of the transferee in the transfer-deed?
8. Does instrument of transfer need stamping?
9. The law requires the instrument of transfer to be delivered to the company along with the certificate relating to the shares transferred. But if no such certificate is in existence, then what should the parties do?
10. When is the instrument to be presented to the company (a) when shares are quoted on a recognised stock exchange and (b) where it is not quoted?
11. When all the requirements relating to transfer are compiled with what should the company do?
12. Can registration of transfer of shares be refused by the company on any ground?
13. State the period within which the notice of refusal must be communicated to both the transferor and the transferee?

14. What is the remedy of the parties in case of refusal?
15. Can the Company Law Board compel the company to register the transfer?

SHORT ANSWER TYPE QUESTIONS

1. Distinguish between transfer and Transmission of Shares
2. Write short notes on the following:
   (a) Blank Transfer
   (b) Forged Transfer
   (c) Certificate of Transfer
3. "A company cannot refuse to register a transfer of shares." Comment

LONG ANSWER TYPE QUESTIONS

1. Explain the procedure for effecting a transfer of shares in a limited company.
2. Explain the legal position of transferor and transferee of shares pending registration of transfer by the company.
3. What is a forged transfer? What would be the legal position of the parties involved in it?
4. When can a company refuse to register a transfer of shares?
5. Explain the law relating to restrictions on the acquisition and transfer of shares.

CHAPTER

10 Membership

1.0 MEMBER AND SHAREHOLDER

1.1 Definition of Member [Section 41]

Section 41 covers the following persons as member:

1. **Subscribers to Memorandum** The subscribers to the Memorandum of a company shall be deemed to have agreed to become members of the company and on its registration, shall be entered as members in its register of members.
2. **Every Other Person** Every other person who agrees in writing to become a member of a company and whose name is entered in its register of members, shall be a member of the company.
3. **Beneficial Owner in Records of Depository** Every person who holds equity share capital of company and whose name is entered as beneficial owner in the records of the depository shall be deemed to be a member of the concerned company.

Note: A person may also become a member through transfer or transmission of shares (to be discussed later on)

1.2 Judicial Rullings

1. The subscriber to the memorandum becomes a member, on registration of the company, even without the shares having been allotted to him and is liable as a contributory when the company is wound up [***Universal Transport Co. v. Jagjit Singh***, (1965) Comp. Case. 36; ***Babulal* v. *Naraina Sugar Mill***, (1958) Comp. Case. 155].
2. Since his agreement needs to be in writing, one cannot be deemed to be a member on ground of estoppel, simply because his name appears in the register of members.
3. Where, however, a person's name is there in the register and he has, in fact, accepted the position and acted as a member, the agreement will be presumed to be in writing until the presumption is rebutted by proof to the contrary

1.3 Definition of Shareholder

The term 'shareholder' refers to a person who holds share in a company.

1.4 Distinction between Member and Shareholder

Though the two terms 'Members' and 'Shareholder' are used synonymously, yet there is a difference between the two. In some cases, a person may be a member but not a shareholder or he may be shareholder but not a member.

1.5 All Shareholders need not be Members

Under the following circumstances, a person is a shareholder and not a member:

(a) Holder of share warrant is a shareholder and not a member because holder's name is struck off from the Register of Members on the issue of share warrants. However, the articles may give membership rights to holders of share warrants. [Section 115(1)]

(b) A transferee or legal representative of a deceased member is a shareholder and not a member unless he applies for registration of transfer/transmission of the shares and his name is entered into the Register of Members.

1.6 All Members Need not be Shareholders

Under the following circumstances, a person is a member and not a shareholder:

(a) Subscribers to the Memorandum of a company become members on registration of the company even before any shares are allotted to them.

(b) Members of a company limited by guarantee having no share capital or an unlimited company having no share capital.

(c) A transferor of shares ceases to be a holder of those shares but continues to be the member of the company until his name is replaced by the name of the transferee.

(d) A deceased member continues to be the member of the company until his name is removed from the register of member.

(e) List 'B' contributories who ceased to be members within 12 months before the commencement of winding up, are treated as part members even though they are not shareholders.

1.7 Distinction Between A Member and a Shareholder

Basis of Distinction	*Member*	*Shareholder*
1. Definition	The term 'member' is defined u/s 2(27) read with Sec. 41.	The term 'shareholder' has not been defined under the Companies Act. 1956.
2. Meaning	The term 'member' generally means a person whose name is entered in the register of members.	The term 'shareholder' means a person who holds shares in a company.
3. Nature of company	**Every company** shall have the minimum number of members, whether it is limited by share capital or guarantee.	**Only a company having a share capital** can have shareholders. A company limited by guarantee and having no share capital does not have any shareholders.
4. Signatory to Memorandum	A person who signs the memorandum is a member even before shares are allotted to him.	A person who signs the memorandum becomes a shareholder only when the shares are actually allotted to him
5. Transferor of shares with change in the register	A transferor of shares continues to be a member until his name is removed from the register of members, although he may not be a shareholder.	Where a person transfers his shares, he immediately ceases to be a shareholder, even though his name continues to appear in the register of members.
6. Bearer of Share Warrant	The bearer of a share warrant is not a member [Sec. 2(27)]	A bearer of a share warrant is a shareholder.

2.0 MODES OF ACQUIRING MEMBERSHIP

The various modes of acquiring membership are shown below:

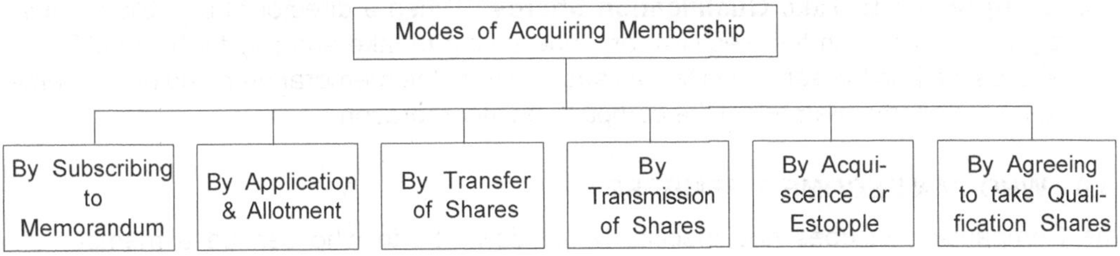

Let us discuss these modes one by one:

1. **By Subscribing to Memorandum** A subscriber to the memorandum automatically becomes a member of the company on its registration.

Notes:

(i) Neither application form nor allotment of shares is necessary. Even an absence of entry in the register of members cannot deprive him of his status as member.
[***Official Liquidator*** **v.** ***Suleman Bhai***, AIR (1955) M.B. 166]

(ii) A subscriber cannot rescind the contract for purchase of shares even on the ground of fraud or misrepresentation on the part of promoters.
[***Re Metal Constituents Co. Lord Husgan's*** **case** (1902) 1 Ch. 707]

(iii) A subscriber cannot refuse to take shares on the ground that his name does not appear in the register of members.

2. **By Application and Allotment of Shares** Every person other than the subscribers to the Memorandum becomes the member on fulfilment of the following two conditions:
   (a) He must have agreed in writing to become a member. In other words, there must be an offer to take shares by way of written application and acceptance of that offer by way of allotment. The general law of contract applies to this agreement. If a person applies for shares subject to certain conditions, the allotment by the company must be made according to those conditions otherwise the allottee shall not be bound to accept the shares. Where a person applies for shares but withdraws his application before acceptance and the company allots the shares and puts his name in the register, he may rescind the contract.
   (b) His name must have entered in the registers of members.
3. **By Transfer** A person may become a member by acquiring shares in the open market and by having the transfer registered and getting his name placed on the register of members. It may be noted that the shares are movable property and are transferable as determined by the Articles of the company.
4. **By Transmission** A person may become a member by operation of law on the happening of such events as the death, insolvency or lunacy of a member when he gives notice of fact of transmission to the company. On the death of a member, his legal representatives have the right to get the shares of the deceased member registered in their name.
   Similarly the Official Receiver or Official Assignee is entitled to be a member in place of member who has been declared insolvent. No instrument of transfer is necessary in this case.
5. **By Acquiescence or Estoppel** A person is deemed to be a member if he allows his name, to be on the register of members or otherwise holds himself out or allows himself

to be held out as a member. In such a case, he is estopped from denying that he is registered with his consent. He can, however, escape liability by taking prompt action to have his name removed from the register on some permissible ground.

6. **By Agreeing to Take Qualification Shares** When a director of a public company signs and files with the Registrar an undertaking to take and pay for his qualification shares, he is in the same position as subscriber to the memorandum and he is deemed to have become member of the company on incorporation.

3.0 WHO CAN BECOME A MEMBER?

The Companies Act does not specifically lay down as to who can be a member of a company. It also does not prescribe any disqualification for any person which would debar him from becoming a member of a company. The Act simply provides that any person who agrees in writing to become a member of a company can become a member. As the contract to purchase shares in a company is like any other contract. Therefore, only such persons can become members of a company who are competent to contract. However, as regards competency of a member, the provisions of The Indian Contract Act, 1872 shall apply. This means that minors, persons of unsound mind and those who have been disqualified by law from contracting, cannot become members of a company.

The membership rights of some special categories of persons are discussed below:

1. **Minor** Can minor become a member?

   (a) **Incompetent to Contract** According to Section 11 of the Indian Contract Act, a minor is incompetent to contract, therefore, he **cannot** enter into an agreement to become a member of the company. In ***Palaniappa* v. *Official Liquidator, Pasupati Bank Ltd.*** an application was made by a father as guardian of his minor daughter describing her as minor. The company went into liquidation. It was held that the allotment was void and neither the minor nor her guardian could be held liable as contributories.

   (b) **Right to Repudiate the Allotment during Minority**

   (i) Both the company and minor can repudiate the allotment.

   (ii) Minor is entitled to receive back the money paid on shares allotted in case of repudiation of allotment.

   (iii) *Neither* minor *nor* Guardian are liable to pay the unpaid amount an shares.

   (iv) The question of whether or not the minor can be compelled to restore the benefits received from the company would be for the court to decide considering the circumstances of each case.

   (v) If neither party repudiates allotment, the name of the minor shall continue to appear on the register of members, but even then a minor incurs no personal liability.

   (c) **Right to Repudiate the Allotment after Attaining Majority**

Case	*Whether Right to Repudiate available*
(a) ***If he has not received dividend after attaining majority***	He **can repudiate** his liability on the shares even if he had received dividends during his minority and if he does so the company cannot plead estoppel on the plea that he had received dividends during his minority or that he had fraudulently misrepresented his age in his application for shares [*Sadiq Ali* vs. *Jay Kishore,* 30 Bomb. L.R. B 46(1)]

Case	*Whether Right to Repudiate available*
(b) ***If he has received dividend after attaining majority***	He **cannot repudiate** his liability on the shares because he would be deemed to have intentionally led the company to believe him to be a shareholder and on the faith of such belief to pay him the dividend [***Fazalbhoy*** **v.** ***The Credit Bank of Public***, (1914) 39 Bom. 331]

(d) Right to become Transferee of Fully Paid Share

There is nothing in the Act to debar a minor from **becoming a transferee of fully paid shares**. *In* ***Miss Nandita Jain*** **v.** ***Bennet Coleman and Company Ltd.***, the Company Law Board held that the contract entered into by a minor for registration of transfer of fully paid shares, through the natural guardian was a valid and binding contract. In such a case the entry in the register of members will be made as follows. "***A, (a minor) through . . . guardian***".

If shares are transferred to a minor, the transferor will continue to remain liable for all future calls on such shares even if he was ignorant of the minority of the transferee. If the company is aware of the minority of the transferee at the time of transfer, it can refuse to register the transfer in favour of a minor unless the shares are fully paid.

2. Company

(a) A company being a legal person **can become** a member of another company if it is so authorised by its Memorandum.

(b) A subsidiary company cannot become a member of its holding company except in the following two cases:

(i) where the subsidiary is concerned as the legal representative of a deceased member,

(ii) where the subsidiary is concerned as trustee and the holding company or its subsidiary is not beneficially interested except as lender of money in the ordinary course of business. [Section 42(2)]

(c) A subsidiary which was a member of its holding company at the commencement of the Act or before becoming a subsidiary, may continue to be a member.

(d) But a subsidiary shall not except in two cases mentioned in Section 42(2), have any voting right at the holding company's meeting.

(e) A subsidiary cannot hold shares in holding company even through its nominee. [Section 42(4)]

3. Partnership Firm A partnership firm **can not become** a member of the company because it has no separate legal entity. A firm may hold shares in the names of individual partners who may be entered as joint holders in the register of members.

Exception: A firm can become member of a non-profit making ompany licensed under Section 25 of the Act and its membership shall cease on dissolution of firm.

4. Hindu Undivided Family A HUF **can not become** a member of the company because it has no separate legal entity. A HUF can have shares in a company in the name of its Karta. Thus, the Karta will be a member of a company as his name alone will be entered in the register of members.

5. Trust A trust **can not become** a member of the company because it has no separate legal entity. Section 153 of the Act lays down that no notice of trust, express or implied or constructive, shall be entered in the register of members. A trustee cannot become a member of a company in his capacity as such.

6. **Insolvent** If any member is declared insolvent, he remains a member of the company till his name appears on company's register of members. He is entitled to vote in respect of shares held by him, but the dividend on shares will be paid to Official Assignee or Official Receiver.
7. **Foreigners** A foreigner may become a member with the general or special permission of the Reserve Bank of India under the Foreign Exchange Management Act, 1973. But if he becomes an alien enemy, his rights as a member shall be suspended.
8. **Co-operative Society** A registered co-operative society **can become** a member of the company because it has separate legal entity.
9. **Society** A society registered under the Societies Registration Act. 1860 **can become** a member of the company because it has separate legal entity.
10. **Govt.** The **Central/State Govt. can become** member of a company.
11. **Trade union** A trade union registered under The Trade Union Act, 1926, **can become** member of the company because it has separate legal entity.
12. **Married Woman** A married women who is competent to contract **can become** a member of a company.

4.0 TERMINATION OF MEMBERSHIP

A person ceases to be a member of a company when his name is removed from the register of members. A person may cease to be a member in any one of the following ways:

1. **Transfer of Shares** When he transfers all of his shares to another person and the transfer is duly registered by the company, the name of the transferor is removed from the register to members.
2. **Transmission of Shares** When he dies and his legal representative(s), transfer the shares or secures their registration in his/their own name. Until the shares are transmitted he continues to be member and his estate to be liable for any money due on shares. The legal representative of deceased member is entitled to receive dividends and notice of the meeting but cannot vote at the meeting.
3. **Forfeiture of Shares** When his shares are forfeited for non-payment of calls and other reasons contained in the articles. The membership terminates on share forfeiture.
4. **Surrender of Shares** When he validly surrenders his shares to the company, he ceases to be a member.
5. **Redemption of Shares** When a member holds redeemable preference shares, his membership terminates on redemption of such shares.
6. **Repudiation of Contract** When he repudiates the contract to take shares on the ground of misrepresentation or mistake in the prospectus or on the ground of irregular allotment.
7. **Insolvency of Member** When he is declared insolvent, his shares vest in the Official Receiver or Official Assignee. The Assignee or Receiver may sell these shares and when the transferee's name is entered in the register of members, insolvent member ceases to be a member.
8. **Winding up of Company** When the winding up of the company, commences, he ceases to a member but he continues to be liable as a contributory.
9. **Issue of Share Warrants** When share warrants are issued in exchange of fully paid shares, his name is removed from the register of members although he continues to be a shareholder of the company.
10. **Court's Order** When the court passes an order for the purchase of shares of a member under Section 402 of the Companies Act, he ceases to be a member.
11. **On Buy-back of Shares**

12. **Enforcement of Lien** When the company has a lien on the shares and the shares are sold by the company to enforce this lien or if the shares are sold in the execution of a decree of the court, the membership terminates.

The Register of members, however is only *prima facie* evidence as to whether a person is a member or not and if a person's name is improperly removed, all his rights and obligations as a member continue to remain the same.

5.0 RIGHTS OF MEMBERS

A number of rights have been conferred on the members by the Companies Act, some of the important rights are as under:

1. Right to receive copies of memorandum and Articles of Association on request and on payment of the prescribed fee. [Section 39]
2. Right of priority to have shares offered in case of increase of capital. [Section 81]
3. Right to transfer his shares according to the Articles of Association. [Section 82]
4. Right to apply to the court to have any variation or abrogation to his rights set aside by the court. [Section 107]
5. Right to appeal to the Company Law Board where the company refuses or fails to register the transfer of shares. [Section 111]
6. Right to apply to the Company Law Board for rectification of register of members.
7. Right to receive share/stock certificate within the prescribed period. [Section 113]
8. Right to inspect register of members, register of debentureholders, Index and copies of annual returns and to obtain extracts or copy thereof.
9. Right to receive a copy of Statutory Report. [Section 165]
10. Right to make requisition to convene an extra ordinary meeting. [Section 169]
11. Right to request the Central Govt. for calling an annual general meeting when the Board of directors fail to call such meeting [Sections 167].
12. Right to request the Company Law Board for calling an Extraordinary meeting [Section 186]
13. Right to have his name entered in the register of members.
14. Right to receive notice of meetings, to attend, to appoint a proxy and vote at the meeting.
15. Right to demand poll. [Section 179]
16. Right to receive proper notice of resolutions requiring special notice. [Section 196(2)]
17. Right to have on request minutes of proceedings at a general meeting. [Section 192(2)]
18. Right to receive copies of Balance Sheet, Profit and Loss Account and Director's report before the annual general meeting. [Section 210 and 219]
19. Right to participate in the appointment of auditors at the annual general meeting. [Sections 224 and 225]
20. Right to inspect the Auditor's Report at AGM [Section 230]
21. Right to apply to the Company Law Tribunal for ordering an investigation into the affairs of the company. [Section 235 and 237]
22. Right to remove a director by joining with others. [Section 284]
23. Right to present petition to the Company Law Tribunal for relief in cases of oppression and mismanagement. [Section 397 and 398]
24. Right to present petition to High Court for the winding up of the company. [Sections 433 and 484(1) (b)]
25. Right to share in the surplus assets of the company on winding up. [Sections 475 and 511]
26. Right to associate in the declaration of dividends and to apply to the court for an injunction restraining the directors from paying dividends on an ultra vires declaration or out of capital.

27. Right to participate in appointmet and in fixation of remuneration of one or more liquidators in the case of a Member's Voluntary Winding up and to fill any vacancy in the office of a liquidator so appointed by him. [Sections 490 and 492]

6.0 DUTIES AND LIABILITIES OF MEMBERS

6.1 Duties of Members

1. To take shares when they are allotted in due time and in compliance with the provisions of the Act, unless the refusal to accept the shares has been sent on the ground of non-compliance with the provisions of the Act as regards the issue of the prospectus or as regards allotment.
2. To abide by the doing of the majority of members unless the majority acts vindictively, oppressively, *mala fide* or fraudulently.

6.2 Liabilities of Members

1. **In Case of Unlimited Company** Every member of such a company is liable for all debts contracted by the company during the period when he was a member.
2. **In Case of Company Limited by Guarantee** Every member is liable to contribute to the extent of the amount guaranteed by him which is given in the liability clause of the memorandum.
3. **In Case of Company Limited by Shares** The majority of the companies belong to this category. In the case of such companies, the liability of a member is limited to the amount unpaid on the shares held by him. If he has paid full amount on shares, his liability is nil.
4. It may be noted that all money payable by any member to the company under the memorandum or articles are a debt due from him to the company [Section 36]. If a shareholder dies and he was holding partly paid-up shares, then his estate will be liable or the legal representatives will be liable for the unpaid amount.
5. **Unlimited Liability on Reduction of Membership below Minimum:** If at any time the number of members is reduced below the statutory number (7 for public company and 2 for private company), and the company carries on business for more than 6 months while the number is so reduced, every member becomes personally liable for the **debts** of the company **contracted after** the said period of 6 months.

7.0 IS A CONTRACT TO TAKE SHARES IN A COMPANY GOVERNED BY THE SAME RULES AS ANY OTHER CONTRACT?

The same rules which govern the contract under the law of contracts also apply to a contract to take shares.

1. **Offer by Applicant** An application to subscribe shares/debentures in response to a prospectus (which is an invitation to make an offer) is treated as an offer made by the applicant to the company.
2. **Revocation of Offer**
   (a) The applicant can revoke his application, before the notice of the allotment is put in the course of transmission to him e.g. by post. [*Wallance's* case (1920)].
   (b) The aforesaid application generally cannot be revoked untill after the expiry of the 6th day after the opening of the subscription list, or the giving, of a public notice by some responsible person u/s 62 having the effect of excluding, limiting or diminishing the responsibility of that person before the expiry of said 5th day.

3. **Acceptance of an Offer** Allotment to the applicant with the notice thereof constitutes an acceptance of an offer. Acceptance must be communicated to the applicant in some way whether by writing or verbally or conduct. [*Gun's* case (1867)]
   (a) Even a notice of allotment brought to the applicant, not from the company but elsewhere will be binding on him. [*Wall's* case (1863]
   (b) Where shares have been applied for prior to the company's incorporation, allotment and notice thereof after incorporation in response to such application constitute a complete contract because the application operates as a continuing offer and when the company accepts it after incorporarion, it matures into a binding contract. [*Lawarence's* case (1866)]
4. **Application Subject to Condition**
   (a) Where the application has been made subject to a condition precedent, the applicant becomes a member only when the condition is complied with
   (b) where the application has been subject to a condition subsequent, the applicant becomes a member in present, when he accepts the notice of allotment and his name is placed on the Register of Members. If the company goes into liquidation before the fulfilment of condition by the company, he cannot escape his liability as contributory. He may be entitled to damages against the company for its failure in carrying out the condition. [*Fishes's* case (1885)]

   Since the liability of a contributory arises *exlege and net ex contracts*, he cannot set up the non-fulfilment of the condition as a defence against his statutory liability as a contributory, which is the direct result of his being a member of the company. [*Hansraj* v. *Astana* 35]
5. **Entry on Register of Members** The applicant by agreeing to take shares, merely agrees to become a member but does not actually become a member, he becomes a member only when his name is entered on the Register of Members. [*Odessa Tramways Co.* v. *Mande* (1878)]

Conclusion Now it may be conclued that the statement that "a contract to take shares in a company is governed by the same rules as any other contract" is fully correct.

VERY SHORT ANSWER TYPE QUESTIONS

1. Who is called a member?
2. Who is called a shareholder?

SHORT ANSWER TYPE QUESTIONS

1. Name the persons who are called members.
2. All shareholders need not be members. Comment.
3. All members need not be shareholders. Comment.
4. Enumerate the various modes of acquiring membership.
5. Who can become a member?
6. A subsidiary company can become member of its holding company. Comment.
7. Comment on the following:
   (a) A minor may become a member of a company.
   (b) A company cannot become a member of another company.
   (c) Every shareholder is a member but every member is not necessarily a shareholder.
   (d) A firm may become a member of a company.
8. When does the liability of a member of a limited company become unlimited?
9. Distinguish between a member and shareholder.

LONG ANSWER TYPE QUESTIONS

1. Explain the various modes of acquiring membership.
2. (a) Can minor or lunatic become a member?
   (b) State the position when shares are allotted to a minor and his name appears on the Registers of Members.
   (c) State the position after attaining majority.
   (d) State the position of minor as transferee of fully paid shares.
3. State the position of a company as a member of another company.
4. Explain the ways in which a person may cease to be a member.
5. Enumerate any 10 statutory rights of members.
6. Explain the liabilities of members.
7. In what ways may a person (i) become (ii) cease to be a member of a company.
8. State giving reasons as to whether the following can become member in a company:
   (a) A Minor (b) A Company (c) A Firm
   (d) A Foreigner (e) An Insolvent

CHAPTER 11

Borrowing Powers and Debentuares

1.0 POWER TO BORROW

1.1 Has Every Company Implied Power to Borrow?

(a) A **trading company** has **implied power** to borrow even though there is no express authority in its Memorandum of Association. In fact, the power to borrow is incidental to the objects of a trading company. The ground for the rule is that "the exigencies of the commerce render such a power necessary".

(b) A **non-trading company** has **no implied power** to borrow. There **must be an express power** to borrow in its Memorandum of Association.

1.2 When can Power to Borrow be exercised?

(a) A **private company** can exercise its borrowing power immediately **after** obtaining the **certificate of incorporation**

(b) A **public company** having share capital can exercise its borrowing powers only **after** obtaining the **Certificate of Commencement of Business**.

(c) However, the provisions do not prevent a simultaneous offer for subscription or allotment of any shares and debentures in case of public companies. [Section 149(5)]

2.0 ULTRA-VIRES BORROWINGS

2.1 Borrowing Ultra Vires the Company

(a) Meaning Where the company has no borrowing power, any borrowing and where the memorandum fixes a limit on borrowing powers of the Board of Directors of a Company, any borrowing in excess of that limit is known as *ultra vires borrowing*.

(b) Void and cannot be ratified Such borrowings are void and the securities given for them are inoperative. In such a case the lender cannot sue the company because it does not create any relation of debtor and creditor. The borrowings which are *ultra vires cannot be ratified by a resolution* passed at a general meeting.

(c) Effect The effect on *ultra vires* borrowing by company depends upon whether the money borrowed has been expended or not.

Case	*Effect*
(a) ***If ultra vires borrowings have not been used.***	**Right of Restitution** The lender may bring injunction against the company to restrain it from using the amount of loan since the lender remains the owner of the money which is *ultra vires* the company, he can take back the property in specie. [***Sinclair*** v. ***Broughman,*** (1914) A.C. 398]

Case	Effect
(b) ***If ultra vires borrowings have been used to pay-off lawful debt of the company***	**Right of Subrogation** The lender steps into the shoes of paid off creditor and consequently he would be entitled to recover his loan to that extent from the company. [***Neeth Building Society* v. *Luce.*** (1889) 43 Ch. D. 158]. But he cannot claim any right to any securities held by the original creditor. [***Re Wrexham Rly. Co.,*** (1889) 1 Ch. 440]
(c) ***If ultra vires borrowings have been used for the purchase of any asset or assets***	The lender may claim repayment of his money out of the asset or assets purchased out of his money. In addition to aforesaid rights, the lender can sue the directors for breach of warranty of authority.

2.2 Borrowings Ultra Vires the Director

(a) Meaning Borrowings which are beyond the powers of the directors but are within the powers of the company are termed as borrowings *ultra vires* the director. Such borrowings are not altogether void.

(b) Not void and can be ratified Such acts can be ratified and made valid by altering its Articles by a special resolution at its general meeting with retrospective effect so as to give directors the powers beyond which they have exceeded.

(c) Effects of Ratification When the acts are so ratified the company becomes liable for such acts. *For example*, if the company has power to borrow, but it restricts the authority of the directors to borrow upto a certain sum. If the directors exceed their authority and borrow more than what they are authorised to borrow, then the company may, if it wishes, ratify the directors' act, in which case the loan binds both the lender and the company as if it has been made with the company's authority in the first place.

(d) Effect of No Ratification If the borrowings *ultra vires* the director are not ratified and are not made valid by altering Articles, the concerned directors shall be liable.

(e) The lender shall have all the rights to recover the money form the company, relying on the doctrine of indoor management as laid down in ***Royal British Bank V Turquand.*** However, if the lender knew about the restrictions imposed on the powers of directors, he shall have no right to recover the money from the company (***Haward v Patent Ivory Mfr.***)

3.0 WHO CAN EXERCISE POWER TO BORROW [SEC. 292]

(a) ***Power to borrow Money by Issue of Debentures***	Such power shall be exercised only by passing a resolution at Board Meeting.
(b) ***Power to borrow money otherwise than by Issue of Debentures***	• Such power can be exercised by the Board or person to whom such power has been delegated. • Such power may be delegated by the Board provided: (a) the resolution delegating the power to borrow money is passed at Board's meeting (b) the Board's resolution specifies total amount that may be borrowed.

4.0 LIMITS ON BORROWINGS [Sec. 293]

The borrowings must be within the statutory limits as per sec 293 and limits if any specified in the Articles. As per sec. 293, the board of directors of a public company shall not borrow money exceeding the aggregate of paid up capital and free reserves unless the approval of shareholders is obtained by passing ordinary resolution at general meeting.

5.0 MEANING OF DEBENTURES

5.1 Literary Meaning

The term '*Debenture*' implies a written acknowledgement of a debt.

5.2 Legal Meaning

According to Section 2(12) of the Companies Act, 1956 "*debenture includes debentures, stock, bonds and any other securities of a company whether constituting a charge on the assets of the company or not.*"

The above definition is not exhaustive because it does not reveal the characteristics of the debentures.

5.3 Other Definitions

1. **According to Palmer,** "*the word 'Debenture' signifies "any instrument under seal, evidencing a deed, the essence of it being the admission of indebtedness.*"
2. **According to Chitty J.,** "*Debenture means a document which either creates a debt or acknowledges it and any document which fulfils either of these conditions is a debenture.*"

5.4 Characteristics of a Debenture

On analysing the aforesaid definitions, the following characteristics of a debenture are revealed:

1. It is an acknowledgement of indebtedness by the company to its holder for the amount stated in it.
2. It is issued under the common seal of the company.
3. It provides for a fixed rate of interest.
4. It provides for repayment of principal sum at the fixed date or dates except in case of perpetual (or irredeemable) debentures.
5. It may or may not be secured.
6. It is expressed to be one of a series of like debentures except where single debenture is issued to one person. [*Robson* v. *Smith,* (1895) 2 Ch. 118]

6.0 DEBENTURE STOCK

6.1 Meaning of Debenture Stock

Debenture stock is the description of debt secured by an instrument which carries interest at a fixed rate. It provides for repayment of principal at the fixed date except in case of perpetual stock which is payable only in the case of winding up or in case of default in paying interest. According to Lord Lindley, 'debenture stock is borrowed capital consolidated into one mass for the sake of convenience'. A company may raise the loan capital in the form of Debenture Stock by issuing Debenture Stock Certificate. Unlike share stock, debenture stock can be issued directly without first issuing debentures.

6.2 Difference between a Debenture and Debenture Stock

The difference between a debenture and debenture stock may be noted as under:

(a) Debentures are transferable only in its entirety while debenture stock is transferable in fractions also.
(b) Debentures need not be fully paid up but debenture stock must always be fully paid up.
(c) Debentures are serially numbered but debenture stock is not.
(d) Debenture is the description of an instrument but debenture stock is the description of debt or sum secured by instrument.

7.0 KINDS OF DEBENTURES

Depending upon the terms and conditions of the issue and redemption, the debentures may of the following types:

7.1 From the Point of View of security

1. **Unsecured Debentures** or **Naked Debentures** are those which are not secured on any asset.
2. **Fully Secured Debentures** are those which are secured *either* on a particular asset *or* on all the assets of the company in general.
   (i) **Secured Debentures having Fixed Charge** When the charge is created against specific assets of the company then such a charge is called a fixed charge. This charge is created against those assets which are held by the company for use in operations and are not meant for sale.
   (ii) **Secured Debentures having Floating Charge** A floating charge is a kind of security for which no specific asset is given, but all assets of the company (excluding those given by way of specific charge to secured creditors) are under charge for such creditors. This implies that before anything is paid to unsecured creditors, creditors holding a floating charge will get their claims settled on a priority basis.
3. **Partly Secured Debentures** In case of partly secured debentures/bond, specific assets are given by way of charge but their value is less than the amount owed by the company.

7.2 From the Point of View of Priority of Charge

1. **First Mortgage Debentures** are those which have a **first claim** on the assets charged.
2. **Second Mortgage Debentures** are those which have a **second claim** on the assets charged.

   The assets against which first charge is created are to be first used in paying off the secured lenders holding first charge. The amount of surplus from such assets, if any, will be utilized for paying off the secured lenders holding second charge. In case, the claims of second charge holders are not fully paid-off, the unpaid amount of such lenders is to be treated as unsecured and hence, to that extent, they will be paid-off along with unsecured creditors. In other words, the unpaid amount of partly satisfied secured creditors will rank alongwith unsecured creditors.

7.3 From the Point of View of Tenure

1. **Redeemable Debentures** are those which are repayable after a specified period in lump sum or by instalments during the life time of the company.
2. **Irredeemable Debentures (or Perpetual Debentures)** are those which are redeemable on the happening of specified events which may not happen for an indefinite period. For example when the company goes into liquidation or makes a default in payment of interest.

7.4 From the Point of View of Registration

1. **Registered Debentures** are those which are payable to the persons whose name appear in the Register of Debentureholders. These can be transferred only by executing a transfer deed. Interest is paid to the registered holder.
2. **Bearer Debentures** are those which are payable to bearer thereof. These can be transferred merely by delivery. Interest is paid to the person who produces the interest coupon attached to such debentures. A *bona fide* transferee for value is not affected by the defect in the title of the transferor.

7.5 From the Point of View of Coupon Rate

1. **Debentures Carrying Fixed Rate of Interest** These debentures carry a specified fixed rate of interest. For example, 15% Debentures.
2. **Debenture Carrying Floating Rate of Interest** These debentures carry a floating rate on interest. The floating interest rate is usually tagged with the bank rate and yield on treasury bond plus a reward for risk. Since the bank rate and yield on treasury securities keep on fluctuating over a period of time, any change is compensated in the risk premium. The rate of interest in such a case is quoted as "PLR + 50 basis points. In this case, if we assume a PLR of 9%, the rate of interest would be 9.5%. The + basis points is determined in relation to risk involved.
3. **A Zero Coupon Bond** is one which does not carry a specified rate of interest. In order to compensate the investors, such bonds are then issued at a substantial discount. The different between the Maturity value and issue price is the total amount of interest related to the duration of the bond. In order to calculate the periodic charge of interest, the amount is calculated by using the following formula of compound value:
   Compount Value (or Maturity Value) = Present Value $(1 + r)^n$

   or $$PV = \frac{MV}{(1+r)^n}$$

   PV = Present of zero coupon bond,
   MV = Maturity value of zero coupon bond.
   n = Life of zero coupon bond, r = Required rate of return

ILLUSTRATION

Tulsian Ltd. issues a zero coupon bond having 10 years maturity with face value of Rs 5,000. At what price the company should issue the bond, if the required rate of return is 10% p.a.?

PV = Maturity Value = Present Value $(1 + r)^n$

PV = Rs 5,000/$(1 + 0.1)^{10}$ = Rs 5,000/2.594 = Rs 1,927.50

It implies that the investor should be able to get a zero coupon bond for Rs 1927.50 with a face value of Rs 5,000.

7.6 From the Point of View of Convertibility

1. **Convertible Debentures (CD)** Those debentures which are convertible into equity shares or other securities *or* at the expiry of specified period(s). Convertible debentures are of two types.
   (i) **Fully Convertible Debentures (FCD)** These are the debentures where the full amount is convertible into shares or other securities at agreed terms and conditions. Where the conversion is to be made at or after 18 months from the date of allotment but before 36 months, the conversion is optional on the part of debentureholders as per SEBI Guidelines. These debentures may or may not carry any interest.
   (ii) **Partly Convertible Debenture (PCD)** These are the debentures where only a portion of the amount of debenture is convertible into shares or other securities at a specified time and remaining part of debenture is redeemable on agreed terms. The portion of debenture which is fully convertible into shares is termed as FCD (i.e., Fully Convertible Debenture) portion and the remaining portion which is not convertible into shares is termed as NCD (i.e., Non-convertible Debenture) portion or popularly known as KHOKHA in Stock Market.

2. **Non-convertible Debentures (NCD)** The debentures which cannot be converted into shares or any other securities are called non-convertible debentures. These are redeemable at the expiry of a specified period(s).

8.0 DISTINCTION BETWEEN FULLY CONVERTIBLE AND PARTLY CONVERTIBLE DEBENTURES

Fully convertible debentures differ from the Partly Convertible Debentures in the following respects:

Basis of Distinction	*Fully Convertible Debentures*	*Partly Convertible Debentures*
(i) ***Classification for computing debt equity ratio***	They are fully classified as equity for computing debt equity ratio.	Convertible portion is classified as 'equity' and non-convertible portion as 'debt'.
(ii) ***Impact on debt equity ratio***	These result in lower debt equity ratio.	These result in relatively higher debt equity ratio.
(iii) ***Capital base***	These result in higher equity capital on conversion of debentures.	These result in relatively lower equity capital on conversion of debentures.
(iv) ***Suitability***	These are better suited for companies without established track record.	These are better suited for companies with established track record.
(v) ***Servicing of equity***	These involve higher burden of servicing of equity.	These involve relatively lesser burden of equity servicing.
(vi) ***Debenture redemption reserve (DRR)***	DRR is not required to be created.	DRR is required to be created for 50% of the face value of the non-convertible portion.
(vii) ***Buy-back arrange-ments***	No buy-back arrangement is required	Buy back arrangement may be made for non-convertible portion.

9.0 DISTINCTION BETWEEN A SHARE AND A DEBENTURE

A share differs from a debenture in the following respects:

Basis of Distinction	*Share*	*Debenture*
1. **Capital v. Loan**	Share is a part of *owned capital*.	Debenture constitutes a *loan*.
2. **Reward for investment**	Reward is the payment of *dividend*.	Reward is the payment of *interest*.
3. **Fluctuations in the rate of interest and dividend**	The rate of dividend *may vary* from year to year depending upon the profit, decisions of directors and members.	The rate of interest is *fixed*.
4. **Charge v. Appropriation**	Payment of dividend is an *appropriation* out of profit and this cannot be made if there is no profit.	Payment of interest is a *charge* against profits and is to be made even if there is no profit.
5. **Priority as to payment of interest/dividend**	Payment of dividend gets *no priority* over the payment of interest.	Payment of interest *gets priority* over the payment of dividend.
6. **Priority as to repay-ment of principal during winding up**	Payment of share capital is made *after* the repayment of debentures.	Payment of debentures is made *before* the payment of share capital.
7. **Secured by charge**	Shares are *not secured* by any charge.	Non-convertible debentures for a term exceeding 18 months are always *secured* by a charge.
8. **Restriction on issue at discount**	Section 79 of the Companies Act, 1956, imposes certain *restrictions* on issue of shares at discount.	No *restriction* is imposed on the issue of debentures at discount.
9. **Voting rights**	Shareholders generally *enjoy* voting rights.	Debentureholders do *not have* any voting rights (except at their class meetings).
10. **Convertibility**	Equity shares can *never be convertible*.	Debentures *can be convertible*.
11. **Trust deed**	Share Trust Deed is *not required* to be executed.	Debenture trust deed is *required* to be executed.

10.0 ISSUE OF DEBENTURES

10.1 When can Debentures be Issued?

A **private** company can issue debentures immediately **after** obtaining the **certificate of incorporation** but **a public** company can issue debentures only after obtaining a **certificate of Commencement of Business**.

10.2 Who can Exercise the Power to Issue Debentures and how?

(a) **Only the Board of Directors** of a company can exercise the power to issue debentures by means of resolution passed at meeting of the Board [Section 292(1)(b)] but subject to restrictions if any imposed by Section 293.

(b) According to Section 293(1)(d), except with the consent of the company in General Meeting the Board of Directors of a public company, or of a private company which is a subsidiary of a public company, shall not exercise the power to borrow moneys where the moneys to be borrowed together with the moneys already borrowed by the company (apart from temporary loans) will exceed the aggregate of the paid up capital of the company and its free reserves.

10.3 Debentures with Voting Rights not Permissible [Section 117]

(a) No company can issue any debentures carrying voting rights at any meeting of the company, whether generally or in respect of any particular classes of business. This provision applies to debentures issued after the commencement of the Companies Act [Section 117].

(b) This means, debentures issued before commencement of this Act may continue to have voting rights.

(c) The idea behind prohibition of issue of debentures with voting rights is to ensure that debentureholders are not placed in a much more advantageous position than the holders of equity shares and are not in a position to influence the policy of the company in a manner detrimental to the interest of the general body of shareholders.

10.4 Power to Issue Debentures [Section 120]

A company shall have the power to issue:

(a) irredeemable debentures; *or*

(b) debentures that are redeemable only on the happening of a contingency, however remote; or

(c) debentures that are redeemable on the expiration of a period, however long.

11.0 DEBENTURES TRUST DEED

11.1 Meaning of Debenture Trust Deed

Debentures Trust Deed is a document executed between a company and the trustees acting on behalf of debentureholders to safeguard the interests of the latter. This deed contains the terms and conditions endorsed on the debentures and defines the rights of the debentureholders and the company. It usually empowers the trustees to appoint a receiver on the breach of certain covenants and to call, hold and conduct the meetings of the debentureholders.

11.2 Advantages of Trust Deed

The advantages of executing a trust deed are as under:

(a) The trustees can act expeditiously and effectively in safeguarding the interest of the debentureholders and enforcing the security on their behalf.

(b) They act as watchdogs in seeing and insisting that the company's obligations under the trust deed are carried out properly.

(c) They are generally empowered to appoint a receiver or take possession of the property on the breach of some covenants.
(d) In case of doubt or difficulty, they can convene meetings to appraise them of the position and to enable them to discuss it can authorise the trustees to pursue any course of action to be beneficial to the debentureholders as a whole.

11.3 Form of Debenture Trust Deed [Section 117A]

Debentures trust deed must be in the prescribed form and must be executed within the prescribed period.

11.4 Inspection of Debenture Trust Deed [Section 117A]

(a) A copy of the trust deed must be open to inspection to any member or debenture holder of the company.
(b) Every member or debentureholder is entitled to obtain copies of such trust deed on payment of prescribed fees.
(c) If a copy of the trust deed is not made available for inspection or is not given to any member or debentureholder, the company and its every officer of the company in default, shall be punishable, for each offence, with fine upto Rs 500 for every day continuing offence.

11.5 Appointment and Duties of Debenture Trustees [Section 117B]

(a) **Duty of Company to Appoint**
A company can not issue a prospectus or a letter of offer to the public for subscription of its debentures, unless the company has, **before such issue**, appointed one or more debenture trustees for such debentures and the company has, on the face of the prospectus or the letter of offer, stated that the debenture trustee or trustees have given their consent to the company to be so appointed.
(b) **Who cannot be appointed as a Debenture Trustee**
No person shall be appointed as a debenture trustee, if he—
   (a) beneficially holds shares in the company;
   (b) is beneficially entitled to moneys which are to be paid by the company to the debenture trustee;
   (c) has entered into any guarantee in respect of principal debts secured by the debentures or interest thereon.
(c) **Functions of Debenture Trustees**
To protect the interest of debentureshoIders (including the creation of securities within the stipulated time) and to redress the grievances of holders of debentures effectively, a debenture trustee is required—
   (a) to ensure that the assets of the company issuing debentures and each of the guarantors are sufficient to discharge the principal amount at all times;
   (b) to satisfy himself that the prospectus or the letter of offer does not contain any matter which is inconsistent with the terms of the debentures or with the trust deed;
   (c) to ensure that the company does not commit any breach of covenants and provisions of the trust deed;
   (d) to take such reasonable steps to remedy any breach of the covenants of the trust deed or the terms of issue of debentures;

(e) to take steps to call a meeting of holders of debentures as and when such meeting is required to be held.

(d) **Power of Debenture Trustee to File Petition before CLB**
Where at any time the debenture trustee comes to a conclusion that the assets of the company are insufficient or are likely to become insufficient to discharge the principal amount as and when it becomes due, the debenture trustee may file a petition before the Company Law Board and the Company Law Board may, after hearing the company and any other person interested in the matter, by an order, impose such restrictions on the incurring of any further liabilities as the Company Law Board thinks necessary in the interests of holders of the debentures.

11.6 Liability of Company to Create Security and Debenture Redemption Reserve [Section 117C]

(a) The company must create a debenture redemption reserve for the redemption of such debentures, to which adequate amounts shall be credited, from out of its profits every year until such debentures are redeemed.
(b) The debenture redemption reserve must not be utilised for any purpose other than for redemption of debentures.
(c) The company must pay interest and redeem the debentures as per terms and conditions of their issue.

11.7 Power of CLB to Direct Company for Redemption

(a) Where a company fails to redeem the debentures on the date of maturity, the Company Law Board may, on the application of any or all the holders of debentures shall, after hearing the parties concerned, direct, by order, the company to redeem the debentures forthwith by the payment of principal and interest due thereon.
(b) If default is made in complying with the order of the Company Law Board the company and every officer in default, shall be punishable with imprisonment upto 3 years and with a fine of at least Rs 500 for every day during which such default continues.

11.8 Right to Inspect trust Deed & Copy There of [Sec. 118]

(a) **Who has right** Every debenture holder and member is entitled to inspect the trust deed as per sec 163 and obtain the copy of the trust deed.
(b) **Consequences of Default** If a default is made by the company in allowing inspection or forwarding copy of trust deed, Company Law Board may direct the company to forthwith allow inspection or forward copies.

11.9 Liability of Trustees [Section 119]

(a) Trustees must act with reasonable care and diligence failing which they would be liable for breach of trust.
(b) Any provision in the trust deed which has the effect of exempting a trustee from or indemnifying him against liability for breach of trust shall be void.
(c) But a trustee may be released from liability by the consent of at least three-fourths of the members present in person or by proxy at a meeting summoned for the purpose.

12.0 DEBENTURE CERTIFICATE [SECTION 113 AND SECTION 53]

12.1 Duty of Company to Deliver Certificate within 3 Months [Section 113]

Every company must, within 3 months of allotment of any of its shares, debentures or debenture stock and within 2 months after the application for registration of the transfer of any such debentures or debenture stock, deliver the certificates of all debentures and debenture stock allotted or transferred in accordance with the procedure laid down in Section 53 of the Companies Act, 1956. However, the CLB may extend the period within which the debenture certificate may be delivered to a further period not exceeding 9 months, if it is satisfied that it is not possible for the company to deliver the certificates within the said period.

12.2 Penalty for default

If default is made in complying with the above provisions, every officer of the company who is in default shall be punishable with imprisonment for a term upto 2 years and the company and its every officer in default shall be punishable with fine upto Rs 5,000 per day of default.

12.3 Power of CLB

If a company on which a notice has been served requiring it to make good any default fails to do so within 10 days of the service of the notice, the CLB may on an application made by the aggrieved person, make an order directing the company and any officer of the company to deliver the certificate or debenture within the period mentioned in the order. The order may provide that all costs incidental to the application shall be borne by the company or by the officer of the company responsible for the default.

12.4 Transfer of Debentures

Bearer debentures are negotiable instruments and hence are transferable by delivery, free from nay equities. A *bona fide* transferee for value gets a good title even if there is any defect in the title of the transferor. Transfer of registered debentures takes place exactly in the same way as the transfer of shares.

13.0 *PARI PASSU* CLAUSES FOR DEBENTURE

13.1 Meaning of Pari Passu Clause for Debenture

The term pari-passu means ranking equally among themselves.

(a) When debentures are described as ranking *pari passu* it means all the debentures of a particular series will rank together without any priority of one over the other as regards the charge created. **The effect of such a clause is that the debentures of that series are to be discharged rateably in the event of insufficient funds**.

(b) When there is no *pari passu* clause, a debenture will rank for priority for the purposes of repayment etc. according to the date of issue and if all of them were issued on the same date, then according to their respective numbers.

(c) A company cannot, however, create a new series of debentures to rank *pari passu* with an old series, unless the power to do so is expressly reserved and contained in the debentures trust deed of the prior series. [*Lister* v. *Henery Lister & Son,* (1893) 41 W.R. 330]

13.2 Duty to File Particulars with the Registrar [Section 128]

In the event of the *pari passu* clause being included in the debentures, it is enough if the following particulars are filed with the Registrar within 30 days after the execution of the deed containing the charges or where there is no deed after the execution of any debentures of the series:

(i) the total amount secured by the whole series,

(ii) the dates of the resolutions authorising the issue of the series,

(iii) The date of deed if any, by which security is created, and

(iv) a general description of the property charged and the name of the trustees for debenture holders, if any, together with the deed containing the charges or a certified copy of the deed or, if there is no deed, one of debentures of the series.

(v) Where more than one issue is made of debentures in the series, particulars of the date and the amount of each issue must be filed with the Registrar.

An omission to do so will not affect the validity of the debentures issued.

14.0 BOOKS AND REGISTERS RELATING TO DEBENTURES

The following books and registers relate to debentures:

(a) Register of Charges (in case Debentures are charged);

(b) Register of Debentureholders;

(c) Index of Debenturesholders;

(d) Foreign Register of Debentureholders; and

(e) Debenture Interest Book.

First four books are ***statutory books*** which are required to be kept as per the provisions of Sections 143(1), 152, 157 and 158 of The Companies Act, 1956, where as the last book is a ***statistical book*** which is not compulsorily required to be kept but which the company usually maintains to keep complete records of interest due and payments.

Notes:

(i) The legal requirements as to the prospectus, allotment, issue of certificate etc. applicable to shares shall also apply to debentures as well. However the condition of minimum subscription is not applicable in the case of debentures.

(ii) **No return of allotment is required to be filed incase of allotment of debentures.**

15.0 POWER TO RE ISSUE REDEEMED DEBENTURES [SECTION 21]

1. A company may reissue debentures which have already been redeemed *unless*:
   (a) the articles provide otherwise, or
   (b) the conditions of the issue provide otherwise, or
   (c) the contract entered into by the company provide otherwise, or
   (d) the company decides to cancel the redeemed debentures by passing a resolution.
2. Upon such reissue, the holders of the debentures shall have and shall be deemed always to have had the same rights and priorities as if the debentures had never been redeemed.
3. The reissue of redeemed debentures requires the same stamp as new debentures.

Note: Terms of reissued debentures cannot be different from those in the place of which, these are reissued. [***Anet Eagasta (Chilean) & Bolivia Railway Co. Trust Deed* v. *Schroder,*** (1939)]

16.0 REMEDIES AVAILABLE TO A DEBENTUREHOLDER

16.1 Remedies of an Unsecured Debentureholder

An unsecured creditor may—

(a) sue the company for the recovery of principal and interest and execute the degree against the company's property.

(b) present a petition for winding up of the company under Section 433(e) of the Act on the basis of the liability of the company to pay its debts and prove his debts as an unsecured creditor.

16.2 Remedies of a Secured Debentureholder

A secured Debentureholder may—

(a) The sue the company for the recovery of principal and interest and execute the degree against the company's property.

(b) The present a petition for winding up of the company under Section 433(e) of the Act on the basis of the liability of the company to pay its debts and prove his debts as an unsecured creditor.

(c) appoint a receiver if the condition of the issue so permit.

(d) have the property sold by the trustee if the trust deed so permit.

(e) apply to the court for the appointment of a receiver.

(f) apply to the court for closure of the company's right to redeem the debentures.

Where a company is being wound up and the security is not sufficient to meet the claim in full, a secured debentureholder may either dispose of the security and prove for the balance of his debt or he may give up the security and prove for the whole debt. However, he cannot prove for interest which becomes due after winding up *nor* can he get interest out of his security when arriving at a balance for which he can prove in the winding up.

Note: Even if a debentureholder owes a debt to the company (which is unable to pay its debts) he cannot set off his debt against the debenture. It is based on the rule that a person claiming a share of a fund must first pay up everything he owes to the fund. [*Shephered* v. *Gregory Ltd.*, (1904)].

VERY SHORT ANSWER TYPE QUESTIONS

1. Name the company which has implied power to borrow.
2. Name the company which does not have implied power to borrow.
3. When can a private company exercise its borrowing powers?
4. When can a public company exercise its borrowing powers?
5. Can there be simultaneous offer for subscription or allotment of any shares and debentures in case of a public companies?
6. What is meant by borrowings *ultra vires* the company?
7. What is meant by borrowings *ultra vires* the directors?
8. What is meant by debentures?
9. What is meant by debenture stock?
10. What is meant by unsecured debentures?
11. What is meant by secured debentures?
12. What is meant by first mortgage debentures?
13. What is meant by second mortgage debentures?
14. What is meant by redeemable debentures?

15. What is meant by perpetual debentures?
16. What is meant by registered debentures?
17. What is meant by bearer debentures?
18. What is meant by convertible debentures?
19. What is meant by non-convertible debentures?
20. What is meant by partly convertible debentures?
21. When can a private company issue debentures?
22. When can a public company issue debentures?
23. Who can exercise the power to issue debentures?
24. How can the power to issue debentures be exercised?
25. Can debentures be issued with voting rights?
26. What is debenture trust deed?
27. What is the time limit for issue of debenture certificate?
28. Is the condition of minimum subscription applicable in the case of debentures?
29. Is return of allotment required to be filed in case of allotment of debentures?
30. What is meant by '*pari passu*' clause in debentures?
31. How will the debentures rank if there is *pari passu* clauses?
32. How will the debentures rank if there is no *pari passu* clause?

SHORT ANSWER TYPE QUESTIONS

1. Explain the effects of borrowings which are *ultra vires* (a) the company (b) the directors.
2. State the characteristics of a debenture.
3. Distinguish between the following:
   (a) debentures and debenture stock.
   (b) fully convertible debentures and partly convertible debentures.
   (c) a share and a debenture.
4. State the advantages of executing a Debenture Trust Deed.
5. State the particulars to be filed with the Registrar in case the *pari passu* clause is included in the debentures.
6. Enumerate the statutory book and register relating to debentures.
7. Comment on the following:
   (a) A non-trading company has implied power to borrow.
   (b) A trading company has unlimited power to borrow.
   (c) A company can borrow on the security of its reserve capital.
   (d) A company having share capital can exercise its borrowing powers after obtaining Certificate of Incorporation.

LONG ANSWER TYPE QUESTIONS

1. (a) Has every company implied power to borrow?
   (b) Who is authorised to borrow?
   (c) If a company borrows beyond its powers, what remedies are open to such lender (i) when the money has not been spent (ii) when the money has been spent to pay the debts of the company?
2. (a) What is a debenture?
   (b) Explain the various kinds of debentures?

CHAPTER

12 Fixed and Floating Charges

1.0 MEANING AND KINDS OF CHARGES

1.1 Meaning of Charge

(a) Charge is one of the form in which a title to property is passed by way of security for money borrowed.
(b) Under this form creditor get no legal rights of property but only gets the right to have the security made available by an order of court.
(c) According to Section 124, the expression 'Charge' includes a mortgage. The charge may be fixed or floating.

1.2 Meaning of Mortgage

(a) According to Section 58 of the Transfer of Property Act, 1882, mortgage is a transfer of interest in specific immovable property for the purpose of securing the payment of money advanced or to be advanced to the company by way of loan. Mortgage can be of immovable property only under the Transfer of Property Act.
(b) The essential differences between charge and mortgage is that in the former case, there is only passing of title, while interest in the property remains with the company; in the latter case there is transfer of interest in property.

1.3 Meaning of Fixed Charge or Specific Charge

(a) A charge is said to be fixed or specific when it is made specifically to cover assets which are ascertained and definite or are capable of being ascertained and defined, at the time of creating the charge e.g. land, buildings, or heavy machinery.
(b) A fixed charge, therefore, is against security of certain specific property, and the company losses the right to dispose off that property as unencumbered.
(c) In other words, the company can deal with such property, subject to the condition of fixed charge.

1.4 Meaning of Floating Charge

(a) A floating charge is a charge on a class of assets present and future which in the ordinary course of business is changing from time to time and leaves the company free to deal with the property as it sees fit until the holders of charge take steps to enforce their security.
(b) A floating charge as a type of security, is peculiar to companies and borrowers. A floating charge, is not attached to any definite property but covers property of a fluctuating type e.g. stock-in-trade and is thus necessarily equitable.

(c) When the charge is floating, the company may, in the ordinary course of business, deal with the property in any manner until the charge attaches. Upon the happening of any of the events set out in the deed of the floating charge, the floating charge crystallises or becomes fixed thereafter the asset comprised in the charge are subject to the same restrictions as under a fixed charge.

(d) **Advantage of a Floating Charge** The company may continue to deal in any way with the property which has been charged for. The company may sell, mortgage or lease such property in ordinary course of its business if it is authorised by its memorandum of association. ***Re Borax Co.,*** (1901) 1 CH 325, it has been held that a company may sell the whole of its undertaking if that is one of the objects specified in its memorandum. Unless specifically precluded, the company can create fixed charge subsequent to floating charges over the same property.
[***Wheatly* v. *Silkstone & High Moor Coal Co. Ltd.,*** (1885) 54 L.J. Ch 78].

1.5 Characteristics of Floating Charge

Justice *Romer* in *Re Y.W. Association Ltd.* case summarized the characteristics of a floating charge as follows:

(a) It is a charge upon a ***class of company's assets*** both present and future and not on specific asset.

(b) The class of assets charged is one which in the ordinary course of business of company is ***changing from time to time.***

(c) The company has ***right to deal*** with such class of asset in the ordinary course of its business until some event contempleted in the agreement occurs, e.g. debenture holders enforcing their securities on a default being made by company either in payment of interest or capital or on the company being wound up.

Some Important Judicial Rulings:

(i) Where a company had issued debentures on the security of, 'Undertaking and all sums of money arising therefrom', it was held to be a floating charge as the term 'Undertaking' meant all the property, present and future'.
[***Re Panama New Zealand Etc. Co.,*** (1870) L.R. 5 Ch. 318]

(ii) Where a company borrowed money on the security of 'all its assets including machinery etc. now lying or that may be bought hereafter until repayment it was held to be a floating charge as (a) it covered all assets both present and future, and (b) the company was left free to use them in the course of its business.
[***Re. Indus Film Corporation Ltd.***, AIR 1939 Sind 100]

(iii) The company can create a specific charge of the property already subject to a floating charge without the consent of the holders of the charge and the registered mortgage shall have priority over the charge. [***Theatley* v. *Silkstone Co.,*** (1885) 29 Ch. D 715]

(iv) Where the Company has been prohibited from creating subsequent mortgage, a creditor who takes a subsequent specific mortgage with the notice of the prohibition shall not have priority and the floating charge. [***Wilsen* v. *Kelland,*** (1901) 2 Ch 306]

(v) A company cannot create a fixed charge in priority to the floating charge after it has crystallised.

(vi) Before crystallisation of the floating charge, a company may even sell the whole of the undertaking if that is one of the objects specified in the memorandum.
[***Re. Boreak Co.,*** (1901) 1 Ch. 326]

1.6 Invalidity of Floating Charge [Section 534]

A floating charge created within 12 months immediately preceeding the commencement of the winding up, shall, be invalid **except—**

(a) where it is proved that the company immediately after the creation of the charge was solvent.

(b) to the extent of the amount of any cash actually paid to the company at the time of or after the creating of charge in consideration thereof with interest on that amount @ 5% p.a. or such other rate as may be notified by the Central Government.

1.7 Crystallisation of Floating Charge

(a) **Meaning** Crystallisation means that the rights of the company to deal with the assets subject to floating charge comes to an end.

(b) A floating charge crystallises and the security becomes fixed in the following cases:
   (i) when the company goes into liquidation;
   (ii) when the company ceases to carry on the business;
   (iii) when the creditors or debentureholders take steps to enforce this security e.g. by appointing receiver to take possession of the property charged;
   (iv) on the happening of the event specified in the deed.

(c) In the aforesaid circumstances, the floating charge is said to become fixed or to have crystallised. Until the charge crystallises or attaches or becomes fixed the company can deal with the property so charged in any manner it likes. The company may even sell its whole undertaking if that is otherwise permissible as per the objects specified in the memorandum.

(d) Although a floating charge is a present security, yet leaves the company free to create a specific mortgage on its property having priority over the floating charge. In ***Government Stock Investment Co. Ltd.* v. *Manila Railway Co. Ltd.*,** (1897) A.C 81, the debentures created a floating charge. Three months' interest became due but the debenture holders took no steps and so the charge did not crystallise but remained floating. The company then made a mortgage of a specific part of its property. Held, the mortgage had priority. The debentures remained merely a floating security as the debenture holders had taken no steps to enforce their security.

1.8 Priority of Preferential Creditors Over a Debentureholders' Floating Charge [Section 123]

Where a receiver is appointed on behalf of the debentureholders having floating charge or possession is taken of any property subject to floating charge, the preferential creditors u/s 530 will be ***paid first*** out of any assets coming to the hand of receiver or other person taking possession in priority to any claim for principal or interest in respect of debenture. Payment made in respect of such preferential creditors shall, however, be recouped, as far as may be, out of the assets available for payment of unsecured creditors.

2.0 DISTINCTION BETWEEN FIXED AND FLOATING CHARGE

Basis of Distinction	*Fixed Charge*	*Floating Charge*
1. **Assets subject to charge**	It is created on assets ascertained and definite.	It is created on all assets both present and future.
2. **Can Nature of Assets be changed?**	Cannot be changed.	Change from time to time in ordinary course of business.
3. **Right of company to deal with**	Company cannot deal except with consent of charge holder.	Company can deal until it becomes fixed.
4. **Priority of preferential creditors**	Preferential creditors have no priority over fixed charge holders.	Preferential creditors have priority over floating charge holders where assets are insufficient to meet liability in full u/s 123.
5. **Priority over each other**	Fixed charge holders will have priority over floating charge holder even though it might have been created later in time.	Floating charge holders have no priority.

Some Important Judicial Rulings:

(i) Where the power to create a charge is not given either by the Memorandum or Articles, it may be taken by passing a special resolution.
[***Newton* v. *Debenture- holders of Anglo Australian etc. Co.***, (1895) A.V. 244]

(ii) A company cannot borrow money on the security of reserve capital as the latter can not be called except at the time of winding up of the company.
[***Bartlett* v. *May Fair Property Co.***, (1898) 2 Ch. 28]

(iii) A company cannot borrow on the security of books of account as such books are required to be kept at the registered office of the company and must be open for inspection.

(iv) No charge can be created over the liability of the member of a guarantee company as the guaranteed amount cannot be called except at the time of winding up of the Company. [***Re Pyle Works Ltd.***, (1890) 44 Ch. D 534]

(v) Where the memorandum empowered a company to borrow on any security of the company, it was held that the company could create a charge on its uncalled capital.
[***Newton* v. *Debentureholders of Anglo Australian etc. Co.***, (1895) A.C. 244]

(vi) Where the company could borrow on the security of any property of the company, it was held that it could not create a charge on its uncalled Capital as this becomes property only when it is called up and not before. It is only a property potentially.
[***Irvine* v. *Union Bank of Australia,*** (1877) 2 A.C. 366]

(vii) Where the company has the power to create a charge on 'present and future property', it was held not to be sufficient authority to create a charge on uncalled capital.
[***Re Streatham Estate Co.***, (1897) 1 Ch. 15]

(viii) The power of a company to forfeit shares does not expire by creating a charge on its uncalled capital. [***Re Agency Land & Finance Co.***, (1903) 20 T.L.R. 41]

3.0 REGISTRATION OF CHARGES

3.1 What are the Charges Required to be Registered? [Sec 125(4)]

Section 125(4) provides that the following charges must be registered with the Registrar of Companies:

(a) a charge for the purpose of securing any issue of debentures.
(b) a charge on uncalled share capital of the company.
(c) a charge on any immovable property. (whether situated in *or* outside India)
(d) a charge on any book debts of the company.
(e) a charge, ***not being a pledge,*** on any movable property of the company.
(f) a floating charge on the undertaking or any property of the company including stock-in-trade.
(g) a charge on calls made but not paid.
(h) a charge on a ship or any share in a ship.
(i) a charge on goodwill or a patent or a licence under a patent, on a trade mark or on a copy right or a licence under copyright.

Notes: Pledge of Movable property does not require registration with Registrar.

3.2 Time Limit for Registration of Charges [Sec 125(1)]

(a) Particulars of every charge alongwith copy of instrument creating charge must be filed with the Registrar within **30 days of its creation.**
(b) However, the Registrar, may **extend this period** by a further period of 30 days on payment of such additional fee not exceeding 10 times the amount of fee prescribed in Schedule X to the Act as the Registrar may determine if the Registrar that is satisfied that these was sufficient reason for delay.

Note: Where there is a document, the time runs not from the date of agreement to advance money or the date at which the money is actually advanced, but the date at which document is executed [***Columbia Fire Proofing Co. Ltd.,*** 1912 Ch. 11], ***Capital Countries Bank*** 1913.2. Ch. 336).

3.3 Remedies Available to Company for Failure on its Part to Register with the Registrar within the Prescribed Time Limit

(a) If only 30 days from the date of creation of charge have expired, the company may apply to Registrar for extension of a period for 7 days u/s 125.
(b) If period including extended period of 7 days has already expired, the company or any other interested person may apply to Company Law Board and seek extension of time for filling of the particulars for registration u/s 141(1).

The Company Law Board on being satisfied that:

(a) Such failure was accidental or due to inadvertance or due to some other sufficient cause or was not of nature to prejudice the position of creditors or shareholders of company, or
(b) it is just and equitable to grant relief on the grounds.

CLB may grant the extension of time on such terms and condition as it may deem just and convenient.

3.4 Date of Notice of Charge [Sec 126]

Any person acquiring the property in respect of which any charge has been created and registered, shall be deemed to have acquired the same with the notice of the charge as from the date of registration of charge.

Some Important Judicial Rulings:

(i) The mortgage or charge cannot be invalidated merely because of the delay by the Registrar in registering the particulars which were filed with him on time.
[***Benaras Bank Ltd.* v. *Bank of Bihar,*** I.L.R. 1646 All. 867]

(ii) An equitable mortgage by deposit of the title deed required to be registered.
[***Maneklal* v *Saraspur Mfg. Co.,*** *29* Bom. C.R. 253]

(iii) A simple debenture does not require any registration because such debenture in neither secured by a mortgage nor by a charge but it is a simple unsecured debt.

(iv) A mere lien does not require registration.
[***Ashby Warner Co.* v. *Simmons,*** (1936) All. E.R. 697]

(v) A charge by operating of the law does not require registration.
[***Humkumchand* v. *Pioneer Mills*** AIR (1927) Oudh 55]

3.5 Effects of Non-Registration

If a charge which requires registration under Section 125, is not registered, the consequences are as follows:

1. The charge shall be ***void against the liquidator and any creditor*** of the company. [Section 125(1)]
2. Any contract or obligation for the repayment of the money secured by the charge shall remain unaffected. [Section 125(2)]
3. Money secured by charge ***immediately becomes payable***. [Section 125(3)]
4. The company and its every officer in default shall be punishable with a fine upto Rs 5,000 for every day during which the default continues. [Section 142(1)]
5. The security for the debt may not be valid but the debt itself remains good as simple debt. [*C. Padumji Company* v. *Moose,* 2 Bomb. L.R. 1288]
6. No right of lien can be claimed on the documents of title as they are only ancillary to the charge and were delivered pursuant to the charge.
[***Re Molton Ltd.,*** (1868) Ch. 325 (1968) 53 Cp. case 833]
7. The creditor who lawfully takes possession of the goods before the winding up of the company is not affected by non-registration of floating charge on stock-in-trade.
[***Mercantile Bank of India* v. *Chartered Bank of India,*** (1937) All. E.R. 2311]
8. The company whose properties or goods are charged can not seek to repudiate the charge when the charge becomes void due to non-registration because Section 125(1) does not provide that the charge shall be void against the company.
[***Monolithic Building Co's case,*** (1975) 1 Ch. 643]
9. In case an earlier charge and a subsequent charge have been created in succession of same charge holder and the latter charge becomes void on account of non-registration, the equitable doctrine of revivor will apply so as to revive the earlier charge.
[***United Bank of India* v. *K.C. Mullick and Sons Ltd.,*** *1966]*
10. Registered charge holder shall have priority over unregistered one.
[***Re Mondithic Co.,*** 1915]
11. The company may give a subsequent valid mortgage to secure the same debt.
12. Until liquidation, the person seeking to enforce such a charge, has available to him all remedies of a mortgage against the company, though not against other creditors.
13. During liquidation the chargeholder (creditor) assumes the status of an unsecured creditor, as the charge is void against liquidator and creditors.

3.6 Registration of Charges or Properties Acquired Subject to Charge [Section 127]

(a) Where a company acquires any property which is already subject to a charge, the company must file the particulars of the charge and a copy of the instrument creating the charge with the Registrar for registration within 30 days of the date on which the acquisition is completed.

(b) If default is made in complying with the above provision, the company and every officer of the company who is in default, shall be punishable with a fine upto Rs 5,000.

4.0 REGISTER OF CHARGES TO BE KEPT BY REGISTRAR [SECTION 28 TO 131]

4.1 Duty of Registrar The Registrar must keep a register, in respect of each company, containing the particulars of all the charges requiring registration.

4.2 Duty of Company Every company must forward to the Registrar the particulars of all charges requiring registration in Form No. 13 with a fee of Rs 10 for the purpose of entry in the Register.

4.3 Particulars to be Entered

1. In case of a charge to the benefit of which the holders of a series of debentures are entitled:
   (i) the total amount secured by the whole series;
   (ii) the date of resolution authorising the issue of series;
   (iii) a general description of the property;
   (iv) the names of the trustees, if any, for the debentureholders; and
   (v) particulars of any discount, commission or allowance paid for subscribing or procuring subscription for any debentures of the company. [Secs. 128 and 129]
2. In the case of any other charge:
   (i) If the charge is created by the company, the date of its creation; and if the charge was existing on property acquired by the company, the date of the acquisition of the property;
   (ii) the amount secured by the charge;
   (iii) short particulars of the property charged; and
   (iv) the persons entitled to the charge.

4.4 Numbering The pages of the register must be consecutively numbered.

4.5 Signature The Registrar must sign or initial every page of the register.

4.6 Inspection The register must be open to inspection by any person on payment of Rs 10 for each inspection. [Section 130]

4.7 Index The Registrar must keep a chronological index, in the prescribed form and with the prescribed particulars, of the charges registered with him. [Section 131]

5.0 CERTIFICATE OF REGISTRATION [SECTION 132 AND 133]

(a) The Registrar must give a certificate of registration stating the amount secured by the charge. The certificate shall be conclusive evidence that the legal requirements have been complied with. [Section 132]

(b) The company shall cause copy of every certificate of registration to be endorsed on every debenture or certificate of debenture stock which is issued by the company and payment of which is secured by the charge so registered.

(c) Default is punishable with a fine up to Rs 10,000. [Section 133]

6.0 MODIFICATION OF CHARGE [SECTION 135]

6.1 Duty of Company to Send Particulars of Modification to the Registrar

The company is required to send the particulars of modifications in the terms or conditions or the extent or operation of any registered charge to the Registrar like the registration of a charge.

6.2 Meaning of Modification

The term '*modification*' includes variation of any of the terms of the agreement including variation of rate of interest which may be by mutual agreement or by operation of law. Even if the rights of a charge holder are assigned to a third party, it will be regarded as a modification.

6.3 What constitutes Modification?

1. where the charge is modified by varying any terms and conditions of the existing charge by agreement;
2. where the modification is in pursuance of an agreement for enhancing or decreasing the limits;
3. where the modification is by ceding a *pari passu* charge;
4. change in rate of interest (other than bank rate);
5. change in repayment schedule of loans (this is not applicable in working capital loans which are repayable on demand); and
6. partial release of the charge on a particular asset or property.

6.4 Duty to Notify the Registrar about Appointment of Receiver or Manager

If any person obtains an order for the appointment of a receiver or manager from the court or if any person appoints such a receiver or manager under any powers contained in any instrument in respect of any property of a company, he must give notice of the fact to the Registrar within ***30 days of*** the passing of the order or of making the appointment. The Registrar shall, on payment of the prescribed fee, enter the fact in the register of charges. A similar notice must be given when such a person ceases to act. A defaulter shall be punishable with a fine upto Rs 500 for every day during which the default continues. (Section 137)

6.5 Duties of Company regarding Registration of a Charge or its Modification or its Satisfaction

1. To file with the Registrar for registration complete particulars of every charge created by company and of every issue of debenture of a series. Such registration may also be

effected on an application of an interested person other than the company. In such a case the person shall be entitled to recover from the company the amount of any fees properly paid by him for such registration. (Section 134)

2. To send the Registrar the particulars of modification in terms and condition of any registered charge (if any). (Section 135)
3. To cause a copy of every instrument creating any charge requiring registration to be kept at the registered office of the company. (Section 136)
4. **To intimate the Registrar of the payment or satisfaction in full of any registered charge within 30 days from the date of such payment or satisfaction.** (Section 138)

Note: Part payment of satisfaction need not be intimated.

6.6 Procedure regarding Registration of Satisfaction of Charge in full [Sections 138–139–140]

The procedure regarding registration of satisfaction of charge is discussed below:

1. The company must give intimation to the Registrar of the payment or satisfaction **in full** of any charge within **30 days** from the date of such payment or satisfaction.
2. On receipt of intimation, the Registrar must send a show cause notice to the holder of charge calling upon him to reply within a period **not exceeding 14 days** why payment or satisfaction should not be recorded.
3. If no cause in shown, the Registrar shall order that a memorandum of satisfaction shall be entered in the Register of charges.
4. If cause is shown, the Registrar shall record a note to that effect in the Register and shall inform the company that he has done so.

6.7 Power of Registrar to make Entries without Company's Intimation (Section 139)

The Registrar is empowered to enter a memorandum of satisfaction in whole or in part even if no intimation has been received by him from the company provided he is satisfied that—

(a) the debt for which charge was given has been paid or satisfied in whole or in part, or

(b) part of the property or undertaking has been released from the charge or has ceased to form part of the company's property or undertaking.

6.8 Duty of Registrar to Furnish Memorandum of Satisfaction [Section 140]

Where the Registrar enters a memorandum of satisfaction in whole or in part, he shall furnish the company with a copy of the memorandum.

7.0 POWER OF CLB TO ORDER FOR RECTIFICATION OF REGISTER OF CHARGES [SECTION 141]

7.1 Nature of Relief The Company Law Board may direct the rectification of the register of charges or extend time for registration of the charges on an application by the company or any interested party.

7.2 Condition for Relief CLB may grant relief—

(i) where the omission to register a charge within the required time is accidental or due to inadvertence or to some other sufficient cause or is not of nature to prejudice the position of creditors or shareholders of the company or

(ii) where it is just and equitable to grant relief.

7.3 CLB may make such order as to the costs of an application as it thinks fit.

7.4 Where CLB extends time for the registration of a charge, the order shall not prejudice any rights acquired in respect of the property concerned before the charge is actually registered.

8.0 REGISTER OF CHARGES (SECTION 143)

8.1 Duty of Company Every company must keep at its registered office a register of charges and enter there in all charges specifically affecting any property of the company.

8.2 Particulars to be Entered In each case, the following particulars must be entered namely:

(a) a short description of property charged,
(b) the amount of charges,
(c) except in case of securities to bearer, the names of person entitled to charge.

8.3 Penalty for Default Any officer of the company knowingly in default shall be punishable with fine upto Rs 5,000.

9.0 RIGHT TO INSPECT INSTRUMENTS CREATING CHARGES AND COMPANY'S REGISTER OF CHARGES [SECTION 144]

9.1 Rights [Section 144(1) and (2)]—The copies of instruments creating charges and the register of charges shall be open for at least 2 hours during business hours at registered office to the inspection of—

(a) any creditor or member without fee,
(b) any other person on payment of prescribed fee (i.e. Rs 10 at present).

9.2 Penalty for Default [Section 144(3)] If inspection is refused, the company and its every officer in default shall be punishable with fine upto Rs 500 and with a further fine upto Rs 200 for every day during which the refusal continues.

9.3 Power of CLB [Section 144(4)] CLB may order an immediate inspection of the said copies or register.

VERY SHORT ANSWER TYPE QUESTIONS

1. What is meant by charge?
2. What is meant by mortgage?
3. What is meant by fixed charge?
4. What is meant by floating charge?
5. Can a company borrow on the security of
   (a) reserve capital (b) books of accounts
   (c) book debts (d) uncalled capital
6. Can a charge be created over the liability of members of a guarantee company?
7. Does the power the forfeit shares expire by creating a charge on uncalled capital?
8. What is the time limit for registration of charge created by the company?

9. What is the time limit for registration of charge on properties acquired subject to charge?
10. By whom are the charges created on the property of a company to be registered?
11. Is the pledge of any movable property of the company required to be registered?

SHORT ANSWER TYPE QUESTIONS

1. (a) State the characteristics of a floating charge.
   (b) When shall a floating charge be valid?
   (c) When shall a floating charge created within 12 months preceding the commencement of the winding up not be invalid?
   (d) When does a floating charge crystallise?
   (e) Distinguish between fixed charge and floating charge
2. Write a short note on the following:
   (a) Register of charges to be kept by the Registrar.
   (b) Certificate registration of charges.
   (c) Modification of charge.
   (d) Entry of Appointment of Receiver or Managers.
   (e) Duties of a company in relation to charges.
   (f) Registration of satisfaction of charge.
   (g) Rectification of Register of Charges.
   (h) Remedies available to company for failure on its part to register with the register within the prescribed time limit.
   (i) Register of charges to be kept by the company.
3. Comment on the following: "If a charge is not registered, money secured becomes immediately liable."

LONG ANSWER TYPE QUESTIONS

1. (a) Mention the charges required to be registered.
   (b) State the time limit for registration of charges.
   (c) Explain the effects of non-registration of charge.
2. (a) What is a floating charge?
   (b) How does it differ from a fixed charge?
   (c) When does a floating charge crystallise?

CHAPTER 13 Meetings and Procedures

1.0 MEANING OF MEETING

Meeting is a means of action for the purpose of taking a decision. Unlike a natural person, a company cannot think and express its will or make a decision. A company can express its will and make a decision only through the resolution passed at properly conveyed and constituted meetings. The affairs of a company are conducted by collective action of the members through the general meeting and that of directors through Board meeting.

2.0 CLASSIFICATION OF MEETINGS

Meetings held the Companies Act may be classified as follows:

1. Meetings of shareholders or members:
   - (a) Statutory meeting.
   - (b) Annual general meeting.
   - (c) Extraordinary general meeting.
   - (d) Class meetings.
2. Meeting of debentureholders.
3. Meetings of creditors and contributories in winding up.
4. Meeting of creditors otherwise than in winding up.
5. Meeting of directors:
   - (a) Board meeting:
   - (b) Committee meeting.

3.0 STATUTORY MEETING [SECTION 165]

Statutory meeting is the first meeting of the members of a public limited company having share capital and is held only once during the lifetime of the company.

3.1 Which Company is required to Hold Statutory Meeting?

Every Public limited company having share capital is required to hold such meeting. However, if a private company becomes a public company by virtue of Section 3(i)(iv) or converts itself into a public company 'within period of 6 months from date of its incorporation, it shall be required to hold such meeting.

3.2 To Which Type of Company this Section does not Apply?

(1) Private company (other than banking company) [Section 165(10)]

(2) Government companies

(3) Private company becoming a public company by virtue of Section 3(i)(iv) or on its conversion into a public company after period of 6 months from date of its incorporation
(4) Company not having share capital

3.3 When is to be held?

Such meeting is to be held after the expiry of 1 month but before the expiry of 6 months from the date on which the company is entitled to commence business.
Note: It cannot be held prior to 1 month.

3.4 Object of the Meeting

The object of this meeting is to provide an opportunity to the members of the company to discuss all matters relating to the promotion and formation of the company.

3.5 Place, Date and Hours of Conducting Meeting

Such meeting can be held at **any place, any day and at any time** because the Act is silent on these points.

3.6 At least 21 Clear Days Notice of the Meeting

At least 21 clear days' notice must be given (Section 171). A shorter notice less than 21 days may be given if the consent is obtained thereto—

(a) by the members holding at least 95% of the paid up share capital carrying voting rights in case of the company having share capital.
(b) by member holding at least 95% of the total voting power in case of the company having no share capital.

Note: The notice must state that it is a statutory meeting. [*Gardner* v. *Iredel*]

3.7 Quorum [Section 174]

The term 'Quorum' means the minimum number of members required to constitute a valid meeting and to transact business threat. Unless the articles provide for a larger number, quorum shall be:

Case	*Minimum number required to constitute meeting*
In case of meeting originally held	5 members personally present.
In case of meeting adjourned due to lack of quorum	Members present **Notes:** (i) A single member present shall not constitute quorum at an adjourned meeting. (ii) Even 2 proxies present can constitute quorum at an adjourned meeting.
In case of meeting adjourned due to other reasons	5 members personally present.

In all of the above case, article may provide for the higher number for the purpose of constituting the quorum. But article cannot provide for the shorter number for the purpose of constituting quorum.

3.8 Statutory Report

(i) When to send statutory Report—A statutory report must be sent to every member **at least 21 clear days before the day of the meeting**. Whilst computing the 21 days, the day of service of the notice and day of holding of the meeting are excluded. Each of the 21 days must be a full calendar day and **not a part of the day**. However, such report can be sent at shorter notice if the consent of all the members entitled to attend and vote is obtained in writing prior to or at or even subsequent to meeting concerned.

(ii) Eight Contents of Statutory Report [Section 165(3)]

(a) **Regarding Shares :** (i) The total number of shares allotted, (ii) shares allotted as fully paid or partly paid, (iii) shares issued for consideration otherwise than for cash, (iv) the extent to which shares are paid up, and (v) the consideration for which shares have been allotted.

(b) **Cash :** The total amount of cash received in respect of shares allotted for cash.

(c) **An Abstract of the Receipts and Payment A/c up to date within 7 days of the date of report, showing** (i) the receipts from shares, debentures and other sources, (ii) payments made, (iii) balance in hand, and (iv) an account or estimate of the preliminary expenses of the company, (v) any commission or discount paid, or to be paid on the issue or sale of shares or debentures,

(d) **Particulars of Directors etc.** The names, addresses and occupations of the directors, auditors, manager and secretary, if any and any changes therein, if any occurred since the date of incorporation.

(e) **Contracts** The particulars of any contract, or modifications thereof submitted to the meeting for its approval.

(f) **Underwriting Contract** The extent, if any, to which each underwriting contract has not been carried out and the reasons thereof

(g) **Calls-in-arrears from every director and manager.**

(h) The particulars of any **commission or brokerage paid or payable to any director or manager** in connection with the issue or sale of shares and debentures.

(iii) Certification by at least 2 Directors [Section 165(4)] The statutory report must be certified by at least 2 directors of the company one of them must be managing director if any.

(iv) Certification by Auditors Auditors are required to certify the statutory report after the certification by directors on the following three matters which relates to :

(a) the shares allotted by the company

(b) cash received on such shares and

(c) the receipts and payments (both capital and revenue) of the company.

(v) Delivery of the Report to Registrar [Section 165(5)] After the copies of the report have been sent to the members of the company, then the company must send the copy of the report to the Registrar of the company for registration.

(vi) In Prescribed Form The statutory report must be in Form No. 22 of the General Forms.

3.9 Procedure at the Meeting

(a) **List of Members**—A list showing the names, addresses and occupations of the members of the company and the no. of the shares held by them must be produced at the commencement of the meeting and must be open and accessible to any member during the continuance of the meeting. [Section 165(6)]

(b) **Discussions**—Members present may discuss any matter related to the formation of the company or arising out of the statutory report whether previous notice has been given or not,

(c) **Resolution**—No resolution can be passed unless notice is given in accordance with the provisions of the Act. [Section [165(7)]

(d) **Adjournment of Statutory Meeting**

(i) the statutory meeting may be adjourned from time to time, and at any adjourned meeting, any resolution of which **notice** has been given in accordance with the provisions of the Act, whether **before or after the former meeting,** may be passed; and the adjourned meeting shall have-the same power as an original meeting. [Section 165(8)]

(ii) **Exception to General Rule**—The statutory meeting also provides an exception to the normal rule that only business left unfinished at the original meeting can be transacted at the adjourned meeting [Reg. 53(2), Table A]. Members have a right to introduce new business at the adjourned meeting, since the Act provides that any resolution of which notice has been given in accordance with the provisions of the Act, either *before or after* the former meeting, may be passed, and the adjourned meeting has the same power as an original meeting. If the meeting wishes to pass a resolution on any matter which it is entitled to discuss it may adjourn so that the notice in accordance with the provisions of the Act may be given in the interval.

(iii) The power to adjourn rests with the decision of the meeting Thus, the chairman may not adjourn without the consent of the meeting, and must adjourn if so directed by the meeting, even if any discretionary power is given to the chairman by the articles. Normally, where the chairman is given a discretion he is not bound to adjourn the meeting even if the majority desires it [***Parashuram* v. *Tata Industrial Bank Ltd.*,** (1924)].

(e) The provisions relating to Notice, Quorum, Adjournment, Chairman, Proxies and Voting shall be governed by general sections [Sections 171 to 186] as are applicable to the general meetings.

3.10 Consequences of Default

(a) If the default is made in complying with the provisions of Section 165, every officer who is in default shall be punishable with fine upto Rs 5,000. [Section 165(9)]

(b) The court may order for the compulsory winding up of the company if default is made in delivering the statutory report to the registrar or in holding the statutory meeting [Section 433(b)]; or

The court, instead of winding up order, may direct the company to deliver statutory report or hold statutory meeting. [Section 443(3)]

4.0 ANNUAL GENERAL MEETING [SECTIONS 166 TO 168]

4.1 Which Company is bound to Hold?

Every company must hold an 'Annual General Meeting'. [Section 166(1)]

4.2 When is to be held?

First Annual General Meeting

(i) It must be held **within 18 months of its 'incorporation**. Where the company hold such meeting then the company is not required to hold any annual general meeting in the year of its incorporation or in the following year. [1st Provisio of Section 166(1)]

(ii) It must be held **within 9 months of the end of financial year** [Section 210(3)].
Meaning of Financial year: The financial year means the period for which Profit & Loss Account is prepared. It may be less or more than a calendar year but the period of financial year must **not exceed 15 months and may extend to 18 months** with special permission of the Registrar. [Section 210(4)]

PRACTICAL ILLUSTRATION 1

	I	*II*	*III*
Date of incorporation	31st Dec. 20X1	31st Dec. 20X1	31st Dec. 20X1
Financial year ended	30th Sept. 20X2	31st Mar. 20X3	30th June 20X3*
Last date for holding Annual General Meting	30th June 20X3	30th June 20X3	30th June 20X3

*Here special permission from the Registrar has to be obtained since financial year exceed 15 months.

Subsequent Annual General Meeting

(i) It must be held in **each calendar year**. [Section 166(1)]

(ii) It must be held **within 15 months of date of previous AGM.** [Section 166(1)]

(iii) It must be held **within 6 months of the end of the financial year.**

These three requirements are cumulative and separate. Failure to comply with any of them constitutes an offence unless an extension of time has been granted for holding the meeting by the Registrar of Companies. The period of such extension is limited to 3 months. If extension has been granted the 6 months period will be increased by such extension.

PRACTICAL ILLUSTRATION 2

Case	*Financial year ended*	*Last date for holding AGM*	*AGM held on*
1st	31st Dec. 20X1	30th June 20X2	1st Jan. 20X2
2nd	31st Dec. 20X2	31st Mar. 20X3	30th April 20X3
3rd	31st Dec. 20X3	30th June 20X4	30th Aug. 20X4*

*2 month's extension was granted by the Registrar of companies

In 2nd AGM there is the violation of the Section 166 since the time gap between two AGM is more than 15 months

In 3rd AGM there is no violation of the Section 166 since the time gap of more than 15 months between two AGM of 20X3 and 20X4 has resulted after approval for extension of time from the Registrar.

PRACTICAL ILLUSTRATION 3

Cases	*Financial year ended*	*Last Date for holding AGM*	*AGM held on*
1st	30/09/20X1	31/03/20X2	31/12/20X1
2nd	30/09/20X2	31/03/20X3	01/01/20X3

In 2nd there is the violation of the Section 166 since no AGM could not be held during the calendar year 20X2.

PRACTICAL ILLUSTRATION 4

Cases	*Financial year ended*	*Last Date for holding AGM*	*AGM held on*
1st	30/06/20X1	31/12/20X1	31/12/20X1
2nd	30/06/20X2	31/12/20X2	31/01/20X3*

*1 month's extension was granted by the Registrar of companies

In 2nd AGM there is no violation of the Section 166 since the AGM could not be held in the year 20X2 because of extension granted by the Registrar.

PRACTICAL ILLUSTRATION 5

Cases	*Financial year ended*	*Last Date for holding AGM*	*AGM held on*
1st	30/06/20X1	31/12/20X1	31/ 09/ 20X1
2nd	30/06/20X2	31/12/20X2	31/ 01/ 20X3*

*1 month's extension was granted by the Registrar of companies

In 2nd AGM there is no violation of the Section 166 since gap of more than 15 months resulted and AGM during calendar year 20X2 could not be held because of extension granted by the Registrar.

4.3 Duty of Board to Lay Final Accounts [Section 210(1)]

At every AGM held in pursuance of Section 106, the Board of Directors shall lay before the company.

(a) a Balance Sheet as at the end of period specified in Section 210(3)

(b) a Profit and Loss Account for that period.

4.4 Period for which Profit and Loss shall be Prepared

The Profit and Loss Account shall relate to:

AGM	*Period*
(a) ***In case of the first AGM***	The period beginning with the incorporation of the company and ending with a day which shall not precede the day of meeting by more than 9 months.
(b) ***In the case of any subsequent AGM***	The period beginning with the day immedi-ately after the period for which the account was last submitted and ending on day which shall not precede the day of meetings by more than 6 months, or in case where an extension is granted u/s 166, by more than 6 months and extension so granted.

4.5 Place, Date and Hours of Conducting AGM [Section 166(2)]

(a) **Time**—AGM must be called for **at *any time during business hours***.

(b) **Day**—AGM must be called on a day which is ***not a public holiday,***

(c) **Place**—AGM must be held either **at the *registered office*** of the company *or* at other some *place within* the city, town or village in which the *registered office* of the company is situated.

(d) **Exemption from provisions as to Time, Day and Place of AGM**—The Central Government may exempt any class of companies from this provision subject to such conditions as it may impose. In pursuance of this power, the Central Government has exempted Licensed Companies u/s 25 provided the time, date and place of each AGM are decided before hand by board of directors having regard to the direction if any given in this regard by the company in general meeting.

(e) **Fixing of Time of AGM**—Public company or a private company which is the subsidiary of a public company by its articles can also fix the *time* for its Annual general meeting or by resolution passed in previous Annual general meeting can also fix the time for its subsequent Annual general meeting.

(f) **Fixing of Place of AGM**—An independent Private Company in addition to the power given above can also fix the place for meeting in the similar manner given above. Hence in case of independent private company meeting can be held at any place. It is not a necessary that such a place should be within the city, town or village in which the registered office of the company is situated.

(g) **Meaning of Public Holiday [Section 2(38)]**

(i) "Public holiday" means a public holiday within the meaning of the Negotiable Instrument Act, 1881.

(ii) According to Negotiable Instrument Act the Public Holiday includes Sundays and any other day declared by the Central Government, by notification in the Official Gazette, to be a public holiday.

(iii) If any day is declared by the Central Government as a Public Holiday after the notice calling the meeting has been issued, then such holiday shall not be deemed to be a Public Holiday in relation to such meeting.

4.6 Power of Central Govt. [Section 167]

(i) **Who can invoke Sec. 167**—A member and not a company is empowered to invoke the provision of Section 167. A company cannot seek direction against itself. [***M. Sampath v. AKMN Cylinders Pvt. Ltd.***]

(ii) In case of the default in holding AGM in accordance with Section 166, the CG may on application of any member call/direct the calling of AGM and give such ancillary and consequential direction as the CG think expedient, in relation to the calling, holding and conducting of the meeting.

(iii) Such direction may include a direction that any one member present in member or proxy shall be deemed to be the quorum so as to constitute meeting.

(iv) Such Annual General Meeting subject to any direction of CG shall be deemed to be an annual general meeting of the company.

Notes on Section 167

(i) If the time prescribed by the articles has expired but not the time prescribed by Section 166 then section 167 cannot be invoked.

(ii) If meeting was properly held but some of the resolutions have been challenged then section 167 cannot be invoked.

(iii) When meeting was called but could not be properly commenced because directors abandon it before taking up any business then section 167 can be invoked.

(iv) If meeting of year 20X1 held in year 20X2 as per CG order then it should be treated as the meeting of the year 20X1. It can also be treated as the AGM for both the year i.e. 20X1 and 20X2 provided that the company passes resolution and forward the copy of the resolution to the registrar within 30 days. [Section 192(1)]

4.7 Consequences of Default [Section 168]

If the default is made by the company in holding Annual General Meeting in accordance with Section 166 or in complying in any direction given by CG under Section 167 then the company and its every officer of the company in default shall be punishable with fine upto Rs 50,000 and in case of the continuing default with a further fine upto Rs 2,500 for every day after the first.

4.8 Adjournment

(i) Annual general meeting can be adjourned.

(ii) **Place of Adjourned Meeting**—It must be held either at the registered office of the company or within the city, town or village in which the registered office of a company is situated. But it can not be held at the place different from the place of original Annual General Meeting.

(iii) **Day of Adjourned Meeting**—The Department of company affairs has also clarified that there is no contravention of Section 166(2) if the adjourned meeting comes to be accidentally held on a public holiday. [Department's Letter No. 8/16(1)/61-PR dated 19th May 1961]

(iv) Adjourned meeting can be adjourned again.

(v) **No fresh notice for the adjourned meeting** is necessary provided the date of adjourned meeting is decided in original meeting.

4.9 21 Clear Days Notice

21 clear days' notice in writing must be given. However a **shorter notice** than 21 days may be given **if the consent of ALL** the members entitled to vote had been taken on Form. No. 22A. The notice must state the place, the day and the time of holding the annual general meeting alongwith the details of the business to be transacted.

4.10 Quorum [Section 174]

The term 'Quorum' means the minimum number of members required to constitute a valid meeting and to transact business threat. Unless the articles provide for a larger number, quorum shall be:

Case	*Minimum Number*
In case of a Public company	5 members personally present
In case of a Private company	2 members personally present
In case of meeting adjourned due to lack of quorum	Members present **Notes:** (i) A single member present shall not constitute quorum at an adjourned meeting. (ii) Even 2 proxies present can constitute quorum at an adjourned meeting.
In case of meeting adjourned due to other reasons (i) *Public company* (ii) *Private company*	 5 members personally present 2 members personally present

In all of the above cases article may provide for the higher number for the purpose of constituting the quorum. But article cannot provide for the shorter number for the purpose of constituting quorum.

4.11 Important Judicial Rulings

(i) Meeting held beyond the time prescribed by the Section 166 is not void. As the section only prescribes the limit and is silent about the invalidity of the meeting to be held beyond time. However this act is punishable with a penalty in accordance with section 168. Resolution passed at this AGM are valid.
[***Re El Sombrero Ltd.,*** (1958)]

(ii) Meeting must be held irrespective of the fact that accounts are ready for the consideration or not.
[***Hungerford Investment Trust Ltd. v. Tourner Marrison & Co. Ltd.,*** (1972)]
"In case the annual accounts are not ready for laying at the appropriate AGM, it is open to the company concerned to adjourn the said AGM to a subsequent date when the annual accounts are expected to be ready for laying. This may be done by a suitable resolution adjourning the said meeting to a specific date or to a date to be specified later on". [*Vide Communique No. 35/9/72-CL III dated 2-2-1974 Department of Company Law Affairs*].

PRACTICAL ILLUSTRATION 6

Previous AGM held on 31/12/20X1

Financial year ended on 30/09/20X2

Accounts are not ready for consideration upto 31/12/20X2

Remedy: Hold meeting on or before 31/12/20X2 and adjourn it for future date when the accounts are to be ready for the consideration. But extension of the time by registrar must be obtained.

PRACTICAL ILLUSTRATION 7

Previous AGM held on 30/09/20X1

Financial year ended on 31/03/20X2

Accounts are not ready for consideration upto 30/09/20X2

Remedy: Hold meeting on or before 31/12/20X2 and adjourn it for future date when the accounts are ready for the consideration, but extension of the time by registrar must be obtained. However the adjourned meeting must be held before the expiry of the extended period so as not to attract the penal provision of Section 168.

If Registrar granted 2 months tension then meeting can be held upto 28.02.20X3. As in this case statutory time limit has not been expired so there would be no penalty under Section 168 but penalty will be attracted under Section 210 because statutory limit as per Section 210 is 6 + 2 = 8 months. So meeting should be held before 30.11.20X2.

(iii) Notice for the meeting must be given even when time and place of the meeting is already fixed by the articles.

(iv) Failure to get accounts audited is not the valid excuse for extension of time by the registrar.

(v) Application for extension of time should be admitted before the expiry of statutory period.

(vi) Convened meeting (Notice for which has been given) cannot be postponed.

(vii) Voting right to be considered at the date of the meeting.

(viii) where all the members of the company were also the members of the board of directors, a meeting of the board could be treated as a general meeting of the company. [***P.V. Damodara Reddi* v. *Indian National Agencies Ltd.,*** (1945)]

(ix) If because of circumstances beyond their control (for example, pandemonium in the hall) the directors decided not to hold the meeting, it cannot be said to have been held by mere fact that before the directors' announcement, printed copies of balances sheet and agenda had been distributed to shareholders.
[***Selvaraj* v. *Mylapore Hindu Permanent Fund Ltd.,*** (1968)]

(x) Directors could not be allowed to escape performance of duties regarding the meeting by a mere plea that they had no real control over the affairs of the company and they did not wilfully permit default; if directors were mere passive spectators and did not have the statutory requirements carried out, they may be considered as having wilfully permitted default [***Sarasvati Printers Limited* v. *State,*** (1968)]

(xi) If the registered office is not available, moving to a nearby place and holding meeting there is not a violation of law; It is only an irregularity. [***M.R.S. Rathnavelusami Chettiar* v. *M.R.S. Manickavelu Chettiar,*** (1951) 21 Comp. Cas. 93 (Mad.)]

(xii) The company did not function is no excuse for not holding the AGM.
[***Madan Gopal* v. *State of West Bengal,*** (1968)]

(xiii) Where the account books were seized by the police so on to make it impossible for the directors to hold the meeting, the default was not held punishable.
[***Re Asia Udyog (P) Ltd.,*** (1961)]

(xiv) Failure to place the statement of account before the AGM and the default in holding the AGM are two distinct and separate offences which are punishable separately under the Act.

5.0 EXTRA ORDINARY GENERAL MEETING [SECTION 169]

5.1 Meaning (Regulation 47 of Table A)

All general meetings other than statutory meeting and Annual General Meeting are termed as "extraordinary general meetings".

5.2 Who can Call Extra Ordinary General Meeting?

Extraordinary General Meeting may be called by Board, Requisitionists or Company Law Tribunal.

5.3 Extra Ordinary Meeting by Board of Directors

(a) **On its Own Motion [Regulation 48 of Table A]** The Board may, whenever it thinks fit, call an extraordinary general meeting. If an extraordinary general meeting cannot be convened since number of directors in India is less than the quorum required for Board meeting then any director or any 2 members can call an extraordinary general meeting in the same manner nearly as possible as that in which such a meeting may be called up by the Board. [Regulation 48 of Table A]

Exercise of Directors' Power to Call Extraordinary General Meetings. The directors' power to call general meeting including extraordinary general meeting must, like their other powers, be exercised at a properly convened Board meeting. It is not open to some of the directors to convene a general meeting of their own motion [***Harben* v. *Phillips***, (1883) Ch. D- 14].

If the Articles provide that a resolution in writing signed by all the members of the board without meeting is as effective as a resolution passed at a Board meeting as in normally the case, (Regulation 8 of Table A), a general meeting may be convened on a resolution so signed.

(b) **On Requisition of the Members [Section 169]** The Board on the requisition of the specified number of the members can call an extraordinary general meeting. Specified number of members will be as follows:

Case	*Specified Number of Members*
(i) ***In case of company having share capital***	Members having **at least 10%** of the paid up share capital which carries the voting right as at date of the deposit of requisition.
(ii) ***In case of company having no share capital***	Members having **at least 10%** of the total voting power of all the members having right to vote at the date of the deposit of requisition

PRACTICAL ILLUSTRATION 8

Following data pertains to *X* Ltd.

10,000 shares of Rs 10 each Rs 8 called up	80,000
Less: Call in arrears on 1000 shares @ Rs 2	2,000
Paid up capital	78,000

State the minimum number of members entitled to make requisition in each of the following alternative cases:

Case (i) Where Articles are silent

Case (ii) Where Articles provide that no member shall be entitled to vote at any general meeting unless all calls or other sums presently payable by him in respect of shares in the company have been paid.

Case (iii) Where articles provides that all members whose names appear in the register of member are entitled to vote at general meeting.

Solution:

Case (i) Where articles are silent on particular point then Table A will be applicable and according to Regulation 59 if any calls or sums payable on shares is not paid then that member shall not be entitled to vote. Hence members having 1/10th of the paid up capital (excluding the amount paid up on 1000 shares on which calls are in arrears) i.e. 1/10th of Rs 72,000 (i.e. Rs 78,000 – Rs 6,000) are entitled to make a requisition.

Case (ii) Same Answer as in case (i) because articles provides similar provision as in Table A.

Case (iii) Members having 1/10th of the paid up capital i.e. 1/10th of Rs 78,000 are entitled to make a requisition.

5.4 Provisions as to Requisition

1. **Form of the Requisition** The requisition may be in the form of a letter addressed to the Board of Directors signed by the requisite number of members or there may be several letters in the like form. Although, the letters need not be identical in language but they should be to the same effect.
2. **Contents of Requisition [Section 169(2)]** The requisition must contain all the matters for consideration of which the meeting is to be called. If any special resolution is intended to be passed at the requisitioned meeting, the Board shall be deemed not to have duly convened the meeting if they do not give such notice thereof as is required by Section 189(2). For each item of the agenda explanatory statement must be given.
3. **Signature of the Requisition [Section 169(3)]** The requisition must be signed by **all the requistionists.** In case of joint shareholders, a requisition signed one or some of them for the purpose of this section has the same force and effect as though it has been signed by all of them.
4. **Deposit of Requisition [Section 169(2)]** The requisition must be deposited **at the registered office** of the company. The requisition sent by a registered post properly addressed and received by the company at its registered office will amount to deposit of the requisition at the registered office.
5. **Application of the Section to Each Matter Separately [Section 169(5)]** When there are two more distinct matters covered in the requisition, then the provision of the Section 169(4) shall apply separately to each such matter.
6. **Compliance of Requisition [Section 169(6)]** The Board of Directors must **proceed within 21 days** of the deposit of the requisition to convene a meeting which must be **held within 45 days of** such deposit of the requisition with the company. The Board shall send out notices within 21 days of the deposit of the requisition giving at least 21 days' notice for the meeting.

5.5 Judicial Rulings Relevant for Requisition

1. The Board of Directors cannot refuse to proceed with a requisitioned meeting merely on the ground that the requisition does not disclose sufficient reasons for the resolution to be put to vote at the meeting, in the explanatory statement. [***Life Insurance Corporation of India*** v. ***Escorts Limited,*** 1986, 59 Comp. Cas 548 (SC)]. Section 73(2) requires the management and not the shareholders, calling the meeting to disclose the reasons for the resolution which they purpose to move at meeting.
2. The word or the adjective 'valid' in Section 169 has no reference to the object of the requisition but rather to the requirement in that section itself. If these requirements indicated in the earlier part of section are satisfied, then the requisition deposited with the company must be regarded as a valid requisition on which directors of the company must act. [***Cricket Club of India Ltd.*** **v.** ***Madhav L. Apte,*** (1975) Bom.]
3. The shareholders cannot requisition a meeting to compel the company for withdrawing its petition pending before the court for its sanction under Section 392 where an amalgamation scheme has been approved in a statutory meeting under Section 391. [***Centron Industrial Alliance Ltd.*** v. ***Pravin Kantilal Vakil,*** (1985) Bom.]
4. Shareholders could requisition the meeting for proposing a modification to the scheme pending before the court for its sanction under Section 392. [*Pravin Katilal Vakil* v. *Rohini Ramesh Save*]
5. Where a requisition contained a matter which is illegal and invalid, still directors are liable to hold general meeting, if the requisition made is valid. It is a matter of court to decide on the fact that whether proposal is invalid or contrary to the provision of the Act [***Cricket Club of India Ltd.*** **v.** ***Madhav L. Apte***]. But Judicial opinion outside India is against the view [***Queensland Press Ltd.*** **v.** ***Academy Instrument No. 3 Pvt. Ltd.***].
6. Where a requisition is valid on the ground that it complies with requirements Section 169, still in the case of removal of director a special notice is necessary and the special notice must disclose the grounds for the removal of the director. [***Queens Kuries Loans Pvt. Ltd.*** **v.** ***Sheena Jose,*** (1993) 'Kerala High Court]
7. Where the Articles of Association of a company prohibited any defaulting shareholder from exercising his right to vote at any general meeting, and certain shareholders had not paid a call made on their shares it was held that they were not entitled to requisition an extraordinary general meeting under Section 169. [***Col. Kuldip Singh Dhillon*** v. ***Paragaon Utility Financiers (P) Ltd.***, (1986) 60 Camp. Cas 1075 (Punj. & Har)]
8. Shares the holder of which has died will be excluded in counting 1/10th as they have no power on the date of deposit of the requisition.
9. Preferences shareholders can join in the requisition only if their dividends are in arrears for the specified period or if the proposed resolution is likely to affect their interest, e.g., a resolution for winding up of the company.
10. After requisition if any requisition ceases to be a member or withdraws, it will not invalidate the requisitionist.
11. The right of a member to requisition or vote at a meetings not affected by pledge or attachment of his shares or by appointment of Receiver over his shares.
12. Such rights are also not affected by taking over of management under the Industries (Development and Regulation) Act, of the shareholder company.

    [***Balkrishan Gupta*** v. ***Swadeshi Polytex Ltd.***, (1985) 58 Comp. Cas 563 (SC)]

5.6 Extraordinary Meeting by Requistionists [Section 169(6)]

(a) **Time Period**—If the board did not proceed to convene such a meeting **within 21 days** from the date of receipt of requisition or did not call a meeting **within 45 days** from the date of receipt of the requisition then such meeting may be called **within 3 months** from the date of deposit of requisition:

(b) **Who can call—**
   (a) by the requistionists themselves, or
   (b) ***In the case of a company having share capital*** by the requistionists as representing *either* **majority in value** of the paid up share capital held by all of them ***or* at least 10%** of the paid up share capital which carries the voting rights which ever is less, or
   (c) ***In the case of a company not having a share capital*** by the requistionists representing **at least 10% of** the total voting power of all the members having right to vote.

PRACTICAL ILLUSTRATION 9

7 members (though only 3 members were sufficient to make a requisition) made a requisition to the board who could not proceed to convene the meeting within 21 days from date of requisition. In this case the following members may call the meeting within 3 months from date of deposit of requisition:

(i) 7 members (Requistionist themselves)
(ii) 4 members (Representing majority of the requistionist)
(iii) 3 members (Requisitionist representing at least 10% total voting power)

5.7 Manner of Calling EGM by Requistionists u/s 169(6) [Section (169)(7)]

Where the meeting is called by the requistionists, it shall be called in the same manner as nearly as possible to that in which meetings are to be called by the Board but such meeting must be held **before the expiry of 3 months from the date of deposit of requisition.** However, there is no violation if the meeting is called within 3 months but adjourned to some other date falling after the expiry of the 3 months.

5.8 Consequences of Absence Quorum

If the Quorum is not present within half an hour from the time appointed for holding of the meeting the meeting, shall **stand dissolved** if it is called on the requisition of the members Section 169(6) [Section 174(3)]. But if the articles provide otherwise then articles will apply.

5.9 Consequences of Board's Default [Section 169(9)]

If default is made in calling the meeting by the board then—

(i) The requistionist shall be entitled to claim all reasonable expenses incurred by them for convening a meeting from the company.
(ii) The company shall be entitled to deduct the sum so paid from the remuneration of the defaulting directors

5.10 Important Judicial Rulings

1. Once a final dividend is declared at an annual general meeting no further dividend can be declared at an extraordinary general meeting. [***Biswanath Prasad Khaitan* v. *New Central Jute Mills Co. Ltd.***]
2. In case of a meeting convened by the directors on requisition or on their default, by the requistionists themselves then—
   (a) the meeting cannot transact any business other than the business for which it has been expressly convened. [***Ball* v. *Metal Industries Ltd.***, (1975) S 315]
   (b) the agenda of general meeting cannot include matters which do not appear in the requisition. [***Patent Wood Key Syndicate Ltd.* v. *Pearse***]
3. Where a company cannot convene a meeting due to stay order issued by a court then on Board's inability to call the meeting requistionist themselves also cannot hold meeting. The proper course of action for the requistionist is to apply to the court for convening the meeting. [***Chaudhary (A.D.)* v. *Mysore Paper Mills Ltd.***]

5.11 Power of Company Law Board to Call Extraordinary Meeting [Section 186]

(i) **When to exercise power.** Where for any reason it is impracticable to call a general meeting other than Annual General Meeting, the CLB may either on its own motion *suo moto* or on the application of any director (whether or not the member) or any member of the company who is entitled to vote at a meeting, order a meeting to called, held and conducted in such manner as it thinks fit and give such ancilliary and consequential directions as it thinks expedient in relation to the calling, holding and conducting of such meeting.

(ii) **Direction as to Quorum.** Such directions may include a direction that **one member present in person or by proxy shall be deemed to constitute the meeting**. Such meeting shall be held in the same manner as any other meeting called by the company.

(iii) **Direction as to Modification.** The CLB may direct for the modification of the provisions of the Act or the articles in relation to the calling, holding and conducting of the meeting or that one member of the company present in person or by proxy may be deemed to constitute a meeting.

(iv) **Deemed to be duly called meeting.** Any meeting called, held and conducted in accordance with the order of the CLB will be deemed, for all purpose, to be a meeting of the company duly called, held and conducted.

Note: It may be noted that where a meeting can be called by recourse to Section 169 or Section 167, the CLB will not grant an application under Section 186. For Section 186 the petitioner would at least have to show that there is no other option but to apply under Section 186.

5.12 Judicial Rulings relevant for Section 186

1. On the Word 'Impracticable'

(a) If a petition was filed under Section 186, but in petition there was no allegation that it is impracticable for a company to hold the meeting, such petition would be not valid. [***Siri Ram* v. *Edward Ganj Public Welfare Association Ltd.***]

(b) The word 'impracticable' must be given a practical meaning. It must be understood to be impracticable from the business point of view. It must not be held impracticable on the slightest excuse that the directors do not agree. [***Bengal & Assam Investors Ltd.*** v. ***J.K. Eastern Industries***]

(c) The word impracticable does not mean impossible. Thus where it is possible to hold meeting but impracticable to hold meeting in ordinary manner then it would also be treated as impracticable.
[***Re Passari Floor Mills Ltd.***, (1962) 32. Comp. Cas 896 (M.P.)]

(d) Impracticability of conducting a meeting also includes impracticability of holding a meeting. For example holding of a meeting is impracticable where the registered office of the company is locked and is not available. [***M.R.S. Rathnavelusami Chettiar*** v. ***M.R.S Manickavelu Chettiar,*** (1951) 21 Comp. Cas 93 (Mad.)]

(e) Impracticable also include a case that where due to the Article of Association, it becomes difficult for a company to get a quorum present.
[***Opera Photographic Ltd.*** v. ***BCLC***]

2. Basic Principles which should Guide Company Law Board

Some basic principles that should guide the Company Law Tribunal were set out ***Re. Ruttonjee & Co. Ltd.,*** (1968) 2 Comp. LJ ISS (1970) 40 Com. Cases 491 (Cal.).

(a) CLB would not interfere with the domestic management of a company which should be conducted in accordance with the articles.

(b) The discretion granted under Section 186 should be used sparingly with caution so that CLB does not become either a shareholder or director of a company trying to participate in internecine squabbles of the company.

(c) The word 'impracticable' means impracticable from a reasonable point of view.

(d) CLB should take a common sense view of the matter and must act as a prudent man of business. Prudent means that CLB should in ordinarily circumstances keep itself away from indulging in controversy of rival group of directors or members.

(e) Where there are doubts and controversy about who are the directors and rival group convene their own meeting, the situation may render the holding of the meeting impracticable.

(f) CLB should act in a *bona fide* manner and in a larger interest of a company.

3. An application under Section 186 need not to on behalf of the company since the very language of that section even permits CLB *suo moto* to call meeting of the company if it has become impracticable to call a meeting other than an annual general meeting. An action need not be in the name of the company for actions concerning injuries personal to the petitioner.
[***Smt. Jain*** v. ***Delhi Flour Mills Company Ltd. and others***, (1974) 44 Comp. Cas. 228 (Delhi)]

4. In a petition for an order directing the holding of general meeting under Section 186, CLB will not go to the extent of rectifying the register of member for the purpose of giving directions as to who should vote at such meeting.
[***Smt. Jain*** v. ***Delhi Floor Mills Co. Ltd.***]

5. As directors do not continue to hold office on the failure of calling Annual General Meeting within statutory limits, CLB can invoke Section 186 to call the meeting for election of directors. [***B.R. Kundra*** v. ***Mohan Pictures Association***]

6. A meeting which is not conducted according to the direction issued by the Company Law Board is not a valid meeting.
[***Re Motion Pictures Association***, (1979) 46 Comp. Cas 298 (Delhi)]

7. Company court which is supervising the scheme under Section 392, can convene the meeting for proper supervision and implementation of scheme under Section 392, and it is not necessary to invoke Section 186. In other words Section 186 is not applicable in cases covered by Section 392. [***India Hardware Ltd.* v. *S.K. Gupta***]
8. The Company Law Board's power under Section 186 is discretionary and not mandatory. It is alternative course of action which may be applied on the failure of company management to hold meeting.
[***Bengal & Assam Investors Ltd.* v. *J.K. Eastern Industries***]
9. The use of the word "and" between the word "held" and "conducted" in Section 186(1)(a) clearly shows that the court has no power to make any order regarding the holding and conducting of meeting which has been called up by the board or its members on board's failure to call the meeting. [***Rangachari (R)* v. *S.K. Suppiah***]

5.13 At least 21 Clear Days Notice of the Meeting

At least 21 clear days' notice must be given (Section 171). A **shorter notice** less than 21 days' may be given **if the consent** is obtained there to—

(a) by the members holding **at least 95%** of the share capital carrying voting rights in case of the company having share capital

(b) by member holding at least 95% of the total voting power in case of the company having no share capital.

5.14 Quorum [Section 174]

The term 'Quorum' means the minimum number of members required to constitute a valid meeting and to transact business threat. Unless the articles provide for a larger number, quorum shall be:-

Case	*Minimum number*
In case of Public company	5 members personally present
In case of Private company	2 members personally present
In case of meeting adjourned due to lack of quorum	Members present **Notes:** (i) A single member present shall not constitute quorum at an adjourned meeting. (ii) Even 2 proxies present can constitute quorum at an adjourned meeting.
In case of meeting adjourned due to other reasons (i) *Public company* (ii) *Independent Private company*	 5 members personally present 2 members personally present

In all of the above cases article may provide for the higher number for the purpose of constituting the quorum. But article cannot provide for the shorter number for the purpose of constituting quorum.

5.15 Place, Date and Hours of Conducting Meeting

Such meeting can be held at any place, any day and at any time because the Act is silent on these points.

5.16 Kind of Business [Section 173]

All business to be transacted at a meeting (other than AGM) shall be **special** therefore, an explanatory statement as required by Section 173(2) is required to be annexed to the notice convening such meeting. Such statement shall include amongst other:

(a) All material facts concerning each item of business.
(b) The nature of the concern or interest if any, therein of every director and manager.
(c) If any item of the special business affects any other company, then the extent of shareholding of every director and manager in that company in case their shareholding interest is at least 20% of the paid up share capital of the other company.
(d) The time when and place where the document to be approved at the meeting can be inspected.

Note: The company is not bound to attach any explanatory statement unless the company gives the notice on its own behalf. As long as it is merely forwards the requistionist notice, it does not have to attach any explanatory statements. [*Vijay M. Porwal* v. *Pentokey Organy (India) Ltd.*]

5.17 Kind of Resolution

The resolution can be either ***ordinary* or *special*** depending on the specific provision in this regard incorporated in the Act or Articles.

5.18 Adjournments, Chairman, Proxies and Voting

The provisions relating to Adjournment Chairman, Proxies and Voting shall be governed by general sections [Sections 171 to 186] unless the article provide otherwise. [Section 170]

6.0 CLASS MEETINGS

The class meetings may be of members *or* debentureholders.

6.1 Class Meetings of Members [Sections 106 and 391]

The class meetings of the members may be convened by the company under Section 106 or by the court under Section 391.

(i) Convened by the Company [Section 106] Where the share capital of a company is divided into different classes of shares, the rights attached to the shares of any class may be varied in **any one** of the following two ways:

(a) with the **consent in writing of holders of at least 3/4th** of the issued shares of that class, **or**
(b) with the sanction of **special resolution** at a separate meeting of the holders of the issued shares of that class.

Authority for Variation

(a) Provision with respect to such variation must be contained in the memorandum or articles of the company, or

(b) Such variation must not be prohibited by terms of issue of the shares of that class in the absence of any provision in respect of variation in the memorandum or articles.

(ii) Meeting Convened by the Court [Section 391] Where a compromise or arrangement is proposed either between the company and its creditors or between a company and its members or any class of them, then court may on the application of the company or of any creditor or member of the company, order a meeting of the creditors or members, or class of members, as the case may be, to be called, held and conducted in such manner as the court may direct. If a majority in number representing 3/4th in value of creditors or class of creditors or members or class of members present and voting either in person or by proxy agree to such compromise or arrangement, then such compromise or arrangement if sanctioned by the court shall be binding on the concerned creditors or members as the case may be. The important rules applicable to such meetings are as follows:

(i) Notice is required to be served on all members and creditors by advertisement in the newspaper in the manner to be directed by the court 21 clear days before the date of meeting in addition to individual service of notice.

(ii) the chairman to be appointed by the court,

(iii) Proxies are entitled to attend and vote.

(iv) Decisions must always be ascertained only by taking a poll.

6.2 Class Meetings of Debentureholders

Where the trust deed provides for convening and holding the meeting where it is proposed to vary any condition relating to debentures, appointment of new trustees and to issue new debentures, a class meeting of concerned debentureholders is required to be held.

The objective of such clause in trust deed is to enable the company to deal with debenture holders as a class and prevent a few adversely affected debentureholders from interrupting a necessary or desirable arrangement. However, this power must be exercised in a bona fide manner. [***British America Nickel Corpn.* v. *O' Brien*** (1927)]

Purpose for which Debentureholders' Meeting May be Called These may include the following:

1. to release particular property from the specific charge (with or without the substitution of other property), or
2. to reduce the amount of the debenture interest, or
3. to defer its payment for a time, or
4. to allow the creation of debentures ranking in priority to the existing debentures, or *pari passu* with them, or
5. to release the company for a limited period from all obligations to set apart profits towards a sinking fund, or
6. to effect an exchange of debentures for equity or preference shares.

Applicability of Sections 171 to 186 to Class Meetings [Section 170(2)]
Unless articles otherwise provide, the provision of Sections 171 to 186 with such adaptations and modifications, if any, as may be prescribed, shall apply also with respect to meetings of class of members or of debentureholders or any class of debentureholders in the same manner as they apply to general meetings of such company.

7.0 APPLICABILITY OF SECTIONS 171 TO 186 TO MEETINGS [SECTION 170]

1. The provisions of Sections 171 to 186 shall apply to all public companies and private companies which are subsidiaries of public companies even if anything is contrary in the Articles.
2. The provision of Section 174(1) relating to minimum quorum shall also apply to all independent private companies.
3. The provision of Section 182, (relating to restriction on exercise of voting right) are not applicable to independent private companies.
4. Unless the Articles otherwise provide, the provisions of Sections 171 to 181 and Sections 183 to 186 shall also apply to all independent private company companies. In other words, an independent private company may make special provisions in its articles in respect of any of the matters covered by these sections.
5. Section 176 with such adaptations and modifications if any, may be prescribed shall apply to—
   (a) meetings of any class of members
   (b) meetings of debentureholders
   (c) meetings of any class of debentureholders
6. Unless the Articles otherwise provide or a contract binding on the persons concerned otherwise provide, Sections 171 to 186 apply to—
   (a) meetings of any class of members.
   (b) meetings of debentureholders.
   (c) meetings of any class of debentureholders.

8.0 REQUISITES FOR A VALID GENERAL MEETING OF MEMBERS

1. Proper Authority
2. Proper Notice
3. Proper Place
4. Proper Date
5. Proper Time
6. Proper Quorum
7. Proper Chairmanship
8. Proper Proxies
9. Proper Voting
10. Proper Adjournment
11. Proper Resolution
12. Proper Registration/Filing of Resolution
13. Proper Minutes

Let us discuss the aforesaid points in detail.

9.0 PROPER AUTHORITY

Proper Authority to convene various types of meeting shall be as follows:

Case	*Proper Authority to convene meeting*
(a) ***Statutory Meeting***	**Duly constituted Board of Directors** is normally the proper authority. Neither the Managing director nor the secretary is empowered to convene such meeting unless authorised by the Board. The secretary or the managing director when calling the meeting must quote the authority of the board by adding the words 'By Order of the Board.'
(b) ***Annual General Meeting***	(i) **Duly constituted Board of Directors** where a company does not defaults in holding Annual General Meeting in accordance with Section 166, or (ii) **Company Law Board** where a company defaults in holding Annual General Meeting in accordance with Section 166 and an application is made by any member.
(c) ***Extraordinary General Meeting***	(i) **Duly constituted Board of Directors** whenever it thinks fit. (ii) **One Director/two members** of the company where number of directors in India is less than the quorum required for Board meeting. (Regulation 48) (iii) **Duly constituted Board on deposit of requisition** by requisite number of members under Section 169 (iv) **Requisitionists** if the Board did not proceed to convene the meeting 21 days from the date of deposit of the requisition or did not call a meeting within 45 days from the date of deposit of the requisition under Section 169. (v) **Company Law Board** on its own motion or on the application of a director or any member of the company where for any reason it is impracticable to call extra-ordinary general meeting of the company. [Section 186]

10.0 NOTICE [SECTIONS 171 TO 173 AND SECTION 53]

10.1 By whom Notice must be Given

The notice must be given by the proper summoning authority which would normally be the **Board of Directors**. If however a notice has been issued without authority, the requisite authority may be given by ratification by the proper summoning authority before the meeting is held and notice may thus become good. [*Hooper* v. *Kerr, Stuart & Co.* (1900)]

10.2 Notice in Writing

Notice must be in writing as it is specifically provided in Section 171.

10.3 Length of the Notice [Section 171(1)]

The length of the notice must be 21 clear days i.e. whilst computing the 21 days, the day of service of the notice and day of holding of the meeting are to be excluded. Each of the 21 days must be a full calendar day and not a part of the day.

Where a notice is sent by post, it is deemed to be served by 48 hours from day of posting. Thus, notice to be valid, must be despatched 24 days before the day of holding the meeting.

Shorter Notice [Section 171(2)]

A general meeting may be called by giving a notice shorter than 21 clear days.

(a) ***In case of Annual General Meeting***	If the consent of ***all members*** *entitled to vote* at the meeting is obtained.
(b) ***In case of other general meeting of a company having share capital***	If the consent of members holding **at least 95%** of the *paid up share capital carrying voting rights* is obtained.
(c) ***In case of other general meeting of a company having no share capital***	If the consent of members *having* ***at least 95%*** *of the total voting power* is obtained.

Notes:

(i) Consent of members entitled to attend and vote at that meeting is required and not merely of members entitled to vote and present in person or proxy at that meeting. [***Nagappa (N.V.R) Chettiar*** v. ***Madras Race Club*** (1949)]

Practical Illustration 9

Total No. of members of *X* Ltd. = 100

Total no. of members Present at AGM called by a shorter notice = 60

No. of members present who consented to shorter notice = 60

Although all members present have consented to short notice, it is not sufficient. The consent of total number of members entitled to vote i.e. 100 is required.

(ii) **When should such Consent be Obtained?**

The Act is silent on the point whether such consent should be obtained **prior to or at or even subsequent** to meeting concerned. In case of Self-help Private Industrial Estate (P) Ltd., it has been held that the subsequent consent obtained would validate the resolution passed without proper notice.

(iii) **How should such Consent be Obtained?**

The consent as to shorter notice should be obtained **in writing in Form No. 22A**.

(iv) **Can the Requirement as to Notice be Dispensed with?**

No, unless all the members are present at the meeting since " If you have all the shareholders present then all the requirements in connection with a company are complied with." [*Younger L.J. in Engineering Work* (1920)]

(v) The provisions of Section 171 apply to **Section 25 companies** with the modification that a general meeting may be called by giving a notice in writing of **at least 14 days**.

10.4 Persons Entitled to Receive the Notice [Section 172(2)]

The following persons are entitled to receive the notice:

(i) Every member of the company. [Section 172(2)(i)]
(ii) Legal Representatives of deceased [Section 172(2)(ii)]
(iii) Official Assignees of the Insolvent Members [Section 172(2)(ii)]
(iv) Auditor or auditors of a company. [Section 172(2)(iii)]

Notes:

(i) In case of joint holders, notice is to be served on **the senior or first named** of joint holders.

(ii) Notice is to be sent to members who have given their addresses in India (Section 53). Hence notice need had not be given to members who are residents abroad.

(iii) The words 'every member' seems to suggest that **notice** must be given **even to preference shareholders**. The Department is of the view, the preference share holders have a right to attend the meeting but they may not be allowed to take part in the discussion in the meeting where the meeting does not discuss any matter in which such shareholders have any voting rights. [*Company News & Notes July* 16, 1964]
It may be noted that there is a statutory obligation to send notice to preference shareholders when their dividend is in arrears for more than a certain period [Section 87(2)(b)]. This obligation arises from the fact that preference shareholders whose dividends are in arrears are entitled to attend and vote at the meeting.

(iv) Beneficial owners of shares are not entitled to receive notice.

10.5 Effect of Omission to give of notice [Section 172(3)]

(i) An accidental omission to give notice shall not invalidate the proceedings at the meeting.

(ii) The non-receipt of notice by any member or any other person to whom it should be given shall not invalidate the proceedings of the meeting. [Section 172(3)]

(iii) A **deliberate omission to give notice to even a single member shall invalidate the proceedings at the meeting.**

Important Judicial Rulings:

(i) Omission to serve notice of meeting on a member on the mistaken ground that he is not a shareholder cannot be said to be an accidental omission.
[***Musselwhite* v. *Musselwhite & Sons Ltd.***, (1962) 32 Comp. Cas 804]

(ii) 'Accidental omission' means that the omission must be not only designed but also not deliberate. [***Maharaja Export* v. *Apparels Exports Promotion Council*** (1986) 60 Comp. Cas 353]

(iii) If a meeting is called without notice to a shareholder the omission not being accidental, it is invalid and proceedings therein are also invalid.
[***Eastern Linkers (P) Ltd.* v. *Dina Nath Sodhi*** (1984) (Delhi)]

10.6 Service of Notice [Section 53]

(i) **How to serve Notice**—A notice may be served by the company on any member either personally or by sending it by post

(ii) **Where to serve Notice**—Notice by post, must be sent to his registered **address in India** or if he has no registered address in India to the address in India given by him for the purpose of the giving of the notices to him. [Section 53(1)]

(iii) **When Notice by post deemed to have been served**—Where a notice is sent by post, service shall be deemed to be effected **at the expiration of the 48 hours after the letter containing the same is posted.** [Section 53(2)]

PRACTICAL ILLUSTRATION 10

	Case I	Case II	Case III
Date of Meeting	30th Sep.	30th Sep.	30th Sep.
Date of sending notice by post	5th Sep.	6th Sep.	7th Sep.
No. of days from date of sending notice by Post to date of meeting	26	25	24
Less : Day of meeting	1	1	1
Less: Day of sending notice by post	1	1	1
Less: 2 days (i.e. equivalent to 48 hours) after date of posting	2	2	2
Number of clear days	22	21	20
Length of notice	Proper	Proper	Shorter

10.7 When is Notice Deemed to be Served?

Cases	*Notice shall be deemed to be duly served if ...*
(i) ***In case no particular manner of service of notice has been requested by member.***	The notice is sent by properly addressing, prepaying, and posting to the registered address of the member.
(ii) ***In case particular manner of service has been requested by the member.***	The notice is sent in the manner requested by member.
(iii) ***In case a member who has no registered address in India and has not supplied to the company an address within India for giving notices to him.***	The notice is advertised in a newspaper circulating in the neighbourhood of the registered office of the company at least 21 clear days before the date of meeting. [Section 53] In this case notice is deemed to be served on the day on which advertisement appears in a newspaper.
(iv) ***In case of joint share holdings***	The notice is served on the joint holder whose name appears first in the register of members.

Notes:

(i) The presumption of deemed delivery cannot be raised when at the time of posting the post office was, within the knowledge of the company, on declared strike. [***Bredman* v. *Trinity Estate Plc,*** (1989) BCLC 757 (Ch. D)]

(ii) Section 53 applies to all documents and not merely service of notice of meetings.

(iii) A person who is present and who votes at the meeting will not be entitled to challenge the resolution on the ground of an invalidity in the notice [***Re British Sugar Refining Co.*** (1857) 3 K&J 408]

10.8 Contents of the Notice

Notice must be in writing and signed by a director or manager or the secretary or some other authorised offices of the company and specify the following:

(i) Company's full name and the address of its registered office. [Section 147(1)(c)]

(ii) The place date and hour of the meeting. [Section 172(1)]

(iii) The statement of the business to be transacted (Agenda). [Section 172(1)]

(iv) Where a resolution is to be passed as a special resolution, the intention to propose the resolution as such. [Section 189(2)(a)].

(v) In case of companies having share capital, the notice must also state with reasonable prominence that member entitled to attend and vote is entitled to appoint proxy to attend and vote instead of himself and proxy need not be a member. [Section 176(2)]

10.9 Explanatory Statement Required to be Annexed to Notice [Section 173]

An explanatory statement is required to be annexed to notice in case special business is to be transacted at the general meeting. Such statement shall include amongst other:

(a) The material fact concerning each item of business. [Section 173(2)]
A very minor defect arising out of strict non-conformity with provision contained in Section 173(2) might not render the resolution null and void.
[***Joseph Michael* v. *Travancore Rubber & Tea Co. Ltd.***, (1986)]

(b) The nature of the concern or interest if any, therein of every director and manage. [Section 173(2)]

(c) If any item of the special to be transacted affect any other company then the extent of shareholding of every director and manager in that company in case it is at least 20% of the paid up share capital of the other company. [Proviso to Section 173(2)]

(d) The time and place where the document to be approved at the meeting can be inspected. [Section 173(3)]

10.10 Is it necessary to advertise explanatory statement in the newspaper in case a notice is advertised in the newspaper in case of case of a member who has no registered address in India and has not supplied to the company an address within India for giving notices to him?

No. It would be sufficient compliance if it is mentioned in the advertisement that the explanatory statements has been forwarded of the members. [Proviso to Section 172(2)]

10.11 Purpose of Sec 173

Section 173 is designed to secure that facts having a bearing on the issue on which the shareholders have to form their judgement, are brought to the notice of the shareholders so that they can exercise intelligent judgment.

11.0 PROPER PLACE

Proper place for holding various types of meetings shall be as follows:

Meeting	*Proper place for holding meeting*
(i) ***Annual general Meeting***	An annual general meeting must be held either at the registered office of the company or at other some place within the city, town or village in which the registered office of the company is situated. [Section 166(2)] However an independent private company can fix the place for its annual general meeting and such a place need not be within the city, town or village in which the registered office of the company is situated.
(ii) ***Annual general meeting adjourned due to lack of quorum***	**At the same place where original meeting** was held or at any other place as the board may determine. [Section 174(4)]
(iii) ***Annual general meeting adjourned due to any other reasons other than lack of quorum***	As per Section 166(2) as applicable to original meeting.
(iv) ***Any other meeting***	**At any place** as the board may determine since act is silent about it.

12.0 PROPER DATE

Proper date for holding various types of meetings shall be as follows:

Meeting	*Proper date for holding meeting ...*
(i) ***Annual General meeting***	Original Annual General Meeting must be held on a day which is **not a public holiday.** Public holiday "means a public holiday within the meaning of the Negotiable Instrument Act, 1881. [Section 2(38)] According to Negotiable Instrument Act the Public Holiday includes Sundays and any other day declared by the Central Government, by notification in the Official Gazette, to be a public holiday. If any day declared by the central Government as a public holiday after the notice calling the meeting has been issued, then such holiday shall not be deemed to be a public holiday in relation to such meeting. However 1st April and 30th September shall not be treated as public holiday for the purpose of Section 166.
(ii) ***Annual general meeting adjourned due to lack of quorum***	It may be held on **any other day including public holiday** as the board may determine since the act is silent about it.
(iii) ***Annual general meeting adjourned due to any other reasons other than lack of quorum***	Annual general meeting adjourned for any other reasons other than lack of quorum, must be held **on a day other than public holiday.**
(iv) ***Any other meeting***	It may be held **on any other day including public holiday** as the board may determine since the act is silent about it.

13.0 PROPER HOURS

The Department of Company Affairs has also clarified that there is no contravention of Section 166(2) if the adjourned annual general meeting comes to be accidentally held on a public holiday. [Department's Letter No. 8/16(1)/61-PR]

The proper time for holding various types of meetings are as follows:

Meeting	*Proper time for holding meeting ...*
(i) ***Annual General meeting***	Annual General meeting must be called during **business hours** which means the normal working hours of a company.
(ii) ***Annual general meeting adjourned due to lack of quorum***	It may be called at a **time which may not fall within the business hours** as the board may determine since the act is silent on this point.
(iii) ***Annual general meeting adjourned due to any other reasons other than lack of quorum***	It must be called during **business hours** which means the normal working hours of a company.
(iv) ***General meeting other than Annual General meeting***	It may be called **at a time which may not fall within the business hours as** the board may determine since the act is silent on this point.

14.0 QUORUM (SECTION 174)

14.1 Meaning of Quorum

The term 'Quorum' means the minimum number of members that must be present in order to constitute a valid meeting and to transact business threat.

14.2 Quorum Required for General Meeting

Unless the articles provide for a larger number, quorum shall be:

Case	*Minimum Number*
In case of Public company	5 members personally present
In case of Private company	2 members personally present
In case of meeting adjourned due to lack of quorum	Members present **Notes:** (i) A single member present shall not constitute quorum at an adjourned meeting. (ii) Even 2 proxies present can constitute quorum at an adjourned meeting.
In case of meeting adjourned due to other reasons (i) *Public company* (ii) *Private company*	 5 members personally present 2 members personally present

In all of the above cases article may provide for the higher number for the purpose of constituting the quorum. But article cannot provide for the shorter number for the purpose of constituting quorum.

14.3 Who are/are not Considered as Members Personally Present

Following are considered as members personally present:

(i) a member of the company [Section 176]
(ii) Authorised representative of a body corporate. [Section 187(2)]
(iii) Representative of President/Governor of the state. [Section 187A]

Following are not considered as members personally present:

(i) Proxy appointed by the member. .
(ii) Proxy appointed by authorised representative of a body corporate/ Representative of President/Governor.

14.4 Can Proxy be Counted for the Purpose for the Quorum?

Proxy can be counted for the purpose of the quorum in the following **3 cases:**

(i) **AGM u/s 167** In case of the Annual general meeting convened, conducted and held by the Company Law Board. [Section 167]
(ii) **EGM u/s 186** In case of the General meeting other than Annual General meeting convened, conducted and held by the Company Law Board. [Section 186]
(iii) **Adjourned Meeting** In case of the meeting adjourned due to lack of Quorum.

14.5 Can One Member Constitute Quorum?

One member can constitute quorum in the following **3 cases:**

(i) **AGM u/s 167** In case of the Annual general meeting convened, conducted and held by the Company Law Board. [Section 167]
(ii) **EGM u/s 186** In case of the General meeting other than Annual General meeting convened, conducted and held by the Company Law Board. [Section 186]
(iii) **Class of one Shareholder** In case of class meetings where a class of shares is held by one shareholder. [**East V. Bannet Bros. Ltd.**]
(iv) **Member Representing more than 1 member** A member present in more than one capacity is counted separately in each such capacity.

14.6 Consequences of Absence of Quorum

If the Quorum is not present within half an hour from the time appointed for holding of the meeting the meeting shall stand:

(i) **Dissolved if it is called on the requisition of the members** under Section 169 [Section 174(3)]
(ii) **Adjourned** to the same day in the next week at the same time and same place (if Board does not determine the same) or to such other day, place and time as board may determine. [Section 174(4)]

But if in both 2 cases the articles of the company provide otherwise, then article shall be applied.

14.7 What will be Quorum if at Adjourned Meeting also Quorum is not Present [Section 174(5)]

If at adjourned meeting quorum is not present within half on hour from the time appointed for holding the meeting then **members present shall form quorum** unless articles provides otherwise. **A single member shall not constitute quorum** at an adjourned meeting.

14.8 When is Presence of the Quorum Required?

(i) According to the Regulation 49(1) of the Table A, the Quorum must be present at the time **when the meeting proceed to business.**

(ii) In the American Encyclopaedic Dictionary of Business, "A quorum must be present not only to begin meeting, but to transact business."

(iii) A reasonable conclusion can be drawn from the above statement that if during the meeting a number of members quits, leaving behind the members less than the number required to form quorum then meeting must be adjourned or as articles of the company provides for.

14.9 Effect of Failure of a Quorum

If no quorum is present, then there is no meeting and the proceedings are invalid ***Re Romford Canal Co.,*** (1883) 24 Ch. D 85]. However, acts done creating rights in favour of third parties at a meeting without a quorum being present would not affect the rights of such third parties, provided they had no notice of the irregularity [*For example* debentures issued at a meeting of directors where there was an insufficient quorum—***Re Romford Canal.***]

14.10 When is Quorum Immaterial?

If all the members are present, it is immaterial that the quorum required is more than the total number of members *[**Re Express Engineering Works Ltd.**,* (1920) Ch 466; ***Re Oxted Motor Co. Ltd.*** (1921) 3 KB 32]. If, for example, the articles of a private company provide that four members personally present shall be a quorum, and the number of members is reduced to three then the question of quorum will not arise when all the three members attend a meeting.

14.11 Cases where one Member can be Counted as more than one Member Personally Present

(i) In case where two or more bodies are represented by one person then each of the body corporate shall be deemed to be personally present by the individual representing it.

(ii) If an individual attends the meeting in more than one capacity. *For example* in his individual capacity and as a representative of any body corporate. [***Neil McLeod & Sons, Petitioners*** (1976)]

14.12 Joint Holders and Quorum

(i) In case of the joint holders any one of them may be counted for the purpose of the quorum.

(ii) Two joint holders are each member of the quorum and if they both are present in the meeting then they shall be counted as 2 members personally present. [(***Re Trans-Continental Hotel Ltd.***) & ***Jarnail Singh* v. *Bakshi Singh***]

(iii) If the articles do not provide anything to the contrary, it appears that two or more joint holders when personally present can be counted as so many members for the purpose of forming a quorum.

14.13 Director Who is Not a Member

A director who is not the shareholder of the company cannot be counted for the purpose of the quorum neither he can propose or second a resolution. But by obtaining permission from the chairman he can speak on specific matters.

15.0 PROPER CHAIRMANSHIP [SECTION 175]

15.1 Appointment of Chairman

(a) The chairman shall be appointed as per Articles of the company

(b) If the articles of a company are silent the chairman shall be appointed as per Sec. 175.

(c) The provisions of Sec. 175 are as follows : (i) the members personally present at the meeting shall elect one of themselves to be the chairman thereof on a show of hands. (ii) if a poll is demanded on the election of the chairman (whether before/after the election of chairman on a show of hand) then it shall be taken forthwith (iii) the person elected as chairman on show of hands shall exercise all the powers of chairman. (iv) If some other person is elected chairman as a result of poll he shall be the chairman for the rest of the meeting.

15.2 Is it Necessary for a Chairman to be a Director?

No since according to Section 175(1) members shall elect one of themselves to be the chairman on a show of hands unless the Articles otherwise provides.

15.3 Is it Necessary for a Chairman to be a Member?

No since according to the Regulations of 50 and 51 director may be the chairman of general meeting and according to Section 270, director may not be required to obtain share qualification. Accordingly, the chairman of the general meeting could be a director who may not hold share in the company.

15.4 Chairman must be either a member [As per Sec 175(1)] or Director who may or may not be a member [as per Regulation of 50 and 51 and Sec. 270]

15.5 Voting Rights of a Chairman

Voting rights of a chairman are as follows:

Case	*Voting rights of chairman*
(i) ***In case he is member of the company***	Chairman is entitled to exercise **one vote as a member** of a company and **second/casting vote as a chairman** in case of equality of votes (if articles provides) on a show of hands or a poll.

Case	*Voting rights of chairman*
(ii) ***In case he is not a member of the company***	As he is not a member chairman is entitled to exercise **only second/casting vote as a chairman** in case of equality of votes on a show of a hand or a poll.

15.5 What may Articles Provide Regarding the Appointment of Chairman?

Article may provide—

(i) that the chairman of the Board shall preside as chairman at every general meeting of a company. [*Regulation 50 of Table A*]

(ii) that if no chairman is present or if the chairman is unwilling to act as the chairman of a meeting then the directors shall elect one of them to be the chairman of the meeting. [*Regulation 51 of Table A*]

(iii) Where no director is present within 15 minutes or where the director present are not willing to act as chairman, then the members shall elect one of themselves to be the chairman of the meeting. [*Regulation 52*]

16.0 PROXIES [SECTION 176]

16.1 Meaning of Proxy

A proxy may be defined as an instrument prescribed by the Act by which a member of a company appoints another person to attend a meeting and to vote on his behalf. This term is also used for the person so appointed.

16.2 Who Appoint a Proxy/More than One Proxy? [Section 176(1)]

(i) Every member who is entitled to attend and vote at a meeting of the company shall be entitled to appoint another person (whether a member or not) as his proxy to attend and vote instead of himself.

(ii) Member of company having no share capital is entitled to appoint proxy only if Article of Association so provide,

(iii) Member of a private company having share capital is entitled to appoint more than one proxy if Articles so provide.

16.3 Is proxy is Bound to Vote According to the Directions of the Member Appointing Him?

The relationship between a member and his proxy is that of principal and agent. The proxy is bound to vote according to the directions of the member appointing him. [***Naryan* v. *Kaleshwara Mills Ltd.***, AIR (1952)]

16.4 What are the Rights of a Proxy?

Rights of a proxy are as follows:

(i) A proxy shall be **entitled to vote in case of voting by poll** even if articles does not provide so.

(ii) A proxy may demand for poll or join demanding a poll unless the articles otherwise provide.

(iii) A proxy may vote on show of hands if articles so provide.

16.5 What are the Limitations of a Proxy?

(i) A proxy (if not member) shall **not be entitled to speak** at the meeting. [Section 176(1)]
(ii) A proxy shall not be entitled to vote in case of voting by show of hands unless Articles so provide. [Section 176(1)]
(iii) A proxy is not counted for the purpose of quorum except under Sections 167, 174 (5) and 186.
(iv) A proxy cannot also express his views in writing because it would tantamount to speech.

16.6 Statement Regarding Proxy in Notice [Section 176(2)]

In every notice calling a meeting of a company which has a share capital or the articles of which provides for voting by proxy at the meeting, there shall appear a statement that a "member entitled to attend and vote is entitled to appoint a proxy to attend and vote instead of himself and that a proxy need not be a member of the company."

In the contravention of the aforesaid provision every officer of the company who is in default is punishable with fine upto Rs 5,000.

16.7 Instrument Appointing Proxy

Instrument appointing Proxy must be:

(i) in writing
(ii) signed by the appointer/his attorney duly authorised in writing. If the appointer is body corporate, the instrument should be under its seal or be signed by an officer or an attorney authorised by its incomplete
(iii) properly stamped.
(iv) in the form specified in Schedule IX.

16.8 Form of Proxy [Section 176(6)]

In Schedule IX to the Act the following 2 forms are given:

(i) General Form
(ii) Form for affording member an opportunity of voting for or against a resolution.

An instrument appointing a proxy as set out in Schedule IX shall not be questioned on the ground that it fails to comply with any special requirement specified for such instrument by the articles.

16.9 Deposit of Proxy within 48 hours or Shorter Period [Section 176(3)]

Instrument of Proxy is to be deposited with the company 48 hours before the time for holding meeting or such shorter period as specified by the Articles.

Since, the section speaks about the longer period and not the shorter period the company can provide for shorter period in its article.

PRACTICAL ILLUSTRATION 11

	Case				
	I	*II*	*III*	*IV*	*V*
Date of holding meeting	30/9/20X1	30/9/20X1	30/9/20X1	30/9/20X 1	30/9/20X1
Time of holding meeting	2 p.m.	2 p.m.	2 p.m.	2 p.m.	2 p.m.
Date of deposit of proxy	28/9/20X1	28/9/20X1	28/9/20X1	28/9/20X1	28/9/20X1
Time of deposit of proxy	2 p.m.	3 p.m.	2 p.m.	3 p.m.	4 p.m.
Hours before which Proxy is to be deposited as per articles	49 hours	49 hours	47 hours	47 hours	47 hours

Case I: Deposit of Proxy is valid because it is clear from the Act that if articles provide for a longer period than 48 hours then a period of 48 hours shall be considered.

Case II: Deposit of Proxy is not valid because statutory time limit of 48 hours provided by the Act has been expired.

Case III &
Case IV: Deposit of proxy is valid because the time limit provided by the articles has not been expired.

Case V: Deposit of Proxy is not valid because the time limit provided by the articles has been expired.

There is nothing in law to exclude Sunday in the computation of the 48 hours and therefore a proxy delivered on Sunday for a meeting to be 48 hours later on Tuesday would be valid provided the receipt of the proxies at the time stated could be identified in some way. [***K.P. Chackochan v. Federal Bank*** (1989)]

16.10 Deposit of Proxy at an Adjourned Meeting

Cases	*Provision*
(i) ***In case of Public company limited by shares if its articles are silent***	Proxies may be lodged even before adjourned meeting.
(ii) ***In case of other companies if their articles are silent***	Proxies cannot be lodged before adjourned meeting. Since adjournment is just a continuation meeting, 'it ought to be lodged within the stipulated time before the original meeting. [***Laren* v. *Thompson*,** (1917) 2 Ch. 261]
(iii) ***'Where articles contain provision similar to Regulation 61 of Table A***	Proxies may be lodged even before adjourned meeting.
(iv) ***Where articles prohibit as such***	Proxies cannot be lodged before adjourned meeting.

16.11 Can a Person give Proxies to a Different Person on Different Date to Different Persons?

Yes, he can do so but then the proxy whose date is subsequent to the date of other proxies will be accepted to the exclusion of other proxies.

16.12 Who can Appoint Proxy in Case of Joint Holdings?

Unless articles otherwise provides, in case of joint holdings, senior most joint holder (i.e. **first named joint holder**) sign the proxy.

16.13 Prohibition on Invitation by Company to Members [Section 176(4)]

If an invitation to member to appoint one or more person already specified in the invitation as proxies is sent, the every officer of the company who knowingly issues the invitation as aforesaid or willingly authorises or permits their issues shall be punishable with fine not exceeding Rs 10,000.

However, an officer shall not be punishable in case of issue of form of appointment naming the proxy or of a list of person willing to act as proxies provided:

(i) a request in writing is made by the member, and

(ii) the form/ list is available on request in writing to every member entitled to vote at the meeting by proxy.

16.14 Inspection of Proxy [Section 176(7)]

After giving 3 days' notice to the company, every member entitled to vote, may inspect during business hours the proxies lodged with the company during the period beginning 24 hours before the time fixed for commencement of the meeting and ending with the conclusion of the meeting.

16.15 Revocation of Proxy

A proxy can be revoked at any time and is said to be revoked if:

(i) When a **written intimation of death or insanity of the principal or the revocation** of the proxy or the **transfer of shares** is received by the company at its office before the commencement of meeting or adjourned meeting where articles are silent or contain provision similar to Regulation 63.

(ii) When a member having appointed a proxy, **personally attends** to vote at meeting. [***Cousins* v. *International Bricks Co. Ltd.*** (1931)]

(iii) When a member having appointed a proxy, **appoints another proxy** at a later date. In this case the proxy appointed at later date will supersede the earlier proxies. [***Re Swadeshi Polytex Ltd.***, (1988)]

16.16 Lodging of Proxy at or before Taking Up Poll

Cases	*Provision*
(i) ***In case of Public company limited by shares if its articles are silent***	Proxies may be lodged at or before taking up poll.
(ii) ***In case of other companies if their articles are silent***	Proxies cannot be lodged at or before taking up poll. [*Shaw* v. *Tati Concession Ltd.* (1913)]
(iii) ***Where articles contain provision similar to Regulation 61***	Proxies may be lodged at or before taking up poll.
(iv) ***Where articles prohibit as such***	Proxies cannot be lodged at or before taking up poll.

16.17 Is Proxy entitled to put Question in Writing and Sending the Same to the Chairman?

Yes, a proxy is also entitled to put question in writing and sending the same to the chairman for answer since the Act is silent on this point.

16.18 Members of which Company are not entitled to appoint Proxy

Members of the company having no share capital cannot appoint proxy unless articles otherwise 'provides. [Proviso to Section 176(1)]

16.19 Members of which Company are not Entitled to Appoint more than One Proxy

Members of private company (whether subsidiary of public company or not) cannot appoint more than one proxy unless articles otherwise provide. [Proviso to Section 176(1)]

16.20 Representations of Corporations at Meetings of Companies and of Creditors. [Section 187]

(a) Where a company is a member of another company, it may attend the meeting of any other company through a representative. The representative must be appointed by a resolution of the board of directors or the other governing body. The person so appointed is entitled to exercise the same rights and powers (including the right to vote by proxy) on behalf of the company as the individual member of the company may exercise.

(b) Where a company is a creditor of another company, it may attend the meeting of any other company through a representative. The representative must be appointed by a resolution of the board of directors or the other governing body.

(c) A foreign company can also make the use of this provision or it may appoint a representative by means of power of attorney. [***CEPT* v. *Jeewanlal Ltd.***, (1951)]

(d) In case of company which is in liquidation, the liquidator will be the governing body and may appoint where he is not himself able to be present, a representative. [***Hillman* v. *Crystal Bowl Amusement Ltd.***, (1973)]

16.21 Representation of the President and Governors in Meeting of Companies in which they are Members [Section 187A]

Where a president or Governor is a member of any company, then president or Governor as the case may be, may attend a meeting through representative appointed by the President or Governor. The person so appointed is entitled to exercise the same rights and powers (including the right to vote by proxy) on behalf of the President or Governor as the individual member of the company may exercise.

17.0 PROPER VOTING

17.1 How shall a Resolution at a Meeting be decided?

Section 177 provides that a resolution when put to vote at a meeting shall be decided by a show of hands unless a poll is demanded under Section 179.

The procedure generally followed is that a resolution is proposed either by a chairman or by any other member and is seconded by some other member or members. Chairman can also second a resolution if he has not proposed a resolution. Seconding is necessary if articles requires so otherwise it is not mandatory.

17.2 Voting by show of hands

(a) **Who can Vote on Show by Hands?** The following persons can vote in case of voting by show of hands:

(i) Every member of a company. [Section 87]

(ii) First named member in case of Joint holder. [Regulation 57]

(iii) Authorised representative of a body corporate. [Section 187(2)]

(iv) Representative of President/Governor of the state. [Section 187A]

(v) Preference shareholders if resolution proposed is directly affecting them. [Section 87(2)]

Any resolution for winding up of the company or for the repayment or the reduction of preference share capital shall be deemed directly to affect the rights attached to the preference shares.

(vi) A cumulative preference shareholder in respect of every resolution if his dividend remains unpaid for an aggregate period of at least 2 years preceding the date of the meeting. [Section 87(2)(b)(i)]

(vii) A non-cumulative preference shareholder in respect of every resolution if his dividend remains unpaid for at least 2 years ending with the expiry of financial year immediately preceding the commencement of meeting or for an aggregate period of at least 3 years out of 6 years ending with the expiry of the financial year aforesaid. [Section 87(2)(b)(ii)]

(b) **Who cannot vote in Case of Voting by Show of Hands? Proxy** shall not be entitled to vote in case of voting by show of hands unless the articles provides otherwise. [Section 176]

(c) **What should be the Contents of the Minutes of the Minutes in Case of Voting by Show of Hands? [Section 178]** A declaration by the chairman to the effect that whether the resolution was carried or not, if carried whether unanimously or by majority, is required to be entered in the minute book and such entry shall be conclusive evidence of the fact.

It means, that it is not necessary to indicate in the minutes the number of persons who have voted in favour or against resolution.

It does not mean that shareholder cannot challenge the validity of the passing of the resolution in the court of law.

17.3 Voting by Poll

(a) When may a Poll be Demanded? [Section 179(1)] A poll may be ordered either before or after the declaration of the resolution of a voting on a show of hands.

(b) Who can Demand a Poll? A poll may be demanded by any of the following persons:

(i) Chairman on his own motion

(ii) in case of a public company having share capital, by any member or members present in person or by proxy and holding shares

(a) which carry at least 1/10th of the voting power, or

(b) on which at least Rs 50,000 has been paid up whichever is less.

(iii) In case of a private company, by at least 2 members present in person or by proxy and having right to vote where number of members personally present exceed 7 or by 1 where members personally present does not exceed 7.

(iv) in case any other company, by any member or members present in person or by proxy and having at least 1/10th of total voting power.

(c) When and by Whom the Demand for Poll can be Withdrawn? [Section 179(2)] The demand for poll may be withdrawn at any time by the person or persons who made the demand.

(d) What is Time for Taking Poll? [Section 180]

Case	*Time Limit*
(i) ***A poll demanded on a resolution for the adjournment of the meeting or for the election of chairman.***	It must be taken **immediately.**
(ii) ***A poll demanded on other resolution.***	It must be taken within **48 hours** of demand for poll.

(e) Can the Poll be Continued on the Next Day? Yes. If a poll is not completed on the same day, it will be continued on the next day and the chairman shall not be entitled to close the poll.

(f) Is it Necessary to have Poll for Each of Resolution Separately? Yes, where more than one resolution is to be passed.

(g) Duties of Chairman to Appoint Scrutineers [Section 184] The chairman shall appoint two scrutineers to scrutinise the votes given on the poll and to report thereon to him. At least one of the two scrutineers shall be a member (not being an officer or an employee of the company) present at the meeting provided such a member is available and willing to be appointed.

(h) Powers of Chairman Regarding poll [Sections 184 and 185] The chairman has the following powers :

(i) To remove the scrutineers and to fill up the vacancy arising from such removal any time before the declaration of the result of poll.

(ii) To regulate the manner in which the poll should be conducted.

(i) **How can the Poll be Conducted?** The poll may be taken by ballot/by show of hands.

(j) **Nature of the Result of the Poll [Section 185]** The result of the poll shall be deemed to be the decision of the meeting on which the poll was taken.

(k) **Is Proxy Entitled to Vote on Poll? Yes,** proxy is entitled to vote on poll. [Section 176]

(l) **Can a Proxy Demand for Poll? Yes,** since proxy is entitled to vote on a poll, he is also entitled to demand for poll.

(m) **Voting Rights in Case of Voting by Show of Hands** Each member personally present shall be entitled to **one vote** on show of hands irrespective of his shareholding.

Note: A proxy is not entitled to vote on show of hands unless authorised by the articles.

(n) **Voting rights in case of Voting by Poll**

Case	*Voting Rights*
(i) ***Voting rights of Equity Shareholders***	In the **same proportion as the paid up capital** in respect of equity shares bears to the total paid up equity capital of the company.
(ii) ***Voting rights of Preference Shareholders***	In the same proportion as the paid up capital in respect of preference shares bears to the total paid up equity capital of the company.
(iii) ***Voting rights of Joint Shareholders***	First named shareholder shall be entitled to vote.

PRACTICAL ILLUSTRATION 12

1000 Equity shares of Rs 10 each Rs 8 called and paid up Rs 8,000

500 Preference shares of Rs 10 each Rs 8 called and paid up Rs 4,000

Total Called and Paid up Share Capital Rs 12,000

Additional Information:

100 Equity shares of Rs 10 each Rs 8 paid up hold by Mr. *X*

50 Preference shares of Rs 10 each Rs 8 paid up hold by Mr. *Y*

Determine the voting rights of Mr. *X* and Mr. *Y*.

Answer

Voting Rights of Mr. *X* = (800/8000) *100 = 10%

Voting Rights of Mr. *Y* = (400/8000) *100 = 5%

(o) **Right to Vote on Every Resolution Placed before the Company**

(i) Every member of a company. [Section 87]

(ii) First named member in case of Joint holder. [Regulation 57]

(iii) Authorised representative of a body corporate. [Section 187(2)]

(iv) Representative of President/Governor of the state. [Section 187A]

(v) A cumulative preference shareholder if his dividend remains unpaid for an aggregate period of at least 2 years preceding the date of the meeting. [Section 87(2)(b)(i)]

(vi) A non-cumulative preference shareholder if his dividend remains unpaid for at least 2 years ending with the expiry of financial year immediately preceding the commencement of meeting or for an aggregate period of at least 3 years out of 6 years ending with the expiry of the financial year aforesaid. [Section 87(2)(b)(ii)]

(p) Right of Preference Shareholder to Vote [Section 87(2)]

(i) A preference shareholder shall have a right to vote only on resolution placed before the company which directly affects the rights attached to the preference shares.

(ii) Any resolution for winding up of the company or for the repayment or the reduction of preference share capital shall be deemed directly to affect the rights attached to the preference shares.

(q) Restriction on Exercise of voting rights [Sections 181 and 182]

(i) In case of a Public Company, restriction on exercise of voting rights **on the ground of non-payment of calls or** other sum presently payable in regard to which the company has exercise any right is **valid.** [Section 181] **but on any other ground, is not valid.** [Section 182]

(ii) In case of a private company, restriction or exercise of voting rights may be on any ground contained in its Articles.

(r) Can a Member Use His Votes Differently? [Section 183] A member can use his vote differently (some votes in favour or against the same resolution) in case of voting by poll.

18.0 PASSING OF RESOLUTION BY POSTAL BALLOT [SECTION 192A]

18.1 Meaning of Postal Ballot

"**Postal Ballot**" includes voting by shareholders by postal or electronic mode instead of voting personally by presenting for transacting businesses in a general meeting of the company.

18.2 Power of a Listed Public Company to Pass a Resolution by Postal Ballot

Section 192A permits a listed public company to pass a resolution by postal ballot.

18.3 Procedure to be Followed for Conducting Business through Postal Ballot

1. Provisions as to Notice etc.

(a) Company must send a notice to all members along with a draft resolution stating the reasons therefor. [Section 192A(1)]

(b) The notice must request the members to send their assent or dissent in writing on a postal ballot within 30 days from the date of the posting of the letter. [Section 192A(2)]

(c) The notice must be sent by a registered letter or by any other method as prescribed by the Central Government. [Section 192A(3)]

(d) A postage pre-paid envelope along with the notice must also be sent to all the members to receive their assent or dissent. [Section 192A(3)]

(e) A resolution shall be deemed to have been duly passed at a general meeting if the resolution is assented to by a requisite majority of members by mean of postal ballot. [Section 192A(4)]

Meaning of Requisite Majority—"Requisite Majority" with regard to special resolution means votes cast in favour of the business is three times more than the votes cast against, with regard to ordinary resolution, votes cast in favour is more than the votes cast against.

(f) Any person who defaces or destroys the ballot paper or declaration of the identity of the member shall be punishable with imprisonment upto 6 months or with fine or with both. [Section 192(A)(5)]

(g) **Note below Notice**—The company may make a note below the notice of general meeting for under-standing of members that the transactions(s) at serial number requires consent of shareholders through postal ballot;

2. Other Provisions

(a) **Appointment of Scrutinizer**—The board of directors shall appoint one scrutinizer. The scrutinizer must not be in employment of the company. He may be a retired judge or any person of repute who, in the opinion of the board can conduct the postal ballot voting process in a fair and transparent manner;

(b) **Final Report**—The scrutinizer is to submit final report on or before 35 days (excluding holidays) from the date of issue of notice for annual general meeting.

(c) **Availability of Scrutinizer**—The scrutinizer must be willing to be appointed and he must be available at the registered office of the company for the purpose of ascertaining the requisite majority.

(d) **Register**—The scrutinizer shall maintain a register to record the consent or otherwise received, including electronic media, mentioning the particulars of name, address, folio number, number of shares, nominal value of shares, whether the shares have voting, differential voting or non-voting rights and the scrutinizer shall also maintain record for postal ballot which are received in defaced or mutilated form. The postal ballot and all other papers relating to postal ballot will be under the sate custody of the scrutinizer till the chairman considers, approves and signs the minutes of the meeting. Thereafter, the scrutinizer shall return the ballot papers and other related papers/register to the company so as to preserve such ballot papers and other related papers/register safely till the resolution is given effect to;

(e) **Reply after 35 days to be No Reply**—Consent or otherwise relating to issue mentioned in notice for annual general meeting received after 35 days from the date of issue will be strictly treated as if the reply from the member has not been received.

18.4 Businesses in which the Resolutions May be Passed Through Postal Ballot

1. Alteration in the object clause of Memorandum; [Sec. 17]
2. Alteration of Articles of Associations in relation to deletion or insertion of provisions defining private company; [Sec 3 (1)(iii) and Sec. 31]
3. Buy-back of own shares by the company u/s 77A(1);
4. Issue of shares with differential voting rights as to voting or dividend or otherwise u/s 86(a)(ii);
5. Variation in the rights attached to a class of shares or debentures or other securities as specified u/s 106;
6. Change of registered office out side local limits of any city, town or village but within the same state as specified in u/s 146(2);
7. Election of small shareholders' director u/s 252(1);

8. Sale of whole or substantially the whole of undertaking of a company but within the same state as specified u/s 293(1)(a);
9. Giving loans or extending guarantee or providing security in excess of the limit prescribed u/s 372A(1);
10. Power to compromise or make arrangements with creditors and members as specified u/s 391(2).

18.5 Penalty for Contravention [Section 192A(6)]

The company and its every offices in default shall be punishable with fine upto Rs 5,00,000 in respect of each such default if any of the provisions of Section 192A is not complied with.

18.6 Penalty for Default

If default is made in following this procedure, fine of Rs 50,000 can be levied for each default.

19.0 ORDINARY BUSINESS AND SPECIAL BUSINESS [SECTION 173]

19.1 Ordinary business

The following **four businesses** to be transacted **at Annual General meeting** shall be considered as ordinary business:

(i) Consideration of accounts, balance sheet and the report of Board of Directors and auditors.
(ii) Declaration of Dividend.
(iii) Appointment of Directors in the place of those retiring.
(iv) Appointment of, and fixing of the remuneration of the auditors.

19.2 Special Business

(a) **All businesses except the following four businesses** to be transacted at AGM shall deemed to be special business.
  (i) Consideration of accounts, balance sheet and the report of Board of Directors and auditors.
  (ii) Declaration of Dividend.
  (iii) Appointment of Directors in the place of those retiring.
  (iv) Appointment of, and fixing of the remuneration of the auditors.

(b) All businesses to be transacted at any meeting other than AGM shall be deemed to be special business.

19.3 Explanatory Statement required in case of Special Business [Section 173(2) and (3)]

Where any special business is to be transacted at the meeting, an Explanatory Statement is required to be annexed to the notice. Such statement shall include amongst other:

(a) All material facts concerning each item of business.
(b) The nature of the concern or interest if any, therein of every director and manager.
(c) If any item of the special business affects any other company, then the extent of shareholding of every director and manager in that company in case their share holding interest is at least 20% of the paid up share capital of the other company.

(d) The time when and place where the document to be approved at the meeting can be inspected.

Note: If the notice convening the meeting states no particulars or insufficient particulars as to the special business to be transacted threat, the meeting would be deemed to have been convened irregularly. [*Jain* v. *Kalinga Tubes* (1965)]

19.4 Distinction between Ordinary Business and Special Business

Basis of Distinction	*Special business*	*Ordinary business*
1. *Meaning*	All business except that specified u/s 173(1)(a) shall be deemed to be special business.	Following business shall be ordinary business: (a) Consideration of accounts (b) Declaration of dividend (c) Appointment of directors in the place of those retiring (d) Appointment and fixing of remuneration auditors.
2. *Meeting at which it can be transacted*	At AGM or **any** other **general meeting**	**AT AGM only**
3. *Indication of nature of business*	Notice **must indicate** that the business is special, in case of special business	Notice **need not indicate** that the business is an ordinary business.
4. *Full text of the resolution*	For transacting every item of special business, full text of the resolution **must be given** in the notice.	For transacting ordinary business, full text of the resolution **need not be given** in the notice.
5. *Explanatory Statement*	Explanatory statement is **required** for transacting each item of special business.	Explanatory statement is **not required** for transacting any item of ordinary business.
6. *Nature of resolution required*	The Ordinary/Special resolution may be required depending upon the provisions of the Act applicable.	Ordinary business generally requires an Ordinary Resolution unless Sec. 224A is attracted in which case special resolution is required.

20.0 RESOLUTION

20.1 Meaning Resolution is a formal proposal put to the meeting for approval.

20.2 Two Kinds Basically there are two kinds of resolutions—ordinary and special.

20.3 Ordinary Resolution [Section 189(1)]

A resolution shall be an ordinary resolution when—

(a) the notice of general meeting required under the Act has been duly given,

(b) the **votes cast including the casting vote** if any of the chairman (whether on show of hand or on a poll as the case may be) **exceed the votes if any cast against** the resolution.

PRACTICAL ILLUSTRATION 13

Total number of members	300
Total number of members present at meeting	210
Total votes cast	200
Total votes cast in favour of the resolution	101
Total votes cast against the resolution	99

***Solution*:**

In this case the ordinary resolution will be said to have been passed since votes in favour (i.e. 101) exceeds votes cast against (i.e. 99)

20.4 Matters Requiring only Ordinary Resolution

Subject to the articles, an ordinary resolution is sufficient, for *inter alia* any of the following matters:

1. To rectify the name of company (subject to previous approval of Central Govt.) [Sec. 22]
2. To Authorise variations in terms of any contract contained in the Prospectus/ Statement in lieu of Prospectus [Sec. 61]
3. To authorise an issue of shares at a discount [Section 79];
4. To alter the share capital (if authorised by the articles), apart from its reduction [Sections 94];
5. To adopt annual accounts;
6. To declare dividends;
7. To appoint directors in place of those retiring;
8. To appoint auditors in place of those retiring;
9. To appoint auditors [Section 224(1)]; but in the case of a company in which not less than 25 per cent of the subscribed share capital is held, whether singly or in any combination, by a public financial institution or a Government company or Central or any State Government, or a nationalised bank or an insurance company carrying a general insurance business, the appointment of auditors requires a special resolution [Section 224A];
10. To wind up voluntarily when the period, if any, fixed for the duration of the company by the articles has expired, or the event, if any, has occurred, on the occurrence of which the articles provided that the company is to be dissolved [Section 484(1)];
11. To appoint liquidators in a members 'voluntary winding-up and to fix their remuneration [Section 490];
12. To register an unlimited company as a limited company (Section 32); and generally to do all things for which a special resolution is not specifically required either by the Act or the company's articles.

20.5 Special Resolution [Section 189(2)]

A resolution shall be a special resolution when—

(a) the notice of general meeting required under the Act has been duly given,

(b) the **votes cast including the casting** vote if any of the chairman (whether on show of hand or on a poll as the case may be) **are at least 3 times the number of votes** if any **cast against** the resolution.

(c) the intention to propose the resolution as a special resolution has been duly specified in the notice calling the general meeting or other intimation given to the members.

PRACTICAL ILLUSTRATION 14

Total numbers of members	300
Total numbers of members present at meeting	210
Total votes cast	200
Total votes cast in favour of the resolution	120
Total votes cast against the resolution	40
Total invalid votes	40

Soluton:

In this case the special resolution will be said to have been passed since the number of votes cast in favour (i.e. 120) are 3 times the number of votes cast against (i.e. 40)

20.6 Matters Requiring Special Resolution

The Act requires that the following matters, *inter alia,* have to be resolved by the company, by a special resolution:

1. To alter any provision contained in the memorandum which could lawfully have been contained in the articles instead of the memorandum [Section 16];
2. To alter the objects or the place of registered office of a company (Section 17);
3. To change the name of the company [Section 21];
4. To alter the articles of association [Section 31];
5. To issue further shares to persons other than existing members (Sec. 81)
6. To issue convertible loan or debentures to person other than Govt. [Sec. 81(3)]
7. To create a reserve liability, that is, to determine that a portion of the uncalled capital shall not be capable of being called up, except in the event of a winding up (Section 99);
8. To reduce the share capital [Section 100];
9. To vary the rights of special classes of shares (Sec. 106);
10. To move the company's registered office within the same State but outside the local limits of the city, town or village where such office is situated [Section 146(2)];
11. To commence any new business which is not germane to the business the company is carrying on currently, though covered by the objects clause of the memorandum [Section 149(2A)];
12. To keep statutory registers and return at a place other than the registered office (Sec. 163);
13. To pay interest on shares out of capital [Section 208];
14. To appoint auditors, if at least 25% of the company's subscribed capital is held, whether singly or in any combination, by the Central or any State Government, Government companies, financial institutions, nationalised banks, etc. (Section 224A);

15. To support an application to the Central Government to appoint inspectors to investigate the affairs of the company [Section 237];
16. To appoint sole selling agents, if the company's paid-up capital is Rs 50 lakh or more [Section 294AA(3)];
17. To authorise the payment of remuneration to non-executive directors by way of commission on the basis of a percentage of the net profits, in the case of public company or a private company which is a subsidiary of a public company [Section 309(4)];
18. To authorise directors, etc. to hold office or place of profit under the company [Section 314];
19. To alter the memorandum where the articles permit, to make unlimited the liability of director (Section 323);
20. Investment exceeding the limits prescribed in Section 372A.
21. To have the company wound up by the court [Section 433(a)];
22. To wind up voluntarily for any reason not otherwise provided for by the section (Section 484).
23. To authorise the liquidator to transfer or sell the assets of the company, which is proposed to be, or is in the course of being wound up voluntarily, to another company in exchange for shares [Sections 494 and 507];
24. To authorise the liquidator in a members' voluntary winding up to exercise the powers given by Clauses (a) to (d) Section 457(1) to a liquidator in a winding up by the Court [Section 512(1)(a)]
25. To sanction the exercise by the liquidator in volunteer winding up of powers mention in Section 546;
26. To direct the disposal of books and papers of the company in a members, voluntary winding up [Section 550(3)(a)];
27. To adopt *Table A* in Schedule I in the case of registration of a company under Part IX of the Act [Section 578(3)(a)];
28. To alter the form of constitution of a company registered under Part IX of the Act [Section 579(1)].

In addition to the requirements of the Act, a company's own articles may prescribe for special resolution where the Act requires only an ordinary resolution.

21.0 SPECIAL NOTICE [SECTION 190]

21.1 Length of Special Notice

Where, by any provision contained in the Act or in the Articles, Special Notice is required of any resolution, notice of the intention to move the resolution is given to the company **at least 14 clear days** (exclusive of days on which notice is served or deemed to be served and the day meeting is to be held) before the meeting at which it is to be moved. [Section 190(1)]

21.2 Duty of Company After Receipt of Special Notice

The company immediately after receipt of the notice must give notice of any such resolution to its members in the same manner as it gives notice of meeting or if that is not practicable, give the notice thereof either by advertisement in a newspaper having an appropriate circulation or in any other mode allowed by Articles **at least 7 days before the meeting.** [Section 190(2)]

21.3 Resolutions for which Special Notice is Required Under the Act

(i) To provide that a retiring auditor shall not be re-appointed. [Section 225]
(ii) To appoint an auditor other than retiring one. [Section 225]
(iii) To appoint a director other than retiring one. [Section 257]
(iv) To remove a director before expiry of time of the term. [Section 284(2)]
(v) To appoint another director in place of removed director. [Section 284(2)]
(vi) To appoint certain person who cannot be appointed in the ordinary course as director provided for in Section 261. [Section 261(2)]

The articles of the company may add additional matter in respect of which Special Notice is required.

22.0 CIRCULATION OF MEMBERS' RESOLUTION [SECTION 188]

22.1 Who can make a Requisition for Moving Resolution at AGM or for Circulation of Statement with Regard to any Proposed Resolution or Business to be dealt with at any General Meeting? [Section 188(2)]

The following members can make a requisition for moving resolution at AGM or for circulation of statement with regard to any proposed resolution or business to be dealt with at any general meeting:

(a) members having at least **5% voting power**, or
(b) **at least 100 members** having right to vote who hold shares on which at least Rs 1 lakh has been paid up.

22.2 Duty of Company after Receipt of Requisition [Section 188(1)]

The company on receipt of the written requisition must—

(a) give notice to members entitled to have notice of meeting of any resolution which is intended to be moved at AGM.
(b) circulate to members entitled to have notice of meeting any statement of not more than 1,000 words with regard to any proposed resolution or business to be dealt with at any general meeting

22.3 Service of Notice of Intended Resolution or Circulation of Statement [Section 188(3)]

The notice of intended resolution or circulation of statement must be served by serving a copy of resolution of statement in the same manner and at the same time as the notice of the meeting or where it is not practicable as soon as practicable thereafter.

22.4 When Company not Bound to Give the Notice or Circulate Statement? [Section 188(4)]

A company shall not be bound to give the notice of any resolution or to circulate any statement unless—

(a) a copy of the requisition signed by the requisitionists is deposited at the registered office of the company—
   (i) at least 6 weeks before the meeting in case of requisition requiring notice of resolution.
   (ii) at least 2 weeks before the meeting in case of any other requisition.

(b) a sum reasonably sufficient to meet the company's expenses in giving effect to the requisition has been deposited or tendered with the requisition.

Note: If after a copy of requisition requiring notice of a resolutions has been deposited at the registered office of the co. an AGM called for a date six weeks or less after the copy has been deposited, then the copy although not deposit at time shall be deemed to be deposited properly.

22.5 Other Cases where the Company is not Bound to Circulate Statement [Section 188(5) and (6)]

A company shall not be bound to circulate any statement in the following two cases:
(i) If on the application of the company or any other aggrieved person, the Company Law Tribunal is satisfied that the right is being abused to secure needless publicity for defamatory matter; and
(ii) If it is a banking company and in the opinion of its board of directors, the circulation will injure the interest of the company.

22.6 Effect of Accidental Omission to Serve the Notice [Section 188(7)]

Any accidental omission to serve notice upon one or more members will not invalidate the proceedings.

22.7 Penalty for Default [Section 188(8)]

Every officer of the company who is in default shall be punishable with fine upto Rs 50,000.

22.8 Requirements as to Requisition

Duly signed requisition along with money sufficient to cover company's expenses must be deposited at registered office at least 2 weeks (6 weeks if requisition proposes a resolution).

23.0 REGISTRATION OF CERTAIN RESOLUTIONS AND AGREEMENTS [SECTION 192(4)]

23.1 What is Required to be filed with the Registrar?

The following resolutions/agreements are required to be filed with the registrar:
(a) Special resolution **not passed** by all the members.
(b) Special resolution **passed** by all the members.
(c) Ordinary resolution **passed by all members**.
(d) A resolution of the Board or an agreement executed by a company relating to the appointment, reappointment, renewal of the appointment or variation of the terms of managing directors.
(e) Ordinary resolution passed by the company conferring power under Section 293 upon its directors:

(i) to sell or dispose the whole or any part of the company's undertaking, or
(ii) to borrow money beyond the limits of the paid up capital and free reserves of the company;
(iii) to contribute the charities beyond Rs 50,000 or 5% of profit.

(f) Resolution regarding voluntary winding up of the company under Section 484(1).
(g) Resolution regarding appointment of Sole selling Agent u/s 294 or 294AA
(h) Copies of the terms and conditions of appointment of sole selling agents under section 294 or a sole selling agent or other person under Section 294AA.

23.2 When to be Filed? [Section 192(1)]

The above resolution/agreements duly certified under the signature of an officer of the company, are required to be filed in Form 23 within 30 days after the passing of resolution or making of an agreement, as the case may be in the office of the Registrar.

23.3 Duty of Company Regarding Annexing of a Copy of Resolution and a Copy of Agreement [Section 192(2) and (3)]

(a) Where the articles have been registered, the following are required to be embodied in or annexed to every copy of articles issued after the passing of the resolution or the making of an agreement:
   (i) A copy of every agreement referred to in Section 192(1).
   (ii) A copy of every resolution referred to in Section 192(1) which has the effect of altering the Articles.
(b) However, Section 40 provides that copies of all agreements referred to under Section 192 shall be annexed to every copy of the memorandum and Articles issued after the date of alterations.
(c) Where Articles have not been registered, a printed copy of every resolution and agreement shall be forwarded to any member on his request on payment of Re 1.

23.4 Penalties for Default [Section 192(5) and (6)]

(i) For default in filing with registrar—The company and every officer at default shall be punishable with fine of Rs 200 for every day during which default continues.
(ii) For default in annexing or forwarding a copy of resolution and copy of agreement—The company and every officer at default shall be punishable with fine of Rs 100 for each copy.

24.0 MINUTES [SECTIONS 193 TO 197]

24.1 Meaning of Minute

Minute may be defined as the written record of proceedings at a meeting including decision arrived at such meeting.

24.2 Two Types of Minutes

Minutes are of two kinds:

(a) Minutes of narration which record simple statements of happening which do not require any formal resolution. *For example* "The minutes of the previous Executive committee Meeting held on 10th August 20X1 were read, approved and signed by the chairman as a correct record."

(b) Minutes of resolutions record the formal decisions of the meeting which require passing of a resolution.

24.3 Distinction between Minutes and Reports

(a) Minutes are the records of what was done at meeting but reports are the records of what was said for or against a particular proposition.

(b) Unlike the minutes, reports do not have the same legal significance.

(c) Minutes signed by the chairman, although not conclusive, is *prima facie* evidence of the proceedings thereat and decision recorded therein until the contrary is proved but reports may or may not be prima facie evidence.

24.4 Recording of Minutes within 30 days of Conclusion of Meeting [Section 193(1)]

Every company must prepare minutes of all proceedings of every general meeting or Board meeting or Committee of the Board and such minutes must be recorded in the books kept for this purpose within 30 days from the conclusion of every such meeting and such book must have page **consecutively numbered**.

24.5 Contents of Minutes [Section 193(2), (3), (4), (5)]

(a) The minutes of each meeting shall contain a **fair and correct summary** of the proceedings thereat and the appointment of the officers made thereat.

(b) The **minutes of board** shall also **contain**:

(i) the **names of the directors present**, and

(ii) in case of each **resolution passed** at the meeting names of the directors, if any, dissenting from or not concurring with the resolution.

(c) The minute shall **not contain** any matter which in the opinion of the chairman of the meeting—

(i) is or could reasonably be regarded as defamatory

(ii) is irrelevant or immaterial to the proceedings;

(iii) is detrimental to the interests of the company.

(d) The chairman shall exercise an absolute discretion with regard to the inclusion or non-inclusion of any matter in the minutes on the grounds mentioned above.

24.6 Signature on Minute Book within 30 days of Conclusion of meeting [Section 193(1A)]

Each page of every such minute book should be **initialled or signed** and the **last page** of record of the proceeding of each meeting in such book shall be **dated and signed**:

(a) in the case of minutes of proceedings of a meetings of the Board or of committee thereof, by the chairman of said meeting or the chairman of the succeeding meeting;

(b) in the case of the minutes of proceedings of a general meeting by the chairman of the same meeting **within the period of 30 days of the conclusion** of the meeting or in the event of the death of or inability of that chairman within that period, by a director duly authorised by the board for the purpose.

Notes:

(i) Since there is no prohibition, such a resolution is passed within 30 days so that there is time for the director to sign the minutes within the said period.

(ii) Time gap between the preparation and signing of the minutes of general meeting could be of 30 days.

(iii) Time gap between the preparation and signing of the minutes of Board could be more than 3 months e.g. in case the 1st Board meeting is held on 1st January and 2nd Board meeting is held on 30th June.

24.7 Maintenance of Minutes [Section 193(1B)]

(a) The minutes in no case, shall be attached by pasting or otherwise to the minute books kept for this purpose.

(b) The Central Government has clarified that entering of minutes in bound books by a chemical process which does not amount to attachment to any book by pasting or otherwise is permissible provided on the mechanical impression of the minutes, the original signature of the chairman is given on each page.

(c) The department of company affairs has expressed the view that in certain exceptional cases i.e. in the case of large companies where the minutes of the meeting runs into great lengths, minutes may be kept in a losose leaf binder provided:

  (i) the pages are duly typed and serially numbered;

  (ii) the loose leaves are kept in proper lock for safe custody.

  (iii) the loose leaves are bound up at a reasonable interval not exceeding 6 months; and

  (iv) prior commission of the Company Law Tribunal has been obtained.

24.8 Confirmation of Minutes

(a) The term 'confirmation' means verification. In true technical sense, the decision already taken does not require any ratification or confirmation.

(b) There is no provision in Act which requires the minutes of the Board or general meeting to be read or confirmed at the subsequent meeting but in practice minutes of the Board meeting are read at the next board meeting and request by the chairman is made to the directors present whether they have any comments on the minutes of the previous Board meeting or general meeting which have circulated to them. Normally the minutes covering the confirmation of the minutes of the previous board meeting is usually worded as follows:

"***Minutes of the last Board meeting held on...which were circulated to the directors were read, approved and signed by the chairman as correct record***".

24.9 Penalty [Section 193(6)]

If default is made in complying with aforesaid provision company and every officer of the company who is in default shall punishable with fine which may extend to Rs 500.

24.10 Minutes as Evidence of Proceedings [Section 194]

The minutes of meeting kept in accordance with the provision of Section 193 shall be evidence of the proceedings thereon.

24.11 Presumption [Section 195]

Where the minutes have been duly drawn in accordance with the provision of Section 193, then until the contrary is proved

(i) the meeting shall be deemed to have been duly called and held
(ii) all the proceedings thereat shall be deemed to duly taken place and
(iii) all appointments of directors and liquidators made at the meeting shall be deemed to be valid.

24.12 Inspection of Minutes [Section 196]

(i) **Place and Hours**—The minutes of proceedings of any general meeting of the company shall be:
   (a) kept at the registered office, and
   (b) be open during business hour for inspection by member for at least 2 hours a day without charge subject to such reasonable restrictions as may be imposed by articles.

(ii) **Right to inspect and get copy of Minutes within 7 Days**—Every member is entitled to inspect the minutes and to be furnished with a copy of the minutes of the general meeting **within 7 days** from the date of his request to the company on payment of Re 1 for every hundred words or fractional part thereof required to be copied. [Section 196(2)]

(iii) **No Rights in respect of Board's Minutes**—However, these rights are not available to the member in respect of minutes of Board meetings. But directors, Auditors and investigator appointed by the Central Government are entitled to inspect the minutes of Board and committees thereof.

24.13 Default Regarding Refusal of Inspection/Not Furnishing a Copy of Minute [Section 196(3) and (4)]

In case of default regarding refusal of inspection/not furnishing a copy of minute:

(a) The company and every defaulting officer of the company who is in default shall be punishable with fine upto Rs 5,000 in respect of each default.
(b) The Company Law Board may direct the immediate inspection of the minutes or delivery of the copy of minutes.

24.14 Publication [Section 197]

(a) No document purporting to be a report of the proceeding of any general meeting of the company shall be circulated or advertised at the expense of the company unless it includes matters required by Section 193 to be contained in the minutes of the proceedings of such meetings.
(b) In case of contravention of aforesaid provision, the company and its every officer in default shall be punishable with fine which upto Rs 5,000. It is to be noted that no penalty is attracted when the publication/circulation does not purport to be proceedings of the meeting.
(c) Where any reports of general meetings are published at the expense of the company, all matters required to by Section 193 to be included in the minutes of the proceedings of the meeting, are to be included in publication.

VERY SHORT ANSWER TYPE QUESTIONS

1. (a) "AGM may be held on Public Holiday". Comment
   (b) "AGM may be held on a place other than registered office". Comment
   (c) "AGM may be held at a time outside business hours". Comment
   (d) "Only business left unfinished at the original meeting can be transacted at the adjourned meeting." Comment.
2. (a) "Proxy cannot be counted for the purposes of quorum." Comment.
   (b) "One member cannot constitute quorum." Comment.
   (c) State the consequences of absence of quorum.
3. (a) "Chairman must be a director". Comment.
   (b) "Chairman must be a member". Comment.
   (c) "Chairman can cast two votes in case of equality of votes". Comment
4. Who can demand a poll?
5. Distinguish between:
   (a) Ordinary Business and Special Business.
   (b) Ordinary Resolution and Special Resolution
6. List five matters requiring the
   (a) Ordinary Resolution
   (b) Special Resolution
   (c) Special Notice
7. Write short notes on the following:
   (a) Statutory Report
   (b) Quorum
   (c) Proxy
   (d) Explanatory Statement
   (e) Ordinary and Special Business
   (f) Ordinary and Special Resolution
   (g) Special Notice
8. (a) Are all the provisions of Section 171 to 186 applicable to all companies?
   (b) Is provision of Section 174(1) relating to quorum applicable to a private company which is not a subsidiary company?
   (c) Is provision of Section 182 relating to restriction on exercise of voting right applicable to a private company which is not a subsidiary company?
   (d) Can an independent private company make special provisions in its Articles in respect of any of the matters covered by Section 171 to 186?
   (e) If the Articles of an independent private company are silent, shall the provision of Section 182 apply to it?
   [(a) No. Not applicable to Private company which are not subsidiary of Public company; (b) Yes; (c) No; (d) Yes; (e) No.]

LONG ANSWER TYPE QUESTIONS

1. (a) Name the Companies required to hold Statutory Meeting.
   (b) When is this meeting to be held?
   (c) State the provisions relating to Statutory Report.
   (d) State the consequences of default in holding statutory meeting.
2. (a) When is AGM to be held?
   (b) State the consequences of default in holding AGM
3. (a) Who can call Extra-ordinary Meeting.
   (b) State provisions relating to requisition for Extra-ordinary Meeting.
   (c) When can Company Law Tribunal call Extra-ordinary Meeting?

4. State provisions relating to Class Meetings.
5. (a) What should be the length of notice?
   (b) Can a general meeting be called by giving a shorter notice?
   (c) Who are entitled to receive notice of general meetings?
   (d) State the provisions relating to service of notice.
   (e) State the contents of notice of general meeting.
6. (a) State the rights and limitations of proxy.
   (b) State the provisions relating to deposit of proxy.
   (c) State the provisions relating to revocation of proxy.
7. (a) List the businesses in which the resolution may be passed through postal ballot?
   (b) State the procedure to be followed for conducting business through postal ballot.
8. State the provisions relating to the registration of certain resolution and agreements.
9. State the provisions relating to recording, contents, signature and maintenance of minutes.

CHAPTER 14 Registers, Returns, Service and Authentication of Documents

1.0 REGISTER OF MEMBERS [SECTION 150]

1.1 Which Company is Required to Maintain Register of Member

Every company must keep a register of its members.

1.2 Contents of Register of Members

The Register of Members must contain the following particulars:

(i) the name, address and occupation, if any, of each member.
(ii) the shares held by each member with their individual numbers and the amount paid or agreed to be considered as paid on the shares of each member;
(iii) the date on which each person was entered in the register as a member;
(iv) the date on which each person ceased to be a member; and
(v) where the shares have been converted into stock, the register must show the amount of stock held by each member instead of the amount and particulars relating to shares.

Notes:

(i) In the case of joint shareholders, names of all joint shareholders must be entered in the register and the notices etc., be sent to the first named joint shareholder.
(ii) No notice of any trust, express or implied is allowed to be entered on the register of members.

1.3 Consequences of Default

In case of default, the company and its every officer in default, is punishable with a fine which upto Rs 500 for every day during which the default continues.

The register must be kept up-to-date containing all changes that might be taking place from time to time.

1.4 Place of Keeping the Register [Section 163(1)]

The register must be kept at the **registered office** of the company unless some other place (though it must be in the city, town or village where the registered office is situated) has been approved by a special resolution in the general meeting and the Registrar of Companies has been given in advance a copy of the proposed special resolution.

1.5 Prima Facie but not Conclusive Evidence

Section 164 of the Act provides that the register of members shall be a *prima facie*, but not conclusive, evidence of membership. It is a *prima facie* evidence of matters required or authorised to be contained therein. The court will accept the same as correct until rebutted.

1.6 Form of Register

The form of the register is **prescribed** by the government. The companies can either adopt this form or any other form closely resembling to this. Separate registers in different colours should be maintained for different types of shares.

2.0 INDEX OF MEMBERS

2.1 Which Company is Required to Maintain Index of Members

Every company having more than 50 members must keep an index unless the register serves the purpose of index.

2.2 Place of Keeping the Index

The index must be kept at the **same place** as the register of members.

2.3 Contents of Index of Members

The index must contain sufficient indication to enable the account of each member in the register of members to be easily found.

2.4 Time Limit for Entry of Alteration in the Register of Members in the Index with in 14 days

If any alteration is made in the register of members, the company must make the necessary alteration in the index **within 14 days** after the date on which the alteration is made in the register.

2.5 Consequences of Default

In case of default the company and its every officer in default, is punishable with a fine which upto Rs 500 for every day during which the default continues.

3.0 RESISTER AND INDEX OF BENEFICIAL OWNERS [SECTION 152A]

The register and index of beneficial owners maintained by the depository under Section 11 of Depositories Act, 1996 shall be deemed to a register and index of member.

4.0 INSPECTION OF REGISTER

4.1 Public Document [Section 163(2)]

(a) A company's register of members is a public document and is open to public inspection.
(b) The register of members and index must be open to inspection by members free and by any other person on payment of Rs 10 for each inspection.
(c) The register must remain open for **at least 2 business hours each day** except when the register is closed under the provisions of the Act.
(d) The right to inspect also includes the right to make extracts from the register.

4.2 Duty of Company to Supply copy within 10 days [Sections 163(3) and 163(4)]

The company must supply a copy of the register, index etc. **within 10 days,** exclusive of non-working days on payment of Re 1 for every 100 words or fractional part thereof required to be copied.

4.3 Penality for Default [Section 163(5)]

If inspection is refused or a copy is not sent within a period of 10 days, the company and its every officer in default shall be punishable in respect of each offence with fine upto Rs 500 for every day during which the default continues.

Notes:

(i) The object of inspecting the register is immaterial.

(ii) The right to inspect ceases upon the circumstances of winding up and if an inspection is required after that, an order of the court must be obtained under Section 549. [***Re Rent Coalfield Syndicate***, (1898) 1. Q.B. 754]

5.0 NO NOTICE OF TRUST IN REGISTER OF MEMBER [SECTION 153]

5.1 No notice of trust, express or implied or constructive shall be entered in the Register of members [Section 153]

5.2 This expression means "In the Register of Members only the name of registered shareholder must be entered without mentioning the name of beneficial owner on whose behalf registered shareholder is holding the shares.

Example—If X purchases shares in the name of Y, X wil be beneficial owners and Y will be a trustee. In Register of Member the name of Y only will be included without any mention of his being a trustee on X's behalf.

6.0 CLOSURE OF REGISTER

6.1 Maximum Period for which Register may be Closed [Sec. 154] A company may close the register of members for a period **not exceeding 45 days in a year** but **not exceeding 30 days at any one time.**

6.2 7 Day's Notice For closing the register **at least 7 day's** notice must be given by advertisement in some newspaper circulating in the district in which the registered office of the company is situated.

6.3 Compulsory Closure It is compulsory to close the register of members **before AGM** and **before declaring the bonus issue.**

6.4 No Transfer During the period of closure of the register of members, no transfer of shares is registered.

6.5 Penalty Contravention of these provisions will entail a fine of Rs 5,000 for each day of wrong closure.

7.0 FOREIGN REGISTER OF MEMBERS [SECTION 157]

1. A company, may, if so authorised by its articles, keep in any state or country outside India a branch register (called as foreign register) of its members resident in that state or country.
2. The company must within **30 days from the date of the opening** of any foreign register notify the Registrar about the place where such register is kept.
3. Any change in the situation of the office or of its discontinuance shall be duly notified to the Registrar within 30 days of the date of change or discontinuance.
4. A foreign register shall be deemed to be part of the company's register of members.
5. The company must keep a duplicate of every foreign register.
6. A copy of every entry made in the foreign register must be transmitted to the head office in India.
7. The head office in India must record the same in the duplicate register maintained by it.

8.0 REGISTER AND INDEX OF DEBENTUREHOLDERS [SECTION 152]

8.1 Which Company is Required to Maintain Register of Debentureholders

Every company is required to maintain a register of its debentureholders.

8.2 Contents of Register The Register of Debentureholders must contain the following particulars:

(a) the name and address, and the occupation, if any, of each debentureholder;
(b) the debentures held by each holder, distinguishing each debenture by its number except where such debentures are held with a depository, and the amount paid or agreed to be considered as paid on those debentures;
(c) the date at which each person was entered in the register as a debentureholder; and
(d) the date at which any person ceased to be debentureholder.

8.3 Which Company is Required to Maintain Index of Members

Every company having more than 50 debentureholders shall keep an index of debentureholders along with the register. If the register of debentureholders is in such form that it can serve the purpose of index, then separate index of debentureholders is not required to be maintained.

8.4 Place of Keeping the Index The index must be kept at the **same place** as the Register of Debentureholders.

8.5 Contents of Index The index must contain sufficient indication to enable the account of each debentureholder in the Register of Debentureholders to be easily found.

8.6 Entry of Alteration If any alteration is made in the Register of Debenture-holders the company must make the necessary alteration in the index **within 14 days** after the date on which the alteration is made in the register.

8.7 Consequences of Default If default is made in maintaining the Register and Index, the company, and every officer in default, shall be punishable with fine upto Rs 500.

9.0 REGISTER AND INDEX OF BENEFICIAL OWNERS [SECTION 152A]

The register and index of beneficial owners maintained by a depository under Section 11 of the Depositories Act, 1996, shall be deemed to be register and index of debentureholders, as the case may be.

10.0 FOREIGN REGISTER OF DEBENTURE HOLDERS [SECTION 153 & 158]

10.1 Power A company which has a share capital or which has issued debentures may, if so authorised by its articles, keep in any State or country outside India a branch register of debentureholders resident in that State or country (in this Act called a "foreign register").

10.2 Duty to File Notice of Situation of Regd. Office within 30 days The company must within 30 days from the date of the opening of any foreign register, file with the Registrar notice of the situation of the office where such register is kept; and in the event of any change in the situation of such office or of its discontinuance, shall, within 30 days from the date of such change or discontinuance, as the case may be, file notice with the Registrar of such change or discontinuance.

10.3 Penalty If default is made in complying with the requirements of Sub-section (2), the company, and its every officer in default, shall be punishable with fine which upto Rs 500 for every day during which the default continues.

10.4 Provisions as to Foreign Registers. [Section 158]

(a) A foreign register shall be deemed to be part of the company's register (in this section called the "principal register") of members or of debentureholders, as the case may be.

(b) A foreign register shall be kept, shall be open to inspection and may be closed, and extracts may be taken therefrom and copies thereof may be required, in the same manner, *mutatis mutandis,* as is applicable to the principal register under this Act, except that the advertisement before closing the register shall be inserted in some newspaper circulating in the district wherein the foreign register is kept.

(c) The Central Government may, by notification in the Official Gazette, direct that the provisions of Clause (b) shall apply, or cease to apply, to foreign registers kept in any State or country outside India.

(d) If a foreign register is kept by a company in any State or country to which a direction under Clause (a) applies for the time being, the decision of any competent Court in that State or country in regard to the rectification of the register shall have the same force and effect as if it were the decision of a competent Court in India.

(e) The company shall—

  (a) transmit to its registered office in India a copy of every entry in any foreign register as soon as may be after the entry is made; and

  (b) keep at such office a duplicate of every foreign register duly entered up from time to time.

(f) Every such duplicate shall, for all the purposes of this Act, be deemed to be part of the principal register.

(g) Subject to the provisions of this section with respect to duplicate registers, the shares or debentures registered in any foreign register shall be distinguished from the shares of debentures registered in the principal register and in every other foreign register; and no transaction with respect to any shares or debentures registered in a foreign register shall, during the continuance of that registration, be registered in any other register.

(h) The company may discontinue the keeping of any foreign register; and thereupon all entries, in that register shall be transferred to some other foreign register kept by the company in the same part of the world or to the principal register.

(i) Subject to the provisions of this Act, a company may, by its articles, make such regulations as it thinks fit in regard to its foreign registers.

(j) If default is made in complying with Sub-section (4), the company, and its every officer of the company in default, shall be punishable with fine upto Rs 500.

11.0 ANNUAL RETURN [Sec. 159 to Sec. 161]

11.1 Time Limit for filing—Annual Return is required to be filed within **60 days** of holding general meeting. It may be noted that 60 days will be counted from the date on which the meeting should have held as per the Act and not from the actual date of meeting held.

11.2 Form of Annual Return—Annual Return must be prepared in form as per Schedule V.

11.3 Particulars [Sec. 160]—Annual Return must contain the following particulars :

(a) Complete address of Registered Office
(b) Shares and Debentures (in case of Company having Share Capital)
(c) Indebtedness
(d) Members
(e) Debenture holders (in case of company having share capital & debentures)
(f) Directors, Manager, Secretary

11.4 Signing—Annual Return must be signed by the following :

Case	*Who must sign*
(a) ***If there is Manager or Secretary***	(a) By a Director (b) By the Manger or Secretary and (c) By a Secretary in whole time practice if company is a listed company
(b) ***If there is no Manager and Secretary***	(a) By two Directors and (b) By a Secretary in whole time practice if company is a listed company

12.0 PROVISIONS RELATING TO THE SERVICE OF DOCUMENTS [Sec. 51 to 53]

12.1 Service of Documents on a Company [Sec. 51]

(a) *Where to serve*	A document may be served on the company or on its officer at the **registered office** of the company.
(b) *How to serve*	It may be sent ***either*** **by post under certificate of posting** *or* **registered post**, *or* **hand delivery.**

12.2 Service of Documents on the Registrar

(a) *Where to serve*	A document may be served on a Registrar at the **official address.**
(b) *How to serve*	It may be sent *either* **by post under certificate of posting** *or* **registered post**, *or* **hand delivery.**

12.3 Service of Documents on Members of the Company

(a) *Where to serve*	A document may be served on a Member at his **registered address** or **address in India** supplied for the purpose of giving of notices of general meetings.
(b) *How to serve*	• It may be sent by **post** or **hand delivery** • It must be sent by post under certificate of posting or registered post if the member required the company to send documents by such method and has deposited a sum sufficient to meet the expenses of doing so. • It may be served by advertising in a newspaper circulating in the neighbourhood of the registered office of the company in case of a member who has not supplied an address in India for service of notices.

12.4 Service in case of Joint Holder

A document served on a joint shareholder **named first** in the Registrar of Members shall be deemed to have been served on all the jointholders.

12.5 Service in case of Death or Insolvency

A document may be served on the **person entitled to a share** in consequence of the death or insolvency of a member.

12.6 When shall a document deemed to have been served ?

Mode of Service	*When deemed to have been served*
1. *In case of notice of General Meeting*	**At the expiration of 48 hours after posting.**
2. *In case of service through Advertisement*	The day on which the **advertisement appears** in a vernacular newspaper.
3. *In any other case*	At the time at which the **letter should be delivered in the ordinary course of post.**

13.0 AUTHENTICATION OF DOCUMENTS AND PROCEEDINGS [Sec. 54]

Unless the Act provides otherwise, a document, or proceeding requiring authentication by a company may be signed by a director, the manager, the secretary or other authorised officer of the company and need not be under its common seal.

VERY SHORT ANSWER TYPE QUESTIONS

1. Which company is required to maintain—
   (a) Register of members
   (b) Index of members
   (c) Register of Debentureholders
   (d) Index of Debentureholders
2. State the time limit prescribed for—
   (a) Entry of Alternation in the Register of members in the Index
   (b) Supplying copy of Register, Index etc.
   (c) Filing Annual Return
3. State the maximum period for which Register of members may be closed—
   (a) in a year
   (b) at one time

SHORT ANSWER TYPE QUESTIONS

1. Write short notes on the following:
   (a) Register of members
   (b) Index of members
   (c) Inspection of Register
   (d) Closure of Register
   (e) Rectification of Register
   (f) Foreign Register of Member.
2. Who may apply for rectification of the register of member and under what circumstances?

LONG ANSWER TYPE QUESTIONS

1. What are the provisions of the Companies Act as regards maintenance, location, inspection and closing of the company's register of members?
2. What is meant by rectification of register of members? What are the remedies open to a person where his request for rectification is refused by the company?

CHAPTER

15 Company Law in a Computerized Environment

1.0 WHAT IS MCA 21 PROJECT?

1.1 MCA 21 project is a project initiated by the Ministry of Company Affairs (MCA) to provide MCA services anytime and any where to the Corporates, Professionals and the General Public.

1.2 The project would provide e-services including, registration of new companies, filing of various returns and statutory documents under the Companies Act, 1956. The system would also enable on line filing and access for statutory documents like memorandum of association, articles of association, certificate of incorporation etc.

1.3 The services of the Ministry of Company Affairs with the introduction of MCA 221 will be e-form driven.

1.4 Form filing will be done using freely downloadable software and it can be done offline.

1.5 The prerequisites for using the MCA 21 portal will be P-4 computer with printer, windows 2000/XP, internet explorer 6.0 version, Adobe Acrobat Reader 7.05 version and digital signature certificate.

2.0 KEY BENEFITS OF MCA-21

MCA 21 seeks to fulfill the requirements of the various stakeholders. The key benefits of MCA 21 project are the back office process relates to:

(a) Expeditious incorporation of companies
(b) Simiplified and ease of convenience in filing of Forms/Returns
(c) Better compliance management
(d) Total transparency through e-Governance
(e) Inspection of public documents of companies anytime from anywhere
(f) Registration as well as verification of charges anytime from anywhere
(g) Timely redressal of investor grievances
(h) Building up a centralised database repository of corporate operating
(i) Availability of more time for MCA employees for monitoring and supervision
(j) Enhanced service level fulfillment
(k) Increased usage of professional certificate for ensuring authenticity and reliability of the Forms/Returns
(l) Customer centric approach

3.0 HOW MCA 21 PROGRAM MEETS THE NEEDS OF VARIOUS STATEHOLDERS/ ADVANTAGES OF E-FILING

3.1 Ministry of Company Affairs (MCA), Government of India (GOI) has initiated MCA 21 program, for easy and secure access to MCA services in a manner that best suits the businesses and citizens.

3.2 The program goals have been set as follows keeping in mind stakeholder's needs:

(a) **Business** enabled to register a company and file statutory documents quickly and easily
(b) **Public** to get easy access to relevant records and effective grievances redressal
(c) **Professionals** to be able to offer efficient services to their client companies
(d) **Financial Institutions** to easily find charges registration and verification
(e) **MCA Employees** to ensure proactive and effective compliance of relevant laws and corporate governance

3.3 MCA 21 is envisioned to provide anytime and anywhere services to business. It is a pioneering program being the first mission mode e-goverance project being undertaken in the country. This program builds on the Govt. of India vision to introduce a Service Oriented Approach in the design and delivery of Government services, establish a healthy business ecosystem and make the country globally competitive.

4.0 WHAT IS THE SCOPE OF MCA 21 PROGRAM?

4.1 MCA 21 program will provide for anytime anywhere electronic services with speed and certainty to all the stakeholders. It will include:

(a) Design and development of application system
(b) Setting up of IT infrastructure
(c) Setting up the Digital Signature/PKI delivery mechanisms and associated security requirements
(d) Setting up of Physical Front Offices (PFOs)
(e) Setting up of temporary FOs for the peak periods to meet with the requirements and subsequent shutdown of temporary FOs at the end of such peak periods
(f) Migrating legacy data and digitization of paper documents to the new system
(g) Providing MCA services to all MCA 21 stakeholders in accordance with the Service Oriented Approach
(h) Providing user training at all levels and all offices (Front and Back Offices)

4.2 The MCA 21 is designed to automate processes related to the proactive enforcement and compliance of the legal requirements under the Companies Act, 1956. However, it does not include processes related to OL.

5.0 WHAT IS SET UP OF MCA?

5.1 **Three Tier Set up** MCA has a three tier organizational set-up:

- Headquarters at New Delhi
- Regional Directors (RD) at Mumbai, Kolkata, Chennai and Noida
- Registrar of Companies (RoC) in States and Union Territories

5.2 MCA Headquarters handles cases that require approval of the Govt. of India for citizen related functions. Regional Director supervises the functioning of ROCs and handles the matters delegated by Govt. of India while the ROC offices handle the bulk of citizen functions.

5.3 The Official Liquidators (OL) attached to various High Courts functioning in the country are also under the overall adminstrative control of the MCA. Its headquarters at Delhi also includes two Directors of Inspection and Investigation and Director of Research and Statistics.

6.0 WHAT IS FRONT OFFICE?

6.1 The implementation of Front Offices (FO) is done in two ways. These can be called as Virtual Front Office (VFO) and Physical Front Office (PFO).

6.2 The VFO is what the citizen has in front while accessing the MCA 21 portal.

6.3 The PFO will be a replacement to the existing RoC counters. The PFO will also accept paper documents. However, these will be converted into electronic documents by customer service agents mainning PFO. Also, the authorised person (s) will have to sign these documents digitally. Consequently the authorised signatories for a given document will need to appear in person at the PFO for the purpose of digitally signing the document.

6.4 The user can avail the following services on MCA 21 portal

- e-Filing
- Viewing public document
- Requesting certified copies
- Registering investor complant
- Tracking transaction status

7.0 WHAT IS BACK OFFICE?

The back office is what MCA employee has in front which accessing back office portal. The back office process relates to:

- Dynamic routing of documents that have been electronically filed to the concerned official within MCA based on the types of service request.
- Electronic workflow systems to support speed and certainty in service delivery
- Supporting all routine tasks such as registrations and approvals
- Storing of all approved documents of companies as part of electronic records, including provision of access to electronic records for the stakeholders
- Enhancing identification of defaulters
- Increasing efficiency of Technical Scrutiny
- Ensuring close follow-up on matters related to compliance management including prosecutions
- Enabling quicker responses to investor grievances
- Providing alerts when the tasks are not carried out within stipulated period

8.0 WHAT ARE THE STEPS FOR OFFLINE E-FILING?

Step 1. Read at anytime the related instruction kit to familiarise yourself with the procedures (you can download the instruction kit with e-form or view it under **Help** menu).

Step 2. Select a category to download an e-Form from the MyMCA portal (with or with out the instruction kit.)

Step 3. Fill the downloaded e-Form.

Step 4. Attach the necessary documents as attachments.

Step 5. Use the **Prefill** button in e-Form to populate the greyed out portion by connecting to the Internet.

Step 6. Sign the document using a digital signature.

Step 7. Click the **Check Form** button available in the e-Form. System will check the mandatory fields, mandatory attachment(s) and digital signature(s).

Step 8. Upload the e-Form for pre-scrutiny. The pre-scrutiny service is available under the **Services** tab or under the **e-Forms** tab by clicking the **Upload e-Form** button. The system will verify (pre-scrutinise) the documents. In case of any inadequacies, the user will be asked to rectify the mistakes before getting the document ready for execution (signature).

Step 9. Get the system calculated fee, including late payment fees based on the due date of filing, if applicable.

Step 10. Make Payments through appropriate mechanisms-electronic (credit card, internet banking) or traditional means (at the bank counter through challan).

(a) Electronic payments can be made at the Virtual Front Office (VFO) or at PFO

(b) If the user selects the traditional payment option, the system will generate 3 copies of pre-filled challan in the prescribed format. Traditional payments through cash, cheques can be done at the designated network of banks using the system generated challan. There will be five banks with estimated 200 branches authorised for accepting challan payments.

Notes:

(i) The payment will be exclusively confirmed for all online (Internet) payment transactions using payment gateways.

(ii) Acceptance or rejection of any transaction will be explicity communicated to the applicant (including facility to print a receipt for successful transactions).

(iii) MCA 21 will provide a unique transaction number, the Service Request Number (SRN) which can be used by the applicant for enquiring the status pertaining to that transaction.

(iv) Filing will be complete only when the necessary payments are made.

(v) In case of a rejection, helpful remedial tips will be provided to the applicant.

(vi) The applicants will be provided an acknowledgement through e-mail or alternatively they can check the MCA portal.

9.0 WHAT ARE THE STEPS FOR ONLINE E-FILING?

Step 1. At any time, Read the related instruction kit, available under **Help** menu, to familiarise themselves with the procedures.

Step 2. Enter the username and authentication details-Password/Digital Certificate.

Step 3. The user will be shown a list of e-Forms category-wise under **e-Forms** tab.

Step 4. Fill the appropriate e-Form for the service required. There is an option of pre-fill facility in the e-Forms, where the static details such as name and address of the company will be pre-filled by the system automatically on entering the Corporate Identity Number (CIN).

Step 5. Attach the necessary documents to the e-Form.

Step 6. Option to Avail the pre-scrutiny service of the e-Form. The documents will be verified (pre-scrutinised) by the system. In case of any inadequacies, *for example*, if a mandatory column in the e-Form is not filled in, the user will be asked to rectify before the document is ready for execution (signature).

Step 7. Submit the duly signed documents electronically.

Step 8. Get the system calculated fee, including late payment fees, if applicable.

Step 9. Make Payments through appropriate mechanisms-electronic (credit card, Internet banking) or traditional means (at the bank counter).

(a) Electronic payments can be made at the Virtual Front Office (VFO).

(b) If the user selects the traditional payment option, the system will generate a pre-filled challan in the prescribed format. Traditional payments through cash, cheques can be done at the designated network of banks using the system generated challan. There will be five banks with estimated 200 branches authorised for accepting challan payments.

10.0 SOME FREQUENTLY ASKED QUESTIONS

10.1 How can I apply for a Company Name?

File e-Form 1 A by logging in the portal along with a payment of fees of Rs. 500 and attaching the digital singature of the applicant proposing to incorporate the company. If proposed name is not available apply for a fresh name on the same application.

10.2 Can I apply for a Company Name Online?

Yes, You can avail this service at MCA portal.

10.3 What is the Validity Period of the Name Approved?

The approved name is valid for a period of 6 months from the date of approval. The applicant can renew the name within 6 months by submitting a fresh Name application (Form-1A) along with the fees of Rs. 500, by mentioning that the application is for renewal of the name already approved. Names inadvertently allowed or which are against the guidelines, which have subsequently come to the notice, may be withdrawn by the RoC before or after incorporation of the company.

10.4 What is the Minimum Number of Directors Required to form a Company?

(a) Minimum no. of directors for Private Limited Company: Two

(b) For Public Limited Company: Three.

10.5 What is the Minimum number of Subscribers Required for Registration of a Company?

(a) Minimum no. of subscribers for Private Limited Company: Two.

(b) For Public Limited Company: Seven.

10.6 What is the Minimum Paid-up Capital at the time of Registration of a Company?

The minimum paid up capital for Private Limited Company: Rs. 1,00,000. For Public Limited Company: Rs. 5,00,000. This limit is not applicable to company having licence under section 25.

10.7 What are the Documents to be Filed with ROC Every Year?

Invariably, the Balance Sheet and Annual Return have to be filed every year. Other documents such as, Return of Allotment (Form-2), Change of Registered Office (Form-18), Change among the Directors (Form-32), Charges (Form-8, 10, 17, 13) etc., have to be filed within the due date from the events taking place in the company as per The Companies Act, 1956.

10.8 How do I find SRN for form 1A filed before MCA 21 project?

You may find SRN by entering NIC issued name approval reference number in the "Name Approval Reference Number" service available after logging into MyMCA portal.

10.9 What is e-Filing?

MCA-21 project facilitates e-Filing of various forms and applications under the Companies Act, 1956 and the Rules and Regulations thereunder. The key details relevant to e-Filing are given below:

1. **Meaning of e-Form** An e-Form is nothing but a re-engineered conventional form. It is a document in electronic format for filing with MCA authorities through the Internet. This may be either a form filed for compliance or information purpose or an application seeking approval from the MCA.
2. **General structure of an e-Form** An e-Form contains certain standardized features. Each e-Form contains the form reference and the description as well as the particular section of the Companies Act or the relevant rules or regulations under which it is required to be submitted. It starts with the Corporate Identity Number (CIN), which works as a unique identifier of a company that is required to be filled-up.

10.10 How can User be Registered?

(a) A first time user has to registor with MCA to use the services offered by My-MCA portal. For registration, he has to provide personal information and then choose user ID and password or enter his digital certificate depending upon the user type selected.

(b) Every time the user accesses any service at My-MCA portal, he will be asked to login using the user ID and password/digital certificate selected by him at the time of registration.

10.11 What is Digital Signature?

A digital signature is the electronic signature duly issued by the certifying authority that shows the authenticity of the person signing the same. Every user who is required to sign an e-Form for submission with MCA requires Digital Signature. The persons requiring Digital Singature includes the company representatives, professionals and others who are required affix digital signatures for submitting an e-Form.

EXERCISES

1. What is MCA 21 project?
2. What are the key benefits of MCA 21 project?
3. What is front office and back office in MCA 21 project?
4. What are the advantages of e-filing?

APPENDIX 1

Important Points to Remember — The Indian Contract Act, 1872

CHAPTER 1 MEANING AND ESSENTIALS OF CONTRACT

1.0 MEANING OF CONTRACT

Contract	= An Agreement + Enforceability of an Agreement
Agreement	= Offer (or Proposal) + Acceptance of Offer (or proposal) **Note:** 1. *A proposal when accepted becomes a promise.* 2. *Every promise and every set of promise forming consideration for each other is an agreement.*
Enforceability	An agreement is said to be enforceable by law if it creates some legal obligation.
Usual Presumption	**In Social or Domestic Agreements** – That the parties do not intend to create legal relations.
	In Commercial or Business Agreements – That the parties intend to create legal relations.

2.0 SCOPE OF LAW OF CONTRACT

Not Whole Law of Agreements	The law of contracts is not the whole law of agreements because it is concerned with only those agreements (e.g. Business *or* Commercial Agreements) where parties have the intention to create legal obligations and is not concerned with those agreements (e.g. Social *or* Domestic Agreements) where parties do not have the intention to create legal obligations.
Not Whole Low of Contracts	The law of contracts is not the whole law of obligations because it is concerned with only those obligations which arise out of agreements and is not concerned with those obligations (e.g. obligation to maintain wife & children) which do not arise out of agreements.

3.0 CLASSIFICATION OF CONTRACTS

Type of Contract	Meaning
1. *On the Basis of Creation*	
(a) *Express Contract*	One which is made by words spoken or written
(b) *Implied Contract*	One which is made otherwise than by words spoken or written.
(c) *Tacit Contract*	One which is inferred from the conduct of parties or circumstances of the case
2. *On the Basis of Execution*	
(a) *Executed Contract*	Where both the parties to the contract have performed their respective obligations.
(b) *Executory Contract*	Where both the parties to the contract have still to perform their respective obl igations.
(c) *Partly Executed, Partly Executory*	Where one of the parties to the contract has performed his obligation and the other party has still to perform his obligation.
(d) *Unilateral Contract*	One in which only one party has to perform his Promise or obligation to do forebear.
(e) *Bilateral Contract*	One in which both parties have to perform their respective obligations.
3. *On the Basis of Enforceability*	
(a) *Valid Contract*	Which satisfies all the conditions prescribed by law.
(b) *Void Contract*	A contract which was valid when entered into but which subsequently becomes void due to impossibility of performance due to change of law or any other reason
(c) *Void Agreement*	An agreement not enforceable by law **Note:** *Collateral Agreements do not become void.*
(d) *Voidable Contract*	An agreement which is enforceable by law at the option of one or more of the parties but not at the option of the other or others.
(e) *Illegal Agreement*	One the object or consideration of which is unlawful. **Note:** *Collateral Agreements also become void.*
(f) *Unenforceable Contract*	A contract which is actually valid but cannot be enforced because of some technical defect. Such contract can be enforced if the technical defect is removed.

4.0 ESSENTIAL ELEMENTS OF A VALID CONTRACT

Provisions of Sec. 10	"All agreements are contracts if they are made by the free consent of the parties competent to contract, for a lawful consideration and with a lawful object and are not hereby expressly declared to be void."

Essential Elements of a Valid Contract	1. Proper Offer and its Proper Acceptance 2. Intention to create legal relationship 3. Free Consent 4. Capacity to Contract 5. Lawful Consideration 6. Lawful Object 7. Agreement not expressly declared void 8. Certainity of Meaning 9. Possibility of Performance 10. Legal Formalities

CHAPTER 2 OFFER AND ACCEPTANCE

1.0 MEANING, MODE AND RULES FOR A VALID OFFER

Meaning of Offer	A person is said to have made the proposal when he signifies to another his willingness to do or to abstain from doing anything with a view to obtaining the assent of that offer to such act or abstinence.
Meaning of "Offerer"	The person making the proposal is called the offerer or proposer.
Meaning of "Offeree"	The person to whom the proposal is made is called the 'offeree' or 'proposee'.
How to make an offer? **(a) Express offer**	One which is made by words spoken or written.
(b) Implied offer	One which is made otherwise than in words. It is inferred from the conduct of the person or the circumstances of the particular case.
To Whom Offer can be Made? **(a) Specific Offer**	A specific offer is one which is made to a definite person or particular group of persons. A specific offer can be accepted only by that definite person or that particular group of persons to whom it has been made.
(b) General Offer	A general offer is one which is not made to a definite person, but to the world at large or public in general. A general offer can be accepted by any person by fulfilling the terms of the offer.
Legal Rules for a Valid Offer	1. Intention to create legal relations 2. Certain and unambiguous 3. Different from a mere declaration of intention 4. Different from an invitation to offer 5. Proper communication

	6. No term the non-compliance of which amount to acceptance 7. Communication of special terms
Meaning of Cross Offers	Two offers which are similar in all respects made by two parties to each other, in ignorance of each other's offer are known as 'cross offers'. Cross offers do not amount to acceptance of one's offer by the other. Hence, no contract is entered into on cross offers.
Meaning of Standing Offer	An offer of a continuous nature is known as 'standing offer'. A standing offer is in the nature of a tender. It is the same thing as an invitation to an offer. A contract is said to have been entered into only when an order is placed on the basis of the tender.

2.0 MEANING, MODE AND RULES FOR A VALID ACCEPTANCE

Meaning of Acceptance	Acceptance means giving consent to the offer. "A proposal is said to be accepted when the person to whom the proposal is made signifies his assent thereto. A proposal when accepted becomes a promise."
Who can Accept Offer? **(a) In case of Specific Offer**	An offer made to a definite person or particular group of persons (called specific offer) can be accepted only by that definite person or that particular group of persons to whom it has been made and none else.
(b) In case of General Offer	An offer made to the world at large or public in general (called general offer) can be accepted by any person having knowledge of the offer by fulfilling the terms of the offer.
How to make an Acceptance **(a) Express Acceptance**	Like an offer, an acceptance may also be *either* an 'implied acceptance' *or* 'express acceptance'. An express acceptance is one which is made by words spoken or written.
(b) Implied Acceptance	An implied acceptance is one which is made otherwise than in words. In other words, it is inferred from the conduct of the person or the circumstances of the particular case.
Legal Rules for a Valid Acceptance **1. Absolute and Unqualified**	It must be absolute & unqualified.
2. Prescribed/Usual Manner	The offer must be accepted in the prescribed manner (if any) *or* in same usual and reasonable manner (if not prescribed)
3. Communication to Offerer	It must be communicated to the offerer.

4. Communication by Offeree	It must be communicated by the offeree *or* his authorised agent.
5. Within Prescribed/Reasonable Time	It must be communicated within the time prescribed (if/any) *or* within a reasonable time. (if no time in prescribed).
6. Before Lapse of Offer	It must be made before the offer lapses or is withdrawn.

3.0 COMMUNICATION OF OFFER AND ACCEPTANCE

<table>
<tr><td>Communication of Offer</td><td colspan="2">The communication of offer is complete when it comes to the knowledge of the person to whom it is made. In case an offer is made by post, its communication will complete when the letter containing the offer reaches the offeree.</td></tr>
<tr><td rowspan="4">Communication of Acceptance</td><td>The Communication of Acceptance is Complete</td><td>When does the Communication of Acceptance Complete....</td></tr>
<tr><td>(i) As against the proposer</td><td>When it is put in a course of transmission to him, so as to be out of the power of the acceptor. In case of acceptance made by post, the proposer becomes bound by the acceptance as soon as the properly addressed and stamped letter of acceptance is duly posted even if such letter of acceptance is lost or delayed in post.</td></tr>
<tr><td>(ii) As against the acceptor</td><td>When it comes to the knowledge of the proposer. In case of acceptance made by post, the acceptor becomes bound by the acceptance only when the letter of acceptance is actually received by proposer.</td></tr>
<tr><td colspan="2">Note: The time gap between the date on which the letter of acceptance is posted and the date on which the letter of acceptance is received by the proposer, can be utilized by the acceptor to withdraw his acceptance by a speedier mode of communication so that the revocation notice reaches the proposer before the letter of acceptance.</td></tr>
</table>

4.0 REVOCATION OF OFFER AND ACCEPTANCE

<table>
<tr><td>Meaning of Revocation</td><td colspan="2">The term 'revocation' means 'taking back' or 'withdrawal'.</td></tr>
<tr><td>Time Limit within which Offer can be Revoked</td><td colspan="2">A proposal may be revoked at any time before the communication of its acceptance is complete as against the proposer, but not afterwards. Hence, an offer can be revoked at any time before the letter of acceptance is duly posted by the acceptor.
Notes:
1. Revocation must always be expressed.
2. Revocation must move from the offerer himself or a duly authorised agent.
3. Notice of revocation of a general offer must be given through the same channel by which the original offer was made.
4. Offer cannot be revoked even if the letter of acceptance is lost or delayed in transit.</td></tr>
<tr><td>Time Limit within which Acceptance can be Revoked</td><td colspan="2">"An acceptance may be revoked at any time before the communication of the acceptance is complete as against the acceptor, but not afterwards." Hence, an acceptance can be revoked at any time before the letter of acceptance is actually received by the proposer.</td></tr>
<tr><td>No Revocation in Case of Contract over Telephone or Telex of Fax</td><td colspan="2">In case of contracts over telephone or telex or fax, the question of revocation does not arise because there is instantaneous communication of the offer and its acceptance (i.e. the offer is made and accepted at the same time).</td></tr>
<tr><td rowspan="3">When does Communication of Revocation complete?</td><td>The Communication of Revocation is Complete...</td><td>When does the Communication of Revocation Complete...</td></tr>
<tr><td>1. As against the person who makes it</td><td>When it is put in a course of transmission to the person to whom it is made so as to be out of the power of the person who makes it.</td></tr>
<tr><td>2. As against the person to whom it is made</td><td>When it comes to his knowledge.</td></tr>
<tr><td>When does An Offer come to end? (or Lapse of An offer)</td><td colspan="2">1. By Revocation
2. By Lapse of time
3. By Death or insanity of the offerer/offeree
4. By Failure to accept condition precedent
5. By Counter Offer
6. By Not accepting in the prescribed mode or usual mode
7. By Rejection of offer by offeree
8. By Subsequent illegality or destruction of subject matter of the offer</td></tr>
</table>

CHAPTER 3 CAPACITY OF PARTIES

1.0 WHO IS COMPETENT TO CONTRACT?

Major	Person who is of the age of majority according to the law to which he is subject
Sound Mind	Person who is of sound mind.
Not Disqualified	Person who is not disqualified from contracting by any law to which he is subject **Note:** *A minor whose property has passed under superintendence of the court of wards where a guardian has been appointed under the guardian and wards act, 1890, attains majority on competition of 21 years and in other case minor attains majority on completion of 18 years.*

2.0 POSITION OF AGREEMENTS BY A MINOR

Void-*ab-initio*	An agreement with a minor is *void ab-initio.* **[Mohiri Bibee v. Dharmodas Ghose]**
No Estoppel	A minor is not estopped from setting up the plea of minority. He may plead infancy to escape from being liable.
In case of fraudulent represen tation of age by minor	The Court may award compensation to the other party if the money or property supplied to minor could be traced.
No Ratification on attaining the Age of Majority	An agreement with a minor cannot be ratified even after he attains majority. **Ratification relates back to the date of the making of the agreement** and therefore an agreement which was then void cannot be made valid by subsequent ratification.
Validity of Minor's Agreement jointly with a Major Person	The agreements made by a minor jointly with a major person are void vis-a-vis the minor but can be enforced against the major person who has jointly promised to perform.
Minor as a Partner	A minor cannot become a partner in a partnership firm. However, with the consent of all the partners, minor may be admitted to the benefits of partnership.
Minor can be an Agent and not Principal	A minor can act as an agent and bind his principal by his acts without incurring any personal liability.
Minor can be a Shareholder or Member of a company	A minor can become a shareholder or member of a Company if (a) the shares are fully paid up and (b) the articles of association do not prohibit so.
Minor can not be an Insolvent	A minor cannot be declared insolvent because he is not competent to contract.

Contract for Minor's Benefit	A minor can be a promisee.
Contract by Minor's Guardian	The contracts entered into on behalf of a minor by his guardian or manager of his estate can be enforced by or against the minor if the contract (a) is within the scope of the authority of guardian or manager, and (b) is for the benefit of the minor. It may also be noted that his guardian cannot enter into a valid contract for purchase of the immovable property for his/her service.
Contract for Supply of Necessaries	1. A person who has supplied the necessaries to a minor or to those who are dependent on him is entitled to be reimbursed from the property of such minor. 2. ***Meaning of Necessaries:*** The term 'necessaries' includes articles required to maintain a particular person in the state, degree and station in life in which he is. In India, food, clothing, shelter, education and marriage of a female have been held to be necessaries. 3. Section 68 covers the reimbursement for the supply of such items or loans for the same. Section 68 also covers the rendering of necessary services to a minor. 4. '***Claim against Property and not against Person***' A claim for the payment of necessaries supplied can be made against the minor's property and not against the minor personally. In other words, a minor cannot be asked to expend labour in exchange. 5. ***Liability of Minor's Guardian*** The parent or guardian of a minor cannot be held liable unless those goods/services are supplied/rendered to a minor as the agent of the parent or guardian.
Minor's Liability in Tort	A minor may be held liable in Tort (civil wrong). But if in the course of doing what he is entitled to do under the contract, he is found guilty of negligence, he cannot be made liable on tort if he is not liable on the contract.

3.0 POSITION OF PERSONS OF UNSOUND MIND

Who is a Person of Unsound Mind?	"A person is said to be of sound mind for the purpose of making a contract, if at the time when he makes it, is capable— (a) to understand the terms of the contract, (b) to form a rational judgment as to its effect upon his interests."
When can make Contract?	"A person who is usually of unsound mind but occasionally of sound mind may make a contract when he is of sound mind."

When can not make Contract?	"A person who is usually of sound mind but occasionally of unsound mind may not make a contract when he is of unsound mind."
Position of Contracts with Person of Unsound Mind	The position of contracts with persons of unsound mind is identical with that of contracts with a minor. Thus, (a) He may enforce a contract for his benefit; (b) His properties shall be attachable for realisation of money due against him for the supply of necessaries to him or to any of his dependents.

4.0 POSITION OF PERSONS DISQUALIFIED BY LAW

<table>
<tr><td rowspan="3">Alien Enemy</td><td colspan="2">An alien whose country is at war with the Republic of India is called an alien enemy.</td></tr>
<tr><td>I. Position of Contracts during the war</td><td>An alien enemy can neither enter into any contract nor can be sued in an Indian Court except by licence from the Central Government.</td></tr>
<tr><td>II. Position of Contracts entered into before the war
(a) If such contracts are against the public policy or are such that may benefit the enemy
(b) If such contracts are not against public policy</td><td>(a) Such contracts stand dissolved.
(b) Such contracts are merely suspended for the duration of the war and revived after the war is over unless they have already become time barred under the Law of Limitation Act.</td></tr>
<tr><td>Foreign Sovereigns and Ambassadors</td><td colspan="2">They can enter into contracts and enforce those contracts in our courts but they cannot be sued in our courts without the sanction of the Central Government unless they choose to submit themselves to the jurisdictions of our Courts.</td></tr>
<tr><td>Convicts</td><td colspan="2">A person is called a convict during his period of sentence.</td></tr>
<tr><td>Company</td><td colspan="2">Contractual Capacity is determined by the 'Object Clause' of its Memorandumof Association.</td></tr>
<tr><td>Statutory Corporation</td><td colspan="2">Contractual Capacity is determined by the statute creating it.</td></tr>
<tr><td>Act Ultra vires</td><td colspan="2">Any act done in excess of the power given is ultra vires (i.e. beyond power) and hence void.</td></tr>
<tr><td>Insolvents</td><td colspan="2">When a person's debts exceed his assets, he is adjudged insolvent and his property stands vested in the Official Receiver or Official Assignee appointed by the Court. Such person—
(i) cannot enter into contracts relating to his property,
(ii) cannot sue,
(iii) cannot be sued.</td></tr>
</table>

CHAPTER 4 CONSIDERATION

1.0 MEANING AND ESSENTIAL ELEMENTS OF VALID CONSIDERATION

Meaning	Consideration in simple term means something in return.
Form	Consideration must result *either* (a) a benefit to the promisor and detriment *or* loss to the promisee, (b) a detriment to both promisor *or* promisee.
Essential Elements of Valid Consideration	1. It must be given at the desire of Promisor. 2. It may be given by the promisee or any other person (i.e. stranger). 3. It may be past or present or future. [**Note:** *Past consideration is no consideration in England*] 4. It need not be adequate but it must be of some value in the eye of law. 5. It must be real and not Illusory 6. It must be something which the promisor is not already bound to do. 7. It must be lawful. 8. It must not be opposed to public policy.

2.0 STRANGER TO A CONSIDERATION AND STRANGER TO CONTRACT

Stranger to Consideration	A stranger to consideration can sue because the consideration can be furnished or supplied by any person whether he is the promisee or not.
Stranger to Contract	A stranger to a contract cannot sue because of the absence of **privity of contract** (i.e. relationship subsisting between the parties to a contract).
Exception to above Rule	(a) **In case of Trusts** The beneficiary (i.e. the person for whose benefit the trust has been created) may enforce the contract. (b) **In case of Family Settlement** The person for whose benefit the provision is made under family arrangements may enforce the contract. (c) **Acknowledgments** The person who becomes an agent of third party by acknowledgment or otherwise, can be sued by such third party. (d) **Assignment of a Contract** Where a benefit under a contract has been assigned, the assignee can enforce the contract subject to all equities between the original parties to the contract e.g. the assignee of an insurance policy.

3.0 NO CONSIDERATION, NO CONTRACT

Validity	An agreement made without consideration is void.
Six Exceptions to above Rule	1. **Written & Registered Agreements made on Account of Natural Love and Affection** between parties standing in a near relation to each others. 2. **Promise to Compensate** the person who has already done something voluntarity or has done something which the promisor was legally bound to do. 3. **Written Promise** duly signed by debtor or his authorised agent to pay Time Barred Debt 4. **Completed Gifts [Explanation to Section 25]** The gifts actually made by a donor and accepted by the donee are valid even without consideration. Thus, a completed gift needs no consideration. 5. **Agency**–No consideration is necessary to create an agency. 6. **Gratuitous Bailment**

CHAPTER 5 FREE CONSENT

1.0 CONSENT AND FREE CONSENT

Meaning of Consent	The consent means an act of assenting to an offer. According to Section 13, "Two or more persons are said to consent when they agree upon the same thing in the same sense." Thus, consent involves identity of minds in respect of the subject matter of the contract. In English Law, this is called '***consensus-ad-idem***'.
Effect of Absence of Consent	When there is no consent at all, the agreement is **void ab-initio**, i.e. it is not enforceable at the option of either party.
Meaning of Free Consent	Consent is said to be free when it is not caused by (a) coercion, or (b) undue influence, or (c) fraud, or (d) misrepresentation, or (e) mistake.
Effect of Absence of Free Consent	When there is consent but it is not free (i.e. when it is caused by coercion or undue influence or fraud or misrepresentation), the contract is usually **voidable** at the option of the party whose consent was so caused.

2.0 COERCION

Meaning of Coercion	Coercion means compelling a person to enter into a contract under a pressure or a threat. According to Section 15, a contract is said to be caused by coercion when it is obtained by— (a) committing any act which is forbidden by the Indian Penal Code; or (b) threatening to commit any act which is forbidden by the Indian Penal Code; or

	(c) unlawful detaining of any property; or (d) threatening to detain any property. **Note:** *The Indian Penal Code need not be in force in place where the coercion is employed.*
Against Whom/By Whom	Coercion may proceed from any person, and may be directed against any person, even a stranger.
Threat to file a Suit	A threat to file a suit (whether civil or criminal) does not amount to coercion unless the suit is on false charge. Threat to file a suit on false charge is an act forbidden by the Indian Penal Code and thus will amount to an act of coercion. **Note:** *The Madras High Court held that though a threat to commit suicide is not punishable under the Indian Penal Code, it is deemed to be forbidden by that code. Hence, the threat to commit suicide amounted to coercion and the release deed was therefore, voidable.*
Effects of Coercion	1. Right of aggrieved party to Rescind the contract 2. Obligation of aggrieved party to restore benefit 3. Obligation of other party to repay or return

3.0 UNDUE INFLUENCE

Meaning	The term 'undue influence' means dominating the will of the other person to obtain an unfair advantage over the other. According to Section 16(1), a contract is said to be induced by undue influence— (a) where the relations subsisting between the parties are such that one of them is in a position to dominate the will of the other, and (b) the dominant party uses that position to obtain an unfair advantage over the other.	
Presumption	A person is deemed to be in a position to dominate the will of another in the following **three circumstances**:	
	Circumstances	***Examples***
	(a) ***Where he holds a real or apparent authority over the other***	Master and Servant, Parent and Child, Income Tax Officer and Assessee, Principal and a Temporary Teacher
	(b) ***Where he stands in a fiduciary relation to the other***	Trustee and beneficiary, Spiritual adviser (Guru) and his disciples, Solicitors and Client, Guardian and Ward
	(c) ***Where he makes a contract with a person whose mental capacity is tempo-rarily or perma-nently affected by reason of age, illness or mental or bodily distress***	Medical Attendant and Patient

No Presumption of Domination of Will ?	According to judicial decisions held in various cases, there is no presumption of undue influence in the following relationships: 1. Husband and wife (other than pardanashin) 2. Landlord and tenant 3. Creditor and debtor
Effect of Undue Influence	When Consent to an agreement is caused by undue influence, the agreement is a **contract voidable** at the option of the party whose consent was so caused.
Similarities between Coercion and Undue Influence	In case of both coercion and undue influence, the consent is not free and the contract is voidable at the option of the aggrieved party.

4.0 FRAUD

Meaning	The term 'Fraud' means a false representation of fact made by a party to a contract (i.e., not by a stranger to a contract) wilfully (i.e., with knowledge of its false hood) with a view to deceive the other party who has acted on the basis of such representation and has been actually deceived.
Essential Elements	1. By a party to a contract 2. False representation of fact 3. Intention of deceiving the other party 4. Act of other party on the basis of such representation
Effects of Fraud	1. Right to Rescind the Contract 2. Right to insist Upon Performance 3. Right to Claim Damages
Silence does not amount to Fraud	(a) **General Rule** According to explanation to Section 17, "Mere silence as to facts likely to affect the willingness of a person to enter into a contract is not fraud" (b) **Three Exceptions to the General Rule** 1. Where parties stand in fiduciary relationship like parent-child, trustee-beneficiary. 2. Where the silence itself is equivalent to speech. 3. Half Truth
Conclusion	Fraud is said to have taken place where a party to the contract (i.e. not stranger) made a false representation as to the fact **with** the knowledge of its falsehood **with** the intention of deceiving the other party who actually acted on the faith of such representation and suffered a loss.

5.0 MISREPRESENTATION

Meaning	The term 'Misrepresentation' means a false representation of fact made by a party to a contract (i.e. not by a stranger to a contract) made innocently (i.e. without knowledge of its falsehood) or non-disclosure of a material fact without any intention to deceive the other party who has acted on the basis of such representation.
Essential Elements	1. By a party to a contract 2. False representation of fact 3. Inducing other party to enter into contract without any intention to deceive the other party 4. Act of other party on the basis of such representation
Effects	1. Right to Rescind the Contract 2. Right to Insist upon Performance
Conclusion	Misrepresentation is said to have taken place where a party to the contract (i.e. not stranger) made a false representation as to the fact **without** the knowledge of its falsehood **without** the intention of deceiving the other party who actually acted on the faith of such representation.

6.0 EFFECTS OF MISTAKE

Type of Mistake	***Effect on Validity***
1. Mistake of Indian Law	The contract is not voidable because everyone is supposed to know the law of his country.
2. Mistake of Foreign Law	A mistake of foreign law is treated as mistake of fact, i.e. the contract is void if both the parties are under a mistake as to a foreign law because one cannot be expected to know the law of other country.
3. In case of Bilateral Mis-take as to essential fact (i.e., where both the parties to an agreement are under mistake to essential fact)	The agreement is void.
4. In case of Unilateral Mis-take (i.e. where one of the parties to an agreement in under mistake)	
(i) ***as to the identity of the person contracted with***	The agreement is void.
(ii) ***as to the nature of contract***	The agreement is void.
(iii) ***as to other matter***	The agreement is not void.

CHAPTER 6 LEGALITY OF OBJECT AND CONSIDERATION, AND AGREEMENTS OPPOSED TO PUBLIC POLICY

1.0 FIVE CIRCUMSTANCES UNDER WHICH THE OBJECT OR CONSIDERATION IS DEEMED TO BE UNLAWFUL

1. If it is Forbidden by Law
2. If it Defeats the Provisions of any Law
3. If it is Fraudulent
4. If it Involves or Implies Injury to a Person or Property of Another
5. If the Court Regards it as Immoral or Opposed to Public Policy

Note: *If one of the several considerations or objects of an agreement is unlawful, the agreement is void.*

2.0 ILLEGAL AGREEMENTS

<table>
<tr><td>Meaning</td><td>Illegal agreements are those agreements which are—
(a) void ab-initio, i.e. void from the very beginning, and
(b) punishable by the criminal law of the country or by any special legislation/regulation.</td></tr>
<tr><td>Effects</td><td>(a) The collateral transactions to an illegal agreement also become illegal and hence cannot be enforced.
(b) No action can be taken for the recovery of money paid or property transferred under an illegal agreement and for the breach of an illegal agreement.
(c) In case of an agreement containing the promise, some part of which is legal and other part illegal, the legal position is as under:
<table>
<tr><th>Case</th><th>Provision</th></tr>
<tr><td>1. In the illegal part cannot be separated from the legar part</td><td>The whole agreement is alto gether illegal.</td></tr>
<tr><td>2. If the illegal part can be separated from the legal part</td><td>The Court will enforce the legal part and reject the illegal part.</td></tr>
</table>
</td></tr>
</table>

3.0 AGREEMENTS OPPOSED TO PUBLIC POLICY

1. **Agreements of Trading With Enemy**
2. **Agreement for Stifling Prosecution**
3. **Agreements in the Nature of Maintenance and Champerty** Maintenance is an agreement whereby one party having no interest in suit, agrees to assist another to maintain suit. *For example*, *X* promises to pay *Y* Rs 5,000 if *Y* files a suit against *Z*. This is a maintenance agreement.
   Champerty is an agreement whereby one party agrees to assist another in recovering property and in turn is to share in the proceeds of the action.
4. **Agreement for the Sale/Transfer of Public Offices or to Obtain Public Titles**
5. **Agreements in Restraint of Parental Rights**

6. **Agreements in Restraint of Personal Liberty**
7. **Agreement Tending to Create Monopoly**
8. **Agreements Interfering with Course of Justice**
9. **Marriage Brokerage Contracts**
10. **Agreement in Restraint of Marriage of any person other than a minor is void.**
11. **Agreement in Restraint of any lawful Trade profession, or business, is to that extent void.**
12. **Agreement in Restraint of Legal Proceeding**

CHAPTER 7 VOID AGREEMENTS AND CONTINGENT CONTRACTS

1.0 MEANING AND EXAMPLES OF VOID AGREEMENTS

Meaning	A void agreement is an agreement which is not enforceable by law. The agreements which are not enforceable by law right from the time when they are made, are *void-ab-initio*.
Examples	Agreements which have expressly been declared void: 1. Agreements by or with persons incompetent to contract (Sections 10 & 11). 2. Agreements entered into through a mutual mistake of fact between the parties (Section 20). 3. Agreement, the object or Consideration of which is unlawful (Section 23). 4. Agreement, the Consideration or Object of which is partly unlawful (Section 24). 5. Agreement made without Consideration (Section 25). 6. Agreements in Restraint of Marriage of any person other than minor (Section 26). 7. Agreements in Restraint of Trade (Section 27). 8. Agreements in Restraint of Legal Proceedings (Section 29). 9. Wagering Agreement (Section 30). 10. Impossible Agreement (Section 56). 11. An agreement to enter into an Agreement in the Future.

2.0 AGREEMENTS IN RESTRAINT OF TRADE

Validity	"Every agreement by which anyone is restrained from exercising a lawful profession, trade or business of any kind, is to that extent void."
Meaning of Expression	The expression 'that extent' may be interpreted in the sense that only that portion of such agreement is void which is considered *either* as unreasonable *or*
'that extent'	as opposed to public policy being in restraint of trade. The rest of the agreement would continue to be valid.s

Exceptions	***Under Statutory Provisions***	***Under Judical Interpretations***
	1. Agreement with seller of Goodwill **2. Agreements with Partners** ***(a) Restriction on Existing Partner to carry a any business other than that of firm while he is a partner.*** ***(b) Restrictions on outgoing Partner to carry on similar business within specified period or local limits if restrictions are reasonable.*** ***(c) Restriction on Partners on dissolution of firm to carry on similar business within specified period or local limits if restrictions are reasonable.*** ***(d) Restriction on Partners in case of sale of firm's goodwill, to carry on similar business within specified period or local limits if restrictions are reasonable.***	**1. Trade Combinations to regulate the business or to fix prices (but not to create monopoly)** **2. Sole Dealing Agreements on reasonable terms.** **3. Service Agreements**

3.0 AGREEMENTS IN RESTRAINT OF LEGAL PROCEEDINGS

Restricting Enforcement of Rights	Agreements Restricting Enforcement of Rights is void to that extent.
Limiting Period of Limitation	Agreements Limiting the Period of Limitation is void because its object is to defeat the provisions of law.

4.0 MEANING AND VALIDITY OF VARIOUS AGREEMENTS

Type of Agreement	***Validity***
1. Uncertain Agreement **[An agreement the meaning of which is not certain or capable of being made certain**	Void
2. Wagering Agreement **[An agreement between two persons under which money or money's worth is payable, by one person to another on the happening or non-happening of a future uncertain event is called a wagering event.]**	Void
(a) In the States of Maharastra & Gujrat	Illegal
(b) In Rest of India	Void

3. Agreements collateral to Wagering Agreement ***(a) In the States of Maharastra & Gujrat*** ***(b) In Rest of India***	 Illegal Not Void
4. Contingent Agreement based on Impossible Event **[An agreement to do or not to do anything if an impossible event happens whether impossibility of the event is known or not to the partner to the agreement at the time when it is made]**	Void
5. Agreement to do an Impossible Act	Void
6. Contingent Contract **[A contract to do or not to do something if some event collateral to such contract does or does not happen]** **[or A contract the performance of which depends upon the happening or non happening of some future uncertain event which is collateral to the contract]**	Valid

5.0 RESTITUTION

Meaning	Restitution means "Return or Restoration of Benefit." The provisions relating to 'restitution' are given on next page:	
Provision	***Case***	***Provision***
	(a) When a person at whose option a contract is voidable rescinds it [Section 64].	The party rescinding a voidable contract must restore the benefit to the person from whom he has received it.
	(b) When an agreement is discovered to be void or the contract becomes void [Section 65].	The person who has received any benefit or advantage under such agreement or contract must restore it or compensate for it to the person from whom he has received it.
Non-Applicability	The principle of restitution does not apply to contracts which are void *ab-initio* with the exception where the minor has entered into agreement by misrepresenting his age.	

CHAPTER 8 PERFORMANCE OF CONTRACT

1.0 MEANING AND TYPES OF PERFORMANCE

Meaning of Performance	A contract is said to have been performed when the parties to a contract *either* perform *or* offer to perform their respective promises.
Two Types of Performance	1. **Actual Performance** Where a promisor has made an offer of performance to the promisee and the offer has been accepted by the promisee, it is called an actual performance.

	2. **Attempted Performance (or Tender)** Where a promisor has made an offer of performance to the promisee, and the offer has not been accepted by the promisee, it is called an attempted performance.

2.0 EFFECTS, TYPES AND ESSENTIALS OF A VALID TENDER

Two Effects of Tender	1. The promisor is not responsible for non performance. 2. The promisor does not loose his rights under the contract.
Two Types of Tender	1. Tender of Goods/Services 2. Tender of Money
Essentials of a Valid Tender	1. Unconditional 2. At Proper Time 3. At Proper Place 4. Reasonable Opportunity to Promisee 5. For Whole Obligation 6. To Proper Person

3.0 WHO MAY DEMAND PERFORMANCE AND WHO MAY PERFORM

Who may Demand Performance	1. Promisee 2. Legal Representative 3. Third Party 4. Joint Promisees
Who may Perform the Contract	1. Promisor 2. Promisor's Agent 3. Legal Representatives 4. Third Party 5. Joint Promisors

4.0 DEVOLUTION OF JOINT LIABILITIES AND JOINT RIGHTS

Meaning of Devolution	Devolution means passing over from one person to another.
Meaning of Devolution of Joint Liabilities	The liabilities of joint promisors pass to their legal representatives (in case of death).
Rules Regarding the Performance of Joint Promise	(a) Joint and Several Liability of Joint Promisors (b) Joint Promisor's Right to Claim Contribution (c) Joint Promisor's Duty to Share Loss from Default in Contribution (d) Effect of Release of One Joint Promisor
Meaning of Devolution of Joint Rights	When a person has made a promise to two or more persons jointly, then, unless a contrary intention appears from the contract, the right to claim performance rests, as between him and them, with them during their joint lives, and, after the death of any of them, with the representative of such deceased person jointly, with the survivor or survivors and after the death of the last survivor, with the representatives of all jointly.

5.0 RULES AS TO TIME AND PLACE OF PERFORMANCE OF A CONTRACT

Case where. . .	*Rule as to Performance*
1. Time not specified	Within a reasonable time
2. Time specified but promise is to be performed without promisee's application	During the usual business hours on that particular day
3. Time specified but pro- mises is to be performed on promisee's application	The promisee must apply for performance at a proper place and within usual business hours.
4. Place not specified	The promisor must apply to the promi-see to ap-point a reasonable place for the performance and to perform the promise at such place.
5. Manner for performance prescribed	The promise must be performed in the manner and at the time prescribed by the promisee.

6.0 IS TIME AN ESSENCE OF CONTRACT?

Meaning	Time is an essence of a contract means that it is essential for the parties to a contract to perform their respective promises within the specified time.
When Time Essence?	In the following cases, time is usually considered to be the essence of contract: (a) Where the parties have expressly agreed to treat the time as the essence of the contract. (b) Where the non-performance at the specified time operates as an injury to the party. (c) Where the nature and necessity of the contract requires the performance of the contract within the specified time.
In Commercial Contracts	In commercial contracts time fixed for the delivery of goods and not for the payment of price is considered to be the essence of a contract. Consequences of Non-performance of contract within specified time.

Consequences of Non-Performance of Contract within Specified Time	*Where Time is essence*	*Where Time is not essence*
	1. Contract becomes voidable	1. Contract does not become voidable
	2. Promisee cannot claim compensation	2. Promisee can claim compensation

7.0 RECIPROCAL PROMISES

Meaning	Promises which form the consideration or part of the consideration for each other, are called 'reciprocal promises'.

Types	Lord Mansfield in ***Jones* v. *Barkley*** case have classified the reciprocal promises as under:	
	Types of reciprocal	***Meaning promises***
	(a) Mutual and Independent	When the promises are to be performed by each party independently, without waiting for the other party to perform his promise.
	(b) Mutual and Dependent	When the performance of one party depends on the prior performance of the other party.
	(c) Mutual and Concurrent	When the promises are to be performed simultaneously.

8.0 ASSIGNMENT OF CONTRACTS

Meaning	Assignment of a contract means transfer of contractual rights and liabilities to a third party.	
Mode	***Case***	***Rule***
	(a) By Act of Parties ***1. Assignment of contractual liabilities***	Contractual liabilities cannot be assigned unless Novation takes place. (Novation is a tripartite agreement between promisor, promisee and third party)
	2. Assignment of contractual Rights	Contractual Rights can be assigned subject to all equities between the original parties
	(b) By Operation of law	The rights and obligations (other than those of personal nature) of the deceased/insolvent party pass on to legal represen-tatives/Offical Receiver/Assignee.
Assignment & Succession	Under succession, both benefits and burden attached to the contract devolve upon the legal heir. A son succeeding his father's estate shall be liable to meet the debts and liability of his father to the extent of the property inherited. However, in assignment, only the benefit of a contract can be assigned and not the liabilities attached thereto.	

9.0 MEANING OF APPROPRIATION OF PAYMENT

Meaning	It means application of payment to a particular debt.	
Rules	***Case***	***Rule***
	I. **Where debt to be discharged is indicated,**	The payment, if accepted must be applied accordingly.
	II. **Where debt to be discharged is not indicated**	The creditor has option to apply the payment to any lawful debt due from the debtor even if it is a time barred debt. But he cannot apply to a disputed debt.
	III. **Where neither party makes any appropriation**	The payment shall be applied in discharge of the debts in order of time whether or not they are time barred. If the debt are of equal standing, the payment shall be applied in discharge of each, proportionately. In other words all payments shall be applied towards the payment of first debt till it gets extinguished. Similarly, all subsequent payments applied towards second debt till it gets fully paid and so on and so forth.

CHAPTER 9 DISCHARGE OF CONTRACT

1.0 MEANING AND MODES OF DISCHARGE OF A CONTRACT

Meaning	Discharge of a contract means termination of the contractual relations between the parties to a contract.
Mode	Discharge by Performance. Discharge by Mutual Agreement Discharge by Operation of Law Discharge by Impossibility of Performance Discharge by Lapse of Time as per The Limitation Act, 1963 Discharge by Breach of Contract

2.0 DISCHARGE BY PERFORMANCE

Actual Performance	A contract is said to be discharged by actual performance when the parties to the contract perform their promises in accordance with the terms of the contract.
Attempted Performance or Tender	A contract is said to be discharged by attempted performance when the promisor has made an offer of performance to the promisee but it has not been accepted by the promisee.

3.0 DISCHARGE BY MUTUAL AGREEMENT

Novation	Substitution of a new contract for the original contract.
Rescission	Cancellation of original contract by any party (s) to contract.
Alteration	Change in the terms of a contract with mutual consent
Remission	Acceptance by the promisee of a lesser fulfillment of the promise made.
Waiver	Intentional relinquishment of a right under the contract.

4.0 DISCHARGE BY OPERATION OF LAW

1. **By Death of the Promisor in case of a contract involving the personal skill or ability of the promisor.**
2. **By Insolvency**
3. **By Unauthorised Material Alteration**
4. **By the Identity of Promisor and Promisee**

5.0 DISCHARGE BY IMPOSSIBILITY OF PERFORMANCE

Meaning of Initial Impossibility	Initial impossibility means the impossibility existing at the time of making the contract.	
Effects of Initial Impossibility	***Case***	***Effect***
	I. Where both the Promisor and Promisee know about the initial impossibility	Such agreement is **void *ab-initio.***
	II. Where both the Promisor and Promisee do not know about the initial impossibility	Such agreement is **void** on the ground of mutual mistake.
	III. Where the Promisor alone knows about the initial impossibility	Such promisor **must compensate** for any loss which such promisee sustainsthrough the non-performance of the promise.
Meaning of Supervening Impossibility	Supervening impossibility means impossibility which does not exist at the time of making the contract but which arises subsequently after the formation of the contract.	
Effects of Supervening Impossibility	***Case***	***Effect***
	I. Where an act becomes impossible after the contract is made	The contract to do such an act becomes **void** when the act becomes impossible

	II. **Where an act becomes unlawfulby reason of some event beyond the control of promisor**	The contract to do such an act becomes **void** when the act becomes unlawful.
	III. **Where the promisor alone knows about the impossibility**	Such promisor must compensate the promisee for any loss which such promisee might have suffered on account of non performance of the promise.
	IV. **Where an agreement is discovered to be void or where a contract becomes void**	Any person who has received any benefit under such agreement or contract is bound to restore it or to make compensation for it, to the person from whom he received it.
Cases when a Contract is Discharged on the Ground of Supervening Impossibility	1. Destruction of Subject Matter after the formation of the contract without any fault of either party. 2. Death or Personal Incapacity of a person if the performance of a contract depends on his personal skill or ability. 3. Declaration of War: 4. Change of Law after the formation of the contract. 5. Non-existence or Non-occurrence of a Particular State of Things Necessary for Performance:	
Cases when the Contract is not Discharged on the Ground of Supervening Impossibility	1. Difficulty of Performance 2. Commercial Impossibility 3. Default of a Third Party 4. Strikes, Lockouts and Civil Disturbances 5. Partial Impossibility	

6.0 DISCHARGE BY LAPSE OF TIME AS PER THE LIMITATION ACT, 1963 (E.G., 3 YEARS TO RECOVER A DEBT, 12 YEARS TO RECOVER AN IMMOVABLE PROPERTY)

7.0 DISCHARGE BY BREACH OF CONTRACT

Anticipatory Breah	Anticipatory Breach of Contract occurs when the party declares his intention of not performing the contract before the performance is due.
Actual Breach	Actual Breach of Contract may take place: (a) *On Due Date of Performance:* (b) *During the Course of Performance:*
Consequences of Breach of Contract	The aggrieved party (i.e. the party not at fault) is discharged from his obligation and gets rights to proceed against the party at fault.

CHAPTER 10 REMEDIES FOR BREACH OF CONTRACT

1.0 MEANING AND MODES OF BREACH OF CONTRACT

Meaning	A breach of contract occurs if any party refuses or fails to perform his part of the contract or by his act makes it impossible to perform his obligation under the contract.
Modes	A breach of contact may arise in two ways: (a) anticipatory breach and (b) actual breach.

2.0 ANTICIPATORY BREACH OF CONTRACT

Meaning	Anticipatory breach occurs when the party declares his intention of not performing the contract before the performance is due.	
Modes	A party may declare his intention of not performing the contract in the following two ways: (a) When a party to a contract has refused to perform his promise. (b) When a party to a contract has disabled himself from performing his promise in its entirety.	
Two Options Available to Aggrieved Party	(a) He can rescind the contract and claim damages for breach of contract without waiting until the due date for performance, or (b) He may treat the contract as operative and wait till the due date for performance and claim damages if the promise still remains unperformed.	
Consequences of Treating Contract as Operative	(a) The promisor may perform his promise on or before the due date of performance and the promisee will be bound to accept the performance. (b) The promisor may take advantage of the discharge by supervening impossibility arising between the date of breach and the due date of the performance and in such a case, the promisee shall lose his right to sue for damages.	
Amount of Damages	***Option exercised***	***Amount of Damages***
	I. When the aggrieved party rescinds the contract at the date of breach	Difference between the price prevailing on the date of breach and the contract price.
	II. When the aggrieved party does not rescind the contract at the date of breach	Difference between the price prevailing on the due date of performance and the contract price.

3.0 ACTUAL BREACH OF CONTRACT

<table>
<tr><td>Two Ways of Actual Breach of Contract</td><td colspan="2">Actual breach of contract may take place in any of the following two ways:
(a) Actual Breach on due Date of Performance
(b) Actual Breach during the Course of Performance</td></tr>
<tr><td>Consequences of Actual Breach of Contract</td><td>Where time is the essence of a contract</td><td>Where time is not the essence of a contract</td></tr>
<tr><td>1. Whether the Contract becomes voidable at the option of the promisee.</td><td>Yes</td><td>No</td></tr>
<tr><td>2. Whether the Promisee is entitled to claim the compensation for any loss occasioned to him by the non-performance of the promise at the stipulated time</td><td></td><td></td></tr>
<tr><td>(a) Where performance beyond the stipulated time is not accepted</td><td>Yes</td><td>Yes</td></tr>
<tr><td>(b) Where performance beyond the stipulated time is accepted</td><td>No, unless the promisee gives notice to the promisor of his intention to do so.</td><td>No, unless the promisee gives notice to the promisor of his intention to do so.</td></tr>
</table>

4.0 REMEDIES FOR BREACH OF CONTRACT

<table>
<tr><td>Meaning of Remedy</td><td>A remedy is the course of action available to an aggrieved party (i.e. the party not at default) for the enforcement of a right under a contract.</td></tr>
<tr><td>Remedies for Breach of Contract</td><td>1. Rescission of Contract [Section 39] Rescission means a right not to perform obligation.
2. Suit for Damages
(a) Such damages which naturally arose in the usual course of things from such breach. This relates to ordinary damages arising in the usual course of things.
(b) Such damages which the parties knew, when they made the contract, to be likely to result from the breach. This relates to special damages.
(c) The aforesaid compensation is not to be given for any remote or indirect loss or damage sustained by reason of the breach, and</td></tr>
<tr><td></td><td>3. Suit for Specific Performance i.e. demanding the court's direction to the defaulting party to carry out the promise according to the terms of the contract.</td></tr>
</table>

	4. **Suit for Injunction** i.e. demanding court's stay order. Injunction means an order of the court which prohibits a person to do a particular act.
	5. **Suit for Quantum Meruit** Quantum Meruit means as much as is earned. Right to Quantum Meruit means a right to claim the compensation for the work already done.

5.0 TYPES OF DAMAGES

Ordinary Damages	1. The aggrieved party must suffer by breach of contract, and 2. The damages must be proximate (i.e. direct) consequence of the breach of contract and not the indirect consequence.
Special Damages	Aggrieved party may claim the special damages if the special circumstances resulting in a special loss are communicated to the promisor.
Exemplary or Punitive or Vindictive Damages	Exemplary damages are those which are in the nature of punishment. The court may award these damages in case of: 1. A breach of promise to marry, where damages shall be calculated on the basis of mental injury sustained by the aggrieved party, 2. Wrongful dishonour of a cheque by a banker.
Nominal Damages	Where there is only a technical violation of a legal right but the aggrieved party has not in fact suffered any loss because of breach of contract. *(say, one rupee)*
Damages for Inconvenience and Discomfort suffered	If a party has suffered physical inconvenience and discomfort due to breach of contract, that party can recover the damages for such inconvenience and discomfort.

6.0 LIQUIDATED DAMAGES AND PENALTY

Liquidated Damages	The specified sum payable by the party responsible for breach which represents a fair and genuine preestimate of the damages likely to result due to breach is called liquidated damages.
Penalty	The specified sum payable by the party responsible for breach which is disproportionate to the damages likely to result due to breach.
Position in India	In India, there is no distinction between penalty and liquidated damages. The Courts in India allow only reasonable compensation not exceeding the specified sum [Section 74].
Position in English Law	Under English law, liquidated damages are enforceable and not penalty.

7.0 STIPULATION FOR INTEREST

Stipulation	Whether the stipulation is in the nature of a penalty or not
1. For payment of interest in case of default	It is not in the nature of a penalty if the interest is reasonable.
2. For payment of increased interest from the date of the contract	It is always in the nature of a penalty.
3. For payment of increased interest from the date of default only	It may or may not be in the nature of a penalty depending on the terms and circumstances of the case.
4. For payment of compound interest on default at the same rate as simple interest	It is not in the nature of a penalty.
5. For payment of compound interest on default at the rate higher than that of simple interest	It is in the nature of a penalty.
6. For payment of interest at a rate lower than that of original rate if interest is paid on due date	It is not in the nature of a penalty.

8.0 FORFEITURE OF SECURITY DEPOSIT (OR EARNEST MONEY)

A clause in a contract which provides for forfeiture of security deposit in the event of failure to perform is in the nature of a penalty. In such cases, the court may award reasonable compensation only.

CHAPTER 11 QUASI-CONTRACTS

1.0 MEANING AND KINDS OF QUASI-CONTRACTS

Meaning	A Quasi-contract is an obligation imposed by law upon a person for the benefit of another even in the absence of a contract. It is based on the principle of equity.
Features	(a) It is imposed by law and does not arise from any agreement. (b) The duty of a party and not the promise of any party is the basis of such contract. (c) The right under it is always a right to money and generally, though not always, to a liquidated sum of money. (d) The right under it is available against specific person(s) and not against the world. (e) A suit for its breach may be filed in the same way as in case of a complete contract.
Similarity	The outcome of quasi-contracts resemble that created by a contract. So far as claim for damages are concerned, there is a similarity

	between a Quasi-contracts and contract because in case of breach of a quasi-contract, Section 73 provides for the same remedies as provided in case of breach of a contract.
Kinds	1. **Right to Recover the Price of Necessaries Supplied** to a person who is incapable of contracting or anyone whom such incapable person is legally bound to support, from the property of such incapable person. 2. **Right to Recover Money Paid for Another Person** 3. **Right to Recover for Non-Gratuitous Act** 4. **Responsibility of Finder of Goods as Bailee** 5. **Right to Recover from a Person to whom Money is Paid or thing is Delivered, by Mistake or Under Coercion**
Right of Injured Party	When an obligation created by a Quasi-contract is not discharged, the injured party is entitled to receive the same compensation from the party in default as if such person had contracted to discharge it and had broken his contract.

2.0 QUANTUM MERUIT

Meaning	The term '*quantum meruit*' means as much as merited or 'as much as earned'. In other words, it means payment in proportion to the amount of work done. The right to claim on '*quantum meruit*' does not arise out of a contract as the right to damages does. It is a claim on the quasi contractual obligations which is implied by the circumstances. The claim for *quantum meruit* arises only when the original contract is discharged.
Cases	1. In case of void agreement or contract that becomes void 2. In case of non-gratuitous act 3. In case of act preventing the completion of contract 4. In case of divisible contract 5. In case of indivisible contract performed completely but badly

CHAPTER 12 INDEMNITY AND GUARANTEE

1.0 A CONTRACT OF INDEMNITY

Indemnity	The term 'indemnity' means to make good the loss or to compensate the party who has suffered some loss.
Contract of Indemnity	A contract by which one party promises to save the other from loss caused to him by the conduct of the promisor himself, or by the conduct of any other person, is called a "contract of indemnity".
Indemnifier	The person who promises to make good the loss is called the 'indemnifier'.
Indemnity-Holder	The person whose loss is to be made good is called 'indemnity-holder'.

Insurance Contracts	Indian courts follow the English law in respect of contract of indemnity which covers the contracts of insurance also.
Rights of Indemnity Holder	An indemnity holder is entitled to recover all damages, costs and sums which he may be compelled to pay, from the indemnifier provided he acts within the scope of his authority.
When Liability of Commences?	Although The Indian Contract Act, 1872 is silent on the time of commencement of liability of indemnifier but on the basis of judicial decisions of courts, it can be said that the liability of an indemnifier commences **as soon as the liability of the indemnity-holder becomes absolute and certain.**
Mode of Contract of Indemnity	A contract of indemnity may be express or implied.
Essential Elements	In addition to the implied or express promise to indemnify, all the essentials of a valid contract must also be present.

2.0 A CONTRACT OF GUARANTEE

Meaning	A contract of guarantee is a contract to perform a promise or discharge the liability of a third person in case of his default.
Three Parties	Three parties to a Contract of Guarantee are Principle Debtor, Creditor and Surety.
Essential Features	(a) Tripartite Agreement (b) Consent of Three Parties (c) Existence of a Liability (d) Essentials of a Valid Contract (e) Guarantee not to be Obtained by Misrepresentation (f) Guarantee not to be Obtained by Concealment
Extent of Surety's Liability	Liability of a surety is equal to that of the principal debtor unless otherwise agreed.
Is a Contract of *Uberrimae Fidei* ?	No

3.0 DISTINCTION BETWEEN CONTRACT OF INDEMNITY AND CONTRACT OF GUARANTEE

Basis of Distinction	***Contract of Indemnity***	***Contract of Guarantee***
No. of Parties	There are ***two*** parties—indemnifier and the indemnity-holder.	There are ***three*** parties—principal debtor, creditor and surety.
No. of Contracts	There is only ***one*** contract between indemnifier and indemnity-holder.	There are ***three*** contracts, one between creditor and principal debtor, second between surety and principal debtor, and third between surety and the creditor.

Basis of Distinction	***Contract of Indemnity***	***Contract of Guarantee***
Undertaking	The ***indemnifier*** undertakes to save the indemnity-holder from any loss.	The ***surety*** undertakes for the payment of debts of principal debtor.
Nature of liability	The liability of indemnifier is ***primary and unconditional.***	The liability of surety is ***secondary and conditional.*** Surety's liability is secondary in the sense that the primary liability is of principal debtor. Surety's liability is conditional in the sense that it arises only on default of principal debtor.
Nature of event	The liability arises only on the happening of a contingency.	The liability arises only on the non-performance of an existing promise or non-payment of an existing debt.
Request	The indemnifier need not act at the request of indemnity-holder.	The surety acts at the request of the principal debtor.
Right to sue	The indemnifier cannot sue a third party in his own name because of absence of privity of contract between him and a third party. He can sue the third party in his own name if there in an assignment in his favour.	A surety, on discharging the debt of principal debtor, can sue the principal debtor in his own name.

4.0 KINDS OF GUARANTEE

Specific Guarantee	(a) ***Meaning***–A guarantee which extends to a single debt or specific transaction is called a specific guarantee. (b) ***Surety's Liability***–A Surety's liability comes to an end when the guaranteed debt is duly discharged or the promise is duly performed.
Continuing Guarantee	(a) ***Meaning*** – A guarantee which extends to a series of transactions is called a 'continuing guarantee'. (b) ***Surety's Liability***–*A surety's liability* continues until the revocation of the guarantee. (c) A continuing guarantee may be given for a part of the entire debt or for the entire debt subject to a limit.
Ways of Revocation of Continuing Guarantee	1. By Notice of Revocation 2. By Death of Surety 3. By Modes of Discharging the Surety

5.0 RIGHTS OF A SURETY

Rights Against the Principal Debtor	*Right Against the Creditor*	*Rights against Co-sureties*
(a) Right to Subrogation (b) Right to Indemnity	(a) Right to Securities (b) Right to Claim Set Off	(a) Right to Claim Contribution (b) Right to Share the Security

6.0 MODES OF DISCHARGE OF SURETY

By Revocation of Contract of Guarantee	*By Conduct of Creditor*	*By Invalidation of Contract*
(a) By Notice	(a) By Variance in terms of Contract	(a) Guarantee Obtained by Miserepresentation
(b) By the Death of Surety	(b) By Release or Discharge of Principal Debtor	(b) Guarantee Obtained by Concealment
(c) By Novation	(c) By Arrangment between Principal Debtor and Creditor	(c) Failure of a person to join as Co-surety
	(d) By Creditor's Act or Omission	
	(e) By Loss of Security	

CHAPTER 13 BAILMENT AND PLEDGE

1.0 MEANING OF BAILMENT

Meaning	"the delivery of goods by one person to another for some purpose, upon a contract that they shall, when the purpose is accomplished, be returned or otherwise disposed off according to the directions of the person delivering them."
Essential Elements	(a) Agreement (b) Delivery of Goods (c) Purpose (d) Return of Specific Goods

2.0 DISTINCTION BETWEEN A CONTRACT OF BAILMENT AND A CONTRACT OF SALE

Basis of Distinction	*Bailment*	*Sale*
Transfer of ownership/ possession	There is only a transfer of **possession** of goods from the bailor to the bailee.	There is a transfer of **ownership** of goods from the seller to the buyer.
Consideration	The consideration **need not** be passed between bailor and bailee.	The consideration in terms of price **must** be passed between seller and buyer.

Return of goods	The bailee **must return** the goods to the bailor on the fulfillment of the purpose for which the bailment is made.	There is **no question of such return** of goods in contract of sale.

3.0 KINDS OF BAILMENT

On the Basis on Reward	*On the Basis on Benefit*
(a) Gratuitous Bailment (b) Non-gratuitous Bailment	(a) Bailment for the exclusive benefit of the bailor (b) Bailment for the exclusive benefit of the bailee (c) Bailment for the mutual benefit

4.0 DISTINCTION BETWEEN A GRATUITOUS AND NON-GRATUITOUS BAILMENT

Basis of Distinction	*Gratuitous bailment*	*Non-gratuitous bailment*
Consideration	**No consideration** passes between the bailor and the bailee.	**Some consideration** passes between the bailor and the bailee.
Benefit	It is for the exclusive benefit of the **bailor or bailee.**	It is for the exclusive benefit of the **bailor and bailee.**
Liability of bailor for unknown defects [Section 151]	The bailor is **not liable** to the bailee for the loss due to defect in the goods if he does not know those defects.	The bailor is **liable** to the bailee for the loss due to defects in the goods whether he knows those defects or not.
Bailor's duty to bear expenses [Section 158]	The bailor must repay to the bailee **all the necessary expenses** which the bailee has already incurred for the purposes of bailment.	The bailor must repay to the bailee **only the extraordinary expenses** which the bailee has already incurred for the purpose of bailment.
Termination of Bailment	It can be terminated at **any time** even though the bailment was for a specified period or specified purpose.	It is terminated **on the expiry of specified period** or on the fulfillment of the specified purpose.
Effect of death of bailor/bailee	It is **terminated** by the death of bailor or bailee	It is **not terminated** by the death of bailor or bailee.

5.0 DUTIES OF A BAILOR

(a) Duty to Disclose Defects
(b) Duty to Bear Expenses
(c) Duty to Indemnify the Bailee in case of premature termination of Gratuitous Bailment
(d) Duty to Indemnify the Bailee against the Defective Title of the Bailor
(e) Duty to Receive Back the Goods
(f) Duty to Bear the Risk of Loss

6.0 DUTIES OF A BAILEE

(a) Duty to take Care of the Goods Bailed
(b) Duty not to Make any Unauthorised Use of Goods
(c) Duty not to Mix Bailor's Goods with his Own Goods

(d) Duty to Return the Goods
(e) Duty to Return Accretions to the Goods
(f) Duty not to Set Up any Adverse Title

7.0 RIGHTS OF A BAILOR

Basically, the duties of a bailee are the rights of a bailor and the bailor can enforce his rights against the bailee by suing him in case of a default. The various rights of a bailor are as follows:

(a) Right to Claim Damages in case of Negligence
(b) Right to Terminate the Contract in case of Unauthorised Use
(c) Right to Claim Compensation in case of Unauthorised Use
(d) Right to Claim the Separation of Goods in case of Unauthorised Mixture
(e) Right to Claim Compensation in case of Unauthorised Mixture of Goods which cannot be Separated
(f) Right to Demand Return of Goods
(g) Right to Claim Compensation in case of Unauthorised Retention of Goods
(h) Right to Demand Accretion to Goods

8.0 RIGHTS OF A BAILEE

Basically, the duties of a bailor are the rights of a bailee and the bailee can enforce his rights against the bailor by suing him in case of a default. The various rights of a bailee are as follows:

(a) Right to Claim Damages
(b) Right to Claim Reimbursement of Expenses
(c) Right to be Indemnified in case of Premature Termination of Gratuitous Bailment
(d) Right to Recover Loss in case of Bailor's Defective Title
(e) Right to Recover Loss in case of Bailor's Refusal to take the Goods Back
(f) Right to Deliver Goods to any one of the Joint Bailors
(g) Right to Deliver the Goods to Bailor in case of Bailor's Defective Title
(h) Right to Particular Lien

9.0 MEANING OF LIEN

Lien means the right of a person having possession of goods belonging to another to retain those goods until the satisfaction of sum claimed by the person in possession of the goods.

10.0 DISTINCTION BETWEEN PARTICULAR LIEN AND GENERAL LIEN

Basis of Distinction	***Particular Lien***	***General Lien***
Goods in respect of which lien is available	It is available against **those goods** in respect of which some charges are due.	It is available against **all goods** whether in respect of which claims are due or not.
Purpose	It is available only for **non-payment of remuneration** for the services.	It is available for a **general balance of account**.
To whom available in the absence of contract to contrary	It is available to **every bailee** to whom the goods have been bailed.	It is available only to **specific bailees** like bankers, factors, Wharfingers, attorneys of High Court and policy brokers.

Rendering of service	It is available **only when some service** involving the exercise of labour or skill has been rendered.	It is available **even when no such service** has been rendered.
Purpose of delivery of goods	The purpose of delivery of goods is to **confer an additional value** as the goods bailed.	The purpose of delivery of goods **is to deposit the goods as security.**

11.0 RIGHTS OF A FINDER OF GOODS

(a) Right to Lien
(b) Right to Sue for Reward
(c) Right to Sell

12.0 DUTIES OF A FINDER OF GOODS

A finder of goods is subject to the same responsibility as a bailee. The duties of a finder of goods are as follows:

(a) Duty to take Reasonable care
(b) Duty not to use for Personal Purpose
(c) Duty not to mix with his Own Goods
(d) Duty to find the Owner

13.0 TERMINATION OF BAILMENT

Every Contract of Bailment	(a) On the expiry of Fixed Period (b) On fulfilment of the Purpose (c) Inconsistent Use of Goods (d) Destruction of the Subject Matter of Bailment
Gratuitous Bailment	(a) Before the expiry of a fixed period (b) On Death of Bailor/Bailee

14.0 PLEDGE

Pledge (or Pawn)	The bailment of goods as security for payment of a debt or performance of a promise is called pledge (or pawn).
Pawnor (or Pledgor)	The person who delivers the goods as security for payment of a debt or performance of a promise is called the Pawnor or Pledgor.
Pawnee (or Pledgee)	The person to whom the goods are delivered as security for payment of a debt or performance of a promise is called the Pawnee or Pledgee.
Special Feature of Pledge	It is the special property in goods and not the general property in goods, which passes to the pledgee. General property means the ownership of goods and special property means the possession of goods.

15.0 DISTINCTION BETWEEN PLEDGE AND BAILMENT

Basis of Distinction	***Pledge***	***Bailment***
Purpose	Pledge is bailment of goods for a **specific purpose**, i.e. repayment of a debt or performance of a duty.	Bailment is for a **purpose of any kind.**
Right to use	Pawnee **cannot use** the goods pledged.	Bailee **can use** the goods as per terms of bailment.
Right to sell	Pawnee **can sell** the goods pledged after giving notice to the pawnor in case of default by the pawnor.	Bailee can *either* **retain** the goods *or* **sue** the bailor for his dues.

16.0 DISTINCTION BETWEEN PLEDGE AND HYPOTHECATION

Hypothecation is also one of the modes of providing security. However, it is different from pledge in the following respects:

Basis of Distinction	***Pledge***	***Hypothecation***
Possession of goods	Borrower **transfers** the possession of goods.	Borrower **does not transfer** the possession of goods.
Right to deal with the goods	Borrower has **no right to deal** with the goods pledged.	Borrower has a **right to deal** with the goods hypothecated.

17.0 RIGHTS OF A PAWNEE

A pawnee has almost the same rights as those of a bailee. His rights are as follows:

(a) Right of Retainer
(b) Right to Claim Reimbursement of Extraordinary Expenses
(c) Right to Sue Pawnor
(d) Right to Sell
(e) Right Against True Owner

18.0 DUTIES OF A PAWNEE

The pawnee has almost the same duties as those of the bailee. His duties are as follows:

(a) Duty to take Reasonable Care of the Goods Pledged
(b) Duty not to make Unauthorised Use of Goods
(c) Duty not to Mix Goods Pledged with his Own Goods
(d) Duty to Return Goods
(e) Duty to Return Accretions to the Goods

19.0 RIGHTS OF A PAWNOR

The duties of a pawnee are basically the rights of a pawnor. He has the following rights:

(a) Right to get Pawnee's Duties Duly Enforced
(b) Right to Redeem the goods pledged

20.0 DUTIES OF A PAWNOR

Basically, the pawnor has the following duties:

(a) Duty to Comply with the Terms of Pledge
(b) Duty to Compensate the Pawnee for Extraordinary Expenses

21.0 PLEDGE BY NON-OWNERS

According to the general rule, only the true owner can pledge the goods but under the following cases, even a non-owner can make a valid pledge:

(a) Pledge by a Mercantile Agent
(b) Pledge by Person in Possession under Voidable Contract
(c) Pledge where Pawnor has a Limited Interest
(d) Pledge by a Co-owner in Possession
(e) Pledge by Seller *or* Buyer in Possession

CHAPTER 14 CONTRACT OF AGENCY

1.0 MEANING OF CONTRACT OF AGENCY

Meaning	By a contract of agency, a person employs another person to do any act for him or to represent him in dealing with third persons so as to bind himself by the acts of such another person.
Is Consideration for Agency Necessary	No
Test of Agency	The true test of agency lies in answering the question whether a person has the capacity to create contractual relationship between the principal and a third party and to bind the principal by his acts. If the answer to this question is yes, there exists the relationship of agency, otherwise not.

2.0 AGENT

Meaning	An agent is a person employed to do any act for another or to represent another in dealings with third persons. Thus, an agent establishes a contract between such another person and third person.
Who may be an Agent	Any person (whether he has contractual capacity or not) may become an agent. Thus, a minor or a person of unsound mind can also become an agent.
Agent's Responsibility to his Principal	An agent who is not of the age of majority and who is not of sound mind is not responsible to his principal.

3.0 DISTINCTION BETWEEN AN AGENT AND SERVANT

Basis of Distinction	*An agent*	*Servant*
Authority to create contractual relationship	He has the **authority** to create contractual relationship between the principal and a third party.	He ordinarily has **no such authority.**
Work of several persons	He may work **for several** principal at a time.	He ordinarily works **only for one master.**
Remuneration	He usually gets **commission.**	He usually gets **salary or wages.**

4.0 DISTINCTION BETWEEN AN AGENT AND INDEPENDENT CONTRACTOR

Basis of Distinction	*An agent*	*Independent Contractor*
Control and supervision	He works **under the control** and supervision of the principal	He works **independently** of the control of the person for whom he does the work.
Personal liability	He is **not personally liable for all acts** done by him within the scope of his authority.	He is **personally** liable **for all acts done by him.**
Remmuneration	He usually gets **commission.**	He usually gets the **fixed contracted amount or amount** at a fixed contracted rate.

5.0 PRINCIPAL

Meaning	Principal is the person for whom act is done by an agent or who is represented in dealings with third persons by an agent.
Who may employ an Agent?	Any person who is of the age of majority according to the law to which he is subject, and who is of sound mind, may employ an agent. Thus, a minor or a person of unsound mind cannot appoint an agent. It has been held that a guardian of a minor can appoint an agent to minor. [*Madan Lal* v. *Bheru Lal*]

6.0 MODES OF CREATION OF AGENCY

6.1 **Agency by Express Authority**

6.2 **Agency by Implied Authority** Implied Agency includes the following:

(a) Agency by Estoppel

(b) Agency by Holding

(c) Agency by Necessity

6.3 **Agency by Ratification**

6.4 **Agency by Operation of Law**

7.0 AGENCY BY RATIFICATION

Meaning	Agency by ratification is said to arise when a person, on whose behalf the acts are done without his knowledge or authority, expressly or impliedly accepts such acts.
Effect of Ratification	The effect of ratification is to make the agent's unauthorised acts as authorised as if they had been performed with the principal's authority. It may also be noted that **ratification is tantamount to prior authority.** This means that the **ratification relates back to the date when the act was done by the agent and not to the date when the act is ratified by the principal.** Hence, the agency is deemed to have come into existence from the time when the agent first acted and not from the time when the principal ratified the act.
Essentials of a Valid Ratification	1. Valid Ratification can be done in respect of those acts : (a) which constitute whole transaction

	(b) which does not but a third person to damages or terminate any right/interest of a third person (c) which are done by Agent on behalf of another person (d) which are within the powers of principal (e) which are lawful 2. A valid Ratification can be done only by that principal (a) who has full knowledge of all material facts (b) who exists at the time when the act is done (c) who has contractual capacity both at the time of contract and at the time of ratification. 3. A ratification to be valid must be— (a) done within reasonable time (b) communicated to the third party so as to be binding on the third party.

8.0 CAN AN AGENT DELEGATE HIS AUTHORITY?

'delegatus non potest delegare' means an agent cannot lawfully employ another to perform acts which he has expressly or impliedly undertaken to perform personally.

9.0 APPOINTMENT OF SUB-AGENT

Meaning of Sub-agent [Section 191]	A sub-agent is a person who is employed by the original agent and who acts under the control of the original agent in the business of agency. Thus, a sub-agent is the agent of the original agent. As between the original agent and the sub-agent, the relationship is that of the principal and agent.
Effects of Appointment of Sub-agent [Sections 192 and 193]	The effects of appointment of a sub-agent may be discussed under the following two heads: (i) in case of proper appointment (ii) in case of improper appointment

Basis of Comparison	***Where a sub-agent is properly appointed [Section 192]***	***Where a sub-agent is not properly appointed [Section 193]***
Is principal bound	The principal **is bound** to third parties by the acts of sub-agent.	The principal **is not bound** to third parties by the acts of sub-agent.
Is original agent responsible	The original agent is responsible to the principal for the acts of sub agent.	The original agent is responsible for the acts of sub-agent both to the principal and to the third persons.
Is sub-agent responsible	The sub-agent is responsible to the original agent but not to the principal except incase of fraud or wilful wrong.	The sub-agent is responsible to the original agent but not to the principal even in cases of fraud or wilful wrong.

10.0 DISTINCTION BETWEEN SUB-AGENT AND SUBSTITUTED AGENT

Basis of Distinction	*Sub-agent*	*Substituted Agent*
Work	He works under the control of original agent.	He works under the control of principal.
Privity	There is no privity of contract between a sub-agent and principla and hence both cannot sue each other except that in case of fraud or willful wrong committed by a properly appointed sub-agent, the principal can sue sub-agent.	There is a privity of contract between a substituted agent and principal hence both can sue each other.
Original agent's responsibility	The original agent is responsible for the acts or negligence of the sub-agent.	The original agent is not responsible for the acts or negligence of the substituted agent if in selecting such agent he has exercised the same amount of diligence as a man of ordinary prudence would exercise in his own case.

11.0 RIGHTS OF AN AGENT

1. Right of Retainer 2. Right to Receive Remuneration 3. Right of Lien 4. Right to be Indemnified against consequences of Lawful Acts 5. Right to be Indemnified against consequences of acts done in Good Faith 6. Right to Receive Compensation for Injury caused by Principal's neglect

12.0 DUTIES OF AN AGENT

1. to conduct business as per directions or custom of trade 2. to conduct business with reasonable care and skill 3. to render proper Accounts 4. to communicate with Principal 5. to disclose all Material Circumstances and to obtain Principal's consent in personal dealings 6. to pay sum received for Principal 7. to Protect and Preserve the Interest 8. not to Delegate Authority

13.0 PERSONAL LIABILITY OF AN AGENT

General Rule	In the absence of any contract to that effect, an agent cannot personally enforce contract entered into by him on behalf of his principal, nor is he personally bound by them.
When an Agent becomes Personally liable	(a) In case of Foreign Principal (b) In case of Undisclosed Principal (c) In case of Incompetent Principal (d) In case of Principal not in Existence (e) In case of Acts not Ratified (f) In case of Acts in his Own Name (g) In case of Express Agreement (h) In case of Custom or Usage of traded

14.0 MODES OF TERMINATION OF AGENCY

Termination by Act of the Parties	(a) By Mutual Agreement (b) By Revocation of Authority by the Principal (c) By Renunciation of Agency by the Agent
Termination by Operation of Law	(a) On Completion of the Business of the Agency [Section 201] (b) On Death or on Becoming of Unsound Mind of Principal/Agent [Section 201] (c) On Insolvency of the Principal [Section 201] (d) On Winding up of Company (e) On Principal Becoming an Alien Enemy (f) On Expiry of Fixed Period (g) On Destruction of the Subject-matter

15.0 CIRCUMSTANCES WHEN THE AGENCY IS IRREVOCABLE

(a) Where the Agency is Coupled with Interest
(b) Where the Agent has partly exercised his Authority
(c) Where the Agent has incurred a Personal Liability

APPENDIX 2

Important Points to Remember — The Sale of Goods Act, 1930

IMPORTANT POINTS TO REMEMBER

1.0 THE SALE OF GOODS ACT, 1930

Effective Date	It came into force on 1st July, 1930.
Territory	It extends to the Whole of India except the State of Jammu and Kashmir.
Scope	(a) It deals with sale and not with mortgage *or* pledge *or* hypothecation. (b) It deals with goods but not with other movable property (*e.g.*, actionable claims & money) *or* immovable property.
Not Applicable	(a) It does not apply to Hire Purchase Agreement where possession of goods is transferred immediately but ownership of goods is transferred on the payment of last instalment and the hirer has right to terminate the agreement at any time before the transfer of ownership. (b) It does not apply to Contracts for skill and labour where the rendering of the service and exercise of skill is the essence of contract even though there may be delivery of goods.

2.0 CONTRACT OF SALE

Meaning	Contract of sale of goods is a contract whereby the seller transfers or agrees to transfer the property in goods to the buyer for a price.
Essential Elements	1. There must be Seller as well as Buyer. **Note:** *Distribution of goods among partners on account of dissolution of a firm does not amount to a sale of goods by a firm to partners.* 2. There must be some goods.

	3. There must be *either* a transfer of general property (i.e. ownership) of goods *or* an agreement to transfer the general property (i.e. ownership) of goods. 4. There must be a price (i.e. money consideration) **Note:** *The consideration for the contract of sale can be partly in money and partly in goods.* 5. There must exist all essential elements of a valid contract.
Formation	A Contract of Sale may be implied from the conduct of parties or express (i.e. written or oral or partly written and partly oral)
Includes	A Contract of Sale includes: (a) Sale (i.e. where the transfer of ownership of goods takes place immediately) (b) Agreement to Sell (i.e. where the transfer of ownership of goods is to take place at a future time or subject to fulfillment of same condition)

3.0 DISTINCTION BETWEEN SALE AND AGREEMENT TO SELL

A 'Sale' and an 'Agreement to Sell' can be distinguished as follows:

Basis of Distinction	*Sale*	*Agreement to Sell*
1. *Transfer of Owner-ship*	Transfer of ownership of goods takes place ***immediately***.	Transfer of ownership of goods is to take place at a ***future time*** or subject to fulfilment of some condition.
2. *Executed Contract or Executory Contract*	It is an ***executed*** contract because nothing remains to be done.	It is an ***executory*** contract because something remains to be done.
3. *Conveyance of Property*	Buyer *gets a* ***right to enjoy*** the goods against the whole world including seller. Therefore, a sale creates ***jus in rem*** (Right against property).	Buyer does ***not get*** *such right* to enjoy the goods. It only creates ***jus in personam*** (Right against the person).
4. *Transfer of risk*	Transfer of *risk of loss of goods* **takes place immediately** because ownership is transferred. As a result, in case of destruction of goods, the loss shall be borne by the buyer even though the goods are in the possession of the seller.	Transfer of risk of loss of goods **does not take place** because ownership is not transferred. As a result, in case of destruction of goods, the loss shall be borne by the seller even though the goods are in the possession of the buyer.
5. *Rights of Seller against the Buyer's breach*	Seller can *sue* the buyer *for the* ***price*** even though the goods are in his possession.	Seller can sue the buyer *for* ***damages*** even though the goods are in the possession of the buyer.

Basis of Distinction	*Sale*	*Agreement to Sell*
6. ***Rights of Buyer against the Seller's breach***	Buyer can sue the seller *for* ***damages*** and can sue the third party who bought those goods, for goods.	Buyer can sue the seller for damages only.
7. ***Effect of Insolvency of Seller having possession of goods***	Buyer ***can claim*** the goods from the official receiver or assignee because the ownership of goods has transferred to the buyer.	Buyer **cannot claim** the goods even when he has paid the price because the ownership has not transferred to the buyer. The buyer who has paid the price can only claim rateable dividend.
8. ***Effect of insolvency of the buyer before paying the price***	Seller ***must deliver*** the goods to the official receiver or assignee because the ownership of goods has transferred to the buyer. He can only claim rateable dividend for the unpaid price.	Seller **can refuse to deliver** the goods unless he is paid full price of the goods because the ownership has not transferred to the buyer.

4.0 MEANING AND TYPES OF GOODS

Meaning	The term 'Goods' mean every kind of movable property	
	. . . .and Includes	***. . . .but Excludes***
	(a) Stock and Shares (b) Growing crops, Grass & things agreed to be severed under contract of sale	(a) Actionable claims (b) Money (*i.e.*, legal tender) but not old rare coins
1. Existing Goods		
(a) Specific Goods	Which are identified and agreed upon at the time when a contract of sale is made.	
(b) Ascertained Goods	Which are identified and set aside for a given contract out of a mass of unascertained goods.	
(c) Unascertained Goods	Which are not identified and agreed upon at the time when a contract of sale is made	
2. Future Goods	Which are to be produced or acquired by the seller after making of the contract of sale.	
3. Contingent Goods	The acquisition of which by the seller depends upon a contingency which may or may not happen.	

5.0 SALE/AGREEMENT TO SELL

Sale/Agreement to sell	(a) There can be Sale or Agreement to sell in respect of existing goods. (b) There can only be an agreement to sell in respect of future goods and confingent goods.
Discharge of Contracting Parties	(a) The contracting parties are not discharged on non-acquisition or non-production of future goods. (b) The contracting parties are discharged on non-acquisition of contingent goods.
Effect of Destruction of Goods	(a) The contract of sale *or* an agreement to sell specific goods becomes void. (b) The contract of sale *or* an agreement to sell unascertained goods does not become void even if the entire stock of unascertained goods is destroyed *either* before *or* after making agreement.

6.0 PRICE

Fixation Not Necessary at Time of Sale	Price need not necessarily be fixed at the time of sale.
Fixation by 3rd Party	Price may be fixed by a third party.
Reasorable Price	Where the price is not determined in any manner, the buyer must pay the seller a reasonable price.
Void Agreement	Agreement to sell becomes void if price is to be determined by third party & third party cannot or does not make such valuation.
Sue for Damages	Party not at fault may sue for damages where a third party is prevented from making valuation.
Forfeiture	If the contract is not or cannot be performed by buyer's fault, the seller may forfeit earnest money and not advance payment.
Stipulation as to Time	**Stipulation as to time of payment is** not deemed to be as essence of a contract of sale unless **a different intention appears from the terms of the contract.**

7.0 CONDITION

Meaning	A condition is a stipulation: (a) which is essential to the main purpose of the contract, and (b) the breach of which gives the aggrieved party a right to terminate the contract.
Form	It may be express or implied in a contract of sale.
When treated as Warranty	A breach of condition is treated as breach of warranty in the following 3 cases: (a) when buyer waives a condition (b) when buyer elects to treat breach of condition as breach of warranty (c) where the contract is not several and the buyer has accepted the goods or part thereof.

8.0 WARRANTY

Meaning	A warranty is a stipulation: (a) which is collateral to the main purpose of the contract, and (b) the breach of which gives the aggrieved party a right to claim damages but not a right to reject goods and to terminate the contract
Form	It may be express or implied.

9.0 IMPLIED CONDITIONS

1. Condition as to Title	Seller must have right to sell.
2. Condition as to Sale by Description	Goods must correspond with description. whether or not seen by buyer.
3. Condition as to Sale by Sample	Goods must correspond with the sample.
4. Condition as to Sale by Sample and Description	Goods must correspond with the sample and description.
5. Condition as to Quality or Fitness	Goods must be reasonable fit for a particular purpose if the buyer has disclosed the purpose for which goods are required and relied upon the seller's skill or judgement and the seller's business is to sell such goods. (whether or not buyer has examined the goods) **Note:** *An implied condition as to quality or fitness does not apply:* *(a) If the seller is a casual seller and not a dealer.* *(b) If buyer fails to disclose any abnormal circumstances* *(c) If buyer does not rely upon the seller's skill or judgement.* *(d) If buyer buys a specified article under its patent or other trade name.*
6. Condition as to Merchantable Quality	Goods must of merchantable quality (*i.e.* free from any latent or hidden defects) if goods are bought by description from a seller who deals in goods of that description (whether he is manufacturer or not) **Note:** *An implied condition as to Merchantable Quality does not apply for defects which the buyer could have discovered if he had examined the goods.*
7. Condition as to Wholesomeness	Goods must be fit for human consumption. **Note:** *An implied condition as to merchantable quality applies to goods* *(a) whether or not goods are sold under a patent or trade name* *(b) whether or not buyer relies on the skill/judgement of the seller.*

10.0 CAVEAT EMPTOR

Meaning	It means let tshe buyer beware.
No Seller's Duty	A seller need not disclose the defects of his goods.
Buyer's Duty	It is buyer's duty to satisfy himself about the quality as well as the suitability of the goods.
Not Applicable	The rule of caveat emptor does not apply where the buyer has disclosed the purpose for which the goods are required and relied upon the seller's skills or judgement.

11.0 PASSING OF PROPERTY OR TRANSFER OF OWNERSHIP

Case	***Time when Ownership passes...***
1. Specific Goods	
(a) ***Where there is an unconditional contract for sale of specific goods in a deliverable state***	When the contract is made
(b) ***Where there is a contract for sale of specific goods not in a deliverable state***	(i) When the goods are put into a deliverable state, and (ii) The buyer has notice thereof.
(c) ***Where there is a contract for sale of specific goods in a deliverable state but the seller has to do some act to ascertain the price***	(i) When the seller has done that act to ascertain the price, and (ii) The buyer has notice thereof.
2. Unascertained Goods	When goods are (a) ascertained and (b) unconditionally appropriated by the seller/buyer with the consent of the other **Note:** *Such consent may be before or after appropriation.*
3. Goods sent on approval (a) ***When the buyer signifies his approval or acceptance***	When the approval or acceptance is communicated to the seller.
(b) ***When the buyer does some act adopting the transaction (e.g., pledging of such goods)***	When the act of adoption is done.
(c) ***When the buyer fails to return the goods*** (i) ***If a time has been fixed for the return of goods*** (ii) ***If no time has been fixed for the return of goods***	On the expiry of fixed time. On the expiry of the reasonable time
4. Sale of Standing Trees	When trees are felled and ascertained.
5. Where the seller has reserved the right of disposal of goods (*e.g.*, B/E sent with document of title)	When the conditions imposed by the seller are fulfilled (*e.g.*, when B/E is honoured)

12.0 RESERVATION OF RIGHT OF DISPOSAL

Mode	(a) In case of goods deliverable to the order of seller or his agent (*e.g.*, Railway receipt/Bill of lading/Lorry receipt taken in the name of seller or in the name of buyer but sent through bank). (b) In case of drawing of a Bill of Exchange for the price of goods and sending B/E with R/R, L/R or B/L.
T/F of Ownership	The ownership of goods will not be transferred to the buyer unfill the conditions imposed by the seller are fulfilled.

13.0 PASSING OF RISK

When Passes	Risk passes with property or follows ownership.
Who has to Bear	The person whosoever be the owner at the time of occurrence of loss has to bear the loss whether delivery has been made or not.

14.0 SALE BY NON-OWNERS

Exceptions to The rule "No seller of goods can transfer better title to the buyer of the goods than he himself possesses"

1. Sale by a Mercantile Agent	(a) Possession of Goods/Document of title to goods with the consent of owner (b) Sold in ordinary course of business (c) Buyer must have bought in good faith (d) Buyer must have no knowledge that seller had no authority to sell
2. Sale by One of Joint Owners	(a) Sole Possession with consent of other co owners (b) Same as (c) above in 1 (c) Same as (d) above in 1
3. Sale by Person in possession under Voidable Contract	(a) Possession of goods under voidable contract (b) Sold before contract is rescined (c) Same as (c) in 1 (d) Same as (d) in 1
4. Sale by Seller in Possession after Sale	(a) Possession of goods/documents of title to goods as seller not as bailee (b) same as (c) in 1 (c) same as (d) in 1
5. Sale by a Buyer in Possession before transfer of Ownership	(a) Possession of Goods/Document of title with the consent of original seller (b) same as (c) in 1 (c) same as (d) in 1
6. Sale by an Unpaid Seller	On exercising right of lien *or* stoppage in transit

7. Sale by Finder of Goods	(a) Owner could not be found or (b) Owner refuses to pay (c) Goods of perishable nature (d) Lawful charges – 2/3 of value
8. Sale by a Pawnee/Pledgee	
9. Sale by a Official Receiver/ Assignee	
10. Sale by Owner by Estopple	

15.0 DELIVERY

Meaning	Delivery means voluntary transfer of possession from one person to another.
Types	**(a) Actual delivery** – Where goods are physically handed over to the buyer or his authorised agent. **(b) Symbolic Delivery** – Where some symbol of real possession *or* control over goods is handed to buyer or his authorised agent *e.g.*, delivery of key of a warehouse. **(c) Constructive Delivery** – Where a person in possession of goods acknowledges to hold the goods on behalf of the buyer.
Place	Where there is no contract as to the **place of delivery,** the goods are to be delivered at the **place at which goods are at the time of sale**/agreement to sell (in case of **existing goods**) or at the **manufacturing place** (in case of **future goods**)
Time	Where there is no contract as to the **time of delivery**, the goods are to be delivered within **reasonable time**.
Wrong Qty	(a) Where the seller delivers a quantity of goods larger than contracted for, the buyer may accept/reject the whole or accept the contracted and reject the excess. (b) The buyer may not be allowed to reject the whole goods in case of negligible short or excess delivery. (c) In case of short or excess delivery if the buyer rejects the whole quantity, the contract is not treated as cancelled. The seller still has the right to tender again the quantity of goods as per contract and the buyer is bound to accept the same.
Expenses	The expenses of putting the goods into a deliverable state shall be borne by the seller.
Buyer to Apply	Unless otherwise agreed the buyer must apply for delivery
Payment and Delivery	Unless otherwise agreed there must be simultaneous payment of price and delivery of goods.
Delivery by Instalments	Unless otherwise agreed the buyer is not bound to accept delivery by installments.
Part Delivery	Delivery of part of goods with an intention of giving the delivery of the whole amounts to the delivery of the whole of the goods.

Delivery to Carrier	Delivery of the goods to carrier (whether named by the buyer or not) for the purpose of transmission to the buyer, or delivery of the goods to wharfinger custody, is *prime facie* deemed to be a delivery of the goods to the buyer. The seller is further required to perform the following 2 duties also: 1. To make a reasonable contract with the carrier or wharfinger: 2. To give notice to the buyer to enable him to insure goods during sea transit
Acceptance	**Three Circumstances under which Buyer is deemed to have accepted the goods:** 1. When he intimates to the seller that he has accepted the goods, 2. When the goods have been delivered to him and he does any act in relation to them which shows that he has accepted them (for example resale or pledge of goods by buyer), 3. When he does not inform the seller that he has rejected the goods and retains the goods beyond a reasonable time.

16.0 MEANING OF UNPAID SELLER

The seller of goods is deemed to be an 'unpaid seller':

Whole Price Not Paid	When the whole of the price (not other expenses) has not been paid or tendered
Dishonour	When a bill of exchange or other negotiable instrument (such as cheque) has been received as conditional payment, and it has been dishonoured.
Buyer's Insolvency	When the buyer becomes insolvent during the credit period allowed.

17.0 RIGHT OF LIEN

Meaning	The right of lien means the right to retain the possession of the goods until the full price is received.
Circumstances	**Three Crcumstances under which Right of Lien can be exercised:** 1. Where the goods have been sold without any stipulation to credit, 2. Where the goods have been sold on credit, but the term of credit has expired, 3. Where the buyer becomes insolvent.
Possession as Agent	The seller may exercise his right of lien, even if he possesses the goods as agent or bailee for buyer.
Part Delivery	In case of part delivery, this right of lien can be exercised only where part delivery is not intended as delivery of the whole.
Decree for Price	The seller may exercise his right of lien even though he has obtained a decree for the price of the goods.

18.0 RIGHT OF STOPPAGE OF GOODS IN TRANSIT

Meaning	The right of stoppage in transit means the right of stopping the goods while they are in transit, to regain possession and to retain them till the full price is paid. Right of stoppage in transit is an extention of the right of lien.
Conditions	**Three conditions under which Right of Stoppage in Transit can be exercised:** 1. The seller must have parted with the possession of goods, *i.e.*, the goods must not be in the possession of seller. 2. The goods must be in the course of transit. 3. The buyer must have become insolvent.
Duration of Transit	Goods are deemed to be in course of transit from the time when they are delivered to a carrier or other bailee for the purpose of transmission to the buyer, until the buyer or his agent in that behalf takes delivery of them from such carrier or other bailee. **Note:** *The carrier must hold the goods in the capacity of an independent person and not in the capacity of an agent for the seller or buyer.*

19.0 EFFECT OF SUB-SALE OR PLEDGE BY BUYER

General Rule	The unpaid seller's right of lien or stoppage in transit is not affected by any sale or other disposition of the goods by the buyer.
Exceptions	There are **2 exceptions** to the aforesaid rule as under: 1. Where the sub-sale or other disposition by the buyer has been done with the consent of the seller; 2. Where a document of title to goods (*e.g.*, bill of lading or railway receipt) has been issued or lawfully transferred to any person as buyer and that person transfers the document by way of sale to a person who takes the document in good faith and for consideration,.

20.0 RIGHT OF RESALE

Circumstances	**Three circumstances under which an unpaid seller can resell the goods:** 1. Where the goods are of perishable nature, 2. Where the seller expressly reserves a right of resale if the buyer commits a default in making the payment, **Note:** *As a result of this resale, the original contract will be terminated but the seller will have a right to claim damages.* 3. Where the unpaid seller who has exercised his right of lien or stoppage in transit gives a notice to the buyer about his intention to resell and buyer does not pay or tender within a reasonable time.

Rights in Case of Resale	*In Case of Resale after notice*	*In Case of Resale without notice*
1. Unpaid Seller's right to recover the Loss	Available	Not available
2. Original Buyer's right to recover the Profit	Not Available	Available
3. New Buyer's (who buys in resale) right to acquire a good title	Available	Available

21.0 RIGHTS OF SELLER AND BUYER

Rights of Unpaid Seller aginst Buyer	1. Suit for Price 2. Suit for Interest 3. Suit for Damages for Non-Acceptance of Goods 4. Suit for Damages for Repudiation of the Contract
Rights of buyer against Seller	1. Suit for Damages for non-delivery of goods 2. Suit for Specific Performance 3. Suit for Breach of Warranty 4. Suit for Interest, if any advance has given 5. Right to treat the contract as rescinded or operative in case of repudiation of contract by seller before due date

22.0 AUCTION SALE

Meaning	An auction sale is a public sale where intending buyers *(known as bidders)* offer the purchase price *(known as bids)* at which they are ready to buy the goods and the sale is complete when autioneer announces its completion by the fall of hammer or in other customary manner (*e.g.*, by saying 1, 2, 3)
Advertisement	An advertisement to sell the goods by auction is merely an invitation to make an offer to buy and not an offer to sell and the intending buyers have no right to sue the auctioneer if auctioneer cancels or postpones the sale by auction.
Reserve Price	A sale can be ***subject to reserve*** *price* below which the auctioneer will not sell the goods.
Seller's Right to Bid	A seller can reserve a right to bid at auction.
One Puffer	A seller can appoint ***only one puffer*** to raise the bid.
Bidder's Right to Withdraw Bid	A bid once given can be withdrawn before completion of sale.
Voidable Sale	If a seller makes use of pretended bidding to raise the price, the sale is voidable at the option of the buyer.

Right to Refuse Bid	An auctioneer can refuse to accept even the highest bid because 'bid' is only an offer which may or may not be accepted by the auctioneer.
Dampling	Damping which is intended to discourage the bidders from bidding is an unlawful act.
Knock-out Arrangement	A knock-out arrangement between the bidders not to bid against each others is lawful unless it is made to defraud a third party.
Liabilities of an Auctioneer	On the basis of various decision taken by the court, it can be said that an auctioneer is liable for damages in the following cases: 1. If the auctioneer had no authority to sell the goods. [*Anderson* v. *Creall & Sons Ltd.*] 2. If there is a defect in principal's title. [*Benton* v. *Compbell Parker & Co.*] 3. If the auctioneer refuses to give the possession on the payment of the price 4. If the buyer's possession is disturbed by his principal or himself.

APPENDIX 3

Important Points to Remember — The Indian Partnership Act, 1932

IMPORTANT POINTS TO REMEMBER

1.0 THE INDIAN PARTNERSHIP ACT, 1932

Effective Date	It came into force w.e.f. 1st Oct, 1932 but Sec. 69 came into w.e.f. 1st Oct. 1933.
Territory	It extends to the Whole of India except the State of Jammu & Kashmir.
Scope	The provisions of the Indian Contract Act, 1872 also apply to firms except where the Indian Partnership Act, 1932, specifically provides to the contrary [Section 3].

2.0 MEANING AND ESSENTIAL ELEMENTS OF PARTNERSHIP

Meaning of Partnership	"Partnership is the relation between two or more persons who have agreed to share the profits of a business carried on by all or any of them acting for all." [Section 4]
Five Essential Elements of Partnership	1. At least two persons competent to contract 2. An agreement [whether Implied or Express (*i.e.*, written/oral)] 3. Business (Lawful) 4. Sharing of Profits 5. Mutual Agency {*i.e.*, carrying on of business by all or any of them acting for all) **Note:** *The law of partnership is regarded as an extension of law of agency because of existence of mutual agency.*

3.0 PARTNERS, FIRM, FIRM NAME AND MAXIMUM LIMIT OF PARTNERS

Partners	Persons who have entered into partnership with one another are individually called partners.
Firm	Persons who have entered into partnership with one another are collectively called a firm.
Firm Name	The name under which business is carried on is called firm name.
Maximum Limit of Partners	As per Sec. 11 of Companies Act, 1956 – 10 for banking business, 20 for other business **Note:** *1. If the number of partners exceeds the aforesaid limit, the partnership firm becomes an illegal association.* *2. These statutory limits do not apply to a Hindu Undivided Family. However in case of amalgamation of two or more families these limits apply. (only maj`or persons & not minors are considered for these limits)*

4.0 NATURE OF A PARTNERSHIP FIRM AND TEST OF PARTNERSHIP

Nature of Firm	A partnership firm has no separate legal entity apart from the partners constituting it. **Note:** *Firms themselves cannot enter into a contract for partnership though their partners can. For example, two firms namely, M/s A & B and M/s X & Y, themselves cannot form a new partnership though the partners of the individual firms can form a partnership.*
Test of Partnership	The conclusive evidence of partnership is existence of Mutual Agency relationship *i.e.*, the capacity of a partner to bind other partners by his acts done in firm's name and be bound by the acts of other partners in firm's name and not the sharing of profits which is only a prime facie evidence.
Cases where the Partnership Relation does not exist	1. Joint Owners of some property sharing profit or gross returns arising from the property. 2. Person sharing the profits but not having mutual agency. **For example:** (i) a lender of the firm (who has lent money) who receives a share of profits; (ii) a widow or child of a deceased partner who receives a share of profits; (iii) a servant or an agent who receives a share of profits as part of his remuneration; and (iv) a person who receives a share of profits in consideration of sale of business or goodwill of the business. 3. Members of a Hindu Undivided Family carrying on family business. 4. Burmese Buddhist husband and wife carrying on a business.
Property of Firm	Unless otherwise agreed by the partners, the property of the firm shall be held and used by the partners exclusively for the purposes of the business of the firm.

5.0 CO-OWNERSHIP

Meaning	Co-ownership means joint ownership of some property.
Co-owners	Two or more persons who own some property jointly are called co-owners.
Why Not Partners	Joint Owners of some property sharing profit or gross returns arising from the property do not become partners due to lack of mutual agency relationship.

6.0 HINDU UNDIVIDED FAMILY (HUF)

Meaning	"Hindu undivided family is a family which consists of all persons lineally descended from a common ancestor and includes their wives and unmarried daughters."
Coparceners	Three successive generations in the male line (son, grandson, and great-grandson) who inherit the ancestral property are called 'Coparceners'.
Ancestral Property	The property which a man inherits from any of his three immediate male ancestors (*i.e.*, his father, grandfather and great grandfather), is called 'ancestral property'.
Hindu Law	There are two schools of Hindu Law – Dayabhaga and Mitakshara.
Dayabhaga School	Under Dayabhaga School of Law, which is applicable to West Bengal and Assam, a son acquires an interest in the ancestral property only after the death of his father.
Mitakshara School	Under Mitakshara School of Law, which is applicable to whole of India, (except West Bengal and Assam), each son acquires by birth an interest in the ancestral property.
Maximum Limit	There is no maximum limit of coparceners.
Implied Power	Only Karta has implied power.
Karta's Liability	Only Karta's liability is **unlimited.**
Coparcener's Liability	The liability of other coparceners is limited only to their shares in the family property.
Coparcener's Right	The Coparceners have no right to ask for the account of past dealings.
Effect of Death	The Hindu undivided family continues to operate even after the death of a coparcener.

7.0 PARTNERSHIP DEED

Meaning	The document which contains the terms of a partnership as agreed among the partners is called 'Partnership Deed'.
Stamping	It is required to be duly stamped as per the Indian Stamp Act, 1889.
Signature	It is required to be duly signed by all the partners or their duly authorised agents.
Change	The terms laid down in the partnership deed may be changed with the consent of all partners.
No Contravention	It must not contain any term which is contravention with the provisions of the Indian Partnership Act.

8.0 REGISTRATION OF A FIRM

Optional	It is not compulsory.
Time of Registration	It can be effected at the time of its formation or at any time thereafter.
Effective Date	Registration becomes effective **from the date of filing of the duly signed and verified statement** along with the prescribed form and not from the date of issue of certificate of registration since the act of the Registrar in recording an entry of the statement in the Register of Firms is only a clerical act.
Effects of Non-registration of a Firm	1. A partner can not file a suit against the firm or the other artners to enforce any right arising from contract 2. The firm can not file a suit against third party to enforce any right arising from contract. 3. A firm has no right to claim set off in excess of Rs. 100.
Rights not affected by Non-registration	1. ***Rights of unregistered firm or partners thereof*** (i) Right of firm or partner of a firm having no place of business in India, (ii) Right to file a suit or claim of set-off if the value of suit does not exceed Rs. 100. (iii) Right of a partner to sue (a) for the dissolution of the firm (b) for the accounts of a dissolved firm, or (c) for claiming share of the assets of a dissolved firm (iv) Right to enforce a right arising otherwise than out of a contract *e.g.* , infringement of a Patent right by a third party. The firm may file a suit to restrain the third party from misusing the Patent right. 2. ***Right of a third party to file a suit against the unregistered firm or partners thereof.*** 3. ***Power of an Official Assignee or Receiver or Court to realise the property of an insolvent partner.***

9.0 TYPES OF PARTNERSHIP ON THE BASIS OF DURATION

Partnership at Will	**Meaning:** When there is no provision in partnership agreement for duration of the partnership, the partnership is called 'Partnership at Will'. **Dissolution:** A partnership at will may be dissolved by any partner by giving a notice in writing to *all other* partners of his intention to dissolve the firm.
Particular Partnership	**Meaning:** When a partnership is formed for a specific venture or for a particular period, the partnership is called a 'Particular Partnership'. **Dissolution:** Particular partnership comes to an end on the completion of the venture *or* on the expiry of the period. **Note:** *1. If such partnership is continued after the expiry of term or completion of the venture, it is deemed to be a partnership at will.* *2. A particular partnership may be dissolved before the expiry of the term or completion of the venture only by the mutual consent of all the partners.*

10.0 TYPES OF PARTNERS

Actual or Ostensible Partner	He takes an active part in the conduct of the business.
Sleeping or Dormant Partner	He does not take an active part in the conduct of the business.
Nominal Partner	He lends his name to the firm without having any real interest in the firm. He *neither* contributes to the capital *nor* shares the profits or takes part in the conduct of the business of the firm.
Partner in Profits Only	He shares the profits only and not the losses.
Sub-Partner	He is a third person with whom a partner agrees to share his profits derived from the firm.
Partner by Estoppel or Holding Out	A person is held liable as a partner by estoppel or holding out if the following **two** conditions are fulfilled: (a) He must have represented himself to be a partner by words spoken or written or by his conduct (such type of representation may be called as active representation), ***or*** He must have knowingly permitted himself to be represented as a partner (such type of representation may be called as tacit representation); and

	(b) The other person acting on the faith of such representation must have given credit to the firm. It is immaterial whether the person so representing to be a partner, is aware or not that the representation has reached the other person. **Note:** *Where, after the retirement of a partner, the firm uses the retired partner's name as a partner, the retired partner who has not given public notice of his retirement, is held liable on grounds of holding out to third parties who give credit to the firm on the faith that he is still a partner.*
Two Exceptions to the Principle of Holding Out	The Principle of holding out does not apply in the following two cases: 1. **Deceased Partner:** Where, after the death of a partner, the firm uses the deceased partner's name as a partner, the estate of the deceased partner or his legal representatives cannot be held liable for acts of the firm done after his death. It may be noted that a public notice of a partner's death is not required. 2. **Insolvent Partner:** The estate of the insolvent partner cannot be held liable for the acts of the firm done after the date of the order of adjudication [Section 34]. It may be noted that a public notice of a partner's insolvency is not required.

11.0 POSITION OF MINOR AS A PARTNER [SEC. 30]

How can be admitted?	With the consent of all the partners for the time being, a minor may be admitted to the benefits of partnership.	
Rights and Liabilities of a Minor Partner before attaining Majority	***Rights***	***Liabilities***
	1. He has a **right to share the profits and property** of the firm in accordance with the agreement. [Section 30(2)]	1. He is liable only to the extent of his share in the profits and the property of the firm. He is **not personally liable** to third parties. [Section 30(3)]
	2. He has a **right to have access to, and inspect and copy,** any of the accounts of the firm. But he does not enjoy such rights in respect of books other than account books. [Section 30(2)]	2. He **cannot be declared insolvent** on decla-ration of firm's insolvency, his share vests in the Official Receiver or Official Assignee.

	3. He has a **right to file a suit for his share of profits** or the property of the firm when he is not given his due share of profits. However, he can exercise this right only **when he decides to sever his connections with the firm** [Section 30(4)].	
Minor's Duty to give Public Notice	Within 6 months of date of his attaining majority or date of his obtaining knowledge that he had been admitted to the benefits of firm, whichever is later, the minor partner has to exercise his option whether or not to become a partner by giving a public notice within the said 6 months.	
Effect of Minor's failure to give public notice	If he fails to give a public notice, he is **deemed to have become a partner** in the firm on the expiry of the said six months.	
	When he elects to become a partner	***When he elects not to become a partner***
	1. He becomes **personally liable** to third parties for all acts of the firm since he was admitted to the benefits of partnership [Section 30(7)(a)]. 2. His **share** in the property and profits of the firm **remains the same** as he was entitled as a minor [Section 30(7)(b)].	1. **His rights and liabilities continue to be those of minor up to the date of giving public notice** [Section 30(8)(a)]. 2. His **share is not liable** for any acts of the firm done **after the date of the public notice** [Section 30(8)(b)]. 3. He is **entitled to sue the partners** for his share of the property and profits in the firm [Section 30(8)(c)].
	Note: *1. A partnership intially cannot be formed with a minor because before minor's admission there must be an existence of partnership.* *2. There cannot be a partnership consisting of all minors or of one major and all other minors.*	

12.0 MUTUAL RIGHTS AND DUTIES

Mandatary Duties of Partners	(a) Mandatory duties are prescribed by Sec. 9 and 10. (b) Mandatory duties cannot be changed by mutual agreement amongst partners (c) Every partner has the following **four** mandatory duties: 1. *To carry on the business of the firm to the greatest common advantage,* 2. *To be just and faithfull to each other, i.e. every partner should act in good faith. Good faith requires that a partner should not deceive the other partner by concealment of material facts.* 3. *To render true accounts and full information of all things affecting the firm to any partner or his legal representative.* 4. *To indemnify (i.e., to make good or to compensate) the firm for loss caused to it by his fraud in the conduct of the business of the firm.*
General Duties of Partners	(a) The general duties of partners as provided in the Act are subject to the agreement by partners. (b) These can be changed by an agreement amongst the partners. (c) Unless otherwise agreed by the partners, every partner has the following duties: 1. *To attend deligently (i.e., carefully)* 2. *Not to claim remuneration for taking part* 3. *To contribute equally to the losses* 4. *To indemnify the firm for loss due to his wilful neglect.* 5. *To hold and use firm's property for business purpose* 6. *To account for and pay the personal profits from transactions of firm etc.* 7. *To account for and pay the personal profits from a competing business.*
General Rights of Partners	(a) The rights of partners as provided in the Act are subject to the agreement by partners. (b) These rights can be changed by an agreement amongst the partners. (c) Unless otherwise agreed by the partners, every partner has the following rights: 1. *Right to take part in the conduct of the business* 2. *Right to express opinion before the matter is decided* 3. *Right to have access to and to inspect and copy any of the books of the firm.* 4. *Rights to share profits equally* 5. *Right to receive interest on capital out of profits if the partnership agreement provides.* 6. *Right to claim interest on advances if made by him to the firm @ 6% p.a.* 7. Right to be indemnified against the payments made and liabilities incurred by him:

	(i) *in the ordinary and proper conduct of the business, and* (ii) *in doing act in emergency for the purpose of protecting the firm from loss if he has acted in a manner as a person of ordinary prudence would have acted in similar circumstances in his own case.* 8. *Right to prevent the introduction of a new partner without the consent of all the existing partners.* 9. *Right to retire with the consent of all other partners and in the case of a partnership at will, by giving notice to that effect in writing to all the other partners.* 10. *Right not to be expelled from the firm by any majority of partners unless such power is conferred by partnership agreement and is exercised in good faith.* 11. *Outgoing Partner's Right to carry on competing business and to advertise such business. But, he cannot (i) use the firm's name, (ii) represent the firm, or (iii) solicit the firm's customers.* 12. *Right to share subsequent profits as per Sec. 37* 13. *Right to dissolve the partnership with the consent of all partners and in the case of a partnership at will, by giving notice to that effect in writing to all the other partners.*

13.0 RELATION OF PARTNERS WITH THIRD PARTIES [SEC. 18]

Every Partner An Agent	"Every partner is an agent of the firm for the purposes of the business of the firm" every partner has the capacity to bind other partners by his acts done in firm's name. Therefore, all partners are liable to third parties for the acts of every partner done for the purpose of the business of the firm.

14.0 IMPLIED AUTHORITY OF A PARTNER

Partner's Authority	The authority of a partner means the capacity of a partner to bind the firm by his act.
Mode of Authority	Authority of a partner may be express or implied.
Express Authority	The authority conferred on a partner by mutual agreement is called 'express authority'.
Implied Authority	The authority conferred on a partner by the provisions of Section 19 of the Indian Partnership Act is called 'implied authority'.

Conditions for Implied Authority	Reading together Sections 19(1) and 22. Implied authority covers those acts of partners which fulfill the following **three** conditions: 1. *The act must relate to the normal business of the firm;* 2. *The act must have been done in the usual way of carrying on the business of the firm;* *(It may be noted that the question as to what is usual and what is unusual in a business depends on the nature of business and the usage of trade, e.g. taking loan is considered as usual activity in case of a trading concern but unusual activity in case of a professional concern of solicitors.)* 3. *The act must be done in the firm's name or in any other manner expressing or implying an intention to bind the firm.*
Implied Authority includes 9 Acts	An implied authority of a partner of a trading firm include the following acts: 1. *To purchase goods of the kind that are used in the business of the firm;* 2. *To sell the goods of the firm;* 3. *To settle accounts with the persons dealing with the firm;* 4. *To receive payment of the debts due to the firm and issue receipts for the same;* 5. *To engage servants for the business of the firm;* 6. *To engage a lawyer to defend an action brought against the firm;* 7. *To borrow money for the purpose of the firm's business;* 8. *To pledge the goods of the firm as security for the repayment of borrowings made for the purpose of firm's business;* 9. *To draw, accept, endorse Bill of Exchange and other negotiable instruments in the name of the firm.*
Statutory Restrictions	In the absence of any usage or custom of trade to the contrary, the implied authority of a partner does not empower him to do the following **eight acts** namely— 1. *To submit a dispute to arbitration relating to the business of the firm;* 2. *To open a Bank Account on behalf of the firm in partner's own name;*

	3. *To compromise or relinquish any claim or portion of the claim by the firm;* 4. *To withdraw a suit or proceedings filed on behalf of the firm;* 5. *To admit any liability in a suit or proceedings against the firm;* 6. *To acquire immovable property on behalf of the firm;* 7. *To transfer immovable property belonging to the firm; and* 8. *To enter into partnership on behalf of the firm.* **Note:** *A partner can do any of the above-mentioned acts only if he is expressly authorised to do that act or the usage or custom of the trade permits him to do that act.*
No Liability of the Firm to third party for the Restricted Acts of Partner	The firm is not liable to third party for the above mentioned restricted acts of a partner whether or not the person dealing with the firm knew about such restrictions.
Restrictions Imposed by Mutual Agreement	All partners of a firm by mutual agreement may extend or restrict the scope of implied authority of any partner. But a third party is not bound by any such restriction unless it has the knowledge of such restriction. In other words, the firm is liable to third party if the third party has no knowledge of the restrictions.
Any Admission or Representation by a Partner	Any admission or representation (e.g., acknowledgement signed by a partner) by a partner is sufficient evidence against the firm if the following **two** conditions are fulfilled: 1. Such admission or representation must relate to the affairs of the firm; and 2. Such admission or representation must be made in the ordinary course of business.
Notice to Partner operates as Notice to Firm	Any notice to a partner operates as a notice to the firm if the following **three** conditions are fulfilled: 1. Such notice must relate to the affairs of the firm; 2. Such notice must be given to a working partner and not to a sleeping partner. 3. There must not be any fraud committed by the partners and the third party against the firm.
Nature of Partner's Liability	Every partner is liable jointly with other partners and also severally (i.e., individually) for all those acts of the firm which have been done while he was a partner.
Firm's Liability for Wrongful Act/ommission of a Partner	The firm is liable to the same extent as the partner for any loss or injury caused to any third party or any penalty by the wrongful act or omission of a partner if *either* of the following **two** conditions is fulfilled:

<table>
<tr><td></td><td>1. Such wrongful act or omission must have been done by a partner while he was acting in the ordinary course of business of the firm,
2. Such wrongful act or omission must have been done by a partner with the authority of the other partners.
Note: The term 'wrongful act' includes fraud or negligence of the partners.</td></tr>
<tr><td>Firm's Liability for Misappropriation by a Partner</td><td>The firm is liable to the third parties in the following two cases of misappropriation by a partner:
<table>
<tr><th>Case</th><th>Condition</th></tr>
<tr><td>1. Where a partner receives money or property from a third person and misapplies it.</td><td>The receipt of money or other property by a partner must be an act within the scope of his apparent authority.</td></tr>
<tr><td>2. Where a firm, in the course of its business, receives money or property from a third person and the same is misapplied by any of its partners.</td><td>The partner must have misapplied while the property was in the custody of firm.</td></tr>
</table>
</td></tr>
<tr><td>Partner's Authority in an Emergency</td><td>A partner's authority in an emergency covers those acts which fulfil the following two conditions:
1. The act must be done to protect the firm from loss; and
2. The act must be such as a prudent man would undertake under similar circumstances in his own case.
Note: Acts in emergency do not form part of the implied authority of the partner but, nevertheless, they would bind the firm. A partner's authority in an emergency is similar to that of an agent in similar circumstances u/s 189 of the Indian Contract Act.</td></tr>
</table>

15.0 RECONSTITUTION OF A FIRM

<table>
<tr><td>Modes of Reconstitution</td><td>The various ways in which a firm is reconstituted are:
1. Introduction of a Partner
2. Retirement of a Partner
3. Expulsion of a Partner
4. Insolvency of a Partner
5. Death of a Partner
6. Transfer of a Partner's interest</td></tr>
</table>

	Incoming Partner	***Retiring Partner***	***Insolvent Partner***	***Estate of Deceased Partner***
Liability of Partner For Firm's Acts done before	Not liable unless he assumes by tripartite agreement	Liable unless he is discharged by tripartite agreement	Liable	Liable
For Firm's Acts done after	Liable	He continues to be liable to third party (other than one who deals with the firm without knowing that he was a partner) until public notice of his retirement is given *either* by himself *or* any of the other partners. This liability of a retiring partner is based on the principle of holding out.	Not liable after date of order	Not liable after date of death
Is Public Notice required?	No	Yes	No	No
Is Firm dissolved?	No	No	Unless otherwise agreed, Yes	Unless otherwise agreed, Yes
Expulsion of a Partner [Sec 33]	A partner may be expelled if the following **four conditions** are satisfied: 1. the **power** to expel a partner must have existed **in a contract** between the partners; 2. the power must have been exercised by a **majority** of the partners, and 3. the power must have been exercised in **good faith** without any private animosity. 4. The affected partner must be given an **opportunity to make a representation** before being dismissed. **Note:** *The rights and liabilities of an expelled partner are the same as those of a retired partner.*			
Rights of Transferee of a Partner's Share	A partner may transfer his interest in the firm by sale, mortgage or charge fully or partially. The rights of such a transferee are as follows:			

	(a) During the continuance of the partnership	• **He is entitled to receive:** (a) the share of the profits of the transferring partner and (b) the account of profits agreed to by the partners. • **He is not entitled:** (a) to interfere with the conduct of the business (b) to require accounts; (c) to inspect the books of the firm.
	(b) On the dissolution of firm or on the retirement of the transferring partner	**He is entitled to receive:** (a) the share of the assets of the transferring partner and (b) an account as from the date of the dissolution for the purpose of ascertaining the share.
Revocation of Continuing Guarantee from Date of Change	Unless otherwise agreed by the partners, a continuing guarantee (*i.e.*, a guarantee which extends to a series of transactions) given to a firm or to a third party in respect of the transaction of a firm is revoked as to the future transactions from the date of any change in the constitution of the firm.	
Rights and Duties of Partners	The **rights and duties of the partners of the reconstituted firm** shall be the same as they were before the change in the firm. Section 17 provides for the following **three types of changes** in the firm: (a) Where there is a change in the Constitution of the firm. (b) Where the firm continues after the expiry of the term of the firm. (c) Where the firm carries on an additional undertaking.	

16.0 DISSOLUTION OF FIRM

Meaning of Dissolution	The term 'dissolution' stands for discontinuation. Under the Indian Partnership Act, 1932, the dissolution may be *either* of Partnership *or* of a firm.
Meaning of Dissolution of Partnership	Dissolution of partnership refers to the change in the existing relations of the partners. The firm continues its business after being reconstituted.

Modes of Dissolution of Partnership	1. Admission of a new partner 2. Retirement of a partner 3. Death of a partner 4. Change in profit sharing ratio	
Meaning of Dissolution of Firm	It means dissolution of partnership between all the partners of a firm.	
Modes of Dissolution of Firm	***Without Court's Order***	***By Court's order***
	1. By Mutual Agreement 2. Compulsory Dissolution (a) If all or all but one partner are declared insolvent (b) If some event takes place which makes it unlawful for firm's business to be carried on 3. On happening of certain contingencies – Unless otherwise agreed by partners. (a) On Expiry of fixed term (b) On Completion of venture (c) On Death of a partner (d) On Insolvency of a partner 4. By Notice in writing to all in case of partnership at will	On the following grounds: 1. Insanity of active partner on petition by any other partner or next friend of insane partner 2. Permanent incapacity of Active Partner on a suit by any other partner 3. Misconduct on a suit by any other partner 4. Wilfully or Persistent Breach of Agreement on a suit by any other partner 5. Transfer of whole Interest to a third party 6. Perpetual Losses 7. Any other just and equitable ground
Rights of a Partner on Dissolution	1. Partner's General Lien 2. Right to Claim the Return of Premium on Premature Winding Up 3. Rights of a Partner in Case of Dissolution on Account of Fraud or Misrepresentation 4. Right to Restrain from Use of Firm Name or Firm Property	
Liabilities of a Partner on Dissolution	In general Liability for Acts of Partners done after Dissolution continues: **Exceptions:** Following are not liable for acts of partners done after dissolution. 1. the Estate of a Deceased Partner; 2. the Estate of an Insolvent Partner; 3. a Sleeping or Dormant Partner who has retired from the firm.	
Continuing Authority of Partners After Dissolution	1. to wind up the affairs of the firm, and 2. to complete the unfinished transactions pending at the date of dissolution.	

17.0 SETTLEMENT OF ACCOUNTS

<table>
<tr><td>Treatment of Losses</td><td colspan="3">Losses including deficiencies of capital are to be paid in the following manner:
(i) First out of profits;
(ii) Then out of capital;
(iii) Lastly by partners individually in their profit-sharing ratio. [Section 48(a)]</td></tr>
<tr><td>Application of Assets</td><td colspan="3">The assets of the firm (including the sums, if any, contributed by the partners to make up the deficiencies of capital) shall be applied in the following manner and order:
(i) in paying firm's debts to the third parties;
(ii) in paying to each partner rateably what is due to him on account of advances;
(iii) in paying to each partner rateably what is due to him on account of capital;
(iv) the residue, if any, shall be divided among the partners in their profit-sharing ratio. [Section 48(b)].</td></tr>
<tr><td rowspan="5">Payment of Firm's Debts and Partner's Private Debts</td><td>Basis of Distinction</td><td>Firm's Debts</td><td>Private Debts</td></tr>
<tr><td>1. Who incurs</td><td>Private debts are incurred by in the individual capacity of a household and not in the capacity capacity of a partner of a firm.</td><td>Firm's debts are incurred a partner partner by the firm.</td></tr>
<tr><td>2. Who is liable</td><td>For private debts, only the debts, concerned partner is liable.</td><td>For firm's debts, all partners are jointly and severally liable.</td></tr>
<tr><td>3. Application of firm's property</td><td>For private debts, only the share of concerned partner in the excess of firm's property over firm's debts can be applied.</td><td>For firm's debts, firm's property shall be applied first.</td></tr>
<tr><td>4. Application of private property</td><td>For private debts, private property shall be applied first.</td><td>For firm's debts, only the excess of of partner's private property over his private debts canbe applied.</td></tr>
</table>

Decision in *Garner* v. *Murray* requires	1. that the solvent partners should bring in cash equal to their respective shares of the loss on realisation; 2. that the solvent partners should bear the loss arising due to the insolvency of a partner in the ratio of their Last Agreed Capitals.
Sale of Goodwill	Unless otherwise agreed by the partners, the goodwill shall be included in the assets and may be sold *either* separately *or* alongwith other property of the firm.

18.0 PUBLIC NOTICE

<table>
<tr><td>When required</td><td colspan="2">1. on the Retirement or Expulsion of a partner,
2. on the Dissolution of the Firm,
3. on the Election to become or not to become a partner By a Minor on his attaining majority.</td></tr>
<tr><td>When not required</td><td colspan="2">1. on the Death of a Partner;
2. on the Insolvency of a Partner.</td></tr>
<tr><td rowspan="4">Mode of Giving Public Notice</td><td>In Case of a Registered Firm</td><td>In Case of an Unregistered Firm</td></tr>
<tr><td>(a) in the Official Gazette.</td><td>(a) in the Official Gazette.</td></tr>
<tr><td>(b) in at least one vernacular newspaper</td><td>(b) in at one vernacular newspaper</td></tr>
<tr><td>(c) to the Registrar of Firms.</td><td></td></tr>
<tr><td rowspan="5">Consequences of Not Giving a Public Notice</td><td>Case</td><td>Consequences</td></tr>
<tr><td>(a) On Election to become or not to become a partner by a Minor on his attaining majority</td><td>Minor is deemed to have become a partner on the expiry of said 6 months [Section 30(5)].</td></tr>
<tr><td>(b) On Retirement of a Partner</td><td>Retiring partner and the other partners continues to be liable as partner to the third parties for firm's acts done after retirement [Section 32(3)].</td></tr>
<tr><td>(c) On Expulsion of at Partner</td><td>The expelled partner and the other partners continue to be liable to third parties for firm's acts done after his expulsion [Section 33(2)].</td></tr>
<tr><td>(d) On Dissolution of a Firm</td><td>All the partners continue to be liable to third parties for firm's acts done after the dissolution of firm [Section 45].</td></tr>
</table>

19.0 CONSENT OF PARTNERS REQUIRED

To Expell any Partner	Consent of Majority of partners
To Change the Nature of the Firm's Business	Consent of All Partners
To Change the Terms of Partnership	Consent of All Partners
To Admit Minor	Consent of All Partners
To Introduce a New Partner	Consent of All Partners
To Retire From a Particular Partnership	Consent of All Partners
To Dissolve Particular Partnership	Consent of All Partners

APPENDIX 4

Important Points to Remember — The Negotiable Instruments Act, 1881

THE NEGOTIABLE INSTRUMENTS ACT, 1881 (PART I)

1.0 NEGOTIABLE INSTRUMENT

Meaning	Negotiable Instrument means a promissory note, bill of exchange or cheque, payable *either* to order *or* to the bearer.
Characteristics	(a) Payable to Order or Bearer (b) Freely Transferable (c) Presumption as to Holder (d) Title of Holder in due Course Free from all Defects (e) Presumption as to Consideration
Payable to Order	A promissory note, bill of exchange or cheque is payable to order if, (a) It is expressed to be so payable, *or* (b) It is expressed to be payable to a particular person and it does not contain words which prohibit transfer or indicate an intention that it shall not be transferable.
Payable to Bearer	A promissory note, bill of exchange or cheque is payable to bearer if, (a) It is expressed to be so payable, *or* (b) The only or last endorsement is an endorsement in blank.
Eight Presumptions	(a) Of Consideration (b) As to date (c) As to time of acceptance (d) As to time of transfer (e) As to time of endorsement (f) As to Stamp (g) As to holder in due course (h) As to protest
Types	1. Bearer 2. Order 3. Inland 4. Foreign 5. Ambiguous 6. Inchoate 7. Demand 8. Time 9. Accomodation 10. Fictitious 11. Documentary 12. Clean 13. Escrow 14. Bills in sets

2.0 PROMISSORY NOTE

Meaning	"A promissory note is an instrument in writing (not being a bank note or a currency note) containing an **unconditional undertaking**, signed by the maker to pay a certain sum of money only to, or to the order of a certain person or to the bearer of the instrument." [Sec 4]

Characteristics	1. In writing 2. Express promise to pay 3. Definite and unconditional Promise 4. Signed by the maker 5. Promise to pay certain sum 6. Promise to pay money only 7. Certain payee

3.0 BILL OF EXCHANGE

Meaning	"A bill of exchange is an instrument in writing containing an **unconditional order** signed by the maker directing a certain person to pay a certain sum of money only to, or to the order of a certain person or the bearer of the instrument." [Sec 5]
Characteristics	1. In writing 2. Express order to pay 3. Definite and unconditional Order 4. Signed by the drawer 5. Order to pay certain sum 6. Order to pay money only 7. Certain three parties

4.0 ACCEPTANCE

Essentials	1. Written 2. Signed 3. On the bill 4. Delivery
Types	Acceptance may be *either* general *or* qualified.

5.0 DISTINCTION BETWEEN B/E & PROMISSORY NOTE

Basis of Distinction	***A Bill of Exchange***	***A Promissory Note***
No. of Parties	There are **three** parties—drawer, drawee and payee.	There are **two** parties—maker and payee.
Promise/order	It contains an unconditional **order** given by a creditor to a debtor.	It contains an unconditional **promise** given by a debtor to a creditor.
Nature of liability	The liablity of the drawer is **secondary and conditional.**	The liability of the maker is **primary and absolute.**
Acceptance	It **requires** acceptance to become a valuable instrument.	It **does not require** any acceptance since it is a valuable instrument right from te beginning.
Same identity of payor and payee	The drawer and payee **may be** the same person.	The maker and payee **cannot be** the same person.
Payable to bearer	It **can be** payable to bearer. It cannot be drawen as payable to bearer on demand.	It **cannot be** payable to bearer.

Protest of dishonour	It **requires** the protesting for dishonour.	It **does not** *require* any protesting.
Notice of dishonour	Notice for dishonour **must** be given to all persons (including drawer) liable to pay.	Such notice is ***not required*** to be given to the maker.

6.0 CHEQUE

Meaning	A cheque is a bill of exchange which is (a) drawn upon a specified banker, and (b) payable on demand. [Sec 6]
Characteristics	1. In writing 2. Express order to pay 3. Definite and unconditional order 4. Signed by the drawer 5. Order to pay certain sum 6. Order to pay money only 7. Certain three parties 8. Drawn upon a specified banker 9. Payable on demand.

7.0 DISTINCTION BETWEEN A CHEQUE AND A B/E

Basis of Distinction	***A Cheque***	***A Bill of Exchange***
Drawer	It is always drawn on a **bank.**	It can be drawn upon **any person** (Including a bank.)
Payable on demand	It is **always** payable on demand.	It **need not** always be payable on demand.
Payable to bearer on demand	It ***can be*** drawn payable to bearer on deman.	It **can not** be payable to bearer on demand [Section 31 of the Reserve Bank of India Act, 1934]
Acceptance	It does **not require** an acceptance.	It **requires** an acceptance of the drawee.
Stamp	It does **not require** a stamp.	It requires a stamp.
Three days of grace	It is **not entitled** to three days of grace.	A bill, unless payable on demand is **entitled** to three days of grace.
Crossing	It **can be** crossed.	It **cannot** be crossed.
Fixed Form	Its **fixed from** is honoured by a banker.	There is **no fixed form.**
Notice of dishonour	Notice of dishonour is **not required.**	Notice of dishonour is usually **required.**
Counter-manding	It **can be revoked** by countermanding of payment.	It **cannot be** countermanded.

16.0 CROSSING

Meaning	The Crossing of a Cheque is an instance of an alteration which is authorised by the Act. A cheque is said to be crossed when it bears across its face two parallel transverse lines which are usually drawn on the left hand top corner of the cheque.
Purpose	The purpose of Crossing is to direct the drawee (banker) to pay the amount of cheque only to a banker so that the party who receives the payment of the cheque can be easily traced.
General Crossing	A Cheque is said to be crossed generally where it bears across its face an addition of **two parallel transverse lines with or without** the following words : (a) 'And Company' (b) & Co. (c) Not Negotiable
Special Crossing	A cheque is said to be crossed specially where it bears across its face an addition of the **name of banker with or without** transverse lines or the following words: (a) 'And Company' (b) & Co. (c) Not Negotiable
Can a Cheque be Crossed Specially more than Once?–	Yes

9.0 BOUNCING OR DISHONOUR OF CHEQUE

Meaning	A cheque is said to be bounced or dishonoured by non-payment when the drawee of the cheque makes default in payment upon being duly required to pay the same.
Liability of Drawee [Sec. 31]	The drawee of a cheque must compensate the drawer for any loss or damage caused by non-payment if the following **three conditions** are fulfilled: (a) If the drawee has sufficient **funds of the drawer in his hands;** (b) If the funds are properly applicable to such payment. (c) If the drawee is duly required to pay the cheque. [Sec. 31]
Liability of Drawer [Section 138]	On dishonour of a cheque, the drawer is punishable with **imprisonment** for a term upto **2 years** *or* with **fine not exceeding twice the amount** of a cheque or with both if 5 **conditions** are fulfilled: (a) If the cheque was drawn to discharge a **legally enforceable debt** or other liability; (b) If the cheque is returned by the bank unpaid due to **insufficiency of funds** in the account of drawer; (c) If the cheque has been **presented** to the bank **within** a period of **6 months** from the date on which it is drawn or within the period of its validity, whichever is earlier; (d) If the payee or the holder in due course of the cheque has made a **demand** for the payment of the said amount of money **by giving a notice, in writing,** to the drawer of the cheque **within 30 days of the receipt of information** by him from the bank regarding the return of the cheque as unpaid; and

	(e) If the drawer of such cheque has **failed to make the payment** of the said amount of money to the payee or to the holder in due course of the cheque, **within 30 days of the receipt of the said notice.**
When a Banker *must* refuse to honour	(a) Stop payment (b) Garnishee order (c) Death (d) Insolvency (e) Insanity (f) Assignment (g) Defect in title (h) Loss of Cheque (i) Unauthenticated Material alteration (j) Different signature (k) Notice of closure (l) Irregular endorsement
When a Banker *may* Refuse to Honour	A banker *may* refuse to honour a customer's cheque in the following cases: (a) Insufficient funds (e) Stale cheque (b) Funds not applicable (f) Post dated cheque (c) Presentment at different branch (g) Undated cheque (d) Presentment after banking hours

10.0 HOLDER & HOLDER IN DUE COURSE

Holder [Sec. 8]	A person is called holder of a negotiable instrument if he satisfies the following **two** conditions: (a) He must be entitled to the possession of the instrument in his own name: and (b) He must be entitled to receive/recover the amount due on the instrument from the parties liable under the instrument.
Holder in due Course [Sec. 9]	A person is called a holder in due course if he satisfies the following conditions: (a) Holder (b) For consideration (c) Before its maturity (d) In Good faith (e) Complete and regular on the face of it.
Privileges of Holder in due Course	1. In case of Inchoate Stamped Instrument [Section 20] 2. Liability of prior parties [Section 36] 3. In case of fictious parties to bill [Section 42] 4. In case of instruments without consideration [Section 43] 5. In case of conditional delivery [Section 46] 6. Protection to subsequent holders [Section 53] 7. In case of instrument obtained by unlawful means or for unlawful consideration [Section 58] 8. Estopple against denying original validity of instrument [Section 120] 9. Estoppel against denying capacity of payee to endorse [Section 121]

11.0 DISTINCTION BETWEEN HOLDER & HOLDER IN DUE COURSE

Basis of Distinction	*Holder*	*Holder in due Course*
Consideration	He may become the possessor or payee of an instrument **even without** consideration.	He acquires possession **for consideration.**
Possessor Before maturity	He **need not** become the possessor before the maturity of the instrument.	He must become the possessor **before** the maturity of the instrument.
Good faith	He **need not** become the possessor in good faith	He **must** become the possessor in good faith, i.e. without having sufficient cause to believe that any defect existed in the transferor's title.
Right to have better title than that of transferor	He **cannot** have a better title than of transferor.	He **can have** a better title than that of transferor.
Right to enforce rigthts against all prior parties.	He **cannot** enforce his rights against all the prior parties. He can recover the amount from a person who has signed it and also from the trasferror from whom he obtained.	He **can** enforce his rights against all the prior parties.
Privilleges	He **does not enjoy** all the privileges available to holder in due course	He **enjoys** some privileges under the Act, for example under Sections 20, 36, 42, 43, 46, 58, 120, 121.

12.0 THREE CONDITIONS FOR PAYMENT IN DUE COURSE

1. The payment must be in accordance with the apparent tenor of the instrument
2. The person to whom payment is made must be in possession of the instrument
3. The payment must be made in good faith.

13.0 NEGOTIATION AND ASSIGNMENT

Meaning of Negotiation	An instrument is said to be negotiated when a promissory note, bill of exchange or cheque is transferred to any person so as to constitute that person the holder of the instrument. Thus, the essence of the negotiation is that it must be made with the intention of transferring a title of the instrument to the transferee.
Two Methods of Effecting Negotiation	1. By Delivery, 2. By Endorsement and Delivery.

Duration of Negotiability [Sec. 60]	A negotiable instrument may be negotiated: (a) By person other than the maker, drawer or acceptor until payment. (b) By the maker, drawer or acceptor until maturity.
Meaning of Assignment	An instrument is said to be assigned when a promissory note, bill of exchange or cheque is transferred by means of a **written and registered document** under the provisions of the Transfer of Property Act, 1882. The person who transfers his right to recover the payment of a debt is called an assignor and the person to whom such rights are transferred is called an assignee. The assignee takes the instrument subject to all equities which arise between the party liable and the assignor. Thus, the assignee gets the rights of the assignor only. He does not get the rights of a holder in due course.

14.0 BASIS OF DISTINCTION BETWEEN NEGOTIATION AND ASSIGNMENT

Basis of Distinction	***Negotiation***	***Assignment***
Consideration	Consideration presumed. [Section 118]	Consideration is to be proved.
How to effect	Bearer instruments are negotiated by mere delivery, and instruments order are negotiated by endorsement and delivery.	Assignment is done always by means of a written and registered document under the provisions of Transfer of Property Act, 1882.
Where to effect	Negotiation can be done in respect of **negotiable instruments only.**	Assignment can be done in case of **other documents** in addition to negotiable instruments.
Notice	Notice of transfer to the debtor by the transferee is **not necessary.**	An assignment does not bind the debtor unless notice of assignment has been given by the assignee to the debtor and the debtor in turn expressly or impliedly, has assented.
Title	The transferee acquires **a title better than that of transferor.**	The assignor **does not acquire a title better than that of the assignor** because the title of the assignee is subject to all equities in the title of assignor. In other words, assignee gets the right of assignor only.
Stamp Duty	It does not requires any stamp duty.	It requires payment of stamp duty.

15.0 ENDORSEMENT

Meaning	The process of transferring an instrument is called an endorsement.
Essential Requirements	(a) It must be on the back or face of instrument or on a slip of paper (caller allonge) annexed thereto. (b) It must be signed by the endorser. (c) It must be completed by the delivery of the instrument. (d) It must be made by the holder of the instrument.
Kinds of Endorsement	The meaning and specimen of various kinds of endorsements have been discussed as follows: 1. General 2. Special 3. Restrictive 4. Partial 5. Conditional
Negotiation Back	An instrument is said to be negotiated back to the holder when an endorser, after he has negotiated an instrument, again becomes its holder before its maturity.

14.0 MATERIAL ALTERATION

Meaning	An alteration can be called a material alteration if it alters or attempts to alter the character of the instrument and affects or is likely to affect the contract which the instrument contains or is evidence of. Thus, it totally alters the business effect of the instrument. It makes the instrument speak a language other than that intended.
Material Alterations Authorised by the Act [Sec. 20, 49, 125]	(a) Filling blanks of inchoate instruments (b) Conversion of a blank endorsement into an endorsement in full (c) Crossing of cheques

THE NEGOTIABLE INSTRUMENTS ACT, 1881 (PART II)

1.0 DISTINCTION BETWEEN THE LIABILITY OF DRAWER OF A BILL AND LIABILITY OF ACCEPTOR OF A BILL OR MAKER OF A NOTE

Basis of Distinction	*Liability of Drawer*	*Liability of Acceptor of bill or maker of a note*
Primary or Secondary	The liability of drawer after acceptance is secondary as surety.	The liability of acceptor of a bill or maker of a note is primary as a principal debtor.
Conditional or Uncoditional	The liability of drawer is conditional, in the sense that is arises only in the even of dishonour.	The liability of acceptor of a bill or maker of a note is unconditional and is not dependent on the notice of dishonour.

2.0 DISTINCTION BETWEEN DISHONOUR BY NON-ACCEPTANCE AND BY NON-PAYMENT

On dishonour by non-acceptance, the drawee cannot be sued because he is not a party to the bill, whereas on dishonour by non-payment, the drawee can be sued.

3.0 IMPORTANT TERMS

Noting	Noting is a mode of authenting the fact that a bill or note has been dishonoured.
Protest	Protest is a formal certificate issued by the Notary Public about the dishonour of a bill or note.
Drawee in Case of Need	When in the bill or in any endorsement thereon the name of any person is given in addition to the drawee to be resorted to in case of need, such person is called a "drawee in case of need".
In Case of Need	In Case of need means in the event of the bill being dishonoured by the drawee by non-acceptance or non-payment.
Presentment	Presentment means placing negotiable instrument before a drawee for acceptance or for sight or for payment.
Presentment for Payment	Presentment for payment implies presenting an instrument to the party for payment.

4.0 DISCHARGE OF AN INSTRUMENT

Meaning	An instrument is said to be discharged only *when* ***the party who is ultimately liable thereon is discharged from liability***. All rights of action under the instrument are completely extinguished and the instrument ceases to be negotiable.
Modes	(a) By Payment in due Course (b) By Cancellation (c) By Release (d) By Party Primarily Liable becoming Holder

5.0 DISCHARGE OF A PARTY

Meaning	A party is said to be discharged only when a party or parties (other than a party ultimately liable on instrument) to a negotiable instrument is or are discharged and the instrument continues to be negotiable with the liabilities of undischarged parties attaching thereto.
Modes	(a) By Payment (b) By Cancellation (c) By Release (d) By Allowing Drawee more than 48 hours to Accept (e) By Non-presentment of Cheque within a Reasonable time (f) By Payment of a Cheque Payable to Order or Bearer by the Drawee Banker (g) By Qualified Acceptance (h) By Material Alteration (j) By Acceptor becoming Holder of a Bill at or after Maturity (k) By Operation of Law

6.0 DISTINCTION BETWEEN DISCHARGE OF AN INSTRUMENT AND DISCHARGE OF A PARTY

Basis of Distinction	*Discharge of an Instrument*	*Discharge of a Party*
When takes place	When the party who is ultimately liable, is discharged from liability.	When any party or parties to an instrument is/are discharged.
Negotiability	The instrument ceases to be negotiable.	The instrument continues to be negotiable.
Extinguishment of all rights of action	All rights of action under the instrument are completely extinguished.	All rights of action under the instrument are not completely extinguished.
Discharge of all parties	Discharged of an instrument means discharge of all parties.	Discharge of a party does not mean discharge of all parties.

7.0 HUNDI

Meaning	Hundi is a negotiable instrument drawn in an oriental or vernacular language. The Negotiable Instrument Act, 1872 is ordinarily not applicable to hundies but the parties to the Hundies may agree to be governed by the Negotiable Instrument Act. A hundi may be accepted orally as per local usage. A hundi is assignable without any regular form of endorsement. A hundi is not necessarily a bill of exchange as defined in the Act.
Types	(a) Shahjog Hundi (b) Nam Jog Hundi (c) Dhani Jog Hundi (d) Jokhmi Hundi (e) Jawabee Hundi (f) Zikri Hundi (or Zikri Chit) (g) Darshni Hundi (h) Miadi Hundi (or Muddati Hundi) (i) Peth (j) Perpeth (k) Khoka

APPENDIX 5

Important Points to Remember — The Information Technology Act, 2000

THE INFORMATION TECHNOLOGY ACT, 2000

1.0 IMPORTANT DEFINITIONS

Addressee	Means a person who is intended by the originator to receive the electronic record but does not include any intermediary;
Originator	Means a person who sends, generates, stores or transmits any electronic message; or causes any electronic message to be sent, generated, stored or transmitted to any other person but does not include an intermediary;
Subscriber	Means a person in whose name the Electronic Signature Certificate is issued;
Intermediary	With respect to any particular electronic records, means any person who on behalf of another person receives, stores or transmits that record or provides any service with respect to that record and includes telecom service providers, network service providers, internet service providers, web hosting service providers, search engines, online payment sites, online-auction sites, online market places and cyber cafes.
Key pair	In an asymmetric crypto system, means a private key and its mathematically related public key, which are so related that the public key can verify a digital signature created by the private key;
Private key	Means the key of a key pair used to create a digital signature;
Public key	Means the key of a key pair used to verify a digital signature and listed in the Digital Signature Certificate;
Asymmetric crypto system	Means a system of a secure key pair consisting of a private key for creating a digital signature and a public key to verify the digital signature;
Digital signature	Means authentication of any electronic record by a subscriber by means of an electronic method or procedure in accordance with the provisions of section 3;
Digital Signature Certificate	means a Digital Signature Certificate issued under Sec. 35(4);

Verify	In relation to a digital signature, electronic record or public key, with its grammatical variations and cognate expressions means to determine whether (a) the initial electronic record was affixed with the digital signature by the use of private key corresponding to the public key of the subscriber; (b) the initial electronic record is retained intact or has been altered since such electronic record was so affixed with the digital signature. (2) Any reference in this Act to any enactment or any provision thereof shall, in relation to an area in which such enactment or such provision is not in force, be construed as a reference to the corresponding law or the relevant provision of the corresponding law, if any, in force in that area.
Affixing Electronic signature	With its grammatical variations and cognate expressions means adoption, of any methodology or procedure by a person for the purpose of authenticating an electronic record by means of Electronic Signature;
Certification Practice Statement	Means a statement issued by a Certifying Authority to specify the practices that the Certifying Authority employs in issuing Electronic Signature Certificates;
Secure system	Means computer hardware, software, and procedure that– (a) are reasonably secure from unauthorised access and misuse; (b) provide a reasonable level of reliability and correct operation; (c) are reasonably suited to performing the intended functions; and (d) adhere to generally accepted security procedures;

2.0 HOW IS DIGITAL SIGNATURE CREATED? [SEC 3]

The digital signature is created in two distinct steps:

1. Hash Function 2. Asymmetric Crypto System

3.0 PROVISIONS RELATING TO ELECTRONIC GOVERNANCE

1. Legal Recognition of Electronic Records
2. Legal Recognition of Digital Signatures
3. Use in Government and its Agencies
4. Delivery of Services by Service Provider.
5. Retention of Electronic Records
6. Audit of documents etc. in Electronic form.
7. Publication of Rules, Regulations, etc., in Electronic Gazette
8. No Right to insist that the Document should be accepted in Electronic Form
9. Power of Central Government to make Rules
10. Validity of contracts formed through electronic means.

4.0 PROVISIONS RELATING TO APPLICATION FOR THE ISSUE OF DIGITAL SIGNATURE CERTIFICATE

1. Application to Certifying Authority
2. Application must be accompained by

(a) fee not exceeding Rs. 25,000.

(b) a Certification Practice Statement.

5.0 DIGITAL SIGNATURE CERTIFICATE

Conditions for Grant	No Digital Signature Certificate shall be granted unless the Certifying Authority is satisfied that— (a) the applicant holds the private key corresponding to the public key to listed in the Digital Signature Certificate; (b) the applicant holds a private key, which is capable of creating a digital signature; (c) the public key to be listed in the certificate can be used to verify a digital signature affixed by the private key held by the applicant.
Suspension of Digital Signature Certificate	The Certifying Authority which has issued a Digital Signature Certificate may suspend such Digital Signature Certificate— (a) on receipt of a **request** to that effect from– (i) the subscriber listed in the Digital Signature Certificate; (ii) any person duly authorised to act on behalf of that subscriber; (b) if it is of **opinion** that the Digital Signature Certificate should be suspended in public interest.
Revocation of Digital Signature Certificate	A Certifying Authority may revoke a Digital Signature Certificate issued by it– (a) where the subscriber or any other person authorised by him makes a **request** to that effect; or (b) upon the **death** of the subscriber; or (c) upon the **dissolution** of the firm or winding up of the company where the subscriber is a firm or a company. (d) where it is of **opinion** that– (i) a material fact represented in the Digital Signature Certificate is false or has been concealed; (ii) a requirement for issuance of the Digital Signature Certificate was not satisfied; (iii) the Certifying Autority's private key or security system was compromised in a manner materially affecting the Digital Signature Certificate's reliability; (iv) the subscriber has been declared insolvent or dead or where a subscriber is a firm or company, which has been dissolved, wound-up or otherwise ceased to exist.

6.0 DUTIES OF SUBSCRIBERS

1. Generating Key Pair
2. Acceptance of Digital Signature Certificate
3. Control of Private Key
4. Communication

7.0 PENALTY FOR DAMAGE TO COMPUTER, COMPUTER SYSTEM. ETC

Max. 1 Crore

8.0 PENALTY FOR DEFAULTS

Default	*Maximum Penalty*
1. ***For failure to furnish any document, return or report to the Controller or the Certifying Authority [Sec. 44(a)]***	Rs 1,50,000 for each default
2. ***For failure to file any return or furnish any information, books or other documents within the specified time [Sec. 44(b)]***	Rs 5,000 for every day during which such failure continues
3. ***For failure to maintain books of account or records [Sec. 44(c)]***	Rs 10,000 for every day during which the failure continues
4. ***For the contravention of any rules or regulations for which no specific penalty has been separately provided [Sec. 45]***	The person who contravens shall be liable to pay a compensation not exceeding Rs 25,000 to the person affected by such contravention or a penalty not exceeding Rs 25,000

9.0 THE CYBER REGULATIONS APPELLATE TRIBUNAL [CRAT]

Who can establish	The Central Government
Composition	Chairperson and such other members as appointed by Central Government.
Qualification	**For Chairperson**–Judge of High Court, **for Other Members** — *Either* Add Sec. for at least 2 years in CG/SG or Joint Sec for at least 7 years in CG/SG.
Term of Office	5 years or 65 years whichever is earlier
Terms and Conditions	as may be prescribed.
How to fill Vacancies	Central Government shall appoint another person.
How can be regined	By Notice in writing addressed to be Central Government.
How can be removed	By an order by the Central Government on the ground of proved misbehaviour or incapacity after an inquiry made by a judge of the Supreme Court
Is its Order Final?	No Order of the Central Government shall be called in question.
Staff of CAT	The Central Govt. shall provide such officers and employess as that Government may think fit.

10.0 PROVISIONS RELATING TO TAMPERING WITH COMPUTER SOURCE DOCUMENTS

If any person knowingly, or intentionally conceals, destroys or alters or intentionally or knowingly causes another to conceal, destroy or alter any computer source code used for a computer. Computer programme computer system or computer network, when the computer source code is required to be kept or maintained by law for the time being in force, he shall be punishable **with imprisonment up to 3 years, or with fine up to Rs. 5,00,000 or with both.**

11.0 PROVISIONS RELATING TO HACKING WITH COMPUTER SYSTEM

Whosoever with the intent to cause or knowing that he is likely to cause wrongful loss or damage to public or any person destroys or deletes or alters any information, residing in a computer resource or diminishes its value or utility or affects it injuriously by any means, commits hacking. Whosoever commits hacking shall be punished with **imprisonment up to 3 years, or** with fine upto **Rs. 5,00,000 *or* with both.**

12.0 PROVISIONS RELATING TO PUBLISHING OF INFORMATION WHICH IS OBSCENE IN ELECTRONIC FORM

Whoever publishes or transmits or causes to be published in the electronic form, any material which is lascivious or appeals to the purient interest or if its effect is such as to tend to deprave and corrupt persons who arelikely, having regard to all relevant circumstances, to read, see or hear the matter contained or embodied in it, shall be punished. On first conviction he shall be punishable with imprisonment up to 3 years and with fine up to Rs. 5,00,000. In the event of a second or subsequent conviction he shall be punishable with imprisonment up to 5 years and also with fine up to Rs. 10,00,000.

13.0 SECURING UNAUTHORISED ACCESS TO PROTECTED SYSTEM

The appropriate Government, may, by notification in the Official Gazette declare that any computer, computer system or computer network to be a protected system. It may also by order in writing authorise persons to have access to it. Any person who secures or attempts to secure unauthorised access to a protected system shall be punished with imprisonment upto 10 years and shall also be liable to fine.

14.0 PENALTY FOR VARIOUS DEFAULTS

Default	***Penalty***
Tampering with Computer Source Documents?	Imprisionment upto 3 years or Fine upto Rs. 2,00,000 or both
Hacking with Computer System.	Imprisionment upto 3 years or Fine upto Rs. 5,00,000 or both
Publishing of Information Which is Obscence in Electronic Form.	First–Imprisionment upto 3 years or Fine upto Rs. 5,00,000 or both Subsequent-Imprisionment upto 5 years or Fine upto Rs. 10,00,000 or both
Securing Unauthorised Access to Protected system.	Imprisionment upto 10 years and fine
Misrepresentation of Material Fact	Imprisionment upto 2 years or Fine upto Rs. 1,00,000 or both

Breach of Confidentiality and Privacy	Imprisionment upto 2 years or Fine upto Rs. 1,00,000 or both
Publishing False Digital Signature Certificate in Particulars	Imprisionment upto 2 years or Fine upto Rs. 1,00,000 or both
Publicaton for Fradulent Purposes	Imprisionment upto 2 years or Fine upto Rs. 1,00,000 or both.

APPENDIX 6

Important Points to Remember —The Payment of Bonus Act, 1965

1.0 EFFECTIVE DATE OF THE PAYMENT OF BONUS ACT, 1965— 25TH SEPT. 1965

2.0 TERRITORY OF THE PAYMENT OF BONUS ACT, 1965 – WHOLE OF INDIA.

3.0 CLASSES OF ESTABLISHMENT TO WHICH THE ACT APPLIES

3.1 (a) every factory; and

(b) every other establishment employing at least 20 persons on any day during an accounting year.

3.2 Power of Appropriate Government to apply after giving at least 2 months' notice

3.3 Applicability even in Case Number Falls Below 20

4.0 CLASSES OF EMPLOYEES TO WHICH THE ACT DOES NOT APPLY

Employees of: 1. Any insurer carrying on general insurance business and LIC, 2. Seamen under Merchant Shifting Act, 3. Employees under Dock Workers Act, 4. Employees of an industry carried on by or under the authority of any department of Central/State Government/ Local Authority, 5. Indian Red Cross Society, 6. Education Institutions, 7. Institutions established not for profit, 8. RBI, 9. IFCI, 10. Finance Corporation, 11. Deposit Insurance Corporation, 12. NABARD,14. UTI, 14. IDBI, 15. SIDBI, 17. NHB, 17. Inland water Transport Establishment, 18. Any other financial instituted notified by Central Government.

5.0 ACCOUNTING YEAR [SEC. 2(1)]

In relation to	*Accounting Year means . . .*
(i) *a corporation*	The year ending on the day on which the books and accounts of the corporation are to be closed and balanced;
(ii) *a company,*	The period in respect of which any profit and loss account of the company laid before it in annual general meeting is made up, whether that period is a year or not;
(iii) *in any other case*	(a) the year commencing on the 1st day of April; or (b) if the accounts of an establishment maintained by the employer thereof are closed and balanced on any day other than the 31st day of March, then, at the option of the employer, the year ending on the day on which its accounts are so closed and balanced.

6.0 WHO IS REGARDED AS AN EMPLOYEE? [SECTION 2(13)]

"Employee" means any person (**other than an apprentice**) employed on a salary or wage **not exceeding** Rs 10,000 per mensem in any industry to do any skilled or unskilled manual, supervisory, managerial, administrative, technical or clerical work for hire or reward, whether the terms of employment be express or impiled.

7.0 WHAT IS "SALARY OR WAGE"? [SECTION 2(21)]

7.1 "Salary or Wage" means :

- all remuneration (**other than remuneration in respect of over-time work**)
- capable of being expressed in terms of money,
- which would be payable to an employee in respect of his employment or of work done in such employment.
- if the terms of employment, express or implied where fulfilled.

7.2 Salary or Wage includes :

(a) **Dearness allowance** (*i.e.,* all cash payments, by whatever name called, paid to an employee on account of a rise in the cost of living)

(b) **Free food allowance** or free food by his employer in lieu of salary or wage.

7.3 Salary does not include–

(i) any other allowance which the employee is for the time being entitled to;

(ii) the **value of any house accommodation** *or* of supply of light, water, medical attendance *or* other amenity *or* of any service of any concessional supply of foodgrains *or* other articles;

(iii) any **travelling concession**;

(iv) any **bonus** (including incentive, production and attendance bonus);

(v) any **contribution** paid *or* payable by the employer to any pension **fund or provident fund** *or* for the benefit of the employee under any law for the time being in force;

(vi) any **retrenchment compensation** *or* any gratuity *or* other retirement benefit payable to the employee *or* any ex gratia payment made to him;

(vii) any **commission** payable to the employee;

8.0 WHO IS ELIGIBLE FOR BONUS? [SECTION 8 READ WITH SECTION 2(3)]

Every employee of an establishment provided—

(a) he has worked in that establishment for **at least 30 working days** in that year

(b) he has been employed on a salary or wage **not exceeding Rs 10,000** per mensem (i.e., month)

(c) he is **not disqualified** as per Sec. 9

9.0 WHO ARE DISQUALIFIED FROM RECEIVING BONUS? [SECTION 9]

An employee shall be disqualified from receiving bonus under this Act, if he is dismissed from service for

(a) fraud; or

(b) riotous or violent behaviour while on the premises of the establishment; or

(c) theft, misappropriation or sabotage of any property of the establishment

Effects of Sec. 9

An employee who is dismissed from service on the ground of misconduct as mentioned in Section 9, is disqualified for any bonus (whether for Current Accounting year *or* previous Accounting Year) [*Pandian Roadways Corporation Ltd.* vs. *Presiding Officer* [1996] 2 CLR 1175 (Mad.]

10.0 PAYMENT OF MINIMUM BONUS [SEC 10]

Case	Minimum Bonus
(a) ***Where an employee has completed 15 years of age at the beginning of the accounting year***	8.33% of the salary or wage earned by the employee during the accounting year *or* **Rs. 100** whichever is **higher**.
(b) ***Where an employee has not completed 15 years of age at the beginning of the accounting year***	8.33% of the salary or wage earned by employee during the accounting year *or* **Rs. 60** whichever is **higher**.

Note: The employer is bound to pay minimum bonus u/s 10 even if the employer suffers losses during the accounting year. **[Jalan Trading Co. vs. D.M. Aney AIR 1979 (SC) 233]**

11.0 HOW TO CALCULATE PROPORTIONATE REDUCTION IN BONUS IN CERTAIN CASES

11.1 Bonus shall be proportionately reduced if, an employee has not worked for all the working days in an accounting year.

11.2 Actual Bonus after Proportionate Reduction

Case	Actual Bonus after Proportionate Reduction
(a) ***Where Minimum Bonus of Rs. 100 or Rs. 60 is higher than 8.33% of Salary or Wages***	Rs. 100 or Rs. 60 × $\frac{\text{Actual No. of Working Days}}{\text{Total No. of Working Days}}$
(b) ***In other cases***	83.33% of Salary/Wages× $\frac{\text{Total Working Funds in India}}{\text{Total world Working Funds}}$

12.0 HOW TO COMPUTE NO. OF WORKING DAYS [SEC 14]

Employee is also deemed to have worked on:

(a) Lay off Period

(b) Leave with Salary/Wage

(c) Temporary Disablement

(d) Maternity Leave with Salary or Wage

13.0 PAYMENT OF MAXIMUM BONUS [SECTION 11]

13.1 **When**–Payable where Allocable Surplus exceeds Minimum Bonus

13.2 **Limit**–20% of Salary or Wage

13.3 **Salary or Wage**–as if Rs. 3,500 p.m. where Salary or Wage exceeds Rs. 10,000.

14.0 PAYMENT OF BONUS LINKED WITH PRODUCTION OR PRODUCTIVITY [SECTION 31A]

Bonus linked with production or productivity can neither be less than Minimum Bonus (as per Sec. 10) and nor can be more than Maximum Bonus (as per Sec. 11)

15.0 Adjustment of Customary or Interim Bonus Against Bonus

15.1 Employer's right to deduct Customary/Interim Bonus

The employer shall be entitled to deduct the amount of bonus paid from the amount of bonus payable by him to the employee under this Act in respect of that accounting year if :

(a) an employer has paid any **Puja bonus or other customary bonus** to an employee; *or*

(b) an employer has **paid a part of the bonus** before the due date of bonus.

15.2 Employee's right to receive balance

The employee shall be entitled to receive only the balance.

16.0 DEDUCTION OF CERTAIN AMOUNTS FROM BONUS PAYABLE

16.1 Two Conditions for Deduction

(a) An employee is **found guilty of misconduct causing,** and

(b) There is **financial loss to the employer**, then, the employer can lawfully deduct the amount of loss from the amount of bonus payable by him to the employee under this Act in respect of **that accounting year only**

16.2 Employee's right to receive balance

The employee shall be entitled to receive only the balance.

17.0 WHAT IS THE TIME-LIMIT FOR PAYMENT OF BONUS? [SECTION 19]

Case	*Time Limit*
(a) ***where there is a dispute regarding payment of bonus pending before any authority under Section 22***	Within **1 month** from the date on which the award becomes enforceable or the settlement comes into operation, in respect of such dispute;
(b) ***in any other case***	Within a period of **8 months** from the close of the accounting year or within the period extended by the appropriate Govt. or authority upon an application made by the employer and for sufficient reasons but the total period so extended must **not exceed 2 years.**

18.0 RECOVERY OF THE BONUS DUE FROM AN EMPLOYER [SECTION 21]

Application by Employee or his authorised person (or assignee or heir of deceased employee) within 1 month from the due date of money to the appropriate authority who if safisfied may issue certificate to the collector who will recover the same as arrears of land revenue.

19.0 HOW IS AVAILABLE SURPLUS COMPUTED? [SECTION 5]

Statement Showing the Computation of Available Surplus u/s 6

Particulars		*Rs*
A. Gross Profit as per Section 4		xxx
B. *Less*: Prior charges u/s 6		
(a) Depreciation	xxx	
(b) Development Rebate etc.	xxx	
(c) Direct Tax	xxx	
(d) Sum specified in Third Schedule	xxx	xxx
C. *Add*: Tax saved on account of Bonus in respect of the immediately preceeding accounting year		xxx
D. Available Surplus [A – B + C]		xxx

20.0 WHAT IS AN ALLOCABLE SURPLUS? [SECTION 2(4)]

Case	*Allocable Surplus*
(a) **In relation to an employer, being a company (other than banking company) which has not made the arrangements prescribed under the Income-tax Act, for the declaration and payment within India of the dividends payable out of its profits in accordance with the provisions of Section 194 of that Act,**	(a) **67%** of available surplus in an accounting year.
(b) **In any other case**	(b) **60%** of the available surplus in an accounting year.

21.0 PROVISIONS RELATING TO SET ON/SET OFF

	Provision relating to Set on	*Provision relating to Set off*
When Provision applies	The provision of set on applies where for any accounting year, the **allocable surplus** is **more than** the amount of **maximum bonus** payable to the employees in the establishment under Section 11.	The provision of set-off applies in the following cases: 1. where there is no available surplus 2. where the **allocable surplus** is **less than** the amount of **minimum bonus** paya]ble to the employees in the establishment under Section 10 and there is no amount or sufficient amount carried forward and set on u/s 15(1), which could be utilized for the purposes of payment of the minimum bonus.
Amount which can be carried forward	The excess of allocable surplus over maximum bonus, or 20% of the total salary or wage of the employee employed in the establishment in that accounting year, whichever is lower is to be carried forward for being set on.	The deficiency or the amount of minimum bonus whichever is lower, is to be carried forward for being set-off.
Accounting Years for which amount can be carried forward	Upto 4 Accounting years	Upto 4 Accounting years
Schedule in accordance with amount can be c/f	Fourth Schedule	Fourth Schedule

Conclusions :

1. The Excess (i.e. Difference between Allocable Surplus and Maximum Bonus) not exceeding 20% of salary/wage is to be carried forward for being set on upto 4 accounting years as per Fourth Schedule.
2. The Deficiency (*i.e.* Difference between Available Surplus and Minimum Bonus) is to be carried forward for being set off upto 4 accounting years as per Fourth Schedule.

22.0 HOW IS DIRECT TAX PAYABLE BY THE EMPLOYER CALCULATED? [SECTION 7]

(a) In calculating such tax no account shall be taken of—
   (i) Brought Forward Loss
   (ii) Arrears of Depreciation
   (iii) Exemption u/s 84 or Deduction u/s 101

(b) Charitable/Religious Institution to be treated as widely held company

(c) Establishment income to be treated as only income in case of HUF/Individual

(d) No Rebate on Export Profit

(e) No Rebate for the development of any industry (other than development rebate or investment allowance or development allowance)

23.0 MAINTENANCE OF REGISTERS, RECORDS ETC. [SECTION 26]

22.1 Duty of Employer to Prepare and Maintain prescribed Registers in Form A, B and C.

22.2 Time Limit for filing Returns–30 days from expiry of time limit for Payment of Bonus

24.0 SUMS TO BE DEDUCTED AS PER THIRD SCHEDULE

Employer	*Sum to be deducted as per Third Schedule*
1. ***Non-Banking Co.***	(a) Actual Dividends on Preference Share capital (b) 8.5% of Opening Balance of Paid up Equity Share Capital (c) 6% of Opening Balance of Reserves & Profits c/f **Note:** In case of a foreign company, 8.5% of the aggregate of [Net Fixed Assets + Current Assets – Current Liabilities (other than amount payable to Head office in India)]
2. ***Banking Co.***	(a) Actual Dividends on Preference Share Capital (b) 7.5% of Opening Balance of paid up Equity Share Capital (c) 5% of Opening Balance of Reserves & Profits c/f (d) Amount t/f to Reserve Fund u/s 17(1) or to any Reserves as per RBI's directions whichever is higher. **Note:** In case of Foreign Banking Co., the aggregate of the following: (a) Rate of Pref. Dividend ∞ Pref Share Capital ∞ $\frac{\text{Total Working Funds in India}}{\text{Total world Working Funds}}$ (b) 7.5% ∞ Paidup Equity Share Capital ∞ $\frac{\text{Total Working Funds in India}}{\text{Total world Working Funds}}$ (c) 5% ∞ **Total Disclosed Reserves** ∞ $\frac{\text{Total Working Funds in India}}{\text{Total world Working Funds}}$ (d) **Sum deposited with RBI** u/s 11 (2) (b) (i)

APPENDIX 7
Important Points to Remember —The Payment of Gratuity Act, 1972

1.0 TERRITORY TO WHICH THE PAYMENT OF GRATUITY ACT, 1972 EXTENDS

- It extends to the whole of India:
- It shall not extend to the State of Jammu and Kashmir in so far as it relates to plantations or ports.

2.0 ESTABLISHMENTS TO WHICH THE PAYMENT OF GRATUITY ACT, 1972 APPLIES [SEC. 1(3)]

The Payment of Gratuity Act, 1972 shall apply to—

(a) every factory, mine, oilfield, plantation, port and railway company;

(b) every shop or establishment within the meaning of any law for the time being in force in relation to shops and establishments in a State, in which at least 10 persons are employed, or were employed, on any day of the preceding 12 months;

(c) such other establishments or class of establishments, in which at least 10 employees are employed, or were employed, on any day of the preceding 12 months, as may be specified by the Central Government by notification the Official Gazette.

Under Sec. 1(3)(c), the Central Government has specified Motor Transport undertakings, clubs, chambers of commerce and industry, inland water transport establishments, Solicitors' Officers, Local Bodies and circus industry, in which atleast 10 persons are employed or were employed on any day of the preceding 12 months, as classes of establishments to which the Act shall apply.

Act continues to apply even after No. of Persons falls below 10 [Sec. 1(3A)]

A shop or establishment to which this Act has become applicable shall continue to be governed by this Act even if the number of persons employed therein falls below 10.

Notes :

(i) The expression 'law' used in Section 1(3)(b) means any law in respect of shops, establishments, commercial or non-commercial.

[K. Gangadar vs. Appellate Authority, (1993) 66 FLR 648 (AP)]

(ii) The provisions of Section 1(3)(b) of the Act are very much comprehensive. It also includes Municipal Board.

[Municipal Board vs. Union of India, (1993) 67 FLR 93(All].

Three Eligibility Conditions to receive Gratuity

A person is eligible to receive gratuity under the Act if—

1. He is an employee under the definition of Section 2(e) of the Act
2. He is employed in an establishment to which the Act applies
3. He has rendered continuous service for at least 5 years except in case of death/disablement.

3.0 EMPLOYEE [SEC. 2(E)] MEANS—

- any person (**other than an apprentice**) employed on wages, in any establishment, factory, mine, oilfield, plantation, port, railway company or shop
- to do any skilled, semi-skilled, or unskilled, manual, supervisory, technical or clerical work,
- whether the terms of employment are express or implied, and
- whether or not such person is employed in a managerial or administrative capacity,
- **but does not include** any such person who holds a post under the Central Government or a State Government and is governed by any other Act or by any rules providing for payment of gratuity.

4.0 "WAGES" MEANS [SEC. 2(S)]

- all emoluments which are earned by an employee
- while on duty or on leave
- in accordance with the terms and conditions of his employment and
- which are paid or are payable to him in cash and
- **includes** dearness allowance but
- **does not include** any bonus, commission, house rent allowance, overtime wages and any other allowance.

5.0 CONTINUOUS SERVICE [SEC. 2A]

5.1. An employee shall be said to be in continuous service for a period if he has, for that period, been in uninterrupted service, including service which may be interrupted on account of sickness, accident, leave, absence from duty without leave (not being absence in respect of which an order treating the absence as break in service has been passed in accordance with the standing orders, rules or regulations governing the employees of the establishment), lay-off, strike or a lock-out or cessation of work not due to any fault of the employee, whether such uninterrupted or interrupted service was rendered before or after the commencement of this Act;

5.2. An employee employed in a non-seasonal establishment who is not in continuous service for any period of 1 year *or* 6 months, shall be deemed to be in continuous service for 1 year *or* 6 months if the employee during immediately preceding 12/6 calendar months has actually worked under the employer for at least—

Employees	*Who is not in continuous service for 12 months*	*Who is not in continuous service for 6 months*
(a) *In case of an employee employed below the ground in a mine*	190 days	95 days
(b) *In case of an employee employed in an establishment which works for less than 6 days in a week.*	190 days	95 days
(c) *In case of other employee*	240 days	120 days

5.3. While computing the number of days on which an employee has actually worked under an employer, include the following days :

(i) The days during which employee has been laid-off

(ii) The days during which employee has been on leave with full wages, earned in the previous year;

(iii) The days during which employee has been absent due to temporary disablement caused by accident arising out of and in the course of his employment; and

(iv) The days during which female employee has been on maternity leave not exceeding 12 weeks.

5.4. Where an employee, employed in a seasonal establishment, is not in continuous service of 1 year or 6 months, he shall be deemed to be in continuous service under the employer for such period if he has actually worked for at least 75% of the number of days on which the establishment was in operation during such period. [Sec. 2A]

6.0 WHEN AND TO WHOM IS GRATUITY PAYABLE UNDER THE PAYMENT OF GRATUITY ACT, 1972? [SEC. 4(1)]

Gratuity shall be payable to an employee on the termination of his employment after he has rendered continuous service for atleast 5 years,—

(a) on his superannuation, or

(b) on his retirement or resignation, or

(c) on his death or disablement due to accident or disease:

However the completion of continuous service of 5 years shall not be necessary where the termination of the employment of any employee is due to death or disablement.

7.0 WHAT IS THE AMOUNT OF GRATUITY PAYABLE? [SEC. 4(2)]

Case	*Amount of Gratuity Payable by Employer*
1. In case of an employee of establishment (whether seasonal or non-seasonal), who is employed throughout the year	
(a) *In case of monthly Rated Employee*	Last Drawn Monthly Wages × 15/26 × No. of completed years of service (including part thereof in excess of 6 months.)
(b) *In the case of a piece-rated employee*	$= \dfrac{\text{Total wages (excluding overtime wages) for 3 months immediately preceding the termination of employment}}{\text{Total No. of Actual Working days of Employee in 3 months}} \times 15/26 \times$ No. of completed years of service (including part thereof in excess of 6 months.)
2. In case of an employee of a seasonal establishment who is not employed throughout the year	= Last drawn Monthly Wages × 7/26 × No. of seasons.

8.0 MAXIMUM GRATUITY PAYABLE IS RS 10,00,000.

9.0 WAGES FOR COMPUTING THE GRATUITY PAYABLE TO AN EMPLOYEE WHO IS EMPLOYED AFTER HIS DISABLEMENT [SEC. 4(4)]

Period	*Wages*
1. ***For the period preceding his disablement***	Wages last drawn at the time of disablement
2. ***For the period subsequent to his disablement***	Reduced wages last drawn at the time of termination of services.

10.0 WHAT ARE THE PROVISIONS RELATING TO FORFEITURE OF GRATUITY [SEC. 4(6)]

Reason for Termination of Services	*Extent of Forfeiture of Security*
1. For any act, willful omission or negligence causing any damage or loss to, or destruction of, property belonging to the employer'; [Sec. 4(6)(a)]	1. The gratuity shall be forfeited to the extent of the damage or loss so caused.
2. For his riotous or disorderly conduct or any other act of violence on his part, or	2. The gratuity may be wholly or partially forfeited.
3. For any act which constitutes an offence involving moral turpitude provided that such offence is committed by him in the course of his employment. [Sec. 4(6)(b)]	3. The gratuity may be wholly or partially forfeited.

11.0 WHAT ARE THE PROVISIONS AS TO NOMINATION [SEC. 6]

11.1. Is Nomination compulsory ?

Every employee who has completed 1 year of service, is compulsorily required to make a nomination.

11.2.. Time limit within which Nomination is required to be made

The nomination must be made *within* ***30 days*** of **completion of one year** of service.

11.3. Who can be nominee ?

(a) If, at the time of making nomination, the employee has a family,	the nomination **must** be made in favour of one or more members of the family. (**Note :** Nomination shall be void if it is made in favour of a person who is not a member of his family).
(b) If at the time of making nomination, the employee does not have a family,	the nomination **may** be made in favour of any person. If the employee subsequently acquires a family, such nomination shall forthwith become void, and the employee shall, *within 90 days,* make a fresh nomination in favour of one or more members of his family in duplicate on form 'G'.

11.4. Can there be more than one Nominee ?—Yes

The employee may distribute the amount of gratuity amongst more than one nominee.

11.5. Can nomination be modified ?—Yes

The nomination already made by an employee may be modified by him at any time by giving a written notice to his employer.

11.6. Consequences of death of nominee

If the nominee dies before the death of the employee, the employee shall make a **fresh nomination** in duplicate on from 'H'.

11.7. Safe custody of nomination

- Every nomination, fresh nomination and modification of nomination shall be sent by the employee to the employer, who shall keep the same in safe custody.
- The employer shall verify the service particulars of the employee as given in the nomination form within 30 days of the receipt of nomination form.
- The employer shall return one copy of the nomination form to the employee, as acknowledgment.

11.8. Effective date of nomination

Nomination comes into operation from the **date of receipt** of the same by the employer.

11.9. Submission of Nomination

An employee may submit the nomination form *either* by personal service *or* by registered post with acknowledgment.

12.0. PROVISIONS RELATING TO APPLICATION FOR PAYMENT OF GRATUITY [SEC. 7]

Who is required to make Application?	1. An employee who is eligible for payment of gratuity. 2. Any person authorised in writing by such employee. 3. Nominee (in case nomination exists). 4. Legal heir (in case of no nomination)
To whom Application is to be made	Application shall be made to employer.
Time Limit for Application	• By Nominee within 30 days from the date gratuity becomes payable • By Legal heir within 1 year from the date gratuity becomes payable • By Employee/authorised person within 30 days from the date gratuity becomes payable. **Note :** Employee may apply before 30 days of date of superannuation or retirement if such date is known in advance.
Manner of Making Application	The application shall be made in writing.
Form of Application	For Nominee—Form 'J' or Plain Paper For Legal heirs—Form 'K' or Plain Paper For other—Form 'I'.
Content of Application	The application shall require the employer to pay the gratuity to the employee.
Manner of Presenting Application	The application shall be presented to the employer *either* by personal service *or* by registered post with acknowledgement.
Effect of Delayed Application	An Application even after the prescribed period shall also be entertained by the employer, if the sufficient case for delay has been mentioned in the application. Any dispute in this regard shall be referred to the Controlling Authority for his decision. In any case, the claim for gratuity cannot treated as invalid merely because the claimant failed to submit the application within the prescribed time.

13.0 TIME LIMIT WITHIN WHICH NOTICE FOR PAYMENT OF GRATUITY MUST BE ISSUED

If the claims is found admissible on verification	Within **15 days** of receipt of application, the employer must issue a notice in Form 'L' to the applicant employee, nominee or legal heir, as the case may be, specifying the amount of gratuity payable and fixing a date, not being later than the 30th day after the date of receipt of the application, for payment thereof, or
If the claim for gratuity is not found admissible	Within **15 days** of Receipt of application, the employer must issue a notice in Form 'M' to the applicant employee, nominee or legal heir, as the case may be specifying the reasons why the claim for gratuity is not considered admissible alongwith a copy endorsed to the controlling authority.

14.0 RIGHT OF AGGRIEVED PERSON TO MAKE AN APPEAL [SEC. 7(7)]

Any person aggrieved by an order of Controlling Authority u/s 7(4) may, within 60 days (or extended period if any) from the date of the receipt of the order, prefer an appeal to the Appropriate Government or prescribed authority.

15.0 WHAT ARE THE PROVISIONS RELATING TO RECOVERY OF GRATUITY? [SEC. 8]

If the gratuity payable under the Act is not paid by the employer within 30 days of due date of gratuity the following provisions apply:

1. **Application.**	The aggrieved person is required to make an application in Form 'T' in duplicate to the controlling authority. [Rule 19]
2. **Opportunity of being heard.**	The controlling authority before issuing a certificate must give the employer a reasonable opportunity of showing cause against the issue of such certificate.
3. **Recovery Certificate.**	The controlling authority shall issue a certificate to the controller for that amount together with the compound interest thereon at the prescribed rate from the date of expiry of the prescribed time till the actual date of payment.
4. **Maximum Interest**	The amount of interest payable must not exceed the amount of gratuity payable under this Act.
5. **Recovery by Collector**	The controller shall recover the same as arrears of land revenue and pay the same to the person entitled thereto.

Note: Interest is admissible only if a certificate for recovery of dues as a public demand has been issued; [*Charan Singh* v. *Birla Textiles*, (1988) 57 FLR 534 (SC).]

16.0 PROTECTION OF GRATUITY [SEC. 13]

Gratuity payable to an employee shall not be liable to attachment in execution of any decree or order of the Civil or Revenue or Criminal Court.

It is immaterial as to whether the gratuity is payable to the employee—

(a) under the Act; *or* (b) in an establishment exempted u/s 5.

APPENDIX 8

Important Points to Remember —The Employees Provident Funds & Miscellaneous Provisions Act, 1952

1.0 TERRITORY

Whole of India except the State of Jammu & Kashmir.

2.0 ESTABLISHMENTS TO WHICH THE EPF & MP ACT APPLIES

Subject to the exceptions contained in Section 16, this Act applies to:

(a) every establishment which is a factory engaged in any industry specified in Schedule I and which employs at least 20 persons; and

(b) any other establishment which employs at least 20 persons or class of such establishment which the Central Government may, by notification in Official Gazette specify in this behalf. Thus, this clause empowers the Central Govt. to apply this Act even to an establishment which is not factory.

3.0 BASIC WAGES [SECTION 2(B)]

"*Basic wages*" means all emoluments which are earned by an employee while on duty or on leave or on holidays with wages in either case in accordance with the terms of the contract of employment and which are **paid or payable in cash** to him, but **does not include**

(i) the cash value of any food concessions;

(ii) any dearness allowance (that is to say all cash payments, by whatever name called, paid to an employee on account of rise in the cost of living),

(iii) house rent allowance,

(iv) overtime allowance,

(v) bonus, commission or pay and other similar allowance payable to the employee in respect of his employment or of work done in such employment; and

(vi) any presents made by the employer.

4.0 EMPLOYEE [SECTION 2(F)]

"*Employee*" means any person who is employed for wages in any kind of work, manual or otherwise, in or in connection with work of an establishment, and who gets his wages directly or indirectly from the employer, and includes any person,

(i) employed by or through a contractor in or in connection with the work of the establishment;

(ii) engaged as an apprentice, not being an apprentice engaged under the Apprentice Act, 1961 (52 of 1961), or under the standing orders of the establishment.

5.0 WHO CAN CONSTITUTE CENTRAL BOARD/STATE BOARD OF TRUSTEES

Central Govt.

6.0 NATURE OF CENTRAL/STATE BOARD OF TRUSTEES

Body Corporate having perpetual succession and a Common Seal.

7.0 SETTLEMENT OF PF CLAIMS

P.F. claims must be settled within 30 days from the date of its receipt by the Commissioner otherwise penal interest @ 12% p.a. for delayed period may be recovered from the salary of commissioner.

8.0 DETERMINATION OF MONEYS DUE FROM EMPLOYER [SECTION 7A]

8.1. Who Determines the Moneys Due from an Employer?

1. The Central PF Commissioner
2. Additional Central PF Commissioner
3. Deputy P.F. Commissioner
4. Regional P.F. Commissioner
5. Assistant P.F. Commissioner

8.2. Matters on which Authorities Take Decisions under E.P.F. Act.

1. amount due as contribution.
2. the date from which the same is due.
3. the administrative charges.
4. amount to be transferred under Section 15 or Section 17 of the Act.
5. any other charges payable by the employer under the Act.

9.0 WHO CAN APPLY FOR REVIEW ORDER AND TO WHOM UNDER THE EPF ACT ? [SEC. 7B]

Any person aggrieved by an order under Section 7A(1) may apply **within 45 days of order** for a review of that order to the officer who passed the order provided no appeal has been made against the order under this Act.

10.0 DETERMINATION OF ESCAPED AMOUNT BY REOPENING THE CASE

10.1. Who can Reopen the Case ? [Section 7C]

The Officer who has passed the Order u/s 7A or u/s 7B.

10.2. Time Limit within which Case be Reopened

The case can be reopened **within 5 years** from the date of communication of the order passed u/s 7A or u/s 7B.

11.0 EPF APPELLATE TRIBUNAL

Is constituted by the Central Govt. and consists of 1 person only appointed by Central Govt.

12.0 DEPOSIT OF AMOUNT DUE ON FILING AN APPEAL (SECTION 7-O)

(a) Appeal by the employer can be entertained by a Tribunal only if he has deposited with it **75%** of the amount due from him as determined by an officer referred to in Section 7A.

(b) The Tribunal may, waive or reduce the amount to be deposited for reasons to be recorded in writing.

13.0 PROVIDENT FUND, PENSION AND DEPOSIT LINKED INSURANCE SCHEME [SEC. 6, 6A]

Refer to Para 11.0.

14.0 PROTECTION AGAINST ATTACHMENT OF CREDIT BALANCE IN PF A/C [SECTION 10]

The amount standing to the credit of any member in the Fund or credit of any exempted employee in provident fund

(a) shall not be capable of, being assigned or charged and

(b) shall not be liable to attachment under any decree or order of any court in respect of any debt or liability incurred by the member or the exempted employee.

(c) shall not be capable of being claimed by the Official Assignee or Official Receiver

(d) shall be free from any debt or other liability incurred by the deceased member or the nominee before the death of the member

15.0 PRIORITY OF PAYMENT OF CONTRIBUTION OVER OTHER DEBTS [SECTION 11]

If the employer is adjudged an insolvent or if the employer is a company and an order for winding thereof has been made, the amount due from the employer whether in respect of the employee's contribution or the employer's contribution must be included among the debts which are to be paid in priority to all other debts under Section 49 of the Presidency-Towns Insolvency Act, Section 61 of the Provincial Insolvency Act, Section 530 of the Companies Act, 1956, in the distribution of the property of the insolvent or the assets of the company. In other words, this payment will be a **preferential payment provided the liability therefor has accrued before this order of adjudication or winding up is made.**

16.0 EXEMPTED ESTABLISHMENT [SEC. 17]

	Exemption from Provident Fund Scheme
1. ***Who may grant Exemption ?***	The exemption may be granted by Appropriate Govt.
2. ***Manner of giving Exemption***	The exemption can be given only by way of a notification in the Official Gazette.
3. ***Terms of Exemption***	• The exemption shall be subject to such conditions as may be specified in the notification. • The exemption may be given prospectively or retrospectively. • The exemption may be given from the operation of all or any of the provisions of any Scheme.
4. ***Conditions for giving exemption***	1. Appropriate Govt. must form an opinion that the rules of provident fund with respect to the rates of contribution and other provident fund benefits are **not less** favourable than those specified in the Act or the Scheme; *and* 2. Appropriate Govt. must consult the Central Board. The Central Board shall forward its views within prescribed time limit.
5. ***Applicability of provisions on exempted establishment***	(a) The terms and conditions as may be specified in the notification granting exemption shall apply to the exempted establishment. (b) If the employer contravenes, or makes default in complying with any of the said provisions or conditions or any other provision of this Act, he shall be punishable u/s 14 as if the said establishment had not been exempted.
6. ***Duty of Employer***	The employer shall establish a Board of Trustees for the administration of the Provident Fund.
7. ***Duties of Board of Trustees***	(a) The Board of Trustees shall— (i) maintain detailed accounts to show the contributions credited, withdrawals made and interest accrued in respect of each employee;

	(ii) submit such returns as may be directed from time to time; (iii) invest the PF moneys in accordance with the directions issued by Central Govt. (iv) transfer, where necessary, the PF Account of any employee; and (v) perform such other duties as may be specified in the scheme. (b) If the Trustees contravene, or make default in complying with, any of the duties entrusted to them, they shall be deemed to have committed an offence under section 14 and shall be punishable accordingly.

	Exemption from Pension Scheme u/s 17(1)	***Exemption from Insurance Scheme u/s 17(2A)***
1. ***Who may Grant Exemption ?***	The exemption may be granted by the Appropriate Govt.	The exemption may be granted by the Central Provident Fund Commissioner.
2. ***Manner of Giving Exemption***	The exemption can be given only by way of notification in the Official Gazette.	The exemption can be given only by way of notification in the Official Gazette.
3. ***Terms of Exemption***	Notification may specify the pattern of Investment of Pension Fund.	Notification may specify the pattern of Investment of Insurance fund.
4. ***Conditions for Exemption***	**Appropriate Govt.** must form an opinion that the pensionary benefits available to the employer are **not less favourable** than those specified under the Pension Scheme.	The **Central Provident Fund Commissioner** must form an opinion that the life insurance benefits available to employees are **more favourable** than those specified under the Insurance Scheme.

17.0 Transfer of Accounts [Sec. 17A]

Where an employee of an establishment (Old) leaves his employment and obtain re-employment in another establishment (New), the following provisions are applicable as to transfer of accounts:

If Old Establishment is covered but New Establishment is not covered under P.F. Act [Sec. 17A(1)]	***If Old Establishment is not covered but New Establishment is covered under P.F. Act [Sec. 17A(2)]***	***If both Old and New Establishment are covered under P.F. Act***
The Credit balance of his old Provident Fund A/c **shall** be transferred to his new Provident Fund A/c in New Establishment provided—	The Credit balance of his old Provident Fund A/c **may** be transferred to his new Provident Fund A/c in New Establishment provided—	The Credit balance of his old Provident Fund A/c **may** be transferred to his new Provident Fund A/c in New Establishment provided—

(a) the employee so desires (b) the rules of Old P.F. permit such transfer **Note :** Transfer has to be made within time prescribed by the Central Govt.	(a) the employee so desires (b) the rules of Old P.F. permit such transfer	(a) the employee so desires (b) the rules of Old P.F. permit such transfer

18.0 Liability in case of transfer of establishment [Section 17B]

Where an employer transfers the establishment in whole or in part by sale, gift, lease or licence or in any other manner,

(a) The employer and the transferee shall be jointly or severally liable to pay the contribution and other sum due from the employer under any of the provision of
  (i) the Act
  (ii) the Scheme
  (iii) the Pension Scheme

(b) The liability is limited in respect of period upto the date of such transfer.

(c) The liability of the transferee shall be limited to the value of the assets obtained by him from such transfer.

19.0 Prescribed Time Limits under EPF & MP Act, 1952

(a) **Settlement of Provident Fund Claims.**	(a) 30 days from date of receipt of application by the commissioner.
(b) **Application for Setting aside Ex-parte order.**	(b) 3 months from date of communication of such order.
(c) **Application for Review of order passed u/s 7A.**	(c) 45 days from date of communication of order.
(d) **Reopening the case for determining Escaped Amount.**	(d) 5 years from date of communication of order u/s 7A or 7B.
(e) **Remitting contribution to Employers' Pension Scheme.**	(e) 15 days of the close of every month.

APPENDIX 9

Important Points to Remember — The Companies Act, 1956

CHAPTER 1 DEFINITION AND NATURE OF COMPANY

1. The term 'Body corporate' includes company incorporated outside India.
2. The shares are freely transferable in case of a public company having share capital.
3. The characteristics of every company – separate legal entity, perpetual succession and common seal.
4. (a) Member can be debtor, creditor and director of a company at the same time.
   (b) Members are not co-owners of Company's properties.
   (c) Members can not have any insurable interest in the Company's properties.
   (d) Creditor's remedy for the recovery of their debts lie against the company and not against its members or directors.
5. As per sec 45, if the company carries on business for more than 6 months with no of members reduced below the statutory minimum requirement (i.e. 2 in case of a Pvt. Co and 7 in case of Public Co.) all the persons who were members of the company and were aware of this fact shall be personally liable for debts contracted after those 6 months.
6. (a) Members of a limited company may have unlimited liability as per Sec 45
   (b) A limited liability company can become a partner in a firm since it is a separate legal entity. However, the liability of such limited company shall be unlimited like that of other partners. If may be noted that it is the liability of the members of a limited company which is limited and not that of the company itself. As per department of company affairs, a company can become a partner only if its memorandum of association specifically allows so.
   (c) A limited company can be formed without the word 'limited' as the last word of its name.
   (d) 'Every company need not have minimum paid up capital since company having no share capital need not have minimum paid up share capital.
   (e) A subsidiary company can be member of its holding company if it has acquired the shares of holding Co. before it became subsidiary.
7. The company does not come to an end since it is created by a process of law and can be put to an end only by process of law.
8. **Circumstances when Corporate Veil can be Lifted**

   Under Express Statutory Provisions

   (a) When the no. of members falls below the statutory minimum [Section 45]
   (b) Non-disclosure of Representative capacity [Section 147]
   (c) To examine the relationship of holding and subsidiary [Section 212]
   (d) To investigate into the affairs of related companies [Section. 239]
   (e) To investigate ownership of a company [Section 247]
   (f) When business is carried on to defraud the creditors [Section 542]

   Under Judicial Interpretations

   (a) For determination of the character of the company
   (b) For prevention of fraud or improper conduct

(c) For the protection of revenue
(d) When company is formed to act as an agent of its members
(e) When company is formed to avoid the welfare laws

9. No company can be a citizen of India since Citizenship under the Citizenship Act is available only to an individual.

CHAPTER 2 TYPE OF COMPANIES

1. The Institute of Chartered Accountants of India is a statutory company since it has been created by special Act of parliament.
2. A Private company can be Government company if at least 51% of paid up capital is held by the Central Govt or State Govt. or both as per sec 617.
3. A Public Company includes a Private Company which is subsidiary of a public company as per sec 3(1) (*iv*).
4. In case of a Licensed company with limited liability u/s 25, a partnership firm can become its member as per sec 25.
5. An unlimited company or a company limited by guarantee can be either a public company or a private company.
6. A Government company can be either a public company or a private company as per sec 617.
7. A Government company is one is which at least 51% of the paid up capital is held by the Central Govt or one or more State Govt. or both.
8. After the establishment of business in India foreign company must file the necessary documents with the Registrar of Companies, within 30 days from the date of establishment.
9. A company is deemed to be the holding company of another when former holds more than 50% in the nominal value of equity share capital of latter as per Sec. 4.
10. The Central Govt. by notification in the Official Gazette is empowered to specify an institution as Public financial Institution if at least 51% of its paid up capital is controlled or held by Central Govt. as per sec 4A.
11. Conversation of a private company into a public company requires a special resolution as per sec 44.
12. Conversation of a public company into private company requires a special resolution and approval of Central Govt. as per sec 31.
13. In case of conversion of private company into a public company, a copy of the altered articles must be filed with the Registrar within 30 days of passing the special resolution as per sec 44.
14. In case of conversion of public company into a private company, a copy of the altered articles must be filed with the Registrar within 1 month of date of receipt of approval of the Central Govt. as per sec 31.
15. An Illegal Association is an unregistered association formed for money lending activities with more than 10 persons and for other activities with more than 20 persons as per Sec 11.
16. (a) Illegality of an illegal association can not be cured by subsequent reduction in the number of its members.
    (b) Illegal association can not be wound up under the provisions of the Companies Act.
    (c) Sec 11 does not apply to Single Joint Hindu Family carrying on any business, Stock Exchange and Non-Profit Earning Association.
    (d) Illegal association can not be sued by its members and outsiders as per sec 11.
    (e) When two or more Joint Hindu Families enter into partnership, then all adult members (whether Male or Female) are to counted to determine the limit of 10 or 20 persons as per Sec 11.
17. In case of company limited by guarantee having no share capital, the liability of its members, can be enforced *only by the liquidator* since such liability can be enforced only after the commencement of winding up of the company and not during the life time of the company as per sec 12 (2) (b).

18. A limited liability company can become a partner in a firm. As per sec 25. The Central Govt. may by licence permit an association not for profit to be formed with limited liability without using the word 'limited' or 'private limited' as part of its name The Central Govt. may grant such license if:
    (i) the association about to be formed as a limited company aims at the promotion of commerce, art, science, religion, charity or any other useful object;
    (ii) it intends to apply its profits, if any, for promoting its objects; and
    (iii) it prohibits the payment of dividend to its members.
19. A firm can become a member of a licensed company u/s 25 and ceases to be member on dissolution of him.
20. **Private Company [Section 3(1)(iii)]** A Private Company means a company which has a minimum paid up capital of Rs 1,00,000 or such higher paid up capital as may be prescribed, and by its articles—
    (a) restricts the right to transfer its shares, if any,
    (b) limits the number of its members to 50, and
    (c) prohibits any invitation to the public to subscribe for any shares in or debentures of the company.
    (d) prohibits any invitation or acceptance of deposits from persons other than its members, directors or their relatives.
21. **Holding and Subsidiary:** A company (let us call it Company *S*) is deemed to be a subsidiary of another company (let us call it Company *H*) only in the following **3 cases:**
    (i) When the company (Company *H*) **controls** the composition of Board of Directors of other Company (Company *S*).
    (ii) When the Company *H* holds **more than half** in the nominal value of equity share capital of Company *S*.
    (iii) When Company *S* is a subsidiary of a Company *T*, which in turn is the subsidiary of Company *H*.
22. **Consequences of An Illegal Association [Section 11(4)]**
    (a) **Personal Liability** of Every member
    (b) **Every member Punishable with Fine** not exceeding Rs. 10,000.
    (c) **Cannot Sue** any outsider who has dealt with it.
    (d) **Cannot be sued** by its members *or* outsiders.
    (e) **Can not be wound up** under the provisions of Companies Act because there is nothing to dissolve at all. ***[Mewa Ram* v. *Ram Gopal]***
    (f) **Cannot be made legal by subsequent reduction *[Madanlal* v. *Janki Parshad]***
    (g) Such an association can not enter into any contracts since it has no legal existence.
    (h) No member can sue another member in respect of any matter connected with such association.
    (i) **Outsiders can sue the members** but not such association.
    (j) Contracts made before the registration can not be validated and issued upon by subsequent registration. ***[Gujarat Trading Co.* v. *Tricumji]***
    (k) Illegality or invalidity in the constitution of an association does not effect its liability to tax or its chargeability as a unit of assessment. ***[Kumaraswamy Chettiar* v. *I.T.O.*, 1957]**
    (l) No suit either for administration or partition of assets of an illegal association can be filed by any member of such an association.

    In ***Mewa Ram*** v. ***Ram Gopal***, High Court of Allahabad held that such partition of assets of an illegal association is not possible at all because a decree for partition would amount to be in substance a direction for winding up or a decree for dissolution and accounts.
    (m) A member of an illegal association who has paid any money to such association would be able to recover it from the director or agents or association before the money so paid has been applied to an illegal purpose. **[*Greenpur* v. *Co-operatives* (1926)]**
    (n) Members of an illegal association have a beneficial interest in the property belonging to such association. **[*Queen* v. *Tankard*, (1894)]**

CHAPTER 3 FORMATION OF A COMPANY

1. Persons who buy property with a view to selling it later at profit to a company to be formed by them are regarded as promoters. **(Glucstein v. Barner)**
2. The legal position of a promoter is that he stands in a fiduciary position in relation to the company he promotes. **(Erdanger v. New Sombrero Phosphate Co.)**
3. A promoter is *neither* trustee *nor* agent of the company but he stands in a fiduciary position towards the company. The fiduciary obligation of promoter, means an obligation of promoter to disclose fully all material facts of contracts, profit made or to be made and his personal interest in any transaction/contract with the company. In fiduciary capacity a promoter has duty:
   (a) 'Not to make any secret profit'.
   (b) To make full and fair disclosure of his personal interest in every transaction with the company.
   (c) To give the benefit of Negotiations to the company
   (d) To ensure that prospectus issued at their instance contains all material facts and particulars and does not contain any untrue statement
4. Liability of promoters include liability for not including prescribed matters and reports as per sec 56
5. Promoters can not claim remuneration and reimbursement of expenses incurred by them in promotion—
   (a) as a matter of right
   (b) even if they have already entered into a contract with the prospective Directors
   (c) even if the articles provide for it. Provision in articles merely gives the directors an authority to make such payment but does not give the promoters a right to claim remuneration or to sue the company for the same.
   (d) Unless the company after incorporation makes a contract with promoters.
6. (a) The company is not bound by the preliminary contracts
   (b) The company cannot enforce the preliminary contracts
   (c) The company cannot rectify the preliminary contracts
   (d) The company can not adopt preliminary contracts either by passing special resolution or by making adoption of such contacts as one of the objects of the company in its Memorandum of Association. **[North Sydney Investment Co. V. Higgins]**
   (e) The promoters are personally liable for the preliminarily contracts
7. Notice of situation of registered office in Form No. 18 and Particulars of Directors, Managing Directors, Manager and Secretory in Form No 32 need not be filed at the time of incorporation since these can be filed within 30 days of incorporation as per sec 146 and sec 266.
8. The following forms must be filed with the Registrar within 30 days of incorporation.
   (a) Notice of situation of the registered office in form No 18 and
   (b) Particulars of Directors, Managing Director, Manager and Secretary in form No 32.
9. Statutory Declaration in Form No 1 must be signed by Attorney or a Pleader entitled to appear before a High Court or Advocate of Supreme/High Court
10. The certificate of Incorporation once issued cannot be challenged on any ground whatsoever. Even on the following grounds:
    (a) Where one person has signed on behalf of all the subscribers.
    (b) Where all the signatories to Memorandum are minors
    (c) Where all the signatures on the Memorandum are forged
    (d) Where illegal objects are incorporated in the object clause
11. On issue of certificate of Incorporation every company other than public company having a share capital, can commence its business and can exercise borrowing powers.
12. Certificate to commence business is required to be obtained by a public company having share capital.

13. Declaration to obtain certificate to commence business must be verified by **any one of directors or secretary** of the company **or** any secretary in whole time practice (if company does not have any secretary) as per sec 149
14. Provisional contracts need no rectification since provisional contracts become automatically binding on the company on issue of certificate to commence business.
15. Preliminary contracts are not required to filed at the time of incorporation.
16. The validity of a certificate of incorporation can not be disputed on any ground whatsoever Conclusiveness of Certificate of Incorporation
    (a) **According to Section 35 of the Companies Act** Certificate of incorporation given by the Registrar of Companies in respect of any association shall be conclusive evidence that—
        1. all the requirements of Companies Act have been complied with in respect of its registration as well as matters precedent and incidental thereto,
        2. the association is a company authorized to be registered and duly registered under the Act.

    (b) **Meaning of 'conclusive evidence'** The term 'conclusive evidence' means that no inquiry shall be allowed to be made regarding the correctness or incorrectness of any particulars contained in the certificate of incorporation.

CHAPTER 4 MEMORANDUM OF ASSOCIATION

1. The Memorandum of association of a Public Company Limited by shares must be as per Table B in Schedule I to the Act.
2. The Memorandum of association concludes with association clause as per sec 15(c).
3. **Territorial Limit Clause** In case of companies (other than trading corporations) with object not confined to one state, the states to whose territories the object extends must also be mentioned under object clause as per sec 13(1) (e)
4. Notice of situation of Registered office must be given to the Registrar within 30 days of the date of incorporation.
5. Capital clause and liability clause are not required in Memorandum of Association of unlimited company whether or not having share capital and capital clause is not required in case of companies having no share capital.
6. A company can be signatory to the Memorandum since it is a separate legal entity but a firm cannot.
7. Alteration of name clause involving merely **Rectification of name** as per sec 22(1) requires Ordinary Resolution and approval of Central Govt.
8. Alteration of name clause involving merely **deletion of word 'Private'** on conversion of a Private Company into a Public Company requires only Special Resolution as per sec 21
9. Alteration of name clause of non-Licensed company (other than these involving Rectification of name as per sec 22(1), or deletion of word 'Private') requires Special Resolution and Approval of Central Govt.
10. Registration of Alteration of name requires that a copy of Approval of Central Govt. (whenever, if any required) must be filed with the Registrar within 3 months from the date of Approval as per sec 23.
11. Change of Registered office within the same city, town or village requires **only Board's resolution** as per sec 146 (2)
12. Change of Registered office from one city, town or village to another within the jurisdiction of the same ROC requires **only Special Resolution** as per Provisio to Sec 146 (2)
13. Change of Registered office from the jurisdiction of one ROC to the jurisdiction of another ROC within the same state requires the **Special Resolution and confirmation of Regional Director**.
14. Alteration of Registered Office Clause (i.e, change from one state to another) requires **Special Resolution and confirmation of CLB as per sec 17.**

15. Registration of change of Registered office from the jurisdiction of one ROC to the jurisdiction of another ROC within the same state requires the filing of a certified copy of confirmation of Regional Director and Printed copy of altered Memorandum within **2 months** of the date of confirmation.
16. Registration of Alteration of Registered office clause requires filing of a certified copy of confirmation of Company Law Board and printed copy of altered Memorandum within **3 months** of the date of confirmation as per sec 18.
17. Registration of Alteration of object clause requires filing of a copy of **Special Resolution within 1 months** from the date of resolution as per sec 17(1).
18. To commerce a new business covered under sub-clause 'Others Objects' but not covered under sub-clause 'Main objects', requirement is Ordinary Resolution and Approval of Central Govt as per sec 149 (2B).
19. To commence a new business covered under sub-clause 'Other Objects but not covered under sub-clause 'Main Objects' requirement is Special Resolution as per sec 149 (2A).
20. (a) where the company is a club, its member is bound by alteration increasing his liability even if he does not agree in writing
    (b) where the company is not a club or other association, its member is not bound by alteration increasing his liability unless he agrees in writing
    (c) An unlimited company can be made a registered company as per Sec 32.
    (d) Liability of Directors of a limited company can be made unlimited as per Sec 323 if authorised by Articles.
    (e) Alteration of Memorandum invariably does not involve passing of special resolution since the Rectification of name as per sec 22 and alteration of capital clause as per sec 94 requires passing of ordinary resolution.
    (f) Alteration of Memorandum invariably does not require Articles' Authorisation since alteration of share capital requires Articles' Authorisation as per Sec 94.
21. (a) Acts ultra vires the Companies Act/Memorandum shall be void and can not be ratified even by an unanimous resolution of all the shareholders. **[Ashbury Railway Carriage & Iron Co. v. Riche]**
    (b) Acts ultra vires the Articles of Association/Powers of Directors but within the powers of the company shall not be altogether void and can be rectified and made valid by altering its Articles by a special resolution.
    (c) A company cannot be sued on ultravires transactions.
    (d) A members can bring injunction against the company to restrain it from doing ultravires acts
22. For an act which is ultravires the company,
    (a) The company can not be sued by outsiders
    (b) The company can not sue outsiders
    (c) The directors can not be held liable
    (d) The directors can be held personally liable for breach of warranty of authority.
23. The Memorandum of Association can be altered in cases, in the mode and to the extent for which express provision is made in the Act.
24. The Memorandum of Association is the charter of the company which defines and conifens its objects. The Articles of Association are subordinate to the Memorandum of Association. Hence, in case of conflict between the two the provision of memorandum will be upheld.
25. **Limits on the Power of Alteration of Objects Clause**
    Substantive Limits i.e. Change must be for any of the following specified purposes:
    (a) to carry on its business more economically or more efficiently,
    (b) to attain its main purpose by new or improved means,
    (c) to enlarge or change the local area of its operations.
    (d) to carry on some business which under the existing circumstance may be conveniently or advantageously combined with the business of the company.
    (e) to restrict or abandon any of the objects specified in the memorandum, or

(f) to sell or dispose of the whole, or any part of the undertaking of the company,
(g) to amalgamate with any other company or body of persons.

Procedural Limits

1. Passing of the special resolution.
2. Filing within 1 month from date of resolution the following documents:
   (a) A copy of special resolution
   (b) A printed copy of altered Memorandum.

CHAPTER 5 ARTICLES OF ASSOCIATION

1. A public company limited by shares need not have its own articles since it can adopt table A as per Sec 28
2. If a public company limited by shares does not have its own articles , Table A will apply as per Sec 28
3. Table A contains model form of article of association of company limited by shares per sec 29.
4. A public limited company is not required to get its articles registered if it adopts Table A in full.
5. The articles must also state the number of members with which the company is to be registered in case of every unlimited company as per sec 27(2).
6. The articles must also state the amount of share capital with which the company is to be registered in case of every unlimited company having share capital as per Sec 27 (2).
7. The articles must also state the number of members with which the company is to be registered in case of every company limited by guarantee as per sec 27 (2).
8. Alteration of article involving conversation of public company into private company requires special resolution and approval of Central Govt. as per sec 31(c) and 321 (2A).
9. Any Alteration of articles not involving conversion of public company into private company requires only special resolution as per sec 31(1).
10. (a) Alteration of articles must neither be inconsistent with any of the provisions of Act or Memorandum of Association nor with an order of Company Law Board.
    (b) Alteration having the effect of increasing the liability of a member shall not be binding upon him unless the company is a club any other associations.
    (c) Alteration may have a retrospective effect so long as it does not effect the things already done by the company and alteration is for the benefit of the company as a whole. **[Allen v. Gold Feet of West Africa]**
    (d) Alteration must not constitute a fraud on minority.
    (e) Alteration must not cause a breach of contract with an outsider.
    (f) The power to alter articles is a statutory power and it can not be taken away by any provision in the Memorandum or Articles. **[Walker Vs. London Tramways Co. (1879)]**
11. A outsider is not entitled to sue the company for enforcement to the article even the article provide certain right to him since the memorandum and articles do not constitute a contract between the company and outsider. **[Eley V. Positive Govt. Life Assurance Co. Ltd (1876)]**
12. The memorandum and articles of association are open for inspection by any person as per sec 610.
13. Doctrine of constructive notice is the presumed knowledge of outsiders as to the contents of memorandum & articles of association.
14. Doctrine of indoor management entitles outsiders to assume that the provisions of the articles of association have been duly complied with by the company.
15. There must not be any ultravires act or illegality since the doctrine of Indoor management protects the outsiders against the procedural irregularities and not illegalities. **[Rubben V. Great Fingal Consolidated (1906)]**
16. Binding effects of memorandum and Articles
    (a) Members bound to the Co.
    (b) Company bound to the members.

(c) Between Members Interse
(d) Between company and outsiders

17. **Conditions for Availability of the benefit of Doctrine of Indoor Management**
    (a) The person dealing with the company must have the knowledge of the Memorandum and Articles
    (b) The person dealing with the company must not have knowledge of irregularity.
    (c) The person dealing with the company must not be put upon an enquiry
    (d) There must be some procedural or internal irregularity.
    (e) There must not be any ultra vires act or illegality.
18. **Exceptions to the Doctrine of Indoor Management**
    (a) Knowledge of Irregularity
    (b) Suspicion of Irregularity
    (c) Forgery
    (d) No knowledge of Articles
    (e) Acts beyond Apparent Authority

CHAPTER 6 PROSPECTUS

1. Prospectus is written document inviting deposits from the public or inviting offers from the public for the subscription/purchase of shares/debentures of a body corporate.
2. An offer made to at least 50 persons is treated as an offer to public.
3. Prospectus is required to be issued where shares/debentures are offered to the public.
4. A copy of prospectus to be delivered to the registrar for registration must be signed by every director or proposed director or his agent authorised in writing as per sec 60 (1)
5. A copy of prospectus to be delivered to the registrar for registration on or before the date of its publication as per sec 60(1)
6. Prospectus must be issued within 90 days from the date of its delivery to the Registrar as per Sec 60 (4).
7. (a) Shelf prospectus means a prospectus issued by any financial institution or bank for one or more issue of securities or class of securities specified in that prospectus.
   (b) Red-herring prospectus means a prospectus which does not have complete particulars on the price of the securities offered and the quantum of securities offered as per sec 60 B.
   (c) Deemed prospectus is a document by which offer for sale to public is made by the issuing house to whom the company allots or agrees to allot shares or debentures.
   (d) Abridged prospectus means a memorandum containing prescribed salient features of a prospectus.
8. Every prospectus must state the matters specified in Part I of Schedule II to the Act.
9. Every prospectus must set out the reports specified in Part II of Schedule II to the Act as per sec 56
10. As per SEBI guidelines, rating of a credit agency is mandatory for debentures with maturity period of more than 18 months
11. Prospectus must contain a report from the auditors on Profits & losses, assets & liabilities and rate of dividend of the company for each of the 5 financial years preceding the issue of prospectus.
12. Untrue statement in a prospectus covers both false statement and concealment of material facts as per sec 65.
13. A person who subscribed the shares on the faith of misstatement as to material fact has remedies against the Company and its Directors, Promoters and Experts.
14. A person who purchased in the open market the share of a company whose prospectus contained fraudulent statements has no remedies against any one.

15. In case of misleading prospectus, the right of rescission is not lost if such right is exercised before the company goes into liquidation.
16. (a) A person who subscribed shares on the faith of mis-statement as to material fact has a right to rescind the contract to take shares if there is misrepresentation as to material fact irrespective of the fact whether the misrepresentation was made innocently or fraudulently or the aggrieved party has suffered some loss or not.
    (b) A person who subscribed shares on the faith of mis-statement as to material fact has a right to claim damages if misrepresentation was made fraudulently and the aggrieved partly has suffered some loss.
    (c) Right to claim damages may be exercised against the company only after rescinding the contract of allotment. **[Houldsworth v, City Glargow Bank (1880)] [Derry v. Feek (1889)]**
    (d) Right to claim damages may be exercised against the person who authorized the issue of prospectus even without rescinding the contract of allotment.
17. Right to claim damages for misrepresentation against those who authorised the issue of prospectus may be exercised even if the company goes into liquidation.
18. (a) The company and every person who is knowingly a party to the issue of prospectus without registration shall be punishable with fine upto Rs. 50,000.
    (b) Every person who had authorised the issue of prospectus containing an untrue statement shall be punishable with imprisonment for a term upto 2 years or with fine upto Rs 5,000 or with both.
    (c) Any person who fraudulently induces another person to invest money shall be punishable with imprisonment for a term upto 5 years or with fine upto Rs 1,00,000 or with both
    (d) Any person who makes an application to a company for acquiring shares in a fictitious name shall be punishable with imprisonment for term upto 5 years as per sec 68 A (1).
19. Statement in lieu of prospectus is required to be issued by public company which issue shares privately to friends and relatives, as per sec 70.
20. The statement in lieu of prospectus must contain the particulars and reports as set out in Schedule III to the Act as per sec 70
21. Statement in lieu of prospectus must be delivered to the registrar for registration **at least 3 days** before the allotment of shares/debenture as per sec 70.
22. **Cases in which Right of Recession is lost**
    (i) **Affirmation/Addition of Contract** The aggrieved party must exercise the right to rescind the contract before he affirms his contract for purchase of shares. In the following cases, it has been held that the subscriber has affirmed the contract:
    (a) where he has received dividend or paid calls ***[Scholey* v. *Central Railway]***,
    (b) where he attends and votes at general meetings [***Shrpley* v. *Louth Etc. Co.***],
    (c) where he executes a transfer of his shares [***Crowley's case]***.

    It may be noted that a transfer of part of shares before discovery of misrepresentation does not affect his right as to the rest. [***Re Mount Morgan Etc. Ltd.,***]
    (ii) Lapse of Reasonable Time
    (iii) Commencement of Liquidation of Company

CHAPTER 7 ALLOTMENT OF SHARES

1. (a) Allotment is the acceptance by the company of the offer to take shares made by an applicant.
   (b) Re-issue of forfeited shares (whether to outsider or member) is not an allotment of share since it is sale of forfeited shares which had already been allotted.
   (c) Allotment must be made by proper authority within a reasonable time.
   (d) Allotment must be communicated to the applicants and must be absolute and unconditional

2. Subscription list shall open from the beginning of 5th (or later time specified in prospectus) from date of publication of prospectus to the public
3. The Companies Act is silent about the time for which the subscription list must be kept open.
4. An application for shares is not revocable until the end of 5th day from the opening of subscription list as per sec 75(5).
5. (a) As per the Companies Act, minimum subscription is required in case of first allotment of shares and not subsequent allotment of shares.
   (b) A per SEBI guidelines, the minimum subscription in respect of public and right issues (excluding the offer for sale of securities) is 90% of the issued amount
   (c) Application money of each share must be at least 5% of the nominal value of share as per sec 69(3).
   (d) Application money must be deposited in a scheduled bank until the receipt of minimum subscription or certificate to commence business, whichever is earlier
6. As per the Companies Act, the companies must refund the application money within 130 days without interest and with interest @ 6% p.a, for the delayed period beyond 130 days from the date of issue of prospectus if minimum subscription is not received within 120 days from the date of issue of prospectus
7. As per SEBI guidelines, the company must refund the subscription amount in full within 78 days without interest and with interest @ 15% p.a for the delayed period beyond 78 days from the date of closure of the issue if 90% of the issued amount is not received within 60 days from the date of closure of issue
8. In case of No listing permission within 10 weeks from the date of closing of subscription list the company must repay all moneys received from applicants within 8 days from the day the company becomes liable to pay
9. In case of over subscription, the company must repay excess subscription within 8 days from the day the company becomes liable to pay
10. In case of no listing permission within 10 weeks from the date of closing of subscription list and in case of over subscription, if required money is not paid within 8 days from the day the company becomes listing to pay, the following shall be liable repay money with interest at prescribed rate, (which shall be minimum 4% and maximum 15%) for the delayed period beyond the expiry of 8th day—The company and its directors jointly and severally.
11. (a) An allotment is said to be irregular if it is made in contravention of the provisions of Sec 69 or 70
    (b) An irregular allotment is voidable at the option of the applicant within 2 months , after the holding of statutory meeting and not later where allotment is made before the statutory meeting.
    (c) An irregular allotment is voidable at the option of the applicant within 2 months, after the date of allotment and not later where allotment is made after the statutory meeting.
    (d) Every director who is knowing responsible for the contraventions of any of provisions of sec 69 or sec 70 with respect to allotment shall be liable to compensate the company and the allotee for the loss suffered provided legal proceedings commence within 2 years from the date of allotment.
12. A return of allotment must be in Form No 2.
13. A return of allotment is required to be filed in case of issue of bonus shares as per sec 75
14. A return of allotment must be filed within 30 days of allotment (or period extended by registrar)
15. The payment of underwriting commission requires authorisation in articles.
16. Maximum payment of underwriting commission is 5% of the issue price of shares or amount or rate authorised by articles whichever is less and 2.5% of the issue price of debentures or amount or rate authorised by articles whichever is less
17. Return of Allotment is not required in case of allotment of debentures and issue of shares to signatatories to M/A as per sec 75

CHAPTER 8 SHARES AND SHARE CAPITAL

1. (a) A share is the smallest unit into which the capital of the company is divided.
   (b) A share is not a sum of money but is an interest measured by a sum of money and made up of various rights contained in the contract.
   (c) Stock is an aggregate of fully paid shares which have been legally consolidated which is transferable in fraction also.
   (d) The shares are the movable properties transferable in the manner provided by the articles of the company.
   (e) Articles' Authorisation is required for issue of stock and not for issue of shares as per sec. 94.
2. (a) The company can issue equity shares without voting rights
   (b) The company can issue equity shares with differential voting rights
   (c) The company can issue equity shares with differential dividend rights
   (d) A company can issue equity shares with differential rights as to dividend or voting as per sec. 86.
3. Unless otherwise stated, a preference share is deemed to be cumulative, non-participating and non-convertible.
4. No company limited by shares shall issue any preference share which is redeemable after the expiry of a period of 20 years from the date of issue.
5. Deferred shares can be issued by private company limited by shares.
6. Issue of shares at premium neither requires Articles' Authorisation nor ordinary resolution nor any approval of Central Govt. or Company Law Board.
7. Issue of shares at discount requires ordinary resolution and approval of Company Law Board as per Sec 79.
8. Securities premium may be applied to issue fully paid bonus shares to members as per Sec 78
9. Subject to approval, maximum allowable Rate of discount is 10% as per Sec 79.
10. The shares may be issued at discount only after the expiry of 1 year from the date of certificate to commence business.
11. The issue of shares at discount must be made within 2 months of approval of Central Govt.
12. Issue of Sweat Equity Shares requires only Special Resolution.
13. A valid call on shares can be made by the Board of directors by a resolution passed at its meeting.
14. If Articles of a public company limited by shares are silent, the amount of call must not exceed 25% of the nominal value of the share.
15. Table A specifies the Maximum Rate of 5% p.a. and not the Minimum rate.
16. Table A specifies the Maximum Rate of 6% p.a and not the Minimum rate.
17. (a) A company may accept calls-in -advance if so authorised by its Articles.
    (b) Member is not entitled to voting right in respect of calls in advance.
    (c) A company if so authorised by its Articles may pay dividends in proportion to the amount paid up on each share where a larger amount is paid up on shares than on others.
    (d) Call in advance is refundable only in the event of winding up.
18. Authorised capital is stated in the memorandum of a company limited by shares.
19. That portion of uncalled share capital which shall not be capable of being called up except in the event of winding up of the company is called Reserve Capital.
20. Creation of reserve capital requires Special Resolution.
21. Reserve Capital can be created only by a limited company.
22. (a) Reserve Capital can not be dealt with in any manner under a power in the Memorandum of Association.
    (b) A company can not borrow on the security of its Reserve Capital
    (c) Reserve capital cannot be turned into uncalled capital without the leave of the Court
    (d) Reserve capital is not required to be disclosed in the balance sheet.

23. Financial Assistance for the purchase of its own shares or shares of holding company is justified where loan is made by the company to its employees (other than directors or managers) to enable them to purchase or subscribe for fully paid shares for an amount not exceeding his salary or wages for a period of 6 months as per Sec. 77.
24. A company can not purchase its own shares or other specified securities out of proceeds of an earlier issue of same kind of shares or other specified securities as per Sec. 77A
25. Buy back of shares requires Articles Authorisation and Special Resolution as per Sec. 77A
26. Where buy-back does not exceed 10% of the total equity up capital and free reserves either board's resolution or special resolution is required as per Sec 77A.
27. Minimum time interval between two buy-back must be a period of 365 days as per Sec 77A.
28. The buy-back of shares must not exceed 25% of total paid up capital and free reserves as per Sec 77A.
29. The maximum Debt-Equity Ratio after Buy-back can be 2 : 1 as per Sec 77A.
30. The buy back must be completed within 12 months from date of passing special resolution/ board's resolution as per Sec 77A.
31. On buy back of shares by a listed company, the company must file Solvency Declaration and Buy-back Return with the Registrar and SEBI
32. For the purpose of 77A (Buy back), The term 'Free Reserves includes Securities Premium.
33. Where a company purchases its own shares out of free reserves a sum equal to the nominal value of shares so purchased must be transferred to Capital Redemption Reserves Account.
34. Where a company buys back its own shares, it must not issue same kind of shares including right shares within 6 months as per Sec 77A.
35. Where a company buys back its own shares, it must extinguish and physically destroy the securities so bought back within 7 days of last date of completion of buy back in the presence of Merchant Bankers or Registrar or Statutory Auditor as per Sec 77A.
36. A company limited by shares can issue redeemable preference shares as per Sec. 80
37. Redemption of Redeemable Preference Shares requires Articles Authorisation as per Sec 80.
38. Maximum Period of Redemption of Redeemable Preference Shares can be 20 years.
39. Sources of Redemption of Redeemable Pref. shares are divisible profits and Proceeds of fresh issue of shares as per Sec 80
40. Sources of providing premium payable on redemption of Redeemable Pref. Shares are Profits and Securities Premium as per Sec 80
41. Where Red. Pref. Shares are redeemed out of divisible profits an amount equivalent to the nominal value of shares so redeemed must be transferred to Capital Redemption Reserve Account as per Sec 80
42. The Capital Redemption Reserve may be applied by the company in issuing fully paid bonus shares to members as per Sec 80
43. Proceeds of fresh issue of shares mean issue price (excluding Securities Premium and discount) of only equity or pref shares.
44. Further shares must be offered to the existing equity share holders when it is proposed to increase the subscribed capital of the company by allotment of further shares at any time after the expiry of 2 years from the formation of a company or after the expiry of 1 year from the first allotment of shares whichever is earlier.
45. New shares can be offered to the outsiders before offering them to the existing shareholders if special resolution is passed or ordinary resolution is passed and Approval of Cent. Govt. is taken.
46. The terms of issue of Convertible Debentures/Loan to any person other than Govt. must be approved by Special Resolution and Central Govt.
47. The term of issue of Convertible Debentures/Loan to Govt. must be approved by Central Govt. only.
48. Alteration of Capital Clause requires Articles authorisation and Ordinary Resolution.
49. A notice of alteration of capital clause must be given to the Registrar within 30 days of alteration.
50. Reduction of share capital may involve reduction of subscribed capital.

51. The restrictions as to reduction of share capital apply to every limited company having share capital.
52. Reduction of share capital requires Articles' Authorisation Special Resolution and Court's order
53. Variation of shareholders' rights requires authorisation of Memorandum/articles or no prohibition by the term of issue of such shares and written consent of 75% holders of that class or special resolution at separate meeting of shareholders of that class.
54. Dissentient shareholders can apply to the Court within 21 days to have the variation cancelled if they hold atleast 10% of issued shares of that class.
55. Issue of Bonus Shares requires only Special Resolution.
56. Fully paid bonus shares can be issued out of Securities Premium, Capital Redemption Reserve. and General Reserve.
57. A return of bonus issue must be filed with Registrar within 30 days of allotment.
58. Share certificates must be issued to allottee within 3 months of allotment.
59. Share certificates must be delivered to transferee within 2 months of transfer of shares.
60. Issue of share certificate neither requires Articles Authorisation nor Approval of Central Govt.
61. Issue of share warrant requires Articles' Authorisation and approval of Central Govt as per Sec. 114.
62. Every public company limited by shares can issue share warrants as per Sec 114.
63. The bearer of a share warrant is not a member of the company unless the articles provide otherwise as per Sec 115(5).
64. (a) Share warrant can be issued only in respect of fully paid up shares.
    (b) Share warrant does not constitute qualification for directorship.
    (c) Holder of share warrant can not present petition for winding up.
    (d) Holder of share warrant shall be deemed to be member of the company if the Articles provide as per Sec. 115(5).
65. Forfeiture of shares requires both articles' authorisation and board's resolution.
66. Ex-member whose partly paid up shares have been forfeited may he held liable as contributory if the company goes into liquidation within 1 year of forfeiture.
67. A company can offer new shares to outsiders before offering them to the existing shareholders in the following 4 circumstances only:
    (a) Special Resolution
    (b) Ordinary Resolution and Central Govt's Approval
    (c) No Acceptance of Offer by Offeree/Renouncee
    (d) Allotment before expiry of Statutory Period
68. (a) A preference shareholder shall have a right to vote only on resolution placed before the company which directly affects the rights attached to the preference shares.
    (b) Any resolution for winding up of the company or for the repayment or the reduction of preference share capital shall be deemed directly to affect the rights attached to the preference shares.
69. Surrender of shares is short cut to the long procedure of forfeiture where their forfeiture is justified.
70. The company does not have inherent right of lien on shares since the right of lien must be expressly provided for in the Articles. Regulations 9 to 12 of Table A provide for this right.

CHAPTER 9 TRANSFER AND TRANSMISSION OF SHARES

1. (a) The shares are movable property which are transferable in the manner specified in the Act and the Articles.
   (b) The shares of a public company are freely transferable.
   (c) A private company can not impose absolute prohibition on transferability of shares
   (d) A public company can refuse to transfer shares for sufficient cause.

2. Notice of Refusal to transfer the shares must be given by a private company within 2 Months.
3. An appeal against the refusal to transfer the shares can be filed by transferor or transferee or person giving intimation of transmission with CLB.
4. An appeal against the refusal to transfer the share of a **private** company can be filed within 2 Months of receipt of notice of refusal.
5. An appeal against the refusal to transfer the shares of a **public** company can be filed within Reasonable time.
6. An application for rectification of register of members of a Pvt. co. is to be made to CLB within Reasonable time.
7. An application for rectification of register of members of a public Co. to CLB is to be made within 2 Months.
8. (a) Every member who is an individual can make a nomination.
   (b) Only an Individual can be nominee.
   (c) A minor can be named as a nominee.
   (d) Nomination can be made, or varied or cancelled at any time.
9. (a) In case of joint holding, transmission takes place when all the joint holders die or become insolvent as per Sec 109.
   (b) The need for certification arises where a member intends to transfer only a part of shares or shares of one share certificate to 2 or more persons.
   (c) Forged transfer is transfer of shares made on the basis of a transfer deed on which the transferor's signatures are forged and is nullity (i.e. without any legal effect.)
   (d) A transfer of shares shall be said to be blank if it contains the signature of the transferor but it does not contain the particulars relating to the transferee and shall remain valid only for such period as prescribed u/s 108.
10. A minor can not become a member because he does not have contractual capacity to enter any valid contract. But a minor can become transferee of a fully paid shares through guardian. **[Miss Nandita Jain V. BC & Co.]**
11. The shares of only public company are freely transferable and not of a private company as per Sec 3(1) (*iii*) and Sec 111A.

CHAPTER 10 MEMBERSHIP

1. (a) Every company must have minimum members.
   (b) A company having no share capital does not have any shareholder.
   (c) Subscribers to the memodandum of a company become members on registration of company even before any shares are allotted to them.
   (d) Holder of share warrant is a shareholder and not a member.
2. (a) Minor can not become a member of the company since he is not competent to contract.
   (b) Minor can become a transferee of fully paid shares through guardian.
   (c) A company, Registered Co-operative society, any Registered Society, and Central State Govt. can become member of a company since these are separate legal entities in the eyes of law.
   (d) A Partnership firm, a Hindu Undivided family, and a Trust can not become a member of the company since these are not separate legal entities in the eyes of law.
   (e) A partnership firm can become a member of licensed company as per Sec 25.
   (f) A company can become member of another company if it is so authorised by its M/A since it is a separate legal entity. But a subsidiary company can not become a member of its holding company except in two cases as per Sec 42 (2)
3. Every shareholder need not be member. Holder of share warrant and legal representative of a deceased member are shareholders and not members.

4. Every Member need not be shareholder. Following are Members but not shareholders:
   (a) Members of a Co. Ltd. by guarantee having no share capital, or an unlimited company having no share capital
   (b) List 'B' contributiories who ceased to be members within 12 months before the commencement of winding up of
   (c) A deceased member until removal of his name from register of member
   (d) Subscribers to M/A before allotment of shares.
5. The various modes of acquiring membership are shown below:
   (a) By Subscribing to Memorandum
   (b) By Application and Allotment of Shares
   (c) By Transfer
   (d) By Transmission
   (e) By Acquiescence or Estoppel
   (f) By Agreeing to Take Qualification Shares

CHAPTER 11 BORROWING POWERS AND DEBENTURES

1. (a) A trading company need not have express power to borrow in its memorandum.
   (b) A non-trading company must have an express power to borrow in its memorandum.
   (c) A private company can excercise its borrowing powers immediately after obtaining the certificate of incorporation.
   (d) A public company can exercise its borrowing powers only after obtaining the certificate of commencement of business
2. (a) Borrowings ultravires the Company/Memoradum are void and can not be ratified even by an unanimous resolution passed at a general meeting.
   (b) In case of borrowings ultravires the company, the lender can sue the directors for breach of warranty of authority.
   (c) Borrowings ultravires the directors are not altogether void and can be ratified by altering articles by a special resolution with retrospective effect so as to give directors extra powers.
   (d) The company and not the concerned directors shall be liable when the borrowings ultravires the directors are ratified by the company
3. (a) A private company can issue debentures immediately after obtaining the certificate of Incorporation.
   (b) A public company can issue debentures only after obtaining a certificate of commencement of business.
   (c) Only the board of directors can issue debentures by means of resolution passed at its meeting but subject to Sec 293.
   (d) No company can issue any debentures carrying voting rights.
4. In case of a public company and private company which is subsidiary of a public company, Board's resolution and ordinary resolution are required where the moneys to be borrowed together with the money already borrowed exceed the aggregate of paid up capital and free reserves
5. A person who owes money to the company can be appointed as a debenture trustee.
6. A partnership firm can not be appointed as debenture trustee.
7. Debenture trustees are required to be appointed in case of debentures with maturity of more than 18 Months
8. Creation of debenture redemption reserve is mandatory in case of debentures with a maturity period of more than 18 months
9. (a) Minimum subscription is not required in case of debentures.
   (b) Four statutory books relating to debentures required are Register of Charges, Register of Debentureholders, Index of Debentureholders, Foreign Register of Debentureholders.

(c) Debenture interest book is a statistical book and not a statutory book.

(d) Return of allotment is not required to be filed with the Registrar in case of allotment of debentures.

10. If Pari-passu clause in included in the debentures, then after execution of the deed containing the charges or where these is no deed after the execution of any debentures of the series, the prescribed particulars must be filed with the Registrar within 30 days as per Sec 128

CHAPTER 12 FIXED AND FLOATING CHARGES

1. As per Sec 124 the expression Charge includes a mortgage.
2. Pledge of movable property is not required to be registered (as per sec 125 (4)).
3. Particulars of every charge alongwith copy of instrument creating charge must be filed with the Registrar within 30 days of its creation (extended further period of 30 days) as per sec 125 (1).
4. Where a company acquires any property which is already subject to charge, particulars of every charge alongwith copy of instrument creating charge must be filed with the Registrar within 30 days of its creation (extended further period of 30 days) as per sec 127.
5. In case of non-registration
   (a) The charge shall **be void** against the liquidator and any creditor of the company .
   (b) The charge shall **not be void** against the company.
   (c) Any contract or obligation for the repayment of the money secured by the charge shall remain unaffected.
   (d) Money secured by charge immediately becomes payable.
6. The company must give intimation to the Registrar of the payment or satisfaction of any charge **in full** within 30 days from the date of such payment or satisfaction as per sec 138.
7. Company or any person interested in the charge can register charge.
8. Fixed charge can be created by any person but floating charge can be created only by an incorporated body.
9. Floating charge is an equity charge. Neither ownership nor the possession of the property is passed to the lender. Borrower has the freedom to deal with the asset charged in the ordinary course of the business.

CHAPTER 13 MEETINGS AND PROCEDURES

1. Statutory meeting is to be called by public company having share capital as per sec 165.
2. Statutory meeting is to be held after the expiry of 1 month but before the expiry of 6 months from the date of issue of certificate to commence business as per sec 165.
3. Statutory meeting can be called by Duly Constituted Board as sec 165.
4. Statutory meetings can be called at a notice shorter than of at least 21 clear Days if the consent of members holding 95% paid up capital/voting power is obtained prior to or at or even subsequent to meeting as sec 165.
5. Statutory meeting can be called at any time, any day and at any place since the Act is silent on this point.
6. Statutory report can be sent at notice shorter than of a least 21 clear days with the consent of all members entitled to vote as per sec 165.
7. If quorum is not present within half and hour from the time appointed, extraordinary general meeting shall stand dissolved if it is called on requisition of members as per sec 169.
8. Minimum quorum is 5 members personally present at statutory meeting adjourned due to others reason as per sec 174.
9. Members present personally or by proxy shall constitute quorum at general meeting adjourned due to lack of quorum as per sec 174

10. One member present personally or by proxy shall not constitute quorum at general meeting adjourned due to lack of quorum because sec 174 provides that **members** present personally or by proxy shall constitute quorum. Hence there must be at least 2 members present personally or by proxy.
11. Members are entitled to appoint more than one proxy even if article of association does not provide in case of a public company having share capital as per sec 176.
12. Proxy (if not member) has no right to speak unless articles otherwise provide.
13. Ordinary business can be transacted only at AGM as per sec 173
14. AGM is to be called by every company as per sec 166
15. First AGM is to be held within 18 months of incorporation [as per Sec 166(1)] but within 9 months of end of financial year [as per sec 210 (3)]
16. Subsequent AGM is to be held within 15 months of previous AGM as per sec 166(1) but within 6 months of end of financial year [as per sec 210]
17. The period of financial year of a company must not exceed 15 months but may extend to 18 months with special permission of Registrar as per provisio to Sec 210 (4).
18. AGM can be called by the Central Govt. as per sec 167.
19. AGM can be called at a notice shorter than of at least 21 clear days with **consent of all members** entitled to vote as per sec 171 to 173.
20. AGM can be called at any place within the city, town or village in which Regd. office is situated as per sec 166(2).
21. AGM adjourned due to lack of quorum can be called at any time, any day and at any place as the board may determine.
22. Sec 167 (Power of CG to call/direct AGM) can be invoked by a member and not by company itself if meeting was called but could not be properly commenced because directors abandon it before taking up any business.
23. Extraordinary general meeting by the board on requisition is to be called within 45 days from the date of deposit or requisition by members as per sec 169.
24. Extraordinary general meeting by the requisitionsts is to be called within 21 days and did not call within 45 days from the date of deposit of requisition as per sec 169.
25. Extra ordinary general meeting may be called by the Company Law Board as per sec 186.
26. Extra ordinary general meeting may be called at anytime, any day and at any place since the Act is silent on this point.
27. In case of a public company having share capital the requisition for extraordinary general meeting may be made by any number of members having at least 10% of paid up share capital carrying voting power as per sec 169.
28. A person who holds majority in value of paid up share capital held by all of them can call meeting as per sec 169 (6).
29. Class meeting of members may be convened by the company as per sec 106.
30. Shareholders' rights may be varied with the consent in writing of holders of at least 75% issued shares of that class.
31. Special notice is required to remove director before the expiry of term as per sec 284 (2).
32. Requisition for moving resolution at AGM can be made by member having at least 5% voting power as per sec 188 (2).
33. Ordinary resolutions not passed by all the members are not required to be filed with the Registrar, as per sec 192 (4).
34. Minutes of board meeting can not be inspected by a member of the company as per sec 196.
35. In case of a public company a poll may be demanded by any member or members present personally or by proxy and holding shares which carry at least 10% of voting powers or on which at least Rs. 50,000 has been paid whichever is less as per sec 179.
36. A poll demanded on a resolution for the election of chairman must be taken immediately as per Sec 180.
37. Voting rights on a poll will be in the same proportion as the capital paid up on these shares bears to the total paid up capital. But no voting right in respect of calls in advance unless call becomes presently payable as per Sec 92(2)

38. There can be restriction on exercise of voting right of members who have not paid calls if Article's provide as such as per Sec 181
39. AGM may be held on public holiday in case of AGM of Private Co. and Adjourned AGM of Public Co.
40. AGM may be held on a place other than Regd. Office in case of AGM of Private Co. and Adjourned AGM of Public Co.
41. AGM may be held at a time outside business hours in case of AGM of Private Co. and Adjourned AGM of Public Co.
42. Chairman need not necessarily be member or director. But chairman must be *either* a member *or* a director per Sec 175 (1), Members personally present shall elect one of themselves to be the chairman on show of hands unless the articles otherwise provide. Thus, chairman need not be director. Regulation 50 and 51, permits director to be the chairman. Sec 270 does not require directors to obtain share qualification and hence director need not be member.
43. Proxy cannot cast vote against the wishers of a person who appointed him since the relationship between a shareholder and his proxy is that of principal and agent and thus proxy must act according to the wishes of a shareholder.
44. Proxy appointed by a body corporate is considered as member personally present for the purposes of quorum.
45. Proxy bearing the latest date will supersed the earlier are. The earlier proxy stands revoked on deposit of proxy bearing the latest date.
46. Only business left unfinished at the original meeting can be transacted at the adjoined meeting. This is true with respect to all general meetings other than statutory meeting. At Adjourned statutory meeting, any resolution of which notice has been given before or after the original meeting may be passed as per Sec. 165(8).
47. Chairman cannot always cast two votes in case of equality of votes. Chairman who is not a member can cast only one casting vote as chairman in case of equality of votes. Chairman who is member can cast two votes (one as member and second as chairman) in case of equality of votes.
48. Proxy can be counted as quorum in 3 cases:
    (a) AGM by CLB u/s 167.
    (b) EGM by CLB u/s 186
    (c) Meeting Adjourned due to lock of quorum
49. One member can constitute quorum in 4 cases:
    (a) AGM by CLB u/s 167
    (b) EGM by CLB u/s 186
    (c) Member present in more than one capacity
    (d) Class meeting whose a class of shares is held by one shareholder.

CHAPTER 14 REGISTERS, RETURNS SERVICE AND AUTHENTICATION OF DOCUMENTS

1. Every company is required to have Register of Members as per sec 150.
2. An index of members is required by a company having more than 50 members.
3. The register of member must remain open to inspection by members free and by any other person on payment of prescribed fee
4. A company may close the register of members for a period not exceeding 45 days in a year but not exceeding 30 days at any one time.
5. Annual return is required to be filed within 60 days from date on which general meeting should have been held.
6. Annual return must be prepared in form as per schedule V.
7. A document to be served on the Company must be sent by post under certificate of posting or registered post or hand delivery

8. A document to be served on the Registrar must be sent by post under certificate of posting or registered post or hand delivery.
9. A document to be served on the Members of the company must be sent by post or hand delivery
10. Document need not be served at address abroad as per sec 51.
11. Notice of General Meeting is deemed to have been served at the expiration of 48 hours after posting.
12. Unless the Act provides otherwise, a document or proceeding requiring authentication by a company must be signed by a director or manager or secretory or other authorised officer.
13. Maximum period for closure of register of members in a year is 45 days.
14. Maximum period for closure of register of members at any one time is 30 days.
15. A copy of register of members must be supplied within 10 working days.
16. Alteration in the register of members must be made in index within 14 Days.
17. Minutes books of general meeting and not of board meeting are open for inspection by any members as per sec 193 & 196
18. Register & Index of members and debentureholders is open for inspection by any person.
19. Register of charges is open for inspection by member only.
20. Common seal is not required (a) for actual execution of deed on behalf of company by its attorney as per sec. 48 (b) for a document requiring authentication signed by an authorised officer as per Sec 54.
21. The Articles which contain the provision contrary to Sec. 51 can not be enforced nor can they limit the mode of service to only one of the modes provided by the stature. **[Sadasiv v. Gandhi Seva Samaj]**

Summarised Table I Showing the Various Provisions Applicable to Various Meetings

Basis of Comparison	*Statutory Meeting*	*Annual General Meeting*	*Extra Ordinary General meeting*
1. Persuant to section	Section 165	Section 166 to 168	Section 169
2. Companies required to hold	Public limited company having share capital	Every Company	No Company (Optional)
3. When is to be held	After expiry of 1 month but before expiry of 6 Months from the date of certificate to commence business.	**First AGM**— Within 18 months of incorporation & within 9 months (a) of end of financial year. **Subsequent**—Within 6 months of the end of financial year but within 15 months of previous AGM. It must be held in each calender year. **Note:** The period of Financial year must not exceed 15 months but may extend to 18 months with special permission of the Registrar.	**(a) By B.O.D. on its own Motion [Reg. 48 of Table A]** **(b) By B.O.D. on Requisition:** Convey within 21 days & call within 45 days from the date of deposit of requisition by members. **(c) By Requisitionsts:** Within 3 months if B.O.D. did not convey within 21 days & did not call within 45 days from the date of deposit of requisition.
4. Who can call	Duly Constituted Board	Duly Constituted Board/Central Govt u/s 167 on application of any member if a default is made in holding AGM	Duly Consituted Board/ Requistionists/ Tribunal u/s186
5. Notice [Sec. 171 to 173]	Atleast 21 clear days' notice to all members and auditors	At least 21 clear days' notice to all members and auditors	Same as in case of, SM
6. Can shorter Notice be given?	With consent of members holding at least 95% paid up capital/ voting power obtained prior to or at or even subsequent to meeting.	With consent of **all** members entitled to vote.	Same as in case of Statutory Meeting

Basis of Comparison	*Statutory Meeting*	*Annual General Meeting*	*Extra Ordinary General meeting*
7. Documents with Notice	Statutory Report, Admission Card, Proxy Form	Audited, A/cs, Balance Sheet and Auditor's Report, Directors' Report Proxy Form, Admission Card Explanatory Statement (if special business to be transacted)	Explanatory Statement, Proxy Form, Admission Card
8. Hour, days & place of meeting	Any time, any day & at any place since the Act is silent on this point.	During Business Hours. Day Other than Public Holiday, Regd Office or other place within the city, town or village in which RO is situated. [Sec. 166(2)]	Same as in case of Statutory Meeting
9. Adjournment – Hour, Day & Place	To same day in the next week at the same time and place or to such other day and at such other time and place as the Board may determine if the quorum is not present within half an hour from the time appointed.	(a) To **same day** (even on Public Holiday) at the same **time and place if** AGM is **adjourned due to lack of quorum** (b) **To any day other than public holiday if adjourned due to any other reason**	• Adjorn if meeting has not been called on requisition of members. • Meeting shall stand dissolved if quorum is not present within half an hour from time appoin-ted and it is called on requisition of members.
– Quorum	Members present shall form the quorum.		
10. Consequences of default	**Penalty:** for any default us/165 fine upto Rs 5,000 for every officer in default.	For any default u/s 166 or 167 Fine upto Rs 50,000 & Rs 2,500 per day for continuing default for **company and every officer** in default	—
	Other Consequence: U/s 433— The Tribunal may also order for compulsory winding up if default is made in deliverying Statutory Report or in. holding Statutory Meeting	—	—

Basis of Comparison	*Statutory Meeting*	*Annual General Meeting*	*Extra Ordinary General meeting*
11. Minimum Quorum [Sec. 174] **1. At Original Meeting** **2. At meeting adjourned due to lack of quorum** **3. At meeting adjourned due to other reasons**	5 Members Personally present Members present Personally or by proxy. 5 members personally present	**1. At Original Meeting** (a) **In case of AGM called by Central Govt.** One member present personally or by proxy (b) **In case of other AGM — Public Co : 5** Members Personally present **Other Cos : 2** members personally present **2. Same point as in case of SM** **3. Same point as in (1)(b) above**	**In case of EGM called by Tribunal** one member present personally **In case of class meeting**—Even one shareholder can constitute quorum if that class consists of only one member.
12. Proxies [Sec 176]	(a) Members of public co. having share capital are entitled to appoint more than one proxy even if A/A does not provide so. (b) Members of public company having **no share share capital** are entitled to appoint proxy only if A/A so provides	(a) Members of **public co.** having share capital are entitled to appoint more than one proxy even if A/A does not provide so. (b) Members of **pvt. co.** having capital are entitled to appoint more than one proxy if A/A provides. (c) Members of company having no share capital are entitled to appoint **proxy** only if A/A so provides	Same as in case of AGM
13. Chairman	Unless the articles provide otherwise & poll is demanded. Chairman is to be elected by show of hands.	Same	Same
14. Voting (177 to 185) **1. by Show ofhand**	1. (a) Each member has one vote by show of hands. (b) Proxy may vote by show of hands if A/A so provides	Same	Same

Basis of Comparison	Statutory Meeting	Annual General Meeting	Extra Ordinary General meeting
	(c) Proxy (if not member) has no right to speak unless A/A otherwise provide.		
2. by Poll	2. Voting rights as per A/A & Sec 86 & 89.		
15. Ordinary/Special Business which can be transacted	Special Business	Ordinary as well as Special Business	Special Business
16. Ordinary/Special Resolution which can be passed	**Ordinary:** By simple majority of vote. **Special:** By 3/4th majority	Ordinary & Special Resolution	Ordinary & Special Resolution
17. Special Remark (if any)	(a) Statutory Report can be sent in Form 22 at notice shorter than of atleast 21 clear days' if so agreed by all members. (b) Members may discuss any matter relating to the formation of company or arising out of special resolution whether previous notice has been given or not but no resolution may be passed unless notice is given in accordance with provisions of Act.	—	If default is made in calling the meeting by the Board, then (i) The requisitionists shall be entitled to claim all reasonable expenses incurred for conveining a meeting from the company (ii) The company shall be entitled to retain such sum from the fees or other remuneration due to directors who were in default.

Summarised Table II showing Proper Place, Proper Date, Proper Hours and Quorum for Various Meetings

S. No.	*Proper Place*	*Proper Date*	*Proper Hours*	*Quorum*
1. Original AGM	At Registered Office or at some other place within the city, town or village in which the registered office is situated. Note: An Independent Pvt. Co. can fix any place.	On any day other than Public Holiday.	During Business Hours	**1. Called by Central Govt.**—One member present personally or by proxy **Other AGM** — Public Co.: 5 Members personally present **Pvt. Co.:** 2 Members personally present
2. AGM adjourned due to lack of Quorum	At same place where original AGM was held or at any other place as the Board may determine.	On any day (including public holiday) as the board may determine	At any time (whether or not falling within business hours) as the board may determine.	**2.** Members present personally or by proxy
3. AGM adjourned due to any other reason	As original AGM	As original AGM	As original AGM	**3.** As original AGM
4. Any other General Meeting	At any place as the board may determine	As AGM adjourned due to lack of quorum	As AGM adjourned due to lack of quorum.	**4. EGM called by Tribunal** — one member personally present **Other GM** — As original other AGM.

APPENDIX 10

Procedural Legal Requirements Under the Companies Act, 1956

Sec.	Particulars	Articles' Authorization	Ordinary Resolution	Special Resolution	Postal Bollot	C.G. Approval	CLB Approval	Court's Confirmation
17	Alteration of Object Clause	—	—	Yes	Yes	—	—	—
17	Alteration of Registered Office Clause	—	—	Yes	—	—	Yes	—
21	Change of Name	—	—	Yes	—	Yes	—	—
22	Rectification of Company's Name	—	Yes	—	—	Yes	—	—
31	Alteration of Articles Converting a Public Co. into a Pvt. Co.	—	—	Yes	—	Yes	—	—
31	Alteration of Articles (not involving Conversion of Public Co. into a Pvt. Co.)	—	—	Yes	Yes	—	—	—
77A	Buy Back of Shares	Yes	—	Yes	Yes	—	—	—
79	Issue of Shares at Discount	—	Yes	—	—	—	Yes	—
81	Issue of further shares to persons other than existing members	—	Yes	—	—	Yes	—	—
81	*Alternatively* Issue of further shares to persons other than existing members	—	—	Yes	—	—	—	—
81(3)	Issue of Convertible Loans/Debentures to persons other than Govt.	—	—	Yes	—	Yes	—	—
86	Issue of Shares with Differential voting rights	Yes	—	—	Yes	—	—	—
94	Alteration of Share Capital	Yes	Yes	—	—	—	—	—
99	Creation of Reserve Capital	—	—	Yes	—	—	—	—
100	Reduction of Capital	Yes	—	Yes	—	—	—	Yes
106	Variation of Shareholders Rights	Yes	—	Yes	Yes	—	—	—
114	Issue of Share Warrants	Yes	—	—	—	Yes	—	—
146	Shifting of Regd. Office outside the local limits of city ,town or village but within the same state	—	—	Yes	Yes	—	—	—
149(2A)	Commencement of New business covered under other objects clause	—	Yes	—	—	Yes	—	—
149(2B)	*Alternatively* Commencement of New business covered under other objects clause	—	—	Yes	—	—	—	—
163	To keep Statutory Registers & Returns at a place other than the Regd. Office provided such place is with in the city , town , village in which Regd. Office is situated	—	—	Yes	—	—	—	—
208	Payment of Interest out of Capital	Yes	—	Yes	—	—	—	—

APPENDIX 11

Time Limits Prescribed Under The Companies Act, 1956

Sec	Particulars	Time Limit
17	Filing of Copy of SR in case of alteration of object clause	30 days
18	Filing of Copy of SR in case of alteration of RO clause	30 days
18	Filing of Certified Copy of order of CLB together with printed copy of altered Memorandum in case of change of RO from one state to another	3 Months Of date of order
21&22	Filing of copy of order of Central Govt. in case of change of Name	3 Months of order
21&31	Filing of a certified copy of approval of Central Govt. together with a printed copy of A/A in case of conversion of Public Co. into Pvt. Co.	1 Month of date of Receipt of Approval
60(1)	Delivery of a copy of Prospectus	On/Before Date of Publication
60(4)	Issue of Prospectus to public	90 Days of its delivery to Registrar
69(5)	Refund of application money (in case of non-receipt of minimum subscription within 120 days of date of issue of prospectus)	• 130 days without interest • beyond 130 days with interest @6% p.a.
SEBI	Refund of application money (in case of non-receipt of 90% of issued amount within 60 days from date of closure of issue)	• 78 days without interest • beyond 78 days with interest @15% p.a.
70	Filling of Statement in lieu of Prospectus	At least 3 days before to first allotment of shares
73(2)	Refund of application money (in case of No Listing permission within 10 weeks from date of closing of subscription list)	• 8 days after becomes liable • beyond 8 days with interest between 4% – 15%
73(2A)	Refund of Excess Subscription	8 Days after the Co. to becomes liable
75	Filling of A Return of Allotment	30 days of allotment (or extended period)
77A	Minimum Time Interval between Two buy backs	365 days

Sec	*Particulars*	*Time Limit*
77A	Completion of Buy back	12 months from date of passing SR/Board's Resolution
79	Issue of Shares at Discount	2 Months of CLB approval
80	Maximum Period of Redemption of RPS	20 years
94	Notice of Alteration of Capital Clause to Registrar	30 days of Alteration
103	Filing of Certified Copy of Court's order in case of reduction of share capital	No Time Limit
107(2)	Application to Court by Dissentient Shareholders	21 Days after resolution on consent obtained
107(5)	Filing of Certified copy of Court's Order	30 days after the service of order
108	Intimation of refusal to register a T/F of shares to transferee & transferor	2 Months of its refusal
108	Appeal to CLB against any refusal of company to register a Transfer	2 Months
113	Issue of Share/Debenture Certificate to allottee	3 months of allotment
113	Delivery of Share Certificate in case of Transfer	2 months of Application for valid T/F
125(1)	Filing of Particulars of every charge	30 days of creation (extended period of 30 days)
128	Filling of Particulars in case of *Pari Passu* Clause	30 days after execution
138	Intimation of payment or satisfaction of any charge in full (Not in Part)	30 days of payment/satisfaction
146	Notice of Change of Regd. office	30 days of change
146(2)	Filling of Notice of Situation of registered office	30 days of incorporation
146(2)	Filling of particulars of Directors, Manager or Secretory in Form No 32	30 days of incorporation
146(1)	Mandatory to have regd. office	From the day of commencement of business or from the 30th day after the date of incorporation which ever is earlier
146(2)	Filling of Certified Copy of Confirmation of Regional Director together with printed copy of altered Memorandum	2 Months of date of confirmation
151	Noting of Alteration in the Register of Members/ Debentureholders/in Index	14 Days of making Alteration
154	Maximum Period for which Register of Members can be closed in a year	45 days

Sec	*Particulars*	*Time Limit*
154	Maximum period for which Register of Members can be closed at any one time.	30 days
161	Filing of Annual Return	60 days of date of holding general meeting *or* date on which GM should have held
163	Supply of copy of Register of Members	10 Working Days of demand
165(1)	Holding of Statutory Meeting	After 1 month but before 6 months of Date of Certificate to commence business
165(2)	Sending of Statutory Report to members	21 Clear Days
166(1)	Holding of First AGM	18 months of incorporation
166(1)	Holding of Subsequent AGM	15 months of previous AGM
166(1)	Holding of Subsequent AGM	Each calender year
169(6)	Calling of EGM on requisition by BOD	21 day of deposit of requisition
169(6)	Holding of EGM by BOD	45 days of deposit of requisition
169(6)	Calling of EGM by Requisitionists	3 months from date of deposit of requisition
171	Notice of General Meeting by person	21 Clear days
171	Notice of General Meeting by post	21 Clear days + 48 days after posting
176	Deposit of Instrument of Proxy with company	48 hours before the time for holding meeting **or shorter period as per A/A**
180	Time for taking poll demanded on (*a*) resolution for the adjournment of meeting or election of chairman (*b*) other resolutions	 • Immediately • 48 hours of demand for Poll
190(1)	Special Notice to company	14 clear days
190(2)	Notice of Resolution proposed in Special Notice	7 Days before meeting
192(4)	Registration of Resolutions and Agreements	30 days of passing the resolution/ making agreement
193(1)	Recording of Minutes	30 days of conclusion of meeting
	Filing of prescribed documents by a foreign company	30 days from date of establishment in India
210(3)	Holding of First AGM	9 months of end of financial year
210(4)	Holding of Subsequent AGM	6 months of end of financial year